ROGET'S THESAURUS

OF
SYNONYMS
AND
ANTONYMS

BY

PETER MARK ROGET, M.D., F.R.S.

ENLARGED BY

JOHN LEWIS ROGET, M.A.

NEW EDITION REVISED AND ENLARGED BY

SAMUEL ROMILLY ROGET, M.A.

Roydon Publishing Co. Ltd., London

PLAN OF CLASSIFICATION

TABULAR SYNOPSIS OF CATEGORIES

CLASS I. ABSTRACT RELATIONS

I. EXISTENCE

1°. ABSTRACT..........	1. Existence.	2. Inexistence.
2°. CONCRETE..........	3. Substantiality.	4. Unsubstantiality.
3°. FORMAL...........	*Internal.*	*External.*
	5. Intrinsicality.	6. Extrinsicality.
4°. MODAL............	*Absolute.*	*Relative.*
	7. State.	8. Circumstance.

II. RELATION

	9. Relation.	10. Irrelation.
1°. ABSOLUTE..........	11. Consanguinity.	
	12. Correlation.	
	13. Identity.	14. Contrariety.
	15. Difference.	
2°. CONTINUOUS........	16. Uniformity.	16a. Non-uniformity.
3°. PARTIAL...........	17. Similarity.	18. Dissimilarity.
	19. Imitation.	20. Non-imitation.
	20a. Variation.	
	21. Copy.	22. Prototype.
4°. GENERAL...........	23. Agreement.	24. Disagreement.

III. QUANTITY

	Absolute.	*Relative.*
1°. SIMPLE............	25. Quantity.	26. Degree.
	27. Equality.	28. Inequality.
	29. Mean.	
	30. Compensation.	
	By Comparison with a Standard.	
2°. COMPARATIVE.......	31. Greatness.	32. Smallness.
	By Comparison with a similar Object.	
	33. Superiority.	34. Inferiority.
	Changes in Quantity.	
	35. Increase.	36. Decrease.
	37. Addition.	38. { Non-addition. / Subduction.
	39. Adjunct.	40. Remainder.
		40a. Decrement.
3°. CONJUNCTIVE.......	41. Mixture.	42. Simpleness.
	43. Junction.	44. Disjunction.
	45. Vinculum.	
	46. Coherence.	47. Incoherence.
	48. Combination.	49. Decomposition.

4°. CONCRETE
- 50. Whole.
- 52. Completeness.
- 54. Composition.
- 56. Component.
- 51. Part.
- 53. Incompleteness.
- 55. Exclusion.
- 57. Extraneous.

IV. ORDER

1°. GENERAL
- 58. Order.
- 60. Arrangement.
- 62. Precedence.
- 64. Precursor.
- 59. Disorder.
- 61. Derangement.
- 63. Sequence.
- 65. Sequel.

2°. CONSECUTIVE
- 66. Beginning.
- 68. Middle.
- 69. Continuity.
- 71. Term.
- 67. End.
- 70. Discontinuity.

3°. COLLECTIVE
- 72. Assemblage.
- 73. { Non-assemblage. / Dispersion. }
- 74. Focus.
- 75. Class.

4°. DISTRIBUTIVE
- 76. Inclusion.
- 78. Generality.
- 77. Exclusion.
- 79. Speciality.

5°. CATEGORICAL
- 80. Rule.
- 82. Conformity.
- 81. Multiformity.
- 83. Unconformity.

V. NUMBER

1°. ABSTRACT
- 84. Number.
- 85. Numeration.
- 86. List.
- 87. Unity.
- 88. Accompaniment.

2°. DETERMINATE
- 89. Duality.
- 90. Duplication.
- 92. Triality.
- 93. Triplication.
- 94. Quadruplication.
- 95. Quaternity.
- 98. Five, &c.
- 100. Plurality.
- 91. Bisection.
- 96. Trisection.
- 97. Quadrisection.
- 99. Quinquesection, &c.
- 100a. Fraction.
- 101. Zero.

3°. INDETERMINATE
- 102. Multitude.
- 104. Repetition.
- 105. Infinity.
- 103. Fewness.

VI. TIME

1°. ABSOLUTE
- 106. Time.
- *Definite.*
- 108. Period.
- 108a. Contingent Duration.
- 110. Diuturnity.
- 112. Perpetuity.
- 114. Chronometry.
- 116. Priority.
- 107. Neverness.
- *Indefinite.*
- 109. Course.
- 111. Transientness.
- 113. Instantaneity.
- 115. Anachronism.
- 117. Posteriority.

2°. RELATIVE

1. *to Succession*
- 118. Present time.
- 120. Synchronism.
- 121. Futurity.
- 123. Newness.
- 119. Different time.
- 122. Preterition.
- 124. Oldness.

2. *to a Period*
- 125. Morning.
- 127. Youth.
- 129. Infant.
- 131. Adolescence.
- 126. Evening.
- 128. Age.
- 130. Veteran.

3. *to an Effect or purpose*
- 132. Earliness.
- 134. Occasion.
- 133. Lateness.
- 135. Intempestivity.

3°. RECURRENT
- 136. Frequency.
- 138. Periodicity.
- 137. Infrequency.
- 139. Irregularity.

VII. CHANGE

1°. SIMPLE
- 140. Change.
- 141. Permanence.
- 142. Cessation.
- 143. Continuance.
- 144. Conversion.
- 145. Reversion.
- 146. Revolution.

2°. COMPLEX
- 147. Substitution.
- 148. Interchange.
- 149. Changeableness.
- 150. Stability.
- *Present.*
- *Future.*
- 151. Eventuality.
- 152. Destiny.

VIII. CAUSATION

1°. CONSTANCY OF SEQUENCE
- 153. { *Constant Antecedent.* Cause.
- 154. { *Constant Sequent.* Effect.
- 155. { *Assignment of Cause.* Attribution.
- 156. { *Absence of Assignment.* Chance.

2°. CONNECTION BETWEEN CAUSE AND EFFECT
- 157. Power.
- 158. Impotence.
- *Degrees of Power.*
- 159. Strength.
- 160. Weakness.

3°. POWER IN OPERATION
- 161. Production.
- 162. Destruction.
- 163. Reproduction.
- 164. Producer.
- 165. Destroyer.
- 166. Paternity.
- 167. Posterity.
- 168. Productiveness.
- 169. Unproductiveness.
- 170. Agency.
- 171. Energy.
- 172. Inertness.
- 173. Violence.
- 174. Moderation.

4°. INDIRECT POWER
- 175. Influence.
- 175a. Absence of Influence.
- 176. Tendency.
- 177. Liability.

5°. COMBINATIONS OF CAUSES
- 178. Concurrence.
- 179. Counteraction.

CLASS II. SPACE

I. SPACE IN GENERAL

1°. ABSTRACT SPACE
- 180. { *Indefinite.* Space.
- 180a. Inextension.
- 181. { *Definite.* Region.
- 182. { *Limited.* Place.

2°. RELATIVE SPACE
- 183. Situation.
- 184. Location.
- 185. Displacement.

3°. EXISTENCE IN SPACE
- 186. Presence.
- 187. Absence.
- 188. Inhabitant.
- 189. Abode.
- 190. Contents.
- 191. Receptacle.

II. DIMENSIONS

1°. GENERAL
- 192. Size.
- 193. Littleness.
- 194. Expansion.
- 195. Contraction.
- 196. Distance.
- 197. Nearness.
- 198. Interval.
- 199. Contiguity.
- 200. Length.
- 201. Shortness.

2°. LINEAR
- 202. { Breadth. Thickness.
- 203. { Narrowness. Thinness.
- 204. Layer.
- 205. Filament.
- 206. Height.
- 207. Lowness.
- 208. Depth.
- 209. Shallowness.

SYNOPSIS OF CATEGORIES

	210. Summit.	211. Base.
	212. Verticality.	213. Horizontality.
2°. LINEAR—*continued*...	214. Pendency.	215. Support.
	216. Parallelism.	217. Obliquity.
	218. Inversion.	
	219. Crossing.	
	220. Exteriority.	221. Interiority.
	222. Centrality.	
	223. Covering.	224. Lining.
	225. Investment.	226. Divestment.
1. *General*	227. Circumjacence.	228. Interjacence.
	229. Circumscription.	
	230. Outline.	
3°. CENTRI-CAL	231. Edge.	
	232. Inclosure.	
	233. Limit.	
	234. Front	235. Rear.
2. *Special*	236. Laterality.	237. Contraposition.
	238. Dextrality.	239. Sinistrality.

III. FORM

1°. GENERAL..........	240. Form.	241. Amorphism.
	242. Symmetry.	243. Distortion.
	244. Angularity.	
2°. SPECIAL..........	245. Curvature.	246. Straightness.
	247. Circularity.	248. Convolution.
	249. Rotundity.	
	250. Convexity.	252. Concavity.
	251. Flatness.	
	253. Sharpness.	254. Bluntness.
	255. Smoothness.	256. Roughness.
3°. SUPERFICIAL........	257. Notch.	
	258. Fold.	
	259. Furrow.	
	260. Opening.	261. Closure.
	262. Perforator.	263. Stopper.

IV. MOTION

	264. Motion.	265. Quiescence.
	266. Journey.	267. Navigation.
1°. MOTION IN GENERAL	268. Traveler.	269. Mariner.
	270. Transference.	
	271. Carrier.	
	272. Vehicle.	273. Ship.
2°. DEGREES OF MOTION	274. Velocity.	275. Slowness.
3°. CONJOINED WITH FORCE............	276. Impulse.	277. Recoil.
	278. Direction.	279. Deviation.
	280. Precession.	281. Sequence.
	282. Progression.	283. Regression.
	284. Propulsion.	285. Traction.
	286. Approach.	287. Recession.
	288. Attraction.	289. Repulsion.
4°. WITH REFERENCE TO DIRECTION.....	290. Convergence.	291. Divergence.
	292. Arrival.	293. Departure.
	294. Ingress.	295. Egress.
	296. Reception.	297. Ejection.
	298. Food.	299. Excretion.
	300. Insertion.	301. Extraction.
	302. Passage.	
	303. Overstep.	304. Shortcoming.

4°. WITH REFERENCE TO DIRECTION—*cont*...		
305. Ascent.	306. Descent.
307. Elevation.	308. Depression.
309. Leap.	310. Plunge.
311. Circuition.	
312. Rotation.	313. Evolution.
314. Oscillation.	
315. Agitation.	

CLASS III. MATTER

I. MATTER IN GENERAL

316. Materiality.	317. Immateriality.
318. World.	
319. Gravity.	320. Levity.

II. INORGANIC MATTER

1°. SOLIDS

321. Density.	322. Rarity.
323. Hardness.	324. Softness.
325. Elasticity.	326. Inelasticity.
327. Tenacity.	328. Brittleness.
329. Texture.	
330. Pulverulence.	
331. Friction.	332. Lubrication.

2°. FLUIDS

1. *In General*

333. Fluidity.	334. Gaseity.
335. Liquefaction.	336. Vaporization.
337. Water.	338. Air.
339. Moisture.	340. Dryness.

2. *Specific*...

341. Ocean.	342. Land.
343. Gulf. Lake.	344. Plain.
345. Marsh.	346. Island.
347. Stream.	

3. *In motion*

348. River.	349. Wind.
350. Conduit.	351. Air-pipe.

3°. IMPERFECT FLUIDS...

352. Semiliquidity.	353. Bubble.
354. Pulpiness.	355. Unctuousness.
	356. Oil.
	356a. Resin.

III. ORGANIC MATTER

1°. VITALITY

1. *In General*...

357. Organization.	358. Inorganization.
359. Life.	360. Death.
	361. Killing.
	362. Corpse.
	363. Interment.

2. *Special*

364. Animality.	365. Vegetability.
366. Animal.	367. Vegetable.
368. Zoology.	369. Botany.
370. Cicuration.	371. Agriculture.
372. Mankind.	
373. Man.	374. Woman.

SYNOPSIS OF CATEGORIES

2°. SENSATION

(1) General
- 375. Sensibility.
- 377. Pleasure.
- 379. Touch.
- 376. Insensibility.
- 378. Pain.

(2) Special

1. Touch
- 380. { Sensations of Touch.
- 381. Numbness.

2. Heat
- 382. Heat.
- 384. Calefaction.
- 386. Furnace.
- 388. Fuel.
- 389. Thermometer.
- 383. Cold.
- 385. Refrigeration.
- 387. Refrigeratory.

3. Taste
- 390. Taste.
- 392. Pungency.
- 393. Condiment.
- 394. Savouriness.
- 396. Sweetness.
- 391. Insipidity.
- 395. Unsavouriness.
- 397. Sourness.

4. Odor
- 398. Odor.
- 400. Fragrance.
- 399. Inodorousness.
- 401. Fœtor.

5. Sound

(i.) *Sound in General.*
- 402. Sound.
- 404. Loudness.
- 403. Silence.
- 405. Faintness.

(ii.) *Specific Sounds.*
- 406. Snap.
- 408. Resonance.
- 407. Roll.
- 408a. Non-resonance.
- 409. Sibilation.
- 410. Stridor.
- 411. Cry.
- 412. Ululation.

(iii.) *Musical Sounds.*
- 413. { Melody. Concord.
- 414. Discord.
- 415. Music.
- 416. Musician.
- 417. Musical Instruments.

(iv.) *Perception of Sound.*
- 418. Hearing.
- 419. Deafness.

6. Light

(i.) *Light in General.*
- 420. Light.
- 421. Darkness.
- 422. Dimness.
- 423. Luminary.
- 424. Shade.
- 425. Transparency.
- 426. Opacity.
- 427. Semitransparency.

(ii.) *Specific Light.*
- 428. Color.
- 429. Achromatism.
- 430. Whiteness.
- 431. Blackness.
- 432. Gray.
- 433. Brown.
- 434. Redness.
- 435. Greenness.
- 436. Yellowness.
- 437. Purple.
- 438. Blueness.
- 439. Orange.
- 440. Variegation.

(iii.) *Perceptions of Light.*
- 441. Vision.
- 442. Blindness.
- 443. Dimsightedness.
- 444. Spectator.
- 445. Optical Instruments.
- 446. Visibility.
- 447. Invisibility.
- 448. Appearance.
- 449. Disappearance.

SYNOPSIS OF CATEGORIES

Class IV. INTELLECT

Division (I.). FORMATION OF IDEAS

I. OPERATIONS OF INTELLECT IN GENERAL.....

450. Intellect.	450a. Absence of Intellect.
451. Thought.	452. Incogitancy.
453. Idea.	454. Topic.
455. Curiosity.	456. Incuriosity.
457. Attention.	458. Inattention.
459. Care.	460. Neglect.

II. PRECURSORY CONDITIONS AND OPERATIONS......

461. Inquiry.	462. Answer.
463. Experiment.	
464. Comparison.	
465. Discrimination.	465a. Indiscrimination.
466. Measurement.	
467. Evidence.	468. Counter-evidence.
469. Qualification.	

III. MATERIALS FOR REASONING...........

Degrees of Evidence.

470. Possibility.	471. Impossibility.
472. Probability.	473. Improbability.
474. Certainty.	475. Uncertainty.

IV. REASONING PROCESSES

476. Reasoning.	477. { Intuition. / Sophistry. }
478. Demonstration.	479. Confutation.
480. Judgement.	481. Misjudgement.
480a. Discovery.	
482. Over-estimation.	483. Under-estimation.
484. Belief.	485. { Unbelief. / Doubt. }
486. Credulity.	487. Incredulity.
488. Assent.	489. Dissent.

V. RESULTS OF REASONING

490. Knowledge.	491. Ignorance.
492. Scholar.	493. Ignoramus.
494. Truth.	495. Error.
496. Maxim.	497. Absurdity.

Faculties.

498. { Intelligence. / Wisdom. }	499. { Imbecility. / Folly. }
500. Sage.	501. Fool.
502. Sanity.	503. Insanity.
	504. Madman.

VI. EXTENSION OF THOUGHT — 1°. *To the Past...*

505. Memory.	506. Oblivion.
507. Expectation.	508. Inexpectation.
	509. Disappointment.

2°. *To the Future.*

510. Foresight.	
511. Prediction.	
512. Omen.	
513. Oracle.	

VII. CREATIVE THOUGHT...

514. Supposition.
515. Imagination.

SYNOPSIS OF CATEGORIES
Division (II.). COMMUNICATION OF IDEAS

I. NATURE OF IDEAS COMMUNICATED.......

516. Meaning. | 517. Unmeaningness.
518. Intelligibility. | 519. Unintelligibility
520. Equivocalness.
521. Metaphor.
522. Interpretation. | 523. Misinterpretatic
524. Interpreter.
525. Manifestation. | 526. Latency.
527. Information. | 528. Concealment.
529. Disclosure. | 530. Ambush.
531. Publication.
532. News. | 533. Secret.
534. Messenger.
535. Affirmation. | 536. Negation.

II. MODES OF COMMUNI-CATION............

537. Teaching. | 538. Misteaching.
  | 539. Learning.
540. Teacher. | 541. Learner.
542. School.
543. Veracity. | 544. Falsehood.
  | 545. Deception.
  | 546. Untruth.
547. Dupe. | 548. Deceiver.
  | 549. Exaggeration.

III. MEANS OF COMMUNICATION

1°. Natural Means.......

550. Indication.
551. Record. | 552. Obliteration.
553. Recorder.
554. Representation. | 555. Misrepresentati
556. Painting.
557. Sculpture.
558. Engraving.
559. Artist.
560. Language.
561. Letter.
562. Word. | 563. Neology.
564. Nomenclature. | 565. Misnomer.
566. Phrase.
567. Grammar. | 568. Solecism.

2°. Conventional Means

1. Language generally

569. Style.

Qualities of Style.
570. Perspicuity. | 571. Obscurity.
572. Conciseness. | 573. Diffuseness.
574. Vigour. | 575. Feebleness.
576. Plainness. | 577. Ornament.
578. Elegance. | 579. Inelegance.

2. Spoken Language

580. Voice. | 581. Aphony.
582. Speech. | 583. Stammering.
584. Loquacity. | 585. Taciturnity.
586. Allocution. | 587. Response.
588. Interlocution. | 589. Soliloquy.

3. Written Language

590. Writing. | 591. Printing.
592. Correspondence. | 593. Book.
594. Description.
595. Dissertation.
596. Compendium.
597. Poetry. | 598. Prose.
599. The Drama.

Class V. VOLITION

Division (I.). Individual Volition

I. Volition in General

1°. Acts....

600. Will.	601. Necessity.
602. Willingness.	603. Unwillingness.
604. Resolution.	605. Irresolution.
604a. Perseverance. }	607. Tergiversation.
606. Obstinacy.	
	608. Caprice.
609. Choice.	609a. Absence of Choice.
	610. Rejection.
611. Predetermination.	612. Impulse.
613. Habit.	614. Desuetude.

2°. Causes..

615. Motive.	615a. Absence of Motive.
	616. Dissuasion.
617. Plea.	

3°. Objects..

618. Good.	619. Evil.
620. Intention.	621. Chance.
622. Pursuit.	623. Avoidance.
	624. Relinquishment.

II. Prospective Volition.......

1°. Conceptional..

625. Business.
626. Plan.
627. Method.
628. Mid-Course.   629. Circuit.
630. Requirement.

2°. Subservience to Ends...

1. Actual Subservience.

631. Instrumentality.
632. Means.
633. Instrument.
634. Substitute.
635. Materials.
636. Store.
637. Provision.   638. Waste.
639. Sufficiency.
641. Redundance.   640. Insufficiency.

2. Degree of Subservience.

642. Importance.	643. Unimportance.
644. Utility.	645. Inutility.
646. Expedience.	647. Inexpedience.
648. Goodness.	649. Badness.
650. Perfection.	651. Imperfection.
652. Cleanness.	653. Uncleanness.
654. Health.	655. Disease.
656. Salubrity.	657. Insalubrity.
658. Improvement.	659. Deterioration.
660. Restoration.	661. Relapse.
662. Remedy.	663. Bane.

3. Contingent Subservience.

664. Safety.	665. Danger.
666. Refuge.	667. Pitfall.
668. Warning.	
669. Alarm.	
670. Preservation.	
671. Escape.	
672. Deliverance.	

II. PERSONAL

1°. PASSIVE

827. Pleasure.	828. Pain.
829. Pleasureableness.	830. Painfulness.
831. Content.	832. Discontent.
	833. Regret.
834. Relief.	835. Aggravation.
836. Cheerfulness.	837. Dejection.
838. Rejoicing.	839. Lamentation.
840. Amusement.	841. Weariness.
842. Wit.	843. Dulness.
844. Humorist.	

2°. DISCRIMINATIVE

845. Beauty.	846. Ugliness.
847. Ornament.	848. Blemish.
	849. Simplicity.
850. Taste.	851. Vulgarity.
852. Fashion.	
	853. Ridiculousness.
	854. Fop.
	855. Affection.
	856. Ridicule.
	857. Laughing-stock.

3°. PROSPECTIVE

858. Hope.	859. Hopelessness.
	860. Fear.
861. Courage.	862. Cowardice.
863. Rashness.	864. Caution.
865. Desire.	867. Dislike.
866. Indifference.	
	868. Fastidiousness.
	869. Satiety.

4°. CONTEMPLATIVE

870. Wonder.	871. Expectance.
872. Prodigy.	

5°. EXTRINSIC

873. Repute.	874. Disrepute.
875. Nobility.	876. Commonalty.
877. Title.	
878. Pride.	879. Humility.
880. Vanity.	881. Modesty.
882. Ostentation.	
883. Celebration.	
884. Boasting.	
885. Insolence.	886. Servility.
887. Blusterer.	

III. SYMPATHETIC

1°. SOCIAL

888. Friendship.	889. Enmity.
890. Friend.	891. Enemy.
892. Sociality.	893. Seclusion.
894. Courtesy.	895. Discourtesy.
896. Congratulation.	
897. Love.	898. Hate.
899. Favorite.	
	900. Resentment.
	901. Irascibility.
	901a. Sullenness.
902. Endearment.	
903. Marriage.	904. Celibacy.
	905. Divorce.

2°. DIFFUSIVE.........
- 906. Benevolence.
- 910. Philanthropy.
- 912. Benefactor.

- 907. Malevolence.
- 908. Malediction.
- 909. Threat.
- 911. Misanthropy.
- 913. Evil doer.

3°. SPECIAL...........
- 914. Pity.
- 915. Condolence.
- 916. Gratitude.
- 918. Forgiveness.

- 914a. Pitilessness.
- 917. Ingratitude.

4°. RETROSPECTIVE....
- 919. Revenge.
- 920. Jealousy.
- 921. Envy.

IV. MORAL

1°. OBLIGATIONS.......
- 922. Right.
- 924. Dueness.
- 926. Duty.
- 928. Respect.

- 923. Wrong.
- 925. Undueness.
- 927. Dereliction.
- 927a. Exemption.
- 929. Disrespect.
- 930. Contempt.

2°. SENTIMENTS........
- 931. Approbation.
- 933. Flattery.
- 935. Flatterer.
- 937. Vindication.
- 939. Probity.

- 932. Disapprobation.
- 934. Detraction.
- 936. Detractor.
- 938. Accusation.
- 940. Improbity.
- 941. Knave.

3°. CONDITIONS........
- 942. Disinterestedness.
- 944. Virtue.
- 946. Innocence.
- 948. Good Man.
- 950. Penitence.
- 952. Atonement.
- 953. Temperance.

- 943. Selfishness.
- 945. Vice.
- 947. Guilt.
- 949. Bad Man.
- 951. Impenitence.
- 954. Intemperance.
- 954a. Sensualist.

4°. PRACTICE.........
- 955. Asceticism.
- 956. Fasting.
- 958. Sobriety.
- 960. Purity.

- 957. Gluttony.
- 959. Drunkenness.
- 961. Impurity.
- 962. Libertine.
- 964. Illegality.

5°. INSTITUTIONS......
- 963. Legality.
- 965. Jurisprudence.
- 966. Tribunal.
- 967. Judge.
- 968. Lawyer.
- 969. Lawsuit.
- 970. Acquittal.
- 973. Reward.

- 971. Condemnation.
- 972. Punishment.
- 974. Penalty.
- 975. Scourge.

V. RELIGIOUS

1°. SUPERHUMAN BE-
INGS AND REGIONS..
- 976. Deity.
- 977. Angel.
- 979. Jupiter.
- 981. Heaven.

- 978. Satan.
- 980. Demon.
- 982. Hell.

2°. DOCTRINES........
- 983. Theology.
- 983a. Orthodoxy.
- 985. Revelation.

- 984. Heterodoxy.
- 986. Pseudo-revelation.

3°. SENTIMENTS........
- 987. Piety.

- 988. Impiety.
- 989. Irreligion.

SYNOPSIS OF CATEGORIES

4°. ACTS............
- 990. Worship.
- 991. Idolatry
- 992. Sorcery.
- 993. Spell.
- 994. Sorcerer.

5°. INSTITUTIONS......
- 995. Churchdom.
- 996. Clergy.
- 997. Laity.
- 998. Rite.
- 999. Canonicals.
- 1000. Temple.

ABBREVIATIONS, &c.

Adj.	*adj.*	Adjectives, Participles, and Words having the power of Adjectives.
Adv.	*adv.*	Adverbs and Adverbial Expressions.
Int.	*int.*	Interjections.
Phr.	*phr.*	Phrases.
V.	*v.*	Verbs.

The numbers are those of the headings, or Categories.

Words in italics within parentheses are not intended to explain the meanings of the words which precede them, but to indicate the nature of allied group of words under the numbers which follow them.

THESAURUS

OF

ENGLISH WORDS AND PHRASES

1. Existence.—N. existence, being, entity, *ens, esse,* subsistence, quiddity.

reality, realness, actuality; positiveness etc. *adj.*; fact, matter of fact, sober reality; truth etc. 494; actual existence.

presence etc. (*existence in space*) 186; coexistence etc. 120.

stubborn fact; not a -dream etc. 515; no joke.

substance, essence, prime constituent, hypostatis.

[Science of existence] , ontology.

V. exist, be; have -being etc. *n.*; subsist, live, breathe, stand, obtain, be the case; occur etc. (*event*) 151; have place, rank, prevail; find oneself, pass the time, vegetate.

consist in, lie in, reside in, inhere in.

come into -existence etc. *n.*; arise etc. (*begin*) 66; come forth etc. (*appear*) 446.

become etc. (*be converted*) 144; bring into existence etc. 161; coexist, preexist, endure etc. 141.

Adj. existing etc. *v.*; existent, subsistent, under the sun; in -existence etc. *n.*; extant; afloat, on foot, current, prevalent, rife, in force, -vogue; undestroyed.

real, actual, positive, absolute; true etc. 494; substan-tial, -tive; self-existing, -ent.

well-founded, -grounded; un-ideal, -imagined; not -potential etc. 2.

Adv. actually etc. *adj.*; in -fact, – point of fact, – reality; indeed; *de* –, *ipso-facto.*

2. Nonexistence.—N. nonexistence; inexistence, -subsistence; nonentity, *nil*; negativeness etc. *adj.*; nullity; nihil-ity, -ism; *tabula rasa,* blank; abeyance; absence etc. 187; no such thing etc. 4; nothingness, oblivion, *non esse.*

annihilation; extinction etc. (*destruction*) 162.

V. not -exist etc. 1; have no -existence etc. 1; be null and void; cease to -exist etc. 1; pass away, perish; be –, become-extinct etc. *adj.*; die out; disappear etc. 449; melt away, dissolve, leave not a rack behind, leave no trace; go, be no more; die etc. 360.

annihilate, render null, nullify; abrogate etc. 756; destroy etc. 162; take away; remove etc. (*displace*) 185.

Adj. inexistent, non-existent etc. 1; negative, blank, null and void; missing, omitted; absent etc. 187; visionary etc. 515.

unreal, potential, virtual; baseless, *in nubibus*; unsubstantial etc. 4; vain.

un-born, -created, -begotten, -conceived, produced, -made.

perished, annihilated etc. *v.*; extinct, exhausted, gone, lost, departed; defunct etc. (*dead*) 360; fabulous, ideal etc. (*imaginary*) 515; supposititious etc. 514.

Adv. negatively, virtually, etc. *adj.*

3. Substantiality.—N. substantiality, *hypostasis*; person, thing, object, article; something, a being, an existence; creature, body, substance, flesh and blood, stuff, *substratum*; matter etc. 316; physical nature.

[Totality of existences], world etc. 318; *plenum.*

Adj. substan-tive, -tial, concrete; hypostatic; personal, bodily; tangible etc. (*material*) 316; real, corporeal, evident.

Adv. substantially etc. *adj.*; bodily, essentially.

4. Unsubstantiality.—N. un-, in-substantiality; nothingness, nihility.

nothing, naught, *nil*, nullity, zero, cipher, no one, nobody; never – , ne'er -a one; no such thing, none in the world; nothing -whatever, – at all, – on earth; not a -particle etc. (*smallness*) 32; all - talk, – moonshine, – stuff and nonsense, matter of no import.

thing of naught, man of straw, John Doe and Richard Roe; *nominis umbra,* nonentity, figurehead, lay figure; flash in the pan, *vox et praeterea nihil.*

shadow; phantasm, phantom etc. (*fallacy of vision*) 443; dream etc. (*imagination*) 515; *ignis fatuus* etc. (*luminary*) 423; 'such stuff as dreams are made of;' air, thin air; bubble etc. 353; 'baseless fabric of a vision;' mockery.

hollowness, blank; vacuity, void etc. (*absence*) 187.

inanity, fool's paradise, fatuity, stupidity, emptiness of mind.

V. vanish, evaporate, fade, sink, fly – , die – , melt- away, dissolve, disappear etc. 449; become extinct, become invisible.

Adj. unsubstantial; fleeting; base-, ground-less; ungrounded; without – , having no- foundation. visionary etc. (*imaginary*) 515; immaterial etc. 317; spectral etc. 980; dreamy; shadowy; ethereal, airy, imponderable, tenuous, vague.

vacant, vacuous; empty etc. 187; eviscerated; blank, hollow; nominal; null; inane.

Phr. there's nothing in it.

1

5. Intrinsicality.—N. intrinsicality, inbeing, inherence, inhesion, immanence; subjectiveness; *ego;* essence; essentialness etc. *adj.*; essential part, essential stuff, substance, quintessence, incarnation, quiddity, gist, pith, core, kernel, marrow, sap, life-blood, backbone, heart, soul, life, flower; important part etc. (*importance*) 642.

principle, nature, constitution, character, ethos, type, quality, crasis, *diathesis.*

habit; temper, -ament; spirit, humor, grain, disposition, streak, tendency etc. 176.

endowment, capacity; capability etc. (*power*) 157; moods, declensions, features, aspects; peculiarities etc. (*specialty*) 79; idiosyncrasy; idiocrasy; diagnostics.

V. be –, run- in the blood; be born so; be -intrinsic etc. *adj.*

Adj. derived from within, subjective; idiocratic, idiosyncratic, intrin-sic, -sical; fundamental, cardinal, normal, inherent, essential, natural; in-nate, -born, -bred, -dwelling, -grained; -wrought; radical, incarnate, thoroughbred, hereditary, inherited, immanent; congen-ital, -ite; connate, running in the blood; coeval with birth, genetic, ingenerate, -genite; indigenous; in the -grain etc. *n.*; bred in the bone, instinctive; inward, internal etc. 221; to the manner born; virtual.

characteristic etc. (*special*) 79, (*indicative*) 550; invariable, incurable, ineradicable, fixed, settled, constant, unchanging.

Adv. intrinsically etc. *adj.*; at bottom, in the main, in effect, essentially, practically, virtually, substantially, *au fond;* fairly.

6. Extrinsicality.—N. extrinsicality, objectiveness, *non ego;* extraneousness etc. 57; accident; letter of the law.

Adj. derived from without; objective; extrinsic, -sical; extraneous etc. (*foreign*) 57; modal, adventitious, additional, supervenient, fortuitous; a-, ad-scititious; incidental, casual, accidental, unessential, non-essential, accessory.

implanted, ingrafted; instilled, inculcated. outward etc. (*external*) 220.

Adv. extrinsically etc. *adj.*

7. State.—N. state, condition, category, estate, lot, case, trim, mood, pickle, plight etc. 704; temper; aspect etc. (*appearance*) 448.

constitution, habitude, *diathesis;* frame, fabric etc. 329; stamp, set, fit, mold.

mode, modality, schesis; fettle; form etc. (*shape*) 240.

tone, tenor, turn; trim, guise, fashion, light, complexion, style, character.

V. be in –, possess –, enjoy –, labor under- a -state etc. *n.*; be on a footing, do, fare; come to pass.

Adj. conditional, modal, formal; structural, organic.

Adv. conditionally etc. *adj.*; as -the matter stands, – things are; such being the case etc. 8.

8. Circumstance.—N. circumstance, situation, phase, position, posture, attitude, place, point; terms; *régime;* footing, standing, status.

occasion, juncture, conjuncture; contingency etc. (*event*) 151.

predicament; emergen-ce, -cy; exigency, crisis, pinch, pass, push; turning point; crossroads.

bearings, how the land lies.

Adj. circumstantial; given, conditional, provisional; critical; modal; contingent, incidental; adventitious etc. (*extrinsic*) 6.

Adv. in the circumstances etc. *n.*, under the conditions etc. 7; thus, in such wise.

accordingly; that –, such- being the case; that being so, since, seeing that.

as matters stand; as -things, – times- go.

conditionally, provided, if, in case; if -so, – so be, – it be so; if it so -happen, – turn out; in the event of; in such a -contingency, – case, – event; provisionally, unless, without.

according to -circumstances, – the occasion: as it may -happen, – turn out, – be; as the -case may be, – wind blows; *pro re natâ.*

9. Relation.—N. relation, bearing, reference, connection, apposition, interconnection, concern, cognation; applicability, appositeness; correlation etc. 12; analogy; similarity etc. 17; affinity, intimacy, friendship; homology, alliance, homogeneity, association, rapport; approximation etc. (*nearness*) 197; filiation etc. (*consanguinity*) 11; interest; relevancy etc. 23; relationship, relative position; relativity; interrelation etc. 12.

comparison etc. 464; ratio, proportion.

link, tie, bond, bond of union.

V. be-related etc. *adj.*; have a relation etc. *n.*; relate –, refer- to; bear upon, regard, concern, touch, affect, have to do with; pertain –, belong –, appertain- to; have respect to; answer to; interest.

bring -into relation with, – to bear upon; connect, associate, draw a parallel; link etc. 43.

Adj. relative; correlative etc. 12; cognate; relating to etc. *v.;* relative to, in relation with, referable *or* referrible to; belonging to etc. *v.;* appurtenant to, in common with.

related, connected; implicated, associated, affiliated, akin, allied to; collateral, cognate, congenial, kindred, affinitive, *en rapport*, in touch with.

approxima-tive, -ting; approaching; proportion-al, -ate, -able; allusive, comparable.

in the same -category etc. 75; like etc. 17; relevant etc. (*apt*) 23.

Adv. relatively etc. *adj.;* pertinently etc. 23.

thereof; as -to, – for, – respects, – re-gards; about; concerning etc, *v.;* anent relating –, as relates- to; with -relation, – reference, – respect, – regard-to; in respect of; while speaking –, *à propos* -of; in connection with; by the -way, – by; whereas; for –, in -as much as; in point of, as far as; on the -part, – score- of; *quoad hoc; pro re natâ;* under the -head etc. (*class*) 75- of; in the matter of, *in re.*

Phr. 'thereby hangs a tale.'

10. Irrelation. [Want, or absence of relation.]**—N.** irrelation, dissociation; inapplicability; inconnection; multifariousness; disconnection etc. (*disjunction*) 44; inconsequence, independence; incommensurability; irreconcilableness etc. (*disagreement*) 24; heterogeneity;

unconformity etc. 83; irrelevancy, impertinence, *nihil ad rem;* intrusion etc. 24.

V. have no -relation etc. 9 to, – bearing upon, – concern etc. 9 with, – business with; not -concern etc. 9; have -nothing to do with, – no business there; intrude, etc. 24.

bring –, drag –, haul –, lug- in head and shoulders.

Adj. irrelative, irrespective, unrelated, irrelated; arbitrary; independent, unallied; un-, dis-connected; adrift, isolated, insular; extraneous, strange, alien, foreign, outlandish, exotic.

not comparable, incommensurable, heterogeneous; unconformable etc. 83.

irrelevant; rambling etc. 279; inapplicable; not -pertinent, – to the purpose; impertinent, inapposite, beside the mark, *à propos de bottes;* away from –, foreign to –, beside- the -purpose, – question, – transaction, – point; misplaced etc. (*intrusive*) 24.

remote, far fetched, out of the way, forced, neither here nor there, quite another thing; detached, segregated, segregate.

multifarious; discordant etc. 24.

incidental, parenthetical, *obiter dictum,* episodic.

Adv. parenthetically etc. *adj.;* by the -way, – by; *en passant,* incidentally; irrespecitively etc. *adj.;* without reference, – regard- to; in the abstract etc. 87; *a se.*

11. Consanguinity. [Relations of kindred.]—N. consanguinity, relationship, kindred, blood; parentage etc. (*paternity*) 166; filiation, affiliation; lineage, agnation, connection, cognation, alliance; family -connection, – tie; ties of blood; blood relationship; nepotism.

kins-man, -folk; people; kith and kin; relation, -tive; connection; sib; next of kin; uncle, aunt, nephew, niece; cousin, -german; first –, second- cousin; cousin -once, – twice etc.- removed; near –, distant-relation; brother, sister, one's own flesh and blood.

family, patriarch, matriarch; fraternity; brother-, sister-, cousin-hood.

race, stock, generation; sept etc. 166 ; stirps, side; strain; breed, clan, tribe.

V. be -related etc. *adj.* – to; claim -relationship etc. *n.*- with.

Adj. related, akin, consanguineous, matrilinear, patrilineal, of the blood, family, allied, collateral; cog-, ag-, con-nate; kindred; affiliated, affine; fraternal, avuncular.

intimately –, nearly –, closely –, remotely – distantly--related, – allied; german.

12. Correlation. [Double or reciprocal relation.]—N. reciprocalness etc. *adj.;* recipro-city, - cality, -cation; mutuality, correlation, correspondence, interdependence; interchange etc. 148; exchange, barter; interrelation, interconnection; alternation, see-saw.

V. reciprocate, alternate; interchange etc. 148; exchange; counterchange; interact, correspond, mutualize, give and take.

Adj. reciprocal, mutual, commutual, correlative; alternate; interchangeable; international; correspondent, complementary, analogous.

Adv. *mutatis mutandis; vice versâ;* each other; by turns etc. 148; reciprocally etc. *adj.;* to and fro etc. 314.

13. Identity.—N. identity, sameness, oneness, ditto, homogeneity; unity, coincidence, coalescence; convertibility; equality etc. 27; self-ness, self, oneself; identification.

monotony, tautology etc. (*repetition*) 104. synonym.

fac-simile etc. (*copy*) 21; *alter ego* etc. (*similar*) 17; *ipsissima verba* etc. (*exactness*) 494; same; self –, very –, one and the same; very –, actual-thing, no other.

V. be -identical etc. *adj.;* match, coincide, coalesce.

treat as –, render--the same , –identical; identify; recognize the identity of.

Adj. identical; self, ilk; the -same etc. *n.;* self same; synonymous; one and the same.

coincid-, coalesc-ent, -ing; indistinguishable; one; equivalent etc. (*equal*) 27; much -the same, – of a muchness; unaltered.

Adv. identically etc. *adj.;* on all fours; ibid-, - em.

14. Contrariety. [Non-coincidence.]—N. contrariety, contrast, foil, antithesis, oppositeness; counterpole; contradiction; antagonism etc. (*opposition*) 708; counteraction etc. 179.

inversion etc. 218; the -opposite, – reverse, – inverse, – converse, – antipodes, – other extreme etc. 237.

antonym.

V. be -contrary etc. *adj.;* contrast with, oppose; differ *toto coelo.*

invert, reverse, turn the tables etc. 218.

contra-dict, -vene; antagonize etc. 708.

Adj. contrar-y, -ious, -iant; opposite, counter, dead against; ad-, con-, reverse; opposed, antithetical, contrasted, antipodean, antagonistic, opposing; conflicting, inconsistent, contradictory, at cross purposes; negative; hostile etc. 708.

differing *toto coelo;* diametrically opposite; as opposite as -black and white, – light and darkness, – fire and water, – the poles, as different as chalk from cheese; 'Hyperion to a satyr;' quite the -contrary, – reverse; no such thing, just the other way, *tout au contraire.*

Adv. contrarily etc. *adj.; contra,* contrariwise, *per contra,* on the contrary, nay rather; topsy-turvy; *vice versâ;* on the other hand etc. (*in compensation*) 30.

15. Difference.—N. difference, unlikeness; heterogeneity; vari-ance, -ation, -ety; diversity, dissimilarity etc. 18; disagreement etc. 24; disparity etc. (*inequality*) 28; distinction, contradistinction; distinctness; discrepancy, divergence, contrast etc. 18; nonconformity, incompatibility, antithesis.

discord etc. 713.

modification, moods and tenses.

nice -, – delicate –, subtle- distinction; shade of di rence, *nuance;* discrimination etc. 465; *diffe* 1.

different thing, something else, variant, apple

off another tree, horse of another color, another pair of shoes; this that or the other.
V. be -different etc. *adj.;* differ, vary, ablude, mismatch, contrast; diverge –, depart –, deviate- -from; divaricate; differ *-toto coelo, — longo intervallo.*
disagree etc. 713.
vary, modify etc. (*change*) 140.
discriminate etc. 465.
Adj. differing etc. *v.;* different, diverse, divided, heterogeneous; distinguishable; varied, modified; divergent, incongruous, diversified, various; discrepant, dissentient, differential; divers, all manner of; variform etc. 81; discordant etc. 713.
other, another, not the same; unequal etc. 28; unmatched; widely apart.
distinctive, characteristic; discriminative; distinghishing.
Adv. differently etc. *adj.*
Phr. *il y a fagots et fagots; tot nomines tot sententiae;* one man's meat is another man's poison.

16. Uniformity.—N. uniformity; homogeneity, -ousness; continuity, stability, consistency; connatural-ity, -ness; homology; accordance; conformity etc. 82; agreement etc. 23.
regularity, constancy, even tenor, routine; monotony, evenness, sameness, dead level; steadiness, equability, unity.
V. be -uniform etc. *adj.;* accord with etc. 23; run through.
become -uniform etc. *adj.;* conform to etc. 82.
render uniform etc. *adj.;* assimilate, level, smooth, dress.
Adj. uniform; homo-geneous, -logous; of a piece, consistent, steady; connatural; monotonous, changeless, dreary, even, invariable, equable, level, regular, stereotyped, unchanged, unvarying; methodical etc. 60; habitual etc. 613.
Adv. uniformly etc. *adj.;* uniformly with etc. (*conformably*) 82; in harmony with etc. (*agreeing*) 23; in a -rut, – groove.
always, ever etc. 112; invariably, without exception, never otherwise; by clock-work; endlessly etc. 112.
Phr. *ab uno disce omnes.*

16a. Non-uniformity. [Absence or want of uniformity.]– **N.** diversity, irregularity, unevenness; multiformity etc. 81; unconformity etc. 83; roughness etc. 256; heterogeneity, heteromorphism.
Adj. diversified, varied, irregular, uneven, rough etc. 256; multifarious; multiform etc. 81; of various kinds; all -manner, – sorts, – kinds-of.
Adv. in all manner of ways, here there and everywhere.

17. Similarity.—N. similarity, resemblance, likeness, similitude, semblance; affinity, approximation, parallelism; parity, agreement etc. 23; ana-logy, -logicalness; co.. espondence, equality etc.
connatural-ness, -ity; brotherhood, family likeness.

alliteration, rhyme, pun.
repetition etc. 104; sameness etc. (*identity*) 13; uniformity etc. 16.
analogue; the like; match, *pendant,* fellow, companion, pair, mate, twin, double, counterpart, brother, sister; one's second self, *alter ego,* chip of the old block, *par nobile fratrum, Arcades ambo,* birds of a feather, *et hoc genus omne.*
parallel; simile; type etc. (*metaphor*) 521; image etc. (*representation*) 554; photograph; close –, striking –, speaking –, faithful etc *adj.*
– likeness, – resemblance.
V. be -similar etc. *adj.;* look like, resemble, bear resemblance, favor; savor –, smack- of; approximate; parallel, match, rhyme with; take after; imitate etc. 19; run in pairs.
Adj. similar; resembling etc. *v.;* like, alike; twin.
analog-ous, -ical; parallel, of a piece; such as, so.
connatural, congeneric, allied to; corresponding, cognate; akin to etc. (*consanguineous*) 11.
approximate, much the same, near, close, something like, such like; a show of; mock, *pseudo,* simulating, representing.
exact etc. (*true*) 494; lifelike, faithful, realistic; true to -nature, – the life; the very image – pic-ure- of; for all the world like, *comme deux gouttes d'eau;* as like as -two peas, – it can stare; *instar omnium,* case in the same mold, ridiculously like.
Adv. as if, so to speak; as –, as if- it were; *quasi,* just as, *veluti in speculum.*

18. Dissimilarity.—N. dissimil-arity, -itude; unlikeness, diversity, disparity, dissemblance; divergence, inequality, difference etc. 15; novelty; variation, variety, originality, disguise.
V. be -unlike etc. *adj.;* vary etc. (*differ*) 15; bear no resemblance to, differ *toto coelo.*
render -unlike etc. *adj.;* vary etc. (*diversify*) 140.
Adj. dissimilar, unlike, disparate; of a different kind etc. (*class*) 75; unmatched, unique; new, novel; unprecedented etc. 83; original.
nothing of the kind; no such –, quite anotherthing; far from it, other than, cast in a different mold, *tertium quid,* as like a dock as a daisy, 'very like a whale;' as different as -chalk from cheese, – Macedon and Monmouth; *lucus a non lucendo.*
diversified etc. 16a.
Adv. otherwise, *alias.*

19. Imitation.—N. imitation; copying etc, *v.;* transcription; repetition, mimeograph, mimeotype, duplication, reduplication; quotation; reproduction.
mockery, mimicry, mime, simulation, personation; representation etc. 554; semblance, pretence; copy etc. 21; assimilation.
paraphrase, parody etc. 21.
plagiarism; forgery etc. (*falsehood*) 544.
imitator; echo, cuckoo, parrot, ape, monkey, mocking-bird, mimic, impersonator, copyist.
V. imitate, copy, mirror, reflect, reproduce, repeat, borrow; do like, echo, re-echo, catch; transcribe; match, parallel.

mock, take off, mimic, ape, simulate, personate, impersonate; forge; act etc. (*drama*) 599; represent*etc. 554; counterfeit, duplicate; portray, parody, travesty, caricature, burlesque.

follow -, tread- in the- -steps, - footsteps, - wake- of; pattern after, take pattern by; follow - suit, - the example of; walk in the shoes of, take a leaf out of another's book, strike in with; take -, model -after; emulate.

Adj. imitated etc. *v.*; mock, mimic; counterfeit, false, pseudo; modelled after, molded on, paraphrastic; literal; imitative, apish; secondhand; imitable; sham etc. 545.

Adv. literally, to the letter, strictly, precisely, *verbatim, literatim, sic, totidem verbis,* word for word, *mot à mot.*

Phr. like master like man.

20. Non-Imitation.—N. no imitation, genuineness, originality; creativeness.

Adj. unimitated, uncopied; unmatched, unparalleled; inimitable etc. 33; *unique,* original, primordial, primary, pristine, underived, firsthand, archetypal, prototypal.

20a. Variation.—N. variation; alteration etc. (*change*) 140. modification, moods and tenses; modulation.

divergency etc. 291; deviation etc. 279; aberration; innovation.

V. vary etc. (*change*) 140; deviate etc. 279; diverge etc. 291.

Adj. varied etc. *v.*; modified; dissimilar etc. 18; diversified etc. 16a.

21. Copy. [Result of imitation.]—N. copy, facsimile, counterpart, *effigies,* effigy, symbol, image, form, likeness, similitude, semblance, resemblance, cast, electrotype, stereotype, tracing, ectype; imitation etc. 19; model, representation, adumbration, study; counterfeit presentment, portrait etc. (*representment*) 554.

duplicate; transcript, -ion; reflex, -ion; shadow, echo; chip of the old block; reprint, reproduction, casting, engraving, replica; transfer; second edition etc. (*repetition*) 104; *réchauffé* apograph, fair copy; revise.

parody, caricature, cartoon, burlesque. travesty, paraphrase.

servile -copy, - imitation; counterfeit etc. (*deception*) 545; *pasticcio.*

Adj. faithful; lifelike etc. (*similar*) 17

22. Prototype. [Thing copied.]—N. prototype, original, model, pattern, founding, precedent, standard, scantling, type, arche-, anti-type; protoplast, copy-book, module, exemplar, example, ensample, specimen; paradigm; guide; templet; lay-figure.

text, copy, manuscript, MS., design; fugleman, keynote.

die, mold; matrix, engraving, last, plasm; pro-, proto-plasm; mint; seal, punch, *intaglio,* negative, stamp.

V. be -, set- an example; set a copy; standardize.

23. Agreement.—N. agreement; ac-cord, -cordance; unison, harmony, concord etc. 714; concordance, concert, understanding, convention, *entente -cordiale, consortium,* consensus of opinion, pact, mutual understanding, unanimity.

conformity etc. 82; conformance; uniformity etc. 16; consonance, consentaneousness, consistency; congruity, -ence; keeping; congeniality; correspondence, concinnity, parallelism, apposition, union.

fitness, aptness etc. *adj.*; relevancy; pertinence, -cy; sortance; case in point; aptitude, propriety, applicability, admissibility, commensurability, compatibility, suitability; cognation etc (*relation*) 9.

adaptation, adjustment, arrangement, graduation, accommodation; reconcil-iation -ement; assimilation; attunement.   .'

consent etc. (*assent*) 448; concurrence etc. 178; co-operation etc. 709.

right man in the right place, very thing; quite - just- the thing.

be -accordant etc. *adj.*; agree, accord, harmonize; correspond, tally, respond; meet, suit, fit, befit, do, adapt itself to; fall in -, chime in -, square -, quadrate -, consort -, comport- with; dovetail, assimilate; fit like a glove; fit to a -tittle, - T; match etc. 17; become one.

consent etc. (*assent*) 488.

render -accordant etc. *adj.*; fit, suit, adapt, accommodate; graduate; adjust etc. (*render equal*) 27; dress, regulate, readjust; accord, harmonize, reconcile; fadge, dovetail, square.

Adj. agreeing, suiting etc. *v.*; in accord, accordant, concordant, consonant, congruous, consentaneous, correspondent, corresponding, homologous, congenial; becoming; harmonious, reconcilable, conformable; in -accordance, - harminy, - keeping, - unison, etc. *n.*;-with; at one with, of one mind, of a piece; consistent, compatible, proportionate, answerable; commensurate; on all fours.

. apt, apposite, pertinent, pat; to the -point, - - purpose; happy, felicitous, germane, *ad rem,* in point, bearing upon, applicable, relevant, admissible.

fit, adapted, *in loco, à propos,* appropriate, seasonable; sortable, suitable, idoneous, deft; meet etc. (*expedient*) 646.

at home, in one's proper element.

Adv. *à propos of;* pertinently etc. *adj.*; pro *rata.*

Phr. *rem acu tetigisti,* the cap fits.

24. Disagreement.—N. disagreement, discord, -cordance; disunion, dissonance, dissidence, discrepancy; unconformity etc. 83; incongru-ity, -ence; discongruity, *mésalliance, oxymoron;* jarring etc. *v.*; clash, collision, dissension etc. 713; conflict etc. (*opposition*) 708; controversy etc. 720; falling out, wrangle, argument.

disparity, mismatch, misfit, disproportion; disproportionateness etc. *adj.*; variance, divergence, repugnance.

unfitness etc. *adj.*; inaptitude, impropriety; inapplicability etc. *adj.*; inconsistency, inconcinnity; irrelevancy etc. (*irrelation*) 10.

misjoin-ing, -der; syncretism, intrusion, interference; *concordia discors.*
fish out of water.
V. disagree; clash, quarrel, jar etc. *(discord)* 713; interfere, intrude, come amiss; not concern etc. 10; mismatch; *hymano capiti cervicem jungere equinam.*
Adj. disagreeing etc. v.; discordant, discrepant; at -variance, − war; hostile, antagonistic, repugnant, factious, contradictory, dissentious, incompatible, irreconcilable, inconsistent with; unconformable, exceptional etc. 83; intrusive, incongruous; disproportionate, -ed; unharmonious; unconsonant; divergent, repugnant to.
inapt, unapt, inappropriate, inept, infelicitous, improper; unsuit-ed, -able; inapplicable; un-fit, -fitting, -befitting; unbecoming; ill-timed, illadapted, unseasonable, *mal â propos,* inadmissible; inapposite etc. *(irrelevant)* 10.
uncongenial; ill-assorted, -sorted, -matched; mis-matched, -mated, -joined, -placed; unaccommodating, irreducible, uncommensurable, unsympathetic.
out of -character, − keeping, − proportion, − joint, − tune, − place, − season, − its element; at -odds, − variance with.
Adv. in -defiance, − contempt, − spite-of; discordantly etc. *adj.; à tort et à travers.*

25. Quantity. [Absolute quantity.]—N. quantity, magnitude; size etc. *(dimensions)* 192; amplitude, mass, amount, *quantum,* measure, measurement, substance, strength.
[Science of quantity.] Mathematics, Mathesis.
[Definite or finite quantity] arm-, hand-, mouth-, spoon-, thimble-, capful; stock, batch, lot, dose, ration, quotum, quota, pittance, driblet, part, portion etc. 51.
Adj. quantitative, some, any, more or less.
Adv. to the tune of.

26. Degree. [Relative quantity.]—N. degree, grade, extent, measure, proportion, amount, ratio, stint, standard, height, pitch; reach, amplitude, range, scope, size, caliber; gradation, shade; tenor, compass; sphere, station, rank, standing; rate, way, sort.
point, mark, step, stage etc. *(term)* 71; intensity, strength etc. *(greatness)* 31.
V. compare, graduate, calibrate, measure.
Adj. comparative; gradual, shading off, gradational; within the bounds etc. *(limit),* 233.
Adv. by degrees, gradually, inasmuch, *pro tanto;* how-ever, -soever; step by step, bit by bit, little by little, inch by inch, drop by drop, gradatim; by -inches, − slow degrees, − little and little; in some -degree, − measure; to some extent; just a bit.

27. Equality. [Sameness of quantity or degree.]—N. equality, parity, co-extension, symmetry, balance, poise; evenness, monotony, level.
equivalence; equi-pollence, -poise, -librium, -ponderance; par, quits; not a pin to choose; distinction without a difference, six of one and half a dozen of the other; identity etc. 13; similarity etc. 17; isotropism; coequality.
equalization, equation, equilibration, coordination, adjustment, readjustment.

drawn -game, -battle, draw, stalemate; neck and neck- race; tie, dead heat.
match, peer, compeer, equal, mate, fellow, brother; equivalent.
V. be -equal etc. *adj.;* equal, match, reach, keep pace with, run'abreast; come −, amount −, come upto; be −, lie- on a level with; balance; cope with; come to the same thing; level off.
render -equal etc. *adj.;* equalize, level, dress, balance, equate, handicap, give points, trim, adjust, poise; fit, accommodate; adapt etc. *(render accordant)* 23; strike a balance; establish −, restore- equality, − equilibrium; readjust; stretch on the bed of Procrustes.
Adj. equal, even, level, monotonous, coequal, symmetrical, coordinate; on a -par, − level, − footing- with; up to the mark; equiparent.
equivalent, tantamount; quits; homologous; synonymous etc. 522; resolvable into, convertible, much at one, as broad as long, neither more nor less; much the same −, the same thing −, as good- as; all -one, − the same; equi-pollent, -ponderant, -ponderous, -balanced; equalized etc. *v.;* drawn; half and half; isochronous; isoperimetrical.
Adv. equally etc. *adj.; pari passu, ad eundem, caeteris paribus; in equilibrio;* to all intents and purposes.
Phr. it -comes, -adds up, − amounts- to the same thing.

28. Inequality. [Difference of quantity or degree.]—N. inequality; dis-, im-parity; odds; difference etc. 15; ill-balanced; unevenness; inclination of the balance. partiality; shortcoming; casting −make- weight; superiority etc. 33; inferiority etc. 34.
V. be -unequal etc. *adj.;* countervail; have −, give- the advantage; turn the scale; kick the beam; topple, -over; over-match etc. 33; not come up to etc. 34.
Adj. unequal, uneven, disparate, partial; un-, over-balanced; top-heavy, lop-sided.
Adv. *haud passibus aequis.*

29. Mean.—N. mean, medium, intermedium, average, run of the mill, normal, balance; mediocrity, generality, rule, ordinary -run, -ruck; golden mean etc. *(mid-course)* 628; middle etc. 68; compromise etc. 774; neutrality; middle point, middle course.
V. split the difference; take the -average etc. *n.;* reduce to a -mean etc. *n.;* strike a balance, pair off.
Adj. mean, intermediate; medial; middle etc. 68; average, normal, standard, neutral; middling, moderate.
médiocre, middle-class; *bourgeois,* commonplace etc. *(unimportant)* 643.
Adv. on an average, in the long run; taking -one with another, − all things together, − it for all in all; *communibus annis,* in round numbers.

30. Compensation.—N. compensation, equation; commutation; indemnification; compromise etc. 774; neutralization, nullification; counteraction etc. 179; reaction; measure for measure; retaliation etc. 718; equalization etc. 27; redemption, recoupment, recompense.

set-off, offset; make- casting-weight; counterpoise, equipoise, ballast; indemnity, reparation etc. 790; equivalent, *quid pro quo;* bribe, hushmoney, tribute etc. 784; amends etc. *(atonement)* 952; counterclaim, counterbalance, equiponderance, countervail, cross demand.

V. make -amends; – compensation; compensate, -pense; indemnify; counter-act, -vail, - poise; equiponderate; balance; out-, over-, counterbalance; set off, offset, cancel; hedge, square, give and take; make up -for, – lee way; cover, fill up, neutralize, nullify; equalize etc. 27; make good; redeem etc. *(atone)* 952; recoup, pay etc. 973.

Adj. compensat-ing, -ory; amendatory, reparative, countervailing etc. *v.;* in the opposite scale; equivalent etc. *(equal)* 27.

Adv. in -return, – consideration; but, however, yet, still, notwithstanding; neverthe-, nathless; although, though; al-, how-beit; in spite of, despite; mauger; at -all events, – any rate; be that as it may, for all that, even so, on the other hand, at the same time, *quoad minus, quand même,* however that may be; after all, – is said and done; taking one thing with another etc. *(average)* 29.

31. Greatness.—**N.** greatness etc. *adj.;* magnitude; size etc. *(dimensions)* 192; multitude. etc. *(number)* 102; immensity, enormity, infinity etc. 105; might, strength, intensity, fulness; importance etc. 642; fame etc. 873.

great quantity, quantity, deal, power, sight, pot, volume, world; mass, heap etc. *(assemblage)* 72; stock etc. *(store)* 636; peck, bushel, load, cargo; cart –, wagon –, car –, truck –, shipload; flood, spring tide; abundance etc. *(sufficiency)* 639.

principal –, chief –, main –, greater –, major –, best –, essential- part; bulk, mass etc. *(whole)* 50.

V. be -great etc. *adj.;* run high, soar, loom up, tower, bulk large, transcend; rise –, carry- to a great height; know no bounds; scale, overtop, ascend.

enlarge etc. *(increase)* 35, *(expand)* 194.

Adj. great; greater etc. 33; large, considerable, fair, above par; big, massive, huge etc. *(large in size)* 192; ample; abundant etc. *(enough)* 639; Herculean etc. 159; full, intense, strong, sound, passing, heavy, plenary, deep, high; signal, at its height, in the zenith.

world-wide, wide-spread, extensive; wholesale; many etc. 102.

goodly, noble, precious, mighty; sad, grave, serious; far gone, arrant, downright; utter, -most; crass, gross, arch, profound, intense, consummate; rank, unmitigated, red-hot, desperate; glaring, flagrant, stark staring; thorough-paced, - going; roaring, thumping, thundering, strapping, whacking; extraordinary; important etc. 642; unsurpassed etc. *(supreme)* 33; complete etc. 52.

vast, immense, enormous, extreme; inordinate, excessive, extravagant, exorbitant, outrageous, preposterous, unconscionable, swinging, monstrous, over-grown; towering, stupendous, prodigious, astonishing, incredible; terrific, frightful; marvelous etc. *(wonder)* 870; grand.

unlimited etc. *(infinite)* 105; unapproachable,

unutterable, indescribable, ineffable, unspeakable, inexpressible, beyond expression, fabulous.

un-diminished, -abated, -reduced, -restricted.

absolute, positive, stark, decided, unequivocal, essential, perfect, finished.

remarkable, of mark, marked, pointed, veriest; noticeable, uncommon, noteworthy, eminent etc. 873.

Adv. [in a positive degree] truly etc. *(truth)* 494; decidedly, unequivocally, purely, absolutely, seriously, essentially, fundamentally, radically, downright, in all conscience; for the most part, in the main.

[in a complete degree] entirely etc. *(completely)* 52; abundantly, etc. *(sufficiently)* 639; widely, far and wide.

[in a great or high degree] greatly etc. *adj.;* much, muckle, well, indeed, very, very much, a deal, no end of, most not a little; pretty, – well; enough, in a great measure, passing richly; to a - large, – great, – gigantic- extent; on a large scale; so; never –, ever- so; ever so much; by wholesale; mightily, mighty, powerfully; with a witness, *ultra,* in the extreme, extremely, exceedingly, intensely, exquisitely, acutely, indefinitely, immeasurably; beyond -compare, – comparison, – measure, – all bounds; incalculably, infinitely.

[in a supreme degree] pre-eminently, superlatively etc. *(superiority)* 33.

[in a too great degree] immoderately, unduly, monstrously, grossly, preposterously, inordinately, exorbitantly, excessively, enormously, out of all proportion, with a vengeance.

[in a marked degree] particularly, remarkably, singularly, curiously, uncommonly, unusually, peculiarly, notably, signally, strikingly, pointedly, mainly, chiefly; famously, egregiously, prominently, glaringly, emphatically, strangely, wonderfully, amazingly, surprisingly, astonishingly, incredibly, marvelously, awfully, stupendously.

[in an exceptional degree] peculiarly etc. *(unconformity)* 83.

[in a violent degree] furiously etc. *(violence)* 173; severely, desperately, tremendously, extravagantly, confoundedly, deucedly, devilishly, with a vengeance; *à –, à toute- outrance.*

[in a painful degree] painfully, sadly, grossly, sorely, bitterly, piteously, grievously, miserably, cruelly, woefully, lamentably, shockingly, frightfully, dreadfully, fearfully, terribly, horribly, distressingly, balefully.

32. Smallness.—**N.** smallness etc. *adj.;* littleness etc. *(small size)* 193; tenuity; paucity; fewness etc. *(small number)* 103; meanness, insignificance etc. *(unimportance)* 643; mediocrity, moderation.

small quantity, *modicum, minimum;* vanishing point; material point, electron, atom, particle, molecule, corpuscle, point, dab, fleck, speck, dot, mote, jot, iota, ace; *minutiae,* details; look, thought, idea, *soupçon,* whit, tittle, shade, shadow; spark, *scintilla,* gleam; touch, cast; grain, scruple, granule, globule, minim, sup, sip, sop, spice, drop, droplet; sprinkling, dash, smack, tinge, tincture; inch, patch, scantling, dole; scrap, shred, tag, splinter, rag, tatter, cantlet, flitter, gobbet, mite, bit, morsel, crumb, seed, fritter, shive; snip, -pet; snick, snack, snatch, slip, scrag; chip, -ping; shiver, sliver, driblet, clipping, paring, shaving, hair.

nutshell; thimble-, spoon-, hand-, cap-, mouthful; fragment; fraction etc. (*part*)51; drop in the ocean, drop in the bucket.

animalcule etc. 193.

trifle etc. (*unimportant thing*) 643; mere −, next to- nothing; hardly anything; just enough to swear by; the shadow of a shade.

finiteness, finite quantity.

V. be -shall etc. *adj.*; lie in a nutshell.

diminish etc. (*decrease*) 36, (*contract*) 195.

Adj. small, little, tiny, weeny; diminutive etc. (*small in size*) 193; minute; minikin, fine, inconsiderable, dribbling, paltry etc. (*unimportant*) 643; faint etc. (*weak*) 160; slender, light, slight, scanty, scant, limited; meager etc. (*insufficient*) 640; sparing; few etc. 103; low, so-so, middling, tolerable, no great shakes; below −, under-par, − the mark; at a low ebb; half-way; moderate, modest; tender, subtle; petty, shallow, skin-deep.

inappreciable, evanescent, infinite-simal, homeopathic, very small, atomic, molecular, ultra-, -microscopic.

petty, shallow etc. 499.

mere, simple, sheer, stark, bare; near run.

Adv. [in a small degree] to a small extent, on a small scale; a -little, − wee, − tiny bit; slightly etc. *adj.*; imperceptibly; miserably, wretchedly; insufficiently etc. 640; imperfectly; faintly etc. 160; passably, pretty well, well enough.

[in a certain or limited degree] partially, in part; in −, to a certain degree; to a certain extent; comparatively; some, rather; in some -degree, -measure; some-thing, -what; simply, only, purely, merely; at −, at the- -least, − most; ever so little, as little as may be, *tant soit peu*, in ever so small a degree; thus far, *pro tanto;* within bounds, in a manner, after a fashion.

almost, nearly, well nigh, short of, not quite, all but; near −, close- upon; *peu s'en faut*, near the mark; within an -ace, − inch- of; on the brink of; scarcely, hardly, barely, only just, no more than.

[in an uncertain degree] about, therabouts, somewhere about, nearly, say; be the same -more, − little more- or less.

[in no degree] no- ways, − wise; not -at all, − in the least, − a bit, − a bit of it, − a whit, − a jot, − a shadow; in no -wise, − respect; by no -means, − manner of means; on no account, at no hand.

33. Superiority.—N. superiority, supremacy, majority; greatness etc. 31; advantage, odds, pull; preponderance, -ation; predominance, vantage ground, coign of vantage, prevalence, partiality; personal superiority; sovereignty etc. 737; nobility etc. (*rank*) 875; Triton among the min-nows, *primus inter pares, nulli secundus*, super-man; captain etc. 475.

supremacy, pre-eminence; primacy, lead, *maximum;* record; climax, crest, top; culmination etc. (*summit*) 210; transcendence; *ne plus ultra;* lion's share, Benjamin's mess; excess; bisque, surplus etc. (*remainder*) 40, (*redundance*) 641.

V. be -superior etc. *adj.*; exceed, excel, transcend; out-do, -balance, -weigh, -rival, -Herod, outrank, pass, surpass, surmount, get ahead of; over-top, -ride, -pass, -balance, -weigh, -match; top, o'er-top, cap, beat, win out, cut out; beat hollow; outstrip etc. 303; eclipse, throw into the shade, take the shine out of, put one's nose out of joint; have the -upper hand, − whip hand of, − advantage; turn the scale, play first fiddle etc. (*importance*) 642; preponderate, predominate, prevail; precede, take .precedence, come first; come to a head, culminate; beat etc. all others, bear the palm; break the record, take the cake.

become −, render- -larger, etc. (*increase*) 35, (*expand*) 194.

Adj. superior, greater, major, higher; exceeding etc. *v.*; great etc. 31; distinguished, *ultra;* vaulting; more than a match for.

supreme, greatest, maximal, maximum, utmost, paramount, pre-eminent, foremost, crowning; first-rate etc. (*important*) 642, (*excellent*) 648; unrivalled; peer-, match-less; none such, second to none, *sans pareil;* un-paragoned, -paralleled, -equalled, -approached, -surpassed; superlative, inimitable, *facile princeps*, incomparable, sovereign, without parallel, *nulli secundus, ne plus ultra;* beyond -compare, − comparison; culminating etc. (*topmost*) 210; transcendent, -ental; *plus royaliste que le Roi.*

increased etc. (*added to*) 35; enlarged etc. (*expanded*) 194.

Adv. beyond, more, over; over −, above- the mark; above par; upwards −, in advance- of; over and above; at the top of the scale, on the crest, at it height.

[in a superior or supreme degree] eminently, egregiously, pre-eminently, surpassing, prominently, superlatively, supremely, above all, of all things, the most, to crown all, *par excellence*, principally, especially, particularly, peculiarly, *a fortiori*, even, yea, still more.

Phr. 'we shall not look upon his like again.'

34. Inferiority.—N. inferiority, minority, subordinancy; shortcoming, deficiency; handicap; *minimum;* smallness etc. 32; imperfection, shabbiness.

[personal inferiority] commonalty etc. 876; subordinate, substitute, sub.

V. be -inferior etc. *adj.*; fall −, come- short of; not -pass, −.come up to; want.

become −, render- smaller etc. (decrease) 36, (*contract*) 195; hide its diminished head, retire into the shade, yield the palm, play second fiddle, take a back seat; bow.

Adj. inferior, smaller; small etc. 32; minor, less, lesser, deficient, minus, lower, subordinate, secondary; second-rate etc. (*imperfect*) 651; sub, subaltern; thrown into the shade; weighed in the balance and found wanting; not fit to hold a candle to.

least, smallest etc. (*see* little, small etc. 193); lowest.

diminished etc. (*decreased*) 36; reduced etc. (*contracted*) 195; unimportant etc. 643.

Adv. less; under −, below- -the mark, − par; at -the bottom of the scale, − a low ebb, − a disadvantage; short of, under.

35. Increase.—N. increase; augmentation, addition, enlargement, extension; dilatation etc. (*expansion*) 194; multiplication; increment, accretion; accession etc. 37; production etc. 161; development, growth; aggrandizement, aggravation, intensification; rise; ascent etc. 305; anabasis; ex-aggeration, -acerbation; spread etc. (*dispersion*) 73; flood-, spring-, -tide; gain, produce, profit etc. 618; booty, plunder etc. 793.

V. increase, augment, add to, enlarge; dilate etc. (*expand*) 194; grow, wax, mount, swell, get ahead, gain strength; advance; run –, shoot- up; rise; ascend etc. 305; sprout etc. 194.

aggrandize; raise; exalt; deepen, heighten; lengthen; thicken; strengthen; intensify, enhance, inflate, magnify, double, redouble; multiply; aggravate, exaggerate; ex-asperate, -acerbate; add fuel to the flame, *oleum addere camino,* superadd etc. (*add*) 37; spread etc. (*disperse*) 73.

Adj. increased etc. *v.;* on the increase, undiminished, additional etc. (*added*) 37; increasing etc. *v.;* growing, crescent, intensive, cumulative.

Adv. *crescendo,* increasingly.

Phr. *vires acquirit eundo.*

36. Non-Increase, Decrease.—N. decrease, diminution, lessening etc. *v.;* subtraction etc. 38; reduction, abatement, declension; shrinkage etc. (*contraction*) 195; coarctation; abridgment etc. (*shortening*) 201; extenuation.

subsidence, catabasis, wane, ebb-, neap-tide, decline; descent etc. 306; decrement, reflux, depreciation; erosion, wear and tear, deterioration etc. 659; anticlimax; mitigation etc. (*moderation*) 174.

V. decrease, diminish, lessen; abridge etc. (*shorten*) 201; shrink etc. (*contract*) 195; drop –, fall –, tail- off; fall away, waste, wear, erode; wane, ebb, decline; descent etc. 306; subside; deliquesce, melt –, die -away; retire into the shade, hide its diminished head, fall to a low ebb, run low, languish, decay, crumble, consume away.

bate, abate, dequantitate; discount; depreciate; extenuate, lower, weaken, attenuate, fritter away; mitigate etc.(*moderate*) 174; belittle, minimize; dwarf, throw into the shade; keep down, reduce etc. 195; shorten etc. 201; subtract etc. 38.

Adj. unincreased etc. (*see* increase etc. 35); decreased etc. *v.;* decreasing etc. *v.;* on the -wane etc. *n.;* deliquescent.

Adv. *diminuendo, decrescendo,* decreasingly.

37. Addition.—N. addition, annexation, adjection; junction etc. 43; super-position, -addition, -junction, -fetation; accession, reinforcement; increase etc. 35; increment, supplement; accompaniment etc. 88; interposition etc. 228; insertion etc. 300; summation etc. 85; adjunct etc. 39.

V. add, annex, adject, affix, attach, superadd. subjoin, superpose; clap –, saddle- on; tack to, postfix, append, tag; ingraft; saddle with; sprinkle; introduce etc. (*interpose*) 228; insert etc. 300.

become added, accrue; ad-, supervene; add up etc. 85.

reinforce, strengthen, swell the ranks of; augment etc. 35.

Adj. added etc. *v.;* additional; supplement, -al, -ary; suppletory, subjunctive; adjec-, adsci-, ascititious; additive, extra, spare, further, fresh, more, new, ulterior, other, auxiliary, supernumerary, accessory.

Adv. in addition, more, plus, extra; and, also, likewise, too, furthermore, further, item; and - also, – eke; else, besides, to boot, *et cetera;* etc.; and so -on, – forth; into the bargain, *cum multis aliis,* over and above, moreover.

with, withal; including, inclusive, as well as, not to mention, let alone; together –, along –, coupled –, in conjunction- with; conjointly; jointly etc. 43.

38. Non-Addition. Subduction.—N. sub-traction, -duction; deduction, retrenchment; removal; ab-, sub-lation; abstraction etc. (*taking*) 789; garbling etc. *v.;* mutilation, detruncation; amputation, severance; abs-, ex-, re-cision; curtailment etc. 201; minuend, subtrahend; decrease etc. 36; abrasion.

V. sub-tract, -duct; rebate, de-duct, – duce; bate, retrench; remove, withdraw; take – from, – away; detract.

garble, mutilate, amputate, sever, detruncate; cut -off, – away, – out; expurgate; abscind, excise; pare, thin, prune, decimate; abrade, scrape, file; geld, castrate, emasculate, unman, spay, caponize; eliminate.

diminish etc. 36; curtail etc. (*shorten*) 201; deprive of etc. (*take*) 789; weaken.

Adj. subtracted etc. *v.;* subtractive.

tailless, acaudal.

Adv. in -deduction etc. *n.;* less; short of; minus, without, except, excepting, with the exception of, barring, bar, save, exclusive of, save and except, with a reservation.

39. Adjunct. [Thing added.]—N. adjunct, addit-ion, -ament; *additum,* affix, appendage, annex; augment, -ation; increment, reinforcement, supernumerary, accessory, item; garnish, sauce; accompaniment etc. 88; adjective, *addendum,* accession, complement, supplement; continuation; extension, subscript, tag, appendix, postscript, interlineation, interpolation, insertion.

rider, codicil, off-shoot, episode, side issue, corollary; piece; flap, lapel, label, tab, strip, fold, lappet, apron, skirt, embroidery, trappings, *cortège;* tail, suffix etc. (*sequel*) 65; wing.

Adj. additional etc. 37.

Adv. in addition etc. 37.

40. Remainder. [Thing remaining.]—N. remainder, residue; remains, *remanet,* remnant, rest, relic, relict; leavings, heel-tap, odds and ends, cheese-parings, candle ends, orts; *residuum;* dottle, dregs, etc. (*dirt*) 653; refuse etc. (*useless*) 645; stubble, result, educt; fag-end, stub; ruins, wreck, skeleton, stump; *alluvium.*

surplus, overplus, excess; balance, complement; superfluity etc. (*redundance*) 641; survival, -ance; afterglow.

V. remain; be -left etc. *adj.;* exceed, survive; leave.

Adj. remaining, left; left -behind, – over;

residu-al, -ary; over, odd; unconsumed, sedimentary; surviving; net; exceeding, over and above; outlying, -standing; cast off etc. 782; superfluous etc. (*redundant*) 641.

V. remain; be -left; left -behind, − over; redidual, -ary; over, odd; unconsumed, sedimentary; surviving; net; exceeding, over and above; outlying, -standing; cast off etc. 782; superfluous etc. (*redundant*) 641.

40a. Decrement. [Thing deducted.]—N. decrement, discount, rebate, defect, loss, deduction, eduction, tare; drawback; waste, wastage; reprise.

41. Mixture. [Forming a whole without coherence.]—N. mix-, admix-, commix-ture, -tion, mingling; commixion, immixture, interfusion, intermixture, alloyage, matrimony; junction etc. 43; combination etc. 48; entanglement, interlacing; miscegenation, interbreeding.

impregnation; in-, dif-, suf-, transfusion; infiltration; seasoning, sprinkling, interlarding; interpolation etc. 228; adulteration, sophistication.

[Thing mixed] tinge, tincture, touch, dash, smack, sprinkling, spice, seasoning, infusion, *soupçon*.

[Compound resulting from mixture] alloy, brass, bronze, pewter etc.; amalgam, *magma*, blend, half-and-half, *mélange, tertium, quid*, ·miscellany, *ambigu*, medley, mess, hash, hotchpotch, hodgepodge, *pasticcio*, patchwork, odds and ends, all sorts; jumble etc. (*disorder*) 59; salad, sauce, mash, *omnium gatherum*, gallimaufry, ragout, *olla podrida, olio*, salmagundi, *potpourri*, Noah's ark; texture, mingled yarn; mosaic etc. (*variegation*) 440.

half-blood, -caste, -breed, Eurasian; mulatto; terc-, quart-, quinteron etc.; quad-, octo-roon; *griffo, zambo;* cross, hybrid, mongrel etc. 83.

V. mix; join etc. 43; combine etc. 48; com-, im-, inter-mix; mix up with, mingle; com-, inter-, be-mingle; shuffle etc. (*derange*) 61; pound together; hash −, stir- up; knead, brew; impregnate with; interlard etc. (*interpolate*) 228; inter-twine, -weave etc. 219; associate with, miscegenate, interbreed.

be mixed etc.; get among, be entangled with.

instil, imbue; in-, suf-, trans-fuse; infiltrate, dash, tinge, tincture, season, sprinkle, besprinkle, attemper, medicate, blend, cross; alloy, amalgamate, compound, adulterate, sophisticate, infect.

Adj. mixed etc. *v.;* implex, composite, half-and-half, linsey-wolsey, hybrid, mongrel, heterogeneous; motley etc. (*variegated*) 440; miscellaneous, promiscuous, indiscriminate; miscible.

Adv. among, amongst, amid, amidst, with; in the midst of, in the crowd.

42. Simpleness [Freedom from mixture.]—N. simpleness etc. *adj.;* purity, homogeneity.

elimination; sifting etc. *v.;* purification etc. (*cleanness*) 652.

V. render -simple etc. *adj.;* simplify.

sift, winnow, bolt, eliminate; narrow down; get rid of, exclude etc. 55; clear; purify etc. (*clean*) 652; disentangle etc. (*disjoin*) 44.

Adj. simple, uniform, of a piece, homogeneous, single, pure, clear, sheer, neat; Attic.

un-mixed, -mingled, -blended, -combined, -compounded; elementary, undecomposed; unadulterated, -sophisticated, -alloyed, -tinged, -fortified; pure and simple.

free −, exempt- from; exclusive.

Adv. simply etc. *adj.;* only.

43. Junction.—N. junction; joining etc. *v.;* joinder, union; con-nection, -junction, -jugation, compendency, annex-ion, -ation, -ment; coalition; astriction, attachment, compagination, vincture, ligation, alligation; accouplement; marriage etc. (*wedlock*) 903; infibulation, inosculation, symphysis, anastomosis, confluence, communication, concatenation; concurrence, meeting, reunion; assemblage etc. 72.

copulation, coition, intercourse.

joint, joining, juncture, chiasma, pivot, hinge, articulation, commissure, seam, suture, gusset, stitch, splice; link etc. 45; miter, mortise.

closeness, tightness etc. *adj.;* coherence etc. 46; combination etc. 48.

V. join, unite; con-join, -nect; associate; put −, lay −, clap −, hang −, lump −, hold −, piece −, tack −, fix −, bind up- together; embody, re-embody; roll into one.

attach, fix, affix, saddle on, fasten, bind, secure, clinch, twist, make -fast etc. *adj.;* tie, pinion, string, strap, sew, lace, stitch, tack, paste, knit, button, buckle, hitch, lash, truss, bandage, braid, splice, swathe, gird, tether, moor, picket, harness, chain; fetter etc. (*restrain*) 751; lock, latch, belay, brace, hook, grapple, leash, couple, accouple, link, yoke, bracket; marry etc. (*wed*) 903; bridge over, span.

pin, nail, bolt, hasp, clasp, clamp, screw, rivet; impact, solder, braze, cement, set; weld −, fuse-together; wedge, rabbet, mortise, miter, jam, dovetail, enchase; graft, ingraft, inosculate; en-, in-twine; inter-link, -lace, -twine, -twist, -weave; entangle; twine round, belay; tighten; trice −, screw-up.

be -joined etc.; hang −, hold-'together; cohere etc. 46.

Adj. joined etc. *v.;* joint; con-joint, -junct; corporate, compact; hand in hand.

firm, fast, close, tight, taut, taught, tense, secure, set, intervolved; in-separable, -dissoluble, -secable, -severable.

Adv. jointly etc. *adj.;* in conjunction with etc. (*in addition to*) 37; fast, firmly etc. *adj.;* intimately.

44. Disjunction.—N. dis-junction, -connection, -unity, -union, -association, -engagement, -sociation; discontinuity etc. 70; inconnection; abstraction, -edness; isolation; insul-arity, -ation; oasis; separateness etc. *adj.; disjecta membra;* dispersion etc. 73; apportionment etc. 786.

separation; parting etc. *v.;* detachment, segregation; divorce, sejunction, seposition; diduction, diremption, discerption; elision; *caesura*, division, subdivision, break, fracture, rupture; compartition; dis-memberment, -integration, -location; luxation; sever-, dis-severance; scission; re-, ab-scission; circumcision;

lacer-, dilacer-ation; dis-, ab-ruption; avulsion, divulsion; section, resection, cleavage; fission; separability; separatism.

fissure, breach, rent, split, rift, crack, slit, slot, incision.

dissection, anatomy; decomposition etc. 49; cutting instrument etc. (*sharpness*) 253; saw.

V. be -disjoined etc.; come −, fall- -off, − to pieces; peel off; get loose.

dis-join, -connect, -engage, -unite, -sociate, -pair; divorce, part, dispart, detach, uncouple, separate, cut off, rescind, segregate; set −, keep-apart; insulate, isolate; throw out of gear; cut adrift; loose; un-loose, -do, -bind, -tie, -hitch, -chain, -lock etc. (*fix*) 43, -pack, -ravel; disentangle; set free etc. (*liberate*) 750.

sunder, divide, subdivide, sectionalize, sever, dissever, abscind; cut; segment; in-cide, -cise; circumcise; saw, snip, nib, nip, cleave, rive, rend, slit, split, splinter, chip, crack, snap, break, tear, burst; rend etc. -asunder, − in twain; wrench, rupture, shatter, shiver, cranch, crunch, craunch, chop; rip up; hack, hew, slash; whittle; haggle, hackle, discind, lacerate, scamble, mangle, gash, hash, slice.

cut up, carve, quarter, dissect, anatomize; take −, pull −, pick −, tear- to pieces; tear to tatters, − piecemeal; divellicate; skin etc. 226; dis-integrate, -member, -branch, -band; disperse etc. 73; dis-locate, -joint; break up; mince; comminute etc. (*pulverize*) 330; distribute, apportion etc. 786.

part, − company; separate, leave; alienate, estrange.

Adj. disjoined etc. *v.;* discontinuous etc. 70; bipartite, multipartite, abstract; digitate; disjunctive; isolated etc. *v.;* insular, separate, disparate, discrete, apart, asunder, far between, loose, free; unattached, -annexed, -associated, -connected; distinct; adrift; straggling; rift, reft, cleft, split.

[capable of being divided] scissile, partible, divisible, separable, severable, detachable.

Adv. separately etc. *adj.;* one by one, severally, apart; adrift, asunder, in twain; in the abstract, abstractedly.

45. Vinculum. [Connecting medium.]—**N.** vinculum, link, *nexus*; connec-tive, -tion; junction etc. 43; bond of union, copula, intermedium, hyphen; bracket; bridge, stepping-stone, isthmus.

bond, tendon, tendril; cord, -age; riband, ribbon, rope, guy, cable, line, halser, hawser, painter, moorings, wire, chain; string etc. (*filament*) 205.

fastening, tie; liga-ment, -ture; strap; bowline, halliard, tackle, lanyard, rigging, shrouds; standing −, running- rigging; traces, harness; yoke; band, -age; brace, roller, fillet; inkle; with, withe, withy; thong, braid; girder, tie-beam; girt, cinch, girth, girdle, cestus, garter, braces, suspenders, halter, noose, lasso, lariat, surcingle, knot, hitch, running knot, frog.

pin, corking pin, nail, brad, tack, skewer, staple, cleat, clamp; cramp, screw, button, buckle, clasp, hasp, hinge, hank, catch, latch, bolt, ring, latchet, pawl, tag; tooth; stud; hook, − and eye; morse, lock, holdfast, padlock, rivet; anchor, grappling-iron, drawbar, coupler, draw-

head, coupling, treenail, trennel, stake, pale, pile, post, bollard.

cement, glue, gum, paste, size, wafer, solder, lute, putty, bird-lime, mortar, stucco, plaster, grout.

shackle, rein etc. (*means of restraint*) 752; suspender etc. 214; prop etc. (*support*) 215.

V. bridge over, span; connect etc. 43; hang etc. 214.

46. Coherence.—**N.** co-, ad-herence, -hesion, -hesiveness; concretion, accretion; con-, agglutination, -glomeration; aggregation; consolidation, set, cementation; sticking, soldering etc. *v.;* connection.

tenacity, toughness; stickiness etc. 352; insepara-bility, -bleness; bur, remora.

conglomerate, concrete etc. (*density*) 321.

V. cohere, adhere, stick, cling, cleave, hold, take hold of, hold fast, close with, embrace, clasp, hug; grow −, hang-together; twine round etc. (*join*) 43.

stick like -a leech, − wax; stick close; cling like -ivy, − a bur; adhere like -a remora, − Dejanira's shirt.

glue; ag-, con-glutinate; cement, lute, paste, gum; solder, weld; cake, coagulate, consolidate etc. (*solidify*) 321; agglomerate.

Adj. co-, ad-hesive, -hering etc. *v.;* tenacious, tough; sticky etc. 352.

united, unseparated, sessile, inseparable, inextricable, infrangible; compact etc. (*dense*) 321.

47. Incoherence. [Want of adhesion, non-adhesion, immiscibility.]—**N.** non-adhesion; immiscibility; incoherence; looseness etc. *adj.;* laxity; relaxation; loosening etc. *v.;* freedom; disjunction etc. 44; rope of sand.

V. make -loose etc. *adj.;* loosen, slacken, relax; un-glue etc. 46; detach etc. (*disjoin*) 44.

Adj. non-adhesive, immiscible; incoherent, detached, loose, slack, baggy, lax, relaxed, flapping, streaming; dishevelled; segregated, like grains of sand; un-consolidated etc. 321; -combined etc. 48; non-cohesive.

48. Combination.—**N.** combination; mixture etc. 41; alloy; junction etc. 43; union, unification, synthesis, incorporation, amalgamation, embodiment, coalescence, crasis, fusion, blend, blending, absorption, centralization, federation.

compound, amalgam, composition, *tertium quid;* resultant, impregnation.

V. combine, unite, incorporate, alloy, intertwine etc. 41; amalgamate, embody, absorb, re-embody, blend, merge, fuse, melt into one, consolidate, coalesce, centralize, impregnate; put −, lump- together; federate, associate; fraternize; cement a union, marry, wed, couple, pair, ally.

Adj. combined etc. *v.;* conjunctive, conjugate, conjoint, allied, confederate; impregnated with, ingrained, inoculated.

49. Decomposition.—**N.** decomposition, analysis, diaeresis dissection, resolution, catalysis, electrolysis, hydrolysis, photolysis, dissolution; dispersion etc. 73; disjunction etc. 44;

putrescence, caries, necrosis, corruption etc. (*uncleanness*) 653.

V. decom-pose, -pound; analyze, disembody, dissolve; resolve −, separate- into its elements; electrolyze; dissect, decentralize, break up; disintegrate; disperse etc. 73; unravel etc. (*unroll*) 313; crumble into dust; decay etc. *n.;* deteriorate etc. 659.

Adj. decomposed etc. *v.;* catalytic, analytical.

50. Whole. [Principal part.]—N. whole, totality, integrity; totalness etc. *adj.;* entirety, *ensemble*, collectiveness; unity etc. 87; completeness etc. 52; indivisibility, indiscerptibility; integration, embodiment; integer, integral.

all, the whole, total, aggregate, one and all, gross amount, sum, sum-total, *tout ensemble*, length and breadth of, Alpha and Omega, 'be all and end all,' lock, stock and barrel.

bulk, mass, lump, tissue, staple, body, torso, *compages;* truck, bole, hull, hulk, skeleton; greater −, major −, best −, principal −, mainpart; essential part etc. (*importance*) 642; lion's share, Benjamin's mess; the long and the short; nearly −, almost- all.

V. form −, constitute- a whole; integrate, embody, amass; aggregate etc. (*assemble*) 72; amount to, come to.

Adj. whole, total, integral, entire; complete etc. 52; one, individual.

un-broken, -cut, -divided, -severed, -clipped, - cropped, -shorn; seamless; undiminished; undemolished, -dissolved, -destroyed, -bruised.

in-divisible, -dissoluble, -dissolvable, - discerptible.

wholesale, sweeping, comprehensive.

Adv. wholly, altogether; totally etc. (*completely*) 52; entirely, all, all in all, considering all things, in a body, collectively, all put together; in the -aggregate, − lump; − mass, − gross, − main, − long run; *en masse*, on the whole, as a whole, bodily, *en bloc, in extenso*, throughout, every inch; substantially.

51. Part.—N. part, portion; dose; item, particular; aught, any; division, ward; subdivision, section; chapter, verse; article, clause, count, paragraph, passage; phrase; number, volume, book, fascicule; sector, segment; fraction, fragment; cantle, -t; frustum; detachment, parcel, unit, class etc. 75.

piece, lump, bit; cut, -ting; chip, chunk, collop, slice, scale, shard; lamina etc. 204; moiety; small part; morsel, scrap, crumb; particle etc. (*smallness*) 32; instalment, dividend; share etc. (*allotment*) 786.

débris, odds and ends, oddments, *detritus; excerpta;* member, limb, lobe, lobule, arm, wing, scion, branch, bough, joint, link, offshoot, ramification, twig, stipule, tendril, bush, spray, sprig; runner; leaf, -let; stump; constituent, ingredient, component part etc. 56.

compartment; department etc. (*class*) 75; county etc. (*region*) 181.

V. part, divide, break etc. (*disjoin*) 44; partition etc. (*apportion*) 786.

Adj. fractional, fragmentary; sectional, aliquot; divided etc. *v.;* in compartments, multifid, incomplete, partial, divided etc. 44.

Adv. partly, in part, partially; piecemeal, part by part; by -instalments, − snatches, − inches, − driblets; bit by bit, inch by inch, foot by foot, drop by drop; in -detail, − lots.

52. Completeness.—N. completeness etc. *adj.;* completion etc. 729; integration; integrality.

entirety; universality; totality; perfection etc. 650; solid-ity, -arity; unity; all; *ne plus ultra*, ideal, limit.

complement, supplement, make-weight; filling up etc. *v.*

impletion; satur-ation, -ity; high water; high −, flood −, spring- tide; fill, load, bumper, belly-ful; brimmer; sufficiency etc. 639.

V. be -complete etc. *adj.;* come to a head.

render -complete etc. *adj.;* complete etc. (*accomplish*) 729; fill, charge, load, replenish; make-up, − good; piece −, eke- out; supply deficiencies; fill -up, − in, − to the brim, − the measure of; saturate etc. 869.

go the whole -hog, − length, go all lengths.

Adj. complete, entire;whole etc.50; perfect etc. 650; full, good, absolute, thorough, plenary; solid, undivided; with all its parts.

exhaustive, radical, sweeping, thorough-going; dead.

regular, consummate, unmitigated, sheer, unqualified, unconditional, free; abundant etc. (*sufficient*) 639.

brimming; brim-, top-ful; chock −, choke-full; as full as- an egg is of meat, − a vetch, − a tick; saturated, crammed; replete etc. (*redundant*) 641; fraught, laden; full-laden, -fraught, - charged; heavy laden.

completing etc. *v.;* supplement-al, -ary; ascititious.

Adv. completely etc. *adj.;* altogether, outright, wholly, totally, *in toto*, quite; over head and ears; effectually, for good and all, nicely, fully, through thick and thin, head and shoulders; neck and -heel, − crop; all out; in -all respects, − every respect; at all points, out and out, to all intents and purposes; *toto coelo;* utterly, clean, − as a whistle; to the -full, − utmost, − backbone; hollow, stark; heart and soul, root and branch; down to the ground.

to the top of one's bent, as far as possible. *à outrance.*

throughout; from -first to last, − beginning to end, − end to end, − one end to the other, −Dan to Beersheba, − head to foot, − head to heels, − top to toe, − top to bottom; *de fond en comble; à fond, a capite ad calcem, ab ovo usque ad mala*, fore and aft; every -whit, − inch; *cap-à-pie*, to the end of the chapter; up to the -brim, − ears, − eyes; as ... as can be.

on all accounts; *sous tous les rapports;* with a - vengeance, − witness.

53. Incompleteness.—N. incompleteness etc. *adj.;* deficiency, short -measure, − wieght; shortcoming etc. 304; insufficiency etc. 640; imperfection etc. 651; immaturity etc. (*nonpreparation*) 674; half measures.

[part wanting] defect, deficit, shortage, ullage, defalcation, omission, *caret;* interval etc. 198; break etc. (*discontinuity*) 70; non-completion etc. 730; missing link.

V. be -incomplete etc. *adj.;* fall short of etc. 304; lack etc. (*be insufficient*) 640; neglect etc. 460.

Adj. incomplete; imperfect etc. 651; unfinished; uncompleted etc. (*see* complete etc. 729); defective, deficient, wanting; failing; in -default, – arrear; short, – of; hollow, meagre, lame, half-and-half, perfunctory, sketchy; crude etc. (*unprepared*) 674.

mutilated, garbled, mangled, docked, lopped, truncated; bobtailed, cropped, bobbed, shingled.

in -progress, – hand; going on, proceeding.

Adv. incompletely etc. *adj.;* by halves.

Phr. *caetera desunt; caret.*

54. Composition.—N. composition, constitution, crasis, synthesis; make-up; combination etc. 48; inclusion, admission, comprehension, reception; embodiment, formation, conformation, production.

compilation etc. 72. (*musical*) composition etc. 415; painting etc. 556; writing etc. 590; typography etc. 591.

V. be -composed, – made, – formed, – made up- of; consist of, be resolved into.

include etc. ' (*in a class*) 76; subsume; synthesize; contain, hold, comprehend, take in, admit, embrace, embody; involve; implicate, drag into.

compose, constitute, form, make; make –, fill –, build- up; weave, construct, fabricate; compile; write, draw; set up (*printing*); enter into the composition of etc. (*be a component*) 56.

Adj. containing, constituting etc. *v.*

55. Exclusion.—N. exclusion, non-admission, omission, exception, rejection, repudiation; exile etc. (*seclusion*) 893; preclusion, lock out, ostracism, prohibition; disbarment, expulsion, ban.

separation, segregation, seposition, elimination, coffer-dam.

V. be excluded from etc.

exclude, bar, ban; leave –, shut –, thrust –, bar- out; reject, repudiate, spurn, blackball; ostracize, boycott; lay –, put –, set-apart, – aside; relegate, segregate; throw overboard; strike -off, – out; neglect etc. 460; banish etc. (*seclude*) 893; separate etc. (*disjoin*) 44.

pass over, omit; garble; eliminate, weed, winnow.

Adj. excluding etc. *v.;* exclusive.

excluded etc. *v.;* unrecounted, not included in; inadmissible; preventive, interdictive.

Adv. exclusive of, barring, except; with the exception of; save, bating.

56. Component.—N. component; component –, integral –, integrant-part; element, constituent, ingredient, leaven; part and parcel; contents; appurtenance; feature; member etc. (*part*) 51; personnel.

V. enter into, – the composition of; be a -component etc. *n.;* be –, form- part of; merge –, be merged- in; be implicated in; share in etc. (*participate*) 778; belong –, appertain- to.

form, make, constitute, compose.

Adj. forming etc. *v.;* inclusive; inherent etc. 5.

57. Extraneousness.—N. extraneousness etc. *adj.;* extrinsicality etc. 6; exteriority etc. 220; alienism.

foreign -body, – substance, – element; alien, stranger, intruder, interloper, foreigner, tramontane, *novus homo,* new comer, immi-, emi-grant; creole, Afrikander; outsider, outlander, tenderfoot.

Adj. extraneous, foreign, alien, ulterior; exterior, external, outside, outlandish; oversea; tra-ultra-montane.

excluded etc. 55; inadmissible; exceptional.

Adv. in foreign -parts, – lands; abroad, beyond seas, overseas.

58. Order.—N. order, regularity etc. 80; uniformity, symmetry, *lucidus ordo;* harmony, music of the spheres.

gradation, progression; series etc. (*continuity*) 69.

subordination; course, even tenor, routine; method, disposition, arrangement, array, system, economy, discipline; orderliness etc. *adj.*

rank, place etc. (*term*) 71.

V. be –, become- in order etc. *adj.;* form, fall in, draw up; arrange –, range –, place- itself; adjust; fall into –, take- -one's place, – rank; rally round; arrange etc. 60.

Adj. orderly, regular; in -order, – trim, – apple-pie order, according to Cocker, – its proper place, neat, neat as a pin, tidy, *en règle,* well regulated, correct, methodical, uniform, symmetrical, ship-shape, business-like, systematic; habitual; unconfused etc. (*see* confuse etc. 61) arranged etc. 60.

Adv. in order; methodically etc. *adj.;* in -turn, – its turn; step by step; by regular -steps, – gradations – stages, – intervals; *seriatim,* systematically, by clockwork, *gradatim;* at stated periods etc. (*periodically*)138.

59. Disorder. [Absence, or want of Order, etc.]—N. disorder; derangement etc. 61; irregularity; anomaly etc. (*unconformity*) 83; anar-chy; -chism; want of method; dishevelment, untidiness etc. *adj.;* disunion; discord etc. 24.

confusion; confusedness etc. *adj.;* disarray, jumble, mix-up, huddle, litter, lumber; *cahotage;* farrago; mess, muss, mash, muddle, hash; hotchpotch; *imbroglio,* chaos, *omnium gatherum,* medley; mere -mixture etc. 41; fortuitous concourse of atoms, *disjecta membra, rudis indigestaque moles.*

complexity; complexness etc. *adj.;* com-, implication; intri-cacy, -cation; perplexity; network, maze, labyrinth, wilderness, jungle; involution, ravelling, entanglement; coil etc. (*convolution*) 248; sleave, tangled skein, knot, Gordian know, kink, web; wheels within wheels.

turmoil; ferment, etc. (*agitation*) 315; to do, trouble, pudder, pother, row, disturbance, convulsion, tumult, pandemonium, uproar, riot, rumpus, stour, scramble, *fracas,* embroilment, mêlée, spill and pelt, rough and tumble; whirlwind etc. 349; bear garden, Babel, Saturnalia, Donnybrook Fair, confusion worse confounded, most admired disorder, *concordia discors;* Bedlam –, hell- broke loose; bull in a china shop;

all the fat in the fire, *diable à quatre*, Devil to pay; pretty kettle of fish; pretty piece of -work, — business.

slattern, slut, sloven; draggle-tail.

V. be -disorderly etc. *adj.;* ferment, play at cross purposes.

put out of order; derange etc. 61; ravel etc. 219; ruffle, rumple; bungle, botch.

Adj. disorderly, orderless; out of -order; — place, — gear, — whack; irregular, desultory; anomalous etc. (*unconformable*) 83; acephalous, disorganized, straggling; un-, im-methodical; unsymmetric; unsystematic; untidy, slovenly, bedraggled, messy; dislocated; out of sorts; promiscuous, indiscriminate; chaotic, anarchical, lawless; unarranged etc. 60; confused, tumultuous, turbulent, tempestuous; deranged etc. 61; topsy turvy etc. (*inverted*) 218; shapeless etc. 241; disjointed, out of joint.

com-plex, -plexed; intricate, complicated, perplexed, involved, ravelled, entangled, knotted, tangled, inextricable; irreducible.

troublous; riotous etc. (*violent*) 173.

Adv. irregularly etc. *adj.;* by fits and -snatches, — starts; pell-mell; higgledy-piggledy, helter-skelter, harum-scarum; in a ferment; at -sixes and sevens, — cross purposes; upside down etc. 218.

Phr. the cart before the horse, chaos is come again.

60. Arrangement. [Reduction to Order.]—**N.** arrangement; plan etc. 626; preparation etc. 673; dispos-al, -ition; col-, al-location; distribution; sorting etc. *v.;* assortment, allotment; grouping; apportionment, *taxis*, taxonomy, *syn-taxis*, graduation, organization, grading; re-organization, rationalization.

analysis, classification, division, digestion; systematism.

[Result of arrangement] order, orderliness, form, array; digest, synopsis etc. (compendi-um) 596; *syntagma*, table, atlas; register etc. (*record*) 551; score etc. 415; cosmos, organism, architecture.

[Instrument for sorting] sieve etc. 260; file, card index.

V. reduce to -, bring into- order; introduce order into; rally.

arrange, dispose, place, form; put —, set —, place- in order; straighten up, tidy up; set out, collocate, allocate, pack, marshal, range, size, rank, array, group, parcel out, allot, space, distribute, deal; cast —, assign- the parts; dispose of, assign places to; assort, sort; sift, riddle; put —, set- -to rights, — into shape, — in trim, — in array.

class, -ify; divide; file, string together, thread; register etc. (*record*) 551; list, catalogue, tabulate, index, alphabeticize, graduate, digest, grade, codify; orchestrate, score.

methodize, regulate, systematize, standardize, co-ordinate, organize, settle, fix.

unravel, disentangle, ravel, card; disembroil.

Adj. arranged etc. *v.;* embattled, in battle array; cut and dried; methodical, orderly, regular, systematic, tabular.

61. Derangement. [Subversion of Order; bringing into disorder.]—**N.** derangement etc. *v.;* dis-

order etc. 59; evection, discomposure, disturbance; dis-, de-organization; involvement; dislocation; perturbation, interruption; shuffling etc. *v.;* inversion etc. 218; corrugation etc. (*fold*) 258; insanity etc. 503.

V. derange; dis-, mis-arrange; dis-, mis-place; mislay, discompose, disorder, de-, dis-organize; embroil, unsettle, disturb, confuse, trouble, perturb, jumble, tumble; huddle, shuffle, muddle, toss, hustle, fumble, riot; bring —, put —, throw-into -disorder etc. 59; break the ranks, disconcert, convulse; break in upon.

unhinge, dislocate, put out of joint, throw out of gear.

turn topsy-turvy etc. (*invert*) 218; bedevil; complicate, involve, perplex, confound; im-, embrangle; tangle, en-tangle, ravel, tousle, dishevel, ruffle, rumple etc. (*fold*) 258; dement.

litter, scatter; mix etc. 41.

Adj. deranged etc. *v.;* syncre-tic, -tistic.

62. Precedence.—**N.** precedence; coming before etc. *v.;* the lead, *le pas;* superiority etc. 33; importance etc. 642; anteced-ence, -ency; anteriority etc. (*front*) 234; precursor etc. 64; priority etc. 116; precession etc. 280; anteposition, preference.

V. precede; come -before, — first; forerun, head, lead, take the lead; lead the -way, — dance; introduce, usher in; have the *pas*; set the fashion etc. (*influence*) 175; lead off, kick off, open the ball; take —, have- precedence; outrank; have the start etc. (*get before*) 280.

place before; prefix; premise, prelude, preface.

Adj. preceding etc. *v.;* pre-, antecedent; anterior, prior etc. 116; before; former, foregoing; before-, above-mentioned; aforesaid, said; precurs-ory, -ive; prevenient, preliminary, prefatory, introductory; prelus-ive, -ory; proemial, preparatory.

Adv. before; in advance etc. (*precession*) 280.

Phr. *seniores priores.*

63. Sequence.—**N.** sequence, coming after; going after etc. (*following*) 281; consecution, succession; posteriority etc. 117.

continuation; prolongation, order of succussion; successiveness; Elijah's mantle.

secondariness; subordinancy etc. (*inferiority*) 34.

V. succeed; come -after, — on, — next; follow, ensue, step into the shoes of; alternate.

place after, suffix, append.

Adj. succeeding etc. *v.;* sequent; sub-, consequent; sequacious, proximate, next; consecutive etc. (*continuity*) 69; alternate, amoebaean.

latter; posterior etc. 117.

Adv. after, subsequently; behind etc. (*rear*) 235.

64. Precursor.—**N.** precursor, antecedent, precedent, predecessor; forerunner, van-courier, *avant-coureur*, pioneer, prodrome, *prodromos*, outrider; leader, bell-wether; herald, harbinger; dawn.

prelude, preamble, preface, prologue, foreword, *avant-propos, protasis*, prolusion, proem, *prolepsis, prolegomena*, prefix, introduction;

lead, heading, frontispiece, groundwork; preparation etc. 673; overture, voluntary, *exordium*. symphony, *ritornello;* premises. prefigurement etc. 511; omen etc. 512.

Adj. precursory; prelu-sive, -sory, -dious; proemial, introductory, prefatory, prodromous, inaugural, preliminary; precedent etc. (*prior*) 116.

65. Sequel.—N. sequel, suffix, successor; tail, *queue*, train, wake, trail, rear; retinue, suite; appendix, postscript, subscript; epilogue; conclusion; peroration; codicil; continuation, *sequela;* appendage etc. 39; tail –, heel-piece; tag, more last words; *colophon.*

follower, after-glow, -growth, -crop, -taste, -math.

after-part, -piece, -course, -thought, -game; *arrière pensée*, second thoughts.

66. Beginning.—N. beginning, commencement, opening, outset, incipience, inception, inchoation; introduction etc. (*precursor*) 64; *alpha;* initial; foundation; inauguration, *début, le premier pas*, embarcation, rising of the curtain; zero hour; exordium, curtain raiser; maiden speech; prelude; outbreak, onset, brunt; initiative, move, first move; gambit, narrow –, thin- end of the wedge; fresh start, new departure; forefront.

origin etc. (*cause*) 153; source, rise; bud, germ etc. 153; egg, rudiment; genesis, birth, nativity, cradle, infancy, incunabula; start, starting-point etc. 293; dawn etc. (*morning*) 125.

title-page; head, -ing, caption; van etc. (*front*) 234.

en-trance, -try; inlet, orifice, mouth, chops, lips, porch, portal, portico, *propylon*, door; gate, -way; postern, wicket, threshold, vestibule; skirts, border etc. (*edge*) 231; tee.

first -stage, – blush, – glance, – impression, – sight.

rudiments, elements, outlines, *principia*, grammar, *protasis;* alphabet, ABC.

V. begin, commence, inchoate. rise, arise, originate, institute, conceive, initiate, open, dawn, set in, take its rise, enter upon, start; enter; set out etc. (*depart*) 293; embark in.

usher in; lead -off, – the way; take the -lead, – initiative; inaugurate, head; stand -at the head, – first, – for; lay the foundations etc. (*prepare*) 673; found etc. (*cause*) 153; set -up, – on foot, – agoing, – abroach, – the ball in motion; apply the match to a train; launch, broach; open -up, – the door to; set -about, – to work; make a -beginning, – start; handsel; take the first step, lay the first stone, cut the first turf; break -ground, – the ice, – cover; pass –, cross- the Rubicon; open -fire, – the ball; ventilate, air; undertake etc. 676.

come into -existence, – the world; make one's *début*, take birth; burst forth, break out; spring –, crop- up.

begin -at the beginning, – *ab ovo*, – again, – *de novo;* start afresh, make a fresh start, shuffle the cards, resume, recommence.

Adj. beginning etc. *v.;* initi-al, -atory, -ative; inceptive, introductory, incipient; proemial, inaugural; incho-ate, -ative; embryonic, rudimental; primogenial; primeval etc. (*old*) 124; rudimentary, aboriginal; natal, nascent.

first, foremost, front, leading, head; maiden. begun etc. *v.;* just -begun etc. *v.*

Adv. at –, in- the beginning etc. *n.;* first, in the first place, *imprimis*, first and foremost; *in limine;* in -the bud, – embryo, – its infancy; from -the beginning, – its birth; *ab -initio, – ovo, – incunabilis*, primarily, originally.

67. End.—N. end, close, termination; desinence, conclusion, *finis, finale*, period, term, *terminus*, last, *omega;* extreme, -tremity; gable –, butt –, fagend; tip, nib, point; tail etc. (*rear*) 235; verge etc. (*edge*) 231; tag, epilogue, peroration; *bonne bouche*, bitter end, tail end; terminal; *apodosis;* appendix.

consummation, *dénouement;* finish etc. (*completion*) 729; fate; doom, -sday; crack of doom, day of Judgment, fall of the curtain, wind-up; goal, destination; limit, stoppage, end all, determination; expiration, expiry; death etc. 360; end of all things; finality; eschatology.

break up, *commencement de la fin*, last stage, turning point; *coup de grâce*, death-blow; knock-out.

V. end, close, finish, terminate, conclude, be all over; expire; die etc. 360; come –, draw- to a -close etc. *n.;* have run its course; run out, pass away.

bring to an -end etc. *n.;* put an end to, make an end of; determine; get through; achieve etc. (*complete*) 729; stop etc. (*make to cease*) 142; shut up shop.

Adj. ending etc. *v.;* final, terminal, definitive, conclusive; crowning etc. (*completing*) 729; last, ultimate; hindermost; rear etc. 235; caudal.

contermin-ate, -ous, -able.

ended etc. *v.;* at an end; settled, decided, over, played out, set at rest.

penultimate; last but -one, – two, – etc.

unbegun, uncommenced; fresh.

Adv. finally etc. *adj ;* in fine; at the last; once for all.

68. Middle.—N. middle, midst, mediety; mean etc. 29; medium, middle term; center etc. 222; mid-course etc. 628; *mezzo termine; juste milieu* etc. 628; half-way house, nave, navel, omphalos; nucle-us, -olus.

equidistance, bisection, half-distance; equator, diaphragm, midriff; interjacence etc. 228.

Adj. middle, medial, mesial, mean, mid; middle-, mid-most; middling; median; intermediate etc. (*interjacent*) 228; equidistant; central etc. 222; mediterranean, equatorial.

Adv. in the middle; in the thick; mid-, half-way; midships, *in medias res.*

69. Continuity. [Uninterrupted sequence.]—**N.** continuity; consecu-tion,, -tiveness etc. *adj.;* succession, round, suite, progression, series, train, chain; cat-, concatenation; catena; scale; gradation, course, constant flow, perpetuity.

procession, column; retinue, *cortège*, cavalcade, rank and file, line of battle, array.

pedigree, genealogy, lineage, race etc. 166.

rank, file, line, row, range, tier, string, thread; team; suit; colonnade.

V. follow in –, form- a series etc. *n.;* fall in.

arrange in a -series etc. *n.;* string together, catenate, file, thread, graduate, tabulate.

Adj. continu-ous. -ed; consecutive; progressive, gradual; serial, successive; immediate, unbroken, entire; linear; in a -line, – row etc. *n.;* uninter-rupted, -mitting; unremitting; perennial, evergreen; constant.

Adv. continuously etc. *adj.; seriatim;* in a -line etc. *n.;* in -succession, – turn; running, gradually, step by step; *gradatim,* at a stretch; in -file, – column, – single file, – Indian file.

70. Discontinuity. [Interrupted sequence.]—N. discontinuity; disjunction etc. 44; anacoluthon; interruption, break, fracture, flaw, fault, split, crack, cut; gap etc. *(interval)* 198; solution of continuity, *caesura;* broken thread; parenthesis, episode; rhapsody, patchwork; intermission; alternation etc. *(periodicity)* 138; dropping fire.

V. be -discontinuous etc. *adj.;* alternate, intermit.

discontinue, pause, interrupt; intervene; break, – in upon; interpose etc. 228; break –, snap- the thread; disconnect etc. *(disjoin)* 44.

Adj. discontinuous, unsuccessive, broken, interrupted, *décousu;* dis-, un-connected, discrete, disjunctive; fitful etc. *(irregular)* 139; spasmodic, desultory, intermit-ting etc. *v.;* -tent; alternate; recurrent etc. *(periodic)* 138; few and far between.

Adv. at intervals; by -snatches, – jerks, – skips, – catches, – fits and starts; skippingly, *per saltum; longo intervallo.*

71. Term.—N. term, rank, station, stage, step; degree etc. 26; scale, remove, grade, link, peg, round –, rung- of the ladder, *status,* position, place, point, mark, *pas,* period, pitch; stand, - ing; footing, range.

V. hold –, occupy –, fall into- a place etc. *n.*

72. Assemblage.—N. assemblage; col-lection, location, -ligation; compilation, levy, gathering, ingathering, mobilization, meet, foregathering, muster, *attroupement;* con-course, -flux, - gregation, -tesseration, -vergence etc. 290; meeting, *levée, réunion,* drawing room, at home; conversazione etc. *(social gathering)* 892; assembly, congress, eisteddfod; conven-tion, -ticle; gemote; conclave, etc. *(council)* 696; posse, *posse comitatus;* Noah's ark.

miscellany, *collectanea,* symposium; museum, menagerie, etc. *(store)* 636.

crowd, throng, multitude; flood, rush, deluge; rout, rabble, mob, press, crush, *cohue,* jam, horde, body, tribe; crew, gang, knot, squad, band, party; swarm, shoal, school, covey, flock, herd, drove, kennel; array, bevy, galaxy; *corps,* company, troop, *troupe;* army, force, regiment, etc. *(combatants)* 726; host etc. *(multitude)* 102; populousness.

clan, brotherhood, association etc. *(party)* 712.

volley, shower, storm, cloud.

group, cluster, Pleiades, clump, pencil; set, batch, lot, pack; budget, *dossier,* assortment, bunch; parcel; pack-et, -age; bundle, *fasciculus,* fascine, bale; ser-on, oon; faggot, wisp, truss,

tuft; shock, rick, fardel, stack, sheaf, swath, gavel, haycock, stook.

accumulation etc. *(store)* 636; congeries, heap, lump, pile, *rouleau,* tissue, mass, pyramid; drift; snow-ball, -drift; acervation, cumulation; amassment, glom-, agglom-eration; conglobation; conglomeration, -ate; coacervation, coagmentation, aggregation, concentration, congestion, *omnium gatherum, spicilegium,* black hole of Calcutta; quantity etc. *(greatness)* 31.

collector, gatherer; whip, -per in.

V. [be or come together] assemble, collect, muster; meet, unite, join, rejoin; cluster, flock, swarm, surge, stream, herd, crowd, throng, associate; con-gregate, -glomerate, -centrate; center round, *rendezvous,* resort; come –, flock –, get –, pig- together; forgather; huddle; reassemble.

[get or bring together] assemble, muster, mobilize; bring –, get –, put –, draw –, scrape –, lump- together; col-lect, -locate. -ligate; get –, whip- in; gather; hold a meeting; con-vene, -voke, -vocate; rake up, dredge; heap, mass, pile; pack, put up, truss, cram; acervate; ag-glomerate, -gregate; compile; group, aggroup, concentrate, unite; collect –, bring- into a focus; amass, accumulate etc. *(store)* 636; collect in a drag-net; heap Ossa upon Pelion.

Adj. assembled etc. *v.;* closely packed, dense, serried, crowded to suffocation, teeming, swarming, populous; as thick as hops; all of a heap, fasciculated; cumulative.

Phr. the plot thickens.

73. Non-assemblage. Dispersion.—N. dispersion; disjunction etc. 44; divergence etc. 291; scattering etc. *v.;* dissemination, broadcasting, diffusion, dissipation, distribution; apportionment etc. 786; spread, respersion, circumfusion, interspersion, spargefaction.

waifs and estrays, flotsam and jetsam, *disjecta membra.*

V. disperse, scatter, sow, disseminate, radiate, diffuse, shed, spread, ted, bestrew, overspread, dispense, disband, disembody, demobilize, dismember, distribute; apportion etc. 786; blow off, let out, dispel, cast forth, draught off; strew, straw, strow; spirtle, cast, sprinkle, shatter; issue, deal out, retail; utter; re-, inter-sperse; set abroach, circumfuse.

turn –, cast- adrift; scatter to the winds; sow broadcast.

spread like wildfire, disperse themselves.

Adj. unassembled etc. *(see* assemble etc. 72); dispersed etc. *v.;* sparse, dispread, broadcast, sporadic, widespread; far-flung; epidemic etc. *(general)* 78; adrift, stray; dishevelled, streaming.

Adv. *sparsim,* here and there, *passim.*

74. Focus. [Place of meeting.]—N. focus; point of- convergence etc. 290; corradiation etc. 222; gathering-place, resort; haunt; retreat; *venue, rendezvous;* rallying point, head-quarters, home, club; *dépôt* etc. *(store)* 636; tryst, trysting-place; place of -meeting, – resort, – assignation; *point de –, lieu de- réunion;* issue.

V. bring to- a point, – a focus, – an issue; focus.

75. Class.—N. class, category, *categorema*, head, order, section; division, subdivision; department, province, domain, sphere.

kind, sort, genus, species, variety, branch, family, race, tribe, caste, sept, clan, breed; *clique, coterie;* type, kit, sect, set; assortment; feather, kidney; suit; range; gender, sex, kin.

manner, description, denomination, persuasion, connection, designation, character, stamp; predicament; conviction etc. **484.**

similarity etc. **17.**

76. Inclusion. [Comprehension under, or reference to a class.]—N. inclusion, admission, incorporation, comprehension, reception.

composition etc. (*inclusion in a compound*) **54.**

V. be -included in etc.; come −, fall −, range-under; belong −, pertain- to; range with; merge in.

include, compromise, comprehend, contain, admit, embrace, receive; enclose etc. (*circumscribe*) **229;** incorporate, cover, embody, encircle.

reckon −, enumerate −, number- among; refer to; place −, arrange-under, − with; take into account.

Adj. includ-ed; -ing etc. *v.;* inclusive; comprehensive, all-embracing; congen-er, -erous; of the same -class etc. **75.**

Phr. *et hoc genus omne,* etc.; *et caetera.*

77. Exclusion.*—N. exclusion etc. **55.**

* The same set of words is used to express *Exclusion from a class* and *Exclusion from a compound.* Reference is therefore made to the former at **55.** This identity does not occur with regard to *Inclusion,* which therefore constitutes a separate category.

78. Generality.—N. general-ity, -ization; universality; catholic-ity, -ism; miscel-lany, -laneousness; drag-net.

every-one, -body; all hands, all the world and his wife; any body, N or M, all sorts; *tout le monde.*

prevalence, run.

V. be -general etc. *adj.;* prevail, obtain, be going about, stalk abroad.

render -general etc. *adj.;* generalize; spread, broadcast.

Adj. general, usual, current, generic, collective; broad, comprehensive, sweeping; encyclopedical, panoramic, widespread etc. (*dispersed*) **73.**

universal; catho-lic, -lical; common, world-wide; e-cumenical; transcendental; prevalent, prevailing, rife, epidemic, besetting; all over, covered with.

every, all; indeterminate, indefinite, unspecified, impersonal.

customary etc. (*habitual*) **613.**

Adv. what-ever, -soever; to a man, one and all, without exception.

generally etc. *adj.;* always, for better for worse; in general, generally speaking; speaking generally; for the most part; in the long run etc. (*on an average*) **29.**

79. Speciality.—N. speciality, *spécialité;* individ-uality, -uity; particularity, peculairity;

idiocrasy etc. (*tendency*) **176;** personality, characteristic, mannerism, idiosyncrasy, attribute specificness etc. *adj.;* singularity etc. (*unconformity*) **83;** reading, version, lection; state; *trait;* distinctive feature; technicality; *differentia.*

particulars, details, minutiae, items, counts.

I, self, I myself, *ego;* my-, him-, her-, it-self.

V. specify, particularize, individualize, realize, specialize, designate, differentiate, determine, define, denote, indicate, itemize, detail.

descend to particulars, enter into detail, come to the point.

Adj. special; particular, individual, specific, proper, personal, intimate, original, private, respective, definite, concrete, determinate, especial, certain, esoteric, endemic, partial, party, peculiar, marked, appropriate, several, characteristic, diagnistic, exact, exclusive; singular etc. (*exceptional*) **83;** idiomatic; typical, representative, distinctive.

this, that; yon, -der.

Adv. specially etc. *adj.;* in particular, *in propriâ personâ; ad hominem;* for my part.

each, apiece, one by one; severally, respectively, each to each; *seriatim,* in detail, bit by bit; *pro hac vice, − re natâ.*

namely, that is to say; *videlicet,* viz.; to wit.

80. Rule.—N. regularity, uniformity etc. **16;** clock-work precision; punctuality etc. (*exactness*) **494;** routine etc. (*custom*) **613;** formula; system; rut; canon, convention, maxim; rule etc. (*form, regulation*) **697;** key-note, standard, model; precedent etc. (*prototype*) **22;** conformity etc. **82.**

nature, principle; law; order of things; normal −, natural −, ordinary −, model- -state, − condition; standing -dish, − order; normality; Procrustean law; law of the Medes and Persians; hard and fast rule.

Adj. regular, uniform, symmetrical, constant, steady; according to rule etc. (*conformable*) **82;** customary etc. **613;** orderly etc. **58.**

81. Multiformity.—N. multi-, omniformity; variety, diversity; multifariousness etc. *adj.*

Adj. multi-form, -fold, -farious, -generous; multiplex, variform, manifold, many-sided, multiplicate; omni-form, -genous, -farious; polymorphic; protean; heterogeneous, motley, mosaic; epicene, indiscriminate, desultory, irregular, diversified, different, divers; all manner of; of -every description, − all sorts and kinds; *et hoc genus omne;* and what not? *de omnibus rebus et quibusdam aliis.*

82. Conformity.—N. conform-ity, -ance; observance.

naturalization; conventionality etc. (*custom*) **613;** agreement etc. **23.**

example, instance, specimen, sample, quotation; exemplification, illustration, case in point; object lesson.

conventionalist, formalist, Philistine.

pattern etc. (*prototype*) **22.**

V. conform to, − rule; accommodate −, adapt- oneself to; rub off corners.

be -regular etc. *adj.;* move in a groove; follow
−, observe −, go by −, bend to −, obey- -rules,
− precedents; comply −, tally −, chime in −,
fall in-with; be -guided, − regulated- by; fall into
a -custom, − usage; follow the -fashion, − multitude; pass muster, do as others do, *hurler aves les
loups;* do at Rome as the Romans do; go −,
swim- with the -stream, − current, − tide; tread
the beaten track etc. (*habit*) 613; rubber-stamp;
keep one in countenance.

exemplify, illustrate, cite, quote, put a case;
produce an- instance etc. *n.*

Adj. conformable to rule, adaptable, compliant, consistent, agreeable; regular etc. 80;
according to -regulation, − rule, − Cocker; *en
règle, selon les regles,* well regulated, orderly;
symmetric etc. 242.

conventional commonplace etc. (*customary*)
613; of -daily, − every day- occurrence; in the
natural order of things; ordinary, common, − or
garden, prosaic, habitual, usual.

in the order of the day; naturalized.

typical, normal, formal; canonical, orthodox,
sound, strict, rigid, positive, uncompromising,
Procrustean; point device.

secundum artem, ship-shape, technical.

exemplary, illustrative, in point.

Adv. conformably etc. *adj.;* by rule; agreeably
to; in -conformity, − accordance, − keeping-
with; according to; consistently with; as usual, *ad
instar, instar omnium; more -solito,* − major-
um.

for the sake of conformity; of −, as a matter
of- course; *pro formâ,* for form's sake, by the
card; according to plan.

invariably etc. (*uniformly*) 16.

for -example, − instance; *exempli gratiâ; e.g.,
inter alia.*

Phr. *cela va sans dire, ex pede Herculem.
noscitur a sociis.*

83. Unconformity.—N. non-conformity etc.
82; un-, dis-conformity; unconventionality, informality, abnormity, anomaly; anomalousness
etc. *adj.;* exception, peculiarity, etc. 79; infraction −, breach −, violation −, infringe-
ment- of -law, − custom, − usage; eccentricity,
bizarrerie, oddity, *je ne sais quoi,* monstrosity,
rarity; freak of Nature.

individuality, idiosyncrasy, singularity,
oritinality, mannerism.

aberration; irregularity; variety; singularity;
exemption; salvo etc. (*qualification*) 469.

nonconformist; nondescript, character,
original, nonsuch, monster, prodigy, wonder,
miracle, curiosity, missing link, flying fish, black
swan, *lusus naturae, rara avis,* queer fish;
mongrel; half-caste, -blood, -breed; *métis,* cross
breed, hybrid, mule, mulatto, sacatra, marabou;
tertium quid, hermaphrodite, gynander, an-
drogyn.

phoenix, chimera, hydra, sphinx, minotaur;
griff-in, -on; centaur; hippogriff, -centaur; sagit-
tary; kraken; cockatrice, wyvern, roc, liver,
dragon, sea-serpent; mermaid; unicorn; Cyclops,
'men whose heads do grown beneath their
shoulders;. Teratolgy.

fish out of water; neither -one /thing nor
another, − fish flesh nor fowl nor good red her-

ring; one in a -way, − thousand; out-cast, -law;
Ishmael, pariah; oasis.

V. be -unconformable etc. *adj.;* leave the
beaten -track, − path; infringe −, break −,
violate- a -law, − habit, − usage, − custom;
drive a coach and six through; stretch a point;
have no business there; baffle −, beggar- all description.

Adj. unconformable, exceptional; abnorm-al,
-ous; anomal-ous, -istic; out of -order, − place,
− keeping, − tune, − one's element; irregular,
arbitrary; lawless, informal, aberrant, stray,
wandering, wanton; peculiar, exclusive, unnatural, eccentric, crotchety, egregious; out of
the -beaten track, − common, − common run,
− pale of; misplaced; funny.

un-usual, -accustomed, -customary, -wonted, -
common; rare, singular, *unique,* curious, odd,
extraordinary, strange, monstrous; wonderful
etc. 870; unexpected, unaccountable; *outré,* out
of the way, remarkable, noteworthy; queer,
quaint, nondescript, none such, *sui generis;*
original, unconventional, Bohemian, unfashionable; un-described, -precedented, -paralleled, -
exampled, -heard of, -familiar; fantastic, new-
fangled, grotesque, *bizarre;* outlandish, exotic,
tombé de nues, preternatural; denaturalized.

heterogeneious, heteroclite, amorphous,
mongrel, amphibious, epicene, half-blood,
hybrid; androgyn-ous, -al; unsymmetric etc. 243.

qualified etc. 469.

Adv. unconformably etc. *adj.;* except, unless,
save, barring, beside, without, save and except,
let alone.

however, yet, but.

Int. what -on earth! − in the world!

Phr. never was -seen, − heard, − known- the
like.

84. Number.—N. number, symbol, numeral,
figure, cipher, digit, integer; counter; round
number; formula; function; series.

sum, total, aggregate, difference, complement, subtrahend; product; multipli-cand, -er, -
cator; coefficient, multiple; dividend, divisor,
factor, quotient, sub-multiple, fraction; mixed
number; numerator, denominator; decimal,
circulating decimal, repetend; common measure,
aliquot part; reciprocal; prime number; totitive,
totient.

permutation, combination, variation; election.

ratio, proportion; progression; arithmetical −,
geometrical −, harmonical- progression; percentage.

figurate −, pyramidal −, polvgonal- numbers.

power, root, exponent, index, logarithm, antilogarithm; modulus.

differential, integral, fluxion, fluent.

Adj. numeral, complementary, divisible, aliquot, reciprocal, prime, fractional, decimal,
figurate, incommensurable.

proportional, exponential, logarithmic, logometric, differential, fluxional, integral.

positive, negative; rational, irrational; surd,
radical, real, imaginary, impossible.

85. Numeration.—N. numeration, numbering
etc. *v.;* pagination; tale, tally, recension, enumer-

ation, summation, reckoning, computation, supputation; calcu-lation, -lus; algorithm, rhabdology, dactylonomy; measurement etc. 466; statistics.

arithmetic, analysis, algebra, fluxions; differential −, integral −, infinitesimal-calculus; calculus of differences.

[Statistics] dead reckoning, muster, poll, census, capitation, roll-call, recapitulation; account etc. (*list*) 86.

[Operations] notation, addition, subtraction, multiplication, division, proportion, rule of three, practice, equations, extraction of roots, reduction, involution, evolution, approximation, interpolation, differentiation, integration.

[Instruments] abacus, swan-pan, logometer, sliding −, slide- rule, tallies, Napier's bones, calculating −, adding- machine, difference engine; cash register.

arithmetician, calculator, abacist; mathematician, actuary, statistician, surveyor, geodesist.

V. number, count, tell; call −, run- over, take an account of, enumerate, call the roll, muster, poll, recite, recapitulate; sum; sum −, cast- up; tell off, score, cipher, compute, calculate, set a price, reckon, − up, estimate; suppute, add, subtract, multiply, divide, extract roots.

check, prove, demonstrate, balance, audit, overhaul, take stock; affix numbers to, page, foliate, paginate.

amount −, come- to.

Adj. numer-al, -ical; arithmetical, analytic, algebraic, statistical, numerable, computable, calculable; commensur-able, -ate; incommensur-able, -ate.

86. List.—N. list, catalogue, enumeration, inventory, schedule; register etc. (*record*) 551; account; bill, − of costs, syllabus; terrier, tally, file; almanac, calendar, index, table, atlas, contents, card index; rota, ticket; book, ledger; synopsis, *catalogue raisonné; tableau,* scroll, manifest, invoice, bill of lading; prospectus, *programme;* bill of fare, *menu, carte;* score, census, statistics, returns; Red −, Blue −, Domesday- book; *cadaster;* directory, gazetteer, dictionary, glossary, lexicon, thesaurus, gradus.

roll; check −, chequer −, bead- roll, − of honor; muster -roll, − book; roster, panel; cartulary, diptych.

V. list, enrol, schedule, register etc. *n.;* indent, post, docket; matriculate.

Adj. cadastral, listed etc. *v.*

87. Unity.—N. unity; oneness etc. *adj.;* individuality; solitude etc. (*seclusion*) 893; isolation etc. (*disjunction*) 44; unification etc. 48.

one, unit, ace; item; individual; solo, none else, no other, naught beside.

V. be -one, − alone etc. *adj.;* dine with Duke Humphrey.

isolate etc. (*disjoin*) 44.

render one; unite etc. (*join*) 43, (*combine*) 48.

Adj. one, sole, single, solitary, only- begotten; individual, apart, alone; kithless.

un-accompanied, -attended; *solus,* singlehanded; singular, odd, unique, unrepeated, azygous, first and last; isolated etc. (*disjoined*) 44; insular; unitary.

lone; lone-ly, -some; desolate, dreary.

in-secable, -severable, -discerptible; compact, irresolvable.

Adv. singly etc. *adj.;* alone, by itself, *per se,* only, apart, in the singular number, in the abstract; one -by one, − at a time; simply; one and a half, *sesqui-.*

Phr. *natura il fece, e poi roppe la stampa.*

88. Accompaniment.—N. accompaniment; appurtenance, adjunct etc. 39; context.

coexistence, concomitance, company, association, companionship; part-, copart-ner-ship; coefficiency.

concomitant, accessory, coefficient; companion, attendant, fellow, associate, consort, spouse, colleague, *fidus Achates;* part-, co-partner; satellite, hanger on, shadow; excort, *entourage,* suite, *cortège;* convoy, follower etc. 65; attribute.

V. accompany, coexist, attend, convoy, chaperon; hang −, wait- on; go hand in hand with; synchronize etc. 120; bear −, keep- company; row in the same boat; bring in its train, associate −, couple- with.

Adj. accompanying etc. *v.;* concomitant, fellow, twin, joint; associated −, coupled- with; accessory, attendant, *obbligato.*

Adv. with, withal; together −, along −, in company- with; hand in hand, side by side; cheek by -jowl, − jole; arm in arm; there-, here-with; and etc. (*addition*) 37.

together, in a body, collectively.

89. Duality.—N. dual-ity, -ism; duplicity; biplicity, -formity; span, polarity.

two, deuce, couple, couplet, doublet, brace, pair, cheeks, twins, Castor and Pollux, *gemini.* Siamese twins; fellows; yoke, conjugation, dyad, distich.

V. [unite in pairs] pair, couple, bracket, yoke; conduplicate, mate.

Adj. two, twain; dual, -istic; binary, binomial; twin, biparous; dyadic; conduplicate; duplex etc. 90; *tête-à-tête;* paired; dihedral.

coupled etc. *v.;* conjugate.

both, − the one and the other.

90. Duplication.—N. duplication, doubling etc. *v.;* gemi-, ingemi-nation; reduplication; iteration etc. (*repetition*) 104; renewal.

V. double; re-double, -duplicate; geminate; repeat etc. 104; renew etc. 660; duplicate, copy etc. 21.

Adj. double; doubled etc. *v.;* bicameral, bicapital, bi-fold, -form, -lateral, -farious, -facial; two-fold, -sided, -headed, -edged etc.; duplex; double-faced; twin, duplicate, ingeminate; second; dual etc. 29.

Adv. twice, once more; over again etc. (*repeatedly*) 104; as much again; twofold.

secondly, in the second place, again.

91. Bisection. [Division into two parts.]—N. bi-section, -partition; di-, subdi-chotomy; halving etc. *v.;* dimidiation; *hendiadis.*

bifurcation, forking, branching, furcation, ramification, divarication; fork, prong; fold.

half, moiety.
V. bisect, halve, divide, split, cut in two, cleave, dimidiate, dichotomize, divaricate.
go halves, divide with.
separate, fork, bifurcate; branch -off, – out; ramify.
Adj. bisected etc. *v.;* cloven, cleft; bipartite, biconjugate, bicuspid, bifid; bifur-cous, -cate, -cated; semi-, demi- hemi-

92. Triality.—N. triality, trinity,* triplicity.
three, triad, triplet, trey, trio, ternion, trinomial, leash; tierce; triennium; trefoil, triangle, trident, tripod, triumvirate, *troika.*
third power, cube.
Adj. three; tri-form, -nal, -nomial; tertiary; triune.
Trinity is hardly ever used except in a theological sense; see Deity 976.

93. Triplication.—N. tripli-cation,   -city; trebleness, trine, trilogy.
V. treble, triple, triplicate, cube.
Adj. treble, triple; tern, -ary; triplex, triplicate, threefold, trilogistic; third; trinal; trihedral.
Adv. three -times, – fold; thrice, in the third place, thirdly; trebly etc. *adj.*

94. Trisection. [Division into three parts.]—N. tri-section, -partition, -chotomy; third, – part.
V. trisect, divide into three parts, trifurcate.
Adj. trifid; trisected etc. *v.;* tripartite, -chotomous, -sulcate.

95. Quaternity.—N. quaternity, four, tetrad, quartet, quaternion, square, quadrature, quarter, quadruplet; quadrilateral, quadrangle, quatrefoil; *quadriga.*
V. reduce to a square, square.
Adj. four; quat-ernary, -ernal; quadratic; quartile, quartic, tetractic, tetrad, tetrahedral; quadrennial; quadrivalent.

96. Quadruplication.—N. quadruplication.
V. multiply by four, quadruplicate, biquadrate.
Adj. fourfold; quad-ruple, -ruplicate, -rible; quadruplex; fourth.
Adv. four times; in the fourth place, fourthly.

97. Quadrisection. [Division into four parts.]—N. quadri-section, -partition; quartering etc. *v.;* fourth; quart, -er, -ern; farthing (*i.e.* fourthing); quarto.
V. quarter, divide into four parts, quadrisect.
Adj. quartered etc. *v.;* quadri-fid, -partite.

98. Five, etc.—N. five, cinque, quint, quincunx, quintuplet, quintet, pentagon, pentameter, Pentateuch; six, half-a-dozen; sextet, hexagon, hexameter; seven, Heptarchy; eight, octet, octagon, octave; nine, three times three; ten, decade; eleven; twelve, dozen; thirteen; long –, baker's-dozen.
twenty, score; twenty-four, four and twenty, two dozen; twenty-five, five and twenty, quarter

of a hundred; forty, two score; fifty, half a hundred; sixty, three score, sexagenarian; seventy, three score and ten, septuagenarian; eighty, four score, octogenarian; ninety, four score and ten, nonagenarian.
hundred, centenary, hecatomb, century; hundredweight, cwt.; one hundred and forty-four, gross; bicentenary, tercentenary etc.
thousand, chiliad; myriad, millennium, ·ten thousand; lac, lakh, one hundred thousand, plum; million; thousand million, *milliard.*
billion, trillion etc.
V. centuriate.
Adj. five, quinary, quintuple; fifth; senary, sextuple; sixth; seventh; octuple; eighth; ninefold, ninth; tenfold, decimal, denary, decuple, tenth; eleventh; duo-denary, -denal; twelfth; in one's 'teens, thirteenth.
vices-, viges-imal; twentieth; twenty-fourth etc. *n.*
cent-uple, -uplicate, -ennial, -enary, -urial; secular, hundredth; thousandth; millenary etc.

99. Quinquesection, etc.—N. division by -five etc. 98; quinquesection etc.; fifth etc.; decimation.
V. decimate, quinquesect.
Adj. quinque-fid, -partite; quinquarticular; octifid; decimal, tenth, tithe, teind; duodecimal, twelfth; sexagesimal, -genary; hundredth, centesimal; millesimal etc.

100. Plurality. [More than one.]—N. plurality; a -number, – certain number; one or two, two or three etc.; a few, several; multitude etc. 102.
Adj. plural, more than one, upwards of, some, certain; not -alone etc. 87.
Adv. et cetera, etc., etc.
Phr. non deficit alter.

100a. Fraction [Less than one.]—N. fraction, fractional part, fragment; part etc. 51.
Adj. fractional, fragmentary, partial.

101. Zero.—N. zero, nothing, naught, nought, duck's egg, goose egg; cipher, none, nobody; not a soul; *âme qui vive;* absence etc. 187; unsubstantiality etc. 4.
Adj. not -one, – any.

102. Multitude.—N. multitude; numerousness etc. *adj.;* numer-osity, -ality; multiplicity; profusion etc. (*plenty*) 639; legion, host; great –, large –, round –, enormous- number; a quantity, numbers, array, sight, army, sea, galaxy; scores, peck, bushel, school, shoal, swarm, draft, bevy, cloud, flock, herd, drove, flight, covey, hive, brood, litter, farrow, fry, nest; mob, crowd etc. (*assemblage*) 72; lots, loads, heaps; all the world and his wife.
[Increase of number] greater number, majority; multiplication, multiple.
V. be -numerous etc. *adj.;* swarm –, teem –, crawl –, creep -with; crowd, swarm, come thick upon; outnumber, multiply; people; swarm like -locusts, — bees.
Adj. many, several, sundry, divers, various,

not a few; a -hundred, − thousand, − myriad, − million, − thousand and one; some -ten or a dozen, − forty or fifty etc.; half a -dozen, − hundred etc.; very −, full −, ever so- many; numer-ous, -ose; profuse, in profusion; manifold, multiplied, multitudinous, multiferous, multiple, multinomial, teeming, crawling, populous, peopled, crowded, thick, studded; galore.

thick coming, many more, more than one can tell, a world of; no end -of, − to; *cum multis aliis*; thick as -hops, − hail; plenty as blackberries; numerous as the -stars in the firmament, − sands on the sea-shore, − hairs on the head; and -what not, − heaven knows what; endless etc. (*infinite*) 105.

Phr. their name is 'Legion.'

103. Fewness.—N. fewness etc. *adj.*; paucity, small number; small quantity etc. 32; scarcity, sparsity; rarity; infrequency etc. 137; handfull; maniple; minority; exiguity.

[Diminution of number] reduction; weeding etc. *v.*; elimination, sarculation, decimation.

V. be -few etc. *adj.*

render -few etc. *adj.*; reduce, diminish the number, weed; eliminate, thin, decimate.

Adj. few; scarce; scant, -y; thin, rare, thinly scattered; few and far between; exiguous; infrequent etc. 137; *rari nantes*; hardly −, scarcely-any; to be counted on one's fingers; reduced etc. *v.*; unrepeated.

Adv. here and there.

104. Repetition.—N. repetition, iteration, reiteration, duplication, ding-dong, alliteration; *epistrophe;* harping, recurrence, succession, run; batto-, tauto-logy; monotony, tautophony; rhythm etc. 138; pleonasm, redundancy, diffuseness.

chimes, repetend, echo, *ritornello,* burden of a song, *refrain;* rehearsal; encore; *réchauffé, rifacimento,* recapitulation.

cuckoo etc. (*imitation*) 19; reverberation etc. 408; drumming etc. (*roll*) 407; renewal etc. (*restoration*) 660.

twice-told tale; old -story, − song, chestnut; second −, new- edition; reprint, new impression; return game, return match, reappearance, reproduction; periodicity etc. 138.

V. repeat, iterate, reiterate, reproduce, parrot, echo, re-echo, drum, harp upon, battologize, hammer, redouble.

recur, revert, return, reappear; renew etc. (*restore*) 660.

rehearse; do ¯−, say- over again; ring the changes on; harp on the same string; din −, drum- in the ear; conjugate in all its moods, tenses and inflexions, begin again, go over the same ground, go the same round, never hear the last of; resume, return to, recapitulate, reword.

Adj. repeated etc. *v.*; repetition-al, -ary; recurrent, -ring; ever recurring, thick coming; frequent, incessant, redundant, pleonastic, tautological.

monotonous, harping, iterative; mocking, chiming; retold; aforesaid, -named; above-mentioned, said; habitual etc. 613; another.

Adv. repeatedly, often, again, afresh, anew,

over again, once more; ditto, *encore, de novo, bis, da capo.*

again and again; over and over, − again; many times over; time- and again, − after time; year after year; day by day etc.; many −, several −, a number of- times; many −, full many- a time; times out of number, year in and year out, morning, noon and night; frequently etc. 136.

Phr. *ecce iterum* Crispinus, toujours perdrix, cut and come again; 'tomorrow and tomorrow.'

105. Infinity.—N. infini-ty, -tude, -teness etc. *adj.*; perpetuity etc. 112.

V. be -infinite etc. *adj.*; know −, have- no - limits, − bounds; go on for ever.

Adj. infinite, immense; number-, count-, sum-, measure-less; innumer-, immeasur-, incalcul-, illimit-, intermin-, unfathom-, unapproach-able; exhaustless, inexhaustible, indefinite; without - number, − measure, − limit, − end; incomprehensible; limit-, end-, bound-, termless; un-told, - numbered, -measured, -bounded, -limited; illimited; perpetual etc. 112.

Adv. infinitely etc. *adj.*; *ad infinitum.*

106. Time.—N. time, duration; period, term, stage, space, span, spell, season; the whole -time, − period; course etc. 109.

intermediate, time, while, *interim,* interval, bit, pendency; inter-vention, -mission, -mittence, -regnum, -lude; respite.

era, epoch, eon, cycle; time of life, age, year, date; decade etc. (*period*) 108; moment, etc. (*instant*) 113; reign etc. 737.

glass −, ravages −, whirligig −, noiseless foot- of time; scythe.

V. continue, last, endure, go on, hold out, remain, stay, persist, abide, run; intervene; elapse etc. 109.

take − take up −, fill −, occupy- time.

pass −, pass away −, spend −, while away −, consume −, talk against −, kill- time; tide over; use −, employ- time; tarry etc. 110; seize an opportunity etc. 134; waste time etc. (*be inactive*) 683.

Adj. continuing etc. *v.*; on foot; permanent etc. (*durable*) 110.

Adv. while, whilst, during, pending; during the -time, − interval; in the course of; for the time being, day by day; in the time of; when; meantime, -while; in the -meantime, − interim; *ad interim, pendente lite; de die in diem;* from -day to day, − hour to hour etc.; hourly, always; for a -time, − season; till, until, up to; yet; the whole −, all the- time; all along; throughout etc. (*completely*) 52; for good etc. (*diuturnity*) 110.

here-, there-, where-upon; then; *anno, − Domini;* A.D.; *ante Christum;* A.C.; before Christ; B.C.; *anno urbis conditae;* A.U.C.; *anno regni,* A.R.; once upon a time, one fine morning.

Phr. time -runs, − runs against; *tempus fugit.*

107. Neverness.—N. 'neverness;' absence of time, no time; *dies non;* Tib's eve; Greek Kalends.

Adv. never; at no -time, − period; on no occasion, never in all one's born days, nevermore, *sine die.*

108. Period. [Definite duration, or portion of time.]—N. period; second, minute, hour, day, week, sennight, octave, month, moon, quarter, semester, year, *lustrum, quinquennium*, decade, *decennium*, indiction, lifetime, generation, epoch, era, cycle.

century, age, *millennium; annus magnus.*

Adj. horary; hourly, annual etc. (*periodical*) 138.

108a. Contingent Duration.—Adv. during - pleasure, − good behavior; *quamdiu se bene gesserit.*

109. Course. [Indefinite duration.]—N. course −, progress −, process −, succession −, lapse −, flow −, flux −, effluxion, stream −, tract −, current −, sweep −, tide −, march −, step −, flight- of time; duration etc. 106.

[Indefinite time] aorist.

V. elapse, lapse, flow, run, proceed, advance, pass; roll −, wear −, press −, drag· on; flit, fly, slip, slide, glide, crawl; run -its course.

out; expire; go −, pass- by; be -past etc. 122.

Adj. elapsing etc. *v.;* aoristic; progressive, transient etc. 111.

Adv. in due -time, − season; in -course, − process, − the fulness- of time; in time.

Phr. *labitur et labetur; truditur dies die; fugaces labuntur anni;* 'tomorrow and tomorrow and tomorrow creeps in this petty pace from day to day.'

110. Diuturnity. [Long duration.]—N. diuturnity; a -long −, length of -time; an·age, a century. an eternity, aeons; slowness etc. 275; perpetuity etc. 112; blue moon.

dura-bleness, -bility; persistence, lastingness etc. *adj.;* continuance, assiduity, endurance, standing; permanence etc. (*stability*) 150; survival, -vance; longevity etc. (*age*) 128; distance of time.

protraction −, prolongation −, extension- of time; delay etc. (*lateness*) 133.

V. last, endure, stand, remain, abide, continue, brave a thousand years.

tarry etc. (*be late*) 133; drag -on, − its slow length along, − a lengthening chain; protract, prolong; spin −, eke −, draw −, lengthen- out; temporize; gain −, make −, talk against- time.

out-last, -live; survive; live to fight again.

Adj. durable; perdurable; lasting etc. *v.;* of long -duration, − standing; permanent, chronic, long-standing; intransi-ent, -tive; intransmutable, persistent; life-, live-long; longeval, long-lived, macrobiotic, diuturnal, sempervirent, evergreen, perennial; unin-, ter-, unremitting; perpetual etc. 112.

lingering, protracted, prolonged, spun out etc. *v.;* long-pending, -winded; slow etc. 275.

Adv. long; for -a long time, − an age, − ages, − ever so long, − many a long day; long ago etc. (*in a past time*) 122; *longo intervallo.*

all the -day long, − year round; the livelong day, as the day is long, morning, noon and night; hour after hour, day after day, etc.; for good; permanently etc. *adj.*

111. Transientness. [Short duration.]—N. transientness etc. *adj.;* evanescence, impermanence, fugacity, transitoriness, volatility, caducity, mortality, span; flash in the pan, nine days' wonder, bubble, May-fly; spurt; temporary arrangement, interregnum.

velocity etc. 274; suddenness etc. 113; changeableness etc. 149.

V. be -transient etc. *adj.;* flit, pass away, fly, gallop, vanish, fade, fleet, melt away, evaporate; pass away like a -cloud, − summer cloud, − shadow, − dream.

Adj. transi-ent, -tory, -tive; passing, evanescent, fleeting; flying etc. *v.;* fug-acious, -itive; shifting, slippery; spasmodic.

tempor-al, -ary; provis-ional, -ory; cursory, short-lived, ephemeral, deciduous; perishable, mortal, precarious; impermanent.

brief, quick, brisk; cometary, meteoric, extemporaneous, summary; pressed for time etc. (*haste*) 684; sudden, momentary etc. (*instantaneous*) 113.

Adv. temporarily etc. *adj.; pro tempore;* for - the moment, − a time; awhile, *en passant, in transitu;* in a short time; soon etc. (*early*) 132; briefly etc. *adj.;* at short notice; on the -point, − eve -of; *in articulo;* between cup and lip.

Phr. one's days are numbered; the time is up; her to-day and gone tomorrow; *non semper erit aestas; eheu! fugaces labuntur anni; sic transit gloria mundi.*

112. Perpetuity. [Endless duration.]—N. perpetuity, eternity, timelessness; everness, aye, sempiternity, immortality, athanasia; everlastingness etc. *adj.;* perpetuation; infinite duration.

V. last −, endure −, go on- for ever; have no end.

eternize, eternify, perpetuate, immortalize.

Adj. perpetual, eternal, eterne; everlasting, - living, -flowing; continual, constant, sempiternal; co-eternal; endless, unending; ceaseless, incessant, uninterrupted, indesinent, unceasing; interminable, having no end; unfading, evergreen, amaranthine; neverending, -dying, -fading; deathless, immortal, undying, imperishable.

Adv. perpetually etc. *adj.;* always, ever, evermore, aye; for -ever, − aye, − evermore, − ever and a day, −, ever and ever; in all ages, from age to age; without end; world −, time- without end; *in saecula saeculorum;* to the -end of time, − crack of doom, − 'last syllable of recorded time;' till doomsday; constantly etc. (*very frequently*) 136.

Phr. *esto perpetuum; labitur et labetur in omne volubilis aevum.*

113. Instantaneity. [Point of time.]—N. instantane-ity, -ousness; sudden-, abrupt-ness.

moment, instant, second, minute; twinkling, trice, flash, breath, crack, jiffy, *coup*, burst, flash of lightning, stroke of time.

epoch, time; time of -day, − night; hour, minute; very -minute etc., − time, − hours; present −, right −, true −, exact −, correct-time.

V. be -instantaneous etc. *adj.;* twinkle, flash.

Adj. instantaneous, momentary, extempore, sudden, instant, abrupt; subitaneous, hasty; quick as- thought,* − lightning, − a flash; rapid as electricity.

Adv. instantaneously etc. *adj.*; in — in less than-no time; *presto, subito, instanter,* suddenly, at a stroke, like- a shot, — greased lightning; in a trice, in a moment etc. *n.*; eftsoons, in the twinkling of - ar eye, — a bed post; at one jump, in the same breath, *per saltum, uno saltu*; at — , all at- once; in one's tracks; plump, slap; 'at one fell swoop;' at the same -instant etc. *n.*; immediately etc. (*early*) 132; *ex tempore,* on the -spot, — spur of the moment, — dot; just then; slap- dash etc. (*haste*) 684; before you could -turn round, — say -knife, — Jack Robinson.

> **Phr.** touch and go; no sooner said than done.
*See note on 264.

114. Chronometry. [Estimation, measurement, and record of time.]—**N.** chrono-, horo-metry, -logy; date, epoch; style, era.

almanac, calendar, ephemeris; register, -try; chronicle, annals, journal, diary, chronogram.

[Instruments for the measurement of time] clock, watch; chrono-meter, -scope, -graph; repeater, alarum; time-keeper, -piece; dial, sun-dial, *gnomon, pendule,* horologe, pendulum, hourglass, water clock, clepsydra.

mean — , Greenwich — , solar — , sidereal — , local — , summer- time; daylight saving.

chrono-grapher, -loger, -logist; annalist.

V. fix — , mark- the time; date, register, chronicle; measure — , beat — , mark- time; bear date.

Adj. chrono-logical, -metrical, -grammatical; isochronal.

Adv. o'clock; *a.m., p.m.*

115. Anachronism. [False estimate of time.]—**N.** ana-, meta-, para-, prochronism; *prolepsis,* misdate; anticipation, antichronism.

disregard — , neglect — , oblivion- of time. intempestivity etc. 135.

V. mis-, ante-, post-, over-date; anticipate; take no note of time.

Adj. misdated etc. *v.;* undated; overdue; out of date; anachronous etc. *n.*

116. Priority.—**N.** priority, antecedence; anteriority, pre-existence,- precedence etc. 62; precession etc. 280; precursor etc. 64; the past etc. 122; premises.

V. precede, come before; forerun; antecede, go before etc. (*lead*) 280; pre-exist; dawn; premise, presage etc. 511.

be -beforehand etc. (*be early*) 132; steal a march upon, anticipate, forestall; have — , gain-the start.

Adj. prior, previous; preced-ing, -ent; anterior, antecedent; pre-existing, -existent; foresighted; former,-foregoing; afore — , before-, above-mentioned; aforesaid, said; introductory etc. (*precursory*) 64; pre-war.

Adv. before, prior to; earlier; previously etc. *adj.;* afore, ere, theretofore, erewhile, ere — , before- -then, — now; erewhile, already, yet, beforehand; aforetime; on the eve of, in anticipation.

117. Posteriority.—**N.** posteriority; succession, sequence; following etc. 281; subsequence,

supervention; futurity etc. 121; successor; sequel etc. 65; remainder, reversion.

V. follow etc. 281 — , come — , go- after; ensue, result; succeed, supervene; step into the shoes of.

Adj. subsequent, posterior, following, after, later, succeeding, postliminious, postnate; successive etc. 63; postdiluvial, -an; *puisné;* posthumous; post-war, future etc. 121.

Adv. subsequently, after, afterwards, since, later; at a -subsequent, — later- period; next, in the sequel, close upon, thereafter. thereupon, upon which, eftsoons; from that -time, — moment; after a -while, — time; in process of time.

postcenal, postcibal, postprandial, after-dinner.

118. The Present Time.—**N.** the present -time, — day, — moment, — juncture, — occasion; the times, existing time, time being; twentieth century; nonce, crisis, epoch, day, hour.

age, time of life.

Adj. present, actual, instant, current, latest, existing, that is.

Adv. at this -time, — moment etc. 113; at the - present time etc. *n.;* now, at present.

at this time of day, to-day, now-adays; already; even — , but — , just-now; on the present occasion; for the -time being, — nonce; *pro hâc vice;* on the -nail, — spot; on the spur of the -moment, — occasion.

until now; to -this, — the present day.

119. Different Time. [Time different from the present.]—**N.** different — , other- time.

[Indefinite time] aorist.

Adj. aoristic.

Adv. at that — , at which- -time, — moment, — instant; then, on that occasion, upon.

when; when-ever, -soever; upon which, on which occasion; at -another, — a different, — some other, — any - time; at various times; some — , one- -of these days, — fine morning, — day; sooner or later; some time or other; once upon a time, once.

120. Synchronism.—**N.** synchronism; coexistence, coincidence; simultaneousness etc. *adj.;* concurrence, concomitance, unity of time, interim.

[Having equal times] isochronism, syntony.

contemporary, coetanian.

V. coexist, concur, accompany, go hand in hand, keep pace with; synchronize, isochronize.

Adj. synchron-ous, -al, -ical, -istical; simultaneous, coexisting, coincident, concomitant, concurrent; coev-al; contempora-ry, -neous; coetaneous; coterminous, coeternal; isochronous.

Adv. at the same time; simultaneously etc. *adj.;* together, in concert; during the same time; in the same breath; *pari passu;* in the interim.

at the -very moment etc. 113; just as, as soon as; meanwhile etc. (*while*) 106.

121. Futurity. [Prospective time.]—**N.** futurity, -ition; future, hereafter, time to come; approaching — , coming — , after- -time, — age, — days, — hours, — years, — ages, — life;

morrow, to-morrow, by and by; millennium, doomsday, day of judgment, crack of doom, remote future.

approach of time, advent, time drawing on, womb of time; destiny etc. 152; eventuality.

heritage, heirs, posterity, descendants.

prospect etc. (*expectation*) 507; foresight etc. 510.

V. look forwards; anticipate etc. (*expect*) 507, (*foresee*) 510; forestall etc. (*be early*) 132.

come −, draw- on; draw near; approach, await, threaten; impend etc. (*be destined*) 152.

Adj. future, to come; coming etc. (*impending*) 152; next, near; near −, close- at hand; eventual, ulterior; expectant, prospective, in prospect etc. (*expectation*) 507.

Adv. prospectively, hereafter, on the knees of the gods, in future; to-morrow, the day after to-morrow; in -course, − process, − the fulness- of time; eventually, ultimately, sooner or later; *proxImo; paulo post futurum;* in after time; one of these days; after a -time, − while.

from this time; hence-forth, -forwards; thence; thence-forth, -forward; whereupon, upon which.

soon etc. (*early*) 132; on the -eve, − point, − brink- of; about to; close upon.

122. Preterition. [Retrospective time.]—N. preterition, priority etc. 116; the past, past time; days −, times- -of yore, − of old, − past, − gone by; bygone days, good old days; old −, ancient −, former -times; fore time; yesterdays; the olden −, good old- time; auld lang syne; eld.

antiquity, antiqueness, *status quo;* time immemorial; distance of time; remote -age, − time; ancient history; remote past; rust of antiquity; ancientness.

pale-ontology, -ography, -ology; palaetiol-ogy,* archaeology; archaism, antiquarianism, mediaevalism, pre- Raphaelitism; retrospection, looking back, memory etc. 505.

laudator temporis acti; mediaevalist, pre-Raphaelite; antiqu-ary, -arian; archaeologist etc.; Oldbuck, Dryasdust.

ancestry etc. (*paternity*) 166.

V. be -past etc. *adj.;*have -expired etc. *adj.;* − run its course, − had its day; pass; pass −, go- - by, − away, − off; lapse, blow over.

look −, trace −, cast the eyes- back; exhume.

Adj. past, gone, gone by, over, passed away, bygone, foregone; elapsed, lapsed, preterlapsed, expired, no more, run out, blown over, that has been, whilom, extinct, never to return, exploded, forgotten, irrecoverable; obsolete etc. (*old*) 124; extinct as the dodo.

former, pristine, *quondam, ci-devant,* late; ancestral.

foregoing; last, latter; recent, overnight; past, preterite, preter-perfect, -pluperfect, past perfect.

looking back etc. *v.;* retro-spective, -active; archaelogical etc. *n.*

Adv. formerly; of -old, −yore; erst, whilom, erewhile, time was, ago, over; in -the olden time etc. *n.;* anciently, long -ago, − since; a long -while, − time- ago; years −, ages-ago; some time -ago, − since, − back.

yesterday, the day before yesterday; last -year, − season, − month etc.; *ultimo,* lately etc. (*newly*) 123.

retrospectively; ere −, before −, till- now; hitherto, heretofore; no longer; once, − upon a time; from time immemorial; in the memory of man; time out of mind; already, yet, up to this time; *ex post facto.*

Phr. time was; the time -has, − hath- been. *Whewell.*

123. Newness.—N. newness etc. *adj.;* neologism, neoterism; novelty, recency; immaturity; youth etc. 127; gloss of novelty.

innovation; renovation etc. (*restoration*) 660.

modernist, neologist, neoteric.

modernism, modernity; mushroom; latest fashion, *dernier cri.*

upstart, *parvenu, nouveau riche.*

V. renew etc. (*restore*) 660; modernize.

Adj. new, novel, recent, fresh, green; young etc. 127; evergreen; raw, immature; virgin; un-tried, -handseled, -used, -trodden, -beaten; fledgling.

late, modern, neoteric; new-born, -fashioned, -fangled, -fledged; of yesterday; just out, brand −, span-new, up to date, topical; vernal, renovated; innovatory.

fresh as -a rose, − a daisy, − paint; spick and span.

Adv. newly etc. *adj.;* afresh, anew, lately, just now, only yesterday, the other day; latterly, of late.

not long −, a short time- ago.

124. Oldness.—N. oldness etc. *adj.;* age, antiq-uity; cobwebs of antiquity.

maturity, ripeness; decline, decay; senility etc. 128.

seniority, eldership, primogeniture.

archaism etc. (*the past*) 122; thing −, relic- of the past; megatherium.

tradition, prescription, custom, folklore, immemorial usage, common law.

V. be -old etc. *adj.;* have -had, − seen- its day; become -old etc. *adj.;* age, fade.

Adj. old, olden, ancient, antique; of long standing, time-honored, venerable; eld-er, -est; first-born.

prime; prim-itive, -eval, -igenous; primordi-al, -nate; aboriginal etc. (*beginning*) 66; diluvian, antediluvian; pre-historic; patriarchal, preadamite; paleocrystic; fossil, paleozoic, pre-glacial, ante-mundane; archaic, classic, mediaeval, pre-Raphaelite, ancestral, black-letter.

immemorial, traditional, prescriptive, customary, whereof the memory of man runneth not to the contrary; inveterate, rooted.

antiquated, of other times, rococo, of the old school, after-age, obsolete; fusty, moth-eaten; out of -date, − fashion; stale, old-fashioned, behind the -age, − times; exploded; gone out, − by; *passé,* outworn, run out; disused; senile etc. 128; time-worn; crumbling etc. (*deteriorated*) 659; second-hand.

old as -the hills, − Methuselah, − Adam, − history.

Adv. since the -world was made, − year one, − days of Methuselah.

125. Morning. [Noon.]—N. morning, morn, matins, forenoon, *a.m.,* prime, dawn, daybreak, daylight, sun-up, peep −, break- of day; aurora,

Eos; first blush −, prime- of the morning; twilight, crepuscule, sunrise, cockcrow.

spring; vernal equinox.

noon; mid-, noon-day; noontide, meridian, prime.

summer, midsummer; summer solstice.

Adj. matin, matutinal; vernal, aestival.

Adv. at -sunrise etc. *n.*; with the lark, when the morning dawns.

126. Evening. [Midnight.]—N. evening, eve; decline −, fall −, close- of day; eventide, evensong, vespers; candlelight; nightfall, curfew, dusk, twilight, blind man's holiday; eleventh hour; sun-set, -down; going down of the sun, cock-shut, dewy eve, gloaming, bed-time.

afternoon, *post meridiem, p.m.*

autumn; fall, − of the leaf; autumnal equinox, Indian summer, harvest-time.

midnight; dead −, witching time- of night; winter, − solstice.

Adj. vespertine, autumnal, nocturnal, wintry, brumal, hiemal.

127. Youth.—N. youth; juven- -ility, -escence; juniority; infancy; baby-, child-, boy-, girl-, youth-hood; *incunabula;* minority, immaturity, nonage, teens, tender age, bloom.

cradle, nursery, leading-strings, pupilage, puberty, *pucelage.*

prime −, flower −, spring-tide −, seedtime −, golden season - of life; heyday of youth, school days; rising generation, younger generation.

Adj. young, youthful, juvenile, green, callow, budding, sappy, *puisné*, beardless, unfledged, unripe, under age, in one's teens; *in statu pupillari;* younger, junior.

128. Age.—N. age; oldness etc. *adj.;* old −, advanced- age; sen-ility, -escence; years, anility, grey hairs, climacteric, grand climacteric, declining years, decrepitude, hoary age, caducity, superannuation; second childhood, -ishness; dotage; vale of years, decline of life, 'sear and yellow leaf;' three-score years and ten; green old age, ripe old age; longevity; time of life.

seniority, eldership; elders etc. (*veteran*) 130; firstling; *doyen*, dean, father; primogeniture; nostology.

V. be -aged etc. *adj.;* grow −, get- old etc. *adj.;* age; decline, wane.

Adj. aged; old etc. 124; elderly, senile; matronly, anile; in years; ripe, mellow, run to seed, declining, waning, past one's prime; grey, -headed; hoar, -y; venerable, time-worn, antiquated, *passé*, effete, doddering, decrepit, superannuated; advanced in -life, − years; stricken in years; wrinkled, marked with the crow's foot; having one foot in the grave; doting etc. (*imbecile*) 499.

old-, eld-er, -est; senior; first-born.

turned of, years old; of a certain age, no chicken, old as Methuselah; gerontic; ancestral; patriarchal etc. (*ancient*) 124.

129. Infant.—N. infant, babe, baby; nurse-, suck-, year-, wean-ling; *papoose, bambino.*

child, bairn, little- one, − tot, − mite, chick, brat, chit, pickaninny, kid, urchin; bant-, bratling; elf.

youth, boy, lad, slip, sprig, stripling, youngster, cub, unlicked cub, younker, callant, whipster, whipper-snapper, schoolboy, hobbledehoy, hopeful, cadet, minor, master.

scion; sap-, seed-ling; tendril, olive branch, nestling, chicken, duckling; larva, caterpillar, chrysalis, cocoon; tadpole, whelp, cub, pullet, fry, callow; codlin, -g; *foetus*, calf, colt, pup, foal, kitten; lamb, -kin.

girl; lass, -ie; wench, miss, damsel, *demoiselle*, damozel; maid, -en; virgin; nymph; colleen; minx, baggage, school-girl; tomboy, flapper, hoyden.

Adj. infant-ine, -ile; puerile; boy-, girl-, child-, baby-, kitten-ish; baby; new-born, unfledged, new-fledged, callow.

in -the cradle, − swaddling clothes, − long clothes, − arms, − leading strings; at the breast; in one's teens; young etc. 127.

130. Veteran.—N. veteran, old man, seer, patriarch, greybeard, dugout, grand-father, -sire; grandam, beldam; gaffer, gammer; hag, crone; pantaloon; sexage-, octoge-, nonage-, cente-narian; old stager; dotard etc. 501.

preadamite, Methuselah, Nestor, Rip van Winkle, old Parr; elders; forefathers etc. (*paternity*) 166.

131. Adolescence.—N. adolescence, pubescence, majority; adultness etc. *adj.;* manhood, virility, maturity; flower of age; prime −, meridian- of life.

man etc. 373; woman etc. 374; adult, no chicken.

V. come -of age, − to man's estate, − to years of discretion; attain majority, assume the *toga virilis;* have -cut one's eye-teeth, − sown one's wild oats, settle down.

Adj. adolescent, pubescent, of age; of -full, − ripe- age; out of one's teens, grown up, mature, full- blown, − grown, in one's prime, in full bloom, manly, virile, adult; womanly, matronly; marriageable, nubile.

132. Earliness.—N. earliness etc. *adj.;* morning etc. 125.

punctuality; promptitude etc. (*activity*) 682; haste etc. (*velocity*) 274; suddenness etc. (*instantaneity*) 113.

prematurity, precocity, precipitation, anticipation; prevenience, a stitch in time.

V. be -early etc. *adj.;* − beforehand etc. *adv.;* keep time, take time by the forelock, anticipate, forestall; have −, gain- the start; steal a march upon; gain time, draw on futurity; bespeak, secure, engage, pre-engage.

accelerate; expedite etc. (*quicken*) 274; make haste etc. (*hurry*) 684.

Adj. early, prime, timely, in time, punctual, forward; prompt etc. (*active*) 682; summary.

premature, precipitate, precocious; prevenient, anticipatory; rathe.

sudden etc. (*instantaneous*) 113; unexpected etc. 508; impending, imminent; near, − at hand; immediate.

Adv. early, soon, anon, betimes, rathe; eft, -soons; ere −, before- long; punctually etc. *adj.;* to the minute; in time; in -good, − military, − pudding, − due- time; time enough.

beforehand; prematurely etc. *adj.;* precipitately etc. (*hastily*) 684; too soon; before -its, − one's- time; in anticipation; unexpectedly etc. 508.

suddenly etc. (*instantaneously*) 113; before one can say 'Jack Robinson,' at short notice, extempore; on the spur of the -moment, − occasion; at once; on the -spot, − instant; at sight; off −, out of- hand; *à vue d'oeil;* straight, - way, -forth; forthwith, incontinently, summarily, instanter, immediately, briefly, shortly, quickly, speedily, apace, before the ink is dry, almost immediately, presently, at the first opportunity, in no long time, by and by, in a while, directly.

Phr. touch and go, no sooner said than done.

133. Lateness.—N. lateness etc. *adj.;* tardiness etc. (*slowness*) 275.

de-lay, -lation; cunctation, procrastination; detention; deferring etc. *v.;* filibuster, postponement, adjournment, prorogation, retardation, respite, reprieve, stay; protraction, prolongation, moratorium; contango; demurrage; remand; Fabian policy, *médecine expectante,* chancery suit; leeway; high time.

V. be -late etc. *adj.;* tarry, wait, stay, bide, take time; dawdle etc. (*be inactive*) 683; linger, loiter, saunter, lag behind; bide −, take- one's time; hang -about, − around, − back, − in the balance; gain time; hang fire; stand −, lie-over.

put off, defer, delay, lay over, suspend; shift −, stave- off; waive, retard, remand, postpone, adjourn; procrastinate; dally; prolong, protract; spin −, draw −, lengthen- out; prorogue; keep back; tide over; push −, drive- to the last; let the matter stand over; reserve etc. (*store*) 636; temporize; consult one's pillow, sleep upon it.

shelve, table, lay on the table.

lose an opportunity etc. 135; be kept waiting, dance attendance; kick −, cool- one's heels; *faire antichambre;* wait impatiently; await etc. (*expect*) 507; sit up, − at night.

Adj. late, tardy, slow, behindhand, belated, postliminious, posthumous, backward, unpunctual; dilatory etc. (*slow*), overdue 275; delayed etc. *v.;* in abeyance.

Adv. late; late-, back-ward; late in the day; at -sunset, − the eleventh hour, − length, − last, − long; ultimately; after −, behind- time; too late; too late for etc. 135.

slowly, leisurely, deliberately, at one's leisure; *ex post facto; sine die.*

Phr. *nonum prematur in annum.*

134. Occasion.—N. occasion, opportunity, opening, room, scope, field; suitable −, proper- - time, − season; high time; opportuneness etc. *adj.;* tempestivity.

crisis, turn, juncture, emergency, conjuncture; turning point; given time.

nick of time; golden −, well-timed −, fine −, favorable- opportunity; clear stage, fair field; *mollia tempora; fata Morgana;* spare time etc. (*leisure*) 685.

V. seize etc. (*take*) 789 −, use etc. 677 −, give etc. 784- an -opportunity, − occasion; improve the occasion.

suit the occasion etc. (*be expedient*) 646.

strike the iron while it is hot, *battre le fer sur l'enclume,* make hay while the sun shines, take time by the forelock, *prendre la balle au bond.*

Adj. opportune, timely, well-timed, timeous, timeful, seasonable.

providential, lucky, fortunate, happy, favorable, propitious, auspicious, critical; suitable etc. 23; *obiter dicta.*

Adv. opportunely etc. *adj. ;* in -proper, − due- -time, − course, − season; for the nonce; in the -nick, − fulness- of time; all in good time; just in time, at the eleventh hour, now or never.

by the -way, − by; *en passant, à propos; pro - re natâ,* − *hac vice; par parenthèse,* parenthetically, by way of parenthesis; while -speaking of, − on this subject; *ex tempore;* on the spur of the -moment, − occasion; on the spot etc. (*early*) 132.

Phr. *carpe diem; occasionem cognosce;* one's hour is come, the time is up; that reminds me.

135. Intempestivity.—N. intempestivity; unseasonableness; unsuitable −, improper-time; unreasonableness etc. *adj.;* evil hour; *contretemps;* intrusion; anachronism etc. 115.

V. be -ill timed etc. *adj.;* mistime, intrude, come amiss, break in upon; have other fish to fry; be -busy, − engaged, − tied up, − occupied.

lose −, throw away −, waste −, neglect etc. 460- an opportunity; allow −, suffer- the -opportunity, − occasion- to -pass, − slip, − go by, − escape, − lapse; waste time etc. (*be inactive*) 683; let slip through the fingers, lock the stable door when the steed is stolen.

Adj. ill-, mis-timed; untimely, intrusive, unseasonable; out of -date, − season; inopportune, timeless, untoward, *mal à propos,* unlucky, inauspicious, unpropitious, unfortunate, unfavorable; unsuited etc. 24; inexpedient etc. 647.

unpunctual etc. (*late*) 133; too late for; premature etc. (*early*) 132; too soon for; wise after the event.

Adv. inopportunely etc. *adj.;* as ill luck would have it, in an evil hour, the time having gone by, a day after the fair.

Phr. after meat mustard, after death the doctor.

136. Frequency.—N. frequency, oftness; repetition, etc. 104.

V. recur etc. 104; do nothing but; keep, − on.

Adj. frequent, many times, not rare, thickcoming, incessant, perpetual, continual, constant, recurrent, repeated etc. 104; habitual etc. 613; hourly, etc. 138.

Adv. often, often to be met with, oft; oft-, often-times; frequently; repeatedly etc. 104; unseldom, not unfrequently; in -quick, − rapid- succession; many a time and oft; daily, hourly etc.; every -day, − hour, − moment etc.

perpetually, continually, constantly, incessantly, without ceasing, at all times, daily and hourly, night and day, day and night, day after day, morning, noon and night, ever and anon.

most often; commonly etc. (*habitually*) 613.

sometimes, occasionally, at times, now and then, from time to time, there being times when, *toties quoties*, often enough, again and again etc. 104.

137. Infrequency.—N. infrequency, infrequence, rareness, rarity; fewness etc. 103; seldomness, uncommonness.
V. be -rare etc. *adj.*
Adj. un-, in-frequent; uncommon, sporadic, rare, — as a blue diamond; few etc. 103; scarce; almost unheard of, unprecedented, which has not occurred within the memory of the oldest inhabitant, not within one's previous experience.
Adv. seldom, rarely, scarcely, hardly; not often, unfrequently, infrequently, unoften; scarcely —, hardly- ever; once in a while.
once; once -for all, — in a way; *pro hac vice;* like angels' visits, few and far between.

138. Regularity of recurrence. **Periodicity.**—N. periodicity, intermittence; beat; oscillation etc. 314; pulse, pulsation; rhythm; alternation, -nateness, -nativeness, -nity.
bout, round, revolution, rotation, turn.
anniversary, birthday, jubilee, centenary, bi-, ter-centenary.
[Regularity of return] rota, cycle, period, stated time, routine; days of the week; Sunday, Monday etc.; months of the year; January etc.; feast, fast, saint's day etc.; Christmas, Easter, New Year's Day etc. 998; quarter-, Lady-, Midsummer-, Michaelmas-day; May Day, the King's Birthday; leap year, seasons.
punctuality, regularity, steadiness.
V. recur in regular -order, — succession; return, revolve, rotate; come -again, — in its turn; come round, — again; beat, pulsate; alternate; intermit.
Adj. periodic, -al; serial, recurrent, cyclic-, -al, rhythmic-, -al, even; recurring etc. *V.;* inter-, remittent; alternate, every other.
hourly; diurnal, daily; quotidian, tertian, weekly; ,hebdomad-al, -ary; bi-weekly, fortnightly; monthly, menstrual, catamenial; yearly, annual; biennial, triennial, etc.; bissextile; centennial, secular; paschal, lenten, etc.
regular, steady, punctual, constant, methodical, regular as clockwork.
Adv. periodically etc. *adj.;* at -regular intervals, — stated times; at -fixed, — established-periods; punctually etc. *adj.; de die in diem;* from day to day, day by day.
by turns, in -turn; — rotation; alternately, every other day, off and on, ride and tie, round and round.

139. Irregularity of recurrence.—N. irregularity, uncertainty, unpunctuality; fitfulness etc. *adj.*
Adj. irregular, uneven, uncertain, unpunctual, capricious, erratic, desultory; fitful, flickering; rambling, rhapsodical; spasmodic, unsystematic, unequal, variable, halting.
Adv. irregularly etc. *adj.;* by fits and starts etc. (*discontinuously*) 70.

140. Change. [Difference at different times.]—N. change, alteration, mutation, permutation, variation, modification, modulation, inflexion, mood, qualification, innovation, *metastasis,* deviation, shift, turn; diversion; break.
transformation, transfiguration; metamorphosis; metabolism; transmutation; transsubstantiation; metagenesis, transanimation, transmigration, metempsychosis; version, metathesis, transmogrification; catalysis; *avatar;* alterative.
conversion etc. (*gradual change*) 144; revolution etc. (*sudden or radical change*) 146; inversion etc. (*reversal*) 218; displacement etc. 185; transference etc. 270.
changeableness etc. 149; tergiversation etc. (*change of mind*) 607.
V. change, alter, vary, wax and wane; modulate, diversify, qualify, tamper with; turn, shift, veer, jibe, tack, chop, shuffle, swerve, dodge, warp, deviate, turn aside, evert, intervert; pass to, take a turn, turn the corner, resume.
work a change, modify, vamp, revamp, superinduce; trans-form, —mute, -ume, -figure etc. *n.;* metamorphose, ring the changes; convert, resolve; revolutionize; chop and change; patch, re-shape.
innovate, introduce new blood, shuffle the cards, spin the wheel; give a -turn, — color- to; influence, turn the scale; ,shift the scene, turn over a new leaf.
recast etc. 146; reverse etc. 218; disturb etc. 61; convert into etc. 144.
Adj. changed etc. *v.;* new-fangled; changeable etc. 149; transitional; modifiable; alterative.
Adv. *mutatis mutandis.*
Int. *quantum mutatus!*
Phr. 'a change came o'er the spirit of my dream;' *nous avons changé tout cela; tempora mutantur et nos mutamur in illis; non sum qualis eram.*

141. Permanence. [Absence of change.]—N. stability etc. 150; quiescence etc. 265; obstinacy etc. 606.
permanence, -cy, persistence, fixity, fixity of purpose, endurance, durability; standing, *status quo;* maintenance, preservation, conservation; conservatism; *laissez-faire;* law of the Medes and Persians; standing dish.
V. let -alone, — be; persist, remain, stay, tarry, rest; hold, — on; last, endure, bide, abide, aby, dwell, maintain, keep; stand, — still, — fast; subsist, live, outlive, survive; hold —, keep- one's ground, — footing; hold good.
Adj. stable etc. 150; persisting etc. *v.;* permanent; established, fixed; durable; unchanged etc. (change etc. 140); unrenewed; intact, inviolate; persistent; monotonous, uncheckered; unfailing.
un-destroyed, -repealed, -suppressed; conservative, *qualis ab incepto;* prescriptive etc. (*old*) 124; stationary etc. 265.
Adv. *in statu quo;* for good, finally; at a stand, - still; *uti possidetis;* without a shadow of turning.
Phr. as you were!; *j'y suis j'y reste; esto perpetua; nolumus leges Angliae mutari;* let sleeping dogs lie.

142. Cessation. [Change from action to

rest.]—N. cessation, discontinuance, desistance, desinence.

inter-, re-mission; sus-pense, -pension, interruption, hitch; hartal; stop; stopping etc. *v.;* closure, stoppage, halt; arrival etc. 292.

pause, rest, lull, respite, truce, armistice, drop; interregnum, abeyance.

closure etc. 261.

dead -stop, − stand, − lock; checkmate; comma, colon, semicolon, period, full stop; end etc. 67; death etc. 360; *caesura.*

V. cease, discontinue, desist, stay; break −, leave- off; hold, stop, pull up, stall, stop short, check; stick, deadlock, hand fire; halt; pause, rest.

have done with, give over, surcease, shut up shop; give up etc. (*relinquish*) 624.

hold −, stay- one's hand; rest on one's oars, repose on one's laurels.

come to a -stand, − standstill, − dead lock, − full stop; arrive etc. 292; go out, die away, peter out; wear -away, − off; pass away etc. (*be past*) 122; be at an end.

intromit, interrupt, suspend, interpel; inter-, re-mit; put -an end, − a stop, − a period- to; bring to a stand, -still; stop, cut out, cut short, arrest, avast; stem the -tide, − torrent; pull the check string; switch off.

Int. halt! hold! stop! enough! avast! have done! a truce to! soft! leave off! shut up! give over! chuck it!

143. **Continuance** in action.—N.continu-ance, -ation; run; extension; prolongation; maintenance, perpetuation; persistence etc. (*perseverance*) 604a; repetition etc. 104.

V. continue, persist; go −, jog −, keep −, carry −, run − hold- on; abide, keep, pursue, stick to; endure; take −, maintain- its course; keep up.

sustain, uphold, hold up, keep on foot; follow up, perpetuate. prolong; maintain; preserve etc. 604a; harp upon etc. (*repeat*)104.

keep -going, − alive, − at it, − the pot boiling, − the ball rolling, − up the ball; plod-, plug-along; slog on; die in harness; hold on −, pursue- the even tenor of one's way.

let be; *stare super antiquas vias; quieta non movere;* let things take their course.

Adj. continuing etc. *v.;* uninterrupted, unintermitting, unremitting, unvarying, unshifting; unreversed, unstopped, unrevoked, unvaried; sustained; undying etc. (*perpetual*) 112; inconvertible.

follow-up.

Int. carry on! right away!

Phr. *vestigia nulla retrorsum,· labitur et labetur.*

144. **Conversion.** [Gradual change to something different.]—N. conversion, reduction, transmutation, transformation, development, resolution, assimilation; assumption; naturalization.

chemistry, alchemy; progress, growth, lapse, flux.

passage; transit, -ion; transmigration, shifting etc. *v.;* conjugation; convertibility.

crucible, alembic, caldron, retort, test tube etc.

convert, neophyte, proselyte, pervert, renegade, deserter, apostate, turncoat.

V. be converted into; become, get, wax; come −, turn--to, − into; turn out, lapse, shift; run −, fall −, pass −, slide −, glide −, grow −, ripen −, open −, resolve itself −, settle −, merge- into; melt, grow, come round to, mature, mellow; assume the -form, − shape, − state. − nature, − character- of; illapse; assume a new phase, undergo a change.

convert −, resolve- into; make, render; mold, form etc. 240; remodel, new model, refound, reform, reorganize; assimilate −, bring − reduce- to; transform.

Adj. converted into etc. *v.;* convertible, resolvable into; transitional; naturalized.

Adv. gradually etc. (*slowly*) 275; *in transitu* etc. (*transference*) 270.

145. **Reversion.**—N. reversion, return; revulsion; reaction.

turning point, turn of the tide; *status quo ante bellum;* calm before a storm.

alternation etc. (*periodicity*) 138; inversion etc. 219; recoil etc. 277; regression etc. 283; restoration etc. 660; relapse etc. 661; vicinism, atavism, throwback.

V. revert, turn back, return; relapse etc. 661; recoil etc. 277; retreat etc. 283; restore etc. 660; undo, unmake; turn the -tide, − scale; escheat.

Adj. reverting etc. *v.;* revulsive, reactionary.

Adv. *à rebours,* wrong side out.

146. **Revolution.** [Sudden or violent change.]—N. revolution, *bouleversement,* subversion. break up; destruction etc. 162; sudden −, radical −, sweeping −, organic- change; clean sweep, *coup d'état,* overthrow, *débâcle*; counter-revolution, rebellion etc. 742.

transilience, jump, leap, plunge, jerk, start; explosion; spasm, convulsion, throe, revulsion; storm, earthquake, eruption, upheaval, cataclysm.

legerdemain etc. (*trick*) 545.

V. revolutionize; new model, remodel, recast; strike out something new, break with the past; change the face of, unsex; revert etc. 742.

Adj. unrecognizable.

Revolutionary, Bolshevik etc. 742.

147. **Substitution.** [Change of one thing for another.]—N. substitution, subrogation, commutation; supplanting etc. *v.;* supersession,. metonymy etc. (*figure of speech*) 521.

[Thing substituted.] substitute, *succedaneum,* make-shift, temporary expedient, shift, *pis aller,* stop-gap, jury-mast, *locum tenens,* warming-pan, dummy, goat, scape-goat; double; changeling; *quid pro quo,* alternative; remount; representative etc. (*deputy*) 759; palimpsest.

price, purchase-money, consideration, equivalent.

V. substitute, put in the place of, change for; make way for, give place to; supply −, take- the place of; supplant, supersede, replace, cut out, serve as a substitute; step into −, stand in- the shoes of; make a shift −, put up- with; borrow of Peter to pay Paul; commute, redeem, compound for.

Adj. substituted etc., *v.;* vicarious, subdititious; substitutional.
Adv. instead; in -place, – lieu, – the stead, – the room- of; *faute de mieux.*

148. Interchange. [Double or mutual change.]—N. inter-, ex-change; com-, per-, intermutation; reciprocation, transposal, transposition, shuffling; reciprocity, castling [at chess]; hocus-pocus.
interchange-ableness, -ability.
barter etc. 794; tit for tat etc. (*retaliation*) 718; cross fire, battledore and shuttlecock; *quid pro quo.*
V. inter-; ex-, counter-change; bandy, transpose, shuffle, change hands, swap, trade, permute, reciprocate, commute; give and take, return the compliment; play at -puss in the corner, – battledore and shuttlecock; retaliate etc. 718; barter etc. 794.
Adj. interchanged etc. *v.;* reciprocal, mutual, commutative, interchanged etc. *v.;* interchangeable, intercurrent.
Adv. in exchange, *vice versâ, mutatis mutandis,* backwards and forwards, by turns, turn and turn about, turn about; each –, every one- in his turn.

149. Changeableness.—N. changeableness etc. *adj.;* mutability, inconstancy; versatility, mobility; instability, unstable equilibrium; vacillation etc. (*irresolution*) 605; fluctuation, vicissitude; alternation etc. (*oscillation*) 314.
' restlessness etc. *adj.;* fidgets, disquiet; dis-, inquietude; unrest; agitation etc. 315.
moon, Proteus, chameleon, kaleidoscope, quicksilver, shifting sands, weathercock, harlequin, Cynthia of the minute, April showers; wheel of Fortune; transientness etc. 111.
V. fluctuate, vary, waver, flounder, flicker, flitter, flit, flutter, shift, shuffle, shake, totter, tremble, vacillate, wamble, turn and turn about, ring , the changes; sway –, shift- to and fro; change and change about; oscillate etc. 314; vibrate –, oscillate- between two extremes; alternate; have as many phases as the moon.
Adj. change-able, -ful; changing etc. 140; mutable, variable, checkered, ever changing, kaleidoscopic, prote-an, -iform; versatile.
unstaid, inconstant; un-steady, -stable, -fixed, -settled; fluctuating etc. *v.;* restless; mercurial; agitated etc. 315; erratic, fickle; irresolute etc. 605; capricious etc. 608; touch-and-go; inconsonant, fitful, spasmodic; vibratory; afloat; alternating; alterable, plastic, mobile; fleeting, transient etc. 111.
Adv. see-saw etc. (*oscillation*) 314; off and on.

150. Stability.—N. stability; immutability etc. *adj.;* unchangeableness etc. *adj.;* constancy; stable equilibrium, immobility, soundness, vitality, stabiliment, stabilization, stiffness, ankylosis, solidity, *aplomb.*
establishment, fixture; rock, pillar, tower, foundation, leopard's spots, Ethiopian's skin, law of the Medes and Persians.
stabilimeter, stabilizator.

permanence etc. 141; obstinacy etc. 606.
V. be -firm etc. *adj.;* stick fast; stand –, keep –, remain- firm; weather the storm.
settle, establish, stablish, ascertain, fix, set, stabilitate, stabilize; retain, stet, keep hold; make -good, – sure; fasten etc. (*join*) 43; set on its legs, float; perpetuate.
settle down; strike –, take- root; take up one's abode etc. 184; build one's house on a rock.
Adj. unchangeable, immutable; unalter-ed, -able; not to be changed, constant; permanent etc. 141; invariable, undeviating; stable, durable; perennial etc. (*diuturnal*) 110.
fixed, steadfast, firm, fast, steady, balanced; confirmed, valid, fiducial, immovable, irremovable, riveted, rooted; settled, established etc. *v.;* vested; incontrovertible, stereotyped, indeclinable.
tethered, anchored, moored, at anchor, on a rock, firm as a rock; firmly -seated, – established etc. *v.;* deep-rooted, ineradicable; inveterate; obstinate etc. 606.
transfixed, stuck fast, aground, high and dry, stranded.
indefeasible, irretrievable, intransmutable, · incommutable, irresoluble, irrevocable, irreversible, reverseless, inextinguishable, irreducible; indissol-uble, -vable; indestructible, undying, imperishable, indelible, indeciduous; insusceptible, – of change.
Int. *stet.*

151. Eventuality.—N. eventuality, event, occurrence, incident, affair, transaction, proceeding, fact; matter of –, naked- fact; phenomenon; advent.
business, concern; circumstance, particular, casualty, happening, accident, adventure, passage, crisis, pass, emergency, contingency, consequence etc. 154.
the world, life, things, doings, affairs, matters; things –, affairs- in general; the times, state of affairs, order of the day; course –, tide –, stream –, current –, run –, march- of -things, – events; ups and downs of life; chapter of accidents etc. (*chance*) 156; situation etc. (*circumstances*) 8.
V. happen, occur; take -place, – effect; come, become of; come -off, – about, – round, – into existence, – forth, – to pass, – on; pass, present itself; fall; fall –, turn- out; run, be on foot, fall in; be-fall, -tide, -chance; prove, eventuate, draw on; turn –, crop –, spring –, cast- up; super-, sur-vene; issue, emanate, arrive, ensue, arise, start, hold, take its course; pass off etc. (*be past*) 122.
meet with; experience; fall to the lot of; be one's -chance, – fortune, – lot; find; encounter, undergo; pass –, go- through; endure etc. (*feel*) 821.
Adj. happening etc. *v.;* going on, doing, current; in the wind, afloat; on -foot, – the *tapis;* at issue, in question; incidental.
eventful, momentous, signal; stirring, bustling, full of incident.
Adv. eventually, ultimately, in -the event of, – case; in the course of things; in the -natural, – ordinary- course of things; as -things, – times- go; as the world -goes, – wags; as the -tree falls, – cat jumps; as it may -turn out, – happen.
Phr. the plot thickens.

152. Destiny.—N. destiny etc. (*necessity*) 601; hereafter, future –, post- existence; future state, next world, world to come, after life; futurity etc. 121; everlasting -life, – death; prospect etc. (*expectation*) 507.

V. impend; hang –, lie –, hover- over; threaten, loom, await, come on, approach, stare one in the face; fore-, pre-ordain; predestine, doom, foredoom, foreshadow, have in store for.

Adj. impending etc. *v.;* destined; about to -be, – happen; coming, in store, to come, going to happen, instant, at hand, near; near –, close- at hand; overhanging, hanging over one's head, imminent; brewing, preparing, forthcoming; in the wind, on the cards, in reserve; that -will, – is to-be; in prospect etc. (*expected*) 507; looming in the -distance, – horizon, – future; unborn, in embryo; in the womb of -time; – futurity; on the knees of the gods; pregnant etc.'(*producing*) 161.

Adv. in -time, – the long run; all in good time; eventually etc. 151; whatever may happen etc. (*certainly*) 474; as -chance etc. 156- would have it.

153. Cause. [Constant antecedent.]—N. cause, origin, source, principle, element; occasioner, prime mover, engine, turbine, motor, *primum mobile; vera causa;* author etc. (*producer*) 164; main-spring, agent; dynamo, generator, battery (electric); leaven; groundwork, foundation etc. (*support*) 215.

spring, fountain, well, font; fountain –, spring- head; *fons et origo.* genesis; descent etc. (*paternity*) 166; remote cause; influence.

pivot, hinge, turning-point, lever; key; kernel, core; proximate cause, *causa causans;* last straw that breaks the camel's back.

ground; reason, – why; why and wherefore, rationale, occasion, derivation; final cause etc. (*intention*) 620; *le dessous des cartes;* undercurrents.

rudiment, egg, germ, embryo, fetus, bud, root, *radix,* radical, etymon, nucleus, seed, stem, stalk, stock, *stirps,* trunk, tap-root; latent organism.

nest, cradle, nursery, womb, *nidus,* birth-, breeding-place, hot-bed.

caus-ality, -ation; origination; production etc. 161.

V. be the -cause etc. *n.*- of; originate; give - origin, – rise, – occasion- to; cause, occasion, sow the seeds of, kindle, suscitate; bring -on, – to pass, – about; produce; create etc. 161; set - up, – afloat, – on foot; found, broach, institute, lay the foundation of, inaugurate; lie at the root of.

procure, induce, draw down, open the door to, superinduce, evoke, entail, operate; elicit, provoke.

conduce to etc. (*tend to*) 176; contribute; promote; have a -hand in, – finger in- the pie; determine, decide, turn the scale, give the casting vote; have a common origin; derive its origin etc. (*effect*) 154.

Adj. caused etc. *v.;* causal, original; prim-ary, -itive, -ordial; aboriginal; radical; inceptive, embry-onic, -otic; *in -embryo,* – *ovo;* seminal, germinal; formative, productive etc. 168; at the bottom of; connate, having a common origin.

Adv. because etc. 155; behind the scenes.

154. Effect. [Constant sequent.]—N. effect,

consequence, sequela; derivative, -tion; result; result-ant, -ance; upshot, issue, *dénouement;* outcome; termination, end etc. 67; development, outgrowth, fruit, crop, harvest, product, bud, blossom, florescence, ear.

production, produce, product, finished product, work, handiwork, fabric, performance; creature, creation; offspring, -shoot; first-fruits, -lings; *prémices.*

V. be the -effect etc. *n.*- of; be -due, – owing-to; originate -in, – from; rise –, arise –, take its rise –, spring –, proceed –, emanate –, come –, grow –, bud –, sprout –, germinate –, issue –, flow –, result –, follow –, derive its origin –, accrue- from; come -to, – of, – out of; depend –, hand –, hinge –, turn- upon.

take the consequences, sow the wind and reap the whirlwind.

Adj. owing to; resulting from etc. *v.;* resultant; derivable from; due to; caused etc. by, 153; dependent upon; derived –, evolved- from; derivative; hereditary.

Adv. of course, it follows that, naturally, consequently; as a –, in- consequence; through all, all along of, necessarily, eventually.

Phr. *cela va sans dire,* thereby hangs a tale.

155. Attribution. [Assignment of cause.]—N. attribution, theory, etiology, ascription, reference to, rationale;.accounting for etc. *v.;* imputation, derivation from.

fil-, affil-iation; pedigree etc. (*paternity*) 166. explanation etc. (*interpretation*) 522; reason why etc. (*cause*) 153.

V. attribute –, ascribe –, impute –, refer –, lay –, point –, trace –, bring home- to; put –, set- down- to; charge –, ground- on; invest with, assign as cause, charge with, blame, lay at the door of, father upon; saddle with; affiliate; account-for, derive from, point out the -reason etc. 153; theorize; tell how it comes; put the saddle on the right horse.

Adj. attributed etc. *v.;* attributable etc. *v.;* refer-able, -rible; due to, derivable from; owing to etc. (*effect*) 154; putative.

Adv. hence, thence, therefore, for, since, on account of, because, owing to; on that account; from -this, – that- cause; thanks to, forasmuch as; whence, *propter hoc.*

why? wherefore? whence? how -comes, – is, – happens- it? how does it happen?

in -some, – some such- way; somehow, – or other.

Phr. that is why; *hinc illae lachrymae; cherchez la femme.*

156. Chance.† [Absence of assignable cause.]—N. chance, indetermination, accident, fortune, hazard, hap, haphazard, chance-medley, random, luck, *raccroc,* casualty, fortuity, contingence, coincidence, adventure, hit; fate etc. (*necessity*) 601; equal chance; lottery, raffle, tombola, sweepstake; toss up etc. 621; turn of the -table, – cards; hazard of the die, chapter of accidents; cast –, throw- of the dice; heads or tails, wheel of Fortune, whirligig of chance; *sortes;* – *Virgilianae.*

probability, possibility, contingency, odds, long odds, run of luck; main- chance.

theory of -probabilities, – chances; book-making; assurance; speculation, gamble, gaming etc. 621.

V. chance, hap, turn up; fall to one's lot; be one's -fate etc. 601; stumble on, light –, blunder –, hit- upon; take one's chance etc. 621.

Adj. casual, fortuitous, accidental, haphazard, random, stray, adventitious, adventive, causeless, incidental. contingent, uncaused, undetermined, indeterminate; possible etc. 470; unintentional etc. 621.

Adv. by -chance, – accident; casually; perchance etc. (*possibly*) 470; for aught one knows; as -good, – bad, – ill-luck etc. *n.*- would have it; as it may -be, – chance, – turn up, – happen; as the case may be.

†The word *Chance* has two distinct meanings: the first, the absence of assignable *cause*, as above; and the second, the absence of *design*—for the latter see 621.

157. Power.—N. power; poten-cy, -tiality; puissance, might, force; energy etc. 171; dint; right -hand, – arm; ascendency, sway, control; pre-potency, -pollence; almightiness, omnipotence; authority etc. 737; strength etc. 159.

ability; ableness etc. *adj.;* competency; efficiency, -cacy; validity, cogency; enablement; vantage ground; influence etc. 175; horse power; dynamometer.

pressure; elasticity; gravity; attraction, repulsion; *vis -inertiae,* – *mortua,* – *viva;* friction, suction.

electricity, magnetism, galvanism, voltaic electricity, voltaism, electro-magnetism, electro-statics, electrification; electric – current, – power; potential –, dynamic –, kinetic –, electrical –, chemical –, atomic- energe; electric field, circuit, charge, discharge, shock, polarity, pole; amperage, voltage, wattage, resistance, conduction, induction, electrification, electrolysis.

electronics, radionics, electron physics, electrophysics, avionics, radiometry, photoelectronics; electron, negatron, positron, photoelectron, thermion, barytron; electronic effect; electron emission; electron –, cathode –, anode –, positive – ray; electron – current, ⊤ flow – stream, – beam, – volt; electronic circuit; conductance; electron tube, tube, vacuum tube, photoelectric tube, call; transistor.

capability, capacity; *quid valeant humeri quid ferre recusent;* faculty, quality, attribute, endowment, virtue, gift, property, qualification, susceptibility.

V. be -powerful etc. *adj.;* gain -power etc. *n.* belong –, pertain- to; lie –, be- in one's power; can.

electrify, generate, magnetize.

give –, confer –, exercise- power etc. *n.;* empower, enable, invest; in-, en-due; endow, arm; strengthen etc. 159; compel etc. 744.

Adj. powerful, puissant, potent, -ial; capable, able; equal –, up- to; cogent, valid; effect-ive, -ual; efficient, efficacious, adequate, competent; multi-, pleni-, omni-, armi- potent; mighty, ascendent; almighty.

electric, electrical, electronic etc.

forcible etc. *adj.* (*energetic*) 171; influential etc. 175; productive etc. 168.

Adv. powerfully etc. *adj.;* by -virtue, – dint-of.

158. Impotence.—N. impotence; in-, dis-ability; disablement, impuissance, imbecility, caducity; incapa-city, -bility; inapt-, inept-itude; indocility; invalidity, inefficiency, incompetence, disqualification.

telum imbelle, brutum fulmen, blank cartridge, flash in the pan, *vox et praeterea nihil,* dead letter, bit of waste paper, dummy; scrap of paper.

inefficacy etc. (*inutility*) 645; failure etc. 732.

helplessness etc. *adj.;* prostration, paralysis, palsy, ataxia, apoplexy, syncope, sideration, *deliquium,* collapse, exhaustion, softening of the brain, e nasculation, inanition, senility etc. 128; castrato, eunuch.

cripple, old woman, muff, molly-coddle, milk-sop.

V. be -impotent etc. *adj.;* not have a leg to stand on.

vouloir -rompre l'anguille au genou, – *prendre la lune avec les dents.*

collapse, faint, swoon, fall into a swoon, drop; go by the board; end in smoke etc. (*fail*) 732.

render -powerless etc. *adj.;* deprive of power; decontrol; dis-able, -enable; disarm, incapacitate, disqualify, unfit, invalidate, undermine, deaden, cramp, tie the hands; double up, prostrate, paralyze, muzzle, cripple, be-cripple, maim, lame, hamstring, draw the teeth of; throttle, strangle, *garrotte;* ratten, silence, sprain, clip the wings of, render *hors de combat,* spike the guns; take the wind out of one's sails, scotch the snake, put a spoke in one's wheel; break the -neck, – back; un-hinge, -fit; put out of gear.

unman, unnerve, devitalize, attenuate, enervate; emasculate, spay, caponize, castrate, geld; effeminize.

shatter, exhaust; weaken etc. 160.

Adj. powerless, impotent, unable, incapable, incompetent; ineff-icient, -ective; inept; un-fit, -fitted; un-, dis-qualified; unendowed; in-, un-apt; crippled, decrepit; disabled etc. *v.;* armless.

harmless, unarmed, weaponless, defenceless, *sine ictu,* unfortified, indefensible, vincible, pregnable, untenable.

para-lytic, -lyzed; palsied, imbecile; nerve-, sinew-, marrow-, pith-, lust-less; emasculate, disjointed, out of -joint, – gear; un-nerved, -hinged; water-logged, on one's beam ends, rudderless; laid on one's back; done up, dead beat, exhausted, shattered, demoralized; gravelled etc. (*in difficulty*) 704; helpless, unfriended, fatherless; without a leg to stand on, *hors de combat,* laid on the shelf.

null and void, nugatory, imoperative, good for nothing; dud; invertebrate; ineffectual etc. (*failing*) 732; inadequate etc. 640; inefficacious etc. (*useless*) 645.

159. Strength. (Degree of power.]—N. strength; power etc. 157; energy etc. 171; vigor, force; main –, physical –, brute- force; spring, elasticity, tone, tension, tonicity.

stoutness etc. *adj.;* lustihood, stamina, nerve,

muscle, sinew, thews and sinews, *physique;* pith, - iness; virility, vitality.

athlet-ics, -icism; gymnastics, feats of strength.

adamant, steel, iron, oak, heart of oak; iron grip; grit, bone.

athlete, gymnast, tumbler, acrobat; Atlas, Hercules, Antaeus, Samson, Cyclops, Goliath, Titan; tower of strength; giant refreshed.

strengthening etc. *v.;* invigoration, refreshment, refocillation.

[Science of forces] dynamics, statics.

V. be -strong etc. *adj.*, − stronger; overmatch.

render -strong etc. *adj.;* give -strength etc. *n.;* strengthen, invigorate, brace, nerve, fortify, buttress, sustain, harden, case-harden, steel; gird; screw −, wind −, set- up; gird −, brace- up one's loins; recruit, set on one's legs; vivify; refresh etc. 689; refect; reinforce etc. (*restore*) 660.

Adj. strong, mighty, vigorous, forcible, hard, adamantine, stout, robust, sturdy, hardy, powerful, potent, puissant, valid.

resistless, irresistible, invincible, proof against, impregnable, unconquerable, indomitable, inextinguishable, unquenchable; incontestable; more than a match for; over-powering, - whelming; all-powerful; sovereign.

able-bodied; athletic, gymnastic; Herculean, Cyclopean, Atlantean; muscular, husky, brawny, wiry, well-knit, broad-shouldered, sinewy, strapping, stalwart, gigantic.

man-ly, -like, -ful; masculine, male, virile, in the prime of manhood.

un-weakened, -allayed, -withered, -shaken, - worn, -exhausted; in full -force, − swing; in the plenitude of power.

stubborn, thick-ribbed, made of iron, deep-rooted; strong as -a lion, − a horse, − brandy; sound as a roach; in -fine, − high- feather; in fine fettle; like a giant refreshed.

Adv. strongly etc. *adj.*; by -force etc. *n.*; by main force etc. (*by compulsion*) 744.

Phr. 'our withers are unwrung.'

160. Weakness.—N. weakness etc. *adj.;* debility, atony, relaxation, languor, enervation; impotence etc. 158; infirmity; effeminancy, feminality; fragility, flaccidity; inactivity etc. 683.

declension −, loss −, failure- of strength; delicacy, invalidation, decrepitude, asthenia, adynamy, cachexy, *cachexia,* anemia, bloodlessness, sprain, strain.

reed, thread, rope of sand, broken reed, house -of cards, − built on sand.

soft-, weak-ling; infant etc. 129; youth etc. 127.

V. be -weak etc. *adj.;* drop, crumble, give way, totter, tremble, shake, halt, limp, fade, languish, decline, flag, fail, have one foot in the grave.

render -weak etc. *adj.;* weaken, enfeeble, debilitate, shake, deprive of strength, relax, enervate; un-brace, -nerve; cripple, unman, etc. (*render powerless*) 158; cramp, reduce, sprain, strain, blunt the edge of; dilute, impoverish; decimate; extenuate; reduce -in strength, − the strength of; invalidate; *mettre de l'eau dans son vin.*

Adj. weak, feeble, debile; impotent etc. 158; relaxed, unnerved etc. *v.*; sap-, strength-, powerless; weakly, unstrung, flaccid, adynamic, asthenic; nervous.

soft, effeminate, feminate, womanish.

frail, fragile, shattery, frangible, brittle etc. 328; flimsy, unsubstantial, gimcrack, gingerbread; rickety, cranky; creachy; drooping, tottering etc. *v.;* broken, lame, halt, game, withered, shattered, shaken, crazy, shaky, tumble-down; palsied etc. 158; decrepit; C3.

lanquid, poor, poorly, infirm; faint, -ish; sickly etc. (*disease*) 655; dull, slack, evanid, speñt, short-winded, effete; weatherbeaten; decayed, rotten, worn, seedy, languishing, wasted, washy, wishy-washy, laid low, pulled down, the worse for wear.

un-strengthened etc. 159, -supported, -aided, - assisted; aidless, defenceless etc. 158.

on its last legs; weak as a -child, − baby, − chicken, − cat, − rat; weak as -water, − water gruel, − gingerbread, − milk and water; colorless etc. 429.

Phr. *non sum qualis eram.*

161. Production.—N. production, creation, construction, formation, fabrication, manufacture; building, architecture, erection, edification; coinage; organization; *nisus formativus;* putting togeher etc. *v.;* establishment; workmanship, performance;· achievement etc. (*completion*) 729; effect etc. 154.

flowering, fructification fruition.

bringing forth etc. *v.;* parturition, birth, birth-throe, child-birth, delivery, confinement, *accouchement,* travail, labour, midwifery, obstetrics; geniture; gestation etc. (*maturation*) 673; evolution, development, growth; genesis, fertilization, breeding, conception, germination, generation, *epigenesis,* pro-creation, -generation, -pagation; fecundation, impregnation; spontaneous generation; *arche-genesis, -biosis; bio-, abio-, homo-, xeno-genesis.*

authorship, publication; works, *oeuvre, opus.*

edifice, building, structure, fabric, erection, pile, tower, flower, fruit.

V. produce, perform, operate, do, make, gar, form, construct, fabricate, frame, contrive, manufacture; weave, forge, coin, carve, chisel; build, raise, edify, rear, erect, put together; set −, run- up; establish, constitute, compose, organize, institute, get up; achieve, accomplish etc. (*complete*) 729.

flower, sprout, blossom, burgeon, bear fruit, fructify, spawn, teem, ean, yean, farrow, drop, calf, pup, whelp, kitten, kindle; bear, lay, bring forth, give birth to, lie in, be brought to bed of, evolve, pullulate, usher into the world.

make productive etc. 168; create; beget, conceive, get, generate, fecundate, impregnate; procreate, -generate, -pagate; engender; bring −, call- into -being, − existence; breed, hatch, develop, bring up.

induce, superinduce; suscitate; cause etc. 153; acquire etc. 775.

Adj. produc-ed, -ing etc. *v.;* productive of; prolific etc. 168; creative; formative; gen-etic, - ial, -ital; fertile, pregnant; *enceinte,* big −, fraught-with; with child, in the family way,

teeming, parturient, in the straw, brought to bed of; puerper-al, -ous.
architectonic; constructive.

162. Destruction. [Non-production.]—N. destruction; waste, dissolution, breaking up; di-, dis-ruption; consumption; disorganization.

fall, downfall, ruin, perdition, crash, smash, havoc, *délabrement, débâcle;* break -down, − up; prostration; desolation, *bouleversement,* wreck, crack-up, crash, wrack, shipwreck, cataclysm; Caudine Forks, Sedan.

extinction, annihilation; destruction of life etc. 361; knock-out, knock-down blow; doom, crack of doom.

destroying etc. *v.;* demo-lition, -lishment; biblioclasm; overthrow, subversion, suppression; abolition etc. (*abrogation*) 756; sacrifice; ravage, devastation, *sabotage, razzia;* incendiarism; revolution etc. 146; extirpation etc. (*extraction*) 301; *commencement de la fin,* road to ruin; dilapidation etc. (*deterioration*) 659.

V. be -destroyed etc.; perish; fall, − to the ground; tumble, topple; go −, fall- to pieces; break up; crumble, − to dust; go to -the dogs, − the wall, − smash, − shivers, − wreck, − pot, − wrack and ruin; go -by the board, − all to smash, − to pieces, − under; be all -over, − up- with; totter to its fall.

destroy; do −, make- away with; nullify; annul etc. 756; sacrifice, demolish; tear up; over-turn, -throw, -whelm; upset, subvert, put an end to; seal the doom of, do for, dish, undo; break -, cut- up; break −, cut −, pull −, mow −, blow −, beat-down; suppress, quash, put down; cut short, take off, blot out; dispel, dissipate, dissolve; consume.

smash, − to smithereens, quell, squash, squelch, crumple up, shatter, shiver; batter; tear −, crush −, cut −, shake −, pull −, pick- to pieces; nip; tear to -rags, − tatters; crush −, knock- to atoms; pulverize; ruin; strike out; throw −, knock- -down, − over; lay by the heels; fell, sink, swamp, scuttle, wreck, crash, ship-wreck, engulf, submerge; lay in -ashes, − ruins; sweep away, erase, expunge, strike out, delete, efface, raze; level, − with the -ground, − dust.

deal destruction, lay waste, ravage, gut; disorganize; dismantle etc. (*render useless*) 645; devour, swallow up, desolate, devastate, sap, mine, blast, confound; exterminate, extinguish, quench, annihilate; snuff −, put −, stamp −, trample- out; lay −, trample- in the dust; prostrate; tread −, crush −, trample- under foot; lay the axe to the root of; make -short work, − a clean sweep, − mincemeat- of; cut up root and branch; fling −, scatter- to the winds; throw overboard; strike at the root of, sap the foundations of, spring a mine, blow up; ravage with fire and sword; cast to the dogs; eradicate etc. 301.

Adj. destroyed etc. *v.;* perishing etc. *v.;* trembling −, nodding −, tottering- to its fall; in course of destruction etc. *n.;* extinct.

destructive, subversive, ruinous, incendiary, deletory; destroying etc. *v.;* suicidal; deadly etc. (*killing*) 361.

Adv. with -crushing effect, − a sledge-hammer.

Phr. *delenda est Carthago.*

163. Reproduction.—N. reproduction, renovation; restoration etc. 660; renewal; new edition, reprint etc. 21; revival, regeneration, palingenesia, revivification; apotheosis; resuscitation, reanimation, resurrection, resurgence, re-appearance, atavism; Phoenix; reincarnation.

generation etc. (*production*) 161; multiplication.

V. reproduce; restore etc. 660; revive, renovate, renew, regenerate, revivify, resuscitate, reanimate, refashion, stir the embers, put into the crucible; multiply, repeat, resurge.

crop up, spring up like mushrooms.

Adj. reproduced etc. *v.;* renascent, reappearing; reproductive; resurgent; progenitive; Hydra-headed.

164. Producer.—N. producer, creator, deviser, designer, originator, inventor, author, founder, generator, mover, architect; grower, constructor, maker etc. (*agent*) 690.

165. Destroyer.—N. destroyer etc. (destroy etc. 162); cankerworm etc. (*bane*) 663; iconoclast; assassin etc. (*killer*) 361; executioner etc. (*punish*) 975; Hun, Vandal, nihilist, anarchist.

166. Paternity.—N. paternity; parentage; fatherhood; consanguinity etc. 11.

parent, father, sire, dad, daddy, papa, governor, *pater, paterfamilias, abba;* genitor, progenitor, procreator, begetter; ancestor; grand-sire, -father; great-grandfather.

house, stem, truck, tree, stock, *stirps,* pedigree, lineage, line, family, tribe, sept, race, clan; genealogy, descent, extraction, birth, ancestry; forefathers, forbears, patriarchs.

motherhood, maternity; mother, dam, mamma, *materfamilias;* grand-mother; matriarch.

Adj. paternal, parental; maternal; family, ancestral, linear, matrilinear, patrilineal, patriarchal.

167. Posterity.—N. posterity, progeny, breed, issue, offspring, brood, litter, seed, farrow, spawn, spat; family, children, grandchildren, heirs; great-grandchild.

child, son, daughter; kid; infant etc. 129; bantling, scion; shoot, sprout, olive branch, sprit, branch; off-shoot, -set; ramification; descendant; heir, -ess; heir -apparent, − presumptive; chip of the old block; heredity; rising generation.

straight descent, sonship, line, lineage, filiation, promogeniture.

Adj. filial.

168. Productiveness.—N. productiveness etc. *adj.* fecundity, fertility, luxuriance, uberty.

pregnancy, pullulation, fructification, multiplication, propagation, procreation; superfetation.

milch cow, rabbit, hydra, warren, seed-plot, land flowing with milk and honey; second crop, after-crop, -growth, -math; fertilization.

V. make -productive etc. *adj.;* fructify; procreate, generate, fertilize, spermatize, impregnate; fecund-ate, -ify; teem, pullulate, multiply; produce etc. 161; conceive.

Adj. productive, prolific; teem-ing, -ful; fertile, fruitful, frugiferous, fruit-bearing; fructiferous; fecund, luxuriant; pregnant, uberous.

procre-ant, -ative; generative, life-giving, spermatic; originative; multiparous; omnific; propagable.

parturient etc. (*producing*) 161; profitable etc. (*useful*) 644.

169. Unproductiveness.—N. unproductiveness etc. *adj.;* infertility, steril; ity, infecundity; impotence etc. 158- unprofitableness etc. (*inutility*) 645.

waste, desert, Sahara, wild, wilderness, howling wilderness.

V. be -unproductive etc. *adj.;* hang fire, flash in the pan, come to nothing.

Adj. unproductive, inoperative, barren, addle, unfertile, unprolific, arid, sterile, unfruitful, acarpous, infecund; *sine prole;* fallow; teem-, issue-, fruitless; unprofitable etc. (*useless*) 645; null and void, of no effect.

170. Agency.—N. agency, operation, force, working, strain, function, office, maintenance, exercise, work, swing, play; inter-working, -action, procuration, procurement.

causation etc. 153; instrumentality etc. 631; influence etc. 175; action etc. (*voluntary*) 680; *modus operandi* etc. 627.

quickening −, maintaining- power; home stroke.

V. be -in action etc. *adj.;* operate, work; act, − upon; perform, play, support, sustain, strain, maintain, take effect, quicken, strike.

come −, bring- into -operation, − play; have -play, − free play; bring to bear upon.

Adj. operative, efficient, efficacious, practical, effectual.

at work, on foot; acting etc. (*doing*) 680; in -operation, − force, − action, − play, − exercise; acted −, wrought- upon.

Adv. by the -agency etc. *n.*- of; through etc. (*instrumentality*) 631; by means of etc. 632.

171. Physical Energy.—N. energy, physical energy, force; keenness etc. *adj.;* intensity, vigor, strength, elasticity; go; pep, live wire, high pressure; backbone, mettle, fire, vim.

acri-mony, -tude, -dity; causticity, virulence, poignancy; harshness etc. *adj.;* severity, edge, point; pungency etc. 392.

cantharides; Spanish fly; seasoning etc. (*condiment*) 393, stimulant, excitant.

activity, agitation, effervescence; ferment, -ation; ebullition, splutter, perturbation, stir, bustle; voluntary energy etc. 682; quicksilver.

resolution etc. (*mental energy*) 604; exertion etc. (*effort*) 686; excitation etc. (*mental*) 824.

V. give -energy etc. *n.;* energize, stimulate, kindle, excite, activate, exert; sharpen, pep up, intensify; inflame etc. (*render violent*) 173; wind up etc. (*strengthen*) 159.

strike, − into, − hard, − home; make an impression.

Adj. strong, energetic, forcible, active; strenuous, forceful, mettlesome, enterprising, go ahead; intense, deep-dyed, severe, keen, vivid, sharp, acute, incisive, trenchant, brisk, vigorous, live.

rousing, irritating; poignant; virulent, caustic, corrosive, mordant, harsh, stringent; double-edged, − shotted, − distilled; drastic, escharotic; racy etc. (*pungent*) 392; sarcastic etc. 932.

potent etc. (*powerful*) 157; radio-active.

Adv. strongly etc. *adj.; fortiter in re;* with telling effect.

Phr. the steam is up; *vires acquirit eundo.*

172. Physical Inertness.—N. inertness, dulness etc. *adj.;* inertia, *vis inertiae,* inertion, inactivity, torpor, languor; dormancy, quiescence etc. 265; latency, inaction, passivity.

mental inertness; sloth etc. (*inactivity*) 683; inexcitability etc. 826; irresolution etc. 605; obstinacy etc. 606; permanence etc. 141.

V. be -inert etc. *adj.;* hang fire, smoulder.

Adj. inert, inactive, passive, pacific; torpid etc. 683; sluggish, stagnant, dull, heavy, flat, slack, tame, slow, blunt; lifeless, dead, uninfluential. latent, dormant, smouldering, unexerted.

Adv. inactively etc. *adj.;* in -suspense, -abeyance.

173. Violence.—N. violence, inclemency, vehemence, might, impetuosity; boisterousness etc.; *adj.;* effervescence, ebullition; turbulence, bluster; uproar, riot, row, rumpus, *le diable à quatre,* devil to pay, all the fat in the fire.

severity etc. 739; ferocity, rage, berserk, fury; exacerbation, exasperation, malignity; fit, paroxysm, orgasm; force, brute force; outrage; *coup de main;* strain, shock, shog; spasm, convulsion, 'throe; hysterics, passion etc. (*state of excitability*) 825.

out-break, -burst; burst, bounce, dissilience, discharge, volley, explosion, blow up, blast, detonation, rush, eruption, displosion, torrent.

turmoil etc. (*disorder*) 59; ferment etc. (*agitation*) 315; storm, tempest, rough weather; squall etc. (*wind*) 349; earthquake, volcano, thunderstorm.

fury, dragon, demon, tiger, beldame, Tisiphone, Megaera, Alecto, madcap, wild beast; fire-eater etc. (*blusterer*) 887.

V. be -violent etc. *adj.;* run high; ferment, effervesce; romp, rampage; run -wild, − riot; break the peace; rush, tear; rush head-long, -foremost; run amuck, raise a storm, make a riot; make −, kick up- a row, − a fuss; bluster, rage, roar, riot, storm; boil, − over; fume, foam, come in like a lion, wreak, bear down, ride roughshod, out-Herod Herod; spread like wildfire.

break −, fly −, burst- out; bounce, shock, strain; break-, pry-, force-, prize- open.

render -violent etc. *adj.;* sharpen, stir up, quicken, excite, incite, urge, lash, stimulate; irritate, inflame, exacerbate, kindle, suscitate, foment; accelerate, aggravate, exasperate, convulse, infuriate, madden, lash into fury; fan −, add fuel to- the flame; *oleum addere camino.*

explode, go off, displode, fly, detonate, thunder, blow up, flash, flare, erupt, burst; let - off,. − fly; discharge, detonize, fulminate.

Adj. violent, vehement, forcible; warm; acute, sharp; rough, rude, ungentle, bluff, boisterous, wild, vicious; brusque, abrupt, waspish; impetuous; rampant.

turbulent; disorderly; blustering, raging etc. *v.;* troublous, riotous; tumultu-ary, -ous; obstreperous, uproarious; extravagant; unmitigated; ravening, tameless; frenzied etc. (*insane*) 503; desperate etc. (*rash*) 863; infuriate, towering, furious, outrageous, frantic, hysteric, in hysterics.

fiery, flaming, scorching, hot, red-hot, ebullient.

savage, fierce, ferocious, fierce as a tiger.

excited etc. *v.;* un-quelled, -quenched, -extinguished, -repressed, -bridled, -ruly; headstrong; un-governable, -appeasable, -mitigable; un-, in-controllable; insup-, irre-pressible.

spasmodic, convulsive, explosive; detonating etc. *v.;* volcanic, meteoric; stormy etc. (*wind*) 349.

Adv. violently etc. *adj.;* amain; by -storm, − force, − main force; with might and main; tooth and nail, *vi et armis,* at the point of the -sword, − bayonet; at one fell swoop; with a high hand, through thick and thin; in desperation, with a vengeance; *à −, à touteoutrance;* head-long, -foremost, -first; like a bull at a gate.

174. Moderation.—N. moderation; lenity etc. 740; temperance, temperateness, gentleness etc. *adj.;* sobriety; quiet; mental calmness etc. (*inexcitability*) 826.

moderating etc. *v.;* relaxation, remission, mitigation etc. 834; tranquilization, alleviation, assuagement, appeasement, contemporation, pacification.

measure, *juste milieu,* golden mean etc. 29.

moderator; lullaby, sedative, lenitive, demulcent, rose-water, balm, soothing syrup, poppy, opiate, anodyne, milk, opium, laudanum, 'poppy or mandragora;' wet blanket; palliative, calmative.

V. be -moderate etc. *adj.;* keep within -bounds, − compass; sober −, settle- down; keep the pease, remit, relent; take in sail.

moderate, soften, mitigate, temper, accoy; at-, con-temper; mollify, lenify, dull, take off the edge, blunt, obtund, sheathe, subdue, chasten; sober ´−, tone −, smooth- down; censor, blue-pencil, weaken etc. 160; lessen etc. (*decrease*) 36; check; palliate.

tranquilize, assuage, appease, dulcify, swage, lull, soothe, compose, still, calm, cool, quiet, hush, quell, sober, pacify, tame, damp, lay, allay, rebate, slacken, smooth, alleviate, rock to sleep, deaden, smother; throw -cold water on, − a wet blanket over; slake; curb etc. (*restrain*) 751; tame etc. (*subjugate*) 749; smooth over; pour oil on the -waves, − troubled waters; pour balm into, *mettre de l'eau dans son vin.*

go out like a lamb, 'roar you as gently as any sucking dove.'

Adj. moderate; lenient etc. 740; gentle, mild; cool, sober, temperate, reasonable, measured; tempered etc. *v.;* calm, unruffled, quiet, tranquil,

still; slow, smooth, untroubled; tame; peaceful, -able; pacific, halcyon.

un-exciting, -irritating; soft, bland, oily, demulcent, lenitive, anodyne; hypnotic etc. 683; sedative; assuaging.

mild as mother's milk; milk and water; gentle as a lamb.

Adv. moderately etc. *adj.;* gingerly; *piano;* under easy sail, at half speed; within -bounds, − compass; in reason.

Phr. *est modus in rebus.*

175. Influence.—N. influence; importance etc. 642; weight, pressure, preponderance, prevalence, sway, pull; predomi-nance, -nancy; ascendency; control, dominance, reign; authority etc. 737; capability etc. (*power*) 157; interest; spell, magic, magnetism.

footing; purchase etc. (*support*) 215; play, leverage, vantage ground.

tower of strength, host in himself; protection, patronage, auspices.

V. have -influence etc. *n.;* be -influential etc. *adj.;* carry weight, actuate, sway, bias, weigh, tell; have a hold upon, magnetize, bear upon, gain a footing, work upon; take -root, − hold; strike root in.

run through, pervade, prevail, dominate, predominate, subject; out-, over-weigh; over-ride, -bear, − come; gain head; rage; be -rife etc. *adj.;* spread like wildfire; have −, get −, gain- -the upper hand, − full play.

be -recognized, − listened to; make one's voice heard, gain a hearing; play a -part, − leading part- in; lead, control, rule, master; get the mastery over; make one's influence felt, cut ice with; take the lead, pull the strings; turn −, throw your weight into- the scale; set the fashion, lead the dance.

Adj. influential; important etc. 642; weighty; prevailing etc. *v.;* prevalent, rife, rampant; dominant, regnant, predominant, in the ascendant, hegemonical; authoritative, recognized, telling, with authority.

Adv. with telling effect.

175a. Absence of Influence.—N. impotence etc. 158; inertness etc. 172; irrelevancy etc. 10.

V. have no -influence etc. 175.

Adj. uninfluential; unconduc-ing, -ive, -ting to; powerless etc. 158; irrelevant etc. 10.

176. Tendency.—N. tendency; apt-ness, -itude; proneness, proclivity, bent, turn, tone, bias, set, warp, leaning to, predisposition, inclination, conatus, propensity, susceptibility; liability etc. 177; quality, nature, temperament; characteristic, idio-crasy, -syncrasy; cast, vein, grain; humor, mood; drift etc. (*direction*) 278; conduciveness, -ducement; applicability etc. (*utility*) 644; subservience etc. (*instrumentality*) 631.

V. tend, contribute, conduce, lead, dispose, incline, verge, bend to, warp, turn, trend, affect, carry, redound to, bid fair to, gravitate towards; promote etc. (*aid*) 707.

Adj. tending etc. *v.;* conducive, working to-

wards, in a fair way to, calculated to; liable etc.
177; subservient etc. (*instrumental*) 631; useful
etc. 644; subsidiary etc. (*helping*) 707.
Adv. for, whither.

177. Liability.—N. lia-bility, -bleness; possibility, contingency; suscepti-vity, -bility.
V. be -liable etc. *adj.;* incur, lay oneself open
to; run the —, stand a- chance; lie under, expose
oneself to, open a door to.
Adj. liable, subject; in danger etc. 665; open —,
exposed —, obnoxious- to; answerable, responsible, accountable, amenable; unexempt from; apt
to; dependent on; incident to.
contingent, incidental, possible, on the cards,
within range of, at the mercy of.

178. Concurrence.—N. concurrence, cooperation, coagency; coincidence, consilience;
union; agreement etc. 23; consent etc. (*assent*)
488; alliance; concert etc. 709; partnership etc.
712; collaboration, conformity.
V. con-cur, -duce, -spire, -tribute; agree, unite,
harmonize; hang —, pull- together etc. (*co-operate*) 709; help to etc. (*aid*) 707.
keep pace with, run parallel to; go —, go along
—, go hand in hand- with.
Adj. concurring etc. *v.;* concurrent, conformable, joint, co-operative, concordant, coincident, concomitant, harmonious; in alliance with,
banded together, of one mind, at one with;
parallel.
Adv. with one consent.

179. Counteraction.—N. counteraction, opposition; contrariety etc. 14; antagonism, polarity; clashing etc. *v.;* collision, interference,
resistance, renitency, friction; reaction; retroaction; repercussion etc. (*recoil*) 277; counterblast; neutralization etc. (*compensation*) 30; vis
inertiae; check etc. (*hindrance*) 706.
voluntary -opposition etc. 708, — resistance
etc. 719; repression etc. (*restraint*) 751.
V. counteract; run counter, clash, cross; interfere —, conflict- with; jostle; go —, run —, beat
—, militate- against; stultify; antagonize, frustrate, oppose etc. 708; withstand etc. (*resist*) 719;
hinder etc. 706; repress etc. (*restrain*) 751; react
etc. (*recoil*) 277.
undo, neutralize, cancel; counterpoise etc.
(*compensate*) 30; overpoise.
Adj. counteracting etc. *v.;* antagonistic, conflicting, retroactive, renitent, reactionary; contrary etc. 14.
Adv. although etc. 30; in spite of etc. 708;
malgré; against.

180. Space. [Indefinite space.]—N. space,
extension, extent, superficial extent, expanse,
stretch; capacity, volume, room, accommodation,
scope, range, latitude, field, way, expansion, compass, sweep, play, swing, spread.
dimension, fourth dimension; relativity, geometry.

spare —, elbow —, house- room; stowage,
roomage, margin; opening, sphere, arena; lee-,
sea-, head-way.
open —, free- space; wide open spaces, void etc.
(*absence*) 187; waste; wild-, wilder-ness; up-, bottom-, moor -land; *campagna, veldt,* prairie,
steppe.
abyss etc. (*interval*) 198; unlimited space;
infinity etc. 105; world, wide world; ubiquity etc.
(*presence*) 186; length and breadth of the land.
proportions, acreage; acres, — roods and
perches; square -inches, — yards etc.
V. reach, extend, stretch, sweep, spread,
range, cover, thrust out, reach forth.
Adj. spacious, roomy, extensive, expansive,
capacious, ample; wide-spread, vast, world-wide,
uncircumscribed; boundless etc. (*infinite*) 105;
shore-, track-, path-less; large etc. 192.
spatial, dimensional, proportional; two-,
three-, four-dimensional; stereoscopic.
Adv. extensively etc. *adj.;* wherever; everywhere; far and -near, — wide; right and left, all
over, all the world over; throughout the -world,
— length and breadth of the land; under the sun,
in every quarter; in all -quarters, — lands; here,
there and everywhere; from -pole to pole, —
China to Peru, — Indus to the pole, — Dan to
Beersheba, — end to end; on the face of the earth,
in the wide world, from all points of the compass; to the -four winds, — uttermost parts of the
earth.

180a. Inextension.—N. in-, non-extension;
point; atom etc. (*smallness*) 32; pinprick; limitation etc. 229.

181. Region. [Definite space.]—N. region,
sphere, sphere of influence, corridor, ground,
soil, area, realm, hemisphere, quarter district,
beat, orb, orbit, zone, belt, circuit, circle; pale etc.
(*limit*) 233; com-, department; domain, tract,
territory, terrain, country, canton, county, shire,
province, *arrondissement,* diocese, parish, township, borough, constituency, *commune,* ward,
wapentake, hundred, riding, lathe, garth, soke,
tithing, bailiwick; empire, kingdom, principality,
duchy, grand —, arch- duchy, palatinate, republic,
commonwealth, dominion, colony, state, island.
arena, precincts, *enceinte,* walk, march; patch,
plot, enclosure, etc. 232; close, *enclave,* field,
court; street etc. (*abode*) 189.
clime, climate, zone, meridian, latitude.
Adj. territorial, local, parochial, provincial,
insular.

182. Place. [Limited space.]—N. place, lieu,
spot, point, dot; niche, nook, etc. (*corner*) 244;
hole; pigeonhole etc. (*receptacle*) 191; compartment; premises, precinct, station, confine; area,
court, yard, quadrangle, square, compound;
abode etc. 189; locality etc. (*situation*) 183.
ins and outs; every hole and corner.
Adv. somewhere, in some place, wherever it
may be, here and there, in various places,
passim.

183. Situation.—N. situation, position, locality, *locale, status,* latitude and longitude; footing, standing, standpoint, post; stage, aspect, attitude, posture, *pose.*

place, site, base, station, seat, *venue,* whereabouts, environment, neighborhood; bearings etc. (*direction*) 278; spot etc. (*limited space*) 182.

top-, ge-, chor-ography; map etc. 554.

V. be -situated; – situate; lie; have its seat in.

Adj. situ-ate, -ated; local, topical, topographical etc. *n.*

Adv. *in -situ,* – *loco;* here and there, *passim;* here-, there-, whereabouts; in place, here, there.

in –, amidst- such and such- -surroundings, – *environs,* – *entourage.*

184. Location.—N. loca-tion, -lization; lodgement; de-, re-position; stow-, pack-age; collocation; packing, lading; establishment, settlement, installation; fixation; insertion etc. 300.

anchorage, roadstead, mooring, mooring mast, encampment, camp, bivouac.

plantation, colony, settlement, cantonment, encampment, reservation; colonization, domestication, situation; habitation etc. (*abode*) 189; cohabitation; 'a local habitation and a name;' indenization, naturalization.

. **V.** place, situate, locate, localize, make a place for, put, lay, set, seat, station, lodge, quarter, post, install; storehouse, stow; extablish, fix, pin, root; graft; plant etc. (*insert*) 300; shelve, pitch, camp, lay down, deposit, reposit; cradle; moor, tether, picket; pack, tuck in; embed; vest, invest in.

billet on, quarter upon, saddle with; load, lade, freight; pocket, put up. bag.

inhabit etc. (*be present*) 186; domesticate, colonize, populate, people; take –, strike-root; anchor; cast –, come to an- anchor; sit –, settle-down; settle; take up one's -abode, – quarters; plant –, establish –, locate- oneself; squat, perch, hive, *se nicher,* bivouac, burrow, get a footing; encamp, pitch one's tent; put up -at, – one's horses at; keep house.

indenizen, naturalize, adopt.

put back, replace etc. (*restore*) 660.

Adj. placed etc. *v.;* situate, posited, ensconced, embedded, embosomed, rooted; ˌ domesticated; vested in unremoved; settled, stationed, established.

moored etc. *v.;* at anchor.

185. Displacement.—N. displacement, elocation, transposition.

ejectment etc. 297; exile etc.'(*banishment*) 893; removal etc. (*transference*) 270; unshipment.

misplacement, dislocation etc. 61; fish out of water.

V. dis-place, -plant, -lodge, -nest, -establish; misplace, unseat, disturb; exile etc. (*seclude*) 893; ablegate, set aside, rèmove; take –, cart- away; take –, draft- off; lade etc. 184, unship.

unload, empty etc. (*eject*) 297; transfer etc. 270; dispel.

vacate; depart etc. 293.

Adj. displaced etc. *v.;* un-placed, -housed, -harbored, -established, -settled; house-, homeless; out of -place, – a situation.

misplaced, out of its element.

186. Presence.—N. presence; occupancy, -ation; attendance; whereness.

permeation, pervasion; diffusion etc. (*dispersion*) 73.

ubi-ety, -quity, -quitariness; omnipresence.

bystander etc. (*spectator*) 444.

V. exist in space, be -present etc. *adj.;* assist at; make one -of, – at; look on, attend, remain; find –, present- oneself; show one's face; fall in the way of, occur in a place; lie, stand; occupy.

people; inhabit, dwell, reside, stay, sojourn, live, room, abide, bunk, lodge, nestle, roost, perch; take up one's abode etc. (*be located*) 184; tenant, occupy.

resort to, frequent, haunt; revisit.

fill, pervade, permeate; be -diffused, – disseminated- through; over-spread, -run; run through; meet one at every turn.

Adj. present; occupying, inhabiting etc. *v.;* moored etc. 184; residential, resi-ant, -dent, -dentiary; domiciled.

ubiquit-ous, -ary; omnipresent.

peopled, populous, full of people, inhabited.

Adv. here; there, where, everywhere, aboard, on board, at home, afield; on the spot; here, there and everywhere etc. (*space*) 180; in presence of, before; under the -eyes, –nose- of; in the face of; *in propriâ personâ.*

187. Absence. [Nullibiety.]—N. absence; inexistence etc. 2; non-residence, absenteeism; non-attendance, *alibi.*

emptiness etc. *adj.;* void, *vacuum;* vac-uity, -ancy; *tabula rasa;* exemption; *hiatus* etc. (*interval*) 198; no man's land.

truant, absentee.

nobody; nobody -present, – on earth; no one; not a soul; *âme qui vive.*

V. be -absent etc. *adj.;* keep -away, – out of the way; play truant, absent oneself, stay away.

withdraw, make oneself scarce, vacate; go away, slip out, slip away, retreat etc. 293.

Adj. absent, not present, away, nonresident, gone, from home; missing; lost; wanted, wanting; omitted; nowhere to be found; inexistent etc. 2.

empty, void; blank, vac-ant, -uous; unten-anted, -occupied, -inhabited; tenantless; desert, -ed; devoid; un-, uninhabitable.

exempt from, not having.

Adv. without, *minus,* nowhere; elsewhere; neither here nor there; in default of; *sans;* behind one's back.

Phr. the bird has flown, *non est inventus.*

188. Inhabitant.—N. inhabitant; habitant, resident, -iary; dweller, in-dweller; occup-ier, -ant, farmer, planter; householder, lodger, boarder, paying guest; inmate, tenant, renter, incumbent, sojourner, *locum tenens,* commorant; settler, squatter, backwoodsman, colonist; islander; denizen, citizen; burgher, oppidan, cockney, cit, townsman, burgess; villager; cottager, -tier, -ter; compatriot.

native, indigene, aboriginal, aborigines, autochthones; Briton, Englishman, John Bull; new comer etc. (*stranger*) 57.

garrison, crew; population; people etc. (*mankind*) 372; colony, settlement; household.

V. inhabit etc. (*be present*) 186; indenizen etc. (*locate oneself*) 184.

Adj. indigenous; enchorial; national, nat-ive, -al; autochthonous; British, English; colonial; domestic, domiciliated, -ed; naturalized, vernacular, domesticated; domiciliary.

in the occupation of; garrisoned —, occupied-by.

189. Abode. [Place of habitation, or resort.]—N. abode, dwelling, lodging, -s; diggings, domicile, residence, address, habitation, where one's lot is cast, local habitation, berth, seat, lap, sojourn, housing, quarters, headquarters, resiance, tabernacle, throne, ark.

home, fatherland, mother country, country etc. 181; home-stead, -stall; fireside, chimney corner; hearth, — stone; household gods, *lares et penates,* roof, household, housing, *dulce domum,* paternal domicile; native -soil, — land, blighty.

nest, *nidus,* snuggery; arbor, bower etc. 191; lair, den, cave, hole, hidingplace, cell, *sanctum sanctorum,* aerie, eyry, rookery, hive; *habitat,* haunt, covert, resort, retreat, perch, roost; nidification.

bivouac, camp, encampment, cantonment, castrametation; barrack, casemate, casern.

tent etc. (*covering*) 223; building etc. (*construction*) 161; chamber etc. (*receptacle*) 191.

tenement, messuage, farm, farmhouse, grange, *hacienda.*

cot, cabin, log cabin, shack, hut, *châlet,* croft, shed, booth, stall, hovel, bothy, shanty, igloo, tepee, wigwam; pen etc. (*inclosure*) 232; barn, bawn; kennel, sty, dog-hole, cote, coop, hutch, byre; cowhouse, -shed; stable, dove-cote, shippen.

house, mansion, place, villa, cottage, box, lodge, hermitage, *rus in urbe,* folly, rotunda, tower, *château,* castle, pavilion, hotel, court, manor-house, capital messuage, hall, palace, alcazar; country seat; kiosk, bungalow; temple etc. 1000; home of rest, alms-, poor-, work-house, asylum; boarding-, lodging-house; flat, maisonette, duplex, penthouse, suite of rooms, apartments, rooms, room building etc. 161; Mansion House, town hall, Capitol.

assembly-room, auditorium, coliseum, meeting-house, pump-room, spa, health resort, watering-place; club; theatrè etc. 840; drill hall, gymnasium, church etc. 1000; Houses of Parliament etc. 696; school etc. 542; inn; hostel, -ry; hotel, tavern, caravansary, khan, hospice; public-, ale-, pot-, mug-house; gin-palace, gin mill; coffee-, eating-house; canteen, *restaurant, rotisserie,* cafeteria, grill-room, *buffet, cafe, estaminet, posada, bodega;* bar; saloon, speakeasy, shebeen.

hamlet, village, thorp, dorp, ham, kraal; borough, burgh, town, county-seat, — town, city, capital, metropolis; suburb, quarter, parish etc. 181; ghetto; province, country.

street, place, terrace, parade, esplanade, promenade, pier, embankment, road, villas, row, walk, lane, alley, court, quadrangle, quad, wynd, close, yard, passage, rents, mansions, buildings, mews.

square, polygon, circus, crescent, mall, *piazza,* arcade, colonnade, peristyle, cloister; gardens, grove, residences; block of buildings, market-place, *place.*

anchorage, roadstead, roads; dock, basin, wharf, quay, port; harbor; dry-, graving-, floating-dock.

garden, park, pleasure-ground, pleasance, demesne.

V. take up one's abode etc. (*locate oneself*) 184; inhabit etc. (*be present*) 186.

Adj. urban, oppidan, metropolitan; suburban; provincial, rural, rustic; countrified; regional, parochial, domestic; cosmopolitan; palatial.

190. Contents. [Things contained.]—N. contents; cargo, lading, freight, shipment, load, bale, burden; cart-, ship-load; cup —, basket —, etc. (*receptacle*) 191 - of; inside etc. 221; stuffing, ullage.

V. load, lade, ship, charge, fill, stuff.

191. Receptacle.—N. receptacle, container; inclosure etc. 232; recipient, receiver, reservatory.

compartment; cell, -ule; follicle; hole, corner, niche, recess, nook; crypt, stall, pigeon-hole, cove, oriel; cave etc. (*concavity*) 252.

capsule, vesicle, cyst, pod, calyx, *cancelli,* utricle, bladder, udder.

stomach, paunch, *venter,* abdomen, ventricle, crop, craw, ingluvies, maw, gizzard, bread-basket, belly, little Mary; mouth.

pocket, pouch, fob, sheath, scabbard, socket, bag, vanity bag, compact, sac, sack, saccule, despatch —, attaché-, tachy- case, wallet, scrip, card-, note-, case, billfold, poke, knit, knap-, haver-, ruck-sack, sachel, satchel, reticule, budget, net; ditty-, -box, -bag, kitbag; portfolio; saddlebags, holster; quiver etc. (*magazine*) 636.

chest, box, coffer, caddy, case, casket, pyx, pix, *caisson,* desk, *bureau,* reliquary, shrine; trunk, portmanteau, band-box, *valise,* suitcase, hand-, traveling-, overnight-, Gladstone-, carpet-bag, brief case; boot, imperial; *vache;* cage, manger, rack.

vessel, vase, bushel, barrel, canister, jar; pottle, basket, punnet, pannier, buck-basket, hopper, maund, creel, cran, crate, cradle, bassinet, wisket, whisket, *jardinière, corbeille,* hamper, wastepaper basket, dosser, dorser, tray, hod, scuttle, utensil, spittoon, cuspidor.

[For liquids] cistern etc. (*store*) 636; vat, caldron, barrel, cask, puncheon, keg, rundlet, tun, butt, firkin, hogshead, kilderkin, carboy, amphora, ampulla, bottle, jar, leather bottle, decanter, ewer, cruse, carafe, crock, kit, canteen, flagon; demijohn; flask, -et; stoup, noggin, vial, phial, ampoulé, cruet, caster; gourd; urn, *épergne,* salver, *patella, tazza, patera;* pig-, big-gin; tea-, coffee-pot, percolator, *samovar;* tyg, nipperkin, pocket-pistol; tub, bucket, pail, skeel, pot, tankard, jug, pitcher, toby, mug, pipkin; gal-, gall-ipot, pannikin; matrass, receiver, retort, alembic, bolthead, can, kettle; bowl, basin, jorum, punch-bowl, cup, goblet, chalice, tumbler, glass, wineglass, rummer, beaker, tass, horn, saucepan, skillet, posnet, tureen, terrine, *casserole,* sauce-, gravy-boat.

plate, platter, paten, dish, vegetable —, *entrée-*dish, trencher, calabash, porringer, potager, saucer, pan, crucible.

shovel, trowel, spoon; table-, dessert-, tea-, egg-.

salt-spoon; spatula, ladle; dipper; baler; watch-glass, thimble.

closet, commode, cupboard, cellaret, *chiffonnière*, locker, bin, bunker, *buffet*, press, safe, sideboard, drawer, chest of drawers, till, *scrutoire*, *secrétaire*, *éscritoire*, davenport, book-case, cabinet, canterbury; corner cupboard, wardrobe.

chamber, apartment, room, cabin; office, court, hall, atrium; suite of rooms, flat, story; saloon, *salon*, parlor; presence-chamber; sitting-, drawing-, reception-, state-, living-, work-room; gallery, cabinet, closet, cubicle; pew, box; *boudoir*; *adytum*, *sanctum*; bed-room, dormitory, dressing-room; refectory, dining-room, *salle-à-manger*; nursery, schoolroom; library, study; *studio*; billiard-, bath-, smoking-room; den, canteen, mess, officers' mess; gun-, ward-, mess-room.

attic, loft, garret, cockloft, clerestory; cellar, vault, hold, cockpit; *entre-sol*; mezzanine floor; ground-floor, *rez-de-chaussée*; basement, kitchen, cook-house, galley, pantry, scullery, offices; store-room etc. (*depository*) 636; lumber-room; dust-hole, -bin; dairy, laundry, coachhouse; *garage*; *hangar*; out-, pent-house; lean-to.

portico, porch, piazza, verandah, lobby, court, hall, vestibule, corridor, passage; ante-room, chamber; lounge; *foyer*, *loggia*.

conservatory, green-house, glass-house, vinery, bower, arbor, summer-house, alcove, grotto, hermitage, pergola.

lodging etc. (*abode*) 189; bed etc. (*support*) 215; carriage etc. (*vehicle*) 272.

Adj. capsular; saccu-lar, -lated; recipient; ventricular, cystic, vascular, vesicular, cellular, camerated, locular, multilocular, poly-gastric; marsupial; siliqu-ose, -ous.

192. Size.—N. size, magnitude, dimension, bulk, volume; largeness etc. *adj.*; greatness etc. (*of quantity*) 31; expanse etc. (*space*) 180; amplitude, mass; proportions.

capacity; ton-, tun-nage; caliber, scantling.

turgidity etc. (*expansion*) 194; corpulence, obesity; plumpness, etc. *adj.*; *embonpoint*, corporation, flesh and blood, lustihood.

hugeness etc. *adj.*; enormity, immensity, monstrosity.

giant, Brobdingnagian, Antaeus, Goliath, Gog and Magog, Gargantua, monster, mammoth, Cyclops; whale, porpoise, behemoth, leviathan, elephant, hippopotamus; colossus; tun, lump, bulk, block, loaf, mass, clod, nugget, bushel, thumper, whopper, spanker, strapper; Triton among the minnows.

mountain, mound; heap etc. (*assemblage*) 72. largest portion etc. 50; full-, life-size.

V. ve - large etc. *adj.*; become -large etc. (*expand*) 194.

Adj. large, big; great etc. (*in quantity*) 31; considerable, bulky, voluminous, ample, massive, massy; capacious, comprehensive; spacious etc. 180; mighty, towering, fine, magnificent.

corpulent, stout, fat, plump, squab, full, lusty, strapping, bouncing; portly, burly, well-fed, full-grown; stalwart, brawny, fleshy; goodly; in good -case, - condition; in condition; chopping, jolly; chub-, chubby-faced.

lubberly, hulky, unwieldy, lumpish, gaunt, spanking, whacking, whopping, thumping, thundering, hulking; overgrown; puffy etc. (*swollen*) 194.

huge, immense, enormous, mighty; vast, -y; amplitudinous, stupendous; monst-er, -rous; gigantic, elephantine; giant, -like; colossal, Cyclopean, Brobdingnagian, Garguantuan, Titanic; infinite etc. 105.

large as life; plump as a dumpling, - partridge; fat as -a pig, - a quail, - butter, - brawn, - bacon.

193. Littleness.—N. littleness etc. *adj.*; smallness etc. (*of quantity*) 32; exiguity, inextension; parvi-tude, -ty; duodecimo; Elzevir edition, epitome, microcosm; rudiment; vanishing point; thinness etc. 203.

dwarf, pigmy, atomy, Liliputian, midget, chit, pigwidgeon, urchin, elf; doll, puppet; Tom Thumb, Hop-o'-my thumb, Humpty-dumpty; man-, mannikin; *homunculus*, dapperling, fingerling, dandiprat, cock-sparrow, scalawag.

animalcule, monad, mite, insect, emmet, fly, midge, gnat, shrimp, minnow, worm, maggot, entozoon; *bacillus*, microbe, micro-organism, *bacteria*; *infusoria*; microbe; grub; tit, tomtit, runt, mouse, small fry; millet-, mustard-seed; barleycorn; pebble, grain of sand; mole-hill, button, bubble.

point; atom etc. (*small quantity*) 32; fragment etc. (*small part*) 51; powder etc. 330; point of a pin, mathematical point; *minutiae* etc. (*unimportance*) 643.

micro-graphy, -meter, -scope; vernier; scale.

V. be -little etc. *adj.*; lie in a nutshell; become small etc. (*decrease*) 36, (*contract*) 195.

Adj. little; small etc. (*in quantity*) 32; minute, diminutive, microscopic; inconsiderable etc. (*unimportant*) 643; exiguous, puny, tiny, wee, petty, minikin, miniature, pigmy, elfin; under sized; dwarf, -ed, -ish; spare, stunted, limited; cramp, -ed; pollard, Liliputian, dapper, pocket; port-ative, -able; duodecimo; dumpy, squat; compact, handy; short etc. 201.

impalpable, intangible, evanescent, imperceptible, invisible, inappreciable, infinitesimal, homeopathic; atomic, corpuscular, molecular; rudiment-ary, -al; embryonic.

weazen, scant, scraggy, scrubby; thin etc. (*narrow*) 203; granular etc. (*powdery*) 330; shrunk etc. 195.

Adv. in a -small compass, - nutshell; on a small scale.

194. Expansion.—N. expansion; increase etc. 35 -of size; enlargement, extension, augmentation; ampli-fication, -ation; aggrandizement, spread, increment, growth, development, pullulation, swell, dilation, dilatation, rarefaction; turg-escence, -idness, -idity; obesity etc. (*size*) 192; dropsy, tumefaction, intumescence, swelling, tumor, *diastole*, distension; puff-ing, -iness; inflation; pandiculation.

dilatability, expansibility.

germination, growth, upgrowth; accretion etc. 35.

over-growth, -distension; hypertrophy, tympany.

bulb etc. (*convexity*) 250; plumper; superiority of size.

V. become -larger etc. (large etc. 192); expand, widen, enlarge, extend, grow, increase, incrassate, swell, gather; fill out; deploy, take open . order, dilate, stretch, spread; mantle, was; grow –, spring- up; bud, bourgeon, shoot, sprout, germinate, put forth, vegetate, pullulate, open, burst forth, flower, blow etc. 734; gain –, gather- flesh; outgrow; spread like wildfire, overrun.

be larger than; surpass etc. (*be superior*) 33.
render -larger etc. (large etc. 192); expand, spread, extend, aggrandize, distend, develop, amplify, spread out, widen, magnify, rarefy, inflate, puff, puff out, blow up, stuff, pad, cram; exaggerate; fatten.

Adj. expanded etc. *v.*; larger etc. (large etc. 192); swollen; expansive; wide-open, -spread; fanshaped; flabelliform; overgrown exaggerated, bloated, fat, turgid, tumid, hypertrophied, dropsical; pot-, swag-bellied; edematous, obese, puffy, pursy, blowzy, distended; patulous; bulbous etc. (*convex*) 250; full-blown, -grown, -formed; big etc. 192.

195. Contraction.—N. contraction, reduction, diminution; decrease etc. 36- of size; defalcation, decrement; lessening, shrinkage; collapse, emaciation, attenuation, tabefaction, comsumption, marasmus, atrophy; systole, neck, hourglass.

condensation, compression, constraint, compactness; compendium etc. 596; squeezing etc. *v.* ; strangulation; corrugation; astringency, constringency; astringents, sclerotics; contractility, compressibility; coarctation.

inferiority in size.
V. become -small, – smaller; lessen, decrease etc. 36; grow less, dwindle, shrink, contract, narrow, shrivel, collapse, wither, lose flesh, wizen, fall away, waste, wane, ebb; decay etc. (*deteriorate*) 659.

be smaller than, fall short of; not come up to etc. (*be inferior*) 34.
render smaller, lessen, diminish, contract, draw in, shrink, shrivel, narrow, coarctate; constrict, constringe; condense, compress, boil down, deflate, exhaust, empty; squeeze, corrugate, crush, crumple up, warp, purse up, pack, stow; pinch, tighten, strangle; cramp; dwarf, bedwarf; shorten etc. 201; circumscribe etc. 229; restrain etc. 751; fold etc. 258.

pare, reduce, attenuate, rub down, scrape, file, grind, chip, shave, shear.
Adj. contracting etc. *v.*; astringent; shrunk, contracted etc. *v.*; strangulated, tabid, wizened, stunted, tabescent; marasmic; waning etc. *v.*; neap; compact; shriveled, preshrunk.

unexpanded etc. (expand etc. 194); inswept; contractile; compressible; smaller etc. small etc. 193).

196. Distance.—N. distance; space etc. 180; remoteness, farness; far- cry to; longinquity, elongation; offing, background; removedness; parallax; reach, span, stride; drift.

out-post, -skirt; horizon, sky-line; aphelion; foreign parts, *ultima Thule*, *ne plus ultra*, antipodes; long range, giant's stride.

dispersion etc. 73.
V. be -distant etc. *adj.*; extend –, stretch –, reach –, spread –, go –, get –, stretch away- to; range, outrange, outreach.

remain at a distance; keep –, stand- -away, – off, – aloof, – clear of.
Adj. distant; far -off, away; remote, telescopic, distal, wide of; stretching to etc. *v.*; yon, -der; ulterior; trans-marine, -pontine, -atlantic, -pacific, -continental, -polar, -equatorial, -alpine; tramontane; ultra-montane, -mundane; hyperborean, antihodean; inaccessible, out of the way; unapproached, -able; incontiguous.

Adv. far -off, – away; afar, -off; off; away; a -long, – great, – good- way off; wide away, aloof; wide –, clear- of; out of -the way, – reach; abroad, ' yonder, farther, further, beyond; *outre mer*, over the border, far and wide, over the hills and far away; from pole to pole etc. (*over great space*) 180; to the -uttermost parts, – ends- of the earth; out of -hearing, – range, nobody knows where, *à perte de vue*, out of the sphere of, wide of the mark; a far cry to.

apart, asunder; wide -apart, – asunder; *longo intervallo*; at arm's length.

197. Nearness.—N. nearness etc. *adj.*; proximity, propinquity; vicinity, -age; neighborhood, adjacency; contiguity etc. 199.

short -distance, – step, – cut; earshot, close quarters, brief span; stone's throw; bow –, gun –, pistol- shot; hair's breadth, span; close-up.

purlieus, neighborhood, vicinage, *environs*, *alentours*, suburbs, confines, *banlieue*, borderland; whereabouts.

bystander; neighbor, borderer.
approach etc. 286; convergence etc. 290; perihelion.

V. be -near etc. *adj.*; adjoin, hang about, trench on; border-, verge upon; stand by; approximate, tread on the heels of, cling to, clasp, hug; cuddle, huddle; hang about the skirts of, hover over; burn; abut.

bring –, draw- -near etc. 286; converge etc. 290; crowd etc. 72; place -side by side etc. *adv.*
Adj. near, nigh; close-, near- at hand; close, neighboring, propinquent, bordering upon; adjacent, adjoining, limitrophe; proxim-ate, ~al; at hand, handy; near the mark, near run; home, intimate.

Adv. near, nigh; hard –, 'fast- by; close -to. upon, – up; at the point of; next door to; within -reach, – call, – hearing, – earshot, – range; within an ace of; but a step, not far from, at no great distance; on the -verge, – brink, – skirts- of; in the -environs etc. *n.*; at one's -door, – feet, – elbow, – finger's end, – side; on the tip of one's tongue; under one's nose; within a -stone's throw etc. *n.*; in -sight, – presence- of; at close quarters; cheek by -jole, – jowl; beside, alongside, side by side, *tête-à-tête*; in juxtaposition etc. (*touching*) 199; yard-arm to yard-arm; at the heels of; on the confines of, at the threshold, bordering upon, verging to; in the way.

about; here- there-abouts; roughly, in round

numbers; approxim- -ately,   – atively; as good
as, well nigh.

198. Interval.—N. interval, interspace;
separation etc. 44; break gap, opening; hole etc.
260; chasm, *hiatus*, caesura; inter-ruption,-
regnum; interstice, *lacuna*, cleft, mesh, crevice,
chink, rime, creek, cranny, crack, chap, slit, slot,
fissure, scissure, rift, flaw, breach, fracture, rent,
gash, cut, leak, dike, ha-ha.

gorge, defile, ravine, canon, *crevasse*, abyss,
abysm; gulf; inlet, frith, strait, gully, gulch, nullah;
pass; notch; furrow etc. 259; yawning gulf; *hiatus -
maxime, — valde- deflendus*; parenthesis etc. (*interjacence*) 228; void etc. (*absence*) 187; incompleteness etc. 530.

V. gape etc. (*open*) 260; part, remove.

Adj. with an interval, far between; separated,
spaced, split.

Adv. at intervals etc. (*discontinuously*) 70;
longo intervallo.

199. Contiguity.—N. contiguity, contact,
proximity, apposition, juxtaposition, touching etc.
v.; abutment, osculation; meeting, appulse, ap-
pulsion, *rencontre*, rencounter, syzygy, coincidence, conjunction, coexistence; adhesion etc.
46.

border-land; frontier etc. (*limit*) 233; tangent.

V. be -contiguous etc. *adj.*; join, adjoin, abut
on, march with, border; tick, graze, touch, meet,
osculate, kiss, come in contact; coincide; coexist;
adhere etc. 46.

Adj. contiguous; touching etc. *v.*; in -contact
etc. *n.*, conterminous, end to end, osculatory; pertingent; tangential.

hand to hand; close to etc. (*near*) 197; with no -
interval etc. 198.

200. Length.—N. length, longitude, span, extent, mileage.

line, bar, rule, stripe, streak, spoke, radius.

lengthening etc. *v.*; pro-longation, -duction, -
traction; ten-sion, -sure; extension.

[Measures of length] line, nail, inch, hand,
palm, foot, cubit, yard, ell, fathom, rod, pole,
perch, furlong, mile, league; chain, meter, kilo-,
centi-, milli- etc meter.

pedometer, perambulator, odometer, odograph,
speedometer, cyclometer, log, telemeter, range finder; scale etc. (*measurement*) 466.

V. be -long etc. *adj.*; stretch out, sprawl; extend –, reach –, stretch -to; make a long
arm, 'drag its slow length along.'

render -long etc. *adj.*; lengthen, extend,
elongate; stretch; pro-long, -duce, -tract; let
–, pay –, draw –, spin- out; drawl.

enfilade, look along, view in perspective.

Adj. long, -some; lengthy, lank, wiredrawn, outstretched; stretched, drawn out, lengthened etc. *v.*;
sesquipedalian etc. (*words*) 577; interminable, no
end of.

linc-ar, -al; longitudinal, oblong.

as long as -my arm, —to-day and to-morrow; unshortened etc. (*shorten* etc. 201).

Adv. lengthwise, at length, longitudinally, endlong, along; *tandem*; in a line etc. (*continuously*)
69; in perspective.

from -end to end; —stem to stern, —head to foot,
—the crown of the head to the sole of the foot, —
top to toe, —head to heels; fore and aft.

201. Shortness.—N. shortness etc. *adj.*; brevity;
littleness etc. 193; a span.

shortening etc. *v.*; abbrevia-tion, -ture;
abridgment, concision, retrenchment, curtailment,
decurtation; reduction etc. (*contraction*) 195;
epitome etc. (*compendium*) 596.

abridger, abstractor, epitomiser.

elision, ellipsis; conciseness etc. (*in style*) 572.

V. be -short etc. *adj.*; render -short etc. *adj.*;
shorten, curtail, abridge, abbreviate, take in,
reduce; compress etc. (*contract*) 195; epitomize
etc. 596.

retrench, cut short, obtruncate; scrimp, cut, chop
up, hack, hew; cut –, pare- down; clip, snip, dock,
lop, prune; shear, shave, mow, reap, crop; snub;
truncate, pollard, stunt, nip, nip in the bud, check
the growth of; [in drawing] foreshorten.

Adj. short, brief, curt; compendious, compact;
stubby, scrimp; shorn, stubbed; stumpy, thickset,
podgy, stocky, pug; squab, -by; squat, dumpy; little
etc. 193; curtailed of its fair proportions; short by;
oblate; concise etc. 572; summary.

Adv. shortly etc. *adj.*; in short etc. (*concisely*)
572.

202. Breadth. Thickness.—N. breadth, width,
latitude, amplitude; diameter, bore, calibre, radius;
superficial extent etc. (*space*) 180.

thickness, crassitude; corpulence etc. (*size*) 192;
dilatation etc. (*expansion*) 194.

V. be -broad etc. *adj.*; become –, render- -
broad etc. *adj.*; expand etc. 194; thicken, widen.

Adj. broad, wide, ample, extended; discous; fan-
like; out-spread, -stretched; wide as a church-door.

thick, dumpy, squab, squat, thickset, tubby; thick
as a rope, stubby etc. 201.

203. Narrowness. Thinness.—N. narrowness
etc. *adj.*; closeness, exility; exiguity etc. (*little*)
193.

line; hair's –, finger's -breadth; strip, streak,
vein.

thinness etc. *adj.*; tenuity; emaciation, slen-
derness, macilency, *marcor*.

shaving, slip etc. (*filament*) 205; threadpaper,
skeleton, shadow, scrag, anatomy, spindle-shanks,
barebones, lantern jaws, mere skin and bone.

middle construction, stricture, neck, waist, isthmus, wasp, hour-glass; ridge, *ghaut*, pass; ravine
etc. 198.

narrowing, coarctation, angustation, tapering;
contraction etc. 195.

V. be-narrow etc. *adj.*; narrow, taper, diminish,
contract etc. 195; render -narrow etc. *adj.*

Adj. narrow, close; slender, thin, fine; *svelte*;
thread-like etc. (*filament*) 205; finespun, taper,
slim, gracile, slight, slight-made; scant, -y; spare,
delicate, incapacious; contracted etc. 195; unexpanded etc. (expand etc. 194); slender as a thread,
capillary.

emaciated, lean, meager, gaunt, macilent; lank, -y; weedy, skinny, scrawny, scraggy; starv-ed, -eling; attenuated, shrivelled; wizened, pinched, peaky, skeletal, spindling, spindle- -legged, -shanked; extenuated, tabid, marcid, bare-bone, raw-boned; herring-gutted; worn to a shadow, lean as a rake; thin as a -lath,—whipping post,—wafer; hatchet-faced; lantern-jawed.

204. Layer.—N. layer, stratum, course, bed, zone, *substratum,*floor, flag, stage, story, tier, slab, escarpment, table, tablet, panel, plaque; board, plank; trencher, platter.

plate; lam-ina, -ella; sheet, flake, foil, wafer, scale, coat, peel, pellicle, ply, thickness, membrane, film, leaf, slice, shive, cut, rasher, shaving, integument etc. (*covering*) 223.

V. slice, shave, pare, peel; plate, coat, veneer; cover etc. 223.

Adj. lamell-ar, -ated, -iform; laminated, -iferous; micaceous; schist-ose, -ous; scaly; filmy, membranous, flaky, squamous; folia-ted, -ceous; stratified, -form; tabular, discoid, spathic.

205. Filament.—N. filament, line; fiber, fibril; funicle, vein, hair, capillament, *cilium*, tendril, gossamer; hair-stroke; harl.

wire, string, thread, packthread, cotton, sewing-silk, twine, twist, whip-cord, cord, rope, cable, yarn, hemp, oakum, jute, wool, worsted.

strip, shred, slip, spill, list, band, fillet, *fascia*, ribbon, riband, tape, roll, lath, slat, strake, splinter, shiver, shaving.

beard etc. (*roughness*) 256; ramification; strand.

Adj. fil-amentous, -aceous, -iform; fibr-ous, -illous; thread-like, wiry, stringy, ropy; capill-ary, -iform; funicular, wire-drawn; anguilliform; flagelliform; hairy etc. (*rough*) 256; ligulate.

206. Height.—N. height, altitude, elevation, ceiling; eminence. pitch; loftiness etc. *adj.*; sublimity.

tallness etc. *adj.*; stature, procerity; prominence etc. 250.

colossus etc. (*size*) 192; giant, grenadier, giraffe.

mount, -ain; hill, butte, monticle, fell, knap;· cape; head-, fore-land; promontory; ridge, hog's back, dune; rising – , vantage- ground; down; moor, -land; Alp; up-, table-, high-lands; heights etc. (*summit*) 210; knoll, hummock, hillock, barrow, mound, mole, *kopje*; steeps, bluff, cliff, craig, tor, peak, pike, clough; escarpment, edge, ledge, brae; dizzy height.

tower, pillar, column, pylon, obelisk, monument, steeple, spire, minaret, *campanile*, belfry, turret, roof, dome, cupola, pagoda, pyramid; sky scraper; Eiffel tower.

pole, pikestaff, maypole, flagstaff; mast, top—, topgallant- mast.

ceiling etc. (*covering*) 223.

high water; high—, flood—, spring-tide.

altimetry etc. (*angle*) 244; altimeter, height-finder, hypsometer, barograph.

V. be -high etc. *adj.*; tower, soar, command;

hover; cap, culminate; overhang, hang over, impend, beetle; bestride, ride, mount; perch, surmount; cover etc. 233; overtop etc. (*be superior*) 33; stand on tiptoe.

become -high etc. *adj.*; grow, – higher, – taller; upgrow; rise etc. (*ascend*) 305.

render -high etc. *adj.*; heighten etc. (*elevate*) 307.

Adj. high, elevated, eminent, exalted, lofty, supernal; tall; gigantic etc. (*big*) 192; Patagonian; towering, beetling, soaring, hanging [gardens]; elevated etc. 307; upper; highest etc. (*topmost*) 210; monticulous, perching, hill-dwelling.

up-, moor-land; hilly, mountainous, alpine, subalpine, heaven-kissing; cloud-topt, -capt, -touching; aerial.

overhanging etc. *v.*; incumbent, overlying; super-incumbent, -natant, -imposed; prominent etc. 250.

tall as a -maypole, —poplar,—steeple; lanky etc. (*thin*) 203.

Adv. on high, high up, aloft, up, above, aloof, overhead; up—, above- stairs; in the clouds; on -tiptoe, —stilts,—the shoulders of; over head and ears; breast high.

over, upwards; from top to bottom etc. (*completely*) 52.

207. Lowness.—N. lowness etc. *adj.*; debasement, depression; prostration etc. (*horizontal*) 213; depression etc. (*concave*) 252.

molehill; lowlands; bottomlands; basement-ground-floor; *rez de chaussée* etc. 211; hold; feet, heels.

low water; low—, ebb—, neap—, spring- tide.

V. be -low etc. *adj.*; lie -low, —flat; underlie; crouch, slouch, wallow, grovel; lower etc. (*depress*) 308.

Adj. low, neap, debased; nether, -most; flat, level with the ground; lying low etc. *v.*; crouched, subjacent, squat, prostrate etc. (*horizontal*) 213.

Adv. under; be-, under-neath; below; down, -wards; adown, at the foot of; under-foot, -ground; down—, below-stairs; at a low ebb; below par.

208. Depth.—N. depth; deepness etc. *adj.*; profundity, depression etc. (*concavity*) 252.

hollow, pit, shaft, well, crater, abyss; gulf etc. 198; bowels of the earth, bottomless pit, hell.

soundings, sonar, depth of water, water, draught; submersion; plummet, sound, probe; sounding -rod, – line, – machine; lead; submarine, diving bell, bathysphere; diver.

V. be -deep etc. *adj.*; render -deep etc. *adj.*; deepen.

plunge etc. 310; sound, heave the lead, take soundings; dig etc. (*excavate*) 252.

Adj. deep, -seated; profound, sunk, buried; submerged etc. 310; sub-aqueous, -marine, -terranean, -terrene; underground.

bottom-, sound-, fathom-less; unfathom-ed, -able; abysmal; deep as a well, deep-sea; knee-, ankle-deep.

Adv. beyond—, out of- one's depth; over head and ears, over one's head.

209. Shallowness.—N. shallowness etc. *adj.*; shoals; mere scratch; veneer, gloss, pinprick.

Adj. shallow, superficial; skin–, ankle–, knee-deep; just enough to wet one's feet; shoal, -y.
V. shallow, shoal, skim– over, –the surface, touch on.

210. Summit.—N. summit, -y; top, vertex, apex, zenith, pinnacle, acme, acropolis, culmination, meridian, utmost height, *ne plus ultra,* height, pitch, maximum, climax, apogee; culminating –, crowning –, turning- point; turn of the tide, fountain head; water-shed, -parting; sky, pole.

tip, -top; crest, crow's nest, cap, truck, peak, nib; end etc. 67; crown, brow; head, nob, noddle, pate, skull, cranium.

high places, heights.

top-, top-gallant mast, sky scraper; quarter –, hurricane- deck.

architrave, frieze, cornice, coping, coping-stone, zoophorus, capital, headpiece, capstone, epistyle, sconce, pediment, entablature; tympanum; ceiling etc. (*covering*) 223.

attic, loft, garret, house-top, upper story, roof.

topping, icing, frosting.

V. culminate, cap, crown, top; overtop etc. (*be superior to*) 33.

Adj. highest etc. (high etc. 206); top; top-, upper-most; tip-top; culminating etc. *v.*; meridi-an, -onal; capital, head, polar, supreme, supernal, top-gallant.

Adv. a-top, at the top of – the tree, – the heap.

211. Base.—N. base, -ment; plinth, dado, wainscot, baseboard; foundation etc. (*support*) 215; substructure, *sub · stratum,* sump, ground, earth, pavement, floor, paving, flag, carpet, ground-floor, deck; footing, groundwork, basis; hold, bilge, orlop deck.

bottom, nadir, foot, sole, toe, hoof, keel, kelson, root.

Adj. bottom; under-, nether-most; fundamental; founded –, based –, grounded –, built- on.

212. Verticality.—N. verticality; erectness etc. *adj.*; perpendicularity; right angle, normal; azimuth circle.

wall, palisade, precipice, cliff, steep, bluff.

elevation, erection; square, plumb-line, plummet.

V. be -vertical etc. *adj.*; stand -up, – on end, – erect, – upright; stick –, cock-up.

render -vertical etc. *adj.*; set –, stick –, raise –, cock- up; erect, rear, raise, pitch, raise on its legs.

Adj. vertical, upright, erect, perpendicular, normal, plumb, straight, bolt upright; rampant; straight –, standing- up etc. *v.*; rectangular, orthogonal.

Adv. vertically etc. *adj.*; up, on end; up –, right- on end; *à plomb,* endwise; on one's legs; at right angles.

213. Horizontality.—N. horizontality; flatness; level, plane; stratum etc. 204; dead -level, – flat; level plane.

recumbeney; lying down etc. *v.*; reclination, decumbence; de-, discumbency; proneness etc. *adj.*; accubation, supination, resupination, prostration; azimuth.

plain, floor, platform, bowling-green; cricket-ground; court; gridiron; base-ball diamond; hockey rink; tennis-, croquet-ground, – lawn; billiard table; terrace, estrade, esplanade, *parterre,* table-land, *plateau,* ledge.

spirit-, level; T-square.

V. be -horizontal etc. *adj.*; lie, recline, couch; lie -down, – flat, – prostrate; sprawl, loll; sit down.

render -horizontal etc. *adj.*; lay, – down, – out; level, flatten, even, raze, equalize, smooth, align; prostrate, knock down, floor, fell, ground.

Adj. horizontal, level, even, plane; flat etc. 251; flat as a -billiard table, – bowling green; alluvial; calm, – as a mill-pond; smooth, –as glass.

re-, de-, pro-, ac-cumbent; lying etc. *v.*; prone, supine, couchant, jacent, prostrate.

Adv. horizontally etc. *adj.*; on -one's back. –all fours, – its beam ends.

214. Pendency.—N. pend-, dependency; suspension, hanging etc. *v.*

pendant, drop, tippet, tassel, lobe, tail, train, flap, lappet, skirt, pig-tail, queue, pendulum, hanger, suspender, supporter.

peg, knob, button, hook, nail, stud, ring, staple, tenterhook; davit; fastening etc. 45; spar, horse.

chande-, gase-, electro-lier.

V. be -pendent etc. *adj.*; hang, depend, swing, dangle, droop, sag; swag; daggle, flap, trail, flow.

suspend, hang, sling, hook up, hitch, fasten to, append.

Adj. pend-ent, -ulous; pensile; hanging etc. *v.*; dependent; suspended etc. *v.*; lowering, overhanging, beetling, decumbent; loose, flowing.

having a -peduncle etc. *n.*; pedunculate, tailed, caudate.

215. Support.—N. support, backing, ground, foundation, base, basis; *terra firma*; bearing, fulcrum, *point d'appui,* caudex, purchase, footing, hold, -*locus standi*; landing, – stage, – place; stage, platform; block; rest, resting-place; ground-work, *substratum,* sustentation, subvention; floor etc. (*basement*) 211.

supporter; aid etc. 707; prop, stand, anvil, fulciment; hod, stay, shore, skid, rib, sprag, truss, bandage; sleeper; stirrup, stilts, shoe, sole, heel, splint, lap; bar, rod, boom, sprit, outrigger.

staff, stick, crutch, alpenstock, bourdon; *bâton,* maulstick, colstaff, cowlstaff, staddle; stalk, pedicel, -icle, – uncle.

post, pillar, shaft, column, pilaster; pediment, pedestal; plinth, shank, leg, socle, zocle; buttress, jamb, mullion, abutment; pile, baluster, banister, stanchion, king post; balustrade.

frame, -work, body, *chassis, fuselage*; scaffold, skeleton, beam, rafter, girder, lintel, joist, cantilever, travis, trave, corner-stone, summer, transom; rung, round, step, sill.

columella, back-bone; key-stone; axle, -tree; axis; arch, ogive, mainstay.

trunnion, pivot, rowlock; peg etc. (*pendency*)

214; tie-beam etc. (*fastening*) 45; thole pin.

board, ledge, shelf, hob, bracket, trevet, trivet, arbor, rack, hatrack; mantel, -piece, -shelf; slab, console; counter, dresser; flange, corbel; table, trestle, teapoy; shoulder; perch; horse; easel, desk; retable, predella.

seat, throne, dais; divan, musnud; chair, bench, form, stool, camp-stool, sofa, settee, davenport, stall, miserere, arm –, easy –, elbow –, rocking-chair; couch, day bed, *fauteuil*, woolsack, ottoman, settle, squab, bench, box, dicky; saddle, pannel, pillion; side –, pack- saddle; pommel.

bed, berth, pallet, tester, crib, cot, bassinet, hammock, shakedown, camp bed, bunk, truckle-bed, cradle, litter, stretcher, bedstead; four-poster, French bed; bedding, mattress, *paillasse;* pillow, bolster; mat, rug, cushion.

stool, footstool, hassock, faldstool, *prie-dieu;* tabouret; tripod.

Atlas, Persides, Atlantes, Caryatides, Hercules.

V. be -supported etc.; lie –, sit –, recline –, lean –, loll –, rest –, stand –, step –, repose –, abut –, beat –, be based etc.- on; have at one's back; be-stride, -straddle.

support, bear, carry, hold, sustain, shoulder; hold –, back –, bolster –, shore- up; up-hold, -bear; prop; under-prop,-pin, -set; bandage, etc. 43; brace, truss; cradle, pillow.

give –, furnish –, afford –, supply –, lend- -support, – foundations; bottom, found, base, ground, embed.

maintain, keep on foot; aid etc. 707.

Adj. support-ing, -ed, etc.*v.*; atlantean, columellar; sustentative, fundamental, basal.

Adv. astride on, astraddle; pick-a-back.

216. Parallelism.—N. parallelism; coextension, concentricity, collimation.

V. be –, lie- parallel to; collimate; equate, match.

Adj. parallel; coextensive, collateral, concentric, concurrent, abreast, aligned.

Adv. alongside, abreast etc. (*laterally*) 236.

217. Obliquity.—N. obliquity, inclination, skew, slope, slant; crookedness etc. *adj.*; slopeness; leaning etc. *v.*; bevel, bezel, ramp, tilt; bias, list, twist, warp, swag, cant, lurch; distortion etc. 243; bend etc. (*curve*) 245; tower of Pisa.

acclivity, rise, ascent, grade, gradient, *glacis*, rising ground, hill, bank, declivity, downhill, dip, fall, devexity; gentle –, rapid- slope; easy -ascent, – descent; shelving beach; *talus; montagne Russe; facilis descensus Averni*.

steepness etc. *adj.*; cliff, precipice etc. (*vertical*) 212; escarpment, scarp.

[Measure of inclination]clinometer, theodolite, level, sextant, quadrant, protractor; angle, sine, cosine, tangent etc. hypothenuse.

diagonal; zigzag, chevron.

V. be -oblique etc. *adj.*; slope, slant, lean, incline, shelve, stoop, decline, descent, bend, heel, careen, sag, swag, seel, slouch, cant, sidle.

render -oblique etc. *adj.*; sway, bias; slope, slant; incline, bend, crook; cant, tilt; distort etc. 243.

Adj. oblique, inclined; sloping etc. *v.*; tilted etc.

v.; recumbent, clinal, skew, askew, slant, aslant, bias, plagiedral, indirect, wry, awry, ajee, crooked; knock-kneed etc. (*distorted*) 243; bevel, out of the perpendicular.

uphill, rising, ascending, acclivous; downhill, falling, descending; declining, declivous, devex, anticlinal; steep, abrupt, precipitous, breakneck.

diagonal; trans-verse, -versal; athwart, antiparallel; curved etc. 245.

Adv. obliquely etc. *adj.*; on –, all on- one side; askew, askant, askance, aslope, asquint, edgewise, at an angle; side-long, -ways; slope-, slant-wise; by a side wind.

218. Inversion.—N. in-, e-, sub-, re-, retro-, intro-version; contraposition etc. 237; contrariety etc. 14; reversal; turn of the tide.

overturn; upset, capsize; somer-sault, -set; summerset; *culbute;* revulsion; *pirouette.*

transposition, transposal, anastrophy, *metastasis, hyperbaton, anastrophe, hysteron--proteron,* hypallage, *synchysis, tmesis,* parenthesis; *metathesis;* palindrome; Spoonerism.

pronation and supination.

V. be -inverted etc.; turn –, go –, wheel- -round, – about, – to the right about; turn –, go –, tilt –, topple-over; capsize, turn turtle.

in-, sub-, retro-, intro-vert; reverse; up-, overturn, -set; turn -topsy turvy etc. *adj.*; *calbuter*; transpose, put the cart before the horse, turn the tables.

Adj. inverted etc. *v.*; wrong side -out, – up; inside out, upside down; bottom –, keel- upwards; supine, on one's head, topsy turvy, *sens dessus sens dessous.*

inverse; reverse etc. (*contrary*) 14; opposite etc. 237.

topheavy, unstable.

Adv. inversely etc.*adj.*; hirdie-girdie; heels over head, head over heels.

219. Crossing.—N. crossing etc. *v.*; intersection, – lacement, – twinement, -digitation; decussation, transversion; convolution etc. 248.

reticulation, meshwork, network; inosculation, anastomosis, inter-texture, mortise.

net, *plexus*, web, mesh, twill, skein, sleeve, felt, lace; wicker; mat, ting; plait, trellis, wattle, lattice, grating, *grille*, gridiron, tracery, fretwork, filigree; reticle; tissue, netting, mokes.

cross, crucifix, rood, crisscross, crux; chain, wreath, braid, cat's cradle,knot; entanglement etc. (*disorder*) 59.

[woven fabrics] cloth, linen, muslin, cambric, drill, homespun, tweed, broadcloth etc.

V. cross, decussate; inter-sect, -lace, -twine, -twist, -weave, -digitate, -link.

twine, entwine, weave, inweave, twist, wreathe; anastomose, inosculate, dovetail, splice, link.

mat, plait, plat, braid, felt, twill; tangle, entangle; ravel; net, knot; dishevel, raddle.

Adj. crossing etc.*v.*; crossed, matted etc. *v.*; transverse.

cross, cruciform, crucial; reti-form, -cular, -culated; areolar, cancellated, mullioned, latticed, grated, barred, streaked; textile, secant, plexal; interfretted.

Adv. across, thwart, athwart, transversely, crosswise.

220. Exteriority.—N. exteriority; outside, exterior; surface, superficies; skin etc. (*covering*) 223; *superstratum*; disk, disc; face, facet, external, the open.

excentricity; circumjacence etc. 227.

V. be -exterior etc. *adj.*; lie around etc. 227.

place -exteriorly, — outwardly, — outside; put —, turn- out.

Adj. exter-ior, -nal; extraneous, outer, -most; out-ward, -lying, -side, -door; round about etc. 227; extramural.

superficial, skin-deep; frontal, discoid.

extraregarding; eccentric; outstanding; extrinsic etc. 6.

Adv. externally etc. *adj.*; out, without, over, outwards, *ab extra*, out of doors; *extra muros*.

in the open air; *sub -Jovè*, — *dio; à la belle étoile, al fresco.*

221. Interiority.—N. interiority; inside, -land, interior, endocrine; interspace, subsoil, *substratum*.

contents etc. 190; substance, pith, marrow; backbone etc. (*center*) 222; heart, bosom, breast, abdomen; vitals, viscera, entrails, bowels, belly, intestines, guts, chitterlings, womb, lap; gland, cell; internal organs, *penetralia*, recesses, innermost recesses; cave etc. (*concavity*) 252.

inhabitant etc. 188.

V. be -inside etc. *adj.*, — within etc. *adv.*

place —, keep- within; enclose etc. (*circumscribe*) 229; intern; embed etc. (*insert*) 300.

Adj. inter-ior, -nal; inner, inside, intimate, inward, intraregarding; in-, inner-most; deep-seated; visceral, intestine, -tinal; inland; subcutaneous; interstitial etc. (*interjacent*) 228; inwrought etc. (*intrinsic*) 5; enclosed etc. *v.*

home, domestic, indoor, intramural, vernacular; endemic.

Adv. internally etc. *adj.*; inwards, within, in, inly; here-, there-, where-in; *ab intra*, withinside; in —, within- doors; at home, in the bosom of one's family.

222. Centrality.—N. centrality, centricalness, center; middle etc. 68; focus etc. 74.

core, kernel; nucleus, nucleolus; heart, pole, axis, pivot, fulcrum, bull's eye; hub, nave, navel; *umbilicus*, spine, backbone, marrow, pith; hot-bed; concentration etc. (*convergence*) 290; centralization; symmetry.

center of -gravity, — pressure, — percussion, — oscillation, — buoyancy etc. metacenter.

V. be -central etc. *adj.*; converge etc. 290.

render central, centralize, concentrate; bring to a focus.

Adj. centr-al, -ical; middle etc. 68; axial, pivotal, focal, umbilical, concentric; middlemost, nuclear, centric, centraidal; spinal, vertebral.

Adv. middle; midst; centrally etc. *adj.*

223. Covering.—N. covering, cover; canopy, tilt, awning, baldachin, tent, marquee, *tente d'abri*, umbrella, parasol, sunshade; veil (*shade*) 424; shield etc. (*defense*) 717; hall.

roof, dome, cupola, mansard roof; ceiling; thatch, tile; pan-, pen-tile; tiling, shingles, slates, slating, leads; shed etc. (*abode*) 189.

top, lid, covercle, door, *operculum*, eyelid, blind, curtain.

bandage, plaster, lint, wrapping, dossil, finger stall.

coverlet, counterpane, sheet, quilt, comforter, eiderdown; tarpaulin, blanket, rug, drugget, linoleum, oilcloth; housing.

in-, tegument; skin, pellicle, fleece, fell, fur, ermine, miniver, sable, sealskin etc.; fabrikoid; leather, morocco, calf, pigskin, elk, kid, cowhide etc.; shagreen, hide; pelt, -ry; cuticle, *dermis*, scarf-skin, *epidermis*.

clothing etc. 225; mask etc. (*concealment*) 530.

peel, crust, bark, rind, *cortex*, husk, shell, coat.

capsule; ferrule; sheath, -ing; pod, cod; casing, case, theca; *elytron; involucrum;* wrapp-ing, -er, cellophane; envelope, vesicle; dermatology, conchology.

armor, -plate, armoring; veneer, facing; pavement; scale etc. (*layer*) 204; coating, paint, stain; varnish etc. (*resin*) 356a; anointing etc. *v.*; inunction; incrustation, superposition, obduction, ground, enamel, whitewash, plaster, stucco, rough cast, pebble dash, compo; rendering; cerement; ointment etc. (*grease*) 356.

V. cover; super-pose, -impose; over-lay, -spread; wrap etc. 225; incase; face, case, veneer, pave, paper; tip, cap, bind, revet.

coat, paint, varnish, pay, incrust, stucco, cement, dab, plaster, tar; wash; be-, smear; be-, daub; anoint, do over; gild, plate, electroplate, japan, laquer, lacker, enamel, whitewash; lay it on thick.

over-lie, -arch; conceal etc. 528.

Adj. covering etc. *v.*; cutaneous, dermal, cortical, cuticular, tegumentary, skinny, scaly, squamous; covered etc. *v.*; imbricated, loricated, armor-plated, iron-clad; under cover, hooded, cloaked, cowled.

224. Lining.—N. lining, inner coating; coating etc. (*covering*) 223; stalactite, -agmite.

filling, stuffing, wadding, padding, bushing.

wainscot, *parietes*, wall brattice.

V. line, stuff, incrust, wad, pad, fill.

Adj. lined etc. *v.*

225. Investment.—N. investment; covering etc. 223; dress, clothing, raiment, drapery, costume, attire, guise, toilet, *toilette,* trim; habiliment; vesture, -ment; garment, garb, palliament, apparel, wardrobe, wearing apparel, clothes, things.

array; tailoring, millinery; best bib and tucker; finery etc. (*ornament*) 847; full dress etc. (*show*) 882; garniture; theatrical properties.

outfit, equipment, *trousseau*; uniform, khaki, regimentals; academicals, canonicals etc. 999; livery, gear, harness, turn out, accoutrement, caparison, suit, rigging, trappings, traps, slops, togs, toggery; masquerade.

dishabille, morning dress, lounge suit, tea-gown, *kimono, néglig*é, dressing-gown, *peignoir,* wrapper, undress; shooting-coat; smoking jacket, mufti; rags, tatters, old clothes; mourning, weeds; duds; slippers.

robe, tunic, dolman, *paletot*, habit, gown, coat, coatee, frock, blouse, *pelisse*, middy, sagum, *toga*, smock-frock; frock-, dress-, morning-, tail- coat; dress-suit, — clothes, swallow-tail coat, dinner-, Eton-jacket.

cloak, pall; mantle, mantlet, mantua, shawl, *pelisse*, veil, yashmak; cape, tippet, kirtle, plaid, muffler, comforter, Balaclava helmet, haik, huke, chlamys, mantilla, tabard, housing, horse-cloth, burnous, *roquelaure*, *houppelande*; sur-, top-, over-, great-coat; *surtout*, spencer, cardigan, sweater, blazer; mackintosh, waterproof, slicker, raincoat, oilskin, trench coat, ulster, monkey-, pea-pilot-jacket, redingote; wraprascal, poncho, cardinal, pelerine, talma.

jacket, jumper, vest, jerkin, waistcoat, doublet, *camisole*, gabardine; stays, *corsage*, corset, corselet, bodice; stomacher; skirt, petticoat, slip, far-thingale, kilt, jupe, crinoline, bustle, hobble skirt, *panier*, apron, pinafore; loin cloth.

trousers; breeches, trews, pantaloons, unmentionables, inexpressibles, overalls, pajamas, smalls, small-clothes; tights, pants, shorts, drawers; knickerbockers, knickers, plus fours, bloomers, divided skirt; phil-, fill-ibeg.

head-dress, -gear; cap, *béret*, tam o' shanter, glengarry, topee, sombrero; hat; cocked —, high —, tall —, top —, silk —, opera —; crush - hat, *gibus*, beaver, castor, bonnet, tile, wideawake, billy-cock; bowler; soft felt —, straw —, leghorn- hat, panama; toque; wimple; night-, mob-, skull-cap, biretta; hood, cowl, coif; capote, calach; scull-cap; kerchief, snood; head, *coiffure*; crown etc. (*circle*) 247; *chignon*, pelt, wig, front, peruke, periwig; caftan, turban, fez, *tarboosh*, taj, shako, csako, busby; *képi*, forage cap, bearskin; helmet etc. 717; mask, domino.

body clothes; linen; shirt, sark, smock, shift, *chemise*, *lingerie*; night-gown, -shirt; bed-gown, *sac de nuit*; jersey, guernsey; underclothing, - waistcoat.

neck-erchief, -cloth; tie, ruff, collar, cravat, stock, handkerchief, bandana, scarf; bib, tucker; dicky; boa; girdle etc. (*circle*) 247; cummerbund.

shoe, pump, brogue, boot, slipper, sandal, galoche, galoshes, arctics, rubber boots, overshoes, patten, clog, sabot; high-low; Blucher —, Wellington —, Hessian —, jack —, top- boot; Balmoral; legging, puttee, buskin, greave, galligaskin, moccasin, *gamache*, gambado, gaiter, spatter-dash, spat, antigropeles; stocking, hose, gaskins, trunk-hose, sock, hosiery.

glove, gauntlet, mitten, cuff, muffettee, wristband, sleeve.

swaddling cloth, baby-linen, *layette*; pocket-handkerchief.

shroud, etc. 363.

clothier, tailor, milliner, *costumier*, sempstress, seamstress, snip; dress-, habit-, breeches-, shoemaker; cordwainer, cobbler, Crispin, hosier, hatter; draper, linendraper, haberdasher, mercer.

V. invest; cover etc. 223; envelop, lap, involve; in-, en-wrap; wrap; fold —, wrap —, lap —, muffle-up; overlap; sheathe, swathe, swaddle, roll up in, shroud, circumvest.

vest, clothe, array, dress, dight, drape, robe, enrobe, attire, tire, garb, habilitate, apparel, accouter, rig, fit out; bedizen, deck etc. (*ornament*) 847; perk; equip, harness, caparison; dress up.

wear; don; put —, huddle —, slip- on; mantle.
Adj. invested etc. *v.*; habited; dight, -ed; clad, *costumé*, shod, *chaussé*; *en grande tenue* etc. (*show*) 882.
sartorial.

226. Divestment.—N. divestment; taking off, stripping, removal etc. *v.*
nudity; bareness etc. *adj.*; undress; dishabille etc. 225, altogether; nu-, denu-dation; decortication, depilation, excoriation, desquamation; molting; exfoliation.
baldness, alopecia, acomia.
V. divest; uncover etc. (*cover* etc. 223); denude, bare, strip; undress, unclothe, disrobe etc. (*dress*, *enrobe*, etc. 225); uncoif; dismantle; uncase; put —, take —, cast- off; shed, doff; husk, peel, pare, decorticate, desquamate; excoriate, skin, scalp, flay, bark, expose, lay open; exfoliate, molt, mew; cast the skin.
Adj. divested etc. *v.*; bare, naked, nude; undressed, -draped, -clad, -clothed, -appareled; exposed; in dishabille; *décolleté*; bald, threadbare, ragged, callow, roofless.
in -a state of nature, — nature's garb, — buff, — native buff, — birthday suit; *in puris naturalibus*; with nothing on, stark naked; bald as a coot, bare as the back of one's hand; out at elbows; barefoot; bareback; leaf-, nap-, hairless, shaved, clean shaven, tonsured, beardless, bald-headed, acomous.

227. Circumjacence.—N. circumjacence - ambience; environment, encompassment; atmosphere, medium; surroundings, *entourage*.
outpost; border etc. (*edge*) 231; girdle etc. (*circumference*) 230; outskirts, *boulevards*, suburbs, purlieus, precincts, *faubourgs*, environs, banlieue, neighborhood, vicinity.
V. lie -around etc. *adv.*; surround, beset, compass, encompass, environ, inclose, enclose, encircle, circle, embrace, circumvent, lap, gird; begird, girdle, engird; skirt, twine round; hem in etc. (*circumscribe*) 229; besiege, invest, blockade.
Adj. circum-jacent, -ambient, -fluent; ambient; surrounding etc. *v.*; circumferential, suburban.
Adv. around, about; without; on -every side, — all sides; right and left, all round, round about; in the neighborhood.

228. Interjacence.—N. inter-jacence, -currence, -venience, -location, -digitation, -penetration; permeation.
inter-jection, -polation, -lineation, -spersion, -calation; embolism.
inter-vention, -ference, -position; in-, ob-trusion; insinuation; insertion etc. 300; dovetailing; infiltration; intromission.
intermedi-um, -ary; go-between, agent, middleman, medium, bodkin, intruder, interloper; parenthesis, episode; fly-leaf.
partition, *septum*, diaphragm, mid-riff; partywall, panel, vail, bulkhead, brattice, *cloison*; halfway house.
V. lie —, come —, get- between; intervene, slide in, interpenetrate, permeate.

put between, introduce, intromit, import; throw –, wedge –, edge –, jam –, worm –, foist –, run –, plough –, work- in; interpose, -ject, -calate, -polate, -line, -leave, - sperse, -weave, -lard, -digitate; let in, dovetail, splice, mortise; insinuate, smuggle; infiltrate, ingrain.

interfere, put in an oar, thrust one's nose in; intrude, obtrude; have a finger in the pie; introduce the thin end of the wedge; thrust in etc. (*insert*) 300.

Adj. inter-jacent, -current, -venient, -vening etc. *v.*, -mediate, -mediary, -calary, -sitital, -costal, - mural, -planetary, -stellar; embolismal.

parenthctical, episodic: mediterranean; intrusive; embosomed; merged, mean, middle, medium, median.

Adv. between, betwixt; 'twixt; among, -st; amid, st; 'mid, -st; in the thick of; betwixt and between; sandwich-wise; parenthetically, *obiter dictum*.

229. Circumscription.—N. circumscription, limitation, inclosure; confinement etc. (*restraint*) 751; circumvallation, encincture; envelope etc. 232.

V. circumscribe, limit, bound, confine, restrict, enclose; surround etc. 227; compass about; imprision etc. (*restrain*) 751; hedge –, wall –, rail- in; fence –, hedge- round; embar; picket, corral.

enfold, bury, incase, pack up, enshrine, inclasp; wrap up etc. (*invest*) 225; embosom.

Adj. circumscribed etc. *v.*; begirt, lapt; circumambient; buried –, immersed- in; embosomed, in the bosom of, imbedded, encysted, mewed up; imprisoned etc. 751; land-locked, in a ring fence.

230. Outline.—N. outline, circumference; perimeter, -phery; ambit, circuit, lines, *tournure*, *contour*, profile, *silhouette*, lineaments; bounds, coastline.

zone, belt, girth, band, baldric, zodiac, girdle, tire, cingle, clasp, girt; *cordon* etc. (*inclosure*) 232; circlet etc. 247.

V. outline, delineate, *silhouette*, circumscribe etc. 229; profile, block out.

Adj. outlined etc. *v.*; circumferential, perimetric, peripheral.

231. Edge.—N. edge, verge, brink, brow, brim. margin, border, confines, skirt, rim, felloe, felly, flange, side, mouth; jaws, chops, chaps, *fauces*; lip, muzzle.

threshold, door, porch; portal etc.: (*opening*) 260; coast, shore, strand, beach, bank, wharf, quay, dock.

frame, fringe, flounce, frill, list, trimming, edging, skirting, hem, selvedge, welt; furbelow, valance, exergue.

Adj. border, marginal, skirting; labial; labiated, marginated.

232. Inclosure.—N. inclosure, enclosure, envelope; package, box, crate, case etc. (*receptacle*) 191; wrapper; girdle etc. 230.

pen, fold, croft, sty; pen-, in-, sheep--fold; paddock, pound, corral, kraal; yard, compound; net, seine net.

wall; hedge, -row; *espalier*; fence etc. (*defence*) 717; pale, paling, balustrade, rail, railing, gunwale; quickset hedge, park paling, circumvallation, *enciente*, ring fence.

barrier, barricade; gate; -way; door, hatch, *cordon*; prison etc. 752.

dike, dyke, ditch, fosse, moat, trench.

V. inclose; circumscribe etc. 229.

233. Limit.—N. limit, boundary, bounds, confine, *enclave*, term, bourn, verge, kerb-stone, curb-stone, but, pale; termin-ation, -us; stint, frontier, precinct, marches.

boundary line, landmark; line of -demarcation, – circumvallation; pillars of Hercules; Rubicon, turning-point: *ne plus ultra*; sluice, flood-gate.

V. limit, bound, confine, define, circumscribe, demarcate, delimit, encompass.

Adj. definite; contermin-ate, -able, terminable, limitable; terminal, frontier, border, bordering, boundary.

Adv. thus far, – and no further.

234. Front.—N. front; fore, – part; foreground; forefront, face, disk, disc, frontage, *façade*, *proscenium*, facia, frontispiece; priority, anteriority; obverse [of a medal].

fore –, front- rank, first line; van, -guard; advanced guard; outpost, scout.

brow, forehead, visage, physiognomy, phiz, features, countenance, map, mug; rostrum, beak, bow, stem, prow, prore, jib, bowsprit; forecastle. pioneer etc.(*precursor*) 64; metoposcopy.

V. be –, stand- in front etc. *adj.*; front, face, confront, breast, brave; bend forwards; come to the -front, – fore.

Adj. fore, forward, anterior, front, frontal, head-on, leading, first, primary.

Adv. before; in -front, – the van, – advance; ahead, right ahead; fore-, head-most; in the foreground; before one's -face, – eyes; face to face. *vis-à-vis*.

235. Rear.—N. rear, back, posterior-ity; rear - rank, – guard; background, *hinterland*.

occiput, nape, scruff, chine; heels; tail, rump, croup, buttock, posteriors, bottom, seat, backside, scut, breech, *dorsum*, loin; dorsal –, lumbar-region; hind quarters.

stern poop, after-part, counter; postern, heel-, tail-piece, crupper.

wake; train etc. (*sequence*) 281.

reverse; other side of the shield.

V. be -behind etc. *adv.*; fall astern; bend backwards; bring up the rear; follow etc. 622; tail, shadow.

Adj. back, rear; hind, -er, -most, -ermost; postern, -erior; dorsal, after; caudal, lumbar; mizzen.

Adv. behind; in the -rear, – ruck, – back-

ground; behind one's back; at the -heels. — tail. —
back- of; back to back.
after. -most. aft. abaft. astern. stern- most.
aback, rear-. hind-. back-ward.

236. Laterality.—N. laterality; side. flank.
beam. quarter. lee; hand; cheek. jowl. jole. wing;
profile; temple. *parietes*. loin. haunch. hip.
gable. -end; broadside; lee side.
points of the compass; East. Orient. Levant;
West. occident; orientation.
V. be -on one side etc. *adv.*; flank. outflank;
sidle; skirt. border.
Adj. lateral. sidelong; collateral; parietal.
flanking. skirting; flanked; sideling.
many-sided; multi-. bi-. tri-. quadri- lateral.
East-ern. -ward. -erly; orient. -al. auroral.
Levantine; West-ern. -ward. -erly; occidental.
Hesperian; equatorial.
Adv. side-ways. -long; broadside on; on one
side. abreast, abeam, alongside, beside, aside;
by, — the side of; side by side; cheek by jowl
etc. (*near*) 197; to -windward. — leeward;
laterally etc. *adj.*; right and left; on her beam
ends.

237. Contraposition.—N. contraposition, opposition; polarity; inversion etc. 218; opposite side;
antithesis; reverse. inverse; counterpart; antipodes;
opposite poles. North and South.
V. be -opposite etc. *adj.*; subtend.
Adj. opposite; reverse. inverse; antipodal. sub-
contrary; fronting. facing. diametrically opposite.
Northern. Septentrional. Boreal. arctic;
Southern. Austral, antarctic, polar.
Adv. over. — the way. — against; against; face to
face. vis-à-vis; as poles asunder.

238. Dextrality.—N. dextrality; right. — hand;
dexter. offside. starboard.
Adj. dextral. right-handed; ambidextral; dexterous. dextrorsal etc.

239. Sinistrality.—N. sinistrality; left. — hand;
sinister. nearside. larboard. port.
Adj. sinistral. sinister. sinistrorsal etc.. left-
handed. sinistromanual. sinistrous.

240. Form.—N. form. figure. shape. physique;
con-formation. -figuration; make.. formation.
frame. construction. design. cut. set. build. trim.
cut of one's jib; stamp. type. cast. mold; fashion;
contour etc. (*outline*) 230; structure etc. 329.
feature. lineament. outline. turn; phase etc.
(*aspect*) 448; posture. attitude, *pose*.
[Science of form] morphology.
[Similarity of -form] isomorphism.
forming etc. *v.*; form-. figur-. efform- ation;
sculpture.
V. form. shape. figure. fashion. efform. carve.
cut. chisel. hew. cast; rough-hew. -cast; sketch;
block —. hammer- out; trim; lick —. put- into

shape; model. knead. work up into. set. mold.
sculpture; cast. stamp; built etc. (*construct*) 161.
Adj. formed etc. *v.*
[Receiving form] plastic. fictile. full- fashioned
etc.
[Giving form] plasmic, etc.
[Similar in form] isomorphous etc.

241. Amorphism. [Absence of *form*.]—N.
amorphism, informity. uncouthness; unlicked cub.
rough diamond; *rudis indigestaque moles*; disorder etc. 59; deformity etc. 243.
disfigure-. deface-ment. deformation; mutilation.
V. [Destroy form] deface. disfigure. deform.
mutilate. truncate; derange etc. 61.
Adj. shapeless. amorphous. malformed. formless; un-formed. -hewn. -fashioned. -shapen;
rough. rude. Gothic. barbarous. rugged. in the
rough; misshapen etc. 243.

242. Symmetry. [Regularity of form.]—N.
symmetry, shapeliness, finish; beauty etc. 845;
proportion, eurythmy, eurythmic, uniformity,
parallelism; bi-, tri-, multi-lateral symmetry;
centrality etc. 222.
arborescence, branching, ramification.
Adj. symmetrical, shapely, well set, finished;
beautiful etc. 845; classic, chaste, severe.
regular, uniform. balanced; equal etc. 27;
parallel, coextensive.
arbor-escent, -iform; dendr-iform. -oid; branching; ramous, ramose.

243. Distortion. [Irregularity of form.]—N.
dis-, de-. con-tortion; knot, mop, warp, buckle,
screw, twist; crookedness etc. (*obliquity*) 217;
grimmace; deformity; mal-. malcon-formation;
monstrosity, misproportion, want of symmetry,
anamorphosis; ugliness etc. 846; teratology.
V. distort, contort, twist, warp etc. *n.*; wrest,
writhe, make faces, deform, misshape.
Adj. distorted etc. *v.*; out of shape, irregular, unsymmetric, awry, wry, askew, crooked, sinuous;
anamorphous; not -true, — straight; on one side,
crump. deformed; mis-shapen, -begotten; mis-, ill-
proportioned; ill-made; grotesque, crooked as a
ram's horn; hump-, hunch-, bunch-, crook-backed;
bandy; bandy-, bow-legged; bow-, knock-kneed;
splay-, club-footed; taliped; round-shouldered;
snub-nosed; curtailed of one's fair proportions;
scalene, stumpy etc. (*short*) 201; gaunt etc. (*thin*)
203; bloated etc. 194..
Adv. all manner of ways.

244. Angularity.—N. angular-ity, -ness; aduncity; angle, cusp, bend; fold etc. 258; notch etc.
257; fork, bifurcation.
elbow, knee, knuckle, ankle.. groin, crotch.
crane, fluke, scythe, sickle, zigzag, kimbo.
corner, nook, recess, niche, oriel.
right angle etc. (*perpendicular*) 212; obliquity
etc. 217; angle of 45 degrees, miter; acute —, obtuse —, salient —, re-entrant —, spherical —
solid —, dihedral- angle.

angular -measurement, – elevation, – distance, – velocity; trigon-, goni-ometry; altimetry; clin-, graph-, goni-ometer; theodolite; transit circle; sextant, quadrant; dichotomy.

triangle, trigon, wedge; rectangle, square, lozenge, diamond; rhomb, -us; quadr-angle, -ilateral; parallelogram; quadrature; poly-, penta-, hexa-, hepta-, octa-, deca-gon.

Platonic bodies; cube, rhomboid; tetra-, penta-, hexa-, octa-, dodeca-, icosa-hedron; prism, pyramid; parallelopiped.

V. bend, fork, bifurcate, crinkle, divaricate, branch, ramify.

Adj. angular, bent, crooked, aduncous, un-cinated, aquiline, jagged, serrated; falc-iform, -ated; furcular, furcated, forked, bifurcate, crotch-ed; zigzag; dovetailed; knock-kneed, crinkled, akimbo, kimbo, geniculated; oblique etc. 217.

fusiform, wedge-shaped, cuneiform; tri-angular, -gonal, -lateral; quadr-angular, -ilateral; rec-tangular, square, foursquare, multilateral; polygonal etc. *n.*; cubical, rhomboidal, pyramidal.

245. Curvature.—N. curv-ature, -ity, -ation; incurv-ity, -ation; bend; flex- ure, -ion; conflexure; crook, hook, bought, bending; de-, inflexion; ar-cuation, devexity, turn; deviation, *détour*, sweep; curl, -ing; bough; recurv-ity, -ation; sinuosity etc. 248; aduncity.

curve, arc, arch, arcade, vault, dome, bow, crescent, *meniscus*, half-moon, lunule, horse-shoe, loop, crane-neck; para-, hyper-bola; catenary, festoon; conch-, cardi-oid; caustic, instep; tracery.

V. be -curved etc. *adj.*; sweep, swag, sag; deviate etc. 279; turn; re-enter.

render -curved etc. *adj.*; bend, curve, incurvate; de-, in-flect; crook; turn, round, arch, arcuate, arch over, loop the loop, concamerate; bow, coil, curl, recurve, frizzle.

`Adj.` curved etc. *v.*; curvi-form, -lineal, -linear, devex, devious; recurv-ed, -ous; *retroussé*; crump; bowed etc. *v.*; vaulted; hooked; falc-iform, -ated; semicircular, crescentic; lun-iform, -ular; semi-lunar, meniscal; conchoidal; cord-iform, -ated; cardioid, heart-, bell-, pear-, fig-shaped; reniform; lenti-form, -cular; bow-legged etc. (*distorted*) 243; oblique etc. 217; circular etc. 247.

246. Straightness.—N. straightness, rec-tilinearity, directness; inflexibility etc. (*stiffness*) 323; straight –, right –, direct-, bee- line; short cut.

V. be -straight etc. *adj*; have no turning; not - incline, – bend, – turn, – deviate- to either side; go straight; steer for etc. (*direction*) 278.

render straight, straighten, rectify; set –, put-straight; un-bend, -fold, -curl etc. 248, -ravel etc. 219, -wrap.

Adj. straight; rectiline-ar, -al; direct, even, right, true, in a line; unbent etc. *v.*; un-deviating, -turned, -distorted, -swerving; straight as an arrow etc. (*direct*) 278; inflexible etc. 323.

247. Circularity. [Simple circularity.]—**N.** circularity, roundness; rotundity etc. 249.

circle, circlet, ring, washer, areola, hoop, round-let, *annulus*, annulet, bracelet, armlet, armilla; ringlet; eye, loop, wheel; cycle, orb, orbit, rundle, zone, belt, *cordon*, band; sash, girdle, cestus, cinc-ture, baldric, fillet, *fascia*, wreath, garland; crown, corona, coronet, chaplet, snood, necklace, collar; noose, lasso, lariat.

ellipse, oval, ovule; ellipsoid, cycloid; epi-cycloid, -cycle; semi-circle; quadrant, sextant, sec-tor.

V. make -round etc. *adj.*; round.

go round; encircle etc. 227; describe -a circle etc. 311.

Adj. round, rounded, circular, annular, or-bicular; oval, ovate; elliptic, -al; ovoid, egg-shaped; pear-shaped etc. 245; cycloidal etc. *n.*; spherical etc. 249.

248. Convolution. [Complex circularity.]—**N.** winding etc. *v.*; con-, in-, circum-volution; wave, undulation, tortuosity, anfractuosity; sinu-osity, -ation, sinuousness; meandering, circuit, cir-cumbendibus, twist, twirl, windings and turnings, *ambages*; torsion; inosculation; reticulation etc. (*crossing*) 219.

coil, roll, curl, buckle, spire, spiral, helix, corkscrew, worm, volute, whorl, rundle; tendril; scollop, scallop, escalop; kink.

serpent, snake, eel, maze, labyrinth.

V. be -convoluted etc. *adj.*; wind, twine, turn and twist, twirl; wave, undulate, meander; inosculate; entwine, intwine; twist, coil, roll; wrinkle, curl, crisp, twill; frizz, -le; crimp, crape, indent, scollop, scallop; wring, intort; contort; wreathe etc. (*cross*).219.

Adj. convoluted; winding, twisted etc. *v.*; tortile, tortive; wavy; und-ated, -ulatory; circling, snaky, snake-like, serpentine; serpent-, anguill-, verm-iform; vermicular; mazy, tortuous, anfractuous, sinuous, flexuous, wavy, sigmoidal.

involved, intricate, complicated, perplexed; labyrinth-ic, -ian, -ine; circuitous; peristaltic; daedalian, curly.

wreathy, frizzly, *crêpé*, buckled; ravelled etc. (*in disorder*) 59.

spiral, coiled, helical, turbinated.

Adv. in and out, round and round.

249. Rotundity.—N. rotundity; roundness etc. *adj.*; cylindricity; spher-icity, -oidity; globosity.

cylin-der, -droid; barrel, drum; roll, -er; *rouleau*, column, rolling-pin, rundle; chimney-pot, drain-pipe.

cone, conoid; pear-, egg-, bell-shape.

sphere, globe, orb, orbit, ball, boulder, bowlder; spher-, ellips-, ge-, glob-oid, oblong –, oblate-spheroid; drop, spherule, globule, vesicle, bulb, bullet, pellet, *pelote*, clew, pill, marble, pea, knob, pommel, knot.

V. render -spherical etc. *adj.*; form into a sphere, sphere, roll into a ball; give -rotundity etc. *n.*; round.

Adj. rotund; round etc. (*circular*) 247; cylindr-ic, -ical; -oid; columnar, lumbriciform; conic, -al; spher-ical, -oidal; glob-ular, -ated, -ous, -ose; egg-, bell-, pear-shaped; ov-oid, -iform; gibbous; cam-paniform, -ulate, -iliform; fungiform, bead-like, moniliform, pyriform, bulbous; *teres atque rotundus*; round as -an orange, — an apple, — a ball, — a billiard ball, — a cannon ball.

250. Convexity.—N. convexity, prominence, projection, swelling, gibbosity, bilge, bulge, protuberance, protrusion; excrescency, camber.

intumescence; tumor; tubercle, -osity; excrescence; hump, hunch, bunch, gnarl.

tooth, knob, elbow, process, *apophysis*, condyle, bulb, node, nodule, nodosity, tongue, *dorsum*, boss, embossment, bump, clump; sugar-loaf etc. (*sharpness*) 253; bow; mamelon.

pimple, wen, wheal, *papula*, postule, pock, proud flesh, growth, goiter, *sarcoma*, caruncle, corn, bunion, wart, furnuncle, polypus, adenoid, fungus, fungosity, *exostosis*, bleb, blister, blain; boil etc. (*disease*) 655; bubble, blob.

papilla, nipple, teat, pap, breast, dug, mammilla; proboscis, .ose, neb, beak, snout, nozzle, snozzle; Adam's apple; belly, paunch, corporation; withers, back, shoulder, lip, flange.

peg, button, stud, ridge, rib, jutty, trunnion, snag.

cupola, dome, bee-hive; arch, balcony, eaves; pilaster.

relief, relievo, *cameo*; *basso-*, *mezzo-*, *altorilievo*; low-, bas-, high-relief.

hill etc. (*height*) 206; cape, promontory, mull; fore-, head-land; point of land, naze, ness, mole, jetty, hummock, ledge, spur.

V. be -prominent etc. *adj.*; project, bulge, protrude, bag, belly, pout, bouge, bunch; jut —, stand —, stick —, poke- out; stick —, bristle —, start —, cock —, shoot- up; swell —, hang —, bend-over; beetle.

render -prominent etc. *adj.*; raise 307; emboss, chase.

Adj. convex, prominent, protuberant, underhung, undershot; projecting etc. *v.*; bossed, bossy, nodular, bunchy; clav-ate, -ated; hummocky, *moutonné*, mammiform; papul-ous, -ose; hemispheric, bulbous; bowed, arched; bold; bellied; tuber-ous, -culous; tumorous, cornute, knobby, odontoid; lenti-form, -cular; gibbous.

salient, in relief, raised, *repoussé*; bloated etc. (*expanded*) 194.

251. Flatness.—N. flatness etc. *adj.*; smoothness etc. 255.

plane; level etc. 213; plate, platter, table, tablet, slab.

V. render flat, flatten, squash; level etc. 213.

Adj. flat, plane, even, flush, scutiform, discoid; level etc. (*horizontal*) 213; smooth; flat as -a pancake, — a fluke, — a flounder, — a board, — my hand.

252. Concavity.—N. concavity, depression, dip; hollow, -ness; indentation, *intaglio*, cavity, antrum, dent, dint, dimple, follicle, pit, *sinus*, *alveolus*, *lacuna*; excavation, trench, shaft, sap, mine, tunnel, burrow; trough etc. (*furrow*) 259; honeycomb.

cup, basin, crater, punch-bowl; cell etc. (*receptacle*) 191; socket, faucet.

valley, vale, dale, dell, gap, dingle, combe, bottom, slade, strath, glade, grove, glen, cave, cavern, cove; grot, -to; alcove, *cul-de-sac*, blind alley; gully etc. 198; arch etc. (*curve*) 245; bay etc. (*of the sea*) 343.

excavator, sapper, miner.

V. be -concave etc. *adj.*; retire, cave in.

render -concave etc. *adj.*; depress, hollow; scoop, — out; gouge, dig, delve, excavate, dent, dint, mine, sap, undermine, burrow, tunnel, stave in.

Adj. depressed etc. *v.*; concave, hollow, stove in; dished; spoon-like; retiring; retreating; cavernous; porous etc. (*with holes*) 260; cellular, spongy, spongious; honeycombed, alveolar; infundibul-ar, -iform; funnel-, bell-shaped; campaniform, capsular; vaulted, arched.

253. Sharpness.—N. sharpness etc. *adj.*; acuity, acumination; spinosity.

point, spike, spine, *spiculum*, tine; needle, pin; tack, nail; prick, -le; spur, rowel, barb; spit, cusp; horn, antler; snag; tag; thorn, bristle.

nib, tooth, incisor, tusk; spoke, cog, ratchet.

crag, crest *arête*, cone, peak, sugar-loaf, pike, *aiguille*; spire, pyramid, steeple.

beard, *chevaux de frise*, porcupine, hedgehog, brier, bramble, thistle; comb, awn, bur.

wedge; knife-, cutting- edge; blade, edge-tool, cutlery, knife, penknife, whittle, razor; scalpel, bistoury, lancet; chisel; ploughshare, coulter; hatchet, axe, pick-axe, mattock, pick, adze, bill; billhook, cleaver, cutter; skiver; scythe, sickle, scissors, shears; sword etc. (*arms*) 727; bodkin etc. (*perforator*) 262.

sharpener, hone, strop; grind-, whet-stone; steel, emery.

V. be -sharp etc. *adj.*; taper to a point; bristle with.

render -sharp etc. *adj.*; sharpen, point, aculeate, acuminate, whet, barb, spiculate, set, strop, grind. cut etc. (*sunder*) 44.

Adj. sharp, keen; acute; aci-cular, -form; aculeated, -minated; pointed; tapering; conical, pyramidal; mucron-ate, -ated; spindle-, needle-shaped; spiked, spiky, ensiform, peaked, salient, cusp-ed; -idate, -idated; corn-ute, -uted, -iculate; prickly; spiny, spinous; thorny, bristling, muricated, pectinated, studded, thistly, briery; craggy etc. (*rough*) 256; snaggy; digitated, two-edged, fusiform; denti-form, -culated; toothed; odontoid; star-like; stell-ated, -iform; arrow-headed; arrowy, barbed, spurred, sagittal; spear-shaped, hastate; horned; conical.

cutting; sharp-, knife-edged; sharp —, keen-as a razor; sharp as a needle; sharpened etc. *v.*; set.

254. Bluntness.—N. bluntness etc. *adj.*; abruptness, dullness.

V. be —, render- blunt etc. *adj.*; obtund, dull; take off the -point, — edge; turn.

Adj. blunt, obtuse, dull, bluff.

255. Smoothness.—N. smoothness etc. *adj.*; polish, gloss; lubric-ity, -ation.

down, velvet, silk, satin; slide; bowling green etc. (*level*) 213; glass, ice; asphalt, pavement, flags.

roller, steam-roller; iron, flat-iron, tailor's goose; sand-, emery-paper; burnisher, turpentine and bees-wax.

V. smooth, -en; plane; file; mow, shave; level, roll; macadamize; polish, burnish, planish, levigate, calender, glaze; iron, hot-press, mangle; lubricate etc. (*oil*) 332.

Adj. smooth; polished etc. *v.*; even; level etc. 213; plane etc. (*flat*) 251; sleek, glossy; silken, silky; lanate, downy, velvety; glabrous, slippery, glassy, lubricous, oily, soft; unwrinkled; smooth as -glass, – ice, – velvet, – oil; slippery as an eel; wooly etc. (*feathery*) 256.

256. Roughness.—N. roughness etc. *adj.*; tooth, grain, texture, ripple; asperity, rugosity, salebrosity, corrugation, nodosity; arborescence etc. 242.

brush, hair, beard, shag, mane, whisker, mutton-chops, *moustache, mustachio*, imperial, Van Dyke, tress, lock, curl, ringlet, *fimbriae, cilia, villi*; eye-lashes, eye-brows, love-lock.

plum-age, -osity; plume, *panache*, crest; feather, tuft, tussock, fringe, toupee.

wool, velvet, plush, nap, pile, floss, fluff, fur, down; byssus, moss, bur.

V. be -rough etc. *adj.*; go against the grain.

render -rough etc. *adj.*; roughen, rough cast, knurl; ruffle, crisp, crumple, crinkle, corrugate, engrail; set on edge, stroke – , rub- the wrong way, rumple.

Adj. rough, uneven; scabrous, knotted; nodular; rug-ged, -ose, -ous; asperous, crisp, salebrous, gnarled, unpolished, unsmooth, rough-hewn; knurled, cross-grained, crag-gy, -ged; crankling, scraggy, jagged, unkempt, prickly etc. (*sharp*) 253; arborescent etc. 242; leafy, well-wooded; feathery; plum-ose, -igerous; tufted, fimbriated, hairy, bristly, ciliated, filamentous, hirsute; crin-ose, -ite; bushy, hispid, villous, pappous, bearded, pilous, shaggy, shagged; fringed, befringed; set-ous, -ose, -aceous; 'like quills upon the fretful porcupine;' rough as a -nutmeg grater, – bear.

downy, velvety, flocculent, wolly; lan-ate, -ated; lanugin-ous, ose; tomentous.

Adv. against the grain, in the rough, on edge.

257. Notch.—N. notch, dent, nick, cut; indent, -ation; serration; dimple.

embrasure, battlement, machicolation; saw, tooth, crenelle, scallop, scollop, vandyke.

V. notch, nick, cut, pink, mill, score, dent, indent, jag, scarify, scotch, crimp, scollop, crenulate, vandyke.

Adj. notched etc. *v.*; crenate, -d; dentate, -d; denticulate, -d; toothed, palmated, serrated.

258. Fold.—N. fold, plicature, pleat, plait, ply, crease; tuck, gather; flexion, flexure, joint, elbow, doubling, duplicature, wrinkle, rimple, crinkle, crankle, crumple, rumple, rivel, ruck, ruffle, dog's ear, corrugation, frounce, flounce, lapel; pucker, crow's feet.

V. fold, double, plicate, pleat, plait, crease, wrinkle, crinkle, crankle, curl, smock, cockle up, crocker, rimple, rumple, frizzle, frounce, rivel, twill, corrugate, ruffle, crimple, crumple, pucker; turn –, double- -down, – under; tuck, ruck, hem, gather.

Adj. folded etc. *v.*

259. Furrow.—N. furrow, groove, rut, *sulcus*, scratch, streak, *striae*, crack, score, incision, slit; chamfer, fluting.

channel, gutter, trench, ditch, dike, dyke, moat, fosse, trough, kennel; ravine etc. (*interval*) 198.

V. furrow etc. *n.*; flute, groove, carve, corrugate, plough; incise, chase, enchase, grave, engrave, etch, bite in, cross-hatch.

Adj. furrowed etc. *v.*; ribbed, straited, sulcated, fluted, canaliculated; bisulc-ous, -ate; trisulcate; corduroy.

260. Opening.—N. hole, foramen; puncture, blow-out, perforation; pin-, key-, loop-, port-, peep-, mouse-, pigeon-hole; eye, – of a needle; eyelet; slot.

opening; apert-ure, -ness; hiation, yawning, oscitancy, dehiscence, patefaction, pandiculation; gap, chasm etc. (*interval*) 198.

embrasure, window, casement, light; sky-, fan-light; lattice; bay-, bow-window; oriel; dormer, lantern.

out-, in-let; vent, vomitory; *embouchure*; orifice, mouth, sucker, muzzle, throat, gullet, placket, weasand, wizen, nozzle, *esophagus*.

portal, porch, gate, ostiary, postern, wicket, trap-door, hatch, door; arcade; gate-, door-, hatch-, gang-way; lych-gate.

way, path etc. 627; thoroughfare; channel, passage, tube, pipe; waterpipe etc. 350; air-pipe etc. 351; vessel, tubule, canal, gut, fistula; adjutage, ajutage; chimney, smoke stack, flue, tap, funnel, gully, tunnel, main; mine, pit, adit, shaft; gallery, alley, aisle, glade, lane, vista.

bore, caliber; pore; blind orifice.

por-ousness, -osity; sieve, cullender, colander; grater, shredder; cribble, riddle, screen; honeycomb.

apertion, perforation; piercing etc. *v.*; terebration, empalement, pertusion, puncture, acupuncture, penetration.

opener, corkscrew, can opener, key, master-key, *passe-partout*.

V. open, ope, gape, dehisce, yawn, bilge; fly open.

perforate, pierce, empierce, tap, bore, drill; mine etc. (*scoop out*) 252; tunnel; trans-pierce, -fix; en-filade, impale, spike, spear, gore, spit, stab, pink, puncture, lance, trepan, trephine, stick, prick, riddle, punch; stave in.

cut a passage through; make -way, – room- for, un-cover, -close, -rip; lay –, cut –, rip –, throw-open.

Adj. open; perforated etc. *v.*; perforate; wide open, agape, ajar; un-closed, -stopped; oscitant, gaping, yawning; patent.

tubular, cannular, fistulous; per-vious, -meable; foraminous; vesi-, vas-cular; porous, follicular.

cribriform, honeycombed, infundibular, riddled; tubul-ous, -ated, piped.

opening etc. *v.*; aperient.

Int. *open sesame!*

261. Closure.—N. closure, occlusion, blockade; shutting up etc. *v.*; obstruction etc. (*hindrance*) 706; gag; embolism; contraction etc. 195; infarction; con-, ob-stipation; blind -alley, — corner; *cul-de-sac, caecum*; imperforation, -viousness etc. *adj.*; -meability; stopper etc. 263; *operculum*.

V. close, occlude, plug; block —, stop —, fill —, bung —, cork —, button —, stuff —, shut —, damup, obturate; blockade; obstruct etc. (*hinder*) 706; bar, bolt, stop, seal, plumb; — choke, throttle; ram down, tamp, dam, cram; trap, clinch; put to —, shut- the door; batten down the hatches.

Adj. closed etc. *v.; shut*, operculated; unopened.

unpierced, imporous, caecal; imperforate, -vious, -meable; impenetrable; un-, im-passable; invious; path-, way-less; untrodden.

unventilated; air-, water-tight; hermetically sealed; tight, snug.

262. Perforator.—N. perforator, piercer, borer, auger, gimlet, stylet, drill, wimble, awl, bradawl, scoop, terrier, corkscrew, dibble, trocar, trepan, trephine, probe, bodkin, needle, stiletto, broach, reamer, rimer, warder, lancet; punch, -eon; spikebit, gouge; spear etc. (*weapon*) 727.

263. Stopper.—N. stopper, stopple; plug, cork, bung, spike, spill, stop-cock, tap; rammer; ram, -rod; piston; stopgap; wadding, stuffing, padding, stopping, dossil, pledget, tompion, tourniquet, obturator; wad.

cover etc. 223; valve, slide valve; vent-peg, spigot.

janitor, door —, gate- keeper, porter, commissionaire, *concierge*, warder, beadle, Cerberus, usher, guard, sentry, sentinel; ostiary.

264. Motion. [Successive change of place. *] —N.** motion, movement, move; motivity, motility, going etc. *v.*; unrest.

stream, current, flow, flux, run, course, stir; conduction, evolution; kinematics.

step, rate, pace, tread, stride, gait, clip, port, footfall, cadence, carriage, velocity, angular velocity; progress, locomotion; journey etc. 266; voyage etc. 267; transit etc. 270.

restlessness etc. (*changeableness*) 149; mobility; movableness, motive power; laws of motion; mobilization.

V. be -in motion etc. *adj.*; move, go, hie, gang, budge, stir, pass, flit; hover -round, — about; shift, slide, slither, glide; roll, — on; flow, stream, run, drift, sweep along; wander etc. (*deviate*) 279; walk etc. 266; change —, shift- one's -place, — quarters; dodge; keep -going, — moving.

put —, set- in motion; move; impel etc. 276; propel etc. 284; render movable, mobilize.

Adj. moving etc. *v.*; in motion; motile, transitional; motory, motive; shifting, movable, mobile, mercurial, unquiet; restless etc. (*changeable*) 149; nomadic etc. 266; erratic etc. 279.

Adv. under way; on the -move, — wing, — tramp, — march.

"A thing cannot be said to *move* from one place to another, unless it passes in succession through every intermediate place; hence motion is only such a change of place as is *successive*. 'Rapid, swift, etc., as thought' are therefore incorrect expressions.

265. Quiescence.—N. rest; stillness etc. *adj.*; quiescence; stag-nation, -nancy; fixity, immobility, catalepsy; indisturbance; quietism.

quiet, tranquillity, calm; repose etc. 687; peace; dead calm, anticyclone; statue-like repose; silence etc. 403; not a -breath of air, — mouse stirring; sleep etc. (*inactivity*) 683.

pause, lull etc. (*cessation*) 142; stand, — still; standing still etc. *v.*; lock; dead -lock, — stop, — stand; full stop; fix; embargo.

resting-place; bivouac; home etc. (*abode*) 189; pillow etc. (*support*) 215; haven etc. (*refuge*) 666; goal etc. (*arrival*) 292.

V. be -quiescent etc. *adj.*; stand —, lie- still; keep quiet, repose, hold the breath.

remain, stay; stand, lie to, ride at anchor, remain *in situ*, mark time, tarry; bring —, heave —, lay- to; pull —, draw- up; hold, halt; stop, — short; rest, pause, anchor; cast —, come to an- anchor; rest on one's oars; repose on one's laurels, take breath; stop etc. (*discontinue*) 142.

stagnate, vegetate; *quieta non movere*; let - alone, — well alone; abide, rest and be thankful; keep within doors, stay at home, go to bed.

dwell etc. (*be present*) 186; settle etc. (*be located*) 184; alight etc. (*arrive*) 292.

stick, — fast; stand, — like a post; not stir a -peg, — step; be at a -stand etc. *n.*

quell, becalm, hush, stay, lull to sleep, lay an embargo on; put the brake on.

Adj. quiescent, still; motion-, move-less; fixed; stationary; at -rest, — a stand, — a stand-still, — anchor; stock-still; immotile; standing still etc. *v.*; sedentary, untravelled, stay-at-home; becalmed, stagnant, quiet; un-moved, -disturbed, -ruffled; calm, restful; cataleptic; immovable etc. (*stable*) 150; sleeping etc. (*inactive*) 683; silent etc. 403; still as -a statue; — a post, — a mouse, — death.

Adv. at a stand etc. *adj.; tout court*; at the halt.

Int. stop! stay! avast! halt! hold, — hard! whoa!

Phr. *requiescat in pace.*

266. Journey. [Locomotion by land.]—N. travel, traveling etc. *v.*; wayfaring, campaigning.

journey, excursion, expedition, tour, trip, grand tour, circuit, peregrination, discursion, ramble, pilgrimage, *trek*, course, ambulation, march, walk, hike, promenade, constitutional, stroll, saunter, tramp, jog-trot, turn, stalk, perambulation; noctambulation; somnambulism, sleep walking; outing, ride, drive, airing, jaunt.

equitation, horsemanship, riding, *manège*, ride and tie.

roving, vagrancy, pererration; marching and countermarching; nomadism; vagabond-ism, -age; gadding; flit, -ting; migration; e-, im-, de-, inter-migration.

plan, itinerary, guide; hand-, road- book; Baedeker, Murray, Bradshaw, time table.

procession, parade, cavalcade, caravan, file, *cortège*, column.

[Organs and instruments of locomotion] vehicle etc. 272; locomotive etc. 271; legs, feet, pegs, pins, trotters.

traveler etc. 268.

V. travel, journey, course; tour; take —, go- a journey, take —, go out for- -a walk etc. *n.*; have a run; take the air.

flit, take wing; migrate, emigrate, *trek*; rove, prowl, roam, range, patrol, pace up and down, traverse; scour —, traverse- the country; peragrate; per-, circum-ambulate; nomadize, wander, ramble, stroll, saunter, hover, go one's rounds, straggle; gad; — about; expatiate.

walk, march, step, tread, pace, plod, wend; promenade; trudge, tramp; stalk, stride, straddle, strut, foot it, stump, bundle, bowl along, toddle; paddle; tread —, follow —, pursue- a path.

take horse, ride, drive, trot, amble, canter, prance, fisk, frisk, *caracoler*; gallop etc. (*move quickly*) 274; motor, cycle, taxi; go by -car, — train, — tram, — bus, — plane.

peg —, jog —, wag —, shuffle- on; stir one's stumps; bend one's -steps, - course; make —, find —, wend —, pick —, thread —, plough- one's way; coast, slide, glide, skim, skate, ski; march in procession, file off, defile.

go —, repair —, resort —, hie —, betake oneself-to.

Adj. traveling etc. *v.*; ambulatory, itinerant, peripatetic, perambulatory, roving, rambling, gadding, discursive, vagrant, migratory, nomadic; circumforane-an, -ous; somnambular, nocti-, mundi-vagant; locomotive, automotive, self-moving.

way-faring, -worn; travel-stained.

Adv. on -foot, — horseback, — Shanks's mare; by the Marrowbone-stage; *in transitu* etc. 270; *en route* etc. 282.

Int. come along!

267. Navigation. [Locomotion by water, or air.]—**N.** navigation; aquatics; boating, cruising, yachting; ship etc. 273; oar, scull, sweep, punt pole, paddle, — wheel, screw, propeller, stern wheel, sail, canvas.

natation, swimming; fin, flipper, fish's tail.

aeronautics, aviation, flying, winging, cruising, gliding, ballooning; blind —, instrument — flying; avigation, take-off.

flight, trip, run; solo —, nolo (pilotless) —, supersonic —, test — flight; air -lift, -drop; shuttle, reconnaisence, mission, dry run (coll.), search mission, combat flight, sortie, air raid, bombing mission; air — support, — cover, — umbrella; formation flying, maneuvers, aerobatics, stunt flying (coll.), diving, rolling, barrel roll, spin, tail spin, loop, buzzing, landing, instrument —, crash — landing.

angle, center, axis, stability, load, pressure, torsion, torque, thrust, propulsion, jet propulsion, pitch, lift, dray, yaw, resistance, drift, flow, wash, course, heading, altitude; air -route, -lane.

voyage, sail, cruise, passage, circumnavigation, *periplus*; head-, stern-, lee-way.

astro-, cosmo- nautics; space —, interplanetary — travel; space — exploration, — flight.

mariner, aeronaut etc. 269.

V. sail; put to sea etc. (*depart*) 293; take ship, get under way; spread -sail, — canvas; gather way, have way on; make —, carry- sail; plough the -waves, — deep, — main, — ocean; walk the waters.

navigate, warp, luff, scud, boom, kedge; drift, course, cruise, coast; hug the -shore, — land; circumnavigate.

ply the oar, row, paddle, pull, scull, punt, steam, swim, float; buffet the waves, ride the storm, skim, *effleurer*, dive, wade.

fly, pilot, copilot, astronavigate, solo, take off, taxi, ascend, climb, stunt, spin, loop, roll, dive, buzz, land, descend, level off, bail out, parachute.

Adj. sailing etc. *v.*; seafaring, nautical, maritime, naval; sea-going, coasting; afloat; navigable, aquatic, natatory.

volitant, volant, aerostatic, aerial, aeronautic; alar, alate, pennate.

Adv. under -way, — sail, — canvas, — steam; on the wing.

268. Traveler.—N. traveler, wayfarer, voyager, itinerant, passenger.

tourist, excursionist, globe-trotter; explorer, adventurer, mountaineer, Alpine Club; peregrinator, wanderer, rover, straggler, rambler; bird of passage; gad-about, -ling; vagrant, scatterling, land-loper, waifs and estrays, wastrel, stray; loafer; tramp, -er, hobo, beachcomber, vagabond, nomad, Bohemian, gipsy, Arab, Wandering Jew, Hadji, pilgrim, palmer; peripatetic; somnambulist; sleep walker, noctambulist; emigrant, fugitive, refugee, *émigré*.

runner, courier, King's messenger; Mercury, Iris, Ariel, comet.

pedestrian, walker, foot-passenger; cyclist; wheelman.

rider, horseman, equestrian, cavalier, jockey, rough rider, trainer, breaker, huntsman.

driver, coachman, whip, Jehu, charioteer, postilion, post-boy, carter, wagoner, drayman, truckman; cab-man, -driver; *voiturier*, *vetturino*, *condottiere*; engine-driver; stoker, fireman, guard, brakeman, conductor; chauffeur, automobilist, motorist, motor —, truck —, taxi- driver.

269. Mariner.—N. sailor, mariner, navigator, argonaut; sea-man, -farer, -faring man; yachtsman; tar, jack tar, salt, gob, sea-dog, shellback, able seaman, A.B.; man-of-war's man, bluejacket, marine, jolly; midshipman, middy, reefer; captain, commander, master mariner, skipper, mate; ship-, boat-, ferry-, water-, lighter-, barge- longshore-man, hoveller; bargee, gondolier; oar-, -sman; rower; boat-, cock-swain; coxswain; steersman, helmsman, pilot, crew; lascar.

aerial navigator, navigator; aero-, astro-, cosmo-naut; balloonist, Icarus, aviator, pilot, flyer, copilot, spaceman; fighter —, bomber — pilot; bombardier, gunner; meteorologist; stewardess, aviatrix, aviatress; ground crew, aeromechanic, aeronautical engineer; parachutist, paratrooper.

270. Transference.—N. transfer; -ence; trans-, e-location; displacement; *meta-stasis*, *-thesis*; removal; re-, a-motion; relegation; de-, asportation; extradition, conveyance, draft; carrying, carriage; convection, -duction, -tagion, infection; transfusion; transfer etc. (*of property*) 783.

transit, transition; passage, ferry, gestation; portage, porterage, carting, cartage; shoveling etc. *v.*; vect-ion, -ure, -itation; shipment, freight, wafture; trans-mission, -port, -portation, -umption, - plantation, -lation; shift-, dodg-ing; dispersion etc. 73; transposition etc. (*interchange*) 148; traction etc. 285.

[Thing transferred] drift, alluvium, detritus, *moraine*; gift, legacy, bequest, lease; freight, mails, cargo, luggage, baggage, goods.

V. trans-fer, -mit, -port, -place, -plant; convey, assign, carry, bear, fetch and carry; carry —, ferry-over; hand, pass, forward; shift; conduct, convoy, bring, fetch, reach.

send, delegate, consign, mail post, relegate, turn over to, pass the buck, deliver; ship, embark; waft; switch, shunt; transpose etc. (*interchange*) 148; displace etc. 185; throw etc. 284; drag etc. 285.

shovel, lade, dip, ladle, bale, decant, draft off, transfuse.

Adj. transferred etc. *v.*; drifted; movable, portable, -ative; conductive; contagious, infectious.

transferable, assignable, conveyable, devisable, negotiable, transmissible.

Adv. from -hand to hand, — pillar to post. on —, by- the way; on the -road, — wing; as one goes; *in transitu, en route, chemin faisant, en passant,* in mid-progress.

271. Carrier.—N. carrier, porter, red cap, bearer, messenger, postman, tranter, conveyer; stevedore; coolie; conductor, locomotive, tractor, caterpillar tractor, motor.

beast of burden, cattle, horse steed, nag, palfrey, Arab, blood horse, thorough-bred, galloway, charger, courser, racer, hunter, jument, pony, filly, colt, foal, barb, roan, jade, hack, *bidet*, pad, cob, tit, punch, roadster, goer; race-, pack-, draft-, cart-, dray-, post-horse, mount; Shetland pony, sheltie; garran; jennet, genet, bayard, mare, stallion, gelding; stud.

Pegasus, Bucephalus, Rozinante.

ass, donkey, jackass, mule, hinny; sumpter·-horse, — mule; reindeer; camel, dromedary, mehari, llama, elephant; carrier pigeon.

carriage etc. (*vehicle*) 272; ship etc. 273.

Adj. equine, asinine.

272. Vehicle.—N. vehicle, conveyance, carriage, car, caravan, van, furniture van, pantechnicon; wagon, wain, dray, cart, lorry.

carriole; sledge, sled, sleigh, bob-sleigh, toboggan, *luge*, truck, tram; limber, tumbrel, pontoon; barrow; wheel-, hand- -barrow, — cart, trolley; perambulator; Bath —, wheel —, sedan-chair, jinriksha, rickshaw; ekka; chaise; palankeen, -quin; litter, horse-litter, brancard, crate, hurdle, stretcher, ambulance; velocipede, hobby-horse, coaster, scooter, go-cart; cycle; bi-, tri-, quadri-cycle; tandem, safety; skate, roller —, ice — skate; sled, sleigh; ski, snow-shoe.

equipage, turn-out; coach, chariot; *quadriga*, chaise, phaëton, break, brake, mail-phaëton, wagonette, drag, curricle, tilbury, whisky, landau, *barouche,* victoria, brougham, clarence, calash, *calèche,* britzska, *araba,* kibitka; berlin; sulky, *désobligeant,* sociable, *vis-à-vis, dormeuse;* jaunting —, outside- car; *tarantass;* runabout; shay.

post-chaise; diligence; stage; stage ·—, mail —, hackney —, glass- coach; stage-wagon; car, omnibus, bus, fly, *cabriolet,* cab, hansom, shofle, fourwheeler, growler, *droshki,* drosky.

dog-cart, trap, gig, whitechapel, buggy, four-in-hand, unicorn, random, tandem; shandredhan, *char-à-banc.*

automobile, motor-, auto-, touring-, racing-, cycle-, side-, steam-, electric- car; motor — cycle, — bike; motorized vehicle; bus, mini-bus; buggy, crate, tub, flivver, jalopy, wreck, clunker, dog, heap (all. slang); coupe, coup, sedan, convertible, hard-top; camper, trailer, mobile home; limosine, landaulette, cabriolet, *coupé, voiturette,* runabout, electromobile, taxi, -cab.

train; passenger —, express —, freight —, subway —, special —, corridor —, parliamentary —, luggage —, goods- train, *train de luxe;* 1st-, 2nd-, 3rd- class- -train, — carriage, — compartment; Pullman —, sleeping-, club-, observation-, dining-, restaurant-car; mail-, luggage-, brake-van, coach, car, carriage; rolling stock; horse-box, cattle- truck.

273. Ship.—N. ship, vessel, sail; craft, bottom, navy, marine, fleet, flotilla, squadron; shipping. man of war etc. (*combatant*) 726; transport, tender, store-ship; merchant ship, merchantman; packet, liner; whaler, slaver, collier, coaster, tanker, freighter, freight steamer, cargo boat, lighter; fishing-, pilot- boat; trawler, drifter; cable ship; hulk; yacht; floating palace, ocean greyhound.

ship, bark, barque, brig, snow, hermaphrodite brig; brigantine, barquentine; schooner; topsail —, fore and aft —, three masted- schooner; *chassemarée;* sloop, cutter, corvette, clipper, foist, yawl, dandy, ketch, smack, lugger, barge, hoy, cat-, - boat, buss; sail-er, -ing vessel, wind jammer; steam-er, -boat, -ship; mail—, paddle —, screw —, stern-wheel- steamer; tug; train-ferry; line of steamers etc.

boat, pinnace, launch, motor-boat, picket-boat; hydroplane; life-, long-, jolly-, bum-, fly-, cock-, ferry-, canal- boat, dory, dugout, galliot; shallop, gig, funny, skiff, dingy, scow, cockleshell, wherry, coble, punt, cog, lerret; eight-, four-, pair- oar; randan; out- rigger; float, raft, pontoon; prame, ice-yacht.

state barge, bucentaur.

catamaran, coracle, gondola, carvel, caravel; felucca, caique, canoe; trireme; galley, — foist; bilander, dogger, hooker, howker; argosy, carack; galliass, galleon; galliot, polacca, polacre, corsair, tartane, junk, lorcha, praam, proa, prahu, saick, sampan, xebec, dhow; dahabeah; nuggar, cayak, piroque; trireme.

submarine, submersible.

aircraft (*combatant*) etc. 726; flying machine, air mail, aero-, air-, mono-, bi-, tri-, hydro aero-

plane, plane, cabin –, transport –, propeller –
plane; *avion*, flying boat, glider; helicopter,
rotor –, gyro-plane, whirlybird, autogyro,
gyrodine; sea-, hydro-plane; amphibian; jet.
– plane; turbo-, ram-, pulse-, subsonic –, supersonic –, strato- jet; rocket – plane, – ship,; space
ship; war-. combat – plane; kamikaze, fleet, armada; trainer, fliight simulator; aerostat, dirigible,
blimp (coll.), zeppelin; parachute, chute
(coll.); kite.

rocket, flying –, ballistic –, guided – missile;
projectile; rocket –, robot –, buzz-bomb;
multistage –, step –, test – rocket; booster;
satellite; flying saucer, unidentified flying object.
(UFO).

nacelle, car, gondola, aileron; hangar, airport,
landing field, airdrome; catwalk, controls, rudder,
tail.

Adj. marine, maritime, naval, nautical,
seafaring, sea-, ocean-going, sea-worthy.

aerial, aeronautical, air-worthy, flying etc. *n.*

Adv. afloat, aboard; on -board, – ship board, –
board ship.

274. Velocity.—N. velocity, speed, celerity;
swiftness etc. *adj.*; rapidity, eagle speed; expedition
etc. (*activity*) 682; pernicity; acceleration; haste
etc. 684.

spurt, rush, dash, race, steeplechase; smart –,
lively –, swift etc. *adj.* –, rattling –, spanking –,
strapping- -rate, – pace; round pace; flying, flight.

gallop, canter. trot, round trot, run, scamper;
hand –, full- gallop; swoop.

lightning, light, electricity, wind; cannon-ball,
rocket, arrow, dart, quicksilver; telegraph, express
train; torrent; swallow flight.

eagle, antelope, courser, race-horse, gazelle;
greyhound, hare, doe, squirrel.

Mercury, Ariel, Camilla, Harlequin.

[Measurement of velocity.] speedometer, log, -
line, tachometer.

air speed, speed of sound, sonic –, subsonic –,
supersonic –, ultrasonic –, hypersonic –, tran-
sonic – speed.

V. move quickly, trip, fisk; speed, hie, hasten,
sprint, spurt, post, spank, scuttle; scud, -dle, scurry;
scour, – the plain; scamper, sprint, dash, run, –
-like mad; fly, race, run a race, cut away, cut and
run, shoot, tear, whisk, whiz, sweep, skim, brush;
cut –, bowl- along; rush etc. (*be violent*) 173;
dash -on, – off, – forward; bolt; trot, gallop,
bound, flit, spring, dart, boom; march in -quick, –
double-time; ride hard; et over the ground, scorch.

hurry etc. (*hasten*) 684; accelerate, put on;
quicken; quicken –, mend- one's pace; clap spurs
to one's horse; make-haste, – rapid strides, – forced marches, – the best of one's way; put one's
best leg foremost, stir one's stumps, wing one's
way, set off at a score; carry –, crowd- sail; go off
like a shot, go ahead, gain ground; outstrip the
wind, fly on the wings of the wind.

keep -up, – pace- with; outstrip etc. 303.

Adj. fast, speedy, swift, rapid, quick, fleet; nim-
.ble, agile, expeditious; express; active etc. 682;
flying, galloping etc. *v.*; light- nimble-footed;
winged; eagle-winged, mercurial, electric
telegraphic; light-legged; light of heel; swift as -an
arrow etc. *n.*; quick as -lightning etc. *n.*,
– thought.*

Adv. swiftly etc. *adj.*; with -speed etc. *n.*; apace;
at -a great rate, – full speed, – railway speed; full -
drive, – gallop; post-haste, in full sail, tantivy; trippingly; instantaneously etc. 113; like a shot.

under press of -sale, – canvas, – sail and steam;
velis et remis, on eagle's wing, in double quick
time; with -rapid, – giant- strides; *à pas de géant*;
in seven league boots; whip and spur; *ventre à
terre*; as fast as one's -legs, – heels- will carry one;
as fast on one can lay feet to the ground, at the top
of one's speed; by leaps and bounds; with haste etc.
684; in- high – gear, – speed.

Phr. *vires acquirit eundo.*

*See note on 274.

275. Slowness.—N. slowness etc. *adj.*; languor
etc. (*inactivity*) 683; drawl; creeping etc. *v.*, lentor.

retardation; slackening etc. *v.*; delay etc.
(*lateness*) 133; claudication.

jog-, dog-trot, walk; mincing steps; slow -march,
– time.

slow -goer, – coach, – back; lingerer, loiterer,
sluggard, tortoise, snail; dawdle etc. (*inactive*) 683.

V. move -slowly, etc. *adv.*; creep, crawl, lag,
slug, walk, drawl, linger, loiter, saunter; plod,
trudge, stump along, lumber; trail; drag; dawdle
etc. (*be inactive*) 683; grovel, worm one's way,
steal along; jog –, rub –, bundle- on; toddle,
waddle, wabble, slug; traipse, slouch, shuffle, halt,
hobble, limp, claudicate, shamble; flag, falter, totter, stagger; mince, step short; march in -slow time,
– funeral procession; take one's time; hang fire
etc. (*be late*) 133.

retard, relax; slacken, check, moderate, rein in,
curb; reef; strike –, shorten –, take in- sail; put
on the drag, apply the brake; clip the wings; reduce
the speed, decelerate; slacken -speed, – one's
pace, lose ground; back -water, – pedal, put the
engines astern, throttle down.

Adj. slow, slack; tardy; dilatory etc. (*inactive*)
683; gentle, easy; leisurely; deliberate, gradual; insensible, imperceptible; languid, sluggish,
apathetic, phlegmatic, slow-paced, tardigrade,
snail-like; creeping etc. *v.*

Adv. slowly etc. *adj.*; leisurely; *piano, adagio*;
largo, larghetto; at half speed, under easy sail; at a
-foot's, – snail's, – funeral- pace; slower than
molasses in January; in slow time; with -mincing
steps, – clipped wings; *haud passibus aequis*; in-
low –, gear, – speed.

gradually etc. *adj.*; *gradatim*; by -degrees, –
slow degrees, – inches, – little and little; step by
step; inch by inch, bit by bit, little by little,
seriatim; consecutively.

276. Impulse.—N. impulse, impulsion, im-
petus; momentum; push, pulsion, thrust, shove, jog,
jolt, brunt, booming, boost, throw; explosion etc.
(*violence*) 173; propulsion etc. 284, jet
propulsion; firing, launching, projection, trajection.

percussion, concussion, collision, occursion,
clash, encounter, cannon, *carambole*, appulse,
shock, crash, bump; impact; *élan*; charge etc. (*attack*) 716; beating etc. (*punishment*) 972.

blow, dint, stroke, knock, tap, rap, slap, smack,
pat, dab; fillip; slam, bang; hit, whack, thwack,

clout; cuff etc. 972; squash, dowse, whap, swap, punch, thump, swipe, jab, pelt, kick, punce, calcitration; *ruade*; arietation; cut, thrust, lunge, yerk.

hammer, sledge-hammer, mall, maul, mallet, flail; ram, -mer; battering-ram, monkey, pile-driver, punch, bat, tamper, tamping iron; cudgel etc. (*weapon*) 727; axe etc. (*sharp*) 253.

[Science of mechanical forces] mechanics, dynamics etc.

V. give an -impetus etc. *n.*; impel, push; start, give a start to, set going; drive, urge, boom; thrust, prod, foin; cant; elbow, shoulder, jostle, justle, hustle, hurtle, shove, jog, jolt, bean, encounter; run –, bump –, butt- against; knock –, run- one's head against; impinge.

fire, launch, project, traject, propel, 284.

strike, knock, hit, hash, tap, rap, bat, slap, flap, dab, pat, thump, beat, bang, slam, dash; punch, thwack, whack; hit –, strike- hard; swap, batter, dowse, baste; pelt, patter, skelter, buffet, belabor, tamp; fetch one a blow, swat; poke at, pink, lunge, yerk; kick, calcitrate; butt; strike at etc. (*attack*) 716; whip etc. (*punish*) 972; propel etc. 284.

come –, enter- into collision; collide; foul; fall –, run- foul of.

throw etc.

Adj. impelling etc. *v.*; im-pulsive, -pellent; booming; dynamic, -al; impelled etc. *v.*

277. Recoil.—N. recoil; re-, retro-action; revulsion; rebound, *ricochet*; re-percussion, -calcitration; kick, *contre-coup*; springing back etc. *v.*; elasticity etc. 325; reflexion, reflex, reflux; reverberation etc. (*resonance*) 408; rebuff, repulse; return.

ducks and drakes; boomerang; spring; reactionist, reactionary.

V. recoil, resile, react; spring –, fly –, bound-back; rebound, reverberate, repercuss, recalcitrate, echo, *ricochet*.

Adj. recoiling etc. *v.*; re-fluent, -percussive, -calcitrant, -actionary; retroactive.

Adv. on the -recoil etc. *n.*

278. Direction.—N. direction, bearing, course, set, drift, tenor; tendency etc. 176; incidence; bending, trending etc. *v.*; dip, tack, aim, collimation; steer-ing, -age.

point of the compass, cardinal –, half –, quarter- points; North, East, South, West; N by E, ENE, NE by N, NE etc; rhumb, azimuth, line of collimation.

line, path, road, range, quarter, line of march; alignment; straight shot, bee-line.

course, bearing, heading, altitude, air -route, - lane, angle, center, axis, torsion, torque, pitch, lift, drift, flow, wash.

V. tend –, bend –, point- towards; conduct –, go- to; point -to. – at; bend, trend, verge, incline, dip, determine.

steer –, make- -for, – towards; aim –, level- at; take aim; keep –, hold- a course; be bound for; bend one's steps towards; direct –, steer –, bend –, shape- one's course; align –, align- one's march; go straight, – to the point; march -on, – on a point.

ascertain one's -direction etc. *n.*; *s'orienter*, see which way the wind blows; box the compass.

Adj. directed etc. *v.*, – towards; pointing towards etc. *v.*; bound for; aligned –, with; direct, straight; un-deviating, -swerving; straightforward; North, -ern, -erly, etc. *n.* -

directable etc. *v.*

Adv. towards; on the -road, – high road- to; versus, to; hither, thither, whither; directly; straight, – forwards, – as an arrow; point blank; in a -direct, – straight- line -to, – for, – with; in a line with; full tilt at, as the crow flies.

before –, near –, close to –, against- the wind; windwards, in the wind's eye.

through, *via*, by way of; in all -directions, – manner of ways; *quaqua-versum*, from the four winds.

279. Deviation.—N. deviation; swerving etc. *v.*; obliquation, warp, refraction; flection, flexion; sweep; de-flection, -flexure; declination.

diversion, digression, departure from, aberration, drift, sheer; divergence etc. 291; zigzag; *détour* etc. (*circuit*) 629.

[Desultory motion] wandering etc. *v.*; vagrancy, evagation; by-paths and crooked ways.

[Motion sideways, oblique motion] sidling etc. *v.*; *échelon*, leeway; knight's move (at chess).

V. alter one's course, deviate, depart from, turn, trend; bend, curve, etc. 245; swerve, heel, bear off.

intervert; deflect; divert, – from its course; put on a new scent, shift, shunt, switch, wear, draw aside, crook, warp, short circuit.

stray, straggle; sidle, edge; diverge etc. 291; tralineate, digress, divagate, wander; wind, twist, meander, meander around Robin Hood's barn; veer, tack, sheer; turn -aside, – a corner, – away from; wheel, steer clear of; ramble, rove, drift; go -astray, – adrift; yaw, dodge; step aside, ease off, make way for, shy.

fly off at a tangent; glance off; turn, wheel –, face- about; turn –, face- to the right about; wabble etc. (*oscillate*) 314; go out of one's way etc. (*perform a circuit*) 629; lose one's way.

Adj. deviating etc. *v.*; aberrant, errant; ex-, dis-cursive; devious, desultory, loose; rambling, stray, erratic, vagrant, undirected; circuitous, indirect, zigzag; crab-like.

Adv. astray from, round about, wide of the mark; to the right about; all manner of ways; circuitously etc. 629.

obliquely, sideling, like the move of the knight on a chessboard.

280. Precession. [Going before.]—**N.** precession, leading, heading; precedence etc. 62; priority etc. 116; the lead, *le pas*; van etc. (*front*) 234; precursor etc. 64.

V. go -before, – ahead, – in the van, – in advance; precede, forerun; usher in, introduce, herald, head, take the lead; lead, – the way, – the dance; get –, have- the start; steal a march; get -before, – ahead, – in front of; outstrip etc. 303; take precedence etc. (*first in order*) 62.

Adj. foremost, first, leading etc. *v.*

Adv. in advance, before, ahead, in the van; fore-head-most; in front.

Phr. *seniores priores.*

281. Sequence. [Going after.]—**N.** sequence, run; coming after etc. (*order*) 63; (*time*) 117; following; pursuit etc. 622.

follower, attendant, satellite, shadow, dangler, train.

V. follow; pursue etc. 622; go –, fly- after.

attend, beset, dance attendance on, dog, be-dog; tread -in the steps of, – close upon; be –, go –, follow- in the -wake, –, trail,' – rear- of; trail, follow as a shadow, hang on the skirts of; tread –, follow- on the heels of, tag-after.

lag, get behind.

Adj. following etc. *v.*

Adv. behind; in the -rear etc. 235, – train of, wake of; after etc. (*order*) 63, (*time*) 117.

282. Progression. [Motion forwards; progressive motion.]—**N.** progress, -ion, -iveness; advancing etc. *v.*; advance, -ment; ongoing; flood-tide, headway; march etc. 266; rise; improvement etc. 658.

V. advance; proceed, progress; get -on, – along, – over the ground; gain ground; jog –, rub –, wag- on; go with the stream; keep –, hold on-one's course; go –, move –, come –, get –, pass –, push –, press- -on, – forward, – forwards, – ahead; press onwards; step forward; make –, work –, carve –, push –, force –; edge –, elbow-one's way; make -progress, – head, – way, – headway, – advances. – strides. – rapid strides etc. (*velocity*) 274; go –, shoot- ahead; distance; make up leeway.

Adj. advancing etc. *v.*; pro-gressive, -fluent; advanced.

Adv. forward; onward; forth, on ahead, under way, *en route* for, on -one's way, – the way, – the road, – the high road- to; in -progress, – mid progress; *in transitu* etc. 270.

Phr. *vestigia nulla retrorsum.*

283. Regression. [Motion backwards.]—**N.** regress, -ion; retro-cession, -gression, -gradation, -action; *reculade*; retreat, withdrawal, retirement, remigration; recession etc. (*motion from*) 287; recess; crab-like motion.

re-fluence, -flux; backwater, regurgitation, ebb, return; resilience; reflexion (*recoil*) 277; *volte-face*.

counter -motion, – movement, – march; veering, tergiversation, recidivation, backsliding, fall, relapse; deterioration etc. 659.

turning point etc. (*reversion*) 145.

V. re-cede. -grade, -turn, -vert, -treat, -tire; retro-grade, -cede; back, – down, – out, crawl; withdraw; rebound etc. 277; go –, come –, turn –, hark –, draw –, fall –, get –, put –, run-back; lose ground; fall –, drop- astern; back water, put about; veer, – round; double, wheel, counter-march; ebb, regurgitate; *jib*, shrink, shy.

turn -tail, – round, – upon one's heel, – one's back upon; retrace one's steps, dance the back step; sound –, beat- a retreat; go home.

Adj. receding etc. *v.*; retro-grade, -gressive; regressive, -fluent, -flex, -cidivous, -silient; crab-like; reactionary etc. 277; counter-clockwise.

Adv. back, -wards; reflexively, to the right about; *à reculons, à rebours.*

Phr. *revenons à nos moutons,* as you were.

284. Propulsion. [Motion given to an object situated in front.]—**N.** pro-pulsion, -jection; *vis a tergo*; push etc. (*impulse*) 276; e-, jaculation; ejection etc. 297; throw, fling, toss, shot, discharge, shy.

[Science of propulsion] steam –, gas –, diesel –, jet –, rocket – propulsion, gunnery, ballistics, archery.

missile, projectile, ball, *discus*, javelin, hammer, quoit, brickbat, shot, bullet; arrow, shaft, gun etc. (*arms*) 727.

shooter, shot; gunner, gun-layer; archer, toxophilite; bow-, rifle-, marks- man; good –, crack- shot; sharpshooter etc. (*combatant*) 726.

V. propel, project, throw, fling, cast, pitch, chuck, toss, jerk, heave, shy, hurl; flirt, fillip.

dart, lance, tilt; e-, jaculate; fulminate, bolt, drive, sling, pitchfork.

send; send –, let –, fire- off; discharge, shoot; launch, send forth, let fly; dash.

put –, set- in motion; set agoing, start; give -a start, – an impulse- to; push, impel etc. 276; trun-dle etc. (*set in rotation*) 312; expel etc. 297.

carry one off one's legs; put to flight.

Adj. propelled etc. *v.*; propelling etc. *v.*; pro-pulsive, -jectile.

285. Traction. [Motion given to an object situated behind.]—**N.** traction; drawing etc. *v.*; draft, pull, tug, haul; rake; "a long pull, a strong pull and a pull all together;' towage, haulage.

V. draw, pull, haul, lug, rake, drag, draggle, tug, tow, trail, trawl, train; take in tow.

wrench, jerk, twitch.

Adj. drawing etc. *v.*; tractive, tractile; ductile, pulling, hauling, tugging, towing.

286. Approach. Motion towards.]—**N.** ap-proach, approximation, appropinquation; access; appulse; afflux, -ion; advent etc. (*approach of time*) 121; pursuit etc. 622; convergence etc. 290.

V. approach, approximate; near; get –, go –, draw- near; come, – near, – to close quarters; move –, set in- towards; drift; make up to; gain upon; pursue etc. 622; tread on the heels of; bear up; make the land; hug the -shore, – land.

Adj. approaching etc. *v.*; approximative; convergent; affluent; impending, imminent etc. (*destined*) 152.

Adv. on the road.

Int. come hither! approach! here! come! come near!

287. Recession. [Motion from.]—**N.** recession, retirement, withdrawal; retreat; retrocession etc. 283; departure etc. 293; recoil etc. 277; flight etc. (*avoidance*) 623.

V. recede, go, move from, retire, ebb, withdraw, shrink; come –, move –, go –, get –, drift-away; depart etc. 293; retreat etc. 283; move –, stand –, sheer- off; swerve from; fall back, stand aside; run away etc. (*avoid*) 623.

remove, shunt, side track, switch off.

Adj. receding etc. *v.*

288. Attraction. [Motion towards, ac-tively.]—**N.** attract-ion, -iveness; pull; drawing to,

pulling towards, adduction, magnetism, gravity, attraction of gravitation; lure, bait, decoy.
lode-stone, -star; magnet, siderite, magnetite.
V. attract; draw –, pull –, drag- towards; adduce.
lure, bait, decoy.
Adj. attracting etc. *v.*; attrahent, attractive, adducent, adductive, alluring.

289. Repulsion. [Motion from, actively.]—**N.** repulsion; driving from etc. *v.*; repulse; abduction.
V. repel; push –, drive – etc. 276; from; chase, dispel; retrude; abduce, abduct; send away, repulse, dismiss.
keep at arm's length, turn one's back upon, give the cold shoulder; send packing; send -off, – away- with a flea in one's ear. – about one's business.
Adj. repelling etc. *v.*; repellant, repulsive; abducent, abductive.

290. Convergence. [Motion nearer to.]—**N.** con-vergence, -fluence, -course, -flux, -gress, - currence, -centration; appulse, meeting; corradiation.
assemblage etc. 72; resort etc. (*focus*) 74; asymptote.
V. converge, concur; come together, unite, meet, fall in with; close -with, – in upon; center - round, – in; enter in; pour in.
gather together, unite, concentrate, bring into a focus.
Adj. converging etc. *v.*; con-vergent, -fluent, - current; centripetal; asymptotical.

291. Divergence. [Motion further off.]—**N.** diverg-ence, -ency; divarication, ramification, radiation; separation etc. (*disjunction*) 44; dispersion etc. 73; deviation etc. 279; aberration, declination.
V. diverge, divaricate, radiate; ramify: branch –, glance –, file- off; fly off, – at a tangent; spread, scatter, disperse etc. 73; deviate etc. 279; part etc. (*separate*) 44; splay apart.
Adj. diverging etc. *v.*; divergent, radiant, centrifugal; aberrant.

292. Arrival. [Terminal motion at.]—**N.** arrival, advent; landing; de-, disem-barkation; reception, welcome, *vin d'honneur*.
home, goal, bourn; landing-place, -stage; resting –, stopping -place; destination, harbor, haven, port; terminal, terminus, railway station, depot, airport; halt, halting -place, – ground; anchorage etc. (*refuge*) 666.
return, recursion, remigration; meeting; ren-, en-counter.
completion etc. 729.
V. arrive; get to, come to; come; reach, attain; come up, – with, – to; overtake; make, fetch; complete etc. 729; join, rejoin.
light, alight, dismount; land, go ashore; debark, disembark; put -in, – into; visit, cast anchor, pitch

one's tent; sit down etc. (*be located*) 184; get to one's journey's end; make the land; be in at the death; come –, get- -back, – home; return; come in etc. (*ingress*) 294; make one's appearance etc. (*appear*) 446; drop in; detrain; outspan.
come to hand; come -at, – across; hit; come –, light –; pop –, bounce –, plump –, burst –, pitch- upon; meet; en- ren-counter; come in contact.
Adj. arriving etc. *v.*; homewardbound; terminal.
Adv. here, hither.
Int. welcome! hail! all hail! good- day, – morrow; greetings! hullo! well!

293. Departure. [Initial motion from.]—**N.** departure, decession, decampment; embarkation; take-off; outset, start; removal; exit etc. (*egress*) 295; exodus, Hejira, flight.
leave-taking, *congé*, valediction, valedictory, adieu, farewell, good-bye, stirrup-cup.
starting -point, – post; point –, place- of - departure, – embarkation; port of embarkation.
V. depart; go, – away; take one's departure, set out; set –, march –, put –, start –, be –, move –, get –, whip –, pack –, go –, take oneself-off; start, issue, march out, debouch; go –, sally-forth; sally, set forward; be gone.
leave a place, quit, vacate, evacuate, abandon; go off the stage, make ones' exit; retire, withdraw, remove; go -one's way, – along, – from home; take -flight, – wing; spring, fly, flit, wing one's flight; fly –, whip- away; take off, hop off; embark; go -on board, – aboard; set sail; put –, go-to sea; sail, take ship; hoist blue Peter; get under way, weigh anchor; strike tents, break camp.
decamp; walk one's chalks, make tracks, cut one's stick; cut and run; take leave; say –/bid- -good-bye etc. *n.*; disappear etc. 449; abscond etc. (*avoid*) 623; entrain, embus, emplane; saddle –, harness –, hitch- up; inspan.
Adj. departing etc. *v.*; valedictory; outward bound.
Adv. whence, hence, thence; with a foot in the stirrup; on the -wing, – move.
Int. begone! etc. (*ejection*) 297; to horse! all aboard! farewell! adieu! good-bye, – day! *au revoir! auf wiedersehen!* fare you well! so long! God -bless you, – speed! *bon voyage!*

294. Ingress. [Motion into.]—**N.** ingress; entrance, entry; introgression; influx; intrusion, inroad, incursion, invasion, irruption; pene-, interpene- tration; illapse, import, importation, infiltration; immigration; admission etc. (*reception*) 296; insinuation etc. (*interjacence*) 228; insertion etc. 300.
inlet; way in; mouth, door etc. (*opening*) 260; path etc. (*way*) 627; conduit etc. 350; immigrant, visitor, incomer, newcomer, colonist.
V. have the *entrée*; enter; go –, come –, pour –, flow –, creep –, slip –, pop –, break –, burst- -into, – in; set foot on; burst –, break-in upon; invade, intrude, butt in, horn in, crash; insinuate itself; inter-, penetrate; infiltrate; find one's way –, wriggle –, worm oneself- into.
give entrance to etc. (*receive*) 296; insert etc. 300.

Adj. incoming, ingressive etc. *n.*; inward bound.
Adv. inward.

295. Egress. [Motion out of.]—**N.** egress, exit, issue; emer-sion, -gence; disemboguement; outbreak, -burst; e-, pro-ruption; emanation; evacuation; ex, trans-udation; extravasation, perspiration, sweating, leakage, percolation, distillation, oozing; gush etc. (*water in motion*) 348; outpour, -ing; effluence, effusion; efflux, -ion; drain; dribbling etc. *v.*; defluxion; drainage; outcome, -put; discharge etc. (*excretion*) 299.

export; expatriation; e-, re-migration; *débouche*; exodus etc. (*departure*) 293; emigrant, migrant, *émigré*, colonist.

outlet, vent, spout, tap, sluice, floodgate; pore; vomitory, out-gate, sally-port; way out; mouth, door etc. (*opening*) 260; path etc. (*way*) 627; conduit etc. 350; air-pipe etc. 351.

V. emerge, emanate, issue; go −, come −, move −, pass −, pour −, flow- out of; pass off, evacuate; migrate.

ex-, trans-ude; leak; run, − out, − through; per-, trans-colate; seep; strain, distil; perspire, sweat, drain, ooze; filter, filtrate; dribble, gush, spout, flow out; well, − out; pour, trickle etc. (*water in motion*) 348; effuse, extravasate, disembogue, discharge itself, debouch; come −, breakforth; burst- out, − through; find vent, escape etc. 671.

Adj. effused etc. *v.*; outgoing, outward bound.
Adv. outward.

296. Reception. [Motion into, actively.]—**N.** reception; admission, admittance, *entrée* importation; initiation; intro-duction, -mission, - ception; immission, ingestion, imbibition, absorption, ingurgitation, inhalation; suction, sucking; eating, drinking etc. (*food*) 298; insertion etc. 300; interjection etc. 228.

V. give -entrance to, − admittance to, − the *entrée*; intro-duce, -mit; usher, admit, receive, import, initiate, bring in, open the door to, throw open, ingest, absorb, imbibe, inhale, infiltrate; let −, take −, suck- in; re-admit, -sorb, -absorb; snuff up; swallow, ingurgitate; enfulf, engorge; gulp; eat, drink etc. (*food*) 298.

Adj. admit-ting etc. *v.*, -ted etc. *v.*; admissible; absorbent; introductory, introceptive, intromittent, initiatory.

297. Ejection. [Motion out of, actively.]—**N.** ejection, emission, effusion, rejection, expulsion, eviction, extrusion, trajection; discharge.

egestion, evacuation, vomition, disgorgement, voidance, eruption, eructiveness; ruc-, eruc-tation, blood-letting, venesection, phlebotomy, paracentesis; tapping, drainage; clear-ance, -age, voidance; vomiting, excretion etc. 299.

deportation; banishment etc. (*punishment*) 972; rogue's march; relegation, extradition; dislodgment.

V. give -exit, − vent- to; let −, give −, pour −, send- out; des-, dis-patch; exhale, excern, excrete, disembogue, secrete, secern; extravasate,

shed, void, evacuate, egest, emit; open the -sluices, − floodgates; turn on the tap; extrude, detrude; effuse, spend, expend; pour forth; squirt, spirt, spill, slop; perspire etc. (*exude*) 295; breathe, blow etc. (*wind*) 349.

tap, draw off; bale −, lade- out; let blood, broach.

eject, reject; expel, discard; cut, send to Coventry, boycott, ostracize; *chasser*; banish etc. (*punish*) 972; throw etc. 284 -out, − up, − off, − away, − aside; push etc. 276 -out, − off, − away, − aside; shovel −, sweep- -out, − away; brush −, whisk −, turn −, send- -off, − away; discharge; send −, turn −, cast- adrift; turn −, bundle- out; throw overboard; give the sack to; send -packing, − about one's business, − to the right about; strike off the roll etc. (*abrogate*) 756; turn outneck and heels, − head and shoulders, − neck and crop; pack off; send away with a flea in the ear; send to Jericho; bow out, show the door to, dismiss, fire, sack.

turn out of -doors, − house and home; evict, oust; exorcise, un-house, -kennel; dislodge; un-, dis-people; depopulate; relegate, deport.

empty; drain, − to the dregs; sweep off; clear, − off, − out, − away; such, draw off, extract; clean out, make a clean sweep of, clear decks, purge.

em-, dis-, disem-bowel; eviscerate, gut; unearth, root -out, − up; averruncate; weed −, get out; eliminate, get rid of, do away with, shake off; exenterate.

vomit, spew, puke, keck, retch; belch, − out, eruct, eructate; cast −, bring- up; disgorge; expectorate, salivate, clear the throat, hawk, spit, sputter, splutter, slobber, drool, drivel, slaver, slabber.

unpack, unlade, unload, unship; break bulk.

be let out; ooze etc. (*emerge*) 295.

Adj. emitt-ing, -ed etc. *v.*

begone! get you gone! get −, go- away, − along, − along with you! go your way! away, − with! off with you! go, − about your business! be off! avaunt! aroynt! get out!

298. Food. [Eating.]—**N.** eating etc. *v.*; deglutition, gulp, epulation, mastication, manducation, rumination, gastronomy, gastrology; panto-, hippo-, ichthyo-phagy etc.; gluttony etc. 957; carnivorousness, vegetarianism.

mouth, jaws, mandible, mazard, chops.

drinking etc. *v.*; potation, draught, libation; carousal etc. (*amusement*) 840; drunkenness etc. 959.

food, *pabulum*; aliment, nourishment, nutriment; susten-ance, -tation; nurture, subsistence, provender, feed, fodder, provision, ration, keep, commons, board; commissariat etc. (*provision*) 637; prey, forage, pasture, pasturage; fare, cheer; diet, -ary; regimen; belly timber, staff of life; bread, -and cheese; proteins, carbohydrates, vitamines.

comestibles, eatables, victuals, edibles, *ingesta*; grub, prog, tack, hard tack, meat; bread, -stuffs; cereals; viands, cates, delicacy, dainty, creature comforts, contents of the larder, flesh-pots; festal board; ambrosia; good -cheer, − living.

hors-d'oeuvre; soup, pottage, *potage*, broth,

bouillon, *consommé*, *purée*, *borsch*, stock, skilly, gumbo; fish. − cakes, − pie; joint, *rôti*, *pièce de résistance*, *relevé*, hash, *réchauffé*, stew, *ragoût*, fricassee, mince, *salmi*, *goulash*, *bouillabaisse*, remove, *entrée*, croquette, rissole, sausage, curry, bubble and squeak; haggis, collops, giblets; poultry, game etc.; biscuit, bun, scone, rusk, pancake, pie, pastry, pasty, patty, *patisseria*, tart, turnover, *vol-au-vent*, *soufflé*, dumpling, pudding, duff, compote, fritters, cake, napoleon, blancmange, custard, jelly, jam, sweets etc. 396; *entremet*; oatmeal, porridge, hasty pudding, gruel; eggs, omelet, cheese, matzoon, savory, vegetable, salad, *mayonnaise*, fruit; sauce, condiment etc. 393; kickshaws.

table, *cuisine*, bill of fare, *menu*, *table d'hôte*, ordinary, *à la carte*; cover.

meal, repast, feed, spread; mess; dish, plate, course, side dish; regale; regale-, refresh-, entertain-ment; refection, collation, picnic, feast, banquet, junket; breakfast; lunch, -eon, *déjeuner*, bever, tiffin, tea, dinner, supper, snack, whet, bait, dessert; pot-luck, *table d'hôte*, *déjeuner à la fourchette*; hearty −, square −, substantial −, full-meal; blow out; light refreshment; pemmican.

mouthful, bolus, gobbet, tit-bit, morsel, sop, sippet.

drink, beverage, liquor, broth, soup; potion, dram, draft, drench, swill; nip, peg, sip, sup, gulp.

wine, champagne, spirits, *liqueur* beer, porter, stout, ale, malt liquor, julep, Sir John Barleycorn, stingo, heavy wet, bitter, lager- beer, cider, grog, toddy, flip, purl, punch, negus, cup, bishop, posset, wassail; bitters, *apéritif*, high-ball, cocktail; whisky, rum, absinthe; gin etc. (*intoxicating liquor*) 959; coffee, chocolate, cocoa, tea, *maté*, the cup that cheers but not inebriates.

eating-house etc. 189.

V. eat, feed, fare, devour, swallow, take; gulp, bolt, snap; fall to; despatch, dispatch; discuss; take −, get −, gulp-down; lay −, tuck- in; lick, pick, peck; gormandize etc. 957; bite, champ, munch, cranch, craunch, crunch, chew, masticate, nibble, gnaw, mumble.

live on; feed −, batten −, fatten −, feast- upon; browse, graze, crop, regale; carouse etc. (*make merry*) 840; eat heartily, do justice to, play a good knife and fork, banquet.

break -bread, − one's fast; breakfast; lunch, dine, take tea, sup.

drink, − in, − up, − one's fill; quaff, sip, sup; suck, − up; lap; swig; swill, tipple etc. (*be drunken*) 959; empty one's glass, drain the cup; toss -off, − one's glass; wash down, crack a bottle, wet one's whistle.

cater, purvey etc. 637.

Adj. eatable, edible, esculent, comestible, alimentary; cereal, cibarious; dietetic; culinary; nutri-tive, -tious; succulent; drinkable, pot-able, -ulent; bibulous.

omn-, carn-, herb-, frug-, gran-, gramin-, phytivorous; ichthyophagous.

prandial.

299. Excretion.—N. excretion, discharge, emanation; ejection etc. 297; exhalation, exudation, extrusion, secretion, effusion, extravasation, *ecchymosis*, evacuation, cacation, defecation, dysentery, dejection, *feces*, excrement;

perspiration, sweat; sub-, exud-ation; *diaphoresis*; sewage.

saliva, spittle, rheum; ptyalism, salivation, catarrh, distemper; diarrhea; *ejecta*, *egesta*, *sputum*, *sputa*; excreta; lava; *exuviae* etc. (*uncleanness*) 653.

hemorrhage, bleeding; catamenia, menses; outpouring etc. (*egress*) 295; leucorrhea.

V. excrete etc. (*eject*) 297; emanate etc. (*come out*) 295.

Adj. excretory, fecal, secretory; ejective, eliminant.

300. Insertion. [Forcible ingress.]—N. insertion, implantation, intercalation, embolism, introduction; interpolation, insinuation etc. (*intervention*) 228; planting etc. v.; injection, inoculation, importation, infusion; forcible -ingress etc. 294; immersion; submersion, -gence; dip, plunge; bath etc. (*water*) 337; interment etc. 363.

V. insert; intro-duce, -mit; put −, run- into; import; inject; interject etc. 228; infuse, instil, inoculate, impregnate, imbue, imbrue.

graft, ingraft, bud, plant, implant; dovetail.

obtrude; thrust −, stick −, ram −, stuff −, tuck −, press −, drive −, pop −, whip −, drop −, put- in; impact; empierce etc. (*make a hole*) 260.

embed; immerse, immerge, merge; bathe, soak etc. (*water*) 337; dip, plunge etc. 310.

bury etc. (*inter*) 363.

insert etc. -itself; plunge *in medias res*.

Adj. inserted etc. v.

301. Extraction. [Forcible egress.]—N. extraction; extracting etc. v.; removal, elimination, extrication, eradication, evolution.

evulsion, avulsion; wrench; expression, squeezing; extirpation, extermination; ejection etc. 297; export etc. (*egress*) 295; distillation.

extractor, corkscrew, forceps, pliers.

V. extract, draw, pit; take −, draw −, pull −, tear −, pluck −, pick −, get- out; wring from, wrench; extort; root −, weed −, grub −, rake-up, − out; eradicate; pull −, pluck- up by the roots; averruncate; unroot; uproot, pull up, extirpate, dredge.

remove; educe, elicit; evolve, extricate; eliminate etc. (*eject*) 297; eviscerate etc. 297.

express, squeeze '−, press- out; distil.

Adj. extracted etc. v.

302. Passage. [Motion through.]—N. passage, transmission; permeation; pene-, interpene-tration; transudation, infiltration; osmosis, osmose, endos-, exos-mose; intercurrence; ingress etc. 294; egress etc. 295; path etc. 627; conduit etc. 350; opening etc. 260; journey etc. 266; voyage etc. 267.

V. pass, − through; perforate etc. (*hole*) 260; penetrate, permeate, thread, thrid, enfilade; go-through, − across; go −, pass- over; cut across; ford, cross; pass and repass, work; make −, thread −, worm −, force- one's way; make −, force- a passage; cut one's way through; find its -way. −

vent; transmit, make way, clear the course;
traverse, go over the ground.
   Adj. passing etc. *v.*; intercurrent; osmotic etc. *n.*
   Adv. *en passant* etc. (*transit*) 270.

303. Overstep. [Motion beyond.]—**N.** transcursion, -ilience, -gression; infraction, intrusion;
trespass; encroach-, infringe-ment; extravagation,
transcendence; redundance etc. 641; ingress etc.
294.
   V. transgress, surpass, pass; go beyond, – by;
show in –, come to the- front; shoot ahead of;
steal a march –, gain- upon.
   over-step, -pass, -reach, -go, -ride- -leap, -jump, -
skip, -lap, -shoot the mark; out-strip, -leap, -jump,
-go, -step, -run, -ride, -rival, -do; beat, – hollow;
distance; leave in the -lurch, – rear; go one better,
throw into the shade; exceed, transcend, surmount;
soar etc. (*rise*) 305.
   encroach, intrude, trespass, infringe, invade,
trench upon, intrench on; strain; stretch –, strain-
a point; pass the Rubicon.
   Adj. surpassing etc. *v.*
   Adv. beyond the mark, ahead.

304. Shortcoming. [Motion short of.]—**N.**
shortcoming; failure; delinquency; falling short etc.
v.; de-fault, -falcation; leeway; labor in vain, no
go.
   incompleteness etc. 53; imperfection etc. 651;
insufficiency etc. 640; noncompletion etc. 730;
failure etc. 732.
   V. come –, fall –, stop- -short, – short of; not
reach; want; keep within -bounds, – the mark, –
compass.
   break down, stick in the mud, collapse, come to
nothing; fall -through, – to the ground, – down;
cave in, end in smoke, fizzle out, miss the mark,
fail; lose ground; miss stays, slump.
   Adj. unreached; deficient; short, – of; *minus*;
out of depth; perfunctory etc. (*neglect*) 460.
   Adv. within -the mark, – compass, – bounds;
behindhand; *re infectâ*; to no purpose; far from it.
   Phr. the bubble burst.

305. Ascent. [Motion upwards.]—**N.** ascent,
ascension; rising etc. *v.*; rise, upgrowth; leap etc.
309; acclivity, hill etc. 217; stair, stairs, stair-case, -
way, flight of -steps, – stairs; ladder, companion,
– way; lift, elevator etc. 307.
   rocket, lark; sky-rocket, -lark; Alpine Club.
   V. ascend, rise, mount, arise, uprise; go –, get
–, work one's way –, start –, spring –, shoot-
up; zoom; aspire.
   climb, clamber, ramp, scramble, swarm,
escalade, surmount; scale, – the heights.
   tower, soar, hover, spire, plane, swim, float,
surge; leap etc. 309.
   Adj. rising etc. *v.*; scandent, buoyant; super-
natant, -fluitant; excelsior.
   Adv. uphill.

306. Descent. [Motion downwards.]—**N.**
descent, descension, declension, declination; fall;

falling etc. *v.*; drop, cadence; subsidence, lapse;
come-down, downfall, tumble, slip, tilt, trip, lurch;
cropper, *culbute*; titubation, stumble; fate of
Icarus; dive, nose-dive, *volpané*.
   -*avalanche, débâcle*, landslip, slide.
   V. descend; go –, drop –, come-down; fall,
gravitate, drop, slip, slide, glissade, dive, plunge,
settle; decline, slump, set, sink, droop, come down
a peg.
   dismount, alight, light, get down; swoop; stoop
etc. 308; fall prostrate, precipitate oneself; let fall
etc. 308.
   tumble, trip, stumble, titubate, lurch, pitch,
swag, topple; topple –, tumble- -down, – over;
tilt, sprawl, plump down, come a cropper.
   Adj. descending etc. *v.*; descendent, declivitous;
downcast; decur-rent, sive; labent, deciduous;
nodding to its fall.
   Adv. down, -hill, -wards.

307. Elevation.—**N.** elevation; raising etc. *v.*;
erection, lift; sublevation, upheaval; sublimation,
exaltation; prominence etc. (*convexity*) 250.
   lever etc. 633; crane, derrick, windlass, capstan,
winch, dredger, lift, elevator, escalator, dumb
waiter.
   V. heighten, elevate, raise, lift, erect; set –,
stick –, perch –, perk –, tilt- up; rear, hoist,
heave; up-lift, -raise, -rear, -bear, -cast, -hoist, -
heave; buoy, weigh, mount, give a lift; exalt,
sublimate; place –, set- on a pedestal.
   take –, drag –, fish- up; dredge.
   stand –, rise –, get –, jump- up; spring to
one's feet; hold -oneself, – one's head- up; draw
oneself up to his full height.
   Adj. elevated etc. *v.*; standing up; stilted, attollent, rampant.
   Adv. on -stilts, – the shoulders of, – one's legs,
– one's hind legs.

308. Depression.—**N.** lowering etc. *v.*;
depression; dip etc. (*concavity*) 252; abasement;
detrusion; reduction.
   over-throw, -set, -turn; upset; prostration, subversion, precipitation.
   bow; courtesy, curtsy; genuflexion, *kowtow*,
obeisance, *salaam*.
   V. depress, lower; let –, take- -down, – down
a peg; cast; let -drop, – fall; -sink, debase, bring
low, abase, slash, reduce, detrude, pitch,
precipitate.
   over-throw, -turn, -set; upset, subvert, prostrate,
level, fell; cast –, take –, throw –, fling –, dash
–, pull –, cut –, knock –, hew- down; raze, –
to the ground, humiliate, trample in the dust, pull
about one's ears.
   sit, – down; crouch, squat, crouch, stoop, bend,
bow, courtesy, curtsy; bob, duck, dip, genuflect,
kneel; *kowtow, salaam*, make obeisance, prostrate
oneself; bend, bow- the -head, – knee; incline the
head; bow down; cower; recline etc. (*be horizontal*) 213.
   Adj. depressed etc. *v.*; at a low ebb; prostrate
etc. (*horizontal*) 213; detrusive.

309. Leap.—**N.** leap, jump, hop, spring,
bound, vault, saltation.

dance, caper, gambol; curvet, caracole; *gambade, -bado*; capriole, demivolt; buck, – jump; hop, skip and jump.

kangaroo, jerboa, chamois, goat, frog, grasshopper, flea.

V. leap; jump -up, – over the moon; hop, spring, bound, vault, ramp, cut capers, gambol, trip, skip, dance, caper, curvet, *caracole*; foot it, bob, bounce, flounce, start, frisk etc. (*amusement*) 840; jump about etc. (*agitation*) 315; trip it on the light fantastic toe, dance oneself off one's legs.

Adj. leaping etc. *v.*; saltatory, frisky.

Adv. on the light fantastic toe.

310. Plunge.—N. plunge, dip, dive, header; ducking etc. *v.*; submergence, immersion, diver.

V. plunge, dip, souse, duck; dive, plump; take a -plunge, – header, make a plunge; bathe etc. (*water*) 337.

sub-merge, -merse; immerse, douse, sink, engulf, send to -the bottom, – Davy Jones' locker.

get out of one's depth; go -to the bottom, – down like a stone; founder, welter, wallow.

311. Circuition. [Curvilinear motion.]**—N.** circuition, circulation; turn, curvet; excursion; circum-vention, -navigation, -ambulation; north-west passage; ambit, gyre, lap, circuit etc. 629.

turning etc. *v.*; wrench; evolution; coil, helix, spiral; corkscrew.

V. turn, bend, wheel; go – , put- about; heel; go – , turn -round, – to the right about; turn on one's heel; make – , describe- a -circle, – complete circle; encircle; go – , pass- through -180°, – 360°

circum-navigate, -aviate, -ambulate, -vent; put a girdle round the earth, go the round, make the round of.

turn – , round- a corner; double a point.

wind, circulate, meander; whisk, twirl; twist etc. (*convolution*) 248; make a *détour* etc. (*circuit*) 629.

Adj. turning etc. *v.*; circuitous; circumforaneous, -fluent; devious, roundabout, circumambient, -flex, -navigable.

Adv. round about.

312. Rotation. [Motion in a continued circle.]**—N.** rotation, revolution, gyration, circulation, roll; circum-rotation, -volution, - gyration; volutation, circination, turbination, *pirouette*, convolution.

verticity; whir, whirl, swirl, eddy, vortex, whirlpool, gurge; cyclone, tornado; surge; *vertigo*, dizzy round; Maelstrom, Charybdis; Ixion; wheel of Fortune.

wheel, screw, propeller, whirligig, rolling stone, windmill; top, teetotum, merry-go-round; roller; cog-, fly-wheel, spit; jack; caster.

axis, axle, spindle, spool, pivot, pin, hinge, pole, swivel, gimbals, arbor, bobbin, mandrel, shaft.

[Science of rotatory motion] trochilics, gyrostatics.

V. rotate; roll, – along; revolve, spin; turn, – round; circumvolve; circulate; gyre, gyrate, wheel,

whirl, swirl, twirl, trundle, troll, bowl; slew round.

roll up, furl; wallow, welter; box the compass; spin like a -top, – teetotum.

Adj. rotating etc. *v.*; rota-tory, -ry; circumrotatory, trochilic, vertiginous, gyratory; vortic-al, -ose.

Adv. head over heels, round and round, like a horse in a mill.

313. Evolution. [Motion in a reverse circle.]**—N.** evolution, unfolding, development; eversion etc. (*inversion*) 218.

V. evolve; un-fold, -roll, -wind, -coil, -twist, - furl, -twine, -ravel; disentangle; develop.

Adj. evolving etc. *v.*; evolved etc. *v.*

314. Oscillation. [Reciprocating motion, motion to and fro.]**—N.** oscillation; vibration, libration; motion of a pendulum; nutation; undulation; pulsation; pulse; throb; seismic disturbance.

alternation; coming and going etc. *v.*; ebb and flow, flux and reflux, ups and downs; wave, vibratiuncle, swing; beat, shake, wag, see-saw, dance, lurch, dodge; fluctuation; vacillation etc. (*irresolution*) 605.

seismometer, vibroscope, seismograph.

V. oscillate; vi-, li-brate; alternate, undulate, wave; sway, rock, swing; pulsate, beat; wag, -gle; nod, bob, courtesy, curtsy; tick; play; chatter, wamble, wabble; teeter, dangle, swag.

fluctuate, dance, curvet, reel, quake; quiver, quaver, shake, flicker; wriggle; roll, toss, pitch; flounder, stagger, totter, waddle; move – , bob- up and down etc. *adv.*; pass and repass, ebb and flow, come and go, shuttle; vacillate etc. 605.

brandish, shake, flourish.

Adj. oscillating etc. *v.*; oscill-, undul-, puls-, libr-atory; vibrat-ory, -ile; pendulous, shutterwise; seismic.

Adv. to and fro, up and down, backwards and forwards, see-saw, zigzag, wibble-wabble, in and out, from side to side, like buckets in a well.

315. Agitation. [Irregular motion.]**—N.** agitation, stir, tremor, shake, ripple, jog, jolt, jerk, shock, succession, trepidation, . quiver, quaver, dance; jactit-ation, -ance; shuffling etc. *v.*; twitter, flicker, flutter.

disquiet, perturbation, commotion, turmoil, turbulence; tumult, -uation; hubbub, rout, bustle, fuss, racket, *subsultus*, staggers, megrims, epilepsy, fits, twitching, vellication, St. Vitus' dance.

spasm, throe, throb, palpitation, convulsion, paroxysm; tetanus.

disturbance etc. (*disorder*) 59; restlessness etc. (*changeableness*) 149.

ferment, -ation; ebullition, effervescence, hurly burly, *cahotage*; tempest, storm, ground swell, heavy sea, whirlpool, vortex etc. 312; whirlwind etc. (*wind*) 349.

V. be -agitated etc.; shake; tremble, – like an aspen leaf; quiver, quaver, quake, shiver, twitter, twire, dither, dodder; twitch, writhe, toss, shuffle, tumble, stagger, bob, reel, sway; wag , -gle, wiggle; wriggle, – like an eel; squirm; dance, stumble, shamble, flounder, totter, flounce, flop, curvet, prance.

throb, pulsate, beat, palpitate, go pit-a-pat; flutter, flitter, flicker, bicker; bustle.

ferment, effervesce, foam; boil, – over; bubble, – up; simmer.

toss –, jump- about; jump like a parched pea; shake like an aspen leaf; shake to its -center, – foundations; be the sport of the winds and waves; reel to and fro like a drunken man; move –, drivefrom post to pillar and from pillar to post; keep between hawk and buzzard.

agitate, shake, convulse, toss, tumble, bandy, wield, brandish, flap, flourish, whisk, jerk, hitch, jolt; jog, -gle; hostle, buffet, hustle, disturb, stir, shake up, churn, jounce, wallop, whip, vellicate.

Adj. shaking etc. *v.*; agitated, tremulous; de-, sub-sultory; shambling; giddy-paced, saltatory, convulsive, jerky, unquiet, restless, all of a twitter.

Adv. by fits and starts; subsultorily etc. *adj.*; per saltum; hop, skip and jump; in -convulsions, – fits, pit-a-pat.

316. Materiality.—N. material-ity, -ness; materialization; corpor-eity, -ality; substantiality, material existence, incarnation, flesh and blood, *plenum*; physical condition.

matter, body, substance, brute matter, stuff, element, principle, protoplasm, plasma, *parenchyma*, material, *substratum*, hyle, *corpus*, *pabulum*; frame.

object, article, thing, something; still life; stocks and stones; materials etc. 635.

[Science of matter] physics; somatology, -ics; natural –, experimental- philosophy; physical science, *philosophie positive*, materialism, hylism; applied –, micro-, molecular –, nuclear – physics.

atomics, atomic science, nucleonics, quantum mechanics, radiology.

atom, radical, tracer, isotope, pleiad; atomic – nucleus, – cluster; nuclear particle, neutron, protron, shell, valence electron.

materialist, physicist, atomic scientist, radiologist.

V. materialize, incorporate, incarnate, substantiate, embody.

atomize, split –, smash – the atom; radioactivate.

Adj. material, bodily; corpor-eal, -al; physical; somat-ic, -oscopic; sensible, tangible, ponderable, palpable, substantial; fleshly, incarnate.

physical, bio-, electro-, geo-physical; atomic, nuclear, thermonuclear, radio-active.

objective, impersonal, neuter, unspiritual, materialistic.

317. Immateriality.—N. immaterial-ity, -ness; incorporeity, dematerialization, unsubstantiality, spirituality; inextension; astral plane.

personality; I, myself, me; *ego*, spirit etc. (*soul*) 450; astral body; immaterialism; spiritual-ism, -ist; subliminal –, subconscious- self.

V. disembody, spiritualize, dematerialize.

Adj. immateri-al, -ate; incorpor-eal, -al; asomatous, unextended; un-, dis-embodied; extramundane, supersensible, unearthly;

pneumatoscopic; spiritual etc. (*psychical*) 450; aery.

personal, subjective.

318. World.—N. world, creation, nature, universe; earth, globe, wide world; *cosmos*; terraqueous globe, sphere; macro-, mega-cosm; music of the spheres; strato-, tropo-sphere.

heavens, sky, welkin, empyrean; starry -heaven, – host; firmament; vault –, canopy- of heaven; celestial spaces.

heavenly bodies, stars, luminaries, nebulae; galaxy, milky way, galactic circle, *via lactea*.

sun, orb of day, Apollo, Phoebus; photo-, chromo-sphere; solar system; planet, -oid, asteroid; comet; satellite; moon, orb of night, Diana, Luna; aerolite, meteor; falling –, shootingstar; meteorite.

constellation, zodiac, signs of the zodiac, Charles's wain, Great Bear, Southern Cross, Orion's belt, Cassiopeia's chair, Pleiades etc.

colures, equator, ecliptic, orbit.

[Science of heavenly bodies] astronomy; uranography, -logy; cosmo-logy, -graphy, -gony; *eidouranion*, orrery; geography; geodesy etc. (*measurement*) 466; star-gazing, -gazer; astronomer; cosmogonist, geodesist, geographer; observatory.

Adj. cosmic, cosmical, mundane; terr-estrial, -estrious, -aqueous, -ene, -eous; telluric, earthly, geotic, geodetic, cosmogonal, under the sun; sublunary, -astral.

solar, heliacal; lunar; celestial, heavenly, empyreal, sphery; starry, stellar; sider-eal, -al; astral; nebular.

Adv. in all creation, on the face of the globe, here below, under the sun.

319. Gravity.—N. gravi-ty, -tation; weight; heaviness etc. *adj.*; specific gravity; ponderosity, pressure, load; bur-den, -then; ballast, counterpoise; lump –, mass –, weight- of.

lead, millstone, mountain, Ossa on Pelion.

weighing, ponderation, trutination; weights; avoirdupois –, troy –, apothecaries'- weight; grain, scruple, drachm, ounce, pound, lb., load, stone, hundredweight, cwt., ton, quintal, carat, pennyweight, tod, gram, kilogram etc.

[Weighing instrument] balance, scales, steelyard, beam, weighbridge, spring balance, weighing machine.

[Science of gravity] statics.

V. be -heavy etc. *adj.*; gravitate, weigh, press, cumber, load.

[Measure the weight of] weigh, poise.

Adj. weighty; weighing etc. *v.*; heavy, – as lead; ponder-ous, -able; lump-ish, -y; cumber-, burden-some; cumbrous, unwieldy, massive.

in-, superin-cumbent.

320. Levity.—N. levity; lightness etc. *adj.*; imponderability, imponderables, buoyancy, volatility.

feather, dust, mote, down, thistledown, flue, cobweb, gossamer, straw, cork, bubble; float, bouy; ether, air.

leaven, ferment, barm, yeast, enzyme.
V. be -light etc. *adj.*; float, swim, be buoyed up.
render -light etc. *adj.*; lighten, levitate; leaven.
Adj. light, subtile, subtle, airy; imponder-ous, -
able; astatic, weightless, ethereal, sublimated; un-
compressed, volatile; buoyant, floating etc. *v.*;
barmy, frothy; portable.
light as -a feather, – thistle down, – air.
fermenting etc. *n.*

321. Density.—N. density, solidity; solidness
etc. *adj.*; impenetra-, impermea-bility; in-
compressibility; imporosity; cohesion etc. 46; con-
stipation, consistence, spissitude.
specific gravity; hydro-, areo-meter.
condensation; solid-ation, -ification; consolidation; concretion, caseation, coagulation;
petrifaction etc. (*hardening*) 323; crystallization,
precipitation; deposit, precipitate, silt; inspissation;
thickening etc. *v.*
indivisibility, indiscerptibility, indissolvableness.
solid body, mass, block, knot, lump; con-cretion,
-crete, -glomerate; cake, clot, stone, curd,
coagulum, grume; bone, gristle, cartilage.
V. be -dense etc. *adj.*; become – . render- solid
etc. *adj.*; solid-ify, -ate; concrete, set, take a set,
consolidate, congeal, coagulate; curd, -le; fix, clot,
cake, candy, precipitate, deposit, cohere,
crystallize; petrify etc. (*harden*) 323.
condense, thicken, inspissate, incrassate; compress, squeeze, ram down, constipate.
Adj. dense, solid, solidified etc. *v.*; cohe-rent, -
sive etc. 46; compact, close, serried, thickset; substantial, massive, lumpish; impenetrable, im-
permeable, imporous; incompressible; con-
stipated; concrete etc. (*hard*) 323; knot-ted, -ty;
gnarled; crystal-line, -lizable; thick, grumous,
stuffy.
un-dissolved, -melted, -liquified, -thawed.
in-divisible, -discerptible, -frangible,
dissolvable, -dissoluble, -soluble, -fusible.

322. Rarity.—N. rarity; tenuity; absence of -
solidity etc. 321; subtility; sponginess, compressibility.
rarefaction, expansion, dilatation, inflation, sub-
tilization.
ether etc. (*gas*) 334.
V. rarefy, expand, dilate, subtilize, attenuate,
thin.
Adj. rare, subtile, thin, fine, tenuous, compressible, flimsy, slight; light etc. 320; cavernous,
spongy etc. (*hollow*) 252.
rarefied etc. *v.*; unsubstantial; uncom-pact, -
pressed.

323. Hardness.—N. hardness etc. *adj.*; rigidity,
renitence, inflexibility, temper, callosity, durity.
induration, petrifaction; lapid-ification, -escence;
vitri-, ossi-, corni-fication; crystallization.
stone, pebble, flint, marble, rock, fossil, crag,
crystal, quartz, granite, adamant; bone, cartilage;
heart of oak, block, board, deal board; iron, steel;
cast –, wrought- iron; nail; brick, concrete;
cement.

V. render -hard etc. *adj.*; harden, stiffen, indurate, petrify, temper, ossify, vitrify.
Adj. hard, rigid, stubborn, stiff, firm; starch, -
ed; stark, unbending, unlimber, unyielding; inflexible, tense; indurate, -d; gritty, proof.
adamant-ine, -ean; concrete, stony, rocky, lithic,
granitic, vitreous; crystalline; horny, corneous;
bony; oss-eous, -ific; cartilaginous; hard as a -stone
etc. *n.*; stiff as -buckram. – a poker.

324. Softness.—N. softness, pliableness etc.
adj.; flexibility; pli-ancy, -ability; sequacity,
malleability; flabbiness; duct-, tract-ility; extend-,
extensibility; plasticity; inelasticity; flaccidity,
laxity.
clay, wax, butter, dough, pudding; cushion,
pillow, feather-bed, pad, down, padding, wadding.
mollification; softening etc. *v.*
V. render -soft etc. *adj.*; soften, mollify, mellow,
relax, temper; mash, knead, squash, *massage*.
bend, yield, relent, relax, give.
Adj. soft, tender, supple; pli-ant, -able; flexible, -ile; lithe, -some; lissom, limber, plastic; ductile; tract-ile, -able; malleable, extensile,
sequacious, inelastic, mollient.
yielding etc. *v.*; flabby, limp, flimsy.
flaccid, flocculent, downy; spongy, edematous,
medullary, doughy, argillaceous, mellow.
soft as -butter, – down, – silk; yielding as wax;
tender as a chicken.

325. Elasticity.—N. elasticity, springiness,
spring, resilience, renitency, buoyancy.
india-rubber, caoutchouc, gutta-percha, whale-
bone, gum elastic.
V. be -elastic etc. *adj.*; spring back etc. (*recoil*)
227.
Adj. elastic, tensile, springy, ductile, resilient,
renitent, buoyant.

326. Inelasticity.—N. want of – , absence of-
elasticity etc. 325; inelasticity etc. (*softness*) 324.
Adj. inelastic etc. (*soft*) 324.

327. Tenacity.—N. tenacity, toughness,
strength; cohesion etc. 46; sequacity; stubbornness
etc. (*obstinacy*) 606; viscidity etc. 352.
leather; gristle, cartilage.
V. be -tenacious etc. *adj.*; resist fracture.
Adj. tenacious, tough, cohesive, adhesive, strong,
resisting, sequacious, stringy, gristly, cartilaginous,
leathery, coriaceous, tough as whit-leather; stubborn etc. (*obstinate*) 606.

328. Brittleness.—N. brittleness etc. *adj.*; frag-
, friab-, frangib-, fiss-ility; frailty; house of -cards,
– glass.
V. be -brittle etc. *adj.*; live in a glass house.
break, crack, snap, split, shiver, splinter, crumble, break short, burst, fly, give way; fall to pieces;
crumble -to, – into- dust.

Adj. breakable, brittle, frangible, fragile, frail, friable, delicate, gimcrack, shivery, fissile; splitting etc. *v.*; lacerable, splintery, crisp, crimp, short, brittle as glass.

329. Texture. [Structure.]—**N.** structure, organization, anatomy, frame, mold, fabric, construction; frame-work, carcass, architecture; stratification, cleavage.

substance, stuff, *compages, parenchyma*; constitution, staple, organism.

[Science of structures] organ-, oste-, my- splanchn-, neur-, angi-, aden-ology; angi-, aden-ography.

texture; inter-, con-texture; tissue, grain, web, surface; warp and -woof, – weft; tooth, nap etc. (*roughness*) 256; fineness –, coarseness- of grain. [Science of textures] histology.

Adj. structural, organic; atomic, -al.

text-ural, -ile; fine-, coarse-grained; fine, delicate, subtile, gossamery, filmy; coarse; homespun; linsey-woolsey.

330. Pulverulence. [State of powder.]—**N.** pulverulence; sandiness etc. *adj.*; efflorescence; friability.

powder, dust, sand, shingle; sawdust; grit; attrition; meal, bran, flour, *farina,* spore, sporule; crumb, seed, grain; particle etc. (*smallness*) 32; thermion; limature, filings, *débris, detritus*, scobs, magistery, fine powder; *flocculi.*

smoke; cloud of -dust, – sand, – smoke; puff –, volume -of smoke; sand – , dust- storm.

[Reduction to powder] pulverization, comminution, attenuation, granulation, disintegration, subaction, contusion, trituration, levigation, abrasion, detrition, multure; limation; filing etc. *v.*

[Instruments for pulverization] mill, millstone, grater, rasp, file, pestle and mortar, nutmeg grater, teeth, molar, grinder, chopper, grindstone, kern, quern, muller.

V. come to dust; be -disintegrated, – reduced to powder etc.

reduce –, grind- to powder; pulverize, comminute, granulate, triturate, levigate; scrape, file, abrade, rub down, grind, grate, rasp, pound, bray, bruise; con-tuse, -tund; beat, crush, cranch, craunch, crunch, muller, scranch, crumble, disintegrate; attenuate etc. 195.

Adj. powdery, pulverulent, granular, mealy, floury, farinaceous, branny, furfuraceous, flocculent, dusty, sandy, sabulous; aren-ose, -arious, - aceous; gritty; efflorescent, impalpable.

pulverizable; friable, crumbly, shivery; pulverized etc. *v.*; attrite; in pieces.

331. Friction.—**N.** friction, attrition; rubbing etc. *v.*; erasure; con-frication, -trition; affriction, abrasion, arrosion, limature, frication, rub; elbowgrease; rosin; *massage.*

V. rub, scratch, abrade, scrape, scrub, fray, rasp, graze, curry, scour, polish, rub out, erase, gnaw; file, grind etc. (*reduce to powder*) 330; *massage.*

set one's teeth on edge; rosin.

Adj. anatriptic, abrasive.

332. Lubrication. [Absence of friction. Prevention of friction.]—**N.** smoothness etc. 255; unctuousness etc. 355.

lubri-cation, -fication; anointment; oiling etc. *v.* synovia; lubricant, graphite, glycerine, oil etc. 356; saliva; lather.

V. lubri-cate, -citate; oil, grease, lather, soap; wax.

Adj. lubricated etc. *v.*

333. Fluidity.—**N.** fluidity, liquidity; liquidness etc. *adj.*; gaseity etc. 334; liquefaction etc. 334.

fluid, inelastic fluid; liquid, liquor; lymph, humor, juice, sap, serum, blood, serosity, gravy, rheum, ichor, sanies.

solu-bility, -bleness.

[Science of liquids] hydro-logy, -statics, dynamics, hydraulics, etc.

V. be -fluid etc. *adj.*; flow etc. (*water in motion*) 348; liquefy etc. 335.

Adj. liquid, fluid, serous, juicy, succulent, sappy; fluent etc. (*flowing*) 348.

liquefied etc. 335; uncongealed; soluble, hydrostatic etc. *n.*

334. Gaseity.—**N.** gaseity, gaseousness, vapourousness etc. *adj.*; flatulence, -lency; volatility, aeration, gasification.

elastic fluid, gas, air, vapor, ether, steam, fume, reek, *effluvium, flatus*; cloud etc. 353.

[Science of elastic fluids] pneumat-ics, -ostatics; aero-statics, -dynamics etc.

gas-, gaso-meter.

V. gassify, aerate, aerify; emit vapor etc. 336.

Adj. gaseous, aeriform, ethereal, aerial, airy, vaporous, volatile, evaporable; flatulent; aerostatic etc. *n.*

335. Liquefaction.—**N.** liquefaction; liquescen-ce, -cy, deliquescence; melting etc. (*heat*) 384; colliqu-ation, -efaction; thaw; de-, liquation; lixiviation, dissolution.

solution, apozem, lixivium, infusion, decoction, flux.

solvent, diluent, menstruum, alkahest, *aqua fortis.*

V. render -liquid etc 333; liquefy, run, deliquesce; melt etc. (*heat*) 384; solve; dissolve, resolve; liquate; hold in solution; leach, lixiviate.

Adj. lique-fied etc. *v.*, -scent, -fiable; deliquescent, soluble, colliquative; solvent.

336. Vaporization.—**N.** vapor-, volatilization; gasification; e-, vaporation; distillation, cohobation, sublimation, exhalation; volatility.

vaporizer, still, retort, spray, atomizer; fumigation, steaming.

V. render -gaseous etc. 334; vaporize, volatilize; distil, sublime; evaporate, exhale, smoke, transpire; emit vapor, fume, reek, steam, fumigate.

Adj. volatilized etc. *v.*; reeking etc. *v.*; volatile; evaporable, vaporizable.

337. Water.—N. water; serum, serosity; lymph; rheum; diluent.

dilution, maceration, lotion; washing etc. *v.*; im-, mersion; humectation, infiltration, spargefaction, affusion, irrigation, *douche*, balneation, bath.

deluge etc. (*water in motion*) 348; high water, flood-, spring-tide.

V. be -watery etc. *adj.*; reek.

add water, water, wet; moisten etc. 339; dilute, dip, immerse; merge; im-, sub-merge; plunge, souse, duck, drown; soak, steep, macerate, pickle, wash, sprinkle, sparge, lave, bathe, affuse, splash, swash, douse, slosh, drench; dabble, slop, slobber, irrigate, inundate, deluge; syringe, inject, gargle; infiltrate, percolate.

Adj. watery, aqueous, aquatic, lymphatic; balneal, diluent; drenching etc. *v.*; diluted etc. *v.*; weak; wet etc. (*moist*) 339.

Phr. the waters are out.

338. Air.—N. air etc. (*gas*) 334; common –, atmospheric- air; atmosphere, stratosphere, isothermal layer, troposphere, Heaviside layer.

open; – air; sky, welkin; blue, – sky; cloud etc. 353.

weather, climate, rise and fall of the barometer, isobar.

[Science of air] pneumatics, aero-logy, -scopy, -graphy; meteorology, climatology; eudio-, baro-, aero-meter; aneroid, baro-graph, -scope; weather-gauge, -glass, -cock.

exposure to the -air, – weather; ventilation; aero-station; -nautics; -naut etc. 265 and 269.

V. air, ventilate; fan etc. (*wind*) 349.

Adj. containing air, flatulent, effervescent; windy etc. 349.

atmospheric, airy; aeri-al, -form; pneumatic; meteorological; weather-wise.

Adv. in the open air, out of doors, *à la belle étoile, al fresco*; sub -Jove, – dio.

339. Moisture.—N. moisture; moistness etc. *adj.*; hum-idity, -ectation; madefaction, dew; *serein*; marsh etc. 345; Hygromet-ry, -er.

V. moisten, wet; humect, -ate; sponge, damp, dampen, bedew; imbue, imbrue, infiltrate, saturate; seethe, sop; soak, drench etc. (*water*) 337.

be -moist etc. *adj.*; not have a dry thread; perspire not (*exude*) 295:

Adj. moist, damp; watery etc. 337; undried, humid, wet, dank, muggy, dewy; roric; roscid; juicy.

wringing wet; wet -through, – to the skin; saturated etc. *v.*

swashy, soggy, dabbled; reeking, seething, dripping, soaking, soft, sodden, sloppy, muddy; swampy etc. (*marshy*) 345; irriguous.

340. Dryness.—N. dryness etc. *adj.*; siccity, aridity, drought, ebb-, neap-tide, low water.

drying, ex-, de-siccation; evaporation; dehydration; arefaction, dephlegmation, drainage.

drier, desiccator.

V. be -dry etc. *adj.*; render -dry etc. *adj.*; dry;

dry –, soak- up; sponge, swab, wipe; ex-, de-siccate, dehydrate, anhydrate; drain, parch.

be fine, hold up.

Adj. dry, anhydrous, arid, waterless; dried etc. *v.*; undamped; juice-, sap- less; sear; husky; rainless, without rain, fine; dry as -a bone, – dust, – a stick, – a mummy, – a biscuit; disiccated; dehydrated; water-proof, -tight.

341. Ocean.—N. sea, ocean, main, deep, brine, salt water, waters, waves, billows, high seas, offing, great waters, watery waste, 'vasty deep,' briny ocean, herring pond, steamer track, the seven seas; wave, tide etc. (*water in motion*) 348.

hydrograph-y, -er, oceanography; Neptune, Thetis, Triton, Naiad, Nereid; sea-nymph, Siren, mer-maid, -man; trident, dolphin.

Adj. oceanic; mar-ine, -itime; pleagic, -ian; sea-going, -worthy; hydrographic.

Adv. at –, on- sea; afloat, on the high seas.

342. Land.—N. land, earth, ground, dry land, *terra firma*.

continent, mainland, peninsula, delta; tongue –, neck- of land; isthmus; oasis; promontory etc. (*projection*) 250; highland etc. (*height*) 206.

coast, shore, scar, strand, beach; bank, lea; sea-board, -side, -shore, -bank, -coast, -beach; rock-, iron- bound coast; loom of the land; derelict; innings; *alluvium*, alluvion.

soil, glebe, clay, loam, marl, clodge, chalk, gravel, mold, subsoil, clod, clot; rock, crag, cliff.

acres; real estate etc. (*property*) 780; landsman, land-lubber, farmer.

geography etc. 318; agriculture etc. 371.

V. land, come to land; set foot on -the soil, – dry land; come –, go- ashore.

Adj. earthy; continental, midland; littoral, riparian, ripuarian; alluvial; terrene etc. (*world*) 318; landed, predial, territorial.

Adv. ashore; on -shore, – land.

343. Gulf. Lake.—N. land covered with water, gulf, gulph, bay, inlet, bight, estuary, arm of the sea, fiord, armlet; frith, firth, ostiary, mouth; lagune, lagoon; indraught; cove, creek; natural harbor; roads; strait, narrows; Euripus; sound, belt, gut, kyles.

lake, loch, lough, mere, tarn, plash, broad, pond, pool, lin, puddle, well, artesian well, tank, sump; standing –, dead –, sheet of- water; fish –, mill-pond; race; ditch, dike, dyke, dam; reservoir etc. (*store*) 636.

Adj. lacustrine; land locked.

344. Plain.—N. plain, table land, mesa, face of the country; open –, champaign-country; basin, downs, waste, weary waste, desert, tundra, wild, steppe, pampas, savanna, prairie, champaign, heath, common, wold, veld; moor, -land, uplands, fell; bush; *plateau* etc. (*level*) 213; *campagna*.

meadow, mead, haugh, pasturage, park, field.

lawn, green, plat, plot, grass-plat, greensward, sward, grass, turf, sod, heather; lea, ley, lay; grounds.

Adj. campestrian, champaign, alluvial.

345. Marsh.—N. marsh, swamp, morass, marish, moss, fen, bog, quagmire, slough, sump, wash; mud, squash, slush.

Adj. marsh, -y; swampy, boggy, plashy, poachy, quaggy, soft; muddy, sloppy, squashy, spongy; paludal; moor-ish, -y; fenny.

346. Island.—N. island, isle, islet, eyot, ait, holm, reef, atoll, breaker; archipelago; islander.

Adj. insular, sea-girt.

347. Stream. [Fluid in motion.]—**N.** stream etc. (*of water*) 348, (*of air*) 349.

V. flow etc. 348; blow etc. 349.

348. River. [Water in motion.]—**N.** running water.

jet, spirt, squirt, spout, splash, swash, rush, gush, *jet d'eau*; sluice, chute.

water-spout, -fall; fall, cascade, force, foss; lin, -n, ghyll, Niagara; cata-ract, -dupe, -clysm; *débâcle*, inundation, deluge.

rain, -fall; *serein*; shower, scud; downpour, cloud burst; driving –, pouring –, drenching-rain; hyeto-logy, -graphy; rainy season, monsoon; predominance of Aquarius, reign of St. Swithin; mizzle, drizzle, *stilliciduim*, plash; dropping etc. *v.*

stream, course, flux, flow, profluence; effluence etc. (*egress*) 295; defluxion; flowing etc. *v.*; current, tide, race.

spring; fount, -ain; rill, rivulet, gill, gullet, rillet; stream-, brook-let; runnel, sike, burn, beck, brook, stream, river; reach; tributary.

body of water, torrent, rapids, flush, flood, swash, spate; spring –, high –, full-tide; bore; eagre, *hugre*; fresh, -et; undertow, indraught, reflux, undercurrent, eddy, vortex, gurge, whirlpool, Maelstrom, regurgitation, overflow; confluence, corrivation.

wave, billow, surge, swell, ripple; roller, ground swell, surf, breaker, white horses; comber, beach-comber; rough –, heavy –. cross –, long –, short –, chopping –, choppy- sea, choppiness; tidal wave.

[Science of fluids in motion] Hydrodynamics; Hydraul-ics etc.; raingauge etc.

water-bearer, – carrier, Aquarius.

irrigation etc. (*water*) 337; pump; watering-pot, – cart; hydrant, standpipe, hose, sprinkler, drencher; fire engine, squirt, syringe.

V. flow, run; meander; gush, pour, spout, roll, jet, well, issue; drop, drip, dribble, plash, squirt, spurt, spirtle, trill, trickle, distil, percolate; stream, overflow, inundate, deluge, flow *over*, splash, swash; guggle, murmur, babble, bubble, purl, gurgle, sputter, regurgitate; ooze, flow out etc. (*egress*) 295.

rain, – hard, – in torrents, – cats and dogs, – pitchforks; come down in sheets; pour with rain, drizzle, mizzle, spit, sprinkle, set in.

flow –, fall –, open –, drain- into; discharge itself, desembogue.

[Cause a flow] pour; pour out etc. (*discharge*) 297; shower down; irrigate, drench etc. (*wet*) 337; spill, splash.

[Stop a flow] stanch; dam, -up etc. (*close*).261; obstruct etc. 706.

Adj. fluent; dif-, pro-, af-fluent; tidal; flowing etc. *v.*; meand-ering, -ry, -rous; fluvi-al, -atile; streamy, showery, rainy, drizzly, drizzling, pluvial, pluviose, stillicidous.

349. Wind. [Air in motion.]—**N.** wind, draught, *flatus*, *afflatus*, air; breath, – of air; puff, whiff, zephyr; blow, drift; *aura*; stream, current; under-current.

gust, blast, breeze, squall, gale, half a gale, storm, tempest, hurricane, whirlwind, tornado, samiel, cyclone, typhoon; simoon; harmattan, monsoon, trade wind, sirocco, *mistral*, *bise*, *föhn*, tramontane, levanter; capful of wind; fresh –, stiff- breeze; keen blast; blizzard.

windiness etc. *adj.*; ventosity; rough –, dirty –, ugly –, stress of- weather; dirty-, windy-, mackerel- sky; mare's tail; thick –, black –, white- squall.

anemography, aerodynamics; windgauge, anemometer, weather-cock, vane.

suf-, insuf-, per-, in-, af-flation; blowing, fanning etc. *v.*; ventilation.

sneezing etc. *v.*; sternutation; hic-cup, -cough; catching of the breath; breathing etc.

Eolus, Eurus, Boreas, Zephyr, cave of Eolus.

air-pump, lungs, bellows, blow-pipe, fan, blower; pulmotor, ventilator, punkah, aspirator, exhauster, ejector.

V. blow, waft; blow -hard, – great guns, – a hurricane etc. *n.*; whistle, roar, howl, ring in the shrouds; stream, issue.

respire, breathe, in-, ex-hale, puff; whif, -fle; gasp, wheeze; snuff, -le; sniff, -le; sneeze, cough, belch.

fan, ventilate; in-, per-flate; blow –, pump- up.

Adj. blowing etc. *v.*; windy, airy, aeolian, flatulent; breezy, gusty, squally; stormy, tempestuous, blustering; boisterous etc. (*violent*) 173. pulmon-ic, -ary.

350. Conduit. [Channel for the passage of water.]—**N.** conduit, channel, duct, watercourse, race; head –, tail- race; adit, aqueduct, canal, trough, flume, gutter, pantile; dike, canyon, ravine, gorge, hollow, main, gully, moat, ditch, drain, sewer, culvert, *cloaca*, sough. kennel, siphon, *piscina*; pipe etc. (*tube*) 260; funnel; tunnel etc. (*passage*) 627; water –, waste- pipe; emunctory, gully-hole, artery, aorta, vein, blood vessel; lymphatic; throat, alimentary canal, intestine; pore, spout, scupper; ad-, a-jutage; hose; gar-, gur-goyle; penstock, weir; flood-, water-gate; sluice, lock, valve; rose; waterworks.

Adj. vascular etc. (*with holes*) 260.

351. Air-pipe. [Channel for the passage of air.]—**N.** air-pipe, – shaft, – way, – passage, –

tube; shaft, flue, chimney, funnel, vent, blow-hole. nostril, nozzle, throat, weasand, *trachea*; *bronchus*, *-ia*; larynx, tonsils, wind-pipe, spiracle; ventiduct, -lator; louvre, Venetian blinds; blow-pipe etc. (*wind*) 349; pipe etc. (*tube*) 260.

352. Semiliquidity.—N. semiliquidity; stickiness etc. *adj.*; visc-idity, -osity; gumm-, glutin-, muc-osity; spiss-, crass-itude; lentor; adhesiveness etc. (*cohesion*) 46.

inspiss-, incrass-ation; thickening, coagulation.

jelly, aspic, mucilage, gelatin, isinglass; colloid, mucus, phlegm; pituite, lava; glair, starch, gluten, albumen, milk, cream, protein; syrup, treacle; gum, size, glue, paste; wax, bee's-wax; emulsoid, emulsion, soup; squash, mud, slush, slime, ooze; moisture etc. 339; marsh etc. 345.

V. inspiss-, incrass-ate; coagulate, gelatinize, gelatinify, gel, jell, emulsify, thicken; mash, squash, churn, beat up.

Adj. semi-fluid, -liquid; half-melted, -frozen; milky, muddy etc. *n.*; lact-eal, -ean, -eous, -escent, -iferous; emulsive, curdled, thick, succulent, uliginous.

gelat-, album-, mucilag-, glut-inous; gelatine, mastic, amylaceous, ropy, clammy, clotted; vis-cid, -cous; sticky, tacky; slab, -by; lentous, pituitous; mu-cid, -culent, -cous.

353. Bubble. [Mixture of air and water.] [Cloud.]—**N.** bubble; foam, froth, head, fume, spume, lather, suds, spray, surf, yeast, barm, spindrift.

cloud, vapor, fog, mist, haze, steam; scud, rack, *nimbus*; *cumulus*, woolpack, *cirrus, stratus*; *cirro-, cumulo-stratus*; *cirro-cumulus*; mackerel sky, mare's tail, dirty sky.

[Science of clouds] nephelognosy, nephology. effervescence, fermentation; bubbling etc. *v.*

nebula; cloudiness etc. (*opacity*) 426; nebulosity etc. (*dimness*) 422.

V. bubble, boil, foam, froth, spume, mantle, sparkle, guggle, gurgle; effervesce, ferment, fizzle; aerate; cloud, overcast, befog.

Adj. bubbling etc. *v.*; frothy, nappy, effervescent, sparkling, *mousseux*, up, fizzy, with a head on.

cloudy etc. *n.*; vaporous, nebulous, overcast; nubiferous, nephological; foggy, brumous.

354. Pulpiness.—N. pulpiness etc. *adj.*; pulp, paste, dough, sponge, curd, pap, rob, jam, pudding, mush, fool, poultice, grume.

Adj. pulpy etc. *n.*; pultaceous, grumous.

V. pulp, pulpify, mash.

355. Unctuousness.—N. unctuousness etc. *adj.*; unctuosity, lubricity; ointment etc. (*oil*) 356; anointment; lubrication etc. 332.

V. oil etc. (*lubricate*) 332.

Adj. unctuous, oily, oleaginous, adipose, sebaceous; fat, -ty; greasy; waxy, butyraceous, soapy, saponaceous, pinguid, lardaceous; slippery.

356. Oil.—N. oil, fat, butter, cream, grease, tallow, suet, lard, dripping, margarine, oleomargarine, exunge, blubber; glycerine, stearine, elaine, oleagine; soap; soft soap, wax, cerement; paraffin, spermaceti, adipocere; petroleum, mineral –, rock –, crystal- oil, kerosene, vegetable –; colza –, olive –, linseed –, cotton seed –, rape –, nut –, fusel- oil; animal –, neat's foot –, signal –, train- oil; ointment, unguent, liniment, salve, pomade, pomatum, brilliantine, spike –, nard.

356a. Resin.—N. resin, rosin, colophony; gum; lac, shellac, sealing-wax; amber, -gris; bitumen, pitch, tar, asphalt, -e, -um; varnish, copal, mastic, magilp, lacquer, japan.

V. varnish etc. (*overlay*) 223.

Adj. resinous, bituminous, pitchy, tarry.

357. Organization.—N. organized -world, – nature; living –, animated- nature; living beings; organic remains, organism; fossils; animal and vegetable kingdom, *fauna* and *flora*, biota.

prot-oplasm, -ein; albumen; structure etc. 329; organ-ization, -ism.

[Science of living beings] 'biology; natural history,* organic –, bio-chemistry, anatomy, physiology, embryology, morphology, evolution, Darwinism, Lamarkism, zoology etc. 368; botany etc. 369; naturalist, biologist etc.

Adj. organ-ic, -ized.

*The term *Natural History* is also used as relating to all the objects in Nature whether organic or inorganic, and including therefore *Mineralogy, Geology, Meteorology*, etc.

358. Inorganization.—N. mineral -world, – kingdom; unorganized –, inorganic –, brute –, inanimate- matter.

[Science of the mineral kingdom] mineralogy; geo-logy, -gnosy, -scopy; metall-urgy, -ography; lithology; orycto-logy, -graphy.

V. turn to dust, pulverize.

Adj. in-organic, -animate; unorganized; azoic; mineral.

359. Life.—N. life; vi-tality, -ability; animation; vital -spark, – flame, – force.

respiration, wind; breath -of life, – of one's nostrils; life-blood; Archeus; existence etc. 1.

vivification, vitalization; revivification etc. 163; Prometheus; life to come etc. (*destiny*) 152.

[Science of life] physiology, etiology, embryology, biology; animal economy.

nourishment, staff of life etc. (*food*) 298.

V. be -alive etc. *adj.*; live, breathe, respire; subsist etc. (*exist*) 1; walk the earth; strut and fret one's hour upon a stage; be spared.

see the light, be born, come into the world; fetch –, draw- -breath, – the breath of life; quicken; revive; come to, – life.

give birth to etc. (*produce*) 161; bring to life, put into life, vitalize; vivi-fy, -ficate; reanimate etc. (*restore*) 660; keep -alive, – body and soul together, – the wolf from the door; support life.

have nine lives like a cat.

Adj. living, alive; in -life, – the flesh, – the land of the living; on this side of the grave, above ground, breathing, quick, animated, viable; lively etc. (*active*) 682; alive and kicking; tenacious of life.

vital; vivi-fying; -fied etc. *v.*; Promethean. **Adv.** *vivendi causâ.*

360. Death.—N. death, dying etc. *v.*; de-cease, -mise; dissolution, departure, *obit*, release, rest, *quietus*, fall; loss, bereavement.

end etc. 67 –, cessation etc. 142 –, loss –, extinction –, ebb- of -life etc. 359.

death-warrant, -watch, -rattle, -bed; stroke –, agonies –, shades –, valley of the shadow –, jaws –, hand- of death; last -breath, – gasp, – agonies; dying -day, – breath, – agonies; swan song, *chant du cygne*; *rigor mortis*; Stygian shore; crossing the bar, the great adventure.

King -of terrors, – Death; Death, Angel of Death; mortality; doom etc. (*necessity*) 601.

euthanasia; happy release; break up of the system; natural -death, – decay; sudden –, violent- death; untimely end, watery grave; suffocation, *asphyxia*; heart failure; fatal disease etc. (*disease*) 655; death-blow etc. (*killing*) 361.

necrology, bills of mortality, obituary; death-song etc. (*lamentation*) 839.

V. die, expire, perish; meet one's -death, – end; pass away, be taken; yield –, resign- one's breath; resign one's -being, – life; end one's -days, – life, – earthly career; breathe one's last; cease to -live, – breathe; depart this life; be -no more etc. *adj.*; go –, drop –, pop -off; lose –, lay down –, relinquish –, surrender- one's life; drop –, sink- into the grave; close one's eyes; fall –, drop- dead, – down dead; break one's neck; give –, yield- up the ghost; be all over with one.

pay the debt to nature, shuffle off this mortal coil, take one's last sleep; go the way of all flesh; join the -greater number, – majority, – choir invisible, to life immortal awake; come –, turn- to dust; cross the Stygian ferry; go to -one's long account, – one's last home, – Davy Jones's locker, – the wall; receive one's death warrant, make one's will, die a natural death, go out like the snuff of a candle; come to an untimely end; catch one's death; go off the hooks, kick the bucket, pet out; go West; hop the twig, turn up one's toes; die a violent death etc. (*be killed*) 361; make the supreme sacrifice.

Adj. dead, lifeless; deceased, demised, departed, defunct; late, gone, no more; ex-, in-animate; out of the world, taken off, released; departed this life etc. *v.*; dead and gone; bereft of life, stone dead, dead as -a door nail, – a door post, – mutton, – a herring, – nits; launched into eternity, gathered to one's fathers, numbered with the dead, gone to a better land, behind the veil, beyond the grave, – mortal ken.

dying etc. *v.*; mori-bund, -ent, Acherontic; hippocratic; in -articulo, – extremis; in the -jaws, – agony- of death; going, – off; aux abois; on one's -last legs, – death bed; at -the point of death, – death's door, – the last gasp; near one's end, given over, booked, fey; with one foot in –, tottering on the brink of- the grave.

still-born; mortuary; deadly etc. (*killing*) 361. **Adv.** *post -obit, – mortem.* **Phr.** life -ebbs, – fails, – hangs by a thread; one's -days are numbered, – hour is come, – race is run, – doom is sealed; Death -knocks at the door, – stares one in the face; the breath is out of the body; the grave closes over one; *sic itur ad astra.*

361. Killing. [Destruction of life; violent death.]—**N.** killing etc. *v.*; homicide, manslaughter, murder, assassination, trucidation, occision; lynching, effusion of blood; blood, -shed; gore, slaughter, carnage, butchery; *battue*, gladiatorial combat.

massacre; *fussillade*, *noyade*, *pogrom*; thuggism; racketeering.

death blow, finishing stroke, *coup de grâce*, *quietus*; execution etc. (*capital punishment*) 972; judicial murder; martyrdom.

butcher, slayer, murderer, Cain, assassin, cut-throat, garrotter, *bravo*, thug, racketeer, gunman, mobster, gangster, Moloch, *matador*, *sabreur*; *guet-à-pens*; gallows, executioner etc. (*punishment*) 975; man-eater.

regicide, parricide, fratricide, infanticide, aborticide etc.

suicide, *felo de se*, *suttee*, *hara kiri*, Juggernaut; immolation, holocaust.

suffocation, strangulation, *garrotte*; hanging etc. *v.*

deadly weapon etc. (*arms*) 727; Aceldama; the potter's field, the field of blood.

fatal accident, violent death, casualty.

[Destruction of animals] slaughtering; phthiozoics;* sport, -'ing; the chase, venery; hunting, coursing, shooting, fishing; pig-sticking; sports-, hunts-, fisher-man; hunter, Nimrod; slaughterer, knacker, slaughter-house, shambles, *abattoir.*

V. kill, put to death, slay, shed blood; murder, assassinate, butcher, slaughter; victimize, immolate; massacre; take away –, deprive of- life; make away with, put an end to; despatch, dispatch; burke settle, do, – to death, – for.

strangle, garrotte, hang, lynch, throttle, choke, stifle, suffocate, stop the breath, smother, asphyxiate, drown.

saber; cut -down, – to pieces, – the throat; jugulate, stab, run through the body, bayonet; put to the -sword, – edge of the sword.

shoot, – dead; blow one's brains out; brain, knock on the head; stone, lapidate; give –, deal- a death blow; give a -quietus, – coup de grâce.

behead, bowstring etc. (*execute*) 972.

hunt, shoot etc. *n.*

cut off, nip in the bud, launch into eternity, send to one's last account, bump off, rub out, sign one's death warrant, strike the death knell of.

give no quarter, pour out blood like water; decimate; run amuck, wade knee-deep –, imbrue one's hands- in blood.

die a violent death, welter in one's blood; dash –, blow- out one's brains; commit suicide; kill – -make away with –, put an end to- oneself.

Adj. killing etc. *v.*; murd-, slaught-erous; sanguin-ary, -olent; blood-stained, -thirsty;

homicidal, red-handed; bloody, -minded; en-sanguined, gory, sanguineous.
mortal fatal, lethal; dead-, death-ly; mort-, leth-iferous; unhealthy etc. 657; internecine; suicidal.
sporting; piscator-ial, -y.
Adv. in at the death.
*Bentham, 'Chrestomathia.'

362. Corpse.—N. corpse, corse, carcass, bones, skeleton, dry-bones; defunct, relics, *relinquiae*, remains, mortal remains, dust, ashes, earth, clay; mummy; carrion; food for- worms, – fishes; tenement of clay, this mortal coil.
shade, ghost, *manes*, apparition etc. 980.
organic remains, fossils.
Adj. cadaverous, corpse-like; unburied etc. 363.

363. Interment.—N. interment, burial, inhumation, sepulture, entombment; in-, humation; obs-, ex-equies; funeral, wake, pyre, funeral pile; cremation.
funeral -rite, – solemnity; knell, passing bell, tolling; dirge etc. (*lamentation*) 839; cypress; *obit*, dead march, muffled drum; coroner, mortician, undertaker, mute, mourner, professional mourner, pallbearer; elegy; funeral -oration, – sermon; epitaph.
grave clothes, shroud; winding-sheet, cere-cloth; cerement.
coffin, shell, sarcophagus, urn, pall, bier, hearse, catafalque, cinerary urn.
grave, pit, sepulcher, tomb, vault, crypt, catacomb, mausoleum, *Golgotha*, house of death, narrow house, long home; cemetery, necropolis, boneyard; burial-place, -ground; grave-, church-yard; God's acre; mortuary, tope, cromlech, dolmen,'menhir, barrow, tumulus, cairn; ossuary; bone-, charnel-, dead-house; *Morgue*; lich-gate; crematorium.
sexton, grave-digger.
monument, memorial, cenotaph, shrine; grave-, head-, tomb-stone; *memento mori*; hatchment, stone, cross.
exhumation, disinterment; necropsy, autopsy, *post mortem* examination.
V. inter, bury, lay in – , consign to- the -grave, – tomb; en-, in-tomb; inhume; lay out, prepare for burial, embalm, mummify; conduct a funeral, hold services; toll the knell; put to bed with a shovel.
exhume, disinter, unearth.
Adj. buried etc. *v.*; burial; fune-real, -brial; mor-tuary, sepulchral, cinerary; elegiac; necroscopic.
Adv. *in memoriam*; *post-obit*, *-mortem*; beneath – , under- the sod.
Phr. *hic jacet*, *ci-git*, *requiescat in pace*.

364. Animality.—N. animal life; anima-tion, -lity, -lization; breath.
flesh, – and blood; corporeal nature; *physique*; strength etc. 159.
V. animalize, incorporate.
Adj. fleshly, incarnate, carnal, corporeal, human.

365. Vegetability.—N. vegetable life; vegeta-tion, -bility; herbage.

V. vegetate, germinate, sprout, shoot; cultivate.
Adj. vegetable etc. 367; rank, lush.

366. Animal.*—N. animal, – kingdom; *fauna*; brute creation.
beast, brute, creature, created being; creeping – , living- thing; dumb -animal, – creature.
flocks and herds, live stock; domestic – , wild-animals; game, *ferae naturae*; beasts of the fields, fowls of the air, denizens of the day.
vertebrate, bi-, quadru-ped, mammal, marsupial, bird, reptile, batrachian, amphibian, fish, crus-tacean, shell fish, articulate, mollusc, worm, insect, zoophyte; protozoon, animalcule etc. 193.
horse etc. (*beast of burden*) 271; cattle, kine, ox; bull, -ock; steer, stot; cow, milch-cow, calf, heifer, shorthorn; sheep; lamb, -kin; ewe – , pet-lamb; ewe, ram, tup; pig, swine, boar, hog, shoat, sow; tag, teg, wether.
dog, bitch, hound; pup, -py; whelp, cur, mutt, mongrel; house-, watch-, sheep-, shepherd's, sport-ing-, fancy-, lap-, toy-, bull-, badger-dog; mastiff; blood-, grey-, stag-, deer-, fox-, otter-, hound; harrier, beagle, spaniel, pointer, setter, retriever; Newfoundland; water -dog, – spaniel; pug, poodle; dachshund; Pinscher; turnspit; terrier; fox – , Skye- terrier; Dandie Dinmont; colley.
cat; puss,-y; kitten; grimalkin; gib-, tom-cat; mouser; fox, Reynard, vixen, stag, deer, hart, buck, doe, roe, antelope.
bird; poultry, fowl, cock, hen, chicken, chan-ticleer, partlet, rooster, dunghill cock, barn-door fowl; feathered -tribes, – songster; singing – , dicky- bird; canary; finch; auk, dodo, moa, roc, phoenix.
snake, serpent, viper, adder; newt, eft; asp, ver-min.
Adj. animal, zoological.
equine, bovine, vaccine, canine, feline; fishy; piscator-y, -ial; molluscous, vermicular.
• *Extended lists of names of specific varieties of animals, vegetables, etc., are beyond the scope of this work.*

367. Vegetable.*—N. vegetable, – kingdom; *flora*, verdure.
plant; tree, shrub, bush; creeper; vine; herb, -age; grass.
annual; per-, bi-, tri-ennial; exotic.
timber; primeval – , virgin- forest; wood, -lands; hurst; frith, holt, weald, park, chase, greenwood, brake, grove, copse, coppice, *bocage*, tope, clump of trees, thicket, spinet, spinney; under-, brush-wood; boscage, scrub; the oak and the ash and the bonny ivy tree.
bush, jungle, prairie; heath, -er; fern, bracken, furze, gorse, whin, broom; grass, turf, grassland, greensward, green, lawn, meadow; pas-ture, -turage; turbary; sedge, rush, weed; fungus, mushroom, toadstool; lichen, moss, conferva, mold; seaweed etc.; growth, crop.
foliage, leafage, branch, bough, ramage; spray etc. 51; leaf, frond, flag, petal, shoot, tendril.
flower, blossom, bud, bloom, bine; flowering plant; tree, sapling, pollard; timber-, fruit-tree; palm-, gum-tree; pulse, legume.
Adj. veget-able, -ous; herb-aceous, -al; botanic; sylvan, silvan; arbor- ary, -eous, -escent, -ical; den-

dritic, dendriform; wooœy, grassy; ver-dant, - durous; floral, mossy; lign-ous. -eous; wooden, leguminous; end-, ex-ogenous.
*Extended lists of names of specific varieties of animals, vegetables, etc., are beyond the scope of this work.

368. Zoology. [The science of animals.]—**N.** zoo-logy, -nomy. -graphy, -tomy; anatomy; comparative anatomy; animal –, comparative-physiology; morphology.
anthrop-, ornith-, ichthy-, herpet-, ophi-, malac-, helminth-, entom-, oryct-, paleont-ology; ichthyetc. -otomy; taxidermy.
zo- etc. -ologist.
Adj. zoological etc. *n.*

369. Botany. [The science of plants.]—**N.** botany; phyto-graphy, -logy, -tomy; vegetable physiology, herborization, dendr-, myc-, fung-, algology; flora, pomona; botanist etc.; botanic garden etc. (*garden*) 371; *hortus siccus, herbarium*, herbal.
herb-ist, -arist, -alist, -orist, -arian etc.
V. botanize, herborize.
Adj. botanical etc. *n.*

370. Cicuration. [The economy or management of animals.]—**N.** taming etc. *v.*; cicuration, zoohygiantics; domestication, -ity; *manège*; veterinary art; breeding, pisciculture, apiculture etc.
menagery, vivarium, zoological garden, zoo; bear-pit; aviary, apiary, hive; aquarium, fishery, fish hatchery; duck-, fish-pond; stud-farm; stock farm, dairy.
[Destruction of animals] phthisozoics etc. (*killing*) 361.
neat-, cow-, shep-herd, shepherdess; grazier; drover, cowboy, cowkeeper; trainer, breeder, groom, ostler etc. 746; veterinary surgeon, vet, horse doctor; farrier; keeper; game keeper.
cage etc. (*prison*) 752; hen-coop, bird-cage, cauf; sheep-fold etc. (*inclosure*) 232.
V. tame, domesticate, acclimatize, breed, tend, break in, train, corral, round up; cage, bridle etc. (*restrain*) 751; ride etc. 266.
drive, yoke, harness, hitch; groom, eurry-comb; milk; shear; hatch; incubate.
Adj. pastoral, bucolic; tame, domestic, domesticated, broken in, gentle, docile.

371. Agriculture. [The economy or management of plants.]—**N.** agriculture, cultivation, husbandry, farming; georgics, geoponics; tillage, tilth, agronomy, gardening, spade husbandry, vintage; hort-, arbor-, silv-, citr-, vit-, flor-iculture; intensive culture; landscape gardening; forestry, afforestation.
husbandman, horticulturist, citriculturist, gardener, florist; agricult-or, -urist; yeoman, farmer, cultivator, tiller of the soil, ploughman, sower, reaper; woodcutter, backwoodsman, forester; vine grower, vintager; Boer; Triptolemus.
field, meadow, garden; botanic –, winter –, or-namental –, flower –, kitchen –, truck –, market –, hop- garden; nursery; green-, hot-, glass-house; conservatory, cucumber frame, *cloche*, bed, border, seed-plot; grass-plat, lawn; park etc. (*pleasure ground*) 840; *partere*, shrubbery, plantation, avenue, *arboretum*, pinery, *pinetum*, orchard, vineyard, vinery; orangery; farm etc. (*abode*) 189.
V. cultivate; till, – the soil; farm, garden; sow, plant; reap, mow, cut; manure, dress the ground, dig, delve, dibble, hoe, plough, plow, harrow, rake, weed, lop and top, force, transplant, thin out, bed out, prune, graft.
Adj. agr-icultural, -airan, -estic.
arable; predial, rural, rustic, country, bucolic, Boeotian; horticultural.

372. Mankind.—N. man, -kind; human -race, – species, – nature; humanity, mortality, flesh, generation.
[Science of man] anthropo-logy, -graphy, sophy; ethno-logy, -graphy; humanitarianism.
human being; person, -age; individual, creature, fellow creature, mortal, body, somebody, one; such a –, someone; soul, living soul; earthling; party, head, hand; *dramatis personae*.
people, persons, folk, public, society, world; community, – at large; general public; nation, - ality; state, realm; common-weal, -wealth; republic, body politic; million etc. (*commonalty*) 876; population etc. (*inhabitant*) 188.
cosmopolite; lords of the creation; ourselves.
Adj. human, mortal, personal, individual, national, civic, public, cosmopolitan; anthropoid.

373. Man.—N. man, male, he; manhood etc. (*adolescence*) 131; . gentleman, sir, master; yeoman, wight, swain, fellow, guy, blade, *beau*, chap, gaffer, good man; husband etc. (*married man*) 903; Mr., mister, *monsieur, sahib, Herr, señor, signor*; boy etc. (*youth*) 129; Adonis.
[Male animal] cock, drake, gander, dog, boar, stag, hart, buck, horse, entire horse, stallion; gib-, tom-cat; he-, Billy-goat; ram, tup; bull, -ock; capon, ox, gelding; steer, stot.
Adj. male, he, masculine; manly, virile; unwomanly, -feminine.

374. Woman.—N. woman, she, female, petticoat, skirt, moll, broad.
feminality, feminity, muliebrity; womanhood etc. (*adolescence*) 131; feminism; gynecology, gyniatrics, gynics.
womankind; the -sex, – fair; fair –, softer- sex; weaker vessel; the distaff side.
dame, madam, *madame*, mistress, Mrs., lady, mem-sahib, *Frau, señora, signora, donna, belle*, matron, dowager, goody, gammer; good -woman, – wife; squaw; wife etc. (*marriage*) 903; matronage, -hood.
Venus, nymph, wench, *grisette*; little bit of fluff; girl etc. (*youth*) 129.
inamorata (love) etc. 897; courtesan etc. 962.
spinster, old maid, virgin, bachelor girl, new woman, amazon.

[Female animal] hen, slut, bitch, sow, doe, roe, mare; she-, Nanny-goat; ewe, cow; lioness, tigress; vixen.
gynecaeum, harem, *seraglio*, *zenana*, *purdah.*
Adj. female, she; feminine, womanly, ladylike, matronly, maidenly; womanish, effeminate, unmanly, gynecic.

375. Physical Sensibility.—N. sensibility; sensitiveness etc. *adj.*; physical sensibility, feeling, perceptivity, anaphylaxis, susceptibility, esthetics; moral sensibility etc. 882.
sensation, impression, effect; consciousness etc. (*knowledge*) 490.
external senses.
V. be -sensible etc. *adj.* -of; feel, perceive.
render, -sensible etc. *adj.*; excite, stir, sharpen, cultivate, tutor.
cause sensation, impress; excite -, produce- an impression.
Adj. sens-ible, -itive, -uous; esthetic, perceptive, sentient; conscious etc. (*aware*) 490; impressionable, responsive, alive to.
acute, sharp, keen, vivid, lively, impressive, thin-skinned.
Adv. to the quick.

376. Physical Insensibility.—N. insensibility, physical insensibility; obtuseness etc. *adj.*; palsy, paralysis, *anesthesia*, *analgesia*, *narcosis*, *hypnosis*, twilight sleep, stupor, coma, trance, catalepsy; sleep etc. (*inactivity*) 683; moral insensibility etc. 823; numbness etc. 381.
anesthetic agent, general -, local- anesthetic, opium, ether, chloroform, cocaine, novocaine, chloral; nitrous oxide, laughing gas; refrigeration.
V. be -insensible etc. *adj.*; have a -thick skin, - rhinoceros hide.
render -insensible etc. *adj.*; blunt, pall, obtund, benumb, deaden, paralyze; anesthetize, drug, dope; put under the influence of -chloroform etc. *n.*; hypnotize; stupefy, stun, narcotize.
Adj. insensible, unfeeling, senseless, comatose, dazed, impercipient, callous, thick-skinned, pachydermatous; hard, -ened; case-hardened; proof; obtuse, dull; anesthetic; paralytic, palsied, numb, dead.

377. Physical Pleasure.—N. pleasure; physical -, sensual -, sensuous- pleasure; bodily enjoyment, animal gratification, sensuality; hedonism, luxuriousness etc. *adj.*; dissipation, round of pleasure; titillation, *gusto*, creature comforts, comfort, ease; pillow etc. (*support*) 215; luxury, lap of luxury; purple and fine linen; bed of -down, - roses; velvet, clover; cup of Circe etc. (*intemperance*) 954.
treat; diversion, divertisement, entertainment; refreshment, regale; feast; *délice*; dainty etc. 394; *bonne bouche.*
source of pleasure etc. 829; happiness etc. (*mental enjoyment*) 827.
V. feel -, experience -, receive- pleasure; enjoy, relish; luxuriate -, revel -, riot -, bask -,

swim -, wallow- in; feast on; gloat -over, - on; smack the lips.
live -on the fat of the land, - in comfort etc. *adv.*; bask in the sunshine, *faire ses choux gras.*
give pleasure etc. 829.
Adj. enjoying etc. *v.*; luxurious, voluptuous, sensual, hedonistic, comfortable, cosy, snug, in comfort, at ease.
agreeable etc. 829; grateful, refreshing, comforting, cordial, genial; sensuous; palatable etc. 394; sweet etc. (*sugar*) 396; fragrant etc. 400; melodious etc. 413; lovely etc. (*beautiful*) 845.
Adv. in -comfort etc. *n.*; on -a bed of roses etc. *n.*; at one's ease.

378. Physical Pain.—N. pain; suffering, -ance; bodily - physical -pain, - suffering; mental suffering etc. 828; dolor, ache; aching etc. *v.*; smart; shoot, -ing; twinge, twitch, gripe, head-, ear-, toothache; *migraine*, neuralgia, neuritis, lumbago, gout, sciatica; hurt, cut; sore, -ness; discomfort, *malaise*; *tic douloureux.*
spasm, cramp; nightmare, *ephialtes*; crick, stitch, kink; thrill, convulsion, throe; throb etc. (*agitation*) 315; pang.
sharp -, piercing -, throbbing -, shooting - gnawing -, burning- pain; anguish, agony.
torment, torture; rack; cruci-ation, -fixion; martyrdom; martyr, toad under a harrow, vivisection.
V. feel -, experience -, suffer -, undergo- pain etc. *n.*; suffer, ache, smart, bleed; tingle, shoot; twinge, twitch, lancinate; writhe, wince, make a wry face; sit on -thorns, - pins and needles.
give -, inflict- pain; pain, hurt, chafe, sting, bite, gnaw, gripe, stab, grind; pinch, tweak; grate, gall, fret, prick, pierce, wring, convulse; torment, torture; rack, agonize; crucify; excruciate; break on the wheel, put to the rack; flag etc. (*punish*) 972; grate on the ear etc. (*harsh sound*) 410.
Adj. in -pain etc. *n.*; - a state of pain; pained etc. *v.*
painful; aching etc. *v.*; biting, poignant; sore, raw, tender, with exposed nerve.

379. Touch. [Sensation of pressure.] **—N.** touch; tact, -ion, -ility; feeling; palp-ation, -ability; manipulation; brush, tick, graze, contact etc. 199.
[Organ of touch] hand, finger, fore-finger, thumb, paw, feeler, *antenna.*
V. touch, feel, handle, finger, thumb, paw, fumble, grope, grabble; twiddle, tweedle; pass -, run-the fingers over, massage, rub, knead; palpate, stroke, manipulate, wield; throw out a feeler.
Adj. tact-ual, -ile; tangible, palpable; lambent.

380. Sensations of Touch.—N. itching etc. *v.*; titillation, formication, *aura.*
V. itch, tingle, creep, thrill, sting; prick, -le; tickle, titillate.
Adj. itching etc. *v.*

381. Numbness. [Insensibility to touch.] **—N.**

numbness etc. (*physical insensibility*) 376; pins and needles.
local anesthetic,cocaine novocaine etc.; morphia.
V. benumb etc. 376; freeze, dull, deaden.
Adj. numb; benumbed etc. *v.*; intangible, impalpable.

382. Heat.—N. heat, caloric; temperature, warmth, fervor, calidity; incal-, incand-, recal-, decal-escence; glow, flush, blush; fever, hectic.

phlogiston; fire, spark, scintillation, flash, flame, blaze; arc; bonfire; firework, pyrotechny; wild-fire; sheet of fire, lambent flame; devouring element; conflagration.

summer, dog-days, canicule; baking etc. 384 –, white –, tropical –, Afric –, Bengal –, summer –, blood- heat; heat wave, sirocco, simoon; broiling sun; isolation; warming etc. 384.

sun etc. (*luminary*) 423; fire worshipper etc. 991; furnace etc. 386.

geyser, hot spring, volcano.

: Science of heat. pyrology; thermology, -otics; thermometer etc. 389.

V. be -hot etc. *adj.*; glow, incandesce, flush, sweat, swelter, bask, smoke, reek, stew, simmer, seethe, boil, burn, singe, scorch, scald, grill, broil, blaze, flame; smoulder; parch, fume, pant.

heat etc. (*make hot*) 384; thaw, fuse, melt, give.

Adj. hot, heated, warm, mild, genial, tepid, lukewarm, unfrozen; therm-al, -ic; calorific; fervent, -id; ardent; aglow.

sunny, torrid, tropical, estival, canicular; close, sultry, stifling, stuffy, suffocating, oppressive; reeking etc. *v.*; baking etc. 384.

red –, white –, smoking –, bruning etc. *v.* –, piping- hot; like -a furnace, – an oven; hot as -fire, – pepper; hot enough to roast an ox.

fiery; incand-, incal-escent; candent, ebullient, glowing, smoking; on fire; blazing etc. *v.*; in - flames, – a blaze; alight, afire, ablaze; unquenched, -extinguished; smouldering; in a -heat, – glow, – fever, – perspiration, – sweat; sudorific; swelter-ing, -ed; blood-hot, -warm; warm as -a toast, – wool; recalescent, thermogenic, pyrotechnic, feverish, febrile, inflamed.

volcanic, plutonic, igneous; isother-mal, -mic, -al.

Phr. Not a breath of air.

383. Cold.—N. cold, -ness etc. *adj.*; frigidity, gelidity, algidity, inclemency, *fresco.*.

winter; depth of –, harg- winter; Siberia, Nova Zembla; Ant-, arctic, North –, .South- Pole.

ice; snow, – flake, – crystal – drift; sleet; hail, -stone; rime, frost; hoar –, white –, hard –, sharp- frost; icicle, thick-ribbed ice; fall of snow, snow storm, heavy fall, *avalanche*; ice-berg, -floe; floe, berg; *glacier*; *nevée, serac.*

[Sensation of cold] chilliness etc. *adj.*; chill shivering etc. *v.*; goose- skin, -flesh; *rigor*, horripilation, chattering of teeth; frostbite, chilblain.

V. be -cold etc. *adj.*; shiver, starve, quake, shake, tremble, shudder, didder, quiver; perish with cold; chill etc. (*render cold*) 385.

Adj. cold, cool; chill, -y; gelid, frigid, algid; fresh, keen, bleak, raw, inclement, bitter, biting,

niveous, cutting, nipping, piercing, pinching; claycold; starved etc. (*made cold*) 385; shivering etc. *v.*; aguish, *transi de froid*; frost- bitten, -bound, - nipped.

cold as -a stone, – marble, – lead, – iron, – a frog, – charity, – Christmas; cool as -a cucumber, – custard.

icy, glacial, frosty, freezing, wintry, brumal, hibernal, boreal, arctic, antarctic, polar, Siberian, hyemal; hyperbore-an, -al; ice-bound; frozen out.

un-warmed, -thawed, -heated; isocheimal, - chimenal.

Adv. coldly, bitterly etc. *adj.*; *à pierre fendre.*

384. Calefaction.—N. increase of temperature; heating etc. *v.*; cale-, tepe-, torre-faction; melting, fusion; liquefaction etc. 335; burning etc. *v.*; kindling, combustion; in-, ac-cension; con-, cremation; scorification, cauter-y, -ization; ustulation, calcination; in-, cineration; cupellation; carbonization.

ignition, inflammation, adustion, flagration; de-, con-flagration; empyrosis, incendiarism; arson; *auto da fé*; suttee.

boiling etc. *v.*; coction, ebullition, estuation, elixation, decoction.

furnace etc. 386; blanket, flannel, fur, muffler, wrap; wadding etc. (*lining*) 224; clothing etc. 225.

,match etc. (*fuel*) 388; incendiary, pryomaniac; *pétroleur, pétroleuse*; cauterant, caustic, lunar caustic, apozem, moxa.

sunstroke, *coup de soliel*; insolation, sunburn.

pottery, ceramics, crockery, porcelain, china; earthen-, stone-ware; pot, mug, *terra-cotta*, brick, clinker; cinder, ash, *scoriae*; embers, dress, slag, products of combustion, coke, carbon, charcoal.

inflamma-, combusti-bility.

[Transmission of heat] diathermancy, transcalency, diathermy.

V. heat, warm, chafe, stive, foment; make -hot etc. 382; sun oneself, bask in the sun.

fire; set -fire to, – on fire; kindle, enkindle, light, ignite, strike a light; apply the -match, – torch- to; re-kindle, -lume; fan –, add fuel to- the flame; poke –, stir –, blow- the fire; make a bonfire of; burn at the stake.

melt, thaw, fuse; liquefy etc. 335.

burn, inflame, roast, toast, fry, grill, singe, parch, bake, torrefy, scorch; brand, cauterize, sear, burn in; corrode, char, carbonize, calcine, incinerate; smelt, cupel, scorify; reduce to ashes; burn to a cinder; commit –, consign- to the flames.

boil, digest, stew, cook, seethe, scald; parboil, simmer; do to rags.

take –, catch- fire; blaze etc. (*flame*) 382.

Adj. heated etc. *v.*; molten, sodden; réchauffe; heating etc. *v.*

inflammable, burnable, inflammatory, combustible; diatherm-al, -anous; burnt etc. *v.*; volcanic.

386. Refrigeration.—N. refrigeration, infrigidation, reduction of temperature; cooling etc. *v.*; con-gelation, -glaciation; ice etc. 383; solidification etc. (*density*) 321; refrigerator etc. 387.

extincteur; fire, – engine, – extinguisher, – annihilator, – brigade, – man; sprinkler, hose, hydrant, standpipe.
incombusti-bility, -bleness etc. adj.
V. cool, fan, refrigerate, refresh, ice; congeal, freeze, glaciate; benumb, · starve, pinch, chill, petrify, chill to the marrow, nip, cut, pierce, bite, make one's teeth chatter; damp, slack; quench; put –, stamp- out; extinguish.
go –, burn- out.
Adj. cooled etc. v.; frozen out; cooling etc. v.; frigorific.
incombustible; un-, unin-flammable; fire-proof.

386. Furnace.—N. furnace, blast furnace, fire-box, stove, incinerator, destructor, crematorium, crematory, kiln, oven, oast-house; hot-, bake-, wash-house; laundry; conservatory; hearth, focus; athanor, hypocaust, reverberatory; volcano; forge, fiery furnace; tuyère, brasier, salamander, heater, warming-pan, foot-warmer, hot-water bottle; radiator; boiler, geyser, caldron, seething caldron, pot; urn, kettle; chafing-dish; retort, crucible, alembic, still; saggar.
fire-place, · -dog, -irons; hearth, ingle, grate, range, kitchener; kitchen range; oil-, gas-, electric, -cooker, -stove; fireless cooker; fire; galley; ca-, cam-boose; poker, tongs, shovel, hob, trivet; and-, grid-iron; frying-, stew-pan etc.
hot –, Turkish –, Russian –, vapor –, shower –, warm- bath; *calidarium, tepidarium, sudatorium*, sudatory; *hammam*.

387. Refrigerator.—N. refrigerator, -y; *frigidarium*; cold storage; refrigerating-plant, – machine; ice-house, -pail, -bag, -chest, -pack; cooler, damper; wine-cooler, freezing mixture.

388. Fuel.—N. fuel, firing, combustible, coal, wallsend, anthracite, bituminous coal, slack, culm, cannel coal, lignite, briquette, coke, carbon, char-coal; turf, peat, fire-wood, bobbing, faggot, log, yule log, ember, cinder etc. (*products of combustion*) 384; kindling wood, tinder, touch-wood; fumigator, sulphur, brimstone; incense; port-fire; fire-barrel, -ball, -brand.
fuel oil, gas, gasoline, electricity.
brand, torch, fuse; wick; spill, match, safety match, light, lucifer, congreve, vesuvian, vesta, fusee, locofoco; linstock; illuminant.
candle etc. (*luminary*) 423; oil etc. (*grease*) 356; petrol, gasoline, methylated –, spirit; gas, acetylene.
Adj. carbonaceous; combustible, inflammable.
V. stoke, fire, feed, add fuel to the flames.

389. Thermometer.—N. thermo-meter, -scope, -stat, -pile, differential thermometer; pyro-, calori-meter; radio micrometer etc.

390. Taste.—N. taste, flavor, gust, *gusto*, relish, savor; sapor, sapidity; twang, smack, smatch; after-taste, tang.
tasting; de-, gustation.
palate, tongue, tooth, stomach.
V. taste, savor, smatch, smack, flavor, twang; tickle the palate etc. (*savory*) 394; smack the lips.
Adj. sapid, saporific; gusta-ble, -tory; strong; flavored, spiced, savory; palatable etc. 394

391. Insipidity.—N. insipidity; tastlessness etc. *adj.*
V. be -tasteless etc. *adj.*
Adj. void of -taste etc. 390; insipid; jejune; taste-, gust-, savor-less; ingustible, mawkish, milk ·and water, weak, stale, flat, vapid, *fade*, wishy-washy, mild; untasted.

392. Pungency.—N. pungency, piquancy, poignancy, *haut-goût*, strong taste, twang, race, tang.
sharpness etc. *adj.*; acrimony, acridity; roughness etc. (*sour*) 397; unsavoriness etc. 395.
niter, saltpeter; mustard, cayenne, caviar; seasoning etc. (*condiment*) 393; brine.
dram, cordial, nip, pick-me-up, bracer, potion. nicotine, tobacco, snuff, quid; segar; cigar, -ette, gasper, fag; cheroot; weed; fragrant –, Indian-weed; pipe, clay pipe, churchwarden, brier, meer-schaum, hookah, hubble-bubble.
V. be -pungent etc. *adj.*; bite the tongue.
render -pungent etc. *adj.*; season, spice, salt, pepper, pickle, brine, devil, curry.
smoke, chew, take snuff.
Adj. pungent, strong; high-, full-flavored; high-tasted, -seasoned; gamy; sharp, stinging, rough, *piquant*, racy; biting, mordant; spicy; seasoned etc. *v.*; hot, – as pepper; peppery, vellicating, eschar otic, meracious; acrid, acrimonious, bitter; rough etc. (*sour*) 397; unsavory etc. 395.
salt, saline, brackish, briny; salt as -brine, – a herring, – Lot's wife.

393. Condiment.—N. condiment, flavoring, salt, mustard, pepper, cayenne, curry, seasoning, sauce, spice, cinnamon, chillies, relish, *sauce piquante*, caviare, pot-herbs, onion, garlic, pickle, chutney, nutmeg etc.
V. season etc. (*render pungent*) 392.

394. Savoriness.—N. savoriness etc. *adj.*; relish, zest.
tit-bit, dainty, delicacy, ambrosia, nectar, *bonne bouche*; game, turtle, venison.
V. taste good; be -savory etc. *adj.*; tickle the -palate, – appetite; flatter the palate.
render -palatable etc. *adj.*
relish, like, smack the lips.
Adj. savory, well-tasted, to one's taste, tasty, good, palatable, nice, dainty, delectable; tooth-ful, -some; gustful, appetizing, lickerish, delicate, delicious, exquisite, rich, luscious, ambrosial.
Adv. *per amusare la bocca.*
Phr. *cela se laisse manger.*

395. Unsavoriness.—N. unsavoriness etc. *adj.*; amaritude; acri-mony, -tude; roughness etc. (*sour*) 397; acerbity, austerity; gall and worm-wood, rue, quassia, aloes; sickener.

V. be -unpalatable etc. *adj.*; sicken, disgust, nauseate, pall, turn the stomach.

Adj. un-savory, -palatable, -sweet; ill-flavored, un-appetizing, -eatable, inedible; bitter, – as gall; acrid, acrimonious; rough.

offensive, repulsive, nasty; sickening etc. *v.*; nauseous; loath-, ful-some; unpleasant etc. 830.

396. Sweetness.—N. sweetness, dulcitude, saccharinity.

sugar, cane-, beet-sugar; saccharine, glucose, syrup, treacle, molasses, honey, manna; confection, -ary; sweets, grocery, conserve, preserve, *confiture*, jam, marmalade, julep; sugar-candy, .-plum; licorice, liquorice, plum, lollipop, *bon bon*, *jujube*, comfit, sweetmeat, caramel, toffee, butterscotch.

nectar; hydromel, mead, metheglin, honeysuckle, *liqueur*, sweet wine.

pastry, pie, tart, puff, pudding, cake.

dulc-ification, -oration.

V. be sweet etc. *adj.*

render -sweet etc. *adj.*; sugar, saccharize, sweeten; edulcorate; dulc-orate, -ify; candy; mull.

Adj. sweet, sugary; sacchar-ine, -iferous; dulcet, honied, candied, luscious, nectarious, melliferous; sweetened etc. *v.*

sweet as -a nut, – sugar, – honey.

397. Sourness.—N. sourness etc. *adj.*; acid, -ity; acetous fermentation; acerbity.

vinegar, verjuice, crab, alum.

V. be – , turn- -sour etc. *adj.*; set the teeth on edge.

render -sour etc. *adj.*; acid-ify, -ulate.

Adj. sour; acid, -ulous, -ulated; acerb; tart, crabbed; acet-ous, -ose; sour as vinegar, sourish, acescent, sub-acid; styptic, hard, rough; unripe, green.

398. Odor.—N. odor, smell, odorament, scent, effluvium; eman-, exhal-ation; fume, essence, trail, nidor, redolence.

sense of smell; scent; act of -smeiling etc. *v.*

V. have an -odor etc. *n.*; smell, – of, – strong of; exhale; give out a -smell etc. *n.*; scent.

smell, scent; snuff, – up; sniff, nose, inhale.

Adj. odor-ous, -iferous; smelling, strong-scented; redolent, graveolent, nidorous, pungent.

[Relating to the sense of smell] olfactory, quick-scented..

399. Inodorousness.—N. inodorousness; absence –, want- of smell.

V. be -inodorous etc. *adj.*; not smell.

deodorize.

Adj. inodor-ous, -ate; scentless; without –, wanting- smell etc. 398.

deodoriz-ed, -ing.

400. Fragrance.—N. fragrance, aroma, redolence, perfume, *bouquet*; sweet smell, aromatic perfume.

perfumery; incense; musk, frankincense; pastil, -le; myrrh, perfumes of Arabia, chypre; otto, ottar, attar; bergamot, balm, civet, *pot-pourri*, pulvil; nosegay, *boutonnière*; scent, -bag; *sachet*, scent-bottle, smelling bottle, *vinaigrette*; toilet water, *eau de Cologne*; thurible, censer, thurification.

perfumer; incense bearer.

V. be -fragrant etc. *adj.*; have a -perfume etc. *n.*; smell sweet, scent, perfume, thurify, embalm.

Adj. fragrant, aromatic, redolent, spicy; balmy, scented; sweet-smelling, -scented; perfum-ed, -atory; thuriferous; fragrant as a rose, muscadine, ambrosial.

401. Fetor.—N. fetor, fetidness; bad etc. *adj.*; -smell, – odor; stench, stink; mephitis, foul –, mal- odor; *empyreuma*; mustiness etc. *adj.*; rancidity; foulness etc. (*uncleanness*) 653.

stoat, polecat, skunk; asafetida; fungus, garlic; stink-pot, -bomb.

V. have a -bad smell etc. *n.*; smell; stink, – in the nostrils, – like a polecat; smell -strong etc. *adj.*; – offensively.

Adj. fetid; strong-smelling; high, bad, strong, fulsome, offensive, noisome, rank, rancid, reasty, tainted, musty, fusty, frouzy; olid, -ous; nidorous; smelling, stinking; putrid etc. 653; suffocating, mephitic; empyreumatic.

402. Sound.—N. sound, noise, strain; accent, twang, intonation, tone, tune; cadence; sonority, sonorousness etc. *adj.*; audibility; resonance etc. 408; voice etc. 580.

[Science of sound] acou-, acu-stics; catacoustics; cataphonics; phon-ics, -etics, -ology, -ography; diacoustics, -phonics.

telephone, phonograph etc. 418.

V. produce sound; sound, make a noise; give out –, emit- sound; phonetize, phonate; resound etc. 408.

Adj. sounding; soniferous; sonorific; resonant, audible, acoustic, auditory, distinct; stertorous; phonic, sonant; phonetic.

403. Silence.—N. silence; stillness etc. (*quiet*) 265; peace, hush, lull, rest; muteness etc. 581; solemn –, awful –, dead –, deathlike-silence.

V. be -silent etc. *adj.*; hold one's tongue etc. (*not speak*) 585.

render -silent etc. *adj.*; silence, still, hush; stifle, muffle, gag, stop; muzzle, put to silence etc. (*render mute*) 581.

Adj. silent; still, -y; calm, quiet; noise-, sound-, speech-less; hushed etc. *v.*; mute etc. 581; aphonic.

soft, solemn, awful, deathlike, silent as the grave; inaudible etc. (*faint*) 405.

Adv. silently etc. *adj.*; *sub silentio*; in perfect silence.

Int. hush! 'sh! silence! soft! whist! tush! chut! tut! *pax!* mum's the word! hold your tongue! shut up! be

silent! be quiet! stop that noise! hold your row! dry up! peace, be still!
Phr. one might hear a -feather, — pin- drop.

404. Loudness.—N. loudness, power; loud noise, din; clang, -or; clatter, noise, bombilation, roar, uproar, racket, static, grinders, hubbub, *fracas, charivari,* trumpet blast, blare, flourish of trumpets, fanfare, *tintamarre,* peal, swell, blast, alarum, boom; resonance etc. 408.
vociferation; pandemonium, hullaballoo etc. 411; lungs; Stentor; megaphone; siren.
artillery, cannon, gunfire, shellburst, bomb; thunder.
V. be -loud etc. *adj.*; peal, swell, clang, boom, thunder, fulminate, roar; resound etc. 408; speak up, shout etc. (*vociferate*) 411; bellow etc. (*cry as an animal*) 412; give tongue.
rend the -air, — skies; fill the air; din —, ring —, thunder- in the ear; pierce —, split —, rend-the-ears, — head; deafen, stun; *faire le diable à quatre*; make one's windows shake; awaken — startle- the echoes; make the welkin ring.
Adj. loud, sonorous; high-, big- sounding; blatant; deep, full, powerful, noisy, clangorous, multisonous, *fortisimo*; thundering, deafening etc. *v.*; trumpet-tongued; ear-splitting, -rending, - deafening; piercing; obstreperous, rackety, uproarious; enough to wake the -dead, — seven sleepers.
shrill etc. 410; clamorous etc. (*vociferous*) 411; stentor-ian, -ophonic.
Adv. loudly etc. *adj.*; aloud; at the top of one's voice, lustily, in full cry.
Phr. the air rings with.

405. Faintness.—N. faintness etc. *adj.*; faint sound, whisper, breath; under-tone, -breath; murmur, hum, rustle, buzz, purr; plash; sough, moan, sigh, susurration; tinkle; 'still small voice.'
hoarseness etc. *adj.*; raucity.
silencer, soft pedal, damper, mute, *sourdine.*
V. whisper, breathe, murmur, purl, hum, gurgle, ripple, babble, flow; tinkle; mutter etc. (*speak imperfectly*) 583.
steal on the ear; melt in —, float on- the air. muffle, mute, deaden, damp, stifle.
Adj. inaudible; scarcely —, just- audible; low, dull; stifled, muffled; hoarse, husky; gentle, soft, faint; floating; purling, flowing etc. *v.*; whispered etc. *v.*; liquid; soothing; dulcet etc. (*melodious*) 413.
Adv. in a whisper, with bated breath, *sotto voce,* between the teeth, aside; *pian-o, -issimo; à la sourdine; con sourdine;* out of earshot, inaudibly etc. *adj.*

406. Snap. [Sudden and violent sounds.]—**N.** snap etc. *v.*; rapping etc. *v.*; de-, crepitation; smack, clap, report; thud; burst, explosion, discharge, detonation, blow-out, back-fire, firing, salvo, volley, pistol-shot.
squib, cracker, gun, rifle, pop-gun.
V. rap, snap, tap, knock; click; clash; crack, -

le; crash; pop; slam, bang, clap, thump, plump; toot; back-fire, explode, burst on the ear.
Adj. rapping etc. *v.*
Int. crash! bang!

407. Roll. [Repeated and protracted sounds.]—**N.** roll etc. *v.*; drumming etc. *v.*; tattoo; ding-dong; tantara; rataplan; whirr; rat-a-tat; rub-a-dub; pit-a-pat; quaver, clutter, *charivari,* racket; cuckoo; repetition etc. 104; peal of bells, devil's tattoo; reverberation etc. 408.
drumfire, barrage.
machine gun.
V. roll, drum, rumble, rattle, clatter, rustle, roar, drone, patter, clack.
hum, trill, shake; chime, peal, toll; tick, beat.
drum —, din- in the ear.
Adj. rolling etc. *v.*; monotonous etc. (*repeated*), 104; like a bee in a bottle.

408. Resonance.—N. resonance; ring etc. *v.*; ringing etc. *v.*; tintinnabulation; reflection, reverberation, clangor.
low —, base —, bass —, flat —, grave —, deep —, pedal- note; bass; *basso, — profondo;* bari-. bary-tone; *contralto.*
V. re-sound, -verberate, -echo; ring, ding, sing, jingle, gingle, chink, clink; tink, -le; chime; gurgle etc. 405; plash, guggle, echo, ring in the ear.
Adj. resounding etc. *v.*; resonant, tinnient; tintinnabulary; deep-toned, -sounding, -mouthed; hollow, sepulchral; gruff etc. (*harsh*) 410.

408a. Non-resonance.—N. thud, thump, dead sound; non-resonance; muffled drums, cracked bell; silencer, damper; mute, *sourdine.*
V. sound dead; stop —, damp- the -sound, — reverberations; deaden, muffle.
Adj. non-resonant, dead, muted, muffled.

409. Sibilation. [Hissing sounds.]—**N.** sibilation; hiss etc. *v.*; sternutation; high note etc. 410.
goose, serpent, snake.
V. hiss, buzz, whiz, rustle; fizz, -le, sizzle, swish; wheeze, whistle, snuffle; squash; sneeze.
Adj. sibilant; hissing etc. *v.*; wheezy.

410. Stridor. [Harsh sounds.]—**N.** creak etc. *v.*; creaking etc. *v.*; discord etc. 414; stridor; harshness, roughness, sharpness etc. *adj.*; cacophony.
acute —, high- note; *soprano,* treble, tenor, *alto,* falsetto, *voce di testa;* shriek, cry etc. 411.
piccolo, fife, penny -whistle, — trumpet.
. **V.** creak, grate, jar, burr, pipe, twang, jangle, clank, clink; scream etc. (*cry*) 411; yelp etc. (*animal sound*) 412; buzz etc. (*hiss*) 409.
set the teeth on edge, *écorcher les oreilles;* pierce —, split- the -ears, — head; offend —, grate upon —, jar upon- the ear.
Adj. creaking etc. *v.*; strident, stridulous, harsh,

coarse, hoarse, horrisonous, raucous, metallic, rough, gruff, grum, sepulchral.

sharp, high, acute, shrill, high-pitched; trumpet-toned; piercing, ear-piercing; cracked; discordant etc. 414; cacophonous.

411. Cry.—N. cry etc. *v.*; voice etc. (*human*) 580; bark etc. (*animal*) 412.

vociferation, outcry, hullaballoo, chorus, clamor, hue and cry, plaint; lungs; stentor.

V. cry, roar, shout, bawl, brawl, halloo, halloa, hail, hoop, whoop, yell, bellow, howl, scream, screech, screak, shriek, shrill, squeak, squeal, squall, whine, whinny, pule, pipe, yaup.

cheer, hurrah; hoot; grumble, maon, groan.

snore, snort; grunt etc. (*animal sounds*) 412.

vociferate; raise –, lift up- the voice; call –, sing –, cry- out; exclaim; rend the air; thunder –, shout- at the -top of one's voice, – pitch of one's breath; *s'égosiller*; strain the -throat, – voice, – lungs; give a -cry etc.

Adj. crying etc. *v.*; clam-ant, -orous; vociferous; stentorian etc. (*loud*) 404; open-mouthed.

412. Ululation. [Animal sounds.]—N. cry etc. *v.*; crying etc. *v.*; ululation, latration, belling; reboation; call, note; bark, howl, yelp; twittering, woodnote; insect cry, fritinancy, drone; screech; cuckoo.

V. cry, ululate, howl, roar, bellow, blare, rebellow, bark, yelp; bay, – the moon; yap, growl, yarr, yawl, snarl, howl; grunt, -le; snort, squeak; neigh, bray; mew, mewl; purr, caterwaul, pule; bleat, low, moo; troat, croak, crow, screech, caw, coo, gobble, quack, cackle, gaggle, guggle; chuck, -le; cluck; clack; cheep, chirp, chirrup, twitter, sing, cuckoo; pout, wail, hum, buzz; hiss, blatter; hoot.

Adj. crying etc. *v.*; blatant, latrant; re-, mugient; deep-, full-mouthed.

Adv. in full cry.

413. Melody. Concord.—N. melody, rhythm, measure; rhyme etc. (*poetry*) 597.

pitch, *timbre*, intonation, tone, overtone.

scale, gamut; diapason; diatonic –, chromatic –, enharmonic- scale; key, clef, chords.

modulation, temperament, syncope, syncopation, preparation, suspension, resolution.

staff, stave, line, space, brace; bar, rest; *appogia- to*, -*tura*; acciaccatura, shake, *arpeggio*.

note, musical note, notes of a sclae; sharp, flat, natural; high note etc. (*shrillness*) 410; low note etc. 408; interval; semitone; second, third, fourth etc.; diatessaron.

breve, semibreve, minim, crotchet, quaver; semi-demisemi- quaver; sustained note, drone, burden.

tonic; key-, leading-, fundamental-, note; super-tonic, mediant, dominant; sub-mediant, -dominant, organ-, pedal-point; octave, tetrachord; major –, minor- -mode, – scale, – key; Doric mode, passage, phrase.

concord, harmony; unison, -ance; chime, homophony; euphon-y, -ism; tonality; consonance; concent; part.

orchestration; harmonization, – phrasing.

[Science of harmony] harmon-y, -ics; thorough-fundamental- bass; counterpoint; faburden.

piece of music etc. 415; composer, harmonist, contrapuntist.

V. be -harmonious etc. *adj.*; harmonize, chime, symphonize, transpose; put in tune, tune, accord, string; score, arrange, orchestrate.

Adj. harmoni-ous, -cal; in -concord etc. *n.*, – tune, – concert; unisonant, concentual, sym-phonizing, isotonic, homophonous, assonant, con-sonant.

measured, rhythmical, diatonic, chromatic, enharmonic.

melodious, musical; tuneful, tunable; sweet, dulcet, canorous; mell-ow, -ifluous; soft; clear, – as a bell; silvery; euphon-ious, -ic, -ical; sym-phonious; enchanting etc. (*pleasure-giving*) 829; fine-, full-, silver-toned.

Adv. harmoniously etc. *adj.*

414. Discord.—N. discord, -ance; dissonance, cacaphony, caterwauling; harshness etc. 410; con-secutive fifths.

[Confused sounds] Babel, pandemonium; Dutch –, cat's- concert; marrow-bones and cleavers.

V. be -discordant etc. *adj.* : jar etc. (*sound harshly*) 410.

Adj. discordant; dis-, ab-sonant; out of tune, tuneless; un-musical, -tunable; un-, im-melodious; un-, in-harmonious; sing-song; cacophonous; jarring, harsh etc. 410.

415. Music.—N. music, classical –, modern –, descriptive- music; concert, recital; strain, tune, air, *motif*; melody etc. 413; *aria, arietta*; piece of music, *sonata*; *rond-o*, -*eau*; *pastorale, cavatina*, roulade, *fantasia, toccata, concerto*, overture, symphony, symphonic poem, tone poem, prelude, voluntary, *intermezzo*, variations, *cadenza*; cadence; fugue, canon, serenade, *nocturne*, *not-turno*, rhapsody, romance, *aubade*, dithyramb; opera, operetta; oratorio; composition, movement, stave.

instrumental music; full-, orchestral- score; min-strelsy, tweedledum and tweedledee, band, or-chestra etc. 416; concerted piece, *potpourri*, medley, *capriccio*, incidental music; im-provisation; peal.

vocal music, vocalism; chaunt, chant; psalm, -ody; hymn; song etc. (*poem*) 597; canticle, can-zonet, *cantata, bravura, coloratura*; lay, ballad, ditty, carol, barcarolle, pastoral, recitative, *recitativo, solfeggio*, tonic sol-fa.

Lydian measures; slow -music, – movement; *adagio* etc. *adv.*; minuet; siren strains, soft music, lullaby; *berceuse*, cradle song, dump; dirge etc. (*lament*) 839; pibroch; martial music, march, funeral-, dead- march; dance 'music; waltz etc. (*dance*) 840; rag-time, syncopation, jazz.

solo, duet, *duo*, *trio*; quartet; quintet, sextet, sep-tet; part song, descant, glee, madrigal, catch, round, chorus, *chorale*; antiphon, -y; ac-companiment, second –, alto –, tenor –, bass-part; score, thorough bass; counterpoint.

composer etc. 413; musician etc. 416.

V. compose, perform etc. 416; attune.

Adj. musical; instrumental, orchestral, vocal, choral, lyric, operatic; harmonious etc. 413.

Adv. *adagio*; *largo, larghetto, andan-te, -tino*; *alla capella*; *maestoso, moderato*; *allegr-o, -etto*; *spiritoso, vivace, veloce*; *prest-o, -issimo*; *pian-o, -issimo, fort-e, -issimo, sforzando*; *con brio*; *capriccioso*; *scherz-o, -ando*; *legato, sostenuto, staccato, crescendo*, diminuendo, *rallentando, affettuoso, arioso*; *parlante, cantabile*; *obbligato*; *pizzacato, tremolo, vibrato*.

416. Musician. [Performance of Music.]—**N.** musician, *artiste, virtuoso*, performer, player, minstrel; bard etc. (*poet*) 597; instrumental-, organ-, accompan-, pian-, violin-, flaut-, harp-ist; harper, fiddler, fifer, trumpeter, piper, drummer; catgut scraper.

band, orchestra, waits.

vocal-, melod-ist; singer, warbler; songst-, chaunt-er, -ress; *diva, cantatrice*, coloratura, soprano, mezzo-soprano, alto, contralto, tenor, baritone, bass, *basso, -profundo*.

choir, quire, chorister; chorus, – singer; choral society, festival, *eisteddfod*.

nightingale, philomel, thrush; siren; Orpheus, Apollo, the Muses, Erato, Euterpe, Terpsichore; tuneful -nine, – quire.

composer etc. 413.

performance, virtuosity, execution, touch, expression, solmization.

V. play, pipe, strike – , tune-up, sweep the chords, tickle – , paw- the ivories, vamp, tweedle, fiddle; strike the lyre, beat the drum; blow – , sound – , wind- the horn; grind the organ; touch the -guitar etc. (*instruments*) 417; thrum, strum, twang, drum, beat – , keep- time, conduct.

execute, perform; accompany; sing – , play- a second; compose, write music, set to music, arrange, harmonize, orchestrate.

sing, chaunt, chant, hum, warble, carol, chirp, chirrup, lilt, purl, quaver, trill, shake, twitter, whistle; sol-fa; intone.

have -an ear for music, – a musical ear, – a correct ear, – absolute pitch.

Adj. playing etc. *v.*; musical, lyric.

Adv. *adagio, andante* etc. (*music*) 415.

417. Musical Instruments.—**N.** musical instruments; band; string-, brass-, drum and fife-, military-, bugle-, German-, dance-, jazz-band; orchestra, string quartet; orchestration, orchestrelle.

[Stringed instruments] mono-, poly-chord; harp, lyre, lute, archlute, thearbo; mandol-a, -in, -ine; guitar; *ukulele*; psaltery, zither; bandore, cither, -n; gittern, rebeck, *bandurria*, banjo, zither banjo, *balalaika, samisen*; plectrum.

viol, -in, Cremona, Stradivarius; fiddle; kit; *vielle, viola, – d'amore, – di gamba*, tenor, *violoncello*, cello; bass, bass-, bass-viol; double-bass, *contrabasso, violone*, hurdy-gurdy; strings, catgut; bow, fiddlestick.

piano, -forte; grand – , concert grand – , baby – , upright – , cottage- piano; pianino, pianette; harpsi-, clavi-, clari-, mani-chord; *clavier*, spinet, virginals; dulcimer, *cymbalo*; Eolian harp; piano-

organ, -player, electric piano, player-piano, pianola.

[Wind instruments] organ, church – , pipe – , American- organ; harmoni-um, -phon; accordion, seraphina, concertina; melodeon; barrel- organ; humming top.

flute, fife, piccolo, flageolet, penny-whistle, reed instrument; clari-net, -onet; bass -clarionet; saxophone; basset horn, *corno di bassetto*; musette, shawm, oboe, hautboy, *cor Anglais, corno Inglese*, bassoon, double bassoon, *contrafagotto*; bag-, union-pipes; ocarina, Pandean pipes; calliope; sirene, pipe, pitch-pipe; sourdet; whistle, catcall.

horn, bugle, key bugle, cornet, *cornet-à-pistons*, cornopean, clarion, trumpet, trombone, ophicleide, serpent; English-, French-, bugle-, sax-, flugel-, alt-, helicon-, post-horn; sackbut, euphonium, bombardon, tuba, bass tuba.

[Vibrating surfaces] cymbal, bell, gong, peal of bells, *carillon*; tambour, -ine; drum, tom-tom, tabor, -ret, -ourine, -orin; *sistrum, grand caisse*, bass-, big-, side-, kettle-drum; *tympani*; war drums; tymbal, timbrel, castanet, bones; musical-glasses, - stones; harmonica, sounding- board, rattle; gramophone, phonograph.

[Vibrating bars] reed, tuning-fork, triangle, Jew's harp, musical box, harmonicon, xylophone, marimba, *celeste*.

sord-ine, -et; *sourd-ine, -et;* mute.

418. Hearing. [Sense of sound.]—**N.** hearing etc. *v.*; audition, auscultation; eavesdropping; audibility; acoustics etc. 402.

acute – , nice – , delicate – , quick – , sharp – , correct – , musical -ear; ear for music.

ear, auricle, lug, acoustic organs, auditory apparatus, ear-drum, tympanum; ear-, speaking-trumpet, megaphone; telephone, radiophone, stethoscope, phonograph, gramophone, microphone.

hearer, auditor, listener, eavesdropper; audi-tory, -ence.

V. hear, overhear; hark, -en; list, -en; give – , lend – , bend- an ear; give attention; catch a sound, prick up one's ears; give -a hearing, – audience -to.

hang upon the lips of, be all ear, listen with both ears, monitor.

become audible; meet – , fall upon – , catch – , reach- the ear; be heard; ring in the ear etc. (*resound*) 408.

Adj. hearing etc. *v.*; auditory, auricular, aural, auditive, acoustic.

Adv. *arrectis auribus.*

Int. hark, – ye!.hear! list, -en! *Oyez!* attention! lend me your ears!

419. Deafness.—**N.** deafness, hardness of hearing, surdity; inaudibility.

V. be -deaf etc. *adj.*; have no ear; shut – , stop – . close- one's ears; turn a deaf ear to.

render deaf, stun, deafen.

Adj. deaf, earless, surd; hard – , dull- of hearing; deaf-mute, stunned, deafened; stone deaf; deaf as -a post, – an adder, – a beetle, – a trunk-maker.

inaudible etc. 405; out of hearing.

420. Light.—N. light, ray, beam, stream, gleam, streak, pencil; sun-, moon-beam; dawn, aurora.

day; sunshine; light of -day, – heaven; sun etc. (*luminary*) 432, day-, broad day-, noontide- light; noon-tide, -day; glare.

glow etc. *v.*; afterglow, sunset; glimmering etc. *v.*; glint; play –, flood- of light; phosphorescence, flush, halo, glory, nimbus, aureole, *aureola*.

spark, *scintilla*; *facula*; sparkling etc. *v.*; emication, scintillation, flash, blaze, coruscation, fulguration; flame etc. (*fire*) 382; lightning, *ignis fatuus*, etc. (*luminary*) 423, radio-activity.

luster, sheen, shimmer, reflection; gloss, tinsel, spangle, brightness, brilliancy, splendor; ef-, refulgence; ful-gor, -gidity; dazzlement, resplendence, transplendency; luminousness etc. *adj.*; luminosity; lucidity; renitency; radi-ance, -ation; irradiation, illumination, phosphorescence, luminescence.

radiation, radiant heat, infra-red rays, visible radiation, ultra-violet –, actinic- rays, actinism; X –, Roentgen- rays; phot-, heli-ography; optical instruments etc. 445.

[Science of light] optics; photo-logy, -metry; di-, cat-optrics.

[Distribution of light] *chiaroscuro*, *clairobscur*, clear obscure, breadth, light and shade, black and white, tonality, half-tone, mezzotint.

reflection, refraction, dispersion, double refraction, polarization, diffraction, interference.

illuminant etc. 423.

V. shine, glow, glitter, phosphoresce; glis-ter, -ten; twinkle, gleam; flare, – up; glare, beam, shimmer, glimmer, flicker, sparkle, scintillate, coruscate, flash, fulgurate, blaze; be -bright etc.

adj.; reflect light, daze, dazzle, bedazzle, raidate; shoot out beams.

clear up, brighten.

lighten, enlighten; light, – up; irradiate, shine upon; give –, hang out- a light; cast –, throw –, shed- -luster, – light- upon; illum-e, -ine, -inate; relume, strike a light; kindle etc. (*set fire to*) 384.

Adj. shining etc. *v.*; lumin-ous, -iferous; luc-id, -ent, -ulent, -ific, -iferous; illuminating, light, -some; bright, vivid, splendent, nitid, lustrous, shiny, brilliant, beamy, scintillant, radiant, lambent; sheen, -y; glossy, burnished, glassy, sunny, orient, meridian; noon-day, -tide; cloudless, clear; unclouded, -obscured.

garish; re-, tran-splendent; re-, effulgent; ful-gid, -gent; relucent, splendid, blazing, in a blaze, ablaze, rutilant, meteoric, phosphorescent; aglow.

bright as silver; light –, bright- as -day, – noonday, – the sun at noonday.

optical, actinic; photo-genic, -graphic; heliographic, radioactive.

421. Darkness.—N. darkness etc. *adj.*; blackness etc. (*dark color*) 431; obscurity, gloom, murk; dusk etc. (*dimness*) 422; tenebrosity, umbrageousness.

Cimmerian –, Stygian –, Egyptian- darkness; night; midnight; dead of –, witching- time of-night; blind man's holiday; darkness -visible; – that can be felt; palpable, obscure; Erebus.

shade, shadow, umbra, penumbra; sciagraphy; *silhouette*; radiograph, skiagraph.

obscuration; ad-, ob-umbration; obtenebration, offuscation, caligation; extinction; eclipse, total eclipse; gathering of the clouds.

shading; distribution of shade; *chiaroscuro* etc. (*light*) 420.

noctivagation, noctograph, noctuary.

obscurantist.

V. be -dark etc. *adj.*

darken, obscure, shade; dim; tone down, lower; over-cast, -shadow; cloud, eclipse; ob-, of-fuscate; ob-, ad-umbrate, cast into the shade; be-cloud, -dim, -darken; cast –, throw –, spread- a -shade, – shadow, – gloom.

extinguish; put –, blow –, snuff- out; doubt.

Adj. dark, -some, -ling; obscure, tenebrous, tenebrious, sombrous, pitch dark, pitchy, caliginous; black etc. (*in color*) 431.

sunless, lightless etc. (*see* sun, light etc. 423); somber, dusky; unilluminated etc. (*see* illuminate etc. 420); nocturnal; dingy, lurid, gloomy; murk-y, -some; shady, umbrageous; overcast etc. (*dim*) 422; cloudy etc. (*opaque*) 426; darkened etc. *v.*

dark as -pitch, – a pit, – Erebus.

benighted; noctivag-ant, -ous.

Adv. in the -dark, – shade; at night.

422. Dimness.—N. dimness etc. *adj.*; darkness etc. 421; paleness etc. (*light color*) 429.

half-light, *demi-jour*; partial -shadow, – eclipse; shadow of a shade; glimmer, -ing; nebulosity; cloud etc. 353; eclipse.

aurora, dusk, twilight, gloaming, blind man's holiday, shades of evening, crepuscule, cockshut time; break of day, daybreak, dawn.

moon-light, -beam, -shine; star- owl's-, candle-, rush-, fire-light; farthing candle.

V. be – ,grow- -dim etc. *adj.*; flicker, twinkle, glimmer; loom, lower; fade; darken; pale, – its ineffectual fire.

render -dim etc. *adj.*; dim, bedim, obscure.

Adj. dim, dull, lack-luster, dingy, darkish, shorn of its beams; dark 421.

faint, shadowed forth; glassy; bleary; cloudy; misty etc. (*opaque*) 426; muggy, fuliginous; nebulous, -ar; obnubilated, overcast, crepuscular, twilight, muddy, lurid, leaden, dun, dirty; looming etc. *v.*

pale etc. (*colorless*) 429; confused etc. (*invisible*) 447.

423. Luminary. [Source of light.]—**N.** luminary; light etc. 420; flame etc. (*fire*) 382.

spark, *scintilla*; phosphorescence.

sun, orb of day, day star, Phoebus, Apollo, Helios, Phaethon, Hyperion, Ra, Aurora; star, orb, meteor; falling –, shooting- star; blazing –, dog-star; Sirius, canicula, Aldebaran; morning star, Lucifer, Phosphor, evening star; Hesperus, Venus, planet, moon etc. 318; constellation, galaxy; northern light, *aurora -borealis*, – *australis*, zodiacal light; mock sun, parhelion.

lightning; fork –, sheet –, summer- lightning, St. Elmo's fire; phosphorus; *ignis fatuus*; Jack o' – Friar's- lantern; Will o' the wisp, fire-drake, *Fata Morgana*.

glow-worm, fire-fly.

radium, luminous paint.

[Artificial light] gas; gas –, lime –, electric –, head –, search –, spot –, flash –, flood –, foot-light; lamp, oil –, gas –, arc –, incandescent-lamp; flare; lant-ern, -horn; dark lantern, bull's eye, projector; candle, *bougie*, tallow –, wax- candle; dip, farthing dip; taper, rush-light; oil etc. (*grease*) 356; wick, burner; Argand, moderator, duplex; torch, *flambeau*, link, brand; cresset; gase-, chande-, electro-lier; candelabrum, *girandole*, sconce, luster, candle-stick.

firework, fizgig; pyrotechnics; Roman candle, Very light, star shell, parachute light; rocket, lighthouse etc. (*signal*) 550.

V. illuminate etc. (*light*) 420.

Adj. self-luminous, incandescent; phosphor-ic, -escent; luminescent, fluorescent, radiant etc. (*light*) 420.

424. Shade.—N. shade; awning etc. (*cover*) 223; parasol, sunshade, umbrella; screen, curtain, shutter, blind, gauze, veil, mantle, mask; cloud, mist, gathering of clouds; smoke screen; smoked glasses, colored spectacles; blinkers, blinders. umbrage, glade; shadow etc. 421.

V. draw a curtain; put up –, close- a shutter; veil etc. *v.*; cast a shadow etc. (*darken*) 421; screen, obstruct the view.

Adj. shady, umbrageous, bowery.

425. Transparency.—N. transparen-ce, -cy; translucen-ce, -cy; diaphaneity; luc-, pelluc-, limp-idity.

transparent medium, glass, crystal, mica; lymph, water.

v. be -transparent etc. *adj.*; transmit light.

Adj. transparent, pellucid, lucid, diaphanous; trans-, tra-lucent; limpid, clear, serene, crystalline, clear as crystal, vitreous, transpicuous, glassy, hyaline.

426. Opacity.—N. opacity; opaqueness etc. *adj.*

film; cloud etc. 353.

V. be -opaque etc. *adj.*; obstruct the passage of light; ob-, of-fuscate.

Adj. opaque, impervious to light.

dim etc. 422; turbid, thick, muddy, opacous, ob-fuscated, fuliginous, cloudy, hazy, foggy, vaporous, nubiferous, muggy.

smoky, fumid, murky, dirty.

427. Semitransparency.—N. semitrans-parency, opalescence, milkiness, pearliness; gauze, muslin; film; mist etc. (*cloud*) 353; frosted glass.

Adj. semi-transparent, -pellucid, -diaphanous, -opacous, -opaque; opal-escent, -ine; pearly, milky, frosted, mat; misty.

428. Color.—N. color, hue, tint, tinge, dye, complexion, shade, tincture, cast, livery, coloration, chromatism, glow, flush; tone, key.

pure –, positive –, primary –, primitive –, complementary- color; three primaries; spectrum, chromatic dispersion; broken –, secondary –, ter-tiary- color.

local color, coloring, keeping, tone, value, aerial perspective.

[Science of color] chromatics, spectrum analysis; prism, spectroscope.

pigment, coloring matter, paint, dye, wash, distemper, stain; medium; mordant; oil-paint etc. (*painting*) 556.

V. color, dye, tinge, stain, tint, tinct, tone, paint, wash, ingrain, grain, illuminate, emblazon, imbue; paint etc. (*fine art*) 556; daub.

Adj. colored etc. *v.*; colorific, tingent, tinctorial; chromatic, prismatic; full-, high-, deep-colored; doubly-dyed; polychromatic.

bright, vivid, intense, deep; fresh, unfaded; rich, gorgeous; highly colored; gay; variegated etc. 440.

gaudy, florid; garish; showy, flaunting, flashy; raw, crude; glaring, flaring; discordant, inhar-monious.

mellow, harmonious, pearly, sweet, delicate, ten-der, refined.

429. Achromatism. [Absence of color.]—**N.** achromatism; dis-coloration; pall-or, -idity; paleness etc. *adj.*; etoilation; neutral tint, monochrome, black-and-white.

V. lose -color etc. 428; fade, fly, go; become -colorless etc. *adj.*; turn pale, pale, whiten.

deprive of color, decolorize, bleach, tarnish, achromatize, blanch, etiolate, wash out, tone down.

Adj. uncolored etc. (*see* color etc. 428); colorless, achromatic, hueless, pale, pallid; pale-, tallow-faced; faint, dull, cold, muddy, leaden, dun, wan, sallow, dead, dingy, ashy, ashen, ghastly, cadaverous, glassy, lack-luster; discolored etc. *v.* light-colored, fair, *blond*; white etc. 430.

pale as -death, – ashes, – a witch, – a ghost, – a corpse.

430. Whiteness.—N. whiteness etc. *adj.*; argent.

albification, albescence, albinism, etiolation.

snow, paper, chalk, milk, lily, ivory, silver, alabaster; white lead, chinese –, flake –, ivory –, zinc- white, white-wash, -ning, whiting.

V. be -white etc. *adj.*

render -white etc. *adj.*; whiten- bleach, blanch, etiolate, whitewash, silver, frost.

Adj. white; milky, milk-, snow-white; snowy, niveous, candid, chalky; hoar, -y; frosted, silvery; argent, -ine; canescent.

whitish, creamy, pearly, ivory, fair, *blond*, ash-blond, platinum blond; blanched etc. *v.*; high in tone, light.

white as -a sheet, – driven snow, – a lily, – silver; like -ivory etc. *n.*

431. Blackness.—N. blackness etc. *adj.*; darkness etc. (*want of light*) 421; swarthness, lividity, dark color, tone, color; *chiaroscuro* etc. 420.

nigrification, infuscation, denigration.

jet, ink, ebony, coal, pitch, soot, smudge, charcoal, sloe, raven, crow; black.

[Pigments] lamp –, ivory –, blue-black; writing –, printing –,. printer's –, Indian- ink.

V. be -black etc. *adj.*

render -black etc. *adj.*; blacken, infuscate, denigrate; blot, -ch; smutch; smirch; darken etc. 421.

Adj. black, sable, swarthy, somber, dark, inky, ebon, atramentous, jetty; coal-, jet-black; fuliginous, pitchy, sooty, swart, dusky, dingy, murky, low-toned, low in tone; of the deepest dye.

black as -jet etc. *n.*, – my hat, – a shoe, – a tinker's pot, – November, – thunder, – midnight; nocturnal etc. (*dark*) 421; nigrescent; gray etc. 432; obscure etc. 421.

Adv. in mourning.

432. Gray.—N. gray etc. *adj.*; neutral tint, silver, pepper and salt, *chiaroscuro, grisaille,* grayness.

[Pigments] Payne's gray; black etc. 431.

Adj. gray, grey; steel –, iron- gray, dun, drab, dingy, leaden, livid, somber, sad, pearly; silver, -y, -ed; ash-en, -y; ciner-eous, -itious; grizzl-y, -ed; dove-, slate-, stone-, mouse-, ash-colored; mole; cool.

433. Brown.—N. brown etc. *adj.*

[Pigments] bister, ocher, sepia, Vandyke brown.

Adj. brown, adust, bay, dapple, auburn, chestnut, nutbrown, cinnamon, hazel, fawn, puce, *écru,* russet, tawny, fuscous, chocolate, maroon, foxy, tan, brunette, whitey-brown; snuff-, liver-colored; brown as -a berry, – mahogany; reddish brown; copper-, rust- colored; henna, bronze, khaki; russet, roan, sorrel.

sub-burnt; tanned etc. *v.*

V. render -brown etc. *adj.*; tan, embrown, bronze.

434. Redness.—N. red, scarlet, vermilion, cardinal, Post Office, red, carmine, crimson, pink, lake, *cerise,* cherry red, maroon, carnation, *couleur de rose. rose du Barry*; magenta, damask; flesh -color, – tint; color; fresh –, high- color; warmth; gules.

ruby, garnet, carbuncle; rose; rust, iron-mold.

[Dyes and pigments] cinnabar, cochineal; fuchsine; ruddle, madder, redlead; light –, Venetian- red; red ink, annotto.

redness etc. *adj.*; rub-escence, -icundity, -ification; erubescence, blush.

V. be –, become- -red etc. *adj.*; blush, flush, color up, mantle, redden.

render- red etc. *adj.*; redden, rouge; rub-ify, -ricate; incarnadine; ruddle.

Adj. red etc. *n.*; -dish; rufous, ruddy, florid, incarnadine, sanguine, bloody, gory; ros-y, -eate; blowz-y, -ed; brunt; rubi-cund, -form; lurid, stammel, blood-red; russet, murrey, carroty, sorrel, lateritious.

rose-, ruby-, cherry-, claret-, wine-, plum-,

flame-, flesh-, peach-, salmon-, brick-, brickdust-colored, reddish brown etc. 433.

red as -fire, – blood, – scarlet, – a turkeycock, – a lobster; warm, hot; foxy.

435. Greenness.—N. green etc. *adj.*; blue and yellow; vert.

emerald, verd antique, verdigris, malachite, beryl, aquamarine, reseda.

[Pigments] *terre verte,* verditer, bice, chlorophyl.

greenness, verdure, verdancy; viridity, -escence.

Adj. green, verdant; glaucous, olive; porraceous; green as grass.

emerald –, pea –, grass –, apple –, sea –, olive –, bottle –, leaf- green.

greenish; vir-ent, -escent.

436. Yellowness.—N. yellow etc. *adj.*; or.

[Pigments] gamboge; cadmium –, chrome –, Indian –, lemon- yellow; orpiment, yellow ocher, Claude tint, aureolin.

crocus, saffron, topaz, gold.

jaundice; London fog; yellowness etc. *adj.*

Adj. yellow, aureate, gold, golden, gilt, gilded, flavous, citrine, fallow; fulv-ous, -id; sallow, luteous, fawny, creamy, sandy; xanth-ic, -ous; jaundiced.

gold-, citron-, saffron-, lemon-, sulphur-, amber-, straw-; primrose-, cream-colored; flazen, yellowish, buff.

yellow as a -quince, – guinea, – crow's foot.

437. Purple.—N. purple etc. *adj.*; blue and red, bishop's purple; aniline dyes, gridelin, amethyst; purpure.

livid-ness, -ity.

V. empurple.

Adj. purple, violet, plum-colored, lavender, lilac, puce, *mauve*; livid.

438. Blueness.—N. blue etc. *adj.*; garter-blue; watchet.

[Pigments] ultramarine, smalt, cobalt, cyanogen; Prussian –, syenite- blue; bice, indigo, woad.

lapis lazuli, sapphire, turquoise.

blue-, bluish-ness; bloom

Adj. blue, azure, cerulean; sky-blue, -colored, -dyed; navy-blue, aquamarine, electric blue, royal blue, cyanic; bluish; atmospheric, retiring; cold.

439. Orange.—N. orange, red and yellow; gold; or; flame etc. color, *adj.*

[Pigments] ochre, Mars orange, cadmium.

V. gild, warm.

Adj. orange; ocherous; orange-, gold-, flame-, copper-, brass-, apricot-colored; warm, hot, glowing.

440. Variegation.—N. variegation; di-, tri-chromism; iridescence, irisation, play of colors, polychrome, maculation, spottiness, striae.

spectrum, rainbow, iris, tulip, peacock, chameleon, butterfly, tortoiseshell; mackerel, – sky; zebra, leopard, mother-of-pearl, nacre, opal, marble, batik.

check, plaid, tartan, patchwork; mar-, parquetry; mosiac, *tesserae*, tesselation, chess-board, checkers, chequers; harlequin; Joseph's coat; tricolor; patches, bands, stripes, spots etc of color.

V. be -variegated etc. *adj.*; variegate, stripe, streak, checker, chequer; be-, speckle, fleck; be-, sprinkle; stipple, maculate, dot, bespot; tattoo, inlay, tesselate, damascene; embroider, braid, quilt.

Adj. variegated etc. *v.*; divers-, parti-colored; di-, poly-chromatic; bi-, tri-, versi-color; of all -the colors of the rainbow, – manner of colors; kaleidoscopic.

iridescent; opal-ine, -escent; prismatic, nacreous, pearly, shot, *gorge de pigeon, chatoyant*, irisated.

pied, piebald, skewbald; motley; mottled, marbled; pepper and salt, paned, dappled, clouded, cymophanous.

mosiac, tesselated, chequered, plaid; tortoiseshell etc. *n.*

spott-ed, -y; punctuated, powdered; speckled etc. *v.*; freckled, fleabitten, studded; fleck-ed, -ered; striated, barred, veined; brind-ed, -led; tabby; watered; grizzled; listed; embroidered etc. *v.*; daedal.

441. Vision.—N. vision, sight, optics, eye-sight.

view, look, espial, glance, ken, *coup d'oeil*; glimpse, peep, glint; gaze, stare, leer; perlustration, contemplation; conspect-ion, -uity; regard, survey; in-, intro-spection; *reconnaissance*, speculation, watch, espionage, *espionnage*, autopsy; ocular - inspection, – demonstration; sight-seeing.

macrography, micrography.

point of view; view-, stand- point; gazebo, loophole, *belvedere*, watchtower.

field of view; theater, amphitheater, arena, vista, horizon; commanding –, bird's eye –, panoramic- view; periscope.

visual organ, organ of vision; eye; naked –, unassisted- eye; eye-ball, retina, pupil, iris, cornea, white; optics, orbs; saucer –, goggle –, gooseberry-eyes.

short sight etc. 443; clear –, sharp –, quick –, eagle –, piercing-, –, penetrating- -sight, – glance, – eye; perspicacity, discernment; catopsis.

eagle, hawk; cat, lynx; Argus.

evil eye; basilisk, cockatrice.

spectacles, telescope etc. 445.

V. see, behold, discern, perceive, have in sight, descry, sight, make out, discover, distinguish, recognize, spy, espy, ken; get –, have –, catch- a - sight, – glimpse- of; command of view of; witness, contemplate, speculate; cast –, set- the eyes on; be a -spectator etc. 444- of; look on etc. (*be present*) 186; see sights etc. (*curiosity*) 445; see at a glance etc. (*intelligence*) 498.

look, view, eye; lift up the eyes, open one's eye; look -at, – on, – upon, – over, – about one, – round; survey, scan, inspect; run the eye -over, – through; reconnoiter, glance -round, – on, – over; turn –, bend- one's looks upon; direct the

eyes to, turn the eyes on, cast a glance, make eyes at.

observe etc. (*attend to*) 457; watch etc. (*care*) 459; see with one's own eyes; watch for etc. (*expect*) 507; peek, peep, peer, pry, take a peep; play at bo-peep.

look -full in the face, – hard at, – intently; strain one's eyes; fix –, rivet- the eyes upon; stare, gaze; pore over, gloat -over, – on; leer, ogle, glare; goggle; cock the eye, squint, gloat, look askance; give the glad eye.

Adj. seeing etc. *v.*; visual, ocular, -al; ophthalmic.

far-, clear-sighted etc. *h.*; eagle-, hawk-, lynx-, keen-, Argus-eyed.

visible etc. 446.

Adv. visibly etc. 446; in sight of, with one's eyes open.

at -sight, – first sight, – a glance, – the first blush; *primâ facie*.

Int. look! etc. (*attention*) 457.

Phr. the scales falling from one's eyes.

442. Blindness.—N. blindness, anopsia, cecity, excecation, *amaurosis*, cataract, ablepsy, prestriction; dim-sightedness etc. 443.

V. be -blind etc. *adj.*; not see; lose sight of; have the eyes bandaged; grope in the dark.

not look; close –, shut –, turn away –, avert-the eyes; look another way; wink etc. (*limited vision*) 443; shut the eyes –, be blind- to; wink –, blink- at.

render -blind etc. *adj.*; blind, -fold; hoodwink, dazzle; put one's eyes out; throw dust into one's eyes; *jeter de la poudre aux yeux*; screen from sight etc. (*hide*) 528.

Adj. blind; eye-, sight-, vision-less; dark; stone-, sand-, stark-blind; undiscerning; dim-sighted etc. 443.

blind as -a bat, *– a buzzard, – a beetle, – a mole, – an owl; wall-eyed.

blinded etc. *v.*

Adv. blind-ly, -fold; darkly.

443. Dim-sightedness. [Imperfect vision.] [Fallacies of vision.]—**N.** dim –, dull –, half –, short –, near –, long –, double –, astigmatic –, failing- sight; dim etc -sightedness; snow blindness; purblindness, lippitude; my-, presby-opia; confusion of vision; astigmatism; nystagmus; color-blindness, dichromism, chromato-pseudo-blepsis, Daltonism; nyctalopy; *strabismus*, strabism, squint, cast in the eye, swivel eye, goggle eyes; obliquity of vision.

winking etc. *v.*; nictitation; blinkard, albino.

dizziness, swimming, scotomy; cataract; ophthalmia.

[Limitation of vision] eye shade, blinker, blinder; screen etc. (*hider*) 530.

[Fallacies of vision] *deceptio visûs*; refraction, distortion, illustion, false light, *anamorphosis*, virtual image, *spectrum, mirage*, looming, phasma; phant-asm, -asma, -om; vision; specter, apparition, ghost; *ignis fatuus* etc. (*luminary*) 423; specter of the Brocken; magic mirror; magic lantern etc. (*show*) 448; mirror, lens etc. (*instrument*) 445.

V. be -dim-sighted etc. .; see double; have a - mote in the eye, – mist before the eyes, – film over the eyes; see through a -prism, – glass darkly; wink, blink, nictitate; squint; look ask-ant, -ance; screw up the eyes, glare, glower.

dazzle, glare, blur, swim, loom.

Adj. dim-sighted etc. *n.*; my-, presby-opic; astigmatic; moon-, mope-, blear-, goggle-, gooseberry-, one-eyed; blind of one eye, monoculous; half-, pur-, color-blind; dichromatic.

blind as a bat etc. (*blind*) 442; winking etc. *v.*

444. Spectator.—N. spectator, beholder, observer, inspector, viewer, looker-on, onlooker, witness, eye-witness, bystander, passer by; sight-seer.

spy, scout; sentinel etc. (*warning*) 668.

v. witness, behold etc. (*see*) 441; look on etc. (*be present*) 186.

445. Optical Instruments.—N. optical instruments; lens, meniscus, magnifier, reading –, burning- glass; micro-, mega-, teino-scope; spectacles, glasses, barnacles, goggles, giglamps, eyeglass, *pince-nez*, monocle; periscopic lens; telescope, glass, lorgnette, binocular; spy-, opera-, field-glass, periscope, range finder.

mirror, reflector, speculum; looking-, pier-, cheval-, hand-glass.

prism; camera, *camera-lucida, -obscura*; projector, stereopticon, magic lantern etc. (*show*) 448; chro-, thau-matrope; stereo-, pseudo-, poly-, kaleido-scope.

photo-, opto-, erio-, actino-, luci-, radio-, spectro-meter; polari-, polemo-, spectro-scope, diffraction grating.

optics, optician, optometry, optometrist; microscop-y, -ist; photometry, photography; photographer.

446. Visibility.—N. visibility, perceptibility; conspicuousness, distinctness etc. *adj.*; conspicuity; appearance etc. 448; exposure; manifestation etc. 525; ocular-proof, – evidence, – demonstration; field of view etc. (*vision*) 441.

V. be – , become- -visible etc. *adj.*; appear, emerge, open to the view; meet – , catch- the eye; present – , show – , manifest – , produce – , discover – , reveal – , expose – , betray- itself; stand -forth, – out; show; arise; peep – , peer – , crop- out; start – ; spring – , show – , turn – ; crop- up; glimmer, glitter, glow, loom; glare; burst forth, scintillate; burst upon the -view, – sight; heave in sight; come -in sight, – into view, – out, – forth, – forward; see the light of day; break through the clouds; make its appearance, show its face, materialize, appear to one's eyes, come upon the stage, enter; float before the eyes, speak for itself. etc. (*manifest*) 525; attract the attention etc. 457; reappear; live in a glass house.

expose to view etc. 525.

Adj. visible, perceptible, perceivable, discernible, apparent; in -view, – full view, – sight; exposed to view, *en évidence*; unclouded.

obvious etc. (*manifest*) 525; plain, clear,

distinct, definite; well-defined, -marked; in focus; recognizable, palpable, autoptical; glaring, staring, conspicuous; stereoscopic; in -bold, – strong, – high- relief.

periscopic, panoramic.

before – , under- one's eyes; before one, *à vue d'oeil*, in one's eye, *oculis subjecta fidelibus.*

Adv. visibly etc. *adj.*; in sight of; before one's eyes etc. *adj.*; *veluti in speculum.*

447. Invisibility.—N. invisibility, nonappearance, imperceptibility; indistinctness etc. *adj.*; mystery, delitescence.

concealment etc. 528; latency etc. 526.

V. be -invisible etc. *adj.*; be hidden etc. (*hide*) 528; lurk etc. (*lie hidden*) 526; escape notice.

render -invisible etc. *adj.*; conceal etc. 528; put out of sight.

not see etc. (*be blind*) 442; lose sight of.

Adj. invisible, imperceptible; un-, in-discernible; un-, non-apparent; out of – , not in- sight; *à perte de vue*; behind- the -scenes, – curtain; view-, sightless; in-, un-conspicuous; unseen etc. (*see* see etc. 441); covert etc. (*latent*) 526; eclipsed, under an eclipse.

dim etc. (*faint*) 422; mysterious, dark, obscure, confused; indistin-ct, -guishable; shadowy, indefinite, unde/ined; ill-defined, -marked; blurred, fuzZy, out of focus; misty etc. (*opaque*) 426; veiled etc. (*concealed*) 528; delitescent.

448. Appearance.—N. appearance, phenomenon, sight, spectacle, show, premonstration, scene, species, view, *coup d'oeil*; look-out, out-look, prospect, vista, perspective, bird's-eye view, scenery, landscape, picture, *tableau*; display, exposure, *mise en scène*; scenery, *décor*; rising of the curtain.

phant-asm, -om etc. (*fallacy of vision*) 443.

pageant, *spectacle*; peep-, raree-, gallanty-show; *ombres chinoises*; projector, optical – , magic-lantern, phantasmagoria, dissolving views; cinema, -tograph; bio-scope, -graph; moving pictures, movies, film, screen etc.; pan-, di-, cosm-, georama; *coup – , jeu- de théâtre*; pageantry etc. (*ostentation*) 882; insignia etc. (*indication*) 550.

aspect, phase, *phasis*, seeming; shape etc. (*form*) 240; guise, look, complexion, color, image, mien, air, cast, carriage, port, demeanor; presence, expression, first blush, face of the thing; point of view, light.

lineament, feature, trait, lines; out-line, -side; contour, *silhouette*, face, countenance, physiognomy, visage, phiz, mug, cast of countenance, profile, *tournure*, cut of one's jib, metoposcopy; outside etc. 220.

V. appear; be – , become- visible etc. 446; seem, look, show; present – , wear – , carry – , have – , bear – , exhibit – , take – , take on – , assume- the -appearance, – semblance- of; look like; cut a figure, figure; present to the view; show etc. (*make manifest*) 525.

Adj. apparent, seeming, ostensible; on view.

Adv. apparently; to all -seeming, – appearance; ostensibly, seemingly, as it seems, on the face of it, *primā facie*; at the first blush, at first sight; in the eyes of; to the eye.

449. Disappearance.—N. disappearance, evanescence, eclipse, occultation.　•
departure etc. 293; exit, vanishing point; dissolving views.
V. disappear, vanish, dissolve, fade, melt away, pass, go, avaunt; be -gone etc. *adj.*; leave -no trace, – 'not a rack behind;' go off the stage etc. (*depart*) 293; suffer –, undergo- an eclipse; be lost to –, retire from- -sight, – view.
lose sight of.
efface etc. 552.
Adj. disappearing etc. *v.*; evanescent; missing, lost; lost to -sight, – view; gone; *spurlos versenki.*
Int. vanish! disappear! avaunt! etc. (*ejection*) 297.

450. Intellect.—N. intellect, mind, understanding, reason, thinking principle; rationality; cogitative –, cognitive –, intellectual- faculties; faculties, senses, consciousness, observation, percipience, apperception, mentality, intelligence, intellection, intuition, association of ideas, instinct, flair, conception, judgment, wits, parts, capacity, intellectuality, reasoning power, brains, genius; wit etc. 498; ability etc. (*skill*) 698; wisdom etc. 498.
soul, spirit, ghost, inner man, heart, breast, bosom, *penetralia mentis, divina particula aurae,* heart's core; ego, psyche, pneuma, subconsciousness, subconscious, subliminal self; dual personality.
organ –, seat- of thought; *sensorium,* sensory, brain, gray matter; head, -piece; pate, noddle, skull, scull, *pericranium, cerebrum, cranium,* brain-pan, -box; sconce, upper story.
[Science of mind] metaphysics; psychics, psycho-logy, -metry, -genesis, -analysis, -physics, psychi-atry, -cal research, thought reading etc. 992; ideology; mental –, moral- philosophy; philosophy of the mind; pneumat-, phren-ology; no –, cranio-logy, -scopy.
ideal-ity, -ism; transcendental-, spiritual-ism; immateriality etc. 317.
metaphysician, psychologist etc.
V. note, notice, mark; take -notice, – cognizance- of; be -aware, – conscious- of; realize; appreciate; ruminate etc. (*think*) 451; fancy etc. (*imagine*) 515; conceive, reason, understand.
Adj. [Relating to intellect] intellectual, mental, rational, subjective, metaphysical, nooscopic, spiritual; ghostly; psych-ical, -ological; cerebral. immaterial etc. 317; endowed with reason.
Adv. *in petto.*

450a. Absence or want **of Intellect.—N.** absence –, want- of -intellect etc. 450; imbecility etc. 499; brutality; brute -instinct, – force.
Adj. unendowed with reason.

451. Thought.—N. thought; exercitation –, exercise- of the intellect; reflection, cogitation, consideration, meditation, study, lucubration, speculation, deliberation, pondering; head-, brain-work; cerebration; mentation, deep reflection; close study, application etc. (*attention*) 457.

abstract thought, abstraction, contemplation, musing; brown study etc. (*inattention*) 458; reverie, Platonism; depth of thought, workings of the mind, thoughts, inmost thoughts; self-counsel, communing, -consultation.
association –, succession –, flow –, train –, current- of -thought, – ideas.
after –, mature- thought; reconsideration, second thoughts; retrospection etc. (*memory*) 505; excogitation; examination etc. (*inquiry*) 461; invention etc. (*imagination*) 515.
thoughtfulness etc. *adj.*
V. think, reflect, reason, cogitate, excogitate, consider, deliberate; bestow -thought, – consideration- upon; speculate, contemplate, meditate, ponder, muse, dream, ruminate; brood –, conover; animadvert, study; bend–, apply- the mind etc. (*attend*) 457; digest, discuss, hammer at, weigh, perpend; realize, appreciate; fancy etc. (*imagine*) 515; trow.
take into consideration; take counsel etc. (*be advised*) 695; commune with –, bethink- oneself; collect one's thoughts; revolve –, turn over –, run over- in the mind; chew the cud –, sleep- upon; take counsel of –, advise with- one's pillow.
rack –, ransack –, crack –, beat –, cudgel- one's brains; set one's -brain, – wits- to work.
harbor –, entertain –, cherish –, nurture- an idea etc. 453; take into one's head; bear in mind; reconsider.
occur; present –, suggest- itself; come –, get-into one's head; strike one, flit across the view, come uppermost, run in one's head; enter –, pass in –, cross –, flash on –, flash across –, float in –, fasten itself on –, be uppermost in –, occupy- the mind; have in one's mind.
make an impression; sink –, penetrate- into the mind; engross the thoughts.
Adj. thinking etc. *v.*; thoughtful, pensive, meditative, reflective, cogitative, museful, wistful, contemplative, speculative, deliberative, studious, sedate, introspective, Platonic, philosophical.
lost –, engrossed –, rapt –, absorbed- in thought etc. (*inattentive*) 458; deep musing etc. (*intent*) 457.
in the mind, under consideration, in contemplation.
Adv. all things considered; taking everything into account.
Phr. the mind being on the stretch; the -mind, – head- -turning, – running- upon.

452. Incogitancy. [Absence or want of thought.]—**N.** incogitancy, vacancy, inunderstanding; inanity, fatuity etc. 499; thoughtlessness etc. (*inattention*) 458.
V. not -think of, 451; not think of; dismiss from the -mind, – thoughts- etc. 451.
indulge in reverie etc. (*be inattentive*) 458.
put away thought; unbend –, relax –, divert- the mind.
Adj. vacant, unintellectual, unideal, unoccupied, unthinking, inconsiderate, thoughtless; absent etc. (*inattentive*) 458; diverted; irrational etc. 499; narrow-minded etc. 481.
un-thought of, -dreamt of, -considered; off one's mind; incogitable, not to be thought of, inconceivable.

453. Idea. [Object of thought.]—**N.** idea, notion, conception, thought, apprehension, impression, perception, image, sentiment, reflection, observation, consideration; abstract idea, principle; archetype.

view etc. (*opinion*) 484; theory etc. 514; conceit, fancy; phantasy etc. (*imagination*) 515.

point of view etc. (*aspect*) 448; field of view.

454. Topic. [Subject of thought.]—**N.** subject of –, material for- thought; food for the mind, mental *pabulum.*

subject, -matter; matter, theme, topic, what it is about, *thesis*, text, business, affair, matter in hand, argument; motion, resolution; head, chapter; case, point; proposition, theorem; field of inquiry; moot point, problem, etc. (*question*) 461.

V. float –, pass- in the mind etc. 451.

Adj. thought of; uppermost in the mind; *in petto.*

Adv. under -discussion, – consideration, – advisement; in -question, – the mind; on -foot, – the carpet, – the *tapis*; before the house, relative to etc. 9.

455. Curiosity. [The desire of knowledge.]—**N.** interest, thirst for knowledge; curi-osity, -ousness; inquiring mind; inquisitiveness.

sight-seer, quidnunc, newsmonger, Paul Pry, peeping Tom, eavesdropper; gossip etc. (*news*) 532; questioner, *enfant terrible.*

V. be -curious etc. *adj.*; take an interest in, stare, gape; prick up the ears, see sights, lionize; pry, speer; dig up.

Adj. curious, inquisitive, burning with curiosity, overcurious, nosey; inquiring etc. 461; prying; inquisitorial; agape etc. (*expectant*) 507; attentive etc. 457.

Phr. what's the matter? what next?

456. Incuriosity. [Absence of curiosity.]—**N.** incuriosity; incuriousness etc. *adj.*; *insouciance* etc. 866; indifference, apathy.

V. be -incurious etc. *adj.*; have no -curiosity etc. 455; take no interest in etc. 823; mind one's own business.

Adj. incurious, uninquisitive, uninterested, indifferent, bored; impassive etc. 823.

457. Attention.—N. attention; mindfulness etc. *adj.*; intent-ness, -iveness; thought etc. 451; adverten-ce, -cy observ-ance, -ation; consideration, reflection, perpension; heed; particularity; notice, regard etc. *v.*; circumspection etc. (*care*) 459; study, scrutiny, once-over; in-, intro-spection; revision, -al.

active –, diligent –, exclusive –, minute –, close –, intense –, deep –, profound –, abstract –, labored –, deliberate- -thought, – attention, – application, – study.

minuteness, attention to detail etc. 459. absorption of mind etc. (*abstraction*) 458. indication, calling attention to etc. *v.*

V. be -attentive etc. *adj.*; attend, advert to, observe, look, see, view, remark, notice, regard, take notice, mark; give –, pay- -attention, – heedto; listen in, incline –, lend- an ear to; trouble one's head about; give a thought –, animadvert- to; occupy oneself with; contemplate etc. (*think of*) 451; look -at, – to, – after, – into, – over; see to; turn –, bend –, apply –, direct –, give- the -mind, – eye, – attention- to; have -an eye to, – in one's eye; bear in mind; take into -account, – consideration; keep in -sight, – view; have regard to, heed, mind, take cognizance of, be engaged in, entertain, recognize; make –, take- note of; note.

examine cursorily; glance -at, – upon, – over; cast –, pass- the eyes over; run over, turn over the leaves, dip into, perstringe; skim etc. (*neglect*) 460; take a cursory view of.

examine, – closely, – intently; scan, scrutinize, consider; give –, bend- one's mind to; overhaul, revise, pore over; inspect, review, pass under review; take stock of; fix –, rivet –, focus –, devote- the - eye, – mind, – thoughts, – attention on *or* to; hear –, think- out; mind one's business.

revert –, hark back- to; watch etc. (*expect*) 507. (*take care of*) 459; hearken –, listen- to; prick up the ears; have –, keep- the eyes open; come to the point.

meet with attention; fall under one's -notice, – observation; be -under consideration etc. (*topic*) 454.

catch –, strike- the eye; attract notice; catch –, awaken –, wake –, invite –, solicit –, attract –, claim –, excite –, engage –, occupy –, strike –, arrest –, fix –, engross –, absorb –, rivet-the-attention, – mind, – thoughts; be -present to, – uppermost in- the mind.

bring under one's notice; point -out, – to, – at, – the finger at; lay the finger on, indigitate, indicate; direct –, call- attention to; show; put a mark etc. (*sign*) 550- upon; call soldiers to 'attention;' bring forward etc. (*make manifest*) 525.

Adj. attentive, mindful, heedful, observant, regardful; alive –, awake- to, alert; observing etc. *v.*; taken up –, occupied- with; engaged –, engrossed –, interested –, wrapped- in; absorbed, rapt; breathless; pre-occupied etc. (*inattentive*) 458; watchful etc. (*careful*) 459; intent on, openeyed, breathless, undistracted, upon the stretch; on the watch etc. (*expectant*) 507.

steadfast.

Int. see! look, – here, – out, – alive, – you, – to it! mark! lo! behold! soho! hark, – ye! mind ! halloo! observe! lo and behold!- attention! *nota bene*;N.B.; *,†; I'd have you to know; notice! take notice! O yes! *Oyez!*

Phr. this is –, these are- to give notice.

458. Inattention.—N. in-attention, - consideration; inconsiderateness etc. *adj.*; oversight; inadverten-ce, -cy; non-observance, disregard.

supineness etc. (*inactivity*) 683; *étourderie*; want of thought; heedlessness etc. (*neglect*) 460; *insouciance* etc. (*indifference*) 866.

abstraction; absence —, absorption- of mind; preoccupation, distraction, reverie, brown study, deep musing, fit of abstraction, woolgathering.

V. be -inattentive etc. *adj.*; overlook, disregard; pass by etc. (*neglect*) 460; not -observe etc. 457; think little of.

close —, shut- one's eyes to; wink at; pay no attention to; dismiss —, discard —, discharge- from one's -thoughts, — mind; drop the subject, think no more of; set —, turn —, put- aside; turn -away from, — one's attention from, — a deaf ear to, — one's back upon.

abstract oneself, dream, indulge in reverie.

escape -notice, — attention; come in at one ear and go out at the other; forget etc. (*have no remembrance*) 506.

call off —, draw off —, call away —, divert —, distract- the -attention, — thoughts, — mind; put out of one's head; dis-concert, -compose; put out, confuse, perplex, bewilder, fluster, muddle, dazzle; throw a sop to Cerberus.

Adj. inattentive; un-observant, -mindful, -heeding, -discerning; inadvertent; mind-, regard-, respect-less; listless etc. (*indifferent*) 866; blind, deaf; flighty, hand over head; cur-, percur-sory; giddy-, scatter-, hare-brained; unreflecting, *écervelé*, inconsiderate, off-hand, thoughtless, dizzy, muzzy, brainsick; giddy, — as a goose; wild, harum-scarum, ranipole, high-flying; heed-, care-less etc. (*neglectful*) 460.

absent, absent-minded, abstracted, *distrait*; lost; lost —, wrapped- in thought, woolgathering; rapt, in the clouds, bemused; dreaming —, musing- on other things; pre-occupied; engrossed etc. (*attentive*) 457; in a -reverie etc. *n.*; off one's guard etc. (*inexpectant*) 508; napping; dreamy.

disconcerted, put out etc. *v.*; rattled.

Adv. inattentively, inadvertently etc. *adj.*; *per incuriam*, *sub silentio*.

Int. stand -at ease, — easy!

Phr. the attention wanders; one's wits gone a -woolgathering, — bird's nesting; it never entered into one's head; the mind running on other things; one's thoughts being elsewhere; had it been a bear it would have bitten you.

459. Care. [Vigilance.]—**N.** care, solicitude, heed; heedfulness etc. *adj.*; scruple etc. (*conscientiousness*) 939.

watchfulness etc. *adj.*; vigilance, *surveillance*, eyes of Argus, watch, vigil, look out, watch and ward, *l'oeil du maître*.

alertness etc. (*activity*) 682; attention etc. 457; prudence etc., circumspection etc. (*caution*) 864; forethought etc. 510; precaution etc. (*preparation*) 673; tidiness etc. (*order*) 58, (*cleanliness*) 652; accuracy etc. (*exactness*) 494; minuteness, attention to detail; meticulousness, nicety, circumstantiality.

V. be -careful etc. *adj.*; reck; take care etc. (*be cautious*) 864; pay attention to etc. 457; take care of; look —, see- -to, — after; keep -an eye, — a sharp eye- upon; keep -watch, — watch and ward; mount guard, set watch, watch; keep in -sight, — view; chaperon, play gooseberry; mind, — one's business.

look -sharp, — about one; look with one's own eyes; keep a -good, — sharp- look-out; have all one's -wits, — eyes- about one; watch for etc. (*ex-*

pect) 507; stand to; keep one's eyes —, have the eyes —, sleep with one eye- open.

take precautions etc. 673; protect etc. (*render safe*) 664.

do one's best etc. 682; mind one's Ps and Qs, speak by the card, pick one's steps.

Adj. care-, regard-, heed-ful; taking care etc. *v.*; particular; prudent etc. (*cautious*) 864; considerate; thoughtful etc. (*deliberative*) 451; provident etc. (*prepared*) 673; alert etc. (*active*) 682; sure-footed.

guarded, on one's guard; on the *-qui vive*, - alert, — watch, — look-out; awake, broad awake, vigilant; watch-, wake-, wist-ful; Argus-, lynx-eyed; wide awake etc. (*intelligent*) 498; on the watch for etc. (*expectant*) 507.

tidy etc. (*orderly*) 58, (*clean*) 652; accurate etc. (*exact*) 494; scrupulous etc. (*conscientious*) 939; *cavendo tutus* etc. (*safe*) 664.

Adv. carefully etc. *adj.*; with care, gingerly.

Phr. *quis custodiet ipsos custodes?*

460. Neglect.—N. neglect; carelessness etc. *adj.*; trifling etc. *v.*; negligence; omission, laches, default; remissness, slackness, procrastination; supineness etc. (*inactivity*) 683; inattention etc. 458; nonchalance etc. (*insensibility*) 823; imprudence, recklessness etc. 863; slovenliness etc. (*disorder*) 59; (*dirt*) 653; improvidence etc. 674; non-completion etc. 730; inexactness etc. (*error*) 495.

paraleipsis [in rhetoric].

trifler, slacker, waster, waiter on Providence; Micawber.

V. be -negligent etc. *adj.*; take no care of etc. (take care of etc. 459); neglect; let -slip, — go; lay —, set —, cast —, put- aside; keep —, leave- out of sight; lose sight of.

overlook, disregard, pass -over, — by; let pass; blink; wink —, connive- at; gloss over; take no -note, — notice, — thought, — account- of; pay no regard to; *laisser aller*; allow to lie on the table.

scamp; trifle, fribble; do by halves; skimp; cut; slight etc. (*despise*) 930; play — trifle- with; slur; skim, — the surface; *effleurer*; take a cursory view of etc. 457.

slur —, slip —, skip —, jump- over; pertermit, miss, skip, jump, omit, give the go-by to, push aside, throw into the background, shelve, sink; ignore, shut one's eyes to, refuse to hear, turn a deaf ear to; leave out of one's calculation; not -attend to etc. 457, — mind; not trouble -oneself, — one's head- -with, — about; forget etc. 506; leave a loose thread; let the grass grow under one's feet.

render -neglectful etc. *adj.*; put —, throw- off one's guard.

Adj. neglecting etc. *v.*; unmindful, negligent, neglectful; heedless, careless, thoughtless; perfunctory, remiss, slack.

inconsiderate; un-, in-circumspect; off one's guard; un-wary, -watchful, -guarded; offhand.

supine etc. (*inactive*) 683; inattentive etc 458; *insouciant* etc. (*indifferent*) 823; imprudent, reckless etc. 863; slovenly etc. (*disorderly*) 59, (*dirty*) 653; inexact etc. (*erroneous*) 495; improvident etc. 674.

neglected etc. *v.*; un-heeded, -cared for, -

perceived, -seen, -observed, -noticed, -noted, -marked, -attended to, -thought of, -regarded, - remarked, -missed; shunted, shelved.

un-examined, -studied, -searched, -scanned, - weighed, -sifted, -explored.

Adv. negligently etc. *adj.*; hand over head, anyhow; in an unguarded moment etc. (*unexpectedly*) 508; *per incuriam.*

Int. never mind, no matter, let it pass; it will be all the same a hundred years hence.

461. Inquiry. [Subject of Inquiry. Question.]—**N.** inquiry; request etc. 765; search, research, quest; pursuit etc. 622.

examination, review, scrutiny, investigation, indagation; per-quisition, -scrutation, -vestigation; inqu-est, -isition; exploration; *exploitation*, ventilation.

sifting; calculation, analysis, dissection, resolution, induction; Baconian method.

strict —, close —, searching —, exhaustive- inquiry; narrow —, strict- search; study etc. (*consideration*) 451.

scire facias, ad referendum; trial.

questioning etc. *v.*; interroga-tion, -tory; third degree; interpellation; challenge, examination, cross-examination, catechism; feeler, Socratic method, zetetic philosophy; leading question; discussion etc. (*reasoning*) 476; questionnaire, questionary.

reconnoitering, *reconnaissance*; prying etc. *v.*; espionage, *espionnage*; domiciliary visit, peep behind the curtain; lantern of Diogenes.

question, query, problem, *desideratum*, point to be solved, porism; subject —, field- of -inquiry, — controversy; point —, matter- in dispute; moot-point; issue, question at issue; bone of contention etc. (*discord*) 713; plain —, fair —, open- question; enigma etc. (*secret*) 533; knotty point etc. (*difficulty*) 704; *quod-libet*; threshold of an inquiry.

inquirer, investigator, experimenter, inquisitor, inspector, querist, examiner, catechist; scrut-ator, - ineer; analyst; quidnunc etc. (*curiosity*) 455.

V. make -inquiry etc. *n.*; inquire, seek, search, frisk, speer, look -for, — about for, — out for; scan, reconnoiter, explore, sound, rummage, ransack, pry, peer, look round; look —, go- -over, — through; spy, over-haul.

scratch the head, slap the forehead.

look —, peer —, pry- into every hole and corner; look behind the scenes; trace up; hunt —, fish —, dig —, ferret- out; unearth; leave no stone unturned.

seek a -clue, — clew; hunt, track, trail, shadow, mouse, dodge, trace; follow the -trail, — scent; pursue etc. 622; beat up one's quarters; fish for; feel for etc. (*experiment*) 463.

investigate; take up —, institute —, pursue —, follow up —, conduct —, carry on —, prosecute- -an inquiry etc. *n.*; look -at, — into; pre-examine; discuss, canvass, agitate.

examine, study, consider, calculate; dip —, dive —, delve —, go deep- into; make sure of, probe, sound, fathom; probe to the -bottom, — quick; scrutinize, analyze, anatomize, dissect, parse, resolve, sift, winnow; view —, try- in all its phases; thresh out.

bring in question, subject to examination; put to

the proof etc. (*experiment*) 463; audit, tax, pass in review; take into consideration etc. (*think over*) 451; take counsel etc. 695.

ask, question, demand; put —, pop —, propose — , propound —, moot —, start —, raise —, stir —, suggest —, put forth —, ventilate —, grapple with —, go into- a question.

put to the question, interrogate, catechize, pump, grill; cross-question, -examine; dodge; require an answer; pick —, suck- the brains of; feel the pulse. be -in question etc. *adj.*; undergo examination.

Adj. inquiry etc. *v.*; inquisitive etc. (*curious*) 455; requisit-ive, -ory; catechetical, inquisitorial, analytic; in -search, — quest- of; on the look-out for, interrogative, zetetic; all-searching.

un-determined, -tried, -decided; in -question, — dispute, — issue, — course of inquiry; under - discussion, — consideration, — investigation etc. *n.*, *sub judice*, moot, proposed; doubtful etc. (*uncertain*) 475.

Adv. what? why? wherefore? whence? whither? where? *quaere?* how -comes, — happens, — is- it? what is the reason? what's -the matter, — up, in the wind? what on earth? when? who?

462. Answer.—**N.** answer, response, reply, replication, *riposte*, rejoinder, surrejoinder, rebutter, surrebutter, counter-evidence etc. 468, counter-charge, defence, plea; retort, repartee; contradiction etc. 536; rescript, -ion; antiphon, -y; acknowledgment; password; echo.

discovery etc. 480a; solution etc. (*explanation*) 522; rationale etc. (*cause*) 153; clue etc. (*indication*) 550.

Oedipus; oracle, etc. 513; return etc. (*record*) 551.

V. answer, respond, reply, rebut, retort, rejoin; give —, return for- answer; acknowledge, echo.

explain etc. (*interpret*) 522; solve etc. (*unriddle*) 522; discover etc. 480a; fathom, hunt out etc. (*inquire*) 461; satisfy, set at rest, determine.

Adj. answering etc. *v.*; respon-sive, -dent; oracular; antiphonal; conclusive.

Adv. because etc. (*cause*) 153; on the -scent, — right scent.

Int. *eureka!*

463. Experiment.—**N.** experiment; essay etc. (*attempt*) 675; research etc. (*investigation*) 461; trial, tentative method, *tâtonnement*.

verification, probation, *experimentum crucis*, proof, criterion, diagnostic test, tryout, crucial test, acid test.

crucible, reagent, check, touchstone, pix; assay, ordeal; ring.

empiricism, rule of thumb.

feeler; pilot —, messenger- balloon, *ballon d'essai*; pilot engine; scout; straw to show the wind. speculation, random shot, leap in the dark.

analy-zer, -st; adventurer, explorer, sourdough, prospector; experiment-er, -ist, -alist; assayer.

V. experiment; essay etc. (*endeavor*) 675; try, assay, sample; make -an experiment, — trial of; give a trial to; put upon —, subject to- trial; experiment upon; rehearse; put —, bring —, submitto the -test, — proof; prove, verify, test, touch, practise upon, try one's strength.

grope; feel —, grope- -for, — one's way; fumble; *tâtonner, aller à tâtons*; put —, throw- out a feeler; send up a pilot balloon; see how the -land lies, — wind blows; consult the barometer; feel the pulse; fish —, bob- for; cast —, beat- about for; angle, trawl, cast one's net, beat the bushes.

venture, try one's fortune etc. (*adventure*) 675; explore etc. (*inquire*) 461.

Adj. experimental; probat-ive, ory, -ionary; analytic, docimastic; tentative; empirical; speculative, tentive.

under probation, on one's trial, on trial, on approval.

464. Comparison.—N. comparison, collation, contrast; identification.

sim-ile, -ilitude; allegory etc. (*metaphor*) 521.

V. compare -to, — with; collate, confront; place side by side etc. (*near*) 197; set —, pit- against one another; contrast balance.

identify, draw a parallel, parallel.

compare notes; institute a comparison; *parva componere magnis*.

Adj. comparative, relative; metaphorical etc. 521.

compared with etc. *v.*; comparable.

Adv. relatively etc. (*relation*) 9; as compared with etc. *v.*

465. Discrimination.—N. discrimination, distinction, differentiation, diagnosis, diorism; nice perception; perception —, appreciation- of difference; acuteness; estimation etc. 466; nicety, refinement; taste etc. 850; *critique*, judgement, tact; insight, discernment etc. (*intelligence*) 498; *nuances*.

V. discriminate, distinguish, differentiate, severalize; separate; draw the line, sift; separate —, winnow- the chaff from the wheat; split hairs.

estimate etc. (*measure*) 466; know -which is which, — one's stuff, — one's way about, — what is what, — 'a hawk from a handsaw.'

take into -account, — consideration; give —, allow- due weight to; weigh carefully.

Adj. discriminating etc. *v.*; dioristic, discriminative, critical, distinctive; nice.

Phr. *il y a fagots et fagots*; *rem acu tetigisti*.

465a. Indiscrimination.—N. indiscrimination; promiscuity; indistinctness, -ion; uncertainty etc. (*doubt*) 475; obtuseness.

V. not -indiscriminate etc. 465; overlook etc.' (*neglect*) 460- a distinction; con-found, -fuse, jumble; swallow whole.

Adj. indiscriminate, undiscriminating, promiscuous; undistinguish-ed, -able, -ing; unmeasured.

466. Measurement.—N. measurement, admeasurement, mensuration, survey, valuation, ap-praisment, assessment, assize; estim-ate, -ation; dead reckoning; reckoning etc. (*numeration*) 85; gauging etc. *v.*

metrology, weights and measures, compound arithmetic.

measure, yard measure, standard, rule, foot-rule, chain, tape, staff, compass, callipers; dividers; gage, gauge, planimeter; meter, line, rod, check.

volt, kilowatt, ampere, candle power; horse power; axle load; foot pound.

flood —, high water- mark; Plimsoll mark; index etc. 550.

scale; gradu-ation, -ated scale; nonius; vernier etc. (*minuteness*) 193; pedo (*length*)- 200, sounding line etc. (*depth*) 208, thermo (*heat* etc. 398)-, baro (*air* etc. 338)-, dynamo (*power*)- 276, anemo (*wind* 349)-, gonio (*angle* 244)- meter; landmark etc. (*limit*) 233; balance etc. (*weight*) 310; optical instruments etc. 445.

co-ordinates, ordinate and abscissa, polar co-ordinates, latitude and longitude, declination and right ascension, altitude and azimuth.

geo-, stereo-, hypso-metry; metage; surveying, land surveying; geo-desy, -detics, -desia; ortho-, alti-metry; *cadastre*.

astrolabe, armillary sphere.

land, -surveyor; geometer, topographer, cartographer, hydrographer.

V. measure, meter, mete; value, assess, rate, appraise, estimate, form as estimate, set a value on; appreciate; standardize.

span, pace, step; apply the -compass etc. *n.*; gauge, plumb, probe, calliper, sound, fathom etc. 208; heave the -log, — lead; weigh etc. 319; survey.

take an average etc. 29; graduate.

Adj. measuring etc. *v.*; metric, -al; measurable; geodetical, cadastral, topographical.

467. Evidence. [on one side]—N. evidence; facts, premises, *data*, *praecognita*, grounds.

indication etc. 550; criterion etc. (*test*) 463.

testi-mony, -fication; attestation; deposition etc. (*affirmation*) 535; examination.

admission etc. (*assent*) 488; authority, warrant, credential, diploma, voucher, certificate, docket; record etc. 551; document, muniments; *pièce justificative*; deed, warranty etc. (*security*) 771; signature, seal etc. (*identification*) 550; exhibit, citation, reference.

witness, indicator; eye-, ear-witness; deponent; sponsor.

oral —, documentary —, hearsay —, external —, extrinsic —, internal —, intrinsic —, circumstantial —, cumulative —, *ex parte* —, presumptive —, collateral —, constructive- evidence; proof etc. (*demonstration*) 478; evidence in chief; finger prints, dactylogram.

secondary evidence; confirmation, corroboration, adminicle, support; ratification etc. (*assent*) 488; authentication, verification; compurgation, wager of law, comprobation.

citation, reference.

V. be -evidence etc. *n.*; evince, show, betoken, tell of; indicate etc. (*denote*) 550; imply, involve, argue, bespeak, breathe.

have —, carry- weight; tell, speak volumes; speak for itself etc. (*manifest*) 525.

rest —, depend- upon; repose on.

bear -witness etc. *n.*; give -evidence etc. *n.*; testify, depose, witness, vouch for; sign, seal, undersign, set one's hand and seal, sign and seal, deliver as one's act and deed, certify, attest; acknowledge etc. (*assent*) 488.

make absolute, confirm, ratify, corroborate, endorse, countersign, support, bear out, vindicate, uphold, warrant.

adduce, attest, cite, quote; refer —, appeal- to; call, — to witness; bring -forward, — into court; allege, plead; produce —, confront- witnesses; collect —, bring together —, rake up- evidence.

have —, make out- a case; establish, circumstantiate, authenticate, substantiate, verify, make good, quote chapter and verse; bring -home to, — to book.

Adj. showing etc. *v.*; evidential, indica-tive, -tory; deducible etc. 478; grounded —, founded —, based- on; first hand, authentic, verifiable; corroborative, confirmatory; significant, conclusive.

Adv. by inference; according to, witness, *a fortiori*; still -more, — less; *raison de plus*; in corroboration etc. *n.* of; *valeat quantum*; under - seal, — one's hand and seal.

468. Counter-evidence. [Evidence on the other side, on the other hand.]—**N.** counter-evidence, evidence on the other -side, — hand; disproof; refutation etc. 479; negation etc. 536; conflicting evidence.

plea etc. 617; vindication etc. 937; counter-protest; *tu quoque* argument; other side —, reverse- of the shield.

V. countervail, oppose; run counter; rebut etc. (*refute*) 479; subvert etc. (*destroy*) 162; check, weaken; contravene; contradict etc. (*deny*) 536; tell another story, turn the -tables, — scale; alter the case; cut both ways; prove a negative. *audire alteram partem.*

Adj. countervailing etc. *v.*; contradictory, in rebuttal.

un-attested, -authenticated, -supported by evidence; suppositious, trumped up.

Adv. *per contra*, conversely, on the other hand.

469. Qualification.—**N.** qualification, limitation, modification, coloring.

allowance, grains of allowance, consideration, extenuating circumstances.

condition, proviso, exception; exemption; salvo, saving clause; discount etc. 813.

V. qualify, limit, modify, affect, temper, leaven, give a color to, introduce new conditions.

allow —, make allowance- for; admit exceptions, take into account.

take exception, object.

Adj. qualifying etc. *v.*; conditional; extenuatory; exceptional etc. (*unconformable*) 83.

hypothetical etc. (*supposed*) 514; contingent etc. (*uncertain*) 475.

Adv. provided, — always; if, unless, but, yet; according as; conditionally, admitting, supposing; on the supposition of etc. (*theoretically*) 514; with the understanding, even, although, though, for all that, after all, at all events.

with grains of allowance, *cum grano salis*; *exceptis excipiendis*; wind and weather permitting; if possible etc. 470.

subject to; with this -proviso etc. *n.*

470. Possibility.—**N.** possibility, potentiality; what -may be, — is possible etc. *adj.*; compatibility etc. (*agreement*) 23.

practicability, feasibility; practicableness etc. *adj.*

contingency, chance etc. 156.

V. be -possible etc. *adj.*; stand a chance, have a leg to stand on; admit of, bear.

render -possible etc. *adj.*; put in the way of.

Adj. possible; on the -cards, — dice; *in posse*, within the bounds of possibility, conceivable, credible, imaginable; compatible etc. 23.

practicable, feasible, workable, performable, achievable; within -reach, — measurable distance; accessible, superable, surmountable; at-, obtainable; contingent etc. (*doubtful*) 475.

Adv. possibly, by possibility; perhaps, -chance, - adventure; may be, haply, mayhap.

if possible, wind and weather permitting, God willing, *Deo volente*, D.V.

471. Impossibility.—**N.** impossibility etc. *adj.*; what -cannot, — can never- be; sour grapes; infeasibility, impracticability; hopelessness etc. 859.

V. be -impossible etc. *adj.*; have no chance whatever.

attempt impossibilities; square the circle; discover the -philosopher's stone — elixir of life, — secret of perpetual motion; wash a blackamoor white; skin a flint; make -a silk purse out of a sow's ear, — bricks without straw; have nothing to go upon; weave a rope of sand, build castles in the air, *prendre la lune avec les dents*, extract sunbeams from cucumbers, set the Thames on fire, milk a he-goat into a sieve, catch a weasel asleep, *rompre l'anguille au genou*, be in two places at once.

Adj. impossible; not -possible etc. 470; absurd, contrary to reason; unlikely, at variance with facts; unreasonable etc. 477; incredible etc. 485; beyond the bounds of -reason, — possibility; from which reason recoils; visionary; inconceivable etc. (*improbable*) 473; prodigious etc. (*wonderful*) 870; un-, in-imaginable, unthinkable, not a Chinaman's chance.

impracticable, unachievable; un-, in-feasible; insuperable; un-, in-surmountable; unat-, unobtainable; out of -reach, — the question; not to be - had, — thought of; beyond control; desperate etc. (*hopeless*) 859; incompatible etc. 24; inaccessible, uncomeatable, impassable, impervious, innavigable, inextricable.

out of -, beyond- one's -power, — depth, — reach, — grasp; too much for; *ultra crepidam*.

Phr. the grapes are sour; *non possumus*; *non nostrum tantas componere lites*.

472. Probability.—**N.** probability, likelihood; likeliness etc. *adj.*

vraisemblance, verisimilitude, plausibility;

color, semblance, show of; presumption; presumptive –, circumstantial- evidence; credibility.
reasonable –, fair –, good –, favorable- - chance, – prospect; prospect, well-grounded hope; chance etc. 156.
V. be -probable etc. adj.; give –, lend- color to; point to; imply etc. (evidence) 467; bid fair etc. (promise) 511; stand fair for; stand –, run- a good chance.
presume, infer, suppose, take for granted.
think likely, dare say, flatter oneself; expect etc. 507; count upon etc. (believe) 484.
Adj. probable, likely, hopeful, to be expected, in a fair way.
plausible, specious, ostensible, colorable, ben trovato, well-founded, reasonable, credible, easy of belief, presumable, presumptive, apparent.
Adv. probably etc. adj.; belike; in all - probability, – likelihood; very –, most- likely; as likely as not; like enough; ten etc. to one; apparently, seemingly, according to every reasonable expectation; primâ facie; to all appearance etc. (to the eye) 448.
Phr. the -chances, – odds- are; appearances –, chances- are in favor of; there is reason to -believe, – think, – expect; I dare say; all Lombard Street to a China orange.

473. Improbability.—N. improbability, unlikelihood; unfavorable –, bad –, little –, small –, poor –, scarcely any –, no –, not a ghost of a- chance; bare possibility; long odds; incredibility etc. 485.
V. be -improbable etc. adj.; have a -small chance etc. n.
Adj. improbable, unlikely, contrary to all reasonable expectation, implausible.
rare etc. (infrequent) 137; unheard of, inconceivable; un-, in-imaginable; incredible etc. 485; more than doubtful.
Int. not likely! no fear!
Phr. the chances are against.

474. Certainty.—N. certainty; necessity etc. 601; · certitude, certainness, surety, assurance, sureness; dead –, moral- certainty; infallibleness etc. adj.; infallibility, reliability.
gospel, scripture, church, pope, court of final ap-, peal; res judicata, ultimatum.
positiveness; dogmat-ism, -ist, -izer; doctrinaire, know-all, bigot, -ry; opinionist, Sir Oracle; ipse dixit; zealot.
fact; positive –, matter of- fact; fait accompli.
V. be -certain etc. adj.; stand to reason.
render -certain etc. adj.; in-, en-, as-sure; clinch, make sure; determine, decide, set at rest, ·make assurance double sure;· know etc. (believe) 484; dismiss all doubt.
dogmatize, lay down the law.
Adj. certain, sure; assured etc. v.; solid, well-founded.
unqualified, absolute, positive, determinate, definite, clear, unequivocal, categorical, unmistakable, decisive, decided, ascertained.
inevitable, unavoidable, ineluctable, avoidless.

unerring, infallible; unchangeable etc. 150; to be depended on, trustworthy, reliable, bound.
un-impeachable, -deniable, -questionable; indisputable, -contestable, -controvertible, - defeasible, -dubitable; irrefutable etc. (proven) 478; conclusive, without power of appeal, final.
indubious; without –, beyond a –, without a shade or shadow or- -doubt – question; past dispute; beyond all -question, – dispute; un-doubted, -contested, -questioned, -disputed; question-, doubt-less.
bigoted, fanatical, dogmatic, opinionat-ed, -ive, doctrinaire.
authoritative, authentic; official.
sure as -fate, – death and taxes, – a gun.
evident, self-evident, axiomatic; clear, – as day, – as the sun at noonday; obvious.
Adv. certainly etc. adj.; for certain, certes, sure, no doubt, doubtless, and no mistake, flagrante delicto, sure enough, to be sure, of course, as a matter of course, à coup sur, to a certainty, undoubtedly; in truth etc. (truly) 494; at -any rate, – all events; without fail; coûte que coûte; whatever may happen, if the worst come to the worst; come –, happen- what -may; – will; sink or swim; rain or shine.
Phr. cela va sans dire; there is -no question, – not a shadow of doubt; the die is cast etc. (necessity) 601.

475. Uncertainty.—N. uncertainty, in-certitude, doubt; doubtfulness etc. adj.; dubi-ety, -tation, -tancy, -ousness.
hesitation, suspense; perplexity, embarrassment, dilemma, quandary, Morton's fork, bewilderment; timidity etc. (fear) 860; indecision, vacillation etc. 605; diaporesis, indetermination.
vagueness etc. adj.; haze, fog; obscurity etc. (darkness) 421; ambiguity etc. (double meaning) 520; contingency, double contingency, possibility upon a possibility; conjecture; open question etc. (question) 461; onus probandi; blind bargain, pig in a poke, leap in the dark, something or other; needle in a bottle of hay; roving commission.
fallibility, unreliability, untrustworthiness, precariousness.
V. be -uncertain etc. adj.; wonder whether.
lose the -clue, – clew, – scent; miss one's way.
not know -what to make of, etc. (unintelligibility) 519, – which way to turn, – whether one stands on one's head or one's heels; float in a sea of doubt, hesitate, flounder; lose -oneself, – one's head, – one's way, wander aimlessly; muddle one's brains.
render -uncertain etc. adj.; put out, pose, puzzle, perplex, embarrass; confuse, -found; bewilder, mystify, bother, nonplus, addle the wits, throw off the scent; ambiguas in vulgus spargere voces; keep in suspense.
doubt etc. (disbelieve) 485; hang –, tremble- in the balance; depend.
Adj. uncertain; casual; random etc. (aimless) 621; changeable etc. 149.
doubtful, dubious; indecisive; unsettled, - decided, -determined; in suspense, open to discussion; controvertible; in question etc. (inquiry) 461; insecure, unstable.

vague; in-determinate, -definite; ambiguous,
equivocal; undefin-ed, -able; confused etc. (*indistinct*) 447; mystic, mysterious, veiled, obscure,
cryptic, oracular.

perplexing etc. *v.*; enigmatic, paradoxical;
apocryphal, problematical, hypothetical; experimental etc. 463.

fallible, questionable, precarious, slippery,
ticklish, debatable, disputable; un-reliable, -
trustworthy.

contingent, — on, dependent on; subject to;
dependent on circumstances; occasional;
provisional.

unauth-entic, -enticated, -oritative; un-
ascertained, confirmed; undemonstrated; un-told,
-counted.

in a -state of uncertainty, — cloud, — maze;
ignorant etc. 491; on the horns of a dilemma;
afraid to say; out of one's reckoning, astray, adrift;
as -sea, — fault, — a loss, — one's wit's end, — a
nonplus; puzzled etc. *v.*; lost abroad, *désorienté*;
dis-tracted, -traught.

Adv. *pendente lite*; *sub spe rati*.

Phr. Heaven knows; who can tell? who shall
decide when doctors disagree?

476. Reasoning.—**N.** reasoning; ratio-cination,
-nalism; dialectics, induction, generalization.

discussion, comment; ventilation; inquiry etc.
461.

argumentation, controversy, debate; polemics,
wrangling; contention etc. 720; logomachy; dis-
putation, -ceptation; paper war.

art of reasoning, logic.

process —, train —, chain- of reasoning; de-, induction; systhesis, analysis.

argument; case, plea, *plaidoyer*, opening;
lemma, proposition, terms, premises, postulate,
data, starting point, principle; inference etc.
(*judgment*) 480.

pro-, syllogism; enthymeme, sorites, dilemma,
perilepsis, a priori reasoning, *reductio ad absurdum*, horns of a dilemma, *argumentum ad
hominem*, comprehensive argument.

reasoner, logician, dialectician; disputant; con-
trover-sialist, -tist; wrangler, arguer, debater,
polemic, casuist, rationalist; scientist.

logical sequence; good case; correct —, just —,
sound —, valid —, cogent —, logical —, forcible —,
persuasive —, persuasory —, consectary —, conclusive etc. 478 —, subtle- reasoning; force of
argument; strong -point, — argument.

arguments, reasons, pros and cons.

V. reason, argue, discuss, debate, dispute,
wrangle; bandy -words, — arguments; chop logic;
hold —, carry on- an argument; controvert etc.
(*deny*) 536; canvass; comment —, moralize-upon;
consider etc. (*examine*) 461.

open a -discussion, — case; join —, be at- issue;
moot; come to the point; stir —, agitate —, ventilate
—, torture- a question; try conclusions; take up a -
side, — case.

contend, take one's stand upon, insist, lay stress
on; infer etc. 480.

follow from etc. (*demonstration*) 478.

Adj. rational; reasoning etc. *v.*; rationalistic;
argumentative, controversial, dialectic, polemical;
discurs-ory, -ive; disputations.

debatable, controvertible.

logical; in-, de-ductive; synthetic, analytic;
relevant etc. 23.

Adv. for, because, hence, whence, seeing that,
since, sith, then, thence, so; for -that, — this, —
which- reason; for-, inasmuch as; whereas, *ex concesso*, considering, in consideration of; there-,
where-fore; consequently, *ergo*, thus, accordingly;
a fortiori.

in -conclusion, — fine; finally, after all, *au bout
du compte*, on the whole, taking one thing with
another.

rationally etc. *adj.*

477. Sophistry. [*The absence of reasoning.*]
Intuition. [*False or vicious reasoning; show of
reason.*]—**N.** intuition, instinct, association; presentiment; rule of thumb.

sophistry, paralogy, perversion, casuistry,
jesuitry, equivocation, evasion, mental reservation;
chicane, -ry; quiddit, quiddity; mystification; special
pleading; speciousness etc. *adj.*; nonsense etc. 497;
word-, tongue-fence.

false —, vicious- reasoning; *petitio principii,
ignoratio elenchi; post hoc ergo propter hoc; non
sequitur, ignotum per ignotius.*

misjudgment etc. 481; false teaching etc. 538.

sophism, solecism, paralogism; quibble, quirk,
elenchus, elench, fallacy, *quodlibet*, subterfuge,
subtlety, quillet; inconsistency, antilogy; 'a
mockery, a delusion and a snare;' claptrap, mere
words; 'lame and impotent conclusion.'

meshes —, cobwebs- of sophistry; flaw in an
argument; weak point, bad case.

over-refinement; hair-splitting etc. *v.*

sophist, casuist, paralogist.

V. judge -intuitively, — by intuition; hazard a
proposition, talk at random.

reason -ill, — falsely etc. *adj.*; paralogize;
misjudge etc. 481.

pervert, quibble; equivocate, mystify, evade,
elude; gloss over, varnish; misteach etc. 538;
mislead etc. (*error*) 495; cavil, refine, subtilize,
split hairs; misrepresent etc. (*lie*) 544.

beg the question, reason in a circle, cut blocks
with a razor, beat about the bush, play fast and
loose, blow hot and cold, prove that black is white
and white black, travel out of the record, *parler à
tort et à travers*, put oneself out of court, not have
a leg to stand on.

Adj. intuitive, ·instinctive, impulsive; independent of —, anterior to- reason; gratuitous;
hazarded; unconnected.

unreasonable, illogical, false, unsound, invalid;
unwarranted, not following; inconsequent, -ial; inconsistent, incongruous; abson-ous, -ant; unscientific; untenable, inconclusive, incorrect;
fall-acious, -ible; groundless, unproved.

deceptive, sophistical, sophisticated, casuistical,
jesuitical; illus-ive, -ory; specious, hollow,
plausible, *ad captandum*, evasive; irrelevant etc.
10.

weak, feeble, poor, flimsy, loose, vague,
irrational; nonsensical etc. (*absurd*) 497; foolish
etc. (*imbecile*) 499; frivolous, pettifogging, quibbling; finespun, over-refined.

at the end of one's tether, *au bout de son latin*.

Adv. intuitively etc. *adj.*; by intuition; illogically etc. *adj.*

Phr. *non constat*; that goes for nothing.

478. Demonstration.—N. demonstration, proof; conclusiveness etc. *adj.*; *apodixis*, probation, comprobation.

logic of facts etc. (*evidence*) 467; *experimentum curcis* etc. (*test*) 463; argument etc. 476; irrefragability.

V. demonstrate, prove, establish, make good; show; evince etc. (*be evidence of*) 467; verify etc. 467; settle the question, reduce to demonstration, set the question at rest.

make out, — a case; prove one's point, have the best of the argument; draw a conclusion etc. (*judge*) 480.

follow, — of course; stand to reason; hold -good, — water.

Adj. demonstra-ting etc. *v.*, -tive, -ble; probative, unanswerable, conclusive; apodictic, -al; irre-sistible, -futable, -fragable, undeniable.

→ categorical, decisive, crucial.

demonstrated etc. *v.*; proven; unconfuted, -answered, -refuted; evident etc. 474.

deducible, consequential, consectary, inferential, following.

Adv. of course, in consequence, consequently, as a matter of course.

Phr. *probatum est*; there is nothing more to be said, Q.E.D., it must follow.

479. Confutation.—N. con-, re-futation; answer, complete answer; disproof, conviction, redargution, invalidation; expos-ure, -ition; clincher; retort; *reductio ad absurdum*; knock down — *tu quoque*- argument.

V. con-, re-fute; parry, negative, disprove, redargue, expose, show the fallacy of, rebut, defeat; demolish etc. (*destroy*) 162; over-throw,' -turn; scatter to the winds, explode, invalidate; silence; put —, reduce- to silence; clinch -an argument, — a question; give one a set down, stop the mouth, shut up; have, — on the hip; get the better of; confound, convince.

not leave a leg to stand on, cut the ground from under one's feet.

be confuted etc.; fail; expose —, show- one's weak point.

Adj. confut-ing, -ed etc. *v.*; capable of refutation; re-, con-futable.

condemned -on one's own showing, — out of one's own mouth.

Phr. the argument falls to the ground, *cadit quaestio*, it does not hold water, 'suo sibi gladio hunc jugulo.'

480. Judgment. [Conclusion.]—N. result, conclusion, upshot; deduction, inference, ergotism, illation; corollary, porism; moral.

estimation, valuation, appreciation, judication; di-, ad-judication; arbitr- ament, -ement, -ation; assessment, ponderation.

award, estimate; review, criticism, *critique*, notice, report.

decision, determination, judgment, finding, verdict, sentence, decree, — nisi, — absolute, — interlocutory; dictum; *res judicata*.

plebiscite, referendum, voice, casting vote; vote etc. (*choice*) 609; opinion etc. (*belief*) 484; good judgment etc. (*wisdom*) 498.

judge, jurist, umpire; arbi-ter, -trator; assessor, referee; censor, reviewer, critic; *connoisseur*; commentator etc. 524; inspector, inspecting officer.

V. judge, conclude; come to —, draw —, arrive at- a conclusion; ascertain, determine, make up one's mind.

deduce, derive, gather, collect, draw an inference, make a deduction, weet, ween.

form an estimate, estimate, size up, appreciate, value, count, assess, rate, rank, account; regard, consider, think of; look upon etc. (*believe*) 484.

settle; pass —, give- an opinion; decide, try, pronounce, rule; pass -judgment, — sentence; sentence, doom; find; give —, deliver- judgment; adjud-ge, -icate; arbitrate, award, report; bring in a verdict; make absolute, set a question ar rest; confirm etc. (*assent*) 488.

comment, criticize; review, pass under review etc (*examine*) 457; investigate etc. (*inquire*) 461.

hold the scales, sit in judgment; try —, hear- a cause.

Adj. judging etc. *v.*; judicious etc. (*wise*) 498; determinate, conclusive, censorious, critical etc. 932.

Adv. on the whole, all things considered.

480a. Discovery. [Result of search or inquiry.]—N. discovery, invention, detection, disenchantment, disclosure, find, ascertainment, revelation.

trover etc. 775.

V. discover, find, determine, evolve; fix upon; find —, trace —, make —, hunt —, fish —, worm —, ferret —, root-out; fathom; bring —, draw-out; educe, elicit, bring to light, invent; dig —, grub —, fish- up; unearth, disinter.

solve, resolve; un-riddle, -ravel, -lock; pick —, open- the lock; find a -clue, — clew- to; interpret etc. 522; disclose etc. 529.

trace, get at; hit it, have it; lay one's -finger, — hands- upon; spot; get —, arrive- at the -turth etc. 494; put the saddle on the right horse, hit the right nail on the head.

be near the truth, burn; smoke, scent, sniff, smell a rat.

open the eyes to; see -through, — daylight, — in its true colors, — the cloven foot; detect; catch, — tripping.

pitch —, fall —, light —, hit —, stumble —, pop- upon; come across; meet —, fall in- with.

recognize, realize, verify, make certain of, identify.

Int. *eureka!*

481. Misjudgment.—N. misjudgment, obliquity of —, warped- judgment; mis-calculation, -computation, -conception etc. (*error*) 495; hasty conclusion.

prejud-gment, -ication, -ice; foregone conclusion; pre-notion, -vention, -conception, - dilection, -possession, -apprehension; -sumption, - sentiment; fixed −, preconceived- idea; *idée fixe*; *mentis gratissimus error*; fool's paradise.

esprit de corps, party spirit, race −, class-prejudice, partisanship, clannishness, *prestige*.

bias, warp, twist; hobby, fad, whim, craze, quirk, crotchet, partiality, infatuation, blind side, mote in the eye.

one-sided −, partial −, narrow −, confined −, superficial- -views, − ideas,− conceptions. − notions; narrow mind; bigotry etc. (*obstinacy*) 606; *odium theologicum*; pedantry; hypercriticism.
doctrinaire etc. (*positive*) 474.

V. mis-judge, -estimate, -think, -conjecture, - conceive etc. (*error*) 495; fly in the face of facts; mis-calculate, -reckon, -compute.

overestimate etc. 482; underestimate etc. 483.

pre-, fore-judge; pre-suppose, -sume, -judicate; dogmatize; have a -bias etc. *n.*; have only one idea; *jurare in verba magistri*, run away with the notion; jump −, rush- to a conclusion; look only at one side of the shield; view -with jaundiced eye, − through distorting spectacles; not see beyond one's nose; *dare pondus fumo*; get the wrong sow by the ear etc. (*blunder*) 699.

give a -bias, − twist; bias, warp, twist; pre-judice, -possess.

Adj. misjudging etc. *v.*; ill-judging, wrong-headed; prejudiced, prejudicial, etc. *v.*; jaundiced; short-sighted, pur-blind; partial, one-sided, superficial.

narrow-minded; confined, insular, provincial, parochial, illiberal, intolerant, narrow, besotted, infatuated, fanatical, cracked, warped, *entêté*, positive, dogmatic, dictatorial; conceited; opin-, opini-ative; opinion-ed, -ate, -ative, -ated; self-opinioned, wedded to an opinion, *opinâtre*; bigoted etc. (*obstinate*) 606; crotchety, fussy, impracticable; unreason-able, -ing; stupid etc. 499; credulous etc. 486.

misjudged etc. *v.*

Adv. *ex parte.*

Phr. nothing like leather; the wish the father to the thought.

482. Overestimation.—N. overestimation etc. *v.*; exaggeration etc. 549; vanity etc. 880; optim-, pessim-ism, -ist; megalomania.

much -cry and little wool, − ado about nothing; storm in a teacup; fine talking, rodomontade, gush, hot air, gas, bombast.

egotism etc. 880; boasting etc. 884.

V. over-estimate, -rate, -value, -prize, -weigh, - reckon, -strain, -praise; estimate too highly, attach too much importance to, make mountains of molehills, catch at straws; strain, magnify; exaggerate etc. 549; set too high a value upon; think −, make- -much, − too much- of; outreckon.

extol, − to the skies; make the -most, − best, − worst- of, eulogize, panegyrize, gush, puff, boost; make two bites of a cherry.

have too high an opinion of oneself etc. (*vanity*) 880.

Adj. overestimated etc. *v.*; oversensitive etc.

(*sensibility*) 822; inflated, puffed up, exaggerated etc. 549.

Phr. all his geese are swans; *parturiunt montes.*

483. Underestimation.—N. underestimation; depreciation etc. (*detraction*) 934; pessim-ism, -ist; undervaluing etc. *v.*; modesty etc. 881.

V. under-rate, -estimate, -value, -reckon; depreciate; disparage etc. (*detract*) 934; not do justice to; mis-, dis-prize; ridicule etc. 856; slight etc. (*despise*) 930; neglect etc. 460; slur over, under-state.

make -light, − little, − nothing, − no account-of; minimize, belittle, run down, think nothing of; set -no store by, − at naught; shake off as dewdrops from the lion's mane.

Adj. depreciat-ing, -ed, -ive, -ory, etc. *v.*; unappreciated, -valued, -prized; pejorative.

484. Belief.—N. belief; credence; credit; assurance; faith, trust, troth, confidence, presumption, sanguine expectation etc. (*hope*) 858; dependence on, reliance on.

persuasion, conviction, convincement, plerophory, self-conviction; certainty etc. 474; opinion, mind, view; conception, thinking; impression etc. (*idea*) 453; surmise etc. 514; conclusion etc. (*judgment*) 480.

tenet, dogma, principle, way of thinking; popular belief etc. (*assent*) 488.

firm −, implicit −, settled −, fixed −, rooted −, deep-rooted −, staunch −, unshaken −, steadfast −, inveterate −, calm −, sober −, dispassionate −, impartial −, well-founded- -belief, − opinion etc.; *uberrima fides.*

system of opinions, school, doctrine, articles, canons; declaration −, profession- of faith; tenets, *credenda*, creed; thirty-nine articles etc. (*orthodoxy*) 983a; catechism; assent etc. 488; *propaganda* etc. (*teaching*) 537.

credibility etc. (*probability*) 472.

V. believe, credit; give -faith, − credit, − credence- to; see, realize; assume, receive; set down −, take- for; have −, take- it; consider, esteem, presume.

count −, depend −, calculate −, pin one's faith −, reckon −, lean −, build −, rely −, rest-upon; lay one's account for; make sure of.

make oneself easy -about, − on that score; take on -trust, − credit; take for -granted, − -gospel; allow −, attach- some weight to.

know, − for certain; have −, make- no doubt; doubt not; be − rest- -assured etc. *adj.*; persuade −, assure −, satisfy- oneself; make up one's mind.

give one credit for; confide −, believe −, put one's trust- in; place −, repose- implicit confidence in; take -one's word for, − at one's word; place reliance on, rely upon, swear by, regard to.

think, hold; take, − it; opine, be of opinion, conceive, trow, ween, fancy, apprehend; have −, hold −, possess −, entertain −, adopt −, imbibe −, embrace −, get hold of −, hazard −, foster −, nurture −, cherish- -a belief, − an opinion etc. *n.*

view −, consider −, take −, hold −, conceive −, regard −, esteem −, deem −, look upon − account −, set down- as; surmise etc. 514.

get –, take- it into one's head; come round to an opinion; swallow etc. (*credulity*) 486.

cause to -be believed etc. *v.*; satisfy, persuade, have the ear of, gain the confidence of, assure; convince, -vict, -vert; put across, sell; wean, bring round; bring –, put –, win- over; indoctrinate etc. (*teach*) 537; cram down the throat; produce –, carry- conviction; bring –, drive- home to.

go down, find credence, pass current; be -received etc. *v.*, – current etc. *adj.*; possess –, take hold of –, take possession of- the mind.

Adj. believing etc. *v.*; certain, sure, assured, positive, cocksure, satisfied, confident, unhesitating, convinced, secure.

under the impression; impressed –, imbued –, penetrated- with.

confiding, trustful, suspectless; unsusp-ecting, -icious; void of suspicion; credulous etc. 486; wedded to.

believed etc. *v.*; accredited, putative; unsuspected.

worthy of –, deserving of –, commanding- -belief, – confidence; credible, reliable, trusted, trustworthy, to be depended on, undoubted; satisfactory; probable etc. 472; fiduci-al, -ary; persuasive, impressive.

relating to belief, doctrinal.

Adv. in the -opinion, – eyes- of; *me judice*; me-seems, -thinks; to the best of one's belief; I - dare say, – doubt not, – have no doubt, – am sure; in my opinion; sure enough etc. (*certainty*) 474; depend –, rely- upon it; be –, rest- assured; I'll warrant you etc. (*affirmation*) 535.

485. Unbelief. Doubt.—N. un-, dis-, mis-belief; discredit, miscreance; infidelity etc. (*irreligion*) 989; dissent etc. 489; change of - opinion etc. 484; retraction etc. 607.

doubt etc. (*uncertainty*) 475; skepticism, misgiving, demur; dis-, mis-trust; misdoubt, suspicion, jealousy, scruple, qualm; *onus probandi.*

incredib-ility, -leness; incredulity; unbeliever etc. 487.

V. dis-believe, -credit; not -believe etc. 484; misbelieve; refuse to admit etc. (*dissent*) 489; refuse to believe etc. (*incredulity*) 487.

doubt; be -doubtful etc. (*uncertain*) 475; doubt the truth of; be -skeptical as to etc. *adj.*; diffide; dis-, mis-trust; suspect, smoke, scent, smell a rat; have –, harbor –, entertain- -doubts, -suspicions; have one's doubts.

demur, stick at, pause, hesitate, scruple, waver, stop and consider.

hang in -suspense, – doubt.

throw doubt upon, raise a question; bring –, call- in question; question, challenge, query; dispute; deny etc. 536; cavil; cause –, raise –, start –, suggest –, awake- a -doubt, – suspicion; ergotize.

startle, stagger; shake –, stagger- one's faith, – belief.

Adj. unbelieving; incredulous –, skeptical- as to; distrustful –, shy –, suspicious- of; doubting etc. *v.*

doubtful etc. (*uncertain*) 475; disputable; unworthy –, undeserving- of -belief etc. 484; questionable; sus-pect, -picious; open to -suspicion,

– doubt; staggering, hard to believe, incredible, not to be believed, inconceivable.

fallible etc. (*uncertain*) 475; undemonstrable; controvertible etc. (*untrue*) 495.

Adv. *cum grano salis.*

Phr. *fronti nulla fides*; *nimium ne crede colori*; *'timeo Danaos et dona ferentes;' credat Judaeus Apella*; let those believe who may.

486. Credulity.—N. credul-ity, -ousness etc. *adj.*; gull-, cull-ibility; gross credulity, infatuation; self-delusion, -deception; blind reasoning; superstition; one's blind side; bigotry etc. (*obstinacy*) 606; hyper-orthodoxy etc. 984; misjudgment etc. 481.

credulous person etc. (*dupe*) 547.

V. be -credulous etc. *adj.*; *jurare in verba magistri*; follow implicitly; swallow, – whole, gulp down; take on trust; take for -granted, – gospel; run away with -a notion, – an idea; jump –, rush-to a conclusion; think the moon is made of green cheese; take –, grasp- the shadow for the substance; catch at straws.

impose upon etc. (*deceive*) 545.

Adj. credulous, gullible; easily -deceived etc. 545; simple, green, soft, childish, silly, stupid; over-credulous, -confident; infatuated, superstitious; confiding etc. (*believing*) 484.

Phr. the wish the father to the thought; *credo quia impossibile.*

487. Incredulity.—N. incredul-ous-ness, -ity; skepticism, pyrrhonism; want of faith etc. (*irreligion*) 989.

suspiciousness etc. *adj.*; scrupulosity; suspicion etc. (*unbelief*) 485; dissent etc. 489.

unbeliever, skeptic, aporetic; atheist, agnostic, infidel, disbeliever, misbeliever, pyrrhonist etc. 989; heretic etc. (*heterodox*) 984.

v. be -incredulous etc. *adj.*; distrust etc. (*disbelieve*) 485; refuse to believe; shut one's -eyes, – ears- to; turn a deaf ear to; hold aloof; ignore; *nullis jurare in verba magistri.*

Adj. incredulous, skeptical, unbelieving, inconvincible; hard –, shy- of belief; suspicious, scrupulous, distrustful, heterodox etc. 984.

488. Assent.—N. assent, -ment; acquiescence, admission; nod; ac-, con-cord, -cordance; agreement etc. 23; affirm-ance, -ation; recognition, acknowledgment, avowal; confession, – of faith.

unanimity, common. consent, *consensus*, acclamation, chorus, *vox populi*; popular –, current- -belief, – opinion; public opinion; concurrence etc. (*of causes*) 178; co-operation etc. (*voluntary*) 709.

ratification, confirmation, corroboration, approval, acceptance, *visa*; indorsement etc. (*record*) 551.

consent etc. (*compliance*) 762.

affirmant, consenter, covenantor, subscriber, endorser, upholder.

V. assent; give –, yield –, not- assent; acquiesce; agree etc. 23; receive, accept, accede, accord, concur, lend oneself to, consent, coincide, reciprocate, go with; be -at one with etc. *adj.*; go along –, chime in –, strike in –, close- with; echo, enter into one's views, agree in opinion; vote –, give one's voice- for; recognize; subscribe –, conform –, 'defer- to; say -yes, – ditto, – amen; – aye- to.

acknowledge, own, admit, allow, avow, confess; concede etc. (*yield*) 762; come round to; abide by; permit etc. 760.

come to –, arrive at- -an understanding, – terms, – an agreement.

con-, af-firm; ratify, approve, endorse, countersign; visa; corroborate etc. 467.

go –, swim- with the stream, float with the current; be in the fashion, join in the chorus; be in every mouth.

Adj. assenting etc. *v.*; of one -accord, – mind; of the same mind, at one with, agreed, acquiescent, content; willing etc. 602.

un-contradicted, -challenged, -questioned, - controverted.

carried –, agreed- *-nem. con.* etc. *adv.*; unanimous; agreed on all hands, carried by acclamation.

affirmative etc. 535.

Adv. yes, yea, ay, aye, true; good; well; very - well, – true; well and good; granted; *placet*; even –, just- 'so; to be sure, surely, 'thou hast said;' truly, exactly, precisely, that's just it, indeed, certainly, certes, *ex concesso*; of course, unquestionably, assuredly, no doubt, doubtless, undoubtedly.

be it so; so -be it, – let it be, so mote it be; amen; with all my heart; willingly etc. 602.

with one -consent, – voice, – accord; unanimously, *unâ voce*, by common consent, in chorus, to a man, *nem. con.*; *nemine - contradicente*, – *dissentiente*; without a dissentient voice; as one man, one and all, on all hands.

489. Dissent.—**N.** dissent; discordance etc. (*disagreement*) 24; difference –, diversity- of opinion.

non-conformity etc. (*heterodoxy*) 984; protestantism, recusancy, schism; disaffection; secession etc. 624; recantation etc. 607.

dissension etc. (*discord*) 713; discontent etc. 832; cavilling.

protest; contradiction etc. (*denial*) 536; noncompliance etc. (*rejection*) 764; disapprobation etc. 932; hartal.

dissent-ient, -er; non-juror, -content; recusant, sectary, schismatic, protestant, non-conformist, separatist, non-co-operator, conscientious objector, passive resister.

V. dissent; demur; call in question etc. (*doubt*) 485; differ in opinion, disagree; say -no etc. 536; refuse -assent, – to admit; cavil, protest, raise one's voice against, make bold to differ; repudiate; contradict etc. (*deny*) 536; agree to differ.

have no notion of, differ *toto caelo*; revolt -at, – from the idea.

shake the head, shrug the shoulders; look - askance, – askant.

secede; recant etc. 607.

Adj. dissenting etc. *v.*; negative etc. 536; dissident, -entient; unconsenting etc. (*refusing*) 764;

non-content, -juring; protestant, recusant; unconvinced, -verted.

unavowed, unacknowledged; out of the question. discontented etc. 832; unwilling etc. 603; extorted.

sectarian, denominational, schismatic, heterodox, intolerant.

Adv. no etc. 536; at -variance, – issue- with; under protest; *non placet.*

Int. God forbid! not for the world; not on your life; I beg to differ; I'll be hanged if; never tell me; your humble servant, pardon me; tell that to the marines.

Phr. many men many minds; *quot homines tot sententiae*; *tant s'en faut*; *il s'en faut bien.*

490. Knowledge.—**N.** knowledge; cogn-izance, -ition, -oscence; acquaintance, experience, ken, privity, insight, familiarity; com-, ap-prehension; recognition; appreciation etc. (*judgment*) 480; intuition; consci-ence, -ousness; preception, precognition; acroamatics.

light, enlightenment; glimpse, inkling; side light; glimmer, -ing; dawn; scent, suspicion; impression etc. (*idea*) 453; discovery etc. 480a.

system –, body- of knowledge; science, philosophy, pansophy; theory, Etiology; circle of the sciences; pandect, doctrine, body of doctrine; cy-, ency-clopedia; school etc. (*system of opinions*) 484.

tree of knowledge; republic of letters etc. (*language*) 560.

erudition, learning, lore, scholarship, reading, letters; literature; booklearning, bookishness; biblio-mania, -latry; information, general information; store of -knowledge etc.; education etc. (*teaching*) 537; culture, attainments; acqui-rements, -sitions; accomplishments, proficiency; practical knowledge etc. (*skill*) 698; higher education, liberal education; dilettantism; rudiments etc. (*beginning*) 66.

deep –, profound –, solid –, accurate –, acroatic –, acroamatic –, vast –, extensive –, encyclopedical- -knowledge, – learning; omniscience, pantology.

march of intellect; progress –, advance- of - science, – learning; schoolmaster abroad.

V. know, ken, scan, wot; wot –, be aware etc. *adj.*- of; ween, weet, trow, have, possess.

conceive; ap-, com-prehend; take, realize, understand, appreciate; fathom, make out; recognize, discern, perceive, see, get a sight of, experience.

know full well; have –, possess- some knowledge of; be *-au courant* etc. *adj.*; have -in one's head, – at one's fingers' ends; know by - heart, – rote; be master of; *connaître le dessous des cartes*, know what's what etc. 698.

see one's way; learn, discover etc. 480a.

come to one's knowledge etc. (*information*) 527.

Adj. knowing etc. *v.*; cognitive; acroamatic. aware –, cognizant –, conscious- of; acquainted -ed –, made acquainted- with; privy –, no stranger- to; *au -fait*, – *courant*; in the secret; up –, alive- to; sensible of; behind the -scenes, – curtain; -let into; apprized –, informed- of; undeceived.

proficient –, versed –, read –, forward –

strong –, at home- in; conversant –, familiar-with.

erudite, instructed, learned, lettered, educated; high-brow; well-conned, -informed, -read, -grounded, -educated; enlightened, shrewd, insightful, *savant*, blue, bookish, scholastic, solid, profound, deep-read, book-learned; accomplished etc. (*skilful*) 698; omniscient; self-taught, -educated.

known etc. *v.*; ascertained, well-known, recognized, received, notorious, noted; proverbial; familiar, – as household words, to every schoolboy; hackneyed, trite, commonplace.

knowable, cogn-oscible, -izable.

Adv. to –, to the best of- one's knowledge.

Phr. one's eyes being opened etc. (*disclosure*) 529.

491. Ignorance.—N. ignorance, nescience, *tabula rasa*, crass ignorance, *ignorance crasse*; unacquaintance; unconsciousness etc. *adj.*; dark-, blind-ness; incomprehension, inexperience, simplicity.

unknown quantities, *x, y, z*.

sealed book, *terra incognita*, virgin soil, unexplored ground; dark ages.

[Imperfect knowledge] smattering, superficiality, half-learning, sciolism, glimmering; bewilderment etc. (*uncertainty*) 475; incapacity.

[Affectation of knowledge] pedantry; charlatanry, -ism:

V. be -ignorant etc. *adj.*; not -know etc. 490; know -not, – not what, – nothing of; have no -idea, – notion, – conception; not have the remotest idea; not know chalk from cheese.

ignore, be blind to; keep in ignorance etc. (*conceal*) 528.

see through a glass darkly; have a -film over the eyes, – glimmering etc. *n.*; wonder whether; not know what to make of etc. (*unintelligibility*) 519; not pretend –, not take upon oneself- to say.

Adj. ignorant, nescient; un-knowing, -aware, -acquainted, -apprized, -witting, -weeting, -conscious; wit-, weet-less; a stranger to; unconversant.

un-informed, -cultivated, -versed, -instructed, -taught, -initiated, -tutored, -schooled, -guided, -enlightened; Philistine; behind the age.

shallow, superficial, green, rude, empty, half-learned, illiterate; un-read, -informed, -educated, -learned, -lettered, -bookish; empty-headed; lowbrow; pedantic.

in the dark; be-nighted, -lated; blind-ed, -fold; hoodwinked; misinformed; *au bout de son latin*, at the end of his tether; at fault; at sea etc. (*uncertain*) 475; caught tripping.

un-known, -apprehended, -explained, -ascertained, -investigated, -explored, -heard of, -perceived; concealed etc. 528; novel.

Adv. ignorantly etc. *adj.*; unawares; for -anything, – aught- one knows; not that one knows.

Int. God –, Heaven –, the Lord –, nobody-knows.

Phr. a little learning is a dangerous thing.

492. Scholar.—N. scholar, *connoissuer*, *savant*, pundit, schoolman, professor, graduate,

wrangler, moonshee; academ-ician, -ist; fellow, don, post graduate, advanced student; master –, bachelor- of arts; doctor, licentiate, gownsman; philo-sopher, -math; scientist, clerk; soph, -ist, -ister; linguist, classicist; glosso-, etymo-, philologist; philologer; lexico-, glosso-grapher; scholiast, commentator, annotator, grammarian; *littérateur*, *literati*, *dilettanti*, *illuminati*; Mezzofanti, admirable Crichton, Maecenas.

book-worm, *helluo librorum*, biblio-phile, -maniac; blue-stocking, *bas-bleu*; big-wig, learned Theban.

learned –, literary- man; *homo multarum literarum*; man of -learning, – letters, – education; high-brow, intelligentsia.

antiquar-ian, -y; archeologist; sage etc. (*wise man*) 500.

pendant, *doctrinaire*; pedagogue, Dr. Pangloss; pantologist.

teacher etc. 540; schoolboy etc. (*learner*) 541.

Adj. learned etc. 490; brought up at the feet of Gamaliel.

493. Ignoramus.—N. ignoramus, illiterate, moron, dunce, numskull; wooden spoon; no scholar.

sciolist, smatterer, dabbler, half-scholar; *charlatan*; wiseacre.

novice, griffin; greenhorn etc. (*dupe*) 547; tyro etc. (*learner*) 541.

lubber etc. (*bungler*) 701; fool etc. 501; pedant etc. 492.

Adj. bookless, shallow, simple, dense, dumb, thick, dull, ignorant etc. 491.

494. Truth. [Object of knowledge.]—N. fact, reality etc. (*existence*) 1; plain matter of fact; nature etc. (*principle*) 5; truth, verity; gospel; orthodoxy etc. 983a; authenticity; veracity etc. 543.

accuracy, exactitude; exact-, precise-ness etc. *adj.*; precision, delicacy; rigor, mathematical precision, punctuality; clockwork precision etc. (*regularity*) 80.

orthology; *ipsissima verba*; letter of the law, realism.

plain –, honest –, sober –, naked –, unalloyed –, unqualified –, stern –, exact –, intrinsic- truth; *nuda veritas*; the very thing; not an illusion etc. 495; real Simon Pure; unvarnished tale; the truth, the whole truth and nothing but the truth; just the thing.

V. be -true etc. *adj.*, – the case; stand the test; have the true ring; hold -good, – true, – water; conform to- rule.

render –, prove- -true etc. *adj.*; substantiate etc. (*evidence*) 467.

get at the truth etc. (*discover*) 480a.

Adj. real, actual etc. (*existing*) 1; veritable, true; certain etc. 474; substantially –, categorically- true etc; true -to the letter; – to life, – to scale, – the facts, – as gospel; unimpeachable; veracious etc. 543; unre-, uncon-futed; un-ideal -imagined; realistic.

exact, accurate, definite, precise, well defined, just, right, correct, strict, severe; close etc. (*similar*) 17; literal; rigid, rigorous; scrupulous etc. (*con-*

scientious) 939; religiously exact, punctual, mathematical, scientific; faithful, constant, unerring; curious, particular, punctilious, meticulous, nice, delicate, fine.

genuine, authentic, legitimate, pukka; orthodox etc. 983a; official, ex officio.

pure, natural, sound, sterling; un-sophisticated, -adulterated, -varnished, -colored; in its true colors.

well-grounded, -founded; solid, substantial, tangible, valid; undis-torted, -guised; un-affected, -exaggerated, -romantic, -flattering.

Adv. truly etc.adj.; verily; indeed, in reality; as a matter of fact; beyond -doubt, - question; with truth etc. (veracity) 543; certainly etc. (certain) 474; actually etc. (existence) 1; in effect etc. (intrinsically) 5.

exactly etc. adj. ; ad amussim; verbatim, - et literatim; word for word, literally, literatim, totidem verbis, sic, to the letter, chapter and verse, ipsissimis verbis; ad unguem; to an inch; to a -nicety, - hair, - tittle, - turn, - T; au pied de la lettre; neither more nor less; in -every respect, - all respects; sous tous les rapports; at -any rate, - all events; strictly speaking.

Phr. the -truth, - fact- is; rem acu tetigisti.

495. Error.—N. error, fallacy; misconception, -apprehension, -understanding; inexactness etc. adj.; laxity; misconstruction etc. (misinterpretation) 523; miscomputation etc. (misjudgment) 481; non-sequitur etc. 477; misstatement, -report; anachronism; malapropism.

mistake; miss, fault, blunder, boner, bloomer, howler, quid pro quo, cross purposes, oversight, misprint, erratum, corrigendum, slip, blot, flaw, loose thread; trip, stumble etc. (failure) 732; botchery etc. (want of skill) 699; slip of the -tongue, - pen; lapsus -linguae, - calami, clerical error; bull etc. (absurdity) 497.

il-, de-lusion; false -impression, - idea; bubble; self-deceit, -deception; warped notion; mists of error; superstition, exploded notion.

heresy etc. (heterodoxy) 984; hallucination etc. (insanity) 503; false light etc. (fallacy of vision) 443; dream etc. (fancy) 515; fable etc. (untruth) 546; bias etc. (misjudgment) 481; misleading etc. v.

V. be -erroneous etc. adj.

cause error; mis-lead, -guide; lead -astray, - into error; beguile, misinform etc. (misteach) 538; delude; give a false -impression, - idea; falsify, garble, misstate; deceive etc. 545; lie etc. 544.

err; be -in error etc. adj.; - mistaken etc. v.; be deceived etc. (duped) 547; mistake, receive a false impression, deceive oneself; fall into - , lie under -, labor under- -an error etc. n.; be in the wrong, blunder; mis-apprehend, -conceive, -understand, -reckon, -count, -calculate etc. (misjudge) 481.

play -, be- at cross purposes etc. (misinterpret) 523.

trip, stumble; lose oneself etc. (uncertainty) 475; go astray; fail etc. 732; take the wrong sow by the ear etc. (mismanage) 699; put the saddle on the wrong horse; reckon without one's host; take the shadow for the substance etc. (credulity) 486; dream etc. (imagine) 515.

Adj. erroneous, untrue, false, devoid of truth, fallacious, faulty, apocryphal, unreal, ungrounded,

groundless; unsubstantial etc. 4; heretical etc. (heterodox) 984; unsound; illogical etc. 477; wrong.

in-, un-exact; in-accurate, -correct; indefinite etc. (uncertain) 475.

illus-ive, -ory; delusive; mock; ideal etc. (imaginary) 515; spurious etc. 545; deceitful etc. 544; perverted.

controvertible, unsustain-able, -ed; unauthenticated, untrustworthy.

exploded, refuted, discarded.

in - , under an- error etc. n.; mistaken etc. v.; tripping etc. v.; out, - in one's reckoning; aberrant; beside - , wide of the- -mark, - truth; astray etc. (at fault) 475; on -a false, - the wrongscent; in the wrong box; at cross purposes, all in the wrong, all abroad, at sea.

Adv. more or less.

496. Maxim.—N. maxim, aphorism; apo-, apoph-thegm; dictum, saying, gnome, adage, saw, proverb, epigram; sentence, mot, motto, word, byword, precept, moral, phylactery, protasis, brocard.

axiom, postulate, theorem, scholium, truism.

reflection etc. (idea) 453; conclusion etc. (judgment) 480; golden rule etc. (precept) 697; principle, principia; profession of faith etc. (belief) 484; formula.

wise - , sage - , received - , admitted - , recognized- maxim etc.; true - , common - , hackneyed - , trite - , commonplace- saying etc.

Adj. aphoristic, proverbial, phylacteric; axiomatic, gnomic.

Adv. as -the saying is, - they say.

497. Absurdity.—N. absurd-ity, -ness etc. adj.; imbecility etc. 499; alogy, nonsense, paradox, inconsistency; stultiloqu-y, -ence, futility.

blunder, muddle, bull; Irish-, Hibernic-ism; slipslop; anti climax; bathos; sophism etc. 477.

farce, burlesque, galimatias, amphigouri, rhapsody; farrago etc. (disorder) 59; extravagance, romance; sciomachy.

joke, catch, sell, pun, verbal·quibble, macaronic, jargon, fustian, twaddle etc. (no meaning) 517; exaggeration etc. 549; moonshine, stuff; mare's nest.

vagary, tomfoolery, mummery, monkey trick, practical joke, boutade, escapade.

V. play the fool etc. 499; stultify, blunder, muddle; joke; talk nonsense, parler à tort et à travers; battre la campagne; be -absurd etc, adj.

Adj. absurd, nonsensical, preposterous, egregious, senseless, farcical, inconsistent, ridiculous, extravagant, quibbling, futile; macaronic, punning, paradoxical.

foolish etc. 499; sophistical etc. 477; unmeaning etc. 517; without rhyme or reason; fantastic.

Int. fiddle-de-dee! pish! pish and tush! pho! stuff and nonsense! rubbish! !rot! bosh! in the name of the Prophet—figs!

Phr. credat Judaeus Apella; tell it to the marines.

498. Intelligence. Wisdom.—N. intelligence, capacity, comprehension, understanding, intellect etc. 450; nous, parts, sagacity, mother wit, wit, *esprit*, gumption, quick parts, grasp of intellect; acuteness etc. adj.; acumen, subtlety, penetration; perspica-cy, -city; discernment; long-headedness, due sense of, good judgment; discrimination etc. 465; craftiness, cunning etc. 702; refinement etc. (*taste*) 850.

head, brains, gray matter, headpiece, upper story, long head; eagle -eye, – glance; eye of a - lynx, – hawk.

wisdom, sapience, sense; good –, common –, plain –, horse- sense; clear thinking; rationality, reason; reasonableness etc. adj.; judgment; solidity, depth, profundity, caliber; enlarged views; reach –, compass- of thought; enlargement of mind.

genius, inspiration, *geist*, fire of genius, heaven-born genius, soul; talent etc. (*aptitude*) 698.

[Wisdom in action] prudence etc. 864; vigilance etc. 459; tact etc. 698; foresight etc. 510; sobriety, self-possession, *aplomb*, ballast, mental - poise, – balance.

a bright thought, inspiration, brainwave, not a bad idea.

V. be -intelligent etc. adj.; have all one's wits about one; understand etc. (*intelligible*) 518; catch –, take in- an idea; take a -joke, – hint.

see -through, – at a glance, – with half an eye, – far into, – through a millstone; penetrate; discern etc. (*descry*) 441; foresee etc. 510.

discriminate etc. 465; know what's what etc. 698; listen to reason.

Adj. [Applied to persons] intelligent, quick of apprehension, keen, acute, alive, brainy, awake, bright, quick, sharp; quick-, keen-, clear-, sharp- - eyed, -sighted, -witted; wide awake; canny, shrewd, astute; clear-headed; far-sighted etc. 510; discerning, perspicacious, penetrating, piercing; argute nimble-, needle-witted; sharp as a needle; alive to etc. (*cognizant*) 490; clever etc. (*apt*) 698; arch etc. (*cunning*) 702; *pas si -bête*; acute etc. 682.

wise, sage, sapient, sagacious, reasonable, rational, sound, in one's right mind, sensible, *abnormis sapiens*, judicious, strong-minded.

un-prejudiced, -biassed, -bigoted, -prepossessed; un-dazzled, -perplexed; of unwarped judgment, impartial, equitable, fair, broad-minded.

cool; cool-, long-, hard-, strong-headed; long-sighted, calculating, thoughtful, reflecting; solid, deep, profound.

oracular; heaven-directed, -born.

prudent etc. (*cautious*) 864; sober, staid, solid; considerate, politic, wise in one's generation; watchful etc. 459; provident etc. (*prepared*) 673; in advance of one's age; wise as -a serpent, – Solomon, – Solon.

[Applied to actions] wise, sensible, reasonable, judicious; well-judged, -advised; prudent, politic; expedient etc. 646.

499. Imbecility. Folly.—N. want of - intelligence etc. 498, – intellect etc. 450; shallow-, silli-, foolish-ness etc. adj.; imbecility, incapacity, vacancy of mind, poverty of intellect, clouded perception, poor head, apartments to let; stup-, stolidity; hebetude, dull understanding, meanest capacity; short-sightedness; incompetence etc. (*unskilfulness*) 699.

one's weak side; bias etc. 481; infatuation etc. (*insanity*) 503.

simplicity, puerility, babyhood; dotage, anility, second childishness, senile dementia, fatuity; idio-cy, -tism; driveling.

folly, frivolity, desipience, irrationality, trifling, ineptitude, nugacity, inconsistency, lip-wisdom, conceit; sophistry etc. 477; giddiness etc. (*inattention*) 458; eccentricity etc. 503; extravagance etc. (*absurdity*) 497; rashness etc. 863.

act of folly etc. 699.

V. be -imbecile etc. adj.; have no -brains, – sense etc. 498.

trifle, drivel, *radoter*, dote; ramble etc. (*madness*) 503; play the -fool, – monkey, – goat, take leave of one's senses; not see an inch beyond one's nose; stultify oneself etc. -699; talk nonsense etc. 497.

Adj. [Applied to persons] un-intelligent, - intellectual, -reasoning; mind-, wit-, reason-, brain-less; having no -head etc. 498; not -bright etc. 498; inapprehensible.

weak-, addle-, puzzle-, blunder-, muddle-, muddy-, pig-, beetle-, maggotty-, gross-headed; beef-, fat- -witted, -headed.

weak, feeble-minded; dull-, shallow-, rattle-, lack-brained; half-, nit-, short-, dull-, blunt-witted; shallow-, clod-, addle-pated; dim-, short-sighted; thick-skulled; weak in the upper story.

shallow, *borné*, weak, wanting, soft, nutty, sappy, spoony; dull, – as a beetle; stupid, heavy, insulse, obtuse, blunt, stolid, doltish, asinine; inapt etc. 699; prosaic etc. 843.

child-ish, -like; infant-ine, -ile; baby-, bab-ish; puerile; anile; simple etc. (*credulous*) 486.

fatuous, idiotic, imbecile, moronic, driveling; blatant, babbling; vacant; sottish; bewildered etc. 475.

blockish, unteachable; Boeot-ian, -ic; bovine; un-gifted, -discerning, -enlightened, -wise, - philosophical; apish.

foolish, silly, senseless, irrational, insensate, non-sensical, inept; maudlin.

narrow-minded etc. 481; bigoted etc. (*obstinate*) 606; giddy etc. (*thoughtless*) 458; rash etc. 863; eccentric etc. (*crazed*) 503.

[Applied to actions] foolish, unwise, indiscreet, injudicious, improper, unreasonable, without reason, ridiculous, silly, stupid, -asinine; ill-imagined, -advised, -judged, -devised; inconsistent, irrational, unphilosophical; extravagant etc. (*nonsensical*) 497; sleeveless, idle; useless etc. 645; inexpedient etc. 647; frivolous etc. (*trivial*) 643; absurd etc. 497.

Phr. *Davis sum non Oedipus.*

500. Sage.—N. sage, wise man; pundit; master - mind, – spirit of the age; longhead, thinker, philosopher.

authority, oracle, mentor, luminary, shining light, *esprit fort, magnus Apollo*, Solon, Solomon, Nestor, Magi, 'second Daniel.'

man of learning etc. 492; expert etc. 700; wizard etc. 994.

[Ironically] wiseacre, bigwig.

Adj. wise, learned; authoritative, oracular; erudite etc. 490; venerable, reverenced, revered, *emeritus*.

501. Fool.—N. fool, idiot, tomfool, wiseacre, simpleton, Simple Simon, nit-wit, witling, dizzard, donkey, ass; ninny, -hammer; moron, dolt, booby, Tom Noddy, looby, hoddy-doddy, noddy, nonny, noodle, nizy, owl; goose, -cap; *imbécile*; gaby, *radoteur*, nincompoop, *badaud*, zany; trifler, babbler; pretty fellow; natural, *niais*.

child, baby, infant, innocent, milksop, sop.

oaf, lout, loon, lown, dullard, doodle, calf, colt, buzzard, block, put, stick, stock, numps, tony.

bull-, dunder-, addle-, block-, dull-, logger-, jolt-, jolter-, beetle-, gross-, thick-, giddy-head; num-, thick- skull; lack-, shallow-brain; half-, lack-wit; dunder-pate; fat-head, poor stick.

sawney, gowk; clod, -hopper; clod-, clot-poll, pate; bull-calf; men of Boeotia, wise men of Gotham.

un sot à triple étage, sot; jobbernowl, changeling, mooncalf, *gobemouche*.

dotard, driveller; old -fogey, – woman; crone, grandmother.

greenhorn etc. (*dupe*) 547; dunce etc. (*ignoramus*) 493; lubber etc. (*bungler*) 701; madman etc. 504.

one who -will not set the Thames on fire, – did not invent gunpowder; *qui n'a pas inventé la poudre*; no conjuror.

502. Sanity.—N. sanity; soundness etc. *adj.*; rationality, normality, sobriety, lucidity, lucid interval; senses, sober senses, sound mind, *mens sana*.

V. be -sane etc. *adj.*; retain one's senses, – reason.

become -sane etc. *adj.*; come to one's senses, sober down.

render -sane etc. *adj.*; bring to one's senses, sober.

Adj. sane, rational, reasonable, *compos mentis*, of sound mind; sound, -minded.

self-possessed; sober, -minded.

in one's -sober senses, – right mind; in possession of one's faculties.

Adv. sanely etc. *adj.*

503. Insanity.—N. disordered -reason, – intellect; diseased –, unsound –, abnormal- mind; derangement, unsoundness.

insanity, lunacy; madness etc. *adj.*; mania, *rabies*, *furor*, mental aliénation, paranoia, aberration; *amentiá*, dementation, -tia, -cy; *dementia praecox*; *morosis*, idiocy, phrenitis, frenzy, raving, incoherence, wandering, delirium, calenture of the brain, delusion, hallucination; lycanthropy, brain storm, *delirium tremens*, D.T.'s.

vertigo, dizziness, swimming; sunstroke, *coup de soleil*, siriasis.

fanatism, infatuation, craze; oddity, eccentricity, twist, monomania; klepto-, dipso-mania; hypochondriasis etc. (*low spirits*) 837; *melancholia*, hysteria.

screw –, tile –, slate- loose; bee in one's bonnet, rats in the upper story.

dotage etc. (*imbecility*) 499.

V. be –, become- -insane etc. *adj.*; lose one's senses, – reason, – faculties, – wits; go –, run-

mad, run amuck; rave, dote, ramble, wander; drivel etc. (*be imbecile*) 499; have a -screw loose etc. *n.*, – devil; *avoir le diable au corps*; lose one's head etc. (*be uncertain*) 475.

derange, render –, drive- -mad etc. *adj.*; madden, dementate, addle the wits, derange the head, infatuate, befool; turn -the brain, – one's head.

Adj. insane, mad, lunatic; crazy, crazed, *aliéné*, *non compos mentis*; not right, cracked, touched; bereft of reason; unhinged, deranged, unsettled in one's mind; insensate, reasonless, beside oneself, demented, daft; phren-, fren-zied. -etic; possessed, – with a devil; far gone, maddened, moonstruck; shatterpated; barmy; mad-, scatter-, shatter-, crackbrained, off one's head; bug-house, *loco*.

maniacal; manic, manic-depressive; delirious, light-headed, incoherent, rambling, doting, wandering; frantic, raving, stark staring mad, amok, amuck.

corybantic, dithyrambic; rabid, giddy, vertiginous, dizzy, wild, haggard, mazed; flighty; distracted, -aught; bewildered etc. (*uncertain*) 475.

mad as a -March hare, – hatter; of -unsound mind etc. *n.* touched –, wrong –, not right- in one's -head, – mind, – wits, – upper story; out of one's -mind, – senses, – wits; not in one's right mind.

fanatical, infatuated, odd, eccentric; hypp-ed, -ish.

imbecile, silly etc. 499.

Adv. like one possessed.

Phr. the mind having lost its balance; the reason under a cloud; *tête -exaltée, -montée.*

504. Madman—N. madman, lunatic, maniac, bedlamite, candidate for Bedlam, raver, madcap; energumen; paranoiac; auto-, mono-, pyro-, megalo-, dipso-, klepto-maniac; hypochondriac etc. (*low spirit*) 837.

dreamer etc. 515; rhapsodist, seer, high-flier, enthusiast, crank, eccentric, nut, fanatic, *fanatico*; *exalté*; knight errant, Don Quixote.

idiot etc. 501.

505. Memory.—N. memory, remembrance; reten-tion, -tiveness; tenacity; *veteris vestigia flammae*; tablets of the memory; readiness.

reminiscence, recognition, recurrence, recollection, rememoration; retrospect, -ion; after-thought.

suggestion etc. (*information*) 527; prompting etc. *v.*; hint, reminder, token of remembrance, *memento*, souvenir, keepsake, relic, *memorandum*; remembrancer, flapper; memorial etc. (*record*) 551; commemoration etc. (*celebration*) 883.

things to be remembered, *memorabilia*.

art of –, artificial- memory; *memoria technica*; mnemo-nics, -technics; phrenotypics; Mnemosyne; memorandum-, note-, engagement-, prompt-book.

retentive –, tenacious –, green –, trustworthy –, capacious –, faithful –, correct –, exact –, ready –, prompt- memory.

V. remember, mind; retain the -memory, – remembrance- of; keep in view.

have –, hold –, carry –, keep –, retain- in *or* in the -thoughts, – mind, – memory, – remembrance; be in –, live in –, remain in –, dwell in –, haunt –, impress- one's -memory, – thoughts, – mind.

sink in the mind; run in the head; not be able to get it out of one's head; be deeply impressed with; rankle etc. (*revenge*) 919.

recur to the mind; flash -on the mind, – across the memory.

recognize, recollect, bethink oneself, recall, call up, conjure up, retrace; look –, trace- -back, – backwards; think –, look back- upon; review; call –, recall –, bring- to mind; remembrance; carry one's thoughts back; rake up the past.

suggest etc.'(*inform*) 527; prompt; put –, keep-in mind; remind; fan the embers; call –, summon –, rip- up; renew; *infandum renovare dolorem*; task –, tax –, jog –, flap –, refresh –, rub up –, awaken- the memory; pull by the sleeve; bring back the memory, put in remembrance, memorialize.

get –, have –, learn –, know –, say –, repeat- by -heart, – rote; drive –, get- into -one's head; say one's lesson; repeat, – as a parrot; have at one's finger's ends.

commit to memory; memorize; con, – over; fix –, rivet –, imprint –, impress –, stamp –, grave –, engrave –, store –, treasure up –, bottle up –, embalm –, enshrine- in the memory; load –, store –, stuff –, burden- the memory with.

redeem from oblivion; keep the memory -alive, – green; *tangere ulcus*; keep up the memory of; commemorate etc. (*celebrate*) 883.

make a note of etc. (*record*) 551.

Adj. remember-ing, -ed etc. *v.*; mindful, reminiscential; retained in the memory etc. *v.*; pent up in one's memory; fresh; green, – in remembrance, still vivid; unforgotten, present to the mind; within one's -memory etc. *n.*; indelible; not to be forgotten, unforgettable, enduring; uppermost in one's thoughts; memorable etc. (*important*) 642.

Adv. by -heart, – rote; without book, *memoriter*.

in memory of; *in memoriam*; suggestive.

Phr. *manet altâ mente repostum*; *forsan et haec olim meminisse juvabit*.

506. Oblivion.—N. oblivion; forgetfulness etc. *adj.*; obliteration etc. 552, of –, insensibility etc. 823 to- the past.

short –, treacherous –, loose –, slippery –, failing- memory; decay –, failure –, lapse- of memory; memory like a sieve; waters of -Lethe, – oblivion, *amnesia*.

pardon, acquittal, amnesty, oblivion; absolution.

V. forget; be -forgetful etc. *adj.*; fall –, sink-into oblivion; have -a short memory etc. *n.* – no head.

forget one's own name, have on the tip of one's tongue, come in at one ear and go out at the other.

slip –, escape –, fade from –, die away from-the memory; lose, – sight of.

unlearn; efface etc. 552 –, discharge- from the memory; consign to -oblivion, – the tomb of the Capulets; think no more of etc. (*turn the attention from*) 458; cast behind one's back, wean one's thoughts from; let bygones be bygones etc. (*forgive*) 918.

Adj. forgotten etc. *v.*; unremembered, past recollection, bygone, out of mind; buried –, sunk-in oblivion; clean -forgotten; gone out of one's -head, – recollection.

forgetful, oblivious, mindless, heedless, Lethean; insensible etc. 823- to the past.

Phr. *non mi ricordo*; the memory -failing, – deserting one, – being at (*or* in) fault.

507. Expectation.—N. expect-ation, -ance, -ancy; anticipation, reckoning, calculation; contingency; foresight etc. 510.

contemplation, prospection, look out; prospect, perspective, horizon, vista; destiny etc. 152.

suspense, waiting, abeyance; curiosity etc. 455; anxious –, ardent –, eager –, breathless –, sanguine- expectation; torment of Tantalus.

presumption, hope -etc. 858; trust -etc. (*belief*) 484; prognostication, auspices etc. (*prediction*) 511.

V. expect; look -for, – out for, – forward to; hope for, anticipate; have in -prospect, – contemplation; keep in view; contemplate, promise oneself; not -wonder etc. 870 -at, – if.

wait –, tarry –, lie in wait –, watch –, bargain- for; keep a -good, – sharp- look-out for; await; stand at 'attention,' abide, bide one's –, mark- time, watch.

foresee etc. 510; prepare for etc. 673; forestall etc. (*be early*) 132; count upon etc. (*believe in*) 484; think likely etc. (*probability*) 472; make one's mouth water.

lead one to expect etc. (*predict*) 511; have in store for etc. (*destiny*) 152.

prick up one's ears, hold one's breath.

Adj. expectant; expecting etc. *v.*; in--expectation etc. *n.*; on the watch etc. (*vigilant*) 459; open -eyed, -mouthed; agape, gaping, all agog; on -tenterhooks, – tiptoe, – the tiptoe of expectation; *aux aguets*; ready; curious etc. 455; looking forward to; prepared for; on the rack.

expected etc. *v.*; long expected, foreseen; in prospect etc. *n.*; prospective; in -one's eye, – view, – the horizon; impending etc. (*destiny*) 152.

Adv. expectantly; in the event of; on the watch etc. *adj.*; with -breathless expectation etc. *n.*; – bated breath, – eyes, – ears strained; *arrectis auribus*; on edge.

Phr. we shall see; *nous verrons.*

508. Inexpectation.—N. in-, non-expectation; false expectation etc. (*disappointment*) 509; miscalculation etc. 481; unforeseen contingency, the unforeseen, the unexpected.

surprise, sudden burst, thunderclap, blow, shock; bolt out of the blue; eye-opener; wonder etc. 870.

V. not -expect etc. 507; be taken by surprise; start; miscalculate etc. 481; not bargain for; come –, fall- upon.

be -unexpected etc. *adj.*; come -unawares etc. *adv.*; turn up, pop, drop from the clouds; come –, burst –, flash –, bounce –, steal –, creep- upon one; come –, burst- like a thunder-clap; -bolt; take –, catch- -by surprise, – unawares, – napping.

pounce –, spring a mine- upon.

surprise, startle, take aback, electrify, stun, stagger, take away one's breath, throw off one's guard; astonish etc.' (*strike with wonder*) 870.

Adj. non-expectant; surprised etc. *v.*; un-warned, -aware; off one's guard; inattentive etc. 458.

un-expected, -anticipated, -prepared for, -looked for, -foreseen, -hoped for; dropped from the clouds; beyond –, contrary to –, against- expectation; out of one's reckoning; unheard of etc. (*exceptional*) 83; startling; sudden etc. (*instantaneous*) 113.

Adv. abruptly, unexpectedly, plump, pop, *à l'improviste*, unawares; without -notice, – warning, – saying 'by your leave;' like a -thief in the night, – thunderbolt; in an unguarded moment; suddenly etc. (*instantaneously*) 113.

Int. heyday! etc. (*wonder*) 870.

Phr. little did one -think, – expect; nobody would ever -suppose, – think, – expect; who would have thought?'

509. Disappointment. [Failure of expectation.]—**N.** disappointment, disillusionment; blighted hope, balk; blow; slip 'twixt cup and lip; non-fulfilment of one's hopes; sad –, bitter- disappointment; trick of fortune; afterclap; false –, vain- expectation; miscalculation etc. 481; fool's paradise; much cry and little wool.

V. be disappointed; look -blank, – blue; look –, stand- -aghast etc. (*wonder*) 870; find to one's cost; laugh on the wrong side of one's mouth; find one a false prophet.

disappoint; crush –, dash –, balk –, disappoint –, blight –, falsify –, defeat –, not realize- one's -hope, – expectation; balk, jilt, bilk; play one -false, – a trick; dash the cup from the lips; tantalize; dumb-found, -founder; disillusion, -ize; dissatisfy, disgruntle.

Adj. disappointed etc. *v.*; disconcerted, aghast; out of one's reckoning; disgruntled.

Phr. the mountain brought forth a mouse; *nascitur ridiculus mus*; *parturiunt montes*; *diis aliter visum*, the bubble burst; one's countenance falling.

510. Foresight.—**N.** foresight, prospicience, prevision, longsightedness; anticipation; providence etc. (*preparation*) 673.

fore-thought, -cast; pre-deliberation, -surmise; foregone conclusion etc. (*prejudgment*) 481; prudence etc. (*caution*) 864.

foreknowledge; *prognosis*; pre-cognition, -science, -notion, -sentiment; second sight; sagacity etc. (*intelligence*) 498.

prospect etc. (*expectation*) 507; foretaste; prospectus etc. (*plan*) 626.

V. foresee; look -forwards to, – ahead, – beyond; scent from afar; feel in one's bones; look –, pry –, peep into the future.

see one's way; see how the -land !ies, – wind blows, – cat jumps.

anticipate; expect etc. 507; be beforehand etc. (*early*) 132; predict etc. 511; fore-know, -judge, -cast; surmise; have an eye to the -future, – main chance; *respicere finem*; keep a sharp look-out etc. (*vigilance*) 459; forewarn etc. 668.

Adj. foreseeing etc. *v.*; prescient; anticipatory; far-seeing, -sighted; sagacious etc. (*intelligent*) 498; weather-wise; provident etc. (*prepared*) 673; prospective etc. 507.

Adv. against the time when.

511. Prediction.—**N.** prediction, announcement; program, programme etc. (*plan*) 626; premonition etc. (*warning*) 668; prognosis, prophecy, vaticination, Mantology, prognostication, premonstration, augur-y, -ation; a-ha-riolation; fore-, a-boding; bode-, abode-ment; omin-ation, -ousness; auspices, forecast; sign, presage, prognostic; omen etc. 512; horoscope, nativity; sooth, -saying; fortune-telling; divination; crystal gazing, necromancy etc. 992; prophet etc. 512.

[Divination by the stars] astrology, horoscopy, astromancy, judicial astrology.*

[Place of prediction] *adytum*.

prefigur-ation, -ement; prototype, type.

V. predict, prognosticate, prophesy, vaticinate, divine, foretell, soothsay, augurate, tell fortunes; cast a -horoscope, – nativity; advise; forewarn etc. 668.

presage, augur, bode; a-, fore-bode, -cast; fore-, be-token; pre-figure, -show; portend; fore-show, -shadow, shadow forth, typify, ominate, signify, point to, precurse.

usher in, herald, premise, announce; lower.

hold out –, raise –, excite- -expectation, – hope; bid fair, promise, lead one to expect; be the -precursor etc. 64.

Adj. predicting etc. *v.*; predictive, prophetic, fatidical, vaticinal, oracular, Sibylline, haruspical, weatherwise.

ominous, presageful, portentous; augur-ous, -al, -ial; auspici-al, -ous; prescious, monitory, extispicious, premonitory, precusory, significant of, pregnant with, big with the fate of.

Phr. 'coming events cast their shadows before.'

*The following terms, expressive of different forms of divination, have been collected from various sources, and are here given as a curious illustration of bygone super-stitions:

Divination by oracles, Theomancy; by the Bible, Bibliomancy; by ghosts, Psychomancy; by spirits seen in a magic lens, Cristallomantia; by shadows or manes, Sciomancy; by appearances in the air, Aeromancy, Chaomancy, by the stars at birth, Genethliacs; by meteors, Meteoromancy; by winds, Austromancy; by sacrificial appearances, Aruspicy (or Haruspicy). Hieromancy, Hieroscopy; by the entrails of animals sacrificed, Hieromancy; by the entrails of a human sacrifice, Anthropomancy; by the entrails of fishes, Ichthyomancy; by sacrificial fire, Pyromancy; by red-hot iron, Sideromancy; by smoke from the alter, Capnomancy; by mice, Myomancy; by birds, Orniscopy, Ornithomancy; by a cock picking up grains, Alectryomancy (or Alectoromancy); by fishes, Ophiomancy; by herbs, Botanomancy; by flowers, Hydromancy; by fountains, Pegomancy; by a wand, Rhabdomancy; by dough of cakes, Crithomancy; by meal, Aleuromancy, Alphitomancy; by salt, Halomancy; by dice, Cleromancy; by arrows, Belomancy; by a balanced hatchet, Axinomancy; by a balanced sieve, Coscinomancy; by a suspended ring, Dactyliomancy; by dots made at random on paper, Geomancy; by precious stones, Lithomancy; by pebbles, Pessomancy; by pebbles drawn from a heap, Psephomancy; by mirrors, Catoptromancy; by writings in ashes, Tephramancy; by dreams, Oneiromancy; by the hand, Palmistry, Chiromancy; by nails reflecting the sun's rays, Onychomancy; by finger rings, Dactylomancy; by numbers, Arithmancy; by drawing lots, Sortilege; by passages in books, Stichomancy; by the letters forming the name of the person, Onomancy, Nomancy; by the *features.* Anthroposcopy: *by the mode of laughing.* Geloscopy: *by ventriloquism.* Gastromancy: *by walking in a circle.* Gyromancy: *by dropping melted wax into water.* Ceromancy: *by currents.* Bletonism.

512. Omen.—N. omen, portent, presage, prognostic, augury, auspice; sigh etc. (*indication*) 550; herald, forerunner, harbinger etc. (*precursor*) 64.

bird of ill omen, signs of the times; gathering clouds; warning etc. 668.

prefigurement etc. 511.

513. Oracle.—N. oracle; prophet, -ess; seer, soothsayer, augur, fortune-teller, palmist, medium, clairvoyant, crystal gazer, witch, geomancer, *aruspex*; a-, ha-ruspice; Sibyl; Python, -ess; Pythia; Pythian −, Delphian- oracle; Monitor, Sphinx, Tiresias, Cassandra, Sibylline leaves; Zadkiel, Old Moore; sorcerer etc. 994; interpreter etc. 524.

514. Supposition.—N. supposition, assumption, postulation, condition, pre-supposition, hypothesis, postulate, *postulatum*, theory, *data*; pro-, position; *thesis*, theorem; proposal etc. (*plan*) 626.

bare −, vague −, loose- -supposition, − suggestion; conceit; conjecture; guess, − work; rough guess, shot; conjecturality; surmise, suspicion, inkling, suggestion, suggestiveness, association of ideas, hint; presumption etc. (*belief*) 484; divination, speculation.

theorist, speculator, doctrinarian, hypothesist.

V. suppose, conjecture, surmise, suspect, guess, divine; theorize; pre-sume, -surmise, -suppose; assume, fancy, wis, take it; give a guess, speculate, believe, dare say, take it into one's head, take for granted.

put forth; pro-pound, -pose; moot; hypothesize; start, put a case, submit, move, make a motion; hazard −, throw out −, put forward- a - suggestion; − conjecture.

allude to, suggest, hint, put it into one's head.

suggest itself etc. (*thought*) 451; run in the head etc. (*memory*) 505; marvel −, wonder- -if, − whether.

Adj. supposing etc. *v.*; given, mooted, postulatory; assumed etc. *v.*; supposit-ive, -itious; gratuitous, speculative, conjectural, hypothetical, suppositional, theoretical, academic, supposable, presumptive, putative.

suggestive, allusive, stimulating.

Adv. if, − so be; an; on the -supposition etc. *n.*; *ex hypothesi*; in -case, − the event of; *quasi*, as if, provided; perhaps etc. (*by possibility*) 470; for aught one knows.

515. Imagination.—N. imagination; originality; invention; fancy; inspiration; *verve*; empathy.

warm −, heated −, excited −, sanguine −, ardent −, fiery −, boiling −, wild −, bold −,

daring −, playful −, lively −, fertile- - imagination, − fancy.

'mind's eye;' 'such stuff as dreams are made of.'

ideal-ity, -ism; romanticism, utopianism, castle-building; dreaming; frenzy; ecs-, ex-tasy; calenture etc. (*delirium*) 503; reverie, brown study, trance; somnambulism.

conception, *vorstellung*, ercogitation, 'a fine frenzy,' poetic frenzy, divine afflatus; cloud-, dream-land; flight −, fumes- of fancy; 'thick-coming fancies;' creation −, coinage- of the brain; imagery, word painting.

conceit, maggot, figment, myth, dream, vision, shadow, chimera; phan-tasm, -tasy; fantasy, fancy; whim, -sey; vagary, rhapsody, romance, *extravaganza*; air-drawn dagger, bugbear, nightmare; flying Dutchman, great sea-serpent, man in the moon, castle in the air, *château en Espagne*; Utopia, Atlantis, happy valley, millennium, fairy land; land of Prester John, kingdom of Micomicon; work of fiction etc. (*novel*) 594; poetry etc. 597; drama etc. 599; Arabian nights; *le pot au lait*; dream of Alnaschar etc. (*hope*) 858; day − golden- dream.

illusion etc. (*error*) 495; phantom etc. (*fallacy of vision*) 443; Fata Morgana etc. (*ignis fatuus*) 423; vapor etc. (*cloud*) 353; stretch of the imagination etc. (*exaggeration*) 549.

idealist, romanticist, visionary; mopus; romancer, dreamer; somnambulist; rhapsodist etc. (*fanatic*) 504.

V. imagine, fancy, conceive; ideal-, real-ize; dream, − of; 'give to airy nothing a local habitation and a name.'

create, originate, devise, invent, coin, fabricate; improvise, strike out something new.

set one's wits to work; strain −, crack- one's invention; rack −, ransack −, cudgel- one's brains; excogitate.

give -play, − the reins, − a loose- to the - imagination, − fancy; empathize; indulge in reverie.

conjure up a vision; fancy −, represent −, picture −, figure- to oneself; envisage.

float in the mind; suggest itself etc. (*thought*) 451.

Adj. imagined etc. *v.*; *ben trovato*; air-drawn, - built.

imagin-ing etc. *v.*, -ative; original, inventive, creative, fertile, productive; ingenious.

romantic, high-flown, flighty, extravagant, fanatic, enthusiastic, Utopian, Quixotic; preposterous, rhapsodical.

ideal, unreal; in the clouds, *in nubibus*; unsubstantial etc. 4; illusory etc. (*fallacious*) 495; fictitious, theoretical, hypothetical.

fabulous, legendary; myth-ic, -ological; chimerical; imagin-, vision-ary; notional; fan-cy, - ciful, -tastic, -tastical; whimsical; fairy, -like. dreamy, entranced, vaporous.

516. Meaning. [Idea to be conveyed.] [Thing signified.]**—N.** meaning; signific-ation, -ance; sense, expression; im-, pur-port; drift, tenor, implication, connotation, essence, force, spirit bearing, coloring; scope.

matter; subject, -matter; argument, text, sum and substance; gist etc. 5.

general –, broad –, substantial – colloquial –, literal –, plain –, simple –, accepted –, natural –, unstrained –, true etc. (*exact*) 494 –, honest etc. 543 –, *primâ facie* etc. (*manifest*) 525- meaning.

literality; literal interpretation; after acceptation; allusion etc. (*latency*) 526; suggestion etc. (*information*) 527; synonym; figure of speech etc. 521; acceptation etc. (*interpretation*) 522.

V. mean, signify, express, connote, denote; im-, pur-port; convey, imply, breathe, indicate, bespeak, bear a sense; tell –, speak- of; touch on; point –, allude- to; drive at; involve etc. (*latency*) 526; delcare etc. (*affirm*) 535.

understand by etc. (*interpret*) 522.

Adj. meaning etc. *v.*; expressive, suggestive, meaningful, allusive; signific-ant, -ative, -atory; pithy; full of –, pregnant with- meaning.

declaratory etc. 535; intelligible etc. 518; literal, metaphrastic; synonymous; tantamount etc. (*equivalent*) 27; implied etc. (*latent*) 526; explicit etc. 525; literal etc. 562.

Adv. to that effect; that is to say etc. (*being interpreted*) 522.

literally; evidently, from the context.

517. Unmeaningness. [Absence of meaning.]—**N.** unmeaningness etc. *adj.*; scrabble, scribble, scrawl, daub, (*painting*), strumming (*music*).

empty sound, dead letter, *vox et praeterea nihil*; 'a tale told by an idiot, full of sound and fury, signifying nothing;' 'sounding brass and a tinkling cymbal.'

nonsense, jargon, gibberish, jabber, mere words, hocus-pocus, fustian, rant, bombast, balderdash, palaver, patter, flummery, *verbiage*, babble, *bavardage*, *baragouin*, platitude, *niaiserie*; inanity; rigmarole, rodomontade; truism; *nugae canorae*; twaddle, twattle, fudge, trash; stuff, – and nonsense; bosh, rubbish, rot, drivel, moonshine, wish-wash, fiddle-faddle, flapdoodle; absurdity etc. 497; vagueness etc. (*unintelligibility*) 519.

V. mean nothing; be -unmeaning etc. *adj.*; twaddle, quibble, rant, gabble, scrabble etc. *n.*

Adj. unmeaning; meaning-, sense-less; nonsensical; void of -sense etc. 516.

in-, un-expressive; vacant, fatuous; not significant; insignificant,.

trashy, washy, inane, vague, trumpery, trivial, fiddle-faddle, twaddling, quibbling.

unmeant, not expressed; tacit etc. (*latent*) 526. inexpressible, undefinable, incommunicable.

Int. rubbish! etc. 497.

518. Intelligibility.—**N.** intelligibility, clearness, clarity, explicitness etc. *adj.*; lucidity, perspicuity; legibility, plain speaking etc. (*manifestation*) 525; precision etc. 494; a word to the wise.

V. be -intelligible etc. *adj.*; speak -for itself, – volumes; tell its own tale, lie on the surface.

render -intelligible etc. *adj.*; popularize, simplify, clear up; elucidate etc. (*explain*) 522.

understand, comprehend; take, – in; catch, grasp, recognize, follow, collect, master, make out;

see -with half an eye, – daylight, – one's way; enter into the ideas of; come to an understanding.

Adj. intelligible; clear, – as -day, – crystal, – noonday; lucid; per-, tran-spicuous; luminous, transparent; comprehensible.

easily understood, easy to understand, for the million, -intelligible to the meanest capacity, popularized.

plain, distinct, explicit, clear-cút; positive; definite etc. (*precise*) 494.

graphic, vivid, telling; expressive etc. (*meaning*) 516; illustrative etc. (*explanatory*) 522.

un-ambiguous, -equivocal, -mistakable etc. (*manifest*) 525, -confused; legible, recognizable; obvious etc. 525.

Adv. in plain -terms, – words, – English.

Phr. he that runs may read etc. (*manifest*) 525.

519. Unintelligibility.—**N.** unintelligibility, incomprehensibility, imperspicuity; in-conceivableness, vagueness etc. *adj.*; obscurity; ambiguity etc. 520; doubtful meaning; uncertainty etc. 475; perplexity etc. (*confusion*) 59; spinosity; *obscurum per obscurius*; mystification etc. (*concealment*) 528; latency etc. 526; transcendentalism.

paradox; enigma, riddle etc. (*secret*) 533; *dignus vindice nodus*; sealed book; steganography, freemasonry.

pons asinorum, asses' bridge; double –, high-Dutch, Greek, Hebrew; jargon etc. (*unmeaning*) 517.

obscurantist.

V. be -unintelligible etc. *adj.*; require - explanation etc. 522; have a doubtful meaning, pass comprehension.

render -unintelligible etc. *adj.*; conceal etc. 528; darken etc. 421; confuse etc. (*derange*) 61; perplex etc. (*bewilder*) 475.

not -understand etc. 518; lose, -- the clue; miss; not know what to make of, be able to make nothing of, give it up; not be able to -account for, – make either head or tail of; be at sea etc. (*uncertain*) 475; wonder etc. 870; see through a glass darkly etc. (*ignorance*) 491.

not understand one another; play at cross purposes etc. (*misinterpret*) 523.

Adj. un-intelligible, -accountable, -decipherable, -discoverable, -knowable, -fathomable; in-cognizable, -explicable, -scrutable; inap-, incomprehensible; insol-vable, -uble; impenetrable.

illegible, indecipherable, as Greek to one, unexplained, paradoxical; enigmatic, -al; puzzling, baffling.

obscure, dark, muddy, clear as mud, seen through a mist, dim, nebulous, shrouded in mystery; undiscernible etc. (*invisible*) 447; misty etc. (*opaque*) 426; hidden etc. 528; latent etc. 526; indefinite etc. (*indistinct*) 447; perplexed etc. (*confused*) 59; undetermined, vague, loose, ambiguous; mysterious; mystic, -al; transcendental; occult, recondite, esoteric, abstruse, crabbed.

incon-ceivable, -ceptible; searchless; above –, beyond –, past- comprehension; beyond one's depth; unconceived.

inexpressible, undefinable, incommunicable, unutterable, ineffable, unpronounceable.

520. Equivocalness. [Having a double sense.]—**N.** equivocalness etc. *adj.*; double - meaning etc. 516; ambiguity, *double entendre,* pun, paragram, *calembour,* quibble, *équivoque,* anagram; conundrum etc. (*riddle*) 533; word-play etc. (*wit*) 842; homonym, -y; amphibo-ly, -logy; ambiloquy.

Sphinx, Delphic oracle.

equivocation etc. (*duplicity*) 544; white lie, mental reservation etc. (*concealment*) 528.

V. be -equivocal etc. *adj.*;.have two -meanings etc. 516; equivocate etc. (*palter*) 544.

Adj. equivocal, ambiguous, amphibolous, homonymous; double-tongued etc. (*lying*) 544.

521. Metaphor.—N. figure of speech; *facon de parler,* way of speaking, colloquialism.

phrase etc. 566; figure, trope, metaphor, tralatition, metonymy, enallage, *catachresis,* *synecdoche,* *autonomasia;* irony, satire, figurativeness etc. *adj.*; image, -ry; *metalepsis,* type, anagoge, simile, personification, *prosopopaeia,* allegory, apologue, parable, fable; allusion, adumbration; application; euphemism; euphuism.

V. employ -metaphor etc. *n.*; personify, allegorize, adumbrate, shadow forth, apply, allude –, refer- to.

Adj. metaphorical etc. *n.*; figurative, catachrestical, typical, tralatitious, parabolic, allegorical, allusive, anagogical; ironical; colloquial.

Adv. so to -speak, – say, – express oneself; as it were.

Phr. *mutato nomine de te fabula nattatur.*

522. Interpretation.—N. interpretation, definition; explan-, explic-ation; solution, answer; rationale; plain –, simple –, strict- interpretation; meaning etc. 516.

translation; rend-ering, -ition; reddition; literal –, free- translation; key, crib; secret; clew etc. (*indication*) 550; Rosetta stone.

exegesis; ex-pounding, -position; Hermeneutics; comment, -ary; inference etc. (*deduction*) 480; illustration, exemplification; gloss, annotation, *scholium,* note; e-, di-lucidation, enucleation; *éclaircissement, mot de l'énigme.*

symptomat-, semei-ology; metoposcopy, physiognomy; diagnosis, prognosis; paleography etc. (*philology*) 560.

accept-ion, -ation, -ance; light, reading, lection, construction, version.

equivalent, – meaning etc. 516; synonym; para-, meta-phrase; convertible terms, apposition; dictionary etc. 562; polyglot.

V. interpret, explain, define, construe, translate, render; do –, turn- into; transfuse the sense of.

find out etc. 480*a*- -the meaning etc. 516- of; read; spell –, figure –, make- out; decipher, decode, unravel, disentangle, puzzle out; find the key of, enucleate, resolve, solve; read between the lines.

account for; find –, tell- the cause etc. 153- of; throw –, shed- -light, – new light, – a fresh light- upon; clear up, elucidate.

illustrate, exemplify; unfold, expound, comment upon, annotate; popularize etc. (*render intelligible*) 518.

take –, understand –, receive –, accept- in a particular sense; understand by, put a construction on, be given to understand.

Adj. explanatory, expository; explica-tive, -tory; exegetical; hermeneutic, interpretive, illustrative, elucidative, annotative, scholiastic.

polyglot; literal; para-, meta-phrastic; cosignificative, synonymous; equivalent etc. 27.

Adv. in -explanation etc. *n.*; that is to say, *id est, videlicet,* to wit, namely, in other words.

literally, strictly speaking; in -plain, – plainer- terms, – words, – English; more simply.

523. Misinterpretation.—N. misinterpretation, -apprehension, -understanding, - acceptation, -construction, -application; *catachresis;* cross -reading, – purposes; mistake etc. 495.

misrepresentation, perversion, exaggeration etc. 549; false -coloring – construction; abuse of terms; parody, travesty; falsification etc. (*lying*) 544.

V. mis-interpret,. -apprehend, -understand, - conceive, -judge, -doubt, -spell, -translate, - construe, -apply; mistake etc. 495.

misrepresent, pervert; garble etc. (*falsify*) 544; distort; detort; travesty, play upon words; stretch –, strain –, wrest- the -sense, – meaning; explain away; put a -bad, – false- construction on; give a false coloring, look through -rose colored –, – dark – spectacles.

be –, play- at cross purposes.

Adj. misinterpreted etc. *v.*; untranslat-ed, -able.

Adv. at cross purposes.

524. Interpreter.—N. interpreter, translator, ex-positor, -pounder, -ponent, -plainer; demonstrator.

scholiast, commentator, annotator; meta-, paraphrast.

spokesman, speaker, mouthpiece, prolocutor; diplomat etc. 758.

guide, courier, dragoman, *valet de place, cicerone,* showman; oneirocritic; Oedipus; oracle etc. 513.

525. Manifestation.—N. manifestation; unfolding; plainness etc. *adj.*; plain speaking; expression; showing etc. *v.*; exposition, demonstration, *séance*; exhibition, production; display, showing off etc. 882; premonstration. [Thing shown] exhibit, show.

indication etc. (*calling attention to*) 457; publicity etc. 531; disclosure etc. 529; openness etc. (*honesty*) 543, (*artlessness*) 703; *épachement,* prominence.

V. make –, render- manifest etc, *adj.*; bring - forth, – forward, – to the front, – into view; give notice, express; represent, set forth, exhibit; show,

– up; expose; produce; hold up –, expose- to view; set –, place –, lay- before -one, – one's eyes; tell to one's face; trot out, put through one's paces, unfold, show off, show forth, unveil, bring to light, display, demonstrate, unroll; lay open; draw –, bring- out; bring out in strong relief; call –, bring- into notice; hold up the mirror; wear one's heart upon his sleeve; show one's -face, – colors; manifest oneself; speak out; make no -mystery, – secret- of; unfurl the flag; proclaim etc. (*publish*) 531.

indicate etc. (*direct attention to*) 457; disclose etc. 529; elicit etc. 480*a*; interpret etc. 522.

be -manifest etc. *adj.*; appear etc. (*be visible*) 446; transpire etc. (*be disclosed*) 529; speak for itself, stand to reason; stare one in the face; loom large, appear on the horizon, rear its head; give - token, – sign, – indication of; tell its own tale etc. (*intelligible*) 518; go without saying.

Adj. manifest, apparent; salient, striking, demonstrative, prominent, in the foreground, notable, pronounced.

flagrant; notorious etc. (*public*) 531; arrant; stark staring; unshaded, glaring.

defin-ed, -ite; distinct, conspicuous etc. (*visible*) 446; obvious, evident, incontestable, unmistakable, not to be mistaken, plain, clear, palpable, self-evident, autoptical; intelligible etc. 518; clear as -day, – daylight, – noonday; plain as -a pikestaff, – the sun at noonday, – the nose on one's ~e, – the way to the parish church.

ostensible; open, – as day; overt, patent, express, explicit; naked, bare, literal, downright, undisguised, exoteric.

unreserved; frank, plain spoken etc. (*artless*) 703; barefaced, brazen, bold, shameless, daring, flaunting, loud.

manifested etc. *v.*; disclosed etc. 529; expressible, capable of being shown, producible; in-, un-concealable.

Adv. manifestly, openly etc. *adj.*; before one's eyes, under one's nose, to one's face, face to face, above board, *cartes sur table*, on the stage, in plain sight, in open court, in the open, – streets; at the cross roads; in market overt; in the face of -day, – heaven; in -broad –, open- daylight; without reserve; at first blush, *primâ facie*, on the face of; in set terms.

Phr. *cela saute aux yeux*; he that runs may read; you can see it with half an eye; it needs no ghost to tell us; the meaning lies on the surface; *cela va sans dire*; *res ipsa loquitur*.

526. Latency.—N. latency, inexpression; hidden –, occult- meaning; occultness, occultism, mysticism, mystery, cabala, symbolism, anagoge; silence etc. (*taciturnity*) 585; concealment etc. 528; more than meets the -eye, – ear; Delphic oracle; *les dessous des cartes*, undercurrent.

allusion, insinuation, implication; innuendo etc. 527; adumbration; 'something rotten in the state of Denmark.'

snake in the grass etc. (*pitfall*) 667; secret etc. 533.

darkness, invisibility, impreceptibility.

latent influence, power behind the throne; friend at court, wire puller.

V. be -latent etc. *adj.*; lurk, smoulder, underlie,

make no sign; escape -observation, – detection, – recognition; lie hid etc. 528.

laugh in one's sleeve; keep back etc. (*conceal*) 528.

involve, imply, implicate, connote, import, understand, allude to, infer, leave an inference; symbolize; whisper etc. (*conceal*) 528.

Adj. latent; lurking etc. *v.*; secret etc. 528; occult, symbolic, mystic; implied etc. *v.*; dormant.

un-apparent, -known, -seen etc. 441; in the background; invisible etc. 447; indiscoverable, dark; impenetrable etc. (*unintelligible*) 519; unspied, suspected.

un-said, -written, -published, -breathed, -talked of, -told etc. 527, -sung, -exposed, -proclaimed, -disclosed etc. 529, -pronounced, -mentioned, -expressed; not expressed, tacit.

un-developed, -solved, -explained, -traced, – discovered etc. 480*a*, -tracked, -explored, – invented.

indirect, crooked, inferential; by -inference, – implication; implicit, constructive; allusive, covert, muffled; steganographic; under-stood, -hand, -ground; concealed etc. 528; delitescent.

Adv. by a side wind; *sub silentio*; in the background; behind -the scenes, – one's back, – the veil; below the surface; on the tip of one's tongue; secretly etc. 528; between the lines; by a mutual understanding.

Phr. 'thereb~ ~ gs a tale.' 'that is another ~tor~'

527. Information.—N. information, enlightenment, acquaintance, knowledge etc. 490; publicity etc. 531.

communication, intimation; not-ice, -ification; e-an-nunciation; announcement; representation, round robin, presentment.

case, estimate, specification, report, advice, monition; news etc. 532; return etc. (*record*) 551; account etc. (*description*) 594; statement etc. (*affirmation*) 535.

mention; acquainting etc. *v.*; instruction etc. (*teaching*) 537; outpouring; intercommunication, communicativeness.

informant, authority, teller, announcer, annunciator, harbinger, herald, intelligencer, commentator, columnist, reporter, exponent, mouthpiece; informer, keek, eavesdropper, delator, detective, sleuth; *mouchard*, spy, stool pigeon, newsmonger; messenger etc. 534; *amicus curiae*.

valet de place, cicerone, pilot, guide; guide-, hand-book; *vade mecum*; manual; map, plan, chart, gazetteer; itinerary etc. (*journey*) 266.

hint, suggestion, wrinkle, innuendo, inkling, whisper, passing word, word in the ear, subaudition, cue, by-play; gesture etc. (*indication*) 550; gentle – broad- hint; *verbum sapienti*; word to the wise; insinuation etc. (*latency*) 526.

V. tell; inform, – of; acquaint, – with; impart, – to; make acquainted with, bring to the ears of, apprise, advise, enlighten, awaken.

let fall, mention, express, intimate, represent, communicate, make known; publish etc 531; notify, signify, specify, convey the knowledge of.

let one –, have one to- know; serve notice, give one to understand; give notice; set –, lay –, put-before; point out, put into one's head; put one in possession of; instruct etc. (*teach*) 537; direct the attention to etc. 457.

an-nounce, -nunciate; report, – progress; bring –, send –, leave –, write- word; tele-graph, -phone; ring –, call- up; wire; retail, render an account; give an account etc. (*describe*) 594; state etc. (*affirm*) 535.

disclose etc. 529; show cause; explain etc. (*interpret*) 522.

hint; give an inkling of; give –, drop –, throw out- a hint; insinuate; allude –, make allusion- to; glance at; tip off, tip the wink etc. (*indicate*) 550; suggest, prompt, give the cue, breathe; whisper, – in the ear.

give a bit of one's mind; tell one plainly, – once for all; speak volumes.

un-deceive, -beguile; set right, correct, open the eyes of, disabuse.

be -informed of etc.; know etc. 490; learn etc. 539; get scent of, gather from; awaken –, open one's eyes- to; become -alive, – awake- to; keep posted; hear, overhear, understand.

come to one's -ears, – knowledge; reach one's ears.

Adj. informed etc. *v.*; *communiqué*; reported etc. *v.*; published etc. 531; advisory.

expressive etc. 516; explicit etc. (*open*) 525, (*clear*) 518; plain-spoken etc. (*artless*) 703.

declara-, nuncupa-, exposi-tory; declarative, enunciative, communicat-ive, -ory; oral.

Adv. from information received; according to - rumor, – report; in the air; from what one can gather.

Phr. a little bird told me.

528. Concealment.—N. concealment; hiding etc. *v.*; occultation, mystification.

seal of secrecy; screen etc. 530; disguise etc. 530; masquerade; masked battery; hiding place etc. 530; cipher, code, crypt-, stegan-ography; invisible –, sympathetic- ink; palimpsest; freemasonry.

stealth, -iness; obreption; slyness etc. (*cunning*) 702.

latit-ancy, -ation; seclusion etc. 893; privacy, secrecy, secretness; *incognita*.

reticence; reserve; mental –, reservation, aside; *arrière pensée*, suppression, evasion, white lie, misprision; silence etc. (*taciturnity*) 585; suppression of truth etc. 544; underhand dealing; close-, secretive-ness etc. *adj.*; mystery.

latency etc. 526; snake in the grass; secret etc. 533.

V. conceal, hide, secrete, stow away, put out of sight; lock –, seal –, bottle- up.

cover, screen, cloak, veil, shroud; screen from - sight, – observation; draw the veil; draw –, close- the curtain; curtain, shade, eclipse, throw a veil over; be-cloud, -fog, -mask; mask, disguise; ensconce, muffle, smother; whisper.

keep -from, – back, – to oneself; keep -snug, – close, – secret, – dark; bury; sink, suppress; keep -from, – out of- -view, – sight; keep in –, throw into- the -shade, – background; cover up one's tracks; stifle, hush up, withhold, reserve; fence with a question; ignore etc. 460.

code, codify, use a cipher.

keep -a secret, – one's own counsel; hold one's

tongue etc. (*silence*) 585; make no sign, not let it go further; not breathe a -word, – syllable- about; not let the right hand know what the left is doing; hide one's light under a bushel, bury one's talent in a napkin.

keep –, leave- in -the dark, – ignorance; blind, – the eyes; blindfold, hoodwink, mystify; puzzle etc. (*render uncertain*) 475; bamboozle etc. (*deceive*) 545.

be -concealed etc. *v.*; suffer an eclipse; retire from sight, couch; hide oneself; lie -hid, – in ambush, – low, – *perdu*, – snug, – close; seclude oneself etc. 893; lurk, sneak, skulk, slink, pussyfoot, prowl; steal -into, – out of, – by, – along; play at -bopeep, – hind and seek; hide in holes and corners.

Adj. concealed etc. *v.*; hidden; veiled, secret, recondite, mystic, cabalistic, occult, dark; cryptic, - al, private, privy, *in petto*, auricular, clandestine, close, inviolate.

behind a -screen etc. 530; under -cover, – an eclipse; in -ambush, – hiding, – disguise; in a - cloud, – fog, – mist, – haze, – dark corner; in the -shade, – dark; clouded, wrapt in clouds; invisible etc. 447; buried, underground, *perdu*; incommunicado; secluded etc. 893.

un-disclosed etc. 529; -told etc. 527; covert etc. (*latent*) 526; mysterious etc. (*unintelligible*) 519.

irrevealable, inviolable; confidential; esoteric; not ot be spoken of.

obreptitious, furtive, stealthy, feline; skulking etc. *v.*; surreptitious, underhand, hole and corner; sly etc. (*cunning*) 702; secretive, evasive, non-committal, reserved, reticent, uncommunicative, buttoned up; close, – as wax; taciturn etc. 585.

Adv. secretly etc. *adj.*; in -secret, – private, – one's sleeve, – holes and corners; in the dark etc. *adj.*

januis clausis, with closed doors, *a huis clos*; hugger-mugger, *à la dérobée*; under the -cloak of, – rose, – table; *sub rosâ, en tapinois*, in the background, aside, on the sly, with bated breath, *sotto voce*, in a whisper, without beat of drum, *à la sourdine*.

in –, strict- confidence; confidentially etc. *adj.*; between -ourselves, – you and me; *entre nous, inter nos*, under the seal of secrecy; in -code, – cipher.

underhand, by stealth, like a thief in the night; stealthily etc. *adj.*; behind -the scenes, – the curtain, – one's back, – a screen etc. 530; *incognito*; *in camerâ*.

Phr. it -must, – will- go no further; 'tell it not in Gath,' nobody the wiser.

529. Disclosure.—N. disclosure; retection; un-veiling etc. *v.*; deterration, revealment, revelation; divulgence, expos-ition, -ure; *exposé*; whole truth; tell-tale etc. (*news*) 532.

acknowledgment, avowal; confession, -al; shrift. bursting of a bubble; *dénouement*.

V. dis-close, -cover, -mask; draw –, draw aside –, lift –, raise –, lift up –, remove –, tear- the -veil; – curtain; un-mask, -veil, -fold, -cover, -seal, -kennel; take off –, break- the seal; lay -open, – bare; expose; open, – up; bare, bring to light; evidence; make -clear, – evident, – manifest; evince.

divulge, reveal, break; let into the secret; reveal the secrets of the prison-house; tell etc. (*inform*) 527; breathe, utter, blab, peach; let -out, – fall, – drop, – the cat out of the bag; betray; tell tales, – out of school; come out with; give -vent, – utterance- to; open the lips, blurt out, vent, whisper about; speak out etc. (*make manifest*) 525; make public etc. 531; unriddle etc. (*find out*) 480*a*; split; blow the gaff; break the news.

acknowledge, allow, concede, grant, admit, own, confess, avow, throw off all disguise, turn inside out, make a clean breast; show one's -hand, – cards; unburden –, disburden- one's -mind, – conscience, – heart; open –, lay bare –, tell a piece of- one's mind; unbosom oneself, own to the soft impeachment; say –, speak- the truth; turn – King's, – Queen's, – States's- evidence.

raise –, drop –, lift –, remove –, throw off-the mask; expose; debunk; lay open; un-deceive, - beguile; disabuse, set right, correct, open the eyes of; *désillusionner*.

be -disclosed etc.; transpire, come to light; come in sight etc. (*be visible*) 446; become known, escape the lips; come –, ooze –, creep –, leak –, peep –, crop- out; show its -face, – colors; discover etc. itself; break through the clouds, flash on the mind.

Adj. disclosed etc. *v.*

Int. out with it!

Phr. the murder is out; a light breaks in upon one; the scales fall from one's eyes; the eyes are opened.

530. Ambush. [Means of concealment.]—**N.** hiding-place; secret -place,   drawer; recess, hole, funk hole, holes and corners; closet, crypt, *adytum*, abditory, *oubliette*, safe, – deposit.

am-bush, -buscade; stalking horse; lurking-hole, -place; secret path, backstairs; retreat etc. (*refuge*) 666.

screen, cover, shade, blinder; veil, curtain, blind, *purdah*, cloak, cloud.

mask, vizor, visor, disguise, masquerade dress, domino; *camouflage*.

pitfall etc. (*source of danger*) 667; trap etc. (*snare*) 545.

v. ambush, ambuscade, lie in ambush etc. (*hide oneself*) 528; lie in wait for; set a trap for etc. (*deceive*) 545.

Adv. *aux aguets.*

531. Publication.—**N.** publication; public - announcement etc. 527; promulgation, propagation, proclamation, pronouncement, encylical, *pronunciamento*; circulation, indiction, edition, imprint, impression, printing; hue and cry.

publicity, notoriety, currency, flagrancy, cry, *bruit*; *vox populi*; report etc. (*news*) 532.

the Press, fourth estate, public press, newspaper, periodical, journal, gazette; house organ, trade publication, tabloid, daily, weekly, monthly, quarterly, annual, magazine, monograph, book; review; news sheet, special edition, supplement, feature, rotogravure, comic strips; leaflet, pamphlet; telegraphy; publisher etc. *v.*

circular, – letter; manifesto, advertisement,

puff, placard, bill, *affiche*, broadside, poster; notice etc. 527; program.

V. publish; make -public, – known etc. (*information*) 527; speak –, talk- of; broach; utter; put forward; circulate, propagate, promulgate; spread –, abroad; rumor, diffuse, disseminate, evulgate; put –, give –, send- forth; emit, edit, get out; issue; cover, report; bring –, lay –, drag-before the public; give -out, – to the world; put –, bandy –, hawk –, buzz –, whisper –, bruit –, blaze- about; drag into the -open day, – limelight; voice.

proclaim, herald, blazon; blaze –, noise-abroad; sound a trumpet; trumpet –, thunder-forth; give tongue; announce with -beat of drum, – flourish of trumpets; proclaim -from the housetops, – at Charing Cross, at the cross roads; declare, declaim.

advertise, placard; post, – up; *afficher*, publish in the Gazette, send round the crier.

raise a -cry, – hue and cry, – report; set news afloat.

telegraph, cable, wireless, broadcast.

be -published etc; be –, become- public etc. *adj.*; come out; go –, fly –, buzz –, blow- about; get -about, – abroad, – afloat, – wind; find vent; see the light; go forth, take air, acquire currency, pass current; go -the rounds, – the round of the newspapers, – through the length and breadth of the land; *virum volitare per ora*; pass from mouth to mouth; spread; run –, spread- like wildfire.

Adj. published etc. *v.*; current etc. (*news*) 532; in circulation, public; notorious; flagrant, arrant; open etc. 525; trumpet-tongued; encyclical, promulgatory; exoteric.

Adv. publicly etc. *adj.*; in open court, with open doors; in the limelight.

Int. *Oyez!* O yes! notice!

Phr. notice is hereby given; this is –, these are-to give notice.

532. News.—**N.** news; information etc. 527; piece –, budget- of -news, – information; report, story, yarn, copy, filler, intelligence, tidings; stop press news.

word, advice, *aviso*, message; dis-, des-patch; telegram, cable, wireless telegram, radio-gram, marconi-gram, communication, errand, embassy; *bulletin.*

microphone; public address system, P.A.; walkie talkie, radio -telephone, -phone.

radio, wireless (Eng.), high fidelity, hi fi, radio set, transistor, receiver; speaker, loudspeaker, amplifier, tweeter, woofer; transmitter, broadcaster; AM –, FM –, short wave – transmitter; radio station, studio, control room, network, hookup, circuit; frequency, kilocycles, megacycles; band, channel, modulation, amplification; broadcast, program, newscast, network show, commerical announcement, serial, sound effects; signature, station – identification, – break, radio listener, audiophile.

television, TV, video, color television; television –, live – broadcast, telecast, TV show; televising, telecasting, transmission, television channel, video, audio, beam, reception, image, test pattern; rain, snow, ghost; television –, TV – station, mobile unit, TVmobile, transmitter, televisor, boost, camera; set, monitor, tube, screen.

rumor, hearsay, *on dit*, flying rumor, news stirring, cry, buzz, *bruit*, fame; talk, *oui-dire*, scandal, eavesdropping; town – , table- talk; tittle-tattle; *canard*, topic of the day, idea afloat.

fresh – , stirring – , old – stale- news; glad tidings; old – , stale- story.

narrator etc. (*describe*) 594; news-, scandal-monger; tale-bearer; tell-tale, gossip, tattler, busy-body, chatterer; informer.

broad-, news-, sports-caster; commentator, announcer, master of ceremonies, M.C., programmer, sound man, radioman, ham, radiooperator.

television technician, TV man, cameraman, soundman.

V. transpire etc. (*be disclosed*) 529; rumor etc. (*publish*) 531.

broadcast, radio, transmit, send, release, beam; sign – on, – off; go on – , go off – the air, monitor; listen – , tune – in.

tele-vise, -cast; color cast.

Adj. many-tongued; rumored; publicly – , currently- -rumored, – reported; rife, current, floating, afloat, going about, in circulation, in everyone's mouth, all over the town.

Adv. as the story -goes, – runs; as they say, it is said.

533. Secret.—N. secret; dead – , profound-secret; *arcanum*, mystery; latency etc. 526; Asian mystery; sealed book, secrets of the prison-house; *le dessous des cartes*.

enigma, riddle, puzzle, nut to crack, conun-drum, charade, rebus, logogriph; mono-, ana-gram; acrostic, cross-word puzzle; Sphinx; *crux criti-corum*.

maze, labyrinth, Hyrcynian wood.

problem etc. (*question*) 461; paradox etc. (*difficulty*) 704; unintelligibility etc. 519; *terra incognita* etc. (*ignorance*) 491.

Adj. secret etc. (*concealed*) 528.

534. Messenger.—N. messenger, envoy, emissary, legate; nuncio, internuncio; intermediary; ambassador etc. (*diplomatist*) 758.

marshal, flag-bearer, herald, crier, trumpeter, bellman, pursuivant, *parlementaire*, *apparitor*.

courier, runner, dawk, *estafette*; Hermes, Mercury, Iris, Ariel.

postman, letter carrier, telegraph boy, messenger boy, district messenger; despatch rider, commissionaire, errand-boy.

mail; post, -office; letter-bag; mail -boat, – train, – coach, – van, aerial mail; tele-graph, -phone; cable, wire; carrier-pigeon; wireless tele-graph, -phone; radiotele-graph, -phone.

journalist, newspaperman, reporter; gentleman – , representative- of the press; sob sister; penny-a-liner; special – , war – , own- correspondent; spy, scout; informer etc. 527.

535. Affirmation.—N. affirm-ance, -ation; statement, allegation, assertion, predication, declaration, word, averment.

asseveration, adjuration, swearing, oath, af-fidavit; deposition etc. (*record*) 551; avouchment, assurance; protest, -ation; profession; acknowledg-ment etc. (*assent*) 488; pledge.

vote, voice, suffrage, ballot.

remark, observation; position etc. (*proposition*) 514; saying, *dictum*, sentence, *ipse dixit*.

emphasis, positiveness, peremptoriness; dogmatism etc. (*certainty*) 474; dogmatist etc. 887.

V. assert; make -an assertion etc. *n.*; have one's say; say, affirm, predicate, declare, state, represent; protest, profess.

put -forth, – forward; advance, allege, propose, propound, enunciate, enounce, broach, set forth, hold out, maintain, contend, pronounce, pretend.

depose, depone, aver, avow, avouch, asseverate, swear; make – , take one's- oath; make – , swear – , put in- an affidavit; take one's Bible oath, kiss the book, vow, *vitam impendere vero*; swear till - one is black in the face, – all's blue; be sworn, call Heaven to witness; vouch, warrant, certify, assure, swear by bell, book and candle.

swear by etc. (*believe*) 484; insist – , take one's stand- upon; emphasize, lay stress on; assert - roundly, – positively; lay down, – the law; raise one's voice, dogmatize, have the last word; rap out; repeat; re-assert, -affirm.

announce etc. (*information*) 527; acknowledge etc. (*assent*) 488; attest etc. (*evidence*) 467; adjure etc. (*put to one's oath*) 768.

Adj. asserting etc. *v.*; declaratory, predicatory, pronunciative, affirmative, *soi-disant*; positive; certain etc. 474; express, explicit etc. (*patent*) 525; absolute, emphatic, flat, broad, round, pointed, marked, distinct, decided, confident, assertive, insistent, trenchant, dogmatic, definitive, formal, solemn, categorical, peremptory; unretracted; predicable, affirmable.

Adv. affirmatively etc. *adj.*; in the affirmative. with emphasis, *ex cathedrâ*, without fear of contradiction.

I must say, indeed, i' faith, let me tell you, why, give me leave to say, marry, you may be sure, I'd have you to know; upon my -word, – honor; by my troth, egad, I assure you; by -jingo, – Jove, – George, – etc.; troth, seriously, sadly; in – , in sober- -sadness, – truth, – earnest; of a truth, truly, pardi, perdy; in all conscience, upon oath; be assured etc. (*belief*) 484; yes etc. (*assent*) 488; I'll - warrant, – warrant you, – engage, – answer for it, – be bound, – venture to say, – take my oath; in fact, as a matter of fact, forsooth, joking apart; so help me God; not to mince the matter.

Phr. quoth he; *dixi*.

536. Negation.—N. ne-, abne-gation; denial; dis-avowal, -claimer; abjuration; contra-diction, - vention; recusation, protest; rebuttal; recusancy etc. (*dissent*) 489; flat – , emphatic- -contradiction, – denial; *démenti*.

qualification etc. 469; repudiation etc. 610; retraction etc. 607; confutation etc. 479; refusal etc. 764; prohibition etc. 761.

V. deny; contra-dict, -vene; controvert, give denial to, gainsay, negative, shake the head.

dis-own, -affirm, -claim, -avow; recant etc. 607; revoke etc. (*abrogate*) 756.

dispute, impugn, traverse, rebut, join issue upon; bring –, call- in question etc. (*doubt*) 485.

deny -flatly, – peremptorily, – ˙ emphatically, – absolutely, – wholly, – entirely; give the lie to, belie.

repudiate etc. 610; set aside, ignore etc. 460; rebut etc. (*confute*) 479; qualify etc. 469; refuse etc. 764.

Adj. denying etc. *v.*; denied etc. *v.*; contradictory; negat-ive, -ory; revocatory; recusant etc. (*dissenting*) 489; at issue upon.

Adv. no, nay, not, nowise; not a -bit, – whit, – jot; not -at all, – in the least, – so; no such thing; nothing of the -kind, – sort; quite the contrary, *tout au contraire*, far from it; *tant s'en faut*; on no account, in no respect; by -no, – no manner of-means; negatively.

phr. there never was a greater mistake; I know better; *non haec in foedera.*

537. Teaching.—N. teaching etc. *v.*; instruction; edification; education; pedagogy; tuition; tutor-, tutel-age; direction, guidance.

qualification, preparation; train-, school-ing etc. *v.*; discipline; exer-cise, -citation; drill, practice.

persuasion, proselytism, propagandism, *propaganda*; in-doctrination, -culcation, oculation.

explanation etc. (*interpretation*) 522; lesson, lecture, sermon, homily; apologue, parable; discourse, prelection, preachment, disquisition.

exercise, task; *curriculum*; course, – of study; grammar, three R's, initiation, A.B.C. etc. (*beginning*) 66.

elementary –, primary –, secondary –, grammar school –, high school –, college –, university –, technical –, liberal –, classical –, religious –, denominational –, moral –, secular-education; technical –, vocational- training; university extension lectures; propaedeutics, moral tuition; evening classes, correspondence course.

physical education, gymnastics, calisthenics, eurythmics; *sloyd.*

V. teach, instruct, edify, school, tutor; cram, prime, coach; enlighten etc. (*inform*) 527.

in-culcate, -doctrinate, -oculate, -fuse, -stil, -fix, - graft, -filtrate; im-bue, -pregnate, -plant; graft, sow the seeds of, disseminate, propagandize.

give an idea of; put -up to, – in the way of; set right.

sharpen the wits, enlarge the mind; give new ideas, open the eyes, bring forward, 'teach the young idea how to shoot;' improve etc. 658.

expound etc. (*interpret*) 522; lecture; prelect; read –, give- a -lesson, – lecture, – sermon, – discourse; hold forth, preach; sermon-, moral-ize; point a moral.

train, discipline; bring up, – to; educate, form, ground, prepare, qualify, drill, exercise, practice, habituate, familiarize with, nurture, dry-nurse, breed, rear, take in hand; break, – in; tame; pre-instruct; initiate; inure etc. (*habituate*) 613.

put to nurse, send to school.

direct, guide; direct attention to etc. (*attention*) 457; impress upon the -mind, – memory; beat into, – the head; convince etc. (*belief*) 484.

Adj. teaching etc. *v.*; taught etc. *v.*; educational;

scholastic, academic, doctrinal; disciplinal; instructive, didactic, hortative, pedagogic, tutorial.

Phr. the schoolmaster abroad.

538. Misteaching—N. mis-teaching, -information, -intelligence, -guidance, -direction, -persuasion, -instruction, -leading etc. *v.*; perversion, false teaching; sophistry etc. 477; college of Laputa; the blind leading the blind.

V. mis-inform, -teach, -direct, -guide, -instruct, -correct; pervert; put on a false –, throw off the-scent; deceive etc. 545; mislead etc. (*error*) 495; misrepresent; lie etc. 544; *ambiguas in vulgum spargere voces*, preach to the wise, teach one's grandmother to suck eggs.

render unintelligible etc. 519; bewilder etc. (*uncertainty*) 475; mystify etc. (*conceal*) 528; unteach.

Adj. misteaching etc. *v.*; unedifying.

Phr. *piscem natare doces.*

539. Learning.—N. learning; acquisition of -knowledge etc. 490, – skill etc. 698; acquirement, attainment; edification, scholarship, erudition; lore; information; self-instruction; study, reading, perusal; inquiry etc. 461.

ap-, prenticeship; pupil-age, -arity; tutelage, novitiate, matriculation.

docility etc. (*willingness*) 602; aptitude etc. 698.

V. learn; acquire –, gain –, receive –, take in –, drink in –, imbibe –, pick up –, gather –, get –, obtain –, collect –, glean- -knowledge, – information, – learning.

acquaint oneself with, master; make oneself -master of, – acquainted with; grind, cram; get –, coach- up; learn by -heart, – rote.

read, spell, peruse; con –, pore –, thumb- over; wade through; dip into; run the eye -over, – through; turn over the leaves.

study, be -studious etc. *adj.*; consume the midnight oil, mind one's book.

go to -school, – college, – the university; serve -an (*or* one's) apprenticeship, – one's time; learn one's trade; be -informed etc. 527; be -taught etc. 537.

Adj. studious; schol-astic, -arly; teachable; docile etc. (*willing*) 602; apt etc. 698; industrious etc. 682; learned erudite.

Adv. at one's books; *in statu pupillari* etc. (*learner*) 541.

540. Teacher.—N. teacher, trainer, instructor, institutor, master, tutor, don, director, Corypheus, dry nurse, coach, grinder, crammer; governor, bear-leader; governess, duenna; disciplinarian.

professor, lecturer, reader, prelector, prolocutor, preacher; Boanerges; pastor etc. (*clergy*) 996; schoolmaster, dominie, usher, pedagogue, abecedarian; schoolmistress, dame, monitor, proctor, pupil-teacher.

expositor etc. 524; preceptor, guide; mentor etc. (*adviser*) 695; pioneer, apostle, missionary, propagandist, moonshee; example etc. (*model for imitation*) 22.

professorship etc. (*school*) 542.

tutelage etc. (*teaching*) 537.

Adj. professorial, tutorial etc. 537.

541. Learner.—N. learner, scholar, student, *alumnus, élève,* pupil; ap-, prentice; articled clerk; school-boy, -girl, beginner, tyro, abecedarian, alphabetarian.

recruit, novice, neophyte, tenderfoot, inceptor, *débutant,* catechumen, probationer; undergraduate; freshman, frosh; sophomore, junior, senior; junior –, senior- soph; sophister, questionist, fellow-, commoner, pensioner, exhibitioner, sizar, scholar, fellow, advanced –, post graduate –, research- student.

class, form, grade, standard, remove; pupilage etc. (*learning*) 539.

disciple, follower, apostle, proselyte; fellow student, school-mate, -fellow, class mate, condisciple.

Adj. in statu pupillari, in leading strings, sophomoric.

542. School.—N. school, academy, university, *alma mater,* college, seminary, Lyceum; instit-ute, -ution, *conservatoire; palaestra, gymnasium.*

day –, boarding –, public –, preparatory –, elementary –, primary –, nursery –, dame's –, grammar –, Board –, County –, Council –, parochial –, denominational –, Sunday –, religious –, collegiate –, secondary –, continuation –, night –, correspondence –, secretarial –, military –, law –, medical –, business –, technical- school; technical –, training- college; Polytechnic; training ship; *Kin- dergarten,* nursery, *crèche,* reformatory.

pulpit, desk, reading desk, ambo, class-, lecture- room, theater, amphitheater, forum, stage, rostrum, platform, hustings, tribune.

school –, horn –, text-book; grammar, primer, abecedary, rudiments, manual, *vade mecum,* Lind- ley, Murray, Cocker.

professor-, lecture-, reader-ship; chair; schoolmaster etc. 540.

School Board, Council of Education; *propaganda.*

Adj. scholastic, academic, collegiate; educational.

Adv. ex cathedrâ.

543. Veracity.—N. veracity; truthfulness, frankness etc. *adj.*; truth, sooth, sincerity, candor, honesty, fidelity, plain dealing, *bona fides;* love of truth; probity etc. 939; ingenuousness etc. (*art- lessness*) 703.

the truth the whole truth and nothing but the truth; honest –, sober- truth etc. (*fact*) 494; un- varnished tale; light of truth.

V. speak –, tell- the truth; speak by the card; paint in its –, show oneself in ones -true colors; make a clean breast etc. (*disclose*) 529; speak one's mind etc. (*be blunt*) 703; not -lie etc. 544, – deceive etc. 545.

Adj. truthful, true; ver-acious, -edical; scrupulous etc. (*honorable*) 939; sincere, candid, frank, open, straightforward, unreserved; open-, true-, simple- hearted; honest, trustworthy; un- dissembling etc. (dissemble etc. 544); guileless, pure; unperjured, ture blue, as good as one's word;

unaffected, unfeigned, *bonâ fide;* outspoken, ingenuous etc. (*artless*) 703; undisguised etc. (*real*) 494.

Adv. truly etc. (*really*) 494; on oath; in plain words etc. 703; in –, with –, of a –, in good –, very- truth; as the -dial to the sun, – needle to the pole; honor bright; troth; in good -sooth, – ear- nest; unfeignedly, with no nonsense, in sooth, sooth to say, *bonâ fide, in foro conscientiae;* without equivocation; *cartes sur table,* from the bottom of one's heart; by my troth etc. (*affirmation*) 535.

544. Falsehood.—N. false-hood, -ness; fals-ity, -ification; misrepresentation; deception etc. 545; untruth etc. 546; guile; bad faith; lying etc. *v.*; misrepresentation; mendacity, perjury, false swearing; forgery, invention, fabrication; subrep- tion; covin.

perversion –, suppression- of truth; *suppressio veri;* perversion, distortion, false coloring; exaggeration etc. 549; prevarication, equivocation, shuffling, fencing, evasion, fraud; *suggestio falsi* etc. (*lie*) 546; mystification etc. (*concealment*) 528; simulation etc. (*imitation*) 19; dis-simulation, -sembling; deceit.

sham; pretence, pretending, malingering.

lip-homage, – service; mouth honor; hollowness; mere -show, – outside, eye-wash, win- dow dressing; duplicity, double dealing, insincerity, hypocrisy, cant, humbug, casuistry; jesuit-ism, -ry; pharisaism; Machiavelism, 'organized hypocrisy;' crocodile tears, mealy-mouthedness, quackery; charlatan-ism, -ry; gammon; bun-kum, -come; flam, ban, flim-flam, cajolery, flattery; Judas kiss; perfidy etc. (*bad faith*) 940; *il volto sciolto i pen- sieri stretti.*

unfairness etc. (*dishonesty*) 940; artfulness etc. (*cunning*) 702; misstatement etc. (*error*) 495.

V. be -false etc. *adj.,* – a liar etc. 548; speak - falsely etc. *adv.*; tell a -lie etc. 546; lie, fib; lie like a trooper; swear falsely, forswear, perjure oneself, bear false witness.

mis-state, -quote, -cite, -report, -represent; belie, falsify, pervert, distort; put a false construction upon etc. (*misinterpret*) 523.

prevaricate, equivocate, quibble; palter, – to the understanding; *répondre en Normand;* trim, shuf- fle, fence, mince the truth, beat about the bush, blow hot and cold, play fast and loose.

garble, gloss over, disguise, give a color to; give –, put- a -gloss, – false coloring- upon; color, varnish, cook, dress up, embroider; varnish right and puzzle wrong, exaggerate etc. 549.

invent, fabricate; trump –, get- up; forge, hatch, concoct; romance etc. (*imagine*) 515; cry 'wolf.'

dis-semble, -simulate; feign, assume, put on, pretend, make believe; play -false, – a double game; coquet; act –, play-, a part; affect etc. 855; simulate, pass off for; counterfeit, fake, sham, make a show of; malinger; swing the lead; say the grapes are sour.

cant, play the hypocrite, sham Abraham, *faire pattes de velours,* put on the mask, clean the out- side of the platter, lie like a conjuror; hang out –, hold out –, sail under- false colors; 'commend the poisoned chalice to the lips;' *ambiguas in vulgus spargere voces;* deceive etc. 545.

Adj. false, deceitful, mendacious, unveracious,

fraudulent, untruthful, dishonest; faith-, truth-, troth-less; un-fair, -candid; evasive; un-, disingenuous; hollow, insincere, *Parthis mendacior*; forsworn.

canting; hypocrit-, jesuit-, pharisa-ical; tartuffish; Machiavelian; double-tongued, -faced, -handed, -minded, -hearted, -dealing; two-faced, bare-faced; Janus-faced; smooth-faced, -spoken, -tongued; plausible; mealy-mouthed; affected etc. 855.

collus-ive; -ory; artful etc. (*cunning*) 702; perfidious etc. 940, spurious etc. (*deceptive*) 545; untrue etc. 546; falsified etc. *v.*; covinous.

Adv. falsely etc. *adj.*; *à la Tartufe*, with a double tongue; out of whole cloth; slily etc. (*cunning*) 702.

545. Deception.—N. deception; falseness etc. 544; untruth etc. 546; impos-ition, -ture; fraud, deceit, guile; fraudulen-ce, -cy; covin; knavery etc. (*cunning*) 702; misrepresentation etc. (*falsehood*) 544.

delusion, gullery, bluff, spoof, *blague*; juggl-ing, -ery; sleight of hand, legerdemain; presti-giation, -digitation; magic etc. 992; conjur-ing, -ation; hocus pocus, jockeyship; trickery, coggery, hanky-panky, chicanery, pettifogging, sharp practice; *supercherie*, cozenage, circumvention, ingannation, collusion; treachery etc. 940; practical joke.

trick, cheat, wile, ruse, blind, feint, plant, bubble fetch, catch, chicane, juggle, reach, hocus, bite; thimble-rig, card-sharping, artful dodge, machination, swindle, hoax; tricks upon travellers; confidence trick; strategem etc. (*artifice*) 702; theft etc. 791.

snare, trap, pitfall, decoy, gin; sprin-ge, -gle; noose, hook; bait, decoy-duck, tub to the whale, baited trap, *guet-à-pens*; cobweb, net, meshes, toils, mouse-trap, bird-lime; ambush etc. 530; trap-door, sliding panel, false bottom; spring-net, -gun; mask, -ed battery; mine; booby trap.

Cornish hug; wolf in sheep's clothing etc. (*deceiver*) 548; disguise, -ment; false colors, masquerade, mummery, borrowed plumes; *pattes de velours*.

mockery etc. (*imitation*) 19; copy etc. 21; counterfeit, sham, brummagem, make-believe, forgery, fraud, fake; lie etc. 546; 'a mockery, a delusion, and a snare,' hollow mockery.

whited –, painted- sepulcher; tinsel, paste, false jewelry, scagliola, ormolu, German silver, Britannia metal, paint; jerry building; man of straw.

illusion etc. (*error*) 495; *ignis fatuus* etc. 423; *mirage* etc. 443.

V. deceive, take in; defraud, cheat, jockey, do, cozen, diddle, nab, gyp, chouse, double cross, play one false, bilk, cully, jilt, bite, pluck, swindle, victimize; abuse; mystify; blind one's eyes; blindfold, hoodwink, spoof, bluff; throw dust into the eyes, 'keep the word of promise to the ear and break it to the hope,' 'draw a herring across the trail.'

impose –, practice –, play –, put –, palm –, foist- upon; snatch a verdict.

circumvent, overreach; out-reach, -wit, maneuvre; steal a march upon, give the go-by to, leave in the lurch.

set –, lay- a -trap, – snare- for; bait the hook, forlay, spread the toils, lime; decoy, waylay, lure,

beguile, delude, inveigle; tra-, -tre-pan; kidnap; let-, hook-in; trick; en-, in-trap, -snare, entoil, benet; nick, springe; catch, – in a trap; sniggle, entangle, illaqueate, hocus, practice on one's credulity, dupe, gull, hoax, fool, befool, bamboozle; hum, -bug; gammon, stuff up, dope, sell; play a -trick, – practical joke- upon one; balk, trip up, throw a tub to a whale; fool to the top of one's bent, send on -a wild goose chase, – a fool's errand; make -game, – a fool, – an April fool, – an ass- of; trifle with, cajole, flatter; come over etc. (*influence*) 615; gild the pill, make things pleasant, divert, put a good face upon; dissemble etc. 544.

cog, – the dice, play with marked cards; live by one's wits, play at hide and seek; obtain money under false pretences etc. (*steal*) 791; conjure, juggle, practice chicanery; gerrymander.

play –, palm –, foist –, fob- off.

lie etc. 544; misinform etc. 538; mislead etc. (*error*) 495; betray etc. 940; be -deceived etc. 547.

Adj. deceived etc. *v.*; deceiving etc. *v.*; cunning etc. 702; prestigi-ous, -atory; decept-ive, -ious; deceitful, covinous; delus-ive, -ory; illus-ive, -ory; elusive, insidious, *ad captandum vulgus*.

untrue etc. 546; mock, sham, make-believe, counterfeit, faked, pseudo, spurious, so-called, pretended, feigned, trumped up, bogus, scamped, fraudulent, tricky, factitious, artificial, bastard; surreptitious, illegitimate, contraband, adulterated, sophisticated; unsound, rotten at the core; colorable; disguised; meretricious; tinsel, pinchbeck, plated; catch-penny; Brummagem; simulated etc. 544.

Adv. under -false colors, – the garb of, – cover of; over the left.

Phr. *fronti nulla fides.*

546. Untruth.—N. untruth, falsehood, lie, story, thing that is not, fib, bounce, crammer, taradiddle, whopper.

forgery, fabrication, invention; mis-statement, -representation; perversion, falsification, gloss, *suggestio falsi*; exaggeration etc. 549.

fiction; fable, nursery tale; romance etc. (*imagination*) 515; untrue –, false –, trumped up- -story, – statement; thing devised by the enemy; *canard*; shave, sell, hum, yarn, traveler's tale, Canterbury tale, cock and bull story, fairy tale, clap-trap.

myth, moonshine, bosh, all my eye, -and Betty Martin, mare's nest, farce.

irony; half truth, white lie, pious fraud; mental reservation etc. (*concealment*) 528.

pretence, pretext; false -plea etc. 617; subterfuge, evasion, shift, shuffle, make-believe; sham etc. (*deception*) 545.

profession, empty words; Judas kiss etc. (*hypocrisy*) 544; disguise etc. (*mask*) 530.

V. have a false meaning; not ring true.

pretend, sham, feign, counterfeit, make believe.

Adj. untrue, false, trumped up; void of –, without- foundation; far from the truth, false as dicer's oaths; unfounded, *ben trovato*, invented, fabulous, fabricated, forged; fict-, fact-, supposit-, surrept-itious; e-, il-lusory; ironical; satirical; evasive; *soi-disant* etc. (*misnamed*) 565.

Phr. *se non e vero e ben trovato.*

547. Dupe.—N. dupe, gull, gudgeon, *gobemouche*, cull, cully, victim, sucker, pigeon, April fool; laughing stock etc. 857; Cyclops, simple Simon, flat, mug, greenhorn; fool etc. 501; puppet, cat's paw.
V. be -deceived etc. 545, – the dupe of; fall into a trap; swallow –, nibble at- the bait; bite; catch a Tartar.
Adj. credulous etc. 486; mistaken etc. *(error)* 495.

548. Deceiver.—N. deceiver etc. (deceive etc. 545); dissembler, hypocrite; sophist, Pharisee, Jesuit, Mawworm, Pecksniff, Joseph Surface, Tartufe, Janus; serpent, snake in the grass, cockatrice, Juaas, wolf in sheep's clothing; Molly Maguire; jilt; shuffler.
liar etc. (lie etc. 544; story-teller, perjurer, false-witness, *menteur à triple étage*, Scapin.
imposter, pretender, capper, decoy, fraud, *soi-disant*, humbug; adventurer; Cagliostro, Fernam Mendez Pinto; ass in lion's skin etc. *(bungler)* 701; actor etc. *(stage player)* 599.
quack, *charlatan*, mountebank, saltimbanco, *saltimbanque*, empiric, quacksalver, medicaster.
conjuror, juggler, magician, necromancer, trickster, prestidigitator, medium, jockey; crimp; decoy-duck, stool pigeon; rogue, knave, cheat; swindler etc. *(thief)* 792; jobber.

549. Exaggeration.—N. exaggeration; expansion etc. 194; hyperbole, stretch, strain, coloring; high coloring, caricature, *caricatura*; extravagance etc. *(nonsense)* 497; Baron Munchausen; men in buckram, yarn, fringe, embroidery, traveler's tale; Pelion upon Ossa.
storm in a teacup; much ado about nothing etc. *(over-estimation)* 482; puffery etc. *(boasting)* 884; rant etc. *(turgescence)* 577.
figure of speech, *façon de parler*; stretch of-fancy, – the imagination; flight of fancy etc. *(imagination)* 515.
false coloring etc. *(falsehood)* 544; aggravation etc. 835.
V. exaggerate, magnify, pile up, aggravate; amplify etc. *(expand)* 194; overestimate etc. 482; hyperbolize; over-charge, -state, -draw, -lay, -shoot the mark, -praise; make -much, – the most- of; strain, – a point; stretch, – a point; go great lengths; spin a long yarn; draw –, shoot with- a long-bow; deal in the marvelous.
out -Herod Herod, run riot, talk at random.
heighten, overcolor; color -highly, – too highly; embroider, *broder*; flourish; color etc. *(misrepresent)* 544; puff etc. *(boast)* 884.
Adj. exaggerated etc. *v.*; overwrought; bombastic etc. *(magniloquent)* 577; hyperbolical, on stilts; fabulous, extravagant, preposterous, egregious, *outré*, high-flying.
Adv. hyperbolically etc. *adj.*

550. Indication.—N. indication; symbol-ism, -ization; semeio-logy, -tics; sign of the times.
lineament, feature, *trait*, characteristic, trick,

diagnostic; divining-rod; cloven hoof; footfall; means of recognition; earmark.
sign, symbol; ind-ex, -ice, -icator; point, -er; marker; exponent, note, token, symptom.
type, figure, emblem, cipher, device; representation etc. 554; epigraph, motto, posy.
gest-ure, -iculation; pantomime; wink, glance, leer; nod, shrug, beck; touch, nudge; grip; dactylo-logy, -nomy; freemasonry, telegraphy, chirology, by-play, dumb-show; cue; hint etc. 527; clue, clew, key, scent, tract etc. 551.
signal, -post; rocket, blue light; watch-fire, -tower; telegraph, semaphore, flag-staff; cresset, fiery cross; calumet; heliograph, signal-, flash-lamp; radar, radar signal, pulse –, microwave –, radar; tracing, blips, pips.
mark, line, stroke, dash, score, stripe, streak, scratch, tick, dot, point, notch, nick, blaze; asterisk, red letter, Italics, heavy type, inverted commas, quotation marks, sublineation, underlining, jotting; print; impr-int, -ess, ession; note, annotation, mark of exclamation.
[For identification] badge, criterion; counter-check, -mark, -sign, -foil, duplicate, tally; label, tab, ticket, stub, billet, letter, counter, *tessera*, card, bill, check; witness, voucher; stamp; *cachet*; trade –, Hall- mark; broad arrow; signature; address –, visiting- card; *carte de visite*; credentials etc. *(evidence)* 467; passport, identity book; attestation; hand, – writing, sign-manual; cipher; monogram, – mark, seal, sigil, signet; autograph, -y, paraph, brand; superscription; in-, en-dorsement; title, heading, rubric, docket; *mot -de passe*, – du guet; *passe-parole*; shibboleth; watch-, catch-, pass-word; open *sesame*.
insignia, banner, -et, -ol; bandrol; flag, colors, streamer, standard, eagle, labarum, oriflamb, *oriflamme*, figure-head; ensign; pen-non, -nant, -dant; burgee, blue Peter, jack, ancient, gonfalon, union-jack; tricolor, stars and stripes; bunting.
hearldry, crest; coat of –, arms; armorial bearings, hatchment; e-, scutcheon; shield, supporters; livery, uniform; cockade, *epaulette*, brassard, chevron; garland, chaplet, love-knot, fillet, favor.
[Of locality] beacon, cairn, post, staff, flagstaff, hand, pointer, vane, cock, weathercock; guide-, hand-, finger-, directing-, sign-post; pillars of Hercules, pharos, signal fire; land-, sea-mark; lighthouse, balize; pole-, load-, lode-star; cynosure, guide; address, direction, name; sign, -board.
[Of the future] warning etc. 668; omen etc. 512; prefigurement etc. 511. [Of the past] trace record etc. 551. [Of danger] warning etc. 668; alarm etc. 669. [Of authority] scepter etc. 747. [Of triumph] trophy etc. 733. [Of quantity] gauge etc. 466. [Of distance] mile-stone, -post. [Of disgrace] brand, fool's cap, stigma, mark of Cain. [For detection] check, tell-tale; test etc. *(experiment)* 463.
notification etc. *(information)* 527; advertisement etc. *(publication)* 531.
word of command, call; bugle-, trumpet-call; reveille, taps; bell, alarum, cry; battle –, rallying-cry.
church, bell, angelus, sacring bell; muezzin.
exposition etc. *(explanation)* 522; proof etc. *(evidence)* 463; pattern etc. *(prototype)* 22.
V. indicate; be the -sign etc. *n.*- of; denote,

betoken; argue, testify etc. (*evidence*) 467; bear the -impress etc. *n.*- of; con-note, -notate.

represent, stand for; typify etc. (*prefigure*) 511; symbolize.

put -an indication, – a mark, – etc. *n.*; note, mark, tick, blaze, stamp, earmark; set one's seal upon; label, ticket, docket; dot, spot, score, dash, trace, chalk; print; im-print, -press, surprint; engrave, stereotype, electrotype.

signal, transmit, send, radiate, beam, deflect, echo, bounce back, return.

make a -sign etc. *n.*; signalize; give –, hang out- a signal; beck, -on; gesture; not; wink, glance, leer, nudge, shrug, tip the wink; gesticulate; raise –, hold up- the-finger, – hand; saw the air, suit the action to the word.

wave –, unfurl –, hoist –, hang out- a banner etc. *n.*; wave -the hand, – a kerchief; give the cue etc. (*inform*) 527; show one's colors; give –, sound- an alarm; beat the drum, sound the trumpets, raise a cry.

sign, seal, attest etc. (*evidence*) 467; underline etc. (*give importance to*) 642; call attention to etc. (*attention*) 457; give notice etc. (*inform*) 527.

Adj. indicat-ing etc. *v.*; -ive, -ory; de-, connotative; diacritical, representative, typical, symbolic, pantomimic, pathognomonic, symptomatic, ominous, characteristic, demonstrative, diagnostic, exponential, emblematic, armorial; individual etc. (*special*) 79.

known –, recognizable- by; indicated etc. *v.*; pointed, marked.

[Capable of being denoted] denotable; indelible.

Adv. in token of; symbolically etc. *adj.*; in dumb show.

Phr. *ecce signum*; *ex ungue leonem, ex pede Herculem.*

551. Record.—N. trace, vestige, relic, remains; scar, *cicatrix*, foot-step, -mark, -print; track, mark, wake, trail, spoor, scent, *piste*.

monument, hatchment, escutcheon, slab, tablet, trophy, achievement; obelisk, pillar, column, monolith, cromlech, dolmen; memorial; *memento* etc. (*memory*) 505; testimonial, medal, ribbon, order; commemoration etc. (*celebration*) 883.

record, note, minute; *dossier*; register, -try; census, roll etc. (*list*) 86; cartulary, diptych, Domesday book; entry, memorandum, indorsement, inscription, copy, duplicate, docket; notch etc. (*mark*) 550; muniment, deed etc. (*security*) 771; document; deposition, *procèsverbal*; affidavit; certificate etc. (*evidence*) 467.

note-, memorandum-, pocket-, commonplacebook; portfolio; scoring-board, -sheet; bulletin board; card index, file; pigeon-holes, *excerpta, adversaria*, jottings, dottings.

gazette, -er; newspaper, magazine etc. 531; alman-ac, -ack; calendar, ephemeris, noctuary, diary, log, journal, account-, cash-, day-book, ledger.

archive, scroll, state-paper, Congressional Record, return, blue-book; statistics etc. 86; *compte rendu*; Acts –, Transactions –, Proceedings- of; Hansard's Debates; chronicle, annals; legend; history, biography etc. 594.

registration; en-, in-rolment; tabulation; entry,

booking; signature etc. (*identification*) 550; recorder etc. 553; journalism.

drawing, photograph etc. 554; phonograph –, gramophone- record; music roll.

V. record; put –, place- upon record; go on record; chronicle, calendar, hand down to posterity; keep up the memory of etc. (*remember*) 505; commemorate etc. (*celebrate*) 883; report etc. (*inform*) 527; commit to –, reduce towriting; put –, set down- -in writing, – in black and white; put –, jot –, take –, write –, note –, set-down; note, minute, put on paper; take –, make- a -note, – minute, – memorandum; make a return.

mark etc. (*indicate*) 550; sign etc. (*attest*) 467.

enter, book; post, – up; insert, make an entry of; mark –, tick- off; register, list, docket, enroll, inscroll; file etc. (*store*) 636.

Adv. on record.

552. Obliteration. [Suppression of sign.]—N. obliteration; erasure, rasure; effacement; interference; cancel, -lation; cassation; circumduction; deletion, blot; *tabula rasa*.

V. efface, obliterate, erase, rase, expunge, cancel; blot –, take –, rub –, scratch –, strike –, wipe –, wash –, sponge- out; wipe –, rub- off; wipe away; deface, render illegible; draw the pen through, apply the sponge.

interfere, jam, black-, block-out; clutter, screen.

be -effaced etc.; leave no -trace etc. 449; 'leave not a rack behind.'

Adj. obliterated etc. *v.*; out of print; printless; leaving no trace; intestate; un-recorded, -registered, -written.

Int. *dele*; out with it!

553. Recorder.—N. recorder, notary, clerk; regis-trar, -trary, -ter; prothonotary; amanuensis, secretary, scribe, stenographer, remembrancer, book-keeper, *custos rotulorum*, Master of the Rolls.

annalist; histori-an, -ographer; chronicler, journalist, reporter, columnist; biographer etc. (*narrator*) 594; antiquary etc. (*antiquity*) 122; memorialist.

draughtsman etc. 559; engraver 558; photographer, cinematographer, camera man.

Recording instrument, recorder, camera, phonograph, gramophone, dictaphone, telegraphone, telautograph, printing telegraph, tape recorder, ticker, time recorder, cash register, turnstile, speedometer, voting machine, seismograph, radar, oscilloscope, teletypewriter, pari-mutuel, photostat.

554. Representation.—N. represent-ation, -ment; imitation etc. 19; illustration, delineation, depictment, portrayal; imagery, portraiture, iconography; design, -ing; art, fine arts; painting etc. 556; sculpture etc. 557; engraving etc. 558; photography, radiography, skiagraphy.

person-ation, -ification; impersonation; drama etc. 599.

picture, drawing, sketch, draught, draft; tracing;
copy etc. 21; photo-, helio-graph; daguerreo-,
talbo-, calo-, helio-type; cabinet, *carte-de-visite*,
snapshot; X-ray photograph; radio-gram, -graph,
skia-graph, -gram.
image, likeness, icon, portrait; striking – ,
speaking- likeness; very image; effigy, fac-simile.
figure, – head; puppet, doll, *figurine*, aglet,
manikin, lay-figure, model, *marionnette*, *fantoccini*, bust; waxwork, statue, -tte, automaton,
Robot.
hieroglyphic, anaglyph; dia-, mono-gram,
graph.
map, plan, chart; ground plan, projection,
elevation; ichno-, carto-graphy; atlas; outline,
scheme; view etc. (*painting*) 556.
artist, draughtsman etc. 559.
V. represent, delineate; depict, -ure; portray;
picture; take – , catch- a likeness etc. *n.*; hit off,
photograph, daguerreotype; figure; shadow -forth,
– out; adumbrate; body forth; describe etc. 594;
trace, copy; mold.
dress up; illustrate, symbolize.
paint etc. 556; carve etc. 557; engrave etc. 558.
person-ate, -ify; impersonate; assume a character; pose as; act; play etc. (*drama*) 599; mimic etc.
(*imitate*) 19; hold the mirror up to nature.
Adj. represent-ing etc. *v.*, -ative; illustrative;
represented etc. *v.*; imitative, figurative.
like etc. 17; graphic etc. (*descriptive*) 594.

555. Misrepresentation.—N. misrepresentation, distortion, exaggeration; daubing etc. *v.*;
bad likeness, daub, sign-painting; scratch,
caricature; *anamorphosis.*
V. misrepresent, distort, overdraw, travesty,
parody, burlesque, exaggerate, caricature, daub.
Adj. misrepresented etc. *v.*

556. Painting.—N. painting; depicting;
drawing etc. *v.*; design; perspective, skiagraphy;
chiaroscuro etc. (*light*) 420; composition; treatment, values, atmosphere, tone, technique.
historical – , portrait – , miniature – , landscape – , marine – , flower – , scene- painting;
scenography.
school, style; the grand style, high art, *genre,*
portraiture; ornamental art etc. 847.
mono-, poly-chrome; *grisaille.*
pallet, palette; easel; brush, pencil, stump;
blacklead, charcoal, crayons, chalk, pastel; paint
etc. (*coloring matter*) 428; water-, body-, oil-
color; oils, oil-paint; varnish etc. 356a; *gouache,*
tempera, distemper, fresco, water-glass; enamel;
encaustic painting; *graffito, gesso;* mosiac; tapestry.
picture, painting, piece, *tableau,* canvas; oil etc.-
painting; fresco, cartoon; easel – , cabinet- picture;
drawing, draught, draft; pencil etc. – , watercolor-
drawing; sketch; outline; study.
portrait etc. (*representation*) 554; whole – ; full
– , half- length; kitcat, head; miniature; shade,
silhouette; profile.
landscape, sea-piece, -scape; view, scene,
prospect; interior; bird's- eye view; pan-, di-orama;
still life.

picture – , art- gallery; *studio, atelier.*
V. paint, design, limn, draw, sketch, pencil,
scratch, shade, stipple, hatch, dash off, chalk out,
square up; color, dead-color, wash, varnish; draw
in -pencil etc. *n.*; paint in -oils etc. *n.*; stencil;
depict etc. (*represent*) 554.
Adj. painted etc. *v.*; pictorial, graphic, pic-
turesque, decorative; classical, romantic, pre-
Raphaelite, modern, cubist, futurist, vorticist.
pencil, oil etc. *n.*
Adv. in -pencil etc. *n.*
Phr. *fecit, delineavit.*

557. Sculpture.—N. sculpture, insculpture;
carving etc. *v.*; statuary, ceramics, plastic arts.
high – , low – , bas- relief; relievo; *basso-, alto-
, mezzo-relievo; intaglio,* anaglyph; medal, -lion;
cameo.
marble, bronze, *terra cotta*; ceramic ware, pottery, porcelain, china, earthenware, faïence,
enamel, *cloisonné.*
statue etc. (*image*) 554; cast etc. (*copy*) 21; glyptotheca.
V. sculpture, carve, cut, chisel, model, mold;
cast.
Adj. sculptured etc. *v.*; in relief, anaglyptic,
ceroplastic, ceramic; parian; marble etc. *n.*

558. Engraving.—N. engraving, chalcography;
line – , mezzotint – , stipple – , chalk- engraving;
dry-point, bur; etching, aquatinta; plate – , copper-
plate – , steel – , wood-, process-, photo-
engraving; xylo-, ligno-, glypto-, cero-, litho-,
chromolitho-, photolitho-, zinco-, glypho- -graphy,
-graph.
impression, print, engraving, plate; steel-, copper-plate; etching; mezzo- aqua-, litho-tint; cut,
woodcut, block; stereo-, grapho-, auto-, helio-type;
half-tone; *photogravure, rotogravure.*
graver, *burin,* etching-point, style; plate, stone,
wood-block, negative; die, punch, stamp.
printing; plate – , copper-plate – , intaglio – ,
anastatic – , lithographic – , color – , three color-
printing; type-printing etc. 591.
illustr-, illumin-ation; *vignette,* initial letter, *cul
de lampe,* tail-piece.
V. engrave, grave, stipple, scrape, etch; bite, –
in; lithograph etc. *n.*; print.
Adj. insculptured; engraved etc. *v.*
Phr. *sculpsit, imprimit.*

559. Artist.—N. artist; painter, limner, drawer,
sketcher, delineator; cartoon-, caricatur-ist,
designer, engraver; draughtsman; copyist; enameller, -list.
historical – , landscape – , genre – , marine – ,
flower – , portrait – , miniature – , scene – , sign-
painter; engraver; Apelles; sculptor, carver, chaser,
modeller, lapidary, *figuriste,* statuary; Phidias,
Praxiteles; Royal Academician.
photographer, retoucher.

560. Language.—N. language; phraseology etc.
569; speech etc. 582; tongue, lingo, vernacular,
slang; mother –, vulgar –, native- tongue;
household words; King's or Queen's English;
idiom; dialect etc. 563.
volapuk, esperanto, ido, occidental, Ro.
confusion of tongues, Babel, pasigraphie; pantomime etc. (signs) 550; onomatopaeia.
phil-, gloss-, glott-ology; linguistics,
chrestomathy; paleo-logy; -graphy; comparative
grammar.
literature, letters, polite literature, belles lettres,
muses, humanities, literae humaniores, republic of
letters, dead languages, classics; genius of a
language; scholarship etc. (knowledge) 490.
linguist etc. (scholar) 492.
V. speak, say, express by words etc. 566.
Adj. lingu-al, -istic; dialectic; vernacular,
current, colloquial, slangy; bilingual, polyglot;
literary.

561. Letter.—N. letter; character; hieroglyphic
etc. (writing) 590; type etc. (printing) 591;
capitals; majus-, minus-cule; alphabet, ABC,
abecedary, christcross row, chrisscross row.
consonant, vowel, diphthong; mute, surd;
sonant, liquid, labial, dental, palatal, gutteral.
syllable; mono-, dis-, poly-syllable; affix, prefix,
suffix.
spelling, orthography; phon-ography, -etic
spelling; ana-, meta-grammatism.
cipher, monogram, anagram; double – acrostic.
V. spell.
Adj. literal; alphabetical, abecedarian; syllabic;
uncial etc. (writing) 590; phonetic, voiced, mute
etc. n.

562. Word.—N. word, term, vocable; name
etc. 564; phrase etc. 566; root, etymon; derivative;
part of speech etc. (grammar) 567.
dictionary, vocabulary, word book, lexicon, index, glossary, thesaurus, gradus, delectus, concordance.
etymology, lexicology, derivation; phonology,
orthoepy; gloss-, termin-, orism-ology; paleology
etc. (philology) 560; comparative philology.
lexicograph-er, -y; glossographer etc. (scholar)
492; etymologist; logolept.
verbosity, verbiage, loquacity etc. 584.
Adj. verbal, literal; titular, nominal. [Similarly
derived] conjugate, paraonymous; derivative.
Adv. verbally etc. adj.; verbatim etc. (exactly)
494.

563. Neology.—N. neolo-gy; -gism; newfangled expression; barbarism; caconym; archaism,
black letter, monkish Latin; corruption; missaying,
antiphrasis.
paronomasia, play upon words; wordplay etc.
(wit) 842; double-entente etc. (ambiguity) 520;
palindrome, paragram, clinch; abuse of -language,
– terms.

dialect, brogue, patois, provincialism, broken
English, lingua franca; Brit-, Gall-, Scott-, Hibernicism; American-ism; Gipsy lingo, Romany, pidgin
English.
dog Latin, macaronics, gibberish, confusion of
tongues, Babel; jargon.
colloquialism etc. (figure of speech) 521; byword; technicality, lingo, slang, cant, argot, St.
Giles's Greek, thieves' Latin, peddler's French,
flash tongue, Billingsgate, Wall Street slang.
pseudonym etc. (misnomer) 565; Mr. So-and-so;
what d'ye call 'em, what's his name; thingum-my, -
bob; je ne sais quoi.
neologist, coiner of words.
V. coin words.
Adj. neologic, -al; rare; archaic; obsolete etc.
(old) 124; colloquial, dialectic, slang, cant.

564. Nomenclature.—N. nomenclature;
naming etc. v.; nuncupation, nomination, baptism;
orismology; onomatopaeia; antonomasia.
name; appella-tion, -tive; designation; title;
head, -ing, caption; denomination; by-name,
epithet.
style, proper name; prae-, ag-, cog-nomen;
patronymic, surname; cognomination; compellation, description; empty -title, – name; handle to one's name; namesake, eponym.
synonym, antonym.
term, expression, noun; by-word; convertible
terms etc. 522; technical term; cant etc. 563.
V. name, call, term, denominate, designate,
style, entitle, intitule, clepe, dub, christen, baptize,
nickname, characterize, specify, define, distinguish
by the name of; label etc. (mark) 550.
be -called etc. v.; take –, bear –, go (or be
known) by –, go (or pass) under –, rejoice in- the
name of.
Adj. named etc. v.; hight, yclept, known as;
what one may -well, – fairly, – properly, – fitly-
call.
nuncupa-tory, -tive; cognominal, titular,
nominal; orismological.

565. Misnomer.—N. misnomer; lucus a non
lucendo; Mrs. Malaprop; what d'ye call 'em etc.
(neologism) 563.
nickname, sobriquet, by-name, handle,
moniker; assumed -name, – title; alias; nom de -
guerre, – plume, – theâtre; pseudonym, pen
name, stage name.
V. mis-name, -call, - term; nickname; assume -a
name, – an alias.
Adj. misnamed etc. v.; pseudonymous; soi-
disant; self-called, -styled, -christened; so-called.
nameless, anonymous; without a –, having no-
name; innominate, unnamed.
Adv. in no sense.

566. Phrase.—N. phrase, expression, set
phrase; sentence, paragraph; figure of speech etc.
521; idi-om, -otism; turn of expression.

paraphrase etc. (*synonym*) 522; periphrase etc. (*circumlocution*) 573; motto etc. (*proverb*) 496. phraseology etc. 569.

V. express, phrase; word, – it; give -words, – expression- to; voice; arrange in –, clothe in –, put into –, express by- words; couch in terms; find words to express; speak by the card.

Adj. expressed etc. *v.*; idiomatic.

Adv. in -round, – set, – good, set- terms; in set phrases.

567. Grammar.—**N.** grammar, accidence, syntax, *praxis*, analysis, paradigm, punctuation; parts of speech, inflexion, case, declension, conjugation; *jus et norma loquendi*; Lindley Murray etc. (*school-book*) 542; correct style; philology etc. (*language*) 560.

V. parse, analyze; decline, conjugate; punctuate.

Adj. grammatical; syntactic; inflexional.

568. Solecism.—**N.** solecism; bad –, false –, faulty- grammar; slip, error; slip of the -pen, – tongue; *lapsus calami-*, – *linguae*; *faux pas*; slipslop; bull.

V. use -bad, – faulty- grammar; solecize, commit a solecism; murder the -King's, – Queen's-English; break Priscian's head.

Adj. ungrammatical; in-correct, -accurate; faulty, improper, incongruous, abnormal.

569. Style.—**N.** style, diction, phraseology, wording; manner, strain; composition; mode of expression, choice of words, literary power, ready pen, pen of a ready writer; command of language etc. (*eloquence*) 582; authorship; *la morgue littéraire*.

V. express by words etc. 566; write.

570. Perspicuity.—**N.** perspicuity etc. (*intelligibility*) 518; plain speaking etc. (*manifestation*) 525; defin-iteness, -ition; exactness etc. 494; perspicuousness, logical acuteness.

Adj. lucid etc. (*intelligible*) 518; explicit etc. (*manifest*) 525; exact etc. 494.

571. Obscurity.—**N.** obscurity etc. (*unintelligibility*) 519; involution; hard words; ambiguity etc. 520; vagueness etc. 475, inexactness etc. 495; what d'ye call 'em etc. (*neologism*) 563; cloudiness, confusion.

Adj. obscure etc. *n.*; crabbed, involved, confused.

572. Conciseness.—**N.** conciseness etc. *adj.*; brevity, 'the soul of wit,' laconism; Tacitus; ellipsis; syncope; abridgment etc. (*shortening*) 201; compression etc. 195; epitome etc. 596; monostitch; portmanteau word, telescope word, protogram.

V. be -concise etc. *adj.*; condense etc. 195; abridge etc. 201; abstract etc. 596; come to the point.

Adj. concise, brief, short, terse, close; to the point, exact; neat, compact, condensed, pointed; laconic, curt, pithy, trenchant, summary; pregnant; compendious etc. (*compendium*) 596; succinct; elliptical, epigrammatic, crisp, sententious.

Adv. concisely etc. *adj.*; briefly, summarily; in -brief, – short, – a word, – few words, – a nutshell; for shortness sake; to -come to the point, – make a long story short, – cut the matter short, – be brief; it comes to this, the long and short of it is.

573. Diffuseness.—**N.** diffuseness etc. *adj.*; amplification etc. *v.*; dilating etc. *v.*; verbosity, *verbiage*, wordiness, cloud of words, *copia verborum*; flow of words etc. (*loquacity*) 584.

poly-, tauto-, batto-, perisso-logy; pleonasm, exuberance, redundance; thrice-told tale; prolixity; circumlocution, *ambages*; periphra-se, -sis; roundabout phrases; episode; expletive; penny-a-lining; padding, drivel, twaddle, rigmarole; richness etc. 577.

V. be -diffuse etc. *adj.*; run out on, descant, expatiate, enlarge, dilate, amplify, expand, inflate, pad; launch –, branch- out; rant.

maunder, prose; harp upon etc. (*repeat*) 104; dwell on, insist upon.

digress, ramble, *battre la campagne*, beat about the bush, perorate, spin a long yarn, protract; spin –, swell –, draw- out, drivel.

Adj. dif-fuse; pro-fuse; wordy, verbose, largiloquent, copious, exuberant, effusive, pleonastic, lengthy; long, -some, -winded, -spun, -drawn out; diffusive, spun out, protracted, prolix, prosing, maundering; circumlocutory, periphrastic, ambagious, roundabout; digressive; dis-, ex-cursive, rambling, episodic; flatulent, frothy.

Adv. diffusely etc. *adj.*; at large, *in extenso*; about it and about it.

574. Vigor.—**N.** vigor, power, force; boldness, raciness etc. *adj.*; spirit, point, antithesis, piquancy; verve, glow, fire, warmth, ardor, enthusiasm; 'thoughts that breathe and words that burn;' strong language; punch; gravity, sententiousness; elevation, loftiness, sublimity.

eloquence; command of -words, – language.

Adj. vigorous, nervous, powerful, forcible, trenchant, mordant, biting, incisive, impressive; sensational.

spirited, lively, glowing, sparkling, racy, bold, slashing; pungent, *piquant*, full of point, pointed, pithy, antithetical; sententious.

lofty, elevated, sublime, grand, weighty, ponderous; eloquent; vehement, petulant, impassioned; poetic.

Adv. in -glowing, – good set, – no measured-terms.

575. Feebleness.—**N.** feebleness etc. *adj.*;

Adj. feeble, bald, tame, meager, insipid, nerve-les, jejune, vapid, trashy, cold, frigid, poor, dull, dry, languid; pros-ing, -y, -aic; unvaried, monotonous, weak, frail, washy, wishy-washy, sloppy; sketchy, slight; careless, slovenly, loose, lax; slip-shod, -slop; inexact; dis-jointed, - connected; puerile, childish; flatulent; rambling etc. (*diffuse*) 573.

576. Plainness.—N. plainness etc. *adj.*; simplicity, severity; plain -terms, – English; Saxon English; household words.
V. speak plainly; call a spade 'a spade;' plunge *in medias res*; come to the point.
Adj. plain, simple; un-ornamented, -adorned, - varnished; home-ly, -spun; neat; severe, chaste, pure, Saxon; commonplace, matter of fact, natural, prosaic, sober, unimaginative.
dry, unvaried, monotonous etc. 575.
Adv. in plain -terms, – words, – English, – common parlance; point blank.

577. Ornament.—N. ornament; floridness etc. *adj.*; turg-idity, -escence; altiloquence etc. *adj.*; orotundity; declamation, teratology; well-rounded periods; elegance etc. 578.
inversion, antithesis, alliteration, *paronomasia*; figurativeness etc. (*metaphor*) 521.
flourish; flowers of -speech, – rhetoric; euphuism, -emism.
big-, high-sounding words; macrology, *sesquipedalia verba*, sesquipedalianism; Alexandrine; inflation, pretension; rant, bombast, fustian, bunkum, balderdash, prose run mad; fine writing; Minerva press.
phrasemonger; euph-uist, -emist.
V. ornament, overlay with ornament, overcharge; smell of the lamp.
Adj. ornamented etc. *v.*; beautified etc. 847; ornate, florid, rich, flowery; euph-uistic, -emistic; sonorous; high-, big-sounding; inflated, swelling, tumid; turg-id, -escent; pedantic, pompous, stilted; high-flown, -flowing; sententious, rhetorical, declamatory; grandiose; grand-, magn-, altiloquent; sesquipedal, -ian; Johnsonian, mouthy; bombastic; fustian; frothy, flashy, flaming, flamboyant.
antithetical, alliterative; figurative etc. 521; artificial etc. (*inelegant*) 579.
Adv. *ore rotundo*; with rounded phrase.

578. Elegance.—N. elegance, purity, grace, ease, felicity, distinction, gracefulness, refinement, readiness etc. *adj.*; concinnity, euphony, numerosity, balance, rythym, symmetry, proportion; restraint; good taste, propriety.
well rounded –, well turned –, flowing-periods; the right word in the right place; antithesis etc. 577.
purist, stylist.
V. point an antithesis, round a period.
Adj. elegant, polished, classical, Attic, correct, Ciceronian, artistic; chaste, pure, Saxon, academical.

graceful, easy, readable, fluent, flowing, tripping; unaffected, natural, unlabored; mellifluous; euph-onidus, -emistic; rhythmical, balanced, symmetrical.
felicitous, happy, neat; well –, neatly- put, – expressed.

579. Inelegance.—N. inelegance; vulgarity, bad taste; stiffness etc. *adj.*; unlettered Muse; barbarism; slang etc. 563; solecism etc. 568; mannerism etc. (*affectation*) 855; euphuism; fustian etc. 577; cacophony; want of balance; words that - break the teeth, – dislocate the jaw.
V. be -inelegant etc. *adj.*
Adj. inelegant, graceless, ungraceful, unpolished; harsh, abrupt; dry, stiff, cramped, formal, *guindé*; forced, labored, awkward; artificial, mannered, ponderous; turgid etc. 577; affected, euphuistic; barbarous, uncouth, grotesque, rude, crude, halting; vulgar; offensive to ears polite.

580. Voice.—N. voice; vocality; organ, lungs, bellows; good –, fine –, powerful etc. (*loud*) 404 –, musical etc. 413- voice; intonation; tone etc. (*sound*) 402- of voice.
vocalization; cry etc. 411; strain, utterance, prolation; exclam-, ejacul-, vocifer-ation; enunci-, articul-ation; articulate sound; distinctness; clearness, – of articulation; stage whisper; delivery; attack.
accent, -uation; emphasis, stress; broad –, strong –, pure –, native –, foreign- accent; pronunciation.
[Word similarly pronounced] homonym.
orthoepy; euphony etc. (*melody*) 413.
gastri-, ventri-loquism; ventriloquist; polyphonism, -ist.
[Science of voice] phonology etc. (*sound*) 402.
V. sing, speak, utter, breathe, voice; give - utterance, – tongue; cry etc. (*shout*) 411; ejaculate, rap out; vocalize, prolate, articulate, enunciate, enounce, pronounce, accentuate, aspirate, deliver, mouth; emit, murmur, whisper, – in the ear, croon, yodel.
Adj. vocal, phonetic, oral; ejaculatory, articulate, distinct, stertorous; enunciative; accentuated, aspirated; euphonious etc. (*melodious*) 413.

581. Aphony—N. aphony, *aphonia*; dumbness etc. *adj.*; obmutescence; absence –, want- of voice; dysphony; silence etc. (*taciturnity*) 585; raucity; harsh etc. 410 –, unmusical etc. 414- voice; *falsetto*, 'childish treble;' mute, dummy, deaf mute.
V. keep silence etc. 585; speak -low, – softly; whisper etc. (*faintness*) 405.
silence; render -mute, – silent etc. 403; muzzle, muffle, suppress, smother, gag, strike dumb, dumbfound, -founder; drown the voice, put to silence, stop one's mouth, cut one short.
stick in the throat.
Adj. aphon-ous, -ic, dumb, mute; deaf-mute, –

and dumb; mum; tongue-tied; breath-, tongue-, voice-, speech-, word-less; mute as a ;fish, – stock-fish, – mackerel; silent etc. (*taciturn*) 585; muzzled; in-articulate, -audible.

croaking, raucous, hoarse, husky, dry, hollow, sepulchral, hoarse as a raven.

Adv. with -bated breath, – the finger on the lips; *sotto voce*; in a -low tone, – cracked voice, – broken voice; in an aside.

Phr. *vox faucibus haesit.*

582. Speech.—**N.** speech, faculty of speech; locution, talk, parlance, verbal intercourse, prolation, oral communication, word of mouth, *parole*, palaver, prattle; effusion.

oration, recitation, delivery, say, address, speech, lecture, harangue, sermon, *tirade*, screed, formal speech, salutatory, peroration; prelection; speechifying; soliloquy etc. 589; allocution etc. 586; interlocution etc. 588.

oratory; elo-cution, -quence; rhetoric, declamation; grandi-, multi-loquence; burst of eloquence; facundity; talkativeness; flow –, command- of -words, – language; *copia verborum*; power of speech, gift of the gab; *usus loquendi*.

speaker etc. *v.*; spokesman, pro-, inter-locutor; mouthpiece, Hermes; ora-tor, -trix, -tress; Demosthenes, Cicero; rhetorician; stump –, platform- orator, tub-thumper; elocutionist; speech-maker, patterer, *improvisatore.*

V. speak, – of; say, utter, pronounce, deliver, give utterance to; utter –, pour- forth; breathe, let fall, come out with; rap –, blurt- out; have on one's lips; have at the -end, – tip- of one's tongue.

break silence; open one's -lips, – mouth; lift –, raise- one's voice; give –, wag the- tongue; talk, outspeak; put in a word or two.

hold forth; make –, deliver- -a speech etc. *n.*; speechify, harangue, declaim, stump, flourish, spout, rant, recite, preach, sermonize, discourse, be on one's legs; have –, say- one's say; expatiate etc. (*speak at length*) 573; speak one's mind.

soliloquize etc. 589; tell etc. (*inform*) 527; speak to etc. 586; talk together etc. 588.

be -eloquent etc. *adj.*; have -a tongue in one's head, – the gift of the gab etc. *n.*

pass –, escape- one's lips; fall from the -lips, – mouth.

Adj. speaking etc., spoken etc. *v.*; oral, lingual, phonetic, not written, unwritten, outspoken; elo-quent, -cutionary; orat-, rhetorical; declamatory; grandiloquent etc. 577; talkative etc. 584.

Adv. orally etc. *adj.*; by word of mouth, *viva voce*, from the lips of.

Phr. quoth –, said- he etc.

583. Stammering. [Imperfect Speech.]—**N.** inarticulateness; stammering etc. *v.*; hesitation etc. *v.*; impediment in one's speech; aphasia, titubancy, traulism; whisper etc. (*faint sound*) 405; lisp, drawl, tardiloquence; nasal -tone, – accent; twang; *falsetto* etc. (*want of voice*) 581; broken -voice, – accents, – sentences.

brogue etc. 563; slip of the tongue, *lapsus linguae.*

V. stammer, stutter, hesitate, falter, hammer; balbu-tiate, -cinate; haw, hum and haw, be unable to put two words together.

mumble, mutter; maund, -er; whisper etc. 405; mince, lisp; jabber, gabble, gibber; sp-, spl-utter; muffle, mump; drawl, mouth; croak; speak -thick, – through the nose; snuffle, clip one's words; murder the -language, – King's (*or* Queen's) English; mis-pronounce, -say.

Adj. stammering etc. *v.*; inarticulate, guttural, nasal; tremulous.

Adv. *sotto voce* etc. (*faintly*) 405.

584. Loquacity.—**N.** loquac-ity, -iousness; talkativeness etc. *adj.*; garrulity; multiloquence, much speaking, effusion, wordiness.

jaw; gab, -ble; jabber, chatter; prate, prattle, cackle, clack; twaddle, trattle, rattle; *caquet, -terie*; blabber, *bavardage*, bibble-babble, gibble-gabble; small talk etc. (*converse*) 588.

fluency, flippancy, volubility, flowing tongue; flow, – of words; *flux de -bouche, – mots, – paroles; copia verborum, cacoëthes loquendi*; verbosity etc. (*diffuseness*) 573; gift of the gab etc. (*eloquence*) 582.

talker; chatter-er, -box; babbler etc. *v.*; rattle; ranter; sermonizer, proser, driveller; wind bag; gossip etc. (*converse*) 588; magpie, jay, parrot, poll, Babel; *moulin à paroles.*

V. be -loquacious etc. *adj.*; talk glibly, pour forth, patter; prate, palaver, prose, chatter, prattle, clack, jabber, jaw; rattle, – on; twaddle, twattle; babble, gabble; out-talk; talk oneself -out of breath, – hoarse; maunder, gush, blatter; talk a donkey's hind leg off; expatiate etc. (*speak at length*) 573; gossip etc. (*converse*) 588; din in the ears etc. (*repeat*) 104; talk -at random, – nonsense etc. 497; be hoarse with talking.

Adj. loquacious, talkative, conversational, garrulous, linguacious, multiloquous; chattering etc. *v.*; chatty etc. (*sociable*) 892; declamatory etc. 582; open-mouthed.

fluent, voluble, glib, flippant; long-tongued, -winded etc. (*diffuse*) 573.

Adv. trippingly on the tongue; glibly etc. *adj.*

Phr. the -tongue running -fast, – loose, – on wheels.

585. Taciturnity.—**N.** silence, muteness, ob-mutescence; taciturnity, pauciloquy, costiveness, curtness; reserve, reticence etc. (*concealment*) 528; *aposiopesis.*

man of few words.

V. be -silent etc. *adj.*; keep silence; hold one's -tongue, – peace, – jaw; not speak etc. 582; say nothing; seal –, close –, put a padlock on- the -lips, – mouth; put a bridle on one's tongue; keep one's tongue between one's teeth; make no sign, not let a word escape one; keep a secret etc. 528; not have a word to say; lay –, place- the finger on the lips; render mute etc. 581.

stick in one's throat.

Adj. silent, mute, mum; silent as -a post, – a stone, – the grave etc. (*still*) 403; dumb etc. 581.

taciturn, sparing of words; close, – mouthed, –

tongued; laconic, costive, inconversable, curt; reserved; reticent etc. (concealing) 528.
Int. tush! silence! mum! hush! chut! hist! tut! etc. 403.

586. Allocution.—N. allocution, alloquy, address; speech etc. 582; apostrophe, interpellation, appeal, invocation, salutation; word in the ear. [Feigned dialogue] dialogism.
platform etc. 542; audience etc. (interview) 588.
V. speak to, address, accost, make up to, apostrophize, appeal to, invoke; hail, salute; call to, halloo.
take -aside, – by the button, button-hole; talk to in private.
lecture etc. (make a speech) 582.
Int. soho! halloo! hey! hist! hi!

587. Response etc.; see Answer 462

588. Interlocution.—N. interlocution; collocution, colloquy, converse, conversation, confabulation, talk, discourse, verbal intercourse; communion, oral communication, commerce; dia-, duo-, tria-logue.
causerie, chat, chit-chat; small –, table –, teatable –, town –, village –, idle- talk; tattle, gossip, tittle-tattle; babble, -ment; tripotage, cackle, prittle-prattle, on dit; talk of the -town, – village.
conference, parley, interview, audience, pourparler; tête-à-tête; reception, conversazione; congress etc. (council) 696; pow-wow.
hall of audience, durbar, coliseum, assembly hall, auditorium.
palaver, debate, logomachy, war of words, controversy.
talker, gossip, tattler; Paul Pry; tabby; chatterer etc. (loquacity) 584; interlocutor etc. (spokesman) 582; conversation-ist, -alist; dialogist.
'the feast of reason and the flow of soul;' mollia tempora fandi.
V. talk together, converse, confabulate; hold –, carry on –, join in –, engage in- a conversation; put in a word; shine in conversation; bandy words; parley; palaver; chat, gossip, tattle; prate etc. (loquacity) 584.
discourse –, confer –, commune –, commerce- with; hold -converse, – conference, – intercourse; talk it over; be closeted with; talk with one -in private, – tête-à-tête.
Adj. conversing etc. v.; interlocutory; conversational, -able; discursive, -coursive; chatty etc. (sociable) 892; colloquial, tête-à-tête, confabulatory.

589. Soliloquy.—N. soliloquy, monologue, apostrophe.
solilo-quist, -quizer, monologist.

V. soliloquize; say –, talk- to oneself; say aside, think aloud, apostrophize.
Adj. soliloquizing etc. v.
Adv. aside.

590. Writing.—N. writing etc. v.; chiro-, stelo-, cero-graphy, graphology; stylography; pen-craft, -script, -manship; quill-driving; typewriting.
writing, manuscript, MS., literae scriptae; these presents.
stroke –, dash- of the pen; coup de plume; line; pen and ink.
letter etc. 561; uncial writing, cuneiform character, arrow-head, Ogham, Runes, futhorc; hieroglyphic, hieratic, demotic; script; contraction.
short-hand; steno-, brachy-, tachy-graphy; secret writing, writing in cipher; crypt-, stegan-ography; phono-, pasi-, poly-, logo-graphy.
copy; tran-, re-script; draft, rough –, fair- copy; handwriting; signature, sign-manual; auto-, mono-, holo-graph; hand, fist; mark.
calligraphy; good –, running –, flowing –, cursive –, legible –, copperplate –, round –, bold-hand.
cacography, griffonage, barbouillage; bad –, cramped –, crabbed –, illegible- hand; scribble etc. v.; pattes de mouche; ill-formed letters; pot-hooks and hangers.
stationery; pen, quill, goose-quill, reed; stylographic-, fountain-pen; pencil, style, stylus; paper, foolscap, parchment, vellum, papyrus, pad, tablet, block, note book, slate, marble, pillar, table, black board.
ink-bottle, -pot, -stand, -well, -horn; typewriter.
transcription etc. (copy) 21; inscription etc. (record) 551; superscription etc. (indication) 550.
composition, authorship; cacoethes scribendi.
writer, scribe, amanuensis, scrivener, secretary, clerk, penman, copyist, transcriber; quill-driver; writer for the press etc. '(author) 593.
shorthand writer, stenographer; typewriter, typist.
V. write, pen; copy, engross; write out, – fair; transcribe; scribble, scrawl, scrabble, scratch; interline; stain paper; write down etc. (record) 551; sign etc. (attest) 467; take down, – in shorthand; typewrite, type.
compose, indite, draw up, redact, draft, formulate; dictate; inscribe, throw on paper, dash off; concoct.
take -up the pen, – pen in hand; shed –, spill –, dip one's pen in- ink.
Adj. writing etc. v.; written etc. v.; in -writing, – black and white; under one's hand.
uncial, Runic, cuneiform, hieroglyphical etc. n.
Adv. currente calamo; pen in hand.

591. Printing.—N. printing; block –, type-printing, lino-, mono-type; plate printing etc. (engraving) 558; the press etc. (publication) 531; composition.
print, letterpress, text, matter, standing type; context, note, page, column; over-running; head-, foot-line, title.
typography; stereo-, electro-, apro-type; type,

black letter, heavy type, font, fount; pi, pie; capitals
etc. (*letters*) 561; diamond, pearl, nonpareil,
minion, brevier, bourgeois, long primer, small
pica, pica, english, great primer.
    folio etc. (*book*) 593; copy, impression, pull,
proof, galley –, author's –, page- proof, revise.
printer, compositor, reader; printer's devil.
    V. print; compose; put –, go- to press; pass –,
see- through the press; publish etc. 531; bring out;
appear in –, rush into- print.
    Adj. printed etc. *v.*; in type; typographical etc.
n.

592. Correspondence.—N. correspondence,
letter, epistle, note, *billet*, post-, letter-card,
missive, circular, form letter; favor, *billet-doux*;
des-, dis-patch; *bulletin*, communication etc. 532;
these presents; rescript, -ion; post etc. (*messenger*)
534; letter writer, correspondent.
    V. correspond, – with; write –, send a letter-
to; keep up a correspondence; drop a line to;
despatch; communicate with; circularize.
    Adj. epistolary.

593. Book.—N. book, -let; writing, work,
volume, tome, opuscule; tract, -ate; *livret*;
brochure, libretto, handbook, treatise, text-book,
codex, manual, pamphlet, monograph, enchiridion, circular, publication; book of poems;
novel; chap-book.
    part, issue, number, *livraison*; album, portfolio;
periodical, serial, magazine, *ephemeris*, annual,
journal.
    paper, bill, sheet, broadsheet, screed; leaf, -let;
fly-leaf, page; quire, ream.
    chapter, section, head, article, paragraph,
passage, clause, supplement, appendix; *feuilleton*.
    folio, quarto, octavo; duo-, sexto-, octo-decimo.'
en-, cyclopedia, dictionary, lexicon, thesaurus,
concordance, anthology, bibliography; compilation, compendium, catalogue etc. 86; library,
bibliotheca; the press etc. (*publication*) 531.
    writer, author, *littérateur*, essayist, journalist,
publicist; scribe, penman, war –, special –,
correspondent; pen, scribbler, the scribbling race;
ghost, hack, literary hack, Grub-street writer;
writer for –, gentlemen of –, representative of-
the press; reporter, penny-a-liner; editor, sub-
editor; playwright etc. 599; poet etc. 597.
    bookseller, publisher; biblio-pole, -polist, -
grapher; librarian; book -collector, – worm.
    book -shop, – club, circulating –, lending –,
public- library; publishing house.
    knowledge of books, bibliography; book-
learning etc. (*knowledge*) 490.

594. Description.—N. description, account,
statement, report; *exposé* etc. (*disclosure*) 529;
specification, particulars, scenario, plot; state –,
summary- of facts; brief etc. (*abstract*) 596; return
etc. (*record*) 551; *catalogue raisonné* etc. (*list*) 86;
guide-book etc. (*information*) 527.

delineation etc. (*representation*) 554; sketch,
vignette; monograph; minute –, detailed –, particular –, circumstantial –, graphic- account;
narration, recital, rehearsal, relation.
    histori-, chron-ography; historic Muse, Clio;
history; bi-, autobi-ography; necrology, obituary.
    narrative, history; memoir, memorials; annals
etc. (*chronicle*) 551; tradition, legend, saga, epic,
epos, story, tale, historiette; personal narrative,
journal, letters, life, adventures, fortunes, experiences, confessions; anecdote, ana, *trait*.
    work of fiction, short story, novelette, novel,
romance, penny dreadful, shilling, shocker,
Minerva press; fairy –, nursery- tale; fable,
allegory, parable, apologue.
    relator etc. *v.*; *raconteur*; historian etc. (*recor-
der*) 553; biographer, fabulist, novelist, story teller,
romancer, teller of tales, spinner of yarns, anec-
dotist.
    V. describe; set forth etc. (*state*) 535; draw a
picture, picture; portray etc. (*represent*) 554;
characterize, particularize; narrate, relate, recite,
recount, sum up, run over, recapitulate, rehearse,
fight one's battles over again.
    unfold etc. (*disclose*) 529- a tale; tell; give –,
render- an account of; report, make a report, draw
up a statement.
    detail; enter into –, descend to- -particulars, –
details.
    Adj. descriptive, graphic, narrative, epic,
suggestive, well-drawn; historic; auto-,
biographical, realistic, expository, tradition-al, -ary;
legendary; fabulous, mythical; anecdotic, storied;
described etc. *v.*

595. Dissertation.—N. dissertation, treatise,
essay; *thesis*, theme; tract, -ate, -ation, excursus;
discourse, memoir, disquisition, lecture, sermon,
homily, pandect.
    commentary, review, *critique*, criticism, article;
lead-er, -ing article, editorial; argument, running
commentary.
    investigation etc. (*inquiry*) 461; study etc. (*con-
sideration*) 451; discussion etc. (*reasoning*) 476;
exposition etc. (*explanation*) 522.
    commentator, critic, essayist, pamphleteer;
publicist, reviewer, leader writer, editor, annotator.
    V. dissert –, descant –, write –, touch- upon
a subject; dissertate; treat of –, take up –, ventilate –, discuss –, deal with –, go into –, canvass –, handle –, do justice to- a subject; comment, criticize, interpret-etc. 522.
    Adj. dis-cursive, -coursive; disquisitional,
disquisitionary; expository, critical.

596. Compendium.—N. compend, -ium; abstract, *précis*, epitome, *multum in parvo*, analysis,
pandect, digest, sum and substance, brief,
abridgment, summary, *aperçu*, draft, minute, note;
synopsis, textbook, *conspectus*, outlines, syllabus,
contents, heads, prospectus.
    album; scrap –, note –, memorandum –,
commonplace- book; extracts, *excerpta*, cuttings;
fugitive -pieces, – writings; *spicilegium*, flowers,

anthology, miscellany, *collectanea, analecta*; compilation.
recapitulation, *résumé*, review.
abbrevia-tion, -ture; contraction; shortening etc. 201; compression etc. 195.
V. abridge, abstract, epitomize, summarize; make –, prepare –, draw –, compile- an abstract etc. *n.*
recapitulate, review, skim, run over, sum up. abbreviate etc. (*shorten*) 201; condense etc. (*compress*) 195; compile etc. (*collect*) 72; edit, blue pencil.
Adj. compendious, synoptic, analectic, analytical; abridged etc. *v.*
Adv. in -short, – epitome, – substance, – few words.
Phr. it lies in a nutshell.

597. Poetry.—N. poetry, poetics, poesy, Muse, Calliope, tuneful Nine, Parnassus, Helicon, Pierides, Pierian spring, afflatus, inspiration.
versification, rhyming, making verses; prosody, scansion, orthometry.
poem; epic, – poem; epopee, *epopaea*, ode, epode, idyl, lyric, eclogue, pastoral, bucolic, georgic, dithyramb, anacreontic, sonnet, roundelay, *rondel, rondoletto, rondeau, rondo*, triolet; madrigal, canzonet, *cento*, monody, elegy, palinode; rhapsody.
dramatic –, lyric- poetry; opera; posy, anthology.
song, ballad, lay; love –, drinking –, war –, folk –, sea- song; lullaby; music etc. 415; nursery rhymes.
[Bad poetry] doggerel, Hudibrastic verse, prose run mad; macaronics; macaronic –, leonineverse; runes.
canto, stanza, distich, verse, line, couplet, triplet, quatrain, sestet; *strophe, antistrophe*, refrain, chorus, burden.
verse, rhyme, assonance, crambo, meter, measure, foot, numbers, strain, rhythm; accentuation etc. (*voice*) 580; iambus, dactyl, spondee, trochee, anapaest etc.; hex-, pent-ameter; Alexandrine; blank verse, alliteration.
elegiacs etc. *adj.*; elegiac etc. *adj.* -verse, – meter, – poetry.
poet, – laureate; laureate; minor poet, bard, lyrist, scald, troubadour, *trouvère*; mistrel; minne-, meister-singer; *improvisatore*; versifier, sonneteer; ballad monger; rhym-er, -ist, -ester; poetaster.
V. poetize, sing, versify, make verses, rhyme, scan.
Adj. poetic, -al; lyric, -al; tuneful; epic; dithyrambic etc. *n.*; metrical; a-, catalectic; elegiac, iambic, trochaic, spondaic, anapest; Ionic, Sapphic, Alcaic, Pindaric.

598. Prose.—N. prose, – writer, pros-aism, -aist, -er.
V. prose, write prose.
write -prose, – in prose.
Adj. pros-y, -aic; unpoetical.
rhymeless, unrhymed, in prose, not in verse.

599. Drama.—N. drama, the -drama, – stage,

– theater, – play; theatricals, dramaturgy, histrionic art, buskin, sock, *cothurnus*, Melpomene and Thalia, Thespis.
play, stage-play, piece, five-act play, tragedy, comedy, opera, comic opera, *vaudeville, comedietta, lever de rideau*, curtain raiser, interlude, afterpiece, exode, farce, *divertissement, extravaganza*, burletta, harlequinade, pantomime, mimodrama, burlesque, *opéra bouffe*, musical comedy, review, revue, intimate revue, variety, cabaret entertainment, *ballet, spectacle*, masque, *drame, comédie drame*; melo-drama, -drame; *comédie larmoyante*, emotional drama, sensation drama, tragi-, farcical-comedy; mono-drame, - logue; duologue; trilogy; charade, *proverbe*; mystery, miracle –, morality-, play.
act, scene, *tableau*; in-, intro-duction; pro-, epilogue, curtain; *libretto*, book, script.
performance, representation, show, *mise en scène*, stagery, *jeu de théâtre*, stage-craft; acting; gesture etc. 550; impersonation etc. 554; stage business, gag, patter, buffoonery.
theater; play-, opera-house; house; music hall; *cabaret*; amphitheater, circus, hippodrome; puppet-show, *fantoccini; marionnettes*, Punch and Judy.
cinema, -tograph-, picture –, theater, the pictures, the movies, the talkies.
auditory, *auditorium*, front of the house, stalls, boxes, balcony, dress –, upper- -circle, – boxes, amphitheater, pit, gallery; *foyer*; greenroom; dressing rooms, *coulisses*.
flat; drop, – scene; wing, screen, side-scene; transformation scene, curtain, act-drop, safety –, fire- curtain; *proscenium*, forestage.
stage, revolving stage, scene, the boards; star –, grave –, trap, mezzanine floor; flies; gridiron, floats, battens, footlights; lime –, spot –, flood –, bunch-lights; scenery, set, *décor*; orchestra.
theatrical -costume, – properties, props.
part, *rôle*, character, cast, *dramatis personae*; *répertoire*.
actor, player; stage –, strolling- player; old –, stager, performer; mime, -r; *artiste*; com-, tragedian, straight man; *tragédienne*, Thespian, Roscius, star.
pantomimist, clown, harlequin, *buffo*, buffoon, *farceur, grimacier*, pantaloon, columbine; *Pierrot, Pierrette*; punch, -inello; *pulcinell-o, -a*; mute, *figurante*, general utility; super, -numerary, extra.
mummer, guiser, guisard, gysart riasque.
mountebank, Jack Pudding; tumbler, posturemaster, acrobat, equilibrist, juggler, contortionist; *danseuse, ballerina*, ballet -dancer, – girl, *coryphée; bayadère, geisha*; chorus -singer, – girl.
company; first tragedian, *prima donna*, lead, leading lady, protagonist; *jeune premier*; juvenile lead, *débutant, -e*; light –, genteel –, low- - comedy, – comedian; *soubrette*, walking gentleman, *amoroso*, heavy, heavy father, *ingénue, jeune veuve, commère, compère*.
property man, *costumier*, machinist, stage hand, electrician, prompter, call-boy; director, manager; stage –, acting –, business- manager; *entrepreneur, impresario*, producer, press agent dramatic -author, – writer; play-writer, -wright; dramatist, mimographer; dramatic critic.
V. act, play, perform; stage, produce, put on the stage; personate etc. 554; mimic etc. (*imitate*) 19; enact; play –, act –, go through –, perform- a

part; rehearse, spout, gag, rant; 'strut and fret one's hour upon a stage;' tread the -stage, – boards; come out;, star.

Adj. dramatic; theatric, -al; scenic, histrionic, anctorial, comic, tragic, buskined, farcical, tragicomic, melodramatic, operatic; stagey spectacular; stagestruck.

Adv. on the -stage, – boards; before -the floats, – an audience; in the limelight, behind the footlights; behind the scenes.

600. Will.—N. will, volition, conation, velleity; will and pleasure, free-will; freedom etc. 748; discretion; choice, inclination, intent, purpose, option etc. (*choice*) 609; voluntariness; spontane-ity, -ousness; originality.

pleasure, wish, desire, mind; frame of mind etc. (*inclination*) 602; intention etc. 620; predetermination etc. 611; self-control etc. determination etc. (*resolution*) 604; will-power.

V. will, list; see –, think- -fit; determine etc. (*resolve*) 604; settle etc. (*choose*) 609; volunteer.

have a will of one's own; do what one chooses etc. (*freedom*) 748; have it all one's own way; have one's -will, – own way.

use –, exercise- one's discretion; take -upon oneself, – one's own course, – the law into one's own hands; do -of one's own accord, – upon one's own -responsibility, – authority; take the bit between one's teeth; take responsibility; originate etc. (*cause*) 153.

Adj. voluntary, volitive, volitional, wilful; free etc. 748; optional; discretion-al, -ary; volitient; dictatorial.

minded etc. (*willing*) 602; prepense etc. (*predetermined*) 611; intended etc. 620; autocratic; unbidden etc. (bid etc. 741); spontaneous; original etc. (*causal*) 153.

Adv. voluntarily etc. *adj.*; at -will, – pleasure; *à -volonté, – discrétion; al piacere; ad -libitum, – arbitrium*; as -one thinks proper, – it seems good to.

of one's own -accord, – free will; *proprio –, suo –, ex mero- motu*; out of one's own head; by choice etc. 609; purposely etc. (*intentionally*) 620; deliberately etc. 611.

Phr. *stet pro ratione voluntas; sic volo sic jubeo.*

601. Necessity.—N. involuntariness; instinct, blind –, natural- impulse; inborn –, innate- proclivity; the force of circumstances.

necessi-ty, -tation, necessarianism; obligation; compulsion etc. 744; subjection etc. 749; stern –, hard –, dire –, imperious –, inexorable –, iron –, adverse- -necessity, – fate; what must be.

desti-ny, -nation; fatality, fate, *kismet*, doom, foredoom, election, predestination; pre-, fore- ordination; lot, fortune; fatalism, determinism; inevitableness etc. *adj.*; spell etc. 993.

star, -s; planet, -s; astral influence; sky, Fates, Norns, *Parcae*, Sisters three, Clotho, Lachesis, Atropos; book of fate; God's will, will of Heaven; wheel of Fortune, Ides of March, Hobson's choice.

last -shift, – resort; *dernier ressort; pis aller*

etc. (*substitute*). 147; necessaries etc. (*requirement*) 630.

necess-arian, -itarian; fatalist, determinist; automaton.

V. lie under a necessity; be -fated, – doomed, – destined etc., – in for, – under the necessity of; have no -choice, – alternative; be- obliged –, forced –, driven –, one's -fate etc. *n.*- to; be -pushed to the wall, – driven into a corner, – unable to help, – drawn irresistibly.

destine, doom, foredoom, devote; pre-destine, -ordain; cast a spell etc. 992; necessitate; compel etc. 744.

Adj. necessary; needful etc. (*requisite*) 630. fated; destined etc. *v.*; fateful; elect; spell-bound. compulsory etc. (*compel*) 744; uncontrollable, inevitable, unavoidable, irréstible, irrevocable, inexorable, binding; avoid-, resist-less; written in the book of fate.

involuntary, instinctive, automatic, blind, mechanical; un-conscious, -witting, -thinking; unintentional etc. (*undesigned*) 621; impulsive etc. 612.

Adv. necessarily etc. *adv.*; of -necessity, – course; *ex necessitate rei*; needs must; perforce etc. 744; *nolens volens*; will he nil he, willy nilly, *bon gré mal gré*, willing or unwilling, *coûte que coûte*, forcefully.

faute de mieux; by stress of; if need be.

Phr. it cannot be helped; there is no- help for, – helping- it; it -will, – must, – must needs- be, – be so, – have its way; the die is cast; *jacta est alea; che sarà sarà;* 'it is written;' one's- days are numbered, – fate is sealed; *Fata obstant; diis aliter visum.*

602. Willingness.—N. willingness, voluntariness etc. *adj.*; willing mind, heart.

disposition, inclination, leaning, *animus*; frame of mind, humor, mood, vein; bent etc. (*turn of mind*) 820; *penchant* etc. (*desire*) 865; aptitude etc. 698.

doc-ility, -ibleness, tractability; persuasi-bleness, -bility;. pliability etc. (*softness*) 324.

geniality, cordiality; goodwill; alacrity, readiness, earnestness, forwardness, enthusiasm; zeal, eagerness etc. (*desire*) 865.

assent etc. 488; compliance etc. 762; pleasure etc. (*will*) 600.

labor of love, self-appointed task; volunteer, -ing, gratuitous service; unpaid worker, amateur.

V. be -willing etc. *adj.*; incline, lean to, mind, propend; had as lief; lend –, give –, turn- a willing ear; have -a, – half a, – a great- mind to; hold –, cling- to; desire etc. 865.

see –, think- -good, – fit, – proper; acquiescence etc. (*assent*) 488; comply with etc. 762.

swallow –, nibble at- the bait; gorge the hook; swallow hook, line and sinker; have –, make- no scruple of; make no bones of; jump –, catch- at; meet half way; volunteer, offer oneself etc. 763.

Adj. willing, minded, fain, disposed, inclined, favorable, favorably- minded, -inclined, -disposed; nothing loth; in the -vein, – mood, – humor, – mind.

ready, forward, enthusiastic, earnest, eager; bent upon etc. (*desirous*) 865; predisposed, propense.

docile; persua-dable, -sible; suasible, easily persuaded, facile, easy-going; amenable; tractable etc.
(*pliant*) 324; genial, gracious, cordial, hearty; content etc. (*assenting*) 488.
voluntary, gratuitous, spontaneous; unasked etc.
(ask etc. 765); unforced etc. (*free*) 748.
Adv. willing etc. *adj.*; fain, freely, as lief, heart
and soul; with -pleasure, – all one's heart, – open
arms; with -good, – right good- will; *de bonne
volonté, ex animo*; *con amore*, heart in hand,
nothing loth, without reluctance, of one's own accord, graciously, with a good grace, without demur.
à la bonne heure; by all -means, – manner of
means; to one's heart's content; yes etc. (*assent*)
488.
Int. sure, -ly! of course!

603. Unwillingness.—N. unwillingness etc.
adj.; indispos-ition, -edness; disinclination, aver-
sation, aversion; nolleity, nolition; renitence; reluctance; indifference etc. 866; backwardness etc.
adj.; slowness etc. 275; want of -alacrity, –
readiness; indocility etc. (*obstinacy*) 606.
scrupul-ousness, -osity; qualms of conscience,
delicacy, demur, scruple, qualm, shrinking, recoil;
hesitation etc. (*irresolution*) 605; fastidiousness
etc. 868.
averseness etc. (*dislike*) 867; dissent etc. 489;
refusal etc. 764.
slacker, scrimshanker, *embusque*, unwilling
worker, forced labor.
V. be -unwilling etc. *adj.*; nill; dislike etc. 867;
grudge, begrudge; not be able to find it in one's
heart to, not have the stomach to.
demur, stick at, scruple, stickle; hang fire, run
rusty, slack, shirk, scamp, give up, fight shy of, not
pull fair; recoil, shrink, swerve; hesitate etc. 605;
avoid etc. 623.
oppose etc. 708; dissent etc. 489; refuse etc.
764.
Adj. unwilling; not in the vein, loth, shy of,
disinclined, indisposed, averse, reluctant, not content; adverse etc. (*opposed*) 708; laggard, back-
ward, remiss, slack, slow to; renitent; indifferent
etc. 866; scrupulous; squeamish etc. (*fastidious*)
868; repugnant etc. (*dislike*) 867; rest-iff, -ive;
demurring etc. *v.*; unconsenting etc. (*refusing*)
764; involuntary etc. 601; grudging, irreconcilable.
Adv. unwilling etc. *adj.*; grudgingly, with a
heavy heart; with -a bad, – an ill- grace; against
–, sore against- -one's wishes, – one's will, – the
grain; *invitâ Minervâ*; *à contre coeur*; *malgré soi*;
in spite of -one's teeth, – oneself; *nolens volens*
etc. (*necessity*) 601; perforce etc. 744; under
protest; no etc. 536; not for the world, far be it
from me; not if I can help it; if I must I must.

604. Resolution.—N. determination, will; iron
–, unconquerable- will; will of one's own,
decision, resolution, backbone, grit; strength of -
mind, – will; resolve etc. (*intent*) 620; *intransigeance*; firmness etc. (*stability*) 150; energy,
manliness, vigor; game, pluck; resoluteness etc.
(*courage*) 861; zeal etc. 682; *aplomb*; desperation;
devot-ion, -edness.
mastery over self; self-control, -command, -

mastery, -possession, -reliance, -government, -
restraint, -conquest, -denial; moral -courage, –
strength, – fiber; perseverance etc. 604*a*; tenacity;
obstinacy etc. 606; bull-dog; British lion.
V. have -determination etc. *n.*; know one's own
mind; be -resolved etc. *adj.*; make up one's mind,
will resolve, determine; decide etc. (*judgment*)
480; form –, come to- a -determination, –
resolution, – resolve; conclude, fix, seal, determine once for all, bring to a crisis, drive matters to
an extremity; take a decisive step etc. (*choice*) 609;
take upon oneself etc. (*undertake*) 676.
devote oneself –, give oneself up- to; throw
away the scabbard, kick down the ladder, nail
one's colors to the mast, set one's back against the
wall, set one's teeth, put one's foot down, burn
one's bridges, take one's stand; stand firm etc.
(*stability*) 150; steel oneself; stand no nonsense,
not listen to the voice of the charmer.
buckle to; put –, lay –, set- one's shoulder to
the wheel; put one's heart into; run the gantlet,
make a dash at, take the bull by the horns; beard
the lion in his den; rush –, plunge- *in medias res*;
go in for; insist upon, make a point of; set one's
heart, – mind- upon.
stick at nothing; make short work of etc. (*activity*) 682; not stick at trifles; go -all lengths, –
the whole hog; persist etc. (*persevere*) 604*a*; go
down with colors flying, die game; go through fire
and water, ride in the whirlwind and direct the
storm.
Adj. resolved etc. *v.* determined; strong-willed, -
minded; resolute etc. (*brave*) 861; self-possessed,
plucky, tenacious; decided, definitive, peremptory;
un-hesitating, -flinching, -shrinking; firm, cast iron,
indomitable, game to the backbone; inexorable,
relentless, not to be -shaken, – put down; *tenax
propositi*; inflexible etc. (*hard*) 323; obstinate etc.
606; steady etc. (*persevering*) 604*a*; unbending,
unyielding, irrevocable; firm as a rock; grim.
earnest, serious; set –, bent –, intent- upon.
steeled –, proof- against; *in utrumque paratus*.
Adv. resolutely etc. *adj.*; in – , in good- earnest;
seriously, joking apart, earnestly, heart and soul; in
one's metal; manfully, like a man, with a high
hand; with a strong hand etc. (*exertion*) 686.
at any -rate, – risk, – hazard, – price, –
cost, – sacrifice; at all -hazards, – risks, –
events; cost what it may; *coûte que coûte*; *à tort et
à travers*; once for all; neck or nothing; rain or
shine; with colors nailed to the mast.
Phr. *spes sibi quisque*.

604a. Perseverance. —N. perseverance; continuance etc. (*inaction*) 143; permanence etc. (*absence of change*) 141; firmness etc. (*stability*) 150.
constancy, steadiness; singleness –, tenacity- of
purpose; persistence, plodding, patience; sedulity
etc. (*industry*) 682; pertina-cy, -city, -ciousness;
iteration etc. 104.
bottom, game, pluck, stamina, backbone, grit;
indefatiga-bility, -bleness; bulldog courage.
V. persevere, persist; hold -on, – out; die in the
last ditch, be in at the death; stick –, cling –,
adhere- to ; stick to one's text, keep on; keep to –,
maintain- one's -course, – ground; bear –, keep
–, hold-up; plod; stick to work etc. (*work*) 686;

continue etc. 143; foll**ó**w up; die -in harness, – at one's post.

Adj. persevering, constant; stead-y, -fast; undeviating, -wavering, -faltering, -swerving, -flinching, -sleeping, -flagging, -drooping; steady as time; uninter-, un-remitting; plodding; industrious etc. 682; strenuous etc. 686; pertinacious; persisting, -ent.

solid, sturdy, staunch, stanch, ture to oneself; unchangeable etc. 150; unconquerable etc. (*strong*) 159; indomitable, game to the last, indefatigable, untiring, unwearied, never tiring.

Adv. through -evil report and good report, – thick and thin, – fire and water; *per fas et nefas*; without fail, sink or swim, at any price, *vogue la galère*; in sickness and in health.

Phr. never say die; *vestigia nulla retrorsum*.

605. Irresolution.—N. irresolution, infirmity of purpose, indecision; in-, un-determination, loss of will power; unsettlement; uncertainty etc. 475; demur, suspense; hesi-tating etc. *v.*, -tation, -tancy; vacillation; ambivalence; changeableness etc. 149; fluctuation; alternation etc. (*oscillation*) 314; caprice etc. 608; lukewarmness.

fickleness, levity, *légèreté*; pliancy etc. (*softness*) 324; weakness; timidity etc. 860; cowardice etc. 862; half measures.

waverer, ass between two bundles of hay; shuttlecock, butterfly; timeserver, opportunist, turn coat.

V. be -irresolute etc. *adj.*; hang – , keep- in suspense; heave 'ad referendum;' think twice about, pause; dawdle etc. (*inactivity*) 683; remain neuter; dilly dally, hesitate, boggle, hover, wobble, shilly-shally, hum and haw, demur, not know one's own mind; debate, balance; dally – , coquet- with; will and will not, *chasser-balancer*; go half-way, compromise, make a compromise; be thrown off one's balance, stagger like a drunken man; be afraid etc. 860; let 'I dare not' wait upon 'I would;' falter, waver.

vacillate etc. 149; change etc. 140; retract etc. 607; fluctuate; alternate etc. (*oscillate*) 314; keep off and on, play fast and loose; blow hot and cold etc. (*caprice*) 608.

shuffle, palter, blink; trim.

Adj. irresolute, infirm of purpose, double-minded, half-hearted; un-decided, -resolved, -determined; drifting; shilly-shally; fidgety, tremulous; wobbly; hesitating etc. *v.*; off one's balance; at a loss etc. (*uncertain*) 475.

vacillating etc. *v.*; unsteady etc. (*changeable*) 149; unsteadfast, fickle, unreliable, irresponsible, unstable, without ballast; capricious etc. 608; volatile, frothy; light, -some, -minded; giddy; fast and loose.

weak, feeble-minded, frail; timid etc. 860; cowardly etc. 862; facile; pliant etc. (*soft*) 324; unable to say 'no,' easy-going.

revocable, reversible.

Adv. irresolutely etc. *adj.*; irresolvedly; in faltering accents; off and on; from pillar to post; see-saw etc. 314.

Int. 'how happy could I be with either!'

606. Obstinacy.—N. obstinateness etc. *adj.*; obstinacy, tenacity; perseverance etc. 604a; im-

movability; old school; inflexibility etc. (*hardness*) 323; obdur-acy, -ation; dogged resolution; resolution etc. 604; ruling passion; blind side.

self-will, contumacy, perversity; pervica-cy, -city; indocility.

bigotry, intolerance, dogmatism; opinia-try, -tiveness; fixed idea etc.; intractibility, incorrigibility; (*prejudgment*) 481; fanaticism, zealotry, infatuation, monomania, opinionativeness.

mule; opin-ionist, -ionatist, -iator, -ator; stickler, dogmatist, die-hard, bitter-ender; bigot; zealot, enthusiast, fanatic.

V. be -obstinate etc. *adj.*; stickle, take no denial, fly in the face of facts; opinionate, be wedded to an opinion, hug a belief; have one's own way etc. (*will*) 600; persist etc. (*persevere*) 604a; have – , insist on having- the last word.

die -hard, – fighting, fight -against destiny, – to the last ditch; not yield an inch, stand out.

Adj. obstinate, tenacious, stubborn, obdurate, case-hardened; inflexible etc. (*hard*) 323; immovable, not to be moved; inert etc. 172; unchangeable etc. 150; inexorable etc. (*determined*) 604; mulish, obstinate as a mule, pig-headed.

dogged; sullen, sulky; un-moved, -influenced, -affected.

wilful, self-willed, perverse; res-ty, -tive, -tiff; pervicacious, wayward, refractory, unruly; head-y, -strong; *entêté*; contumacious; cross-grained.

arbitrary, dogmatic, opinionated, positive, bigoted; prejudiced etc. 481; prepossessed, infatuated; stiff-backed, -necked, -hearted; hard-mouthed, hidebound; unyielding; im-pervious, -practicable, -persuasible; unpersuadable; in-, untractable; incorrigible, deaf to advice, impervious to reason; crotchety etc. 608.

Adv. obstinately etc. *adj.*

Phr. *non possumus*; no surrender.

607. Tergiversation.—N. change of -mind, – intention, – purpose; afterthought.

tergiversation, recantation; palinode, -ody; renunciation; abjur-ation, -ement; defection etc. (*relinquishment*) 624; going over etc. *v.*; apostasy; retract-ion, -ation; withdrawal, disavowal etc. (*negation*) 536; revo-cation, -kement; reversal; repentance etc. 950; *redintegratio amoris*.

coquetry, flirtation; vacillation etc. 605; backsliding, recidivation.

turn-coat, -tippet; rat, apostate, renegade, mugwump; con-, per-vert; proselyte, deserter; backslider, recidivist; black leg.

time-server, -pleaser; timist, Vicar of Bray, trimmer, ambidexter; weathercock etc. (*changeable*) 149; Janus.

V. change one's -mind, – intention, – purpose, – note; abjure, renounce; withdraw from etc. (*relinquish*) 624; wheel –, turn –, veer- round; turn a *pirouette*; go over –, pass –, change –, skip- from one side to another; go to the right about; box the compass, shift one's ground, go upon another tack; back down, crawl, crawfish.

apostatize, change sides, go over, rat; recant, retract; revoke; rescind etc. (*abrogate*) 756; recall, forswear, abjure, unsay; come -over, – round- to an opinion.

draw in one's horns, eat one's words; eat –

swallow- the leek; swerve, flinch, back out of, retrace one's steps, think better of it; come back –, return- to one's first love; turn over a new leaf etc. (*repent*) 950.

trim, shuffle, play fast and loose, blow hot and cold, coquet, flirt, hold with the hare but run with the hounds; straddle; *nager entre deux eaux*; wait to see how the -cat jumps, – wind blows.

Adj. changeful etc. 149; irresolute etc. 605; ductile, slippery as an eel, trimming, ambidextrous, timeserving; coquetting etc. *v.*

revocatory, reactionary.

Phr. 'a change came o'er the spirit of my dream.'

608. Caprice.—N. caprice, fancy, humor; whim, -sey, -wham; crotchet, *capriccio*, quirk, freak, maggot, fad, vagary, prank, fit, flim-flam, *escapade*, *boutade*, wild-goose chase; capriciousness etc. *adj.*; kink.

V. be -capricious etc. *adj.*; have a maggot in the brain; take it into one's head, strain at a gnat and swallow a camel; blow hot and cold; play -fast and loose, – fantastic tricks.

Adj. capricious; erratic, eccentric, fitful, hysterical; full of -whims etc. *n.*; maggoty; inconsistent, fanciful, fantastic, whimsical, crotchety, particular, humorsome, freakish, skittish, wanton, wayward; contrary; captious; arbitrary; unrestrained, undisciplined; not amenable to reason; uncomfortable etc. 83; penny wise and pound foolish; fickle etc. (*irresolute*) 605; frivolous, sleeveless, giddy, volatile.

Adv. by fits and starts, without rhyme or reason, at one's own sweet will.

Phr. *nil fuit unquam sic impar sibi*; the deuce is in him.

609. Choice.—N. choice, option; discretion etc. (*volition*) 600; preoption; alternative; dilemma; *ambarras de choix*; adoption, co-optation; novation; decision etc. (*judgment*) 480.

election, poll, ballot, vote, voice, suffrage, plumper, cumulative vote; *plebiscitum*, *plébiscite*, *vox populi*; *referendum*, electioneering; voting etc. *v.*; franchise; ballot box; slate, ticket.

selection, excerption, gleaning, eclecticism; *excerpta*, gleanings, cuttings, scissors and paste; pick etc. (*best*) 650.

preference, prelation; predilection etc. (*desire*) 865.

V. offer for one's choice, set before; hold out –, present –, offer- the alternative; put to the vote.

use –, exercise –, one's- -discretion, – option; adopt, take up, embrace, espouse; choose, elect, co-opt; take –, make- one's choice; make choice of, fix upon.

vote, poll, hold up one's hand; divide.

settle; decide etc. (*adjudge*) 480; list etc. (*will*) 600; make up one's mind etc. (*resolve*) 604.

select; pick, – and choose; pick –, single- out, excerpt; cull, glean, winnow; sift –, separate –, winnow- the chaff from the wheat; pick up, pitch upon; pick one's way; indulge one's fancy.

set apart, reserve, mark out for; mark etc. 550.

prefer; have -rather, – as lief; fancy etc. (*desire*) 865; be persuaded etc. 615.

take a -decided, – decisive- step; commit oneself to a course; pass –, cross- the Rubicon; cast in one's lot with; take for better or for worse.

Adj. optional; co-optative; discretional etc. (*voluntary*) 600; on approval.

eclectic; choosing etc. *v.*; preferential; chosen etc. *v.*; choice etc. (*good*) 648.

Adv. optionally etc. *adj.*; at pleasure etc. (*will*) 600; either, – the one or the other; or; at the option of; whether or not; once for all; for one's money.

by -choice, – preference; in preference; rather, before.

609a. Absence of Choice.—N. no –, Hobson's- choice; first come, first served; necessity etc. 601; not a pin to choose etc. (*equality*) 27; any, the first that comes.

neutrality, indifference; indecision etc. (*irresolution*) 605.

V. be -neutral etc. *adj.*; have no choice; waive, not vote; abstain –, refrain- from voting; leave undecided; make a virtue of necessity.

Adj. neu-tral, -ter; indifferent; undecided etc. (*irresolute*) 605.

Adv. either etc. (*choice*) 609.

610. Rejection.—N. rejection, repudiation, exclusion; declination; refusal etc. 764.

V. reject; set –, lay- aside; give up; decline etc. (*refuse*) 764; exclude, except, eliminate; pluck, spin; cast.

repudiate, scout, set at naught; fling –, cast –, thrown –, toss- -to the winds, – to the dogs, – overboard, – away; send to the right about; disclaim etc. (*deny*) 536; discard etc. (*eject*) 297, (*have done with*) 678.

Adj. rejected etc. *v.*; reject-aneous, -itious; not -chosen etc. 609, – to be thought of; out of the question.

Adv. neither, – the one nor the other; no etc. 536.

Phr. *non haec in foedera*.

611. Predetermination.—N. premeditation, -deliberation, -determination, -destination; foreordination; foregone conclusion; *parti pris*; resolve, propendency; intention etc. 620; project etc. 626.

V. pre-determine, -destine, -meditate, -resolve, -concert; foreordain; resolve beforehand.

Adj. pre-pense, -meditated etc. *v.*, -designed; advised, studied, designed, calculated; aforethought; intended etc. 620; foregone.

well-laid, -devised, -weighed; maturely considered; cut and dried; cunning.

Adv. advisedly etc. *adj.*; with premeditation, deliberately, all things considered, with eyes open, in cold blood; intentionally etc. 620.

612. Impulse.—N. impulse, sudden thought; *impromptu*, improvisation; inspiration, hunch, flash, spurt.

improvisatore, *improvisatrice*, improviser, extemporizer; creature of impulse.

V. flash on the mind.

say what comes uppermost; improvise, extemporize; rise to the occasion; spurt.

Adj. extemporaneous, impulsive, indeliberate; improvis-ed, -ate, -atory; un-, unpre-meditated; *improvisé*; unprompted, -guided; natural, unguarded; spontaneous etc. (*voluntary*) 600; instinctive etc. 601.

Adv. extem-pore, -poraneously; offhand, *impromptu, à l'improviste*; improviso; on the spur of the -moment, — occasion.

613. Habit.—N. habit, -ude; assuetude, - faction; wont; run, way.

common –, general –, natural –, ordinary –, habitual- -course, – run, – state- of things; matter of course; beaten -path, – track, – ground.

prescription, custom, use, usage, immemorial usage, practice; tradition; prevalence, observance; conventionalism, -ity; mode, fashion, vogue; *etiquette* etc. (*gentility*) 852; order of the day, cry; conformity etc. 82.

habitué, addict.

one's old way, old school, consuetude, *veteris vestigia flammae; laudator temporis acti.*

rule, standing order, precedent, routine; red-tape, -tapism; pipe-clay; rut, groove.

cacoëthes; bad –, confirmed –, inveterate –, intrinsic etc. 5- habit; addiction, trick.

training etc. (*education*) 537; seasoning, hardening, inurement; radication; second nature, acclimatization; knack etc. (*skill*) 698.

V. be -wont etc. *adj.*

fall into a custom etc. (*conform to*) 82; tread –, follow- the beaten -track, – path; *stare super antiquas vias*; move in a rut, run on in a groove, go round like a horse in a mill, go on in the old job-trot way.

habituate, inure, harden, season, caseharden; accustom, familiarize; naturalize, acclimatize; keep one's hand in; train etc. (*educate*) 537.

get into the -way, – knack- of; learn etc. 539; cling –, adhere- to; repeat etc. 104; acquire –, contract –, fall into- a -habit, – trick; addict oneself –, take- to; accustom oneself to.

be -habitual etc. *adj.*; prevail; come into use, become a habit, take root; gain –, grow- upon one.

Adj. habitual; ac-, customary; prescriptive; accustomed etc. *v.*; traditional; of -daily, – everyday- occurrence; wonted, usual, general, ordinary, common, frequent, every-day, household, jog-trot; well-trodden, -known; familiar, vernacular, trite, commonplace, banal, bromidic, conventional, regular, set, stock, officinal, established, stereotyped; pre-vailing, -valent; current, received, acknowledged, recognized, accredited; of course, admitted, understood.

conformable etc. 82; according to -use, – custom, – routine; in -vogue, '– fashion;' fashionable etc. (*genteel*) 852.

wont; used – given – addicted –, attuned –, habituated etc. *v.*- to; in the habit of; *habitué*; at home in etc. (*skilful*) 698; seasoned; permeated –, imbued- with; devoted –, wedded- to; never free from.

hackneyed, fixed, rooted, deep-rooted, ingrafted, permanent, inveterate, besetting; naturalized; ingrained etc. (*intrinsic*) 5.

Adv. habitually etc. *adj.*; always etc. (*uniformly*) 16.

as -usual, – is one's wont, – things go, – the world goes, – the sparks fly upwards; *more -suo, – solito.*

as a rule, for the most part; generally etc. *adj.*; most often, – frequently.

Phr. *cela s'entend.*

614. Desuetude.—N. desuetude, disusage; disuse etc. 678; want of -habit, – practice; inusitation; newness to; new brooms.

infraction of usage etc. (*unconformity*) 83; non-prevalence; 'a custom more honored in the breach than the observance.'

V. be -unaccustomed etc. *adj.*; leave off –, cast off –, break off –, wean oneself of –, violate –, break through –, infringe- -a habit, – a custom, – a usage; break one's fetters; disuse etc. 678; wear off.

Adj. un-accustomed, -used, -wonted, -seasoned, -inured, -habituated, -trained; new; green etc. (*unskilled*) 699; fresh, original, unhackneyed.

unusual etc. (*unconformable*) 83; un-conventional,- non-observant; disused etc. 678.

Adv. just for once.

615. Motive.—N. motive, springs of action.

reason, ground, call, principle; mainspring, *primum mobile*, key-stone; the why and the wherefore; *pro* and *con*, reason why; secret –, ulterior- motive, *arrière-pensée*; intention etc. 620.

inducement, consideration; attraction etc. 288; loadstone; magnet, -ism, -ic force; allect-ation, -ive; temptation, enticement, *agacerie*, allurement, witchery; bewitch-ment, -ery; charm; spell etc. 993; fascination, blandishment, cajolery; seduc-tion, - ement; honeyed words, voice of the tempter, son of the Sirens; forbidden fruit, golden apple.

persuasi-bility, -bleness; attractability; impress-, suscept-ibility; softness; persuas-, attract-iveness; tantalization.

influence, prompting, dictate, instance; impuls-e, -ion; incit-ement, -ation; press, instigation; provocation etc. (*excitation of feeling*) 824; in-spiration; per-, suasion; encouragement, advocacy; exhortation, advice etc. 695; solicitation etc. (*request*) 765; lobbying.

incentive, stimulus, spur, fillip, whip, goad, rowel, provocative, whet, dram.

bribe, lure; decoy, – duck; bait, trail of a red herring; bribery and corruption; sop, – for Cerberus.

prompter, tempter; seduc-er, -tor; suggester, coaxer, wheedler; instigator, firebrand, incendiary; Siren, Circe; *agent provocateur*; lobbyist.

V. induce, move; draw, – on; bring in its train, give an -impulse etc. *n.*- to; inspire; put up to, prompt, call up; attract, beckon.

stimulate etc. (*excite*) 824; spirit up, inspirit; a-, rouse; ecphorize; animate, incite, provoke, in-stigate, set on, actuate; act –, work –, operate-upon; encourage; pat –, clap- on the -back, – shoulder.

influence, weigh with, bias, sway, incline, dispose, predispose, turn the scale, inoculate; lead, – by the nose; have –, exercise- influence- -with, – over, – upon; go –, come- round one; turn the head, magnetize.

persuade; prevail -with, – upon; overcome, carry; bring -round, – to one's senses; draw –, win –, gain –, come –, talk- over; procure, enlist, engage; invite, court.

tempt, seduce, overpersuade, entice, allure, captivate, fascinate, intrigue, bewitch, carry away, charm, conciliate, wheedle, coax, lure, suggest; inveigle; tantalize; cajole etc. (*deceive*) 545.

tamper with, bribe, suborn, grease the palm, bait with a silver hook, gild the pill, make things pleasant, put a sop into the pan, throw a sop to, bait the hook.

enforce, force; impel etc. (*push*) 276; propel etc. 284; whip, lash, goad, spur, prick, urge; egg –, hound –, hurry- on; drag etc. 285; exhort; advise etc. 695; call upon etc.; press etc. (*request*) 765; advocate.

set -an example, – the fashion; keep in countenance; back up.

be -persuaded etc.; yield to temptation, come round; concede etc. (*consent*) 762; obey a call; follow -advice, – the bent, – the dictates of; act · on principle.

Adj. impulsive, motive; suas-, persuas-, hortative, -ory; protreptical; inviting, tempting etc. *v.*; seductive, attractive, irresistible; fascinating etc. (*pleasing*) 829; provocative etc. (*exciting*) 824.

induced etc. *v.*; disposed; persuadable etc. (*docile*) 602; spellbound; instinct –, smitten- with; inspired etc. *v.*- by.

Adv. because, therefore etc. (*cause*) 155; from - this, – that- motive; for -this, – that- reason; for; by reason –, for the sake –, on the score –, on account- of; out of, from, as, forasmuch as.

for all the world; on principle.

615a. Absence of Motive.—N. absence of motive; caprice etc. 608; chance etc. (*absence of design*) 621.

V. have no motive; scruple etc. (*be unwilling*) 603.

Adj. without rhyme or reason; aimless etc. (*chance*) 621.

Adv. capriciously; out of mere caprice.

616. Dissuasion.—N. dissuasion, dehortation, expostulation, remonstrance; deprecation etc. 766.

discouragement, damper, wet blanket; warning.

cohibition etc. (*restraint*) 751; curb etc. (*means of restraint*) 752; check etc. (*hindrance*) 706.

reluctance etc. (*unwillingness*) 603; contraindication.

V. dissuade, dehort, cry out against, remonstrate, expostulate, warn, contraindicate.

disincline, indispose, shake, stagger; dispirit; discourage, -hearten, -enchant; deter; hold –, keep- back etc. (*restrain*) 751; render -averse etc. 603;

repel; turn aside etc. (*deviation*) 279; wean from; act as a drag etc. (*hinder*) 706; throw cold water on, damp, cool, chill, blunt, calm, quiet, quench; deprecate etc. 766.

Adj. dissuading etc. *v.*; dissuasive; dehortatory, expostulatory; monit-ive, -ory.

dissuaded etc. *v.*; uninduced etc. (*induce* etc. 615); unpersuadable etc. (*obstinate*) 606; averse etc. (*unwilling*) 603; repugnant etc. (*dislike*) 867.

617. Plea. [Ostensible motive, ground, or reason assigned.]—**N.** plea, pretext; allegation, advocation; ostensible -motive, – ground, – reason; excuse etc. (*vindication*) 937; color; gloss, guise.

loop-, starting-hole; how to creep out of, salvo, come off.

handle, peg to hang on room, *locus standi*; stalking horse, *cheval de bataille*, cue.

pretence etc. (*untruth*) 546; put off, subterfuge, dust thrown in the eyes; blind; moonshine; mere –, shallow- pretext; lame -excuse, – apology, tub to a whale; flase plea, sour grapes; makeshift, shift, white lie; special pleading etc. (*sophistry*) 477; soft sawder etc. (*flattery*) 933.

V. plead, allege; shelter oneself under the plea of; excuse etc. (*vindicate*) 937; gloss over; lend a color to; furnish a -handle etc. *n.*; make a -pretext, – handle- of; use as a plea etc. *n.*; take one's stand upon, make capital out of; pretend etc. (*lie*) 544.

Adj. ostensible etc. (*manifest*) 525; excusing; alleged, apologetic; pretended etc. 545.

Adv. ostensibly; under -color, – the plea, – the pretence- of.

618. Good.—N. good, benefit, advantage; improvement etc. 658; interest, service, behoof, behalf; weal; main chance, *summum bonum*, common weal; 'consummation devoutly to be wished;' gain, boot; profit, harvest.

boon etc. (*gift*) 784; good turn; blessing, benison; world of good; piece of good -luck, – fortune; nuts, prize, windfall, godsend, waif, treasure trove.

good fortune etc. (*prosperity*) 734; happiness etc. 827.

[Source of good] goodness etc. 648; utility etc. 644; remedy etc. 662; pleasure-giving etc. 829.

Adj. commendable etc. 931; useful etc. 644; good etc., beneficial etc. 648.

V. benefit, profit, advantage, serve, help, avail; do good to, gain, prosper, flourish.

Adv. well, aright, satisfactorily, favorably, not amiss; all for the best; to one's -advantage etc. *n.*; in one's -favor, – interest etc. *n.*

Phr. so far so good.

619. Evil.—N. evil, ill, harm, hurt, mischief, nuisance; machinations of the devil, Pandora's box, ills that flesh is heir to.

blow, buffet, stroke, scratch, bruise, wound, gash, mutilation; mortal -blow, – wound; im-

medicabile vulnus; damage, loss etc. (*deterioration*) 659.

disadvantage, prejudice, drawback.

disaster, accident, casualty; mishap etc. (*misfortune*) 735; bad job, devil to pay; calamity, bale, woe, catastrophe, tragedy; ruin etc. (*destruction*) 162; adversity etc. 735.

mental suffering etc. 828. [Evil spirit] demon etc. 980. [Cause of evil] bane etc. 663. [Production of evil] badness etc. 649; painfulness etc. 830; evil doer etc. 913.

outrage, wrong, injury, foul play; bad –, ill-turn; disservice; spoliation etc. 791; grievance, crying evil.

V. be in trouble etc. (*adversity*) 735; harm, injure, hurt, do disservice to.

Adj. disastrous, bad etc. 649; awry, out of joint; disadvantageous, injurious, harmful.

Adv. amiss, wrong, ill, to one's cost.

620. Intention.—**N.** intent, -ion, -ionality; purpose; *quo animo*; project etc. 626; undertaking etc. 676; predetermination etc. 611; design, ambition.

contemplation, mind, *animus*, view, purview, proposal; study; look out.

final cause; *raison d'être*; *cui bono*; object, aim, end; 'the be all and the end all;' drift etc. (*meaning*) 516; tendency etc. 176; destination, mark, point, butt, goal, target, bull's-eye, quintain; prey, quarry, game.

decision, determination, resolve; set –, settled-purpose; *ultimatum*; resolution etc. 604; wish etc. 865; *arrière-pensée*; motive etc. 615.

[Study of final causes] teleology.

V. intend, purpose, design, mean; have to; propose to oneself; harbor a design; have in -view, – contemplation, – one's eye, – *petto*; have an eye to.

bid –, labor- for; be –, aspire –, endeavour-after; be –, aim –, drive –, point –, level- at; take aim; set before oneself; study to.

take upon oneself etc. (*undertake*) 676; take into one's head; meditate, contemplate; think –, dream –, talk- of; premeditate etc. 611; compass, calculate; dest-ine, -inate, propose.

project etc. (*plan*) 626; have a mind to etc. (*be willing*) 602; desire etc. 865; pursue etc. 622.

Adj. intended etc. *v.*; intentional, advised, express, determinate; prepense etc. 611; bound for; intending etc. *v.*; minded, disposed, inclined; bent upon etc. (*earnest*) 604; at stake, on the -anvil, – *tapis*; in -view; – prospect, – the breast of; *in petto*; teleological.

Adv. intentionally etc. *adj.*; advisedly, wittingly, knowingly, designedly, purposely, on purpose, by design, studiously, pointedly; with -intent etc. *n.*; deliberately etc. (*with premeditation*) 611; with one's eyes open, in cold blood.

for; with -a view, – an eye- to; in order -to, – that; to the end –, with the intent- that; for the purpose –, with the view –, in contemplation –, on account- of.

in pursuance of, pursuant to; *quo animo*; to all intents and purposes.

621. Chance.†[Absence of purpose in the succession of events.]—**N.** chance etc. 156; lot, fate

etc. (*necessity*) 601; luck; good luck etc. (*good*) 618; bad luck etc. 735; wheel of fortune; mascot; swastika.

speculation, venture, stake, flutter, flier, gamble, game of chance; mere –, random- shot; blind bargain, leap in the dark; pig in a poke etc. (*uncertainty*) 475; fluke, pot-luck.

drawing lots; sorti-legy, -tion; . *sortes*, – *Virgilianae*; *rouge et noir*, hazard, *roulette*, pitch and toss, chuck-farthing, cup-tossing, heads or tails, cross and pile, wager; bet, -ting; risk, stake, plunge; gambling; the turf.

stock exchange, bourse, board of trade, curb exchange.

gaming-, gambling-, betting-house; hell; betting ring, totalizator; dice, – box; dicer; gam-bler, -ester, plunger, stock operator, manipulator, punter; man of the turf; adventurer, speculator; book-maker, layer, backer.

V. chance etc. (*hap*) 156; stand a chance etc. (*be possible*) 470.

toss up; cast –, draw- lots; leave –, trust- -to chance, – to the chapter of accidents; tempt fortune; chance it, take one's chance; run –, incur –, encounter- the -risk, – chance; stand the hazard of the die.

speculate, try one's luck, set on a cast, raffle, put into a lottery, buy a pig in a poke, shuffle the cards.

risk, venture, hazard, stake; lay, – a wager; make a bet, wager, bet, gamble; game, play for; play at chuck-farthing.

Adj. fortuitous etc. 156; unintentional, -ded; accidental; not meant; un-designed, -purposed; unpremeditated etc. 612; never thought of.

indiscrim:nate, promiscuous; undirected, random; aim-, drift-, design-, purpose-, cause-less; without purpose.

possible etc. 470.

Adv. casually etc. 156; unintentionally etc. *adj.*; unwittingly.

en passant, by the way, incidentally; as it may happen; at -random, – a venture, – haphazard; as luck would have it, by -chance, – good fortune; un-, -luckily.

† See note on 156.

622. Pursuit. [Purpose in action.]—**N.** pursuit; pursuing etc. *v.*; prosecution; pursuance; enterprise etc. (*undertaking*) 676; business etc. 625; adventure etc. (*essay*) 675; quest etc. (*search*) 461; scramble, hue and cry, game; hobby.

chase, hunt, *battue*, race, steeplechase, hunting, coursing; ven-ation, -ery; fox-chase; sport, -ing; shooting, angling, fishing, hawking.

pursuer; hunt-er, -sman; sportsman, Nimrod, the field; hound etc. 366.

V. pursue, prosecute, follow; run –, make –, be –, hunt – prowl- after; shadow; carry on etc. (*do*) 680; engage in etc. (*undertake*) 676; set about etc. (*begin*) 66; endeavor etc. 675; court etc: (*request*) 765; seek etc. (*search*) 461; aim at etc. (*intention*) 620; follow the trail etc. (*trace*) 461; fish for etc. (*experiment*) 463; press on etc. (*haste*) 684; run a race etc. (*velocity*) 274.

chase, give chase, course, dog, hunt, hound, stalk; tread –, follow- on the heels of etc. (*sequence*) 281.

rush upon; rush headlong etc. (*violence*) 173;

ride –, run- full tilt at; make a leap –, jump –, snatch- at; run down; start game.

tread a path; take –, hold- a course; shape –, direct –, bend- one's -steps, – course; play a game; fight –, elbow- one's way; follow up; take - to, – up; go in for; ride one's hobby.

Adj. pursuing etc. *v.*; in quest of etc. (*inquiry*) 461; in -pursuit, – full cry, – hot pursuit; on the scent.

Adv. in pursuance of etc. (*intention*) 620; after.

Int. tally-ho! yoicks! so-ho!

623. Avoidance. [Absence of pursuit.]—**N.** abst-ention, -inence; forbearance; refraining etc. *v.*; inaction etc. 681; neutrality.

avoidance, evasion, elusion; seclusion etc. 893.

avolation, flight; escape etc. 671; retreat etc. 287; recoil etc. 277; departure etc. 293; rejection etc. 610.

shirker etc. *v.*; slacker; truant; fugitive, refugee; runa-way, -gate; renegade; deserter.

V. abstain, refrain, spare, not attempt; not do etc. 681; maintain the even tenor of one's way.

eschew, keep from, let alone, have nothing to do with; keep –, stand –, hold- -aloof, – off; take no part in, have no hand in.

avoid, shun; steer –, keep- clear of; fight shy of; keep -one's, – at a respectful- distance; keep –, get- out of the way; evade, elude, turn away from; set one's face against etc. (*oppose*) 708; deny oneself.

shrink; hang –, hold –, draw- back; recoil etc. 277; retire etc. (*recede*) 287; flinch, blink, blench, shy, shirk, dodge, parry, make way for, give place to.

beat a retreat; turn -tail, – one's back; take to one's heels; run, -away, – for one's life; cut and run; be off, – like a shot; fly, flee; fly –, flee –, run away- from; take –, take to- flight; desert, elope; make –, scamper –, sneak –, shuffle –, sheer- off; break –, burst –, tear oneself –, slip –, slink –, steal- -away, – away from; slip cable, part company, take to one's heel; sneak out of, play truant, give one the go by, give leg bail, take French leave, slope, decamp, flit, bolt, abscond, levant, skedaddle, absquatulate, cut one's stick, walk one's chalks, show a light pair of heels, make oneself scarce; escape etc. 671; go away etc. (*depart*) 293; abandon etc. 624; reject etc. 610.

lead one a -dance, – a merry chase, – pretty dance; throw off the scent, play at hide and seek.

Adj. unsought, unattempted; avoiding etc. *v.*; neutral; shy of etc. (*unwilling*) 603; elusive, evasive, distant; fugitive, runaway; shy, wild.

Adj. lest, in order to avoid.

Int. forebear! keep –, hands- off! *sauve qui peut!* devil take the hindmost.

624. Relinquishment.—**N.** relinquish-, aban-don-ment; desertion, defection, secession, with-drawal; cave of Adullam; *nolle prosequi.*

discontinuance etc. (*cessation*) 142; renun-ciation etc. (*recantation*) 607; abrogation etc. 756; resignation etc. (*retirement*) 757; desuetude etc. 614; cession etc. (*of property*) 782.

V. relinquish, give up, abandon, desert, forsake, leave in the lurch; depart –, secede –, withdraw-from; back – out of, – down from, leave, go back on one's word, quit, take leave of, bid a long farewell; vacate etc. (*resign*) 757.

renounce etc. (*abjure*) 607; forego, have done with, drop; write off; disuse etc. 678; discard etc. 782; wash one's hands of; drop all idea of; *nolle-pros.*; lose interest in.

break –, leave- off; desist; stop etc. (*cease*) 142; hold –, stay- one's hand; quit one's hold; give over, shut up shop.

throw up the -game, – cards; give up the -point, – argument; pass to the order of the day, move the previous question, table the motion.

Adj. unpursued; relinquished etc. *v.*; relinquishing etc. *v.*

Int. avast etc.! (*stop*) 142.

625. Business.—**N.** business, occupation, em-ployment; pursuit etc. 622; what one is doing-, - about; affair, concern, matter, case, undertaking.

matter in hand, irons in the fire; thing to do, *agendum*, task, work, job, chore, errand, trans-action, commission, mission, charge, care; duty etc. 926.

part, *rôle*, cue; province, function, look-out, department, capacity, sphere, orb, field, line; walk, – of life; beat, round, routine; race, career.

office, place, post, incumbency, living situation, appointment, billet, berth, employ; service etc. (*servitude*) 749; engagement; undertaking etc. 676.

vocation, calling, profession, *métier*, cloth, faculty; industry, art; industrial arts; craft, mystery, handicraft; trade etc. (*commerce*) 794.

exercise; work etc. (*action*) 680; avocation; press of business etc. (*activity*) 682.

V. pass –, employ –, spend- one's time in; em-ploy oneself -in, – upon; occupy –, concern-oneself with; make it one's -business etc. *n.*; un-dertake etc. 676; enter a profession; betake oneself to, turn one's hand to; have to do with etc. (*do*) 680.

drive a trade; carry on –, do –, transact- -business, – a trade etc. *n.*; keep a shop; ply one's task, – trade; labor in one's vocation; pursue the even tenor of one's way; attend to -business, – one's work.

officiate, serve, act; act –, play- one's part; do duty; serve –, discharge –, perform- the -office, – duties, – functions- of; hold –, fill- -an office, – a place, – a situation; hold a portfolio.

be –, doing –, engaged in, – employed in, – occupied with, – at work on; have one's hands in, have in hand; have on one's -hands, – shoulders; bear the burden; have one's hands full etc. (*activity*) 682.

be -in the hands of, – on the stocks, – on the anvil; pass through one's hands.

Adj. business-like; work-a-day; professional; of-ficial, functional; busy etc. (*actively employed*) 682; on –, in- -hand, – one's hands; afoot; on - foot, – the anvil; going on; acting.

Adv. in the course of business, all in a day's work; professionally etc. *adj.*

626. Plan.—**N.** plan, scheme, design, project; propos-al, -ition; suggestion; resolution, motion;

precaution etc. (*provision*) 673; deep-laid etc. (*premeditated*) 611- plan etc.; racket.

system etc. (*order*) 58; organization etc. (*arrangement*) 60; germ etc. (*cause*) 153; Five Year Plan.

sketch, skeleton, outline, draught, draft, *ébauche, brouillon*; rough-cast, – draft, – draught, – copy; proof, revise.

forecast, *programme*, prospectus, scenario; *carte du pays*; card; bill, protocol; order of the day, list of agenda, *memorandum*; bill of fare etc. (*food*) 298; base of operations; platform, plank.

rôle; policy etc. (*line of conduct*) 692.

contrivance, invention, expedient, receipt, nostrum, artifice, device, gadget; stratagem etc. (*cunning*) 702; trick etc. (*deception*) 545; alternative, loophole, shift etc. (*substitute*) 147; last shift etc. (*necessity*) 601.

measure, step; stroke, – of policy; master stroke; trump-, court-card; *chaval de bataille*, great gun; *coup*, – *d'état*; clever –, bold –, good- -move, – hit, – stroke; bright -thought, – idea, great idea.

intrigue, cabal, plot, frame-up, conspiracy, complot, machination; under-, counter-plot.

schem-ist, -atist; stragetist, machinator, schemer; projector, author, builder, artist, promoter, designer etc. *v.*; conspirator; *intrigant* etc. (*cunning*) 702.

V. plan, scheme, design, frame, contrive, project, forecast, sketch; conceive, devise, invent etc. (*imagine*) 515; set one's wits to work etc. 515; spring a project; fall –, hit- upon; strike –, chalk –, cut –, lay –. map-out; lay down a plan; shape –, mark- out a course; predetermine etc. 611; concert, preconcert, preestablish; prepare etc. 673; hatch, – a plot; concoct; take -steps, – measures.

cast, recast, systematize, organize; arrange etc. 60; digest, mature.

plot; counter-plot, -mine; dig a mine; lay a train; intrigue etc. (*cunning*) 702.

Adj. planned etc. *v.*; strategic, -al; planning etc. *v.*; in course of preparation etc. 673; under consideration; on the *-tapis*, – carpet, – table.

627. Method. [Path.]—**N.** method, way, manner, wise, gait, form, mole, fashion, tone, guise; *modus operandi*; procedure etc. (*line of conduct*) 692.

path, road, route, course; line of -way, – road; trajectory, orbit, track, beat, tack.

steps, stair, -case; flight of stairs, ladder, stile.

bridge, viaduct, gauntry, pontoon, stepping stone, plank, gangway, catwalk, drawbridge; pass, ford, ferry, tunnel, subway, elevated; pipe etc. 260.

door; gateway etc. (*opening*) 260; channel, passage, avenue, means of access, approach, perron, adit, entrance; artery, lane, alley, aisle. lobby, corridor, cloister; back- door, -stairs; secret passage; covert-way.

road-, path-, stair-way; thoroughfare; highway, pike, turnpike, trail, parkway, *boulevard*; turnpike –, royal –, coach- road; broad –, King's –, Queen's- highway; beaten -track, – path; horse –, bridle- road, – track, – path; pathway; walk, *trottoir*, foot-path, pavement, flags, side-walk; by –, cross- -road, – path, – way; cut; short -cut

etc. (*mid-course*) 628; *carrefour*; private –, occupation- road; highways and byways; rail-, tramroad, -way; funicular, ropeway, causeway; defile, cutting; canal etc. (*conduit*) 350; street etc. (*abode*) 189.

Adv. how; in what -way, – manner; by what mode; so, in this way, after this fashion, on these lines.

one way or another, anyhow; somehow or other etc. (*instrumentality*) 631; by way of; *viâ*; *in transitu* etc. 270; on the high road to.

Phr. *hae tibi erunt artes.*

628. Mid-course.—**N.** middle-, mid-course; moderation, mean etc. 29; middle etc. 68; *juste milieu, mezzo termine*, golden mean, *aurea mediocritas*.

straight etc. (*direct*) 278 -course, – path; short –, cross- cut; short- circuit; great circle sailing.

neutrality; half –, half and half- measures; compromise.

V. keep in –, steer –, preserve- -a middle, – an even- course; go straight etc. (*direct*) 278.

go half way, compromise, make a compromise.

Adj. neutral, average, even, impartial, moderate, straight etc. (*direct*) 278.

629. Circuit.—**N.** circuit, round-about way, digression, divagation, *détour*, circum-ambience, - ambulation, bendibus, *ambages*, loop; winding etc. (*circuition*) 311; zigzag etc. (*deviation*) 279.

V. perform –, make- a circuit; go -round about, – out of one's way; make a *détour*; meander etc. (*deviate*) 27; circumambulate.

lead a pretty dance; beat about, – the bush; make two bites of a cherry.

adj. circuitous, indirect, round-about; zig-zag etc. (*deviating*) 279; circum-ambient, -ambulatory.

Adv. by -a side wind, – an indirect course; in a roundabout way; from pillar to post.

630. Requirement.—**N.** requirement, need, wants, necessities; necessaries, – of life; stress, exigency, pinch, *sine quâ non*, matter of necessity; case of -need, – life or death.

needfulness, essentiality, necessity, indispensability, urgency, prerequisite.

requisition etc. (*request*) 765, (*exaction*) 741; run upon; demand –, call- for.

desideratum etc. (*desire*) 865; want etc. (*deficiency*) 640.

charge, claim, command, injunction, requisition, mandate, order, *ultimatum*.

V. require, need, want, have occasion for, entail; not be able to -do without, – dispense with; prerequire.

render necessary, necessitate, create a necessity for, call for, put in requisition; make a requisition etc. (*ask for*) 765, (*demand*) 741.

stand in need of; lack etc. 640; desiderate; desire etc. 865; be -necessary etc. *adj.*

Adj. required etc. *v.*; requisite, needful,

necessary, imperative, essential, indispensable, prerequisite; called for; in -demand, – request.
urgent, exigent, pressing, instant, crying, absorbing.
in want of; destitute of etc. 640.
Adv. *ex necessitate rei* etc. (*necessarily*) 601; of –, out of stern- necessity; at a pinch.
Phr. there is no time to lose; it cannot be - spared, – dispensed with.

631. Instrumentality.—N. instrumentality; aid etc. 707; subservien-ce, -cy; mediation, intervention, -mediacy, medium, inter-medium, -mediary, vehicle, hand; agency etc. 170.
minister, handmaid, servant, slave, maid, valet; midwife, *accoucheur*, obstetrician; go-between; cat's paw; stepping-stone.
key; master –, pass –, latch- key; 'open seseme;' passport, *passe partout*, safe-conduct; influence.
instrument etc. 633; expedient etc. (*plan*) 626; means etc. 632.
V. subserve, minister, tend, mediate, intervene; come –, go- between; interpose; pull the strings; be -instrumental etc. *adj.*; pander to.
Adj. instrumental; useful etc. 644; ministerial, subservient, mediatorial; inter-mediate, -vening; conducive.
Adv. through, by, *per*; where-, there-, here-by; by the -agency etc. 170- of; by dint of; by –, in- virtue of; through the -medium etc. *n.*- of; along with; on the shoulders of; by means of etc. 632; by –, with- -the aid etc. (*assistance*) 707- of.
per fas et nefas, by fair means or foul; somehow, – or other; by hook or by crook.

632. Means.—N. means, resources, revenue, wherewithal, ways and means, income; capital etc. (*money*) 800; stock in trade etc. 636; provision etc. 637; a shot in the locker; appliances etc. (*machinery*) 633; means and appliances; conveniences; cards to play; expedients etc. (*measures*) 626; two strings to one's bow; sheet anchor etc. (*safety*) 666; aid etc. 707; medium etc. 631.
V. find –, have –, possess- means etc. *n.*; provide the wherewithal.
Adj. instrumental etc. 631; mechanical etc. 633.
Adv. by means of, with; by -what, – all, – any, – some- means; where-, here-, there-with; wherewithal.
how etc. (*in what manner*) 627; thróugh etc. (*by the instrumentality of*) 631; with –, by- the aid etc. (*assistance*) 707; by the -agency etc. 170- of.

633. Instrument.—N. machinery, mechanism, engineering.
instrument, organ, tool, implement, utensil, contrivance, machine, motor, engine, lathe, gin, mill, pump.
gear; tack-le, -ling, trice, rigging, gear, apparatus, appliances; plant, *matériel*; harness, trap-

pings, fittings, accouterments; equip-ment, -age; appointments, furniture, upholstery; chattels; paraphernalia etc. (*belongings*) 780; *impedimenta*.
mechanical powers; lever, -age; mechanical advantage; crow, -bar; handspike, gavelock, jemmy, arm, limb, wing; oar, paddle; pulley, sheave; parbuckle; wheel and axle; wheel-, clock-work; wheels within wheels; piñion, gear wheel, spur –, bevelgearing, chains, belting, crank, winch, capstan, windlass, crane, derrick, hoist, lift etc. 307; cam; pedal; wheel etc. (*rotation*) 312; inclined plane; wedge; screw; jack; spring, mainspring.
handle, hilt, haft, shaft, heft, shank, blade, trigger, tiller, helm, treadle, key; turnscrew, screwdriver, spanner, wrench.
hammer etc. (*impulse*) 276; edge tool etc. (*cut*) 253; borer etc. 262; vice, teeth etc. (*hold*) 781; nail, rope etc. (*join*) 45; peg etc. (*hang*) 214; support etc. 215; spoon etc. (*vehicle*) 272; arms etc. 727; oar etc. (*navigation*) 267.
Adj. instrumental etc. 631; mechanical, machinal, automatic, self-acting; brachial.

634. Substitute.—N. substitute etc. 147; deputy etc. 759; proxy, alternative, understudy.

635. Materials.—N. material, raw material, stuff, stock, staple; building materials, bricks and mortar; metal; stone; clay, brick; crockery etc. 384; compo, -sition; reinforced –, ferro-, concrete; cement; wood, ore, timber; gravel, cobbles, macadam,‘asphalt, tarmac.
materials; supplies, munition, fuel, grist, household stuff; *pabulum* etc. (*food*) 298; ammunition etc. (*arms*) 727; contingents; relay, reinforcement; baggage etc. (*personal property*) 780; means etc. 632.
Adj. raw etc. (*unprepared*) 674; wooden etc. *n.*

636. Store.—N. stock, fund, mine, vein, lode, quarry; spring; fount, -ain; well, -spring; milchcow.
stock in trade, supply; heap etc. (*collection*) 72; treasure; reserve, *corps de réserve*, reserve fund, nest-egg, savings, *bonne bouche*.
crop, harvest, mow, vintage; yield, product, gleanings.
store, accumulation, hoard, rick, stack; lumber; relay etc. (*provision*) 637.
store-house, -room, -closet; depository, *dépôt*, cache, safe deposit, vault, pantechnicon, repository, -servatory, -pertory; *repertorium*; promptuary, warehouse, *entrepôt*, magazine, dump, buttery, larder, pantry, panary, lanary, still-room, spence;°crib, garner, granary, silo, barn; bunker; thesaurus; bank etc. (*treasury*) 802; armoury; arsenal; dock; gallery, museum, library, conservatory, hot-house; manag-ery, -erie, aquarium, zoological gardens.
reservoir, cistern, tank, sump, pond, mill-pond; gasometer.
budget, quiver, bandolier, portfolio; coffer etc. (*receptacle*) 191.

conservation; storing etc. *v.*; storage.
dictionary etc. 562; list etc. 86.

V. store; put –, lay –, set- by; stow away; set –, lay- apart; store –, hoard –, treasure –, lay –, heap –, put –, garner –, save- up; *cache*; accumulate, amass, hoard, fund, garner, save, bank.

conserve, reserve; keep –, hold- back; husband, – one's resources.

deposit; stow, stack, load, dump; harvest; heap, collect etc. 72; lay -in, – down, – by, store etc. *adj.*; keep, file [papers] lay in etc. (*provide*) 637; preserve etc. 670; put by for a rainy day.

Adj. stored etc. *v.*; in -store, – reserve, – ordinary; spare, supernumerary.

637. Provision.—N. provision, supply; grist, – to the mill; subvention etc. (*aid*) 707; resources etc. (*means*) 632.

provising etc. *v.*; purveyance; reinforcement; commissary, commissariat.

rations; iron –, emergency- rations; provender etc. (*food*) 298; *viaticum*; ensilage.

caterer, purveyor, commissary, quartermaster, steward, housekeeper, manciple, feeder, batman, victualler, storekeeper, grocer, provision merchant, green-, grocer, *comprador*, *restaurateur*; sutler etc. (*merchant*) 797; innkeeper, publican, confectioner, baker, butcher, wine merchant, vintner.

V. provide; make -provision, – due provision for; lay in, – a stock, – a store.

sup-ply, -peditate; furnish; find, – one in; arm.

cater, victual, provision, purvey, forage; beat up for; stock, – with; make good, replenish; fill, – up; recruit, feed, ration.

have in -store, – reserve; keep, – by one, – on foot; have to fall back upon; store etc. 636; provide against a rainy day etc. (*economy*) 817.

638. Waste.—N. consumption, expenditure, exhaustion; dispersion etc. 73; ebb; leakage etc. (*exudation*) 295; loss etc. 776; wear and tear; waste; prodigality etc. 818; misuse etc. 679; wasting etc. *v.*; rubbish etc. (*useless*) 645.

mountain in labor.

v. spend, expend, use, consume, swallow up, exhaust, deplete; impoverish; spill, drain, empty; disperse etc. 73.

cast –, throw –, fling –, fritter- away; burn the candle at both ends, waste; squander etc. 818.

'waste its sweetness on the desert air;' cast -one's bread upon the waters, – pearls before swine; employ a steam engine to crack a nut, waste powder and shot, break a butterfly on a wheel; labor in vain etc. (*useless*) 645; cut a whetstone with a razor, pour water into a sieve; tilt at windmills.

leak etc. (*run out*) 295; run to waste; ebb; melt away, run dry, dry up.

Adj. wasted etc. *v.*; at a low ebb.

wasteful etc. (*prodigal*) 818; penny wise and pound foolish.

Phr. *magno conatu magnas nugas; le jeu n'en vaut pas la chandelle.*

639. Sufficiency.—N. sufficiency, adequacy, enough, withal, *quantum sufficit*, satisfaction, competence; no less.

mediocrity etc. (*average*) 29.

fill; fullness etc (*completeness*) 52; plen-itude, -ty; abundance; copiousness etc. *adj.*; amplitude, galore, lots, profusion; full measure; 'good measure pressed down, shaken together and running over.'

luxuriance etc. (*fertility*) 168; affluence etc. (*wealth*) 803; fat of the land; 'a land flowing with milk and honey;' cornucopia; horn of -plenty, – Amalthaea; mine etc. (*stock*) 636.

outpouring; flood etc. (*great quantity*) 31; tide etc. (*river*) 348; repletion etc. (*reduncance*) 641; satiety etc. 869; rich man etc. 803.

V. be -sufficient etc. *adj.*; suffice, do, just do, satisfy, pass muster; have -enough etc. *n.*; eat –, drink –, have- one's fill; roll –, swim- in; wallow in etc. (*superabundance*) 641.

abound, exuberate, teem, flow, stream, rain, shower down; pour, – in; swarm; bristle with.

render -sufficient etc. *adj.*; replenish etc. (*fill*) 52.

Adj. sufficient, enough, adequate, up to the mark, commensurate, competent, satisfactory, valid, tangible.

measured; moderate etc. (*temperate*) 953.

full etc. (*complete*) 52; ample; plen-ty, -tiful, -teous; plenty as blackberries; copious, abundant; abounding etc. *v.*; replete, enough and to spare, flush; choke-full; well-stocked, -provided; liberal; unstint-ed, -ing; stintless; without stint; un-sparing, -measured; lavish etc. 641; wholesale.

rich, luxuriant etc. (*fertile*) 168; affluent etc. (*wealthy*) 803; wantless; big with etc. (*pregnant*) 161.

un-exhausted, -wasted; exhaustless, inexhaustible.

Adv. sufficiently, amply etc. *adj.*; full; in -abundance etc. *n.*; with no sparing hand; to one's heart's content; *ad libitum*, without stint.

Phr. cut and come again.

640. Insufficiency.—N. insufficiency; inadequa-cy, -teness; incompetence etc. (*impotence*) 158; deficiency etc. (*incompleteness*) 53; imperfection etc. 651; shortcoming etc. 304; paucity; stint; scantiness etc. (*smallness*) 32; none to spare; bare subsistence.

scarcity, dearth; want, need, lack, poverty, exigency, inanition, starvation, famine, drought.

dole, pittance, mite; short -allowance, – commons; half-rations; banyan –, fast- day, Lent.

emptiness, poorness etc. *adj.*; depletion, vacancy, flaccidity; ebb-tide; low water; 'a beggarly account of empty boxes;' indigence etc. (*poverty*) 804; insolvency etc. (*non-payment*) 808; poor man etc. 804; bankrupt etc. 808.

V. be -insufficient etc. *adj.*; not -suffice etc. 639; come short of etc. 304; run dry.

want, lack, need, require; caret; be in want etc. (*poor*) 804; live from hand to mouth.

render- insufficient etc. *adj.*; drain of resources; impoverish etc. (*waste*) 638; stint etc. (*begrudge*) 819; put on short -commons, – allowance.

do -insufficiently etc. *adv.*; scotch the snake.

Adj. insufficient, inadequate; too -little etc. 32; not -enough etc. 639; unequal to; incompetent etc. (*impotent*) 158; 'weighed in the balance and found wanting;' perfunctory etc. (*neglect*) 460; deficient etc. (*incomplete*) 53; wanting etc. *v.*; imperfect etc. 651; ill-furnished, -provided, -stored, -off.

slack, at a low ebb; empty, vacant, bare; short –, out –, destitute –, devoid –, bereft etc. 789 –, denuded- of; dry, drained.

un -provided, -supplied, -furnished; unreplenished, -fed; un-stored, -treasured; emptyhanded.

meager, poor, thin, scrimp, sparing, spare, stinted, stunted; skimpy; starv-ed, -eling; half-starved, emaciated, famine-stricken, famished, underfed, undernourished; jejune.

scant etc. (*small*) 32; scarce; not to be had, – for love or money, – at any price; scurvy; stingy etc. 819; at the end of one's tether; without - resources etc. 632; in want etc. (*poor*) 804; in debt etc. 806.

Adv. insufficiently etc. *adj.*; in default –, for want- of; failing.

641. Redundance.—N. redundance; too - much, – many; superabundance, -fluity, -fluence, -saturation; nimiety, transcendency, exuberance, profuseness; profusion etc. (*plenty*) 639; repletion, enough in all conscience, *satis superque*, lion's share; more than -enough etc. 639; plethora, engorgement, congestion, load, surfeit, sickener; turgescence etc. (*expansion*) 194; over-dose, - measure, -supply, -flow; inundation etc. (*water*) 348; avalanche.

accumulation etc. (*store*) 636; heap etc. 72; drug, – in the market; glut; crowd; burden.

excess; sur-, over-plus, epact; margin; remainder etc. 40; duplicate; surplusage; expletive; work of –, supererogation; *bonus*, bonanza.

luxury; intemperance etc. 954; extravagance etc. (*prodigality*) 818; exorbitance, lavishment.

pleonasm etc. (*diffuseness*) 573; too many irons in the fire; embarrassment of riches; money to burn.

V. super-, over-abound; know no bounds, swarm; meet one at every turn; creep – , bristlewith; overflow; run – , flow – , well – , brim-over; run riot; over-run, -stock, -lay, -charge, -dose, - feed, -burden, -load, -do, -whelm, -shoot the mark etc. (*go beyond*) 303; surcharge, supersaturate, gorge, glut, load, drench, whelm, inundate, deluge, flood; drug, – the market.

choke, cloy, accloy, suffocate; pile up, lay it on, – with a trowel, lay on thick; impregnate with; lavish etc. (*squander*) 818.

send – , carry- coals to Newcastle, – owls to Athens; teach one's grandmother to suck eggs; *pisces natare docere*; kill the slain, 'gild refined gold,' 'paint the lily;' butter one's bread on both sides, put butter upon bacon; employ a steamengine to crack a nut etc. (*waste*) 638.

exaggerate etc. 549; wallow in; roll in etc. (*plenty*) 639; remain on one's hands, hang heavy on hand, go a begging.

Adj. redundant; too -much, – many; exuberant, inordinate, superabundant, excessive, overmuch, replete, profuse, lavish; prodigal etc. 818; exorbitant; overweening; extravagant; overcharged etc. *v.*; supersaturated, drenched, overflowing; running -over, – to waste, – down.

crammed – , filled- to overflowing; gorged, stuffed, ready to burst; dropsical, turgid, plethoric, full-blooded; obese etc. 194; voluminous.

superfluous, unnecessary, needless, supervacaneous, uncalled for, to spare, in excess; over and above etc. (*remainder*) 40; *de trop*; adscititious etc. (*additional*) 37; supernumerary etc. (*reserve*) 636; on one's hands, spare, duplicate, supererogatory, expletive; *un peu fort*.

Adj. over, too, over and above; over – , too-much; too far; without – , beyond – out ofmeasure; with ... to spare; over head and ears; up to one's eyes, – ears; *extra*; beyond the mark etc. (*transcursion*) 303; over one's head.

Phr. It never rains but it pours.

642. Importance.—N. importance, consequence, moment, prominence, consideration, mark, materialness.

import, significance, concern; emphasis, interest. greatness etc. 31; superiority etc. 33; notability etc. (*repute*) 873; weight etc. (*influence*) 175; value etc. (*goodness*) 648; usefulness etc. 644.

gravity, seriousness, solemnity; no -joke, – laughing matter; pressure, urgency, stress; matter of life and death.

memorabilia, notabilia, great doings; red-letter day.

great -thing, – point; main chance, 'the be all and end all,' cardinal point, outstanding feature; substance, gist etc. (*essence*) 5; sum and substance, *gravamen*, head and front; important – , principal –, prominent – , essential- part; half the battle; *sine quâ non*; breath of one's nostrils etc. (*life*) 359; cream, salt, core, kernel, heart, nucleus; key, - note, -stone; corner stone; trumpcard etc. (*device*) 626; salient points.

top-sawyer, first fiddle, *prima donna*, chief, bigwig; triton among the minnows.

V. be -important etc. *adj.*, – somebody, – something; import, signify, matter, be an object; carry weight etc. (*influence*) 175; make a figure etc. (*repute*) 873; be in the ascendant, come to the front, lead the way, take the lead, play first fiddle, throw all else into the shade; lie at the root of; deserve – , merit – , be worthy- of notice, – regard, – consideration.

attach – , ascribe – , give- importance etc. *n.* to; value, care for; set store -upon, – by; mark etc. 550; mark with a white stone, underline; write – , put – , print- in -italics, – capitals, – large letters. – !large type, – letters of gold; accentuate, emphasize, lay stress on.

make -a fuss, – a stir, – a piece of work, – much ado- about; make -of, – much of.

Adj. important; of -importance etc. *n.*; momentous, material; to the point; not to be -overlooked, – despised, – sneezed at; egregious; weighty etc. (*influential*) 175; of note etc. (*repute*) 873; notable, prominent, salient, signal; memorable, remarkable; worthy of -remark, – notice; never to be forgotten; stirring, eventful.

grave, serious, earnest, noble, grand, solemn, impressive, commanding, imposing.

urgent, pressing, critical, instant.

paramount; essential, vital, all-absorbing, radical, cardinal, chief, main, prime, primary, principal, leading, capital, foremost, overruling; of vital etc. importance.

in the front rank, first-rate, A1; superior etc. 33; considerable etc. (*great*) 31; marked etc. *v.*; rare etc. 137.

significant, telling, trenchant, emphatic, pregnant; *tanti*.

Adv. materially etc. *adj.*; in the main; above all, *par excellence*, to crown all.

643. Unimportance.—N. unimportance, insignificance, nothingness, immateriality.

triviality, trivia, fribble, levity, frivolity; paltriness etc. *adj.*; poverty; smallness etc. 32; vanity etc. (*uselessness*) 645; matter of - indifference etc. 866; no object; side issue.

nothing, – to signify, – worth speaking of, – particular, – to boast of, – to speak of; small –, no great –, trifling etc. *adj.*-matter; mere -joke, – nothing; hardly –, scarcely- anything; nonentity, cipher, figurehead; no great shakes, *peu de chose*; child's play; small beer.

toy, plaything, popgun, paper pellet, gimcrack, geegaw, bauble, trinket, *bagatelle*, kickshaw, knicknack, whim-wham, trifle, 'trifles light as air.'

trumpery, trash, rubbish, stuff, *fatras*, frippery; 'leather or prunello;' chaff, drug, froth, bubble, smoke, cobweb; weed; refuse etc. (*inutility*) 645; scum etc. (*dirt*) 653.

joke, jest, snap of the fingers; fudge etc. (*unmeaning*) 517; fiddlestick, – end; pack of nonsense, mere farce.

straw, pin, fig, continental, button, rush; bulrush, feather, halfpenny, farthing, brass farthing, doit, peppercorn, jot, rap, pinch of snuff, old song.

minutiae, details, minor details, small fry; dust in the balance, feather in the scale, drop in the ocean, flea-bite, molehill; fingle-fangle.

nine days' wonder, *ridiculus mus*; flash in the pan etc. (*impotence*) 158; much ado about nothing etc. (*overestimation*) 482; storm in a teacup.

V. be -unimportant etc. *adj.*; not -matter etc. 642; go for –, matter –, signify- -little, – nothing, – little or nothing; not matter a -straw etc. *n.*

make light of etc. (*underestimate*) 483; catch at straws etc. (*overestimate*) 482.

Adj. unimportant; of -little, – small, – no- - account, – importance etc. 642; immaterial; un-, non-essential; not vital; irrelevant, incidental, indifferent.

subordinate etc. (*inferior*) 34; *médiocre* etc. (*average*) 29; passable, fair, respectable, tolerable, commonplace; uneventful, mere, common; ordinary etc. (*habitual*) 613; inconsiderable, so-so, insignificant, inappreciable, nugatory.

trifling, trivial; slight, slender, light, flimsy, frothy, idle; puerile etc. (*foolish*) 499; airy, shallow; weak etc. 160; powerless etc. 158; frivolous, petty, niggling; pid-, ped-dling; fribble, inane, ridiculous, farcical; fini-cal, -kin; fiddle-faddle, namby-pamby, wishy-washy, milk and water.

poor, paltry, pitiful; contemptible etc. (*contempt*) 930; sorry, mean, meager, shabby, miserable, wretched, vile, scrubby, scrannel; weedy, niggardly, scurvy, putid, beggarly, worthless, twopenny-half penny, cheap, trashy, catchpenny, gimcrack, trumpery, one-horse; toy.

not worth -the pains, – while, – mentioning, – speaking of, – a thought, – a curse, – a straw, – rap etc. *n.*; beneath –, unworthy of- -notice, –

regard, – consideration, – contempt; *de lanâ caprinâ*; vain etc. (*useless*) 645.

Adv. slightly etc. *adj.*; rather, somewhat, pretty well, fairly well, tolerably.

for aught one cares.

Int. no matter! pish! tush! tut! pshaw! pugh! pooh, -pooh! fudge! bosh! humbug! fiddle-stick, – end! fiddlededee! never mind! *n'importe!* what - signifies, – matter, – boots it, – of that, – 's the odds! a fig for! stuff ! nonsense! stuff and nonsense!

Phr. *magno conatu magnas nugas*; *le jeu n'en vaut pas la chandelle*; it -matters not, – does not signify; it is of no -consequence, – importance.

644. Utility.—N. utility; usefulness etc. *adj.*; efficacy, efficiency, adequacy; service, use, stead, avail; help etc. (*aid*) 707; applicability etc. *adj.*; subservience etc. (*instrumentality*) 631; function etc. (*business*) 625; value; worth etc. (*goodness*) 648; money's worth; productiveness etc. 168; *cui bono* etc. (*intention*) 620; utilization etc. (*use*) 677; step in the right direction.

common weal, public good; utilitarianism etc. (*philanthropy*) 910.

V. be -useful etc. *adj.*; avail, serve; subserve etc. (*be instrumental to*) 631; conduce etc. (*tend*) 176; answer –, serve- -one's turn, – a purpose.

act a part etc. (*action*) 680; perform –, discharge- -a function etc. 625; do –, render- -a service, – good service, – yeoman's service; bestead, stand one in good stead; be the making of; help etc. 707.

bear fruit etc. (*produce*) 161; bring grist to the mill; profit, remunerate; benefit etc. (*do good*) 648.

find one's -account, – advantage- in; reap the benefit of etc. (*be better for*) 658.

render useful etc. (*use*) 677.

Adj. useful; of -use etc. *n.*; serviceable, usable, proficuous, good for; subservient etc. (*instrumental*) 631; conducive, (*tending*) 176; subsidiary etc. (*helping*) 707.

advantageous etc. (*beneficial*) 648; profitable, gainful, remunerative, worth one's salt; in-, valuable; prolific etc. (*productive*) 168.

adequate; ef-ficient, -ficacious; effect-ive, -ual; practicable, expedient etc. 646.

applicable, available, ready, handy, at hand, tangible; commodious, adaptable; of all work.

Adv. usefully etc. *adj.*; pro bono publico.

645. Inutility.—N. inutility; uselessness etc. *adj.*; inefficacy, futility; inep-, inap-titude; unsubservience; inadequacy etc. (*insufficiency*) 640; inefficiency etc. (*incompetence*) 158; unskilfulness etc. 699; disservice; unfruitfulness etc. (*unproductiveness*) 169; labor -in vain, – lost, – of Sisyphus; lost -trouble, – labor; work of Penelope; sleeveless errand, wild goose chase, mere farce.

tautology etc. (*repetition*) 104; supererogation etc. (*redundance*) 641.

vanitas vanitatum, vanity, inanity, worthlessness, nugacity; triviality etc. (*unimportance*) 643.

caput mortuum, waste paper, dead letter; blunt tool.

litter, rubbish, lumber, odds and ends, cast-off clothes; button-top; shoddy; rags, orts, trash, refuse, sweepings, scourings, off-scourings, dross, slag, waste, rubble, dottle, drast, *débris*; stubble, leavings; broken meat; dregs etc. (*dirt*) 653; weeds, tares; rubbish heap, dust hole; *rudera*, deads. *fruges consumere natus* etc. (*drone*) 683.

V. be -useless etc. *adj.*; go a begging etc. (*redundant*) 641; fail etc. 732.

seek –, strive- after impossibilities; use vain efforts, labor in vain, roll the stone of Sisyphus, beat the air, lash the waves; *battre l'eau avec un bâton, donner un coup d'épée dans l'eau*, fish in the air, milk the ram, drop a bucket into an empty well, sow the sand; bay the moon; preach –, speak- to the winds; whistle jigs to a milestone; kick against the pricks, *se battre contre des moulins*; lock the stable door when the steed is stolen etc. (*too late*) 135; hold a farthing candle to the sun; cast pearls before swine etc. (*waste*) 638; carry coals to Newcastle etc. (*redundance*) 641; wash a blackamoor white etc. (*impossible*) 471.

render -useless etc. *adj.*; dis-mantle, -mast, -mount, -qualify, -able; unrig; cripple, lame etc. (*injure*) 659; spike guns, clip the wings; put out of gear.

Adj. useless, inutile, inefficacious, futile, unavailing, bootless; inoperative etc. 158; inadequate etc. (*insufficient*) 640; in-, un- subservient; inept, inefficient etc.(*impotent*) 158; of no -avail etc. (*use*) 644; inetfectual etc. (*failure*) 732; incompetent etc. (*unskilful*) 699; 'stale, flat and unprofitable;' superfluous etc. (*redundant*) 641; dispensable; thrown away etc. (*wasted*) 638; abortive etc. (*immature*) 674.

worth-, value-less; unsaleable; not worth a straw etc. (*trifling*) 643; dear at any price.

vain, empty, inane; gain-, profit-, fruit-less; unserviceable, -profitable; ill-spent; unproductive etc. 169; *hors de combat*; barren, sterile, impotent, unproductive; effete, past work etc. (*impaired*) 659; obsolete etc. (*old*) 124; fit for the -dust-hole, –wastepaper basket; good for nothing; of no earthly use; not worth -having, – powder and shot; leading to no end, uncalled for; un-necessary, -needed, superfluous.

Adv. uselessly etc. *adj.*; to -little, – no, – little or no- purpose.

Int. *cui bono?* what's the good!

646. Expedience. [Specific subservience.]—N. expedien-ce, -cy; desirableness, -bility etc. *adj.*; fitness etc. (*agreement*) 23; utility etc. 644; propriety; advantage; opportunism, pragmatism.

high time etc. (*occasion*) 134.

V. be -expedient etc. *adj.*; suit etc. (*agree*) 23; befit; suit –, befit- the -time, – season, – occasion.

conform etc. 82.

Adj. expedient; desir-, advis-, accept-able; convenient; worth while, meet; fit, -ting; due, proper, eligible, seemly, becoming; befitting etc. *v.*; opportune etc. (*in season*) 134; *in loco*; suitable etc. (*accordant*) 23; applicable etc. (*useful*) 644; practical, effective, pragmatical; suitable, handy.

Adv. in the right place; conveniently etc. *adj.*; in the nick of time.

Phr. *operae pretium est.*

647. Inexpedience.—N. enexpedien-ce, -cy; undesira-bleness, -bility etc. *adj.*; discommodity, impropriety; unfitness etc. (*disagreement*) 24; inutility etc. 645; inconvenience, inadvisability; disadvantage.

V. be -inexpedient etc. *adj.*; come amiss etc. (*disagree*) 24; embarrass etc. (*hinder*) 706; put to inconvenience; pay too dear for one's whistle.

Adj. inexpedient, undesirable; un-, in-advisable; objectionable; troublesome, in-apt, -eligible, -admissable, -convenient; in-, dis-commodious; disadvantageous; inappropriate, unsuitable, unfit etc. (*inconsonant*) 24.

ill-contrived, -advised; unsatisfactory; unprofitable etc., unsubservient etc. (*useless*) 645; inopportune etc. (*unseasonable*) 135; out of – , in the wrong- place; improper, unseemly.

clumsy, awkward; cum-brous, -bersome; lumbering, unwieldy, hulky; unmanageable etc. (*impracticable*) 704; inepedient (*in the way*) 706.

unnecessary etc. (*redundant*) 641.

Phr. it will never do.

648. Goodness. [Capability of producing good. Good qualities.]—N. goodness etc. *adj.*; excellence, merit; virtue etc. 944; value, worth, price.

super-excellence, -eminence; superiority etc. 33; perfection. 650; *coup de maître*; master-piece, *chef d'oeuvre*, prime, flower, cream, *élite*, pick, Al, none such, *nonpareil, crême de la crême*, flower of the flock, cock of the roost, salt of the earth; champion.

tid-bit; gem, – of the first water; *bijou*, precious stone, jewel, pearl, diamond, ruby, brilliant, treasure; good thing; *rara avis*, one in a thousand.

beneficence etc. 906; good man etc. 948.

V. be -beneficial etc. *adj.*; produce – , do- good etc. 618; profit etc. (*be of use*) 644; benefit; confer a -benefit etc. 618.

be the making of, do a world of good, make a man of.

produce a good effect; do a good turn, confer an obligation; improve etc. 658.

do no harm, break no bones.

be -good etc. *adj.*; excel, transcend etc. (*be superior*) 33; bear away the bell.

stand the -proof, – test; pass -muster, – an examination.

challenge comparison, vie, emulate, rival.

Adj. harm-, hurt-less; unobnoxious; in-nocuous, -nocent, -offensive.

beneficial, valuable, of value; serviceable etc. (*useful*) 644; advantageous, profitable, edifying; salutary etc. (*healthful*) 656.

favorable; propitious etc. (*hopegiving*) 858; fair.

good, – as gold; excellent; better; superior etc. 33; above par; nice, fine; genuine etc. (*true*) 494.

best, choice, select, picked, elect, eximious, *recherché*, rare, priceless; unpara-goned, -lleled etc. (*supreme*) 33; superlatively etc. 33- good; super-fine, -excellent; bonzer; of the first water; first-rate, -class; high-wrought; exquisite, very best, crack, prime, tip-top, gilt-edged, capital, cardinal; standard etc. (*perfect*) 650; inimitable.

admirable, estimable; praiseworthy etc. (*approve*) 931; pleasing etc. 829; *couleur de rose*, precious, of great price; costly etc. (*dear*) 814; worth -its weight in gold, – a Jew's eye, – a king's ransom; matchless, peerless, invaluable, inestimable, precious as the apple of the eye.

tolerable etc. (*not very good*) 651; up to the mark, un-exceptionable, -objectionable; satisfactory, tidy.

in -good, − fair- condition; fresh; unspoiled; sound etc. (*perfect*) 650.

Adv. beneficially etc. *adj.*; well etc. 618.

649. Badness. [Capability of producing evil. Bad qualities.]—**N.** hurtfulness etc. *adj.*; virulence.

evil doer etc. 913; bane etc. 663; plague-spot etc. (*insalubrity*) 657; evil star, ill wind; snake in the grass, skeleton in the closet; *amari aliquid*. thorn in the side; Jonah, jinx, hoodoo.

malignity; malevolence etc. 907; tender mercies [ironically].

ill-treatment, annoyance, molestation, abuse, oppression, persecution, outrage; misusage etc. 679; injury etc. (*damage*) 659.

badness etc. *adj.*; peccancy, abomination; painfulness etc. 830; pestilence etc. (*disease*) 655; guilt etc. 947; depravity etc. 945.

V. be -hurtful etc. *adj.*; cause −, produce −, inflict −, work −, do- evil etc. 619; damnify, endamage, hurt, harm, scathe; injure etc. (*damage*) 659; pain etc. 830.

wrong, aggrieve, oppress, persecute; trample −, tread −, bear hard −, put-upon; overburden; weigh ;down, − heavy on; victimize; run down; molest etc. 830.

maltreat, abuse; ill-use, -treat; thwart, buffet, bruise, scratch, maul; smite etc. (*scourge*) 972; do - violence, − harm, − a mischief; stab, pierce, outrage.

do −, make- mischief; bring −, get- into trouble.

destroy etc. 162.

Adj. hurt-, harm-, scath-, bane-, bale-ful; injurious, deleterious, detrimental, noxious, pernicious, mischievous, full of mischief, mischief-making, malefic, malignant, nocuous, noisome; prejudicial; dis-serviceable, advantageous; wide-wasting.

unlucky, sinister; obnoxious, untoward, disastrous.

oppressive, burdensome, onerous; malign etc. (*malevolent*) 907.

corrupting etc. (corrupt etc. 659) virulent, venomous, envenomed, corrosive; poisonous etc. (*morbific*) 657; deadly etc. (*killing*) 361; destructive etc. (*destroying*) 162; inauspicious etc. 859.

bad, ill, arrant, as bad bad can be, dreadful; horrid, -rible; dire; rank, peccant, foul, fulsome; rotten, − at the core.

vile, base, villainous; mean etc. (*paltry*) 643; injured etc., deteriorated etc. 659; unsatisfactory, exception, -able, indifferent; below par etc. (*imperfect*) 651; ill-contrived, -conditioned; wretched, sad, grievous, deplorable, lamentable; piti-ful, -able, woeful etc. (*painful*) 830.

evil, wrong; depraved etc. 945; shocking; reprehensible etc. (*disapprove*) 932.

hateful, − as a toad; abominable, detestable, execrable, cursed, accursed, confounded; damn-ed, -able; infernal; diabolic etc. (*malevolent*) 907.

inadvisable etc. (*inexpedient*) 647; unprofitable etc. (*useless*) 645; incompetent etc. (*unskilful*) 699; irremediable etc. (*hopeless*) 859.

Adv. badly etc. *adj.*; wrong, ill; to one's cost; where the shoe pinches.

Phr. bad is the best; the worst come to the worst.

650. Perfection.—N. perfection; perfectness etc. *adj.*; indefectibility; inpecc-ancy, -ability.

pink, *beau idéal*, phoenix, paragon; pink −, acme- of perfection; *ne plus ultra*; summit etc. 210.

cygne noir; philosopher's stone; chrysolite, Koh-i-noor, black tulip.

model, standard, pattern, mirror, admirable Crichton; trump; very prince of.

master-piece, -stroke, super-excellence etc. (*goodness*) 648; transcendence etc. (*superiority*) 33.

V. be -perfect etc. *adj.*; transcend etc. (*be supreme*) 33.

bring to perfection, perfect, ripen, mature; consummate, complete etc. 729; put in trim etc. (*prepare*) 673; put the finishing touch to.

Adj. perfect, faultless, ideal; indefective, -ficient, -fectible; immaculate, spotless, impeccable; free from -imperfection etc. 651; un-blemished, - injured etc. 659; sound, − as a roach; in perfect condition; scathless, intact, harmless; seaworthy etc. (*safe*) 644; right as a trivet; *in seipso totus teres atque rotundus*; consummate etc. (*complete*) 52; finished etc. 729; complete in itself.

best etc. (*good*) 648; model, standard; inimitable, unparagoned, unparalleled etc. (*supreme*) 33; superhuman, divine; beyond all praise etc. (*approbation*) 931; *sans peur et sans reproche*.

Adj. to perfection, to the limit; perfectly etc. *adj.*; *ad unguem*; clean, − as a whistle.

651. Imperfection.—N. imperfection; imperfectness etc. *adj.*; deficiency; inadequacy etc. (*insufficiency*) 640; peccancy etc. (*badness*) 649; immaturity etc. 674.

fault, defect, weak point; screw loose; rift within the lute; fly in the ointment; flaw etc. (*break*) 70; gap etc. 198; twist etc. 243; taint, attainder; bar sinister, hole in one's coat; blemish etc. 848; weakness etc. 160; half-blood, touch of the tar brush; shortcoming etc. 304; drawback; seamy side.

mediocrity; no great -shakes, − catch; not much to boast of.

V. be -imperfect etc. *adj.*; have a -defect etc. *n.*; lie under a disadvantage; spring a leak.

not −, barely- pass muster; fall short etc. 304.

Adj. imperfect; not -perfect etc. 650; de-ficient, -fective; faulty, unsound, mutilated, tainted; out of -order, − tune; cracked, leaky; sprung; warped etc. (*distort*) 243; lame, injured etc. (*deteriorated*) 659; peccant etc. (*bad*) 649; frail etc. (*weak*) 160; inadequate etc. (*insufficient*) 640; crude etc. (*unprepared*) 674; incomplete etc. 53; found wanting; below par; shorthanded; below −, under- its full - strength, − complement.

indifferent, middling, ordinary, mediocre; average etc. 29; so-so; *cosi-cosi*, milk and water; tolerable, fair, passable; pretty -well, – good; rather –, moderately- good; good –, well-enough; decent; not -bad, – amiss; inobjectionable, admissable, bearable, only better than nothing.

secondary, inferior; second-rate, -best, one-horse.

Adv. almost etc.; to a limited extent, rather etc. 32; pretty, moderately; only; considering, all things considered, enough.

Phr. *surgit amari aliquid.*

652. Cleanness.—N. cleanness etc. *adj.*; purity; cleaning etc. *v.*; purification, defecation etc. *v.*; purgation, lustration; de-, abs-tersion; epuration, mundation, ablution, lavation, colature; disinfection etc. *v.*; drain-, sewerage.

lavatory, bath, -room; swimming pool, natatorium; public baths; hot –, cold –, Turkish –, Swedish –, Russian – vapor- bath; *hammam*, laundry, washhouse; washerwoman, laundress, laundryman; scavenger, cleaner, sweeper, goodie; crossing sweeper, white wings, dustman, sweep.

brush; broom, besom, carpet-sweeper, vacuum-cleaner, mop, squilgee, rake, shovel, sieve, riddle, screen, filter; scraper, strigil.

napkin, *serviette*, cloth, table-, carving-cloth, table-linen, napery, maukin, handkerchief, towel, sudary; doyley, doily, duster, sponge, mop, swab. cover, drugget, mat, doormat.

soap, wash, lotion, detergent, cathartic, purgative; purifier etc. *v.*; dentifrice, tooth-powder, -paste; mouth wash; disinfectant.

V. be –, render- clean etc. *adj.*

clean, -se; mundify, rinse, wring, flush, full, wipe, mop, sponge, scour, swab, scrub, holystone, brush up.

wash, shampoo, lave, launder, buck; abs-, deterge; clear, purify; de-purate, -spumate, -fecate; purge, expurgate; Bowdlerize; elutriate, lixiviate, edulcorate, clarify, refine, rack; fil-ter, -trate; drain, strain.

disinfect, sterilize, pasteurize, fumigate, ventilate, deodorize; whitewash.

sift, winnow, screen, riddle, pick, weed, comb, rake, brush, sweep.

rout –, clear –, sweep etc.- out; make a clean sweep of.

Adj. clean, -ly; pure; immaculate; spot-, stain-taint-less; without a stain, un-stained, -spotted, -soiled, -sullied, -tainted, -infected, -adulterated; aseptic; sweet, – as a nut.

neat, spruce, tidy, trim, gimp, clean as a new penny, like a cat in pattens; cleaned etc. *v.*; kempt.

Adv. neatly etc. *adj.*; clean as a whistle.

653. Uncleanness.—N. uncleanness etc. *adj.*; impurity; immundi-ty, -city; impurity etc. [of mind] 961.

defilement, contamination etc. *v.*; defedation; soil-ure, -iness; abomination; leaven; taint, -ure; fetor etc. 401.

decay; putre-scence, -faction; corruption; mold, must, mildew, dry-rot, *mucor*, rubigo, caries.

slovenry; slovenliness etc. *adj.*; squalor.

dowdy, drab, slut, malkin, slattern, sloven, slammerkin, scrub, draggletail, mudlark, dustman, sweep; beast.

dirt, filth, soil, slop; dust, cobweb, flue; smoke, soot, smudge, smut, grime, raff.

sordes, dregs, grounds, lees; sedi-, settle-ment; heel-tap; dross, -iness; mother, precipitate, *scoria*, ashes, cinders, recrement, slag; scum, froth.

hog-wash, swill, ditch-, dish-, bilge-water; rinsings, cheese-parings; sweepings etc. (*useless refuse*) 645; off-, out-scourings; off-scum; *caput mortuum*, *residuum*, sprue, feculence, clinker, draff; scurf, -iness; *exuviae*, morphew; fur, -fur; dandruff; tartar.

riffraff; vermin, louse, cootie, flea, bug.

mud, mire, quagmire, *alluvium*, silt, sludge, slime, slush, slosh.

spawn, offal, garbage, carrion; *excreta* etc. 299; slough, peccant humor, pus, matter, suppuration, *lienteria*; *feces*, excrement, ordure, dung; sew-, sewer-age; muck, coprolite; guano, manure, compost.

dunghill, *coluvies*, mixen, midden, bog, laystall, sink, w.c., water-, earth-closet, latrine, privy, jakes, John's, cess, -pool; sump, sough, *cloaca*, drain, sewer, common sewer; Cloacina; dust-hole.

sty, pig-sty, lair, den, Augean stable, sink of corruption; slum, rookery.

V. be –, become- unclean etc. *adj.*; rot, putrefy, fester, rankle, reek; stink etc. 401; mold, -er; go - bad etc. *adj.*

render -unclean etc. *adj.*; dirt, -y; soil, smoke, tarnish, slaver, spot, smear, daub, blot, blur, smudge, smutch, smirch; d-, dr-abble, -aggle; spatter, slubber; be-smear etc.; -mire, -slime, -grime, -foul; splash,·stain, distain, maculate, sully, pollute, defile, debase, contaminate, taint, leaven; corrupt etc.(*injure*) 659; cover with -dust etc; *n.*; drabble in the mud.

wallow in the mire; slob-, slab-ber.

Adj. unclean, dirty, filthy, grimy; soiled etc. *v.*; not to be handled with kid gloves; dusty; snuffy, smutty, sooty, smoky; thick, turbid, dreggy; slimy.

uncleanly, slovenly, untidy, sluttish, dowdy, slatternly, draggletailed; un-combed, -kempt, -scoured, -swept, -wiped, -washed, -strained, -purified; squalid.

nasty, coarse, foul, impure, offensive, abominable, beastly, reeky, reechy; fetid etc. 401.

moldy, lentiginous, musty, mildewed, rusty; moth-eaten, mucid, rancid, bad, gone bad, touched, fusty, reasty, rotten, corrupt, tainted, high, fly-blown, maggoty; putr-id, -escent, -efied; purulent, carious, peccant, fec-al, -ulent; stercoraceous, excrementitious; scurfy, impetiginous; gory, bloody; rotting etc. *v.*; rotten as a pear, – cheese.

crapulous etc. (*intemperate*) 954; gross etc. (*impure in mind*) 961.

654. Health.—N. health, sanity; soundness etc. *adj.*; vigor; good –, perfect –, excellent –, rude –, robust- health; bloom, *mens sana in corpore sano*; Hygeia; incorrupti-on, -bility; good state –, clean bill- of health, eupepsia.

V. be in health etc. *adj.*; bloom, flourish.

keep -body and soul together, – on one's legs; enjoy -good, – a good state of - health; have a clean bill of health.

return to health; recover etc. 660; get better etc. (*improve*) 658; take a -new, – fresh- lease of life; convalesce, be convalescent, recruit; restore to health; cure etc. (*restore*) 660.

Adj. health-y, -ful; in -health etc. *n.*; well, sound, strong, fit, hearty, hale, fresh, blooming, green, whole; florid, flush, hardy, stanch, staunch, brave, robust, vigorous, weather-proof; convalescent.

un-scathed, -injured, -maimed, -marred, - tainted; sound of wind and limb, safe and sound; without a scratch.

on one's legs; sound as a -roach, – bell; fresh as -a daisy, – a rose, – April; picture of health; bursting with health; fit as a fiddle; hearty as a buck; in -fine, – high- feather; in -good case, – full bloom; in fine fettle; pretty bobbish, tolerably well, as well as can be expected.

sanitary etc. (*health-giving*) 656; sanatory etc. (*remedial*) 662.

655. Disease.*—N. disease, illness, sickness etc. *adj.*; ailing etc. *v.*; 'the ills that flesh is heir to;' morb-idity, -osity; infirmity, ailment, indisposition; complaint, disorder, malady; distemper, -ature.

visitation, attack, seizure, stroke, fit, epilepsy, apoplexy, shock, shell-shock.

delicacy, loss of health, valetudinarianism, invalidism, cachexy; *cachexia*, atrophy, *marasmus*; indigestion, *dyspepsia*; decay etc. (*deterioration*) 659; malnutrition, decline, consumption, palsy, paralysis, prostration; occupational diseases.

taint, pollution, infection, contagion, septicity, septicaemia, blood poisoning, pyaemia, epi-, endemic; murrain, plague, pestilence, virus, pox.

sore, ulcer, abscess, fester, boil; pimple etc. (*swelling*) 250; carbuncle, gathering, whitlow, imposthume, peccant humor, issue; rot, canker, cancer, *carcinoma, caries*, mortification, corruption, gangrene, *sphacelus*, leprosy, eruption, rash, breaking out, venereal disease.

fever, calenture; inflammation.

fatal etc. (*hopeless*) 859- -disease etc.; dangerous illness, galloping consumption, churchyard cough; general breaking up, break up of the system.

[Disease of the mind] neurasthenia; idiocy etc. 499; insanity etc. 503.

martyr to disease; cripple; 'the halt, the lame and the blind;' valetudinar-y, -ian; invalid, patient, case; sick-room, -chamber, hospital etc. 662.

[Science of disease] path-, eti-, nos-ology, therapeutics, diagnosis, prognosis.

V. be -ill etc. *adj.*; ail, suffer, labor under, be affected with, complain of; droop, flag, languish, halt; sicken, peak, pine, waste away, fail, lose strength; gasp.

keep one's bed; feign sickness etc. (*falsehood*) 544; malinger.

lay -by, – up; take –, catch- -a disease etc. *n.*, – an infection; be stricken by; break out.

Adj. diseased; ailing etc. *v.*; ill, – of; taken ill, seized with; indisposed, unwell, sick, squeamish, poorly, seedy; affected –, afflicted- with illness; laid up, confined, bed-ridden, invalided, in hospital, on the sick list; out of -health, – sorts; valetudinary.

un-sound, -healthy; sickly, morbose, healthless,

infirm, chlorotic, unbraced, drooping, flagging, lame, halt, crippled, halting.

morbid, tainted, vitiated, peccant, contaminated, poisoned, septic, tabid, mangy, leprous, cankered; rotten, – to, – at- the core; withered, palsied, paralytic, tuberculous; dyspeptic.

touched in the wind, broken-winded, spavined, gasping; *hors de combat* etc. (*useless*) 645.

weak-ly, -ened etc. (*weak*) 160; decrepit; decayed etc. (*deteriorated*) 659; incurable etc. (*hopeless*) 859; in declining health; cranky; in a bad way, in danger, prostrate; moribund etc. (*death*) 360.

morbific, epidemic etc. 657.

*Extended lists of different diseases are beyond the scope of this work.

656. Salubrity.—N. salubrity, salubriousness; healthiness etc. *adj.*

fine -air, – climate; eudiometer.

[Preservation of health] *hygiène*; valetudinarian, -ism, preventorium, sanitarian; *sanitarium, sanitorium*, immunity.

V. be -salubrious etc. *adj.*; agree with, be good for; assimilate etc. 23.

Adj. salu-brious, -tary, -tiferous, wholesome; health-y, -ful; sanitary, prophylactic, benign, bracing, tonic, invigorating, good for, nutritious, hyg-eian, -ienic.

in-noxious, -nocuous, -nocent; harmless, uninjurious, uninfectious; immune.

sanative etc. (*remedial*) 662; restorative etc. (*reinstate*) 660; useful etc. 644.

657. Insalubrity.—N. insalubrity, unhealthiness etc. *adj.*; non-naturals; plague spot; malaria etc. (*poison*) 663; death in the pot, contagion.

Adj. insalubrious; un-healthy, -wholesome; noxious, noisome, foul; morbi-fic, -ferous; mephitic, septic, azotic, deleterious; pesti-lent, -ferous, -lential; virulent, venomous, envenomed, poisonous, toxic, narcotic.

contagious, infectious, catching, taking, communicable, epidemic, zymotic, sporadic, endemic, pandemic, epizoötic.

innutritious, indigestible, ungenial; uncongenial etc. (*disagreeing*) 24.

deadly etc. (*killing*) 361.

658. Improvement.—N. improvement; a-, melioration; betterment; mend, amendment, emendation; mending etc. *v.*; advancement; advance etc. (*progress*) 282; ascent etc. 305; promotion, preferment; elevation etc. 307; increase etc. 35.

cultiv-, civiliz-ation; menticulture, culture, march of intellect; eugenics, euthenics, meliorism, telesis.

reform, -ation; revision, radical reform; second thoughts, correction, *limae labor*, refinement, elaboration; purification etc. 652; repair etc. (*restoration*) 660; recovery etc. 660.

revise; revised –, new- edition.

reformer, radical, progressive.
V. improve; be –, become –, get- better;
mend, amend.
advance etc. (*progress*) 282; ascend etc. 305; increase etc. 35; fructify, ripen, mature; pick up,
come about, rally, take a favorable turn; turn -over
a new leaf, – the corner; raise one's head, sow
one's wild oats; recover etc. 660.
be -better etc. *adj.*, – improved by; turn to -
right, – good, – best- account; profit by, reap the
benefit of; make -good use of, – capital out of;
place to good account; take advantage of.
render better, improve, emend, make over, better; a-, meliorate; correct.
improve –, refine- upon; rectify; enrich,
mellow, elaborate, fatten.'
promote, cultivate, advance, forward, enhance;
bring -forward, – on; foster etc. 707; invigorate
etc. (*strengthen*) 159.
touch –, rub –, brush –, furbish –, bolster
–, vamp –, brighten –, warm- up; polish, cook,
make the most of, set off to advantage; prune;
repair etc. (*restore*) 660; put in order etc. (*arrange*)
60.
review, revise, edit, redact; make -corrections, –
improvements etc. *n.*; doctor etc. (*remedy*) 662;
purify etc. 652.
relieve, refresh, revive, infuse new blood into,
recruit, re-invigorate, renew, revivify, freshen;
build -afresh, – anew; uplift, inspire.
re-form, -model, -organize; new model, civilize.
view in a new light, think better of, appeal from
Philip drunk to Philip sober.
palliate, mitigate; lessen etc. 36- an evil.
Adj. improving etc. *v.*; progressive, improved
etc. *v.*; better, – off, – for; all the better for; better advised.
reform-, emend-atory; reparatory etc.
(*restorative*) 660; remedial etc. 662.
corrigible, improvable, curable, accultural.
Adv. on -consideration, – reconsideration, –
second thoughts, – better advice; *ad melius
inquirendum*; on the -mend, – up grade.

659. Deterioration.—N. deterioration,
debasement; want, ebb; recession etc. 287;
retrogradation etc. 283; decrease etc. 36.
degenera-cy, -tion, -teness; degradation; deprav-
ation, -ement; depravity etc. 945; demoralization,
retrogression.
impairment, inquination, injury, damage, loss,
detriment, delaceration, outrage, havoc, inroad,
ravage, scath; perversion, prostitution, vitiation,
discoloration, oxidation, pollution, defedation,
poisoning, venenation, leaven, contamination,
canker, corruption, adulteration, alloy.
decl-ine, -ension, -ination, decadence, -cy;
falling off etc. *v.*; caducity, decrepitude, senility.
decay, dilapidation, ravages of time, wear and
tear; cor-, e-rosion; mouldi-, rotten-ness; moth and
rust, dry-rot, blight, marasmus, atrophy, collapse;
disorganization; *délabrement* etc. (*destruction*)
162.
wreck, mere wreck, honeycomb, *magni nominis
umbra*.
V. be –, become- -worse, – deteriorated etc.
adj.; have seen better days, deteriorate, degenerate,

fall off; wane etc. (*decrease*) 36; ebb; retrograde
etc.: 283; decline, droop; go down etc. (*sink*) 306;
go -downhill, – on from bad to worse, – farther
and fare worse; jump out of the frying pan into the
fire.
run to -seed, – waste; swale, sweal; lapse, be the
worse for; break, – down; spring a leak, crack,
start; shrivel etc. (*contract*) 195; fade, go off,
wither, molder, rot, rankle, decay, go bad; go to –
fall into- decay; 'fall into the sear and yellow leaf,'
rust, crumble, shake; totter, – to its fall; perish etc.
162; die etc. 360.
[Render less good] deteriorate; weaken etc.
160; put back; taint, infect, contaminate, poison,
empoison, envenom, canker; corrupt, exulcerate,
pollute, vitiate, inquinate; de-, em-base;
denaturalize, leaven; de-flower, -bauch, -file, -
prave, -grade; stain etc. (*dirt*) 653; discolor; alloy,
adulterate, sophisticate, tamper with, prejudice.
pervert, prostitute, demoralize, brutalize; render
vicious etc. 945; compromise.
embitter, ex-, acerbate, aggravate.
injure, impair, labefy, damage, harm, hurt,
shend, scathe, spoil, mar, despoil, dilapidate,
waste; overrun; ravage; pillage etc. 791.
wound, stab, pierce, maim, lame, subrate, cripple, hough, hamstring, hit between the wind and
water, scotch, mangle, mutilate, disfigure, blemish,
deface, warp.
blight, rot; cor-, e-rode, eat away; wear -away,
– out; gnaw, – at the root of; sap, mine, undermine, shake, – sap the foundations of, break up;
dis-organize, -mantle, -mast; destroy etc. 162.
damnify etc. (*aggrieve*) 649; do one's worst;
knock down; deal a blow to; play -havoc, – sad
havoc, – the mischief, – the deuce, – the very
devil- -with, – among; decimate.
Adj. unimproved etc. (improve etc. 658);
deteriorated etc. *v.*; altered, – for the worse; injured etc. *v.*; sprung; withering, spoiling, etc. *v.*; on
the -wane, – decline; tabid; degenerate; worse; the
–, all the- worse for; out of -repair, – tune; imperfect etc. 651; the worse for wear; battered;
weather-ed, -beaten; stale, *passé*, shaken,
dilapidated, frayed, faded, wilted, shabby, second-
hand, second-rate, threadbare; worn, – to- -a
thread, – a shadow, – the stump, rags; reduced,
– to a skeleton, skeletonized; far gone.
decayed etc. *v.*; moth-, worn-eaten; mildewed,
rusty, moldy, spotted, seedy, time-worn, moss-
grown; discolored; effete, wasted, crumbling,
moldering, rotten, cankered, blighted, tainted;
depraved etc. (*vicious*) 945; decrep-id, -it; broken
down; done, – for, – up; worn out, used up; fit
for the -dust-hole, – wastepaper basket; past work
etc. (*useless*) 645.
at a low ebb, in a bad way, on one's last legs,
washed -up; – out; undermined, deciduous; nodding to its fall etc. (*destruction*) 162; tottering etc.
(*dangerous*) 665; past cure etc. (*hopeless*) 859;
fatigued etc. 688; backward, retrograde etc.
(*retrogressive*) 283; deleterious etc. 649; behind
the times.
Adv. on the down grade; beyond hope.
Phr. out of the frying pan into the fire;
aegrescit medendo.

660. Restoration.—N. restor-ation, -al; reinstatement, -placement, -habilitation,

establishment, -construction; reproduction etc.
163; re-novation, -newal; reviv-al, -escence;
refreshment etc. 689; re-suscitation, -animation, -
vivification, -viction; Phoenix; reorganization.

renaissance, renascence, rebirth, second youth,
rejuvenation, rejuvenescence, new birth; regenera-,
tion, -cy, -teness; palingenesis, reconversion,'
resurgence, resurrection.

redress, retrieval, reclamation, recovery; convalescence; resumption, *résumption*.

recurrence etc. (*repetition*) 104; *réchauffé*,
rifacimento.

cure, recure, sanation; healing etc. *v*.; redin-
tegration; rectification, instauration.

repair, reparation, mending; recruiting etc. *v*.;
cicatrization; disinfection; tinkering.

reaction; redemption etc. (*deliverance*) 672;
restitution etc. 790; relief etc. 834.

mender, repairer, renewer; tinker, cobbler; doctor etc. 662; *vis medicatrix* etc. (*remedy*) 662.
curableness.

V. return to the original state; recover, rally,
revive; come -to, – round, – to oneself; pull
through, weather the storm, be oneself again; get -
well, – round, – the better of, – over, – about;
rise from -one's ashes, – the grave; resurge,
resurrect; survive etc. (*outlive*) 110; resume, reappear; come to, – life again; live –, rise- again;
relive.

heal, skin over, cicatrize; right itself.

restore, put back, place *in statu quo*; re-instate, -
place, -seat, -habilitate, -establish, -estate, -install.

re-construct, -build, -organize, -constitute;
reconvert; re-new, -novate; recondition; regenerate;
rejuvenate.

re-deem, -claim, -cover, -trieve; rescue etc.
(*deliver*) 672.

redress, recure; cure, heal, remedy, doctor,
physic, medicate; break of; bring round, set on
one's legs.

re-suscitate, -vive, -animate, -vivify, -call to life;
reproduce etc. 163; warm up; reinvigorate, refresh
etc. 689.

redintegrate, make whole; recoup etc. 790; make
-good, – all square; rectify; put – , set- -right, –
to rights, – straight; set up, correct; put in order
etc. (*arrange*) 60; refit, recruit; fill up, – the ranks;
reinforce.

repair, mend; put in -repair, – thorough repair,
– complete repair; retouch, botch, vamp, tinker,
doctor, cobble; do – , patch – , plaster – , vamp-
up; darn, fine-draw, heel-piece; stop a gap, stanch,
staunch, caulk, calk, careen, splice, bind up
wounds.

Adj. restored etc. *v*.; *redivivus*, convalescent; in
a fair way; none the worse; rejuvenated, renascent.

restoring etc. *v*.; restorative, recuperative; sana-,
repara-tive, -tory; curative, remedial.

restor-, recover-, san-, remedi-, retriev-, cur-able.

Adv. *in statu qho*; as you were.

Phr. *revenons a nos moutons.*

661. Relapse.—N. relapse, lapse; falling back
etc. *v*.; retrogradation etc. (*retrogression*) 283;
deterioration etc. 659.

[Return to, or recurrence of a bad state]
backsliding, recidivation, recrudescence.

V. relapse, lapse; fall – , slide –, sink- back;

have a relapse; return; retrograde etc. 283;
recidivate; fall off etc. 659- again.

662. Remedy.—N. remedy, help, redress; antidote, anti-toxin, -biotic; anti-, counter-poison,
prophylactic, antiseptic, germicide, bactericide,
corrective, restorative, stimulant, pick-me-up,
tonic; sedative etc. 174; palliative; febrifuge; alter-
ant, ative; specific; emetic, carminative; narcotic
etc. *adj*.; Nepenthe, Mithridate.

cure; radical – , perfect – , certain- cure;
sovereign remedy.

physic, medicine, patent medicine, Galenicals,
simples, drug, wonder – , miracle – drugs; potion,
draught, dose, pill, bolus, lozenge, tablet, tabloid,
capsule; electuary; linct-us, -ure; medicament.

nostrum, receipt, recipe, prescription;
catholicon, panacea, elixir, *elixir vitae*,
philosopher's stone; balm, balsam, cordial, theriac,
ptisan.

salve, ointment, cerate, oil, lenitive, lotion,
cosmetic; plaster; epithem, embrocation, liniment,
cataplasm, sinapism, arquebusade, traumatic,
vulnerary, pepastic, poultice, collyrium, depilatory,
compress, pledget; bandage etc. (*support*) 215.

treatment, medical treatment, regimen; diet-ary,
-etics; *vis medicatrix*, – *naturae*; *médicine expectante*; seton, blood-letting, bleeding, venesection, phlebotomy, cupping, leeches; operation,
surgical operation; tonsillectomy, appendectomy;
injection, electrolysis, massage.

pharma-cy, -cology, -ceutics; acology; materia
medica, pharmacopoeia, therapeutics, therapy,
posology, pathology etc. 655; home-, hetero-, all-,
hydr-opathy; cold water – , open air- cure;
dietetics; sur-, chirur-gery, osteopathy; healing art,
leechcraft, practice of medicine; ortho-paedy, -
praxy; dentistry, midwifery, obstetrics, gynecology.

faith -cure, – healing, Christian science; psycho-
therapy, -analysis, psychiatry.

hospital, infirmary, clinic; pest-, lazar-house;
lazaretto, lazaret; lock hospital; *maison de santé*;
ambulance; dispensary; *sanatorium, sanitarium*,
spa, baths, pump-room, well; *hospice*; Red Cross;
nursing home; asylum.

doctor, physician, surgeon; medical – , general-
practitioner, consultant, specialist; medical attendant; medical student, medico; chemist,
apothecary, pharmacopolist, druggist; leech;
Aesculapius, Hippocrates, Galen; *accoucheur*,
gynecologist, midwife, oculist, aurist, dentist;
operator; osteopath, bonesetter; nurse, monthly
nurse, sister; dresser; *masseur, masseuse*.

V. apply a -remedy etc. *n*.; doctor, dose, physic,
nurse, minister to, attend, dress the wounds,
plaster, bandage, poultice; heal, cure, work a cure,
kill or cure, remedy, stay (disease), snatch from the
jaws of death; prevent etc. 706; relieve etc. 834;
palliate etc. 658; restore etc. 660; drench with
physic; consult, operate, extract, deliver; bleed,
cup, let blood, transfuse; electrolyse; psycho-
analyse.

Adj. remedial; restorative etc. 660; corrective,
palliative, healing; sana-tory, -tive; prophylactic;
salutiferous etc. (*salutary*) 656; medic-al, -inal;
therapeutic, surgical, chirurgical, orthopedic,
epulotic, paregoric, tonic, corroborant, analeptic,
balsamic, anodyne, hypnotic, neurotic, narcotic,

sedative, lenitive, demulcent, emollient; depuratory; deter-sive, -gent; abstersive, disinfectant, febrifugal, alternative; traumatic, vulnerary.

dietetic, alimentary; nutrit-ious, -ive; peptic; alexi-pharmic, -teric; remedi-, cur-able.

663. Bane. —**N.** bane, curse, thorn in the -side, -flesh, bugbear, *bête noire*; evil etc. 619; hurtfulness etc. (*badness*) 649; painfulness etc. (*cause of pain*) 830; scourge etc. (*punishment*) 975; *damnosa hereditas*; white elephant.

sting, fang, thorn, tang, bramble, briar, nettle.

poison, leaven, virus, venom; intoxicant; arsenic, Prussic acid, antimony, tartar emetic, strychnine, nicotine, cyanide of potassium, corrosive sublimate; curare; hyoscine etc.; poison-, mustard-, tear-gas; carbon di-, mon-oxide; ptomaine poisoning, botulism; miasm, mephitis, malaria, azote, sewer gas; pest, stench etc. 401.

rust, worm, moth, moth and rust, fungus, mildew; dry-rot; canker, -worm; cancer; torpedo; viper etc. (*evil-doer*) 913; demon etc. 980.

hemlock, hellebore, nightshade, *belladonna*, henbane, aconite; Upas tree.

drugs, dope, opium, morphia, morphine, cocaine, heroin, hashish, bhang.

[*Science of poisons*] Toxicology.

Adj. baneful etc. (*bad*) 649; poisonous etc. (*unwholesome*) 657.

664. Safety. —**N.** safety, security, impregnability; invulnera-bility, -bleness etc. *adj.*; danger -past, – over; storm blown over; coast clear; escape etc. 671; means of escape, safety-valve; safeguard, palladium, sheet anchor, rock, tower of strength.

guardian-, ward-, warden-ship; tutelage, custody, safe keeping; preservation etc. 670; protection, auspices.

safe-conduct, escort, convoy; guard, sheild etc. (*defense*) 717; guardian angel, tutelary -god, ,– deity, – saint; *genius loci*.

protector, guardian; ward-en, -er; preserver, custodian, *duenna chaperon*, third person.

watch-, ban-dog; Cerberus; watch-, patrol-, police-man, constable, peeler, bobby, copper, cop, bull, flat-foot, detective, armed guard; sentinel, sentry, scout etc. (*warning*) 668; garrison; guard-ship.

[Means of safety] refuge etc., anchor etc. 666; precaution etc. (*preparation*) 673; quarantine, *cordon sanitaire*. [Sense of security] confidence etc. 858.

V. be -safe etc. *adj.*; keep one's head above water, tide over, save one's bacon; ride out –, weather- the storm; light upon one's feet; bear a charmed life; escape etc. 671; possess nine lives.

make –, render- -safe etc. *adj.*; protect, watch over; take care of etc. (*care*) 459; preserve etc. 670; cover, screen, shelter, shroud, flank, ward; guard etc. (*defend*) 717; secure etc. (*restrain*) 751; intrench, fence round etc. (*circumscribe*) 229; house, nestle, ensconce; take charge of.

escort, convoy; garrison; watch, mount guard, patrol, scout, spy.

make assurance double sure etc. (*caution*) 864; take up a loose thread; take precautions etc. (*prepare for*) 673; take in a reef; double reef top-sails.

seek safety; take –, find- shelter etc. 666; run into port.

Adj. safe, secure, sure; in -safety, – security; have an anchor to windward; on the safe side; under the -shield of, – shade of, – wing of, – shadow of one's wing; under -cover, – lock and key; out of -danger, – the meshes, – harm's way; in -harbor, – port; on sure ground, at anchor, high and dry, above water, on *terra firma*; unthreatened, -molested; protected etc. *v.*; cavendo tutus; panoplied etc. (*defended*) 717.

snug, sea-, air-worthy; weather-, water-, fire-, bomb-proof.

defensible, tenable, proof against, invulnerable; un-assailable, -attackable; im-pregnable, -perdible; founded on a rock; inexpugnable.

safe and sound etc. (*preserved*) 670; harmless; scathless etc. (*perfect*) 650; unhazarded; not -dangerous etc. 665.

protecting etc. *v.*; guardian, tutelary; perservative etc. 670; trustworthy etc. 939.

Adv. *ex abundanti cautela*; with impunity.

Phr. all's well; all clear; *salva res est*; *suave mari magno*; safety first.

665. Danger. —**N.** danger, peril, insecurity, jeopardy, risk, hazard, venture, precariousness, slipperiness; instability etc. 149; defenselessness etc. *adj.*

exposure etc. (*liability*) 177; vulnerability; vulnerable point, heel of Achilles; forlorn hope etc. (*hopelessness*) 859.

[Dangerous course] leap in the dark etc. (*rashness*) 863; road to ruin, *facilis descensus Averni*, hair-breadth escape.

cause for alarm; source of danger etc. 667. [Approach of danger] rock – , breakers- ahead; storm brewing; clouds -in the horizon, – gathering; warning etc. 668; alarm etc. 669. [Sense of danger] apprehension etc. 860.

V. be -in danger etc. *adj.*; be exposed to – , run into – , incur – , encounter- -danger etc. *n.*; run a risk; lay oneself open to etc. (*liability*) 177; lean on – , trust to- a broken reed; feel the ground sliding from under one, have to run for it; have the -chances, – odds- against one.

hang by a thread, totter; tremble on the -verge, – brink; sleep – stand -on a volcano; sit on a barrel of gunpowder, live in a glass house.

bring – , place – , put- in -danger etc. *n.*; endanger, expose to danger, imperil; jeopard, -ize; compromise; sail too near the wind etc. (*rash*) 863; put one's head in the lion's mouth.

adventure, risk, hazard, venture, stake, set at hazard; run the gauntlet etc. (*dare*) 861; engage in a forlorn hope.

threaten etc. 909- danger; run one hard; lay a trap for etc. (*deceive*) 545.

Adj. in -danger etc. *n.*; endangered etc. *v.*; fraught with danger; danger-, hazard-, peril-. parl-, pericul-ous; unsafe, unprotected etc. (*safe, protect* etc. 664); insecure, untrustworthy, unreliable; built upon sand, on a sandy basis.

defence-, fence-, guard-, harbor-less; unshielded; vulnerable, expugnable, unsheltered, exposed; open to etc. (*liable*) 177.

aux abois, at bay; on -the wrong side of the wall, − a lee shore, − the rocks.

at stake, in question; precarious, aleatory, critical, ticklish; slip-pery, -py; hanging by a thread etc. *v.*; with a halter round one's neck; between - the hammer and the anvil, − Scylla and Charybdis, − two fires; on the -edge, − brink, − verge of a- -precipice, − volcano; in the lion's den, on slippery ground, under fire; not out of the wood.

un-warned, -admonished, -advised; unprepared etc. 674; off one's guard etc. (*inexpectant*) 508.

tottering; un-stable, -steady; shaky, top-heavy, tumble-down, ramshackle, crumbling, waterlogged; help-, guide-less; in a bad way; reduced to − , at- the last extremity; trembling in the balance; nodding to its fall etc. (*destruction*) 162.

threatening etc. 909; ominous, ill-omened; alarming etc. (*fear*) 860; explosive; poisonous etc. 657.

adventurous etc. (*rash*) 863, (*bold*) 861.

Int. stop! look out! beware! take care!

Phr. *incidit in Scyllam qui vult vitare Charybdim; nam tua res agitur paries dum proximus ardet.*

666. Refuge. [Means of safety.]—**N.** refuge, sanctuary, retreat, fastness; stronghold, keep, last resort; ward; prison etc. 752; asylum, ark, home, almshouse, refuge for the destitute; hiding-place etc. (*ambush*) 530; *sanctum sanctorum* etc. (*privacy*) 893.

roadstead, anchorage; breakwater, mole, port, haven; harbor, − of refuge; sea-port; pier, jetty, embankment, quay.

covert, shelter, abri, screen, lee-wall, wing, shield, umbrella; splash-, dash-board, mudguard.

wall etc. (*inclosure*) 232; fort etc. (*defence*) 717.

anchor, kedge; grap-nel, -pling iron; sheet-, mushroom-anchor, main-stay; support etc. 215; check etc. 706; ballast.

jury-mast; vent-peg; safety -valve, − lamp; lightning conductor.

means of escape etc. (*escape*) 671; life-boat, swimming belt, cork jacket; life preserver, breeches buoy; parachute, plank, stepping-stone.

safeguard etc. (*protection*) 664.

V. seek − , take − , find- refuge etc. *n.*; seek − , find- safety etc. 664; throw oneself into the arms of; claim sanctuary; take to the -hills, − woods; make port, reach shelter, bar − , bolt − , lock -the door, − gete; let the portcullis down; raise the drawbridge.

667. Pitfall. [Source of danger.]—**N.** rocks, reefs, coral reef, sunken rocks, snags; sands, quicksands, Goodwin sands, sandy foundation; slippery ground; breakers, shoals, shallows, bank, shelf, flat, lee shore, iron-bound coast; rock − breakers- ahead; derelict.

precipice; abyss, chasm, pit, crevasse; maelstrom, whirlpool, eddy, vortex, rapids, current, bore, tidal wave; storm, squall, hurricane, whirlwind; volcano;

ambush etc. 530; pitfall, trap-door; trap etc. (*snare*) 545.

sword of Damocles; wolf at the door, snake in the grass, viper in one's bosom, death in the pot; latency etc. 526.

ugly customer, dangerous person, *le chat qui dort*; firebrand, hornet's nest.

Phr. *latet anguis in herbâ; proximus ardet Ucalegon.*

668. Warning.—**N.** warning, caution, *caveat*; notice etc. (*information*) 527; premoni-tion, - shment; prediction etc. 511; contraindication; symptom; lesson, dehortation; admonition, monition; alarm etc. 669.

handwriting on the wall, *tekel upharsin*, yellow flag; fog-signal, -horn; siren; monitor, warning voice, Cassandra, signs of the times, Mother Carey's chickens, stormy petrel, bird of ill omen, gathering clouds, clouds in the horizon, cloud no bigger than a man's hand, death-watch.

watch-tower, beacon, signal-post; light-house etc. (*indication of locality*) 550.

sent-inel, -ry; watch, -man; watch and ward; watch-, ban-, house-dog; patrol, vedette, picket, bivouac, scout, spy, spial; advanced − , rear-guard, lookout, flagman.,

cautiousness etc. 864.

V. warn, caution; fore-, pre-warn; ad-, premonish; give -notice, − warning; menace etc. (*threaten*) 909; put on one's guard; sound the alarm etc. 669; croak.

beware, ware; take -warning, − heed at one's peril; watch out for; keep watch and ward etc. (*care*) 459.

Adj. warning etc. *v.*; premonitory, monitory, cautionary; admonitory, -tive; ominous, threatening, lowering, minatory, symptomatic.

warned etc. *v.*; on one's guard etc. (*careful*) 459; (*cautious*) 864.

Adv. *in terrorem* etc. (*threat*) 909.

Int. beware! ware! take care! mind − , take care-what you are about; mind! look out!

Phr. *ne reveillez pas le chat qui dort; foenum habet in cornu.*

669. Alarm. [Indication of danger.]—**N.** alarm; alarum, larum, alarm bell, tocsin, *alerte*, beat of drum, sound of trumpet, note of alarm, hue and cry, signal of distress, S.O.S.; blue-lights; war-cry, -whoop; warning etc. 668; fog-signal, -horn; siren; yellow flag; danger signal; red -light, − flag; fire -bell, − alarm; burglar alarm, police whistle, watchman's rattle.

false alarm, cry of wolf; bug-bear, -aboo.

V. give − , raise − , sound − , beat- the *or* an - alarm etc. *n.*; alarm; warn etc. 668; ring the tocsin; *battre la générale*; cry wolf.

Adj. alarming etc. *v.*

Int. *sauve qui peut! qui vive?* who goes there?

670. Preservation.—**N.** preservation; safe keeping; conservation etc. (*storage*) 636; maintenance, upkeep, support, sustentation, conservatism; *vis conservatrix*; salvation etc. (*deliverance*) 672; drying etc. *v.*

[Means of preservation] prophylaxis; preserv-er, -ative; canned goods; cold pack; hygi-astics, -antics; cover, durgget; *cordon sanitaire*.

[Superstitious remedies] charm etc. 993.

V. preserve, maintain, keep, sustain, support; keep -up, – alive; not willingly let die; shore –, bank- up; nurse; save, rescue; be –, make- safe etc. 664; take care of etc. (*care*) 459; guard etc. (*defend*) 717.

stare super antiquas vias; hold one's own; hold –, stand- -one's ground etc. (*resist*) 719.

embalm, dry, cure, smoke, salt, pickle, season, kyanize, bottle, pot, tin, can; husband etc. (*store*) 636.

Adj. preserving etc. *v.*; conservative; prophylatic; preserva-tory, -tive; hygienic.

preserved etc. *v.*; un-impaired, -broken, -injured, -hurt, -singed, -marred; safe, – and sound; intact, with a whole skin, without a scratch.

Phr. *nolumus leges Angliae mutari*.

671. Escape.—N. escape, scape; avolation, elopment, flight, get-away; evasion etc. (*avoidance*) 623; retreat; narrow –, hairbreadth- escape; close –, near- shave; come off, impunity.

[Means of escape] loophole etc. (*opening*) 260; path etc. 627; secret -door, – passage; refuge etc. 666; vent, – peg; safety-valve; drawbridge, fire-escape.

reprieve etc. (*deliverance*) 672; liberation etc. 750.

refugee etc. (*fugitive*) 623.

V. escape, scape; make –, effect –, make good- one's escape, make a get-away; get -off, – clear off, – well out of; *échapper belle*, save one's bacon; weather the storm etc. (*safe*) 664; escape scot-free.

elude etc., make off etc. (*avoid*) 623; march off etc. (*go away*) 293; give one the slip; slip through the -hands, – fingers; slip the collar, wriggle out of; break -loose, – from prison; break –, slip –, get- away; find -vent, – a hole to creep out of.

Adj. escap-ing, -ed etc. *v.*; stolen away, fled.

Phr. the bird has flown.

672. Deliverance.—N. deliverance, extrication, rescue; repriev-e, -al; respite; ransom; liberation etc. 750; truce, armistice; redemption, salvation; riddance; gaol delivery; exemption, day of grace; redeemableness.

V. deliver, extricate, rescue, save, redeem, ransom, free, -liberate, release, set free, redeem, emancipate; bring -off, – through; *tirer d'affaire*, get the wheel out of the rut; snatch from the jaws of death, come to the rescue; rid; retrieve etc. (*restore*) 660; be –, get- rid of.

Adj. saved etc. *v.*; extric-, redeem-, rescu-able.

Phr. to the rescue!

673. Preparation.—N. preparation; providing etc. *v.*; provi-sion, -dence; anticipation etc. (*foresight*) 510; precaution, -concertation,

disposition; forecast etc. (*plan*) 626; rehearsal, not of preparation.

[Putting in order] arrangement etc. 60; clearance; adjustment etc. 23; tuning; equipment, outfit, accoutrement, armament, array.

ripening etc. *v.*; maturation, evolution; elaboration, concoction, digestion; gestation, hatching, incubation, sitting.

groundwork, datum, first stone, cradle, stepping-stone; foundation, scaffold etc. (*support*) 215; scaffolding, *échafaudage*.

[Preparation -of men] training etc. (*education*) 537; inurement etc. (*habit*) 613; novitiate; [– of food] cook-ing, -ery; brewing, culinary art; [– of the soil] till-, plough-, sow-ing; semination, cultivation.

[State of being prepared] prepared-, readi-, ripe-, mellow-ness; maturity; *un impromptu fait à loisir*.

[Preparer] preparer, teacher, coach, trainer, pioneer; *avant-courrier*, *-coureur*; sappers and miners, paver, navvy; packer, stevedore; warming-pan; precursor etc. 64.

V. prepare; get –, make- ready; make preparations, settle preliminaries, get up, sound the note of preparation; address oneself to.

set –, put- in order etc. (*arrange*) 60; forecast etc. (*plan*) 626; prepare –, plough –, dress- the ground; till –, cultivate- the soil; predispose, sow the seed, lay a train, dig a mine; lay –, fix- the -foundations, – basis, -groundwork; dig the foundations, erect the scaffolding; lay the first stone etc. (*begin*) 66.

rough-hew; cut out work; block –, hammer-out; lick into shape etc. (*form*) 240.

elaborate, mature, ripen, mellow, season, bring to maturity; nurture etc.

(*aid*) 707; hatch, cook, brew; temper; anneal, smelt; dry, cure etc. 670.

equip, arm, man; fit-out, -up; furnish, rig, dress, garnish, betrim, accouter, array, fettle, fledge; dress –, furbish –, brush –, vamp- up; refurbish; sharpen one's tools, trim one's foils, set, prime, attune; whet the -knife, – sword; wind –, screw- up; adjust etc. (*fit*) 27; put in- trim, – train, – gear, – working order, – tune, – a groove for, – harness; pack, stow away, store.

train etc. (*teach*) 537; inure etc. (*habituate*) 613; breed; prepare etc.- for; rehearse; make provision for; take -steps, – measures, – precautions; provide, – against; beat up for recruits; open the door to etc. (*facilitate*) 705.

set one's house in order, make all snug; clear - decks, – for action; close one's ranks; shuffle the cards.

prepare oneself; serve an apprenticeship etc. (*learn*) 539; lay oneself out for, get into harness, gird up one's loins, buckle on one's armor, *reculer pour mieux sauter*, prime and load, shoulder arms, get the steam up, put the horses to.

guard –, make sure- against; forearm, make sure, prepare for the evil day, have a rod in pickle, provide against a rainy day, feather one's nest; lay in provisions etc. 637; make investments; keep on foot.

be -prepared, – ready etc. *adj.*; hold oneself in readiness, watch and pray, keep one's powder dry; lie in wait for etc. (*expect*) 507; anticipate etc. (*foresee*) 510; *principiis obstare*; *veniente occurrere morbo*.

Adj. preparing etc. *v.*; in -preparation, – course

of preparation, – agitation, – embryo, – hand, – train; afoot, afloat; on -foot, – the stocks, – the anvil; under consideration etc. (*plan*) 626; brewing, hatching, forthcoming, brooding; in -store for, – reserve.

precautionary, provident; prepara-tive, -tory; provisional, inchoate, under revision; preliminary etc. (*precedent*) 62.

prepared etc. *v.*; in readiness; ready, – to one's hand, – made, cut and dried; ready for use, reach me down; made to one's hand, handy, on the table, made to order; in gear; in working -order, – gear; snug; in practice.

ripe, mature, mellow; practiced etc. (*skillet*) 698; labored, elaborate, highly-wrought, smelling of the lamp, worked up.

in -full feather, – best bib and tucker; in –, at-harness; in – the saddle, – arms, – battle array, – war paint; up in arms; armed -at all points, – to the teeth, – *cap-à-pie*; sword in hand; booted and spurred.

in utrumque –, *semper- paratus*; on the alert etc. (*vigilant*) 459; at one's post.

Adv. in -preparation, – anticipation of; afoot, astir, abroad; abroach.

674. Non-preparation.—N. non-, absence of –, want of- preparation; unpreparedness; in-culture, inconcoction, improvidence.

immaturity, crudity; rawness etc. *adj.*; abortion; disqualification.

[Absence of art] nature, state of nature; virgin soil, unweeded garden; rough diamond, neglect etc. 460.

rough copy etc. (*plan*) 626; germ etc. 153; raw material etc. 635.

improvisation etc. (*impulse*) 612.

V. be -unprepared etc. *adj.*; want –, lack-preparation; lie fallow; *s'embarquer sans biscuits*; live from hand to mouth.

[Render unprepared] dismantle etc. (*render useless*) 645; undress etc. 226.

extemporize, improvise.

surprise, pay a surprise visit, take by surprise, drop in upon, take unawares; take pot-luck.

Adv. un-prepared etc. prepare etc. 673] without -preparation etc. 673; incomplete etc. 53; rudimental, embryonic, abortive; immature, unripe, raw, green, crude; coarse; rough, -cast, -hewn; in the rough; un-hewn, -formed, -fashioned, -wrought, -labored, -blown, -cooked, -boiled, -concocted, -cut, -polished.

callow, un-hatched, -fledged, -nurtured, -licked, -taught, -educated, -cultivated, -trained, -tutored, -drilled, -exercised; precocious, premature; un-, in-digested; un-mellowed, -seasoned, -leavened.

fallow; un-sown, -tilled; natural, in a state of na-ture; undressed; in dishabille, *en déshabille*, *en négligé*.

un-, dis-qualified; unfitted; ill-digested; un-begun, -ready, -arranged, -organized, -furnished, · provided, -equipped, -trimmed; out of -gear, – or-der; dismantled etc. *v.*

shiftless, improvident, unthrifty, thoughtless, unguarded; happy-go-lucky; caught napping etc. (*inexpectant*) 508; unpremeditated etc. 612.

Adv. extempore etc. 612.

675. Essay.—N. essay, trial, endeavor, aim, at-tempt; venture, adventure, speculation, coup *d'essai*, *début*; probation etc. (*experiment*) 463.

V. try, essay; experiment etc. 463; endeavor, strive; tempt, tackle, take on, attempt, make an at-tempt; venture, adventure, speculate, take one's chance, tempt fortune; try one's -fortune, – luck, – hand; use one's endeavor; feel –, grope –, pick- one's way.

try hard, push, make a bold push, use one's best endeavor; do one's best etc. (*exertion*) 686.

Adj. essaying etc. *v.*; experimental etc. 463; tentative, empirical, probationary.

Adv. experimentally etc. *adj.*; on trial, at a ven-ture; by rule of thumb.

if one may be so bold.

676. Undertaking.—N. undertaking, compact etc. 769; engagement etc. (*promise*) 768; enter-, em-prise; venture etc. 675; pilgrimage; matter in hand etc. (*business*) 625; move; first move etc. (*beginning*) 66.

V. undertake; engage –, embark- in; launch –, plunge- into; volunteer; apprentice oneself to; engage etc. (*promise*) 768; contract etc. 769; take upon -oneself, – one's shoulders; devote oneself to etc. (*determination*) 604.

take -up, – in hand; tackle; set –, go- about; set –, fall- -to, – to work; launch forth; set up shop; put in -hand, – execution; set forward; break the neck of a business, be in for; put one's hand to; betake oneself to, turn one's hand to, go to do; begin etc. 66; broach, institute, etc. (*originate*) 153; put –, lay- one's -hand to the plough, – shoulder to the wheel.

have in hand etc. (*business*) 625; have many irons in the fire etc. (*activity*) 682.

Adj. undertaking etc. *v.*; on the anvil etc. 625; adventurous, venturesome.

Int. here goes!

677. Use.—N. use; employ, -ment; exer-cise, citation; appli-cation, -ance; adhibition, disposal; consumption; agency etc. (*physical*) 170; usufruct; usefulness etc. 644; recourse, resort, avail, pragmatism.

[Conversion to use] utilization, service, wear.

[Way of using] usage.

V. use, make use of, employ, put to use; apply, put in -action, – operation, – practice; set -in motion, – to work.

ply, work, wield, handle, manipulate; play, – off; exert, exercise, practice, avail oneself of, profit by; resort –, have recourse –, recur –, take –, betake oneself- to; take -up with, – advantage of; lay one's hands on, try.

render useful etc. 644; mold; turn to -account, – use; convert to use, utilize, administer; work up; call –, bring- into play; put into requisition; call –, draw- forth; press –, enlist- into the service; bring to bear upon, devote, dedicate, consecrate, apply, adhibit, dispose of; make a -handle, – cat's paw- of.

fall beak upon, make a shift with; make the -most, – best- of.

use –, swallow- up; consume, absorb, expend; tax, task, wear, put to task.

Adj. in use; used etc. *v.*; well-worn, -trodden. useful etc. 644; subservient etc. (*instrumental*) 631; utilitarian; pragmatical.

678. Disuse.—N. forbearance, abstinence; disuse; relinquishment etc. 782; desuetude etc. (*want of habit*) 614.

V. not use; do without, dispense with, let alone, not touch, forbear, abstain, spare, waive, neglect; keep back, reserve.

lay -up, – by, – on the shelf, – up in a napkin; shelve; set –, put –, lay- aside; disuse, leave off, have done with; supersede; discard etc. (*eject*) 297; dismiss, give warning.

throw aside etc. (*relinquish*) 782; make away with etc. (*destroy*) 162; cast –, heave –, throw-overboard; cast to the -dogs, – winds; dismantle etc. (*render useless*) 645.

lie –, remain- unemployed etc. *adj.*

Adj. not used etc. *v.*; un-employed, -applied, disposed of, -spent, -exercised, -touched, -trodden, -essayed, -gathered, -culled; uncalled for, not required.

disused etc. *v.*; done with; run down, used up, cast off.

679. Misuse.—N. mis-use, -usage, employment, -application, -appropriation.

abuse, profanation, prostitution, desecration; waste etc. 638.

V. mis-use, -employ, -apply, -appropriate.

desecrate, abuse, profane, prostitute; waste etc. 638; over-task, -tax, -work; squander etc. 818.

cut a whetstone with a razor, employ a steam-engine to crack a nut; catch at a straw.

Adj. misused etc. *v.*

680. Action.—N. action, performance; doing etc. *v.*; perpetration; exercise, -citation; movement, operation, evolution, work; labor etc. (*exertion*) 686; *praxis*, execution; procedure etc. (*conduct*) 692; handicraft; business etc. 625; agency etc. (*power at work*) 170.

deed, act, overt act, stitch, touch, gest; trans-action, job, doings, dealings, proceeding, measure, step, maneuver, bout, passage, move, stroke, blow; *coup*, – *de main*, – *d'état*; *tour de force* etc. (*display*) 882; feat, exploit, stunt; achievement etc. (*completion*) 729; handiwork, workmanship, crafts-manship; manufacture; stroke of policy etc. (*plan*) 626.

actor etc. (*doer*) 690.

V. do, perform, execute; achieve etc. (*complete*) 729; transact, enact; commit, perpetrate, inflict; exercise, prosecute, carry on, work, practice, play.

employ oneself, ply one's task; officiate, have in hand etc. (*business*) 625; labor etc. 686; be at work; pursue a course; shape one's course etc. (*conduct*) 692.

act, operate; take -action, – steps; strike a blow, lift a finger, stretch forth one's hand; take in hand etc. (*undertake*) 676; put oneself in motion; put in practice; carry into execution etc. (*complete*) 729; act upon.

be -an actor etc. 690; take –, act –, play –, perform- a part in; participate in; have a -hand in, – finger in the pie; have to do with; be a -party to, – participator in; bear –, lend- a hand; pull an oar, run in a race; mix oneself up with etc. (*meddle*) 682.

be in action; come into operation etc. (*power at work*) 170.

Adj. doing etc. *v.*; acting; in action; in harness; on duty; at work; in operation etc. 170; up to one's ears in work, in the midst of things.

Adv. in the -act, – midst of, – thick of; red-handed, *in flagrante delicto*; while one's hand is in.

681. Inaction.—N. inaction, passiveness, ab-stinence from action; non-interference; Fabian –, conservative- policy; neglect etc. 460; stagnation, vegetation; loafing.

inactivity etc. 683; rest etc. (*repose*) 687; quiescence etc. 265; want of –, in- occupation; unemployment; idle hours, time hanging on one's hands, *dolce far niente*; sinecure.

V. not -do, – act, – attempt; be -inactive etc. 683; abstain from doing, do nothing, hold, spare; not -stir, – move, – lift- a -finger, – foot, – peg; fold one's -arms, – hands; leave –, let- alone; let -be, – pass, – things take their course, – it have its way, – well alone; *quieta non movere*; *stare super antiquas vias*; rest and be thankful, live and let live; lie –, rest- upon one's oars; *laisser -aller*, – *faire*; stand aloof; refrain etc. (*avoid*) 623; keep oneself from doing; remit –, relax- one's efforts; desist etc. (*relinquish*) 624; stop etc. (*cease*) 142; pause etc. (*be quiet*) 265.

wait, lie in wait, bide one's time, take time, tide it over.

cool –, kick- one's heels; loaf, while away the -time, – tedious hours; pass –, fill –, beguile- the time; talk against time; waste time etc. (*inactive*) 683.

lie -by, – on the shelf, – in ordinary, – idle, – to, – fallow; keep quiet, slug; have nothing to do, whistle for want of thought; twiddle one's thumbs.

undo, do away with; take -down, – to pieces; destroy etc. 162.

Adj. not doing etc. *v.*; not done etc. *v.*; undone; passive; un-occupied, -employed; out of -employ, – work, – a job; fallow; *désœuvré*.

Adv. *re infectâ*, at a stand, *les bras croisés*, with folded arms; with the hands -in the pockets, – behind one's back; *pour passer le temps*.

Int. so let it be! stop! etc. 142; hands off!

Phr. nothing doing; *cunctando restituit rem*.

682. Activity.—N. activity; briskness, liveliness etc. *adj.*; animation, life, vivacity, spirit, verve, dash, energy, go.

nimbleness, agility; smartness, quickness etc. *adj.*; velocity etc. 274; alacrity, promptitude; des-, dis-patch; expedition; haste etc. 684; punctuality etc. (*early*) 132.

eagerness, zeal, ardor, *perfervidum ingenium*, *empressement*, earnestness, intentness; *abandon*; vigor etc. (*physical energy*) 171; devotion etc. (*resolution*) 604; exertion etc. 686.

industry, assiduity; assiduousness etc. *adj.*; sedulity; laboriousness; drudgery etc. (*labor*) 686; painstaking, diligence; perseverance etc. 604*a*; indefatigation; habits of business.

vigilance etc. 459; wakefulness; sleep-, restlessness; *pervigilium, insomnia*; racketing.

movement, bustle, hustle, stir, fuss, ado, bother, pottering; fidget, -iness; flurry etc. (*haste*) 684.

officiousness; dabbling, meddling; inter-ference, -position, -meddling, butting in, intrusiveness; tampering with, intrigue.

press of business, no sinecure, plenty to do, many irons in the fire, great doings, busy hum of men, battle of life, thick of -things, – the action; the madding corwd.

housewife, busy bee; new brooms; sharp fellow, blade; hustler, devotee, enthusiast, fan, zealot, fanatic; meddler, intermeddler, intriguer, busybody, kibitzer, pickthank.

V. be -active etc. *adj.*; busy oneself in; stir, -about, – one's stumps; bestir –, rouse- oneself; speed, hasten, peg away, lay about one, bustle, fuss; raise –, kick up- a dust; push; make a -push, – fuss, – stir; go ahead, push forward; flight –, elbow- one's way; make progress etc. 282; toil etc. (*labor*) 686; drudge, plod, persist etc. (*persevere*) 604*a*; keep -up the ball, – the pot boiling.

look sharp; have all one's eyes about one etc. (*vigilance*) 459; rise, arouse oneself, get up early, hustle, push; be about, keep moving, steal a march, kill two birds with one stone; seize the opportunity etc. 134; lose no time, not lose a moment, make the most of one's time, not suffer the grass to grow under one's feet, improve the shining hour, make short work of; dash off; make haste etc. 684; do one's best, take pains etc. (*exert oneself*) 686; do –, work- wonders.

have -many irons in the fire, – one's hands full, – much on one's hands; have other -things to do, – fish to fry; be busy; not have a moment -to spare, – that one can call one's own.

have one's fling, run the round of; go all lengths, stick at nothing, run riot.

outdo; over-do, -act, -lay, -shoot the mark; make a toil of a pleasure.

have a hand in etc. (*act in*) 680; take an active part, put in one's oar, have a finger in the pie, mix oneself up with, trouble one's head about, intrigue; agitate.

tamper with, meddle, moil; inter-meddle, -fere, -pose; obtrude; poke –, thrust- one's nose in, butt in.

Adj. active; brisk, – as a lark, – as a bee; lively, animated, vivacious; alive, – and kicking; frisky, spirited, stirring.

nimble, – as a squirrel; agile; light-, nimble-footed; featly, tripping.

quick, prompt, yare, instant, ready, alert, spry, sharp, smart, slick, go-ahead; fast etc. (*swift*) 274; quick as a lamplighter, expeditious; awake, broad awake; wide awake etc. (*intelligent*) 498.

forward, eager, ardent, strenuous, zealous, enterprising, pushing, in earnest; resolute etc. 604.

industrious, assiduous, diligent, sedulous, notable, painstaking; intent etc. (*attention*) 457; indefatigable etc. (*persevering*) 604*a*; unwearied, unsleeping, sleepless, never tired; plodding, hard-working etc. 686; business-like, workaday.

bustling; restless, – as a hyena; fussy, fidgety, pottering, busy, – as a hen with one chicken.

working, laboring, at work, on duty, in harness; up in arms; on one's legs, at call; up and -doing, – stirring.

busy, occupied; hard at -work, – it; up to one's ears in, full of business, busy as a bee.

meddling etc. *v.*; meddlesome, pushing, officious, overofficious, *intrigant*.

astir, stirring; a-going, -foot; on foot; in full swing; eventful; on the alert etc. (*vigilant*) 459.

Adv. actively etc. *adj.*; with -life and spirit, – might and main etc. 686, – haste etc. 684, – wings; full tilt, *in mediis rebus.*

Int. be –, look- -alive, – sharp! move –, push-on! keep moving! go ahead! stir your stumps! *age quod agis!*

Phr. *carpe diem* etc. (*opportunity*) 134; *nulla dies sine lineâ*; *nec mora nec requies*; no sooner said than done etc. (*early*) 132; catch a weasel asleep.

683. Inactivity.—N. inactivity; inaction etc. 681; inertness etc. 172; obstinacy etc. 606.

lull etc. (*cessation*) 142; quiescence etc. 265; rust, -iness.

idle-, remiss-ness etc. *adj.*; sloth, indolence, indiligence; otiosity, dawdling etc. *v.*

dullness etc. *adj.*; languor; segni-ty, -tude; lentor; sluggishness etc. (*slowness*) 275; procrastination etc. (*delay*) 133; torp-or, -idity, -escence; stupor etc. (*insensibility*) 823; somnolence; drowsiness etc. *adj.*; nodding etc. *v.*; oscit-ation, -ancy; pandiculation, hypnotism, lethargy; heaviness, heavy eye-lids, sand in the eyes.

sleep, slumber; sound –, heavy –, balmy- sleep; Morpheus, dreamland; coma, trance, catalepsy, hypnosis, *ecstasis*, dream, hibernation, nap, doze, snooze, *siesta*, wink of sleep, forty winks, snore; Hypnology.

dull work; pottering; relaxation etc. (*loosening*) 47; Castle of Indolence.

[Cause of inactivity] lullaby, *berceuse*; anesthetic, sedative etc. 174; torpedo.

idler, drone, droil, dawdle, mopus; do-little, *fainéant*, dummy, sleeping partner; afternoon farmer; truant etc. (*runaway*) 623; lounger, *lazzarone*, floater, loafer, tramp, beggar, cadger; lubber, -bard; slow-coach etc. (*slow*) 275; opium –, lotus- eater; slug; lag-, slug-gard, lie-abed; slumberer, dormouse, marmot; waiter on Providence, *fruges consumere natus.*

V. be -inactive etc. *adj.*; do nothing etc. 681; move slowly etc. 275; let the grass grow under one's feet; take one's time, dawdle, poke, drawl, droil, lag, hang back, slouch; loll, -op; lounge, loaf, loiter; go to sleep over; sleep at one's post; *ne battre que d'une aile.*

take -it easy, – things as they come; lead an easy life, vegetate, swim with the stream, eat the bread of idleness; loll in the lap of -luxury, – indolence; waste –, consume –, kill –, lose time; burn daylight, waste the precious hours.

idle –, trifle –, fritter –, fool- away time; spend –, take- time in; ped-, pid-dle; potter, putter, dabble, faddle, fribble, fiddle-faddle; dally, dilly-dally.

sleep, slumber, be asleep; hibernate; oversleep; sleep like a -top, – log, – dormouse; sleep - soundly, – heavily; doze, drowze, snooze, nap; take a -nap etc. *n.*; dream; snore; settle –, go –,

go off- to sleep; drop off; fall −, drop- asleep; close −, seal up- -the -eyes, − eyelids; weigh down the eyelids; get sleepy, nod, yawn; go to bed, turn in.
languish, expend itself, flag, hang fire; relax.
render -idle etc. *adj.*; sluggardize; mitigate etc. 174.

Adj. inactive; motionless etc. 265; unoccupied etc. (*doing nothing*) 681.

indolent, lazy, slothful, idle, otiose, lusk, remiss, slack, inert, torpid, sluggish, languid, supine, heavy, dull, leaden, lumpish; exanimate, soulless; listless; dron-y, -ish; lazy as Ludlam's dog.

dilatory, laggard; lagging etc. *v.*; slow etc. 275; rusty, flagging; lackadaisical, maudlin, fiddle-faddle; pottering etc. *v.*; shilly-shally etc. (*irresolute*) 605.

sleeping etc. *v.*; alseep; fast −, dead −, sound-alseep; in a sound sleep; sound as a top, dormant, comatose; in the -arms, − lap- of Morpheus.

sleep-y, -ful; dozy, drowsy, somnolent, torpescent; lethargic, -al; heavy, − with sleep; napping; somni-fic, -ferous; sopor-ous, -ific, -iferous; hypnotic; balmy, dreamy; un-, una-wakened.

sedative etc. 174.

Adv. inactively etc. *adj.*; at leisure etc. 685.

Phr. the eyes begin to draw straws.

684. Haste.—**N.** haste, urgency; des-, dis-patch; acceleration, spurt, spirt, forced march, rush, dash; velocity etc. 274; precipit-ancy, -ation, -ousness etc. *adj.*; impetuosity; *brusquerie*; hurry, scurry, scuttle drive, scramble, push, hustle, bustle, fuss, fidget, flurry, flutter, splutter.

V. haste, hasten; make -haste, − a dash etc. *n.*; hurry −, dash −, whip −, push −, press- -on, − forward; hurry, skurry, scuttle along, bundle on, dart to and fro, bustle, flutter, scramble; plunge, − headlong; run, race, speed; dash off; rush etc. (*violence*) 173.

bestir oneself etc. (*be active*) 682; lose -no time, − not a moment, − not an instant; make short work of; make the best of one's -time, − way.

be -precipitate etc. *adj.*; jump at; be in -haste, − a hurry etc. *n.*; have -no time, − not a moment- -to lose, − to spare; work -under pressure, − against time.

quicken etc. 274; accelerate, expedite, put on, precipitate, urge, whip, spur, flog, goad.

Adj. hasty, hurried, *brusque*; scrambling, cursory, precipitate, headlong, furious, boisterous, impetuous, hot-headed; feverish, fussy; pushing.

in -haste, − a hurry etc. *n.*; in -hot, − all- haste; breathless, pressed for time, hard pressed, urgent.

Adv. with -haste, − all haste, − breathless speed; in haste etc. *adj.*; apace etc. (*swiftly*) 274; amain; all at once etc. (*instantaneously*) 113; at short notice etc., immediately etc. (*early*) 132; posthaste; by -express, − telegraph, − wire, − wireless, − air mail.

hastily, precipitately etc. *adj.*; helter-skelter, hurry-skurry, holusbolus; slap-dash, -bang; full-tilt, -drive; heels over head, head and shoulders, headlong, *à corps perdu*.

by -fits and starts, − spurts; hop, skip and jump.

Phr. *sauve qui peut*, devil take the hindmost, no time to be lost; no sooner said than done etc. (*early*) 132; a word and a blow.

Int. hurry up! look alive! get a move on! buck up! double march! rush! urgent!

685. Leisure.—**N.** leisure; spare -time, − hours, − moments; vacant hour; time, − to spare, − on one's hands; holiday etc. (*rest*) 687; *otium cum dignitate*, ease.

V. have -leisure etc. *n.*; take one's -time, − leisure, − ease; repose etc. 687; move slowly etc. 275; while away the time etc. (*inaction*) 681; be -master of one's time, − an idle man; *desipere in loco*.

Adj. leisurely; slow etc. 275; deliberate, quiet, calm, undisturbed; at -leisure, − one's ease, − a loose end.

Phr. time hanging heavy on one's hands.

686. Exertion.—**N.** exertion, effort, strain, tug, pull, stress, force, pressure, throw, stretch, struggle, spell, spurt, spirt; stroke −, stitch- of work.
'a stong pull, a long pull and a pull all together;' dead lift; heft; gymnastics, sports; exer-cise, -citation; wear and tear; ado; toil and trouble; uphill −, hard −, warm- work; harvest time.

labor, work, toil, travail, manual labor, sweat of one's brow, swink, operoseness, drudgery, slavery, fagging, hammering; *limae labor*.

trouble, pains, duty; resolution etc. 604; energy etc. (*physical*) 171.

V. exert oneself; exert −, tax- one's energies; use exertion.

labor, work, toil, moil, sweat, fag, drudge, slave, drag a lengthened chain, wade through, strive, strain; make −, stretch- a long arm; pull, tug, ply; ply −, tug at- the oar; do the work; take the laboring oar.

bestir oneself (*be active*) 682; take trouble, trouble oneself.

work hard; rough it; put forth -one's strength, − a strong arm; fall to work, bend the bow; buckle to, set one's shoulder to the wheel etc. (*resolution*) 604; work like a -Briton, − horse, − carthorse, − galley-slave, − coalheaver; labor −, work-day and night; redouble one's efforts; do double duty; work double -hours, − tides; sit up, burn the -midnight oil, − candle at both ends; stick to etc. (*persevere*) 604a; work −, fight- one's way; lay about one, hammer at.

take pains; do one's -best, − level best, − utmost; do -the best one can, − all one can, − all in one's power, − as much as in one lies, − what lies in one's power; use one's -best, − utmost- endeavor; try one's -best, − utmost; play one's best card; put one's -best, − right- leg foremost; have one's whole soul in one's work, put all one's strength into, strain every nerve; spare no -efforts, − pains; go all lengths; go through fire and water etc. (*resolution*) 604; move heaven and earth, leave no stone unturned.

Adj. laboring etc. *v.*

laborious, operose, elaborate; strained; toil-, trouble-, burden-, weari-some; uphill; herculean, gymnastic, athletic, palestric.

hardworking, painstaking, strenuous, energetic.

hard at work, on the stretch.

Adv. laboriously etc. *adj.*; lustily; with -might and main, − all one's might, − a strong hand, − sledge-hammer, − much ado; to the best of one's abilities, *totis viribus, vi et armis, manibus pedibusque*, tooth and nail, *unguibus et rostro*,

hammer and tongs, heart and soul; through thick and thin etc. (*perseverance*) 604*a*.
by the sweat of one's brow, *suo Marte*.

687. Repose.—N. repose, rest, silken repose; sleep etc. 683.
relaxation, breathing time; halt, pause etc. (*cessation*) 142; respite.
day of rest, *dies non*, Sabbath, Lord's day, holiday, red-letter day, vacation, recess.
V. repose; rest, – and be thankful; take -rest, – one's ease.
relax, unbend, slacken; take breath etc. (*refresh*) 689; rest upon one's oars; pause etc. (*cease*) 142; stay one's hand.
lie down; recline, – on a bed of down, – on an easy chair; go to -rest, – bed, – sleep etc. 683.
take a holiday, shut up shop; lie fallow etc. (*inaction*) 681.
Adj. reposing etc. *v.*; unstrained.
Adv. at rest.

688. Fatigue.—N. fatigue; weariness etc. 841; yawning, drowsiness etc. 683; lassitude, tiredness, fatigation, exhaustion; sweat.
anhelation, shortness of breath, panting; faintness; collapse, prostration, swoon, fainting, *deliquium*, syncope, lipothymy.
V. be -fatigued etc. *adj.*; yawn etc. (*get sleepy*) 683; droop, sink, flag; lose -breath, – wind; gasp, pant, puff, blow, drop, swoon, faint, succumb.
fatigue, tire, weary, bore, irk, fag, jade, harass, exhaust, knock up, wear out, prostrate.
tax, task, strain; over-task, -work, -burden, -tax, -strain.
Adj. fatigued etc. *v.*; weary etc. 841; drowsy etc. 683; drooping etc. *v.*; haggard; toil-, way-worn; footsore, surbated, weatherbeaten; faint; done –, used –, knock- up; exhausted, prostrate, spent; over-tired, -spent, -fatigued; forspent; unre-freshed, -stored.
worn, – out; battered, shattered, pulled down, seedy, altered.
breath-, wind-less; short of – , out of -breath, – wind; blown, puffing and blowing; short-breathed; anhelous; broken-, short-winded.
ready to drop, more dead than alive, dog -tired; – weary, walked off one's legs, tired to death, on one's last legs, played out, *hors de combat*.
fatiguing etc. *v.*; tire-, irk-, weari-some; weary; trying.

689. Refreshment.—N. bracing etc. *v.*; recovery of -strength etc. 159; restoration, revival etc. 660; repair, refection, refocillation, refreshment, regalement, bait; relief etc. 834.
V. brace etc. (*strengthen*) 159; reinvigorate; air, freshen up, refresh, recruit; repair etc. (*restore*) 660; fan, revocillate.
breathe, respire; draw –, take –, gather –, take a long –, regain –, recover- breath; get better, raise one's head; recover –, regain –, renew-one's strength etc. 159; perk up.

come to oneself etc. (*revive*) 660; feel like a giant refreshed.
Adj. refreshing etc. *v.*; recuperative etc. 660.
refreshed etc. *v.*; un-tired, -wearied.

690. Agent.—N. doer, actor, agent, performer, perpetrator, operator; execu-tor, -trix; practitioner, worker, stager.
bee, ant, working bee, laboring oar, shaft horse, servant –, maid- of all work, general servant, factotum.
workman, artisan; crafts-, handicrafts-man; mechanic, operative; working –, laboring- man; hewers of wood and drawers of water, laborer, navvy; hand, man, day laborer, journeyman, hack; mere -tool etc. 633; porter, docker, stevedore, beast of burden, drudge, fag.
maker, artificer, artist, wright, manufacturer, architect, contractor, builder, mason, bricklayer,. smith, forger, Vulcan; black-, tin-smith; carpenter; ganger, platelayer.
machinist, mechanician, engineer, electrician, plumber, gasfitter etc.
semp-, sem-, seam-stress; needle-, char-, work-woman; tailor, cordwainer.
minister etc. (*instrument*) 631; servant etc. 746; representative etc. (*commissioner*) 758; (*deputy*) 759.
co-worker, fellow-worker, party to, participator in, co-operator, colleague, associate, collaborator, *particeps criminis, dramatis personae; personnel.*
Phrs. '*quorum pars magna fui.*'

691. Workshop.—N. work-shop, -house; laboratory; manufactory, mill, factory, armory, arsenal, mint, forge, loom; cabinet, *studio, bureau, atelier* hive, – of industry; nursery; hot-house, -bed; kitchen, kitchenette; dock, -yard; slip, yard, wharf; found-ry, -ery; furnace; vineyard, orchard, farm, kitchen garden.
melting pot, crucible, alembic, caldron, mortar, *matrix.*

692. Conduct.—N. dealing, transaction etc. (*action*) 680; business etc. 625.
tactics, game, policy, polity; general-, statesman-, seaman-ship; strate-gy, -gics; plan etc. 626.
husbandry; house-keeping, -wifery; stewardship; *ménage*; regimen, *régime*; econom-y, -ics; political economy; management; government etc. (*direction*) 693.
execution, manipulation, treatment, campaign. career, life, course, walk, race.
conduct; behavior; de-, com-portment; carriage *maintien*, demeanor, guise, bearing, manner, mien air, observance.
course –, line- of -conduct, – action, – proceeding; *rôle*; process, ways, practice procedure, *modus operandi*; method etc., path etc 627.
V. transact, execute; des-, dis-patch; proceed with, discharge; carry -on, – through, – out, - into effect; work out; go –, get- through; enact; pt into practice; officiate etc. 625.

behave −, comport −, demean −, carry −, bear −, conduct −, acquit- oneself.

run a race, lead a life, play a game; take −, adopt- a course; steer −, shape- one's course; play one's- part, − cards; shift for oneself; paddle one's own canoe.

conduct; manage etc. (*direct*) 693.

deal −, have to do- with; treat, handle a case; take -steps, − measures.

Adj. conducting etc. *v.*; strategical, business-like, practical, economic, executive.

693. Direction.—N. direction; manage-ment, -ry; government, gubernation, conduct, legislation, regulation, guidance; steer-, pilot-age; reins, − of government; helm, rudder, controls, joy stick, needle, compass, binnacle; guiding −, load −, lode −, pole- star; cynosure.

super-vision, -intendence; *surveillance*, oversight; eye of the master; control, charge, auspices; board of control etc. (*council*) 696; command etc. (*authority*) 737.

premier-, senator-ship; director etc. 694; chair, seat, portfolio.

statesmanship; state-, king-craft.

minis-try, -tration; administration; steward-, proctor-ship; agency.

V. direct, manage, govern, conduct; order, prescribe, cut out work for; head, lead; lead −, show- the way; take the lead, lead on; regulate, guide, steer, pilot; take −, be at- the helm; have −, handle −, hold −, take- the reins, handle the ribbons; drive, tool; tackle.

super-intend, -vise; overlook, control, keep in order, look after, see to, oversee, legislate for; administer, ministrate; patronize; have the -care, − charge- of; have −, take- the direction; pull the -strings, − wires; rule etc. (*command*) 737; have −, hold- -office, − the portfolio; preside, − at the board; take −, occupy −, be in- the chair; pull the stroke oar.

Adj. directing etc. *v.*; executive, supervisory, hegemonic.

Adv. at the -helm, − head of, in charge of; under the auspices of.

694. Director.—N. director, manager, governor, rector, comptroller; super-intendent, -visor; intendant; over-seer, -looker; foreman, boss, straw boss; supercargo, husband, inspector, visitor, ranger, surveyor, aedile, moderator, monitor, task-master; master etc. 745; leader, ringleader, demagogue, corypheus, conductor, fugleman, precentor, bellwether, agitator.

guiding star etc. (*guidance*) 693; adviser etc. 695; guide etc. (*information*) 527; pilot; helmsman; steers-man, -mate; man at the wheel; wire-puller.

driver, whip, Jehu, charioteer; coach-, car-, cabman, jarvey; postilion, *vetturino*, muleteer, teamster; whipper in; engineer, engine driver, motorman, *chauffeur.*

head, − man; principal, president, speaker; chair, -man; captain etc. (*master*) 745; superior; dean; mayor etc. (*civil authority*) 745; vice-

president, prime minister, premier, vizier, grand vizier; dictator.

officer, functionary, minister, official, red-tapist, bureaucrat; man −, Jack- in office; office-bearer; person in authority etc. 745.

statesman, strategist, legislator, lawgiver, politician, administrator, statist, statemonger; Minos, Draco; arbiter etc. (*judge*) 967; king maker, power behind the throne.

board etc. (*council*) 696.

secretary, − of state; Reis Effendi; vicar etc. (*deputy*) 759; steward; factor; agent etc. 758; bailiff, middleman; ganger, clerk of works; land-reeve; factotum, major-domo, seneschal, house-keeper, shepherd, *croupier*; proctor, procurator, curator, librarian.

Adv. *ex officio.*

695. Advice.—N. advice, counsel, adhortation; word to the wise; suggestion, submonition, recommendation, advocacy, consultation.

exhortation etc. (*persuasion*) 615; expostulation etc. (*dissuasion*) 616; admonition etc. (*warning*) 668; guidance etc. (*direction*) 693.

instruction, charge, injunction.

adviser, prompter; counsel, -lor; monitor, mentor, Nestor, *magnus Apollo*, senator; teacher etc. 540.

guide, manual, chart etc. (*information*) 527.

physician, leech, archiater; arbiter etc. (*judge*) 967.

refer-ence, -ment; consultation, conference, parley, *pourparler* etc. 696.

V. advise, counsel; give -advice, − counsel, − a piece of advice; suggest, prompt, submonish, recommend, prescribe, advocate; exhort etc. (*persuade*) 615.

enjoin, enforce, charge, instruct, call; call upon, etc. (*request*) 765; dictate.

expostulate etc. (*dissuade*) 616; admonish etc. (*warn*) 668.

advise with; lay heads −, consult- together; compare notes; hold a council, deliberate, be closeted with.

confer, consult, refer to, call in; take −, follow-advice; follow implicitly; be advised by, have at one's elbow, take one's cue from.

Adj. recommendatory; hortative etc. (*persuasive*) 615; dehortatory etc. (*dissuasive*) 616; admonitory etc. (*warning*) 668; consultative.

Int. go to!

696. Council.—N. council, committee, sub-committee, *comitia*, court, chamber, cabinet, board, bench, staff; consultation.

senate, *senatus*, parliament, house, − of Lords, − Peers, − Commons, legislature, legislative assembly, federal council, chamber of deputies, directory, *reichsrath*, *rigsdag*, *musnud*, *sanhedrim*, witenagemote, *junta*, divan, *musnud*, *sanhedrim*, Amphictyonic council; *duma*, *zemstvo*, *soviet*, *cheka*, *ogpu*; Dáil Eireann; caput, consistory, chapter, syndicate; court of appeal etc. (*tribunal*) 966; board of -control, − works; vestry; county −, borough −, district −, parish −, town- council, local board.

cabinet –, privy- council, royal commission; cockpit, convocation, synod, congress, congregation, convention, diet, states-general,.aulic council.

League of Nations, assembly, *caucus*, conclave, *clique*, conventicle; meeting, sitting, *séance*, conference, session, hearing, palaver, *pourparler, durbar*, pow-wow, house; *quorum*.

senator; member, – of parliament; councilor, M.P., representative of the people.

Adj. senatorial, curule, parliamentary.

697. Precept.—N. precept, direction, instruction, charge; prescript, -ion; *recipe*, receipt; golden rule; maxim etc. 496.

commandment, rule, ruling, canon, law, code, *corpus juris, lex scripta*, common –, unwritten –, canon- law; the Ten Commandments; act, statute, convention, rubric, stage direction, regulation; form, -ula, -ulary; technicality; nice point.

order etc. (*command*) 741.

698. Skill.—N. skill, skilfulness, address; dexter-ity, -ousness; adroitness, expertness etc. *adj* ; proficiency, competence, craft, callidity, facility, knack, trick, sleight; master-y. -ship; excellence, panurgy; ambidext-erity, -rousness; sleight of hand etc. (*deception*) 545.

sea-, air-, marks-, horse-manship; tight-, rope-dancing.

accomplish-, acquire-, attain-ment; art, science; techn-icality, -ology, -ique; practical –, technical-knowledge; technocracy; finish, technic.

knowledge of the world, world wisdom, *savoir-faire*; tact; mother wit etc. (*sagacity*) 498; discretion etc. (*caution*) 864; *finesse*; craftiness etc. (*cunning*) 702; management etc. (*conduct*) 692; *ars celare artem*; self-help.

cleverness, talent, ability, ingenuity, capacity, parts, talents, faculty, endowment, *forte*, turn, gift, genius, flair, feeling; intelligence etc. 498; sharpness, readiness etc. (*activity*) 682; invention etc. 515; apt-ness, -itude; turn –, capacity –, genius-for; felicity, capability, *curiosa felicitas*, qualification, habilitation.

proficient etc. 700.

masterpiece, *coup de maître, chef- d'oeuvre, tour de force*; good stroke etc. (*plan*) 626.

V. be -skilful etc. *adj* ; excel in, be master of; have -a turn for etc. *n.*

know -what's what, – a hawk from a handsaw, – what one is about, – on which side one's bread is buttered, – what's o'clock, – a thing or two; have cut one's -eye, – wisdom- teeth.

see -one's way, – where the wind lies, – which way the wind blows; have -all one's.wits about one, – one's hand in; *savoir vivre*; *scire quid valeant humeri quid ferre recusent*

look after the main chance; cut one's coat according to one's cloth; live by one's wits; exercise one's discretion, feather the oar, sail near the wind; stoop to conquer etc. (*cunning*) 702; play one's -cards well, – best card; hit the right nail on the head, put the saddle on the right horse.

take advantage of, make the most of; profit by etc. (*use*) 677; make a hit etc. (*succeed*) 731; make a virtue of necessity; make hay while the sun shines etc. (*occasion*) 134.

Adj. skilful, dexterous, adroit, expert, apt, slick, handy, quick, deft, ready, resourceful, gain; smart etc. (*active*) 682; proficient, good at, up to, at home in, master of, a good hand. at, *au fait*, thoroughbred, masterly, crack, accomplished; conversant etc. (*knowing*) 490.

experienced, practiced, skilled; up –, well up-in; in -practice, – proper cue; competent, efficient, qualified, capable, fitted, fit for, up to the mark, trained, initiated, prepared, primed, finished.

clever, able, ingenious, felicitous, gifted, talented, endowed, cute, inventive etc. 515; shrewd, sharp etc. (*intelligent*) 498; cunning etc. 702; alive to, up to snuff, not to be caught with chaff; discreet.

neat-handed, fine-fingered, ambidextrous, sure-footed; cut out –, fitted- for.

technical, artistic, scientific, daedalian, ship-shape; workman-, business-, statesman-like.

Adv. skilfully etc. *adj* ; well etc. 618; artistically; with -skill, – consummate skill; *secundum artem, suo Marte*; to the best of one's abilities etc. (*exertion*) 686; like a machine.

699. Unskillfulness.—N. unskillfulness etc. *adj* ; want of -skill etc. 698; incompeten-ce, -cy; in-ability, -felicity, -dexterity, -experience; clumsiness; disqualification, unproficiency; quackery.

folly, stupidity etc. 499; indiscretion etc. (*rashness*) 863; thoughtlessness etc. (*inattention*) 458, (*neglect*) 460.

mis-management, -conduct; impolicy; malad-ministration; mis-rule, -government, -application, -direction, -feasance.

absence of rule, rule of thumb; bungling etc. v ; failure etc. 732; screw loose; too many cooks.

blunder etc. (*mistake*) 495; *étourderie, gaucherie*, act of folly, *balourdise*; botch, -ery; bad job, sad work.

sprat sent out to catch a whale, much ado about nothing, wildgoose chase.

bungler etc. 701; fool etc. 501.

layman, amateur.

V. be -unskillful etc. *adj*; not see an inch beyond one's nose; blunder, bungle, boggle, fumble, muff, botch, bitch, flounder, loppet, stumble, trip; hobble etc. 275; put one's foot in it; make a -mess, – hash, – sad work- of; overshoot the mark.

play -tricks with, – Puck; mismanage, -conduct, -direct, -apply, -send.

stultify –, make a fool of –, commit- oneself; act foolishly; play the fool; put oneself out of court; lose one's -head, – cunning.

begin at the wrong end; do things by halves etc. (*not complete*) 730, make two bites of a cherry; play at cross purposes; strain at a gnat and swallow a camel etc. (*caprice*) 608; put the cart before the horse; lock the stable door when the horse is stolen etc. (*too late*) 135.

not know -what one is about, – one's own interest, – on which side one's bread is buttered; stand in one's own light, quarrel with one's bread and butter, throw a stone in one's own garden, kill the goose which lays the golden eggs, pay dear for one's whistle, cut one's own throat, burn one's fingers; knock –, run- one's head against a stone wall; fall into a trap, catch a Tartar, bring the house about one's ears; have too many -eggs in one basket (*imprudent*) 863, – irons in the fire.

mistake etc. 495; take the shadow for the substance etc. (*credulity*) 486; be in the wrong box, aim at a pigeon and kill a crow; take –, get- the wrong sow by the ear, – the dirty end of the stick; put -the saddle on the wrong horse, – a square peg into a round hole, – new wine into old bottles.

cut a whetstone with a razor; hold a farthing candle to the sun etc. (*useless*) 645; fight with –, grasp at- a shadow; catch at straws, lean on a broken reed, reckon without one's host, pursue a wildgoose chase; go on a fool's –, sleeveless-errand; go further and fare worse; loose –, miss- one's way; fail etc. 732.

Adj. un-skillful etc. 698; unskilled, inexpert; bungling etc. *v.* ; awkward, clumsy, unhandy, lubberly, *gauche, maladroit*; left-, heavy-handed; slovenly, slatternly; gawky.

adrift, at fault.

in-, un-apt; inhabile; un-tractable, -teachable; giddy etc. (*inattentive*) 458; inconsiderate etc. (*neglectful*) 460; stupid etc. 499; inactive etc. 683; incompetent; un-, dis-, ill-qualified; unfit; quackish; raw, green, inexperienced, rusty, out of practice.

un-accustomed, -used, -trained etc. 537; - initiated, -conversant etc. (*ignorant*) 491; shiftless; unbusinesslike, unpractical; unstatesmanlike.

un-, ill-, mis-advised; ill-devised, -imagined, -judged, -contrived, -conducted; un-, mis-guided; misconducted, foolish, wild; infelicitous; penny wise and pound foolish etc. (*inconsistent*) 608.

Phr. one's fingers being all thumbs; the right hand forgets its cunning.

il se noyerait dans une goutte d'eau.

incidit in Scyllam qui vult vitare Charybdim; out of the frying pan into the fire.

700. Proficient.—N. proficient, expert, adept, dab; *connoisseur* etc. (*scholar*) 492; master, -hand; top-sawyer, *prima donna*, first fiddle, *chef de cuisine*; protagonist; past master; profess-or, -ional, specialist.

picked man; medalist, prizeman.

veteran; old -stager, – campaigner, – soldier, – file, – hand; man of -business, – the world.

nice –, good –, clean- hand; practised –, ex-perienced- -eye, – hand; marksman; good –, dead –, crack- shot; rope-dancer, funambulist, acrobat, contortionist; cunning man; conjuror etc. (*deceiver*) 548; wizard etc. 994.

genius; master-mind, – head, – spirit.

cunning –, sharp -blade, – fellow; jobber; cracksman etc. (*thief*) 792; politician, tactician, diplomat, -ist, strategist.

pantologist, admirable Crichton, Jack of all trades; prodigy of learning; walking encyclopedia; mine of information.

701. Bungler.—N. bungler; blunderer, -head; marplot, fumbler, lubber, lout, oaf, duffer, stick, clown; bad –, poor- -hand, – shot; butter-fingers.

no conjuror, flat, muff, slow coach, looby, lub-

ber, swab; clod, yokel, hick, awkward squad, novice, greenhorn, jaywalker, *blanc-bec*.

land lubber; fresh water –, fair weather- sailor; horse-marine; fish out of water, ass in lion's skin, jackdaw in peacock's feathers; quack etc. (*deceiver*) 548; Lord of Misrule.

sloven, slattern, trapes,

Phr. *il n'a pas inventé la poudre*; he will never set the Thames on fire.

702. Cunning.—N. cunning, craft; cun-ningness, craftiness etc. *adj.*; subtlety, artificiality; maneuvring etc. *v.*; temporization; circumvention.

chicane, -ry; sharp practice, knavery, jugglery; concealment etc. 528; nigger in the woodpile; guile, duplicity etc. (*falsehood*) 544; foul play.

diplomacy, politics; Machiavellism; jobbery, back-stairs influence, gerrymandering.

art, -ifice; device, machination; plot etc. (*plan*) 626; maneuver, stratagem, dodge, artful dodge, wile; trick, -ery etc. (*deception*) 545; *ruse, – de guerre; finesse*, side-blow, thin end of the wedge, shift, go by, subterfuge, evasion; white lie etc. (*un-truth*) 546; juggle, *tour de force*; tricks -of the trade, – upon travelers; imposture, deception; *ex-pie-glerie*, net, trap etc. 545.

Ulysses, Machiavel, sly boots, fox, reynard; Scotch-, Yorkshire-man; Jew, Yankee; intriguer, *intrigant*, schemer, trickster.

V. be -cunning etc. *adj.*; have cut one's eye-teeth; contrive etc. (*plan*) 626; live by one's wits; maneuver; intrigue, gerrymander, *finesse*, double, temporize, stoop to conquer, *reculer pour mieux sauter*, circumvent, steal a march upon; overreach etc. 545; throw off one's guard; surprise etc. 508; outdo, get the better of, snatch from under one's nose; snatch a verdict; waylay, undermine, in-troduce the thin end of the wedge; play -a deep game, – tricks with; have an axe to grind; *am-biguas in vulgum spargere voces*; flatter, make things pleasant.

Adj. cunning, crafty, artful; skilful etc. 698; sub-tle, feline, vulpine; cunning as a -fox, – serpent; deep, – laid; profound; designing, contriving; in-triguing etc. *v.*; strategic, diplomatic, politic, Machiavellian, time-serving; artificial; trick-y, -sy; wily, sly, slim, insidious, stealthy, foxy; underhand etc. (*hidden*) 528; subdolous; deceitful etc. 545; double-tongued, -faced; shifty; crooked, arch, pawky, shrewd, acute; sharp, – as a needle; canny, astute, leery, knowing, up to snuff, too clever by half, not to be caught with chaff.

Adv. cunningly etc. *adj.*; slily, on the sly, by a side wind.

Phr. diamond cut diamond.

703. Artlessness.—N. artlessness etc. *adj.*; nature, simplicity; innocence etc. 946; *bonhomie, naïveté, abandon*; candor, sincerity; singleness of - purpose, – heart; honesty etc. 939; plain speaking; *épanchement*.

rough diamond, matter of fact man; *le palais de vérité; enfant terrible.*

V. be -artless etc. *adj.*; look one in the face; wear one's heart upon his sleeves for daws to peck at; think aloud; speak -out, – one's mind; be free with one, call a spade a spade.

Adj. artless, natural, pure, native, simple, plain, martificial, untutored, unsophisticated, *ingenu*, unaffected, *naive*; sincere, frank; open, – as day; candid, ingenuous, guileless, unsuspicious, childlike; honest etc. 939; innocent etc. 946; Arcadian; undesigning, straightforward; unreserved, unvarnished, above-board; simple-, single-minded; frank-, open-, single-, simple-hearted; open and above-board.

free-, plain-, out-spoken; blunt, downright, direct, matter of fact, unpoetical; unflattering.

Adv. in plain -words, – English; without mincing the matter; not to mince the matter etc. (*affirmation*) 535.

Phr. *Davus sum non Oedipus; liberavi animam meam.*

704. Difficulty.—**N.** difficulty; hardness etc. *adj.*; impracticability etc. (*impossibility*) 471; tough –, hard –, uphill- work; hard –, Herculean –, Augean- task; task of Sisyphus, Sisyphean labor, tough job, teaser, rasper, dead lift.

dilemma, embarrassment; perplexity etc. (*uncertainty*) 475; involvement; intricacy; entanglement etc. 59; cross fire; awkwardness, delicacy, ticklish card to play, deadlock, knot, Gordian knot, *dignus vindice nodus*, net, meshes, maze; coil etc. (*convolution*) 248; crooked path.

nice –, delicate –, subtle –, knotty-point; vexed question, *vexata quaestio*, poser; puzzle etc. (*riddle*) 533; paradox; hard –, nut to crack; bone to pick, *crux, pons asinorum*, where the shoe pinches.

nonplus, quandary, strait, pass, pinch, pretty pass, stress, brunt; critical situation, crisis; trial, rub, emergency, exigency, scramble.

scrape, hobble, slough, quagmire, hot water, hornet's nest; sea –, peck- of troubles; pretty kettle of fish; pickle, stew, *imbroglio*, mess, muddle, botch, fuss, bustle, ado; false position; set fast, stand; dead -lock, – set; fix, horns of a dilemma, *cul de sac*; hitch; stumbling block etc. (*hindrance*) 706.

V. be -difficult etc. *adj.*; run one hard, go against the grain, try one's patience, put one out; put to one's -shifts, – wit's end; go hard with –, try- one; pose, perplex etc. (*uncertain*) 475; bother, nonplus, gravel, bring to a dead lock; be -impossible etc. 471; be in the way of etc. (*hinder*) 706.

meet with –, labor under –, get into –, plunge into –, struggle with –, contend with –, grapple with- difficulties; labor under a disadvantage; be -in difficulty etc. *adj.*

fish in troubled waters, buffet the waves, swim against the stream, scud under bare poles.

have -much ado with, – a hard time of it; come to the -push, – pinch; bear the brunt.

grope in the dark, lose one's way, weave a tangled web, walk among eggs.

get into a -scrape etc. *n.*; bring a hornet's nest about one's ears; be put to one's shifts; flounder, boggle, struggle; not know which way to turn etc. (*uncertain*) 475; get -tangled up, – wound up; *perdre son latin*; stick - at, – in the mud, – fast; come to a -stand, – dead lock; hold the wolf by the ears.

render -difficult etc. *adj.*; encumber, embarrass, ravel, entangle; put a spoke in the wheel etc. (*hinder*) 706; lead a pretty dance.

Adj. difficult, not easy, hard, tough; trouble-, toil-, irk-some; operose, laborious, onerous, arduous, Herculean, formidable; sooner –, more easily- said than done; difficult –, hard- to deal with; ill-conditioned, crabbed; not -to be handled with kid gloves, – made with rosewater.

awkward, unwieldy, unmanageable; intractable, stubborn etc. (*obstinate*) 606; perverse, refractory, plaguy, trying, thorny, rugged; knot-ted, -ty; invious; path-, track-less; labyrinthine etc. (*convoluted*) 248; intricate, complicated etc. (*tangled*) 59; impracticable etc. (*impossible*) 471; not -feasible etc. 470; desperate etc. (*hopeless*) 859.

embarrassing, perplexing etc. (*uncertain*) 475; delicate, ticklish, critical; beset with –, full of –, surrounded by –, entangled by –, encompassed with- difficulties.

under a difficulty; in -difficulty, – hot water, – the suds, – a cleft stick, – a fix, – the wrong box, – a scrape etc. *n.*; – deep water, – a fine pickle; *in extremis*; between -two stools, – Scylla and Charybdis; surrounded by -shoals, – breakers, – quicksands; at cross purposes; not out of the wood.

reduced to straits; hard –, sorely- pressed; run hard; pinched, put to it, straitened; hard -up, – put to it, – set; put to one's shifts; puzzled, at a loss etc. (*uncertain*) 475; at -the end of one's tether, – one's wit's end, – a nonplus, – a standstill; graveled, nonplussed, stranded, aground; stuck –, set- fast; up a tree, at bay, *aux abois*, driven -into a corner, – from post to pillar, – to extremity, – to one's wit's end, – to the wall; *au bout de son latin*; out of one's -depth, – reckoning; put –, thrown -out.

accomplished with difficulty; hard-fought, -earned.

Adv. with -difficulty, – much ado; hardly etc. *adj.*; uphill; against the -stream, – grain; *à rebours*; *invitâ Minervâ*; in the teeth of; at –, upon- a pinch; at long odds.

Phr. ay there's the rub; *hic labor hoc opus*; things are come to a pretty pass.

705. Facility.—**N.** facility, ease; easiness etc. *adj.*; capability; feasibility etc. (*practicability*) 470; flexibility, pliancy etc. 324; smoothness etc. 255; convenience.

plain –, smooth –, straight- sailing; mere child's play, holiday task.

smooth water, fair wind; smooth – royal- road; clear -coast, – stage; *tabula rasa, full play* etc. (*freedom*) 748.

disen-cumbrance, -tanglement; deoppilation; permission etc. 760.

V. be -easy etc. *adj.*; go on –, run- smoothly; have -full play etc. *n.*; go –, run- on all fours; obey the helm, work well.

flow –, swim –, drift –, go- with the- -stream, – tide; see one's way; have -it all one's own way, – the game in one's own hands; walk over the course, win -at a canter, – hands down; make -light of, – nothing of; be at home in etc. (*skilful*) 698.

render -easy etc. *adj.*; facilitate, smooth, ease; popularize; lighten, – the labor; free, clear; disencumber, -embarrass, -entangle, -engage; deobstruct, unclog, extricate, unravel; untie –, cut- the knot; disburden, unload, exonerate, emancipate, free from, deoppilate; humor etc. (*aid*) 707; lubricate etc. 332; relieve etc. 834.

leave -a hole to creep out of, – a loophole, – the matter open; give -the reins to, – full play, – full swing; make way for; open the -door to, – way; prepare –, smooth –, clear- the -ground, – way, – path, – road; pave the way, bridge over; permit etc. 760.

Adj. easy, facile; feasible etc. (*practicable*) 470; easily -managed, – accomplished; within reach, accessible, easy of access, for the million, open to.

manageable, wieldy; towardly, tractable; submissive; yielding, ductile; pliant etc. (*soft*) 324; glib, slippery; smooth etc. 255; on -friction wheels, – velvet; convenient.

un-, dis-burdened, -encumbered, -embarrassed; exonerated; un-loaded, -obstructed, -trammeled, -impeded, -restrained etc. (*free*) 748; at ease, light.

at – , quite at- home; in -one's element, – smooth water.

Adv. easily etc. *adj.*; readily, smoothly, swimmingly, *ad lib.*, on easy terms, single-handed.

Phr. touch and go.

Int. all clear!

706. Hindrance.—N. prevention, preclusion, obstruction, stoppage; prohibition; inter-ruption, -ception, -clusion; hindrance, impedition; retardment, -ation; constriction; embarrassment, oppilation; coarctation, stricture, restriction; anchor etc. 666; restraint etc. 751 & 752; inhibition etc. 761; blockade etc. (*closure*) 261; picketing.

inter-ference, -position; obtrusion; discouragement, -countenance, -approval, approbation; opposition etc. 708.

impedimen·, let, obstacle, obstruction, knot, knag; check, hitch, *contretemps, impasse,* screw loose, grit in the oil.

bar, stile, barrier; turn-stile, -pike; gate, portcullis; bulwark, parapet, barricade etc. (*defence*) 717; wall, dead wall, breakwater, groyne; bulkhead, block, buffer; stopper etc. 263; boom, dam, weir, burrock.

drawback, objection; stumbling-block, -stone; lion in the path; snag; snags and sawyers.

en-, in-cumbrance; clog, skid, shoe, spoke; brake, drag, – chain, – weight; stay, stop; preventive, prophylactic; contraception; load, burden, fardel, *onus,* millstone round one's neck, *impedimenta;* dead weight; lumber, pack; nightmare, Ephialtes, incubus, old man of the sea; remora.

difficulty etc. 704; insuperable etc. 471- obstacle; estoppel; ill wind; head wind etc. (*opposition*) 708; trammel, tether etc. (*means of restraint*) 752; hold back, counterpoise; damper, wet blanket, hinderer, marplot, kill-joy, dog in the manger, interloper; trail of a red herring; opponent etc. 710.

V. hinder, impede, impedite, embarrass.

keep –, stave –, ward- off; picket; obviate; a-, ante-vert; turn aside, draw off, prevent, forefend, nip in the bud; retard, slacken, check, let; counteract, -check; preclude, debar, foreclose, estop;

inhibit etc. 761; shackle etc. (*restrain*) 751; restrict, restrain, cohibit.

obstruct, filibuster, stop, stay, bar, bolt, lock; block, – up; belay, barricade; block – , stop- the way; dam up etc. (*close*) 261; put on the -brake etc. *n.*; scotch –, lock –, put a spoke in- the wheel; put a stop to etc. !42; traverse, contravene; inter-rupt, -cept; oppose etc. 708; hedge -in, – round; cut off; interclude.

inter-pose, -fere, -meddle etc. 682.

cramp, hamper; clog, – the wheels; cumber; en-in-cumber; handicap; choke; saddle – , load-with; overload, lay; lumber, trammel, tie one's hands, put to inconvenience; in-, discommode; discompose; hustle, drive into a corner; choke off.

run – , fall- foul of; cross the path of, break in upon.

thwart, frustrate, disconcert, balk, foil, baffle, snub, override, circumvent; defeat etc. 731; spike guns etc. (*render useless*) 645; spoil, mar, clip the wings of; cripple etc. (*injure*) 659; put an extinguisher on; damp; dishearten etc. (*dissuade*) 616; discountenance, throw cold water on, spoil sport; lay – , throw- a wet blanket on; cut the ground from under one, take the wind out of one's sails, undermine; be – , stand- in the way of; act as a drag; hang like a millstone round one's neck.

Adj. hindering etc. *v.*; obstr-uctive, -uent; impedi-tive, -ent; intercipient; prophylactic etc. (*remedial*) 662.

in the way of, unfavorable; onerous, burdensome; cumb-rous, -ersome; obtrusive.

hindered etc. *v.*; wind-bound, water-logged, heavy laden; hard pressed.

unassisted etc. (*see* assist etc. 707); single-handed, alone; deserted etc. 624.

707. Aid.—N. aid, -ance; assistance, help, opitulation, succor; support, lift, advance, furtherance, promotion; coadjuvancy etc. (*co-operation*) 709.

patronage, championship, countenance, favor, interest, advocacy, auspices.

sustentation, subvention, subsidy, bounty, alimentation, nutrition, nourishment, maintenance; manna in the wilderness; food etc. 298; means etc. 632.

ministr-y, -ation; subministration; accommodation.

relief, rescue; help at a dead lift; supernatural aid; *deus ex machinâ.*

supplies, reinforcements, succors, contingents, recruits; support etc. (*physical*) 215; adjunct, ally etc. (*helper*) 711.

V. aid, assist, help, succor, lend one's aid; come to the aid etc. *n-* of; contribute, subscribe to; bring – , give – , furnish – , afford – , supply- -aid etc. *n.*; render assistance; give – , stretch – , lend – , bear – , hold out- a -hand, – helping hand; give one a -lift, – cast, – turn; take -by the hand, – in tow; help a lame dog over a stile, lend wings to.

relieve, rescue; set -up, – agoing, – on one's legs; bear – , pull- through; give new life to, be the making of; reinforce, recruit; set – , put – , push-forward; give -a lift, – a shove, – an impulse- to; promote, further, forward, advance; speed, expedite, quicken, hasten.

support, sustain, uphold, prop, hold up, bolster.

cradle, nourish; nurture, nurse, dry nurse, suckle, put out to nurse; manure, cultivate, force; foster; cherish, foment; feed −, fan- the flame.

serve; do service to, tender to, pander to; ad-, sub-, minister to; tend, attend, wait on; take care of etc. 459; entertain; smooth the bed of death.

oblige, accomodate, consult the wishes of; humor, cheer, encourage.

second, stand by; back, − up; pay the piper, abet; work −, make interest −, stick up −, take up the cudgels- for; take up −, espouse −, adopt- the cause of; advocate, beat up for recruits, press into the service; squire, give moral support to, keep in countenance, countenance, patronize; lend - oneself; favor, befriend, take up, take in hand, enlist under the banners of; side with etc. (co-operate) 709.

be of use to; subserve etc. (instrument) 631; benefit etc. 648; render a service etc. (utility) 644; conduce etc. (tend) 176.

Adj. aiding etc. v; auxiliary, adjuvant, helpful; coadjuvant etc. 709; subservient, ministrant, ancillary, accessory, subsidiary.

at one's beck; friendly, amicable, favorable, propitious, well-disposed; neighborly; obliging etc. (benevolent) 906.

Adv. with −, by- -the aid etc. n.- of; on −, in-behalf of; in -aid, − the service, − the name, − favor, − furtherance- of; on account of; for the sake of, on the part of; non obstante.

Int. help! save us! to the rescue! S.O.S.!

708. Opposition.—N. opposition, antagonism, oppug-nancy, -nation; impugnation; contravention; counteraction etc. 179; counterplot.

cross-fire, under-current, head-wind.

clashing, collision, conflict, lack of harmony, contest.

competition, two of a trade, rivalry, emulation, race; war to the knife.

absence of -aid etc. 707; resistance etc. 719; restraint etc. 751; hindrance etc. 706.

V. oppose, conteract, run counter to; withstand etc. (resist) 719; control etc. (restrain) 751; hinder etc. 706; antagonize, oppugn, fly in the face of, go dead against, kick against, fall foul of; set −, pit- against; face, confront, cope with; make a -stand, − dead set- against; set -oneself, one's face- against; protest −, vote −, raise one's voice- against; disfavor, turn one's back upon; set at naught, slap in the face, slam the door in one's face.

be −, play- at cross purposes; counter-work, - mine; thwart, overthwart.

stem, breast, encounter; stem −, breast- the - tide, − current, − flood; buffet the waves; beat up −, make head- against; grapple with; kick against the pricks etc. (resist) 719; contend etc. 720 −, do battle etc. (warfare) 722- -with, − against.

contra-dict, -vene; belie; go −, run −, beat − militate- against; come in conflict with.

emulate etc. (compete) 720; rival, spoil one's trade.

Adj. oppos-ing, -ed etc. v; adverse, antagonistic; ambivalent; contrary etc. 14; at variance etc. 24; at issue, at war with; in opposition; 'agin the Government.'

un-favorable, -friendly; hostile, inimical, cross, unpropitious.

in hostile array, front to front, with crossed bayonets, at daggers drawn; up in arms; resistant etc. 791.

competitive, emulous.

Adv. against, versus, counter to; in conflict with, at cross purposes.

against the -grain, − current, − stream, − wind, − tide; with a headwind; with the wind - ahead, − in one's teeth.

in spite of, in despite, in defiance; in the -way, − teeth, − face- of; across; a-, over-thwart; where the shoe pinches.

though etc. 30; even; quand même; per contra.

Phr. nitor in adversum.

709. Co-operation.—N. co-operation; coadjuvancy, -tancy; coagency, coefficiency; concert, concurrence, complicity, participation; union etc. 43; amalgamation, combination etc. 48; collusion.

association, alliance, colleagueship, jointstock, copartnership, trust, cartel, pool, ring, combine, interlocking directorate; confederation etc. (party) 712; federation, coalition, fusion; a long pull, a strong pull and a pull all together; log-rolling, freemasonry.

unanimity etc. (assent) 488; esprit de corps, party spirit; clan-, partisan-ship; reciprocity, concord etc. 714.

V. co-operate, co-adjute, concur; conduce etc. 178; combine, cartelize, unite one's efforts; keep −, draw −, pull −, club −, hang −, hold −, league −, band −, be banded- together; stand −, put- shoulder to shoulder; act in concert, join forces, fraternize, cling to one another, conspire, concert, lay one's heads together; confederate, be in league with; collude, understand one another, play into the hands of, hunt in couples.

side −, take side −, go along −, go hand in hand −, join hands −, make common cause −, strike in −, unite −, join −, mix oneself up −, take part −, play along −, cast in one's lot- with; join −, enter into- partnership with; rally round, follow the lead of; come to, pass over to, come into the views of; be −, row −, sail- in the same boat; sail on the same tack.

be a party to, lend oneself to; participate; have a -hand in, − finger in the pie; take −, bear- part in; second etc. (aid) 707; take the part of, play the game of; espouse a -cause, − quarrel.

Adj. co-operating etc. v; in -co-operation etc. n., − league etc. (party) 712; coadju-vant, -tant; hand and glove with.

favorable etc. 707- to; un-opposed etc. 708.

Adj. as one man etc. (unanimously) 488; shoulder to shoulder; in co-operation with.

710. Opponent.—N. opponent, antagonist, adversary; adverse party, opposition; enemy etc. 891; assailant.

oppositionist, obstructive; obscurantist; brawler, wrangler, brangler, disputant, extremist, irreconcilable, diehard, bitter-ender.

malcontent; Jacobin, Fenian etc. 742; demagogue, reactionist.

passive resister, conscientious objector.

rival, competitor, contestant.

711. Auxiliary.—N. auxiliary; recruit; assistant; adju-vant, -tant; adjunct; help, er, -mate, -ing hand; midwife; colleague, partner, mate, *confrère*, co-operator; coadju-tor, -trix; collaborator.

ally; friend etc. 890; confidant, *fidus Achates*, pal, chum, buddy, *alter ego*.

confederate; ac-, complice; accessory, – after the fact; *particeps criminis*.

aide-de-camp, secretary, clerk, associate, marshal; right-hand; candle-, bottle-holder; hand-maid; servant etc. 746; puppet, cat's-paw; stooge, dependent, creature, jackal; tool, *âme damnée*; satellite, adherent, parasite.

votary, disciple; secta-rian, -ry; seconder, backer, upholder, supporter, abettor, advocate, partisan, champion, patron, friend at court, mediator.

friend in need, Jack at a pinch, *deus ex machinâ*, guardian angel, fairy godmother; special providence, tutelary genius.

712. Party.—N. party, faction, side, denomination, class, communion, set, crowd, crew, band, horde, posse, phalanx; regiment etc. 726; family, clan etc. 166.

Tories, Conservatives, Unionists, Whigs, Liberals, Radicals, Labour party, Socialists, Communists etc.; Republicans, Democrats, Farmer-Labor; *Fascisti*, Revolutionaries etc. 742.

community, body, fellowship, sodality, solidarity; con-, fraternity; sorority; brother-, sister-hood.

Freemasons, Knights Templars, Odd Fellows, Ku Klux Klan etx.

knot, gang, *clique*, ring, circle; *coterie*, club, *casino*.

corporation, corporate body, guild; establishment, company, copartnership, firm, house, joint concern, joint-stock company, trust, investment trust, combine etc. 709.

society, association; instit-ute, -ution; union; trade-union; league, syndicate, alliance, *Verein*, *Bund*, *Zollverein*, combination; league –, alliance- offensive and defensive; coalition; federation; confedera -tion, -cy; junto, cabal, *camarilla*, *camorra*, *brigue*; freemasonry; party spirit etc. (*co-operation*) 709.

staff; cast, *dramatis personae*.

V. unite, join; club together etc. (*co-operate*) 709; cement –, form- a party etc. *n.*; associate etc. (*assemble*) 72.

Adj. in -league, – partnership, – alliance etc. *n.*

bonded –, banded –, linked etc. (*joined*) 43- together; embattled; confederated, federative, joint, corporate, leagued, fraternal, masonic, cliquish.

Adv. hand in hand, side by side, shoulder to shoulder, *en masse*, in the same boat.

713. Discord.—N. disagreement etc. 24; discord, -accord, -sidence, -sonance; jar, clash, shock; jarring, jostling etc. *v.*; screw loose.

variance, difference, dissension, misunderstanding, cross purposes, odds, *brouillerie*; division, split, rupture, disruption, division in the camp, house divided against itself, rift within the lute; disunion, breach; schism etc. (*dissent*) 489; feud, faction.

quarrel, dispute, rippet, spat, tiff, *tracasserie*, squabble, altercation, words, high words; wrangling etc. *v.*; jangle, brabble cross questions and crooked answers, snip-snap; family jars.

polemics; litigation; strife etc. (*contention*) 720; warfare etc. 722; outbreak, open rupture; breaking off of negotiations, recall of ambassadors; declaration of war.

broil, brawl, row, racket, hubbub, rixation; embroilment, embranglement, *imbroglio*, *fracas*, breach of the peace, piece of work, scrimmage, rumpus; breeze, squall; riot, disturbance etc. (*disorder*) 59; commotion etc. (*agitation*) 315; bear garden, Donnybrook Fair.

subject of dispute, ground of quarrel, battle ground, disputed point; bone -of contention, – to pick; apple of discord, *casus belli*; question at issue etc. (*subject of inquiry*) 461; vexed question, *vexata quaestio*, brand of discord.

troublous times; cat-and-dog life; contentiousness etc. *adj.*; enmity etc. 889; hate etc. 898; Kilkenny cats; disputant etc. 710; strange bedfellows.

V. be -discordant etc. *adj.*; disagree, come amiss etc. 24; clash, jar, jostle, pull different ways, conflict, have no measures with, misunderstand one another; live like cat and dog; differ; dissent etc. 489; have a -bone to pick, – crow to pluck- with.

fall out, quarrel, dispute; litigate; controvert etc. (*deny*) 536; squabble, wrangle, jangle, brangle, bicker, nag; spar etc. (*contend*) 720; have -words etc. *n.* with; fall foul of.

split; break –, break squares –, part company-with; declare war, try conclusions; join –, put in-issue; pick a quarrel, fasten a quarrel on; sow –, stir up- -dissension etc. *n.*; embroil, estrange, entangle, disunite, widen the breach; set -at odds, – together by the ears; set –, pit- against; rub up the wrong way.

get into hot water, fish in troubled waters, brawl; kick up a -row, – dust; turn the house out of window.

Adj. discordant; disagreeing etc. *v.*; out of tune, dissonant, inharmonious, harsh, grating, jangling, ajar, on bad terms; dissentient etc. 489; inconsistent, contradictory, incongruous, discrepant; un- reconciled, -pacified.

quarrelsome, unpacific; gladiatorial, controversial, polemic, disputatious; factious; liti-gious, -gant; pettifogging.

at odds, at loggerheads, at daggers drawn, at variance, at issue, at cross purposes, at sixes and sevens, at feud, at high words; up in arms, together by the ears, in hot water, embroiled.

torn, disunited.

Phr. *quot homines tot sententiae*; no love lost between them, *non nostrum tantas componere lites*.

714. Concord.—N. concord, accord, harmony, symphony, homology; aggreement etc. 23; sympathy etc. (*love*) 897; response; union, unison, unity; bonds of harmony; peace etc. 721; unanimity etc. (*assent*) 488; league etc. 712; happy family.

rapprochement; *réunion*; amity etc. (*friendship*) 888; reciprocity; alliance, *entente cordiale*, good understanding, conciliation, arbitration, peacemaker etc. 724.

V. agree etc. 23; accord, harmonize with; fraternize; be -concordant etc. *adj.* ; go hand in hand; blend –, tone in- with; run parallel etc. (*concur*) 178; understand one another; pull together etc. (*co-operate*) 709; put up one's horses together, sing in chorus.

side –, sympathize –, go –, chime in –, fall in- with; come round; be pacified etc. 723; assent etc. 488; enter into the -ideas, – feelings- of; reciprocate.

hurler avec les loups; go –, swim- with the stream.

pour oil on troubled waters, keep in good humor, render accordant, put in tune; come to an understanding, meet half-way; keep the –, remain at- peace.

Adj. concordant, congenial; agreeing etc. *v.*; in-accord etc. *n.*; harmonious, united, cemented; banded together etc. 712; allied; friendly etc. 888; fraternal; conciliatory; at one with; of one mind etc. (*assent*) 488.

at peace, in still water; tranquil etc. (*pacific*) 721.

Adv. with one voice etc. (*assent*) 488; in concert with, hand in hand; on one's side, unanimously.

715. Defiance.—N. defiance; daring etc. v.; dare, challenge, *cartel*; threat etc. 909; war-cry, -whoop.

V. defy, dare, beard; brave etc. (*courage*) 861; bid defiance to; set at -defiance, – naught; hurl defiance at; dance the war dance; snap the fingers at, laugh to scorn; disobey etc. 742.

show -fight, – one's teeth, – a bold front; bluster, look big, stand akimbo; double –, shake- the fist; threaten etc 909.

challenge, call out; throw –, fling- down the -gauntlet, – gage, – glove.

Adj. defiant; defying etc. v.; with arms akimbo; rebellious, insolent; reckless, greatly daring.

Adv. in -defiance, – the teeth- of; under one's very nose.

Int. do your worst! come if you dare! come on! marry come up! hoity toity!

Phr. *noli me tangere*; *nemo me impune lacessit*.

716. Attack.—N. attack; assault, – and battery; onset, onslaught, charge.

aggression, drive, offence; incursion, inroad; invasion; irruption; outbreak; *estrapade*, *ruade*; *coup de main*, sally, *sortie*, *camisade*, raid, foray; run -at, – against; dead set at.

storm, -ing; boarding, *escalade*; siege, investment, obsession, bombardment, cannonade; air raid.

fire, volley; platoon –, file –, rapid-fire; *fusillade*; sharp-shooting, sniping; broadside; raking –, cross –, machine gun- fire; – volley of grapeshot, *feu d'enfer*; salvo.

cut, thrust, lunge, pass, *passado*, *carte* and tierce, home thrust, *coup de pied*; kick, punch, etc. (*impulse*) 276.

battue, *razzia*, *Jacquerie*, *dragonnade*; devastation etc. 162.

assailant, aggressor, invader.

base of operations, point of attack.

V. attack, assault, assail; set –, fall- upon; charge, impugn, break a lance with, enter the lists.

assume –, take- the offensive; be –, become- the aggressor; strike the first blow, fire the first shot, throw the first stone at; lift a hand –, draw the sword- against; take up the cudgels; advance –, march- against; march upon, invade, harry; come on, show fight.

strike at, poke at, thrust at; aim –, deal- a blow at; give –, fetch- one a -blow, – kick; have a -cut, – shot, – fling, – shy- at; be down –, pounce-upon; fall foul of, pitch into, launch out against; bait, slap on the face; make a -thrust, – pass, – set, – dead set- at; dunt; bear down upon.

close with, come to close quarters, bring to bay.

ride full tilt against; let fly at, dash at, run a tilt at, rush at, tilt at, run at, fly at, hawk at, have at, let out at; make a -dash, – rush at; attack tooth and nail; strike home; drive –, press- one hard; be hard upon, run down, strike at the root of.

lay about one, run amuck.

fire -upon, – at, – a shot at; shoot at, pop at, level at, let off a gun at; open fire, pepper, bombard, shell, pour a broadside into; fire -a volley, – red-hot shot; spring a mine.

throw -a stone, – stones- at; stone, lapidate, pelt; hurl -at, – against, – at the head of.

beset, besiege, beleaguer; lay siege to, invest, open the trenches, plant a battery, sap, mine; storm, board, scale the walls.

cut and thrust, bayonet, butt; kick, strike etc. (*impulse*) 276; whip etc. (*punish*) 972.

Adj. attacking etc. v.; aggressive, offensive, obsidional.

up in arms; on the warpath; over the top.

Adv. on the offensive.

Int. 'up and at them!'

717. Defense.—N. defense, protection, guard, ward; shielding etc. v.; propugnation; preservation etc. 670; guardianship.

self-defense, -preservation; resistance etc. 719. safeguard etc. (*safety*) 664; screen etc. (*shelter*) 666, (*concealment*) 530; barrage; fortification; muni-tion, -ment; bulwark, fosse, moat, ditch, trenchment, trench, dugout, gas mask; dike, dyke; parapet, parados, sunk fence, embankment, mound, mole, bank; earth- field-work, gabions; fence, wall, dead wall, contravallation; paling etc. (*inclosure*) 232; palisade, haha, stockade, *stoccado*, *laager*, *sangar*; barri-er, -cade; boom; portcullis, *chevaux de frise*; aba-, abat-, abba-tis; *vallum*, circumvallation, battlement, rampart, scarp; e-, counter-scarp; glacis, casemate.

mine, countermine.

buttress, abutment; shore etc. (*support*) 215.

breastwork, *banquette*, curtain, mantlet, bastion, demilune, redan, ravelin; advanced –, horn –, out- work, lunette; barb-acan, -ican; redoubt; fort-elage, -alice; lines; coast defense.

loop-hole, machicolation; sally-port, postern gate.

hold, stronghold, fastness; asylum etc. (*refuge*) 666; keep, donjon, fortress, citadel; capitol, castle; tower, – of strength; fort, barracoon, pah, sconce, martello tower, peel-house, block-house, rath; wooden walls; turret, barbette.

buffer, corner-stone, fender, apron, mask, gauntlet, thimble, carapace, armor, shield, buckler; target, targe, aegis, breastplate, cuirass, plastron, habergeon, mail, coat of mail, brigandine, hauberk, lorication, helmet, helm, basinet, sallet, salade, heaume, morion, murrion, armet, cabaset, vizor, casquetel, siege-cap, head-piece, casque, steel helmet, tin hat; *pickelhaube*, csako; shako etc. (*dress*) 225; bearskin; panoply; truncheon etc. (*weapon*) 727.

garrison, picket, piquet; defender, protector; guardian etc. (*safety*) 664; trabant, body guard, champion; knight-errant, Paladin; propugner.

V. defend, forfend, fend; shield, screen, shroud; fence round etc. (*circumscribe*) 229; fence, intrench; guard etc. (*keep safe*) 664; guard against; take care of etc. (*vigilance*) 459; bear harmless; keep –, ward –, beat- off; hinder etc. 706.

parry, repel, propugn, put to flight; give a warm reception to [*ironical*]; hold –, keep- at -bay, – arm's length.

stand –, act- on the defensive; show fight; maintain –, stand- one's ground; stand by; hold one's own; bear –, stand- the brunt; fall back upon, hold, stand in the gap.

Adj. defending etc. *v.*; defensive; mural; armed, – at all points, – *cap-à-pie*, – to the teeth; panoplied; accoutred, harnessed; iron-plated, -clad; loop-holed, castellated, machicolated; casemated; defended etc. *v.*; proof against, bomb-, bullet-proof; protective.

Adv. defensively; on the -defense, – defensive; in defense; at bay, *pro aris et focis*.

Int. no surrender! *il ne passeront pas!*

Phr. defense not defiance.

718. Retaliation.—**N.** retaliation, reprisal, retort; counter-stroke, -blast, -plot, -project; retribution, *lex talionis*; reciprocation etc. (*reciprocity*) 12.

requital, desert, tit for tat, give and take, blow for blow, *quid pro quo*, a Roland for an Oliver, measure for measure, an eye for an eye, diamond cut diamond, the biter bit, a game at which two can play; boomerang.

recrimination etc. (*accusation*) 938; revenge etc. 919; compensation etc. 30; reaction etc. (*recoil*) 277.

V. retaliate, retort, turn upon; pay -off, – back; pay in -one's own, – the same- coin; cap; reciprocate etc. 148; turn the tables upon, return the compliment; give -a *quid pro quo* etc. *n.*, – as much as one takes; give and take, exchange -blows, – fisticuffs; be -quits, – even- with; pay off old scores.

serve one right, be hoist on one's own petard, throw a stone in one's own garden, cathch a Tartar.

Adj. retaliating etc. *v.*; retalia-tory, -tive; retributive, recriminatory, reciprocal.

Adv.. in retaliation; *en revanche*.

Phr. *mutato nomine de te fabula narratur; par pari refero; tu quoque*; you're another; *suo sibi gladio hunc jugulo*.

719. Resistance.—**N.** resistance, stand, front, oppugnation; opposition etc. 708; renitence, reluctation, recalcitration, recalcitrance; repugnance; kicking etc. *v.*

repulse, rebuff.

insurrection etc. (*disobedience*) 742; strike; turn –, lock –, barring- out; *levée en masse, Jacquerie*; riot etc. (*disorder*) 59.

V. resist; not -submit etc. 725; repugn, reluctate, withstand; stand up –, strive –, bear up –, be proof –, make head- against; stand, – firm, – one's ground, – the brunt of, – out; hold -one's ground, – one's own, – out.

breast the -wave, – current; stem the -tide, – torrent; face, confront, grapple with; show a bold front etc. (*courage*) 861; present a front; make a –, take one's- stand.

kick, – against; recalcitrate, kick against the pricks; oppose etc. 708; fly in the face of; lift the hand against etc. (*attack*) 716; rise up in arms etc. (*war*) 722; strike, turn out; draw up a round robin etc. (*remonstrate*) 932; revolt etc. (*disobey*) 742; make a riot.

prendre le mors aux dents; take the bit between the teeth; sell one's life dearly, die hard, keep at bay; repel, repulse.

Adj. resisting etc. *v.*; resist-ive, -ant; refractory etc. (*disobedient*) 742; recalcitrant, re-nitent, -pulsive, -pellant; up in arms.

proof against; unconquerable etc. (*strong*) 159; stubborn, unconquered; indomitable etc. (*persevering*) 604a; unyielding etc. (*obstinate*) 606.

Int. hands off! keep off!

720. Contention.—**N.** contention, strife; contest, -ation; struggle; belligerency; opposition etc. 708.

controversy, polemics; debate etc. (*discussion*) 476; war of words, logomachy, litigation; paper war, ink slinging; high words etc. (*quarrel*) 713; sparring etc. *v.*

competition, rivalry; corrival-ry, -ship; agonism, *concours*, match, race, horse-racing, heat, steeple chase, point-to-point race, handicap; boat race, regatta; field-day; sham fight, Derby day; turf, sporting, bull-fight, tauromachy, *gymkhana*, rodeo, Olympiad.

wrestling, *ju-jitsu*, pugilism; boxing, fisticuffs, spar, mill, set-to, scrap, round, bout, event; prize-fighting; quarter-staff, single stick; gladiatorship, gymnastics; athletic-s, – sports; games of skill etc. 840.

shindy; *fracas* etc. (*discord*) 713; clash of arms; tussle, scuffle, broil, fray; affray, -ment; velitation; col-, luctation; brabble, *brique*, scramble, *mêlée*, scrimmage, stramash, bush-fighting.

free –, stand up –, hand to hand –, running-fight.

conflict, skirmish; ren-, en-counter; *rencontre*, collision, affair, brush, fight; battle, – royal; combat, action, engagement, joust, tournament; tilt, - ing; tourney, list; pitched battle, guerilla warfare.

death-struggle, struggle for life or death, Armageddon; hard knocks, sharp contest, tug of war.

naval -engagement, – battle; *naumachia*, sea-fight.

duel, -lo; single combat, monomachy, satisfaction, *passage d'armes*, passage of arms, affair of honor; triangular duel; hostile meeting, digladiation; appeal to arms etc. (*warfare*) 722.

deeds –, feats- of arms; pugnacity; combativeness etc. *adj.*; bone of contention etc. 713.

V. contend; contest, strive, struggle, scramble, wrestle; spar, square; exchange -blows, – fisticuffs; scrap, mix with, fib, justle, tussle, tilt, box, stave, fence; skirmish; fight etc. (*war*) 722; wrangle etc. (*quarrel*) 713.

contend etc. –, grapple –, engage –, close –, buckle –, bandy –, try conclusions –, have a brush etc. *n.* . –, tilt- with; encounter, fall foul of, pitch into, clapperclaw, run a tilt at; oppose etc. 708; reluct.

join issue, come to blows, be at loggerheads, set-to, come to the scratch, exchange shots, measure swords, meet hand to hand; take up the -cudgels, – glove, – gauntlet; enter the lists; couch one's lance; give satisfaction; appeal to arms etc. (*warfare*) 722.

lay about one; break the peace.

compete –, cope –, vie –, race- with; outvie, emulate, rival; run a race; contend etc. –, stipulate –, stickle- for; insist upon, make a point of.

Adj. contending etc. *v.*; together by the ears, at loggerheads, at war, at issue.

competitive, rival; belligerent; contentious, combative, bellicose, unpeaceful; warlike etc. 722; quarrelsome etc. 901; pugnacious; pugilistic, gladiatorial; palestric, -al.

Phr. *a verbis ad verbera*; a word and a blow.

721. Peace.—N. peace; amity etc. (*friendship*) 888; harmony etc. (*concord*) 714; tranquility etc. (*quiescence*) 265; truce etc. (*pacification*) 723; pacificism; pipe –, calumet- of peace.

piping time of peace, quiet life; neutrality.

V. be at peace; keep the peace etc. (*concord*) 714; make peace etc. 723.

Adj. pacific; peace-able, -ful; calm, tranquil, untroubled, halcyon; bloodless; neutral.

Phr. the storm blown over; the lion lies down with the lamb.

722. Warfare.—N. warfare; fighting etc. *v.*; hostilities; war, arms, the sword; Mars, Bellona, grim visaged war, *horrida bella*, Armageddon.

appeal to -arms, – the sword; ordeal –, wager- of battle; *ultima ratio regum*, arbitrament of the sword.

battle array, campaign, crusade, expedition; mobilization; state of siege; battle-field etc. (*arena*) 728; warpath.

art of war, tactics, strategy, castrametation; general-, soldier-ship; aerial –, submarine –, naval –, chemical-, atomic-, guerilla- warfare; military evolutions; ballistics, gunnery; chivalry; poison gas; gun-powder, shot, – and shell.

battle, tug of war etc. (*contention*) 720; service, campaigning, active service, tented field; fiery cross, trumpet, clarion, bugle, pibroch, slogan; war-cry, -whoop; battle cry, beat of drum, rappel, tom-tom; word of command; pass-, watch-word.

war to the -death, – knife; *guerre à -mort, - outrance*; open –, internecine –, civil- war.

V. arm; raise –, mobilize- troops; raise up in arms; take up the cudgels etc. 720; take up –, fly to –, appeal to- -arms, – the sword; draw –, unsheathe- the sword; dig up the hatchet; go to –, declare –, wage –, let slip the dogs of- war; cry havoc; kindle –, light- the torch of war; raise one's banner, send round the fiery cross; hoist the black flag; throw –, fling- away the scabbard; enrol, enlist, join up; take the field; take the law into one's own hands; do –, give –, join –, engage in –, go to- battle; flesh one's sword; set to, fall to, engage, measure swords with, draw the trigger, cross swords; come to -blows, – close quarters; fight; combat; contend etc. 720; battle –, break a lance- with.

serve; see –, be on- -service, – active service; campaign; wield the sword, shoulder a musket, smell powder, be under the fire; spill –, imbrue the hands in- blood; be on the warpath.

carry on -war, – hostilities; keep the field; fight the good fight; go over the top; cut one's way through; fight -it out, – like devils, – one's way, – hand to hand; sell one's life dearly.

Adj. conten-ding, -tious etc. 720; armed, – to the teeth, – cap-à-pie; sword in hand; in –, under –, up in- arms; at war with; bristling with arms; in -battle array, – open arms, – the field; embattled.

unpacific, unpeaceful; belligerent, combative, armigerous, bellicose, martial, warlike; mili-tary, -tant; soldier-like, -ly; chivalrous; strategical, internecine.

Adv. *flagrante bello*, in the -thick of the fray, – cannon's mouth; at the -swords's point, – point of the bayonet.

Int. *vae victis!* to arms! to your tents O Israel!

Phr. the battle rages.

723. Pacification.—N. pacification, conciliation; reconcil-iation, -ement; shaking of hands, accomodation, arrangement, adjustment; terms, compromise; amnesty, deed of release.

peace-offering; olive-branch; overtures; pipe –, calumet –, preliminaries- of peace.

truce, armistice; suspension of -arms, – hostilities; breathing-time; convention; *modus vivendi*; flag of truce, white flag, *parlementaire, cartel*.

hollow truce, *pax in bello*; drawn battle.

V. pacify, tranquilize, compose; allay etc. (*moderate*) 174; reconcile, propitiate, placate, conciliate, meet half-way, hold out the olive-branch, heal the breach, make peace, restore harmony, bring to terms.

settle –, arrange –, accommodate- -matters, – differences; set straight; make up a quarrel, *tantas componere lites*; come to -an understanding, – terms; bridge over, hush up; make -it, – matters- up; shake hands.

raise a siege; put up –, sheathe- the sword; bury the hatchet, lay down one's arms, turn swords into ploughshares; smoke the calumet of peace, close the temple of Janus; keep the peace etc. (*concord*) 714; be -pacified etc.; come round.

Adj. conciliatory, pacificatory; composing etc *v.*; pacified etc. *v.*

Phr. *requiescat in pace*.

724. Mediation.—**N.** media-tion, -torship, -tization; inter-vention, -position, -ference, -meddling, -cession; parley, negotiation, arbitration; flag of truce etc. 723; good offices, peace -offering; diploma-tics, -cy; compromise etc. 774.

mediator, intercessor, peacemaker, make-peace, negotiator, go-between; diplomatist etc. (*consignee*) 758; moderator, propitiator, umpire, arbitrator.

V. media-te, -tize; inter-cede, -pose, -fere, -vene; step in, negotiate; meet half-way; arbitrate; *magnas componere lites.*

Adj. mediatory, propitiatory, diplomatic.

725. Submission.—**N.** submission, yielding, acquiescence, compliance; non-resistance; obedience etc. 743; submissiveness, 'deference.

surrender, cession, capitulation, resignation.

obeisance, homage, kneeling, genuflexion, courtesy, curtsy, *salaam, kowtow*, prostration.

V. succumb, submit, yield, bend, resign, defer to, accede.

lay down –, deliver up- one's arms; hand over one's sword; lower –, haul down –, strike- one's flag, – colors; deliver the keys of the city.

surrender, – at discretion; cede, capitulate, come to terms, retreat, beat a retreat; draw in one's horns etc. (*humility*) 879; give -way, – ground, – in, – up; cave in; suffer judgment by default; bend, – to one's yoke, – before the storm; reel back; bend –, knuckle- -down, – to, – under; knock under.

humble oneself; eat -dirt, – the leek, – humble pie; bite –, lick- the dust; be –, fall- at one's feet; craven; crouch before, throw oneself at the feet of; swallow the -leek, – pill; kiss the rod; turn the other cheek; *avaler des couleuvres*, gulp down.

obey etc. 743; kneel to, bow to, pay homage to, cringe to, truckle to; bend the -neck, – knee; kneel, fall on one's knees, bow submission, courtesy, curtsy, *kowtow*; make obeisance.

pocket the affront; make -the best of, – a virtue of necessity; grin and abide, shrug the shoulders, resign oneself; submit with a good grace etc. (*bear with*) 826.

Adj. surrendering etc. *v.*; submissive, resigned, crouching; down-trodden; down on one's marrow bones; on one's bended knee; weak-kneed, un-, non-resisting; pliant etc. (*soft*) 324; undefended.

untenable, indefensible; humble etc. 879.

Phr. have it your own way; it can't be helped; amen etc. (*assent*) 488.

726. Combatant.—**N.** combatant; disputant, controversialist, polemic, belligerent; competitor, rival, corrival; fighter, assailant, aggressor; champion, Paladin; moss-trooper; swashbuckler, fire-eater, duellist, bully, bludgeon-man, rough, fighter, fighting-man, prize-fighter, pugilist, pug, boxer, bruiser, the fancy, gladiator, athlete, wrestler; fighting-, game-cock; swordsman, *sabreur.*

warrior, soldier, Amazon, man-at-arms, armigerent; campaigner, veteran; red-coat, military man, *rajpoot*, brave.

armed force, troops, soldiery, military, forces, sabaoth, the army, standing army, regulars, the

line, troops of the line, militia, territorials, yeomanry, volunteers, trainband, fencible; auxiliary –, reserve- forces; reserves, *posse comitatus*, national guard, *gendarme*, beefeater; guards, -man; yeoman of the guard, life guards, household troops.

janissary; myrmidon; Mama-, Mame-luke; spahee, *spahi*, Cossack, Croat, Pandour; irregular, free lance, *franc-tireur, bashi-bazouk, guerilla, condottiere*; mercenary.

levy, draught, commando; *Land-wehr, -sturm*; conscript, recruit, rookie, cadet, raw levies.

private, – soldier; Tommy Atkins, rank and file, peon, trooper, doughboy, sepoy, *askari, legionnaire*, legionary, food for powder, cannon fodder; officer etc. (*commander*) 745; subaltern, ensign, shave-tail, standard bearer, non-com; spear-pike-man; halberdier, lancer; musketeer, carabineer, rifleman, sharpshooter, yager, skirmisher; grenadier, fusileer; archer, bowman.

horse and foot; horse –, foot- soldier; cavalry, horse, artillery, horse –, field –, heavy –, mountain- artillery, infantry, light horse, *voltigeur, Uhlan*, mounted rifles, dragoon, hussar, trooper; light –, heavy- dragoon; heavy; *cuirassier*; gunner, cannoneer, bombardier, artillery-man, matross; sapper, – and miner; engineer; light infantry, rifles, *chasseur, zouave*; military train, supply and transport, coolie.

army, – corps, *corps d'armée*, host, division, column, wing, detachment, *escadrille*, garrison, flying column, brigade, regiment, *corps*, battalion, squadron, company, platoon, battery, subdivision, section, squad; piquet, picket, guard, rank, file; legion, phalanx, cohort; cloud of skirmishers; impi.

war-horse, charger, *destrier*.

armored -train, – car; tank.

marine, man of war's man etc. (*sailor*) 269; navy, first line of defense, wooden walls; naval forces, fleet, flotilla, armada, squadron.

man-of-war, warship; H.M.S., U.S.S.; capital ship; line-of-battle ship, battle ship; super-, dreadnought, battle –, armored –, protected – light-cruiser; scout, flotilla leader; destroyer, torpedo boat; submarine, submersible, U-boat; submarine chaser, eagle boat, mystery ship, Q-boat; mine-layer, -sweeper; ship of the line, iron-clad, turret-ship, ram, Monitor, floating battery; first-rate, frigate, sloop of war, corvette, gunboat, bomb-vessel, fire-boat; flag ship, guard ship, cruiser; airplane carrier; privateer; tender; depot –, parent-ship; store –, troop- ship; transport, catamaran.

aircraft etc. 273; air force, scout, fighter, bomber, troop carrier, aerial patrol, seaplane, flying boat, torpedo plane; airship, Zeppelin; rigid –, semi-rigid –, non-rigid- airship; dirigible –, free –, captive –, kite –, observation- balloon.

anti-aircraft guns, searchlights, sound locators; catapult.

727. Arms.—**N.** arm, -s; weapon, deadly weapon; arma-ment, -ture; panoply, stand of arms; armor etc. (*defense*) 717; armory etc. (*store*) 636.

ammunition; powder, – and shot; explosive; propellant; gun-powder, -cotton; dynam-, melin-, cord-, lydd-ite; trinitrotoluene, T.N.T., ammonal; cartridge; ball cartridge, *cartouche*, fire-ball; dud, black Marie; 'villainous saltpeter;' poison –, mustard –, lachrymatory –, tear- gas.

sword, saber, broadsword, cutlass, falchion, scimitar, cimeter, brand, whinyard, bilbo, glaive, glave, rapier, skean, Toledo, Ferrara, tuck, claymore, creese, kris, *kukri*, dagger, dirk, hanger, poniard, stiletto, stylet, dudgeon, bayonet; sword-bayonet, -stick; side arms, foil, blade, steel; axe, bill; pole-, battle-axe; gisarm, halberd, partisan, tomahawk, bowie-knife; at-, att-, yat-aghan; yatachan; good –, trusty –, naked- sword; cold –, naked-steel.

club, mace, truncheon, staff, bludgeon, cudgel, life-preserver, shillelagh, sprig; hand-, quarter-staff; bat, cane, stick, knuckle-duster, sand bag.

gun, piece; fire-arms; artillery, ordnance; siege –, battering-train; park, battery; cannon, gun of position, heavy –, siege –, field –, mountain –, anti-aircraft –, breech loading –, quick firing-gun; field piece, mortar, trench mortar; mine –, flame- -thrower, napalm; howitzer, carronade, culverin, basilisk; falconet jingal, swivel, *pederero, bouche à feu*; smooth bore, rifled cannon; Armstrong –, Lancaster –, Paixhan –, Whitworth –, Parrott –, Krupp –, Gatling –, Maxim –, Vickers –, Hotchkiss –, Lewis –, machine- gun; tommy gun, Thompson's submachine gun; *mitrailleu-r, -se*; pompom; blow pipe.

small arms; musket, -ry, firelock, flintlock, fowling-piece, shot gun, rifle, *fusil*, caliver, carbine, blunderbuss, musketoon, Brown Bess, matchlock, harquebuss, *arquebuse*, haguebut; petronel; smallbore; breech-, muzzle-loader; Minié –, En-field –, Westly Richards –, Snider –, Springfield –, Martini-Henry –, Lee-Metford –, Lee-Enfield –, Mauser –, Mannlicher –, magazine –, repeating- rifle; needle-gun, *chassepot*; pis-tol, -et; revolver, automatic pistol, automatic; wind-, air-gun; flame –, gas- projector.

bow, cross-bow, arbalest, balister, catapult, sling; battering-ram etc. (*impulse*) 276; gunnery; ballistics etc. (*propulsion*) 284.

missile, bolt, projectile, shot, pellet, ball; grape; grape –, canister –, bar –, cannon –, langrel –, langrage –, round –, chain- shot; explosive; incendiary –, expanding –, soft-nosed –, dum-dum- bullet; slug, stone, brickbat; hand –, rifle-grenade; high explosive –, incendiary –, stink-, A-, H-, atomic –, hydrogen – bomb; petard, torpedo, carcass, rocket; congreve, – rocket; shrapnel, *mitraille*; thunderbolt; mine, land mine, infernal machine.

pike, lance, spear, spontoon, javelin, assagai, throwing stick, dart, djerrid, arrow, reed, shaft, bolt, boomerang, harpoon, gaff.

728. Arena.—N. arena, field, platform; scene of action, theater; walk, course; hustings; stage, boards etc. (*playhouse*) 599; amphitheater; Coli-, Colos-seum; Flavian amphitheater, hippodrome, circus, race-course, track, *stadium, corso*, turf, cockpit, bear-garden, play-ground, playing fields, *gymnasium, palaestra*, ring, lists; tilt-yard, -ing ground; *Campus Martius, Champ de Mars*; aerodrome, airport, air base, flying field.

theater –, seat- of war; battle-field, -ground; field of -battle, – slaughter; no man's land; Aceldama, camp; the enemy's camp; trysting- place etc. (*place of meeting*) 74.

729. Completion.—N. completion; accomplish-, achieve-, fulfil-ment; performance, execution; des-, dis-patch; consummation, culmination, climax; finish, conclusion, effectuation; close etc. (*end*) 67; terminus etc. (*arrival*) 292; winding up; *finale, dénouement,* catastrophe, issue, upshot, result; final –, last –, crowning –, finishing- -touch, – stroke; last finish, *coup de grâce*; crowning of the edifice; coping-, keystone; missing link etc. 53; super-structure, *ne plus ultra*, work done, *fait accompli*.

elaboration; finality; completeness etc. 52.

V. effect, -uate; accomplish, achieve, compass, consummate, hammer out; bring to -maturity, – perfection; perfect, complete; elaborate.

do, execute, make; go –, get- through; work out, enact; bring -about, – to bear, – to pass, – through, – to a head.

des-, dis-patch; knock –, finish –, polish- off; make short work of; dispose of, set at rest; perform, discharge, fulfil, realize; put in -practice, – force; carry -out, – into effect, – into execution; make good; be as good as one's word.

do thoroughly, not do by halves, go the whole hog; drive home; be in at the death etc. (*persevere*) 604a; carry through, play out, exhaust, deliver the goods, fill the bill.

finish, bring to a close etc. (*end*) 67; wind up, stamp, clinch, seal, set the seal on, put the seal to; give the -final touch etc. *n.* to; put the -last, – finishing- hand to; crown, – all; cap.

ripen, culminate; come to a -head, – crisis; come to its end; die a natural death, – of old age; run -its course, – one's race; touch –, reach –, attain- the goal; reach etc. (*arrive*) 292; get in the harvest.

Adj. completing, final; conclu-ding, -sive; crowning etc, *v.*; exhaustive, complete, mature, perfect, consummate.

done, completed etc. *v.*; done for, sped, wrought out; highly wrought etc. (*preparation*) 673; thorough etc. 52; ripe etc. (*ready*) 673.

Adv. completely etc. (*thoroughly*) 52; to crown all, out of hand.

Phr. the race is run; *actum est; finis coronat opus; consummatum est; c'en est fait*; it is all over; the game is played out, the bubble has burst.

730. Non-Completion.—N. non-completion, -fulfilment; shortcoming etc. 304; incompleteness etc. 53; drawn -battle, – game; work of Penelope, task of Sisyphus.

non-performance, inexecution; neglect etc. 460.

V. not -complete etc. 729; leave -unfinished etc. *adj.*, – undone; neglect etc. 460; let -alone, – slip; lose sight of.

fall short of etc. 304; do things by halves; scotch the snake, not kill it; hang fire; be slow to; collapse etc. 304.

Adj. not completed etc. *v.*; incomplete etc. 53; uncompleted, unfinished; unaccomplished; un-performed, unexecuted; sketchy, addle.

in progress, in hand; going on, proceeding; on one's hands; on the fire; on the stocks; in preparation; lacking the finishing touch.

Adv. *re infectâ*.

731. Success.—N. success, -fulness; speed; advance etc. (*progress*) 282.

trump card; hit, stroke; lucky –, fortunate –, good- -hit, – stroke; bold –, master- stroke; *coup de maître*, checkmate; half the battle, prize; profit etc. (*acquisition*) 775; best seller.

continued success; good fortune etc. (*prosperity*) 734; time well spent.

advantage over; edge; upper-, whiphand; ascendancy, mastery; expugnation, conquest, victory, subdual; subjugation etc. (*subjection*) 749.

triumph etc. (*exultation*) 884; proficiency etc. (*skill*) 698; conqueror, victor, winner, champion; master of the -situation, – position.

V. succeed; be, -successful etc. *adj.*; gain one's - end, – ends; crown with success.

gain –, attain –, carry –, secure –, win- -a point, – an object; put over; make a go of; manage to, contrive to; accomplish etc. (*effect, complete*) 729; do –, work- wonders.

come off -well, – successfully, – with flying colors; make short work of; take –, carry- by storm; bear away the bell; win -one's spurs, – the battle; win –, carry –, gain- the -day, – prize, – palm; climb on the bandwagon; have -the best of it, – it all one's own way, – the game in one's own hands, – the ball at one's feet, – one on the hip; walk over the course; carry all before one, remain in possession of the field; score a success, win hands down.

speed; make progress etc. (*advance*) 282; win –, make –, work –, find- one's way; strive to some purpose; prosper etc. 734; drive a roaring trade; make profit etc. (*acquire*) 775; reap –, gather- the -fruits, – benefit of, – harvest; make one's fortune, get in the harvest, turn to good account; turn to account etc. (*use*) 677.

triumph, be triumphant; gain –, obtain- -a victory, – an advantage; chain victory to one's car.

surmount –, overcome –, get over- -a difficulty, – an obstacle etc. 706; *se tirer d'affaire*; make head against; stem the -torrent, – tide, – current; weather -the storm, – a point; turn a corner, keep one's head above water, tide over; master; get –, have –, gain- the -better of, – best of, – upper hand, – ascendancy, – whip hand, – start of; distance; surpass etc. (*superiority*) 33.

defeat, conquer, vanquish, discomfit; over-come, throw, -power, -master, -match, -set, -ride, -reach; out-wit, -do, -flank, -maneuver, -general, -vote; take the wind out of one's adversary's sails; beat, – hollow; rout, lick, drub, floor, worst; put -down, – to flight, – to the rout, – hors de combat; – out of court.

silence, quell, nonsuit, checkmate, upset, confound, nonplus, trump; baffle etc. (*hinder*) 706; circumvent, elude; trip up – the heels of; drive - into a corner, – to the wall; run hard, put one's nose out of joint.*

settle, do for; break the -neck of, – back of; capsize, sink, shipwreck, drown, swamp; subdue; subjugate etc. (*subject*) 749; reduce; make the enemy bite the dust; victimize, roll in the dust, trample under foot, put an extinguisher upon.

answer, – the purpose; avail, prevail, take effect, do, turn out well, work well, take, tell, bear fruit; hit -it, – the mark, – the right nail on the head; nick it; turn up trumps, make a hit; find one's account in.

Adj. succeeding etc. *v.*; successful; prosperous

etc. 734; triumphant; flushed –, crowned- with success; victorious; set up; in the ascendant; unbeaten etc. (*see* beat etc. *v.*); well-spent; felicitous, effective, in full swing.

Adv. successfully etc. *adj.*; with flying colors, in triumph, swimmingly; *à merveille*, beyond all hope; to some –, good- purpose; to one's heart's content.

Phr. *veni vidi vici*, the day being one's own, one's star in the ascendant; *omne tulit punctum*.

732. Failure.—N. failure; non-success, -fulfilment; dead failure, successlessness; abortion, miscarriage; *brutum fulmen* etc. 158; labor in vain etc. (*inutility*) 645; no go; inefficacy; inefficaciousness etc. *adj.*; vain –, ineffectual –, abortive- -attempt, – efforts; flash in the pan, 'lame and impotent conclusion;' frustration; slip 'twixt cup and lip etc. (*disappointment*) 509.

blunder etc. (*mistake*) 495; fault, omission, miss, oversight, slip, trip, stumble, claudication, footfall; false –, wrong- step; *faux pas*, titubation, *bévue*, *faute*, lurch; botchery etc. (*want of skill*) 699; scrape, jam, mess, muddle, foozle, *fiasco*, breakdown.

mishap etc. (*misfortune*) 735; split, collapse, smash, blow, explosion.

repulse, rebuff, defeat, rout, overthrow, discomfiture; beating, drubbing; *quietus*, nonsuit, subjugation; check-, fool's-mate.

fall, downfall, ruin, perdition; wreck etc. (*destruction*) 162; death-blow; bankruptcy etc. (*non-payment*) 808.

losing game, *affaire flambée*.

victim, prey; bankrupt.

V. fail; be -unsuccessful etc. *adj.*; not -succeed etc. 731; make -vain efforts etc. *n.*; do –, labor –, toil- in vain; lose one's labor, take nothing by one's motion; bring to naught, make nothing of; wash a blackamoor white etc. (*impossible*) 471; roll the stone of Sisyphus etc. (*useless*) 645; do by halves etc. (*not complete*) 730; lose ground etc. (*recede*) 283; flunk; fall short of etc. 304.

miss, – one's aim, – the mark, – one's footing, – stays; slip, trip, stumble; make a -slip etc. *n.*, – blunder etc. 495, – mess of, – botch of; bitch it, miscarry, abort, go up like a rocket and come down like the stick, reckon without one's host; get the wrong sow by the ear etc. (*blunder, mismanage*) 699.

limp, halt, hobble, titubate; fall, tumble; lose one's balance; fall -to the ground, – between two stools; flounder, falter, stick in the mud, run aground, split upon a rock; run –, knock –, dash- one's head against a stone wall; break one's back; break down, sink, drown, founder, have the ground cut from under one; get into -trouble, – a mess, – a scrape; come to grief etc. (*adversity*) 735; go to - the wall, – the dogs, – pot; lick –, bite- the dust; be -defeated etc. 731; have the worst of it, lose the day, come off second best, lose; fall a prey to; succumb etc. (*submit*) 725; not have a leg to stand on.

come to nothing, end in smoke; fall -to the ground, – through, – dead, – still-born, – flat; slip through one's fingers; hang –, miss- fire; flash in the pan, collapse; topple down etc. (*descent*) 305; go to wrack and ruin etc. (*destruction*) 162.

go amiss, go wrong, go cross, go hard with, go on a wrong tack; go on –, come off --, turn out

−, work- ill; take -a wrong, − an ugly- turn; gang agley.

be all -over with, − up with; explode; dash one's hopes etc. (*disappoint*) 509; defeat the purpose; upset the apple cart; sow the wind and reap the whirlwind, jump out of the frying pan into the fire.
Adj. unsuccessful, successless; failing, tripping etc. *v.*; at fault; unfortunate etc. 735.

abortive, addle, still-born; fruitless, sterile, bootless; ineffect-ual, -ive; inefficient etc. (*impotent*) 158; inefficacious; lame, hobbling, *décousu*; insufficient etc. 640; unavailing etc. (*useless*) 645; of no effect.

aground, grounded, swamped, stranded, cast away, wrecked, foundered, capsized, shipwrecked, non-suited; foiled; defeated etc. 731; struck −, borne −. broken- down; down-trodden; over-borne, -whelmed; all up with; beaten to a frazzle.

lost, undone, ruined, broken; bankrupt etc. (*not paying*) 808; played out; done -up, − for; dead beat, ruined root and branch, *flambé*, knocked on the head; destroyed etc. 162.

frustrated, thwarted, crossed, unhinged, disconcerted, dashed; thrown -off one's balance, − on one's back, − on one's beam ends; unhorsed, in a sorry plight; hard hit.

stultified, befooled, dished, hoist on one's own petard, victimized, sacrificed.

wide of the mark etc. (*error*) 495; out of one's reckoning etc. (*inexpectation*) 508; left in the lurch; thrown away etc. (*wasted*) 638; unattained; uncompleted etc. 730.
Adv. unsuccessfully etc. *adj.*; to little or no purpose, in vain, *re infectâ*.
Phr. the bubble has burst, the game is up, all is lost; the devil to pay; *parturiunt montes* etc. (*disappointment*) 509.

733. Trophy.—N. trophy; medal, prize, palm; ribbon, blue ribbon, *cordon bleu*; citation; cup, laurel, -s; bays, crown, chaplet, wreath, civic crown; Victoria Cross, V.C., *Croix de Guerre*, Iron Cross; Distinguished Service Cross, Medal of Honor, Congressional Medal; insignia etc. 550; feather in one's cap etc. (*honor*) 873; decoration etc. 877; garland, triumphal arch.

triumph etc. (*celebration*) 883; flying colors etc. (*show*) 882.

monumentum aere perennius.

734. Prosperity.—N. prosperity, welfare, well-being; affluence etc. (*wealth*) 803; success etc. 731; thrift, roaring trade; chicken in every pot, the full dinner paid; good −, smiles of- fortune; blessings, godsend.

luck; good −, run of- luck; sunshine; fair -weather, − wind; palmy −, bright −, halcyon-days; piping times, tide, flood, high tide.

Saturnia regna, Saturnian age; golden -time, − age; bed of roses; fat of the land, milk and honey, loaves and fishes, fleshpots of Egypt.

made man, lucky dog, *enfant fâté*, spoiled child of fortune.

upstart, *parvenu, nouveau riche,* profiteer, skipjack, mushroom.

V. prosper, thrive, flourish; be -prosperous etc. *adj.*; drive a roaring trade; go on -well, − smoothly, − swimmingly; sail before the wind, swim with the tide; run -smooth, − smoothly, − on all fours.

rise −, get on- in the world; work −, make-one's way; look up; lift −, raise- one's head, make one's -fortune, − pile, feather one's nest.

flower, blow, blossom, bloom, fructify, bear fruit, fatten, batten.

keep oneself afloat; keep −, hold- one's head above water; light −, fall- on one's -legs, − feet; drop into a good thing; bask in the sunshine; have a -good, − fine- time of it; have a run, − of luck; have the -good fortune etc. *n.* to; take a favorable turn; live -on the fat of the land, − in clover.

Adj. prosperous; thriving etc. *v.*; in a fair way, buoyant; well -off, − to do, − to do in the world; set up, at one's ease; rich etc. 803; in good case; in -full, − high- feather; fortunate, lucky, in luck; born -with a silver spoon in one's mouth, − under a lucky star; on the sunny side of the hedge.

auspicious, propitious, providential.

palmy, halcyon; agreeable etc. 829; *couleur de rose.*

Adv. prosperously etc. *adj.*; swimmingly; as good luck would have it; beyond all -expectation, − hope, − one's wildest dreams.

Phr. one's star in the ascendant, all for the best, one's course runs smooth.

735. Adversity.—N. adversity, evil etc. 619; failure etc. 732; bad −, ill −, evil −, adverse −, hard- -fortune, − hap, − luck, − lot; frowns of fortune; evil -dispensation, − star, − genius; ups and downs of life, broken fortunes; hard -case, − lines, − life; sea −, peck- of troubles; hell upon earth; slough of despond; jinx.

trouble, humiliation, hardship, curse, blight, blast, load, pressure.

pressure of the times, iron age, evil day, time out of joint; hard −, bad −, sad- times; rainy day, cloud, dark cloud, gathering clouds, ill wind; visitation, infliction; affliction etc. (*painfulness*) 830; bitter -pill, − cup; care, trial; the sport of fortune.

mis-hap, -chance, -adventure, -fortune; disaster, calamity, catastrophe; accident, casualty, cross, reverse, check, *contretemps*, rub, pinch, setback.

losing game; falling etc. *v.*; fall, down-fall, come-down; ruin-ation, -ousness; undoing; extremity; ruin etc. (*destruction*) 162.

V. be -ill off etc. *adj.*; go hard with; fall on evil, − days; go on ill; not -prosper etc. 734.

go -downhill, − to rack and ruin etc. (*destruction*) 162, − to the dogs; fall, − from one's high estate; decay, sink, decline, go down in the world; have seen better days; bring down one's grey hairs with sorrow to the grave; come to grief; be all -over, − up- with; bring a -wasp's, − hornet's- nest about one's ears.

Adj. unfortunate, unblest, unhappy, unlucky; im-, un-prosperous; luck-, hap-less; out of luck; in trouble, in a bad way, in an evil plight; under a cloud; clouded; ill −, badly- off; in adverse circumstances; poor etc. 804; behindhand, down in the world, decayed, undone; on the road to ruin, on its last legs, on the wane; in one's utmost need.

planet-struck, devoted; born -under an evil star, — with a wooden ladle in one's mouth; ill-fated, -starred, -omened; inconspicuous, ominous, doomed, unpropitious.

adverse, untoward; disastrous, calamitous, ruinous, dire, deplorable.

Adv. if the worst come to the worst, as ill luck would have it, from bad to worse, out of the frying pan into the fire.

Phr. one's star is on the wane; one's luck -turns, — fails; the game is up, one's doom is sealed, the ground crumbles under one's feet, *sic transit gloria mundi, tant va la cruche à l'eau qu'à la fin elle se casse.*

736. Mediocrity.—N. moderate —, average-circumstances; respectability; middle classes, *bourgeoisie*; mediocrity; golden mean etc. (*midcourse*) 628, (*moderation*) 174.

V. jog on; go —, get on- -fairly, — quietly, — peaceably, — tolerably, — respectably; steer a middle course etc. 628.

Adj. middling, so-so, fair, medium, moderate, mediocre, second-, third- etc. -rate.

737. Authority.—N. authority; influence, patronage, power, preponderance, credit, *prestige*, prerogative, jurisdiction; right etc. (*title*) 924.

divine right, dynastic rights, authoritativeness; absolut-eness, -ism; despotism, tyranny; *jus nocendi.*

command, empire, sway, rule; domin-ion, -ation; sovereignty, supremacy, suzerainty; lord-, head-ship; chiefdom; seignior-y, -ity, hegemony, patriarchate, patriarchy; master-y, -ship, -dom; government etc. (*direction*) 693; dictation, control.

hold, grasp; grip, -e; reach; iron sway etc. (*severity*) 739; fangs, clutches, talons; rod of empire etc. (*scepter*) 747.

reign, regnancy, *régime*, dynasty; director-, dictator-ship; protector-ate, -ship; caliphate, pashalic, electorate; presiden-cy, -tship; administration; pro-, consulship; prefecture; seneschalship; magistra-ture, -cy; raj.

empire; monarchy; king-hood, -ship; royalty, regality, autocracy, monocracy, arist-archy, -ocracy; oligarchy, democracy, demogogy; republic, -anism, federalism; socialism, collectivism; communism, bolshevism, syndicalism; mob law, mobocracy, ochlocracy, ergatocracy; *vox populi, imperium in imperio*; bureaucracy; beadle-, bumble-dom; stratocracy; martial law, military -power, — government; feodality, feudal system, feudalism.

Thearchy, diarchy; du-, tri-, heter-archy; du-, tri-umvirate; auto-cracy, -nomy; limited monarchy; constitutional -government, — monarchy; home rule, autonomy; self-government, -determination; representative government; Soviet government.

gyn-archy, -ocracy, -aeocracy; petticoat government, matriarchate, matriarchy.

[Vicarious authority] commission etc. 755; deputy etc. 759; permission etc. 760.

country, state, realm, commonwealth, canton, constituency, toparchy, municipality, polity, body politic, *posse comitatus.*

person in authority etc. (*master*) 745; judicature etc. 965; cabinet etc. (*council*) 696; usurper; seat of -government, — authority; head-quarters.

[Acquisition of authority] accession; installation etc. 755; usurpation.

V. authorize etc. (*permit*) 760; warrant etc. (*right*) 924; dictate etc. (*order*) 741; have —, hold —, possess —, exercise —, exert —, wield- -authority etc. *n.*

be -at the head of etc. *adj.*; hold —, be in —, fill an- office; hold —, occupy- a post; be -master etc. 745.

rule, sway, command, control, administer; govern etc. (*direct*) 693; lead, preside over, reign; possess —, be seated on —, occupy- the throne; sway —, wield- the scepte wear the crown.

have —, get- the -upper, whip- hand; gain a hold upon, preponderate, dominate, boss, rule the roost; over-ride, -rule, -awe; lord it over, hold in hand, keep under, make a puppet of, lead by the nose, hold in the hollow of one's hand, turn round one's little finger, bend to one's will, hold one's own, wear the breeches; have -the ball at one's feet, — it all one's own way, — the game in one's own hand, — on the hip, — under one's thumb; be master of the situation; take the lead, play first fiddle, set the fashion; give the law to; carry with a high hand; lay down the law; 'ride in the whirlwind and direct the storm;' rule with a rod of iron etc. (*severity*) 739.

ascend —, mount- the throne, take the reins, — into one's hand; assume -authority etc. *n.*, — the reins of government; take —, assume the- command.

be -governed by, — in the power of; be under -the rule of, — the domination of.

Adj. ruling etc. *v.*; regnant, at the head, dominant, paramount, supreme, predominant, preponderant, in the ascendant, influential; gubernatorial; imperious; authoritative, executive, administrative, clothed with authority, official, *ex officio*, ministerial, bureaucratic, departmental, imperative, peremptory, overruling, absolute; hegemonic, -al; arbitrary; compulsory etc. 744; stringent.

regal, sovereign; royal, -ist; monarchical, kingly; imperial, -istic; princely; feudal; aristo-, auto-cratic; oligarchic etc. *n.*; democratic, republican, dynastic.

at one's command; in one's -power, — grasp; under control; authorized etc. (*due*) 924.

Adv. in the name of, by the authority of, *de par le Roi*, in virtue of; under the auspices of, in the hands of.

at one's pleasure; by a -dash', — stroke- of the pen; *ex mero motu*; *ex cathedrâ.*

Phr. the grey mare the better horse; 'every inch a king.'

738. Laxity. [Absence of authority.]—N. laxity; lax-, loose-, slack-ness; toleration etc. (*lenity*) 740; freedom etc. 748.

anarchy, interregnum; relaxation; loosening etc. *v.*; remission; dead letter, *brutum fulmen*, misrule; license, licentiousness; insubordination etc. (*disobedience*) 742; lynch law etc. (*illegality*) 964; nihilism.

[Deprivation of power.] dethronement, deposition, usurpation, abdication.

V. be -lax etc. adj ; laisser -faire, – aller; hold a loose rein; give -the reins to, – rope enough, – a loose to; tolerate; relax; misrule.

go beyond the length of one's tether; have one's - swing, – fling; act without -instructions, – authority; act on one's own responsibility, usurp authority.

dethrone, depose; abdicate.

Adj. lax, loose; slack; remiss etc. (careless) 460; weak.

relaxed; licensed; reinless, unbridled; anarchical; unauthorized etc. (unwarranted) 925.

739. Severity.—N. severity; strictness, formalism, harshness etc. adj.; rigor, stringency, austerity; inclemency etc. (pitilessness) 914a; arrogance etc. 885.

arbitrary power; absolut-, despot-ism; dictatorship, autocracy, tyranny, domineering, oppression; assumption, usurpation; inquisition, reign of terror, martial law; iron -heel, – rule, – hand, – sway; tight grasp; brute -force, – strength; coercion etc. 744; strong –, tight- hand.

hard -lines, – measure; tender mercies [ironical.]; sharp practice; bureaucracy, red tape; pipe-clay, officialism.

tyrant, disciplinarian, martinet, stickler, formalist, bashaw, despot, hard master, Draco, oppressor, inquisitor, extortioner, harpy, vulture, bird of prey.

V. be -severe etc. adj.

assume, usurp, arrogate, take liberties; domineer, bully etc. 885; tyrannize, inflict, wreak, stretch a point, put on the screw; be hard upon; bear –, lay a heavy hand on; be –, come- down upon; illtreat; deal-hardly with, – hard measure to; rule with a rod of iron, chastise with scorpions; dye with blood; oppress, override; trample –, tread- -down, – upon, – under foot; crush under an iron heel, ride roughshod over; rivet the yoke; hold –, keep a tight hand; force down the throat; coerce etc. 744; give no quarter etc. (pitiless) 914a.

Adj. severe; strict, hard, harsh, dour, rigid, stiff, stern, rigorous, uncompromising, exacting, exigent, exigeant, inexorable, inflexible, obdurate, austere, relentless, Spartan, Draconian, stringent, strait-laced, puritanical, prudish, searching, unsparing, ironhanded, hard-headed, peremptory, absolute, positive, arbitrary, imperative; coercive etc. 744; tyrannical, despotic, masterful, extortionate, grinding, withering, oppressive, inquisitorial; inclement etc. (ruthless) 914a; cruel etc. (malevolent) 907; haughty, arrogant etc. 885.

Adv. severely etc. adj.; with a -high, – strong, – tight, – heavy-hand.

at the point of the -sword, – bayonet.

Phr. Delirant reges plectuntur Achivi.

740. Leniency.—N. leni-ency, -ence, -ty; moderation etc. 174; toler-ance, -ation; mildness, gentleness; favor; indulgen-ce, -cy; clemency, mercy, forbearance, quarter; compassion etc. 914.

V. be -lenient etc. adj.; tolerate, bear with; parcere subjectis, give quarter.

indulge, allow one to have his own way, spoil.

Adj. lenient; mild, – as milk; gentle, soft; tolerant, indulgent, easy-going; clement etc. (compassionate) 914; forbearing; complaisant, longsuffering.

741. Command.—N. command, order, ordinance, act, fiat, bidding, dictum, hest, behest, call, beck, nod.

des-, dis-patch; message, direction, injunction, charge, instructions; appointment, fixture.

demand, exaction, imposition, requisition, claim, reclamation, revendication; ultimatum etc. (terms) 770; request etc. 765; requirement.

dictation; dict-, mand-ate; caveat, decree, decree -nisi, – absolute, senatus consultum; precept; pre-, re-script; writ, ordination, bull, edict, decretal, dispensation, prescription, brevet, placet, ukase, firman, hatti-sheriff, warrant, passport, mittimus, mandamus, summons, subpoena, nisi prius, interpellation, citation; word, – of command; mot d'ordre; bugle –, trumpet- call; beat of drum, tattoo; order of the day; enactment etc. (law) 963; plébiscite etc. (choice) 609.

V. command, order, decree, enact, ordain, dictate, direct, give orders.

prescribe, set, appoint, mark out; set –, prescribe –, impose- a task; set to work, put in requisition etc. 926.

bid, enjoin, charge, call upon, instruct; require, – at the hands of; exact, impose, tax, task; demand; insist on etc. (compel) 744.

claim, lay claim to, revendicate, reclaim.

cite, summon; call –, send- for; subpoena; beckon.

issue a command; make –, issue –, promulgate- -a requisition, – a decree, – an order etc. n.; give the -word of command, – word, – signal; call to order; give –, lay down- the law; assume the command etc. (authority) 737; remand.

be -ordered etc.; receive an order etc. n.

Adj. commanding etc. v.; authoritative etc. 737; decret-ory, -ive, -al; imperative, jussive, decisive, final.

Adv. in a commanding tone; by a -stroke, – dash- of the pen; by order, at beat of drum, on the first summons; at the word of command.

Phr. the decree is gone forth; sic volo sic jubeo; le Roi le veut.

742. Disobedience.—N. disobedience, insubordination, contumacy; infraction, -fringement; violation, non-compliance; non-observance etc. 773.

revolt, rebellion, mutiny, outbreak, rising, uprising, putsch, insurrection, émeute; riot, tumult etc. (disorder) 59; strike etc. (resistance) 719; barring out; defiance etc. 715.

mutinousness etc. adj.; mutineering; sedition, treason; high –, petty –, misprison of- treason; premunire; lèse- majesté; violation of law etc. 964; defection, secession, revolution, sabotage, bolshevism, Sinn Fein.

insurgent, mutineer, rebel, revolter, rioter, traitor, *carbonaro*, *sansculottes*, red republican, communist, Fenian, chartist, *frondeur*; seceder, runagate, brawler, anarchist, demagogue; suffragette; Spartacus, Masaniello, Wat Tyler, Jack Cade; bolshevist, bolshevik, maximalist, ringleader.

V. disobey, violate, infringe; shirk; set at defiance etc. (*defy*) 715; set authority at naught, run riot, fly in the face of, bolt, take the law into one's own hands; kick over the traces.

turn −, run- restive; champ the bit; strike etc. (*resist*) 719; rise, − in arms; secede; mutiny, rebel.

Adj. disobedient; uncompl-ying, -iant; unsubmissive; unruly, ungovernable; insubordinate, impatient of control; rest-iff, -ive; refractory, contumacious; recusant etc. (*refuse*) 764; recalcitrant; resisting etc. 719; lawless, mutinous, seditious, insurgent, riotous, revolutionary.

disobeyed, unobeyed; unbidden.

743. Obedience.—N. obedience; observance etc. 772; compliance; submission etc. 725; subjection etc. 749; non-resistance; passiveness, passivity, resignation.

allegiance, loyalty, fealty, homage, deference, devotion, fidelity, constancy.

submiss-ness, -iveness; ductility etc. (*softness*) 324; obsequiousness etc. (*servility*) 886.

V. be -obedient etc. *adj.*; obey, bear obedience to; submit etc. 725; comply, answer the helm, come at one's call; do -one's bidding, − what one is told, − suit and service; attend to orders, serve - devotedly, −, loyally, − faithfully.

follow, − the lead of, − to the world's end; serve etc. 746; play second fiddle.

Adj. obedient; compl-ying, -iant; law-abiding, loyal, faithful, leal, devoted; at one's -call, − command, − orders, − beck and call; under - beck and call, − control.

restrainable; resigned, passive; submissive etc. 725; henpecked; pliant etc. (*soft*) 324.

unresist-ed, -ing.

Adv. obediently etc. *adj.*; in compliance with, in obedience to.

Phr. to hear is to obey; as −, if- you please; at your service.

744. Compulsion.—N. compulsion, coercion, coaction, constraint, eminent domain, duress, enforcement, press, conscription.

force; brute −, main −, physical- force; the sword, *ultima ratio*; club −, mob −, lynch- law; *argumentum baculinum*, *le droit du plus fort*, martial law.

restraint etc. 751; necessity etc. 601; *force majeure*; Hobson's choice; the spur of necessity.

V. compel, force, make, drive, coerce, constrain, enforce, necessitate, oblige.

force upon, press; cram −, thrust −, force-down the throat; say it must be done, make a point of, insist upon, take no denial; put down, dragoon.

extort, wring from; put −, turn- on the screw; drag into; bind, − over; pin −, tie- down; require, tax, put in force; commandeer; restrain etc. 751.

Adj. compelling etc. *v.*; coercive, coactive; inexorable etc. 739; compuls-ory, -atory; obligatory, stringent, peremptory, binding.

forcible, not to be trifled with; irresistible etc. 601; compelled etc. *v.*; fain to.

Adv. by -force etc. *n.*, − force of arms; on compulsion, perforce; *vi et armis*, under the lash; at the point of the -sword, − bayonet; forcibly; by a strong arm.

under protest, in spite of one's teeth; against one's will etc. 603; *nolens volens* etc. (*of necessity*) 601; by stress of -circumstances, − weather; under press of; *de rigueur*.

745. Master.—N. master, *padrone*; lord, − paramount; command-er, -ant; captain; chief, -tain; *sahib*, sirdar, sachem, sheik, head, senior, governor, *duce*, ruler, dictator; leader etc. (*director*) 694.

lord of the ascendant; cock of the -walk, − roost; grey mare; mistress.

potentate; liege, − lord; suzerain, sovereign, monarch, autocrat, despot, tyrant, oligarch, overlord.

crowned head, emperor, king, anointed king, majesty, *imperator*, protector, president, stadtholder, judge.

caesar, kaiser, czar, sultan, grand Turk, caliph, imaum, shah, padishah, sophi, mogul, great mogul, khan, cham; lama, tycoon, mikado, inca, cazique; domn; vaivode; wai-, way-wode; landamman; seyyid, cacique.

prince, duke etc. (*nobility*) 875; arch-duke, doge, elector; seignior; mar-, land-grave; rajah, emir, nizam, nawab, negus.

empress, queen, sultana, czarina, princess, infanta, duchess, margravine, begum, maharani.

regent, viceroy, exarch, palatine, khedive, hospodar, beglerbeg, three-tailed bashaw, pasha, pashaw, bashaw, bey, beg, dey, scherif, tetrarch, satrap, mandarin, subhadar, nabob, maharajah; burgrave; laird etc. (*proprietor*) 779; High Commissioner.

the -authorities, − powers that be, − government; staff, *état major*, aga, official, man in office, person in authority.

[Naval authorities] admiral, -ty, − of the fleet; rear-, vice-, port-admiral; senior-, naval officer, S.N.O., commodore, captain, commander, lieutenant-commander, lieutenant, sub-lieutenant, midshipman, warrant −, petty- officer, leading seaman; skipper, mate, master.

[Military authorities] marshal, field-marshal, *maréchal*; general, -issimo; commander-in-chief, *seraskier*, *hetman*; lieutenant-, major-general; commandant; colonel, lieutenant-colonel, major, captain, centurion, skipper, lieutenant, second-lieutenant, officer, staff-officer, *aide de camp*, brigadier, brigade-major, adjutant, *jemidar*, ensign, cornet, cadet, subaltern, warrant officer, quartermaster, noncommissioned officer, N.C.O.; sergeant, -major; top-sergeant, color sergeant; corporal, -major; lance-, acting-corporal; drum major; shavetail.

[Air authorities] air -marshal, − commodore; group captain, squadron leader, wing commander, flight lieutenant, flying −, pilot- officer.

[Civil authorities] judge etc. 967; mayor, -alty; prefect, chancellor, archon, provost, magistrate, syndic; alcalde, alcaid; burgomaster, *corregidor*, seneschal, alderman, warden, constable, portreeve; lord mayor, sheriff; officer etc. (*executive*) 965.

746. Servant.—N. subject, liegeman; servant, retainer, follower, henchman, servitor, domestic, menial, help, lady help, *employé, attaché*; official. retinue, suite, *cortège*, staff, court.

attendant, squire, usher, page, buttons, donzel, footboy; dog robber; train-, cup-bearer; waiter, busboy, tapster, butler, livery servant, lackey, footman, flunkey, valet, *valet de chambre*; boots; scout, gyp; equerry, groom; jockey, hostler, ostler, tiger, orderly, messenger, cad, gillie, caddie; *wallah*; journeyman, herdsman, swineherd.

bailiff, castellan, seneschal, chamberlain, *major-domo*, groom of the chambers.

secretary; under –, assistant- secretary; clerk; clerical staff, stenographer, subsidiary; agent etc. 758; subaltern; under-ling, -strapper; man.

maid, -servant, waitress; handmaid; *confidente*, lady's maid, abigail, *soubrette*; nurse, *bonne*, ayah; nurse-, nursery-, house-, parlor-, waiting-, chamber-, kitchen-, scullery-, between –, laundry –, dairy-maid; *femme* –, *fille- de chambre*; *camarista*; *chef de cuisine*, *cordon bleu*, cook, scullion, Cinderella; maid –, servant- of all work, tweeny, general servant, girl, slavey; laundress, bed-maker, goodie, char-woman etc. (*worker*) 690.

serf, vassal, slave, negro, helot; bondsman, -woman; bondslave; *âme damnée, odalisque*, ryot, *adscriptus glebae*; vill-ain, -ein; bead-, bede-sman; sizar; pension-er, -ary; client; dependant, -ent; hanger on, stooge, satellite; parasite etc. (*servility*) 886; led captain; *protégé*, ward, hireling, mercenary, puppet, creature.

badge of slavery; bonds etc. 752.

V. serve; minister to, wait –, attend –, dance attendance –, pin oneself- upon; squire, tend, hang on the sleeve of, char, do for; fag; valet.

Adj. in the train of; in one's -pay, – employ; at one's call etc. (*obedient*) 743; in bonds.

747. Scepter. [Insignia of authority.]—N. scepter, regalia, rod of empire, sword of state, mace, *fasces*, wand; staff, – of office; *bâton*, truncheon; flag etc. (*insignia*) 550; ensign –, emblem –, badge –, insignia- of authority, rank marks, brassard, badge, sash; cocked –, brass- hat.

epaulette, aiguilette, crown, star, eagle, bar, double bar, pip, stripe, chevron, curl, ring, anchor, shoulder-strap, tab.

throne, chair, musnud, divan, dais, woolsack. *toga*, pall, mantle, robes of state, ermine, purple.

crown, coronet, diadem, tiara, triple crown, miter, crozier, cardinal's hat etc.; cap of maintenance; decoration; title etc. 877; portfolio.

key, signet, seals, talisman; helm; reins etc. (*means of restraint*) 752.

748. Freedom.—N. freedom, liberty, independence; license etc. (*permission*) 760; facility etc. 705.

scope, range, latitude, play; free –, full- -play, – scope; free stage and no favor; swing, full swing, elbow-room, margin, rope, wide berth; Liberty Hall.

franchise, denization; free –, freed-, liveryman; denizen.

autonomy, self-government, homerule, self-

determination, liberalism, free trade; non-interference etc. 706.

immunity, exemption; emancipation etc. (*liberation*) 750; en-, af-franchisement; rights, privileges.

free land, freehold; allodium; frankalmoigne, mortmain.

independent, free-lance, -thinker, -trader.

V. be -free etc. *adj.*; have -scope etc. *n.*, – the run of, – one's own way, – a will of one's own, – one's fling; do what one -likes, – wishes, – pleases, – chooses; go at large, feel at home, paddle one's own canoe; stand on one's -legs, – rights; shift for oneself.

take a liberty; make -free with, – oneself quite at home; use a freedom; take -leave, – French leave.

set free etc. (*liberate*) 750; give the reins to etc. (*permit*) 760; allow –, give- scope etc. *n.* to; give a horse his head.

make free of; give the -freedom of, – franchise; en-, af-franchise.

laisser -faire, – aller; live and let live; leave to oneself; leave –, let- alone; mind one's own business.

Adj. free, – as air; out of harness, independent, at large, loose, scot free; left -alone, – to oneself.

in full swing; uncaught, unconstrained, unbuttoned, unconfined, unrestrained, unchecked, unprevented, unhindered, unobstructed, unbound, uncontrolled, untrammeled.

unsubject, ungoverned, unenslaved, unenthralled, unchained, unshackled, unfettered, unreined, unbridled, uncurbed, unmuzzled, unimpeded.

unrestricted, unlimited, unconditional; absolute; discretionary etc. (*optional*) 600.

unassailed, unforced, uncompelled.

unbiassed, unprejudiced, uninfluenced, spontaneous.

free and easy; at –, at one's- ease; *dégagé*, quite at home; wanton, rampant, irrepressible, unvanquished.

exempt; freed etc. 750; freeborn; autonomous, freehold, allodial; *gratis* etc. 815.

unclaimed, going a begging.

Adv. freely etc. *adj.*; *ad libitum* etc. (*at will*) 600.

749. Subjection.—N. subjection; depend-ence, -ance, -ency; subordination; thrall, thraldom, enthralment, subjugation, bondage, serfdom; feudal- - ism, -ity; vassalage, villenage; slavery, enslavement, involuntary servitude.

service; servi-tude, -torship; tendence, employ, tutelage, clientship; liability etc. 177; constraint etc. 751; oppression etc. (*severity*) 739; yoke etc. (*means of restraint*) submission etc. 725; obedience etc. 743.

V. be -subject etc. *adj.*; be – , lie- at the mercy of; depend –, lean –, hang- upon; fall -a prey to, – under; play second fiddle.

be a -mere machine, – puppet, – football; not dare to say one's soul is his own; drag a chain. serve etc. 746; obey etc. 743; submit etc. 725. break in, tame; subject, subjugate; master etc. 731; tread -down, – under foot; weigh down; drag at one's chariot wheels; reduce to -subjection, –

slavery; en-, in-, be-thral; enslave, lead captive; take into custody etc. (*restrain*) 751; rule etc. 737; drive into a corner, hold at the sword's point; keep under; hold in -bondage, – leading strings, – swaddling clothes.

Adj. subject, dependent, subordinate; feud-al, - atory; in subjection to, under control; in -leading strings, – harness; subjected, enslaved etc. *v.*; constrained etc. 751; subservient, servile, fawning, slavish, obsequious, cringing; down-trodden; overborne, -whelmed; under the lash, on the hip, led by the nose, henpecked; the -puppet, – sport, – plaything- of; under one's -orders, – command, – thumb; like dirt under one's feet; a slave to; at the mercy of; in the -power, – hands, – clutches- of; at the feet of; at one's beck and call etc. (*obedient*) 743; liable etc. 177; parasitical; stipendiary.

Adv. under.

750. Liberation.—N. liberation, disengagement, release, disenthrallment, enlargement, emancipation; af-, en-franchisement; manumission; discharge, dismissal.

deliverance etc. 672; redemption, extrication, acquittance, absolution; acquittal etc. 970; escape etc. 671.

V. liberate, free; set -free, – clear, – at liberty; render free, emancipate, release; en-, af-franchise; manumit; enlarge; dis-band, -charge, -miss, – enthral; let -go, – loose, – out, – slip; cast –, turn- adrift; deliver etc. 672; absolve etc. (*acquit*) 970; reprieve.

unfetter etc. 751; untie etc. 44; loose etc. (*disjoin*) 44; loosen, relax; un-bolt, -bar, -close, - cork, -clog, -hand, -bind, -latch, -chain, -harness; dis-engage, -entangle; clear, extricate, unloose.

gain –, obtain –, acquire- one's -liberty etc. 748; get -rid, – clear- of; deliver oneself- from; shake off the yoke, slip the collar; break -loose, – prison; tear asunder one's bonds, cast off trammels; escape etc. 671.

Adj. at -liberty, – large, free, liberated etc. *v.*; out of harness etc. 748; adrift.

Int. unhand me! let me go!

751. Restraint.—N. restraint; hindrance etc. 706; coercion etc. (*compulsion*) 744; cohibition, constraint, repression; discipline, control, self-restraint etc. 604.

confinement; durance, duress; im-, prisonment; incarceration, coarctation, entombment, mancipation, durance vile, thrall, -dom, limbo, captivity; blockade; quarantine; detention.

arrest, -ation; custody, keep, care; charge, ward, restringency.

curb etc. (*means of restraint*) 752; *lettres de cachet.*

limitation, restriction, protection, monopoly; prohibition etc. 761; economic pressure.

prisoner etc. 754.

V. restrain, check; put –, lay- under restraint; en-, in-, be-thral; restrict; debar etc. (*hinder*) 706; constrain; coerce etc. (*compel*) 744; curb, control; hold –, keep- -back, – from, – in, – in check, – within bounds; hold in -leash, – leading strings; withhold.

keep under; repress, suppress; smother; pull in, rein in; hold, – fast; keep a tight hand on; prohibit etc. 761; in-, co-hibit.

enchain; fasten etc. (*join*) 43; fetter, shackle; en-, trammel; bridle, muzzle, gag, pinion, manacle, handcuff, tie one's hands, hobble, bind hand and foot; swathe, swaddle; pin –, peg- down; tether, picket; tie, – up, – down; secure; forge fetters.

confine; shut –, clap –, lock –, box –, mew –, bottle –, cork –, seal –, button- up; shut –, hem –, bolt –, wall –, rail- in; impound, pen, coop; enclose etc. (*circumscribe*) 229; cage; in-, en-cage; close the door upon, cloister; imprison, immure; incarcerate, entomb; clap –, lay- under hatches; put in -irons, – a strait waistcoat; throw –, cast- into prison; put into bilboes.

arrest; take -up, – charge of, – into custody; take –, make- -prisoner, – captive; captivate; lead -captive, – into captivity; send –, commit- to prison; commit; give in -charge, – custody; subjugate etc. 749.

Adj. re-, con-strained; imprisoned etc. *v.*; pent up; jammed in, wedged in; under -restraint, – lock and key, – hatches; serving –, doing- time; in swaddling clothes; on *parole*; in custody etc. (*prisoner*) 754; cohibitive; coactive etc. (*compulsory*) 744.

stiff, restringent, straitlaced, hide-bound.

ice-, wind-, weather-bound; 'cabined, cribbed, confined;' in Lob's pound, laid by the heels.

Adv. in captivity, under arrest, behind the bars, in -prison, – jail, – durance vile.

752. Prison. [Means of restraint.]—**N.** prison, -house; jail, gaol, cage, coop, den, death house, condemned –, cell; stronghold, fortress, keep, donjon, dungeon, *Bastille, oubliette,* bridewell, house of correction, bulks, tool-booth, panopticon, penitentiary, guard-room, clink, can, stir, tronk, jug, lock-up, hold; round –, watch –, station –, sponging-house; station; house of detention, black hole, pen, fold, pound; enclosure etc. 232; penal settlement; chain gang; debtors' prison; reformatory; federal penitentiary, state prison; criminal lunatic asylum; bilboes, stocks, limbo, quod.

Dartmoor, Newgate, Fleet, Marshalsea; King's (*or* Queen's) Bench; Sing Sing, Dannemora.

bond; strap, bandage, splint, tourniquet; irons, pinion, gyve, fetter, shackle, trammel, manacle, handcuff, bracelets, darbies, strait waistcoat, strait-jacket.

yoke, collar, halter, harness; muzzle, gag, bit, brake, curb, snaffle, bridle; rein, -s; ribbons, lines, bearing-rein; martingale, leading string; tether, picket, band, guy, chain; cord etc. (*fastening*) 45.

bolt, bar, lock, padlock, rail, wall; paling, palisade; fence; barrier, barricade.

brake, drag etc. (*hindrance*) 706.

753. Keeper.—N. keeper, custodian, *custos,* ranger, warder, jailer, gaoler, turnkey, castellan, guard; watch, -dog, -man; Charley; sen-try, -tinel; watch and ward; *concierge,* coast-guard, *guarda costa,* gamekeeper.

escort, body guard, convoy.

protector, governor, duenna; guardian; governess etc. (*teacher*) 540; nurse, *bonne, ayah, amah.*

754. Prisoner.—N. prisoner, captive, *détenu*, close prisoner.

jail-bird, ticket-of-leave man.

V. stand committed; be -imprisoned etc. 751.

Adj. imprisoned etc. 751; in -prison, – quod, – durance vile, – limbo, – custody, – charge, – chains; under -lock and key, – hatches; on *parole*; detained at his Majesty's pleasure.

755. Commission. [Vicarious authority.]—**N.** commission, delegation; con-, as-signment; procuration; deputation, legation, mission, embassy; agency, agentship; power of attorney, proxy; clerkship.

errand, charge, *brevet*, diploma, *exequatur*, permit etc. (*permission*) 760.

appointment, nomination, return; charter; ordination; installation, inauguration, investiture; accession, coronation, enthronement.

vicegerency; regency, regentship.

viceroy etc. 745; consignee etc. 758; deputy etc. 759.

V. commission, delegate, depute; consign, assign; charge; in-, en-trust; turn over to; commit, – to the hands of; authorize etc. (*permit*) 760.

put in commission, accredit, engage, hire, bespeak, appoint, name, nominate, return, ordain; install, induct, inaugurate, invest, crown; en-roll, -list.

employ, empower; give power of attorney to; set –, place- over; send out.

be commissioned, be accredited; represent, stand for; stand in the -stead, – place, – shoes- of.

Adj. commissioned etc. *v.*

Adv. per procuratione.

756. Abrogation.—N. abrogation, annulment, nullification; cancelling etc. *v.*; cancel; revo-cation, -kement; repeal, rescission, defeasance.

. dismissal, *congé*, demission; depos-al, -ition; sack, dethronement; disestablish-, disendow-ment; deconsecration.

aboli-tion, -shment; dissolution.

counter-order, -mand; repudiation, retractation; recantation etc. (*tergiversation*) 607.

V. abrogate, annul, cancel; destroy etc. 162; abolish; revoke, repeal, rescind, reverse, retract, recall; over-rule, -ride; set aside; disannul, dissolve, quash, nullify, declare null and void; dis-establish, -endow; deconsecrate.

disclaim etc. (*deny*) 536; ignore, repudiate; recant etc. 607; divest oneself, break off.

counter-mand, -order; do away with; sweep –, brush- away; throw -overboard, – to the dogs; scatter to the winds, cast behind.

dismiss, discard; cast –, turn- -off, – out, – adrift, – out of doors, – aside, – away; send -off, – away, – about one's business; discharge, get rid of, fire out, fire etc. (*eject*) 297; jilt.

cashier; break; oust; set down, unseat, -saddle; un-, de-, disen-throne; depose, uncrown; unfrock, strike off the roll; dis-bar, -bench.

be -abrogated etc.; receive its quietus.

Adj. abrogated etc. *v.*; *functus officio.*

Int. get along with you! begone! go about your business! away with!

757. Resignation.—N. resignation, retirement, abdication, renunciation, abjuration, disclaimer, abandonment, relinquishment.

V. resign; give –, throw- up; lay down, throw up the cards, wash one's hands of, abjure, renounce, forego, disclaim, abandon, relinquish, retract, demit; deny etc. 536.

abrogate etc. 756; desert etc. (*relinquish*) 624; get rid of etc. 782.

abdicate; vacate, – one's seat; accept the stewardship of the Chiltern Hundreds; retire; tender –, send in –, hand in- one's resignation.

Adj. abdicant, renunciatory etc. *v.*

Phr. 'Othello's occupation's gone.'

758. Consignee.—N. consignee, trustee, nominee, committee.

delegate; commiss-ary, -ioner; emissary, envoy, commissionaire; messenger etc. 534.

diplomatist, diplomat, *corps diplomatique*, embassy; am-, em-bassador; representative, resident, consul, legate, nuncio, internuncio, *chargé d' affaires, attaché.*

vicegerent etc. (*deputy*) 759; plenipotentiary.

functionary, placeman, curator; treasurer etc. 801; agent, factor, bailiff, steward, clerk, secretary, attorney, solicitor, proctor, broker, underwriter, commission agent, auctioneer, one's man of business; factotum etc. (*director*) 694; caretaker.

negotiator, go between; middleman; under agent, *employé*; servant etc. 746.

salesman; commercial, – traveler; bagman, *commis-voyageur*, touter.

newspaper –, own –, war –, special-correspondent; reporter.

759. Deputy.—N. deputy, substitute, vice, proxy, *locum tenens*, delegate, representative, next friend, surrogate, secondary.

regent, vicegerent, vizier, minister, vicar; premier etc. (*director*) 694; chancellor, prefect, provost, warden, lieutenant, archon, consul, proconsul; viceroy etc. (*governor*) 745; commissioner etc. 758; plenipotentiary, *alter ego.*

team, eight, eleven; champion.

V. be -deputy etc. *n.*; stand –, appear –, hold a brief –, answer- for; represent; stand –, walk- in the shoes of; stand in the stead of.

substitute, ablegate, accredit; commission, empower, delegate etc. 755.

Adj. acting; vice, -regal; accredited to.

Adv. in behalf of, by proxy.

760. Permission.—N. permission, leave; allow-, suffer-ance; toler-ance, -ation; liberty, law, license, concession, grace; indulgence etc. (*lenity*) 740; favor, dispensation, exemption; release; connivance; vouchsafement.

authorization, warranty, accordance, admission.

permit, warrant, *brevet*, precept, sanction, authority, *firman*; pass, -port; furlough, license, *carte blanche*, ticket of leave; grant, charter, patent.

V. permit; give -permission etc. *n.*, – power;

let, allow, admit; suffer, bear with, tolerate, recognize; concede etc. 762; accord, vouchsafe, favor, humor, gratify, indulge, stretch a point; wink at, connive at; shut one's eyes to.

grant, empower, charter, enfranchise, privilege, confer a privilege, license, authorize, warrant; sanction; entrust etc. (*commission*) 755.

give *-carte blanche*, – the reins to, – scope to etc. (*freedom*) 748; leave *-alone*, – it to one, – the door open; open the -door to, – floodgates; give a loose to.

let off; absolve etc. (*acquit*) 970; release, exonerate, dispense with.

ask –, beg –, request- -leave, – permission.

Adj. permitting etc. *v.*; permissive, indulgent; permitted etc. *v.*; patent, chartered, permissible, allowable, lawful, legitimate, legal; legalized etc. (*law*) 963; licit; unforbid, -den; unconditional.

Adv. permissibly; by –, with –, on- -leave etc. *n.*; *speciali gratiâ*; under favor of; *pace*; *ad libitum* etc. (*freely*) 748, (*at will*) 600; by all means etc. (*willingly*) 602; yes etc. (*assent*) 488.

761. Prohibition.—N. pro-, in-hibition; *veto*, disallowance; interdict, -ion; injunction; embargo, ban, *verboten*, taboo, proscription; *index expurgatorius*; restriction etc. (*restraint*) 751; hindrance etc. 706; forbidden fruit.

V. pro-, in-hibit; forbid, put one's *veto* upon, disallow; bar; debar etc. (*hinder*) 706, forefend.

keep -in, – within bounds; restrain etc. 751; cohibit, withhold, limit, circumscribe, clip the wings of, restrict, narrow; interdict, taboo; put –, place- under -an interdiction, – the ban; proscribe, censor; exclude, shut out; shut –, bolt –, show- the door; warn off; dash the cup from one's lips; forbid the banns.

Adj. prohibit-ive, -ory; interdictive; proscriptive; restrictive, exclusive; forbidding etc. *v.*

prohibited etc. *v.*; not -permitted etc. 760; unlicensed, contraband, under the ban of; illegal etc. 964; unauthorized, not to be thought of.

Adv. on no account etc. (*no*) 536.

Int. forbid it heaven! etc. (*deprecation*) 766. hands –, keep- off! hold! stop! avast!

Phr. that will never do.

762. Consent.—N. consent; assent etc. 488; acquiescence; approval etc. 931; compliance, agreement, concession; yield-ance, -ingness; accession, acknowledgment, acceptance, agnition.

settlement, ratification, confirmation, adjustment.

permit etc. (*permission*) 760; promise etc. 768.

V. consent; assent etc. 488; yield assent, admit, allow, concede, grant, yield; come -over, – round; give in to, acknowledge, agnize, give consent, comply with, acquiesce, agree to, fall in with, accede, accept, embrace an offer, close with, take at one's word, have no objection.

satisfy, meet one's wishes, settle, come to terms etc. 488; not -refuse etc. 764; turn a willing ear etc. (*willingness*) 602; jump at; deign, vouchsafe; promise etc. 768.

Adj. consenting etc. *v.*; agreeable, compliant; agreed etc. (*assent*) 488; unconditional.

Adv. yes etc. (*assent*) 488; by all means etc. (*willingly*) 602; if –, as- you please; be it so, so be it, well and good, of course.

763. Offer.—N. offer, proffer, presentation, tender, bid, overture; propos-al, -ition; motion, invitation; candidature; offering etc. (*gift*) 784.

V. offer, proffer, present, tender; bid; propose, move; make -a motion, – advances; start; invite, hold out, place- at one's disposal, – in one's way, put forward.

hawk about; offer for sale etc. 796; press etc. (*request*) 765; lay at one's feet.

offer –, present- oneself; volunteer, come forward, be a candidate; stand –, bid- for; seek; be at one's service; go a begging; bribe etc. (*give*) 784.

Adj. offer-ing, -ed etc. *v.*; in the market, for sale, to let, disengaged, on hire.

764. Refusal.—N. refusal, rejection; non-, incompliance; denial; declining etc. *v.*; declension; peremptory –, flat –, point blank- refusal; repulse, rebuff; discountenance.

recusancy, renunciation, abnegation, negation, protest, disclaimer; dissent etc. 489; revocation etc. 756.

V. refuse, reject, deny, decline; nill, negative; refuse –, withhold- one's assent; shake the head; close the -hand, – purse; grudge, begrudge, be slow to, hang fire.

be deaf to; turn -a deaf ear to, – one's back upon; set one's face against, discountenance, not hear of, have nothing to do with, wash one's hands of, stand aloof, forswear, set aside, cast behind one; not yield an inch etc. (*obstinacy*) 606.

resist, cross; not -grant etc. 762; repel, repulse; shut –, slam- the door in one's face; rebuff; send -back, – to the right about, – away with a flea in the ear; deny oneself, not be at home to; discard etc. (*repudiate*) 610; rescind etc. (*revoke*) 756; disclaim, protest; dissent etc. 489.

Adj. refusing etc. *v.*; rest-ive, -iff; recusant; uncomplying, noncompliant, unconsenting, uncomplaisant, protestant; not willing to hear of, deaf to.

refused etc. *v.*; ungranted, out of the question, not to be thought of, impossible.

Adv. no etc. 536; on no account, not for the world; no thank you.

Phr. *non possumus*; [ironically] your humble servant; *bien obligé*.

765. Request.—N. requ-est, -isition; claim etc. (*demand*) 741; petition, suit, prayer; begging letter, round-robin.

motion, overture, application, canvass, address, appeal, apostrophe; imprecation; rogation; proposal, proposition.

orison etc. (*worship*) 990; incantation etc. (*spell*) 993.

mendicancy; asking, panhandling, begging etc. *v.*; postulation, solicitation, invitation, entreaty, importunity, supplication, instance, impetration, imploration, obsecration, obtestation, invocation, interpellation.

V. request, ask; beg, crave, sue, pray, petition, solicit, invite, pop the question, make bold to ask; beg -leave, – a boon; apply to, call to, put to; call -upon, – for; make –, address –, prefer –, put up- a -request, – prayer, – petition; make - application, – a requisition; ask –, trouble- one for; claim etc. (*demand*) 741; offer up prayers etc. (*worship*) 990; whistle for.

beg hard, entreat, beseech, plead, supplicate, implore, apostrophize; conjure, adjure; obtest; cry to, kneel to, appeal to; invoke, evoke; impetrate, imprecate, ply, press, urge, beset, importune, dun, tax, clamor for; cry -aloud, – for help; fall on one's knees; throw oneself at the feet of; come down on one's marrow-bones.

beg from door to door, send the hat round, go a begging; mendicate, mump, cadge, panhandle, beg one's bread.

dance attendance on, besiege, knock at the door.

bespeak, canvass, tout, make interest, court; seek, bid for etc. (*offer*) 763; publish the banns.

Adj. requesting etc. *v.*; precatory; suppli-ant, -cant, -catory; invoc-, imprec-, rog-atory; postulant, mendicant.

importunate, clamorous, urgent; solicitous; cap in hand; on one's -knees, – bended knees, – marrow-bones.

Adv. prithee, do, please, pray; be so good as, be good enough; have the goodness, vouchsafe, will you, I pray thee, if you please.

Int. for -God's, – heaven's, – goodness', – mercy's- sake.

766. Deprecation. [Negative request.]—**N.** deprecation, expostulation; remonstrance; intercession, mediation.

V. deprecate, protest, expostulate, enter a protest, intercede for.

Adj. deprecatory, expostulatory, intercessory, mediatorial.

deprecated, protested.

un-, unbe-sought; unasked etc: (*see* ask etc. 765).

Int. cry you mercy! God forbid! forbid it Heaven! Heaven -forefend, – forbid! far be it from! hands off! etc. (*prohibition*) 761.

767. Petitioner.—**N.** petitioner, solicitor, applicant; suppli-ant, -cant; suitor, candidate, claimant, postulant, aspirant, competitor, bidder; place –, pot- hunter; prizer.

beggar, mendicant, mumper, sturdy beggar, cadger, panhandler.

canvasser, barker, touter etc. 768.

sycophant, parasite etc. 886.

768. Promise.—**N.** promise, undertaking, word, troth, plight, pledge, *parole*, word of honor, vow; oath etc. (*affirmation*) 535; profession, assurance, warranty, guarantee, insurance, obligation; contract etc. 769.

engagement, pre-engagement; affiance; betroth, -al, -ment; marriage -compact, – vow.

V. promise; give a -promise etc. *n.*; undertake, engage; make –, form- an engagement; enter -into, – on- an engagement; bind –, tie –, pledge –, commit –, take upon- oneself; vow; swear etc. (*affirm*) 535; give –, pass –, pledge –, plight- one's -word, – honor, – credit, – troth; betroth, plight faith; take the vows.

assure, warrant, guarantee, vouch for, avouch, covenant etc. 769; attest etc. (*bear witness*) 467.

hold out an expectation; contract an obligation; become -bound to, – sponsor for; answer –, be answerable- for; secure; give security etc. 771; underwrite.

adjure, administer an oath, put to one's oath, swear a witness.

Adj. promising etc. *v.*; promissory; votive; under hand and seal; upon -oath, – affirmation.

promised etc. *v.*; affianced, pledged, bound; committed, compromised; in for it.

Adv. as one's head shall answer for; upon my honor.

Phr. in for a penny, in for a pound.

768a. Release from engagement.—**N.** release etc. (*liberation*) 750.

Adj. absolute; unconditional etc. (*free*) 748.

769. Compact.—**N.** compact, contract, agreement, bargain, deal, transaction; affidation; pact, -ion; bond, covenant, indenture.

stipulation, settlement, convention; compromise, *cartel*.

protocol, treaty, *concordat, Zollverein, Son-derbund*, charter, *Magna Charta*, Pragmatic Sanction.

negotiation etc. (*bargaining*) 794; diplomacy etc. (*mediation*) 724; negotiator etc. (*agent*) 758.

ratification, completion, signature, seal, sigil, signet.

V. contract, covenant, agree for, engage etc. (*promise*) 768.

treat, negotiate, stipulate, make terms; bargain etc. (*barter*) 794.

make –, strike- a bargain; come to -terms, – an understanding; compromise etc. 774; set at rest; close, – with; conclude, complete, settle; confirm, ratify, clench, subscribe, underwrite; en-, in-dorse; put the seal to; sign, seal etc. (*attest*) 467; indent.

take one at one's word, bargain by inch of candle.

Adj. contractual, agreed etc. *v.*; conventional; under hand and seal; signed, sealed and delivered.

Phr. *caveat emptor.*

770. Conditions.—**N.** conditions, terms; articles, – of agreement.

clauses, provisions; proviso etc. (*qualification*) 469; covenant, stipulation, obligation, *ultimatum, sine quâ non; casus foederis.*

V. make –, come to- -terms etc. (*contract*) 769; make it a condition, stipulate, insist upon, make a point of; bind, tie up.

Adj. conditional, provisional, guarded, fenced, hedged in.

Adv. conditionally etc. (*with qualification*) 469; provisionally, *pro re natâ*; on condition; with a reservation.

771. Security.—N. security; guaran-ty, -tee; gage, waranty, bond, tie, pledge, plight, mortgage, debenture, hypothecation, bill of sale, lien, pignus, pawn, pignoration; real security; bottomry; collateral, vadium.

stake, deposit, earnest, handsel, caution.

promissory note; bill, – of exchange; I.O.U.: personal security, covenant, specialty; *parole* etc. (*promise*) 768.

acceptance, indorsement, signature, execution, stamp, seal.

spon-sor, -sion, -sorship; surety, bail; main-pernor, hostage.

recognizance; deed –, covenant- of indemnity.

authentication, verfication, warrant, certificate, voucher, docket, doquet; record etc. 551; probate, attested copy.

receipt; ac-, quittance; discharge, release.

muniment, title-deed, instrument; deed, – poll; assurance, insurance, indenture; charter etc. (*compact*) 769; charter-poll; paper, parchment, settlement, will, testament, last will and testament, codicil.

V. give -security, – bail, – substantial bail; go bail; pawn, impawn, hock, spout, mortgage, hypothecate, impignorate.

guarantee, warrant, assure; accept, indorse, underwrite, insure.

execute, stamp; sign, seal etc. (*evidence*) 467.

let, set; grant –, take –, hold- a lease; hold in pledge; lend on security etc. 787.

Adj. secure, -ed; pledged etc. *v.*; in pawn, on deposit.

772. Observance.—N. observance, performance, compliance; obedience, etc. 743; fulfilment, satisfaction, discharge; acquit-tance, -tal.

adhesion, acknowledgment; fidelity etc. (*probity*) 939; exact etc. 494- observance.

V. observe, comply with, respect, acknowledge, abide by; cling to, adhere to, be faithful to, act up to; meet, fulfil; carry -out, – into execution; execute, perform, keep, satisfy, discharge; do one's office.

perform –, fulfill –, discharge –, acquit oneself of- an obligation; make good; make good –, keep- one's -word, – promise; redeem one's pledge; keep faith with, stand to one's engagement.

Adj. observant, faithful, true, loyal; honorable etc. 939; true as the -dial to the sun, – needle to the pole; punct-ual, -ilious; meticulous; literal etc. (*exact*) 494; as good as one's word.

Adv. faithfully etc. *adj.*

773. Non-observance.—N. non-observance etc. 772; evasion, inobservance, failure, omission, neglect, laches, laxity, informality.

infringement, infraction; violation, transgression.

retractation, repudiation, nullification; protest; forfeiture.

lawlessness; disobedience etc. 742; bad faith etc. 940.

V. fail, neglect, omit, elude, evade, give the go by to, cut, set aside, ignore; shut –, close- one's eyes to, avoid.

infringe, transgress, pirate, violate, break, trample under foot, do violence to, drive a coach and six through.

discard, protest, repudiate, fling to the winds, set at naught, nullify, declare null and void; cancel etc. (*wipe off*) 552.

retract, go back from, be off, forfeit, go from one's word, palter; stretch –, strain- a point.

Adj. violating etc. *v.*; lawless, transgressive; elusive, evasive; lax, casual; non-observant. unfulfilled etc. (*see* fulfil etc. 772).

774. Compromise.—N. com-promise, -mutation, -position; middle term, *mezzo termine*; compensation etc. 30; adjustment, mutual concession.

V. com-promise, -mute, -pound; take the mean; split the difference, meet one half way, give and take; come to terms etc. (*contract*) 769; submit to –, abide by- arbitration; patch up, bridge over, fix up, arrange; adjust, – differences; agree; make -the best of, – a virtue of necessity; take the will for the deed.

775. Acquisition.—N. acquisition; gaining etc. *v.*; obtainment; procur-ation, -ement; purchase, descent, inheritance; gift etc. 784.

recovery, retrieval, revendication, replevin; redemption, salvage, trover; find, *trouvaille*, foundling.

gain, thrift; money-making, -grubbing; lucre, filthy lucre, loaves and fishes, the main chance, pelf; emolument etc. 973; wealth etc. 803.

profit, earnings, winnings, innings, clean-up, pickings, perquisite, net profit; income etc. (*receipt*) 810; pro-ceeds, -duce, -duct; out-come, -put; return, fruit, crop, harvest, tilth; second crop, aftermath; benefit etc. (*good*) 618.

sweepstakes, trick, prize, pool.

[Fraudulent acquisition] subreption; theft, stealing etc. 791.

V. acquire, get, gain, win, earn, obtain, procure, gather, annex; collect etc. 72; pick, – up; glean, take etc. 789.

find; come –, pitch –, light- upon; scrape -up, – together; get in, reap and carry, net, bag, sack, bring home, secure, come across, derive, draw, get in the harvest.

profit; make –, draw- profit; turn to -profit, – account; make -capital out of, – money by; obtain a return, reap the fruits of; reap –, gain- an advantage; turn -a penny, – an honest penny; make the pot boil, bring grist to the mill; make –, coin –, raise- money; raise -funds, – the wind; fill one's pocket etc. (*wealth*) 803.

treasure up etc. (*store*) 636; realize, clear; produce etc. 161; take etc. 789.

get back, recover, regain, retrieve, revendicate, replevy, redeem, come by one's own.

come -by, – in for; receive etc. 785; inherit; step into, – a fortune, – the shoes of; succeed to.

get -hold of, – between one's finger and thumb, – into one's hand, – at; take –, come into –, enter into- possession.

be -profitable etc. *adj.*; pay, answer. accrue etc. (*be received*) 785.

Adj. acquir-ing, -ed etc. *v.*; acquisitive; productive, profitable, advantageous, gainful, remunerative, paying, lucrative.

776. Loss.—N. loss; de-, perdition; forfeiture, lapse.

privation, bereavement; deprivation etc. (*dispossession*) 789; riddance.

V. lose; incur –, experience –, meet with- a loss; miss; mislay, let slip, allow to slip through the fingers, squander; be without etc. (*exempt*) 777a; forfeit.

get rid of etc. 782; waste etc. 638. be lost, lapse.

Adj. losing etc. *v.*; not having etc. 777a.

shorn of, deprived of; denuded, bereaved, bereft, *minus*, cut off; dispossessed etc. 789; rid of, quit of; out of pocket.

lost etc. *v.*; long lost; irretrievable etc. (*hopeless*) 859; irredentist; off one's hands.

Int. farewell to! adieu to! good riddance!

777. Possession.—N. possession, seisin; ownership etc. 780; occupancy; hold, -ing; tenure, tenancy, feodality, dependency; villenage; socage, chivalry, knight service.

exclusive possession, impropriation, monopoly, corner; retention etc. 781; pre-possession, -occupancy; nine points of the law.

future possession, heritage, inheritance, heirship, reversion, fee, seigniority, feud, fief.

bird in hand, *uti possidetis*, *chose* in possession.

V. possess, have, hold, occupy, enjoy; be - possessed of etc. *adj.*; have -in hand etc. *adj.*; own etc. 780; command.

inherit; come -to, – in for.

engross, monopolize, forestall, regrate, impropriate, have all to oneself, corner; have a firm hold of etc. (*retain*) 781; get into one's hand etc. (*acquire*) 775.

belong to, appertain to, pertain to; be -in one's possession etc. *adj.*; vest in.

Adj. possessing etc. *v.*; worth; possessed of, seized of, master of, in possession of; endowed –, blest –, instinct –, fraught –, laden –, charged –, instilled –, with.

possessed etc. *v.*; on hand, by one; in hand, in store, in stock; in one's -hands, – grasp, – possession; at one's -command, – disposal; one's own etc. (*property*) 780.

unsold, unshared.

777a. Exemption.—N. exemption; exception, immunity, privilege, release etc. 927a; absence etc. 187.

V. not -have etc. 777; be -without etc. *adj.*

Adj. exempt from, devoid of, without, unpossessed of, unblest with, 'immune from.

not -having etc. 777; unpossessed; untenanted etc. (*vacant*) 187; without an owner.

unobtained, unacquired.

778. Participation. [Joint possession.]—N. participation; co-, joint-tenancy; possession –, tenancy- in common; joint –, common- stock; co-, partnership; communion; community of - possessions, – goods; communalism, communism, socialism, collectivism; co-operation etc. 709; profit sharing.

snacks, co-portion, picnic, hotchpotch; co-heirship, -parceny, -parcenary; gavelkind.

participator, sharer; co-, partner; shareholder; co-, joint-tenant; tenants in common; co-heir, - parcener.

communist, socialist.

V. par-ticipate, -take; share, – in; come in for a share; go -shares, – snacks, – halves; share and share alike.

have –, possess –, be seized- -in common, – as joint tenants etc. *n.*

join in; have a hand in etc. (*co-operate*) 709.

Adj. partaking etc. *v.*; communistic, socialistic, co-operative, profit sharing.

Adv. share and share alike.

779. Possessor.—N. possessor, holder; occupant, -ier; tenant; person –, man- -in possession etc. 777; renter, lodger, lessee, under-lessee; zemindar, ryot; tenant -on sufferance, – at will, – from year to year, – for years, – for life.

owner; propriet-or; -ress, -ary; impropriator, master, mistress, lord.

land-holder, -owner, -lord, -lady; lord -of the manor, – paramount; heritor, laird, vavasor, landed gentry, mesne lord.

cestui-que-trust, beneficiary, mortgagor.

grantee, feoffee, relessee, devisee; legat-ee, -ary. trustee; holder etc.- of the legal estate; mortgagee.

right –, rightful- owner.

[Future possessor] heir, – apparent; – presumptive; heiress; inherit-or, -ress, -rix; reversioner, remainder-man.

780. Property.—N. property, possession, *suum cuique*, *meum et tuum*.

owner-, proprietor, lord-ship; seignority; empire etc. (*dominion*) 737.

interest, stake, estate, right, title, claim, demand, holding; tenure etc. (*possession*) 777; vested –, contingent –, beneficial –, equitable- interest; use, trust, benefit; legal –, equitable- estate; seisin.

absolute interest, paramount estate, freehold; fee, – simple, – tail; estate -in fee, – in tail, – tail; estate in tail -male, – female, – general.

limitation, term, lease, settlement, strict settlement, particular estate; estate -for life, – for years, – *pur autre vie*; remainder, reversion, expectancy, possibility.

dower, dowry, *dot*, jointure, marriage portion, appanage, inheritance, heritage, patrimony, alimony; legacy etc. (*gift*) 784.

assets, belongings, means, resources, circumstances; wealth etc. 803; money etc. 800; what one -is worth, – will cut up for; estate and effects.

landed –, real- -estate, – property; realty; land, -s; subdivision; plot, site; tenements; hereditaments; corporeal –, incorporeal- hereditaments; acres; ground etc. (*earth*) 342; acquest; messuage.

territory, state, kingdom, principality, realm, empire, protectorate, margravate, dependancy, colony, sphere of influence, mandate.

manor, honor, domain, demesne; farm, ranch, plantation, *hacienda*; allodium etc. (*free*) 748; fieff, feoff, feud, zemindary, dependency.

free-, copy-, lease-holds; chattels real; fixtures, plant, heirloom easement; folkland; right of - common, – user.

personal -property, – estate, – effects; personalty, chattels, goods, effects, movables; stock, – in trade; things, traps, rattle-traps, paraphernalia; equipage etc. 633.

parcels, appurtenances.

impedimenta; lug-, bag-gage; bag and baggage; pelf; cargo, lading.

rent-roll; income etc. (*receipts*) 810.

patent, copyright; *chose* in action; credit etc. 805; debt etc. 806.

V. possess etc. 777; be the -possessor etc. 779- of own; have for one's own, – very own; come in for, inherit; enfeoff.

savor of the realty.

be one's own -property etc. *n.*; belong to; ap-, pertain to.

Adj. one's own; landed, predial, manorial, allodial, seignorial; free-, copy-, lease-hold; feu-, feo-dal; hereditary, entailed, personal.

Adv. to one's -credit, – account; to the good.

to one and -his heirs for ever, – the heirs of his body, – his heirs and assigns, – his executors, administrators and assigns.

781. Retention.—N. retention; retaining etc. *v.*; keep, detention, custody; tenacity, firm hold, grasp, gripe, grip, iron grip.

fangs, teeth, claws, talons, nail, hook, tentacle, *tenaculum*; bond etc. (*vinculum*) 45.

clutches, tongs, forceps, pincers, nippers, pliers, tweezers, vise.

paw, hand, finger, wrist, fist, neaf, neif.

bird in hand; captive etc. 754.

V. retain, keep; hold, – fast, – tight, – one's own, – one's ground; clinch, clench, clutch, grasp, gripe, hug, have a firm hold of.

secure, withold, detain; hold –, keepback; keep close; husband etc. (*store*) 636; reserve; have –, keep- in stock etc. (*possess*) 777; enfail, tie up, settle.

Adj. retaining etc. *v.*; retentive, tenacious.

unforfeited, undeprived, undisposed, uncommunicated.

incommunicable, inalienable; in mortmain; in strict settlement.

Phr. *uti possidetis.*

782. Relinquishment.—N. relinquishment, abandonment etc. (*of a course*) 624; renunciation,

expropriation, dereliction; cession, surrender, dispensation; resignation etc. 757; riddance.

derelict etc. *adj.*; jetsam; waif, foundling, orphan.

v. relinquish, give up, surrender, yield, cede; let -go, – slip; spare, drop, resign, forego, renounce, abjure, abandon, expropriate, give away, dispose of, part with; lay -aside, – apart, – down, – on the shelf etc. (*disuse*) 678; set – , put- aside; make away with, cast behind; discard, cast off, dismiss; maroon.

give -notice to quit, – warning; supersede; be –, get- -rid of, – quit of; eject etc. 297.

rid –, disburden –, divest –, dispossess- oneself of; wash one's hands of; divorce, desert; disinherit, cut off.

cast –, throw –, pitch –, fling- -away, – aside, – overboard, – to the dogs; cast –, throw –, sweep- to the winds; put –, turn –, sweep- away; jettison.

quit one's hold.

Adj. relinquished etc. *v.*; cast off, derelict; unowned, unappropriated, unculled; left etc. (*residuary*) 40; divorced; disinherited.

Int. away with!

783. Transfer.—N. transfer, conveyance, assignment, alienation, abalienation; demise, limitation; conveyancing; transmission etc. (*transference*) 270; enfeoffment, bargain and sale, lease and release; exchange etc. (*interchange*) 148; barter etc. 794; substitution etc. 147.

succession, reversion; shifting -use, – trust; devolution.

V. transfer, convey; alien, -ate; assign; grant etc. (*confer* 784; consign; make –, hand- over; pass, hand, transmit, negotiate; hand down; exchange etc. (*interchange*) 148.

change -hands, – from one to another; devolve, succeed; come into possession etc. (*acquire*) 775; take over.

abalienate; disinherit; dispossess etc. 789; substitute etc. 147.

Adj. alienable, negotiable, transferable, reversional.

Phr. estate coming into possession.

784. Giving.—N. giving etc. *v.*; bestowal, donation; present-ation, -ment; accordance; con-, cession; delivery, consignment, dispensation, communication, endowment; invest-ment, -iture; award.

almsgiving, charity, liberality, generosity; philanthropy etc. 910.

[Thing given] gift, donation, present, *cadeau*; fairing; free gift, boon, favor, benefaction, grant, offering, oblation, sacrifice, immolation.

grace, act of grace, *bonus, bonanza*.

allowance, contribution, subscription, subsidy, tribute, subvention.

bequest, legacy, devise, will, dotation, appanage; dowry; voluntary -settlement, – conveyance etc. 783; amortization.

alms, largess, bounty, dole, sportule, donative, help, oblation, offertory, Peter's pence, *honorarium*, gratuity, Maundy money, Christmas box, Easter offering, vail, tip, *douceur*, drink money, *pourboire, trinkgeld, backsheesh*; fee etc. (*recompense*) 973; consideration.

bribe, bait, ground-bait; peace-offering, handsel.

giver, grantor etc. *v.*; donor, feoffer, settlor; almoner; testator; investor, subscriber, contributor; fairy godmother; Santa Claus, benefactor etc. 816.

V. deliver, hand, pass, put into the hands of; hand –, make –, deliver –, pass –, turn- over.

present, give away, dispense, dispose of; give –, deal –, dole –, mete –, fork –, shell –, squeeze- out.

pay etc. 807; render, impart, communicate.

concede, cede, yield, part with, shed cast; spend etc. 809.

give, bestow, confer, grant, accord, award, assign.

entrust, consign, vest in.

make a present; allow, contribute, subscribe, donate, furnish its quota.

invest, endow, settle upon; bequeath, leave, devise.

furnish, supply, help; ad-, minister to; afford, spare; accommodate –, indulge –, favor- with; shower down upon; lavish, pour on, thrust upon; tip, bribe; tickle –, grease- the palm; offer etc. 763; sacrifice, immolate.

Adj. giving etc. *v.*; given etc. *v.*; allow-ed, -able; concessional; communicable; charitable, eleemosynary, sportulary, tributary; *gratis* etc. 815.

785. Receiving.—N. receiving etc. *v.*; acquisition etc. 775; reception etc. (*introduction*) 296; suscipiency, acceptance, admission.

re-, ac-cipient; assignee, devisee; lega-tee, -tary; grantee, feoffee, donee, relessee, lessee.

sportulary, stipendiary; beneficiary; pension-er, - ary; almsman.

income etc. (*receipt*) 810.

v. receive; take etc. 789; acquire etc. 775; ad-mit.

take in, catch, touch; pocket; put into one's - pocket, – purse; accept; take off one's hands.

be received; come -in, – to hand, pass –, fall- into one's hand; go into one's pocket; fall to one's - lot, – share; come –, fall- to one; accrue; have - given etc. 784 to one.

Adj. receiving etc. *v.*; re-, suscipient.

received etc. *v.*; given etc. 784; second-hand.

not given, unbestowed etc. (*see* give, bestow etc. 784).

786. Apportionment.—N. apportion-, allot-, consign-, assign-, appoint-ment; appropriation; dispensation, -tribution; allocation, division, deal; repartition; administration.

dividend, portion, contingent, share, allotment, lot, cut, split, measure, dose; dole, meed, pittance; *quantum*, ration; ratio, proportion, quota, *modicum*, mess, allowance.

V. apportion, divide; cut, split, divvy; distribute, administer, dispense; billet, allot, detail, cast, share, mete; portion –, parcel –, dole- out; deal, carve.

partition, assign, appropriate, appoint.

come in for one's share etc. (*participate*) 778.

Adj. apportioning etc. *v.*; respective.

Adv. respectively, each to each.

787. Lending.—N. lending etc. *v.*; loan, advance, accommodation, feneration; mortgage etc. (*security*) 771; investment.

mont de piété, pawnshop, hock shop, spout, my uncle's.

lender, pawnbroker, money lender, usurer, Jew, Shylock.

V. lend, advance, loan, accommodate with; lend on security; pawn etc. (*security*) 771.

intrust, invest; place –, put- out to interest; sink, risk.

let, demise, lease, set, under-, sub-let.

Adj. lending etc. *v.*; lent etc. *v.*; unborrowed etc. (*see* borrowed etc. 788).

Adv. in advance; on -loan, – security.

788. Borrowing.—N. borrowing, pledging, pawning.

borrowed plumes; plagiarism etc. (*thieving*) 791. replevin.

V. borrow, desume; pawn.

hire, rent, farm; take a -lease, – demise; take –, hire- by- the -hour, – mile, – year etc.

raise –, take up- money; float bonds; raise the wind; fly a kite, borrow of Peter to pay Paul; run into debt etc. (*debt*) 806.

make use of, plagiarize, pirate.

replevy.

789. Taking.—N. taking etc. *v.*; reception etc. (*taking in*) 296; deglutition etc. (*taking food*) 298; appropriation, prehension, prensation; capture, caption; ap-, de-prehension; abreption, seizure; abduction, -lation; subtraction etc. (*subduction*) 38; abstraction, ademption.

dispossession; depriv-ation, -ement; bereavement; divestment; disherison; distraint, distress; sequestration, confiscation, attachment, execution; eviction etc. 297.

rapacity, extortion, vampirism, predacity, blood-sucking; theft etc. 791.

resumption; repris-e, -al; recovery etc. 775.

clutch, swoop, wrench; grip etc. (*retention*) 781; haul, take, catch; scramble.

taker, captor, capturer; vampire; extortioner.

V. take, catch, hook, nab, bag, sack, pocket, put into one's pocket; scrounge; receive; accept.

reap, crop, cull, pluck; gather etc. (*get*) 775; draw.

ap-, im-propriate; assume, possess oneself of; take possession of; commandeer; lay –, clap- one's hands on; help oneself to; make free with; dip one's hands into, lay under contribution; intercept; scramble for; deprive of.

take –, carry –, bear- -away, – off; abstract; hurry off –, run away- with; abduct; steal etc. 791; ravish; seize; pounce –, spring- upon; swoop -to, – down upon; take by -storm, – assault; snatch, reave.

snap up, nip up, whip up, catch up; kidnap; crimp, capture, lay violent hands on.

get –, lay –, take –, catch –, lay fast –, take firm- hold of; lay by the heels, take prisoner; fasten upon, grip, grapple, embrace, gripe, clasp, grab, clutch, collar, throttle, take by the throat, claw, clinch, clench, make sure of.

catch at, jump at, make a grab at, snap at, snatch at; reach, make a long arm, stretch forth one's hand.

take -from, – away from; deduct etc. 38; retrench etc. (*curtail*) 201; dispossess, ease one of, snatch from one's grasp; tear –, tear away –, wrench –, wrest –, wring- from; extort; deprive of, bereave; disinherit, cut off with a shilling.

oust etc. (*eject*) 297; divest; levy, distrain, confiscate; sequest-er, -rate, accroach; usurp; despoil, strip, fleece, shear, displume, impoverish, eat out of house and home; drain, – to the dregs; gut, dry, exhaust, swallow up; absorb etc. (*suck in*) 296; draw off; suck, – like a leech, – the blood of.

retake, resume; recover etc. 775.

Adj. taking etc. *v.*; privative, prehensile; pred-aceous, -al, -atory, -atorial; rap-acious, -torial; ravenous; parasitic; all-devouring, -engulfing.

bereft etc. 776.

Adv. at one fell swoop.

Phr. give an inch and take an ell.

790. Restitution.—N. restitution, return; ren-, red-dition; reinstatement, restoration; reinvestment, recuperation; repatriation; rehabilitation etc. (*reconstruction*) 660; reparation, atonement, indemnity, compensation, recompense.

release, replevin, redemption; recovery etc. (*getting back*) 775; remitter, reversion.

V. return, restore; recondition; give –, carry – bring- back; render, – up; give up; let go, unclutch; dis-, re-gorge; regurgitate; recoup, reimburse, repay, indemnify, reinvest, remit, rehabilitate; repair etc. (*make good*) 660.

redeem, recover etc. (*get back*) 775; take back again; revest, revert.

Adj. restoring etc. *v.*; recuperative etc. 660; in full restitution, to compensate for.

Phr. *suum cuique*.

791. Stealing.—N. stealing etc. *v.*; theft, thievery, robbery, latrociny, direption; abstraction, appropriation; plagiar-y, -ism; rape, kidnapping, depredation; raid, hold up.

spoliation, plunder, pillage; sack, -age; rapine, *brigandage*, highway robbery, foray, *razzia*; blackmail; piracy, privateering, buccaneering; filibustering, -ism; burglary; house-breaking; cattle-stealing, -rustling, -lifting.

peculation, embezzlement; fraud etc. 545; larceny, petty larceny, pilfering, shop-lifting.

thievishness, rapacity, kleptomania, Alsatia; den of -Cacus, – thieves.

license to plunder, letters of marque.

V. steal, thieve, rob, purloin, pilfer, filch, lift, prig, bag, nim, crib, cabbage, palm; abstract; appropriate, plagiarize.

convey away, carry off, abduct, kidnap, shanghai, impress, crimp; make –, walk –, runoff with; run away with; spirit away; seize etc. (*lay violent hands on*) 789.

plunder, pillage, rifle, sack, loot, ransack, spoil, spoliate, despoil, strip, sweep, gut, forage, levy black-mail, pirate, pickeer, maraud, lift cattle, rustle, poach, smuggle, run.

stick –, hold- up.

swindle, peculate, embezzle; sponge, mulct, rook, bilk, pluck, pigeon, skin, fleece, diddle; defraud etc. 545; obtain under false pretences; live by one's wits

rob –, borrow of- Peter to Paul; set a thief to catch a thief.

disregard the distinction between *meum* and *tuum*.

Adj. thieving etc. *v.*; thievish, light-fingered; fur-acious, -tive; piratical; pred-aceous, -al, -atory, -atorial; raptorial etc. (*rapacious*) 789.

stolen etc. *v.*

Phr. *sic vos non. vobis*.

792. Thief.—N. thief, robber, *homo trium literarum*, pilferer, rifler, filcher, plagiarist.

spoiler, depredator, pillager, marauder; harpy, shark, land-shark, falcon, moss-trooper, bushranger, Bedouin, brigand, freebooter, bandit, thug, dacoit, pirate, corsair, viking, Paul Jones; buccan-eer, -ier; piqu-, pick-eerer; rover, ranger, privateer, filibuster; rapparee, wrecker, picaroon; smuggler, poacher, plunderer; racketeer.

highwayman, Dick Turpin, Claude Duval, Macheath, knight of the road, footpad, sturdy beggar; abductor, kidnapper.

cut-, pick-purse; pick-pocket, light-fingered gentry; sharper; card-, skittle-sharper; crook; thimblerigger; rook, Greek, blackleg, leg, welsher, defaulter; Autolycus, Cacus, Barabbas, Jeremy Diddler, Robert Macaire, artful dodger, trickster; swell mob, *chevalier d'industrie*; shop-lifter.

swindler, peculator, forger, coiner, counterfeiter, shoful; fence, receiver of stolen goods, duffer; smasher.

burglar, housebreaker; cracks-, mags-man; Bill Sikes, Jack Sheppard, Jonathan Wild, Raffles, cat burglar.

793. Booty.—N. booty, spoil, plunder, price, loot, graft, swag, pickings, boodle; *spolia opima*, prey; blackmail; stolen goods.

Adj. looting etc. *n.*; manubial, spoliative.

794. Barter.—N. barter, exchange, scorse, truck system; interchange etc. 148.

a Roland for an Oliver; *quid pro quo*; commutation, -position.

trade, commerce, mercature, buying and selling, bargain and sale; traffic, business, nundination, custom, shopping; commercial enterprise, speculation, jobbing, stock-jobbing, *agiotage*, brokery, arbitrage.

dealing, transaction, negotiation, bargain.

free trade.

V. barter, exchange, truck, scorse, swop; interchange etc. 148; commutate etc. (*substitute*) 147; compound for.

trade, traffic, buy and sell, give and take, nundinate; carry on –, ply –, drive- a trade; be in -

business, – the city; keep a shop, deal in, employ one's capital in.

trade –, deal –, have dealings- with; transact –, do- business with; open –, keep- an account with.

bargain; drive –, make- a bargain; negotiate, bid for; dicker, haggle, higgle; chaffer, huckster, cheapen, beat down; stickle, – for; out-, under-bid; ask, charge; strike a bargain etc. (*contract*) 769.

speculate, give a sprat to catch a herring; buy in the cheapest and sell in the dearest market; rig the market.

Adj. commercial, mercantile, trading; interchangeable, marketable, staple, in the market, for sale.

wholesale, retail.

Adv. across the counter; on 'change.

795. Purchase.—N. purchase, emption; buying, purchasing, shopping; pre-emption, refusal.

coemption, bribery; slave trade.

buyer, purchaser, *emptor*, vendee; patron, employer, client, customer, *clientèle*.

V. buy, purchase, invest in, procure; rent etc. (*hire*) 788; repurchase, buy in.

keep in one's pay, bribe, suborn; pay etc. 807; spend etc. 809.

make –, complete- a purchase; buy over the counter; pay cash for.

shop, market, go a shopping.

Adj. purchased etc. *v.*

Phr. *caveat emptor.*

796. Sale.—N. sale, vent, disposal; auction, roup, Dutch auction; custom etc. (*traffic*) 794.

vendi-bility, -bleness.

seller, salesman; peddler, smous; vender, vendor, consignor; merchant etc. 797; auctioneer.

V. sell, vend, dispose of, effect a sale; sell -over the counter, – by auction etc. *n.*; dispense, retail; deal in etc. 794; sell -off, – out; turn into money; realize; bring -to, – under- the hammer; put up to auction; auction, offer –, put up- for sale; hawk, peddle, bring to market; offer etc. 763; undersell; dump, unload.

let; mortgage etc. (*security*) 771.

Adj. under the hammer, in the market, for sale.

saleable, marketable, vendible, in demand, having a ready sale; unsaleable etc., unpurchased, unbought; on one's hands.

797. Merchant.—N. merchant, trader, dealer, monger, chandler, salesman; changer; regrater; shop-keeper, -man; trades-man, -people, -folk.

retailer; chapman, hawker, huckster, higgler; peddler, smous, pedlar, *colporteur*, cadger, Autolycus; sutler, *vivandière*; coster-man, -monger; market woman; cheap jack; caterer etc. 637; tallyman.

money-broker, -changer, -lender; stock-broker, -jobber; cambist, usurer, moneyer, banker.

jobber; broker etc. (*agent*) 758; buyer etc. 795; seller etc. 796.

concern; firm etc. (*partnership*) 712.

798. Merchandise.—N. merchandise, ware, commodity, effects, goods, article, stock, produce, staple commodity; stock in trade etc. (*store*) 636; cargo etc. (*contents*) 190.

799. Mart.—N. mart; market, -place, *forum*; fair, bazaar, staple; stock –, exchange; 'change, *bourse*, Wall Street, Rialto, hall, guildhall; toll-booth, custom-house; Tattersalls.

shop, stall, booth; wharf; office, chambers, counting-house, *bureau*; coun-, comp-ter.

ware-house, -room; *dépôt*, interposit, *entrepôt*, *emporium*, establishment; store etc. 636.

open market, market-overt.

800. Money.—N. money -matters, – market; finance; accounts etc. 811; funds, treasure; capital, stock; assets etc. (*property*) 780; wealth etc. 803; supplies, ways and means, wherewithal, sinews of war, almighty dollar, needful, cash.

sum, amount; balance, -sheet; sum total; proceeds etc. (*receipts*) 810.

currency, circulating medium, specie; coin, – of the realm; piece, hard cash, dollar, sterling coin; pounds, shillings and pence; L s. d., guineas; pocket, breeches pocket, purse; money in hand; the best, ready, – money; filthy lucre, shekels, roll, jack, rhino, blunt, dust, bawbees, brass, dibs, dough, mopus, tin, salt, chink, oof, spondulics, pile, wads.

precious metals, gold, silver, copper, nickel; bullion, bar, ingot, nugget.

petty cash; pocket-, pin-money; small –, change; small coin, loose cash; doit, stiver, rap, mite, farthing, *sou*, penny, shilling, bob, tanner, tester, groat, guinea, ducat; *rouleau*; *wampum*; good –, round –, lump- sum; power –, mint –, tons- of money; plum, lac of rupees, millions, money-bags, miser's hoard, stocking, mine of wealth etc. 803.

[Science of coins] numismatics, chrysology.

paper-money; money –, postal –, Post Office-order; note, – of hand; bank –, treasury- note; Bradbury; promissory note; I.O.U., bond; bill, – of exchange; draft, check, order, warrant, *coupon*, debenture, exchequer bill, *assignat*, greenback, gold –, silver- certificate.

copper, nickel, dime, quarter, two bits, half a dollar, dollar, buck, simoleon, fiver, tenner, a twenty, a sawbuck, a century, a grand; eagle, double eagle.

gold standard, bimetallism, fiat money; rate of –, exchange; in-, de-flation.

remittance etc. (*payment*) 807; credit etc. 805; liability etc. 806; solvency etc. 803.

draw-er, -ee; oblig-or, -ee; moneyer, coiner, counterfeiter, forger.

false –, bad- money; base –, counterfeit- coin, flash note, slip, kite; Bank of Elegance.

argumentum ad crumenam.

V. amount to, come to, mount up to; touch the pocket; draw, – upon; endorse etc. (*security*) 771; issue, utter, circulate; discount etc. 813.

forge, counterfeit, coin, circulate –, pass- bad money.

Adj. monetary, pecuniary, crumenal, fiscal, financial, sumptuary, numismatical; sterling; solvent etc. 803.

801. Treasurer.—N. treasurer; bursar, -y; purser, purse-bearer; cash-keeper, banker; depositary; questor, receiver, steward, trustee, chartered –, accountant; Accountant-General, almoner, liquidator, paymaster, cashier, teller; cambist; money-changer etc. (*merchant*) 797.

financier, Chancellor of the Exchequer, minister of finance; Secretary of the Treasury, Director of the Budget, Controller of Currency.

802. Treasury.—N. treasury, bank, exchequer, almonry, fisc, hanaper, bursary; safe; strong-box, - hold, -room; coffer; chest etc. (*receptacle*) 191; depository etc. 636; till, -er; cash-box, -register, purse, pocketbook, wallet; money-bag, -belt, -box, *porte-monnaie*.

purse-strings; pocket, breeches pocket.

sinking fund; stocks; government –, public –, parliamentary- -stocks, – funds, – securities, bonds; gild-edged securities; Consols, Liberty bonds, government bonds, *crédit mobilier*.

803. Wealth.—N. wealth, riches, fortune, handsome fortune, opulence, affluence; good –, easy- circumstances; independence; competence etc. (*sufficiency*) 639; solvency, soundness, solidity.

provision, livelihood, maintenance; alimony, dowry; means, resources, substance; property etc. 780; command of money.

income etc. 810; capital, money; round sum etc. (*treasure*) 800; mint of money, mine of wealth, *El Dorado*, Pactolus, Golconda, Potosi, *bonanza*; philosopher's stone.

long –, full –, well lined –, heavy- purse; purse of Fortunatus.

pelf, Mammon, lucre, filthy lucre; loaves and fishes; fleshpots of Egypt.

rich –, moneyed –, warm- man; man of substance; capitalist, millionaire, Nabob, Croesus, Midas, Plutus, Dives, Timon of Athens; Timo-, Pluto-cracy; Danaë.

V. be -rich etc. *adj.*; roll –, wallow- in -wealth, – riches; have money to burn.

afford, well afford; command -money, – a sum; make both ends meet, hold one's head above water.

become -rich etc. *adj.*; fill one's -pocket etc. (*treasury*) 802; feather one's nest, clean up –, make- a fortune; make money etc. (*acquire*) 775.

enrich, imburse.

worship -Mammon, – the golden calf.

Adj. wealthy, rich, affluent, opulent, moneyed, monied, worth -a great deal, – much; well -to do, – off; warm; well –, provided for.

made of money; rich as Croesus; rolling in - riches, – wealth.

flush, – of -cash, – money, – tin; in -funds, – cash, – full feather; solvent, solid, sound, pecunious, out of debt, all straight; able to pay 20s in the L.

Phr. one's ship coming in.

804. Poverty.—N. poverty, indigence, penury, pauperism, destitution, want; need, -iness; lack,

necessity, privation, distress, difficulties, wolf at the door.

bad –, poor –, needy –, embarrassed –, reduced –, straitened- circumstances; slender –, narrow- means; straits; hand to mouth existence, *res angusta domi*, low water, impecuniosity.

beggary; mendi-cancy, -city; broken –, loss of-fortune; insolvency etc. (*non-payment*) 808.

empty -purse, – pocket; light purse; beggarly account of empty boxes.

poor man, pauper, mendicant, mumper, beggar, starveling; *pauvre diable.*

V. be -poor etc. *adj.*; want, lack, starve, live from hand to mouth, have seen better days, go down in the world, be on one's uppers, come upon the parish; go to -the dogs, – wrack and ruin; not have a -penny etc. (*money*) 800, – shot in one's locker; beg one's bread; *tirer le diable par la queue*; run into debt etc. (*debt*) 806.

render -poor etc. *adj.*; impoverish; reduce, – to poverty; pauperize, fleece, ruin, bring to the parish.

Adj. poor, indigent; poverty-stricken; badly –, poorly –, ill- off; poor as -a rat, – a church mouse, – Job's turkey, – Job; fortune-, dower-, money-, penni-less; unportioned, unmoneyed; impecunious; broke, flat; out –, short- of -money, – cash; without –, not worth- a rap etc. (*money*) 800; *qui n'a pas le sou*, out of pocket, hard up; out at -elbows, – heels; seedy, bare-footed; beggar-ly, - ed; destitute; fleeced, strapped, stripped; bereft, bereaved; reduced.

in -want etc. *n.*; needy, necessitous, distressed, pinched, straitened; put to one's -shifts, – last shifts; unable to -keep the wolf from the door, – make both ends meet; embarrassed, under hatches; involved etc. (*in debt*) 806; insolvent etc. (*not paying*) 808.

Adv. *in formâ pauperis.*

Phr. *zonam perdidit.*

805. Credit.—N. credit, trust, tick, score, tally, account.

letter of credit, circular note; duplicate; mortgage, lien, debenture, paper credit, floating capital; draft; securities.

creditor, lender, lessor, mortgagee; dun; usurer.

V. keep –, run up- an account with; entrust, credit, accredit.

place to one's -credit, – account; give –, take-credit; fly a kite.

Adj. credit-ing, -ed; accredited.

Adv. on -credit etc. *n.*; to the -account, – credit- of.

806. Debt.—N. debt, obligation, liability, indebtment, debit, score.

arrears, deferred payment, deficit, default; insolvency etc. (*non-payment*) 808; bad debt.

interest; usance, usury; premium; floating -debt, – capital.

debtor, debitor; mortgagor; defaulter etc. 808; borrower.

V. be -in debt etc. *adj.*; owe; incur –, contract- a debt etc. *n.*; run up -a bill, – a score, – an account; go on tick, put on the cuff; borrow etc. 788; run –, get- into debt; outrun the constable.

answer –, go bail- for; back one's note.

Adj. indebted; liable, chargeable, answerable for.

in -debt, – embarrassed circumstances, – difficulties; incumbered, involved; involved –, plunged –, deep –, over head and ears- in debt; deeply involved; fast tied up; insolvent etc. (*not paying*) 808; *minus*, out of pocket.

unpaid; unrequieted, unrewarded; owing, due, in arrear, outstanding.

807. Payment.—N. pay-, defray-ment; discharge; ac-, quittance; settlement, clearance, liquidation, satisfaction, reckoning, arrangement.

acknowledgment, release; receipt, – in full, – in full of all demands; voucher.

repayment, reimbursement, retribution; pay etc. (*reward*) 973; money paid etc. (*expenditure*) 809.

ready money etc. (*cash*) 800; stake, remittance, instalment.

payer, liquidator etc. 801.

V. pay, defray, make payment; pay -down, – on the nail, – ready money, – at sight, – in advance; cash, honor a bill, acknowledge; redeem; pay in kind.

pay one's -way, – shot, – footing;' pay -the piper, – sauce for all, – costs; do the needful; come across; shell –, fork- out; come down with, – the dust; tickle –, grease- the palm; expend etc. 809; put –, lay- down.

discharge, settle, quit, acquit oneself of; account –, reckon –, settle –, be even –, be quits- with; strike a balance; settle –, balance –, square- accounts with; quit scores; foot the bill; wipe –, clear- off old scores; satisfy; pay in full; satisfy –, pay in full of- all demands; clear, liquidate; pay - up, – old debts.

disgorge, make repayment; repay, refund, reimburse, retribute; make compensation etc. 30.

Adj. paying etc., paid etc. *v.*; owing nothing, out of debt, all straight, clear of -debt, – encumbrance; unowed, never indebted.

Adv. to the tune of; on the nail; money –, cashdown; cash on delivery.

808. Non-payment.—N. non-payment; default, defalcation; protest, repudiation; application of the sponge; whitewashing.

insolvency, bankruptcy, failure; overdraft, overdrawn account; insufficiency etc. 640; run upon a bank.

waste paper bonds; dishonored –, protested-bills; bogus cheque.

bankrupt, insolvent debtor, lame duck, man of straw, welsher, stag, defaulter, absconder, levanter.

V. non -pay etc. 807; fail, break, stop payment; become -insolvent, – bankrupt; be gazetted.

protest, dishonor, repudiate, nullify.

pay under protest; button up one's pockets, draw the purse strings; apply the sponge; pay over the left shoulder, get whitewashed; swindle etc. 791; run up bills, fly kites.

Adj. not paying; in debt etc. 806; behindhand, in arrear; beggared etc. (*poor*) 804; unable to make both ends meet; *minus*; worse than nothing.

insolvent, bankrupt, in the gazette, gazetted, ruined.

unpaid etc. (*outstanding*) 806; *gratis* etc. 815; unremunerated.

809. Expenditure.—N. expenditure, money going out; out-goings, -lay; expenses, disbursement; prime cost etc. (*price*) 812; circulation; run upon a bank.

[Money paid] payment etc. 807; pay etc. (*remuneration*) 973; bribe etc. 973; fee, footing, garnish; subsidy; tribute, Peter's pence; contingent, quota; donation etc. 784.

pay in advance, earnest, handsel, deposit, instalment.

investment; purchase etc. 795.

V. expend, spend; run –, get- through; pay, disburse; open –, loose –, untie- the purse strings; lay –, shell –, fork- out; bleed; make up a sum, invest, sink money.

fee etc. (*reward*) 973; pay one's way etc. (*pay*) 807; subscribe etc. (*give*) 784; subsidize, bribe.

Adj. expend-ing, -ed etc. *v.*; sumptuary, liberal etc. 816; openhanded, lavish etc. 818; extensive etc. 814.

810. Receipt—N. receipt, accountable –, conditional –, binding –, return- receipt; value received, money coming in; income, incomings, innings, revenue, return, proceeds; gross receipts, net profit; earnings etc. (*gain*) 775.

rent, – roll; rent-al, -age; rack-rent.

premium, *bonus*; sweepstakes, tontine, prize, drawing.

pension, annuity; jointure etc. (*property*) 780; alimony, pittance, emolument etc. (*remuneration*) 973.

V. receive etc. 785; take money; draw –, derive- from; get, be in receipt of, acquire etc. 775; take etc. 789.

bring in, yield, afford, pay, return; accrue etc. (*be received from*) 785.

Adj. receiv-ing, -ed etc. *v.*; profitable etc. (*gainful*) 775.

811. Accounts.—N. accounts, accompts; commercial –, monetary- arithmetic; statistics etc. (*numeration*) 85; money matters, finance, budget, bill, score, reckoning, account.

books, account book, ledger; day –, cash -, pass- book; journal; debtor and creditor –, cash –, petty cash –, running- account; account-current; balance, – sheet; *compte rendu*, account settled.

book-keeping, audit; double –, single- entry; reckoning etc. 85.

chartered –, certified public –, accountant; auditor, actuary, bookkeeper; financier etc. 801; accounting party.

V. keep accounts, enter, post, book, credit, debit, carry over; take stock; balance –, make up –, square –, settle –, wind up –, cast up –, add up –, tot up- accounts; make accounts square.

bring to book, audit, tax, surcharge and falsify.

falsify –, garble –, cook ∟, doctor- an account.

Adj. monetary etc. 800; account-able, -ing; statistical.

812. Price.—N. price, amount, cost, expense, prime cost, charge, figure, demand, damage, fare, hire; wages etc. (*remuneration*) 973.

dues, duty, toll, tax, impost, cess, sess, tallage, levy, capitation-, poll-, income-, sur-, sales-, super-tax; gabel, *gabelle*; gavel, *octroi*, custom, tariff, ex-cise, assessment, taxation, benevolence, tithe, tenths, exactment, ransom, salvage; broker-, wharf-, lighter-, ton-, freight-age.

worth, rate, value, valuation, appraisement, money's worth, par value; penny etc. -worth; price current, market price, quotation; what it will -fetch etc. *v.*

bill etc. (*account*) 811; shot.

V. bear –, set –, fix- a price; appraise, assess, price, charge, demand, ask, require, exact, run up; distrain; run up a bill etc. (*debt*) 806; have one's price; liquidate.

amount to, come to, mount up to; stand one in. fetch, sell for, cost, bring in, yield, afford.

Adj. priced etc. *v.*; to the tune of, *ad valorem*; mercenary, venal.

Phr. no penny, no paternoster; *point d'argent, point de Suisse*, no longer pipe, no longer dance, no song, no supper.

one may have it for.

813. Discount.—N. discount, abatement, con-cession, reduction, depreciation, allowance, qualification, set off, drawback, poundage, *agio*, percentage; rebate, -ment; backwardation, con-tango; salvage; tare and tret.

V. discount, bate; a-, re-bate; deduct, reduce, mark down, take off, allow, give, make allowance; tax, depreciate.

Adj. discounting etc. *v.*

Adv. at a discount, below par.

814. Dearness.—N. dearness etc. *adj.*; high –, famine –, fancy- price; overcharge; extravagance; exorbitance, extortion; heavy pull upon the purse; Pyrrhic victory.

V. be -dear etc. *adj.*; cost -much, – a pretty penny; rise in price, look up.

overcharge, bleed, fleece, skin, extort.

pay -too much, – through the nose, –, too dear for one's whistle.

Adj. dear; high, -priced; of great price, ex-pensive, costly, precious, worth a Jew's eye, dear bought; unreasonable, extravagant, exorbitant, ex-tortionate.

at a premium; not to be had, – for love or money; beyond –, above- price; priceless, of priceless value.

Adv. dear, -ly; at great –, heavy- cost; *à grands frais*.

Phr. prices looking up; *le jeu ne vaut pas la chandelle*.

815. Cheapness.—N. cheapness, low price; depreciation; bargain; good penny etc.- worth, *bon marché*.

[Absence of charge] gratuity; free -quarters, – seats, – admission, – warren; pass, Annie Oakley; run of one's teeth; nominal price, peppercorn rent; labor of love.

drug in the market.

V. be -cheap etc. *adj.*; cost little; come down –, fall- in price.

buy for -a mere nothing, – an old song; have one's money's worth; cheapen, beat down.

Adj. cheap; low, – priced; moderate, reasonable; in-, un-expensive; well –, worth the money; *magnifique et pas cher*; good –, cheap- at the price; dirt –, dog- cheap; cheap, -as dirt, – and nasty; catchpenny.

reduced, marked down, half-price, depreciated, unsaleable.

gratuitous, *gratis*, free, for love, – nothing; cost-expense-less; without charge, not charged, un-taxed; scot –, shot –, rent- free; free of -cost, – expense; honorary, unbought, unpaid, com-plimentary.

Adv. for a mere song; at -cost price, – prime cost, – a reduction, – a bargain; on the cheap.

816. Liberality.—N. liberality, generosity, munificence; bount-y, -eousness, -ifulness; hospitality; charity etc. (*beneficence*) 906.

benefactor, free giver, Lady Bountiful.

V. be -liberal etc. *adj.*; spend –, bleed- freely; shower down upon; open one's purse strings etc. (*disburse*) 809; spare no expense, give -with both hands, – carte blanche.

Adj. liberal, free, generous; charitable etc. (*beneficent*) 906; hospitable; bount-iful, -eous; handsome; unsparing, ungrudging; open-, free-, full-handed; open-, large-, free-hearted; munificent, princely, unstinting.

overpaid.

Adv. liberally, ungrudgingly, with open hand.

.817. Economy.—N. economy, frugality; thrift, -iness; prudence, care, husbandry, good housewifery, savingness, retrenchment.

savings; prevention of waste, save-all; cheese parings and candle ends; parsimony etc. 819.

V. be -economical etc. *adj.*; economize, save; retrench; cut- down expenses, – one's coat ac-cording to one's cloth, make both ends meet, keep within compass, meet one's expenses, pay one's way; keep one's head above water; husband etc. (*lay by*) 636; save –, invest- money; put out to in-terest; provide –, save- -for, – against- a rainy day; feather one's nest; look after the main chance.

Adj. economical, frugal, careful, thrifty, saving, chary, spare, sparing; parsimonious etc. 819. underpaid.

Adv. sparingly etc. *adj.*; *ne quid nimis*.

818. Prodigality.—N. prodi-gality, -gence; un-thriftiness, waste, -fulness; profus-ion, -eness; ex-travagance; squandering etc. *v.*; lavishness; malver-sation.

prodigal; spend-, waste-thrift; losel, play-boy, spender, squanderer, locust.

V. be -prodigal etc. *adj.*; squander, lavish, sow broadcast; pour forth like water; pay through the nose etc. (*dear*) 814; spill, waste, dissipate, exhaust, drain, eat out of house and home, overdraw, outrun the constable; run -out, – through; misspend; throw -good money after bad, – the helve after the hatchet; burn the candle at both ends; make ducks and drakes of one's money;

squander one's substance, spend money like water; fool –, potter –, muddle –, fritter –, throwaway one's money; pour water into a sieve, kill the goose that lays the golden eggs; *manger son blé en herbe.*

Adj. prodigal, profuse, thriftless, unthrifty, improvident, wasteful, losel, extravagant, lavish, dissipated, over liberal; full-handed etc. (*liberal*) 816.

penny wise and pound foolish:

Adv. with an unsparing hand; money burning one's pocket; recklessly profuse.

Int. hang the expense!

819. Parsimony.—N. parsimony, parcity; parsimoniousness, stinginess etc. *adj.*; stint; illiberality, avarice, tenacity, avidity, rapacity, extortion, venality, cupidity; selfishness etc. 943; *auri sacra fames.*

miser, niggard, churl, screw, tightwad, skinflint, crib, codger, muckworm, money-grubber, pinchfist, scrimp, lickpenny, hunks, curmudgeon, *Harpagon*, Silas Marner, harpy, extortioner, Jew, usurer.

V. be -parsimonious etc. *adj.*; grudge, begrudge, stint, skimp, pinch, gripe, screw, dole out, hold back, withhold, starve, famish, live upon nothing, skin a flint.

drive a -bargain, – hard bargain; cheapen, beat down; stop one hole in a sieve; have an itching palm, grasp, grab.

Adj. parsimonious, penurious, stingy, miserly, mean, shabby, peddling, scrubby, pennywise, near, niggardly, frugal to excess; close; fast-, close-, strait-handed; close-, hard-, tight-fisted; tight, sparing; chary, grudging, griping etc. *v.*; illiberal, ungenerous, churlish, hidebound, sordid, mercenary, venal, covetous, usurious, avaricious, greedy, extortionate, rapacious.

Adv. with a sparing hand.

820. Affections.—N. affections, character, qualities, disposition, nature, spirit, tone; temper, - ament; *diathesis*, idiosyncrasy; cast –, habit –, frame- of -mind, – soul; predilection, turn; natural –, turn of mind; bent, bias, predisposition, proneness, proclivity; propen-sity, -sedness, -sion, -dency; vein, humor, mood, grain, mettle; sympathy etc. (*love*) 897.

soul, heart, breast, bosom, inner man; heart's - core, – strings, – blood; heart of hearts, *penetralia mentis*; secret and inmost recesses of the –, cockles of one's- heart; inmost -heart, – soul; back-bone.

passion, pervading spirit; ruling –, masterpassion; *furore*; fulness of the heart, heyday of the blood, flesh and blood, flow of soul, force of character.

V. have –, possess- -affections etc. *n.*; be of a - character etc. *n.*; be -affected etc. *adj.*; breathe.

Adj. affected, characterized, formed, molded, cast; at-, tempered; framed; pre-, disposed; prone, inclined; having a -bias etc. *n.*; tinctured –, imbued –, penetrated –, eaten up- with.

inborn, inbred, ingrained, in the grain, congenital, inherent, bred in the bone; deep-rooted, ineffaceable, inveterate; pathoscopic.

Adv. in one's -heart etc. *n.*; at heart; heart and soul etc. 821; in the -vein, – mood.

821. Feeling.—N. feeling; suffering etc. *v.*; endurance, tolerance, sufferance, supportance, experience, response; sympathy etc. (*love*) 897; impression, inspiration, affection, sensation, emotion, pathos, deep sense.

fire, warmth, glow, unction, *gusto*, vehemence; ferv-or, -ency; heartiness, cordiality; earnestness, eagerness; *empressement*, ardor, zeal, passion, enthusiasm, *verve, furore*, fanaticism; excitation of feeling etc. 824; fulness of the heart etc. (*disposition*) 820; passion etc. (*state of excitability*) 825; ecstasy etc. (*pleasure*) 827.

blush, suffusion, flush; hectic; tingling, thrill, kick, turn, shock; agitation etc. (*irregular motion*) 315; quiver, heaving, flutter, flurry, fluster, twitter, tremor; throb, -bing; pulsation, palpitation, painting; trepid-, perturb-ation; ruffle, hurry of spirits, pother, stew, ferment.

V. feel; receive an -impression etc. *n.*; be - impressed with etc. *adj.*; entertain –, harbor –, cherish- -feeling etc. *n.*

respond; catch the -flame, – infection; enter the spirit of.

bear, suffer, support, sustain, endure, brook, thole, aby; abide etc. (*be composed*) 826; experience etc. (*meet with*) 151; taste, prove; labor –, smart- under; bear the brunt of, brave, stand.

swell, glow, warm, flush, blush, change color, mantle; turn -color, – pale, – red, – black in the face; blench; crimson, whiten, pale, tingle, thrill, heave, pant, throb, palpitate, go pit-a-pat, tremble, quiver, flutter, twitter; stagger, reel; shake etc. 315 be -agitated, – excited etc. 824; look -blue, – black; wince, draw a deep breath.

impress etc. (*excite the feelings*) 824.

Adj. feeling etc. *v.*; sentient; sensuous; sensorial, -y; emo-tive, -tional; of –, with- feeling etc. *n.*

warm, quick, lively, smart, strong, sharp, acute, cutting, piercing, incisive; keen, – as a razor; trenchant, pungent, racy, *piquant*, poignant, caustic.

impressive, deep, profound, indelible; deep-, home-, heart-felt; swelling, soul-stirring, deep-mouthed, heart-expanding, electric, thrilling, rapturous, ecstatic.

earnest, wistful, eager, breathless; fer-vent, -vid; gushing, passionate, warmhearted, hearty, cordial, sincere, zealous, enthusiastic, glowing, ardent, burning, red-hot, fiery, flaming; boiling, – over.

pervading, penetrating, absorbing; rabid, raving, feverish, fanatical, hysterical; impetuous etc. (*excitable*) 825; overmastering.

impressed –, moved –, touched –, affected –, penetrated –, seized –, imbued etc. 820- with; devoured by; wrought up etc. (*excited*) 824; struck all of a heap; rapt; in a -quiver etc. *n.*; enraptured etc. 829.

Adv. heart and soul, from the bottom of one's heart, *ab imo pectore, de profundis*, at heart, *con amore*, heartily, devoutly, over head and ears.

Phr. the heart -big, – full, – swelling, – beating, – pulsating, – throbbing, – thumping, – beating high, – melting, – overflowing, – bursting, – breaking.

822. Sensibility.—N. sensi-bility, -bleness, -tiveness; moral sensibility; impress-, affect-ibility; suscepti-bleness, -bility, -vity; mobility; viva-city, -ciousness; tender-, soft-ness; sentiment-ality, -ism.

excitability etc. 825; fastidiousness etc. 868; physical sensibility etc. 375.

sore -point, – place; where the shoe pinches.
V. be -sensible etc. *adj.*; have a -tender, –
warm. – sensitive- heart.
take to –, treasure up in the- heart; shrink.
'die of a rose in aromatic pain;' touch to the
quick.
Adj. sensi-ble, -tive; impressi-ble, -onable;
suscepti-ve, -ble; alive to, impassion-able, -ed;
gushing; warm-, tender-, soft-hearted; tender –, as
a chicken; soft, sentimental, romantic; enthusiastic,
highflying, spirited, mettlesome, vivacious, lively,
expressive, mobile, tremblingly alive; excitable etc.
825; over-sensitive, without skin, thin-skinned;
fastidious etc. 868.
Adv. sensibly etc. *adj.*; to the -quick, – inmost
core.

823. Insensibility.—N. insensi-bility, -bleness;
moral insensibility; inertness, *inertia, vis inertiae*;
impassi-bility, -bleness; inappetency, apathy,
phlegm, dulness, hebetude, supineness, lukewarmness, insusceptibility, unimpressibility.
cold -fit, – blood, – heart; cold-, cool-ness;
frigidity, *sang-froid*; stoicism, imperturbation etc.
(*inexcitability*) 826; nonchalance, unconcern, dry
eyes; *insouciance* etc. (*indifference*) 866;
recklessness etc. 863; callousness; heart of stone,
stock and stone, marble, deadness.
torp-or, -idity; obstupefaction, lethargy, coma,
trance; sleep etc. 683; suspended animation; stup-
or, -efaction; paralysis, palsy; numbness etc.
(*physical insensibility*) 376:
neutrality; quietism, vegetation.
V. be -insensible etc. *adj.*; have a rhinoceros
hide; show -insensibility etc *n.*; not -mind, – care.
– be affected by; have no desire for etc. 866; have
–, feel –, take- no interest in; *nil admirari*; not care
a -straw etc. (*unimportance*) 643 for; disregard etc.
(*neglect*) 460; set at naught etc. (*make light of*)
483; turn a deaf ear to etc. (*inattention*) 458;
vegetate.
render -insensible, – callous; blunt, obtund,
numb, benumb, paralyze, chloroform, deaden,
hebetate, stun, stupefy; brut-ify, -alize.
inure; harden, – the heart; steel, case-harden,
sear.
Adj. insensible, unconscious, impassi-ve, -ble;
blind to, deaf to, dead to; un-, in-susceptible; unim-
press-ionable, -ible; passion-, spirit-, heart-, soulless; unfeeling, unmoral.
apathetic; leuco-, phlegmatic; dull, frigid; cold, -
blooded, -hearted; unemotional; cold as charity;
flat, obtuse, inert, supine, sluggish, torpid; sleepy
etc. (*inactive*) 683; languid, half-hearted, tame;
numb, -ed; comatose; anesthetic etc. 376;
stupefied, chloroformed, palsy-stricken.
indifferent, lukewarm; Laodicean; careless, mindless, regardless; inattentive etc. 458; neglectful
etc. 460; disregarding.
unconcerned, *nonchalant, pococurante, insouciant, sans souci*; unambitious etc. 866.
un-affected, -ruffled, -impressed, -inspired, -
excited, -moved, -stirred, -touched, -shocked, -
struck; unblushing etc. (*shameless*) 885;
unanimated; vegetative.
callous, thick-skinned, pachydermatous, impervious; hard, -ened; inured, case-hardened;
steeled –, proof- against; imperturbable etc. (*inexcitable*) 826; unfelt.

Adv. insensibly etc. *adj.*; *aequo animo*; without
being -moved, – touched, – impressed; in cold
blood; with -dry eyes, – withers unwrung.
Phr. never mind; it is of no consequence etc.
(*unimportant*) 643; it cannot be helped; nothing
coming amiss; it is all -the same, – one- to.

824. Excitation.—N. excitation of feeling;
mental –, excitement; suscitation, galvanism,
stimulation, piquancy, provocation inspiration,
calling forth, infection; interest, animation,
agitation, perturbation; subjugation, fascination,
intoxication; en-, ravishment; entrancement, high
pressure.
unction, impressiveness etc. *adj.*; emotional appeal; melodrama; psychological moment, crisis;
sensationalism.
trail of temper, *casus belli*; irritation etc. (*anger*)
900; passion etc. (*state of excitability*) 825; thrill
etc. (*feeling*) 821; repression of feeling etc. 826.
V. excite, affect, touch, move, impress, strike, interest, intrigue, animate, inspire, impassion, smite,
infect; stir –, fire –, warm- the blood; set astir; a-,
wake; a-, waken; call forth; e-, pro-voke; raise up,
summon up, call up, wake up, blow up, get up,
light up; raise; get up steam, rouse, arouse, stir, fire,
kindle, enkindle, apply the torch, set on fire, inflame, illuminate.
stimulate; ex-, suscitate; inspirit; spirit up, stir up,
work up; infuse life into, five new life to; bring –,
introduce- new blood; quicken; sharpen, whet;
work upon etc. (*incite*) 615; hurry on, give a fillip,
put on one's mettle.
fan the -fire, – flame; blow the coals, stir the
embers; fan, – into a flame; foster, heat, warm,
foment, raise to a fever heat; keep -up, – the pot
boiling; revive, rekindle; rake up, rip up.
stir –, play on –, come home to- the feelings;
touch -a string, – a chord, – the soul, – the
heart; go to one's heart, penetrate, pierce, go
through one, touch to the quick, open the wound;
possess –, pervade –, penetrate –, imbrue –,
absorb –, affect –, disturb- the soul.
absorb, rivet the attention; sink into the -mind,
– heart; prey on the mind; intoxicate; over-whelm,
-power; *bouleverser*, upset, turn one's head.
fascinate; enrapture etc. (*give pleasure*) 829.
agitate, perturb, ruffle, fluster, flutter, shake,
disturb, faze, startle, shock, stagger; give one a -
shock, – turn; strike -dumb, – all of a heap; stun,
astound, electrify, galvanize, petrify.
irritate, sting; cut, – to the -heart, – quick; try
one's temper; fool to the top of one's bent, pique;
infuriate, madden, make one's blood boil; lash into
fury etc. (*wrath*) 900.
be -excited etc. *adj.*; flash up, flare up; catch the
infection; thrill etc. (*feel*) 821; mantle; work
oneself up; seethe, boil, simmer, foam, fume,
flame, rage, rave; run mad etc. (*passion*) 825.
Adj. excited etc. *v.*; wrought up, on the *qui vive*,
astir, sparkling; in a -quiver etc. 821, – fever, –
ferment, – blaze, – state of excitement; in
hysterics; black in the face, over-wrought; hot, red-
hot, flushed, feverish; all -of a twitter, – of a flutter, – of a dither, – in a pucker; with -quivering
lips, – tears in one's eyes.
flaming, boiling, – over; ebullient, seething;
foaming, – at the mouth; fuming, raging, carried
away by passion, wild, raving, frantic, mad, dis-

tracted, distraught, beside oneself, out of one's wits, amuck, ready to burst, *bouleversé*, demoniacal.

lost, *eperdu*, tempest-tossed; haggard; ready to sink.

stung to the quick, up, on one's high ropes.

exciting etc. *v.*; impressive, warm, glowing, fervid, swelling, imposing, spirit-stirring, thrilling; high-wrought; soul-stirring, -subduing; heart-swelling, -thrilling; agonizing etc. (*painful*) 830; telling, sensational, melodramatic, hysterical; overpowering, -whelming; more than flesh and blood can bear.

piquant etc. (*pungent*) 392; spicy, appetizing, provocative, *provaquant*, tantalizing.

Adv. till one is black in the face.

Phr. the heart -beating high, – going pit-a-pat, – leaping into one's mouth; the blood -being up, – boiling in one's veins; the eye -glistening. – 'in a fine frenzy rolling;' the head turned.

825. Excitability. [Excess of sensitiveness.]—**N.** excitability, impetuosity, vehemence; boisterousness etc. *adj.*; turbulence; impatience, intolerance, non-endurance; irritability etc. (*irascibility*) 901; itching etc. (*desire*) 865; wincing; disquiet, -ude; restlessness; fidge-ts, -tiness; agitation etc. (*irregular motion*) 315.

trepidation, perturbation, ruffle, hurry, -skurry, fuss, flurry; fluster, flutter; pother, stew, ferment; whirl; thrill etc. (*feeling*) 821; state –, fever- of excitement; transport.

passion, excitement, flush, heat; fever, -heat; fire, flame, fume, blood boiling; tumult; effervescence, ebullition; boiling, – over; whiff, gust, storm, tempest; scene, breaking out, burst, fit, paroxysm, explosion; out-break, -burst; agony.

violence etc. 173; fierceness etc. *adj.*; rage, fury, *furor*, *furore*, desperation, madness, distraction, raving, delirium, brain storm; frenzy, hysterics; intoxication; tearing –, raging- passion, towering rage; anger etc. 900.

fascination, infatuation, fanaticism; Quixot-ism, -ry; *tête montée*.

V. be -impatient etc. *adj.*; not be able to -bear etc. 826; bear ill, wince, chafe, champ the bit; be in a -stew etc. *n.*; be out of all patience, fidget, fuss, not have a wink of sleep; toss, – on one's pillow.

lose one's temper etc. 900; break –, burst –, fly- out; go –, fly- -off, – off the handle, – off at a tangent; explode; flare up, flame up, fire up, burst into a flame, take fire, fire, burn; boil, – over; foam, fume, rage, rave, rant, tear; go –, run- -wild, – mad; run -riot, – amuck; *battre la campagne, faire le diable à quatre*, play the deuce; raise -Cain, – the devil.

Adj. excitable, easily excited, in an excitable state; high strung; irritable etc. (*irascible*) 901; impatient, intolerant.

feverish, febrile, hysterical; delirious, mad, moody, maggoty-headed.

unquiet, mercurial, electric, galvanic, hasty, hurried, restless, fidgety, fussy; chafing etc. *v.*

startlish, mettlesome, high mettled, skittish.

vehement, demonstrative, violent, wild, furious, fierce, fiery, hot-headed, mad-cap.

over-zealous, enthusiastic, impassioned, fanatical; rabid etc. (*eager*) 865.

rampant, clamorous, uproarious, turbulent, tempestuous, tumultuary, boisterous.

impulsive, impetuous, passionate; uncontroll-ed, -able; ungovernable, irrepressible, stanchless, inextinguishable, burning, simmering, volcanic, ready to burst forth.

excit-ed, -ing etc. 824.

Int. pish! pshaw!

Phr. *noli me tangere*.

826. Inexcitability. [Absence of excitability, or of excitement.]—**N.** inexcit- imperturb-, inirritability; even temper, tranquil mind, dispassion; tolerance, toleration, patience.

passiveness etc. (*physical inertness*) 172; hebetude, -ation; impassibility etc. (*insensibility*) 823; stupefaction.

coolness, calmness etc. *adj.*; composure, placidity, indisturbance, imperturbation, *sang-froid*, tranquility, serenity; quiet, -ude; peace of mind, mental calmness.

staidness etc. *adj.*; gravity, sobriety, Quakerism; philosophy, equanimity, stoicism, command of temper; self-possession, -control, -command, -restraint; presence of mind.

submission etc. 725; resignation; suffer-, support-, endur-, long-suffer-, forbear-ance; longanimity; fortitude; patience -of Job, – 'on a monument,' – 'sovereign o'er transmuted ill;' moderation; repression –, subjugation- of feeling; restraint etc. 751.

tranquilization etc. (*moderation*) 174.

V. be -composed etc. *adj.*

laisser -faire, – aller; take things -easily, – as they come; take it easy, run on, live and let live; take -easily, – cooly, – in good part; *aequam serva e mentem*.

bear – well, – the brunt; go through, support, endure, brave, disregard.

tolerate, suffer, stand, bide; abide, aby; bear –, put up –, abide- with; acquiesce; submit etc. (*yield*) 725; submit with a good grace; resign –, reconcile- oneself to; brook, digest, eat, swallow, pocket, stomach; make -light of, – the best of, – a virtue of necessity; put a good face on, keep one's countenance; carry -on, – through; check etc. 751- oneself.

compose, appease etc. (*moderate*) 174; propitiate; repress etc. (*restrain*) 751; render insensible etc. 823; overcome –, allay –, repress-one's -excitability etc. 825; master one's feelings.

make -oneself, – one's mind- easy; set one's mind at -ease, – rest.

calm –, cool- down; thaw, grow cool.

be -borne, – endured; go down.

Adj. in-, un-excitable; imperturbable; un-susceptible etc. (*insensible*) 823; un-, dis-passionate; cold-blooded, inirritable; enduring etc. *v.*; stoical, Platonic, philosophic, staid, stayed; sober, – minded; grave; sober –, grave- as a judge; sedate, demure, cool-, level-headed; steady.

easy-going, peaceful, placid, calm; quiet, – as a mouse; tranquil, serene; cool, – as -a cucumber, – custard; undemonstrative.

temperate etc. (*moderate*) 174; composed, collected; un-excited, -stirred, -ruffled, -disturbed, -perturbed, -impassioned; unoffended; unresisting.

meek, tolerant, patient, – as Job; submissive etc. 725; tame; content, resigned, chastened, subdued, lamblike; gentle, – as a lamb; *suaviter in modo*; mild, – as mother's milk; soft as peppermint; armed with patience, bearing with, clement, forbearant, long-suffering.

Adv. 'like patience on a monument smiling at grief;' *aequo animo*, in cold blood etc. 823; more in sorrow than in anger.

Int. patience! and shuffle the cards.

827. Pleasure.—N. pleasure, gratification, enjoyment, fruition; ob-, de-lectation; relish, zest; *gusto* etc. (*physical pleasure*) 377; satisfaction etc. (*content*) 831; complacency.

well-being; good etc. 618; snugness, comfort, ease; cushion etc. 215; *sans souci*, mind at ease.

joy, gladness, delight, glee, cheer, sunshine; cheerfulness etc. 836.

treat, refreshment; frolic, fun, lark, gambol, merry-making; amusement etc. 840; luxury etc. 377; hedonism.

mens sana in corpore sano.

happiness, felicity, bliss; beati-tude, -fication; enchantment, transport, rapture, ravishment, ecstasy; *summum bonum*; paradise, elysium etc. (*heaven*) 981; third –, seventh- heaven; unalloyed - happiness etc.

honeymoon; palmy –, halcyon- days; golden - age, – time; *Saturnia regna*, Eden, Arcadia, happy valley, Agapemone; Cockaigne.

V. be pleased etc. 829; feel –, experience-pleasure etc. *n*.; joy; enjoy –, hug- oneself; be in - clover etc. 377, – elysium etc. 981; tread on enchanted ground; fall –, go- into raptures.

feel at home, breathe freely, bask in the sunshine.

be -pleased etc. 829- with; receive –, derive-pleasure etc. *n*.- from; take -pleasure etc. *n*.- in; delight in, rejoice in, indulge in, luxuriate in; gloat over etc. (*physical pleasure*) 377; enjoy, relish, like; love etc. 897; take -to, – a fancy to; have a liking for; enter into the spirit of.

take in good part.

treat oneself to, solace oneself with.

Adj. pleased etc. 829; not sorry; glad, -some; pleased as Punch.

happy, blest, blessed, blissful, beatified; happy as -a king, – the day is long; thrice happy, *ter quaterque beatus*; enjoying etc. *v*.; joyful etc. (*in spirits*) 836; hedonic.

in -a blissful state, – paradise etc. 981; – raptures, – ecstasies, – a transport of delight.

comfortable etc. (*physical pleasure*) 377; at ease; content etc. 831; *sans souci*, in clover.

overjoyed, entranced, enchanted; enraptured; en-, trans-ported; fascinated, captivated.

with -a joyful face, – sparkling eyes.

pleasing etc. 829; ecstatic, beat-ic, -ific; painless, unalloyed, without alloy, cloudless.

Adv. happily etc. *adj*.; with pleasure etc. (*willingly*) 60; with -glee etc. *n*.

phr. one's heart leaping with joy.

828. Pain.—N. mental suffering, pain, dolor; suffer-ing, -ance; ache, smart etc. (*physical pain*) 378; passion.

displeasure, dissatisfaction, discomfort, discomposure, disquiet; *malaise*; inquietude, uneasiness, vexation of spirit; taking; discontent etc. 832.

dejection etc. 837; weariness etc. 841.

annoyance, irritation, worry, infliction, visitation; plague, bore; bother, -ation; stew, vexation, mortification, chagrin, *esclandre*; *mauvais quart d'heure*.

care, anxiety, solicitude, trouble, trial, ordeal, fiery ordeal, shock, blow, cark, dole, fret, burden, load.

concern, grief, sorrow, distress, affliction, woe, bitterness, gloom, heartache; heavy –, aching –, bleeding –, broken- heart; heavy affliction, gnawing grief; unhappiness, infelicity, misery, tribulation, wretchedness, desolation; despair etc. 859; extremity, prostration, depth of misery.

nightmare, *ephialtes*, incubus.

anguish, agony; throe, tor-ture, -ment; crucifixion, martyrdom; pang, twinge, stab; the rack, the stake; purgatory etc. (*hell*) 982.

hell upon earth; iron age, reign of terror; slough of despond etc. (*adversity*) 735; peck –, sea- of troubles; ills that flesh is heir to etc. (*evil*) 619; miseries of human life; unkindest cut of all.

sufferer, victim, prey, martyr, object of compassion, wretch, shorn lamb.

V. feel –, suffer –, experience –, undergo –, bear –, endure- pain etc. *n*.; smart, ache etc. (*physical pain*) 378; suffer, bleed, ail; be the victim of; bear – take up- the cross.

labor under afflictions; quaff the bitter cup, have a bad time of it; fall on evil days etc. (*adversity*) 735; go hard with, come to grief, fall a sacrifice to, drain the cup of misery to the dregs, sup full of horrors.

sit on thorns, be on pins and needles, wince, fret, chafe, worry oneself, be in a taking, fret and fume, take -on, – to heart.

grieve; mourn etc. (*lament*) 839; yearn, repine, pine, droop, languish, sink; give way; despair etc. 859; break one's heart; weigh upon the heart etc. (*inflict pain*) 830.

Adj. in –, in a state of –, full of- pain etc. *n*.; suffering etc. *v*.; pained, afflicted, worried, displeased etc. 830; aching, griped, sore etc. (*physical pain*) 378; on the rack; in limbo; between hawk and buzzard.

un-comfortable, -easy; ill at ease; in a -taking, – way; disturbed; discontented etc. 832; out of humor etc. 901a; weary etc. 841.

heavy laden, stricken, crushed, a prey to, victimized, ill-used.

unfortunate etc. (*hapless*) 735; to be pitied, doomed, devoted, accursed, undone, lost, stranded.

unhappy, infelicitous, poor, wretched, miserable, woe-begone; cheerless etc. (*dejected*) 837; careworn.

concerned, sorry; sorrow-ing, -ful; cut up, chagrined, horrified, horror-stricken; in –, plunged in –, a prey to- grief etc. *n*.; in tears etc. (*lamenting*) 839; steeped to the lips in misery; heart-stricken, -broken, -scalded; broken-hearted; in despair etc. 859.

Phr. 'the iron entered into our soul;' *haeret lateri lethalis arundo;*' one's heart bleeding.

829. Pleasurableness. [Capability of giving pleasure; cause or source of pleasure.]**—N.** pleasurable-, pleasant-, agreeable-ness etc. *adj*.; pleasure giving, jocundity, delectability; amusement etc. 840.

attraction etc. (*motive*) 615; attractiveness, –

ability; invitingness etc. *adj.*; charm, fascination, captivation, enchantment, witchery, seduction, winsomeness, winning ways, amenity, amiability, sweetness.

loveliness etc. (*beauty*) 845; sunny –, brightside; sweets etc. (*sugar*) 396; goodness etc. 648; manna in the wilderness, land flowing with milk and honey.

treat; regale etc. (*physical pleasure*) 377; dainty; tit-, tid-bit; nuts, *sauce piquante*.

V. cause –, produce –, create –, give –, afford –, procure –, offer –, present –, yield-pleasure etc. 827.

please, charm, delight; gladden etc. (*make cheerful*) 836; take, captivate, fascinate; enchant, entrance, enrapture, transport, bewitch; en-, ravish.

bless, beatify; satisfy; gratify –, desire etc. 865; slake, satiate, quench; indulge, humor, flatter, tickle; tickle the palate etc. (*savory*) 394; regale, refresh; enliven; treat; amuse etc. 840; take –, tickle –, hit- one's fancy; meet one's wishes; win –, gladden –, rejoice –. warm the cockles of- the heart; do one's heart good.

attract, allure etc. (*move*) 615; stimulate etc. (*excite*) 824; interest, intrigue.

make things pleasant, popularize, gild the pill, sweeten.

Adj. causing pleasure etc. *v.*; pleasure-giving; pleas-ing, -ant, -urable; agreeable, cushy; grat-eful, -ifying; leef, lief, acceptable; welcome, – as the roses in May; welcomed; favorite; to one's -taste, – mind, – liking, – heart's content; satisfactory etc. (*good*) 648.

refreshing; comfortable; cordial; genial; glad, -some; sweet, delectable, nice, dainty; delic-ate, -ious; dulcet; luscious etc. 396; palatable etc. 394; luxurious, voluptuous; sensual etc. 377.

attractive etc. 615; inviting, prepossessing, engaging; win-ning, -some; taking, fascinating, captivating, seducing, -tive; alluring, enticing; appetizing etc. (*exciting*) 824; cheering etc. 836; bewitching; interesting, absorbing, enchanting, entrancing, enravishing.

charming; delightful, felicitous, exquisite; lovely etc. (*beautiful*) 845; ravishing, rapturous; heartfelt, thrilling, ecstatic; beat-ic, -ific; seraphic; empyrean; elysian etc. (*heavenly*) 981.

palmy, halcyon, Saturnian.

Phr. *decies repetita placebit.*

830. Painfulness. [Capability of giving pain; cause or source of pain.]—N. painfulness etc. *adj.* ; trouble, care etc. (*pain*) 828; trial; af-, in-fliction; cross, blow, stroke, burden, load, curse; bitter -pill,' – draught, – cup; waters of bitterness.

annoyance, grievance, nuisance, vexation, mortification, sickener; bore, bother, pother, hot water, sea of troubles, hornet's nest, plague, pest.

cancer, ulcer, sting, thorn; canker etc. (*bane*) 663; scorpion etc. (*evil-doer*) 913; dagger etc. (*arms*) 727; scourge etc. (*instrument of punishment*) 975; carking –, canker worm of- care.

mishap, misfortune etc. (*adversity*) 735; *désagrément, esclandre*, rub.

source of -irritation, – annoyance; wound, sore subject, skeleton in the closet; thorn in -the flesh, – one's side; where the shoe pinches, gall and wormwood.

sorry sight, heavy news, provocation; affront etc. 929; head and front of one's offending.

infestation, molestation; malignity etc. (*malevolence*) 907.

V. cause –, occasion –, give –, bring –, induce –, produce –, create –, inflict- pain etc. 828; pain, hurt, wound.

pinch, prick, gripe etc. (*physical pain*) 378; pierce, lancinate, cut.

hurt –, wound –, grate upon –, jar upon- the feelings; wring –, pierce –, lacerate –, break –, rend- the heart; make the heart bleed; tear –, rend- the heart-strings; draw tears from the eyes.

sadden; make -unhappy etc. 828; plunge into sorrow, grieve, fash, afflict, distress; cut -up, – to the heart.

displease, annoy, incommode, discommode, discompose, trouble, disquiet, disturb, thwart, cross, perplex, molest, tease, rag, tire, irk, vex, mortify, wherret, worry, plague, bother, pester, bore, pother, harass, harry, badger, heckle, bait, beset, infest, persecute, importune, be troublesome.

wring, harrow, torment, torture; put to the -rack, – question; break on the wheel, rack, scarify; cruci-ate, -fy; convulse, agonize; barb the dart; plant a -dagger in the breast, – thron in one's side.

irritate, provoke, sting, nettle, try the patience, pique, fret, rile, tweak the nose, chafe, gall; sting –, wound –, cut- to the quick; aggrieve, affront, enchafe, enrage, ruffle, sour the temper; give offence etc. (*resentment*) 900.

maltreat, bite, snap at, assail, bully; smite etc. (*punish*) 972.

sicken, disgust, revolt, nauseate, disenchant, repel, offend, shock, stink in the nostrils; go against –, turn- the stomach; make one sick, set the teeth on edge; go against the grain, grate on the ear; stick in one's -throat, – gizzard; rankle, gnaw, corrode, horrify, appal, freeze the blood; chill the spine; make the -flesh creep, – hair stand on end; make the blood -curdle, – run cold; make one shudder.

haunt, – the memory; weigh –, prey- on the -heart, – mind, – spirits; bring one's grey hairs with sorrow to the grave; add a nail to one's coffin.

Adj. causing pain, hurting etc. *v.*; hurtful etc. (*bad*) 649; painful; dolor-ific, -ous; unpleasant; un-, dis-pleasing; disagreeable, unpalatable, bitter, distasteful; uninviting; unwelcome; undesir-able, -ed; obnoxious; unacceptable, unpopular, thankless.

unsatisfactory, untoward, unlucky, uncomfortable.

distressing; afflict-ing, -ive; joy-, cheer-, comfort-less; dismal, disheartening; depress-ing, -ive; dreary, melancholy, grievous, piteous; woeful, rueful, mournful, deplorable, pitiable, lamentable; sad, affecting, touching, pathetic.

· irritating, provoking, stinging, annoying, aggravating, mortifying, galling; unaccommodating, invidious, vexatious; trouble-, tire-, irk-, weari-some; plagu-ing, -y; awkward.

importunate; teas-, pester-, bother-, harass-, worry-, torment-, cark-ing.

in-toler-, -suffer-, -support-able; un-bear-, -endur-able; past bearing; not to be -borne, – endured; more than flesh and blood can bear; enough to -drive one mad, – provoke a saint, – make a parson swear, – try the patience of Job.

shocking, terrific, grim, appalling, crushing; dreadful, fearful, frightful; thrilling, tremendous, dire; heart-breaking, -rending, -wounding, -corroding, -sickening; harrowing, rending.

odious, hateful, execrable, repulsive, repellent, abhorrent; horri-d, -ble, -fic, -fying; offensive; nause-ous, -ating; disgust-, sicken-, revolt-ing; nasty; loath-some, -ful; fulsome; vile etc. (*bad*) 649; hideous etc. 846.

sharp, acute, sore, severe, grave, hard, harsh, cruel, biting, acrimonious, caustic; cutting, corroding, consuming, racking, excruciating, searching, searing, grinding, grating, agonizing; envenomed.

ruinous, disastrous, calamitous, tragical; desolating, withering; burdensome, onerous, oppressive; cumb-rous, -ersome.

Adv. painfully etc. *adj.*; with -pain etc. 828; deuced.

Int. *hinc illae lachrymae!* woe is me!

Phr. *surgit amari aliquid*; the place being too hot to hold one; the iron entering the soul.

831. Content.—N. content, -ment, -edness; complacency, satisfaction, entire satisfaction, ease, heart's ease, peace of mind; serenity etc. 826; cheerfulness etc. 836; ray of comfort; comfort etc. (*well-being*) 827.

re-, conciliation; resignation etc. (*patience*) 826.
waiter on Providence.

V. be -content etc. *adj.*; rest -satisfied, – and be thankful; take the good the gods provide, let well alone, feel oneself at home, hug oneself, lay the flattering unction to one's soul.

take -up with, – in good part; assent etc. 488; be reconciled to, make one's peace with; get over it; take -heart, – comfort; put up with etc. (*bear*) 826.

render -content etc. *adj.*; set at ease, comfort; set one's -heart, – mind- at -ease, – rest; speak peace; conciliate, reconcile, win over, propitiate, disarm, beguile; content, satisfy; gratify etc. 829.

be -tolerated etc. 826; go down, – with; do.

Adj. content, -ed; satisfied etc. *v.*; at -ease, – one's ease, – home; with the mind at ease, *sans souci, sine curâ*, easy-going, not particular; conciliatory; unrepining, of good comfort; resigned etc. (*patient*) 826; cheerful etc. 836.

un-afflicted, -vexed, -molested, -plagued; serene etc. 826; at rest; snug, comfortable; in one's element.

satisfactory, satisfying, ample, sufficient, adequate, tolerable.

Adv. to one's heart's content; *à la bonne heure*; all for the best.

Int. amen etc. (*assent*) 488; very well, so much the better, well and good; it –, that- will do; it cannot be helped.

Phr. nothing comes amiss.

832. Discontent.—N. discontent, -ment; dissatisfaction; dissent etc. 489; labor unrest.

disappointment, mortification; cold comfort; regret etc. 833; repining, taking on etc. *v.*; inquietude, vexation of spirit, soreness; heart-burning, -grief; querulousness etc. (*lamentation*) 839; hypercriticism.

malcontent, grumbler, growler, croaker, *laudator temporis acti*; censurer, complainer,

faultfinder, murmurer, Adullamite, Diehard, Bitterender.

the Opposition, cave of Adullam, indignation meeting, 'winter of our discontent.'

V. be -discontented etc. *adj.*; quarrel with one's bread and butter; repine; regret etc. 833; wish one at the bottom of the Red Sea; take -on, – to heart; shrug the shoulders; make a wry –, pull a longface; knit one's brows; look -blue, – black, – black as thunder, – blank, – glum.

take -in bad part, – ill; fret, chafe, make a piece of work; grumble, croak, grouse; lament etc. 839.

cause -discontent etc. *n.*; dissatisfy, disappoint, mortify, put out, disconcert; cut up; dishearten.

Adj. discontented; dissatisfied etc. *v.*; unsatisfied, ungratified; dissident; dissentient etc. 489; malcontent, exigent, exacting, hypercritical.

repining etc. *v.*; regretful etc. 833; down in the mouth etc. (*dejected*) 837.

in -high dudgeon, – a fume, – the sulks, – the dumps, – bad humor; glum, sulky; sour, – as a crab; soured, sore; out of -humor, – temper.

disappointing etc. *v.*; unsatisfactory.

Int. so much the worse!

Phr. that –, it- will never do.

833. Regret.—N. regret, repining; home sickness, nostalgia; *mal –, maladie- du pays*; lamentation etc. 839; contrition, compunction, penitence etc. 950.

bitterness, heart-burning.

laudator temporis acti etc. (*discontent*) 832.

V. regret, deplore; bewail etc. (*lament*) 839; repine, cast a longing lingering look behind; rue, – the day; repent etc. 950; *infandum renovare dolorem*.

prey –, weigh –, have a weight- on the mind; leave an aching void.

Adj. regretting etc. *v.*; regretful; home-sick.

regretted etc. *v.*; much to be regretted, regrettable; lamentable etc. (*bad*) 649.

Int. what a pity! hang it!

Phr. 'tis -pity, – too true.

834. Relief.—N. relief; deliverance; refreshment etc. 689; easement, softening, alleviation, mitigation, palliation etc. 174; soothing, lullaby; cradle song, *berceuse*.

solace, consolation, comfort, encouragement.

lenitive, restorative etc. (*remedy*) 662; poultice etc. *v.*; cushion etc. 215; crumb of comfort, balm in Gilead; aspirin.

V. relieve, ease, alleviate, mitigate, palliate, soothe, adduce; salve; soften, – down; foment, stupe, poultice; assuage, allay.

cheer, comfort, console; encourage, bear up, pat on the back, give comfort, set at ease; enliven, gladden –, cheer- the heart.

remedy; cure etc. (*restore*) 660; refresh; pour -balm into, – oil on.

smoothe the ruffled brow of care, temper the wind to the shorn-lamb, lay the flattering unction to one's soul.

disburden etc. (*free*) 705; take off a load of care.

be relieved; breathe more freely, draw a long breath; take comfort; dry –, wipe- the -tears, – eyes.

Adj. relieving etc. *v.*; consolatory, soothing; assua-ging, -sive; bal-my, -samic; lenitive, palliative; anodyne etc. (*remedial*) 662; curative etc. 660.

835. Aggravation.—**N.** aggravation, heightening; exacerbation; exasperation; overestimation etc. 482; exaggeration etc. 549.

V. aggravate, render worse, heighten, embitter, sour; ex-, acerbate; exasperate, envenom; tease, provoke, enrage.

add fuel to the -fire, – flame; fan the flame etc. (*excite*) 824; go from bad to worse etc. (*deteriorate*) 659.

Adj. aggravated etc. *v.*; worse, unrelieved; aggravable; aggravating etc. *v.*

Adv. out of the frying pan into the fire, from bad to worse, worse and worse.

Int. so much the worse!

836. Cheerfulness.—**N.** cheerfulness etc. *adj.*; geniality, gaiety, *l'allegro*, cheer, good humor, spirits; high –, animal –, flow of- spirits; glee, high glee, light heart; sunshine of the -mind, – breast; *gaieté de coeur*, *bon naturel*.

liveliness etc. *adj.*; life, alacrity, vivacity, animation, *allégresse*; jocundity, joviality, jollity; levity; jocularity etc. (*wit*) 842.

mirth, merriment, hilarity, exhilaration; laughter etc. 838; merry-making etc. (*amusement*) 840; heyday, rejoicing etc. 838; marriage bells.

nepenthe, Euphrosyne.

optimism etc. (*hopefulness*) 858; self-complacency.

V. be -cheerful etc. *adj.*; have the mind at ease, smile, put a good face upon, keep up one's spirits; view -the bright side of the picture, – things *en couleur de rose*; *ridentem dicere verum*, cheer up, brighten up, light up, bear up; chirp, take heart, cast away care, drive dull care away, perk up.

rejoice etc. 838; carol, chirrup, lilt; frisk, rollick, give a loose to mirth.

cheer, enliven, elate, exhilarate, gladden, inspirit, animate, raise the spirits, inspire; put in good humor; cheer –, rejoice- the heart; delight etc. (*give pleasure*) 829.

Adj. cheerful; happy etc. 827; cheer-y, -ly; of good cheer, smiling; blithe; in –, in good- spirits; in high -spirits, – feather; happy as -the day is long, – a king; gay, – as a lark; *allegro*; light, - some, -hearted; buoyant, *débonnaire*, bright, free and easy, airy; janty, jaunty, canty; spright-ly, -ful; spry; spirit-ed, -ful; lively, animated, breezy, vivacious; brisk, – as a bee; sparkling; sportive; full of -play, – spirit; all alive.

sunny, palmy; hopeful etc. 858.

merry, – as a -cricket, – grig, – marriage bell; joyful, joyous, jocund, jovial; jolly, – as a thrush. – as a sandboy; blithesome; glee-ful, -some; hilarious, rattling.

winsome, bonny, hearty, buxom.

play-ful, -some; *folâtre*, playful as a kitten, tricksy, frisky, frolicsome; gamesome; jocose, jocular, waggish; mirth-, laughter-loving; mirthful, rollicking.

elate, -d; exulting, jubilant, flushed; rejoicing etc. 838; cock-a-hoop.

cheering, inspiriting, exhilarating; cardiac, -al; pleasing etc. 829; flourishing, halcyon.

Adv. cheerfully etc. *adj.*

Int. never say die! come! cheer up! hurrah! etc. 838; 'hence loathed melancholy!' begone dull care! away with melancholy!

837. Dejection.—**N.** dejection; dejectedness etc. *adj.*; depression, prosternation; lowness –, depression- of spirits; weight –, oppression –, damp- on the spirits; low –, bad –, drooping –, depressed- spirits; heart sinking; heaviness –, failure- of heart.

heaviness etc. *adj.*; infestivity, gloom; weariness etc. 841; *taedium vitae*, disgust of life; *mal du pays* etc. (*regret*) 833.

melancholy; sadness etc. *adj.*; *il penseroso*, *melancholia*, dismals, mumps, mopes, lachrymals, dumps, blues, blue devils, doldrums, vapors, megrims, spleen, horrors, hypochondriasis, pessimism; despondency, slough of Despond; disconsolateness etc. *adj.*; hope deferred, blank despondency.

prostration, – of soul; broken heart; despair etc. 859; cave of -despair, – Trophonius.

demureness etc. *adj.*; gravity, solemnity; long –, grave- face.

hypochondriac, seek-sorrow, self-tormentor, *heautontimorumenos*, *malade imaginaire*, *médecin tant pis*; croaker, pessimist; mope, mopus. [Cause of dejection] affliction etc. 830; sorry sight; *memento mori*; damper, wet blanket, Job's comforter; death's head, skeleton at the feast.

V. be -dejected etc. *adj.*; grieve; mourn etc. (*lament*) 839; take on, give way, lose heart, despond, droop, sink.

lower, look downcast, frown, pout; hang down the head; pull –, make- a long face; laugh on the wrong side of the mouth; grin a ghastly smile; look -blue, – like a drowned man; lay –, take- to heart.

mope, brood over; fret; sulk; pine, – away; yearn; repine etc. (*regret*) 833; despair etc. 859. refrain from laughter, keep one's countenance; be –, look- grave etc. *adj.*; repress a smile, keep a straight face.

depress; dis-courage, -hearten; dis-pirit; damp, dull, deject, lower, sink, dash, knock down, un- man, prostrate, break one's heart; frown upon; cast a -gloom, – shade- on; sadden; damp –, dash –, wither- one's hopes; weigh –, lie heavy –, prey- on the -mind, – spirits; damp –, depress- the spirits.

Adj. cheer-, joy-, spirit-less; uncheer-ful, -y; unlively; unhappy etc. 828; melancholy, dismal, somber, dark, gloomy, adust, *triste*, clouded, murky, lowering, frowning, lugubrious, Acheron-tic, funereal, mournful, lamentable, dreadful.

dreary, flat; dull, – as -a beetle, – ditchwater; depressing etc. *v.*

'melancholy as a gib cat;' oppressed with –; a prey to- melancholy; down-cast, -hearted; down -in the mouth, – on one's luck; heavy-hearted; in the -dumps, – suds, – sulks, – doldrums; in doleful dumps, in bad humor; sullen; mumpish, dumpish; mopish, moping; moody, glum; sulky etc. (*discontented*) 832; out of -sorts, – humor, – heart, – spirits; ill at ease, low-spirited, in low spirits, a cup too low; weary etc. 841; dis-couraged, -heartened; desponding; chop-, jaw-, crest-fallen.

sad, pensive, *penseroso*, tristful; dole-some, -ful; woebegone, lachrymose, in tears, melancholic, hypped, hypochondriacal, bilious, jaundiced, atrabilious, saturnine, splenetic; lackadaisical.

serious, sedate, staid, stayed; grave, – as -a judge, – an undertaker, – a mustard pot; sober, solemn, demure; grim; grim-faced, -visaged; rueful, wan, long-faced.

disconsolate; un-, in-consolable; forlorn, comfortless, desolate, *désolé*, sick at heart; soul-, heart-sick; *au désepoir*; in despair etc. 859; lost.

overcome; broken-, borne-, bowed-down; heart-stricken etc. (*mental suffering*) 828; cut up, dashed, sunk; unnerved, unmanned; down-fallen, -trodden; broken-hearted; care-worn.

Adv. with -a long face, – tears in one's eyes; sadly etc. *adj.*

Phr. the countenance falling; the heart -failing. – sinking within- one.

838. Rejoicing. [Expression of pleasure.]—**N.** rejoicing, exultation, triumph, jubilation, heyday, flush, revelling; merry-making etc. (*amusement*) 840; jubilee etc. (*celebration*) 883; *paean, Te Deum* etc. (*thanksgiving*) 990; congratulation etc. 896; applause etc. 971.

smile, simper, smirk, grin; broad –, sardonic-grin.

laughter, giggle, titter, crow, cheer, chuckle, snicker, snigger, shout; Homeric laughter, horse – hearty- laugh; guffaw; burst –, fit –, shout – roar –, peal- of laughter; cachinnation.

risibility; derision etc. 856.

Momus; Democritus the Abderite; rollicker; Laughter holding both his sides.

V. rejoice; thank –, bless- one's **stars**; congratulate –, hug- oneself; rub –, clap- one's hands; smack the lips, fling up one's cap; dance, skip, caleer; sing, carol, chirrup, chirp; hurrah; cry for –, leap with- joy; exult etc. (*boast*) 884; triumph; hold jubilee etc. (*celebrate*) 883; make merry etc. (*sport*) 840; sing a paean of joy.

smile, simper, smirk; grin, – like a Cheshire cat; mock, laugh in one's sleeve; laugh, – outright; giggle, titter, snigger, crow, smicker, chuckle, snicker, cackle; burst -out, – into a fit of laughter; shout, split, roar.

shake –, split –, hold both- one's sides; roar –, die- with laughter.

raise laughter etc. (*amuse*) 840.

Adj. rejoicing etc. *v.*; jubilant, exultant, triumphant; flushed, elated; laughing etc. *v.*; risible; ready to -burst, – split, – die with laughter; convulsed with laughter.

laughable etc. (*ludicrous*) 853.

Int. hip, hip, -hurrah! huzza! aha! hail! tolderolloll! tra-la la! Heaven be praised! *io triumphe! tant mieux!* so much the better.

Phr. the heart leaping with joy.

839. Lamentation. [Expression of pain.]—**N.** lament, -ation; wail, complaint, plaint, murmur, mutter, grumble, groan, moan, whine, whimper, sob, sigh, suspiration, heaving, deep sigh.

cry etc. (*vociferation*) 411; scream, howl; outcry, wail of woe, frown, scowl.

tear; weeping etc. *v.*; flood of tears, fit of crying, lachrymation, melting mood, weeping and gnashing of teeth.

plaintiveness etc. *adj.*; languishment; condolence etc. 915.

mourning, weeds, willow, cypress, crêpe, crape, deep mourning; sackcloth and ashes; knell etc. 363; dump, deathsong, dirge, coronach, keen, *nenia*, requiem, elegy, *epicedium*; threne; mon-, thren-ody; jeremiad; ululation.

mourner, professional mourner, keener; grumbler etc. (*discontent*) 832; Niobe; Heraclitus.

V. lament, mourn, deplore, grieve, weep over; be-wail, -moan; keen; condole with etc. 915; fret etc. (*suffer*) 828; wear –, go into –, put on-mourning; wear -the willow, – sackcloth and ashes; *infandum renovare dolorem* etc. (*regret*) 833; give sorrow words.

sigh; give –, heave –, fetch- a sigh; 'waft a sigh from Indus to the pole;' sigh 'like furnace;' wail.

cry, weep, sob, greet, blubber, pipe, snivel, bibber, whimper, pule; pipe one's eye; drop –, shed- -tears, – a tear; melt –, burst- into tears; *fondre en larmes*; cry -oneself blind, – one's eyes out.

scream etc. (*cry out*) 411; mew etc. (*animal sounds*) 412; groan, moan, whine, yammer; roar; roar –, bellow- like a bull; cry out lustily, rend the air, yell.

frown, scowl, make a wry face, grimace, gnash one's teeth, wring one's hands, tear one's hair, beat one's breast, roll on the ground, burst with grief.

complain, murmur, mutter, grumble, growl, clamor, make a fuss about, croak, grunt, maunder; deprecate etc. (*disapprove*) 932.

cry out before one is hurt, complain without cause.

Adj. lamenting etc. *v.*; in mourning, in sackcloth and ashes; crying, sorrowing, -ful etc. (*unhappy*) 828; mourn-, tear-ful; lachrymose; plaint-ive, -ful, quer-ulous, -imonious; in the melting mood.

in tears, with tears in one's eyes; with -moistened, – watery- eyes; bathed –, dissolved-in tears; 'like Niobe all tears.'

elagiac, epicedial, threnetic.

Adv. *de profundis; les larmes aux yeux.*

Int. heigh-ho! alas! alack! O dear! ah –, woe is-me! lackadaisy! well –, lack –, alack- a day! well-a-way! alas the day! *O tempora! O mores!* what a pity! *miserabile dictu!* O lud lud! too true!

Phr. tears -standing in, – starting from- the eyes; eyes -suffused, – swimming, – ; brimming –, over- flowing- with tears.

840. Amusement.—**N.** amuse-, entertain-ment; diver-sion, -tissement; reaction, relaxation, solace; pastime, *passetemps*, sport; labor of love; pleasure etc. 827.

fun, frolic, merriment, whoopee, jollity; jovial-ity, -ness; heyday; laughter etc. 838; jocos-ity, -eness; droll-, buffoon-, tomfool-ery; mummery, masquing, pleasantry; wit etc. 842; quip, quirk.

play; game, – at romps; gambol, romp, prank, antic, rig, lark, spree, skylarking, vagary, trick, monkey trick, *gambade, fredaine, escapade, échappée*, bout, *espièglerie*; practical joke etc. (*ridicule*) 856.

dance; round –, square –, solo –, step –, tap –, clog –, skirt –, sand –, folk –, morris-dance, *pas seul*, step, turn, *chassé*, cut, shuffle, double shuffle; hop, reel, rigadoon, saraband, hornpipe, bolero, fandango, pavan, tarantella, minuet, waltz, polka; galop, -ade; Schottische, *pas de quatre*, Boston, one-, two-step, rumba, tango, maxixe, fox-, turkey-trot, shimmy, ragtime, cakewalk, jazz, blues, Charleston; jig, breakdown, fling, strathspey; *allemande*; gavot, -te; mazurka, morisco; quadrille, lancers, country dance, cotillon, polonaise, Sir Roger de Coverley, Swedish dance; *ballet* etc. (*drama*) 599; ball; *bal*, – *masqué*, – *costumé*; masquerade, fancy dress ball; *thé dansant*; Terpsichore, choreography, Russian ballet, classical dancing; eurythmics; nautch dance, *danse du ventre*, cancan.

festivity, merry-making; party etc. (*social gathering*) 892; *fête*, festival, gala, *ridotto*; revel-s, -ry, -ling; carnival, brawl, saturnalia, high jinks; feast, banquet etc. (*food*) 298; regale, *symposium*, wassail; carous-e, -al; jollification, junket, wake, pic-nic, *fête champêtre*, garden party, gymkhana, regatta, track meet, field day, jamboree, treat.

round of pleasures, dissipation, a short life and a merry one, racketing, holiday making, high jinks.

rejoicing etc. 838; jubilee etc. (*celebration*) 883.

bonfire, fireworks, *feu-de-joie*, rocket, catherine wheel, roman candle etc.

holiday; gala –, red letter –, play- day; high days and holidays; high –, Bank- holiday; May –, Derby- day; Saint –, Easter –, Whit- Monday; King's birthday, Empire Day; *mi-carême*; *Bairam*; wayzgoose, bean feast, beano.

place of amusement, theater 'etc. 599; concert-, ball-, assembly-room; music-hall, cinema, movies, talkies, vaudeville; hippodrome, circus, rodeo; *casino*, *kursaal*; winter garden; park, pleasance, arbor; garden etc. 371; pleasure-, play-, cricket-, football-, polo-, croquet-, archery-, hunting-ground; golf links, race course, stadium, gridiron, bowl, speedway, racing track, ring; gymnasium, swimming pool; shooting gallery; tennis-, racket-court; bowling-green, -alley; croquet-lawn, rink, skating rink; roller-coaster, roundabout, carousel, merry-go-round; swing; *montagne russe*; switchback, scenic railway etc.

game, – of -chance, – skill; athletic sports, gymnastics; fencing; archery, rifle-shooting; tournament, pugilism etc. (*contention*) 720; sporting etc. 622; horse-racing, the turf; aquatics etc. 267; skating, roller skating; ski-running, -joring, - jumping, bobsleighing, luging, tobogganing, winter sports; sliding; cricket, tennis, lawn –, table –, deck-tennis, rackets, fives, squash, ping pong, trap bat and ball, battledore and shuttlecock, badminton, *la grâce*; pall mall, tip-cat, croquet, golf, curling, hockey, basketball, soccer, football, Rugby, Association, *pallone*, polo; tent-pegging, tilting at the ring, quintain, greasy pole; quoits, *discus*; throwing the hammer, putting the -weight, – shot, tossing the caber; knurr and spell; leap-frog; hop, skip and jump; French and English, tug of war; blind man's buff, hunt the slipper, hide-and-seek, kiss in the ring; snapdragon; cross questions and crooked answers; jig-saw puzzle; rounders, base-ball, *la crosse* etc.; angling; swimming, diving, water-polo.

billiards, pool, pyramids, snooker, bagatelle; bowls, skittles, ninepins, kail, American bowls.

cards; bridge, auction, contract, whist, rubber;

round game, coon-can, loo, cribbage, *bésique*, pinocle, euchre, drole, *écarté*, skat, picquet, all-fours, quadrille, ombre, reverse, Pope Joan, commit; bo-, boa-ston; *vingt-et-un*; *quinze*, thirty-one, put-and-take, speculation, connections, brag, cassino, lottery, commerce, snip-snap-snorem, lift smoke, blind hookey, Polish bank, poker, banker; faro; Earl of Coventry, Napoleon, nap, patience, pairs; old maid, fright, beggar-my-neighbor; *baccarat*, *chemin de fer*, *monté*, *roulette*.

chess, draughts, backgammon, dominoes, checkers, mah jong, merelles, nine men's morris, go-bang, solitaire; game of – , fox and-goose; lotto; etc.

morra; gambling etc. (*chance*) 621.

toy, plaything, bauble; doll etc. (*puppet*) 554; teetotum; knick-knack etc. (*trifle*) 643; magic lantern etc. (*show*) 448; peep-, puppet-, raree-, gallanty-show; marionettes, Punch and Judy; toy-shop; 'quips and cranks and wanton wiles, nods and becks and wreathed smiles.'

sportsman, gamester, gambler etc. 621; reveler, master of the -ceremonies, – revels; *arbiter elegantiarum*.

V. amuse, entertain, divert, enliven; tickle, – the fancy; titillate, raise a smile, put in good humor; cause –, create –, occasion –, raise –, excite –, produce –, convulse with- laughter; set the table in a roar, be the death of one.

recreate, solace, cheer, rejoice; please etc. 829; interest; treat, regale.

amuse oneself; game; play, – a game, – pranks, – tricks; sport, disport, toy, wanton, revel, junket, feast, carouse, banquet, make merry; drown care; drive dull care away; frolic, gambol, frisk, romp; caper; dance etc. (*leap*) 309; keep up the ball; run a rig, sow one's wild oats, have one's fling, paint the town red, take one's pleasure; see life; *desipere in loco*, play the fool.

make –, keep- holiday; go a Maying.

while away –, beguile- the time; kill time, dally.

Adj. amusing, entertaining, diverting etc. *v.*; recreative, lusory; pleasant etc. (*pleasing*) 829; laughable etc. (*ludicrous*) 853; witty etc. 842; festive, -al; jovial, jolly, jocund, roguish, rompish; sporting; playful – as a kitten; sportive, ludibrious.

amused etc. *v.*; 'pleased with a feather, tickled with a straw.'

Adv. 'on the light fantastic toe,' at play, in sport.

Int. *vive la bagatelle! vogue la galère!*

Phr. *Deus nobis haec otia fecit; dum vivimus vivamus.*

841. Weariness.—N. weariness, defatigation, boredom, *ennui*; lassitude etc. (*fatigue*) 688; drowsiness etc. 683.

disgust, nausea, loathing, sickness; satiety etc. 869; *taedium vitae* etc. (*dejection*) 837.

wearisome-, tedious-ness etc. *adj.*; dull work, tedium, monotony, twice told tale.

bore, button-hole, proser, wet blanket; heavy hours, 'the enemy' [time].

V. weary; tire etc. (*fatigue*) 688; bore; bore – weary –, tire- -to death, – out of one's life, – out of all patience; set –, send- to sleep.

pall, sicken, nauseate, disgust.

harp on the same string; drag its -slow, – weary-length along.

never hear the last of; be -tired etc. *adj*. -of, – with; yawn; died with *ennui*.

Adj. wearying etc. *v*.; wearing; weari-, tire-, irksome; uninteresting, stupid, bald, devoid of interest, dry, monotonous, dull, arid, tedious, humdrum, mortal, flat; pros-y, -ing; slow; soporific, somniferous, dormitive.

disgusting etc. *v*.; unenjoyed.

weary; tired etc. *v*.; drowsy etc. (*sleepy*) 683; uninterested, flagging, used up, worn out, *blasé*, life-weary, weary of life; sick of.

Adv. wearily etc. *adj*.; *usque ad nauseam*.

Phr. time hanging heavily on one's hands; *toujours perdrix*; *crambe repetita*.

842. Wit.—N. wit, -tiness; attic -wit, – salt; atticism; salt, *esprit*, point, fancy, whim, humor, drollery, pleasantry.

farce, buffoonery, fooling, tomfoolery; harlequinade etc. 599; broad -farce, – humor; fun, *espièglerie*; *vis comica*.

jocularity; jocos-ity, -eness; facetiousness; waggery, -ishness; whimsicality, comicality etc. 853.

smartness, ready wit, banter, *badinage*, *persiflage*, retort, repartee, *quid pro quo*; ridicule etc. 856.

facetiae, quips and cranks; jest, joke, capital joke; standing -jest, – joke; conceit, quip, quirk, crank, quiddity, *concetto*, *plaisanterie*, brilliant idea; merry –, bright –, happy- thought; sally; flash, – of wit, – of merriment; scintillation; *mot*, – pour rire; witticism, smart saying, *bon mot*, *jeu d'esprit*, epigram; jest book; dry joke, *quodlibet*, cream of the jest.

word-play, *jeu de mots*; play -of, – upon- words; pun, -ning; *double entente* etc. (*ambiguity*) 520; quibble, verbal quibble; conundrum etc. (*riddle*) 533; anagram, acrostic, double acrostic, *nugae canorae*, trifling, idle conceit, *turlupinade*.

old joke, Joe Miller, chestnut, hoary-headed jest.

V. joke, jest, cut jokes; crack a joke; perpetrate a -joke; – pun; make -fun of, – merry with; set the table in a roar etc. (*amuse*) 840; scintillate.

retort, flash back; banter etc. (*ridicule*) 856; *ridentem dicere verum*; joke at one's expense.

Adj. witty, attic, salty; quick-, nimble-witted; keen, clever, smart, brilliant, pungent, jocular, jocose, funny, waggish, facetious, whimsical, humorous, gilbertian; playful etc. 840; merry and wise; pleasant, sprightly, *spirituel*, sparkling, epigrammatic, full of point, *ben trovato*; comic etc. 853.

Adv. in joke, in jest, in sport, in play.

843. Dullness.—N. dullness, heaviness, flatness; infestivity etc. 837; stupidity etc. 499; want of originality, dearth of ideas.

prose, matter of fact; heavy book, *conte à dormir debout*; platitude.

V. be -dull etc. *adj*.; prose, platitudinize, take *au sérieux*, be caught napping.

render -dull etc. *adj*.; damp, depress, throw cold water on, lay a wet blanket on; fall flat upon the ear; hang fire.

Adj. dull, – as ditch water; dry, insipid, jejune; unentertaining, uninteresting, unlively,

unimaginative; heavisome, heavy-gaited; insulse; dry as dust; pros-y, -ing, -aic; matter of fact, commonplace, banal, pointless; 'weary, flat, stale and unprofitable.'

stupid, slow, flat, sluggish, ponderous, humdrum, monotonous; melancholic etc. 837; stolid etc. 499; plodding.

Phr. *Davus sum non Oedipus.*

844. Humorist.—N. humorist, wag, wit, reparteeist, epigrammatist, gag man, punster; *bel esprit*, life of the party; wit-snapper, -cracker, - worm; joker, jester, jokesmith, Joe Miller, *drôle de corps*, *gaillard*, spark, *persiffleur*, banterer.

buffoon, *farceur*, merry-andrew, mime, tumbler, acrobat, mountebank, charlatan, posturemaster, harlequin, punch, *pulcinella*, scaramouch, clown; wearer of the -cap and bells, – motley; motley fool; pantaloon, gipsy; jack -pudding, – in the green, – a dandy; zany; mad-cap, pickle-herring, witling, caricaturist, *grimacier*.

845. Beauty.—N. beauty, the beautiful, *le beau ideal*, loveliness.

[Science of the perception of beauty] Callaesthetics.

form, elegance, grace, beauty unadorned; symmetry etc. 242; comeliness, fairness etc. *adj*.; pulchritude, polish, gloss; good -effect, – looks; *belle tournure*; bloom, brilliancy, radiance, splendor, gorgeousness, magnificence; sublimi-ty, -fication.

concinnity, delicacy, refinement; charm, *je ne sais quoi*, style, *chic*, swank.

Venus, – of Milo; Aphrodite, Hebe, the Graces, Peri, Houri, Cupid, Apollo, Hyperion, Adonis, Antinous, Narcissus; Helen of Troy.

peacock, butterfly; flower, flow'ret gay, rose, lily, asphodel; garden; flower of, pink of; *bijou*; jewel etc. (*ornament*) 847; work of art.

pleasurableness etc. 829.

beautifying; landscape gardening; decoration etc. 847; calisthenics.

V. be -beautiful etc. *adj*.; shine, beam, bloom; become one etc. (*accord*) 23; set off, grace, flatter one.

render -beautiful etc. *adj*.; beautify; polish, burnish; gild etc. (*decorate*) 847; set out.

'snatch a grace beyond the reach of art.'

Adj. beaut-iful, -eous; handsome; pretty; lovely, graceful, elegant; delicate, dainty, refined, exquisite; fair, personable, comely, seemly; bonny; good-looking; well-favored,-made,-formed, -proportioned; proper, shapely; symmetrical etc. (*regular*) 242; harmonious etc. (*color*) 428; sightly.

fit to be seen, passable, not amiss.

goodly, dapper, tight, jimp; gimp; janty, jaunty; natty, quaint, trim, tidy, neat, spruce, smart, tricksy.

bright, -eyed; rosy-, cherry-cheeked; rosy, ruddy; blooming, in full bloom.

brilliant, shining; beam-y, -ing; sparkling, swanky, splendid, resplendent, dazzling, glowing; glossy, sleek.

showy, specious; rich, gorgeous, superb, magnificent, grand, fine, sublime, imposing; majestic 873.

artistic, -al; aesthetic; pict-uresque, -orial; *fait à piendre*, paintable; well-composed, -grouped, -varied; curious.

enchanting etc. (*pleasure-giving*) 829; attractive etc. (*inviting*) 615; becoming etc. (*accordant*) 23; ornamental etc. 847.

undeformed, undefaced, unspotted; spotless etc. (*perfect*) 650.

846. Ugliness.—**N.** ugliness etc. *adj.*; deformity, inelegance; disfigurement etc. (*blemsih*) 848; want of symmetry, inconcinnity; distortion etc. 243; squalor etc. (*uncleanness*) 653.

forbidding countenance, vinegar aspect, hanging look, wry face, '*spretae injuria formae.*'

eyesore, object, figure, sight, fright, specter, scarecrow, hag, harridan, satyr, witch, toad, baboon, monster, Caliban, Aesop, '*monstrum horrendum informe ingens cui lumen ademptum.*'

V. be -ugly etc. *adj.*; look ill, grin horribly a ghastly smile, make faces.

render -ugly etc. *adj.*; deface; dis-, de-figure; deform, spoil, distort etc. 243; blemish etc. (*injure*) 659; soil etc. (*render unclean*) 653.

Adj. ugly, - as -sin, - a toad, - a scarecrow, - a dead monkey; plain, bald etc. 226; homely etc. (*unadorned*) 849; ordinary, unornamental, inartistic; unsightly, unseemly, uncomely, unshapely, unlovely; sightless, seemless; not fit to be seen; unbeaut-eous, -iful; beautiless; shapeless etc. (*amorphous*) 241; course; garish, over-decorated etc. 882.

mis-shapen, -proportioned; monstrous; gaunt etc. (*thin*) 203; dumpy etc. (*short*) 201; curtailed of its fair proportions; ill-made, -shaped, -proportioned; crooked etc. (*distorted*) 243; hard-featured, -visaged; ill-, hard-, evil-favored; ill-looking; unprepossessing.

graceless, inelegant; ungraceful, ungainly, uncouth; stiff; rugged, rough, gross, rude, awkward, clumsy, slouching, rickety; gawky; lump-ing, -ish; lumbering; hulk-y, -ing; unwieldy.

squalid, haggard; grim, -faced, -visaged; grisly, ghastly; ghost-, death-like; cadaverous, gruesome.

frightful, hideous, odious, uncanny, forbidding, repellant, repulsive; horri-d, -ble; shocking etc. (*painful*) 830.

foul etc. (*dirty*) 653; dingy etc. (*colorless*) 429; gaudy etc. (*color*) 428; disfigured etc. *v.*; discolored (*blemished*) etc. 848.

847. Ornament.—**N.** ornament, -ation, -al art; ornat-ture, -eness; adorn-ment, decoration, embellishment; architecture.

garnish, polish, varnish, French polish, gilding, japanning, lacquer, ormolu, enamel.

cosmetics, rouge, powder, lipstick, lip salve, mascara; manicure; nail polish; permanent -, Marcel -, finger-wave.

pattern, diaper, powdering, panelling, graining, pargeting, inlay, detail; texture etc. 329; richness; tracery, molding, beading, reeding, fillet, listel, strapwork, *coquillage*, flourish, *fleur-de-lis*; arabesque, fret, *anthemion*; egg and -tongue, - dart; *astragal*, zigzag, *acanthus, cartouche*; pilaster etc. (*projection*) 250; cyma, ogee.

em-, broidery, needlework; knitting, crochet, tatting, brocade, *brocatelle*, beads, bugles; galloon, lace, gimp, *guipure*, fringe, trapping, border, edging, insertion, *motif*, trimming; *passementerie*; drapery, hanging, tapestry, arras; millinery, ermine.

wreath, festoon, garland, lei, chaplet, flower, nosegay, *bouquet*, posy, 'daisies pied and violets blue.'

tassle, knot; shoulder-knot, *épaulette*, epaulet, aigulet, *aiguilette*, frog; star, rosette, bow; feather, plume, *panache, aigrette*.

jewel, -ry, -lery; bijoutry; *bijou, -terie*; diadem, tiara; pendant, trinket, locket, necklace, armilla, bracelet, bangle, armlet, anklet, ear-, nose- ring, carcanet, chain, *châtelaine*, albert, brooch, torque.

gem, precious stone; diamond, brilliant, beryl, aquamarine, alexandrite, cat's eye, emerald, calcedony, chrysoprase, cornelian, jasper, bloodstone, agate, heliotrope; girasol, -e; onyx, plasma; sard, -onyx; garnet, lapis-lazuli, opal, peridot, chrysolite, sapphire, ruby; spinel, -le; balais; oriental -, topaz; turquois, -e; zircon, jacinth, hyacinth, carbuncle, amethyst; moonstone; pearl, coral.

finery, frippery, gewgaw, gimcrack, knick-knack, tinsel, spangle, sequin, *clinquant*, pinch-beck, paste; excess of ornament etc. (*vulgarity*) 851; gaud, pride, ostentation; frills and furbelows.

illustration, illumination, *vignette; fleuron*; head-, tail-piece; *cul-de-lampe*; flowers of rhetoric etc. 577; work of art, article of vertu, *bric-à-brac*, curio, *bibelot*.

V. ornament, embellish, enrich, decorate, adorn, beautify, adonize.

smarten, furbish, polish, gild, varnish, whitewash, enamel, japan, lacquer, paint, grain.

garnish, trim, dizen, bedizen, prink, prank; trick -, fig- out; deck, bedeck, dight, bedight, array; dress, - up, preen, spruce up, titivate; spangle, bespangle, powder; embroider, work; chase, tool, emboss, fret; emblazon, blazon, illuminate; illustrate.

become etc. (*accord with*) 23.

Adj. ornamented, beautified etc. *v.*; ornate, rich, gilt, begilt, tesselated, enamelled, inlaid; festooned; topiary.

smart, gay, tricksy, flowery, glittering; new-gilt, -spangled; fine, - as -a Mayday queen, - fivepence, - a carrot fresh scraped; pranked out, bedight, well-groomed.

in full dress etc. (*fashion*) 852; *en grande - tenue, - toilette*; in best bib and tucker, in Sunday best, *endimanché*; dressed to advantage.

showy, flashy; gaudy etc. (*vulgar*) 851; garish; gorgeous.

ornamental, decorative; becoming etc. (*accordant*) 23.

848. Blemish.—**N.** blemish, disfigurement, deformity; defect etc. (*imperfection*) 651; flaw; injury etc. (*deterioration*) 659, spots on the sun; eyesore.

stain, blot, slur; spot, -tiness; speck, -le; blur, freckle, mole, *macula*, patch, blotch, birthmark, blain, maculation, tarnish, smudge, smear; dirt etc. 653; bruise, black eye, scar, wem; pustule, excrescence, pimple etc. (*protuberance*) 250.

V. disfigure etc. (*injure*) 659; speckle; render ugly etc. 846.

Adj. pitted, freckled, discolored, bloodshot, bruised, disfigured; stained etc. *n.*; imperfect etc. 651; injured etc. (*deteriorated*) 659.

849. Simplicity.—**N.** simplicity; plain-, homeli-ness; undress, nudity, nakedness, beauty unadorned, chastity, chasteness.
V. be -simple etc. *adj.*
render -simple etc. *adj.*; simplify, chasten, strip of ornament.
Adj. simple, plain; home-ly, -spun; ordinary, household.
natural, unaffected; free from -affectation, - ornament; *simplex munditiis*; *sans façon, en déshabillé*, nude, naked.
chaste, inornate, severe.
un-adorned, -ornamented, -decked, -garnished, -arranged, -trimmed, -varnished.
bald, flat, dull, blank.

850. Taste. [Good taste.]—**N.** taste; good –, refined –, cultivated- taste; delicacy, refinement, fine feeling, gust, *gusto*, tact, *finesse*; nicety etc. (*discrimination*) 465; polish, elegance, grace.
virtu; dilettanteism, virtuosity; fine art; cul-ture, -ivation.
[Science of taste] esthetics.
man of -taste etc.; *connoisseur*, judge, critic, *conoscente, virtuoso, amateur, dilettante*, Aristarchus, Corinthian, *arbiter elegantarum*, stagirite, euphemist.
'caviar to the general.'
V. appreciate, judge, criticize, discriminate etc. 465.
Adj. in good taste; tasteful, tasty; unaffected, pure, chaste, classical, attic; cultivated, refined; dainty; esthetic, artistic; elegant etc. 578; euphemistic.
to one's -taste, – mind; after one's fancy; *comme il faut*; *tiré à quatre épingles*.
Adv. elegantly etc. *adj.*
Phr. *nihil tetigit quod non ornavit.*

851. Vulgarity. [Bad taste.]—**N.** vulgar-ity, -ism; barbar-, Vandal-, Gothic-ism; *mauvais goût*, bad taste; Babbittry; *gaucherie*, awkwardness, want of tact; ill-breeding etc. (*discourtesy*) 895; ungentlemanly behavior.
coarseness etc. *adj.*; indecorum, misbehavior.
low-, homeli-ness; low life, *mauvais ton*, rusticity; boorishness etc. *adj.*; brutality; rowdy-, ruffian-, blackguard-ism; ribaſdry; slang etc. (*neology*) 563.
bad joke, *mauvaise plaisanterie*.
[Excell of ornament] gaudi-, tawdri-ness; false ornament; finery, frippery, trickery, tinsel, gewgaw, *clinquant*.
rough diamond, tomboy, hoyden, cub, unlicked cub; clown etc. (*commonalty*) 876; Hun, Goth, Vandal, Boeotian; vulgarian; snob, cad, bounder, gent; *parvenu* etc. 876; frump, dowdy; slattern etc. 653.
V. be -vulgar etc. *adj.*; misbehave; talk –, smell of the- shop.
Adj. in bad taste, vulgar, unrefined, gutter.
coarse, indecorus, ribald, gross; unseemly, un-beseeming, unpresentable; *contra bonos mores*; ungraceful etc. (*ugly*) 846.
dowdy, slovenly etc. (*dirty*) 653; ungenteel, shabby genteel; low etc. (*plebeian*) 876;uncourtly; uncivil etc. (*discourteous*) 895; ill-bred, -mannered; underbred; ungentleman-ly, -like; unladylike, unfeminine; wild, – as an unbacked colt.
unkempt, uncombed, untamed, unlicked, un-polished, uncouth, plebeian; incondite; heavy, rude, awkward; home-ly, -spun, -bred; provincial, hick, countrified, rustic, uncultivated, freshwater; boorish, clownish; savage, brutish, blackguard; rowdy, snobbish; barbar-ous, -ic; Gothic, un-classical, doggerel, heathenish, tramontane, out-landish; Bohemian.
obsolete etc. (*antiquated*) 124; unfashionable, old-fashioned, out of date; new-fangled etc. (*un-familiar*) 83; fantastic, odd etc. (*ridiculous*) 853.
particular; affected etc. 855; meretricious; ex-travagant, monstrous, horrid; shocking etc. (*pain-ful*) 830.
gaudy, tawdry, bedizened, tricked out, ginger-bread; obtrusive, flaunting, loud, flashy, garish, showy.

852. Fashion.—**N.** fashion, style, *ton, bon ton*, society; good –, polite- society; drawing room, civilized life, civilization, town, *beau monde*, high life, court; world; fashionable –, gay- world; Vanity Fair; show etc. (*ostentation*) 822.
manners, breeding etc. (*politeness*) 894; air, demeanor etc. (*appearance*) 448; *savoir faire*; gen-tlemanliness, gentility, decorum, propriety, *bien-séance*; conventions –, dictates- of society; Mrs. Grundy; convention, -ality; punctilio; form, -ality; etiquette, point of etiquette; custom etc. 613; mode, vogue, style, go; rage etc. (*desire*) 865; prevailing taste, *dernier cri*, dress etc. 225.
man –, woman- of -fashion, – the world; height –, pink –, star –, glass –, leader- of fashion; *arbiter elegantiarum* etc. (*taste*) 850; up-per ten thousand etc. (*nobility*) 875; *élite* etc. (*distinction*) 873.
V. be -fashionable etc. *adj.*, – the rage etc. *n.*; have a run, pass current.
follow –, conform to –, fall in with- the fashion etc. *n.*; go with the stream etc. (*conform*) 82; *savoir -vivre*, – *faire*; keep up appearances, behave oneself.
set the –, bring into- fashion; give a tone to –, cut a figure in- society, rub shoulders with nobility, keep one's carriage.
Adj. fashionable; in -fashion etc. *n.*; *à la mode, comme il faut*; admitted –, admissible- in -society etc. *n.*; presentable, decorous, punctilious, con-ventional etc. (*customary*) 613; genteel; well-bred, -mannered, -behaved, -spoken; gentleman-like, -ly; ladylike; civil, polite etc. (*courteous*) 894.
polished, refined, thoroughbred, courtly; *distingué*, aristocratic, unembarrassed, poised, *dégagé*; ja-, jau-nty; dashing, fast, showy, high toned, toney.
modish, stylish, in the latest style, *recherché*; new-fangled etc. (*unfamiliàr*) 83.
in -court, – full, – evening- dress; *en grande tenue* etc. (*ornament*) 847.
Adv. fashionably etc. *adj.*; for fashion's sake.

853. Ridiculousness.—N. ridiculousness etc. *adj.*; comical-, odd-ity etc. *adj.*; extravagance, drollery.

farce, comedy; burlesque etc. (*ridicule*) 856; buffoonery etc. (*fun*) 840; frippery; doggerel verses; Irish bull, Hibernianism, Hibernicism; Spoonerism; absurdity etc. 497; bombast etc. (*unmeaning*) 517; anticlimax, bathos; monstrosity etc. (*unconformity*) 83; laughing stock etc. 857.

V. be -ridiculous etc. *adj.*; pass from the sublime to the ridiculous; make one laugh; play the fool, make a fool of oneself, commit an absurdity.

play a joke on, make a -fool of, – sucker of, – monkey of.

Adj. ridiculous, ludicrous; comic, -al; droll, funny, laughable, *pour rire*, grotesque, farcical, odd; whimsical, – as a dancing bear; fanciful, fantastic, queer, rum, quizzical, waggish, quaint, *bizarre*; eccentric etc. (*unconformable*) 83; strange, outlandish, out of the way, *baroque*, *rocaille*, rococo; awkward etc. (*ugly*) 846.

absurd, extravagant, *outré*, monstrous, preposterous, bombastic, inflated, stilted, burlesque, mock heroic.

drollish; serio-, tragic-comic; gimcrack, contemptible etc. (*unimportant*) 643; doggerel; ironical etc. (*derisive*) 856; risible.

Phr. *'risum teneatis amici?'* rideret Heraclitus.

854. Fop.—N. fop, fine gentleman; swell; dand-y, -iprat; exquisite, coxcomb, toff, beau, macaroni, blade, blood, buck, man about town, fast man; fribble, jemmy, spark, popinjay, puppy, prig, *petit maître*; jacka-napes, -dandy; man milliner; Jemmy Jessamy, carpet-knight, masher, Dundreary, Johnnie, dude.

belle, fine lady, *coquette*, flirt.

855. Affectation.—N. affectation; affectedness etc. *adj.*; acting a part etc. *v.*; pretence etc. (*falsehood*) 544; (*ostentation*) 882; boasting etc. 884.

charlatanism, quakery, shallow profundity, humbug, pretension, airs, pedantry, purism, precisianism, euphuism, prunes and prisms; teratology etc. (*altiloquence*) 577.

mannerism, *simagrée*, grimace.

conceit, foppery, dandyism, man millinery, coxcombry, puppyism.

stiffness, formality, buckram; prudery, demureness, coquetry, mock modesty, *minauderie*, sentimentalism; *mauvaise honte*, false shame.

affector, performer, actor; pedant, pedagogue, *doctrinaire*, purist, euphuist, mannerist, shoneen; *grimacier*; lump of affectation, *précieuse ridicule*, *bas bleu*, blue stocking, poetaster; prig, hypocrite; charlatan etc. (*deceiver*) 548; *petit maître* etc. (*fop*) 854; flatterer etc. 935; *coquette*, prude, puritan; precisian, formalist.

V. affect, act a part, put on; give oneself airs etc. (*arrogance*) 885; boast etc. 884; coquet; simper, mince, attitudinize, strike a pose, pose; flirt a fan; over-act, -play, -do.

Adj. affected, full of affectation, pretentious, pedantic, stilted, stagey, theatrical, big-sounding, *ad captandum*, canting, insincere.

not natural, unnatural; self-conscious; *maniéré*; artificial; over-wrought, -done, -acted; euphuistic etc. 577.

stiff, starch, formal, prim, smug, demure, *tiré à. quatre épingles*, quakerish, puritanical, prudish, pragmatical, priggish, conceited, coxcomical, foppish, dandified; fini-cal, -kin, -cky, mincing, simpering, namby-pamby, sentimental, languishing.

856. Ridicule.—N. ridicule, derision; sardonic -smile, – grin; irrision; snigger; scoffing etc. (*disrespect*) 929; mockery, quiz, banter, irony, *persiflage*, raillery, chaff, *badinage*; quizzing etc. *v.*

squib, satire, skit, quip, quib, grin.

parody, burlesque, travesty; farce etc. (*drama*) 599; caricature, take-off.

buffoonery etc. (*fun*) 840; practical joke, horse-play.

V. ridicule, deride; laugh at, grin at, smile at; snigger; laugh in one's sleeve; banter, rally, chaff, joke, twit, quiz, poke fun at, jolly, roast, rag; fleer; play –, play tricks- upon; fool, – to the top of one's bent; show up.

satirize, parody, caricature, burlesque, travesty.

turn into ridicule; make merry with; make -fun, – game, – a fool, – an April fool- of; rally; scoff etc. (*disrespect*) 929.

raise a laugh etc. (*amuse*) 840; play the fool, make a fool of oneself.

be ridiculous etc. 853.

Adj. deris-ory, -ive; mock; sarcastic, ironical, quizzical, burlesque, Hudibrastic; scurrilous etc. (*disrespectful*) 929.

Adv. in -ridicule etc. *n.*

857. Laughing-stock. [Object and cause of ridicule.]—N. laughing-, jesting-, gazing-stock; butt, game, fair game; April fool etc. (*dupe*) 547.

original, oddity; queer –, odd- fish; quiz, square toes; old –, fogey *or* fogy..

monkey; buffoon etc. (*jester*) 844; pantomimist etc. (*actor*) 599.

jest etc. (*wit*) 842.

858. Hope.—N. hope, -s; desire etc. 865; fervent hope, sanguine expectation, trust, confidence, reliance; faith etc. (*belief*) 484; affiance, assurance; secur-eness, -ity; reassurance.

good -omen, – auspices; promise; well-grounded hopes; good –, bright- .prospect; clear sky.

as-, pre-sumption; anticipation etc. (*expectation*) 507.

hopefulness, buoyancy, optimism, enthusiasm, heart of grace, aspiration; optimist, utop-ian, -ist; Pollyanna.

castles in the air, *châteaux en Espagne*, hope chest, *le pot au lait*, Utopia, millennium; day –, golden- dream; dream of Alnaschar; airy hopes, fool's paradise; *mirage* etc. (*fallacies of vision*) 443; fond hope.

beam –, ray –, gleam –, glimmer –, dawn –, flash –, star- of hope; cheer; bit of blue sky, silver lining of the cloud, bottom of Pandora's box, balm in Gilead.

anchor, sheet-anchor, main-stay; staff etc. (*support*) 215; heaven etc. 981.

·V. hope, trust, confide, rely on, put one's trust in, lean upon; pin one's -hope, – faith- upon etc. (*believe*) 484.

feel –, entertain –, harbor –, indulge –, cherish –, feed –, foster –, nourish –, encourage –, cling to –, live in- hope etc. *n.*; see land; feel –, rest- -assured, – confident etc. *adj.*

presume; promise oneself; expect etc. (*look forward to*) 507.

hope for etc. (*desire*) 865; anticipate.

be -hopeful etc. *adj.*; look on the bright side of, view on the sunny side, make the best of it, hope for the best; put -a good, – a bold, – the best-face upon; keep one's spirits up; take heart, – of grace; be of good -heart, – cheer; flatter oneself, lay the flattering unction to one's soul.

catch at a straw, hope against hope, count one's chickens before they are hatched.

give –, inspire –, raise –, hold out- hope etc. *n.*; raise expectations; encourage, hearten, cheer, assure, reassure, buoy up, embolden; promise, bid fair, augur well, be in a fair way, look up, flatter, tell a flattering tale.

Adj. hoping etc. *v.*; in -hopes etc. *n.*; hopeful, confident; secure etc. (*certain*) 484; sanguine, in good heart, buoyed up, buoyant, elated, flushed, exultant, enthusiastic; utopian.

unsus-pecting, -picious; fearless, free –, exempt from- -fear, – suspicion, – distrust, – despair; undespairing, self-reliant.

probable, on the high road to; within sight of -shore, – land; promising, propitious; of –, full of-promise; of good omen; auspicious, *de bon augure*; reassuring; encouraging, cheering, inspiriting, looking up, bright, roseate, *couleur de rose*, rose-colored.

Adv. hopefully etc. *adj.*

Phr. *nil desperandum*; never say die, *dum spiro spero*, *latet scintillula forsan*, all is for the best, *spero meliora*; the wish being father to the thought; 'hope told a flattering tale;' *rusticus expectat dum defluat amnis*.

859. Hopelessness. [Absence, want, or loss of hope.] —**N.** hopelessness etc. *adj.*; despair, desperation; despondency etc. (*dejection*) 837; pessimism.

hope deferred, dashed hopes; vain expectation etc. (*disappointment*) 509.

airy hopes etc. 858; forlorn hope; bad -job, – business; *enfant perdu*; gloomy –, black spots in the- horizon; slough of Despond, cave of Despair. Job's comforter; bird of -bad, – ill-omen.

V. despair; lose –, give up –, abandon –, relinquish- -all hope, – the hope of; give -up, – over; yield to despair; falter; despond etc. (*be dejected*) 837; *jeter le manche après la cognée*.

inspire –, drive to- despair etc. *n.*; disconcert; dash –, crush –, shatter –, destroy- one's hopes; hope against hope.

Adj. hopeless, desperate, despairing, in despair, *au désespoir*, forlorn; inconsolable etc. (*dejected*) 837; broken-hearted.

out of the question, not to be thought of; im-

practicable etc. 471; past -hope, – cure, – mending, – recall; at one's last gasp etc. (*death*) 360; given -up, – over.

incurable, cureless, immedicable, remediless, beyond remedy; incorrigible; irre-parable, - mediable, -coverable, -versible, -trievable, -claimable, -deemable, -vocable; ruined, undone; immitigable.

unpromising, unpropitious; inauspicious, ill-omened, threatening, clouded over, lowering, ominous.

Phr. *'lasciate ogni speranza voi ch' entrate;'* its days are numbered; the worst come to the worst.

860. Fear.—**N.** fear, timidity, diffidence, want of confidence; apprehensive-, fearful-ness etc. *adj.*; solicitude, anxiety, care, apprehension, misgiving; mistrust etc. (*doubt*) 485; suspicion, qualm; hesitation etc. (*irresolution*) 605.

nervous-, restless-ness etc. *adj.*; in-, dis-quietude; flutter, trepidation, fear and trembling, perturbation, tremor, quivering, shaking, trembling, throbbing heart, palpitation, ague fit, cold sweat; abject fear etc. (*cowardice*) 862; mortal funk, heart-sinking, despondency; despair etc. 859.

fright; affright, -ment; alarm, pavor, dread, awe, terror, horror, dismay, consternation, panic, scare, stampede [of horses].

intimidation, terrorism, reign of terror.

[Object of fear] bug-bear, -aboo; scarecrow; hobgoblin etc. (*demon*) 980; daymare, nightmare, Gorgon, Medusa, mormo, ogre, Hurlothrumbo, raw head and bloody bones, fee faw fum, *bête noire*, *enfant terrible*.

alarmist etc. (*coward*) 862.

V. fear, stand in awe of; be -afraid etc. *adj.*; have -qualms etc. *n.*; apprehend, sit upon thorns, eye askance; distrust etc. (*disbelieve*) 485.

hesitate etc. (*be irresolute*) 605; falter, funk, cower, crouch; skulk etc. (*cowardice*) 862; let 'I dare not' wait upon 'I would;' take -fright, – alarm; start, wince, flinch, shy, shrink; fly etc. (*avoid*) 623.

tremble, shake; shiver, – in one's shoes; shudder, flutter; shake –, tremble- -like an aspen leaf, – all over; quake, quaver, quiver, quail; get the wind up.

grow –, turn- pale; blench, stand aghast; not dare to say one's soul is one's own.

inspire –, excite- -fear, – awe; raise apprehensions; give –, raise –, sound- an alarm; alarm, startle, scare, cry 'wolf,' disquiet, dismay; fright, -en; affright, terrify; astound; frighten from one's propriety; frighten out of one's -wits, – senses, – seven senses; awe; strike -all of a heap, – an awe into, – terror; harrow up the soul, appal, unman, petrify, horrify.

make one's -flesh creep, – hair stand on end, -- blood run cold, – teeth chatter; chill one's spine; take away –, stop- one's breath; make one -tremble etc.

haunt, obsess, beset; prey –, weigh- on the mind.

put in -fear, – bodily fear; terrorize, intimidate, cow, daunt, over-awe, abash, deter, discourage; browbeat, bully; threaten etc. 909.

Adj. fearing etc. *v.*; frightened etc. *v.*; in -fear, – a fright etc. *n.*; haunted with the -fear etc. *n.*- of.

afraid, fearful; tim-id, -orous; nervous, diffident, coy, faint-hearted, tremulous, shaky, afraid of one's shadow, apprehensive, restless, fidgety; more frightened than hurt.

aghast; awe-, horror-, terror-, panic- -struck, - stricken; frightened to death, white as a sheet; pale, – as -death, – ashes, – a ghost; breathless, in hysterics.

inspiring fear etc. *v.*; alarming; formidable, redoubtable; perilous etc. (*danger*) 665; portentous; fear-ful, -some; dread, -ful; fell; dire, -ful; shocking; terri-ble, -fic; tremendous; horri-d, -ble, -fic; ghastly; awful, awe-inspiring, eerie, weird; revolting etc. (*painful*) 830.

Adv. *in terrorem.*

Int. 'angels and ministers of grace defend us!'

Phr. *ante tubam trepidat*; *horresco referens,* one's heart failing one, *obstupui steteruntque comae et vox faucibus haesit.*

861. Courage. [Absence of fear.]—N. courage, bravery, valor; resolute-, bold-ness etc. *adj.*; spirit, daring, gallantry, intrepidity; contempt –, defiance- of danger; derring-do; audacity; rashness etc. 863; dash; defiance etc. 715; confidence, self-reliance.

man-liness, -hood; nerve, pluck, mettle, game; heart, – of grace; spunk, gameness, grit, face, virtue, hardihood, fortitude; firmness etc. (*stability*) 150; heart of oak; bottom, backbone etc. (*perseverance*) 604*a*.

resolution etc. (*determination*) 604; tenacity, bull-dog courage.

prowess, heroism, chivalry.

exploit, feat, achievement; heroic -deed, – act; bold stroke.

man, – of mettle; hero, demigod, paladin, heroine, Amazon, Hector, Joan of Arc; lion, tiger, panther, bulldog; game-, fighting-cock; bully, fire-eater etc. 863; dare-devil.

V. be -courageous etc. *adj.*; dare, venture, make bold; face –, front –; affront –, confront –, brave –, defy –, despise –, mock- danger; look in the face; look -full, – boldly, – danger- in the face; face; meet, – in front; brave, beard; defy etc. 715.

take –, muster –, summon up –, pluck up-courage; nerve oneself, take heart; take –, pluck up- heart of grace; hold up one's head, screw one's courage to the sticking place; come -to, – up to- the scratch; stand, – to one's guns, – fire, – against; bear up – against; hold out etc. (*persevere*) 604*a*.

put a bold face upon; show –, present- a bold front, face the music; envisage; show fight.

bell the cat, take the bull by the horns, beard the lion in his den, march up to the cannon's mouth, go through fire and water, run the gauntlet, go over the top.

give –, infuse –, inspire- courage; reassure, encourage, embolden, inspirit, cheer, hearten, nerve, put upon one's mettle, rally, raise a rallying cry; pat on the back, make a man of, keep in countenance.

Adj. courageous, brave; val-iant, -orous; gallant, intrepid; spirit-ed, -ful; high-spirited, -mettled; mettlesome, game, plucky; man-ly, -ful; resolute; stout, -hearted; iron-, lion-hearted; heart of oak; Penthesilean.

bold, – spirited; daring, audacious; fear-, daunt-, dread-, awe-less; un-daunted, -appalled, -dismayed, -awed, -blenched, -abashed, -alarmed, -flinching, -shrinking, -blenching; apprehensive; confident, self-reliant; bold as -a lion, – brass.

enterprising, adventurous; ventur-ous, -esome; dashing, chivalrous; soldierly etc. (*warlike*) 722; heroic.

fierce, savage; pugnacious etc. (*bellicose*) 720.

strong-minded, hardy, doughty; firm etc. (*stable*) 150; determined etc. (*resolved*) 604; dogged, indomitable etc. (*persevering*) 604*a*.

up to, – the scratch; upon one's mettle; reassured etc. *v.*; unfeared, undreaded.

Phr. one's blood being up.

862. Cowardice. [Excess of fear.]—N. cowardice, pusillanimity; cowardliness etc. *adj.*; timidity, effeminacy.

poltroonery, baseness; dastard-ness, -y; abject fear, funk; Dutch courage; fear etc. 860; white feather, faint heart.

coward, poltroon, dastard, sneak, recreant; shy –, dunghill- cock; coistril, milksop, white-liver, nidget, cur, craven, one that cannot say 'Boo' to a goose; Bob Acres, Jerry Sneak.

alarm-, terror-, pessim-ist; runagate etc. (*fugitive*) 623; shirker.

V. quail etc. (*fear*) 860; be -cowardly etc. *adj.*; – a coward etc. *n.*; funk; cower, skulk, sneak; flinch, shy, fight shy, slink, turn tail; run away etc. (*avoid*) 623; show the white feather, have cold feet, show a yellow streak.

Adj. coward, -ly; fearful, shy; tim-id, -orous; skittish; poor-spirited, spirit-less, soft, effeminate.

weak-minded; infirm of purpose etc. 605; weak-, faint-, chicken-, lily-, pigeon-hearted; yellow; white-, lily-, milk-livered; milksop, smock-faced; unable to say 'Boo' to a goose.

dastard, -ly; base, craven, sneaking, dunghill, recreant; unwar-, unsoldier-like.

'in face a lion but in 'heart a deer.'

unmanned; frightened etc. 860.

Int. *sauve qui peut!* devil take the hindmost!

Adv. in fear and trembling, in fear of one's life, in a blue funk.

Phr. *ante tubam trepidat*, one's courage oozing out.

863. Rashness.—N. rashness etc. *adj.*; temerity, want of caution, imprudence, indiscretion; over-confidence, presumption, audacity.

precipit-ancy, -ation; impetuosity; levity; foolhardi-hood, -ness; heed-, thought-lessness etc. (*inattention*) 458; carelessness etc. (*neglect*) 460; desperation; Quixotism, knight-errantry; fire-eating.

gam-ing, -bling; blind bargain, leap in the dark, fool's paradise; too many eggs in one basket.

desperado, rashling, mad-cap, dare-devil, Hotspur, fire-eater, bully, *bravo*, Hector, scapegrace, *enfant perdu*; Don Quixote, knight-errant, Icarus; adventurer; gam-bler, -ester; dynamitard.

V. be -rash etc. *adj.*; stick at nothing, play a desperate game; run into danger etc. 665; play with -fire, – edge tools.

carry too much sail, sail too near the wind, ride at single anchor, go out of one's depth.

take a leap in the dark, buy a pig in a poke. *donner tête baissée*; knock one's head against a wall etc. (*be unskilful*) 699; rush on destruction; kick against the pricks, tempt Providence, go on a forlorn hope.

count one's chickens before they are hatched; reckon without one's host; catch at straws; trust to – , lean on- a broken reed.

Adj. rash, incautious, indiscreet, injudicious; imprudent, improvident, temerarious; uncalculating; heedless; careless etc. (*neglectful*) 460; without ballast, heels over head; giddy etc. (*inattentive*) 458; wanton, reckless, wild, madcap; desperate, devil-may-care.

hot-blooded, -headed, -brained; head-long, -strong; break-neck; fool-hardy; harebrained; precipitate, impulsive.

over-confident, -weening; ventur-esome, -ous; adventurous, Quixotic; fire-eating, cavalier; free-and-easy.

off one's guard etc. (*inexpectant*) 508.

Adv. post haste, *à corps perdu*, hand over head, *tête baissée*, head- foremost; happen what may.

Phr. neck or nothing, the devil being in one.

864. Caution.—N. caution; cautiousness etc. *adj.*; discretion, prudence, cautel, heed, circumspection, calculation, deliberation; safety first.

foresight etc. 510; vigilance etc. 459; warning etc. 668.

coolness etc. *adj.*; self-possession, -command; presence of mind, *sang froid*; well-regulated mind; worldly wisdom, Fabian policy.

V. be -cautious etc. *adj.*; take -care, – heed, – good care; have a care; mind, – what one is about; be on one's guard etc. (*keep watch*) 459; make assurance double sure; ca' canny.

bespeak etc. (*be early*) 132.

think twice, look before one leaps, keep one's weather eye open, count the cost, look to the main chance, cut one's coat according to one's cloth; feel one's -ground, – way; see how the land lies etc. (*foresight*) 510; wait to see how the cat jumps; bridle one's tongue; *reculer pour mieux sauter* etc. (*prepare*) 673; let well alone, let sleeping dogs lie, *ne pas réveiller le chat qui dort.*

keep out of -harm's way, – troubled waters; keep at a respectful distance, stand aloof; keep – be- on the safe side.

husband one's resources etc. 636.

caution etc. (*warn*) 668.

Adj. cautious, wary, guarded; on one's guard etc. (*watchful*) 459; *cavendo tutus; in medio tutissimus.*

care-, heed-ful; cautelous, stealthy, chary, shy of, circumspect, prudent, canny, safe, non-committal, discreet, politic; sure-footed etc. (*skilful*) 698.

unenterprising, unadventurous, cool, steady, self-possessed; over-cautious.

suspicious, leery, vigilant.

Adv. cautiously, gingerly etc. *adj.*

Int. have a care! look out! *cave canem!*

Phr. *timeo Danaos; festina lente.*

865. Desire.—N. desire, wish, fancy, fantasy; want, need, exigency.

mind, inclination, leaning, bent, *animus*, partiality, *penchant*, predilection; propensity etc. 820; willingness etc. 602; liking, love, fondness, relish.

longing, hankering; solicitude, anxiety; yearning, coveting; aspiration, ambition, vaulting ambition; eagerness, zeal, ardor, *empressement*, breathless impatience, over-anxiety; solicitude, impetuosity etc. 825.

appet-ite, -ition, -ence, -ency; sharp appetite, keenness, hunger, stomach, twist; thirst, -iness; drouth, mouth-watering; itch, -ing; prurience, *cacoëthes*, cupidity, lust, concupiscence.

edge of -appetite, – hunger; torment of Tantalus; sweet – , lickerish- tooth; itching palm; longing – , wistful – , sheep's-eye.

avidity; greed, -iness; covetous-, ravenous-ness etc. *adj.*; grasping, craving, canine appetite, rapacity; voracity etc. (*gluttony*) 957.

passion, rage, *furore*, mania, *manie*; inextinguishable desire; dips-, klept-, mon-omania.

[Person desiring] desirer, lover, *amateur*, votary, devotee, aspirant, solicitant, candidate; cormorant etc. 957; sycophant.

[Object of desire] *desideratum*; want etc. (*requirement*) 630; 'consummation devoutly to be wished;' attraction, magnet, allurement, fancy, temptation, seduction, lure, fascination, *prestige*, height of one's ambition, idol; whim, -sey; maggot; hobby, -horse.

Fortunatus's cap, wishing cap, love potion.

V. desire; wish, – for; be -desirous etc. *adj.*; have a -longing etc. *n.*; hope etc. 858.

care for, affect, like, list; take to, cling to, take a fancy to; fancy; prefer etc. (*choose*) 609.

have -an eye, – a mind- to; find it in one's heart etc. (*be willing*) 602; have a fancy for, set one's eyes upon; cast a sheep's eye – , look sweet- upon; take into one's head, have a heart, be bent upon; set one's -cap at, – heart upon, – mind upon; covet.

want, miss, need, lack, desiderate, feel the want of; would fain -have, – do; would be glad of.

be -hungry etc. *adj.*; have a good appetite, play a good knife and.fork; hunger – , thirst – , crave – , lust – , itch – , hanker – , run mad- after; raven – , die- for; burn to.

desiderate; sigh – , cry – , gape – , gasp – , pine – , pant – , languish – , yearn – , long – , be on thorns – , hope- for; aspire after; catch at, grasp at, jump at.

woo, court, solicit; fish – , spell – , whistle – , put up- for; ogle.

cause – , create – , raise – , excite – , provoke-desire; whet the appetite; appetize, titillate, allure, attract, take one's fancy, tempt; hold out – temptation, – allurement; tantalize, make one's mouth water, *faire venir l'eau à la bouche.*

gratify desire etc. (*give pleasure*) 829.

Adj. desirous; desiring etc. *v.*; orectic, appetitive; inclined etc. (*willing*) 602; partial to; fain, wishful, optative; anxious, wistful, curious; at a loss for, sedulous, solicitous.

craving, hungry, sharp-set, peckish, ravening, with an empty stomach, esurient, lickerish, thirsty, athirst, parched with thirst, pinched with hunger, famished, dry, drouthy; hungry as a -hunter, – hawk, – horse, – church mouse.

greedy, – as a hog; over-eager, voracious; ravenous, – as a wolf; open-mouthed, covetous, rapacious, grasping, extortionate, exacting, sordid, *alieni appetens*; insati-able, -ate; unquenchable, quenchless; omnivorous.

unsatisfied, unsated, unslaked.

eager, avid, keen; burning, fervent, ardent; agog; all agog; breathless; impatient etc. (*impetuous*) 825; bent −, intent −, set- -on, − upon; mad after, *enragé*, rabid, dying for, devoured by desire.

aspiring, ambitious, vaulting, sky-aspiring.

desirable; popular; desired etc. *v.*; in demand; pleasing etc. (*giving pleasure*) 829; appeti-zing, -ble; tantalizing.

Adv. wistfully etc. *adj.*; fain.

Int. would -that, − it were! O for! *esto perpetua!* if only!

Phr. the wish being the father to the thought; *sua cuique voluptas*; *hoc erat in votis*, the mouth watering, the fingers itching; *aut Caesar (ut nullus*.

866. Indifference.—**N.** indifference, neutrality; coldness etc. *adj.*; unconcern, *insouciance, nonchalance*; want of -interest, − earnestness; anorexy, inappetency; apathy etc. (*insensibility*) 823; supineness etc. (*inactivity*) 683; disdain etc. 930; recklessness etc. 863; inattention etc. 458.

V. be -indifferent etc. *adj.*; stand neuter; take no interest in etc. (*insensibility*) 823; have no -desire etc. 865, − taste, − relish- for; not care for; care nothing -for, − about; not care a -straw etc. (*unimportance*) 643 -about, − for; not mind.

set at naught etc. (*make light of*) 483; spurn etc. (*disdain*) 930.

Adj. indifferent, cold, frigid, lukewarm; cool, − as a cucumber; unconcerned, *insouciant*, phlegmatic, *pococurante*, easy-going, devil-may-care, careless, listless, lackadaisical, feckless; half-hearted; un-ambitious, -aspiring, -desirous, - solicitous, -attracted.

un-attractive, -alluring, -desired, -desirable, - cared for, -wished, -valued, all one to.

insipid etc. 391; vain.

Adv. for aught one cares.

Int. never mind.

867. Dislike.—**N.** dis-like, -taste, -relish, - inclination, -placency.

reluctance; backwardness etc. (*unwillingness*) 603.

repugnance, disgust, queasiness, turn, nausea, loathing; avers-eness, -ation, -ion; abomination, antipathy, abhorrence, horror; mortal −, rooted- -antipathy, − horror; hatred, detestation; hate etc. 898; animosity etc. 900; hydrophobia.

sickener; gall and wormwood etc. (*unsavory*) 395; shuddering, cold sweat.

V. dis-, mis-like, -relish; mind, object to; have rather not, not care for; have −, conceive −, entertain −, take- -a dislike, − an aversion- to; have no -taste, − stomach- for.

shun, avoid etc. 623; eschew; withdraw −, shrink −, recoil- from; not be able to -bear, − abide, − endure; shrug the shoulders at, shudder at, turn up the nose at, look askance at; make a - mouth, − wry face, − grimace; make faces.

loathe, nauseate, abominate, detest, abhor; hate etc. 898; take amiss etc. 900; have enough of etc. (*be satiated*) 869.

cause −, excite- dislike; disincline, repel, sicken; make −, render- sick; turn one's stomach, nauseate, wamble, disgust, shock, stink in the nostrils; go against the -grain, − stomach; stick in the throat; make one's blood run cold etc. (*give pain*) 830; pall.

Adj. disliking etc. *v.*; averse to, loth, adverse; shy of, sick of, out of conceit with; disinclined; heart-, dog-sick; queasy.

disliked etc. *v.*; uncared for, unpopular; out of favor; repulsive, repugnant, repellent; abhorrent, insufferable, fulsome, nauseous; loath-some, -ful; offensive; disgusting etc. *v.*; disagreeable etc. (*painful*) 830; unsavory etc. 395.

Adv. *usque ad nauseam.*

Int. faugh! foh! ugh!

868. Fastidiousness.—**N.** fastidiousness etc. *adj.*; nicety, meticulosity, hypercriticism, difficulty in being pleased, *friandise*, epicurism, *omnia suspendens naso*.

discrimination, discernment, good taste, perspicacity.

epicure, gourmet.

[Excess of delicacy] prudery, prudishness, primness.

V. be -fastidious etc. *adj.*; split hairs, discriminate, have a sweet tooth.

mince the matter; turn up one's nose at etc. (*disdain*) 930; look a gift horse in the mouth, see spots on the sun.

Adj. fastidious, meticulous, exacting, nice, delicate, *délicat*, finical, finicky, difficult, dainty, lickerish, squeamish, thin-skinned; s-, queasy; hard −, difficult- to please; querulous, particular, over-particular, straitlaced, prudish, prim, scrupulous; censorious etc. 932; hypercritical, discriminating, discerning, perspicacious.

Phr. *noli me tangere.*

869. Satiety.—**N.** satiety, satisfaction, saturation, repletion, glut, surfeit; weariness etc. 841.

spoiled child; *enfant gâté*; too much of a good thing, *toujours perdrix*; *crambe repetita*.

V. sate, satiate, satisfy, saturate; cloy, quench, slake, pall, glut, gorge, surfeit; bore etc. (*weary*) 841; tire etc. (*fatigue*) 688; spoil.

have -enough of, − quite enough of, − one's fill, − too much of; be -satiated etc. *adj.*

Adj. satiated etc. *v.*; overgorged; *blasé*, used up, sick of, heart-sick.

Int. enough! hold! *eheu jam satis!*

870. Wonder.—**N.** wonder, marvel; astonish-, amaze-, wonder-, bewilder-ment; amazedness etc. *adj.*; admiration, awe; stup-or, -efaction; stound, fascination; sensation; surprise etc. (*inexpectation*) 508; cynosure.

note of admiration; thaumaturgy etc. (*sorcery*) 992.

V. wonder, marvel, admire; be -surprised etc. *adj.*; start; stare; open −, rub −, turn up- one's eyes; gloar; gape, open one's mouth, hold one's breath; look −, stand- -aghast, − agog; look blank etc. (*disappointment*) 509; *tomber des nues*; not believe one's -eyes, – ears, – senses.

not be able to account for etc. (*unintelligible*) 519; not know whether one stands on one's head or one's heels.

surprise, astonish, amaze, astound; dumbfound, -er; startle, dazzle; strike, – with -wonder, – awe; electrify; stun, stupefy, petrify, confound, bewilder, flabbergast; stagger, throw on one's beam ends, fascinate, turn the head, take away one's breath, strike dumb; make one's -hair stand on end, – tongue cleave to the roof of one's mouth; make one stare.

take by surprise etc. (*be unexpected*) 508.

be -wonderful etc. *adj.*; beggar –, baffle-description; stagger belief.

Adj. surprised etc. *v.*; aghast, all agog, breathless, agape; open-mouthed; awe-, thunder-, moon-, planet-struck; spell-bound; lost in -amazement, – wonder, – astonishment; struck all of a heap, unable to believe one's senses, like a duck in thunder.

wonderful, wondrous; surprising etc. *v.*; unexpected etc. 508; unheard of; mysterious etc. (*inexplicable*) 519; miraculous; *foudroyant*.

in-describable, -expressible, -effable; un-utterable, -speakable.

monstrous, prodigious, stupendous, marvelous; in-conceivable, -credible; in-, un-imaginable; strange etc. (*uncommon*) 83; passing strange.

striking etc. *v.*; over-whelming; wonder-working.

Adv. wonderfully etc. *adj.*; fearfully; for a –, in the name of- wonder; strange to say; *mirabile -dictu*, – visu; to one's great surprise.

with -wonder etc. *n.*, – gaping mouth, – open eyes, – upturned eyes; eyes starting out of one's head.

Int. lo, – and behold! O! hey-day! halloo! what! indeed! really! surely! humph! hɒm! good -lack, – heavens, – gracious! – lord! by jove! gad so! well a day! dear me! only think! lack-a-daisy! my -stars, – goodness! gracious goodness! goodness gracious! mercy on us! heavens and earth! God bless me! bless -us, – my heart! odzookens! *O gemini!* adzooks! hoity-toity! strong! Heaven save –, bless-the mark! can such things be! zounds! 'sdeath! what -on earth, – in the world! who would have thought it! etc. (*inexpectation*) 508; fancy! did you ever? you don't say so! what do you say to that! how now! where am I? well I'm blowed! etc.

Phr. *vox faucibus haesit*; one's hair standing on end.

871. Expectance. [Absence of wonder.]—**N.** expectan-ce, -cy etc. (*expectation*) 507; calmness, composure, tranquillity, serenity, coolness, imperturbability etc. 826.

nine days' wonder.

V. expect etc. 507; not -be surprised, – wonder etc. 870; *nil admirari*, make nothing of.

Adj. expecting etc. *v.*; unamazed, astonished at nothing; *blasé* etc. (*weary*) 841; unimaginative, calm, serene, imperturbable etc. 826; expected etc. *v.*; foreseen.

common, ordinary etc. (*habitual*) 613.

Int. no wonder; of course; why not?

872. Prodigy.—**N.** prodigy, phenomenon; wonder, -ment; genius, marvel, miracle; freak, monster

etc. (*unconformity*) 83; curiosity, lion, infant prodigy, sight, spectacle; *jeu* –, *coup- de théâtre*; gazing-stock; sign; portent etc. 512.

bursting of a -shell, – bomb; volcanic eruption, peal of thunder; thunder-clap, -bolt.

what no words can paint; wonders of the world; *annus mirabilis*; *dignus vindice nodus*.

873. Repute.—**N.** distinction, mark, name, figure; repute, reputation, character; good – , high-repute; note, notability, notoriety, *éclat*, 'the bubble reputation,' vogue, celebrity; fame, famousness; renown; popularity, *aura popularis*; esteem, approval, approbation etc. 931; credit, *succès d'estime*, *prestige*, talk of the town; name to conjure with.

glory, honor; luster etc. (*light*) 420; illustriousness etc. *adj.*

account, regard, respect; reputableness etc. *adj.*; respectability etc. (*probity*) 939; good -name, – report; fair name.

dignity; stateliness etc. *adj.*; solemnity, grandeur, splendor, nobility, majesty, sublimity.

rank, standing, brevet rank, precedence, *pas*, station, place, *status*; position, – in society; order, degree, *locus standi*, caste, condition.

greatness etc. *adj.*; eminence; height etc. 206; importance etc. 642; pre-, super-eminence; high mightiness, primacy; top of the -ladder, – tree.

elevation; ascent etc. 305; super-, ex-altation; dignification, aggrandizement.

dedication, consecration, enthronement, canonization, apotheosis, deification, celebration, enshrinement, glorification.

hero, man of mark, great card, celebrity, worthy, lion, *rara avis*, notability, somebody; man of rank etc. (*nobleman*) 875; pillar of the -state, – society, – church.

chief etc. (*master*) 745; first fiddle etc. (*proficient*) 700; scholar etc. 492; cynosure, mirror; flower, pink, pearl; paragon etc. (*perfection*) 650; choice and master spirits of the age; *élite*; star, sun, constellation, galaxy.

ornament, honor, feather in one's cap, halo, aureole, nimbus; halo –, blaze- of glory; blushing honors; laurels etc. (*trophy*) 733.

memory, posthumous fame, niche in the temple of fame; immor-tality, -tal name; *magni nominis umbra*.

V. be conscious of glory; be proud of etc. (*pride*) 878; exult etc. (*boast*) 884; be vain of etc. (*vanity*) 880.

be -distinguished etc. *adj.*; shine etc. (*light*) 420; shine forth, figure; make –, cut- a -figure, – dash, – splash.

rival, surpass; out-shine, -rival, -vie, -jump; emulate, vie with, eclipse; throw –, cast- into the shade; overshadow.

live, flourish, glitter, scintillate, flaunt; gain –, acquire- honor etc. *n.*; play first fiddle etc. (*be of importance*) 642; bear the -palm, – bell; lead the way; take -precedence, – the wall of; gain –, win-laurels, – spurs, – golden opinions etc. (*approbation*) 931; graduate, take one's degree, pass one's examination, win a -scholarship, – fellowship.

make -a, – some- -noise, – noise in the world; leave one's mark, exalt one's horn, star, have a run, be run after; enjoy popularity, come -into vogue, – to the front; raise one's head.

enthrone, signalize, immortalize, deify, exalt to the skies; hand one's name down to posterity.

consecrate; dedicate to, devote to; enshrine, inscribe, blazon, lionize, blow the trumpet, crown with laurel.

confer –, reflect- honor etc. *n.* on; shed a luster on; redound to one's honor, ennoble.

give –, do –, pay –, render- honor to; honor, accredit, pay regard to, dignify, glorify; sing praises to etc. (*approve*) 931; look up to; exalt, aggrandize, elevate, nobilitate.

Adj. distinguished, *distingué*, noted; of -note etc. *n.*; honored etc. *v.*; popular; fashionable etc. 852.

in good odor; in –, in high- favor; reput-, respect-, credit-able.

remarkable etc. (*important*) 642; notable, notorious; celebrated, renowned, in every one's mouth, talked of; fam-ous, -ed; far-famed; conspicuous, to the front; foremost; in the -front rank, – ascendant.

imperishable, deathless, immortal, never fading, *aere perennius*; time-honored.

illustrious, glorious, splendid, brilliant, radiant; bright etc. 420; full-blown; honorific.

eminent, prominent; high etc. 206; in the zenith; at the -head of, – top of the tree; peerless, of the first water; superior etc. 33; super-, pre-eminent.

great, dignified, proud, noble, honorable, worshipful, lordly, grand, stately, august, princely, imposing, solemn, transcendent, majestic, sacred, sublime, heaven-born, heroic, *sans peur et sans reproche*; sacrosanct.

Int. hail! all hail! *ave! viva! vive!* long life to! glory –, honor- be to!

Phr. one's name -being in every mouth, – living for ever; *sic itur ad astra, fama volat, aut Caesar aut nullus*; not to know him argues oneself unknown; none but himself could be his parallel, *palmam qui meruit ferat*.

874. Disrepute.—N. disrepute, discredit; ill-, bad- -repute, -name, -odor, -favor; disapprobation etc. 932; in-gloriousness, derogation; a-, debasement; abjectness etc. *adj.*; degradation, dedecoration; 'a long farewell to all one's greatness;' odium, obloquy, opprobrium, ignominy.

dishonor, disgrace; shame, humiliation; scandal, baseness, vileness; perfidy, turpitude etc. (*improbity*) 940; infamy.

tarnish, taint, defilement, pollution.

stain, blot, spot, blur, stigma, brand, reproach, imputation, slur.

crying –, burning- shame; *scandalum magnatum*, badge of infamy, blot in one's escutcheon; bend –, bar- sinister; champain, point champain; by- word of reproach; Ichabod.

argumentum ad verecundiam; sense of shame etc. 879.

V. be -inglorious etc. *adj.*; incur -disgrace etc. *n.*; have –, earn- a bad name; put –, wear- a halter round one's neck; disgrace –, expose-oneself.

play second fiddle; lose caste; pale one's ineffectual fire; recede into the shade; fall from one's high estate; keep in the background etc. (*modesty*) 881; be conscious of disgrace etc. (*humility*) 879; look -blue, – foolish, – like a fool; cut a -poor,

– sorry- figure; laugh on the wrong side of the mouth; make a sorry face, go away with a flea in one's ear, slink away.

cause -shame etc. *n.*; shame, disgrace, put to shame, dishonor; throw –, cast –, fling –, reflect- dishonor etc. *n.* upon; be a -reproach etc. *n.* to; derogate from.

tarnish, stain, blot, sully, taint; discredit, degrade, debase, defile; beggar; expel .etc. (*punish*) 972.

impute shame to, brand, post, stigmatize, vilify, defame, slur, cast a slur upon; hold up to shame, send to Coventry; tread –,' trample- under foot; show up, drag through the mire, heap dirt upon; reprehend etc. 932.

bring low, put down, snub; take down a peg, – lower, – or two.

obscure, eclipse, outshine, take the shine out of; throw –, cast- into the shade; overshadow; leave –, put- in the background; push into a corner, put one's nose out of joint; put out, – of countenance.

upset, throw off one's center; discompose, disconcert; put to the blush etc. (*humble*) 879.

Adj. disgraced etc. *v.*; blown upon; shorn of -its beams, – one' glory; overcome, down-trodden; loaded with -shame etc. *n.*; in -bad repute etc. *n.*; out of -repute, – favor, – fashion, – countenance; at a discount; under -a cloud, – an eclipse; unable to show one's face; in the -shade, – background; out at elbows, down in the world, down and out.

inglorious; nameless, renownless, obscure, unknown to fame; un-noticed, -noted, -honored, -glorified.

shameful; dis-graceful, -creditable, -reputable; despicable; questionable; unbecoming, unworthy; derogatory; degrading, humiliating, *infra dignitatem*, dedecorous; scandalous, infamous, too bad, unmentionable; ribald, opprobrious; arrant, shocking, outrageous, notorious, shady.

ignominious, scrubby, dirty, abject, vile, beggarly, pitiful, low, mean, shabby; base etc. (*dishonorable*) 940.

Adv. to one's shame be it spoken.

Int. fie! shame! for shame! *proh pudor! O tempora! O mores!* ough! *sic transit gloria mundi!*

875. Nobility.—N. nobility, rank, condition, distinction, optimacy, blood, *pur sang*, birth, high descent, order; quality, gentility; blue blood of Castile; *ancien régime*.

high life, *haut monde*; upper -classes, – ten thousand; *élite*, aristocracy, great folks; fashionable world etc. (*fashion*) 852; salariat.

peer, -age; house of -lords, – peers; lords, – temporal and spiritual; *noblesse*; baronage, knightage; noble, -man; lord, -ling; grandee, *magnifico, hidalgo*; don, -ship; aristocrat, swell, three-tailed bashaw; gentleman, squire, squireen, patrician, laureate.

gentry, gentlefolk; squirarchy, better sort, *magnates, primates, optimates*.

king etc. (*master*) 745; prince, crown prince, *Dauphin*; duke; marquis, -ate; earl, viscount, baron, thane, banneret; baronet, -cy; knight, -hood; count, armiger, laird; sig-, seig-nior; esquire, boyar, margrave, vavasor, sheik, emir, ameer, scherif, *pasha*, effendi, sahib.

queen etc. 745; princess, begum, duchess, marchioness; countess etc.; lady, dame.

personage –, man- of -distinction, – mark, – rank; nota-bles, -bilities; celebrity, big-wig, magnate, great man, star; *magni nominis umbra*; 'every inch a king;' grand Panjandrum
V. be -noble etc. *adj.*
Adj. noble, exalted; of -rank etc. *n.*; princely, titled, patrician, aristocratic; high-, well-born; of gentle blood; genteel, *comme il faut*, gentlemanlike, courtly etc. (*fashionable*) 852; highly respectable.
Adv. in high quarters.

876. Commonalty.—N. commonalty, democracy; obscruity; low -condition, – life, – society, – company; *bourgeoisie*; mass of -the people, – society; Brown, Jones, and Robinson; Tom, Dick, and Harry; lower –, humbler- classes, – orders; vulgar –, common- herd; rank and file, *hoc genus omne*; the -many, – general, – crowd, – people, – populace, – multitude, – million, – masses, – mobility, – peasantry; king Mob; proletariat, *fruges consumere nati*, great unwashed; man in the street

mob; rabble, – rout; chaff, rout, horde, *canaille*; scum –, *residuum* –, dregs- of -the people, – society; swinish multitude, *faex populi*; *profanum* –, *ignobile- vulgus*; vermin, riff-raff, tag-rag and bobtail; small fry.

commoner, one of the people, democrat, plebeian, republican, proletary, *prolétaire*, *roturier*, Mr. Snooks, *bourgeois*, *épicier*, Philistine, cockney; *grisette, demi-monde*.

peasant, countryman, boor, carle, churl; vill-ain, -ein; serf, kern, tyke, tike, chuff, ryot, fellah; longshoreman; swain, clown, hind; clod, -hopper; hobnail, yokel, hick, rube, cider squeezer, bog-trotter, bumpkin; ploughman, -boy; rustic, chawbacon, tiller of the soil; hewers of wood and drawers of water, groundling; gaffer, loon, put, cub, Tony Lumpkin, looby, lout, under-ling; *gamin*, guttersnipe, street arab, mudlark; rough, rowdy, ruffian, roughneck; pot-wallopper, slubberdegullion; vulgar –, low- fellow; cad, curmudgeon.

upstart, *parvenu, nouveau-riche*, skipjack; nobody, ' – one knows; *hesterni quirites, pessoribus orti; bourgeois gentilhomme, novus homo*, snob, gent, mushroom, no one knows who, adventurer; man of straw.

beggar, panhandler, gaberlunzie, muckworm, mudlark, *sans-culotte*, raff, tatterdemalion, caitiff, ragamuffin, Pariah, outcast of society, tramp, weary Willie, bum, vagabond, *chiffonaier*, rag-picker, Cinderella, cinderwench, scrub, jade; boots, gossoon.

Goth, Vandal, Hottentot, savage, barbarian, Yahoo; unlicked cub, rough diamond.

barbat-ousness, -ism; Boeotia.
V. be -ignoble etc. *adj.*, – nobody etc. *n.*
Adj. ignoble, common, mean, low, base, vile, sorry, scrubby, beggarly, below par; no great shakes etc. (*unimportant*) 643; home-ly, -spun; vulgar, low-minded; snobbish, *parvenu*.

plebeian, proletarian; of -low, – mean- parentage, – origin, extraction; low-,base-, earth-born, low bred; mushroom, dunghill, risen from the ranks; unknown to fame, obscure, untitled.

rustic, uncivilized; lout-, boor-, clown-, churl-, brut-, raff-ish; rude, unlicked, unpolished.

barbar-ous, -ian, -ic, -esque; cockney, born within sound of Bow bells.

underling, menial, servile, subaltern.
Adv. below the salt.

877. Title.—N. title, honor; knighthood etc. (*nobility*) 875.

royal –, serene- highness, excellency, grace; lordship, worship, Rt. Hon., rever-ence, -end; esquire, sir; madam, *madame*; master, mistress, Mr., Mrs., *signor, señor, Mein Herr, mynheer*; your –, his- honor; handle to one's name.

decoration, laurel, palm, wreath, garland, bays, medal, ribbon, riband, blue ribbon, *cordon*, cross, crown, coronet, star, garter; feather, – in one's cap; chevron, epaulet, *épaulette*, colors, cockade; livery; order, arms, armorial bearings, shield, scutcheon, crest, reward etc. 973.

878. Pride.—N. dignity, self-respect, *mens sibi conscia recti*.

pride; haughtiness etc. *adj.*; high notions, *hauteur*; vainglory, crest; arrogance etc. (*assumption*) 885; pomposity etc. 882.

proud man, highflier; fine -gentleman, – lady; *grande dame*.
V. be -proud etc. *adj.*; put a good face on; look one in the face; stalk abroad, perk oneself up; presume, swagger, strut; rear –, lift up –, hold up- one's head; hold one's head high, look big, take the wall, 'bear like the Turk no rival near the throne,' carry with a high hand; ride the –, mount on one's- high horse; set one's back up, bridle, toss the head; give oneself airs etc. (*assume*) 885; boast etc. 884.

pride oneself on; glory in, take pride in; pique –, plume –, hug- oneself; stand upon, be proud of; put a good face on; not -hide one's light under a bushel, – put one's talent in a napkin; not think small beer of oneself etc. (*vanity*) 880.
Adj. dignified; stately; proud, -crested; lordly, baronial; lofty-minded; high-souled, -minded, - mettled, -handed, -plumed, -flown, -toned.

haughty, paughty, insolent, lofty, high, mighty, swollen, puffed up, flushed, blown; vain-glorious; purse-proud, fine; proud as -a peacock, Lucifer; bloated with pride.

supercilious, disdainful, bumptious, magisterial, imperious; high-handed, – and mighty; overweening, consequential; arrogant etc. 885; unblushing etc. 880.

stiff, -necked; starch; perked –, stuck- up; in buckram, straitlaced; prim etc. (*affected*) 855.

on one's -high horses, – tight ropes, – high ropes; on stilts; *en grand seigneur*.
Adv. with head erect, with one's nose in the air.
Phr. *odi profanum vulgus et arceo*.

879. Humility.—N. hum-ility, -bleness; meek-, low-ness; lowli-ness, -hood; abasement, self-abasement, -effacement; submission etc. 725; resignation.

condescension; affability etc. (*courtesy*) 894.
modesty etc. 881; verecundity, blush, suffusion, confusion; sense of -shame, – disgrace; humiliation, mortification; let –, set- down.

V. be -humble etc. *adj.*; deign, vouchsafe, condescend; humble –, demean- oneself; stoop, – to conquer; carry coals; submit etc. 725; submit with a good grace etc. (*brook*) 826; yield the palm.

lower one's -tone, – note; sing small, draw in one's horns, sober, down; hide one's -face, – diminished head; not dare to show one's face, take shame to oneself, not have a word to say for oneself; feel –, be conscious of- -shame, – disgrace; drink the cup of humiliation to the dregs; eat -humble pie, – one's words, – dirt; be humiliated, receive a snub.

blush -for, – up to the eyes; redden, change color; color up; hang one's head, look foolish, feel small.

render humble; humble, humiliate; let –, set –, take –, tread –, frown- down; snub, abash, abase, make one sing small, strike dumb; teach one -his distance, – his place; take down a peg, – lower; throw –, cast- into the shade etc. 874; stare –, put- out of countenance; put to the blush; confuse, ashame, mortify, disgrace, crush; send away with a flea in one's ear.

get a set down.

Adj. humble, lowly, meek; modest etc. 881; humble-, sober-minded; unoffended; submissive etc. 725; servile etc. 886.

condescending; affable etc. (*courteous*) 894.

humbled etc. *v.*; bowed down, resigned; abashed, ashamed, dashed; out of countenance; down in the mouth; down on one's -knees, – marrow-bones; humbled in the dust, brow-beaten; chap-, crest-fallen; dumbfoundered, flabbergasted, struck all of a heap.

shorn of one's glory etc. (*disrepute*) 874.

Adv. with -downcast eyes, – bated breath, – bended knee; on all fours, on one's feet.

under correction, with due deference.

Phr. I am your -obedient, – very humble- servant; my service to you.

880. Vanity.—**N.** vanity; conceit, -edness; self-conceit, -complacency, -confidence, -sufficiency, -esteem, -love, -approbation, -praise, -glorification, -laudation, -gratulation, -applause, -admiration; *amour-propre*; selfishness etc. 943.

airs, pretensions, mannerism; egotism; prigg-ism, -ishness; coxcombry, gaudery, vainglory, elation; pride etc. 878; ostentation etc. 882; assurance etc. 885.

vox et praeterea nihil; *cheval de bataille.*

ego-ist, -tist; peacock, coxcomb etc. 854; Sir Oracle etc. 887.

V. be -vain etc. *adj.*, – vain of; pique oneself etc. (*pride*) 878; lay the flattering unction to one's soul.

have -too high, – an overweening- opinion of -oneself, – one's talents; blind oneself as to one's own merit; not think -small beer, – *vin ordinaire*-of oneself; put oneself forward; fish for compliments; give oneself airs etc. (*assume*) 885; boast etc. 884.

render -vain etc. *adj.*; inspire with -vanity etc. *n.*; inflate, puff up, turn up, turn one's head.

Adj. vain, – as a peacock; conceited, assured, overweening, pert, forward, perky; vain-glorious, high-flown; ostentatious etc. 882; puffed up, inflated, flushed.

self-satisfied, -confident, -sufficient, -flattering, -admiring, -applauding, -glorious, -opinionated; *entêté* etc. (*wrong-headed*) 481; wise in one's own conceit, pragmatical, overwise, pretentious, priggish; egotistic, -al; *soi-disant* etc. (*boastful*) 884; arrogant etc. 885.

un-abashed, -blushing; un-constrained, - ceremonious; free and easy.

Adv. vainly etc. *adj.*

Phr. how we apples swim!

881. Modesty.—**N.** modesty; humility etc. 879; diffidence, timidity; retiring disposition, unobtrusiveness, bashfulness etc. *adj.*; *mauvaise honte*; blush, -ing; verecundity; self-knowledge.

reserve, constraint; demureness etc. *adj.*; blushing honors.

V. be -modest etc. *adj.*; retire, reserve oneself; give way to; draw in one's horns etc. 879; hide one's face.

keep -private, – in the background, – one's distance; pursue the noiseless tenor of one's way, 'do good by stealth and blush to find it fame,' hide one's light under a bushel, cast a sheep's eye.

Adj. modest, diffident; humble etc. 879; timid, timorous, bashful; shy, nervous, skittish, coy, sheepish, shamefaced, blushing, over-modest.

unpreten-ding, -tious; un-obtrusive, -assuming, - ostentatious, -boastful, -aspiring; poor in spirit.

out of countenance etc. (*humbled*) 879.

reserved, constrained, demure.

Adv. humbly etc. *adj.*; quietly, privately; without -ceremony, – beat of the drum; *sans facon.*

882. Ostentation.—**N.** ostentation, display, show, flourish, parade, *étalage*, pomp, array, state, solemnity, dash, splash, glitter, strut, swank, side, swagger, pomposity; preten-se, -sions; showing off; fuss.

magnificence, splendor; *coup d'oeil*; grand doings.

coup de théâter; stage -effect, – trick; clap-trap; *mise en scène*; *tour de force*; *chic.*

demonstration, flying colors; tomfoolery; flourish of trumpets etc. (*celebration*) 883; pageant, -ry; spectacle, exhibition, procession; turn –, set- out; grand function; *fête*, gala, field-day, review, march past, promenade, insubstantial pageant.

dress; court –, full –, evening –, ball –, fancy- dress; tailoring, millinery, man-millinery, frippery; foppery; equipage.

ceremon-y, -ial; ritual; form, -ality; etiquette; punct-o, -ilio, -ilious-ness; starched-, stateli-ness.

mummery, solemn mockery, mouth honor.

attitudinarian; fop etc. 854.

V. be -ostentatious etc. *adj.*; come –, put oneself- forward; attract attention, star it.

make –, cut- a -figure, – dash, – splash; strut, blow one's own trumpet; figure, – away; make a show, – display; glitter.

show -off, – one's paces; parade, march past;

display, exhibit, put forward, hold up; trot –, hang- out; sport, brandish, blazon forth; dangle, – before the eyes.

cry up etc. (*praise*) 931; *prôner*, flaunt, emblazon, prink, set off, mount, have framed and glazed.

put a good, – smiling- face upon; clean the outside of the platter etc. (*disguise*) 544.

Adj. ostentatious, showy, dashing, pretentious ja-, jau-nty; grand, pompous, palatial; high sounding; turgid etc. (*big-sounding*) 577; garish, gorgeous; gaudy, – as a -peacock, – butterfly, – tulip; flaunting, flashing, flaming, glittering; gay etc. (*ornate*) 847; colorful.

splendid, magnificent, sumptuous.

theatrical, dramatic, spectacular, scenic, ceremonial, ritual, -istic.

solemn, stately, majestic, formal, stiff, ceremonious, punctilious, starch-ed, -y.

en grande tenue, in best bib and tucker, in Sunday best, *endimanché*.

Adv. with -flourish of trumpet, – beat of drum, – flying colors, – a brass band.

ad captandum vulgus.

883. Celebration.—N. celebration, solemnization, jubilee, diamond jubilee, commemoration, ovation, paean, triumph, jubilation.

triumphal arch, bonfire, salute; salvo, – of artillery; *feu de joie*, flourish of trumpets, *fanfare*, colors flying, illuminations, fireworks.

inauguration, installation, presentation; *début*, coming out, birthday anniversary, bi-, ter-, centenary; silver –, golden –, diamond- wedding, - day; coronation; Lord Mayor's show; harvest home, red letter day, festival; trophy etc. 733; *Te Deum* etc. (*thanksgiving*) 990; fete etc. 882; holiday etc. 840.

V. celebrate, keep, signalize, do honor to, commemorate, solemnize, hallow, mark with a red letter, hold high festival, maffick.

pledge, drink to, toast, hob and nob.

inaugurate, install, instate, induct, chair.

rejoice etc. 838; kill the fatted calf, hold jubilee, roast an ox, fire a salute.

Adj. celebrating etc. *v.*; commemorative, celebrated, immortal.

Adv. in -honor, – commemoration, – celebration of.

Int. hail! all hail! *io -paean, – triumphe!* 'see the conquering hero comes!'

884. Boasting.—N. boasting etc. *v.*; boast, vaunt, crake; preten-ce, -sions; puff, -ery; flourish, fanfaronnade; gasconade; bluff, swank, brag, - gardism; bravado, bunkum, Buncombe; high-falutin; jact-itation, -ancy; bounce, rant, bluster; venditation, vaporing, rodomontade, bombast, fine talking, tall talk, magniloquence, teratology, heroics; jingoism, Chauvinism; exaggeration etc. 549; gas, hot air.

vanity etc. 880; *vox et praeterea nihil*; much cry and little wool, *brutum fulmen*.

exultation; glorification; flourish of trumpets; triumph etc. 883.

boaster; bragg-art, -adocio; hot air merchant;

Gascon, *fanfaron*, pretender, fourflusher, *soi-disant*; windbag, blowhard, bluffer; chauvinist; blusterer etc. 887; charlatan, jack-pudding, trumpeter; puppy etc. (*fop*) 854.

V. boast, make a boast of, brag, vaunt, puff, show off, flourish, crake, crack, trumpet, strut, swagger, vapor, bluff; draw the long bow.

exult, crow over, neigh, chuckle, triumph; glory, gloat, jubilate; throw up one's cap; talk big, *se faire valoir, faire claquer son fouet*, take merit to oneself, make a merit of, sing *Io triumphe*, holloa before one is out of the wood.

Adj. boasting etc. *v.*; magniloquent, flaming, Thrasonic, stilted, gasconading, braggart, boastful, pretentious, *soi-disant*; vain-glorious etc. (*conceited*) 880.

elate, -d; jubilant, triumphant, exultant; in high feather; flushed, – with victory; cock-a-hoop; on stilts.

vaunted etc. *v.*

Adv. vauntingly etc. *adj.*; with a brass band.

Phr. 'let the galled jade wince.'

885. Insolence. [Undue assumption of superiority.]—**N.** insolence; haughtiness etc. *adj.*; arrogance, airs; overbearance, brashness, bumptiousness, contumely, disdain; domineering etc. *v.*; tyranny etc. 739.

impertinence; cheek, nerve, sauce; sauciness-etc. *adj.*; flippancy, dicacity, petulance, procacity, bluster; swagger, -ing etc. *v.*; bounce; terrorism; jingoism, chauvinism.

as-, pre-sumption; beggar on horseback; usurpation.

impudence, assurance, audacity, self-assertion, hardihood, front, face, brass; shamelessness etc. *adj.*; effrontery, hardened front, face of brass.

assumption of infallibility.

malapert, saucebox etc. (*blusterer*) 887.

V. be -insolent etc. *adj.*; bluster, vapor, swagger, swell, give oneself airs; snap one's fingers, kick up a dust; swear etc. (*affirm*) 535; rap out oaths; roister.

arrogate; as-, pre-sume; make -bold, – free; take a liberty, give an inch and take an ell.

domineer, bully, dictate, hector; lord it over, bulldoze; *traiter de haut, regarder de haut en bas*; exact; snub, huff, beard, fly in the face of; put to the blush; bear –, beat- down; browbeat, intimidate; trample –, tread- down,   under foot; dragoon, ride roughshod over, terrorize.

out-face, -look, -stare, -brazen, -brave; stare out of countenance; brazen out; lay down the law; teach one's grandmother to suck eggs; assume a lofty bearing; talk –, look- big; put on big looks, act the *grand seigneur*; mount –, ride- the high horse; toss the head, carry with a high hand.

tempt Providence, want snuffing.

Adj. insolent, haughty, arrogant, imperious, magisterial, dictatorial, arbitrary; high-handed, high and mighty; contumelious, supercilious, overbearing, intolerant, domineering; overweening, high-flown.

flippant, pert, cavalier, saucy, forward, impertinent, fresh, malapert.

precocious, assuming, would-be, bumptious.

bluff; brazen-, browed-faced, shameless, aweless, unblushing, unabashed; bold-, bare-faced; dead –, lost- to shame.

impudent, audacious, presumptuous, free and easy, devil-may-care, rollicking; janty, jaunty; roistering, blustering, hectoring, swaggering, vaporing; thrasonic, fire-eating, 'full of sound and fury.'

Adv. insolently, with a high hand; *ex cathedrâ*.

Phr. one's bark being worse than his bite.

886. Servility.—N. servility; slavery etc. (*subjection*) 749; obsequiousness etc. *adj.*; subserviency; abasement; pros-tration, -ternation; genuflexion etc. (*worship*) 990; fawning etc. *v.*; tuft-hunting, time-serving, flunkeyism; sycophancy etc. (*flattery*) 933; humility etc. 879.

sycophant, parasite, yes-man; toad, -y, -eater; tuft-hunter; snob, flunkey, lap-dog, spaniel, lick-spittle, smell-feast, *Graeculus esuriens*, hanger on, stooge, *cavaliere servente*, led captain, carpet knight; time-server, fortune-hunter, Vicar of Bray, Sir Pertinax Mac Sycophant, pick-thank; flatterer etc. 935; doer of dirty work; *âme damnée*, tool; reptile; slave etc. (*servant*) 746; courtier; sponge, jackal; truckler.

V. cringe, bow, stoop, kneel, bend the knee; fall on one's knees, prostrate oneself; worship etc. 990.

sneak, crawl, crouch, cower, truckle to, grovel, fawn, toady, lick the feet of, kiss the hem of one's garment.

pay court to; feed –, fatten –, batten- on; dance attendance on, pin oneself upon, hang on the sleeve of, *avaler des couleuvres*, keep time to, fetch and carry, do the dirty work of.

go with the stream, follow the crowd, worship the rising sun, hold with the hare and run with the hounds.

Adj. servile, obsequious; supple, – as a glove; soapy, oily, pliant, cringing, fawning, slavish, groveling, sniveling, mealy-mouthed; beggarly, sycophantic, parasitical; abject, prostrate, down on one's marrow-bones; base, mean, sneaking; crouching etc. *v.*

Adv. hat –, cap- in hand.

887. Blusterer.—N. bluster-, swagger-, vapor-, roister-, brawl-er; brazen-face; *fanfaron*; braggart etc. (*boaster*) 884; bully, terrorist, rough, rough-neck; hooligan, hoodlum, larrikin, ruffian; Mohock, -hawk; drawcansir, swashbuckler, Captain Boabdil, Sir Lucius O'Trigger, Thraso, Pistol, Parolles, Bombastes Furioso, Hector, Chrononhotonthologos; jingo; desperado, dare-devil, fire-eater; fury etc. (*violent person*) 173; rowdy.

puppy etc. (*fop*) 854; prig; Sir Oracle, dogmatist, *doctrinaire*, stump orator, jack-in-office; saucebox, malapert, jackanapes, minx; bantam-cock.

888. Friendship.—N. friendship, amity; friendliness etc. *adj.*; brotherhood, fraternity, sodality, confraternity, sorosis, sisterhood; harmony etc. (*concord*) 714; peace etc. 721.

firm –, staunch –, intimate –, familiar –, bosom –, cordial –, tried –, devoted –, lasting –, fast –, sincere –, warm –, ardent- friendship.

cordiality, fraternization, *entente cordiale*, good

understanding, *rapprochement*, sympathy, fellow-feeling, response, welcomeness; *camaraderie*.

affection etc. (*love*) 897; favoritism; goodwill etc. (*benevolence*) 906; partiality.

acquaintance, familiarity, intimacy, intercourse, fellowship, knowledge of; introduction.

V. be -friendly etc. *adj.*, – friends etc. 890; – acquainted with etc. *adj.*; know; have the ear of; keep- company with etc. (*sociality*) 892; hold communication –, have dealings –, sympathize- with; have a leaning to; bear good will etc. (*benevolence*) 906; love etc. 897; make much of; befriend etc. (*aid*) 707; introduce to.

set one's horses together; hold out –, extend the right hand of -friendship, – fellowship; become -friendly etc. *adj.*; make -friends etc. 890 with; break the ice, be introduced to; make –, pick –, scrape- acquaintance with; get into favor, gain the friendship of.

shake hands with, fraternize, embrace; receive with open arms, throw oneself into the arms of; meet half way, take in good part.

Adj. friendly, amic-able, -al; well affected, unhostile, neighborly, brotherly, fraternal, sisterly, sympathetic, harmonious, hearty, cordial, warm-hearted, devoted.

friends –, well –, at home –, hand in hand-with; on -good, – friendly, – amicable, – cordial, – familiar, – intimate- -terms; – footing; on -speaking, – visiting- terms; in one's good - graces, – books.

acquainted, familiar, intimate, thick, hand and glove, hail fellow well met, free and easy; welcome.

Adv. amicably etc. *adj.*; with open arms; *sans cérémonie*; arm in arm.

889. Enmity.—N. enmity, hostility; un-friendliness etc. *adj.*; discord etc. 713.

alienation, estrangement; dislike etc. 867; hate etc. 898; antagonism.

heartburning; animosity etc. 900; malevolence etc. 907.

V. be -inimical etc. *adj.*; keep –, hold- at arm's length; be at loggerheads; bear malice etc. 907; fall out; take umbrage etc. 900; harden the heart, alienate, estrange.

Adj. inimical, unfriendly, hostile; at -enmity, – variance, – swords points, – daggers drawn, – open war with; up in arms against; in bad odor with.

on bad –, not on speaking- terms; cool; cold, -hearted; estranged, alienated, disaffected, irreconcilable.

890. Friend.—N. friend, – of one's bosom, intimate acquaintance, neighbor, well-wisher; *alter ego*; best –, bosom –, fast- friend; *amicus usque ad aras*; *fidus Achates*; *persona grata*.

favorer, *fautor*, patron, backer, Maecenas; tutelary saint, good genius, advocate, partisan, sympathizer; ally; friend in need etc. (*auxiliary*) 711.

associate, compeer, comrade, mate, companion, *confrère*, *camarade*, *confidante*, colleague; old –, crony, side-kick; chum, buddy, bunkie, roommate, pal; play-fellow, -mate; classmate, schoolfellow; bed-fellow, -mate; maid of honor.

compatriot; fellow –, countryman, – townsman.

shop-, ship-, mess-mate; fellow –, boon –, pot-companion; co-partner.

Arcades ambo, Pylades and Orestes, Castor and Pollux, Nisus and Euryalus, Damon and Pythias, *par nobile fratrum.*

host, Amphitryon, Boniface; guest, visitor, frequenter, *habitué; protégé.*

891. Enemy.—N. enemy; antagonist, foeman; open –, bitter- enemy; opponent etc. 710; back friend.

public enemy, enemy to society, traitor, anarchist etc. 743.

Phr. every hand being against one.

892. Sociality.—N. soci-ality, -ability, -ableness etc. *adj.;* social intercourse; consociation; intercourse, -community; consort-, companion-, fellow-, comrade-ship; clubbism; *esprit de corps.*

conviviality; good -fellowship, – company, *camaraderie;* joviality, jollity, *savoir -vivre,* festivity, festive board, merry-making; loving cup; hospitality, heartiness; cheer.

welcome, -ness; greeting; hearty –, warm –, welcome- reception; urbanity etc. *(courtesy)* 894; intimacy, familiarity.

good –, jolly- fellow, good mixer, Rotarian; *bon enfant.*

social –, family- circle; circle of acquaintance, *coterie,* society, company.

social -gathering, – *réunion;* assembly etc. *(assemblage)* 72; party, entertainment, reception, *levée,* at home, *conversazione, soirée, matinée,* evening –, morning –, afternoon –, garden –, dinner –, tea –, cocktail- party; symposium, sing-song; kettle-, drum; *partie carrée,* dish of tea, *ridotto,* rout, housewarming; ball, prom, hop, dance, *thé dansant;* festival etc. *(amusement)* 840; wedding breakfast; 'the feast of reason and the flow of soul.'

visit, -ing; round of visits; call, morning call; interview etc. *(interlocution)* 588; assignation; tryst, -ing place; appointment.

club etc. *(association)* 712.

V. be -sociable etc. *adj.;* know; be -acquainted etc. *adj.;* associate –, sort –, keep company –, walk hand in hand -with; eat off the same trencher, club together, consort, bear one company, join; make acquaintance with etc. *(friendship)* 888; make advances, fraternize, embrace; intercommunicate.

be –, feel –, make oneself- at home with; make free with; crack a bottle with; take pot luck with, receive hospitality, live at free quarters.

visit, pay a visit; interchange -visits, – cards; call -at, – upon; leave a card; drop in, look in; look one up, beat up one's quarters.

entertain; give a -party etc. *n.;* be at home, see one's friends, hang out, keep open house, do the honors; receive, – with open arms; welcome; give a warm reception etc. *n.* to; kill the fatted calf.

Adj. sociable, companionable, clubbable, clubby, conversable, cosy, cosey, chatty, conversational; homiletical.

convivial; fest-ive, -al; jovial, jolly, hospitable.

welcome, – as the roses in May; *fêté,* entertained.

free and easy, hail fellow well met, familiar, on visiting terms, acquainted.

social, neighborly; international, cosmopolitan, gregarious.

Adv. *en famille,* in the family circle; *sans -facon,* – *cérémonie,* arm in arm.

893. Seclusion. Exclusion.—N. seclusion, privacy; retirement; concealment; reclusion, recess; snugness etc. *adj.;* delitescence; rustication, *rus in urbe;* solitude; solitariness etc. *(singleness)* 87; isolation; loneliness etc. *adj.;* estrangement from the world, anchoritism, voluntary exile; aloofness.

cell, hermitage; convent etc. 1000; *sanctum sanctorum;* study, library, den; hide-out.

depopulation, desertion, desolation; wilderness etc. *(unproductive)* 169; howling wilderness; rotten borough, Old Sarum.

exclusion, excommunication, banishment, exile, ostracism, proscription; cut, – direct; dead cut.

inhospit-ality, -ableness etc. *adj.;* un-, dissociability; domesticity, Darby and Joan.

recluse, hermit, eremite, cenobite; anchor-et, -ite; Simon Stylites; Troglodyte, Timon of Athens, Santon, *solitaire,* ruralist, disciple of Zimmermann, closet cynic, Diogenes; outcast, Pariah, casta ᷣᷣ outsider, pilgarlic; wastrel, foundling, orphan.

V. be –, live- secluded etc. *adj.;* keep –, stand –, hold oneself- -aloof, – in the background; keep snug; shut oneself up; deny –, seclude-oneself; creep into a corner, rusticate, *aller planter ses choux;* retire, – from the world; hermetize, take the veil; abandon etc. 624.

cut, – dead; refuse to -associate with, – acknowledge; look cool –, turn one's back –, shut the door- upon; repel, blackball, excommunicate, exclude, exile, expatriate; banish, outlaw, maroon, ostracize, proscribe, cut off from, send to Coventry, keep at arm's length, draw a cordon round; boycott, blockade, lay an embargo on, isolate.

depopulate; dis-, un-people.

Adj. secluded, sequestered, retired, delitescent, private, bye; out of the -world, -way; in a backwater; 'the world forgetting by the world forgot.'

snug, domestic, stay-at-home.

unsociable; un-, dis-social; inhospitable, cynical, inconversable, unclubbable, *sauvage,* eremetic.

solitary; lone-ly, -some; isolated, single.

excluded, estranged; unfrequented; uninhabit-able, -ed; tenantless; un-tenanted, -occupied; abandoned; deserted, – in one's utmost need; un-friended; kith-, friend-, home-less; lorn, forlorn, desolate.

un-visited, -introduced, -invited, -welcome; under a cloud, left to shift for oneself, derelict, outcast, outside the gates.

banished etc. *v.;* under an embargo.

Phr. *noli me tangere.*

894. Courtesy.—N. courtesy; respect etc. 928; good -manners, – behavior, – breeding; manners; politeness etc. *adj.; bienséance,* urbanity, comity, gentility; gentle –, breeding; polish, presence, cultivation, culture; civili-ty, -zation; amenity, suavity; good -temper, – humor; amiability, easy temper, complacency, soft tongue, mansuetude; condescension etc. (*humility*) 879; affability, complaisance, *prévenance*, amiability, gallantry, chivalry; pink of -politeness, – courtesy.

compliment; fair –, soft –, sweet- words; honeyed phrases, flattering remarks, ceremonial; salutation, reception, presentation, introduction, *accueil*, greeting, recognition; welcome, *abord*, respects, *devoir*, regards, remembrances; kind -regards, – remembrances; love, best love, duty; deference.

obeisance etc. (*reverence*) 928; bow, courtesy, curtsy, scrape, *salaam*, *kow-tow*, bowing and scraping; kneeling; genuflexion etc. (*worship*) 990; obsequiousness etc. 886; capping, shaking hands etc. *v.*; grip of the hand, embrace, hug, squeeze, *accolade*, loving cup, *vin d'honneur*, pledge; love token etc. (*endearment*) 902; kiss, buss, salute.

mark of recognition, not; 'nods and becks and wreathed smiles;' valediction etc. 293; condolence etc. 915.

V. be -courteous etc. *adj.*; show -courtesy etc. *n.*

mind one's P's and Q's, behave oneself, be all things to all men, conciliate, speak one fair, take in good part; make –, do- the amiable; look as if butter would not melt in one's mouth; mend one's manners.

receive, do the honors, usher, greet, hail, bid welcome; welcome, – with open arms; shake hands; hold out – press –, squeeze- the hand; bid God speed; speed the parting guest; cheer, serenade.

salute; embrace etc. (*endearment*) 902; kiss, – hands; drink to, pledge, hob and nob; move to, nod to; smile upon.

uncover, cap; touch –, take off- the hat; doff the cap; pull the forelock; present arms; make way for; bow; make one's bow; scrape, curtsy, courtesy; bob a -curtsy, – courtesy; kneel; bow –, bend- the knee; salaam, *kowtow*.

visit, wait upon, present oneself, pay one's respects, pay a visit etc. (*sociability*) 892; dance attendance on etc. (*servility*) 886; pay attentions to; do homage to etc. (*respect*) 928.

prostrate oneself etc. (*worship*) 990.

give –, send- one's duty etc. *n.* to.

render -polite etc. *adj.*; polish, civilize, humanize.

Adj. courteous, polite, civil, mannerly, urbane; well-behaved, -mannered, -bred, -brought up, gently bred, of gentle -breeding, – manners, good-mannered, polished, civilized, cultivated; refined etc. (*taste*) 850; gentlemanlike etc. (*fashion*) 852; gallant, chivalrous, on one's good behavior.

fine –, fair –, soft- spoken; honey-mouthed, -tongued; oily, unctuous, bland, suave; obliging, conciliatory, complaisant, complacent; obsequious etc. 886.

ingratiating, winning; gentle, mild; good-humored, cordial, genial, amiable, tactful, addressful, affable, genial, friendly, familiar; neigh-borly.

Adv. courteously etc. *adj.*; with a good grace; with -open, – outstretched- arms; *à bras ouverts*; *suaviter in modo*, in good humor.

Int. hail! welcome! well met! *ave!* all hail! good -day, – morning etc., – morrow! God speed! *pax vobiscum!* may your shadow never be less! *chin-chin!*

895. Discourtesy.—N. discourtesy; ill-breeding; ill –, bad –, ungainly- manners; insuavity; grouchiness; un-courteousness etc. *adj.*, tactlessness; rusticity, inurbanity; illiberality, incivility, displacency.

disrespect etc. 929; procacity, impudence; barbar-ism, -ity; misbehavior, brutality, blackguard--ism, conduct unbecoming a gentleman, *grossièreté*, *brusquerie*; vulgarity etc. 851.

churlishness etc. *adj.*; spinosity, perversity; moroseness etc. (*sullenness*) 901a.

bad-, ill-temper; sternness etc. *adj.*; austerity; moodishness, captiousness etc. 901; cynicism; tartness etc. *adj.*; acrimony, acerbity, virulence, asperity.

scowl, black looks, frown; short answer, rebuff; hard words, contumely; unparliamentary language, personality.

bear, bruin, brute, grouch, blackguard, beast; unlicked cub; frump, cross-patch; saucebox etc. 887.

V. be -rude etc. *adj.*; insult etc. 929; treat with discourtesy; take a name in vain; make -bold, – free- with; take a liberty; stare out of countenance, ogle, point at, put to the blush.

cut; turn -one's back upon, – on one's heel; give the cold shoulder; keep at -a distance, – arm's length; look -cool, – coldly, – black- upon; show the door to, send away with a flea in the ear.

lose one's temper etc. (*resentment*) 900; sulk etc. 901a; frown, scowl, glower, pout; snap, snarl, growl.

render -rude etc. *adj.*; brut-alize, -ify.

Adj. dis-, un-courteous; uncourtly; ill-bred, -mannered, -behaved, -conditioned, unbred; un-manner-ly, -ed; im-, un-polite; un-polished, -civilized, -genteel; ungentleman-like, -ly; unladylike; blackguard; vulgar etc. 851; dedecorous; foul-mouthed, -spoken; abusive.

un-civil, -gracious, -ceremonious; cool; pert, forward, obtrusive, impudent, rude, saucy, precocious; insolent etc. 885.

repulsive; un-complaisant, -accommodating, -neighborly, -gallant; inaffable; un-gentle, -gainly; rough, rugged, bluff, blunt, gruff; churl-, boor-, bear-ish; brutal, *brusque*; stern, harsh, austere; cavalier.

tart, sour, crabbed, sharp, short, trenchant, sarcastic, crusty, biting, caustic, virulent, bitter, acrimonious, venomous, contumelious; snarling etc., *v.*; surly, – as a bear; perverse; grim, sullen etc. 901a; peevish etc. (*irascible*) 901.

Adv. discourteously etc. *adj.*; with -discourtesy etc. *n.*, – a bad grace.

896. Congratulations.—N. con-, gratulation; felicitation; salute etc. 894; condolence etc. 915; compliments of the season; good –, best- wishes.

V. con-, gratulate; felicitate; compliment; give –, wish one- joy; tender –, offer- one's congratulations; wish -many happy returns of the day, – a merry Christmas and a happy new year.

congratulate oneself etc. (*rejoice*) 838.

Adj. con-, gratulatory.

897. Love.—N. love; fondness etc. *adj.*; liking; inclination etc. (*desire*) 865; regard, dilection, admiration, fancy.

affection, sympathy, fellow-felling; tenderness etc. *adj.*; heart, brotherly love; benevolence etc. 906; attachment.

yearning, tender passion, *affaire de coeur*, *amour*, gallantry, passion, flame, devotion, fervor, enthusiasm, transport of love, rapture, enchantment, infatuation, adoration, idolatry.

narcissism, Oedipus complex, Electra complex.

Cupid, Venus, Eros; myrtle; true lover's knot; love -token, – suit, – affair, – tale, – story; the old story, plighted love; courtship etc. 902; *amourette*.

maternal love.

attractiveness, charm; popularity; favorite etc. 899.

lover, suitor, follower, admirer, adorer, wooer, amoret, beau, sweetheart, inamorato, swain, young man, flame, love, truelove; leman, Lothario, gallant, paramor, *amoroso, cavaliere servente*, captive, *cicisbeo*; *caro sposo*, Don Juan, sheik, ladies' man, squire of dames, Knave of Hearts.

inamorata, lady-love, idol, darling, duck, Dulcinea, angel, goddess, *cara sposa*; mistress.

betrothed, affianced, *fiancée*.

flirt, *coquette*; amorette; pair of turtle doves; abode of love, *agapemone*.

V. love, like, affect, fancy, care for, take an interest in, be partial to, sympathize with; be -in love etc. *adj.*- with; have –, entertain –, harbor –, cherish- a -love etc. *n.* for; regard, revere; take to, bear love to, be wedded to; set one's affections on; make much of, feast one's eyes on; hold dear, prize, treasure; hug, cling to, cherish, pet, caress etc. 902.

burn; adore, idolize, love to distraction, *aimer eperdument*; dote -on, – upon.

take a fancy to, fall for, be stuck on, look sweet upon; become -enamored etc. *adj.*; fall in love with, lose one's heart; desire etc. 865.

excite love; win –, gain –, secure –, engage-the -love, – affections, – heart; take the fancy of; have a place in –, wind round- the heart; attract, attach, endear, charm, fascinate, captivate, bewitch, seduce, enamor, enrapture, turn the head.

get into favor; ingratiate –, insinuate –, worm-oneself; propitiate, curry favor with, pay one's court to, make a date with, *faire l'aimable*, set one's cap at, flirt, coquet.

Adv. loving etc. *v.*; fond of; taken –, struck-with; smitten, bitten; attached to, wedded to; enamored; charmed etc. *v.*; in love; lovesick; over head and ears in love.

affectionate, tender, sweet upon, sympathetic, loving, fond, amorous, amatory; erotic, uxurious, ardent, passionate, rapturous, devoted, motherly.

loved etc. *v.*; beloved; well –, dearly- beloved; dear, precious, darling, pet, little; favorite, popular.

congenial; to –, after- one's -mind, – taste, – fancy, – own heart.

in one's good -graces etc. (*friendly*) 888; dear as the apple of one's eye, nearest to one's heart.

lovable, adorable; lovely, sweet; attractive, seductive, winning; charming, engaging, interesting, enchanting, captivating, fascinating, intriguing, bewitching; amiable, like an angel, angelic, seraphic.

898. Hate.—N. hate, hatred, vials of hate; Hymn of Hate.

dis-affection, -favor; alienation, estrangement, coolness; enmity etc. 889; animosity etc. 900.

umbrage, pique, grudge; dudgeon, spleen; bitterness, – of feeling; ill –, bad- blood; acrimony; malice etc. 907; implacability etc. (*revenge*) 919.

repugnance etc. (*dislike*) 867; odium, unpopularity; loathing, detestation, antipathy; object of -hatred, – execration; abomination, aversion, *bête noire*; enemy etc. 891; bitter pill; source of annoyance etc. 830.

V. hate, detest, abominate, abhor, loathe; recoil –, shudder- at; shrink from, view with horror, hold in abomination, revolt against, execrate; scowl etc. 895; disrelish etc. (*dislike*) 867.

owe a grudge; bear -spleen, – a grudge, – malice etc. (*malevolence*) 907; conceive an aversion to.

excite –, provoke- hatred etc. *n.*; be -hateful etc. *adj.*; stink in the nostrils; estrange, alienate, repel, set against, sow dissension, set by the ears, envenom, incense, irritate, rile, ruffle, vex; horrify etc. 830.

Adj. hating etc. *v.*; abhorrent; averse from etc. (*disliking*) 867; set against.

bitter etc. (*acrimonious*) 895; implacable etc. (*revengeful*) 919.

un-loved, -beloved, -lamented, -deplored, -mourned, -cared for, -endured, -valued; disliked etc. 867.

crossed in love, forsaken, rejected, love-lorn, jilted.

obnoxious, hateful, odious, abominable, repulsive, offensive, shocking, disgusting etc. (*disagreeable*) 830.

invidious, spiteful; malicious etc. 907.

insulting, irritating, provoking.

[Mutual hate] at -daggers drawn, – swords points; not on speaking terms etc.. (*enmity*) 889.

Phr. no love lost between.

899. Favorite.—N. favorite, pet, cosset, minion, idol, jewel, spoiled child, *enfant gâté*; led captain; crony; fondling; apple of one's eye, man after one's own heart; *persona grata*.

love, dear, darling, duck, honey, jewel; mopsey, moppet; sweetheart etc. (*love*) 897.

general –, universal- favorite; idol of the people; matinée idol, movie –, radio- star.

900. Resentment.—N. resentment, displeasure, animosity, anger, wrath, indignation; vexation, exasperation, bitter resentment, wrathful indignation.

pique, umbrage, huff, miff, soreness, dudgeon, acerbity, virulence, bitterness, acrimony, asperity, spleen, gall; heart-burning, -swelling; rankling.

ill –, bad -humor, – temper; irascibility etc. 901; ill blood etc. (*hate*) 898; revenge etc. 919.

excitement, irritation; warmth, bile, choler, ire, fume, pucker, dander, ferment, ebullition; towering -passion, – rage, *acharnement*, angry mood, taking, pet, tiff, passion, fit, tantrums.

burst, explosion, paroxysm, storm, rage, fury, desperation; violence etc. 173; fire and fury; vials of wrath; gnashing of teeth, hot blood, high words.

scowl etc. 895; sulks etc. 901a.

[Cause of umbrage] affront, provocation, offence; indignity etc. (*insult*) 929; grudge, crow to pluck, sore subject; red rag to a bull; *casus belli*.

Furies, Erinys, Eumenides, Alecto, Megaera, Tisiphone.

buffet, slap in the face, box on the ear, rap on the knuckles.

V. resent; take -amiss, – ill, – to heart, – offence, – umbrage, – huff, – exception; take in - ill part, – bad part, – dudgeon; *ne pas entendre raillerie*; breathe revenge, cut up rough.

fly –, fall –, get- into a -rage, – passion; bridle –, oristle –, froth –, fire –, flare- up; open –, pour out- the vials of one's wrath.

pout, knit the brow, frown, scowl, lower, snarl, growl, gnarl, gnash, snap; redden, color; look - black, – black as thunder, – daggers; bite one's thumb; show –, grind- one's teeth; champ the bit.

chafe, mantle, fume, kindle, fly out, take fire; boil, – over; boil with -indignation, – rage; rage, storm, foam; vent one's -rage, – spleen; lose one's temper, stand on one's hind legs, stamp the foot, kick up a row, fly off the handle, cut up rough; stamp –, quiver –, swell –, foam- with rage; burst with anger; raise Cain, breathe fire and fury.

have a fling at; bear malice etc. (*revenge*) 919.

cause –, raise- anger; affront, offend; give offence, – umbrage; anger; hurt the feelings; insult, discompose, fret, ruffle, nettle, heckle, huff, pique; excite etc. 824; irritate, stir the blood, stir up bile; sting, – to the quick; rile, provoke, chafe, wound, incense, inflame, enrage, aggravate, add fuel to the flame, fan into a flame, widen the breach, envenom, embitter, exasperate, infuriate, kindle wrath; stick in one's gizzard; rankle etc. 919.

put out of humor; put one's -monkey, – backup; set –, get- one's back up; raise one's -gorge, – dander, – choler; work up into a passion; make - one's blood boil, – the ears tingle; throw into a ferment, madden, drive one mad; lash into -fury, – madness; fool to the top of one's bent; set by the ears.

· bring a hornet's nest about one's ears.

Adj. angry, wrath, irate; ire-, wrath-ful; cross etc. (*irascible*) 901; sulky etc. 901a; bitter, virulent; acrimonious etc. (*discourteous*) etc. 895; violent etc. 173.

warm, burning; boiling, – over; fuming, raging; foaming, – at the mouth; convulsed with rage.

offended etc. *v.*; waxy, *acharné*; wrought, worked up; indignant, hurt, sore, peeved; set against.

fierce, wild, rageful, furious, mad with rage, fiery, infuriate, rabid, savage; relentless etc. 919.

flushed with -anger, – rage; in a -huff, – stew, – fume, – pucker, – passion, – rage, – fury; on one's high ropes, up in arms; in high dudgeon.

Adv. angrily etc. *adj.*; in the height of passion; in the heat of -passion, – the moment.

Phr. one's -blood, – back, – monkey- being up; *fervens difficili bile jecur*; the gorge rising, eyes flashing fire; the blood -rising, – boiling; *haeret lateri lethalis arundo*.

901. Irascibility.—N. irascibility, temper; crossness etc. *adj.*; susceptibility, procacity,

petulance, irritability, tartness, acerbity, protervity; pugnacity etc. (*contentiousness*) 720.

excitability etc. 825; bad –, fiery –, crooked – , irritable etc. *adj.*- temper; *genus irritabile*; hot blood.

ill humor etc. (*sullenness*) 901a; asperity etc., churlishness etc. (*discourtesy*) 895.

huff etc. (resentment) 900; a word and a blow.

Sir Fretful Plagiary; brabbler, Tartar; shrew, vixen, virago, termagant, dragon, scold, Xanthippe; porcupine; spit-fire; fire-eater etc. (*blusterer*) 887; fury etc. (*violent person*) 173.

V. be -irascible etc. *adj.*; have a -temper etc. *n.*, – devil in one; fire up etc. (*be angry*) 900.

Adj. irascible; bad-, ill-tempered; irritable, susceptible; excitable etc. 825; thin-skinned etc. (*sensitive*) 822; fretful, fidgety; on the fret.

hasty, over-hasty, quick, warm, hot, testy, touchy, techy, tetchy; like -touchwood, – tinder; huffy; pet-tish, -ulant; waspish, snapp-y, -ish, peppery, fiery, passionate, choleric, shrewish, 'sudden and quick in quarrel.'

querulous, captious, mood-y, -ish; quarrelsome, contentious, disputatious; pugnacious etc. (*bellicose*) 720; cantankerous, exceptious, restive etc. (*perverse*) 901a; churlish etc. (*discourteous*) 895.

cross, – as -crabs, – two sticks, – a cat, – a dog, – the tongs; like a bear with a sore head; fractious, peevish, *acariâtre*.

in a bad temper; sulky etc. 901a; angry etc. 900. resent-ful, -ive; vindictive etc. 919.

Int. pish!

901a. Sullenness.—N. sullenness etc. *adj.*; morosity, spleen; churlishness etc. (*discourtesy*) 895; irascibility etc. 901.

moodiness etc. *adj.*; perversity; obstinacy etc. 606; torvity, spinosity; crabbedness etc. *adj.*

ill –, bad- -temper, – humor; sulks, dudgeon, mumps, doleful dumps, doldrums, fit of the sulks, *bouderie*, black looks, scowl, huff etc. (*resentment*) 900.

V. be -sullen etc. *adj.*; sulk; frown, scowl, lower, glower, grouse, grouch, crab, gloam, pout, have a hang-dog look, glout.

Adj. sullen, sulky; ill-tempered, -humored, - affected, -disposed; in -an ill, – a bad, – a shocking- -temper, – humor; out of -temper, – humor; knaggy, torvous, crusty, crabbed; sore as a boil; surly etc. (*discourteous*) 895.

moody; spleen-ish, -ly; splenetic, cankered.

cross, -grained; perverse, wayward, humorsome; restive; cantankerous, refractory, intractable, exceptious, sinistrous, deaf to reason, unaccommodating, rusty, crust, froward.

dogged etc. (*stubborn*) 606.

grumpy, glum, grim, grum, morose, frumpish; in the -sulks etc. *n.*; out of sorts; scowl-, glower-, growl-ing.

peevish etc. (*irascible*) 901.

902. Endearment. [Expression of affection or love.]**—N.** endearment, caress; blandish-, blandiment; *épanchement*, fondling, billing and cooing, dalliance.

embrace, salute; kiss, buss, smack, osculation,

deosculation; amorous glances; ogle, side glance, sheep's eyes.

courtship, wooing, suit, addresses, the soft impeachment; love-making; an affair; serenading; caterwauling.

flirting etc. *v.*; flirtation, gallantry; coquetry, spooning.

ture lover's knot, plighted love, engagement, bethrothal; love -tale, – token, – letter; *billet-doux*, valentine.

honeymoon; Strephon and Chloe, 'Arry and Arriet.

V. caress, fondle, pet, dandle, nurse; pat, – on the -head, – cheek; chuck under the chin, smile upon, coax, wheedle, cosset, coddle, cocker; make -of, – much of, pamper; cherish, foster, kill with kindness.

clasp, hug, cuddle; fold –, strain- in one's arms; nestle, nuzzle, neck, embrace, kiss, buss, smack, blow a kiss; salute etc. (*courtesy*) 894.

bill and coo, spoon, toy, dally, flirt, coquet; galli-, gala-vant; philander; make love; pay one's - court, – addresses, – attentions- to; serenade; court, woo; set one's cap at; be –, look- sweet upon; ogle, cast sheep's eyes upon; *faire les yeux doux*.

fall in love with, win the affections etc. (*love*) 897; die for.

propose; make –, have- an offer; pop the question; plight one's -troth, – faith; become - engaged, – betrothed.

Adj. caressing etc. *v.*; 'sighing like furnace;' love-sick, spoony.

carressed etc. *v.*

903. Marriage.—N. marriage, matrimony, wedlock, union, intermarriage, *vinculum matrimonii*, nuptial tie, knot.

married state, coverture, bed, cohabitation.

match; betrothment etc. (*promise*) 768; wedding, nuptials, Hymen, bridal; e-, spousals; leading to the altar etc. *v.*; nuptial benediction, *epithalamium*.

torch –, temple- of Hymen; hymeneal altar; honeymoon.

bride, bridegroom;. brides-maid; -man.

best –, grooms-man, page, usher.

married -man, – woman, – couple; neogamist, Benedick, partner, spouse, mate, yokemate; husband, man, consort, baron; old –, good- man; wife of one's bosom; help-meet, -mate, rib, better half, grey mare, old woman, good wife; feme, – . coverte; squaw, lady; matron, -age, -hood; man and wife; wedded pair, Darby and Joan.

affinity, soul-mate.

mono-, bi-, di-, deutero-, tri-, poly-gamy; mormonism; poly-andry; Turk, Bluebeard.

unlawful –, left-handed – , companionate –, morganatic –, ill-assorted- marriage; *mésalliance*; *mariage de convenance*; an affair.

match-maker, marriage broker, matrimonial agent.

V. marry, wive, take to oneself -a wife; be - married, – spliced; go –, pair- off; wed, espouse, lead to the hymeneal altar, take 'for better, for worse,' give one's hand to, bestow one's hand upon; remarry; intermarry.

marry, join, handfast; couple etc. (*unite*) 43; tie

the nuptial knot; give -away, – in marriage; affy, affiance; betroth etc. (*promise*) 768; publish – bid- the banns; be asked in church.

Adj. married etc. *v.*; one, – bone and one flesh, marriageable, nubile.

engaged, betrothed, affianced.

matrimonial, marital, conjugal, connubial, wedded; nuptial, hymeneal, spousal, bridal.

Phr. the gray mare the better horse.

904. Celibacy.—N. celibacy, singleness, single blessedness; bachelor-hood, -ship; miso-gamy, - gyny.

virginity, *pucelage*; maiden-hood, -head.

unmarried man, bachelor, agamist, old bachelor; miso-gamist, -gynist; celibate.

unmarried woman, spinster; maid, -en; virgin, *feme sole*, old maid; bachelor girl; nun etc.

V. live single; keep bachelor hall.

Adj. un-married, -wedded; wife-, spouse-less; single, virgin, celibate.

905. Divorce.—N. divorce, -ment; separation; judicial separation, separate maintenance; *separatio a -mensâ et thoro, – vinculo matrimonii.*

widowhood, viduage, viduity, weeds.

widow, -er; relict; dowager; *divorcée*; cuckold.

V. live -separately, – apart; separate, divorce, disespouse, put away; wear the horns.

906. Benevolence.—N. benevolence, Christian charity; God's -love, – grace; good-will; philanthropy etc. 910; unselfishness etc. 942.

good -nature, – feeling, – wishes; kind-, kindliness etc. *adj.*; lovingkindness, benignity, brotherly love, charity, humanity, fellow-feeling, sympathy; goodness –, warmth- of heart; *bon-homie*; kindheartedness; amiability, milk of human kindness, tenderness; love etc. 897; friendship etc. 888.

toleration, consideration, generosity; mercy etc. (*pity*) 914.

charitableness etc. *adj.*; bounty, alms-giving; good works, beneficence, the luxury of doing good.

acts of kindness, a good turn; good –, kind— offices, – treatment.

good Samaritan, sympathizer, well-wisher, philanthropist, *bon enfant*; altruist.

V. be -benevolent etc. *adj.*; have one's heart in the right place, bear good will; wish -well, – God speed; view – regard- with an eye of favor; take in good part; take –, feel- an interest in; be –, feel-interested- in; sympathize with, feel for; fraternize etc. (*be friendly*) 888.

enter into the feelings of others, do as you would be done by, meet halfway.

treat well; give comfort, smooth the bed of death; do -good, – a good turn; benefit etc. (*goodness*) 648; render a service, be of use; aid etc. 707.

Adj. benevolent; kind, -ly; wellmeaning; amiable, obliging, accommodating, indulgent, considerate, gracious, complacent, good-humored.

warm-, soft-, kind-, tender-, large-, broad-hearted; merciful etc. 914; philanthropic etc. 910; charitable, beneficent, humane, benign, benignant; bount-eous, -iful etc. 816.

good-, well-natured; spleenless; sympath-izing, -etic; complaisant etc. (*courteous*) 894; kindly, well-meant, -intentioned.

fatherly, motherly, brotherly, sisterly; pat-, mat-, frat-ernal; friendly etc. 888.

Adv. with -a good intention, – the best intentions.

Int. God speed! much good may it do!

907. Malevolence.—N. malevolence; bad intent, -ion; un-, dis-kindness; ill -nature, – will, – blood; bad blood; enmity etc. 889; hate etc. 898; malignity; malice, – aforethought, – prepense; maliciousness etc. *adj.*; spite, despite; resentment etc. 900.

uncharitableness etc. *adj.*; incompassionateness etc. 914*a*; gall, venom, rancor, rankling, virulence, mordacity, acerbity; churlishness etc. (*discourtesy*) 895.

hardness of heart, heart of stone, obduracy; cruelty; cruelness etc. *adj.*; brutality, savagery; ferity, -ocity; barbarity, inhumanity, immanity, truculence, ruffianism; evil eye, cloven -foot, – hoof; Inquisition; torture.

ill –, bad- turn; affront etc. (*disrespect*) 929; outrage, atrocity; ill usage; intolerance, bigotry, persecution; tender mercies [ironical]; 'unkindest cut of all.'

V. be -malevolent etc. *adj.*; bear –, harbor- -spleen, – a grudge, – malice; betray –, show- the cloven foot.

hurt etc. (*physical pain*) 378; annoy etc. 830; injure, harm, wrong; do -harm, – an ill office- to; outrage; disoblige, malign, plant a thorn in the breast.

molest, worry, harass, haunt, harry, bait, tease, throw stones at; play the devil with; hunt down, dragoon, hound; persecute, oppress, grind; maltreat; ill-treat, -use.

wreak one's malice on, do one's worst, break a butterfly on the wheel; dip –, imbrue- one's hands in blood; have no mercy etc. 914*a*.

Adj. male-, unbene-volent; unbenign; ill-disposed, -intentioned, -natured, -conditioned, -contrived; evil-minded, -disposed.

malicious; malign, -ant; rancorous; de-, spiteful; mordacious, caustic, bitter, envenomed, acrimonious, virulent; un-amiable, -charitable; maleficent, venomous, grinding, galling.

harsh, disobliging; un-kind, -friendly, -gracious; treacherous; inofficious, invidious; uncandid; churlish etc. (*uncourteous*) 895; surly, sullen etc. 901*a*.

cold, -blooded, -hearted; hard-, flint-, marble-, stony-hearted; hard of heart, unnatural; ruthless etc. (*unmerciful*) 914*a*; relentless etc. (*revengeful*) 919.

cruel; brut-al, -ish; savage, – as a -bear, – tiger; ferine, feral, ferocious; inhuman; barbarous, fell, untamed, tameless, truculent, incendiary; blood-thirsty etc. (*murderous*) 361; atrocious;

fiend-ish, -like; demoniacal; diabolic, -al; devilish, infernal, hellish, Satanic.

Adv. malevolently etc. *adj.*; with -bad intent etc. *n.*

908. Malediction.—N. malediction, malison, curse, imprecation, denunciation, execration, anathema, ban, proscription, excommunication, commination, thunders of the Vatican, fulmination, *maranatha*, aspersion, vilification, vituperation, scurrility.

abuse; foul –, bad –, strong –, unparliamentary- language, Limehouse; Billingsgate, sauce, evil speaking; cursing etc. *v.*; profane swearing, oath.

threat etc. 909; more bark than bite; invective etc. (*disapprobation*) 932.

V. curse, accurse, imprecate, damn, swear at; slang; curse with bell, book and candle; invoke –, call down- curses on the head of; devote to destruction.

execrate, beshrew, scold; anathematize etc. (*censure*) 932; hold up to execration, denounce, proscribe, excommunicate, fulminate, thunder against; threaten etc. 909; curse up hill and down dale.

curse and swear; swear, – like a trooper; fall a cursing, rap out an oath, damn, cuss.

Adj. curs-ing, -ed etc. *v.*; maledictory.

Int. woe to! beshrew! *ruat coelum!* ill –, woe-betide! confusion seize! damn! confound! blast! curse! devil take! hang! out with! a plague –, out-upon! aroynt! *honi soit!*

Phr. *delenda est Carthago.*

909. Threat.—N. threat, menace; defiance'etc. 715; abuse, minacity, intimidation; fulmination;-commination etc. (*curse*) 908; gathering clouds etc. (*warning*) 668.

V. threat, -en; menace; snarl, growl, gnarl, mutter, bark, bully.

defy etc. 715; intimidate etc. 860; keep –, hold up –, hold out- *in terrorem*; shake –, double –, clinch- the fist at; thunder, talk big, fulminate, use big words, bluster, look daggers.

Adj. threatening, menacing; mina-tory, -cious; comminatory, abusive; *in terrorem*; ominous etc. (*predicting*) 511; defiant etc. 715; under the ban.

Int. *vae victis!* at your peril! do your worst!

910. Philanthropy.—N. philanthropy; altruism, humanit-y, -arianism; universal benevolence; *deliciae humani generis;* cosmopolitanism, utilitarianism, the greatest happiness of the greatest number, social science, sociology.

common weal, public welfare, socialism, communism.

patriotism, civism, nationality, love of country, *amor patriae*, public spirit.

chivalry, knight errantry; generosity etc. 942. philanthropist, altruist etc. 906; utilitarian, Benthamite, socialist, communist, cosmopolite, citizen of the world, *amicus humani generis*; knight errant; patriot.

Adj. philanthropic, altruistic, humanitarian, utilitarian, cosmopolitan; public-spirited, patriotic; humane, large-hearted etc. (*benevolent*) 906; chival-ric, -rous, generous etc. 942.

Adv. pro -bono publico, – aris et focis.

Phr. 'humani nihil a me alienum puto.'

911. Misanthropy.—N. misanthropy, incivism; egotism etc. (*selfishness*) 943; moroseness etc. 901*a*; cynicism; defeatism.

misanthrope, misanthropist, egotist, cynic, man-hater, Timon, Diogenes.

woman-hater, misogynist.

Adj. misanthropic, antisocial, unpatriotic; egotistical etc. (*selfish*) 943; morose etc. 901a.

912. Benefactor.—N. benefactor, savior, good genius, tutelary saint, patron, guardian angel, fairy godmother, good Samaritan; *pater patriae*; salt of the earth etc. (*good man*) 948; auxiliary etc. 711.

913. Evil-doer. [*Maleficent being.*] —**N.** evil--doer, – worker; wrong doer etc. 949; mischief maker, marplot; oppressor, tyrant; firebrand, incendiary, pyromaniac, anarchist, destroyer. Hun. Boche, Vandal, iconoclast; communist; terrorist, *apache*, gunman, gangster, racketeer.

savage, brute, ruffian, barbarian, semi-barbarian, caitiff, desperado; Mo-hock, -hawk; bludgeon man, bully, rough, hooligan, larrikin, dangerous classes, ugly customer; thief etc. 792.

cockatrice, scorpion, hornet; viper, adder; snake, – in the grass; serpent, cobra, asp, rattlesnake, anaconda; canker-, wire-worm; locust, Colorado beetle; torpedo; bane etc. 663.

cannibal; Anthropophag-us, -ist; bloodsucker, vampire, ogre, ghoul, gorilla; vulture; gyr-, ger-falcon.

wild beast, tiger, hyaena, butcher, hangman; cut-throat etc. (*killer*) 361; blood-, sleuth-, hell-hound.

hag, hellhag, beldam, Jezebel.

monster; fiend etc. (*demon*) 980; homicidal maniac, devil incarnate, demon in human shape; Frankenstein's monster.

harpy, siren, vampire; Furies, Eumenides etc. 900.

Attila, scourge of the human race.

Phr. *foenum habet in cornu.*

914. Pity.—N. pity, compassion, commiseration; bowels, – of compassion; condolence etc. 915; sympathy, fellow-feeling, tenderness, yearning, forbearance, humanity, mercy, clemency, exorability; leniency etc. (*lenity*) 740; charity, ruth, long-suffering.

melting mood; *argumentum ad misericordiam*; quarter, grace, *locus poenitentiae.*

sympathizer, champion, partisan.

V. pity; have –, show –, take- pity etc. *n.*; commiserate, compassionate; condole etc. 915; sympathize; feel –, be sorry –, yearn- for; weep, melt, thaw, enter into the feelings of.

forbear, relent, relax, give quarter, wipe the tears, *parcere subjectis*, give a *coup de grâce*, put out of one's misery; be cruel to be kind.

raise –, excite- pity etc. *n.*; touch, soften; melt, – the heart; appeal to one's better feelings; propitiate, disarm.

ask for -mercy etc. *n.*; supplicate etc. (*request*) 765; cry for quarter, beg one's life, kneel, deprecate.

Adj. pitying etc. *v.*; pitiful, compassionate, sympathetic, touched.

merciful, clement, ruthful; humane; humanitarian etc. (*philanthropic*) 910; tender, –

hearted, – as a chicken; soft, – hearted; unhardened; lenient etc. 740; exorable, forbearing; melting etc. *v.*; weak.

Int. for pity's sake! mercy! have –, cry you-mercy! God help you! poor -thing, – dear, – fellow! woe betide! *quis talia fando temperet a lachrymis!*

Phr. one's heart bleeding for; *haud ignara mali miseris succurrere disco.*

914a. Pitilessness.—N. pitilessness etc. *adj.*; inclemency; inexorability, hardness of heart; inflexibility; severity etc. 739; malevolence etc. 907.

V. have no –, shut the gates of- mercy etc. 914; give no quarter.

Adj. piti-, merci-, ruth-, bowel-less; unpitying, unmerciful, inclement; in-, un-compassionate; inexorable, inflexible; harsh etc. 739; cruel etc. 907; unrelenting etc. 919.

915. Condolence.—N. condolence; lamentation etc. 839; sympathy, consolation.

V. condole with, console, sympathize etc. 914; share one's misery; feel for; express –, testify- pity; afford –, supply- consolation; lament etc. 839- with; send one's condolences.

916. Gratitude.—N. gratitude, thankfulness, gratefulness, feeling of obligation.

acknowledgement, recognition, thanksgiving, giving thanks.

thanks, praise, benediction; paean; *Te Deum* etc. (*worship*) 990; grace, – before, – after-meat; thank-offering.

requital.

V. be -grateful etc. *adj.*; thank; give –, render –, return –, offer –, tender- thanks etc. *n.*; acknowledge, requite.

feel –, be –, lie- under an obligation; *savoir gré*; not look a gift horse in the mouth; never forget, overflow with gratitude; thank –, bless-one's stars; fall on one's knees.

Adj. grateful, thankful, obliged, beholden, indebted to, under obligation.

Int. thanks! many thanks! gramercy! much obliged! thank you! thank Heaven! Heaven be praised!

917. Ingratitude.—N. ingratitude, thanklessness, oblivion of benefits; unthankfulness 'benefits forgot;' thankless -task, – office.

V. be -ungrateful etc. *adj.*; forget benefits; look a gift horse in the mouth.

Adj. un-grateful, -mindful, -thankful; thankless, ingrate, wanting in gratitude, insensible of benefits forgotten; un-acknowledged, -thanked, requited, -rewarded; ill-requited.

Int. thank you for nothing! *'et tu Brute!'*

918. Forgiveness.—N. forgiveness, pardon, condonation, grace, remission, absolution, amnesty, oblivion; indulgence; reprieve.

conciliation; reconciliation etc. (*pacification*) 723; propitiation.

excuse, exoneration, quittance, release, indemnity; bill –, act –, covenant –, deed- of indemnity; exculpation etc. (*acquittal*) 970.

longanimity, placability, forbearance; *amantium irae; locus poenitentiae.*

V. forgive, – and forget; pardon, condone, think no more of, let bygones be bygones, shake hands; forget an injury, bury the hatchet; clean the slate.

excuse, pass over, overlook; wink at etc. (*neglect*) 460; bear with; allow –, make allowances- for; let one down easily, not be too hard upon, pocket the affront; blot out one's transgression.

let off, remit, absolve, give absolution, reprieve; acquit etc. 970.

beg –, ask –, implore- pardon etc. *n.*; conciliate, propitiate, placate; make up a quarrel etc. (*pacify*) 723; let the wound heal.

Adj. forgiving, placable, conciliatory.

forgiven etc. *v.*; un-resented, -avenged, revenged.

Adv. cry you mercy.

Phr. *veniam petimusque damusque vicissim*; more in sorrow than in anger.

919. Revenge.—**N.** revenge, -ment; vengeance; avenge-ment, -ance; sweet revenge, *vendetta*, death-feud, eye for an eye, blood for blood, a Roland for an Oliver; retaliation etc. 718; day of reckoning.

rancor, vindictiveness, implacability; malevolence etc. 907; ruthlessness etc. 914*a*.

avenger, vindicator, Nemesis, Eumenides.

V. re-, a-venge; take –, have one's- revenge; breathe -revenge, – vengeance; wreak one's - vengeance, – anger; give no quarter.

have -accounts to settle, – a crow to pluck, – a rod in pickle; pay off old scores.

keep the wound green; harbor -revenge, – vindictive feeling; bear malice; rankle, – in the breast; have at one's mercy.

Adj. revenge-, venge-ful; vindictive, rancorous; pitiless etc. 914*a*; ruthless, rigorous, avenging, retaliative.

unforgiving, unrelenting; inexorable, stony-hearted, implacable; relent-, remorse-less.

aeternum servans sub pectore vulnus; rankling, immitigable.

Phr. *manet -cicatrix,-- altâ mente repostum.* revenge is sweet.

920. Jealousy.—**N.** jealous-y, -ness; jaundiced eye, heartburning; green-eyed monster; yellows; Juno.

V. be -jealous etc. *adj.*; view with -jealousy, – a jealous eye.

Adj. jealous, – as a Barbary pigeon; jaundiced, yellow-eyed, horn-mad.

921. Envy.—**N.** envy; enviousness etc. *adj.*; rivalry; *jalousie de métier.*

V. envy, covet, lust after, crave, burst with envy, regard with envious eyes.

Adj. envious, invidious, covetous; *alieni appetens.*

922. Right.—**N.** right; what -ought to, – should- be; fitness etc. *adj.*; *summum jus.*

justice, equity; equitableness etc. *adj.*; propriety; fair play, impartiality, measure for measure, give and take, *lex talionis*, square deal.

Astraea, Nemesis, Themis.

scales of justice, even-handed justice, retributive justice, *suum cuique*; clear stage –, fair field- and no favor; Queensberry rules.

morals etc. (*duty*) 926; law etc. 963; honor etc. (*probity*) 939; virtue etc. 944.

V. be -right etc. *adj.*; stand to reason.

see -justice done, – one righted, – fair play; do justice to; recompense etc. (*reward*) 973; hold the scales even, give and take; serve one right, put the saddle on the right horse; give -every one, – the devil- his due; *audire alteram partem.*

deserve etc. (*be entitled to*) 924.

Adj. right, good; just, reasonable; fit etc. 924; equi-al, -able, -itable; evenhanded, fair, – and square.

legitimate, justifiable, rightful; as it -should, – ought to- be; lawful etc. (*permitted*) 760, (*legal*) 963.

deserved etc. 924.

Adv. rightly etc. *adj.*; in -justice, – equity, – reason.

without -distinction of, – regard to, – respect to- persons; upon even terms.

Int. all right!

923. Wrong.—**N.** wrong; what -ought not to, – should not- be; *malum in se*; unreasonableness, grievance; shame.

injustice; unfairness etc. *adj.*; iniquity, foul play, partiality, leaning; favor, -itism; nepotism, party spirit, partisanship; undueness etc. 925; unlawfulness etc. 964.

robbing Peter to pay Paul etc. *v.*; the wolf and the lamb; vice etc. 945.

a custom more honored in the breach than the observance.

V. be -wrong etc. *adj.*; cry to heaven for vengeance.

do -wrong etc. *n.*; be -inequitable etc. *adj.*; favor, lean towards; encroach; impose upon; reap where one has not sown; give an inch and take an ell; rob Peter to pay Paul.

Adj. wrong, -ful; bad, too bad; unjust, -fair; in-, un-equitable; unequal, partial, one-sided.

objectionable; un-reasonable, -allowable, - warrantable, -justifiable; not cricket, not playing the game; improper, unfit; unjustified etc. 925; illegal etc. 964; iniquitous, criminal; immoral etc. 945; injurious etc. 649.

in the wrong, – box.

Adv. wrongly etc. *adj.*

Phr. it will not do; this is too bad.

924. Dueness.—**N.** due, -ness; right, privilege, prerogative, prescription, title, claim, pretension, demand, birthright.

immunity, license, liberty, franchise; vested - interest, – right; licitness.

sanction, authority, warranty, charter; warrant etc. (*permission*) 760; constitution etc. (*law*) 963; tenure; bond etc. (*security*) 771.

deserts, merits, dues.

claimant, appellant; plaintiff etc. 938.

V. be -due etc. *adj.*to, – the due etc. *n.*of; have -right, – title, – claim- to; be entitled to; have a claim upon; belong to etc. (*property*) 780.

deserve, merit, be worthy of, richly deserve.

demand, claim; call upon –, come upon –, appeal to- for; re-vendicate, -claim; exact; insist -on, – upon; challenge; take one's stand, make a point of, require, lay claim to, assert, assume, arrogate, make good; substantiate; vindicate a -claim, – right; make out a case.

give –, confer- a right; sanction, entitle; authorize etc. 760; sanctify, legalize, ordain, prescribe, allot.

give every one his due etc. 922; pay one's dues; have one's -due, – rights; stand upon one's rights.

use a right, assert, enforce, put in force, lay under contribution.

Adj. having a right to etc. *v.*; entitled to; claiming; deserving, meriting, worthy of.

privileged, allowed, sanctioned, warranted, authorized; ordained, prescribed, constitutional, chartered, enfranchised.

prescriptive, presumptive; absolute, indefeasible; un-, in-alienable.

imprescriptible, inviolable, unimpeachable, unchallenged; sacrosanct.

due to, merited, deserved, condign, richly deserved, *emeritus*.

allowable etc. (*permitted*) 760; lawful, licit, legitimate, legal; legalized etc. (*law*) 963.

square, unexceptionable, right; equitable etc. 922; due, *en règle*; fit, -ting; correct, proper, meet, befitting, becoming, seemly; decorous; creditable, up to the mark, right as a trivet; just –, quite- the thing; *selon les règles*.

Adv. duly, *ex officio*, *de jure*; by -right, – divine right; as is -fitting, – proper, – fitting and proper; *jure divino*, *Dei gratiâ*, in the name of.

Phr. *civis Romanus sum*.

925. Undueness. [Absence of right.]—**N.** undueness etc. *adj.*; *malum prohibitum*; impropriety; illegality etc. 964.

falseness etc. *adj.*; emptiness –, invalidity- of title; illegitimacy.

loss of right, disfranchisement, forfeiture.

usurpation, assumption, tort, violation, breach, encroachment, presumption, seizure, stretch, exaction, imposition, lion's share.

usurper, pretender, Carlist; imposter.

V. be -undue etc. *adj.*; not be -due etc. 924.

infringe, encroach, trench on, exact; arrogate, – to oneself; give an inch and take an ell; stretch –, strain- a point; usurp, violate, do violence to; sail under false colors.

dis-franchise, -entitle, -qualify; invalidate.

relax etc. (*be lax*) 738; misbehave etc. (*vice*) 945; misbecome.

Adj. undue; unlawful etc. (*illegal*) 964; unconstitutional, *ultra vires*; illicit; un-authorized, - warranted, -allowed, -sanctioned, -justified; un-, dis-entitled, -qualified; un-privileged, -chartered.

illegitimate, bastard, spurious, false; usurped, tortious.

un-deserved, -merited, -earned; unfulfilled. forfeited, disfranchised.

improper; un-meet, -fit, -befitting, -seemly; un-, mis-becoming; seemless; *contra bonos mores*; not the thing, out of the question, not to be thought of; preposterous, pretentious, would- be.

926. Duty.—**N.** duty, what ought to be done, moral obligation, accountableness, liability, *onus*, responsibility; bounden –, imperative- duty; call, – of duty.

allegiance, fealty, tie; engagement etc. (*promise*) 768; part; function, calling etc. (*business*) 625.

morality, morals, decalogue; case of conscience; conscientiousness etc. (*probity*) 939; conscience, inward monitor, still small voice within, sense of duty, tender conscience.

dueness etc. 924; propriety, fitness, seemliness, amenableness, decorum; the -thing, – proper thing; the -right, – proper- thing to do.

[Science of morals] eth-ics, -ology; deon-, aretology; moral –, ethical-philosophy; casuistry, polity.

observance, fulfilment, discharge, performance, acquittal, satisfaction, redemption; good behavior.

V. be -the duty of, – incumbent etc. *adj.*on, – responsible etc. *adj.*; behoove, become, befit, beseem; belong –, pertain- to; fall to one's lot; devolve on; lie -upon, – on one's head, – at one's door; rest -with, – on the shoulders of.

take upon oneself etc. (*promise*) 768.

be –, become- -bound to, – sponsor for; be responsible for; incur a -responsibility etc. *n.*; be –, stand –, lie- under an obligation; have to answer for, owe it to oneself.

impose a -duty etc. *n.*; enjoin, require, exact; bind, – over; saddle with, prescribe, assign, call upon, look to, oblige.

enter upon –, perform –, observe –, fulfil –, discharge –, adhere to –, acquit oneself of –, satisfy- -a duty, – an obligation; act one's part, redeem one's pledge, do justice to, be at one's post; do duty; do one's duty etc. (*be virtuous*) 944.

be on one's good behavior, mind one's P's and Q's.

Adj. obligatory, binding; imperative, peremptory; stringent etc. (*severe*) 739; behooving etc. *v.*; incumbent –, chargeable- on; under obligation; obliged –, bound –, tied- by; saddled with.

due –, beholden –, bound –, indebted- to; tied down; compromised etc. (*promised*) 768; in duty bound.

amenable, liable, accountable, responsible, answerable.

right, meet etc. (*due*) 924; moral, ethical, casuistical, conscientious, ethological.

Adv. with a safe conscience, as in duty bound, on one's own responsibility, at one's own risk, *suo periculo*; *in foro conscientiae*; *quamdiu se bene gesserit*; at one's post, on duty.

Phr. *dura lex sed lex*.

927. Dereliction of Duty.—**N.** dere; liction of duty; fault etc. (*guilt*) 947- sin etc. (*vice*) 945; non-observance, -performance, -co-operation; neglect, carelessness, laziness, incompetence, eye-service, relaxation, infraction, violation, transgression, failure, evasion, indolence; dead letter.

slacker, loafer, striker, non-co-operator.

V. violate; break, – through; infringe; set - aside, – at naught; trample -on, – under foot; slight, neglect, evade, renounce, forswear, repudiate; wash one's hands of; escape, transgress, fail.

call to account etc. (*disapprobation*) 932.

927a. Exemption.—N. exemption, freedom, irresponsibility, immunity, liberty, license, release, exoneration, excuse, dispensation, absolution, franchise, renunciation, discharge; exculpation etc. 970; *aegrotat*.

V. be -exempt etc. *adj.*

exempt, release, acquit, discharge, quit-claim, remise, remit; free, set at liberty, let off, pass over, spare, excuse, dispense with, give dispensation, license; stretch a point; absolve etc. (*forgive*) 918; exonerate etc. (*exculpate*) 970; save the necessity.

Adj. exempt, free, immune, at liberty, scot free; released etc. *v.*; unbound, unencumbered; irresponsible, unaccountable, not answerable; excusable.

928. Respect.—N. respect, regard, consideration; courtesy etc. 894; attention, deference, reverence, honor, esteem, estimation, veneration, admiration; approbation etc. 931.

homage, fealty, obeisance, genuflexion, kneeling, prostration; obsequiousness etc. 886; salaam, *kowtow*, bow, presenting arms, salute.

respects, regards, duty, *devoirs*, *égards*.

devotion etc. (*piety*) 987.

V. respect, regard; revere, -nce; hold in reverence, honor, venerate, hallow; esteem etc. (*approve of*) 931; think much of; entertain –, bear- respect for; have a high opinion of; look up to, defer to; pay -attention, – respect etc. *n.* - to; do –, render- honor to; do the honors, hail; show courtesy etc. 894; salute, present arms; do –, pay- homage to; pay tribute to; kneel to, bow to, bend the knee to; fall down before, prostrate oneself, kiss the hem of one's garment; worship etc. 990.

keep one's distance, make room, observe due decorum, stand upon ceremony.

command –, inspire- respect; awe, impose, overawe, dazzle.

Adj. respecting etc. *v.*; respectful, deferential, decorous, reverential, obsequious, ceremonious, bare-headed, cap in hand, on one's knees; prostrate etc. (*servile*) 886.

respected etc. *v.*; in high -esteem, – estimation; time-honored, venerable, *emeritus*.

Adv. in deference to; with -all, – due, – the highest- respect; with submission.

saving your -grace, – presence; *salva sit reverentia; pace tanti nominis.*

Int. hail! all hail! *esto perpetua!* may your shadow never be less!

929. Disrespect.—N. dis-respect, -esteem, -estimation, -favor, -repute; low estimation; disparagement etc. (*dispraise*) 932; (*detraction*) 934.

irreverence; slight, neglect; *spretae injuria formae*; superciliousness etc. (*contempt*) 930.

vilipendency, contumely, affront, dishonor, insult, indignity, outrage, discourtesy etc. 895; practical joking; scurrility, scoffing, sibilation; ir-, derision; mockery; irony etc. (*ridicule*) 856; sarcasm.

hiss, hoot, gibe, flout, jeer, scoff, gleek, taunt, sneer, quip, fling, wipe, slap in the face.

V. hold in disrespect etc. (*despise*) 930; misprize, disregard, slight, undervalue, depreciate, trifle with, set at naught, pass by, push aside, overlook, turn one's back upon, laugh in one's sleeve; be -disrespectful etc. *adj.*, – discourteous etc. 895; treat with -disrespect etc. *n.*; set down, browbeat.

dishonor, desecrate; insult, affront, outrage.

speak slightingly of; disparage etc. (*dispraise*) 932; vilipend, call names: throw – , fling- dirt; drag through the mud, point at, indulge in personalities; make -mouths, – faces; bite the thumb; take – , pluck- by the beard; toss in a blanket, tar and feather.

have – , hold- in derision; deride, scoff, sneer, laugh at, snigger, ridicule, gibe, mock, jeer, taunt, twit, niggle, gleek, gird, flout, fleer; roast, turn into ridicule; guy, burlesque etc. 856; laugh to scorn etc. (*contempt*) 930; smoke; fool; make -game, – a fool, – an April fool- of; play a practical joke; rag; lead one a dance, run the rig upon, have a fling at, scout, hiss, hoot, mob.

Adj. disrespectful; aweless, irreverent; disparaging etc. 934; insulting etc. *v.*; supercilious etc. (*scornful*) 930; rude, derisive, contemptuous, sarcastic; scurri-le, -lous; contumelious.

un-respected, -worshipped, -envied, -saluted; undis-regarded.

Adv. disrespectfully etc. *adj.*

930. Contempt.—N. contempt, disdain, scorn, sovereign contempt; despi-sal, -ciency; vilipendency, contumely; slight, sneer, spurn, by-word.

contemptuousness etc. *adj.*; scornful eye; smile of contempt; derision etc. (*disrespect*) 929.

[State of being despised] despisedness.

V. despise, contemn, scorn, disdain, feel contempt for, view with a scornful eye, disregard, slight, not mind; pass by etc. (*neglect*) 460.

look down upon; hold -cheap, – in contempt, – in disrespect; think -nothing, – small beer- of; make light of; underestimate etc. 483; esteem -slightly, – of small or no account; take no account of, care nothing for; set no store by; not care a -straw etc. (*unimportance*) 643; set at naught, laugh in one's sleeve, snap one's fingers at, shrug one's shoulders, turn up one's nose at, pooh-pooh, damn with faint praise; sneeze –, whistle –, sneer- at; curl up one's lip, toss the head, *traiter de haut*; laugh at etc. (*be disrespectful*) 929.

point the finger of – , hold up to – , laugh to- scorn; scout, hoot, flout, hiss, scoff at.

turn -one's back, – a cold shoulder- upon; tread – , trample- -upon, – under foot; spurn, kick; fling to the winds etc. (*repudiate*) 610; send away with a flea in the ear.

Adj. contemptuous; disdain-, scorn-ful; withering, contumelious, supercilious, cynical, haughty, bumptious, cavalier; derisive.

contemptible, despicable; pitiable; pitiful etc. (*unimportant*) 643; despised etc. *v.*; downtrodden; unenvied.

Adv. contemptuously etc. *adj.*

Int. a fig for etc. (*unimportant*) 643; bah! never mind! away with! hang it! fiddle-de-dee!

931. Approbation.—N. approbation; approval, -ement; sanction, advocacy; nod of approbation; esteem, estimation, good opinion, golden opinions, admiration; love etc. 897; appreciation, regard, account, popularity, *kudos*, credit; repute etc. 873.

commendation, praise; laud, -ation; good word; meed –, tribute- of praise; encomium; eulog-y, -ium; *éloge*, panegyric; homage, hero worship; benediction, blessing, benison.

applause, plaudit, clap; clapping, – of hands; accl-aim, -amation; cheer; paean, hosannah; shout –, peal –, chorus –, thunders- of -applause etc. Kentish fire; Prytaneum; blurb.

V. approve; think -good, – much of, – well of, – highly of; esteem, value, prize; set great store - by, – on.

do justice to, appreciate; honor, hold in esteem, look up to, admire; like etc. 897; be in favor of, wish God speed; hail, – with satisfaction.

stand –, stick- up for; uphold, hold up, countenance, sanction; clap –, pat- on the back; keep in countenance, endorse, give credit, recommend; mark with a white -mark, – stone.

commend, praise; be-, laud; compliment, pay a tribute, bepraise; clap, – the hands; applaud, cheer, acclaim, acclamate, encore; panegyrize, eulogize, cry up, *prôner*, puff; extol, – to the skies; magnify, glorify, exalt, boost, swell, make much of; flatter etc. 933; bless, give a blessing to; have –, say- a good word for; speak -well, – highly, – in high terms- of; sing –, sound –, chaunt –, resound- the praises of; sing praises to; cheer –, applaud- to the -echo, – very echo.

redound to the -honor, – praise, – credit- of; do credit to; deserve -praise etc. *n.*; recommend itself; pass muster.

be -praised etc.; receive honorable mention; be in -favor, – high favor- with; ring with the praises of, win golden opinions, gain credit, find favor with, stand well in the opinion of; *laudari a laudato viro.*

Adj. approving etc. *v.*; in favor of; lost in admiration.

commendatory, complimentary, benedictory, laudatory, panegyrical, eulogistic, encomiastic, acclamatory, lavish of praise, uncritical.

approved, praised etc. *v.*; un-censured, - impeached; popular, in good odor; in high esteem etc. (*respected*) 928; in –, in high- favor.

deserving –, worthy of- praise etc. *n.*; praiseworthy, commendable, of estimation; good etc. 648; meritorious, estimable, creditable, plausible, unimpeachable; beyond all praise.

Adv. commendably, with credit, to admiration; well etc. 681; with three times three.

Int. hear, hear! well done! *brav-o! -a! -i! bravissimo! euge! macte virtute!* so far so good, that's right, quite right; *optime!* one cheer more; may your shadow never be less! *esto perpetua!* long life to! *viva! enviva!* God speed! *valete et plaudite! encore! bis!*

Phr. *probatum est.*

932. Disapprobation.—N. disappro-bation, -val; improbation; dis-esteem, -valuation, - placency; odium; dislike etc. 867; dissent etc. 489.

dis-praise, -commendation; blame, censure, obloquy; detraction etc. 934; disparagement, depreciation; denunciation; condemnation etc. 971; ostracism; boycott; black-list, -ball; *index - expurgatorius, – librorum prohibitorum.*

animadversion, reflection, stricture, objection, exception, criticism; sardonic -grin, – laugh; sarcasm, insinuation, innuendo; bad –, poor –, left-handed- compliment.

satire; sneer etc. (*contempt*) 930; taunt etc. (*disrespect*) 929; cavil, carping, censoriousness; hypercriticism etc. (*fastidiousness*) 868.

reprehension, remonstrance, expostulation, reproof, reprobation, admonition, increpation, reproach; rebuke, reprimand, castigation, jobation, lecture, curtain lecture, blow up, wigging, dressing, – down; rating, scolding, trimming; correction, set down, rap on the knuckles, *coup de bec*, rebuff; slap, – on the face; home thrust; hit; frown, scowl, black look.

diatribe; jeremiad; *tirade*, philippic.

clamor, outcry, hue and cry; hiss, -ing; sibilation, cat-call; execration etc. 908.

chiding, upbraiding etc. *v.*; exprobration, abuse, vituperation, invective, objurgation, contumely, personal remarks; hard –, cutting –, bitter-words.

evil-speaking; bad language etc. 908; personality.

V. disapprove; dislike etc. 867; lament etc. 839; object to, take exception to; be scandalized at, think ill of; view with -disfavor, – dark eyes, – jaundiced eyes; *nil admirari*, disvalue, improbate.

frown upon, look grave; bend –, knit- the brows; shake the head at, shrug the shoulders; turn up the nose etc. (*contempt*) 930; look -askance, – black upon; look with an evil eye; make a wry - face, – mouth- at; set one's face against.

dis-praise, -commend, -parage; deprecate, speak ill of, not speak well of, slate, condemn etc. (*find guilty*) 971.

blame; lay –, cast- blame upon; censure, *fronder*, reproach, pass censure on, reprobate, impugn.

remonstrate, expostulate, recriminate.

reprehend, chide, admonish; bring –, call- -to account, – over the coals, – to order; take to task, reprove, lecture, bring to book; read a -lesson, – lecture- to; rebuke, correct.

reprimand, chastise, castigate, lash, blow up, trounce, trim, *laver la tête*, overhaul; give it one, – finely; gibbet.

accuse etc. 938; impeach, denounce; hold up to - reprobation, – execration; expose, brand, gibbet, stigmatize; show –, pull –, take- up; cry 'shame' upon; be outspoken; raise a hue and cry against.

execrate etc. 908; exprobrate, speak daggers, vituperate; abuse, –, like a pickpocket; scold, rate, objurgate, upbraid, fall foul of; jaw; rail, – at, – in good set terms; bark at; anathematize, call names; call by -hard, – ugly- names; a-, re-vile; vili-fy, - pend; bespatter; backbite; clapperclaw; rave –, thunder –, fulminate- against; load with reproaches; lash with the tongue.

exclaim –, protest –, inveigh –, declaim –, cry out –, raise one's voice- against.

decry; cry –, run –, frown- down; clamor, hiss,

hoot, mob, ostracize; draw up –, sing- a round robin; black-ball, -list.

animadvert –, reflect- upon; glance at; cast - reflection, – reproach, – a slur- upon; insinuate, damn with faint praise; 'hint a fault and hesitate dislike;' not to be able to say much for.

scoff at, point at; twit, taunt etc. (disrespect) 929; sneer at etc. (despise) 230; satirize, lampoon; defame etc. (detract) 934; depreciate, find fault with, criticize, cut up; pull –, pick- to pieces; take exception; cavil; peck –, nibble –, carp- at; be - censorious etc. adj.; pick -holes, – a hole, – a hole in one's coat; make a fuss about.

take –, set- down; snub, snap one up, give a rap on the knuckles; throw a stone -at, – in one's gar- den; have a -fling, – snap- at; have words with, pluck a crow with; give one a -wipe, – lick with the rough side of the tongue.

incur blame, excite disapprobation, scandalize, shock, revolt; get a bad name, forfeit one's good opinion, be under a cloud, come under the ferule, bring a hornet's nest about one's ears.

take blame, stand corrected; have to answer for.

Adj. disapproving etc. v.; scandalized.

disparaging, condemnatory, damnatory, denun- ciatory, reproachful, abusive, objurgatory, clamorous, vituperative; defamatory etc. 934.

satirical, sarcastic, sardonic, cynical, dry, sharp, cutting, biting, severe, virulent, withering, trench- ant, hard upon; censorious, critical, captious, carping, hypercritical; fastidious etc. 868; sparing of –, grudging- praise.

disapproved, chid etc. v.; in bad odor, blown upon, unapproved; unblest; at a discount, ex- ploded; weighed in the balance and found wanting.

blameworthy, reprehensible etc. (guilt) 947; to –, worthy of- blame, answerable, un- commendable, exceptionable, not to be thought of, bad etc. 649; vicious etc. 945.

un-lamented, -bewailed, -pitied.

Adv. with a wry face; reproachfully etc. adj.

Int. it is too bad! it -won't, – will never- do! marry come up! Oh! come! 'sdeath!

forbid it Heaven! God –, Heaven- forbid! out –, fie- upon it! away with! tut! O tempora! O mores! shame! fie, – for shame! out on you!

tell it not in Gath!

933. Flattery.—N. flattery, adulation, gloze; bland-ishment, -iloquence; cajolery; fawning, wheedling etc. v.; captation, coquetry, sycophancy, obsequiousness, flunkeyism, toad-eating, tuft- hunting; snobbishness.

incense, honeyed words, flummery; bun-kum, - combe; blarney, placebo, butter; soft -soap, – sawder; rose water.

voice of the charmer, mouth honor; lip-homage; euphemism; unctuousness etc. adj.

V. flatter, praise to the skies, puff; wheedle, cajole, glaver, coax; fawn, –, upon; humor, gloze, soothe, pet, coquet, slaver, butter; be-spatter, - slubber, -plaster, -slaver; lay it on thick, overpraise; earwig, cog, collogue; truckle –, pander or pandar –, pay court- to; court; creep into the good graces of; curry favor with, hang on the sleeve of; fool to the top of one's bent; lick the dust.

lay the flattering unction to one's soul, gild the pill, make things pleasant.

overestimate etc. 482; exaggerate etc. 549.

Adj. flattering etc. v.; adulatory; mealy-, honey- mouthed; honeyed; smooth, – tongued; soapy, oily, unctuous, blandiloquent, specious; fine-, fair- spoken; plausible, servile, sycophantic, fulsome; courtier-ly, -like.

Adv. ad captandum.

934. Detraction.—N. detraction, disparagement, depreciation, vilification, obloquy, scurrility, scandal, defamation, aspersion, traducement, slander, calumny, obtrectation, evil- speaking, backbiting, scandalum magnatum.

personality, libel, squib, lampoon, skit, pasquinade; chronique scandaleuse.

sarcasm, cynicism; criticism (disapprobation) 932; invective etc. 932; envenomed tongue; spretae injuria formae.

detractor etc. 936.

V. detract, derogate, decry, depreciate, disparage; run –, cry- down; minimize, make light of; belittle, sneer at etc. (contemn) 930; criticize, pull to pieces, pick a hole in one's coat, asperse, cast aspersions, blow upon, bespatter, blacken; vili- fy, -pend; avile; give a dog a bad name, brand, malign, backbite, libel, lampoon, traduce, slander, defame, calumniate, bear false witness against; speak ill of behind one's back.

'damn with faint praise, assent with civil leer; and without sneering, others teach to sneer.'

fling dirt etc. (disrespect) 929; anathematize etc. 932; dip the pen in gall, view in a bad light.

Adj. detracting etc. v.; defamatory, detractory, derogatory; disparaging, libellous; scurril-e, -ous; abusive; foul-spoken, -tongued, -mouthed; slan- derous; calumni-ous, -atory; sar-castic, -donic; satirical, cynical.

935. Flatterer.—N flatterer, adulator; eu- logist, -phemist; optimist, encomiast, laudator, whitewasher, booster.

toad-y, -eater; sycophant, courtier, pickthank, Sir Pertinax MacSycophant; flâneur, prôneur; puffer, touter, claqueur; claw-back, ear-wig, doer of dirty work; parasite, hanger on etc. (servility) 886.

936. Detractor.—N. detractor, reprover; cens- or, -urer; cynic, critic, caviller, carper, word- catcher.

defamer, backbiter, slanderer, knocker, Sir Ben- jamin Backbite, lampooner, satirist, traducer, libeller, calumniator, dearest foe, dawplucker, Thersites; Zoilus; good-natured –, candid- friend [satirically]; reviler, vituperator, castigator; shrew etc. 901.

disapprover, laudator temporis acti.

937. Vindication.—N. vindication, justification, warrant, exoneration, exculpation; acquittal etc. 970; whitewashing.

extenuation; pallia-tion, -tive; softening, mitigation.

reply, defense; recrimination etc. 938.

apology, gloss, varnish; plea etc. 617; salvo; excuse, extenuating circumstances; allowance, – to be made; *locus poenitentiae.*

apologist, vindicator, justifier; defendant etc. 938.

justifiable charge, true bill.

V. justify, warrant; be an -excuse etc. *n.*- for; lend a color, furnish a handle; vindicate; ex-, disculpate; acquit etc. 970; clear, set right, exonerate, whitewash.

extenuate, palliate, excuse, soften, apologize, varnish, slur, gloze; put a -gloss, – good faceupon; mince; gloss over, bolster up, help a lame dog over a stile.

advocate. defend, plead one's cause; stand –, stick –, speak- up for; contend –, speak- for; bear out, keep in countenance, support; plead etc. 617; say in defense; plead ignorance; confess and avoid, propugn, put in a good word for.

take the will for the deed, make allowance for, do justice to; give -one, – the Devil- his due.

make good; prove -the truth of, – one's case; be justified by the event.

Adj. vindicat-ed, -ing etc. *v.*; vindicat-ive, -ory; palliative; exculpatory; apologetic.

excusable, defensible, pardonable; veni-al, -able; specious, plausible, justifiable.

Phr. *'honi soit qui mal y pense.'*

938. Accusation.—**N.** accusation, charge, imputation, slur, inculpation, exprobration, delation; crimination; in-, ac-, re-crimination; *tu quoque* argument; invective etc. 932.

de-nunciation, -nouncement; libel, challenge, citation, arraignment; im-, ap-peachment; indictment, bill of indictment, true bill; lawsuit etc. 969; condemnation etc. 971.

gravamen of a charge, head and front of one's offending, *argumentum ad hominem*; scandal etc. (*detraction*) 934; *scandalum magnatum.*

accuser, prosecutor, plaintiff, complainant, petitioner; relator, informer; appellant.

accused, defendant, prisoner, panel, co-, respondent; litigant.

V. accuse, charge, tax, impute, twit, taunt with, reproach.

brand with reproach; stigmatize, slur; cast a - stone at, – slur on; incriminate; inculpate, implicate; call to account etc. (*censure*) 932; take toblame, – task; put in the black book.

inform against, indict, denounce, arraign; im-, ap-peach; have up, show up, pull up, challenge, cite, lodge a complaint; prosecute, bring an action against etc. 969.

charge –, saddle- with; lay to one's -door, – charge;, lay the blame on, bring home to; cast –, throw- in one's teeth; cast the first stone at.

have –, keep- a rod in pickle for; have a crow to pluck with.

trump up a charge.

Adj. accusing etc. *v.*; accusat-ory, -ive; imputative, denunciatory; re-, criminatory.

accused etc. *v.*; suspected; under -suspicion, – a cloud, – surveillance; in -custody, – detention; in the -lock up, – watch house, – house of detention.

accusable, imputable; in-defensible, -excusable; un-pardonable, -justifiable; vicious etc. 945.

Int. look at home; *tu quoque* etc. (*retaliation*) 718.

939. Probity.—**N.** probity, integrity, rectitude; uprightness etc. *adj.*; honesty, faith; honor; good faith, *bona fides*; purity, clean hands.

fairness etc. *adj.*; fair play, justice, equity, impartiality, principle; grace.

constancy; faithfulness etc. *adj.*; fidelity, loyalty; incorrupt-ion, -ibility.

trustworthiness etc. *adj.*; truth, candor, singleness of heart; veracity etc. 543; tender conscience etc. (*sense of duty*) 926.

punctil-iousness, -io; delicacy, nicety; scrupulosity, -ousness etc. *adj.*; scruple; point, – of honor; punctuality.

dignity etc. (*repute*) 873; respectability, -bleness etc. *adj.*; gentleman; man of -honor, – his word; *fidus Achates, preux chevalier; galantuomo*; truepenny, trump, brick; true Briton, white man, sportsman.

court of honor, a fair field and no favor; *argumentum ad verecundiam.*

V. be -honorable etc. *adj.*; deal -honorably, – squarely, – impartially, – fairly; speak the truth etc. (*veracity*) 543; tell the truth and shame the devil, *vitam impendere vero*; show a proper spirit, make a point of; do one's duty etc. 944; play the game.

redeem one's pledge etc. 926; keep –, be as good as- one's -promise, – word; keep faith with, not fail.

give and take, *audire alteram partem*, give the devil his due, put the saddle on the right horse.

redound to one's honor.

Adj. upright; honest, – as daylight; veracious etc. 543; virtuous etc. 944; honorable; fair, right, just, equitable, impartial, even-handed, square; fair –, open- and aboveboard.

constant, – as the northern star; faithful, loyal, staunch; true, – blue, – to one's colors, – to the core, – as the needle to the pole; true-hearted, trust-y, -worthy; as good as one's word, to be depended on, incorruptible.

manly, straightforward etc. (*ingenuous*) 703; frank, candid, open-hearted.

conscientious, tender-conscienced, right-minded; high-principled, -minded; scrupulous, religious, strict; nice, punctilious, correct, punctual; respect-, reput-able; gentlemanlike.

inviol-able, -ate; un-violated, -broken, -betrayed; un-bought, -bribed.

innocent etc. 946; pure; stainless; un-stained, -tarnished, -sullied, -tainted, -perjured; incorrupt, -ed; unde-filed, -praved, -bauched; *integer vitae scelerisque purus; justus et tenax propositi.*

chivalrous, jealous of honor, *sans peur et sans reproche*; high-spirited.

supra-mundane, unworldly, overscrupulous.

Adv. honorably etc. *adj.*; *bona fide*; on the square, in good faith, honor bright, *foro conscientiae*, with clean hands; by fair means.

940. Improbity.—**N.** improbity; dishon-esty, -our; deviation from rectitude; disgrace etc. (*disrepute*) 874; fraud etc. (*deception*) 545; lying etc. 544; bad –, Punic- faith; *mala –, Punica, fides*; infidelity; faithlessness etc. *adj.*; Judas kiss, betrayal; scrap of paper.

breach of -promise, – trust, – faith; prodition, disloyalty, divided allegiance, treason, high treason; apostacy etc. (*tergiversation*) 607; non-observance etc. 773.

shabbiness etc. *adj.*; villainy; baseness etc. *adj.*; abjection, debasement, turpitude, moral turpitude, laxity, trimming, shuffling.

perfidy; perfidiousness etc. *adj.*; treachery, double-dealing; unfairness etc. *adj.*; knavery, roguery, rascality, foul-play; jobb-ing, -ery; Tammany, graft; venality, nepotism; corruption, job, shuffle, fishy transaction, barratry; sharp practice, heads I win, tails you lose; mouth-honor etc. (*flattery*) 933.

V. be -dishonest etc. *adj.*; play false; break one's -word, – faith, – promise; jilt, betray, forswear; shuffle etc. (*lie*) 544; live by one's wits, sail near the wind; play with marked cards.

disgrace –, dishonor –, demean –, degrade-oneself; derogate, stoop, grovel, sneak, lose caste; sell oneself, go over to the enemy; seal one's infamy.

Adj. dishon-est, -orable; un-conscientious, -scrupulous; fraudulent etc. 545; knavish; disgraceful etc. (*disreputable*) 874; wicked etc. 945.

false-hearted, disingenuous; unfair, one-sided; double, -tongued, -faced; time-serving, crooked, tortuous, insidious, Machiavellian, dark, slippery; questionable; fishy; perfidious, treacherous, perjured.

infamous, arrant, foul, base, vile, low, ignominious, blackguard:

contemptible, abject, mean, shabby, little, paltry, dirty, scurvy, scabby, sneaking, groveling, scrubby, rascally, pettifogging; beneath one; not cricket.

low-minded, -thoughted; base-minded.

undignified, indign; unbe-coming, -seeming, fitting; de-rogatory, -grading; *infra dignitatem*; ungentleman-ly, -like; un-knightly, -chivalric, -manly, -handsome; recreant, inglorious.

corrupt, venal; debased, mongrel.

faithless, of bad faith, false, unfaithful, disloyal; untrustworthy; trust-, troth-less; lost to shame, dead to honor.

Adv. dishonestly etc. *adj.*; *malâ fide*, like a thief in the night, by crooked paths; by foul means.

Int. *O tempora! O mores!*

941. Knave.—**N.** knave, rogue, villain; Seapin, rascal; Lazarillo de Tormes; bad man etc. 949; blackguard etc. 949.

traitor, betrayer, arch-traitor, conspirator, stool pigeon, Judas, Catiline; reptile, serpent, snake in the grass, wolf in sheep's clothing, sneak, Jerry Sneak, tell-tale, squealer, mischief-maker, trimmer; renegade etc. (*tergiversation*) 607; truant, recreant; sycophant etc. (*servility*) 886.

942. Disinterestedness.—**N.** disinterestedness etc. *adj.*; generosity; liberal-ity, -ism; altruism; benevolence etc. 906; elevation, loftiness of purpose, exaltation, magnanimity; chival-ry, -rous spirit; heroism, sublimity.

self-denial, -abnegation, -effacement, -sacrifice, -immolation, -control etc. (*resolution*) 604; stoicism, devotion, martyrdom, *suttee*.

labor of love.

V. be -disinterested etc. *adj.*; make a sacrifice, lay one's head on the block; put oneself in the place of others, do as one would be done by, do unto others as we would men should do unto us.

Adj. disinterested; unselfish; self-denying, -sacrificing, -devoted; generous.

handsome, liberal, noble; noble-, high-minded; princely, great, high, elevated, lofty, exalted, spirited, stoical, magnanimous; great-, large-hearted, chivalrous, heroic, sublime.

un-bought, -bribed; uncorrupted etc. (*upright*) 939.

943. Selfishness.—**N.** selfishness etc. *adj.*; self-love, -indulgence, -worship, -interest; ego-tism, -ism; egocentrism, narcissism; *amour propre* etc. (*vanity*) 880; nepotism.

worldliness etc. *adj.*; world wisdom.

illiberality; meanness etc. *adj.*

time-server; tuft-, fortune-hunter; self-seeker; jobber, worldling; egotist, egoist, monopolist, nepotist, profiteer; temporizer, trimmer; dog in the manger, charity that begins at home.

V. be -selfish etc. *adj.*; please –, indulge –, coddle- oneself; consult one's own -wishes, – pleasure; look after one's own interest; feather one's nest; take care of number one, have an eye to the main chance, know on which side one's bread is buttered; give an inch and take an ell; wangle.

Adj. selfish; self-seeking, -indulgent, -interested; wrapt up –, centered- in self; egotistic, -al; egoistical; egocentric.

illiberal, mean, ungenerous, narrowminded; mercenary, venal; covetous etc. 819.

unspiritual; earthly, -minded; mundane; worldly, -minded, -wise; time-serving.

interested; *alieni appetens sui profusus*.

Adv. ungenerously etc. *adj.*; to gain some private ends; from selfish –, interested- motives.

Phr. *après nous le déluge.*

944. Virtue.—**N.** virtue; virtuousness etc. *adj.*; morality; moral rectitude; integrity etc. (*probity*) 939; nobleness etc. 873.

morals; ethics etc. (*duty*) 926; cardinal virtues.

merit, worth, desert, excellence, credit; self-control etc. (*resolution*) 604; self-denial etc. (*temperance*) 953.

well-doing; good -actions, – behavior; discharge –, fulfilment –, performance- of duty; well spent life; innocence etc. 946.

V. be -virtuous etc. *adj.*; practice -virtue etc. *n.*; do –, fulfil –, perform –, discharge- one's duty; redeem one's pledge etc. 926; act well, – one's part; fight the good fight; acquit oneself well; command –, master- one's passions; keep -straight, – in the right path.

set -an, – a good- example; be on one's -good, – best- behavior.

Adj. virtuous, good; innocent etc. 946; meritorious, deserving, worthy, desertful, correct; dut-iful, -eous; moral; right, -eous, -minded; well-intentioned, creditable, laudable, commendable, praiseworthy; above –, beyond- all praise; excellent, admirable; sterling, pure, noble.

exemplary; match-, peer-less; saint-ly, -like; heaven-born, angelic, seraphic, godlike.

Adv. virtuously etc. *adj.*; *e merito,*

945. Vice.—N. vice; evil-doing, – courses; wrong doing; wickedness, viciousness etc. *adj.*; iniquity, peccability, demerit; sin, Adam; old – offending- Adam.

immorality, impropriety, indecorum, scandal, laxity, looseness of morals; want of -principle, – ballast; obliquity, backsliding, infamy, demoralization, pravity, depravity, pollution; hardness of heart; brutality etc. (*malevolence*) 907; corruption etc. (*debasement*) 659; knavery etc. (*improbity*) 940; profligacy; lust etc. 961; flagrancy, atrocity; cannibalism.

infirmity; weakness etc. *adj.*; weakness of the flesh, frailty, imperfection; error; weak side; foible; fail-ing, -ure; crying –, besetting- sin; defect, deficiency, shortcoming; cloven foot.

lowest dregs of vice, sink of iniquity, Alsatian den; *gusto picaresco*.

fault, crime; criminality etc. (*guilt*) 947. sinner etc. 949.

V. be -vicious etc. *adj.*; sin, commit sin, do amiss, err, transgress; misdemean –, forget –, misconduct- oneself; mis-do, -behave; fall, lapse, slip, trip, offend, trespass; deviate from the -line of duty, – path of virtue etc. 944; take a wrong course, go astray; hug a -sin, – fault; sow one's wild oats.

render -vicious etc. *adj.*; demoralize, brutalize; corrupt etc. (*degrade*) 659.

Adj.* vicious; sinful; sinning etc. *v.*; wicked, iniquitous, bad, immoral, unrighteous, wrong, criminal; naughty, incorrect; undut-eous, -iful.

unprincipled, lawless, disorderly, *contra bonos mores*, indecorous, unseemly, improper; dissolute, profligate, scampish; unworthy; worth-, desert-less; disgraceful, recreant; reprehensible, blameworthy, uncommendable; dis-creditable, -reputable.

base, sinister, scurvy, foul, gross, vile, black, grave, facinorous, felonious, nefarious, shameful, scandalous, infamous, villainous, of a deep dye, heinous; flag-rant, -itious; atrocious, incarnate, accursed.

Mephistophelian, satanic, diabolic, hellish, infernal, stygian, fiend-ish, -like; hell-born, demoniacal, devilish.

mis-created, -begotten; demoralized, corrupt, depraved.

evil-minded, -disposed; ill-conditioned; malevolent etc. 907; heart-, grace-, shame-, virtueless; abandoned, lost to virtue; unconscionable; sunk –, lost –, deep –, steeped- in iniquity.

incorrigible, irreclaimable, obdurate, reprobate, past praying for; culpable, reprehensible etc. (*guilty*) 947.

unjustifiable; in-defensible, -excusable; inexpiable, unpardonable, irremissible.

weak, frail, lax, infirm, imperfect, indiscreet; demoralizing, degrading.

Adv. wrong; sinfully etc. *adj.*; without excuse.

Int. *O tempora! O mores!*

*Most of these adjectives are applicable both to the act and to the agent.

946. Innocence.—N. innocence; guiltlessness etc. *adj.*; incorruption, impeccability.

clean hands, clear conscience, *mens sibi conscia recti*.

innocent, new born babe, lamb, dove.

V. be -innocent etc. *adj.*; *nil conscire sibi nullâ pallescere culpâ.*

acquit etc. 970; exculpate etc. (*vindicate*) 937.

Adj. innocent, not guilty, unguilty; guilt-, fault-, sin-, stain-, blood-, spot-less; clear, immaculate; *rectus in curiâ*; un-spotted, -blemished, -erring; undefiled etc. 939; unhardened, Saturnian; Arcadian etc. (*artless*) 703.

in-, un-culpable; unblam-ed, -able; blameless, inerrable, above suspicion; irrepr-oachable, -ovable, -ehensible; un-exceptionable, -objectionable, -impeachable; salvable; venial etc. 937.

harmless; in-offensive, -noxious, -nocuous; dove-, lamb-like; pure, harmless as doves; innocent as -a lamb, – the babe unborn; more sinned against than sinning.

virtuous etc. 944; un-reproved, -impeached, -reproached.

Adv. innocently etc. *adj.*; with clean hands; with a -clear, – safe- conscience.

947. Guilt.—N. guilt, -iness; culpability; crimin-ality, -ousness; deviation from rectitude etc. (*improbity*) 940; sinfulness etc. (*vice*) 945; peccability.

mis-conduct, -behavior, -doing, -deed; malpractice, fault, sin, error, transgression; dereliction, delinquency; indiscretion, lapse, slip, trip, *faux pas, peccadillo*; flaw, blot, omission; fail-ing, -ure.

offence, trespass; mis-demeanor, -feasance, -prision, tort; mal-efaction, -feasance, -versation; crime, felony.

enormity, atrocity, outrage; deadly –, mortal –, unpardonable- sin; died without a name.

corpus delicti.

Adj. guilty, to blame, culpable, peccable, in fault, censurable, reprehensible, blameworthy, uncommendable, illaudable; weighed in the balance and found wanting; exceptionable, objectionable.

Adv. *in flagrante delicto*; red-handed, in the very act.

948. Good Man.—N. good man, worthy.

good woman, goddess, *madonna*, virgin.

model, paragon etc. (*perfection*) 650; good example; hero, demigod, seraph, angel; innocent etc. 946; saint etc. (*piety*) 987; benefactor etc. 912; philanthropist etc. 910; Aristides.

brick, trump, rough diamond, ugly duckling.

salt of the earth; one in ten thousand; one of the best.

Phr. *si sic omnes!*

949. Bad Man.—N. bad man, wrongdoer, worker of iniquity; evil-doer etc. 913; sinner; the -wicked etc. 945; bad example.

rascal, scoundrel, villain, miscreant, caitiff; wretch, reptile, viper, serpent, cockatrice, basilisk, urchin; tiger, monster; devil etc. (*demon*) 980; devil incarnate; demon in human shape, Nana Sahib; hell-hound, -cat; rake-hell.

bad woman, jade, Jezebel, adultress, etc. 962.

scamp, scapegrace, rip, runagate, ne'er-do-well, reprobate, *roué*, rake; limb; one who has sold himself to the devil, fallen angel, *âme damnée*, *vaurien*, *mauvais sujet*, loose fish, sad, dog; lost −, black-sheep; castaway, recreant, defaulter; prodigal etc. 818; libertine etc. 962.

rough, rowdy, ugly customer, ruffian, hoodlum, bully; Jonathan Wild; hangman; incendiary; thief etc. 792; murderer etc. 361.

culprit, delinquent, criminal, melefactor, misdemeanant; felon; convict, jail-bird, ticket-of-leave man; outlaw.

blackguard, *polisson*, loafer, sneak; raps-, rascallion; cullion, mean wretch, varlet, kern, *âme-de-boue, drôle*; cur, dog, hound, whelp, mongrel; lown, lpon, runnion, outcast, vagabond; rogue etc. (*knave*) 941; scum of the earth, riff-raff; *Arcades ambo*.

Int. sirrah!

950. Penitence.—N. penitence, contrition, compunction, repentance, remorse; regret etc. 833.

self-reproach, -reproof, -accusation, -condemnation, -humiliation; stings −, pangs −, qualms −, prickings −, twinge −, twitch −, touch −, voice- of conscience; compunctious visitings of nature.

acknowledgment, confession etc. (*disclosure*) 529; apology etc. 952; recantation etc. 607; penance etc. 952; resipiscence.

awakened conscience, deathbed repentance, *locus poenitentiae*, stool of repentance, cutty stool.

penitent, Magdalen, prodigal son, returned prodigal, a sadder and wiser man.

V. repent, be sorry for; be -penitent etc. *adj.*; rue; regret etc. 833; think better of; recant etc. 607; knock under etc. (*submit*) 725; plead guilty; sing *miserere*, − *de profundis*; cry *peccavi*; own oneself in the wrong; acknowledge, confess etc. (*disclose*) 529; humble oneself; beg pardon etc. (*apologize*) 952; turn over a new leaf, put on the new man, turn from sin; reclaim; repent in sackcloth and ashes etc. (*do penance*) 952; learn by experience.

Adj. penitent; repenting etc. *v.*; repentant, contrite; conscience-smitten, -stricken; self-accusing, -convicted.

penitenti-al, ·ary; chastened, reclaimed; not hardened; un-hardened.

Adv. *meâ culpâ*.

Phr. *peccavi; erubuit; salva res est; vous l'avez voulu, Georges Dandin.*

951. Impenitence.—N. impenitence, irrepentance, recusance.

hardness of heart, seared conscience, induration, obduracy.

V. be -impenitent etc. *adj.*; steel −, harden- the heart; die -game, − and make no sign.

Adj. impenitent uncontrite, obdurate; hard, -ened; seared, recusant; unrepentant; relent-; remorse-, grace-, shrift-less.

lost, incorrigible, irreclaimable.

unre-claimed, -formed; unrepented, unatoned.

952. Atonement.—N. atonement, reparation; compromise, composition; compensation etc. 30; quittance, quits; indemni-ty, -fication; expiation,

redemption, reclamation, conciliation, propitiation.

amends, apology, *amende honorable*, satisfaction; peace −, sin −, burnt- offering; scapegoat, sacrifice.

penance, fasting, maceration, sackcloth and ashes, white sheet, shrift, flagellation, lustration; purga-tion, -tory.

V. atone, − for; expiate; propitiate; make -amends, − good; reclaim, redeem, repair, ransom, absolve, purge, shrive, do penance, stand in a white sheet, repent in sackcloth and ashes.

set one's house in order, wipe off old scores, make matters up; pay the -forfeit, − penalty.

apologize, beg pardon, express regret, *faire amende honorable*, give satisfaction; come −, fall-down on one's -knees, − marrow bones.

Adj. propitiatory, expiatory; sacrific, -ial, -atory; piacul-ar, -ous.

953. Temperance.—N. temperance, moderation, sobriety, soberness.

forbearance, abnegation; self-denial, -restraint, -control etc. (*resolution*) 604.

frugality; vegetarianism, teetotalism, total abstinence, prohibition; abst-inence, -emiousness, asceticism etc. 955; system of -Pythagoras, − Cornaro; Pythagorism, Stoicism.

vegetarian; Pythagorean, gymnosophist; teetotaler etc. 958; abstainer.

V. be -temperate etc. *adj.*; abstain, forbear, refrain, deny oneself, spare; know when one has had enough; take the pledge; look not upon the wine when it is red.

Adj. temperate, moderate, sober, frugal, sparing; abst-emious, -inent; within compass; measured etc. (*sufficient*) 639.

Pythagorean; vegetarian; teetotal, pussy-foot.

954. Intemperance.—N. intemperance; sensuality, animalism, carnality; pleasure; effeminacy, silkiness; luxur-y, -iousness; lap of -pleasure, − luxury.

indulgence; high-, free- living, in-abstinence, self-indulgence; voluptuousness etc. *adj.*; epicurism, -eanism; sybaritism.

dissipation; licentiousness etc. *adj.*; debauchery; crapulence.

revel-s, -ry; debauch, carousal, jollification, drinking bout, wassail, Saturnalia, orgies; excess, too much; intoxication etc. 959.

Circean cup; drug habit etc. 663.

V. be -intemperate etc. *adj.*; indulge, exceed; live -well, − high, − on the fat of the land; give a loose to -indulgence etc. *n.*; dine not wisely but too well; wallow in -voluptuousness etc. *n.*; plunge into dissipation.

revel, rake, live hard, run riot, sow one's wild oats; slake one's -appetite, − thirst; swill; pamper.

Adj. intemperate, inabstinent, intoxicated etc. 958; sensual, self-indulgent; voluptuous, luxurious, licentious, wild, dissolute, rakish, fast, debauched.

brutish, crapulous, swinish, piggish, hoggish, bestial.

Paphian, Epicurean, Sybaritical; bred −, nursed- in the lap of luxury; indulged, pampered, full-fed.

954a. Sensualist.—N. Sybarite, voluptuary, Sardanapalus, man of pleasure, carpet knight; epicure, -an; *gourm-et, -and;* gormandizer, gutling, glutton, pig, hog; votary – , swine- of Epicurus; sensualist; Heliogabalus; free – , hard- liver; libertine etc. 962; hedonist.

955. Asceticism.—N. asceticism, puritanism, sabbatarianism; cynicism, austerity; total abstinence.

mortification, maceration, sackcloth and ashes, flagellation; penance etc. 952; fasting etc. 956; martyrdom.

ascetic; anchor-et, -ite; martyr; *Heautontimorumenos;* hermit etc. (*recluse*) 893; puritan, sabbatarian, cynic.

Adj. ascetic, austere, puritanical; cynical; over-religious.

956. Fasting.—N. fasting; exrophagy; famishment, starvation; banting.

fast, *jour maigre;* fast .– , banyan-day; Lent, quadragesima; Rama-dan, -zan; spare – , meager-diet; lenten -diet, – entertainment; *soupe maigre,* short -rations, – commons; Barmecide feast; hunger strike.

V. fast, starve, clem, famish, perish with hunger; dine with Duke Humphrey; make two bites of a cherry.

Adj. lenten, quadragesimal; unfed; starved etc. *v.;* half-starved; fasting etc. *v.;* hungry etc. 865.

957. Gluttony.—N. gluttony; greed; greediness etc. *adj.;* voracity.

epicurism; good – , high- living; edacity, gulosity, crapulence; gutt-, guzz-ling; over-indulgence.

good cheer, blow out; feast etc. (*food*) 298; gastronomy.

epicure, *bon vivant, gourmand;* glutton, cormorant, hog, belly-god, Apicius, gastronome, gormandizer.

V. gormandize, gorge; over-gorge, -eat- oneself; engorge, eat one's fill, cram, stuff, stodge, glut, satiate; gutt-le, guzz-le; bolt, devour, gobble up; gulp etc. (*swallow food*) 298; raven, eat out of house and home.

have the stomach of an ostrich; play a good knife and fork etc. (*appetite*) 865.

Adj. gluttonous, greedy; gormandizing etc. *v.;* edacious, omnivorous, crapulent, swinish, voracious, devouring.

pampered; over-fed, -gorged.

958. Sobriety.—N. sobriety; teetotalism, temperance etc. 953.

water-drinker; teetotal-er, -ist; abstainer, Good Templar, Rechabite, band of hope; prohibitionist, pussyfoot.

V. take the pledge.

Adj. sober, – as a judge; dry, on the water wagon.

959. Drunkenness.—N. drunkenness etc. *adj.;* intemperance; drinking etc. *v.;* inebri-ety, -ation; ebri-ety, -osity; befuddlement; insobriety; intoxication; temulency, bibacity, wine-bibbing; compotation; deep potations, bacchanals, *bacchanalia,* libations.

oino-, dipso-mania; *delirium tremens,* d.t., alcohol, -ism.

drink; alcoholic drinks, alcohol, booze; gin, blue ruin, grog, brandy, port wine; punch, -bowl; cup, rosy wine, flowing bowl; drop, – too much; dram; beer, wine, spirits etc. (*beverage*) 298; cocktail, nip, peg; stirrup cup.

drunkard, sot, toper, tippler, bibber, wine-bibber; hard – , gin – , dram- drinker; soak, soaker, sponge, tun; love-, toss-pot; thirsty soul, reveller, carouser; Bacchanal, -ian; Bacch-al, -ante; devotee to Bacchus, dipsomaniac.

V. get – , be- drunk etc. *adj.;* see double; take a -drop, – glass- too much; drink, tipple, tope, booze, bouse, guzzle, swill, soak, sot, lush, bib, swig, carouse; sacrifice at the shrine of Bacchus; take to drinking; drink -hard, – deep, – like a fish; have one's swill, drain the cup, splice the main brace, take a hair of the dog that bit you.

liquor, – up; wet one's whistle, take a whet; lift one's elbow; crack a – , pass the- bottle; toss of etc. (*drink up*) 298; go to the -ale, – public house.

make one-drunk etc. *adj.;* inebriate, fuddle, fuzzle, get into one's head.

Adj. drunk, tipsy; intoxicated; inebri-ous, -ate, -ated; in one's cups; in a state of -intoxication etc. *n.;* temulent, -ive; fuddled, mellow, cut, boosy, fou, fresh, merry, elevated, squiffy; plastered, befuddled, sozzled; flush, -ed; flustered, disguised, groggy, beery, topheavy; potvaliant, glorious; potulent; over-come, -taken; whittled, screwed, tight, primed, oiled, corned, raddled, sewed up, lushy, nappy, muddled, muzzy, bosky, obfuscated, maudlin; crapulous, dead – , blind- drunk.

inter pocula; in – , the worse for- liquor, having had a drop too much, half seas over, three sheets in the wind; under the table, blind to the world, one over the eight.

drunk as -a piper, – a fiddler, – a lord, – Chloe, – an owl, – David's sow, – a wheelbarrow.

drunken, bibacious, bibulous, sottish; given – , addicted- to -drink, – the bottle; toping etc. *v.;* wet.

Phr. *nunc est bibendum.*

960. Purity.—N. purity; decency, decorum, delicacy; continence, chastity, honesty, virtue, modesty, shame; pudicity, *pucelage,* virginity.

vestal, virgin, Joseph, Hippolytus; Lucretia, Diana; prude.

Adj. pure, undefiled, modest, delicate, decent, decorous; *virginibus puerisque;* chaste, continent, virtuous, honest, Platonic.

961. Impurity.—N. impurity; uncleanness etc. (*filth*) 653; immodesty; grossness etc. *adj.;* indelicacy, indecency; impudicity; obscenity, ribaldry, smut, bawdry, *double entendre, équivoque;* Aretinism; pornography.

concupiscence, lust, carnality, flesh, salacity; pruriency, lechery, lasciviency, lubricity, lewdness.

incontinence, intrigue, *faux pas*; *amour*, *-ette*; gallantry; dabauchery, libertinism, *libertinage*, fornication; *liaison*; wenching, venery, dissipation.

seduction; defloration, defilement, abuse, violation, rape; incest.

social evil, harlotry, stupration, whoredom, concubinage, cuckoldom, adultery, advoutry, *crim. con.*; free love.

seraglio, harem, zenana; brothel, bagnio, stew, bawdy-house, *lupanar*, house of ill fame, *bordel*, kip.

V. be -impure etc. *adj.*; intrigue; debauch, defile, assault, attack, seduce; prostitute; abuse, violate, deflower; commit -adultery etc. *n.*

Adj. impure; unclean etc. (*dirty*) 653; not to be mentioned to ears polite; immodest, shameless; indecorous, -delicate, -decent; loose, suggestive. *risqué*, coarse, gross, broad, free, equivocal, smutty, fulsome, ribald, obscene, bawdy, pornographic.

concupiscent, prurient, lickerish, rampant, lustful; carnal, -minded; lewd, lascivious, lecherous, libidinous, erotic, ruttish, salacious; Paphian; voluptuous; incestuous.

· unchaste, light, wanton, licentious, adulterous, debauched, dissolute; of -loose character, – easy virtue; frail, gay, riggish, incontinent, meretricious, rakish, gallant, dissipated; no better than she should be; on the -town, – streets, – *pavé*, – loose.

adulterous, incestuous, bestial.

962. Libertine.—N. libertine; voluptuary etc. 954*a*; rake, debauchee, loose fish, rip, rake-hell, fast man; *intrigant*, gallant, seducer, fornicator, lecher, satyr, goat, whoremonger, *paillard*, adulterer, gay deceiver, Lothario, Don Juan, Bluebeard.

adulteress, advoutress, courtesan, prostitute, strumpet, tart, hustler, chippy, broad, harlot, whore, punk, *fille de joie*; woman, – of the town; street-walker, Cyprian, miss, piece; frail sisterhood, fallen woman; demirep, wench, trollop, trull, baggage, hussy, drab, bitch, jade, skit, rig, quean, mopsy, slut, minx, harridan; woman -of easy virtue etc. (*unchaste*) 961; wanton, fornicatress; Jezebel, Messalina, Delilah, Thaïs, Phryne, Aspasia, Lais, *lorette*, *cocotte*, *petite dame*, *grisette*; *demimonde*; white slave.

concubine, mistress, fancy woman, kept woman, doxy, *chère amie*, *bona roba*.

pimp; pand-er, -ar; bawd, *conciliatrix*, procuress, mackerel; wittol.

963. Legality.—N. legality; legitima-cy, teness, legitimization.

legislature; law, code, *corpus juris*, constitution, pandect, charter, act, enactment, statute, rule; canon etc. (*precept*) 697; ordinance, institution, regulation; by-, bye-law, rescript; decree etc. (*order*) 741; *ordonnance*; standing order; *plébiscite* etc. (*choice*) 609.

legal process; form, -ula, -ality; rite; arm of the law; *habeas corpus*.

[Science of law] jurisprudence, nomology; legislation, codification.

equity, common law; *lex* –, *lex nonscripta*, unwritten law; law of nations, international law, *jus gentium*; *jus civile*; civil –, criminal –, canon –, statute –, ecclesiastical- law; *lex mercatoria*.

constitutional-ism, -ity; justice etc. 922.

V. legalize, legitimize; enact, ordain; decree etc. (*order*) 741; pass a law; legislate; codify, formulate; authorize.

Adj. legal, legitimate; according to law; vested, constitutional, chartered, legalized; lawful etc. (*permitted*) 760: statut-able, -ory; legislat-orial, -ive.

Adv. legally etc. *adj.*; in the eye of the law; *de jure*.

964. Illegality. [Absence or violation of law.]—**N.** lawlessness; breach –, violation- of law; disobedience etc. 742; unconformity etc. 83.

arbitrariness etc. *adj.*; antinomy, violence, brute force, despotism, outlawry.

mob –, lynch –, club –, Lydford –, martial –, drumhead- law; *coup d'état*; *le droit du plus fort*; *argumentum baculinum*.

illegality, informality, unlawfulness, illegitimacy, bar sinister.

trover and conversion; smuggling, boot-legging, rum-running, poaching; simony.

speakeasy, speakie, blind pig.

V. offend against –, violate- the law; set the law at defiance, ride rough-shod over, drive a coach and six through a statute; make the law a dead letter, take the law into one's own hands.

smuggle, run, poach.

Adj. illegal; prohibited etc. 761; not allowed, unlawful, illegitimate, illicit, contraband, actionable.

unchartered, unconstitutional; unwarrant-ed, -able; unauthorized; informal, unofficial; in-, extrajudicial.

lawless, arbitrary; despotic, -al; summary, irresponsible; un-answerable, -accountable.

null and void; a dead letter.

Adv. illegally etc. *adj.*; with a high hand, in violation of law.

965. Jurisdiction. [Executive.]—**N.** jurisdiction, judicature, administration of justice, soc; executive, commission of the peace; magistracy etc. (*authority*) 737.

judge etc. 967; tribunal etc. 966; municipality, corporation, bailiwick, shrievalty; lord lieutenant; lord –, mayor, city manager, alderman etc. 745; sheriff, bailie, shrieve, chief –, constable; police, – force; constabulary, bumbledom.

officer; proctor, high –, commissioner; bailiff, tipstaff, bum-bailiff, catchpoll, beadle; police-man, -constable, -sergeant; *sbirro*, *alguazil*, *gendarme*, kavass, *lictor*, macebearer, *huissier*, bedel.

press-gang; exciseman, gauger; custom-house officer, *douanier*.

coroner, edile, aedile, portreeve, paritor; *posse comitatus*.

V. judge, sit in judgment.

Adj. executive, administrative, municipal;

inquisitorial, causidical; judic-atory, -iary, -ial; juridical.

Adv. *coram judice.*

966. Tribunal.—N. tribunal, court, board, bench, judicatory, curia; court of -justice, – law, – arbitration; inquisition; guild.

justice –, judgment –, mercy- seat; woolsack; bar, – of justice; dock; forum, hustings, *bureau*, drum-head; jury-, witness-box.

senate-house, town-hall, theater; House of - Lords, – Commons.

assize, eyre; ward-, burgh-mote; superior courts of Westminister; court of -record, – oyer and ter- miner, – assize, – appeal – error; High court of -Judicature, – Appeal; Judicial Committee of the Privy Council; Star-Chamber; Court of -Chancery, – King's *or* Queen's Bench, – Exchequer, – Common Pleas, – Probate, – Arches, – Ad- miralty, – Criminal Appeal; Lords Justices' –, Rolls –, Vice Chancellor's –, Stannary –, Divorce –, Palatine –, ecclesiastical –, county –, police- court; sessions; quarter –, petty- sessions; court -leet, – baron, – of pie poudre, – of common council; board of green cloth.

court-martial; drum-head court-martial; *durbar*, divan; Areopagus; *rota.*

Adj. judicial etc. 965; appellate; curial.

967. Judge.—N. judge; justi-ce, -ciar, -ciary; chancellor; justice –, judge- of assize; recorder, common serjeant; puisne –, assistant –, county court- judge; conservator –, justice- of the peace, J.P.; court etc. (*tribunal*) 966; grand –, petty –, coroner's- jury; panel, juror, juryman; twelve men in a box; magistrate, police magistrate, stipendiary, the great unpaid, beak; his -worship, – honor, – lordship; deemster, moderator.

Lord -Chancellor, – Justice; Master of the Rolls, Vice-Chancellor; Lord Chief -Justice, – Baron; Mr. Justice; Baron, – of the Exchequer.

jurat, assessor; arbi-ter, -trator; umpire; refer-ee, -endary; revising barrister; domesman; censor etc. (*critic*) 480; official –, receiver.

archon, tribune, praetor, *ephor*, syndic, *podestà*, mullah, ulema, mufti, cadi, kadi; Rhadamanthus.

litigant etc. (*accusation*) 938.

V. adjudge etc. (*determine*) 480; try a -case, – prisoner.

Adj. judicial etc. 965.

Phr. 'a Daniel come to judgment.'

968. Lawyer.—N. lawyer, jurist, legist, civilian, pundit, publicist, jurisconsult, legal adviser, ad- vocate; barrister, – at law; counsel, -lor; King's *or* Queen's counsel; K.C.; Q.C.; silk gown, leader; junior, – counsel; stuff gown, serjeant-at-law; bencher, tubman; judge etc. 967.

bar, legal profession, gentleman of the long robe; junior –, outer –, inner- bar; Inns of Court; equity draftsman, conveyancer, pleader, special pleader.

solicitor, attorney, proctor; notary, – public; scrivener, cursitor; writer, – to the signet; S.S.C.; limb of the law; pettifogger.

V. practice -at, – within- the bar; plead; call – to called- -to, – within- the bar; take silk.

Adj. learned in the law; at the bar; forensic.

969. Lawsuit.—N. lawsuit, suit, action, cause, petition; litigation; dispute etc. 713.

citation, arraignment, prosecution, im- peachment; accusation etc. 938; presentment, true bill, indictment.

apprehension, arrest; committal; imprisonment etc. (*restraint*) 751.

writ, summons, subpoena, *latitat, nisi prius*; *habeas corpus*.

pleadings; declaration, bill, claim; *procès- verbal*, bill of right, information, *corpus delicti*; affidavit, state of facts; answer, replication, plea, demurrer, rebutter, rejoinder; surre-butter, - joinder.

suitor, party to a suit; litigant etc. 938; libellant.

hearing, trial; verdict etc. (*judgment*) 480; ap- peal, – motion; writ of error; *certiorari*.

case, decision, precedent, ruling; decided case, reports.

V. go to –, appeal to the- law; bring to -justice, – trial, – the bar; put on trial, pull up; accuse etc. 938; prefer –, file- a claim etc. *n.*; take the law of, inform against.

serve with a writ, cite, apprehend, arraign, sue, prosecute, bring an action against, indict, impeach, attach, distrain, commit; arrest; summon, -s; give in charge etc. (*restrain*) 751.

empanel a jury, implead, join issue; close the pleadings; set down for hearing.

try, hear a cause; sit in judgment; adjudicate etc. 480.

Adj. litigious etc. (*quarrelsome*) 713; *qui tam*; *coram* –, *sub- judice.*

Adv. *pendente lite.*

Phr. *adhuc sub judice lis est.*

970. Acquittal.—N. acquit-tal, -ment; clearance, exculpation, exoneration; discharge etc. (*release*) 750; *quietus*, absolution, compurgation, reprieve, respite; pardon etc. (*forgiveness*) 918.

[Exemption from punishment] impunity, im- munity.

V. acquit, exculpate, exonerate, clear; absolve, whitewash, assoil, discharge, release; liberate etc. 750.

reprieve, respite; pardon etc. (*forgive*) 918; let off, – scot free.

Adj. acquitted etc. *v.*: un-condemned, punished, -chastised; recommended to mercy.

971. Condemnation.—N. condemnation, con- viction, proscription, damnation; death warrant; penalty etc. 974.

attain-der, -ture, -tment.

V. condemn, convict, cast, bring home to, find guilty, damn, doom, sign the death warrant, sen- tence, pass sentence on, attaint, confiscate, proscribe, sequestrate; non-suit.

disapprove etc. 932; accuse etc. 938.

stand condemned.

Adj. condem-, dam-natory; condemned etc. *v.*; non-suited etc. (*failure*) 732; self-convicted.

Phr. *mutato nomine de te fabula narratur.*

972. Punishment.—N. punishment, punition; chast-isement, -ening; correction, castigation.

discipline, infliction, trial; judgment; penalty etc. 974; retribution; thunderbolt, Nemesis; requital etc. (*reward*) 973; penology; retributive justice.

lash, scaffold etc. (*instrument of punishment*) 975; imprisonment etc. (*restraint*) 751; chain gang; transportation, banishment, expulsion, deportation, exile, involuntary exile, ostracism; penal servitude, hard labor; galleys etc. 975; beating etc. *v.*; flagellation, fustigation, gantlet, *strappado, estrapade, bastinado, argumentum baculinum*, stick law, rap on the knuckles, box on the ear; blow etc. (*impulse*) 276; stripe, cuff, kick, buffet, pummel; slap, – in the face; wipe, douse; *coup de grâce*; torture, rack; picket, -ing; *dragonnade*; capital punishment, extreme penalty; execution; hanging etc. *v.*; de-capitation, -collation; *garrot-te, -to*; electrocution, lethal chamber; crucifixion, impalement; martyrdom, *auto-da-fé*; *noyade; hara-kiri*, happy despatch.

V. punish; chast-ise, -en; castigate, correct, inflict punishment, administer correction, deal retributive justice.

visit upon, pay; pay – , serve- out; settle with, get even with, get one's own back; do for; make short work of, give a lesson to, strafe, serve one right, make an example of; have a rod in pickle for; give it one.

strike etc. 276; deal a blow to, administer the lash, smite; slap, – the face; smack, cuff, box the ears, spank, thwack, thump, beat, lay on, swinge, buffet; thresh, thrash, pummel, drub, leather, trounce, baste, belabor; lace, – one's jacket; dress, give a -dressing, – down; trim, warm, wipe, tund, cob, bang, strap, comb, lash, lick, larrup, whallop, whop, flog, scourge, whip, birch, cane, give the stick, switch, flagellate, horsewhip, *bastinado*, towel, rub down with an oaken towel, rib roast, dust one's jacket, fustigate, pitch into, lay about one, beat black and blue; beat to a -mummy, – jelly; give a black eye; hit on the head; sandbag.

tar and feather; pelt, stone, lapidate; mast-head, keelhaul.

execute; bring to the -block, – gallows; behead; de-capitate, -collate; guillotine; hang, turn off, gibbet, bowstring, hang, draw and quarter; shoot; decimate; burn; electrocute; break on the wheel, crucify; em-, im-pale; flay; lynch; put to death.

torture; put -on, – to- the rack; picket.

banish, exile; trans-, de-port; expel, ostracize; rusticate; drum out; dismiss, -bar, -bench; strike off the roll, unfrock; post.

suffer, – for, – punishment; be -flogged, – hanged etc.; come to the gallows, dance upon nothing, die in one's shoes, be rightly served.

Adj. punishing etc. *v.*; penal; puni-tory, -tive; inflictive, castigatory; punished etc. *v.*

Int. *à la lanterne!*

973. Reward.—N. reward, recompense, remuneration, prize, meed, guerdon, reguerdon; indemni-ty, -fication, price; quittance; compensation; reparation, *ersatz*, assythment, redress; retribution, reckoning, acknowledgment, requital, amends, sop; atonement; consideration, return, *quid pro quo*; salvage, perquisite; vail etc. (*donation*) 784; *douceur*, bribe, bait, baksheesh,

tip; hush-, smart-money; black-mail; carcelage; *solatium*.

allowance, salary, stipend, wages; pay, -ment; emolument; tribute; batta, shot, scot; premium, fee, *honorarium*; hire.

crown etc. (*decoration of honor*) 877.

V. re-ward, -compense, -pay, -quite; re-, munerate; compensate; fee, tip, bribe; pay one's footing etc. (*pay*) 807; make amends, indemnify, atone; satisfy, acknowledge.

get for one's pains, reap the fruits of.

Adj. remunerat-ive, -ory; munerary, compensatory, retributive, reparatory.

974. Penalty.—N. penalty; retribution etc. (*punishment*) 972; pain, pains and penalties; *peine forte et dure*; penance etc. (*atonement*) 952; the devil to pay.

fine, mulct, amercement; forfeit, -ure; escheat, damages, deodand, sequestration, confiscation, *premunire*.

V. penalize, fine, mulct, amerce, sconce, confiscate; sequest-rate, -er; escheat; estreat, forfeit.

975. Scourge. [Instrument of punishment.]—**N.** scourge, rod, cane, stick; ra-, rat-tan; birch, – rod; rod in pickle; switch, ferule, cudgel, truncheon; rubber hose.

whip, lash, strap, thong, cowhide, knout; cat, – o'-nine-tails, *sjambok*, quirt; rope's end.

pillory, stocks, whipping-post; cuck-, duck-ing stool; brank; triangle, wooden horse, maiden, thumbscrew, boot, rack, wheel, iron heel; treadmill, crank, galleys.

scaffold; block, axe, *guillotine*; stake; cross; gallows, gibbet, Tyburn tree; drop, noose, rope, halter, bowstring; electric chair, lethal chamber.

house of correction etc. (*prison*) 752.

gaol-, jail-er; executioner; hang-, heads-man; Jack Ketch; lyncher.

976. Deity.—N. Deity, Divinity; God-head, -ship; Omnipotence, Providence.

[Quality of being divine] divin-eness, -ity.

God, Lord, Jehovah, *Deus*; The -Almighty, – Supreme Being, – First Cause; *Ens Entium*; Author –, Creator- of all things; Author of our being; The -Infinite, – Eternal; The All-powerfull, -wise, -merciful, -holy; The Omni-potent, -scient.

[Attributes and perfections] infinite -power, – wisdom, – goodness, – justice, – truth, – love, – mercy; omni-potence, -science, -presence; unity, immutability, holiness, glory, majesty, sovereignty, infinity, eternity.

The -Trinity, – Holy Trinity, – Trinity in Unity, – Triune God; Three in One and One in Three.

God the Father; The -Maker, – Creator, – Preserver.

[Functions] creation, preservation, divine government; The-ocracy, -archy; providence; ways –, dealings –, dispensations –, visitations- of Providence.

God the Son, Jesus, Christ; The -Messiah, – Anointed, – Savior, – Redeemer, – Mediator,

– Intercessor, – Advocate, – Judge; The Son of - God, – Man, – David; The Only Begotten; The Lamb of God, The Word; Em-, Im-manuel; The - King of Kings and Lord of Lords, – King of Glory, – Prince of Peace, – Good Shepherd, – Way, – Truth, – Life, – Bread of Life, – Light of the World; The -Lord our, – Sun of- Righteousness.

The -Incarnation, – Hypostatic Union, – Word made Flesh.

[Functions] salvation, redemption, atonement, propitiation, mediation, intercession, judgment.

God the Holy Ghost, The Holy Spirit, Paraclete; The -Comforter, – Consoler, – Spirit of Truth, – Dove.

[Functions] inspiration, unction, regeneration, sanctification, consolation.

eon, aeon, special providence, *Deus ex machinâ*; *Avatar*.

V. create, uphold, preserve, govern etc.

atone, redeem, save, propitiate, mediate etc.

predestinate, elect, call, ordain, bless, justify, sanctify, glorify etc.

Adj. almighty, holy, hallowed, sacred, divine, heavenly, celestial; messianic; sacrosanct; all-powerful, -wise, -seeing, -knowing; omnipotent, omniscient; supreme.

super-human, -natural; ghostly, spiritual, hyper-physical, unearthly; the-istic, -ocratic, deistic; anointed.

Adv. *jure divino*, by divine right; *Deo volente*, D.V.

977. Angel. [Beneficent spirits.]—**N.** angel, archangel; heavenly host, choir invisible, host of heaven, sons of God; Michael, Gabriel etc.; seraph, -im; cherub, -im; ministering spirit, morning star; saint, *Madonna*; Our Lady, the Blessed Virgin, the Virgin Mary.

Adj. angelic, seraphic, cherubic.

978. Satan. [Maleficent spirits.]—**N.** Satan, the Devil, Lucifer, Ahrimanes, Belial; Sammael, Zamiel, Beelzebub, the Prince of the Devils; Mephistopheles, his satanic majesty.

the tempter; the evil -one, – spirit; the -author of evil, – wicked one; – old Serpent; the Prince of -darkness, – this world, – the power of the air; the -foul, – arch- fiend; the devil incarnate; the - common enemy, – angel of the bottomless pit; Abaddon, Apollyon, Mammon.

fallen angels, unclean spirits, devils; the -rulers, – powers- of darkness; inhabitants of Pan-demonium; demon etc. 980.

diabolism; devil-ism, -ship, -dom, -ry, -worship; *diablerie*; satanism, manicheism; the cloven foot; black magic etc. 992.

Adj. satanic, diabolic, devilish, infernal, hell-born.

979. Jupiter.—**N.** god, -dess; heathen gods and goddesses; Pantheon; Jupiter, Jove, Zeus, Apollo, Mars, Mercury, Neptune, Vulcan, Bacchus, Pluto, Saturn, Cupid, Eros, Pan; Juno, Ceres, Proserpina, Dina, Minerva, Pallas, Athenae, Venus, Aphrodite, Vesta; The Fates etc. 601.

Allah, Brahma, Vishnu, Siva, Shiva, Krishna, Juggernaut, Buddha; Ra, Isis, Osiris; Belus, Bel, Baal, Asteroth etc.; Thor, Odin; Mumbo Jumbo; good –, tutelary- genius; demiurge, familiar, – spirit; Sibyl; fairy, fay; sylph, -id; Ariel, peri, nymph, nereid, dryad, oread, sea-maid, Banshee, Benshie, Ormuzd; Oberon, Titania, Mab, hamadryad, naiad, mermaid, kelpie, Ondine, nix, nixie, sprite; denizens of the air; pixy etc. (*bad spirit*) 980.

mythology; heathen –, fairy- mythology; Lem-prière, folklore.

Adj. fairy-, sylph-like; sylphic.

980. Demon.—**N.** demon, -ry, -ism, -ology; evil genius, fiend, familiar, – spirit, devil; bad –, un-clean- spirit; cacodemon, incubus, Frankenstein's monster, succubus and succuba, Titan, Shedim, Mephistopheles, Asmodeus, Moloch, Belial, Ahriman, fury, The Furies etc. 900; harpy; Friar Rush.

vampire, ghoul; af-, ef-freet; afrite; ogre, -ss; gnome, gin, djinn, imp, deev, *lamia*; bo-gie, -gle; nis, kobold, flibbertigibbet, fairy, brownie, pixy, elf, dwarf, urchin, Puck, Robin Goodfellow; lepre-, cluri-chaune; troll, dwerger, sprite, oaf, changeling, bad fairy, nixe, pigwidgeon, Will-o'-the-wisp; Erl King.

[Supernatural appearance] ghost, specter, ap-parition, genie, spirit, shade, shadow, vision, phan-tom etc. 443; materialization (*spiritualism*) 992; hob-, goblin; wraith, spook, werwolf, boggart, ban-shee, *loup-garou*, *lemures*; evil eye.

nisse, necks; mer-man, -maid, -folk; siren, Lorelei; satyr, faun.

Adj. supernatural, weird, uncanny, unearthly, spectral; ghost-ly, -like; elf-in, -like; fiend-ish, -like; impish, demoniacal; haunted.

981. Heaven.—**N.** heaven; kingdom of - heaven, – God; heavenly kingdom; throne –, presence- of God; inheritance of the saints in light.

Paradise, Eden, abode of the blessed; Holy City, New Jerusalem; celestial bliss, glory.

[Mythological -heaven] Olympus; [– paradise] Elysium, Elysian fields, Arcadia, bowers of bliss, garden of the Hesperides, Islands of the Blessed; happy hunting-ground; third –, seventh-heaven; Valhalla (Scandinavian); Nirvana (Bud-dhist).

future state, eternity, eternal life, life after death, eternal home, resurrection, translation; resuscitation etc. 660; apotheosis, deification.

Adj. heavenly, celestial, supernal, unearthly, from on high, paradisiacal, beatific, elysian, Olym-pian, Arcadian.

982. Hell.—**N.** hell, bottomless pit, place of torment; habitation of fallen angels; Pan-demonium, Abaddon, Domdaniel.

hell fire; everlasting -fire, – torment; lake of fire and brimstone; fire that is never quenched, worm that never dies.

purgatory, limbo, gehenna, abyss.

[Mythological hell] Tartarus, Hades, Avernus, Styx, Stygian creek, pit of Acheron, Cocytus,

Phlegethon, Lethe; infernal regions, *inferno*, shades below, realms of Pluto.

Pluto, Rhadamanthus, Erebus, Charon, Cerberus; Tophet.

Adj. hellish, infernal, stygian.

983. Theology. [Religious Knowledge.]—**N.** Theology (natural and revealed); Theo-gony, -sophy; Divinity; Hagio-logy, -graphy; Caucasian mystery; monotheism; religion; religious -persuasion, – sect, – denomination; cult; creed etc. (*belief*) 484; articles –, declaration –, profession –, confession- of faith.

theolog-ue, -ian; divine, schoolman, canonist, monotheist.

Adj. theological, religious; canonical; denominational; sectarian etc. 984.

983a. Orthodoxy.—N. orthodoxy; strictness, soundness, religious truth, true faith; truth etc. 494.

Christian-ity, -ism; Catholic-ism, -ity; 'the faith once delivered to the saints;' hyperorthodoxy etc. 984; iconoclasm.

the Holy –, the Orthodox- Church; Catholic –, Universal –, Apostolic –, Established- Church; temple of the Holy Ghost; Church –, body –, members –, disciples –, followers- of Christ; Christian, – community; true believer; canonist etc. (*theologian*) 983; Christendom, collective body, the Christians, the Church Militant.

canons etc. (*belief*) 484; thirty-nine articles; Apostles' –, Nicene –, Athanasian- Creed; Church Catechism; textuary.

Adj. orthodox, sound, literal, strict, faithful, catholic, schismless, Christian, evangelical, scriptural, divine, monotheistic; true etc. 494.

984. Heterodoxy. [Sectarianism.]—**N.** heterodoxy; error etc. 495; false doctrine, heresy, schism; schismantic-ism, -alness; recusancy, backsliding, apostasy; atheism etc. (*irreligion*) 989.

bigotry etc. (*obstinacy*) 606; fanaticism, iconoclasm; hyperorthodoxy, precisianism, bibliolatry, hagiolatry, sabbatarianism, puritanism; idolatry etc. 991; superstition etc. (*credulity*) 486; dissent etc. 489.

sectar-ism, -ianism; nonconformity; secularism; syncretism, religious sects; the clash of creeds.

protestant-, advent-, Arian-, Erastian-, Calvin-, quaker-, method-, anabapt-, Pusey-, tractarian-, ritual-, Origen-, Sabellian-, Socinian-, De-, The-, mon-, material-, positiv-, latitudinairan-ism etc.

High –, Low –, Broad –, Free- Church; ultramontanism; monasticism; pap-ism, -istry; papacy; Anglican-, Catholic-, Roman-ism; popery; Scarlet Lady, Church of Rome, Greek Church; Christian Science, The Church of Christ Scientist.

pagan-, heathen-, ethic-ism; mythology; animism; poly-, di-, tri-, pan-theism; dualism; heathendom.

Juda-, Gentil-, Mahometan-, Islam-, Turc-, Brahmin-, Hindoo-, Buddh-, Lama-, Confucian-, Shinto-, Sabian-, Gnostic-. Soofee-, Hylothe-, Mormon-ism.

Theosophy; Spiritualism, Occultism.

heretic, antichrist; pagan, heathen; pai-, pay-nim; *giaour*; gentile; pan-, poly-theist; idolator; misbeliever, apostate, backslider.

bigot etc. (*obstinacy*) 606; fanatic, dervish, abdal, iconoclast.

latitudinarian, limitarian, Deist, Theist, Unitarian; positivist, materialist; agnostic, sceptic etc. 989.

schismatic; sectar-y, -ian, -ist; seceder, separatist, recusant, dissenter; non-conformist, -juror; Huguenot, Protestant; orthodox dissenter, Congregationalist, Independent; Episcopalian, Presbyterian; Lutheran, Calvinist, Quaker, Methodist, Weslayan; Ana-, Baptist; Dunker; Mormon, Latter-day Saint, Irvingite, Sandemanian, Glassite, Erastian; Sub-, Supra-lapsarian; Gentoo, Antinomian, Swedenborgian, Adventist, Plymouth Brother; Theosophist etc.

Catholic, Roman Catholic, Romanist, papist, ultramontane; Old Catholic, tractarian, Anglican, Puseyite, ritualist; Puritan.

Jew, Hebrew, Rabbist; Mahometan, Mohammedan, Mussulman, Moslem, Islamite, Osmanli; Brahm-in, -an; Parsee, Sofi, Soofee; Buddhist; Zoroastrian, Magi, Gymnosophist, fire-worshipper, Sabian, Gnostic, Sadducee, Rosicrucian etc.

Adj. heterodox, heretical; un-orthodox, scriptural, -canonical; antiscriptural, apocryphal; un-, anti-christian; schismatic, recusant, iconoclastic; sectarian; dis-senting, -sident; secular etc. (*lay*) 997.

pagan; heathen, -ish; ethnic, -al; gentile, painim; pan-, poly-theistic; agnostic, sceptic.

Judaical, Mohammedan, Moslem, Brahminical, Buddhist etc. n.; Romish, Protestant etc. *n.*

bigoted etc. (*prejudiced*) 481; (*obstinate*) 606; superstitious etc. (*credulous*) 486; fanatical; idolatrous etc. 991; visionary etc. (*imaginative*) 515.

985. Revelation.—N. revelation, inspiration, *afflatus*.

Word, – of God; Scripture; the -Scriptures, – Bible, – Book of Books; Holy -Writ, – Scriptures; inspired writings, Gospel.

Old Testament, Septuagint, Vulgate, Pentateuch; Octateuch; the -Law, – Jewish Law, – Prophets; major –, minor- Prophets; Hagio-grapha, -logy; Hierographa; Apocrypha.

New Testament; Gospels, Evangelists, Acts, Epistles, Apocalypse, Revelations.

Talmud; Mishna, Masorah.

prophet etc. (*seer*) 513; evangelist, apostle, disciple, saint; the –, the Apostolical- fathers; Holy Men of old, inspired -writers, – penmen.

Adj. scriptural, biblical, sacred, prophetic; evangel-ical, -istic; apostolic, -al; inspired, theopneustic, apocalyptic, ecclesiastical, canonical, textuary.

986. Pseudo-Revelation.—N. the -Koran, – Alcoran; Ly-king, Shaster, Vedas, Zendavesta, Vedidad, Purana, Edda; Go-, Gau-tama; Book of Mormon.

[False prophets and religious founders] Buddha, Zoroaster, Zerdhusht, Confucius, Mahomet.

[Idols] golden calf etc. 991; Baal, Moloch, Dagon.

987. Piety.—N. piety, religion, theism, faith; religiousness, holiness etc. *adj.*; saintship; religionism; sanctimony etc. (*assumed piety*) 988; reverence etc. (*respect*) 928; humility, veneration, devotion; prostration etc. (*worship*) 990; grace, unction, edification; sancti-ty, -tude; consecration. spiritual existence, odor of sanctity, beauty of holiness.

theopathy, beatification, adoption, regeneration, conversion, justification, sanctification, salvation, inspiration, bread of life; Body and Blood of Christ.

believer, convert, theist, Christian, devotee, pietist; the -good, – righteous, – just, – believing, – elect; Saint, *Madonna*.

the children of -God, – the kingdom, – light.

V. be -pious etc. *adj.*; have -faith etc. *n.*; believe, receive Christ; revere etc. 928; worship etc. 950; be -converted etc.

convert, edify, sanctify, hallow, keep holy, beatify, regenerate, inspire, consecrate, enshrine.

Adj. pious, religious, devout, devoted, reverent, godly, heavenly minded, humble; pure, – in heart; holy, spiritual, pietistic; saint-ly, -like; seraphic, sacred, solemn.

believing, faithful, Christian, Catholic.

elected, adopted, justified, sanctified, regenerated, inspired, consecrated, converted, unearthly, not of the earth.

988. Impiety.—N. impiety; sin etc. 945; irreverence; profan-eness etc. *adj.*, -ity, -ation; blasphemy, desecration, sacrilege; scoffing etc. *v.*

[Assumed piety] hypocrisy etc. (*falsehood*) 544; pietism, cant, pious fraud; lip-devotion, -service, -reverence; mis-devotion, formalism, austerity; sanctimon-y, -iousness etc. *adj.*; pharisaism, precisianism; sabbat-ism, -arianism; *odium theologicum*, sacerdotalism; bigotry etc. (*obstinacy*) 606, (*prejudice*) 481.

hardening, backsliding, declension, perversion, reprobation apostacy, recusancy.

sinner etc. 949; scoffer, blasphemer; sacrilegist; worldling; hypocrite etc. (*dissembler*) 548; Scribes and Pharisees; Tartufe, Maw-worm.

bigot; saint [ironically] ; Pharisee, sabbatarian, formalist, methodist, puritan, pietist, precisian; religionist, devotee, ranter, fanatic, wowser.

the -wicked, – evil, – unjust, – reprobate; son of -men, – Belial, – the wicked one; children of darkness.

V. be -impious etc. *adj.*; profane, desecrate, blaspheme, revile, scoff; swear etc. (*malediction*) 908; commit sacrilege.

snuffle; turn up the whites of the eyes; idolize.

Adj. impious; irreligious etc. 989; desecrating etc. *v.*; profane, irreverent, sacrilegious, blasphemous.

un-hallowed, -sanctified, -regenerate; hardened, perverted, reprobate.

hypocritical etc. (*false*) 544; canting, pietistical, sanctimonious, unctuous, pharisaical, over-righteous, righteous over much.

bigoted, fanatical etc. 481 and 606; priest-ridden.

Adv. under the -mask, – cloak, – pretence, – form, – guise- of religion.

989. Irreligion.—N. irreligion, indevotion; ungodliness etc. *adj.*; laxity, quietism, apathy, indifference, passivity.

scepticism, doubt; un-, dis-belief; incredul-ity, -ousness etc. *adj.*; want of -faith, – belief; pyrrhonism; doubt etc. 485; agnosticism.

atheism, deism; hylotheism; materialism; positivism; nihilism.

infidelity, freethinking, antichristianity, rationalism.

atheist, anti-christian, sceptic, unbeliever, deist, infidel, pyrrhonist; *giaour*, heathen, alien, gentile, Nazarene; *esprit fort*, freethinker, latitudinarian, rationalist; materialist, positivist, nihilist, agnostic.

V. be -irreligious etc. *adj.*; disbelieve, lack faith; doubt, question etc. 485.

dechristianize; serve Mammon, love darkness better than light.

Adj. irreligious; in-, un-devout; devout-, god-, grace-less; un-godly, -holy, -sanctified, -hallowed; atheistic, without God.

sceptical, free-thinking; un-believing, -converted; incredulous, faithless, lacking faith; deistical; un-, anti-christian.

worldly, mundane, earthly, carnal, unspiritual; worldly etc.- minded.

Adv. irreligiously etc. *adj.*

990. Worship.—N. worship, adoration, devotion, aspiration, latria, homage, service, humiliation; kneeling, genuflexion, prostration.

prayer, invocation, supplication, rogation, intercession, orison, holy breathing; petition etc. (*request*) 765; collect, litany, Lord's prayer, paternoster, *Ave Maria*, rosary; bead-roll; latria, dulia, hyperdulia, vigils; revival; cult.

thanksgiving; giving –, returning- thanks; grace, praise, glorification, benediction, doxology, hosanna; h-, allelujah; *Te Deum, non nobis Domine, nunc dimittis*; paean.

psalm, -ody; hymn, plainsong, chant, chaunt, response, anthem, motet; antiphon, -y.

oblation, sacrifice, incense, libation; burnt –, votive –, thank-offering; offertory, collection.

discipline; self-discipline, -examination, -denial; fasting.

divine service, office, duty; morning prayer; mass, matins, evensong, vespers, compline; holy day etc. (*rites*) 998.

worshipper, congregation, communicant, celebrant.

V. worship, lift up the heart, aspire; revere etc. 928; adore, do service, pay homage; humble oneself, kneel; bow –, bend- the knee; fall -down, – on one's knees; prostrate oneself, bow down and worship, recite the rosary.

pray, invoke, supplicate; put –, offer- up - prayers, – petitions; beseech etc. (*ask*) 765; say one's prayers, tell one's beads.

return –, give- thanks; say grace, bless, praise, laud, glorify, magnify, sing praises; give benediction, lead the choir, intone, chant, sing.

propitiate, offer sacrifice, fast, deny oneself; vow, offer vows, give alms.

work out one's salvation; go to church; attend - service, – mass; communicate etc. (*rite*) 998.

Adj. worshipping etc. *v.*; devout, devotional, reverent, pure, solemn; fervid etc. (*heartfelt*) 821.

Int. h-, allelujah! hosanna! glory be to God! O Lord! pray God that! God -grant, – bless, – save, – forbid! *sursum corda.*

991. Idolatry.—N. idol-atry, -ism; demon-ism, -olatry; idol –, demon –, devil – , fire- worship; zoolatry, fetishism, Mari-, Bibli-, ecclesi-, heli-olatry.
deification, apotheosis, canonization; hero worship.
sacrifices, hecatomb, holocaust; human sacrifices, immolation, mactation, infanticide, self-immolation, *suttee.*
idol, golden calf, graven image, fetish, *avatar*, Juggernaut, joss, *lares et penates*; Baal etc. 986.
idolator etc. *n.*
V. worship -idols, – pictures, – relics; put on a pedestal, bow down to, prostrate oneself before, make sacrifice to; deify, canonize, idolize.
Adj. idolatrous.

992. Sorcery.—N. sorcery; superstition; occult -art, – sciences; black –, magic; the black art, necromancy, theurgy, thaumaturgy; demon-ology, -omy, -ship; *diablerie*, bedevilment; witch-craft, -ery; glamor; fetis-hism, -ism; ghost dance; hoodoo, voodoo; Shamanism [Esquimaux], vampirism; conjuration; bewitchery, exorcism, enchantment, incantation, obsession, possession, mysticism, second sight, mesmerism, animal magnetism; od –, odylic- force; electro-biology, *clairvoyance*; spiritualism, spirit-rapping, table-turning; thought reading, telepathy, thought transference, automatic writing, *planchette*, ouija board; crystal gazing; spirit manifestation, materialization, astral body, ectoplasm etc.
divination etc. (*prediction*) 511; sortilege, ordeal, *sortes Virgiliance*; hocus-pocus etc. (*deception*) 545; oracle etc. 513.
V. practice -sorcery etc. *n.*; cast a -horoscope, – nativity; conjure, exorcise, charm, enchant; bewitch, -devil; overlook, look on with the evil eye; entrance, mesmerize, magnetize; fascinate etc. (*influence*) 615; taboo; wave a wand; rub the -ring, – lamp; cast a spell; call up spirits, – from the vasty deep; raise spirits from the dead; raise –, lay-ghosts; command genii.
Adj. magic, -al; mystic, weird, cabalistic, talismanic, phylacteric, incantatory; charmed etc. *v.*

993. Spell.—N. spell, charm, incantation, exorcism, weird, cabala, exsufflation, cantrap, runes, abracadabra, hocus-pocus, open *sesame*, counter-charm, Ephesian letters, bell, book and candle, Mumbo-jumbo, evil-eye, fee-faw-fum.
talisman, amulet, periapt, telesm, phylactery, philter, wish-bone, merry-thought, mascot, scarab, swastika; fetish; *agnus Dei.*
wand, caduceus, rod, divining rod, lamp of Aladdin, magic carpet, seven-league boots; magic ring; wishing –, Fortunatus's- cap.

994. Sorcerer.—N. sorcerer, magician; thaumat-, the-urgist; conjuror, necromancer, seer,

wizard, witch; fairy etc. 980; *lamia*, hag, warlock, charmer, exorcist, voodoo, mage, diviner, dowser; cunning –, , medicine- man, witch doctor; Shaman, figure-flinger, ecstatica, medium, *clairvoyant*, mesmerist, hypnotist; *deus ex machinâ*; astrologer; soothsayer etc. 513.
Katerfelto, Cagliostro, Merlin, Comus, Mesmer, Rosicrucian; Hecate, Circe, Lilith, siren, weird sisters; witch of Endor.

995. Churchdom.—N. church, -dom; ministry, apostleship, priesthood, prelacy, hierarchy, church government, christendom, pale of the church.
clerical-, sacerdotal-, episcopalian-, ultramontan-ism; Theocracy; ecclesiolog-y, -ist; priestcraft, *odium theologicum.*
monach-ism, -y; monasticism, monkhood.
[Ecclesiastical offices and dignities] pontificate; primacy, archbishopric, archiepiscopacy; prelacy; bishop-ric, -dom; episcop-ate, -acy; see, diocese; deanery, stall; canon-ry, -icate; prebend, -aryship; benefice, incumbency, glebe, advowson, living, cure, – of souls; rectorship; vicar-iate, -ship; pastor-ate, -ship; deacon-ry, -ship; -curacy; chaplain, -cy, -ship; cardinal-ate, -ship; abbacy, presbytery.
holy orders, ordination, institution, consecration, induction, reading in, preferment, translation, presentation.
popedom, papacy; the -Vatican, – apostolic see, – see of Rome; religious sects etc. 984.
council etc. 696; conclave, college of cardinals, convocation, synod, consistory, chapter, vestry, presbytery; sanhedrim, *congé d'élire*; ecclesiastical courts, consistorial court, court of Arches.
V. call, ordain, induct, prefer, translate, consecrate, present, elect, bestow.
take -orders, – the veil, – vows.
Adj. ecclesi-astical, -ological; clerical, sacerdotal, priestly, prelatical, pastoral, ministerial, capitular, theocratic; hierarchical, archiepiscopal; episcopal, -ian; canonical; mon-astic, -achal; monkish; abbati-al, -cal; pontifical, papal, apostolic; untramontane, priest-ridden.

996. Clergy.—N. clergy, clericals, ministry, priesthood, presbytery, the cloth, the pulpit.
clergyman, divine, ecclesiastic, churchman, priest, presbyter, hierophant, pastor, shepherd, minister, clerk in holy orders; father, – in Christ; *padre, abbé, curé*; patriarch; reverend; black coat; confessor; sky pilot.
dignitaries of the church; ecclesi-, hier-arch; eminence, reverence, elder, primate, metropolitan, archimandrite, archbishop, bishop, prelate, diocesan, suffragan, dean, subdean, archdeacon, prebendary, canon, rural dean, rector, parson, vicar, perpetual curate, residentiary, beneficiary, incumbent, chaplain, curate, – in charge; deacon, -ess; preacher; lay reader, lecturer; capitular; missionary, propagandist, Jesuit, revivalist, field preacher.
churchwarden, sidesman; clerk, precentor, choir; almoner, *suisse*, verger, beadle, sexton, sacristan; acol-yth, -othyst, -yte; thurifer; chorister, choir boy.
[Roman Catholic priesthood] Pope, *Papa*, Holy

Father, pontiff, high priest, cardinal; ancient –, flamen; confessor, penitentiary; spiritual director.

cenobite, conventual, abbot, prior, monk, friar, lay brother, beadsman, mendicant, pilgrim, palmer; canon-regular, -secular; Jesuit, Franciscan, Friars minor, Minorites; Observant, Capuchin, Dominican, Carmelite; Augustinian; Gilbertine; Austin-, Black-, White-, Grey-, Crossed-, Crutched- Friars; Bonhomme, Carthusian, Benedictine, Cistercian, Trappist, Cluniac, Premonstratensian, Maturine; Templar, Hospitaller.

abb-, prior-, canon-ess; mother superior; *religieuse*, nun, sister, *beguine*, novice, postulant.

[Under the Jewish dispensation] prophet, priest, high priest, Levite; Rabbi, -n; scribe.

[Mohammedan etc.] mullah, ulema, imauam, sheik; so-fi, -phi; mufti, hadji, muezzin, dervish; fakir, -quir; brahmin, gooroo, druid, bonze, santon, abdal, Lama, talapoin, caloyer etc.

V. take orders etc. 995.

Adj. the –, the very –, the Right- Reverend; ordained, in orders, called to the ministry.

997. Laity.—N. laity, flock, fold, congregation, assembly, brethren, people.

temporality, secularization.

layman, civilian; parishioner, catechumen; secularist.

V. secularize.

Adj. secular, lay, laical, civil, temporal, profane.

998. Rite.—N. rite; ceremon-y, -ial; ordinance, observance, function, duty; form, -ulary; solemnity, sacrament; incantation etc. (*spell*) 993; service, psalmody etc. (*worship*) 990; liturgies.

ministration; preach-ing, -ment; predication, sermon, homily, exhortation, lecture, discourse, pastoral.

baptism, christening, chrism; immersion; baptismal regeneration; font; circumcision.

confirmation; imposition –, laying on- of hands; churching, purification, ordination etc. (*churchdom*) 995; excommunication.

Eucharist, Lord's supper, communion; the –, the holy- sacrament; celebration, high celebration; *missa cantata*; offertory; introit; consecration; con-, tran-substantiation; real presence; elements, bread and wine; mass; high –, low –, dry- mass.

matrimony etc. 903; burial etc. 363; visitation of the sick.

seven sacraments, impanation, extreme unction, last rites, *viaticum*, invocation of saints, canonization, transfiguration, auricular confession; fasting; maceration, flagellation, sackcloth and ashes; penance etc. (*atonement*) 952; absolution; telling of beads, reciting the rosary, processional; thurification, incense, holy water, aspersion.

relics, rosary, beads, reliquary, host, cross, rood, crucifix, pax, pix, pyx, *agnus Dei*, censer, thurible, patera, urceole; chalice, patten, Holy Grail, sangrail; seven-branch candle stick, monstrance, sacring bell.

ritual, rubric, canon, ordinal; liturgy, prayerbook, book of common prayer, pietas, euchology.

litany, lectionary; missal, breviary, mass-book, bead-roll.

psalter; psalm –, hymn- book; hymn-al, -ology; psalmody.

ritual-, ceremonial-ism; sabbat-ism, -arianism; ritualist, sabbatarian.

holyday, feast, fast; Sabbath, Passover, Pentecost; Advent, Christmas, Noel, Epiphany, Lent, Shrove Tuesday, Ash Wednesday, Maundy Thursday; Passion –, Holy- week; Good Friday, Easter, Ascension Day, Whitsuntide; Trinity Sunday, Corpus Christi; All-Saints' –, – Souls'- Day; Candle-, Lam-, Martin-, Michael-mas; hogmanay; Ramadan, -zan; Bairam etc. etc.

V. perform service, do duty, minister, officiate, baptize, dip, sprinkle; confirm, lay hands on; give –, administer –, take –, receive –, attend –, partake of- the -sacrament, – communion; communicate; celebrate mass; administer –, receive-extreme unction; anele, shrive, absolve, confess; do penance; genuflect; cross oneself, make the sign of the cross.

excommunicate, ban with bell, book and candle.

preach, sermonize, predicate, lecture.

Adj. ritual, -istic; ceremonial, liturgic; baptismal, eucharistical; paschal.

999. Canonicals.—N. canonicals, vestments; robe, gown, Geneva gown, frock, pallium, surplice, cassock, dalmatic, scapulary, cope, scarf, tunicle, chasuble, alb, *alba*, stole; fan-on, -nel; tonsure, cowl, hood; calo-te, -tte; bands; capouch, amice, orarium, ephod; apron, lawn sleeves, pontificals, pall; miter, tiara, triple crown; shovel –, cardinal's- hat; biretta; crosier; pastoral staff; costume etc. 225.

1000. Temple.—N. place of worship; house of -God, – prayer.

temple, cathedral, minister, church, kirk, chapel, meeting-house, bethel, tabernacle, conventicle, *basilica*, fane, holy place, chantry, oratory.

synagogue; mosque; marabout; pantheon; pagoda; joss-house; dagobah, tope; kiosk.

parsonage, rectory, vicarage, manse, deanery, glebe, church house; Vatican; bishop's palace; Lambeth.

altar, shrine, sanctuary, Holy of Holies, *sanctum sanctorum*, sacrarium, -isty; communion –, holy –, Lord's- table; table of the Lord; pyx; baptistery, font; piscina, stoup; aumbry; sedile; reredos; rood-loft, – screen; jube.

chancel, quire, choir, nave, aisle, transept, lady chapel, vestry, crypt, cloisters, porch; triforum, clerestory, churchyard, *golgotha*, calvary, Easter sepulcher; stall, pew, sitting; pulpit, ambo, lectern, reading-desk, confessional, prothesis, credence, baldachin, *baldacchino*; jesse, apse, belfry; chapter-house; presbytery.

monastery, priory, abbey, friary, convent, nunnery, cloister.

Adj. claustral, cloistered; monast-ic, -erial; conventual.

INDEX

The numbers refer to the headings under which the words or phrases occur. When the same word or phrase may be used in various senses, the several headings under which it, or its synonyms, will be found, according to those meanings, are indicated by the words printed in Italics. These words in Italics are not intended to explain the meaning of the word or phrase to which they are annexed, but only to assist in the required reference.

When the word given in the Index is itself the title or heading of a category, the number of reference is printed in blacker type, thus: **abode 189.**

abundanti cautelâ,
ex – 664
abuse *deceive* 545
ill-treat 649
misuse 679
malediction 908
threat 909
upbraid 932
violate 961
– of language 563
– of terms 523
abusive 895, 934
abut *near* 197 *touch*
199, 215
abutment 717
aby *remain* 141
endure 821, 826
abysmal *deep* 208
abyss *space* 180
depth 208
interval 198
danger 667
hell 982
A.C. 106
academic
teaching 537, 542
theory 514
academical
style 578
academicals
225 *robes*
academician 492
Royal – 559
academy 542
acanthus 847
a capite ad calcem
52
acariâtre 901
acarpous 169
acatalectic 597
acaudal 38
accede 488, 725, 762
accelerate
early 132
stimulate 173
velocity 274
hasten 684
accension 384
accent *sound* 402
tone of voice 580
rhythm 597
accentuate 642
accentuated 580
accept *assent* 488
consent 762
receive 785
take 789
acceptable 646, 829
acceptance 771
acceptation 522
acception 522
access 286
easy of – 705
means of – 627
accessible 470, 705
accession
adjunct 39
increase 35
addition 37
– *to office* 737, 755
consent 762
accessory
extrinsic 6
additive 37
adjunct 39
accompanying 88
aid 707
auxiliary 711

acciaccatura 413
accidence 567
accident *event* 151
chance 156
disaster 619
misfortune 735
fatal – 361
accidental
extrinsic 6
fortuitous 156
undesigned 621
accidents,
trust to the chap-
ter of – 621
accipient 785
acclamation
assent 488
approbation 931
acclimatize 370, 613
acclivity 217
accloy 641
accolade 894
accommodate
suit 23
adjust 27
aid 707
reconcile 723
give 784
lend 787
– oneself to 82
accommodation
space 180
accommodating
kind 906
accompaniment
adjunct 39
coexistence 88
musical 415
accompany
add 37
coexist 88
concur 120
music 416
accompli, fait – 729
accomplice 711
accomplish
execute 161
complete 729
succeed 731
accomplishment
490, 698
accompts 811
accord
uniform 16
agree 23
music 413
assent 488
concord 714
grant 760
give 784
of one's own – 602
according
– *as qualification*
469
– *to evidence* 467
– *to circumstances*
8
– *to law* 963
– *to rule*
conformably 82
– *rumor* 527
accordingly
logically 476
accordion 417
accost 586
accoucheur 631, 662
accouchment 161
account *list* 86

adjudge 480
description 594
credit 805
money - 811
fame 873
approbation 931
call to – 932
find one's – *in*
useful 644
success 731
make no – *of* 483,
930
not – *for* 519
on – *of motive* 615
behalf 707
on no – 536
send to one's – 361
take into – 457,
469
small – 643
to one's – 780
turn to –
improve 658
use 677
success 731
gain 775
– *as deem* 484
– *book* 551
– *for* 155, 522
– *with* 794, 807
accountable
liable 177
debit 811
duty 926
accountant 301, 811
certified public –
811
accounts 811
accouple 43
accoutered
armed 717
accouterment
dress 225
appliance 633
equipment 673
accoy 174
accredit
commission 755,
759
money 805
honor 873
accredited 484, 613
– *to* 755, 759
accretion 35, 46
accrimination 938
accroach 789
accrue *add* 37
result 154
acquire 775
be received 785,
810
accubation 213
accueil 894
accultural 35
accumbent 213
accumulate
collect 72
store 636
redundance 641
accurate 494
– *knowledge* 490
accurse 908
accursed
disastrous 649
undone 828
vicious 945
accusation 938
accuse

disapprove 932
charge 938
lawsuit 969
accustom 613
ace *small* 32
unit 87
within an – 197
aceldama *kill* 361
arena 728
acephalous 59
acerbate 659, 835
acerbity
acrimony 395
sourness 397
rudeness 895
spleen 900, 901
malevolence 907
acervate 72
acetous 397
acetylene 388
acharné 900
Achates, fidus –
890, 939
ache *physical* 378
mental 828
Acheron
pit of – 982
Acherontic
moribund 360
gloomy 837
achievable 470
achieve *end* 67
produce 161
do 680
accomplish 729
achievement 551,
861
Achilles, heel of –
vulnerable 665
achromatism 429
acicular 253
acid 397
acid test 463
acknowledge
answer 462
assent 488
disclose 529
avow 535
consent 762
observe 772
pay 807
thank 916
repent 950
reward 973
acknowledged
custom 613
acme 210
– *of perfection* 650
Acology 662
acolyte 996
acomous 226
aconite 663
acoustic 418
– *organs* 418
acoustics 402
acquaint
– *oneself with* 539
– *with* 527
acquaintance
knowledge 490
information 527
friend 890
make – *with* 888
acquiesce
assent 488
willing 488
consent 762
tolerate 826

acquire
develop 161
get 775
receive 785
– *a habit* 613
– *learning* 539
acquirement
knowledge 490
learning 539
talent 698
receipt 810
acquisition
knowledge 490
gain 775
acquit
liberate 750
exempt 927a
vindicate 937
innocent 946
absolve 970
acquit oneself
behave 692
– *of a debt* 807
– *of a duty* 926
– *of an obligation*
772
acquittal 506, 970
acquittance 771
acres *space* 180
land 342
property 780
Acres, Bob 862
acrid 392, 395
acridity 171
acrimony
physical 171
caustic 830
– *discourtesy* 895
hatred 898
anger 900
malevolence 907
acroamatism 490
acrobat
strength 159
actor 599
proficient 700
mountebank 844
Acropolis 210
across 219, 708
acrostic 533, 561,
842
act *imitate* 19
physical 170
- *of a play* 599
personate 599
voluntary 680
statute 697
in the – 680, 947
– *a part feign* 544
– *one's part* 625,
926
– *upon*
physical 170
mental 615
take steps 680
– *up to* 772
– *well one's part*
944
– *without author-*
ity 738
acting *deputy* 759
actinic 420
actinometer 445
action *physical* 170
voluntary 680
battle 720
law 969
line of – 692

put in – 677
suit the – to the
  word 550
thick of the – 682
activate 171
actionable 964
active *physical* 171
  voluntary 682
  – *service* 722
  – *thought* 457
activity 682
actor
  impostor 548
  player 599
  agent 690
  affectation 855
Acts *record* 551
  Apostolic 985
actual *existing* 1
  present 118
  real 494
actuary 85, 811
actuate 176, 615
actum est 729
acu tetigisti, rem
  465, 494
acuity 253
aculeated 253
acumen 498
acuminated 253
acupuncture 260
acustics 402
acute *energetic* 171
  physically violent
  173
  pointed 253
  physically sensible
  375
  musical tone 410
  perspicacious 498
  cunning 702
  strong feeling 821
  morally painful
  830
  – *angle* 244
  – *ear* 418
  – *note* 410
acutely 31
acuteness 465
ad
  – **eundem** 27
  – **hominem** 79
  – **infinitum** 105
  – **instar** 82
  – **interim** 106
  – **lib** 705
  – **rem** 23
A.D. 106
adage 496
adagio *music* 415
  slow 275
Adam *sin* 945
  – 's apple 250
adamant 159, 323
adapt 23, 27
  – *oneself to* 82
adaptable
  conformable 82
  useful 644
add *increase* 35
  join 37
  numerically 85
  – up 811
addendum 39
adder 913
addict *habit* 613
adding machine 85
additament 39

addition
  extrinsical 6
  increase 35
  adjunction 37
  thing added 39
  arithmetical 85
addle *barren* 169
  incomplete 730
  abortive 732
  – *the wits*, 475, 503
addlehead 501
addleheaded 499
address
  residence 189
  direction 550
  speech 582
  speak to 586
  skill 698
  request 765
  – *oneself to* 673
addresses
  courtship 902
addressful 894
adduce
  bring to 288
  evidence 467
addulce 834
ademption 789
adenoid 250
adenology 329
adept 700
adequate *power* 157
  sufficient 639
  for a purpose 644
adhere *stick* 46
  – *to* 604a, 613
  – *to an obligation*
  772
  – *to a duty* 926
adherent
  follower 711
adhesive, 46, 327,
  352
adhibit 677
adhortation 695
adieu *departure* 293
  loss 776
adipocere 356
adipose 355
adit *orifice* 260
  conduit 350
  passage 627
adjacent 197
adjection 37
adjective 39
adjoin 197, 199
adjourn 133
adjudge 480
adjudicate 480
adjunct
  thing added 39
  accompaniment 88
  aid 707
  auxiliary 711
adjuration 535, 536
adjure 765, 768
adjust *adapt* 23
  equalize 27
  order 58
  prepare 673
  settle 723, 762
  – *differences* 774
adjutage 260, 350
adjutant
  auxiliary 711
  military 745
adjuvant *helping*
  707

  auxiliary 711
admeasurement
  466
adminicle 467
administer
  utilize 677
  conduct 693
  exercise authority
  737
  distribute 786
  – *correction* 972
  – *oath* 768
  – *sacrament* 998
  – *to aid* 707
  give 784
administration of
  justice 965
administrative 737,
  965
administrator 694
admirable 648, 744
admiral 745
Admiralty, court of
  – 966
admirari, nil – 871,
  932
admiration
  wonder 870
  love 897
  respect 928
  approval 931
admired disorder 59
admirer 897
admissible
  relevant 23
  receivable 296
  tolerable 651
  – *in society* 852
admit
  composition 54
  include 76
  let in 296
  assent 488
  acknowledge 529
  permit 760
  concede 762
  accept 785
  – *exceptions* 469
  – *of* 470
admitted
  customary 613
  – *maxim &c.* 496
admixture 41
admonish
  warn 668
  advise 695
  reprove 932
ado *activity* 682
  exertion 686
  difficulty 704
  make much –
  about 542
  much – about
  nothing
  overestimate 482
  unimportant 643
  unskilful 699
adolescence 131
Adonis 845
adonize 847
adopt
  naturalize 184
  choose 609
  – *a cause aid* 707
  – *a course* 692
  – *an opinion* 484
adoption
  religious 987

adore 897, 990
adorn 847
adown 207
adrift *unrelated* 10
  disjoined 44
  dispersed 73
  uncertain 475
  unapt 699
  free 750
  go – *deviate* 279
  turn – *disperse* 73
  liberate 750
  dismiss 756
adroit 698
adscititious
  extrinsic 6
  added 37
  redundant 641
adscriptus glebae
  746
adulation 933
adulator 935
Adullam, cave of
  624, 832
Adullamite 832
adult 131
adulterate *mix* 41
  deteriorate 659
adulterated 545
adulterer 962
adultery 961
adumbrate
  darkness 421
  allegorize 521
  represent 554
adumbration
  semblance 21
  allusion 526
aduncity 244, 245
adust
  color 433
  gloomy 837
adustion 384
advance *increase* 35
  course 109
  progress 282
  assert 535
  improve 658
  aid 707
  succeed 731
  lend 787
  in – *precedence* 62
  front 234
  precession 280
  in – *of* 33
  in – of one's age
  498
  – *against* 716
  – *of learning &c.*
  490
advanced 282
  – *in life* 128
  – *guard* 234
  – *student* 541
  – *work* 717
advances, make –
  offer 763
  social 892
advantage
  superiority 33
  influence 175
  good 618
  expedience 646
  mechanical – 633
  dressed to – 847
  find one's – in 644
  gain an – 775
  set off to – 658

  take – of 677, 698
  – over *success* 731
advantageous
  beneficial 648
  profitable 775
advene 37
advent
  futurity 121
  event 151
  approach 286
  arrival 292
Advent 998
adventism 984
adventitious 6, 156
adventive 156
adventure *event* 151
  chance 156
  pursuit 622
  danger 665
  trial 675
  the great – 360
adventurer
  traveler 268
  deceiver 548
  experimenter 463
  gambler 621
  rash 863
  ignoble 876
adventures 594
adventurous
  undertaking 676
  bold 861
  rash 863
adversaria 551
adversary 710
adverse
  contrary 14
  opposed 708
  unprosperous 735
  disliking 867
  – *party* 710
adversity 735
advert 457
advertise 531
advice *notice* 527
  news 532
  counsel **695**
advisable 646
advise *predict* 511
  inform 527
  counsel 695
  – with one's pillow
  451
advised *predeter-*
  mined 611
  intended 620
  better – 658
adviser 540, 695
advocacy 931
advocate
  prompt 615
  recommend 695
  aid 707
  auxiliary 711
  friend 890
  vindicate 937
  counsellor 968
Advocate, the – 976
advocation 617
advoutress 962
advoutry 961
advowson 995
adynamic 160
adytum *room* 191
  prediction 511
  secret place 530
adze 253
adzooks 870

aidless 160
aigrette 847
aiguille 253
aiguillette 747, 847
aigulet 847
ail 655, 828
aileron 267, 273
ailment 655
aim 278, 620, 675
- a blow at 716
aimable 894
faire l' - 897
aimer éperdument 897
aimless *without motive* 615a
chance 621
air *unsubstantial* 4
broach 66
lightness 320
gas 334
atmospheric **338**
wind 349
tune 415
appearance 448
refresh 689
demeanor 692
fashionable 852
beat the - 645
fill the - 404
fine - *salubrity* 656
fish in the - 645
fowls of the - 366
in the - 527
rend the - 404
take - 531
air-balloon 273
air base 728
air-commodore 745
aircraft 273, 726
air-drawn 515
airdrome 273
air-force 726
air-gun 727
airing 266
air-mail 273
airman 269
airmanship 698
air-marshal 745
air-passage 351
air-pipe 351
airport 273, 292, 728
air-pump 349
air-raid 716
airs *affectation* 855
pride 878
vanity 880
arrogance 885
air-shaft 351
air service 267
airship 273, 726
air-tight 261
airways 267
airworthy 273, 664
airy [*see air*]
windy 349
unimportant 643
gay 836
- hopes 858, 859
give to - nothing
a local habitation &c. 515
aisle *passage* 260
way 627
in a church 1000
ait 346
ajar *open* 260

discordant 713
ajee 217
ajutage 260, 350
akimbo *angular* 244
stand - 715
akin *related* 9
consanguineous 11
similar 17
al fresco 220
alabaster *white* 430
alack! 839
alacrity *willing* 602
active 682
cheerful 836
Aladdin's lamp 993
alar 267
alarm *warning* 668
notice of danger 669
fear 860
cause for - 665
give an - *indicate* 550
alarmist 862
alarum 114, 550, 669
alas! 839
alate 267
alb 999
albeit 30
albert
chain 847
albification 430
albinescence 430
albinism 430
albino 443
album 593, 596
albumen
semi-liquid 352
protein 357
Alcaic 597
alcaid 745
alcalde 745
alcazar 189
alchemy 144
alcohol 995
Alcoran 986
alcove 191, 252
Aldebaran 423
alderman 745
ale 298
alea, jacta est - 601
aleatory 665
Alecto 173
alectromancy 511
alehouse 189
go to the - 959
alembic
conversion 144
vessel 191
furnace 386
laboratory 691
alentours 197
alert *watchful* 457, 459
active 682
alerte 669
aleuromancy 511
Alexandrine
ornate style 577
verse 597
alexandrite 848
alexipharmic 662
alexiteric 662
algebra 85
algid 383
algology 369
algorithm 85
alguazil 965

alias
otherwise 18
pseudonym 565
alibi 187
alien *irrelevant* 10
foreign 57
transfer 783
gentile 989
alienable 783
alienate
transfer 783
estrange 44, 889
set against 898
alienation
mental - 503
alieni appetens
grasping 865
envious 921
selfish 943
alienism 54
align 278
alight *stop* 265
arrive 292
descend 306
on fire 382
alike 17
share and share - 778
aliment *food* 298
alimentary 662
- canal 350
alimentation
aid 707
alimony
property 780
provision 803
income 810
aliquot 51, 84
aliter visum, diis - 601
alive
living 359
intelligent 498
active 682
cheerful 836
be - with 102
keep - *continue* 143
keep the memory - 505
look - 684
- to *attention* 457
cognizant 490
informed 527
able 698
sensible 822
alkahest 335
all *whole* 50
complete 52
generality 78
- absorbing 642
in - ages 112
- aboard 495
- agog 865
- in all 50
- along 106
- along of 154
- but 32
- colors 440
- considered 451, 480
- day long 110
- devouring 190
in - directions 278
- engrossing 190
at - events *compensation* 30
qualification 469

true 494
resolve 604
- fours *easy* 705
cards 840
- in good time 152
- hail! *welcome* 292
honor to 873
celebration 883
courtesy 894
- hands *everybody* 78
on - hands 488
- of a dither 824
- of a heap 72
- knowing 976
- manner of *difference* 15
multiform 81
with - one's might 686
- at once 113
- one 27, 866
- out 52
- over *end* 67
universal 78
destruction 162
space 180
at - points 52
- in one's power 686
- powerful
mighty 159
God 976
in - quarters 180
with - respect 928
in - respects 52, 494
- right! 922
- Saints' day 998
- searching 461
- seeing 976
on - sides 227
- sorts *diverse* 16a
mixed 41
multiform 81
- talk 4
- things to all men 894
- the time 106
at - times 136
- together 50
- ways 243, 279
- wise 976
- the world and his wife 78
of - work
useful 644
maid - 746
Allah 979
allay
moderate 174
pacify 723
relieve 834
- excitability 826
allective 615
allege *evidence* 467
assert 535
plea 617
allegiance 743, 926
allegory 464, 521, 594
allegro *music* 415
cheerful 836
allelujah 990
allemande 840
all-embracing 76
alleviate 174, 834
alley *court* 189

passage 26
way 627
alliance *relation* 9
kindred 11
physical co-operation 178
voluntary co-operation 709
party 712
union 714
allied to *like* 17
alligation 43
allign 278
alliteration
similarity 17
style in writing 577
poetry 597
allocation 60, 786
allocution **586**
allodium *free* 748
property 780
allopathy 662
alloquy 586
allot *arrange* 60
distribute 786
due 924
allow *assent* 488
admit 529
permit 760
consent 762
give 784
- to have one's own way 740
allowable 760, 924
allowance
qualification 469
gift 784
allotment 786
discount 813
salary 973
with grains of - 485
make - for *forgive* 918
vindicate 937
alloy *mixture* 41
combination 48
debase 659
allude *hint* 514
mean 516
refer to 521
latent 526
inform 527
allure *move* 615
create desire 865
alluring 829
allusive
relative 9
alluvial *level* 213
land 342
plain 344
alluvium
deposit 40
land 342
soil 653
ally *combine* 48
auxiliary 711
friend 891
alma mater 542
almanac
list 86
chronometry 114
record 551
almighty 157
Almighty, the - 976
almoner
treasurer 801

giver 784
church officer 996
almonry 802
almost *nearly* 32
not quite 651
– all 50
– *immediately* 132
alms *gift* 784
benevolence 906
worship 990
almshouse 189, 666
almsman 785
Alnaschar's dream 515, 858
aloes 395
aloft 206
alogy 497
alone *single* 87
unaided 706
let – not use 678
not restrain 748
along 200
get – progress 282
go – depart 293
go – with-concur 178
assent 488
co-operate 709
– *of caused by* 154
– *with added* 37
together 88
by means of 631
alongside *near* 197
parallel 216
laterally 236
aloof *distant* 196
high 206
secluded 893
stand – inaction 681
refuse 764
cautious 864
alopecia 226
aloud 404
think – 589
naïveté 703
Alp 206
alpenstock 215
Alpha 66
– *and Omega* 50
alphabet
beginning 66
letters 561
alphabetarian 541
alphabeticize 60
alphitomancy 511
alpine *high* 206
Alpine Club 268, 305
already
antecedently 116
even now 118
past time 122
Alsatia 791, 945
also 37
altar 903, 1000
alter 140
– *the case* 468
– *one's course* 279
alter ego *similar* 17
auxiliary 711
deputy 759
friend 890
alterable 149
alteram partem, *audire –* 468, 922
alterative
substitute 634
remedy 662

altercation 713
altered *worn* 688
– *for the worse* 659
alternate
reciprocal 12
sequence 63
discontinuous 70
periodic 138
changeable 149
oscillate 314
alternative
substitute 147
choice 609
plan 626
although
compensation 30
counteraction 179
unless 469
altiloquence 577
altimetry
height 206
angle 244
measurement 466
altitude *height* 206
– *and azimuth* 466
alto 410, 416
– *part* 415
alto-rilievo 250, 557
altogether 50, 51
nude 226
altruism 910, 942
altruist 906
alum 397
alumnus 541
alveolus 252
always
uniformly 16
generally 78
during 106
perpetually 112
habitually 613
a.m. 114, 125
amability 829, 894
amah 753
amain 173, 684
amalgam, -ate 41, 48
amalgamation 709
Amalthea's horn 639
amantium iræ 918
amanuensis 553, 590
amaranthine 112
amari aliquid
bad 649
imperfect 651
painful 830
amaritude 395
amass *whole* 50
collect 72
store 636
amateur *volunteer* 602
layman 699
taste 850
votary 865
amatory 897
amaurosis 442
amaze 870
amazingly 31
Amazon
woman 374
warrior 726
courage 861
ambages
convolutions 248
circumlocution

573
circuit 629
ambagious 573
ambassador
messenger 534
representative 758
recall of –s 713
amber 356a
– *color* 436
ambidexter
right and left 238
fickle 607
clever 698
ambient 227
ambigu 41
ambiguas spargere voces
uncertain 475
misteach 538
false 544
cunning 702
ambiguous
uncertain 475
unintelligible 519
equivocal 520
obscure 571
ambiloquy 520
ambit 230
ambition 620, 865
ambivalence 605, 708
amble 266
ambo *school* 542
pulpit 1000
ambo, Arcades – *alike* 17
friends 890
bad men 949
ambrosia 298
ambrosial 394, 490
ambulance
vehicle 272
hospital 662
ambulation 266
ambuscade 530
ambush 530, 667
lie in – 528
âme – de boue 949
– *damnée*
catspaw 711
servant 746
servile 886
bad man 949
– *qui vive* 101, 187
ameer 875
ameliorate 658
amen *assent* 488
submission 725
content 831
amenable 177, 602, 926
not – *to reason* 608
amend 658
amendatory 20
amende honorable 952
amends
compensation 50
atonement 952
reward 973
amenity 829, 894
amentia 503
amerce 974
American organ 417
Americanism 563
amethyst
purple 437
jewel 847

amiable
courteous 894
loving 897
kind 906
amicable 707, 888
amice 999
amicus – curiæ 527
– *humani generis* 910
– *usque ad aras* 890
amidships 68
amidst 41, 228
amiss 619
come – *disagree* 24
mistime 135
inexpedient 647.
do – 945
nothing comes – 823
take – 867, 900
amity *concord* 714
peace 721
friendship 888
ammunition 635, 727
amnesia 506
amnesty 506, 723, 918
amnis, rusticus expectat dum defluat – *hope* 858
amœbæan 63
amok 503
among 41, 228
amor patriæ 910
amore, con – 602, 821
amoroso 599
amorous 897
– *glances* 902
amorphous 83, 241
amorphism 241
amortization 784
amotion 270
amount
quantity 25
degree 26
sum of money 800
price 812
gross – 50
– *to* 27, 85
amour 897, 961
– *propre* 880
ampere 466
amphibian 366
amphibious 83
amphibology 520
Amphictyonic council 696
amphigouri 497
amphitheatre
prospect 441
school 542
theater 599
arena 728
Amphitryon 890
amphora 191
ample *much* 31
spacious 180
large 192
broad 202
copious 639
amplify
expand 194
exaggerate 549
diffuse style 573
amplitude

quantity 25
degree 26
size 192
breadth 202
enough 639
ampoulé 191
ampulla 191
amputate 38
amuck 824
run – 503
amulet 247, 993
amusare la bocca, per – 394
amuse 829, 840
amusement 840
place of – 840
amussim, ad – 494
amylaceous 352
an *if* 514
ana 594
Anabaptist 984
anabasis 35
anachronism
false time 115
inopportune 135
error 495
anacoluthon 70
anaconda 913
anacreontic 597
anaglyph 554, 557
anagoge 521, 526
anagram
double sense 520
secret 533
letter 561
wit 842
analecta 596
analeptic 662
analgesia 376
analogy 9, 17
analogous 12
analysis
decomposition 49
arrangement 60
algebra 85
inquiry 461
experiment 463
reasoning 476
grammar 567
compendium 596
analyst 461, 463
anamorphosis
distortion 243
optical 443
misrepresentation 555
anapest 597
anaphylaxis 375
anarchist
destroyer 165
disobedient 742
evil-doer 913
anarchy 59, 738
anastatic printing 558
anastomosis 43, 219
anastrophe 218
anathema 908
anathematize 908
censure 932
detract 934
anatomize *dissect* 44
investigate 461
anatomy
dissection 44
leanness 203
texture 329
anatomy

science 357
comparative – 368
anatriptic 331
ancestral
  bygone 122
  old 124
  aged 128
ancestry 166
anchor
  connection 45
  stop 265
  safeguard 666
  badge 747
  hope 858
  at – fixed 150
  stationed 184
  safe 664
  cast – settle 184
  arrive 292
  have an – to wind-
    ward 664
  sheet – means 632
anchorage
  location 184
  roadstead 189
  refuge 866
anchored 150
anchorite 893, 955
ancien régime 875
ancient old 124
  flag 550
  – times 122
ancientness 122
ancillary 707
and 37, 88
andante 415
andiron 386
androgynous 83
anecdote 594
anele 998
anemia 160
anemography 349
ἀνεμώλια βάζειν 497
anemometer
  wind 349
  measure 466
anent 9
aneroid 338
anesthesia 376,
  381, 683
anew again 104
  newly 123
anfractuosity 248
angel
  object of love 897
  good person 948
  supernatural
    being 977
  fallen –
    bad man 949
    devil 978
  guardian –
    safety 664
    auxiliary 711
    benefactor 912
  – of Death 362
  – 's visits 137
angelic 944
angels and minis-
  ters of grace de-
  fend us! 860
angelus 550
anger 900
  more in sorrow
    than in – 826,
    918
angiology 329
angle 244

try 463
  at an – 217
Anglicanism 984
angling 622, 840
anguille au genou,
  rompre l' – 158,
  471
anguilliform 205,
  248
anguis in herbâ 667
anguish
  physical 378
  moral 828
angular 244
  – velocity 264
angularity 244
angusta domi, res
  – 804
angustation 203
anhelation 688
anhydrate 340
anhydrous 340
aniline dyes 437
anility 128, 499
animadvert
  consider 451
  attend to 457
  reprehend 932
animal 366
  female – 374
  – cries 412
  – economy 359
  – gratification 377
  – life 364
  – physiology 368
  – spirits 836
  – and vegetable
    kingdom 357
animalcule 193, 366
animalism
  sensuality 954
animality 364
animate
  induce 615
  excite 824
  enliven 836
animation
  life 359
  animality 364
  activity 682
  vivacity 836
  suspended – 823
animism 984
animo, ex – 602
  quo – 620
animosity
  dislike 867
  enmity 889
  hatred 898
  anger 900
animus
  willingness 602
  intention 620
  desire 865
ankle 244
  – deep 208, 209
anklet 847
ankylosis 150
annalist 114, 553
annals
  chronology 114
  record 551
  account 594
anneal 673
annex
  addition 37
  adjunct 39
  junction 43

acquire 775
Annie Oakley 815
annihilate 2, 162
anniversary 138
anno 106
Anno Domini
  era 106
  old age 124
annotation 522, 550
annotator 524
  scholar 492
  interpreter 524
  editor 595
annotto 434
announce
  predict 511
  inform 527
  publish 531
  assert 535
announcer 527
annoy
  molest 649, 907
  disquiet 830
annoyance 828
  source of – 830
annual periodic 138
  plant 367
  book 593
annuity 810
annul 162, 750
annular 247
annunciate 527
annus magnus 108
anodyne
  lenitive 174
  remedial 662
  relief 834
anoint coat 223
  lubricate 332
  oil 355
anointed
  deity 976
  king 745
anomaly 59, 83
  disorder 59
  irregularity 83
anon 132
anonymous 565
anopsia 442
anorexy 866
another
  different 15
  repetition 104
  – story 468, 526
  go upon – tack 507
  – time 119
answer
  to an inquiry 462
  confute 479
  solution 522
  succeed 731
  pecuniary profit
    775
  pleadings 969
  require an – 461
  – for deputy 759
  promise 768
  go bail 806
  I'll – for it 535
  – the helm 745
  – the purpose 731
  – to correspond 9
  – one's turn 644
answerable
  agreement 23
  liable 177
  bail 806
  duty 926

censurable 932
ant 690
Antaeus 159, 192
antagonism
  difference 14
  physical 179
  voluntary 708
  enmity 889
antagonist 710, 891
antagonistic 24
antarctic 237
antecedence 62, 116
antecedent 64
antechamber 191
ante Christum 106
antedate 115
antediluvian 124
antelope 274
antemundane 124
antenna 379
anteposition 62
anterior
  in order 62
  in time 116
  in place 234
  – to reason 477
anteroom 191
antevert 706
anthem 990
anthemion 847
anthology
  book 533
  collection 596
  poem 597
anthracite 388
anthropoid 372
anthropology
  zoology 368
  mankind 372
anthropomancy 511
anthropophagi 913
anthroposcopy 511
anthroposophy 372
antic 840
anti-aircraft gun
  564, 727
antichambre,
  faire – 133
antichristian 984,
  989
antichronism 115
anticipate
  anachronism 115
  priority 116
  future 121
  early 132
  expect 507
  foresee 510
  prepare 673
  hope 858
  in – 116
anticlimax
  decrease 36
  bathos 497, 853
anticlinal 217
anticyclone 265
antidote 662
antigropelos 225
antilogarithm 84
antilogy 477
antimony 663
Antinomian 984
antinomy 964
Antinous 845
antiparallel 217
antipathy 867, 898
antiphon music 415
  answer 462

worship 990
antiphrasis 563
antipodes
  difference 14
  distance 196
  contraposition
    237
antipoison 660
antiquary
  past times 122
  scholar 492
  historian 553
antiquas vias,
  stare super –
    613, 670
antiquated 128
antique 124
antiquity 122
antiscriptural 984
antiseptic 652, 662
antisocial 911
antistrophe 597
antithesis
  contrast 14
  difference 15
  opposite 237
  style 574, 577
antitoxin 662
antitype 22
antler 253
antonomasia
  metaphor 521
  nomenclature 564
antonym 14
antrum 252
anvil support 215
  on the –
    intended 620
    in hand 625
    preparing 673
anxiety pain 828
  fear 860
  desire 865
anxious expectation
  507
any some 25
  part 51
  no choice 609a
  at – price 604a
  at – rate
    certain 474
    true 494
  at all hazards 604
anybody 78
anyhow 460, 627
anything one
  knows, for – 491
aorist 109, 119
aorta 350
apace early 132
  swift 274
apache 913
apart 44, 87
  set – 636
  wide – 196
apartment 191
  -s 189
  -s to let
    imbecile 499
apathetic 275
apathy
  indifference 465
  insensibility 823
  irreligion 989
ape imitate 19
Apelles 559
aperçu 596
aperture 260

apex 210
aphasia 583
aphelion 196
aphonic 403
aphony 581
aphorism 496
aphrodite 845, 979
apiary 370
apiculture 370
Apicius 957
apiece 79
apish 19, 499
aplanatic 429
aplomb
  stability 150
  self-possession 498
  resolution 604
Apocalypse 985
Apocrypha 985
apocryphal
  uncertain 475
  erroneous 495
  heterodox 984
apodictic 478
apodosis 67
apogee 210
apograph 21
Apollo *sun* 318
  music 416
  luminary 423
  beauty 845
  god 979
  magnus – 500, 695
Apollyon 978
apologue
  metaphor 521
  teaching 537
  description 594
apology *excuse* 617
  vindication 937
  penitence 950
  atonement 952
apophthegm 496
apophysis 250
apoplexy 158, 655
aporetic 487
aposiopesis 585
apostasy
  recantation 607
  dishonor 940
  heterodoxy 984
apostate
  convert 144
  turncoat 607
  impiety 988
apostle *teacher* 540
  disciple 541
  inspired 985
  –'s creed 983*a*
apostolic 985
  – church 983*a*
  – see 995
apostrophe
  address 586
  soliloquy 589
  appeal 765
apothecary 662
  –'s weight 319
apothegm 496
. apotheosis
  resuscitation 163
  canonization 873
  heaven 981
  hero worship 991
apozem 335, 384
appal 830, 860
appanage

property 780
gift 784
apparatus 633
apparel 225
apparent
  visible 446
  appearing 448
  probable 472
  manifest 525
  heir – 779
apparition
  fallacy of vision 443
  spirit 980
apparitor 534
appeach 938
appeal 586, 765
  court of – 966
  – to arms 722
  – motion 969
  – from Philip drunk to Philip sober 658
  – to *call to witness* 467
  – to for (*claim*) 924
appear 446, 525
  – for 759
  – in print 591
appearance 448
  make one's – 292
  to all – 448
  probable 472
appearances
  keep up – 852
appellant 924, 938
appellate 966
appellation 564
append *add* 37
  sequence 63
  hang 214
appendage 39
appendectomy 662
appendix
  adjunct 39
  sequel 65
  end 67
  book 593
appertain
  related to 9
  component 56
  belong 777
  property 780
appetite 865
  tickle the –
  savory 394
appetizing 865
  exciting 824
applaud 931
apple – of discord 713
  golden –
  allurement 615
  – of one's eye *good* 648
  love 897
  favorite 899
  – off another tree 15
  how we –s swim! 880
apple-green 435
apple-pie order 58
appliance *use* 677
  –s *means* 632
  machinery 633
applicable *relevant*

23
  useful 644
  expedient 646
applicability 9
applicant 767
application *study* 457
  metaphor 521
  use 677
  request 765
apply, *use* 677
  – a match 384
  – the match to a train 66
  – the mind 457
  – a remedy 662
appoggiatura 413
appointment
  employment 625
  order 741
  charge 755
  assignment 786
  interview 892
appointments
  gear 633
apportion *arrange* 60
  disperse 73
  allot 786
apportionment 786
appositeness 9
apposition
  relation 9
  relevancy 23
  closeness 199
  paraphrase 522
appraise 466, 812
appreciate
  realize 450, 451
  measure 466
  judge 480
  know 490
  taste 850
  approve 931
apprehend
  believe 484
  know 490
  fear 860
  seize 789
apprehension
  idea 453
  taking 789
apprentice 541
  – oneself 676
apprenticeship 539, 673
apprise 527
apprised of 490
approach
  of time 121
  impend 152
  nearness 197
  move 286
  path 627
approaching 9
approbation 931
appropinquation 286
appropriate *fit* 23
  peculiar 79
  expedient 646
  assign 786
  take 789
  steal 791
approval 488, 931
  on – 609
approximate
  related to 9

resemble 17
  in mathematics 85
  nearness 197
  approach 286
appulse *meeting* 199
  collision 276
  approach 286
  convergence 290
appurtenance
  part 51
  component 56
  belongings 780
  accompaniment 88
appurtenant 9
après nous le déluge 943
apricot *color* 439
April
  – fool 547, 857
  make an – fool of 545
  – showers 149
apron *extension* 39
  clothing 225
  defence 717
  canonicals 999
àpropos [*see* à]
aprotype 591
apse 1000
apt *consonant* 23
  tendency 176, 177
  docile 539
  willing 602
  clever 698
aqua-fortis 335
aquamarine 435
aquarium 370
Aquarius 348, 636
aquatic *water* 337
aquatics 267
aquatinta 558
aqueduct 350
aqueous 337
aquiline 244
A.R. 106
Arab *wanderer* 268
  horse 271
  street – 876
araba 272
arabesque 847
Arabian
  – *perfumes* 400
  – *nights* 515
arable 371
arbalest 727
arbiter *critic* 480
  director 694
  adviser 695
  judge 967
  – *elegantiarum*
  revels 840
  taste 850
  fashion 852
arbitrage 794
arbitrament 480
  judgment 480
  – *of the sword* 722
arbitrary
  without relation 10
  irregular 83
  wilful 606
  capricious 608
  authoritative 737
  severe 739
  insolent 885
  lawless 964

– *power* 739
arbitrate
  adjudicate 480
  mediate 724
arbitration
  court of – 966
  submit to – 774
arbitrium, ad – 600
arbor 215, 312
arbor *abode* 189
  summer-house 191
  plaisance 840
arborescent
  ramifying 242
  rough 256
  trees 367
arboriculture 371
arc 245
  heat 382
arcade *street* 189
  curve 245
  gateway 260
Arcades ambo
  alike 17
  friends 890
  bad men 949
Arcadia 827, 981
Arcadian 703, 946
arcanum 533
arch *great* 31
  support 215
  curve 245
  convex 250
  concave 252
  clever 498
  cunning 702
  triumphal – 733, 883
archaic *old* 124
archaism 122, 563
archangel 977
archbishop 996
archbishopric 995
archdeacon 996
archduchy 181
archduke 745
archegenesis 161
archeologist
  pastimes 122
  scholar 492
archeology 122
archer 726
archery 840
Arches, court of – 966, 995
archetype 22
archetypal 20
Archeus 359
archfiend 978
archiater 695
archiepiscopal 995
archimandrite 996
archipelago 346
architect 164, 690
architectonic 161
architecture
  arrangement 60
  construction 161
  fabric 329
  ornament 847
architrave 210
archive 551
archlute 417
archon *ruler* 745
  deputy 759
  judge 967
archtraitor 941

arctic *northern* 237
  cold 383
arctics 225
arcuation 245
ardent *fiery* 382
  eager 682
  feeling 821
  loving 897
  – *expectation* 507
  – *imagination* 515
ardet, proximus –
  665, 667
ardor *vigor* 574
  activity 821
  feeling 821
  desire 865
arduous 704
area 181, 182
arefaction 340
arena *space* 180
  region 181
  field of view 441
  field of battle **728**
arenaceous 330
areola 247
areolar 219
areometer 321
Areopagus 966
arête 253
aretinism 961
aretology 926
Argand lamp 423
argent 430
argillaceous 324
argosy 273
argot 563
argonaut 269
argue *evidence* 467
  reason 476
  indicate 550
  dissectation 595
argument *disagree-*
  ment 24
  topic 454
  discussion 476
  meaning 516
  have the best of
  an – 478
argumentum
  – baculinum
  compel 744
  lawless 964
  punish 972
  – ad crumenam
  800
  – ad hominem
  reasoning 476
  accuse 938
  – ad verecundiam
  939
Argus-eyed 441, 459
argute 498
aria 415
arianism 984
arid 340
  unproductive 169
  uninteresting 841
Ariel *courier* 268
  swift 274
  messenger 534
  spirit 979
arietation 276
arietta 415
aright *well* 618
Ariman [*see* Ahri-
  manes]
ariolation 511
arioso 415

aris et focis, pro –
  defence 717
  philanthropy 910
arise *exist* 1
  begin 66
  happen 151
  mount 305
  appear 446
  – *from* 154
Aristarchus 850
Aristides
  good man 948
aristocracy
  power 737
  fashion 852
  nobility 875
ἄριστον μέτρον 628
Arithmancy 511
arithmetic 85
ark *abode* 189
  asylum 666
arm *part* 51
  power 157
  instrument 633
  provide 637
  prepare 673
  war 722
  weapon 727
  make a long – 200
  – chair 215
  – in arm
  together 88
  friends 888
  sociable 892
  – of the law 963
  – of the sea 343
armada 726
Armageddon 720,
  722
armament 673, 727
armed 717
  – at all points 673
  – force 726
  – guard 664
armet 717
armful 25
armiger 875
armigerent 726
armigerous 722
armilla 247, 847
armillary sphere
  466
armipotent 157
armistice
  cessation 142
  respite 672
  pacification 723
armless 158
armlet *ring* 247
  gulf 343
  ornament 847
armor *cover* 223
  defence 717
  arms 727
  buckle on one's –
  673
  – plated 223
armored
  – car 726
  – cruiser 726
  – train 726
armorial bearings
  550, 877
armory *store* 636
  workshop 691
arm's length
  at – 196
  keep at –

repel 289
defence 717
enmity 889
seclusion 893
discourtesy 895
arms 727 [*see* arm]
  heraldry 550
  war 722
  honors 877
  clash of – 720
  deeds of – 720
  with folded – 681
  in – *infant* 129
  throw oneself into
  the – of 666, 880
  under – 722
  up in – *active* 682
  discord 713
  résistance 719
  resentment 900
  enmity 889
Armstrong gun 727
army *collection* 72
  multitude 102
  troops 726
aroma 400
around 227
  lie – 220
arouse *move* 615
  excite 824
  – oneself 682
aroynt *begone* 297
  malediction 908
arquebusade 662
arquebuse 727
arraign 938, 969
arrange
  set in order 60
  plan 626
  compromise 774
  – with creditors
  807
  – itself 58
arrange – matters
  pacify 723
  – music 413, 416
  – in a series 69
  – under 76
arrangement 23, 60
  [*see* arrange]
  order 58
  temporary – 111
arrant *identical* 31
  manifest 525
  notorious 531
  bad 649
  disreputable 874
  base 940
arras 847
array *order* 58, 60
  series 69
  assemblage 72
  multitude 102
  dress 225
  prepare 673
  adorn 847
  ostentation 882
  battle – 722
arrear, in – 53, 808
arrears *debt* 806
arrectis auribus
  hear 418
  expect 507
arrest *stop* 142
  restrain 751
  in law 969
  – the attention 457
arrière-pensée

after-thought 65
mental reservation
  528
motive 615
set purpose 620
arrival **292**
arrive *happen* 151
  reach 292
  complete 729
  – at a conclusion
  480
  – at the truth 480a
arrogant *severe* 739
  proud 878
  insolent 885
arrogate 885, 924
  – to oneself
  undue 925
arrondissement 181
arrosion 331
arrow *swift* 274
  missile 284
  arms 727
  broad – 550
arrow-head
  form 253
  writing 590
'Arry and 'Arriet
  902
ars celare artem
  698
ars, hae tibi
  erunt – 627
artesian well 343
artful 544, 702
  – dodge 545, 702
article *thing* 3
  part 51
  matter 316
  chapter 593
  review 595
  goods 798
articled clerk 541
articles
  thirty-nine – 983a
  – of agreement
  770
  – of faith 484, 983
articulate 366
articulation
  junction 43
  speech 580
articulo, in –
  transient 111
  dying 360
artifice 626, 702
artificer 690
artificial
  fictitious 545
  cunning 702
  affected 855
  – language 579
artillery
  explosion 404
  arms 727

artilleryman 726
artisan 690
artist *painter* &c.
  559
  contriver 626
  agent 690
artiste *music* 416
  drama 599
artistic *skilful* 698
  beautiful 845
  taste 850
  – language 578
artlessness 703
aruspex 513
aruspicy 511
arundo, haeret
  lateri lethalis –
  828
as *motive* 615
  – broad as long 27
  – can be 52
  – good as 27
  – if *similar* 17
  suppose 514
  – little as may be
  32
  – it may be
  circumstance 8
  event 151
  chance 156
  – much again 90
  – soon as 120
  – they say 496, 532
  – things are 7
  – things go 151,
  613
  – to 9
  – usual 82
  – it were 17, 521
  – you were 141,
  283
  – well as 37
  – the world wags
  151
ascend *be great* 31
  increase 35
  rise 305
  improve 658
ascendancy
  power 157
  influence 175
  success 731
ascendant
  lord of the – 745
  in the –
  influence 175
  important 642
  success 731
  authority 737
  repute 873
  one's star in the –
  prosperity 734
ascension
  [*see* ascend]
  calefaction 384
  – Day 998
ascent
  [*see* ascend]
  gradient 217
  rise **305**
  glory 873
ascertain *fix* 150
  determine 480
ascertained 474,
  490
ascertainment 480a
asceticism **955**
ascititious

intrinsic 6
additional 37
supplementary 52
ascribe 155
aseptic 652
ash 384
– colored 432
– blond 430
ashen 429
Ash Wednesday 998
ashamed 879
ashes *corpse* 362
dirt 653
lay in – 162
pale as – 429, 860
rise from one's – 660
ashore 342
go – *arrive* 292
ashy 429
Asian mystery 533
aside *laterally* 236
whisper 405
private 528
say – 589
set &c. – *displace* 185
neglect 460
negative 536
reject 610
disuse 678
abrogate 756
discard 782
step – 279
asinine *ass* 271
fool 499
ask *inquire* 461
request 765
for sale 794
price 812
– leave 760
askance 217
eye – *fear* 860
look – *vision* 441, 443
dissent 489
dislike 867
disapproval 932
askari 726
asked in church 903
askew 217, 243
aslant 217
asleep 683
aslope 217
Asmodeus 980
asomatous 317
asp *animal* 366
evil-doer 913
Aspasia 962
aspect *feature* 5
state 7
situation 183
appearance 448
aspen leaf
shake like an – 315, 860
asperity
roughness 256
discourtesy 895
anger 900
irascibility 901
asperse 934
aspersion
malediction 908
rite 998
asphalt
smooth 255

resin 356a
material 635
asphodel 845
aspic 352
asphyxia 360
asphyxiate 361
aspirant 767, 865
aspirate 580
aspirator 349
aspire *rise* 305
hope 858
desire 865
worship 990
aspirin 834
asportation 270
asquint 217
ass *beast of burden* 271
fool 501
make an – of
delude 545
– between two bundles of hay 605
–'s bridge 519
– in lion's skin
cheat 548
bungler 701
assafetida 401
assagai 727
assail 716, 830
assailant 710, 726
assassin, –ate 361
assault 716, 961
take by – 789
assay 463
asseguay 727
assemblage 72
assembly
council 696
society 892
religious 997
assembly hall 588
assembly room 189
assent *belief* 484
agree 488
willing 602
consent 762
content 831
assert 535, 924
assess *measure* 466
determine 480
tax 812
assessor
judge 967
assets 780, 800
asseverate 535
assiduity 110
assiduous 682
assign
commission 755
transfer 270, 783
give 784
allot 786
– as cause 155
– a duty 926
– places 60
assignat 800
assignation 892
place of – 74
assignee *donee* 785
assimilate
uniform 16
resemble 17
imitate 19
agree 23
transmute 144
assist 707

– at 186
assistant 711
assister *be present* 186
assize *measure* 466
tribunal 966
justice of – 967
associate *mix* 41
unite 43
collect 72
accompany 88
colleague 690
auxiliary 711
friend 890
– with 892
association
[*see* associate]
relation 9
combination 48
co-operation 709
partnership 712
– of ideas
intellect 450
thought 451
intuition 477
hint 514
– football 840
assoil *acquit* 970
assonance
music 413
poetry 597
assort *arrange* 60
assortment 72, 75
assuage 174, 834
assuetude 613
assume *believe* 484
suppose 514
falsehood 544
take 789
insolent 885
right 924
– authority 737
– a character 554
– command 741
– a form 144
– the offensive 716
assumed name 565
assumption
[*see* assume]
severity 739
hope 858
usurpation 925
assurance
speculation 156
certainty 474
belief 484
assertion 535
promise 768
security 771
hope 858
vanity 880
insolence 885
make – double
sure *safe* 664
caution 864
assuredly
assent 488
assythment 973
astatic 320
asterisk 550
astern 235
put the engines – 275
fall – 283
asteroid 318
Asteroth 979
asthenia 160
astigmatism 443

astir 682
set – 824
astonish 870
astonished
– at nothing 871
astonishing
great 31
astound *excite* 824
fear 860
surprise 870
astra, sic itur ad – 360, 873
astraddle 215
Astraea 922
astragal 847
astral 318
– body 717, 992
– influence 601
– plane 317
astray 475, 495
go – *deviate* 279
sin 945
astriction 43
astride 215
astringent 195
astrolabe 466
astrologer 994
astrology 511
astromancy 511
astronomy 318
astute 498, 702
asunder 44, 196
as poles – 237
asylum *hospital* 663
retreat 666
defence 717
asymptote 290
at, be – 620
up and – them! 716
ataghan 727
atavism 144, 163
ataxia 158
atelier 556, 691
athanasia 112
Athanasian creed 983a
athanor 386
atheism 989
atheist 487
Athenae 979
Athens, owls to – 641
athirst 865
athlete *strong* 159
gladiator 726
athletic *strong* 159
strenuous 686
– sports
contest 720
games 840
athwart
oblique 217
crossing 219
opposing 708
Atkins, Tommy 726
Atlantis 515
Atlas *arrangement* 60
list 86
strength 159
support 215
maps 554
atmosphere
circumambience 227
air 338
painting 556

atmospheric blue 438
atoll 346
atom *small* 32, 193
atomic energy 157
atomics 316
atomizer 336
atoms
crush to – 162
atomy 193
atonement
restitution 790
expiation 952
amends 973
religious 976
atony 160
atrabilious 837
atramentous 431
atrium 191
atrocity
malevolence 907
vice 945
guilt 947
atrophy
shrinking 195
disease 655
decay 659
atropos 601
attach *join* 43
love 897
legal 969
– importance to 642
attaché
employé 746
diplomatic 758
– case 191
attack *singing* 580
disease 655
assault 716
debauch 961
attaghan 727
attain *arrive* 292
succeed 731
– majority 131
attainable 470
attainder
taint 651
at law 971
attainment
knowledge 490
learning 539
skill 698
attar 400
attempter 41, 174
attempered 820
attempt 675
vain – 732
– impossibilities 471
attend
accompany 88
be present 186
follow 281
apply the mind 457
medically 662
aid 707
serve 746
– to business 625
– to orders 743
attendance on
dance – 886
attendant
[*see* attend]
attention 457
care 459
respect 928

attract – 882
call to – 457
call – to 550
give – 418
pay –s to 894
pay one's –s to
  902
attenuate
  decrease 36
  weaken 158
  reduce 195
  rarefy 322
attenuated 203
attest
  bear testimony 467
  affirm 535
  adjure 768
attested copy 771
attic *simple* 42
  garret 191
  summit 210
  style 578
  wit 842
  taste 850
Attila 913
attire 225
attitude
  circumstance 8
  situation 183
  posture 240
attitudinarian 882
attitudinize 855
attollent 307
attorney
  consignee 758
  at law 968
  power of – 755
attract
  bring towards 288
  induce 615
  allure 865
  excite love 897
  – the attention
  457
  visible 446
attraction
  [see attract]
  natural power 157
  bring towards
  288
attractive
  [see attract]
  pleasing 829
  beautiful 845
attrahent 288
attribute
  speciality 79
  accompaniment
  88
  power 157
  –s of the Deity 976
  – to 155
attribution **155**
attrite 330
attrition 330, 331
attroupement 72
attune *music* 415
  prepare 673
attuned to
  habit 613
attunement 23
auburn 433
A.U.C. 106
auction 796, 840
auctioneer 758, 796
auctorial 599
audacity
  courage 861

rashness 863
insolence 885
audible 402
  become – 418
  scarcely – 405
audience
  hearing 418
  conversation 588
  before an – 599
audire alteram
  partem
  counter-evidence
  468
  right 922
  justice 939
audit
  numeration 85
  examination 461
  accounts 811
auditive 418
auditor
  hearer 418
  accountant 811
auditorium 189, 588
auditory
  sound 402
  hearing 418
  theater 599
  – *apparatus* 418
au fait 698
au fond 5
auf wiedersehen
  293
Augean
  – *stable* 653
  – *task* 704
auger 262
aught 51
for – one cares
  unimportant 643
  indifferent 866
for – one knows
  ignorance 491
  conjecture 514
augment
  increase 35
  thing added 39
  expand 194
augur 513
  – *well* 858
augurate 511
augury 512
august 873
Augustinian 996
auk 366
auld lang syne 122
aulic council 696
aumbry 1000
aunt 11
aura *wind* 349
  sensation 380
aurea mediocritas
  628
aureate 436
aureola 420
aureole 420, 873
aureolin 436
auribus, arrectis –
  418
auricular *hearing*
  418
  clandestine 528
  – *confession* 998
auri sacra fames
  819
aurist 662
aurora
  dawn 125

light 420, 423
  twilight 422
  – *australes* 423
  – *borealis* 423
Auroral 236
ausculation 418
auspice *omen* 512
auspices
  influence 175
  prediction 511
  protection 664
  direction 693
  aid 707
  under the – of 693,
  737
auspicious
  opportune 134
  prosperous 734
  hopeful 858
austerity
  harsh taste 395
  severe 739
  discourteous 895
  ascetic 955
  pietism 988
austral 237
austromancy 511
authentic 467
  certain 474
  true 494
authentication
  evidence 467
  security 771
author 164, 593
  projector 626
  dramatic – 599
  – of our being 976
  – of evil 978
  – 's proof 591
authoritative 474,
  741
authority
  testimony 467
  sage 500
  informant 527
  power **737**
  permission 760
  right 924
  ensign of – 747
  person in – 745
  do upon one's own
  – 600
authorized *due* 924
  legalized 963
authorship
  production 161
  style 569
  writing 590
autobiography 594
autocar 272
autochthonous 188
autocracy 737, 739
autocrat 745
autocratic 600, 737
auto-da-fe 384, 972
autograph 550, 590
Autolycus *thief* 792
  pedlar 797
automaniac 504
automatic 601, 633
  – *pistol* 727
  – *writing* 992
automaton 554, 601
automobile 272
automobilist 268
automotive 266
autonomasia 521
autonomy 737, 748

autopsy
  post-mortem 363
  vision 441
autoptical 446, 535
autotype 558
autumn 126
auxiliary **711**
  additional 34
  helpful 707
  – *forces* 726
avail *benefit* 618
  useful 644
  succeed 731
  of no – 645
  – oneself of 677
avalanche *fall* 306
  snow 383
  redundance 641
avaler les couleu-
  vres 725, 886
avant-courier 64,
  673
avant-propos 64
avarice 819
avast! *stop* 142, 265
  desist 624
  forbid 761
avatar *change* 140
  deity 976
  idol 991
avaunt! 297, 449
ave! *honor* 873
  courtesy 894
Ave maria 990
avenge 919
avenue
  plantation 371
  way 627
aver 535
average *mean* 29,
  628
  médiocre 651
  – *circumstances*
  736
  take an – 466
Averni, facilis de-
  scensus – 217,
  665
Avernus 982
averruncate 297,
  301
aversion *unwilling-*
  ness 603
  dislike 867
  hate 898
avert 706
  – the eyes 442
aviary 370
aviation 267
aviator 269
avidity *avarice* 819
  desire 865
airette 273
avile 932, 934
avion 273
aviso 532
avocation 625
avoidance **623**
avoidless 474, 601
avoirdupois 319
avolation 623, 671
avouch 535, 768
avow *assent* 488
  disclose 529
  assert 535
avulsion 44, 301
avuncular 11
await *future* 121

be kept waiting
  133
  impend 152
  expect 507
awake *attentive* 457
  careful 459
  intelligent 498
  active 682
  – to life immortal
  360
awaken *inform* 527
  excite 824
  – the attention 457
  – the memory 505
award *adjudge* 480
  give 784
aware 490
away 187, 196
  break – 623
  fly – 293
  move – 287
  take – from 789
  get &c. – 671
  throw &c. –
  eject 297
  reject 610
  waste 638
  relinquish 782
  – from *unrelated* 10
  – with! 930, 932
  do – with *undo* 681
  abrogate 756
awe *fear* 860
  wonder 870
  respect 928
aweless *fearless* 861
  insolent 885
  disrespectful 329
awful 31, 860
  – *silence* 403
awhile 111
awkward
  inelegant 579
  inexpedient 647
  unskilful 699
  difficult 704
  painful 830
  ugly 846
  vulgar 851
  ridiculous 853
  – *squad* 701
awl 262
awn 253
awning 223, 424
awry *oblique* 217
  distorted 243
  evil 619
axe *edge tool* 253
  impulse 276
  weapon 727
  for beheading 975
  have an – to grind
  702
Axinomancy 511
axiom 496
axiomatic 474
axis *support* 215
  center 222
  rotation 312
axle 312
  wheel and – 633
axle load 466
axletree 215
ay 488
ayah 746, 753
aye *ever* 112
  yes 488
azimuth

relief 834
Balmoral *boot* 225
balmy
  sleep 683
balneal 337
balourdise 699
balsam 662
balsamic
  salubrious 834
balustrade
  support 215
  inclosure 232
bam 544
bambino 129
bamboozle 545
ban *exclude* 55
  prohibit 761
  denounce 908
  under the – 909
  – with bell, book,
    and candle 998
banal 613, 843
band *ligature* 45
  assemblage 72
  filament 205
  belt 230
  ring 247
  music 415, 416,
    417
  party 712
  shackle 752
  – of hope 958
  – together 709
  – with 720
bandage 43, 45
  support 215
  cover 223
  remedy 662
  restraint 752
  the eyes -d 442
bandana 225
bandbox 191
banded together
  178, 712
bandit 792
bandog 664, 668
bandolier 636
bandore 417
bandrol 550
bands 999
bandurria 417
bandy
  exchange 148
  agitate 315
  – about 531
  – legged 243
  – words 476, 588
bane 619, **663**
baneful 649
bang *impel* 276
  sound 406
  beat 972
bangle 847
banish *eject* 297
  seclude 893
  punish 972
banister 215
banjo 417
bank *acclivity* 217
  side of lake 342
  store 636
  sand 667
  fence 717
  money 802
  sea – 342
  – of elegance 800
  – holiday 840
  – up 670

banker 797, 801
  game 840
bank-note 800
bankruptcy 732, 808
banlieue 197, 227
banner 550
  enlist under the -s
    of 707
  raise one's – 722
banneret 875
banns
  forbid the – 761
  publish the –
    ask 765
  marriage 903
banquet 298, 840
banquette 717
banshee 979, 980
bantam *cock* 887
banter 842, 856
banterer 844
banting 956
bantling 129, 167
banyan *stint* 640
  fast 956
baptism *name* 564
  rite 998
Baptist 984
baptistery 1000
bar *except* 38
  exclude 55
  hotel 189
  line 200
  support 215
  inclosure 232
  close 261
  music 413
  hindrance 706
  insignia 747
  prison 752
  prohibit 761
  ingot 800
  tribunal 966
  legal profession
    968
  – sinister *flaw* 651
  disrepute 874
  illegal 964
  crossing the – 360
Barabbas 792
baragouin 517
barb *spike* 253
  nag 271
  – the dart *pain* 830
barbacan 717
barbarian
  uncivilized 876
  evil-doer 913
barbaric 851, 876
barbarism
  neology 563
  bad style 579
  vulgarity 851
  discourtesy 895
barbarous
  unformed 241
  plebeian 876
  maleficent 907
barbette 717
barbican 717
barbouillage 590
barcarolle 415
bard 416, 597
bare *mere* 32
  nude 226
  manifest 525
  disclose 529
  scanty 640

– back 226
– bone 203
– faced *deceitful*
  544, *insolent* 885
– foot 226, 804
– headed 928
  scud under - poles
    704
– possibility 473
– supposition 514
bargain
  compact 769
  barter 794
  cheap 815
  into the - 37
  - for 507
  - and sale *transfer*
    of property 783
barge 273
bargee 269
baritone 408
bark *rind* 223
  strip 226
  ship 273
  yelp 412
  - at *threaten* 909
  censure 932
  more - than bite
    908
  worse than bite
    885
barker 767
barleycorn
  little 193
Barleycorn, Sir
  John - 298
barm *leaven* 320
  bubbles 353
Barmecide feast
  956
barmy 320, 503
barn 189
barnacles 445
barndoor *fowl* 366
barograph 206, 338
barometer *air* 338
  measure 466
  consult the – 463
baron *peer* 875
  husband 903
  court – 966
  - of the Exchequer
    967
baronet 875
baronial 878
baroque 853
baroscope 338
barouche 272
barque 273
barrack 189
barracoon 717
barrage 407, 717
barratry 940
barred 219, 440
barrel 191, 249
  - organ 417
barren 169, 645
barricade *fence* 232
  obstacle 706
  defence 717
  prison 752
barrier [*see* barri-
  cade]
barring *save* 38
  excluding 55
  except 83
  - out *resist* 719
  disobey 742

barrister 968
  revising - 967
barrow
  mound 206
  vehicle 272
  grave 363
barter
  reciprocate 12
  interchange 148
  commerce **794**
barytone 408
basal 215
bas-bleu
  scholar 492
  affectation 855
base
  site 183
  lowest part **211**
  support 215
  bad 649
  cowardly 862
  shameful 874
  servile 886
  dishonorable 940
  vicious 945
  - ball 840
  - born 876
  - coin 800
  - note 408
  - of operations
    plan 626
  attack 716
  - viol 417
baseball diamond
  213
baseboard 211
based on *ground of*
  belief 467
baseless 2, 4
basement *cellar* 191
  lowest part 207,
    211
bash 276
bashaw 739, 745
bashful 881
bashi bazouk 726
basilica 1000
basilisk *sight* 441
  cannon 737
  serpent 949
basin *dock* 189
  vessel 191
  hollow 252
  plain 344
basinet 717
basis
  lowest part 211
  support 215
  preparation 673
bask *physical enjoy-*
  ment 377
  warmth 382
  prosperity 734
  moral enjoyment
    827
basket 191
  - of 190
bas-relief 250, 557
bass *music* 415
  - note 408
  - viol 417
basset horn 417
bassinet 191, 215
bassoon 417
basso-profondo 408
basso-rilievo 250,
  557
bastard 545, 925

baste *beat* 276
  punish 972
Bastille 752
bastinado 972
bastion 717
bat 276, 727
batch 25, 72
bate *diminish* 36
  subtract 38
  reduce price 813
bated breath
  with - *faint sound*
    405
  expecting 507
  hiding 528
  whisper 581
  humble 879
bath 337, 652
  public -s 652
  warm – 386
  - room 191, 652
Bath chair 272
bathe *immerse* 300
  plunge 310
  water 337
bathos 497
bathysphere 208
batik 440
batman 637
bâton *support* 215
  scepter 747
batrachian 366
batta 973
battalion 726
batten
  feed 298
  stage lighting 599
  - down the
    hatches 261
  - on 886
batter *destroy* 162
  beat 276
battered 659, 688
battering-ram 276
battering-train 727
battery *electric* 153
  artillery 726
  guns 727
  floating – 726
  plant a – 716
battle 720, 722
  half the – 642
  win the – 731
  - array *order* 60
  prepare 673
  war 722
  - axe 727
  - cruiser 726
  - cry 550, 722
  - field *arena* 728
  - ground *discord*
    713
  - ship 726
  - with *oppose* 708
battledore and
  shuttlecock
  interchange 148
  game 840
battlement 257, 717
battre
  - la campagne
    nonsense 497
  diffuse style 573
  excitable 825
  - l'eau avec un
    bâton 645
  - le fer sur l'en-
    clume 134

- la générale 669
se — contre des
moulins 645
ne – que d'une aile
683
battology
repeat 104
diffuse style 373
battue *pursuit* 622
attack 716
kill 361
bauble 643, 840
bavardage 517, 584
bawd 962
bawdy, – **house** 961
bawl 411
bawn 189
bay *concave* 252
gulf 343
cry 412
brown 433
at – *danger* 665
difficulty 704
defence 717, 719
bring to – 716
– *the moon* 645
– *window* 260
bayadère 599
bayard 271
bayonet *kill* 361
attack 716
weapon 727
crossed –s 708
at the point of the
– *war* 722
severity 739
coercion 744
bays *trophy* 733
crown 877
bazaar 799
B.C. 106
be 1
– *all* and *end all*
whole 50
intention 620
importance 642
– *off depart* 293
eject 297
retract 773
– *it so* 488
– *that as it may* 30

on – ends
powerless 158
horizontal 213
side 236
fail 732
wonder 870
beaming
beautiful 845
bean 276
beanfeast 840
bear *produce* 161
sustain 215
carry 270
admit of 470
suffer 821
endure 826
bring to – 677
*more than flesh
and blood can* –
824
unable to –
excited 825
dislike 867
– *away* 789
– *away the bell*
648, 731
– *the brunt* 704,
717
– *the burden* 625
– *the cross* 828
– *company* 88
– *down* 173, 885
– *down upon* 716
– *false witness* 544
– *fruit produce* 161
– *useful* 644
success 731
prosper 734
– *a hand* 680
– *hard upon* 649
– *harmless* 717
– *ill* 825
– *off deviate* 279
– *on* 215
– *oneself* 692
– *out evidence* 467
vindicate 937
– *pain* 828
– *the palm* 33
– *a sense* 516
– *through* 707
– *up approach* 286
persevere 604a
relieve 834
cheerful 836
– *up against* 719,
861
– *upon*
relevant 9, 23
influence 175
– *with*
tolerate 740
permit 760
take coolly 826
forgive 918
bear
savage 907
surly 895
*had it been a – it
would have bit-
ten you* 458
– *garden*
disorder 59
discord 713
arena 728
– *leader* 540
– *pit* 370
– *skin cap* 225

helmet 717
– *with a sore back*
901
bearable 651
beard *hair* 205
prickles 253
rough 256
defy 715
brave 861
insolence 885
pluck by the –
disrespect 929
– *the lion* 604
beardless 127, 226
bearer 271, 363
bearing *relation* 9
support 215
direction 278
meaning 516
demeanor 692
– *rein* 706, 752
bearings
circumstances 8
situation 183
armorial – 550
beast *animal* 366
unclean 653
discourteous 895
– *of burden* 271,
690
beat *be superior* 33
periodic 138
region 181
impulse 276
surpass 303
oscillate 314
agitation 315
crush 330
sound 407
line of pursuit 625
path 627
overcome 731
strike 972
– *about*
circuit 629
– *the air* 645
– *against* 708
– *one's breast* 839
– *about the bush*
try for 463
evade the point 477
prevaricate 544
diffuse style 573
– *down destroy* 162
cheapen 794, 819
insolent 885
– *of drum*
music 416
publish 531
alarm 669
wear 722
command 741
pomp 882
without – *of*
drum 528
– *into teach* 537
– *off* 717
– *a retreat*
retire 283
avoid 623
submit 725
– *time clock* 114
music 416
– *up churn* 352
– *up against*
oppose 708
– *up for cater* 637
– *up one's quarters*

seek 461
visit 892
– *up for recruits*
prepare 673
aid 707
beaten track
habit 613
way 627
leave the – 83
tread the – 82
beatic 827
beatific 829, 981
beatification 827,
987
beating high
the heart – 824
beatitude 827·
beau *man* 373
fop 854
admirer 897
– *idéal* 650, 845
– *monde* 852
beautify 845, 847
beautiless 846
beauty 845
beaver *hat* 225
becalm 265
because *cause* 153
attribution 155
answer 462
reasoning 476
motive 615
bechance 151
beck *rill* 348
sign 550
mandate 741
at one's – *aid* 707
obey 743
beckon *sign* 550
motive 615
call 741
becloud *dark* 421
hide 528
become
change to 144
accord with 23
behove 926
– *of* 151
becoming
accordant 23
proper 646
beautiful 845, 847
due 924
becripple 158
bed *lodgment* 191
layer 204
support 215
garden 371
marriage 903
brought to – 161
death – 360
smooth the – *of
death* 707
go to – 265, 683
keep one's – 655
– *of down* 687
– *gown* 255
– *maker* 746
– *out* 371
– *ridden* 655
– *room* 191
– *of roses* 377, 734
put to – *with a
shovel* 363
– *time* 126
bedarken 421
bedaub 223, 653
bedazzle 420

bedding 215
bedeck 847
bedel 965
bedesman
[*see* **beadsman**]
bedevil *derange* 61
sorcery 992
bedew 339
bedight 847
bedim 421, 422
bedizen *clothe* 225
ornament 847
vulgar 851
Bedlam
– *broke loose* 59
candidate for –
504
be-dog 281
Bedouin 792
bedraggled 59
bedwarf 195
bee 690
busy – 682
swarm like –s 102
– *in one's bonnet*
503
– *in a bottle* 407
– *line* 246, 278
–'s *wax* 352
beef-eater 726
beef-headed 499
beehive 250
Beelzebub 978
beer 298
beery 959
beetle *overhang* 206,
214
project 250
blind as a – 442
Colorado – 913
– *head* 501
befall 151
befit *agree* 23
expedient 646
due 924, 926
befog 353, 528
befool *mad* 503
deceive 545
befooled
victimized 732
before *in order* 62
in time 116
presence 186
in space 234
precession 280
preference 609
set – *one* 525
– *Christ* 106
– *long* 132
– *mentioned* 62,
116
– *now* 122
– *one's eyes* 446,
525
– *one's time* 132
– *you could* –*turn
round,* – *say
Jack Robinson*
113
beforehand
prior 116
early 132
foresight 510
resolve – 611
befoul 653
befriend 707, 888
befuddlement 959
beg *Turk* 745

by instalments 51
in detail 79
slowly 275
– between the
  teeth 600, 719
bitch *animal* 366
female 374
clumsy 699
fail 732
impure 962
bite *eat* 298
physical pain 378
cold 385
cheat 545
dupe 547
etch 558
mental pain 830
– the dust 725
– in 259
– the thumb 900,
  929
– the tongue 392
biter *bit* 718
biting *pain* 378
cold 383
pungent 392
painful 830
discourteous 895
censorious 932
bitten 897
bitter *beer* 298
cold 383
taste 392, 395
painful 830
acrimonious 895
hate 898
angry 900
malevolent 907
– end 67
– ender 606, 710,
  832
– pill 735
– words 932
bitterly *greatly* 31
bitterness
  [*see* bitter]
pain 828
regret 833
bitumen 356a
bituminous coal
  388
bivouac
encamp 184
camp 189
repose 265
watch 668
bi-weekly 138
bizarre 83, 853
blab 529
blabber 584
black *color* 431
crime 945
look – *feeling* 821
discontent 832
angry 900
– art 992
– and blue
  beat 972
– board 590
– book 938
– eye 848, 972
– in the face
  swear 535
excitement 821,
  824
– flag 722
– hole *crowd* 72
prison 752

– lead 556
– letter *old* 124
barbarism 563
print 591
– list 932
– looks
discourteous 895
sullen 901a
disapprove 932
magic 998
– mail *theft* 791
booty 793
bribe 973
– sheep 949
– spots in the hori-
  zon 859
– swan 83
– and white
chiaroscuro 420
colorless 429
record 551
writing 590
prove that – *is*
white 477
blackamoor 431
wash a – *white* 471
blackball 55, 893,
  932
blackcoat 996
blacken [*see* black]
defame 934
blackguard
vulgar 851
rude 895
base 940
vagabond 949
blackleg 792
black Maria 727
blackness 431
blacksmith 690
bladder 191
blade *edge tool* 253
man 373
instrument 633
sharp fellow 682
proficient 700
sword 727
fop 854
blague 545
blain 250, 848
blame 155, 932
lay – *on* 938
take – 932
blameless 946
blameworthy
disapprove 932
vice 945
guilt 947
blanc-bec 701
blancmange 298
blanch 429, 430
bland 174, 894
blandiloquence 933
blandishment
inducement 615
endearment 902
flattery 933
blank 2, 4
empty 187
simple 849
look –
disappointed 509
discontent 832
wonder 870
point – 576
– cartridge 158
– verse 597
blanket 223, 384

wet – 174
toss in a – 929
blare 404, 412
blarney 933
blasé 841, 869
blasphemy 988
blast
destroy 162
explosion 173
wind 349
sound 404
adversity 735
curse 908
– furnace 386
blatant *loud* 404
cry 412
silly 499
blather 584
blatter 412
blaze *heat* 382
light 420
mark 550
excitement 824
– abroad 531
blazer 225
blazing
luminary 423
blazon *publish* 531
repute 873
ornament 847
ostentation 882
blé: *manger son* –
  on herbe 818
bleach 429, 430
bleak 383
blear-eyed 443
bleary 422
bloat 412
blob 250
bleed
physical pain 378
remedy 662
spend money 809
extort money 814
moral pain 828
make the heart –
  830
– freely *liberal* 816
bleeding
hemorrhage 299
remedy 662
– heart 828
blemish
imperfection 651
injure 659
ugly 846
defect **848**
blench *avoid* 623
whiten 821
fear 860
blend 41, 48
– with 714
bless
give pleasure 829
approve 931
divine function
  976
worship 990
– my heart 870
– one's stars 838,
  916
blessed 827
abode of the – 981
blessedness
single – 904
blessing *good* 618
approval 931
blessings 734

blest 827
– with 177
bletonism 511
blight
deteriorate 659
adversity 735
– hope 509
blighty 189
blimp 273
blind 223
shade 424
cecity 442
inattentive **458**
ignorant 491
conceal 528
screen 530
deception 545
instinctive 601
pretext 617
insensible 823
drunk 959
– alley 261
– bargain
uncertain 475
purposeless 62
rash 863
– the eyes *hide* 528
deceive 545
– hookey 840
– lead the blind
  538
– man's buff 840
– man's holiday
evening 126
dark 421, 422
– to one's own
  merit 880
– to the world 959
– of one eye 443
– reasoning 486
– side *prejudice*
  481
credulity 486
obstinacy 606
blinders 424, 443
blindness **442**
blind pig 964
blink *wink* 443
neglect 460
falter 605
avoid 623
– at *blind to* 442,
  458
blinkard 443
blinker 424, 530
bliss 827
celestial 981
blister 250
blithe 836
blizzard 349
bloated
expanded 194
misshapen 243
convex 250
– with pride 878
blob 250
block *mass* 192
support 215
dense 321
hard 323
fool 501
engraving 558
writing 590
hinder 706
execution 975
bring to the – 972
wood – 558
– of buildings 189

– out 230, 240, 973
– printing 591
– up 261, 706
blockade
surround 227
close 261
restrain 751
exclude 893
blockhead 501
blockhouse 717
blockish 499
blond 429, 430
blood
consanguinity 11
fluid 333
kill 361
fop 854
nobility 875
dye with –
severe 739
hands in – *cruel*
  907
in the – 5
life – 359
new – 658, 824
spill – *war* 722
– for blood 919
– boil *excite* 824,
  825
anger 900
– run cold 830,
  860
– heat 382
– horse 271
– hound 913
– letting 297, 662
– poisoning 655
– red 434
– stained 361
– sucker 789, 913
– thirsty
murderous 361
cruel 907
– up *excited* 824
angry 900
bloodless 160
peace 721
virtue 946
bloody [*see* blood]
red 434
unclean 653
cruel 907
bloom *youth* 127
flower 367
blue 438
health 654
prosperity 734
bloomer 495
bloomers 225
blooming 654, 845
blossom
flower 154, 161,
  367
prosperity 734
blot *blacken* 431
error 495
obliterate 552
dirty 653
blemish 848
disgrace 874
guilt 947
– out *destroy* 162
forgive 918
blotch 848
blouse 225
blow *expand* 194
knock 276
wind 349

accuse 938
– comparison 648
cham 745
chamber *room* 191
  council 696
  mart 799
  sick – 655
chamberlain 746
chambermaid 746
chameleon 149, 440
chamfer 259
chamois 309
champ 298
– the bit *disobedient* 742
  chafe 825
  angry 900
champagne 298
champaign 344
champain 874
Champ de Mars 728
champêtre, fête 840
champion
  best 648
  auxiliary 711
  defence 717
  combatant 726
  representative 759
  sympathizer 914
championship 707
chance 156, 621
  be one's – 151
  game of – 840
  great – 472
  small – 473
  stand a – 177, 470
  take one's – 675
  –s against one 665
  whirligig of – 156
  as – would have it 152
chancel 1000
chancellor
  president 745
  deputy 759
  judge 967
  – of the exchequer 801
chancery
  court of – 966
  – suit *delay* 133
chandelier 214, 423
chandelle, le jeu n'en vaut pas la – 638, 643
  dear 814
chandler 797
change
  alteration 140
  mart 799
  small coin 800
  inter– 148
  radical – 146
  sudden – 146
  – about 149
  – color 821
  – for 147
  – hands 783
  – of mind 607
  – of opinion 485
  – of place 264
changeableness 149, 605
changeful
  fickle 607
changeling

substitute 147
  fool 501
changeless 16
changer 797
channel
  furrow 259
  opening 260
  conduit 350
  way 627
chant *song* 415
  sing 416
  worship 990
chant du cygne 360
chanter 416
chanticleer 366
chantry 1000
chaomancy 511
chaos 59
chap *crack* 198
  jaw 231
  fellow 373
  – *book* 593
chapel 1000
chaperon
  accompany 88
  watch 459
  protect 664
chapfallen 878
chaplain 995, 996
chaplet *circle* 247
  garland 550
  trophy 733
  ornament 847
chapman 797
chapter *part* 51
  topic 454
  book 593
  council 696
  church 995
  – of accidents 156, 621
  – house 1000
  – and verse 467, 494
char *burn* 384
  serve 746
char-à-banc 272
character
  nature 5
  state 7
  class 75
  oddity 83
  letter 561
  drama 599
  disposition 820
  reputation 873
characteristic
  intrinsic 5
  special 79
  tendency 176
  mark 550
characterize 564, 594
characterized 820
charade 533, 599
charcoal *fuel* 384, 388
  black 431
  drawing 556
charge *fill* 52
  contents 190
  business 625
  requisition 630
  direction 693
  advice 695
  precept 697
  attack 716
  order 741

custody 751
  commission 755
  bargain for 794
  price 812
  accusation 938
  in – *prisoner* 754
  justifiable – 937
  take – *of* 664
  take in – 751
  – on *attribute* 155
  – with 155, 777
chargé d'affaires 758
chargeable *debt* 806
  – on *duty* 926
charger
  carrier 271
  fighter 726
Charing Cross, proclaim at – 531
chariot 272
  drag at one's – wheels 749
charioteer 268, 694
charity *give* 784
  liberal 816
  beneficent 906
  pity 914
  Christian – 906
  cold as – 823
  – that begins at home 943
charivari 404, 407
charlatan
  ignoramus 493
  imposter 548
  mountebank 844
  boaster 884
charlatanism
  ignorance 491
  falsehood 544
  affectation 855
Charles's wain 318
Charleston 840
Charley 753
charm *motive* 615
  please 829
  beauty 845
  love 897
  conjure 992
  spell 993
  bear a –ed life 644, 734
charmer 994
  voice of the – 933
  not listen to voice of – 604
charnel-house 363
Charon 982
chart 527, 554
charter
  commission 755
  permit 760
  compact 769
  security 771
  privilege 924
chartered
  legal 963
  – *accountant* 801, 811
  – *libertine* 962
Chartist 742
charwoman 690, 746
chary
  economical 817
  stingy 819
  cautious 864

Charybdis 312, 665
chase *emboss* 250
  furrow 259
  drive away 289
  killing 361
  forest 367
  pursue 622
  ornament 847
  wild goose – 645
chaser 559
chasm *interval* 198
  opening 260
chassé 840
chassemarée 273
chassepot 727
chasser 297
  – *balancer* 605
chasseur 726
chassis 215
chaste
  shapely 242
  language 576, 578
  simple 849
  good taste 850
  pure 960
chasten
  moderate 174
  punish 972
chastened
  subdued spirit 826
  penitent 950
chastise 932, 972
  – with scorpions 739
chasuble 999
chat 588
chat qui dort 667, 668
château 189
  – *en Espagne* 858
chatelaine 847
chatoyant 440
chattels 633, 789
chatter 314, 584
chatterbox 584
chattering of teeth *cold* 383
chatty 584, 892
chauffeur 268
chaunt
  song 415
  sing 416
  worship 990
chaussé 225
Chauvinism 884, 885
chawbacon 876
cheap 643, 815
  hold – 930
  – *jack* 797
cheapen *haggle* 794
  begrudge 819
cheapness 815
cheat 545, 548
check
  numerical 85
  stop 142
  moderate 174
  counteract 179
  slacken 275
  plaid 440
  experiment 463
  measure 466
  evidence 468
  ticket 550
  dissuade 616
  hinder 706

misfortune 735
  restrain 751
  money order 800
  – the growth 201
  – oneself 826
checkered 149
checkers 440, 840
checkmate
  stop 142
  success 731
  failure 732
check-roll 86
check-string
  pull the – 142
cheek *side* 236
  impertinence 885
  – by jowl *with* 88
  near 197
cheeks *dual* 89
cheep 412
cheer *repast* 298
  cry 411
  aid 707
  pleasure 827
  relief 834
  mirth 836
  rejoicing 838
  amusement 840
  courage 861
  sociality 892
  welcome 894
  applaud 931
  good – *hope* 858
  high living 957
cheerfulness 836
cheerless 830, 837
cheeseparings
  remains 40
  dirt 653
  economy 817
chef de cuisine
  proficient 700
  servant 746
chef-d'oeuvre 648, 698
cheka 696
chemin
  – de fer *game* 840
  – faisant 270
chemise 225
chemist 662
Chemistry 144
  organic – 357
cheque 800
chequer 440
  – roll 86
cherchez la femme 155 c
chère amie 962
cherish *aid* 707
  love 897
  endearment 902
  – a belief 484
  – feelings &c. 821
  – an idea &c. 451
cherry
  – *red* 434
  two bites of a – *overrate* 482
  roundabout 629
  clumsy 699
cherry-cheeked 845
cherry-colored 434
cheroot 392
cherub 977
Cheshire cat 838

circumfluent
lie round 227
move round 311
circumforaneous
traveling 266
circuition 311
circumfuse 73
circumgyration 312
circumjacence 227
circumlocution 573
circumnavigate
navigation 267
circuition 311
circumrotation 312
circumscribe
surround 229
limit 233, 761
circumscription 229
circumspection
attention 457
care 459
caution 459
circumstance
phase 8
event 151
circumstances
property 780
bad – 804
depend on – 475
good – 803
under the – 8
circumstantial 8
– *account* 594
– *evidence* 467
probability 472
circumstantiality 459
circumstantiate 467
circumvallation
enclosure 229, 232
defence 717
line of – 233
circumvent
environ 227
move round 311
cheat 545
cunning 702
hinder 706
defeat 731
circumvest 225
circumvolution
winding 248
rotation 312
circus
buildings 189
drama 599
arena 728
amusement 840
cirrus 353
cistern
receptacle 191
store 636
Cistercian 996
cit 188
citadel 717
citation 467, 733
cite
quote as example 82
as evidence 467
summon 741
accuse 938
arraign 969
cithern 417
citizen 188
– *of the world* 910
citriculture 371

citrine 436
city 189
in the – 794
city manager 965
civet 400
civic 372
civil *courteous* 894
laity 997
– *authorities* 745
– *crown* 733
– *law* 963
– *war* 722
civilian *lawyer* 968
layman 997
civilization
improvement 658
fashion 852
courtesy 894
civilized life 852
civism 910
clack *clatter* 407
animal cry 412
talkative 584
clad 225
claim *requisition* 630
demand 741
property 780
right 924
lawsuit 969
– *the attention* 457
claimant
petitioner 767
right 924
clair-obscur 420
clairvoyance 992
clairvoyant 513, 994
clamant 411
clamber 305
clammy 352
clamor *cry* 411
wail 839
– *against* 932
– *for* 765
clamorous
[see clamor]
loud 404
excitable 825
clamp *fasten* 43
fastening 45
clan *race* 11
class 75
family 166
party 712
clandestine 528
clangor 404
clank 410
clannishness 481
clanship 709
clap *explosion* 406
applaud 931
thunder –
prodigy 872
– *the hands*
rejoice 838
– *on* 31
– *on the shoulder* 615
– *together* 43
– *up imprison* 751
clapperclaw
contention 720
censure 932
claptrap
pretence 546
display 882
claquer 935

faire – *son fouet* 884
clarence 272
claret color 434
clarify 652
clarinet 417
clarion *music* 417
war 722
clarity 518
clash *disagree* 24
cross 179
concussion 276
sound 406
oppose 708
discord 713
– *of arms* 720
clasp *fasten* 43
fastening 45
stick 46
come close 197
belt 230
embrace 902
class *arrange* 60
category 75
learners 541
party 712
– *prejudice* 481
– *room* 542
classic *old* 124
symmetry 242
classical
elegant writing 578
taste 850
– *art* 556
– *dancing* 840
– *education* 537
– *music* 415
classicist 492
classics 560
classify 60
classmate 890
clatter 404, 407
claudication
slowness 275
failure 732
clause *part* 51
passage 593
condition 770
clausis, januis – 528
claustral 110
clavate 250
clavichord 417
clavier 417
claw *hook* 781
grasp 789
– *back* 935
clay *soft* 324
earth 342
corpse 362
material 635
– *pipe* 392
clay-cold 383
claymore 727
clean
entirely 52
perfect 650
unstained 652
– *bill of health* 654
– *breast*
disclose 529
– *forgotten* 506
– *hand*
proficient 700
with – *hands*
honesty 939
innocence 946

– *out empty* 297
– *shaven* 226
– *sweep*
revolution 146
destruction 162
clean-up 775
clear *simple* 42
sound 413
light 420
transparent 425
visible 446
certain 474
intelligible 518
manifest 525
easy 705
liberate 750
profit 775
vindicate 937
innocent 946
acquit 975
all – 664, 705
coast – 664
get – *off* 671
keep – *of* 623
make – 529
– *for action*
prepare 673
– *articulation* 580
– *conscience* 946
– *the course* 302
– *cut* 518
– *the ground*
facilitate 705
– *of distant* 196
– *off pay* 807
– *out empty* 297
clean 652
– *sighted*
vision 441
shrewd 498
– *sky hope* 858
– *stage*
occasion 134
easy 705
right 922
– *thinking* 498
– *the throat* 297
– *up light* 420
intelligible 518
interpret 522
clearheaded 498
clear-obscure 420
cleat 45
cleavage
cutting 44
structure 329
cleave *sunder* 44
adhere 46
bisect 91
cleaver 253
cledge 342
clef 413
cleft *divided* 44
bisected 91
chink 198
in a – *stick*
difficulty 704
clem 956
clement
lenient 740
long-suffering 826
compassionate 914
clench *compact* 769
retain 781
take 789
clepe 564

clepsydra 114
clerestory 191, 1000
clergy 996
clerical 995, 996
– *error* 495
– *staff* 746
clerk *scholar* 492
recorder 553
writer 590
helper 711
servant 746
agent 758
clergy 996
articled – 541
– *in holy orders* 995
– *of works* 694
clerkship
commission 755
cleromancy 511
clever
intelligent 498
skilful 698
smart 842
too – *by half* 702
clew *ball* 249
interpretation 522
indication 550
seek a – 461
click 406
client
dependant 746
customer 795
clientship
subjection 749
cliff *height* 206
vertical 212
steep 217
land 342
climacteric 128
climate *region* 181
weather 338
fine – 656
climatology 338
climax
supremacy 33
summit 210
culmination 729
climb 305
– *on the bandwagon* 731
clime 181
clinal 217
clinch *fasten* 43
close 261
certify 474
pun 563
complete 729
clutch 781
snatch 789
– *an argument* 47
– *the fist at* 909
clincher 479
cling *adhere* 46
– *to near* 197
willing 602
persevere 604a
habit 613
observe 772
desire 865
love 897
– *to hope* 858
– *to one another* 709
clinic 662
clink
resonance 408
stridor 410

prison 752
clinker brick 384
  dirt 653
clinometer
  oblique 217
  angle 244
clinquant
  ornament 847
  vulgar 851
Clio 594
clip shorten 201
  – the wings
  powerless 158
  speed 264
  slow 275
  useless 645
  hinder 706
  prohibit 761
  – one's words 583
clipper 273
clipping
  small piece 51
clique conclave 696
  party 712
cloaca conduit 350
  foul 653
Cloacina 653
cloak dress 225
  conceal 528
  disguise 530
cloaked 223
cloche 371
clock 114
clockwork 633
  by – uniform 16
  order 58
  regular 80
clod lump 192
  earth 342
  fool 501
  bungler 701
clodhopper 876
clodpated
  stupid 499
clog shoe 225
  hinder 706
  – dance 840
cloison 228
cloisonné 557
cloister arcade 189
  way 627
  restraint 751
  convent 1000
close similar 17
  tight 43
  end 67
  field 181
  court 189
  near 197
  narrow 203
  shut 261
  dense 321
  warm 382
  hidden 528
  concise 572
  taciturn 585
  complete 729
  stingy 819
  examine –ly 457
  keep – hide 528
  retain 781
  tread – upon 281
  – the door upon
  restrain 751
  – the ears 419
  – the eyes
  die 360
  not see 442

– one's eyes to
  not attend 458
  set at naught 773
– at hand
  to-morrow 121
  imminent 152
  near 197
– the hand
  refuse 764
– in upon 290
– inquiry 461
–ly packed 72
– prisoner 754
– quarters 197
  approach 286
  attack 716
  battle 722
– one's ranks 673
– study
  thought 451
  attention 457
– up 197, 290
– with cohere 46
  assent 488
  attack 716
  contend 720
  consent 762
  compact 769
close-mouthed 585
closet
  receptacle 191
  ambush 530
closeted with
  conference 588
  advice 695
close-up 197
closure 142, 261
clot solidify 321
  earth 342
cloth vocation 625
  napkin 652
  clergy 996
clothes 225
  grave – 363
  – basket 191
clothier 225
Clotho 601
clotpoll 501
clotted 352
cloud
  assemblage 72
  multitude 102
  mist 353
  shade 424
  screen 520
  break through the
  –s 446
  drop from the –s
  508
  in a – 475, 528
  in the –s
  lofty 206
  inattentive 458
  dreaming 515
  under a –
  insane 503
  adversity 735
  disrepute 874
  secluded 893
  censured 932
  accused 938
– burst 348
–capt 206
– of dust 330, 353
–s gathering
  dark 421
  danger 665
  warning 668

– no bigger than a
  man's hand 668
– of skirmishers
  726
– of smoke 353
– of words 573
clouded
  variegated 440
  dejected 837
  hopeless 859
– perception 499
cloudiness 571
cloudland 515
cloudless
  light 420
  happy 827
cloudy dim 422,
  426
clough 206
clout 276
cloven 91
cloven foot
  mark 550
  malevolence 907
  vice 945
  Satan 978
  see the – 480a
  show the – 907
clover
  luxury 377
  prosperity 734
  comfort 827
clown
  pantomime 599
  bungler 702
  buffoon 844
  vulgar 851
  rustic 876
cloy 641, 869
club
  place of meeting
  74
  house 189
  association 712
  weapon 727
  sociality 892
  – law
  compulsion 744
  lawless 964
  – together
  co-operate 709
clubby 892
club car 272
clubfooted 243
cluck 412
clue 550
  seek a – 461
clump
  assemblage 72
  projecting mass
  250
  – of trees 367
clumsy
  unfit 647
  awkward 699
  ugly 846
Cluniac 996
clurichaune 980
cluster 72
clutch retain 781
  seize 789
clutches 737
  in the – of 749
clutter 407
coacervation 72
coach
  carriage 272
  teach 537

tutor 540, 673
– painter 540
– road 627
drive a – and six
  through 964
– up 539
coachhouse 191
coachman 268, 694
coaction 744
coadjutant 709
coadjutor 711
coadjuvancy 709
coagency 178, 709
coagmentation 72
coagulate
  cohere 46
  density 321
  semi-liquid 352
coal 388
  call over the –s
  932
  carry –s 879
  – black 431
  carry –s to New-
  castle 641
coalesce
  identity 13
  combine 48
coalheaver
  work like a – 686
coalition 43, 709,
  712
coaming 232
coaptation 23
coarctation
  decrease 36
  contraction 195
  narrow 203
  impede 706
  restraint 751
coarse harsh 410
  dirty 653
  unpolished 674
  garish 846
  vulgar 851
  impure 961
  – grain 329
coast border 231
  slide 266
  navigate 267
  land 342
  – defence 717
  – line 230
coaster 273
coastguard 753
coat layer 204
  paint 223
  habit 225
  cut – according to
  cloth 698
  – of arms 550
  – of mail 717
coating, inner –
  224
coax persuade 615
  endearment 902
  flatter 933
cob horse 271
  punish 972
cobalt 438
cobble mend 660
cobbler 225
cobbles 635
coble 273
cobra 913
cobweb light 320
  fiction 545
  flimsy 643

dirt 653
–s of antiquity
  124
–s of sophistry
  477
cocaine 376, 381,
  663
cochineal 434
cock bird 366
  male 373
  game – 861
  – boat 273
  – and bull story
  546
  – the eye 441
  – of the roost
  best 648
  master 745
  – up vertical 212
  convex 250
cockade badge 550
  title 877
cock-a-hoop
  gay 836
  exulting 884
Cockaigne 827
cockatrice
  monster 83
  piercing eye 548
  evil-doer 913
  miscreant 949
cockcrow 125
cocked hat 225, 745
cocker fold 258
  caress 902
Cocker
  school book 542
  according to – 82
cockle fold 258
  – of one's heart
  820
cockleshell 273
cockloft 191
cockney
  Londoner 188
  plebeian 876
cockpit hold 191
  council 696
  arena 728
cockshut
  morning 125
  evening 126
  dusk 422
cock-sparrow 193
cocksure 484
cockswain 269
cocktail 298, 959
  – party 892
cocoa 298
cocotte 962
coction 384
Cocytus 982
cod shell 223
coddle 902
  – oneself 943
code conceal 528
  precept 697
  law 963
codex 593
codger 819
codicil sequel 65
  testament 771
codify 60, 963
codlin 129
coefficient
  factor 84
  accompany 88

- of 154
- off *event* 151
disjoin 44
loop-hole 617
escape 671
- on *future* 121
destiny 152
I defy you 715
attack 716
- to oneself 660
- into operation
170
- out
disclosure 529
publication 531
on the stage 599
- out of *effect* 154
egress 295
- out with
disclose 529
speak 582
- over
influence 615
consent 762
- to pass *state* 7
event 151
- to pieces 44
- to the point
speciality 79
attention 457
concise 572
- to the rescue
672
- round
period 138
conversion 144
belief 484
assent 488
change of mind
607
influence 615
restoration 660
be pacified 723
consent 762
- to the same
thing 27
- short of
inferior 34
fall short 304
- to one's senses
502
- to a stand 142
- to terms
assent 488
contract 769
it -s to this
concisely 572
- to *equal* 27
whole 50
arithmetic 85
become 144
effect 154
inherit 777
money 800
price 812
- together
assemble 72
converge 290
- under 76
- upon
unexpected 508
acquire 775
claim 924
- into use 613
- into view 446
- into the views of
co-operate 709
- off *well* 731

- into the world
359
come-down 306,
735
comedy
drama 599
comic 853
comely 845
comestible 298
comet
wanderer 268
star 318
cometary 111
comfit 396
comfort
pleasure 377
delight 827
content 831
relief 834
give - 906
comfortable
pleasing 829
comforter
covering 223
Comforter 976
comfortless
painful 830
dejected 837
comic *wit* 842
ridiculous 853
- opera 599
- strips 531
coming [see come]
impending 152
- events
prediction 511
- out 883
- time 121
comitia 696
comity 894
comma 142
inverted -s 550
command *high* 206
requisition 630
authority 737
order 741
possess 777
at one's -
obedient 743
- belief 484
- of language
writing 574
speaking 582
- of money 803
- one's passions
944
- respect 928
- one's temper
826
- a view of 441
commandant 745
commander 269
commandeer 744,
789
commanding
[see command]
important 642
commando 726
commandment 697
comme deux
gouttes d'eau 17
comme il faut
taste 850
fashion 852
genteel 875
commemorate 883
commence 66
commencement de

la fin *end* 67
destruction 162
commend 931
- the poisoned
chalice 544
commendable 944
commensurate
accordant 23
numeral 85
adequate 639
comment
reason 476
judgment 480
interpretation 522
criticize 595
commentary 595
commentator 492,
524, 527
commerce
conversation 588
barter 794
cards 840
commercial 811
- arithmetic 811
- traveler 758
commère 599
commination 908,
909
commingle 41
comminute 330
commiserate 914
commissariat 637
commissary
provisions 637
consignee 758
commission
task 625
delegate 755, 759
Royal - 696
- of the peace 965
commissioner 758
commissionaire
doorkeeper 263
messenger 534
consignee 758
commissure 43
commis-voyageur
758
commit *do* 680
delegate 755
cards 840
arrest 969
- an absurdity 853
- oneself to a
course 609
- to the flames
384
- to memory 505
- oneself
clumsy 699
promise 768
- to prison 751
- sin 945
- to writing 551
committee
council 696
consignee 758
(*director* 694)
commix 41
commode 191
commodious 644
commodity 798
commodore 745
common
general 78
ordinary 82
plain 344
habitual 613

trifling 643
base 876
in - *related* 9
participate 778
right of - 780
short -s 640
tenant in - 778
make - *cause* 709
- consent 488
- council 966
- course 613
- herd 876
- law *old* 124
law 697, 963
- measure 84
- origin 153
- parlance 576
- place 82
- place book
, *record* 551
compendium 596
- saying 496
- sense 498
- sewer 653
- stock 778
- weal
mankind 372
good 681
utility 644
philanthropy 910
Common Pleas
Court of - 966
commonalty 876
commoner 876
commonplace
usual 82
known 490
plain 576
habit 613
unimportant 643
dull 843
commons 298
commonwealth
territory 181
community 372
authority 737
commorant 188
commotion 315
communalism 778
commune
township 181
commune with 588
- oneself 451
communibus annis
29
communicant 990
communicate
join 43
tell 527
correspond 592
give 784
sacrament 998
communication
news 532
of disease 657
oral - 582, 588
communion
discourse 588
society 712
participation 778
sacrament 998
hold - with 888
- table 1000
communiqué 527
communism 737
communist
party 712
rebel 742

participation 778
philanthropy 910
evil doer 913
community
party 712
- at large 372
- of goods 778
commutation
compensation 30
substitution 147
interchange 148
compromise 774
barter 794
commutual 12
compact
joined 43
united 87
receptacle 191
small 193
compressed 195
compendious 201
dense 321
bargain **769**
compages
whole 50
structure 329
compagination 43
companion *match*
17
accompaniment
88
ladder 305
friend 890
companionable 892
companionship 892
companionway 305
company
assembly 72
actors 599
*party, partner-
ship* 712
troop 726
sociality 892
bear - 88
in - with 88
comparable 9
comparative 464
degree 26
- anatomy 368
comparatively 32
compare 464
- notes 695
comparison 464
compartition 44
compartment
part 51
region 181
place 182
cell 191
carriage 272
compass
degree 26
space 180
surround 227
measure 466
intend 620
guidance 693
achieve 729
box the -
azimuth 278
rotation 312
keep within -
moderation 174
fall short 304
economy 817
points of the - 236
in a small - 193
- about 229

- of thought 498
compassion 914
 object of - 828
compatible
 consentaneous 23
 possible 470
compatriot
 inhabitant 188
 friend 890
compeer *equal* 27
 friend 890
compel 744
compellation 564
compendency 43
compendious 201
compendium 596
 book 593
compensate
 make up for 30
 requite 973
compensation 30
compère 599
competence
 power 157
 sufficiency 639
 skill 698
 wealth 803
competition
 opposition 708
 contention 720
competitor
 opponent 710
 combatant 726
 candidate 767
compilation
 collect 72
 book 593
 compendium 596
compile 54
complacent
 pleased 827
 content 831
 courteous 894
 kind 906
complain 839
complainant 938
complaint
 illness 655
 murmur 839
 lodge a - 938
 - without cause
 839
complaisant
 lenient 740
 courteous 894
 kind 906
complement
 adjunct 39
 remainder 40
 part 52
 arithmetic 84
complementary
 correlation 12
 colour 428
complete
 entire 52
 accomplish 729
 compact 769
 - *answer* 479
 - *circle* 311
 in a - degree 31
/**completeness 52**
completion 729
complex 59
complexion
 state 7
 color 428
 appearance 448

compliance
 conformity 82
 obedience 743
 consent 762
 observance 772
complicate
 derange 61
complicated
 disorder 59
 convolution 248
complice 711
complicity 709
compliment
 courtesy 894, 896
 praise 931
 poor - 932
 -s of season 896
complimentary
 free 815
complot 626
comply [*see* compli-
 ance]
compo *coating* 223
 material 635
component 56
componere lites
 723, 724
comport
 - *oneself* 692
 - *with* 23
compos mentis 502
compose
 make up 54, 56
 produce 161
 moderate 174
 music 416
 write 590
 printing 591
 pacify 723
 assuage 826
composed
 self-possessed 826
composer
 music 413
composite 41
composition 54
 [*see* compose]
 combination 48
 piece of music 415
 picture 556
 style 569
 writing 590
 building material
 635
 compromise 774
 barter 794
 atonement 952
compositor
 printer 591
compost 653
composure 826, 871
compotation 959
compote 298
compound
 mix 41
 combination 48
 limited space 182
 enclosure 232
 compromise 774
 - *arithmetic* 466
 - *for substitute* 147
 barter 794
comprador 637
comprehend
 compose 54
 include 76
 know 490
 understand 518

comprehension [*see*
 comprehend]
 intelligence 498
comprehensive 76
 complete 50
 general 78
 wide 192
 - *argument* 476
compress
 contract 195
 curtail 201
 condense 321
 remedy 662
compressible 322
comprise 76
comprobation
 evidence 467
 demonstration 478
compromise
 dally with 605
 mid-course 628
 taint 659
 danger 665
 pacify 723
 compact 769
 compound 774
 atone 952
compromised
 promised 768
compter 799
compte rendu
 record 551
 accounts 811
comptroller 694
compulsion 744
compunction 833,
 950
compurgation
 evidence 467
 acquittal 970
compute 85
comrade 890
comradeship 892
con *think* 451
 get by heart 505
 learn 539
conation 600
conatu magnas
 nugas, magno -
 waste 638
 unimportance 643
conatus 176
concamerate 245
concatenation
 junction 43
 continuity 69
concavity 252
conceal
 invisible 447
 hide 528
 cunning 702
concealment 528,
 893
concede
 assent 488
 admit 529
 permit 760
 consent 762
 give 784
conceit *idea* 453
 folly 499
 supposition 514
 imagination 515
 wit 842
 affectation 855
 vanity 880
conceited
 dogmatic 481

conceivable 470
conceive *begin* 66
 beget 161
 teem 168
 believe 484
 understand 490
 imagine 515
 plan 626
concent 413
concentrate
 assemble 72
 centrality 222
 converge 290
concentric 216, 222
conception
 [*see* conceive]
 intellect 450
 idea 453
concern
 relation 9
 event 151
 business 625
 importance 642
 firm 797
 grief 828
 - *oneself with* 625
concert
 agreement 23
 synchronism 120
 music 415
 act in - 709
 in - *musical* 413
 concord 714
 - *measures* 626
concertina 417
concerto 415
concert-room 840
concession
 permission 760
 consent 762
 compromise 774
 giving 784
 discount 813
concesso, ex -
 reasoning 476
 assent 488
concetto 842
conchoid 245
conchology 223
concierge 163, 753
conciliate
 talk over 615
 pacify 723
 satisfy 831
 courtesy 894
 atonement 952
conciliatory [*see*
 conciliate]
 concord 714
 forgiving 918
conciliatrix 962
concinnity
 agreement 23
 style 578
 beauty 845
conciseness 572
concision 201
conclave
 assembly 72
 council 696
 church 995
conclude
 end 67
 infer 480
 resolve 604
 complete 729
 compact 769
conclusion

conceivable 470
[*see* conclude]
 sequel 65
 germination 161
 judgment 480
 try -s 476
 forgone - 611
 hasty - 481
conclusive
 [*see* conclude]
 answer 462
 evidence 467
 certain 474
 proof 478
 - *reasoning* 476
concoct *lie* 544
 write 590
 plan 626
 prepare 673
concomitant
 accompany 88
 same time 120
 concurrent 178
concord *agree* 23
 music 413
 assent 488
 harmony 714
concordance 562
 book 593
concordant 173
concordat 769
concordia discors
 24, 59
concours 720
concourse
 assemblage 72
 convergence 290
concremation 384
concrete *existent* 3
 mass 46
 definite 79
 density 321
 hardness 323
 materials 635
concubinage 961
concubine 926
concupiscence 865,
 961
concur
 co-exist 120
 causation 178
 converge 290
 assent 488
 concert 709
concurrence 178,
 216
concussion 276
condemnation 932,
 971
condemned cell 752
condense
 compress 195
 dense 321
condensed
 concise 572
condescend 879
condign 924
condiment 393
condisciple 541
condition *state* 7
 modification 469
 supposition 514
 term 770
 repute 873
 rank 875
 in - *plump* 192
 in good - 648
 on - 770
 in perfect - 650

physical – 316
conditional 8
conditions 770
condolence 914, **915**
condone 918
condottiere
  traveller 268
  fighter 726
conduce
  contribute 153
  tend 176
  concur 178
  avail 644
conducive 631
conduct
  transfer 270
  music 416
  procedure **692**
  lead 693
  safe –
    passport 631
  safety 664
  – a funeral 363
  – an inquiry 461
  – to 278
conduction 264
conductor 269
  conveyer 271
  director 694
  lightning – 666
conduit 350
conduplicate 89
condyle 250
cone *round* 249
  pointed 253
confabulation 588
confection 396
  confectionary 396
confectioner 637
confederacy
  co-operation 709
  party 712
confederate 711
confer *advise* 695
  give 784
  – benefit 648
  – power 157
  – privilege 760
  – right 924
  – with 588
conference [*see*
  confer]
  council 696
confess *assent* 488
  avow 529
  penitence 950,
  998
  – and avoid 937
confession [*see*
  confess]
  auricular – 998
  – of faith 983
confessional 1000
confessions
  biography 594
confessor 996
confidant 711
confidante
  servant 746
  friend 890
confidence
  trust 484
  hope 858
  courage 861
  in – 528
  – trick 545
confident 535
configuration 240

confine
  region 182
  circumscribe 229
  limit 231, 233
  imprison 751
confined
  narrow judgment
  481
  ill 655
confinement
  childbed 161
confines of
  on the – 197
confirm
  corroborate 467
  assent 488
  consent 762
  compact 769
  rite 998
confirmed 150
  – habit 613
confiscate *take* 789
  condemn 971
  penalty 974
confiture 396
conflagration 382,
  384
conflexure 245
conflict
  opposition 708
  discord 713
  contention 720
conflicting
  contrary 14
  counteracting 179
  – evidence 468
confluence
  junction 43
  convergence 290
  river 348
conflux
  assemblage 72
  convergence 290
conform *assent* 488
  – to rule 494
conformable 23,
  178
conformation 54,
  240
conformity **82,** 178
confound
  disorder 61
  destroy 162
  not discriminate
  465a
  perplex 475
  defeat 731
  astonish 870
  curse 908
confounded
  great 31
  bad 649
confraternity
  party 712
  friendship 888
confrère
  colleague 711
  friend 890
confrication 331
confront *face* 234
  compare 464
  oppose 708
  resist 719
  – danger 861
  – witnesses 467
confucianism 984
Confucius 986
confuse *derange* 61

  perplex 458
  obscure 519
  not discriminate
  465a
  abash 879
confused *disorder*
  59
  invisible 447
  uncertain 475
  style 571
confusion
  [*see* confuse]
  – seize 908
  – of tongues 560,
  563
  – of vision 443
  – worse-con-
  founded 59
confutation **479**
congé 293, 756
  – d'élire 995
congeal *dense* 321
  cold 385
congeneric
  similar 17
  included 76
congenial
  related 9
  agreeing 23
  concord 714
  love 897
congenital 5, 820
congeries 72
congestion 641
conglaciation 385
conglobation 72
conglomerate
  cohere 46
  assemblage 72
  council 696
  dense 321
conglutinate 46
congratulate 896
  – oneself 838
congratulation **896**
congregation
  assemblage 72
  worshippers 990
  laity 997
Congregationalist
  984
congress
  assembly 72
  convergence 290
  conference 588
  council 698
Congressional
  Medal 733
Congressional
  Record 551
congreve *fuel* 388
  – rocket 727
congruous
  agreeing 23
  (*expedient* 646)
conical *round* 249
  pointed 253
conjecture 475, 514
conjoin 43
conjoint 48
conjointly 37
conjugal 903
conjugate
  words 562
  grammar 567
  – in all its tenses
  &c. 104
conjugation

  junction 43
  pair 89
  phase 144
  grammar 567
conjunction 43
  in – with 37
conjuncture
  contingency 8
  occasion 134
conjure *deceive* 545
  entreat 765
  – up *recall* 505
  – up a vision 505
conjuror
  deceiver 548
  sorcerer 994
connaître les des-
  sous des cartes
  490
connate
  intrinsic 5
  kindred 11
  cause 153
connatural
  uniform 16
  similar 17
connect *relate* 9
  link 43
connection
  [*see* connect]
  kin 11
  in – with 9
connections
  cards 840
connective 45
conned, well – 490
connive
  overlook 460
  co-operate 709
  allow 760
connoisseur
  critic 480
  scholar 492
  taste 850
connotate 550
connote 516, 550
  imply 526
connubial 903
connuted 9
conoscente 850
conquer 731
conquered
  (*failure* 732)
conquering hero
  comes 883
conqueror 731
consanguinity 11
consciarecti, mens-
  pride 878
  innocence 946
conscience
  knowledge 490
  moral sense 926
  in all – *great* 31
  affirmation 535
  awakened – 950
  qualms of – 603
  clear – 946
  stricken – 950
  tender – 926
  honor 939
conscientious 926
  scrupulous 939
  – objector 489
conscious

  intuitive 450
  knowledge 490
  – of disgrace 874
  – of glory 873
conscript 726
conscription 744
consecrate *use* 677
  dedicate 873
  sanctify 987
  holy orders 995
consecration
  rite 998
consectory 478
  – reasoning 476
consecution 63
consecutive
  following 63
  continuous 69
  – fifth 414
consecutively
  slowly 275
consensus 488
  – of opinion 23
consent *assent* 488
  compliance **762**
  with one – 178
consentaneous
  agreeing 23
  (*expedient* 646)
consequence
  event 151
  effect 154
  importance 642
  in – 478
  of no – 643
  take the –s 154
consequent 63
consequential
  deducible 478
  arrogant 878
consequently
  reasoning 476
  effect 154
conservation
  permanence 141
  storage 636
  preservation 670
conservatism 141,
  670
conservative 141,
  712
  – policy 681
conservatoire 542
conservator
  of the peace 967
conservatory
  receptacle 191
  floriculture 371
  furnace 386
  store 636
conserve 396, 636
consider *think* 451
  attend to 457
  examine 461
  adjudge 480
  believe 484
considerable
  in degree 31
  in size 192
  important 642
considerate
  careful 459
  judicious 498
  benevolent 906
consideration
  purchase money
  147
  thought 451

contrition
  abrasion 331
  regret 833
  penitence 950
contrivance 633
contrive
  produce 161
  plan 626
  – *to succeed in* 731
contriving
  cunning 702
control
  power 157
  influence 175
  regulate 693
  authority 737
  restrain 751
  board of – 696
  under –
  obedience 743
  subjection 749
controller of
  currency 801
controls 273, 693
controversial
  discussion 476
  discordant 713
controversialist
  476, 726
controversy
  disagreement 24
  discussion 476
  debate 588
  contention 720
controvert
  deny 536
controvertible
  uncertain 475
  debatable 476
  untrue 495
contumacy
  obstinacy 606
  disobedience 742
contumely
  arrogance 885
  rudeness 895
  disrespect 929
  scorn 930
  reproach 932
contund 330
contuse 330
conundrum *pun*
  520
  riddle 533
  wit 842
convalescence 654,
  660
convection 270
convenance
  mariage de – 903
convene 72
conveniences 632
convenient 646, 705
convent 1000
conventicle
  assembly 72
  council 696
  chapel 1000
convention
  agreement 23
  assembly 72
  rule 80
  council 696
  precept 697
  treaty of peace
  723
  compact 769

–s of society 852
conventional 82,
  613
conventual 996,
  1000
convergence 290
convergent 286
conversable
  talk 588
  sociable 892
conversant
  know 490
  skilful 698
conversation 588
conversational
  loquacious 584
  interlocution 588
  sociable 892
conversazione 588,
  892
converse
  reverse 14
  talk 588
conversely 468
conversion 144
  trover and – 964
convert
  change to 140, 144
  opinion 484
  tergiversation 607
  religion 987
  – *to use* 677
convertible 13, 27
  – terms 522
convexity 250
convey
  transfer 270
  mean 516
  assign 783
  – *away* 791
  – the knowledge
  of 527
conveyance
  [*see* convey]
  vehicle 272
conveyancer 968
conveyancing 783
convict
  convince 484
  condemned 949
  condemn 971
convicted, self –
  950
conviction
  confutation 479
  belief 484
  prove guilty 971
convince
  belief 484
  confute 479
  teach 537
convivial 892
convocate 72
convocation
  council 696
  church 995
convoke 72
convolution
  coil 248
  rotation 312
convoy
  accompany 88
  transfer 270
  guard 664
  escort 753
convulse
  derange 61

violent 173
  agitate 315
  bodily pain 378
  mental pain 830
convulsed with
  – laughter 838
  – rage 900
convulsion
  [*see* convulse]
  disorder 59
  revolution 146
  in – s 325
coo 412
cook *heat* 384
  falsify 544
  improve 658
  prepare 673
  servant 746
  too many –s 699
  – accounts 811
cool *moderate* 174
  cold 383
  refrigerate 385
  grey 432
  dissuade 616
  cautious 864
  indifferent 866
  unamazed 871
  unfriendly 889
  discourteous 895
  look – upon
  unsocial 893
  take –ly 826
  – down 826
  – one's heels
  kept waiting 133
  inaction 681
cooler 387
coolheaded
  judicious 498
  unexcitable 826
coolie
  bearer 271
  military 726
coolness
  insensibility 823
  estrangement 898
coon-can 840
coop *abode* 189
  restrain 751
  prison 752
co-operation
  physical 178
  voluntary 709
  participation 778
co-operator 690, '11
co-optation 609
co-ordinate
  equal 27
  arrange 60
  measure 466
cootie 653
cop 664
copal 356a
coparcener 778
copartner
  accompanying 88
  participator 778
  associate 890
copartnership
  co-operation 709
  party 712
cope *equal* 27
  oppose 708
  contend 720
  canonicals 999
copia verborum

diffuse 573
  loquacious 584
coping stone
  top 210
  completion 729
copious
  diffuse style 573
  abundant 639
coportion 778
copper *money* 800
  policeman 664
copper-colored
  433, 439
copper-plate
  engraving 558
  writing 590
coppice 367
coprolite 653
copse 367
copula 45
copulation 43
copy
  imitate 19
  facsimile 21
  prototype 22
  news 532
  record 551
  represent 554
  write 590
  for the press 591
  plan 626
  – *book* 22
copyhold 780
copyist
  imitator 19
  artist 559
  writer 590
copyright 780
coquet *lie* 544
  change the mind
  607
  affected 855
  endearment 902
  flattery 933
  – with
  irresolute 605
coquette
  affected 854, 855
  flirt 897
coquillage 847
coracle 273
coral 847
  – reef 667
coram judice
  jurisdiction 965
  lawsuit 969
cor Anglais 417
corbeille 191
corbel 215
cord *tie* 45
  filament 205
cordage 45
cordated 245
cordial
  pleasure 377
  dram 392
  willing 602
  remedy 662
  feeling 821
  grateful 829
  friendly 888
  courteous 894
cordiform 245
cordite 727
cordon
  inclosure 232
  circularity 247

decoration 877
  – bleu 733, 746
  – sanitaire
  safety 664
  preservation 670
corduroy 259
cordwainer
  shoemaker 225
  artificer 690
core *gist* 5
  source 153
  center 222
  gist 642
  true to the – 939
coriaceous 327
Corinthian 850
co-rival
  [*see* corrival]
cork *plug* 263
  lightness 320
  – *jacket* 666
  – up *close* 261
  restrain 751
corking pin 45
corkscrew
  spiral 248
  perforator 262
  circuition 311
cormorant
  desire 865
  gluttony 957
corn
  projection 250
Cornaro 953
cornea 441
corned 959
cornelian 847
corneous 323
corner *place* 182
  receptacle 191
  angle 244
  monopoly 777
  – creep into a –
  893
  in a dark – 528
  drive into a – 706
  push into a – 874
  rub off –s 82
  – turn a – 311
  turn the – 658
  – stone
  support 215
  importance 642
  defence 717
cornet *music* 417
  officer 745
cornice 210
corniculate 253
cornification 323
Cornish hug 545
corno 417
cornopean 417
cornucopia 639
cornute
  projecting 250
  sharp 253
corollary
  adjunct 39
  deduction 480
corona 247
coronach 839
coronation
  enthronement 755
  celebration 883
coroner 363, 965
  –'s jury 967
coronet *hoop* 247

insignia 747
title 877
\ corporal
  corporeal 316
  officer 745
corporate 43
  – body 712
corporation
  bulk 192
  convex 250
  association 712
  jurisdiction 965
corporeal 3, 316, 364
  – hereditaments 780
corporeity 316
corps assemblage 72
  troops 726
  à – perdu
  haste 684
  rash 863
  – de reserve 636
corpse 362
corpulence 192
corpus 316
  – Christi 998
  – delicti
  guilt 947
  lawsuit 969
  – juris
  precept 697
  law 963
corpuscle
  small 32
  little 193
corradiation
  focus 74
  convergence 290
corral 232, 370
correct
  orderly 58
  true 494
  inform 527
  disclose 529
  improve 658
  repair 660
  due 924
  censure 932
  honorable 939
  virtuous 944
  punish 972
  – ear 416, 418
  – memory 505
  – reasoning 476
  – style
  grammatical 567
  elegant 578
correction
  [see correct]
  house of – 752
  under – 879
corrective 662
corregidor 745
correlation
  relation 9
  reciprocity 12
correspondence
  correlation 12
  similarity 17
  agreement 23
  writing 592
  – course 537
correspondent
  messenger 534
  journalist 593
  consignee 758
corresponding

similar 17
agreeing 23
corridor region 181
  place 191
  passage 627
  – train 272
corrigendum 495
corrigible 658
corrival 726
corrivalry 720
corrivation 348
corroborant 662
corroboration
  evidence 467
  assent 488
corrode burn 384
  erode 659
  afflict 830
corrosive
  [see corrode]
  acrid 171
  destructive 649
  – sublimate 663
corrugate
  derange 61
  constrict 195
  roughen 256
  rumple 258
  furrow 259
corruption
  decomposition 49
  neology 563
  foulness 653
  disease 655
  deterioration 659
  improbity 940
  vice 945
corrupting
  noxious 649
corsage 225
corsair 273, 792
corse 362
corselet 225
corset 225
corso 728
cortège
  adjunct 39
  continuity 69
  accompaniment 88
  journey 266
  suite 746
cortes 696
cortex
  cortical 223
coruscate 420
corvette 273, 726
corybantic 503
coryphée 599
Corypheus
  teacher 540
  director 694
coscinomancy 511
cosey 892
cosignificative 522
cosine 217
cosmetic
  remedy 662
  ornament 847
cosmic 318
cosmogony &c. 318
cosmopolitan
  abode 189
  mankind 372
  philanthropic 910
  sociality 892
cosmorama 448
cosmos 60, 318

Cossack 726
cosset
  darling 899
  caress 902
cost 812
  pay –s 807
  to one's –
  evil 619
  badness 649
  – what it may 604
  – price 815
costermonger 797
costless 815
costly 814
costive
  taciturn 585
costume 225
  theatrical – 599
costumé 225
  bal – 840
costumier 225
  theatrical 599
cosy snug 377
  sociable 892
cot abode 189
  bed 215
cote 189
cotenancy 778
coterie class 75
  junto 712
  society 892
coterminous 120
cothurnus 599
cotillon 840
cottage 189
  – piano 417
cottager 188
cotter 188
cotton 205
  – seed oil 356
couch lie 213
  bed 215
  stoop 308
  lurk 528
  – one's lance 720
  – in terms 566
couchant 213
couci-couci 651
cough 349
  churchyard – 655
couleur de rose
  good 648
  prosperity 734
  view en – 836
coulisses 599
coulter 253
council
  senate 696
  church 995
  hold a – 695
  – of education 542
  – school 542
councillor 696
counsel
  advice 695
  lawyer 968
  keep one's own – 528
  take – think 451
  inquire 461
  be advised 695
count clause 51
  item 79
  compute 85
  estimate 480
  lord 875
  – one's chickens before they are

hatched 858, 863
  – the cost 864
  – upon
  believe 484
  expect 507
  to be –ed on one's fingers 103
countenance
  face 234
  appearance 448
  favor 707
  approve 931
  keep in –
  conform 82
  induce 615
  encourage 861
  vindicate 937
  keep one's –
  brook 826
  not laugh 837
  out of –
  abashed 879
  put out of – 874
  stare out of – 885
  – falling
  disappointment 509
  dejection 837
counter contrary 14
  number 84
  table 215
  stern 235
  token 550
  shop-board 799
  over the –
  barter 794
  buy 795
  sell 796
  run – 179
  – to 708
counteract
  compensate 30
  physically 179
  hinder 706
  voluntarily 708
counteraction 14, 179
counterbalance 30
counterblast
  counteract 179
  retaliate 718
countercharge 462
counterchange
  correlation 12
  interchange 148
countercharm 993
countercheck
  mark 550
  hindrance 706
counterclaim 30
counter-evidence 468
counterfeit
  imitate 19
  copy 21
  simulate 544
  sham 545
  coinage 792
counterfoil 550
countermand 756
countermarch 266, 283
countermark 550
countermine
  plan 626
  oppose 708
countermotion 283

counterorder 756
counterpane 223
counterpart
  match 17
  copy 21
  reverse 237
counterplot
  plan 626
  oppose 708
  retaliate 718
counterpoint 415
counterpoise
  compensate 30
  weight 319
  hinder 706
counter-poison 662
counterpole 14
counter-project 718
counter-protest 468
counter-revolution 146
counterscarp 717
countersign
  evidence 467
  assent 488
  mark 550
counterstroke 718
countervail
  outweigh 28
  compensate 30
  evidence 468
counterwork 708
countess 875
counting-house 799
countless 105
countrified 189
  vulgar 851
country
  region 181
  abode 189
  rural 371
  authority 737
  love of – 910
country-dance 840
countryman
  commonalty 876
  friend 890
county 181
  – seat 189
  – town 189
  – school 542
  – council 696
  – court 966
coup
  instantaneous 113
  action 680
  – de bec
  attack 716
  censure 932
  – d'épée dans l'eau 645
  – d'essai 675
  – d'état
  revolution 146
  plan 626
  action 680
  lawless 964
  – de grâce
  end 67
  death-blow 361
  completion 729
  punishment 972
  – de main
  violence 173
  action 680
  attack 716
  – de maître
  excellent 648

skilful 698
success 731
– d'œil
sight 441
appearance 448
display 882
– de plume 590
– de soleil
hot 384
mad 503
à – sûr 474
– de théâtre
appearance 448
display 882
coupé 272
couple
unite 43
two 89
–d with
added 37
accompanied 88
coupler 45
couplet 89, 597
coupling 45
coupon 800
courage 861
moral – 604
– oozing out 862
courant, au – 490
coureur, avant –
673
courier
traveler 268
guide 524
messenger 534
course order 58
continuity 69
time 106, 109
layer 204
motion 264
locomotion 266,
267
direction 278
dinner 298
river 348
pursuit 622
way 627
conduct 692
arena 728
bend one's – 266
in due – 134
hold a – 278
in the – of
during 106
keep one's –
progress 282
persevere 604a
let things take
their –
continue 143
inaction 681
follow as of – 478
mark out a – 626
of –
conformity 82
effect 154
certain 474
assent 488
necessity 601
willingly 602
custom 613
consent 762
expect 871
race – 840
run its –
end 67
complete 729
take a – 622

take its – 151
– of action 692
– of business 625
– of events 151
– of inquiry 461
– of preparation
673
– runs smooth 734
– of study 537
– of things 151
– of time 121
courser
horse 271
swift 274
coursing
kill 361
pursue 622
court close 181, 182
house 189
hall 191
flatness 213
invite 615
pursue 622
council 696
retinue 746
solicit 765
gentility 852
wish 865
woo 902
flatter 933
tribunal 966
bring into – 467
friend at – 526,
711
pay – to
servile 886
love 897, 902
flatter 933
put out of – 731
– card 626
– of honor 939
courteous 894
courtesan 962
courtesy
stoop 308, 314
submit 725
politeness 894
show –
respect 928
courtier
servile 886
flatterer 935
–like 933
courtly 852
courtship 902
courtyard 182
cousin 11
coûte-que-coûte
certainly 474
necessary 601
resolution 604
cove cell 191
hollow 252
bay 343
covenant
compact 769
condition 770
security 771
covenanter 488
Coventry
Earl of –
cards 840
send to –
eject 297
disrepute 874
seclusion 893
cover
compensate 30

include 76
superpose, lid 223
dress 225
stopper 263
meal 298
conceal 528
retreat 530
report 531
keep clean 652
keep safe 664
preserve 670
under –
hidden 528
pretence 545
safe 664
with dust 653
covercle 223
covering 223
coverlet 223
Coverley, Sir Roger
de – 840
covert abode 189
invisible 447
latent 526
refuge 666
feme -e 903
– way 627
coverture 903
covet desire 865
envy 921
covetous
miserly 819
covey
assemblage 72
multitude 102
cow
animal 366
female 374
intimidate 860
coward 862
cowardice 862
cowboy 370
cower stoop 308
fear 860
cowardice 862
servile 886
cowherd 370
cowhide 223, 975
cowhouse 189
cowkeeper 370
cowl sacerdotal 999
dress 225
cowled 223
cowl-staff 215
co-worker 690
coxcomb 854
coxcombry
affectation 855
vanity 880
coxswain 269
coy timid 860
modest 881
cozen 545
crab sourness 397
–like motion
deviation 279
regression 283
grouch 901a
crabbed sour 397
unintelligible 519
obscure style 571
difficult 704
uncivil 895
sulky 901a
crack split 44
discontinuity 70
instantaneous 113
fissure 198

furrow 259
brittle 328
sound 406
excellent 648
injure 659
skilful 698
boast 884
– a bottle
food 298
social 892
drunken 959
– of doom
end 67
future 121
destruction 162
– one's invention
515
– a joke 842
– shot 700
crackbrained 503
cracked
unmusical 410
fanatical 481
mad 503
faulty 651
– bell 408a
– voice 581
cracker 406
crackle 406
cracksman 792
crack-up 162
cradle
beginning 66
infancy 127
origin 153
placing 184
bed 215
training 673
aid 707
in the – 129
– song 415
craft shipping 273
business 625
skill 698
cunning 702
craftiness 498
craftsman 690
craftsmanship 680
crag pointed 253
hard 323
land 342
craggy
rough 256
craig height 206
crake 884
cram crowd 72
stuff 194
choke 261
teach 537
learn 539
gorge 957
– down the throat
induce belief 484
compel 744
crambe repetita
weariness 841
satiety 869
crambo 597
crammed 52
– to overflowing
641
crammer lie 546
teacher 537
cramp
fastening 45
paralyze 158
weaken 160
little 193

compress 195
spasm 378
hinder 706
cramped style 579
cran 191
cranch
[see craunch]
crane angle 244
elevate 307
instrument 633
– neck 245
craniology &c. 450
cranium 450
crank
fanatic 504
instrument 633
wit 842
treadmill 975
crankle fold 258
crankling
rough 256
cranky weak 160
ill health 655
cranny 198
crape
crinkle 248
mourning 839
crapulence
intemperance 954
gluttony 957
drunken 959
crash
destruction 162
collision 276
gain entrance 294
sound 406
crasis nature 5
coherence 48
composition 54
crass 31
– ignorance 491
crassitude
breadth 202
thickness 352
crate
receptacle 191
vehicle 272
crater deep 208
hollow 252
craunch
shatter 44
chew 298
pulverize 330
cravat 225
crave ask 765
desire 865
envy 921
craven submit 725
cowardly 862
craw 191
crawfish 607
crawl time 109
creep 275
back down 283,
606
servile 886
– with 102
crawling 102
crayons 556
craze 481
crazy weak 160
mad 503
creachy 160
creak 410
cream
emulsion 352
oil 356
important part

642
best 648
– color
  white 430
  yellow 436
– of the jest 842
creamy 352
crease 258
create *cause* 153
  produce 161
  imagine 515
created *being* 366
creation
  [*see* create]
  effect 154
  world 318
Creator 976
creator 164
creature *thing* 3
  effect 154
  animal 366
  man 372
  parasite 711
  slave 746
  – comforts
    food 298
    pleasure 377
crèche 542
credat Judaeus
  Apella
  unbelief 485
  absurdity 497
credence *belief* 484
  church 1000
credenda 484
credential 467
credible
  possible 470
  probable 472
  belief 484
credit *belief* 484
  influence 737
  pecuniary 805
  account 811
  repute 873
  approbation 931
  desert 944
  to one's –
  property 780
crédit mobilier 802
creditable *right* 924
creditor 805
credo quia
  impossibile 486
credulity 486
credulous *person*
  dupe 547
creed *belief* 484
  theology 983
  Apostles' – 983a
creek *interval* 198
  water 343
creel 191
creep *crawl* 275
  tingle 380
  (*inactivity* 683)
  – in 294
  – into a corner 893
  – into the good
    graces of 933
  – out 529
  – upon one 508
  – with
    multitude 102
    redundance 641
creeper 367
creeping
  sensation 380

– thing 366
creese 727
cremation
  of corpses 363
  burning 384
crematorium 363,
  386
crematory 386
creme de la crême
  648
Cremona 417
crenate 257
crenele 257
crenulate 257
creole 57
crêpé 248, 839
crepidam, ultra –
  471
crepitation 406
crepuscule
  dawn 125
  dusk 422
crescendo
  increase 35
  musical 415
crescent
  growing 35
  street 189
  curve 245
cresset 423, 550
crest *supremacy* 33
  summit 210
  pointed 253
  tuft 256
  sign 550
  armorial 877
  pride 878
  on the – 33
crest-fallen
  dejected 837
  humble 879
crevasse 198, 667
crevice 198
crew *assemblage* 72
  inhabitants 188
  mariners 269
  party 712
crib *bed* 215
  key 522
  granary 636
  steal 791
  parsimony 819
cribbage 840
cribbed, confined,
  cabined – 751
cribble 260
cribriform 260
Crichton,
  Admirable –
  scholar 492
  perfect 650
  proficient 700
crick *pain* 378
cricket *game* 840
  not – 940
  – ground 213
crier 534
  send round the –
  531
crim. con. 961
crime 945, 947
criminal 923, 945
  culprit 949
  – law 963
  court of – appeal
  966
criminality 947
criminate 938

crimp *crinkle* 248
  notch 257
  brittle 328
  deceiver 548
  take 789
  steal 791
crimple 258
crimson 434, 821
cringe *submit* 725
  subject 749
  servility 886
crinite 256
crinkle *angle* 244
  convolution 248
  roughen 256
  fold 258
crinoline 225
cripple *disable* 158
  weaken 160
  injure 659
crippled
  disease 655
crisis
  conjuncture 8
  present time 118
  opportunity 134
  event 151
  strait 704
  excitement 824
  bring to a – 604
  come to a – 729
crisp *rumpled* 248
  rough 256
  brittle 328
  style 572
Crispin 225
criss-cross 219
cristallomantia 511
criterion *test* 463
  evidence 467
  indication 550
crithomancy 511
critic *judge* 480
  taste 850
  detractor 936
critical
  contingent 8
  opportune 134
  discriminating
    465
  important 642
  dangerous 665
  difficult 704
  censorious 932
criticism
  judgment 480
  dissertation 595
  disapprobation
    932
  detraction 934
critique
  [*see* criticism]
croak *cry* 412
  hoarseness 581
  stammer 583
  warning 668
  discontent 832
  lament 839
croaker 832, 837
Croat 726
crochet 847
crock 191
crockery 384
crocodile tears 544
crocus *yellow* 436
Croesus 803
croft 189, 232
Croix de Guerre 733

cromlech 363, 551
crone *veteran* 130
  fool 501
crony *friend* 890
  favourite 899
crook *curve* 245
  deviation 279
  thief 792
crooked
  sloping 217
  distorted 243
  angular 244
  latent 526
  crafty 702
  ugly 846
  dishonorable 940
  – path 704
  – temper 901
  – ways 279
croon 580
crop
  stomach 191
  harvest 154
  shorten 201
  eat 298
  vegetable 367
  store 636
  gather 775
  take 789
  second – 167, 775
  – out *visible* 446
  disclose 529
  – up *begin* 66
  take place 151
  reproduction 163
cropper *fall* 306
  – ground *level* 213
croquette 298
crosier 747, 999
cross *mix* 41
  across 219
  pass 302
  grave 363
  oppose 708
  failure 732
  disaster 735
  refuse 764
  pain 830
  decoration 877
  fretful 901
  punishment 975
  rites 998
  fiery – 722
  proclaim at the –
    roads 531
  red – 662
  –ed bayonets 708
  – breed 63
  – cut 628
  – fire *interchange*
    148
  difficulty 704
  opposition 708
  attack 716
  –ed in love 898
  – the mind 451
  – the path of 706
  – and pile 621
  – purposes 14
  disorder 59
  error 495
  misinterpret 523
  unskilful 699
  difficulty 704
  opposition 708
  discord 713
  – oneself 998

– questions
  inquiry 461
  discord 713
  game 840
  – road 627
  – the Rubicon 609
  – sea 348
  – swords 722
crossbow 727
cross-examine 461
cross-grained 256
  obstinate 606
  sulky 901a
crossing 219
  – sweeper 652
crosspatch 895
crossroads 8
cross-word puzzle
  533
crotch 244
crotchet
  eccentric 83
  music 413
  misjudgment 481
  obstinacy 606
  caprice 608
crouch *lower* 207
  stoop 308
  fear 860
  servile 886
  – before 725
croup 235
croupier 694
crow *cry* 412
  black 431
  rejoice 838
  boast 884
  pluck a – with 932
  as the – flies 278
  –'s foot (*age*) 128
  –'s nest 210
  – to pluck
  discord 713
  anger 900
  accuse 938
crowbar 633
crowd 72
  multitude 102
  close 197
  redundance 641
  party 712
  vulgar 876
  in the – mixed 41
  madding – 682
crown *top* 210
  circle 247
  complete 729
  trophy 733
  scepter 747
  install 755
  decoration 877
  reward 973
  to – all 33, 642
  –ed head 745
  – with laurel 873
  – with success 731
crowning
  [*see* crown]
  superior 33
  end 67
  – point 210
cruche à l'eau &c.
  tant va la – 735
crucial
  crossing 219
  proof 478
  – test 463
cruciate

curry-comb 370
curse *bane* 663
  adversity 735
  painful 830
  malediction 908
cursed *bad* 649
cursitor 968
cursive 590
cursory
  transient 111
  inattentive 458
  hasty 684
  take a – view of
    457
  neglect 460
curst 901*a*
curt *short* 201
  concise 572
  taciturn 585
curtail *retrench* 38
  shorten 201
  -ed of its fair pro-
    portions
  distorted 243
  ugly 846
curtain 223
  shade 424
  hide 528, 530
  theatre 599
  fortification 717
  behind the –
  invisible 447
  inquiry 461
  knowledge 490
  close the – 528
  raise the – 529
  rising of the – 448
  – lecture 932
  – raiser 66, 599
curtsy
  stoop 308, 314
  submit 725
  polite 894
curule 696
curvature **245**
curvet *leap* 309
  turn 311
  oscillate 314
  agitate 315
curvilinear 245
  – motion 311
cushion *pillow* 215
  soft 324
  relief 834
cushy 829
cusp *angle* 244
  sharp 253
cuspidor 191
cuss 908
custard 298
custodes? quis cus-
  todiet – 459
custodian 753
custody *safe* 664
  captive 751
  retention 781
  in – *prisoner* 754
  accused 938
  take into – 751
custom *old* 124
  habit 613
  barter 794
  sale 796
  tax 812
  fashion 852
  – honored in
    breach 614
customary

[*see* custom]
  regular 80
customer 795
custom-house 799
  – officer 965
custos 753
  – rotulorum 553
cut *divide* 44
  bit 51
  discontinuity 70
  interval 198
  curtail 201
  layer 204
  form 240
  notch 257
  blow 276
  eject 297
  reap 371
  physical pain 378
  cold 385
  neglect 460
  carve 557
  engraving 558
  road 627
  attack 716
  portion 786
  affect 824
  mental pain 830
  dance step 840
  decline acquaint-
    ance 893
  discourtesy 895
  tipsy 959
  – short 628
  unkindest – of all
  pain 828
  malevolence 907
  – across 302
  – adrift 44
  – along 274
  have a – at 716
  – away 274
  – a whetstone with
    a razor
  sophistry 477
  waste 638
  misuse 679
  – both ways 468
  – capers 309
  – according to
    cloth
  economy 817
  caution 864
  – and come again
  repeat 104
  enough 639
  – dead 893
  – direct 893
  – down *destroy* 162
  shorten 201
  fell 308
  kill 361
  – down expenses
    817
  – and dried
  arranged 60
  prepared 673
  – a figure
  appearance 448
  fashion 852
  repute 873
  display 882
  – the first turf 66
  – the ground from
    under one
  confute 479
  hinder 706
  – to the heart 824,

830
  – ice with
  influence 175
  – of one's jib 448
  – jokes 842
  – the knot 705
  – off *subduct* 38
  disjoin 44
  kill 361
  impede 706
  bereft 776
  secluded 893
  – off with a shil-
    ling 789
  – open 260
  – out *surpass* 33
  stop 142
  substitute 147
  plan 626
  – out for 698
  – out work
  prepare 673
  direct 693
  – to pieces
  destroy 162
  kill 361
  – a poor figure 874
  – to the quick 830
  – up root and
    branch 162
  – up rough 900
  – and run 274
  depart 293
  escape 623
  – short *stop* 142
  destroy 162
  shorten 201
  silence 581
  – one's stick
  depart 283
  avoid 623
  – one's own throat
    699
  – and thrust 716
  – in two 91
  – up *divide* 44
  destroy 162
  pained 828
  give pain 830
  discontented 832
  dejected 837
  censure 932
  what one will – up
    for 780
  – one's way
    through 302
cutaneous 223
cute 698
cuticle 223
cutlass 727
cutlery 253
cut-purse 792
cutter 273
cut-throat
  killer 361
  evil-doer 913
cutting *sharp* 253
  cold 383
  path 627
  affecting 821
  painful 830
  reproachful 932
cuttings
  excerpta 596
  selections 609
cutty stool 950
cwt. 98, 319
cyanogen 438

cyanide of potas-
  sium *poison* 663
cycle *time* 106
  period 138
  circle 247
  ride 266
  vehicle 272
  – car 272
cyclist 268
cycloid 247
cyclometer 200
cyclone
  rotation 312
  wind 349
Cyclopean
  strong 159
  huge 192
cyclopedia
  knowledge 490
  book 593
Cyclops
  monster 83
  mighty 159
  huge 192
  dupe 547
cygne
  chant du – 360
  – *noir* 650
cylindric 249
cyma 847
cymbal 417
cymbalo 417
cymophanous 440
cynic
  misanthrope 911
  detractor 936
  ascetic 955
  closet – 893
cynical
  contemptuous 930
  censorious 932
  detracting 934
cynicism
  discourtesy 895
  contempt 930
cynosure *sign* 550
  direction 693
  wonder 870
  repute 873
Cynthia of the
  minute 149
cypher [*see* cipher]
cypress
  interment 363
  mourning 839
Cyprian 962
cyst 191
czar 745

D

da capo 104
dab *small* 32
  paint 223
  slap 276
  clever 700
dabble *water* 337
  dirty 653
  meddle 682
  fribble 683
dabbled *wet* 339
dabbler 493
dachshund 366
dacoit 792
dactyl 597
dactylogram 467
dactyliomancy 511

dactylonomy
  numeration 85
  symbol 550
dad 166
daddy 166
dado 211
daedal
  variegated 440
daedalion
  convoluted 248
  artistic 698
daft 503
dagger 727
  look –s *anger* 900
  threat 909
  air drawn – 515
  plant – in breast
  give pain 830
  speak –s 932
  at –s drawn
  opposed 708
  discord 713
  enmity 889
  hate 898
daggle *hang* 214
  dirty 653
dagobah 1000
Dagon 986
daguerreotype
  represent 554
  paint 556
dahabeah 273
Dail Eireann 696
daily
  frequent 136
  periodic 138
  – occurrence
  normal 82
  habitual 613
  – paper 531
dainty *food* 298
  savory 394
  pleasing 829
  delicate 845
  tasty 850
  fastidious 868
dairy 191, 370
  – maid 946
dais *support* 215
  throne 747
daisy
  fresh as a – 654
  – pied 847
dale 252
dally *delay* 133
  irresolute 605
  inactive 683
  amuse 840
  fondle 902
dalmatic 999
Daltonism 443
dam *parent* 166
  close 261
  pond 343
  obstruct 706
damage *evil* 619
  injure, spoil 659
  price 812
damages 974
damascene 440
damask 434
dame
  woman 374
  teacher 540
  lady 875
damn
  malediction 908
  condemn 971

- to *insensible* 823
deafen *loud* 404
deafness 419
deal *much* 31
  arrange 60
  bargain 768
  allot 786
  - a blow
  injure 659
  attack 716
  punish 972
  - board 323
  - in 794
  - out *scatter* 73
  give 784
  - with
  treat of 595
  handle 692
  barter 794
dealer 797
dealings *action* 680
  have – with
  trade 794
  friendly 888
dean 128, 694, 996
deanery *office* 995
  house 1000
dear
  high-priced 814
  loved 897
  favorite 899
  O – ! *lament* 839
  - at any price 646
  - me *wonder* 870
  pay – for whistle
  647
dearest foe 936
dearness 814
dearth 640
  - of ideas 843
death 360
  house of – 363
  in at the –
  arrive 292
  kill 361
  persevere 604a
  pale as –
  colorless 429
  fear 860
  put to – 361, 972
  still as – 265
  violent – 361
  be the – of one
  amuse 480
  -'s head 837
  - in the pot
  unhealthy 657
  hidden danger
  667
deathbed repent-
  ance 950
death-blow
  end 67
  killing 361
  failure 732
death-house 752
deathless
  perpetual 112
  fame 873
deathlike
  silent 403
  hideous 846
death-song 839
death-struggle 720
death-warrant 971
death-watch 668
débâcle 145
  destruction 162

downfall 306
  torrent 348
debar *hinder* 706
  restrain 751
  prohibit 761
debark 292
debase *depress* 308
  foul 653
  deteriorate 659
  degrade 874
debased
  lowered 207
  dishonored 940
debate *reason* 476
  talk 588
  hesitate 605
  dispute 720
debatable 475
debauch
  spoil 659
  intemperance 954
  impurity 961
debauchee 962
debenture
  security 771
  money 800
  credit 805
debility 160
debit *debt* 806
  accounts 811
debitor 806
débonnaire 836
debouch 293, 295
débris
  fragments 51
  crumbled 330
  useless 645
debt 806
  out of – 803
  get out of – 807
  - of nature 360
debtor 806
  - and creditor 811
debunk 529
début *beginning* 66
  essay 675
  celebration 883
débutant
  learner 541
  drama 599
decade *ten* 98
  period 108
decadence 659
decagon 244
decalescence 382
decalogue 926
decamp
  go away 293
  run away 623
decant 270
decanter 191
decapitate *kill* 361
  punish 972
decay *decrease* 36
  decompose 49
  shrivel 195
  unclean 653
  disease 655
  spoil 659
  adversity 735
  natural – 360
  - of memory 506
decayed
  [*see* decay]
  old 124
  rotten 160
decease 360
deceit

falsehood 544
  deception 545
  cunning 702
deceived
  in error 495
  duped 547
deceiver 548
  gay – 962
decelerate 275
decennium 108
decent
  mediocre 651
  pure 960
decentralize 49
deceptio visûs 443
deception 545
deceptive reason-
  ing 477
decession 293
dechristianize 989
decide
  turn the scale 153
  judge 480
  choose 609
decided *great* 31
  ended 67
  certain 474
  resolved 604
  take a – step 609
deciduous
  transitory 111
  falling 306
  spoiled 659
decies repetita
  placebit 829
decimal 84, 98, 99
decimate
  subtract 38
  tenth 99
  few 103
  weaken 160
  kill 361
  play havoc 659
  punish 972
decipher 522
decision
  judgment 480
  resolution 604
  intention 620
  law case 969
decisive
  certain 474
  proof 478
  commanding 741
  take a – step 609
deck *floor* 211
  beautify 847
declaim 531, 582
  - against 932
declamatory
  style 577
  speech 582
declaration
  affirmation 535
  law pleadings 969
  - of faith
  belief 484
  theology 983
  - of war 713
declaratory
  meaning 516
  inform 527
declare
  publish 531
declension
  [*see* decline]
  grammar 567
  backsliding 988

declensions 5
declination
  [*see* decline]
  deviation 279
  measurement 466
  rejection 610
decline *decrease* 36
  old 124
  weaken 160
  descent 306
  grammar 567
  be unwilling 603
  reject 610
  disease 655
  become worse 659
  adversity 735
  refuse 764
  - of day 126
  - of life 128
declivity *slope* 217
  descent 306
decoction 335, 384
decode 522
decollate 972
décolleté 226
decoloration 429
decomposition 49
deconsecrate 756
decontrol 158
décor 448, 599
decoration
  insignia 747
  ornament 847
  title 877
decorative 556
decorous
  [*see* decorum]
  fashionable 852
  proper 924
  respectful 928
decorticate 226
decorum
  fashion 852
  duty 926
  purity 960
décousu
  discontinuous 70
  failure 732
decoy *attract* 288
  deceive 545
  deceiver 548
  entice 615
decrease 36, 195
decree
  judgment 480
  order 741
  law 963, 969
decrement
  decrease 36
  thing deducted 40a
  contraction 195
decrepit *old* 128
  weak 158, 160
  disease 655
  decayed 659
decrepitate 406
decrescendo 36
decretal 741
decry *underrate* 483
  censure 932
  detract 934
decumbent 213
decuple 98
decursive 306
decurtation 201
decussation 219
dedecorous
  disreputable 874

discourteous 895
dedicate *use* 677
  inscribe 873
deduce *deduct* 38
  infer 480
deducible
  evidence 467
  proof 478
deduct *retrench* 38
  deprive 789
  subtract 813
deduction
  [*see* deduce]
  decrement 40a
  reasoning 476
deed *evidence* 467
  record 551
  act 680
  security 771
  -s of arms 720
  - without a name
  947
deem 484
deemster 967
deep *great* 31
  profound 208
  sea 341
  sonorous 404
  cunning 702
  plough the – 267
  - color 428
  - in debt 806
  - game 702
  - knowledge 490
  - mourning 839
  - note 408
  - potations 959
  - reflection 451
  - sense 821
  - sigh 839
  - study 457
  in – water 704
deepen 35
deep-dyed
  intense 171
  black 431
  vicious 945
deep-felt 821
deep-laid *plan* 626
deep-mouthed
  resonant 408
  bark 412
  thrilling 821
deep-musing 458
deep-read 490
deep-rooted
  stable 150
  strong 159
  belief 484
  habit 613
  affections 820
deep-sea 208
deep-seated 208,
  221
deer 366
  in heart a – 862
deev 980
deface
  destroy form 241
  obliterate 552
  injure 659
  render ugly 846
defalcation
  incomplete 53
  contraction 195
  shortcoming 304
  non-payment 808
defame *shame* 874

expedition 682
haste 684
conduct 692
complete 729
command 741
happy – 972
– case 191
– food 298
– rider 534
desperado
rash 863
blusterer 887
evil-doer 913
desperate great 31
violent 173
impossible 471
resolved 604
difficult 704
excitable 825
hopeless 859
rash 863
anger 900
despicable
trifling 643
shameful 874
contemptible 930
despise 930
– danger 861
despite 30, 907
in – 708
despoil injure 659
take 789
rob 791
despond 837, 860
despot 745
despotism
authority 737
severity 739
arbitrary 964
despumate 652
desquamation 226
dessert 298
dessous des cartes
cause 153
latent 526
secret 533
connaître le – 490
dessus dessous
sens – 218
destination end 67
arrival 292
intention 620
destiny chance 152
fate 601
fight against – 606
destitute
insufficient 640
poor 804
refuge for – 666
destrier 726
destroy
demolish 162
injure 659
– hopes 859
– life 361
destroyed
[see destroy]
inexistent 2
failure 732
destroyer 165
warship 726
evil-doer 913
destructive
bad 649
destructor 383
desuetude 614
disuse 678
desultory

disordered 59
fitful 70
multiform 81
irregular in time 139
changeable 149
deviating 279
agitated 315
desume 788
detach 44
detached
irrelated 10
loose 47
detachment
part 51
army 726
detail describe 594
special portions 79
allot 786
ornament 847
attention to – 457, 459
in – 51
details
minutiæ 32
unimportant 643
detain 781
detect 480a
detective 527, 664
detention 133, 751, 781
house of – 752
in house of – 938
détenu 754
deter dissuade 616
alarm 860
deterge clean 652
detergent
remedy 662
deterioration 659
determinate
special 79
exact 474
conclusive 480
intended 620
determine end 67
define 79
cause 153
direction 278
satisfy 462
make sure 474
judge 480
discover 480a
resolve 604
determined
resolute 604
determinism 601
deterration 529
detersion 652
detersive 662
detest dislike 867
hate 898
detestable 649
dethronement
anarchy 738
abrogation 756
detonate
explode 173
sound 406
detortion form 243
meaning 523
détour curve 245
circuit 629
detract subduct 38
underrate 483
defame 934
slander 938

detraction 934
detractor 936
detrain 292
detriment
evil 619
deterioration 659
detrimental 649
detrition 330
detritus
fragments 51
deposit 270
powder 330
detrude
cast out 297
cut down 308
detruncate 38
deuce two 89
devil 978
play the – 825
– is in him 608
deuced great 31
painful 830
deus 976
– ex machinâ
aid 707
auxiliary 711
deity 976
sorcerer 994
deuterogamy 903
devastate
destroy 162
havoc 659
develop
increase 35
produce 161
expand 194
evolve 313
development 144, 154
devexity
bending 217
curvature 245
deviate vary 20a
change 140
turn 279
diverge 291
circuit 629
– from 15
– from rectitude 940
– from virtue 945
deviation 279
device motto 550
expedient 626
artifice 702
devil
seasoned food 392
evil-doer 913
bad man 949
Satan 978
demon 980
fight like –s 722
have a – 503
machinations of the – 619
play the – with
injure 659
malevolent 907
printer's – 591
raise the – 828
– may care
rash 863
indifferent 866
insolent 885
give the – his due
right 922
vindicate 937
fair 939

– in one
headstrong 863
temper 901
– to pay
disorder 59
violence 173
evil 619
failure 732
penalty 974
– take 908
– take the hindmost
run away 623
haste 684
cowardice 862
–'s tattoo 407
devilish great 31
bad 649
malevolent 907
devious curved 245
deviating 279
circuitous 311
devisable 270
devise imagine 515
plan 626
bequeath 784
devised by the enemy 546
devisee possess 779
receive 785
deviser 164
devitalize 158
devoid absent 187
empty 640
not having 777a
devoir courtesy 894
respect 928
devolve 783
– on 926
devote destine 601
employ 677
consecrate 873
– to destruction 908
– the mind to 457
– oneself to 604
devoted
habit 613
ill-fated 735
obedient 743
undone 828
friendship 888
love 897
devotee
zealot 682
aspirant 865
pious 987
fanatic 988
devotion [see devotee, devoted]
love 897
piety 987
worship 990
self – 942
devour
destroy 162
eat 298
gluttony 957
devoured by
feeling 821
devouring element 382
devout 987, 990
devoutless 989
devoutly 821
dew 339
shake as –drops from lion's

mane 483
dewy eve 126
dexterous 238, 698
dextrality 238
dey 745
dhow 273
diable:
avoir le – au corps 503
– à quatre
disorder 59
violence 173
loud 404
excitement 825
tirer le – par la queue 804
diablerie 978, 992
diabolic
bad 649
malevolent 907
wicked 945
Satanic 978
Diacoustics 402
diacritical 550
diadem 747, 847
diaeresis 49
diagnosis 465, 655
diagnostic
special 79
experiment 463
indication 550
(intrinsic 5)
diagonal 217
diagram 554
dial 114
as the – to the sun
veracious 543
faithful 772
dialect 563
dialectic
argument 476
language 560
dialogism 586
dialogue 588
diameter 202
diametrically
opposite
contrariety 14
contraposition 237
diamond
lozenge 244
type 591
goodness 648
ornament 847
rough – 703
– cut diamond
cunning 702
retaliation 718
– jubilee 883
– wedding 883
Diana moon 318
chaste 960
goddess 979
diapason 413
diaper 847
diaphanous 425
diaphonics 402
diaphoresis 299
diaphragm 68, 228
diaporesis 475
diarchy 737
diarrhea 299
diary 114, 551
diastole 194
diatessaron 413
diathermancy 384
diathesis

discover 480a
disinterested 942
disjecta membra
　separate 44
　disorder 59
　dispersed 73
　– *poetae* 597
disjoin 44
disjointed
　disorder 59
　powerless 158
　style 575
disjunction 44
disjunctive 70
diskindness 907
dislike 867
　reluctance 603
　hate 898
dislocate
　separate 44
　put out of joint 61
dislocated
　disorder 59
dislodge
　displace 185
　eject 297
disloyal 940
dismal
　depressing 830
　dejected 837
dismantle
　destroy 162
　divest 226
　render useless 645
　injure 659
　disuse 678
dismask 529
dismast
　render useless 645
　injure 659
　disuse 678
dismay 860
dismember
　separate 44
　disperse 73
dismiss
　send away 289
　discharge 297
　discard 678
　liberate 750
　abrogate 756
　relinquish 782
　punish 972
　– *from the mind*
　　452, 458
dismount
　arrive 292
　descend 306
　render useless 645
disnest 185
disobedience 742
　non-observance
　　773
disoblige 907
disorder
　confusion **59**
　derange 61
　turbulent 173
　disease 655
　–ed *intellect* 503
disorderly
　unprincipled 945
disorganize
　derange 61
　destroy 162
　spoil 659
disorganized 59
'**disown** 536

dispair 44
disparage
　underrate 483
　disrespect 929
　dispraise 932
　detract 934
disparity
　different 15
　dissimilar 18
　disagreeing 24
　unequal 28
　isolated 44
dispart 44
dispassionate 826
　– *opinion* 484
dispatch
　[*see* despatch]
dispel *scatter* 73
　destroy 162
　displace 185
　repel 289
dispensable
　useless 645
dispensary 662
dispensation
　[*see* dispense]
　command 741
　licence 760
　relinquishment
　　782
　exemption 927a
　–s *of Providence*
　　976
dispense
　disperse 73
　give 784
　apportion 786
　retail 796
　– *with*
　　disuse 678
　　permit 760
　　exempt 927a
　cannot be –d *with*
　　630
dispeople
　eject 297
　expatriate 893
disperse
　separate 44
　scatter 73
　diverge 291
　waste 638
dispersion 73
　– *of light* 420
　chromatic – 428
dispirit
　discourage 616
　sadden 837
displacement
　derange 61
　remove **185**
　transfer 270
displacency
　dislike 867
　incivility 895
　disapprobation
　　932
displant 185
display *appear* 448
　show 525
　parade 882
displease 830
displeasure 828
　anger 900
displosion 173
displume 789
disport 840
disposal

[*see* dispose]
　at one's – 763, 777
dispose
　arrange 60
　tend 176
　induce 615
　– *of use* 677
　complete 729
　relinquish 782
　give 784
　sell 796
disposed 620
disposition
　nature 5
　order 58
　arrangement 60
　inclination 602
　mind 820
dispossess
　transfer 783
　take away 789
　– *oneself of* 782
dispraise 932
dispread 73
disprize 483
disproof
　counter-evidence
　　468
　confutation 479
disproportion
　irrelation 10
　disagreement 24
disprove 479
disputable 475, 485
disputant 710, 726
disputatious 901
dispute
　discuss 476
　doubt 485
　deny 536
　discord 713
　in – 461
disqualification
　incapacitate 158
　useless 645
　unprepared 674
　unskilful 699
　disentitle 925
disquiet
　changeable 149
　agitation 315
　excitement 825
　uneasiness 828
　give pain 830
disquietude
　apprehension 860
disquisition 539,
　　595
disregard
　overlook 458
　neglect 460
　make light of 483
　insensible to 823,
　　826
　disrespect **929**
　contempt 930
　– *of time* 115
disrelish 867, 898
disreputable 874
　vicious 945
disrepute **874,** 929
disrespect 929
　despise 930
disrobe 226
disruption
　disjunction 44
　destruction 162
　discord 713

dissatisfaction
　disappointment
　　509
　sorrow 828
　discontent 832
dissect
　anatomize 44, 49
　investigate 461
dissemblance 18
dissemble 544
dissembler 548
disseminate
　scatter 73
　pervade 186
　publish 531
　teach 537
dissension 713
　sow – 898
dissent
　disagree **489**
　refuse 764
　heterodoxy 984
dissentient 15
dissentious 24
dissertation 595
disservice
　disadvantage 619
　useless 645
disserviceable 649
dissever 44
dissidence
　disagreement 24
　dissent 489
　discord 713
　discontent 832
　heterodoxy 984
dissilience 173
dissimilarity 18
dissimulate 544
dissipate *scatter* 73
　destroy 162
　pleasure 377
　prodigality 818
　amusement 840
　intemperance 954
　dissolute 961
dissocial 893
dissociate 44
dissociation
　irrelation 10
　separation 44
dissolute 961
　profligate 945
　intemperate 954
dissolution
　[*see* dissolve]
　decomposition 49
　destruction 162
　death 360
dissolve *vanish* 2, 4
　liquefy 335
　disappear 449
　abrogate 756
dissolving views
　　448, 449
dissonance
　disagreement 24
　unmusical 414
　discord 713
dissuasion **616**
dissyllable 561
distaff
　– *side* 374
distain *dirty* 653
　ugly 846
distal 196
distance **196**
　overtake 282

go beyond **303**
defeat 731
　angular – 244
　keep at a –
　　discourtesy 895
　keep one's –
　　avoid 623
　　modest 881
　　respect 928
　teach one his – 879
　– *of time*
　　long time 110
　　past 122
distaste 867
distasteful 830
distemper 299, 428
　color 428
　painting 556
　disease 655
distend 194
distended 192
distich 89, 597
distil *come out* 295
　extract 301
　evaporate 336
　drop 348
distinct
　disjoined 44
　audible 402
　visible 446
　intelligible 518
　manifest 525
　express 535
　articulate 580
distinction
　difference 15
　discrimination
　　465
　style 578
　fame 873
　rank 875
　– *without a differ-*
　　ence 27
distinctive 15
　– *feature* 79
distinctness 15
distingué 852, 873
distinguish
　perceive 441
　discriminate 465
　– *by the name of*
　　564
distinguishable 15
distinguished
　superior 33
　repute 873
Distinguished
　　Service Cross
　　733
distortion
　obliquity 217
　twist **243**
　of vision 443
　misinterpret 523
　falsehood 544
　misrepresent 555
　ugly 846
distract 458
distracted
　confused 475
　insane 503
　excited 824
distraction
　passion 825
　love to – 897
distrain *take* 789
　appraise 812
　attach 969

dolt 501	*death* 360	dotation 784	*blow* 972	doxology 990
doltish 499	*judgment* 480	dottle 40, 645	Dove	doxy 897
domain	*necessity* 601	dote *drivel* 499, 503	*Holy Ghost* 976	doyer 128
class 75	*sentence* 971	– upon 897	dove	doyley 652
region 181	– sealed	douanier 965	*innocent* 946	doze 683
property 780	*death* 360	double	roar like sucking –	dozen 98
Domdaniel 982	*adversity* 735	*similar* 17	174	drab *color* 432
dome *high* 206	doomed 735, 828	*increase* 35	dovecote 189	*slut* 653
roof 223	doomsday	*duplex* 90	dovetail	*hussy* 962
curvature 245	*end* 67	*substitute* 147	*agree* 23	drabble 653
convex 250	*future* 121	*fold* 258	*join* 43	drachm 319
Domesday book	*till* – 112	*turn* 283	*intersect* 219	Draco 694, 739
list 86	door *entrance* 66	*finesse* 702	*intervene* 228	draff 653
record 551	*cover* 223	march at the – 274	*angle* 244	draft [*see also*
domesman 967	*brink* 231	see –	*insert* 300	draught]
domestic	*barrier* 232	*dim sight* 443	dowager 374, 905	*multitude* 102
inhabitant 188	*opening* 260	*drunk* 959	dowdy 653, 851	*drawing* 554, 556
home 189	*passage* 627	– acrostic	dower 780, 803, 810	*write* 590
interior 221	at one's – 197	*letters* 561	dowerless 804	*abstract* 596
servant 746	beg from door to –	*wit* 842	down	*plan* 626
secluded 893	765	– dutch 518	*below* 207	*cheque* 800
– animals 366	bolt the – 666	– entry 811	*light* 320	*credit* 805
domesticate	close the – upon	– the fist 909	bear – upon 716	– off *displace* 185
locate 184	751	– march 684	bed of –	*transfer* 270
acclimatize 613	death's – 360	– meaning 520	*pleasure* 377	draft-horse 271
– animals 370	keep within –s 265	– a point 311	*repose* 687	drag *carriage* 272
domicile 189	lie at one's – 926	in – quick time	*come* – 306	*crawl* 275
domiciled 186	lock the – 666	274	*get* – 306	*traction* 285
domiciliary 188	open a – to	– reef topsails 664	*go* –	*impediment* 706
– visit 461	*liable* 177	– sure 474	*sink* 306	put on the – 275
dominant 175	open the – to	work – tides 686	*calm* 826	– a chain
note in music 413	*receive* 296	– up	*keep* – 36	*tedious* 109, 110
domination 737	*facilitate* 705	*render powerless*	*money* – 807	*exertion* 686
dominical 998	*permit* 760	158	*take* –	*subjection* 749
domineer	show the to	double bar 747	*lower* 308	– into
tyrannize 739	*eject* 297	double-bass 417	*rebuff* 874	*implicate* 54
insolence 885	*discourtesy* 895	doublecross 545	*humble* 879	*compel* 744
Domini, anno – 106	– mat 652	double-dealing	– on one's mar-	– through mire
Dominican 996	doorkeeper 263	*lie* 544	row-bones 886	*disrepute* 874
Dominie 540	doorway 260	*cunning* 940	– in the mouth 837	*disrespect* 929
dominion 181, 737	dope 376, 545, 663	double-distilled 171	– and out 874	– on *tedious* 110
domino *dress* 225	doquet	double-dyed 428	– in price 815	– into open day
mask 530	*security* 771	double-eagle 800	go – like a stone	531
game 840	Dorado, El – 803	double-edged 90,	310	– towards
domn 745	Doric mode 413	171	be – upon	*attract* 288
don *put on* 225	dormant	double entendre	*attack* 716	– slow length
scholar 492	*inert* 172	*ambiguity* 520	*severe* 739	*long* 200
teacher 540	*latent* 526	*impure* 961	downcast 306, 837	*weary* 841
noble 875	*asleep* 683	double-faced	– eyes 879	draggle 285, 653
Don Juan 897	dormer 260	*lie* 544	downfall	– tail 59
donation 784	dormeuse 272	*cunning* 702, 940	*destruction* 162	drag-net
done *finished* 729	dormir debout,	double-headed 90	*fall* 306	*all sorts* 78
work – 729	conte à – 843	double-minded 605	*failure* 732	dragoman 524
– for *spoilt* 659	dormitive 841	double-shotted 171	*misfortune* 735	dragon *monster* 83
failure 732	dormitory 191	doublet 225	downhill 217, 306	*violent* 173
– up	dormouse 683	double-tongued	go –	*animal* 366
impotent 158	dorp 189	*lie* 544	*adversity* 735	*irascible* 901
tired 688	dorsal 235	*cunning* 702, 940	downpour 348	dragonnade
have – with	dorser 191	doubt	downright	*attack* 716
cease 142	dorsum 235, 250	*uncertain* 475	*absolute* 31	*punish* 972
relinquish 624	dory 273	*disbelieve* 485	*manifest* 525	dragoon
disuse 678	dose *quantity* 25	*sceptic* 989	*sincere* 703	*soldier* 726
donee 785	*part* 51	doubtful 475	downs 206, 344	*compel* 744
donjon 717, 752	*medicine* 662	more than – 473	down-trodden	*insolent* 885
donkey *ass* 271	*apportion* 786	– meaning	*submission* 725	*worry* 907
fool 501	dosser 191	*unintelligible* 519	*vanquished* 732	drain
talk a –'s hind leg	dossier *bundle* 72	doubtless	*subject* 749	*flow out* 295
off 584	*record* 551	*certain* 474	*dejected* 837	*empty* 297
donna 374	dossil 223, 263	*belief* 484	*disrepute* 874	*dry* 340
Donnybrook Fair	dot *small* 32	*assent* 488	*contempt* 930	*conduit* 350
disorder 59	*place* 182	douceur 784, 973	downwards 306	*waste* 638
discord 713	*little* 193	douche 337	downy	*clean* 652
donor 784	*variegate* 440	dough 324, 354, 800	*smooth* 255	*unclean* 653
donzel 746	*mark* 550	doughty 861	*plumose* 256	*exhaust* 789
doodle 501	*dowry* 780	dour 739	*soft* 324	*dissipate* 818
doom *end* 67	on the – 113	douse	dowry 780, 784	– the cup
fate 152	dotage 128, 499	*immerse* 310	dowse 276	*drink* 298
destruction 162	dotard 130, 501	*splash* 337	dowser 994	*drunken* 959

sleepy 683
weary 841
drub
defeat 731, 732
punish 972
drudge *labour* 686
worker 682, 690
drug
render insensible 376
superfluity 641
trash 643
remedy 662
bane 663
– in the market 815
drugget
cover 223
clean 652
preserve 670
druggist 662
druid 996
drum
repeat 104
cylinder 249
sound 407
music 417
party 892
beat of –
signal 550
alarm 669
war 722
command 741
parade 882
ear – 418
muffled –
funeral 363
non-resonance 408a
– *and fife band* 417
– *fire* 407
– *out* 972
drum-head 964, 966
drum-major 745
drummer 416
drunken 959
reel like a – *man* 315
drunkenness 959
dry *arid* 340
style 575, 576, 579
hoarse 581
scanty 640
preserve 670
exhaust 789
tedious 841
dull 842
thirsty 865
cynical 932
teetotal 958
run – 640
with – *eyes* 823
– *dock* 189
– *joke* 842
– *land* 342
– *the tears* 834
– *up* 340, 638
dryad 979
dry-as-dust
antiquarian 122
dull 843
dryness 340
dry-nurse
teach 537
teacher 540
aid 707
dry-point 558

dry-rot
dirt 653
decay 659
bane 663
dualism 984
duality 89
duarchy 737
dub 564
dubious 475
ducat 800
duce 745
duchess 745, 875
duchy 181
duck *stoop* 308
plunge 310
water 337
darling 897, 899
play –s *and drakes*
recoil 277
prodigality 818
–'s *egg*
zero 101
– *in thunder* 870
ducking-stool 975
duckling 127
duck-pond 370
duct 350
ductile
elastic 323
flexible 324
trimming 607
easy 705
docile 743
dud 158, 727
dude 854
duds 225
dudgeon
dagger 727
discontent 832
churlishness 895
hate 898
anger 900
sullenness 901a
due
expedient 646
owing 806
proper 924, 926
give his – *to*
right 922
vindication 937
fair 939
in – *course* 109
occasion 134
– *respect* 928
– *sense of* 498
– *time*
soon 132
– *to*
cause and effect 154, 155
give – *weight* 465
duel 720
duelist 726
dueness 924
duenna
teacher 540
guardian 664
keeper 753
dues 812
duet 415
duff 298
duffer
bungler 701
smuggler 792
dug 250
dug-out
old man 130

boat 273
defence 717
duke *ruler* 745
noble 875
dulce domum 189
dulcet
sweet 396
sound 405
melodious 413
agreeable 829
dulcify 174, 396
dulcimer 417
Dulcinea 897
dulcorate 396
dulia 990
dull *weak* 160
inert 172
moderate 174
blunt 254
insensible 376, 381
sound 405
dim 422
colorless 429
ignorant 493
stolid 499
style 575
inactive 683
unapt 699
callous 823
dejected 837
weary 841
prosing 843
simple 849
– *of hearing* 419
– *sight* 443
dullard 501
dullness 843
duly 924
duma 696
dumb 581
– *animal* 366
– *show* 550
– *waiter* 307
strike –
ignorant 493
astonish 870
humble 879
dumbfounder
disappoint 509
silence 581
astonish 870
humble 879
dummy
substitute 147
impotent 158
speechless 581
inactive 683
dump *music* 415
store 636
lament 839
undersell 796
dumpling 298
dumps
discontent 832
dejection 837
sulk 901a
dumpy *little* 193
short 201
thick 202
dun *dim* 422
colorless 429
grey 432
importune 765
creditor 805
dunce
ignoramus 493
fool 501

dunderhead 501
dune 206
dung 653
dungeon 752
dunghill
dirt 653
cowardly 862
baseborn 876
– *cock* 366
Dunker 984
dunt 716
duo 415
duodecimal 99
duodecimo
little 193
book 593
duodenary 98
duologue
interlocution 588
drama 599
dupe
credulous 486
deceive 545
deceived 547
duplex 90, 189
duplicate
imitate 19
copy 21
double 90
tally 550
record 551
redundant 641
pawn 805
duplication
imitation 19
doubling 90
repetition 104
duplicature
fold 258
duplicity
duality 89
falsehood 544
dura lex sed lex 926
durable
long time 110
stable 150
durance 141, 751
in – 754
duration 106
contingent – 108a
infinite – 112
durbar
conference 588
council 696
tribunal 966
duress
compulsion 744
restraint 751
during 106
– *pleasure &c.* 108a
durity 323
dusk
evening 126
half-light 422
dusky
dark 421
black 431
dust *levity* 320
powder 330
corpse 362
trash 643
dirt 653
money 800
come to –
die 360
come down with the – 807

humbled in the – 879
kick up a – 885
level with the – 162
lick the –
submit 725
fail 732
make to bite the – 731
turn to –
deorganized 358
die 360
– *in the balance* 643
throw – *in the eyes*
blind 442
deceive 545
plead 617
– *one's jacket* 972
duster 652
dust-bin, dust-hole 191, 645
fit for the –
useless 645
dirty 653
spoilt 659
dustman
cleaner 652
dust-storm 330
dusty
powder 330
dirt 653
Dutch
double – 519
high – 519
– *auction* 796
– *courage* 862
Dutchman, flying 515
dutiful 944
duty
business 625
work 686
tax 812
courtesy 894
obligation 926
respect 928
worship 990
rite 998
do one's –
virtue 944
on – 680, 682
duumvirate 737
Duval, Claude – 792
D.V. 470, 976
dwarf
lessen 36
small 193
elf 980
dwell
reside 186
abide 265
– *upon*
descant 573
dweller 188
dwelling 184, 189
dwindle *lessen* 36
shrink 195
dyad 89
dye 428
dying 360
dyke [*see* dike]
dynamic energy 157
dynamics 276

complete 729
carry into – 692
with crushing –
  162
in – 5
take – 731
to that – 516
effective
  capable 157
  useful 644
effectuation 729
expedient 646
effects 780, 798
effectual 731
effectually 52
effectuate 729
effeminate
  weak 160
  womenlike 374
  timorous 862
  sensual 954
effeminize 158
effendi 875
effervesce
  energy 171
  violence 173
  agitate 315
  bubble 353
  excited 825
effervescent 338
effete *old* 128
  weak 160
  useless 645
  spoiled 659
efficacious
  [*see* efficient]
efficient
  power 157
  agency 170
  utility 644
  skill 698
effigy 21, 554
effleurer *skim* 267,
  460
efflorescence 330
effluxion of time
  109
effluence *egress* 295
  flow 348
effluvium 334, 398
efflux 295
efformation 240
effort 686
effreet 980
effrontery 885
effulgence 420
effuse
  pour out 295, 297
  excrete 299
  speech 582
  loquacity 584
effusion of blood
  361
effusive 573
eft 366
eftsoons 117
egad 535
égards 928
egesta 299
egestion 297
egg *beginning* 66
  cause 153
  food 298
  walk among –s
  704
  too many –s in
  one basket
  unskilful 699

(*imprudent* 863)
– and dart
  ornament 847
– on 615
egg-shaped 247,
  249
ego *intrinsic* 5
  speciality 79
  immaterial 317
  non – 6
egocentrism 943
egotism
  vanity 880
  cynicism 911
  selfishness 943
egregious
  exceptional 83
  absurd 497
  exaggerated 549
  important 642
egregiously 31, 33
egress **295**
Egyptian darkness
  421
eheu! fugaces
  labuntur anni
  111
eiderdown 223
eidouranion 318
Eiffel tower 206
eight *number* 98
  boat 273
  representative 759
eisteddfod 72, 416
eighty 98
either *choice* 609
  happy with – 605
ejaculate
  propel 284
  utter 580
ejection 185, **297**
ejecta 299
ejector 349
eke *also* 37
  – out *complete* 52
  spin out 110
ekka 272
El Dorado 803
elaborate
  improve 658
  prepare 673
  laborious 686
  work out 729
elaine 356
élan 276
elapse 109, 122
elastic fluid 334
elasticity
  power 157
  strength 159
  energy 171
  spring **325**
elate *cheer* 836
  rejoice 838
  hope 858
  vain 880
  boast 884
elbow *angle* 244
  projection 250
  push 276
  at one's –
  near 197
  advice 695
  lift one's –
  drink 959
  out at –s
  undress 226
  poor 804

disrepute 874
· one's way
  progress 282
  pursuit 622
  active 682
elbow-chair 215
elbow-grease 331
elbow-room 180,
  748
elder *older* 124
  aged 128
  veteran 130
  clergy 996
elect *choose* 609
  good 648
  predestinate 976
  pious 987
  clergy 996
election
  numerical 84
  necessity 601
electioneering 609
elector 745
electorate 737
Electra complex
  897
electric
  swift 274
  sensation 821
  excitable 825
  car 272
  – blue 438
  – chair 974
  – light 423
  – piano 417
electrician 599, 690
electricity 157, 388
electrify
  unexpected 508
  excite 824
  astonish 870
electro-biology 992
electrocution 972
electrolier 214, 423
electrolyze 49
electro-magnetism
  157
electromobile 272
electron 32
electronics 157
electroplate 223
electrotype 21, 591
electuary 662
eleemosynary 784
elegance
  in style 578
  beauty 845
  taste 859
  Bank of – 800
elegy *interment* 363
  poetry 597
  lament 839
element
  component 56
  beginning 66
  cause 153
  matter 316
  in one's –
  facility 705
  content 831
  devouring – 382
  out of its – 195
elementary 42
  – education 537
  – school 542
elements
  Eucharist 998
elench 477

elephant
  large 192
  carrier 271
  white – *bane* 663
elevated
  tipsy 959
elevation
  height 206
  vertical 212
  raising **307**
  plan 554
  – of style 574
  improvement 658
  glory 873
  – of mind 942
  angular – 244
élève 541
eleven 98
  representative 759
eleventh hour
  evening 126
  late 133
  opportune 134
elf *infant* 129
  little 193
  imp 980
elicit *cause* 153
  draw out 301
  discover 480a
  manifest 525
eligible 646
Elijah's mantle 63
eliminant 299
eliminate
  subduct 38
  simplify 42
  exclude 55
  weed 103
  extract 301
  reject 610
elision 44, 201
élite *best* 648
  distinguished 873
  aristocratic 875
elixation 384
elixir 662
  – of life 471
elk 223
ell 200
  take an –
  take 789
  insolence 885
  wrong 923
  undue 925
  selfish 943
ellipse 247
ellipsis *shorten* 201
  style 572
ellipsoid 247, 249
elocation 185, 270
elocution 582
éloge 931
elongation 196, 200
elopement 623, 671
eloquence 572, 582
else 37
elsewhere 187
elucidate 522
elude
  sophistry 477
  avoid 623
  escape 671
  succeed 731
  palter 773
elusive 545
elusory 546
elutriate 652
elysian 829, 981

Elysium 827, 981
elytron 223
Elzevir. edition 193
emaciation 195,
  203, 640
emanate 151
  go out of 295
  excrete 299
  – from 544
emanation 398
emancipate
  facilitate 705
  free 748, 750
emasculate
  impotent 158
embalm
  interment 363
  perfume 400
  preserve 670
  – in the memory
  505
embankment
  esplanade 189
  refuge 666
  fence 717
embar 229
embargo
  stoppage 265
  prohibition 761
  exclusion 893
embark
  transfer 270
  depart 293
  – in *begin* 66
  engage in 676
embarquer sans
  biscuits, s' – 674
embarras de
  – *choix* 609
embarrass 641,
  704, 706
embarrassed 804,
  806
embarrassing 475
embase 659
embassy
  errand 532
  commission 755
  consignee 758
embattled
  arranged 60
  leagued 712
  war array 722
embed
  locate 184
  base 215
  enclose 221
  insert 300
embellish 847
embers 384
embezzle 791
embitter
  deteriorate 659
  aggravate 835
  acerbate 900
emblazon
  color 428
  ornament 847
  display 882
emblem 550, 747
embody
  join 43
  combine 48
  form a whole 50
  compose 54
embolden
  hope 858
  encourage 861

embolism 228, 261,
  300
embonpoint 192
embosomed
  lodged 184
  interjacent 228
  circumscribed 229
emboss *convex* 250
  ornament 847
embouchure 260
embowel 297
embrace
  cohere 46
  compose 54
  include 76
  enclose 227
  choose 609
  take 789
  friendship 888
  sociality 892
  courtesy 894
  endearment 902
  – *an offer* 760
embrangle 61
embranglement 713
embrasure 257, 260
embrocation 662
embroider
  variegate 440
  lie 544
  ornament 847
embroidery
  adjunct 39
  exaggeration 549
embroil *derange* 61
  discord 713
embroilment 59
embrown 433
embryo
  beginning 66
  cause 153
  in – *destined* 152
  preparing 673
embryology 357
embryonic 193, 674
embus 293
embusqué 603
emendation 658
emerald *green* 435
  jewel 847
emerge 295, 446
emergency
  circumstance 8
  event 151
  difficulty 704
emeritus 500, 928
emersion 295, 446
emery
  sharpener 253
  – *paper*
  smooth 255
emetic *remedy* 662
émeute 742
emication 420
emigrant 57, 268
emigrate 266, 295
emigré 268, 295
eminence
  height 206
  fame 873
  church dignitary
  996
eminent domain
  744
eminently 33
emir 745, 875
emissary
  messenger 534

consignee 758
emission 297
emit *eject* 297
  publish 531
  voice 580
  – *vapour* 336
Emmanuel 976
emmet 193
emollient 662
emolument
  acquisition 775
  receipt 810
  remuneration 973
emotion 821
  –al *appeal* 824
  –al *drama* 599
empale 260, 972
empanel 86, 969
empathy 515
emperor 745
emphasis 580
emphatic 535, 642
emphatically 31
empierce
  perforate 260
  insert 300
empire 737, 789
  – *day* 840
empiric 548
empirical 463, 675
empiricism 463
emplane 293
employ
  business 625
  use 677
  servitude 749
  commission 755
  in one's – 746
  – one's capital in
  794
  – oneself 680
  – one's time in
  625
employé
  servant 746
  agent 758
employer 795
empoison 659
emporium 799
empower
  power 157
  commission 755
  accredit 759
  permit 760
empress 745
empressement
  activity 682
  emotion 821
  desire 865
emprise 676
emption 795
emptor 795
  caveat – 769
empty *clear* 185
  vacant 187
  deflate 195
  drain 297
  ignorant 491
  waste 638
  deficient 640
  useless 645
  beggarly account
  of – *boxes*
  poverty 804
  – one's glass 298
  – *purse* 804
  – *sound* 517
  – *stomach* 865

– *title name* 564
  undue 925
  – *words* 546
empty-handed 640
empty-headed 4,
  491
empurple 437
empyrean *sky* 318
  blissful 829
empyreuma 41
empyrosis 384
emulate *imitate* 19
  goodness 648
  rival 708
  compete 720
  glory 873
emulsion 352
emunctory 350
en – *bloc* 50
  – *masse* 50
  – *passant*
  parenthetical 10
  transient 111
  à *propos* 134
  – *rapport* 9
  – *règle order* 58
  conformity 82
  – *route*
  journey 266
  progress 282
enable 157
enact *drama* 599
  action 680
  conduct 692
  complete 729
  order 741
  law 963
enallage 521
enamel *coating* 223
  painting 556
  ornament 847
enameller 559
enamor 897
encage 751
encamp 184, 189
encampment 184
encaustic 556
enceinte
  with child 161
  region 181
  inclosure 232
enchafe 830
enchain 751
enchant *please* 829
enchanted 827
enchanting 845,
  897
enchantment
  sorcery 992
enchase 43, 259
enchiridion 593
enchorial 188
encincture 229
encircle 76, 227,
  311
enclave *close* 181
  boundary 233
enclose 227, 229
enclosure
  region 181
  envelope 232
  fence 752
encomiast 935
encomium 931
encompass 227, 233
  –ed with difficul-
  ties 704
encore 104, 931

encounter
  undergo 151
  clash 276
  meet 292
  withstand 708
  contest 720
  – *danger* 665
  – *risk* 621
encourage
  animate 615
  aid 707
  comfort 834
  hope 858
  embolden 861
encroach
  transcursion 303
  do wrong 923
  infringe 925
encumber 704, 706
encumbrance
  clear of – 807
encyclical 531
encyclopedia 490,
  593
  walking – 700
encyclopedical
  general 78
  – *knowledge* 490
encysted 229
end
  termination 67
  effect 154
  object 620
  at an – 142
  come to its – 729
  one's journey's –
  292
  on – 212
  put an – to
  destroy 162
  kill 361
  begin at the
  wrong – 699
  – one's days 360
  –s of the earth 196
  – to end *space* 180
  touching 199
  length 200
  – of life 360
  – in smoke 732
  – of one's tether
  sophistry 477
  ignorant 491
  insufficient 640
  difficult 704
endamage 649
endanger 665
endear 897
endearment 902
endeavor
  pursue 622
  attempt 675
  use one's best –
  686
  – after 620
endemic
  special 79
  interior 221
  disease 657
endimanché 847,
  882
endless
  multitudinous
  102
  infinite 105
  perpetual 112
endlessly 16
endlong 200

endocrine 221
endogenous 367
endorse
  evidence 467
  assent 488
  compact 769
  - *a bill* 800
  approve 931
endorsement 550
endosmose 302
endow
  confer power 157
endowed with
  possessed of 777
endowment
  intrinsic 5
  power 157
  talent 698
  gift 784
endrogynous 83
endue 157
endure *time* 106
  last 110
  persist 143
  continue 141
  undergo 151
  feel 821
  submit to 826
  unable to – 867
  – for ever 112
  – *pain* 828
enduring
  indelible 505
endwise 212
enemy *time* 841
  foe 891
  the common – 978
  thing devised by
  the – 546
  – to society 891
energumen 504
energy *power* 157
  strength 159
  physical 171
  resolution 604
  activity 682
enervate 158, 160
enfant, bon – 906
  – *gate*
  prosperity 734
  satiety 869
  favorite 899
  – *perdu*
  hopeless 859
  reckless 863
  – *terrible*
  curiosity 455
  artless 703
  object of fear 860
enfeeble 160
enfeoff 780, 783
Enfield *rifle* 727
enfilade
  lengthwise 200
  pierce 260
  pass through 302
enfold 229
enforce *urge* 615
  advise 695
  compel 744
  require 924
enfranchise
  free 748
  liberate 750
  permit 760
enfranchised 924
engage
  bespeak 132

epicurean 954
Epicurus, system
  of – 954
epicy-cle, -cloid
  247
epidemic
  general 78
  disease 655
  insalubrity 657
epidermis 223
epigenesis 161
epigram 496, 842
epigrammatic 572
epigrammatist 844
epigraph 550
epilepsy 315, 655
epilogue
  sequel 65
  end 67
  drama 599
èpingles, tire a
  quatre – 855
Epiphany 998
episcopal 995
Episcopalian 984
episcopate 995
episode
  adjunct 39
  discontinuity 70
  interjacence 228
episodic
  irrelative 10
  style 573
epistle 592
Epistles 985
epistrophe 104
epistyle 210
epitaph 363
epithalamium 903
epithem 662
epithet 564
epitome
  miniature 193
  short 201
  concise 572
epizoötic 657
epoch *time* 106
  instant 113
  date 114
  present time 118
epode 597
eponym 564
epopoea 597
epos 594
epulation 298
epulotic 662
epuration 652
equable 16, 922
equal *even* 27
  equitable 922
  – *chance* 156
  – *times* 120
  – *to power* 157
equality 13, 27
equalize 213
equate 27, 30
equations 85
equator 68, 318
equatorial 68, 236
equerry 746
equestrian 268
equibalanced 27
equidistant 68
equilibration 27
equilibrist 599
equilibrium 27
equine *carrier* 271

horse 366
equinox 125, 126
equip 225, 673
equipage
  vehicle 272
  instruments 633
  display 882
equiparent 27
equipment 633
equipoise &c. 27, 30
equitable *wise* 498
  just 922
  due 924
  honorable 939
  – *interest* 780
equitation 266
equity *right* 922
  honor 939
  law 963
  in – 922
  – *draftsman* 968
equivalent
  identical 13
  equal 27
  compensation 30
  substitute 147
  translation 522
equivocalness
  dubious 475
  double meaning
    520
  impure 961
equivocate
  sophistry 477
  palter 520·
  lie 544
equivocation
  [*see* equivocate]
  without – 543
équivoque
  double meaning
    520
  impure 961
era *time* 106, 108
  date 114
eradicate
  destroy 162
  extract 301
erase *destroy* 162
  obliterate 331, 552
Erastian 984
erasure 552
Erato 416
ere 116
  – *long* 132
  – *now* 116
  past 122
Erebus *dark* 421
  hell 982
erect *build* 161
  vertical 212
  raise 307
  with head – 878
  – *the scaffolding*
    673
erewhile 116, 122
ergatocracy 737
ergo 476
ergotism 480
ergotize 485
eriometer 445
Erinys 900
Erl King 980
ermine
  badge of authority
    747
  ornament 847

erode 36, 659
Eros 897, 979
erosion 36
erotic 897, 961
err – *in opinion* 495
  – *morally* 945
errand
  message 532
  business 625
  commission 755
errand-boy 534
errant 279
erratic
  irregular 139
  changeable 149
  wandering 279
  capricious 608
erratum 495
erroneous 495
error *fallacy* **495**
  vice 945
  guilt 947
  court of – 966
  writ of – 969
ersatz 973
erst 122
erubescence 434
erubuit salva res
  est 95
eruct 297
eructate 297
erudition 490, 539
eruption
  upheaval 146
  violence 173
  egress 295, 297
  disease 655
  volcanic – 872
escadrille 726
escalade
  mounting 305
  attack 716
escalator 307
escalop 248
escapade
  absurdity 497
  freak 608
  prank 840
escape
  flight **671**
  liberate 750
  evade 927
  means of – 664,
    666
  – *the lips*
    disclosure 529
    speech 582
  – *the memory* 506
  – *notice* &c.
    invisible 447
    inattention 458
    latent 526
escarp 717
escarpment
  stratum 204
  height 206
  oblique 217
escharotic
  caustic 171
  pungent 392
eschatology 67
escheat 144, 974
eschew
  avoid 623
  dislike 867
esclandre 828, 830
escort
  accompany 88

safeguard 664
  keeper 753
escritoire 191
esculent 298
escutcheon 550
esophagus 260
esoteric
  private 79
  concealed 528
Espagne, château
  en – *fancy* 515
espalier 232
especial 79
especially 33
espial 441
espiéglerie
  cunning 702
  fun 840
espionnage 441,
  461
esplanade
  houses 189
  flat 213
espouse
  choose 609
  marriage 903
  – *a cause aid* 707
  co-operate 709
esprit
  shrewdness 498
  wit 842
  bel – 844
  – de corps
    bias 481
    co-operation 709
    sociality 892
    (*party* 712)
  – fort
    thinker 500
    irreligious 989
espy 441
esquire 875, 877
essay
  experiment 463
  dissertation 595
  endeavor **675**
essayist 593, 595
esse 1
essence
  nature 5
  scent 398
essential
  intrinsic 5
  great 31
  required 630
  important 642
essentially
  intrinsically 5
  substantially 3
essential stuff 5
establish
  settle 150
  create 161
  place 184
  evidence 467
  demonstrate 478
  – *equilibrium* 27
established
  permanent 141
  habit 613
  – *church* 983a
establishment
  party 712
  shop 799
estafette 534
estaminet 189

estate *condition* 7
  property 780
  come to man's –
    131
esteem
  believe 484
  repute 873
  approve 931
  in high – 928
estimable 648
estimate
  measure 466
  adjudge 480
  information 527
  – *too highly* 482
estimation
  [*see* esteem,
  estimate]
estime
  succès d' – 873
estival 382
esto perpetua!
  perpetuity 112
  permanence 141
  desire 865
estop 706
estrade 213
estrange
  alienate 44, 889
  discord 713
  hate 898
estranged
  secluded 893
estrapade
  attack 716
  punishment 972
estreat 974
estuary 343
estuation 384
esurient 865
et – cetera
  add 37
  include 76
  plural 100
  – hoc genus omne
    similar 17
    include 76
    multiform 81
étalage 882
état major 745
etch *furrow* 259
  engraving 558
eternal 112
  – *home* 981
Eternal, the – 976
eterne 112
eternify 112
eternity 112
  an – 110
  launch into – 360,
    361
ether
  lightness 320
  rarity 322
  vapor 334
  anesthetic 376
ethereal 4
ethicism 984
ethics 926
Ethiopian 431
  –'s skin 150
Ethiopian's skin
  unchangeable 150
ethnology 372
ethnic 984
ethology 926
ethos 5
etiolate 429, 430

etiology *causes* 155,
  359
  knowledge 490
  disease 655
etiquette
  custom 613
  fashion 832
  ceremony 882
étoile, à la belle –
  out of doors 220
  in the air 338
Eton jacket 225
étourderie
  inattention 458
  unskilfulness 699
etymological 560
etymology 562
etymon *origin* 153
  verbal 562
Eucharist 998
euchology 998
euchre 840
eudiometer
  air 338
  salubrity 656
euge! 931
eugenics 658
eulogist 935
eulogize 482
eulogy 931
Eumenides *fury*
  900
  evil-doers 913
  revenge 919
eunuch 158
eupepsia 654
euphemism
  metaphor 521
  style 577, 578
  flattery 933
euphemist
  man of taste 850
  flatterer 935
euphony 413, 578
Euphrosyne 836
euphuism
  metaphor 521
  elegant style 577
  affected style 579
  affectation 855
Eurasian 41
eureka! 462, 480a
Euripus 343
Eurus 349
eurythmics 537,
  840
eurythmy 242
Euterpe 416
euthanasia 360
euthenics 658
evacuate
  quit 293
  excrete 295
  emit 297
evacuation 299
evade *sophistry* 477
  avoid 623
  not observe 773
  exempt 927
evagation 279
evanescent
  small 32
  transient 111
  little 193
  disappearing 449
evangelical 983a,
  985
Evangelists 985

evanid 160
evaporable 334
evaporate
  unsubstantial 4
  transient 111
  vaporize 336
evaporation 340
evasion
  sophistry 477
  concealment 528
  falsehood 544
  untruth 546
  avoidance 623
  escape 671
  cunning 702
  non-observance
    773
  dereliction 927
eve 126
  on the – of
  transient 111
  prior 116
  future 121
evection 61
even
  uniform 16
  equal 27
  still more 33
  regular 138
  level 213
  straight 246
  flat 251
  smooth 255
  although 469
  in spite of 708
  – course 628
  – now 118
  – so
  for all that 30
  yes 488
  – temper 826
  – terms 922
  – tenor
  uniform 16
  order 58
  continuity 58
  pursue the –
    tenor
  continue 143
  avoid 623
  business 625
  be – with
  retaliate 718
  pay 807
  get – with 972
even-handed 922,
  939
evening 126
  shades of – 422
  – classes 537
  – star 423
evenness 16
evensong 126, 990
event 151
  bout 720
  in the – of
  circumstance 8
  expectation 507
  supposition 514
  justified by the –
    937
eventful 151
  remarkable 642
  stirring 682
eventide 126
eventual 121
eventuality 151
eventually

effect 154
ever 16, 112
  did you – ? 870
  – and anon 136
  – changing 149
  – recurring 104
ever so 31
  – little 32
  – long 110
  – many 102
evergreen
  continuous 69
  lasting 110
  always 112
  fresh 123
everlasting 112
  – life 152
  – fire 982
evermore 112
eversion 218
evert 140
every 78
  – hand against
    one 891
  – day
  conformity 82
  frequent 136
  habit 613
  – description 81
  – inch 50
  in – mouth
  assent 488
  news 532
  repute 873
  – other 138
  in – quarter 180
  in – respect 494
  on – side 227
  at – turn 186
  – whit 52
everybody 78
everyone 78
  – his due 922
  – in his turn 148
everywhere 180,
  186
evict 297
evidence 467
  disclose 529
  ocular – 446
évidence, en – 446
evident
  concrete 3
  visible 446
  certain 474
  manifest 525
evidently 516
evil *harm* 619
  badness 649
  impious 988
  – day
  prepare for – 673
  adversity 735
  – eye *vision* 441
  malevolence 907
  disapprobation
    932
  demon 980
  sorcery 992
  spell 993
  – favored 846
  – fortune 735
  – genius 980
  – hour 135
  – one 978
  – plight 735
  through – report
    &c. 604a

– star 649
evil-doer 913
evil-doing 945
evil-minded 907,
  945
evil-speaking
  malediction 908
  censure 932
  detraction 934
evince *show* 467
  prove 478
  disclose 529
eviscerate 297, 301
eviscerated 4
evoke *cause* 153
  call upon 765
  excite 824
evolution
  numerical 85
  production 161
  motion 264
  extraction 301
  circuition 311
  turning out 313
  organization 357
  training 673
  action 680
  military –s 722
evolve
  discover 480a
evolved from 154
  [*and see*
    evolution]
evulgate 531
evulsion 301
evviva! 931
ewe 366, 374
  – lamb 366
ewer 191
ex
  – animo 602
  – cathedra 542
  – officio 494, 924
  – parte 467
  – pede Herculem
    82
  – post facto 122,
    133
  – tempore .
  instant 113
  occasion 134
exacerbate
  increase 35
  exasperate 173
  aggravate 659,
    835
exact *similar* 17
  special 79
  true 494
  style 572
  require 741
  tax 812
  insolence 885
  claim 924, 926
  – meaning 516
  – memory 505
  – observance 772
  – truth 494
exacting
  severe 739
  discontented 832
  grasping 865
  fastidious 868
exaction
  [*see* exact]
  undue 925
exactly
  just so 488

exaggeration
  increase 35
  expand 194
  overestimate 482
  magnify 549
  misrepresent 555
exalt
  increase 35
  elevate 307
  extol 931
  – one's horn 873
exalté 504
  tête –e 503
exalted *high* 206
  repute 873
  noble 875
  magnanimous
    942
examination
  [*see* examine]
  evidence 467
  undergo – 461
examine 457, 461
example
  pattern 22
  instance 82
  bad – 949
  good – 948
  make an – of 974
  set a good – 944
exanimate
  dead 360
  supine 360
exarch 745
exasperate
  exacerbate 173
  aggravate 835
  enrage 900
excavate 252
excecation 442
exceed *surpass* 33
  remain 40
  transgress 303
  intemperance 954
excel *surpass* 33
  – in *skilful* 698
excellence 648, 944
excellence, par –
    642
excellency 877
excelsior 305
except *subduct* 38
  exclude 55
  reject 610
exception
  unconformity 83
  qualification 469
  exemption 777a
  disapproval 932
  take –
  qualify 469
  resent 900
exceptionable
  bad 649
  guilty 947
exceptional
  original 20
  extraneous 57
  unconformable 83
  in an – degree 31
exceptious 901,
    901a
exceptis
  excipiendis 469
excern 297
excerpt 609
excerpta *parts* 51
  compendium 596

selections 609
excerption 609
excess
 remainder 40
 redundance 641
 intemperance 954
excessive 31
exchange
 reciprocity 12.
 interchange 148
 transfer 783
 barter 794
 mart 799
 bill of – 771
 rate of – 800
 – blows &c.
 retaliation 718
 battle 720
Exchequer 802
 Baron of – 967
 Court of – 966
 – bill 800
excise 812
exciseman 965
excision 38
excitability 825,
 901
excitation 824
excite energy 171
 violence 173
 – morally 824
 – attention 457
 – desire 865
 – hope 811
 – an impression
 375
 – love 897
excited fancy 515
excitement 824, 825
 anger 900
exclaim 411
 – against 932
exclamation 580
 mark of – 550
exclude
 leave out 42, 55
 reject 610
 prohibit 761
 banish 893
exclusion 55, 57
exclusive
 simple 42
 omitting 55
 special 79
 irregular 83
 forbidding 761
 – of 38
 – possession 777
 – thought 457
excogitate 451, 515
excommunicate
 banish 893
 curse 908
 rite 998
excoriate 226
excrement
 excretion 299
 dirt 653
excrescence
 projection 250
 blemish 848
excreta
 excretion 299
 dirt 653
excretion 297, 299
excruciating 378,
 830
exculpate

forgive 918
 vindicate 937
 acquit 970
excursion 266, 311
excursionist 268
excursive
 deviating 279
 – style 573
excursus 595
excuse plea 617
 forgive 918
 exempt 927a
 vindicate 937
execrable 649, 830
execrate 898, 908
execution
 music 416
 action 680
 conduct 692
 signing 771
 observance 772
 punishment 972
 carry into –
 complete 729
 put in –
. undertaking 676
executioner 975
executive
 conduct 692
 direction 693
 authority 737
 judicature 965
executor 690
 to one and his –s
 &c., property
 780
exegetical 522
exemplar 22
exemplary 944
exemplify
 quote 82
 illustrate 522
exempt free 748
 dispensation 927a
 – from absent 187
 unpossessed 777a
exemption
 exception 83
 qualification 469
 deliverance 692
 permission 760
 non-possession
 777a
 non-liability 927a
exenterate 297
exequatur 755
exequies 363
exercise
 operation 170
 teach 537
 task 625
 use 677
 act 680
 exert 686
 – authority 737
 – discretion 600
 – the intellect 451
 – power 157
exergue 231
exert use 677
 – authority 737
 – oneself 686
exertion 171, 686
exfoliate 226
exhalation
 ejection 297
 excretion 299
 vapor 336

breath 349
 odor 398
exhaust
 paralyze 158
 empty 195
 waste 638
 fatigue 688
 complete 729
 drain 789
 squander 818
exhausted
 inexistent 2
exhauster 349
exhaustive
 complete 52
 – inquiry 461
exhaustless
 infinite 105
 enough 639
exhibit evidence 467
 show 525
 display 882
exhilarate 836
exhort
 persuade 615
 advise 695
exhortation 998
exhume
 past times 122
 disinter 363
exigeant 739
exigency crisis 8
 requirement 630
 dearth 640
 difficulty 704
 need 865
exigent
 exacting 739
 discontented 832
exiguous 103, 193
exile
 transport 185
 banish 893
 punish 972
 voluntary – 893
exility 203
eximious 648
existence being 1
 thing 3
 – in time 118
 – in space 186
 come into – 151
exit
 departure 293
 egress 295
 disappear 449
 give – to 297
 ἐξοχήν, κατ'
 supreme 33
 important 642
exode 599
exodus 293
exogenous 367
exonerate
 disburden 705
 release 760
 forgive 918
 exempt 927a
 vindicate 937
 acquit 970
exorable 914
exorbitant
 enormous 31
 redundant 641
 dear 814
exorcise 297
exorcism 992, 993
exorcist 994

exordium 64, 66
exosmose 302
exostosis 250
exoteric 525, 531
exotic alien 10
 exceptional 83
 plant 367
expand increase 35
 swell 194
 – in breadth 202
 rarefy 322
 – in writing 573
expanse 180, 192
expansion 194
expatiate
 range 266
 – in writing &c.
 573
 – in discourse 584
expatriate 295, 893
expect
 look forward to
 507
 hope 858
 not wonder 871
 future 121
 reason to – 472
expectance 871
expectancy 780
expectante,
 médecine –
 wait 133
 remedy 662
expectation 507
 beyond – 508
 hold out an – 768
expected
 as well as can be –
 654
expectorate 297
expedience 646
expedient
 plan 626
 means 632
 useful 646
 temporary – 147
expedite early 132
 quickening 274
 hasten 684
 aid 707
expedition
 [see expedite]
 march 266
 activity 682
 war 722
expel push 284
 eject 297
 punish 972
expend waste 638
 use 677
 pay 809
 – itself 683
expenditure 809
expense price 812
 joke at one's –
 842
 spare no – 816
expenseless 315
expenses 806
expensive 814
experience
 meet with 151
 knowledge 490
 undergo 821
 learn by – 950
experienced 698
 – eye &c. 700
experiences

narrative 594
experiment 463,
 675
Experimental
 Philosophy 316
experimentum
 crucis test 463
 proof 478
expert 698, 700
expiate 952
expire end 67
 run its course 109
 die 360
expired past 122
explain 462, 522
 – away 523
explainer 524
expletive 573, 641
explication 522
explicit clear 518
 potent 525
explode.burst 173
 confute 479
 failure 732
 passion 825
exploded past 122
 antiquated 124
 error 495
 blown upon 932
exploit 680, 861
exploitation 461
explore 461, 463
explorer 268
explosion
 [see explode]
 revolution 146
 violence 173
 sound 406
 anger 900
explosive
 dangerous 665
 ammunition 727
exponent
 numerical 84
 interpreter 524
 informant 527
 index 550
export 295
expose denude 226
 confute 479
 disclose 529
 censure 932
 – to danger 665
 – oneself
 disreputable 874
 – to view
 visible 446
 manifest 525
exposé
 disclosure 529
 description 594
exposed to
 liable 177
exposition [see
 expose]
 explanation 522
expositor 524, 540
expository
 explaining 522
 informing 527
 describing 594
 disserting 595
expostulate
 dissuade 616
 advise 695
 deprecate 766
 reprehend 932
exposure [see

expose]
appearance 448
- to weather 338
expound
  interpret 522
  teach 537
expounder 524
express
  rapid 274
  squeeze out 301
  mean 516
  declare 525
  inform 527
  journal 531
  intentional 620
  by - haste 684
  - train 272
  - by words 566
expressed, well -
  578
expressible 525
expression [see
  express]
  musical 416
  aspect 448
  nomenclature 564
  phrase 566
  mode of - 569
  new fangled - 563
expressive
  meaning 516
  sensibility 822
exprobation 932,
  938
expropriation 782
expugnable 665
expugnation 731
expulsion 55 [see
  expel]
expunge 162, 552
expurgate 38, 652
expurgatorious,
  index - 761
exquisite
  savory 394
  excellent 648
  pleasurable 829
  beautiful 845
  fop 854
exquisitely 31
exsiccate 340
exsudation 299
exsufflation 993
exsuscitate 824
extant 1
extasy [see ecstasy]
extemporaneous
  [see extempore]
  transient 111
extempore
  instant 113
  early 132
  occasion 134
  off-hand 612
  unprepared 674
extend
  expand 194
  prolong 200
  - to 196
extended 202
extensibility 324
extensile 324
extension [see
  extend] 35, 142,
  180
  - of time 110
extensive 31, 180
  - knowledge 490

extenso, in -
  whole 50
  diffuse 573
extent 26, 180
extenuate
  decrease 36
  weaken 160
  excuse 937
extenuated 203
extenuating cir-
  cumstances
  469, 937
extenuatory 469
exteriority 220
exterminate 162
extermination 301
external 57, 220
  - evidence 467
  - senses 375
extinct
  inexistent 2
  past 122
  destroyed 162
  darkness 421
  become - 4
extincteur 385
extinction of life
  360
extinguish
  destroy 162
  blow out 385
  darken 421
extinguisher 165
  put an - upon
  hinder 706
  defeat 731
extirpate 301
extispicious 511
extol
  over-estimate 482
  praise 931
extort extract 301
  compel 744
  despoil 789
extorted
  dissent 489
extortion 814, 819
extortionate 739,
  865
extra 37, 599, 641
  ab - 220
extract
  draw off 297
  take out 301
  quotation 596
  remedy 662
extraction 301
  paternity 166
  - of roots 85
extractor 301
extradition 270, 297
extrajudicial 964
extramundane 317
extramural 220
extraneous
  extrinsic 6
  not related 10
  foreign 57
  outside 220
extraneousness 57
extraordinary
  great 31
  exceptional 83
extraregarding 220
extravagant
  inordinate 31
  violent 173
  absurd 497

foolish 499
  fanciful 515
  exaggerated 549
  excessive 641
  high-priced 814
  prodigal 818
  vulgar 851
  ridiculous 853
extravagation 303
extravaganza
  fanciful 515
  drama 599
extravasate 295,
  297
extreme
  inordinate 31
  end 67
  - unction 998
extremis, in -
  dying 360
  difficulty 704
extremist 710
extremity end 67
  adversity 735
  tribulation 828
  drive matters to
  an - 604
  at the last - 665
extricate
  take out 301
  deliver 672
  facilitate 705
  liberate 750
extrinsicality 6
extrinsic evidence
  467
extrusion 297, 299
exuberant
  - style 573
  redundant 639
exudation 295, 299
exulcerate 659
exult 838, 884
exultant 858
exulting 836
exunge 356
exuviae 653
eye circle 247
  opening 260
  organ of sight 441
  all my - and
  Betty Martin
  546
  appear to one's
  - 446
  before one's -s
  front 234
  visible 446
  manifest 525
  cast the -s on
  see 441
  cast the -s over
  attend to 457
  catch the - 457
  close the -s
  blind 442
  death 360
  sleep 683
  dry -s 823
  fix the -s on 457
  have an - to
  attention 457
  intention 620
  desire 865
  in one's -
  visible 446
  expectant 507
  in the -s of

appearance 448
  belief 484
  keep an - upon
  459
  look with one's
  own -s 459
  make -'s at 441
  mind's - 515
  with moistened -s
  839
  open the -s to
  480a
  with open -s 870
  set one's -s upon
  865
  shut one's -s to
  inattention 458
  permit 760
  to the -s 448
  under the -s of
  186
  up to one's -s
  641
  have one's -s
  about one 459
  - askance 860
  -s draw straws 683
  an - for an - 718,
  919
  - glistening 824
  in the - of the law
  963
  - of the master
  693
  - of a needle 260
  -s open
  attention 457
  care 459
  intention 620
  -s opened
  disclosure 529
  -s out 442
eye-ball 441
eyebrows 256
eyeglass 445
eyelashes 256
eyeless 442
eyelet 260
eyelid 223
eye-shade 443
eye-sight 441
eyesore 846, 848
eye-teeth
  have cut one's -
  adolescence 131
  skill 698
  cunning 702
eye-wash 544
eye-witness
  spectator 444
  evidence 467
eyot 346
eyre 966
eyry 189

F

Fabian policy
  delay 133
  inaction 681
  caution 864
fable error 495
  metaphor 521
  fiction 546
  description 590
fabric state 7
  effect 154

texture 329
fabricate
  composition 54
  make 161
  invent 515
  falsify 544
fabrication lie 546
fabula narratur, de
  te - retaliate 718
  condemn 971
fabulist 594
fabulous
  enormous 31
  imaginary 515
  untrue 546
  exaggerated 549
faburden 413
façade 234
face exterior 220
  covering 223
  front 234
  aspect 448
  oppose 708
  resist 719
  brave 861
  impudence 885
  change the - of
  146
  fly in the - of
  disobey 742
  put a good - upon
  sham 545
  calm 826
  cheerful 836
  hope 858
  pride 878
  display 882
  vindicate 93
  in the - of
  presence 186
  opposite 708
  look in the -
  see 441
  proud 878
  make -s
  distort 243
  ugly 846
  disrespect 929
  on the - of
  manifest 525
  show -
  present 186
  visible 446
  not show -
  disreputable 874
  bashful 879
  to one's - 525
  wry - 378
  - about 279
  set one's - against
  708
  - of the country
  344
  on the - of the
  earth
  space 180
  world 318
  - to face front 234
  contraposition
  237
  manifest 525
  - of the thing
  appearance 448
facet 220
facetiae 842
facetious 842
facia 234
facile willing 602

irresolute 605
easy 705
facile princeps 33
facilis descensus
Averni
sloping 217
danger 665
facilitate 705
facility skill 698
easy 705
facing covering 223
facinorous 945
façon de parler 521,
549
fac-simile 21, 554
fact existence 1
event 151
certainty 474
truth 494
in – 535
faction 712, 713
factious 24
factitious 545, 546
factor
numerical 84
director 694
consignee 758
factory 691
factotum
agent 690
manager 694
employé 758
facts evidence 467
summary of – 594
at variance with –
471
facula 420
faculties 450
in possession of
one's – 502
faculty
power 157
profession 625
skill 698
facundity 582
fad 481, 608
faddle 683
fade vanish 4
transient 111
become old 124
droop 160
grow dim 422
lose color 429
disappear 449
spoil 659
– from the
memory 506
fade 391
fadge 23
faex populi 876
fag cigarette 392
labor 686
fatigue 688
drudge 690, 746
– end
remainder 40
end 67
faggot 72, 388
fagots et fagots 15,
465
faïence 557
fail droop 160
shórtcoming 304
be confuted 479
illness 655
not succeed 732

not observe 773
not pay 808
dereliction 927
failing [see fail]
incomplete 53
insufficient 640
vice 945
guilt 947
– heart 837
– luck 735
– memory 506
– sight 443
– strength 160
failure 732
heart – 360
fain willing 602
compulsive 744
wish 865
fainéant 683
faint
small in degree 32
impotent 158
weak 160
sound 405
dim 422
color 429
swoon 688
– heart fear 860
cowardice 862
damn with –
praise 930, 932,
934
faintness 405
fair in degree 31
pale 429
white 430
wise 498
important 643
good 648
moderate 651
mart 799
beautiful 845
just 922
honorable 939
– chance 472
– copy copy 21
writing 590
– field
occasion 134
– game 857
by – means 631,
940
– name 873
– play 922, 923
– question 461
– sex 374
in a – way
tending 176
probable 472
convalescent 658
prosperous 734
hopeful 858
– weather 734
– weather sailor
701
– wind 705
– words 894
fairing 784
fairly
intrinsically 5
get on – 736
– well 643
fair-spoken
courtesy 894
flattery 933
fairy fanciful 515
fay 979

imp 980
– godmother 711,
784, 912
– tale 545, 594
fairy-land 515
fait: au –
knowledge 490
skilful 698
– accompli
certain 474
complete 729
faith belief 484
hope 858
honor 939
piety 987
declaration of –
983
bad – 544
i' – 535
keep – with
observe 772
plight –
promise 768
love 902
true –
orthodox 983a
want of –
incredulity 487
irreligious 989
– healing 662
faithful [see faith]
like 17
copy 21
exact 494
obedient 743
– memory 505
– to 772
faithless false 544
dishonorable 940
sceptical 989
fake 544, 545
fakir 996
falcate 244, 245
falchion 727
falciform
[see falcate]
falcon 792
falconet 727
faldstool 215
fall autumn 126
happen 151
perish 162
slope 217
regression 283
descend 306
die 360
fail 732
adversity 73
vice 945
let – lower 308
inform 527
water– 348
– asleep 683
– astern 235, 283
– away 105
– back return 283
recede 287
relapse 661
– back upon 677,
717
have to – back
upon 637
– a cursing 908
– of the curtain 67
– into a custom 82
– of day 125
– dead 360

– into decay 659
– down 990
– down before 928
– upon the ear 418
– flat on the ear
843
– at one's feet 725
– foul of blow 276
hinder 706
oppose 708
discord 713
attack 716
contention 720
censure 932
– for 897
– to the ground
be confuted 479
fail 732
– into a habit 613
– from one's high
estate
adversity 735
disrepute 874
– in order 58
continuity 69
event 151
– into
conversion 144
river 348
– in with agree 23
conform 82
converge 2
discover 480a
concord 714
consent 762
– on one's knees
submit 725
servile 886
gratitude 916
worship 990
– of the leaf 126
– from the lips 582
– in love with 897
– to one's lot
event 151
chance 156
receive 785
duty 926
– under one's
notice 457
– into oblivion 506
– off decrease 36
deteriorate 659
– off again 661
– out happen 151
quarrel 713
enmity 889
– into a passion
900
– to pieces
disjunction 44
destruction 162
brittle 328
– a prey to 732,
749
– in price 815
– into raptures
827
– short inferior 32
contract 195
shortcoming 304
– of snow 383
– through fail 734
– to eat 298
take in hand 676
do battle 722
– into a trap 547

– under
inclusion 76
subjection 749
– upon
discover 480a
unexpected 508
devise 626
attack 716
– in the way of 186
– to work 686
fallacy sophistry
477
error 495
show the – of 497
fallen angel 949,
978
fallible 475, 477
falling-out 24
falling star 318, 423
fallow
unproductive 169
yellow 436
unready 674
inactive 681
false imitation 10
sophistry 477
error 495
untrue 544, 546
spurious 925
dishonorable 940
– alarm 669
– coloring
misinterpretation
523
falsehood 544
– construction
523, 544
– doctrine 984
– expectation 509
– hearted 940
– impression 495
– light vision 443
– money 800
– ornament 851
– plea untruth 546
plea 617
– position 704
– pretences 791
– prophet
disappoint 509
pseudo-revelation
986
– reasoning 477
– scent 495, 538
– shame 855
– statement 546
– step 732
– teaching 538
– witness
deceiver 548
detraction 934
falsehood 544, 546
falsetto squeak 410
want of voice 581
falsify error 495
falsehood 544,
546
– accounts 811
– one's hope 509
falter slow 275
stammer 583
hesitate 605
slip 732
hopeless 859
fear 860
faltering accents
605

fame *greatness* 31
  news 532
  renown 873
familiar
  known 490
  habitual 613
  sociable 892
  affable 894
  – *spirit* 979, 980
  on – *terms* 888
familiarize
  teach 537
  habit 613
famille, en – 892
family
  kin 11
  class 75
  ancestors 166
  posterity 167
  party 712
  in the bosom of
    one's – 221
  happy – 714
  – *circle* 892
  – *jars* 713
  – *likeness* 17
  – *tie* 11
  in the – *way* 161
famine 640
  – *price* 814
famine-stricken
  640
famish
  stingy 819
  fasting 956
famished
  insufficient 640
  hungry 865
famous 873
famously 31
fan *blow* 349
  cool 385
  refresh 689
  stimulate 824
  flirt a – 855
  – the embers 505
  – the flame
    violence 173
    heat 384
    aid 707
    excite 824
  – into a flame
    anger 900
  –shaped 194
fanatic
  madman 504
  imaginative 515
  zealot 682
  religious – 988
fanatical
  misjudging 481
  insane 503
  emotional 821
  excitable 825
  heterodox 984
  over-righteous 988
fanaticism 606
fanciful
  imaginative 515
  capricious 608
  ridiculous 853
fancy *think* 451
  idea 453
  believe 484
  suppose 514
  imagine 515
  caprice 608

choice 609
pugilism 726
wit 842
desire 865
wonder 870
love 897
after one's – 850
indulge one's –
  609
take a – to
  delight in 827
  desire 865
take one's –
  please 829
– *dog* 366
– *dress* 840
– *price* 814
– *woman* 962
fandango 840
fandi, mollia tem-
  pora – 588
fane 1000
fanfare *loudness*
  404
  celebration 883
fanfaron 887
fanfaronnade 884
fangs *venom* 663
  rule 737
  retention 781
fan-light 260
fan-like 202
fannel 999
fanon 999
fantasia 415
fantastic *odd* 83
  absurd 497
  imaginative 515
  capricious 608
  unfashionable 851
  ridiculous 853
fantasy
  imagination 515
  desire 865
fantoccini 554, 599
faquir 996
far – *away* 196
  – be it from
    unwilling 603
    deprecation 766
  – between
    disjunction 44
    few 103
    interval 198
  – from it
    unlike 18
    shortcoming 304
    no 536
  – from the truth
    546
  – and near 180
  – off 196
  – and wide 31,
    180, 196
farce
  absurdity 497
  untruth 546
  drama 599
  wit 842
  ridiculous 853
  mere –
    unimportant 643
    useless 645
farceur
  actor 599
  humorist 844
fardel

bundle 72
hindrance 706
fare *state* 7
  food 298
  price 812
  bill of –
    list 86
farewell
  departure 293
  relinquishment
    624
  loss 776
  – to greatness 874
far-famed 873
far-fetched 10
far-flung 73
far-gone
  much 31
  insane 503
  spoiled 654
farinaceous 330
farm *till* 371
  property 780
  rent 788
farmer 188, 342,
  371
  afternoon – 683
farm-house 189
Farmer-Labor 712
faro 840
farrago 59
farrier 370
farrow
  produce 161
  litter 167
  multitude 102
far-sighted 442, 510
farther 196
  [and see **further**]
farthing
  quarter 97
  worthless 643
  coin 800
  – *candle* 422
farthingale 225
fasces 747
fascia 205, 247
fascicule 51
fasciculated 72
fascinate
  influence 615
  excite 824
  please 829
  astonish 870
  love 897
  conjure 992
fascinated
  pleased 827
fascination [*see*
  fascinate]
  infatuation 825
  desire 870
fascine 72
Fascisti 712
fas et nefas, per –
  604a, 631
fash 830
fashion
  state 7
  form 240
  custom 613
  method 627
  ton **852**
  after a –
    middling 32
  after this – 617
  follow the – 82

be in the – 488
man of – 852
set the –
  influence 175
  authority 737
for –'s sake 852
fast *joined* 43
  steadfast 150
  rapid 274
  fashionable 852
  intemperate 954
  not eat 956
  worship 990
  rite 998
  stick – 704
  – *asleep* 683
  – *by* 197
  – *day* 956
  – *friend* 890
  – and loose
    sophistry 477
    falsehood 544
    irresolute 605
    tergiversation 607
    caprice 608
  – man *fop* 854
    libertine 962
fasten *join* 43
  hang 214
  restrain 751
  – on the mind 451
  – a quarrel upon
    713
  – upon 789
fastening 45
fast-handed 819
fastidious
  censorious 932
fastidiousness **868**
fasting
  insufficiency 640
  worship 990
  penance 952
  abstinence **956**
fastness
  asylum 666
  defence 717
fat *corpulent* 192
  expansion 194
  unctuous 355
  oleaginous 356
  kill the –ted calf
    celebration 883
    sociality 892
  – in the fire
    disorder 59
    violence 173
  – of the land
    pleasure 377
    enough 639
    prosperity 734
    intemperance 95
fata – Morgana
  occasion 134
  ignis fatuus 423
  – *obstant* 601
fatal 361
  – *disease* 655
fatalism 601
fatality 601
fate *end* 67
  necessity 601
  chance 621
  be one's – 156
  sure as – 474
Fates 601, 979
fat-head 501

father *eldest* 128
  paternity 166
  priest 996
  Apostolical –s 985
  gathered to one's
    –s 360
  heavy – 599
  – upon 155
Father, God the –
  976
fatherland 189
fatherless 158
fatherly 906
fathom
  length 200
  investigate 461
  solve 462
  measure 466
  discover 480a
  knowledge 490
fathomless 208
fatidical 511
fatigation 688
fatigue **688**
fatras 643
fatten
  expand 194
  improve 658
  prosperous 734
  – on *parasite* 886
  – upon
    feed 298
fatuity 4, 499
fatuous 517
fat-witted 499
faubourg 227
fauces 231
faucet 252
faugh! 867
fault
  break 70
  error 495
  imperfection 651
  failure 732
  vice 945
  guilt 947
  at –
    uncertain 475
    ignorant 491
    unskilful 699
  find – with 932
faultless 650, 946
faulty 495, 651
faun 980
fauna 366
faut: comme il –
  taste 850
  fashion 852
  il s'en – bien 489
  tant s'en – 536
faute 732
  – de mieux
    substitution 147
    necessity 601
fauteuil 215
fautor 890
faux pas
  error 568
  failure 732
  misconduct 947
  intrigue 961
favor
  resemble 16
  badge 550
  letter 592
  aid 707
  indulgence 740

permit 760
gift 784
partiality 923
appearances in –
of 472
get into –
friendship 888
love 897
in – repute 873
approbation 931
in – of
approve 931
under – of 760
view with – 906
– with 784
favorable
occasion 134
willing 602
good 648
aid 707
– prospect 472
– to 709
take a – turn
improve 658
prosperity 734
favorably
well 618
favorer 890
favorite
pleasing 829
beloved 897, **899**
favoritism
friendship 888
wrong 923
fawn color 433
cringe 749, 886
flatter 993
fay 979
fealty
obedience 743
duty 926
respect 928
fear 860
fearful
painful 830
timid 862
fearfully 31, 870
fearless hope 858
courage 861
fearsome 860
feasible 470, 705
feast period 138
repast 298
pleasure 377
revel 840
rite 998
– one's eyes 897
feast of reason
conversation 588
– and flow of soul
sociality 892
feat action 680
courage 861
– of arms 720
– of strength 159
feather
class 75
tuft 256
light 320
trifle 643
ornament 847
decoration 877
in full –
prepared 673
prosperous 734
rich 803
hear a – drop 403

in high –
health 654
cheerful 884
pleased with a –
840
– in one's cap
honor 873
decoration 877
– one's nest
prepare 673
prosperity 734
wealth 803
economy 817
selfish 943
– the oar 698
– in the scale 643
feather-bed 324
feathered tribes
366
feathery 256
featly 682
feature
character 5
component 56
form 240
appearance 448
press 531
lineament 550
– in 56
features
face 234
febrifuge 662
febrile 382, 825
fecal 653
feces 299, 653
fecit 556
feckless 866
feculence 653
fecund 168
fecundate 161
federal council 696
– penitentiary 752
federalism 737
federation 48, 709,
712
fee possession 777
property 780
pay 809
reward 973
feeble weak 160
illogical 477
feeble-minded 497,
605
feebleness
style 575
feed eat 298
supply 637
– the flame 707
fee-faw-fum
bugbear 860
spell 993
feel sense 375
touch 379
emotion 821
– for try 463
benevolence 906
pity 914
condole with 915
– the pulse 461
– the want of 865
– one's way
essay 675
caution 864
feeler 379
inquiry 461
experiment 463
feeling 698, **821**

feet low 207
walkers 266
at one's –
near 197
subjection 749
humility 879
fall at one's –
submit 725
fall on one's –
prosper 734
lick the – of
servile 886
light upon one's
safe 664
spring to one's –
307
throw oneself at
the – of
entreat 765
feign 544, 546
feigned 545
feint 545
felicitas, curiosa –
698
felicitate 896
felicitous
agreeing 23
- style 578
skilful 698
successful 731
pleasant 829
felicity 827
feline cat 366
stealthy 528
cunning 702
fell destroy 162
mountain 206
lay flat 21
skin 223
lay low 308
moor 344
dire 860
malevolent 907
fellah 876
felloe 231
fellow similar 17
equal 27
companion 88
dual 89
man 373
scholar 492, 541
fellow-commoner
541
fellow-companion
890
fellow-countryman
890
fellow-creature 372
fellow-feeling
friendship 888
love 897
benevolence 906
pity 914
fellowship
partnership 712
distinction 873
friendship 888
companionship
890
good – 892
fellow-student 541
fellow-worker 690
felly 231
felo-de-se 361
felon 949
felonious 945
felony 947

felt texture 219
heart– 821
felucca 273
female 374
feme coverte 903
feme sole 904
femininity
weakness 160
woman 374
feminine 374
feminism 374
femme de chambre
746
fen 345
fence enclose 232
evade 544
defence 717
fight 720
prison 752
thief 792
– round 229
– with a question
528
fenced 770
fenceless 665
fencible 726
fencing 840
feneration 787
fend 717
fender 717
Fenian 710, 742
fenum habet in
cornu 668, 913
feodal 780
feodality 737, 777
feoff property 780
feoffee 779, 785
feoffer 784
ferae naturae 366
feral 907
ferine 907
ferment
disorder 59
energy 171
violence 173
agitation 315
lightness 320
effervesce 353
emotion 821
excitement 824,
825
anger 900
fermentation,
acetous – 397
fern 367
ferocity 173, 907
Ferrara
sword 727
ferret out 461, 480a
ferro-concrete 635
ferrule 223
ferry 270, 627
ferry-boat 273
ferry-man 269
fertile 161, 168
– imagination 515
ferule 975
come under the –
932
fervent hot 382
desirous 865
– hope 858
fervid hot 382
heartfelt 821
excited 824
fervour heat 382
animation 821
love 897

festal eating 298
social 892
fester 653, 655
festina lente 864
festival
music 416
celebration 883
festivity 840, 892
festoon 245, 847
fetch bring 270
arrive 292
evasion 545
sell for 812
– one a blow
strike 276
attack 716
– and carry
servile 886
– a sigh 839
fête 840, 882
fêté 892
fetishism 992
fetid 401
fetish 991, 993
fetter 751, 752
fettle 673
state 5
prepare 673
in fine – 159, 654
fetus 129, 153
feu
– d'enfer 716
– de joie
amusement 840
celebration 883
feud discord 713
possess 777
property 780
death – 919
feudal 737, 780
feudatory 749
feuilleton 593
fever heat 382
disease 655
excitement 825
feverish hurry 684
animated 821
excited 824
few
a – 100
– and far between
70
– words
concise 572
taciturn 585
compendium 596
fewness 103
fey 360
fez 225
fiancée 897
fiasco 732
fiat 741
– money 800
fib falsehood 544,
546
thump 720
fiber link 45
filament 205
moral – 60
fickle 149, 605
fictile 240
fiction untruth 546
work of – 594
fictitious 515, 546
fiddle 416, 417
fiddle-de-dee
absurd 497

unimportant 643
  contempt 930
fiddlefaddle
  unmeaning 517
  trifle 643
  dawdle 683
fiddler 416
fiddlestick 417
  - end 643
fidelity
  veracity 543
  obedience 743
  observance 772
  honor 939
fidget *changes* 149
  activity 682
  hurry 684
  excitability 825
fidgety
  irresolute 605
  fearful 860
  irascible 901
fiducial 156
fiduciary 484
fidus Achates
  auxiliary 711
  associate 743
  friend 890
fie *disreputable* 874
  - upon it
  censure 932
fief 777
field *opportunity*
  134
  scope 180
  region 181
  plain 344
  agriculture 371
  business 625
  arena 728
  property 780
  the - *hunting* 622
  beasts of the - 366
  playing -s 728
  the potter's - 361
  take the - 722
  - artillery 726
  the - of blood 361
  - of inquiry
    topic 454
    inquiry 461
  - of view
    vista 441
    idea 453
field-day
  contention 720
  amusement 840
  display 882
field-glass 445
field-marshal 745
field-piece 727
field-preacher 996
field-work 717
fiend 913, 980
fiend-like
  malevolent 907
  wicked 945
  fiend 980
fierce *violent* 173
  passion 825
  daring 861
  angry 900
fiery *violent* 173
  hot 382
  strong feeling 821
  excitable 825
  angry 900
  irascible 901

- cross 550, 722
- furnace 386
- imagination 515
- ordeal 828
fife 417
fifer 416
fifth 98, 99
fifty 98
fig
  unimportance 643
  in the name of the
    prophet -s! 497
  - out 847
fight
  contention 720
  warfare 722
  show -
    defence 717
    courage 861
  - one's battles
    again 594
  - against destiny
    606
  - the good fight
    944
  - it out 722
  - shy *avoid* 603,
    623
  coward 862
  - one's way
    pursue 622
    active 682
    exertion 686
fighter 726
fighting-cock 726,
  861
fighting-man 726
figment 515
figurante 599
figurate number 84
figuration 240
figurative
  metaphorical 521
  representing 554
  - *style* 577
figure
  number 84
  form 240
  appearance 448
  metaphor 521
  indicate 550
  represent 554
  price 812
  ugly 846
  cut a -
    repute 873
    display 882
  poor - 874
  - to oneself 515
  - of speech 521
  - out 522
  exaggeration 549
figure-flinger 994
figure-head 4, 550,
  554, 643
figurine 554
figuriste 559
filaceous 205
filament 205
filamentous 256
filch 791
filcher 762
file *subduct* 38
  arrange 60
  row 69
  assemblage 72
  list 86
  reduce 195

smooth 255
  pulverize 330
  record 551
  store 636
  soldiers 726
  - a claim &c. 969
  - off *march* 266
  diverge 291
file-fire 716
filial 167
filiation
  consanguinity 11
  attribution 155
  posterity 167
filibuster 133, 706,
  792
filibustering 791
filiform 205
filigree 219
filings 330
fill *complete* 52
  occupy 186
  contents 190
  stuff 224
  provision 637
  eat one's - 957
  have one's -
    enough 639
    satiety 869
  - the bill 229
  - an office
    business 625
    government 737
  - out
    expand 194
    -ed to overflow-
      ing 641
  - one's pocket 803
  - time 106
  - up *compensate*
    30
    compose 54
    close 261
    restore 660
  - up the time
    inaction 681
fille
  - de chambre 746
  - de joie 962
filled
  - to overflowing
    641
filler 532
fillet *band* 45
  filament 205
  circle 247
  insignia 550
  ornament 847
fillibeg 225
filling 224
fillip
  impulse 276
  propulsion 284
  stimulus 615
  excite 824
filly 271
film *layer* 204
  opaque 426
  semitransparent
    427
  - over the eyes
    dim sight 443
    cinema 448
    ignorant 491
filmy *texture* 329
filter *percolate* 295
  clean 652
filth 653

-y lucre 800
filtrate 652
fimbriated 256
fin 267
final *ending* 67
  conclusive 474
  completing 729
  court of - appeal
    474
  - cause 620
  - stroke 729
  - touch 729
finale *end* 67
  completion 729
finality 67, 729
finally
  for good 141
  on the whole 476
finance 800, 811
  minister of - 801
financier 801
finch 366
find
  eventuality 151
  adjudge 480
  discover 480a
  acquire 775
  - one's account in
    644
  - the cause of 522
  - a clue to 480a
  - to one's cost 509
  - credence 484
  - it in one's heart
    602
  - in *provide* 637
  - the key of 522
  - the meaning 522
  - means 632
  - oneself *be* 1
    present 186
  - out 480a
  - vent 671
  - one's way 731
  - one's way into
    294
finding
  judgment 480
fine *small* 32
  large 192
  thin 203
  rare 322
  not raining 340
  exact 494
  good 648
  beautiful 845
  adorned 847
  proud 878
  mulct 974
  in - *end* 67
  after all 476
  - air 656
  - arts 554
  - feather 159, 654
  - feeling 850
  - frenzy 515
  - gentleman
    fop 854
    proud 878
  - grain 329
  - lady 854, 878
  one - morning 106
  some - morning
    119
  - powder 330
  - talking
    overrate 482

boast 884
  - writing 577
  - time of it 734
  - voice 580
fine-draw 660
fine-fingered 698
fine-spoken 894,
  933
fine-spun *thin* 203
  sophistry 477
fine-toned 413
finem, respicere -
  510
finery 847, 851
finesse *tact* 698
  artifice 702
  taste 850
finger *touch* 379
  hold 781
  lay the - on
    point out 457
    discover 480a
  lift a - 680
  not lift a - 681
  point the - at 457
  turn round one's
    little - 737
  -'s breadth 203
  at one's -s' end
    near 197
    know 490
    remember 505
  - on the lips
    aphony 581
    taciturnity 585
  - in the pie
    cause 153
    interfere 228
    act 680
    active 682
    co-operate 709
fingerling 193
finger-post 550
finger-print 467
finger-stall 223
fingle-fangle 643
finical
  trifling 643
  affected 855
  fastidious 868
finicky 855, 868
finikin 643
finis 67
  - coronat opus
    729
finish *lend* 67
  symmetry 242
  complete 729
  skill 698
finished
  absolute 31
  perfect 650
  skilled 698
finishing
  - stroke 361
  - touch 729
finite 32
fiord 343
fire *energy* 171
  heat 382
  make hot 384
  stoke 388
  vigor 574
  discharge 756
  enthusiasm 821
  excite 824, 825
  catch - 384

hell – 982
on – 382
open – *begin* 66
play with – 863
signal – 550
take –
  excitable 825
  angry 900
between two –s
  665
under – 665, 722
 – at 716
 – the blood 824
 – and fury 900
 – the first shot 716
 – of genius 498
 – off 284
 – a salute 883
 – and sword 162
 – up *excite* 825
  anger 900
 – a volley 716
go through – and
  water
  resolution 604
  perseverance 604a
  courage 861
fire-alarm 669
fire-annihilator 385
fire-arms 727
fire-ball *fuel* 388
  arms 727
fire-balloon 273
fire-barrel 388
fire-bell 669
fire-boat 726
fire-brand
  fuel 388
  instigator 615
  dangerous man
   667
  incendiary 913
fire-brigade 385
fire-curtain 599
fire-drake 423
fire-eater
  fighter 726
  blusterer 887
fire-eating
  rashness 863
  insolence 885
fire-engine 348
fire-escape 671
fire-extinguisher
  385
fire-fly 423
fireless cooker 386
fire-light 422
firelock 727
fireman *stoker* 268
  extinguisher 385
fire-place 386
fire-proof 385, 644
fireside 189
firewood 388
firework
  fire 382
  luminary 423
  celebration 883
  amusement 840
fire-worship 991
fire-worshipper 984
firing *fuel* 388
  explosion 406
firkin 191
firm
  junction 43

stable 150
hard 323
resolute 604
partnership 712
merchant 797
brave 861
stand – 719
 – as a rock 604
 – belief 484
 – hold 781
firmament 318
firman 741, 760
first 66
 – blush
morning 125
leading 280
vision 441
appearance 448
manifest 525
 – blow 716
 – cause 976
 – that comes 609a
 – fiddle
  importance 642
  proficient 700
  authority 737
 – come first
  served 609a
 – and foremost 66
 – impression 66
 – and last 87
 – line 234
come back to –
  love 607
 – move 66
 – opportunity 132
at – sight 448
 – stage 66
 – stone
  preparation 673
  attack 716
on the – summons
  741
of the – water
  best 648
  repute 873
first-born 124 128
first-fruits 154
first-hand 20, 467
firstlings 128, 154
first-rate
  important 642
  excellent 648
  man-of-war 726
firth 343
fisc 802
fiscal 800
fish *food* 298
  sport 361, 622
  animal 366
food for –es 362
other – to fry
  ill-timed 135
  busy 682
queer – 857
 – in the air 645
 – for compliments
  880
 – for *seek* 4
  experiment 463
  desire 865
 – hatchery 370
 – out *inquire* 461
  discover 480a
 – in troubled
  waters
  difficult 704

discord 713
 – up *raise* 307
  find 480a
 – out of water
  disagree 24
  unconformable 83
  displaced 185
  bungler 701
fisherman 361
fishery 370
fishing *kill* 361
  pursue 622
fishing-boat 273
fishpond 343, 370
fish-trail 267
fishy *transaction*
  940
fisk 266, 274
fissile 328
fission 44
fissure 44
  chink 198
fist
  handwriting 590
  grip 781
shake the –
  defy 515
  threat 909
fisticuffs 720
fistula 260
fit *state* 7
  agreeing 23
  equal 27
  paroxysm 173
  agitation 315
  caprice 608
  expedient 646
  healthy 654
  disease 655
  excitement 825
  anger 900
  right 922
  due 924
  duty 926
in –s 315
 – think – 600
 – of abstraction
  458
 – of crying 839
 – for 698
 – out *dress* 225
  prepare 673
 – to be seen 845
by –s and starts
  irregular 59
  discontinuous 70
  agitated 315
  capricious 608
  haste 684
fitful
  irregular 139
  changeable 149
  capricious 608
fittings 633
five 98
  division by – 99
 – act play 599
 – and twenty 98
Five Year Plan 626
fiver 800
fives *game* 840
fix *join* 43
  arrange 60
  establish 150
  place 184
  immovable 265
  solidify 321

resolve 604
difficulty 704
 – the eyes upon
  441
 – the foundations
  673
 – the memory 505
 – the time 114
 – the thoughts
  457
 – up 774
 – upon *discover*
  480a
  choose 609
fixed *intrinsic* 5
  permanent 141
  stable 150
  quiescent 265
  habitual 613
 – idea 481
 – opinion 484
 – periods 138
fixity 141
fixity of purpose
  141
fixture
  appointment 741
  property 780
fizgig 423
fizz 409
fizzle 353
 – out 304
flabelliform 194
flabbergast 870
  879
flabby 324
flabbiness 324
flaccid *weak* 160
  soft 324
  empty 640
flag *weak* 160
  flat stone 204
  floor 211
  smoothness 255
  slow 275
  leaf 367
  sign 550
  path 627
  infirm 655
  inactive 683
  tired 688
  weary 841
lower one's – 725
  red – *alarm* 669
  yellow –
   warning 668
   alarm 669
 – man 668
 – ship 726
 – of truce 723
flag-bearer 534
flagellation
  penance 952
  asceticism 955
  flogging 972
  rile 998
flagelliform 205
flageolet 417
flagitious 945
flagon 191
flagrant
  great 31
  manifest 525
  notorious 531
  atrocious 945
flagrante
 – *bello* 722

 – *delicto*
  sure enough 474
  act 680
  guilt 947
flagration 384
flagstaff *tall* 206
  signal 550
flail 276
flair 450, 698
flake 204
  snow – 383
  – white 430
flam 544
flambé 732
flambeau 423
flamboyant 577
flame *fire* 382
  light 420
  luminary 423
  passion 824, 825
  love 897
  catch the –
   emotion 821
  consign to the –s
   384
  add fuel to the –
   173
  in –s 382
  – up 825
  –colored
   red 434
   orange 439
flame-projector 527
flamen 996
flaming *violent* 173
  feeling 821
  excited 824
  ostentatious 882
  boasting 884
flâneur 935
flange *support* 215
  rim 231
  projection 250
flank *side* 236
  protect 664
flannel 384
flap *adjunct* 39
  hanging 214
  move to and fro
   315
  – the memory 505
flapdoodle 517
flapper *girl* 129
flapping *loose* 47
flare *violent* 173
  glare 420
  light 423
  – up
   excited 824, 825
   angry 900
flaring *color* 428
flash *instant* 113
  violent 173
  fire 382
  light 420
  eyes – *fire* 900
  – lamp 550
  – light 423
  – across the mem-
   ory 505
  – on the mind
   thought 451
   disclose 529
   impulse 612
  – note 800
  – in the pan
   unsubstantial 4
   transientness 111

foozle 732
fop **854**
foppery 882
foppish 855
for *cause* 155
  tendency 176
  reason 476
  motive 615
  intention 620
  preparation 673
  have –
    price **812**
  – all t'hat
  notwithstanding
    30
  qualification 469
  – all the world
    like 17
  – aught one
    knows 156
  – better for worse
    78
  – ever 112
  – example 82
  – form's sake 82
  – good
    complete 52
    diuturnity 110
    permanence 141
  – the most part
    great 31
    general 78
    special 79
  – the nonce 118
  – nothing 815
  – a season 106
  – a time 111
  – the time being
    106
forage
  food 298
  provision 637
  steal 791
forage-cap 225
foramen 260
foraminous 260
forasmuch as
  relating to 9
  cause 155
  reason 476
  motive 615
foray *attack* 716
  robbery 791
forbear
  avoid 623
  spare 678
  lenity 740
  sufferance 826
  pity 914
  abstain 953
  forbearance 918
forbid 761
  God –
  dissent 489
  deprecation 766
  censure 932
  prayer 990
forbidden fruit
  seduction 615
  prohibition 761
forbidding
  ugly 846
force *corps* 72
  power 157
  strength 159
  agency 170
  energy 171

violence 173
cultivate 371, 707
cascade 348
– *of style* 574
urge 615
exertion 686
compulsion 744
armed – 726
brute – 964
put in – 924
– of argument 476
– of arms 744
– of character 820
– down the throat
severe 739
compel 744
– majeure 744
– open 173
– one's way
progression 282
passage 302
forced *irrelative* 10
– *style* 579
be – to 601
– labor 603
– march 744
forcefully 601
forceps
  extraction 301
  grip 781
forces 726
forcible [*see* force]
ford 302, 627
fore 234
fore and aft
  complete 52
  lengthwise 200
  – schooner 273
fore part 234
forearm 673
forebears 166
forebode 511
forecast
  foresight 510
  prediction 511
  plan 626
foreclose 706
foredoom 152, 601
forefathers 166
forefend
  prohibit 761
forefinger 379
forego
  relinquish 624
  renounce 757
  surrender 782
foregoing 62, 116
foregone
  past 122
  – conclusion
  prejudged 481
  predetermined
    611
foreground 234
  in the –
  manifest 525
forehead 234
foreign
  alien 10
  extraneous 57
  – accent 580
  – parts 196
foreigner 57
forejudge
  prejudge 481
  foresight 510
foreknow 510

foreland 206, 254
forelay 545
fore ock
  pull the – 894
  take time by the –
    early 132
  occasion 134
foreman 694
foremost
  superior 33
  beginning 66
  front 234
  in advance 280
  important 642
  reputed 873
forenoon 125
forensic 968
foreordain 152
foreordination 601,
  611
forerun 62, 116, 280
forerunner 64, 512
foresee 507, 510
foreseen 871
foreshadow 152,
  511
foreshorten 201
foreshow 511
foresight 116, **510**
  caution 864
forest 367
forestage 599
forestry 371
forestall
  prior 116
  early 132
  possession 777
foretaste 510
foretell 511
forethought 459,
  510
foretoken 511
forewarn 511, 668
foreword 64
forfeit *fail* 773
  lose 776
  penalty 974
  – one's good
    opinion 932
forfeiture
  disfranchisement
    925
forfend 706, 717
forgather 72
forge *imitate* 19
  produce 161
  furnace 386
  trump up 544
  workshop 691
  – fetters 751
forged
  false 546
forger
  maker 690
  thief 792
forgery
  deception 545
forget 506
  hand – cunning
    699
  – benefits 917
  – injury 918
  – oneself 945
forgive 918
forgo
  relinquish 624
  renounce 757

surrender 782
forgotten
  past 122
  ingratitude 917
  not to be – 505
  – by the world ,
    893
fork *bifid* 91
  pointed 244
  – lightning 423
  – out
  give 784
  pay 807
  expenditure 809
forlorn
  dejected 837
  hopeless 859
  deserted 893
  – hope
  danger 665
  rashness 863
form *state* 7
  likeness 21
  make up 54
  order 58
  arrange 60
  convert 144
  produce 161
  bench 215
  shape 240
  educate 537
  pupils 541
  manner 627
  beauty 845
  fashion 852
  etiquette 882
  law 963
  rite 998
  – letter 592
  – part of 56
  – a party 712
  – a resolution 604
formal [*see* form]
  regular 82
  definitive 535
  – *style* 579
  affected 855
  stately 882
  – speech 582
formalism 739, 988
formalist 82
formality ·[*see*
  formal]
  ceremony 852
  affectation 855
  law 963
formation
  composition 54
  production 161
  shape 240
formative 153
formed [*see* form]
  attempered 820
former
  in order 62
  prior in time 116
  past 122
formication 380
formidable 704, 860
formless 241
formula *rule* 80
  arithmetic 84
  maxim 496
  precept 697
  law 963
formulary 998
formulate 590

fornication 961
fornicator 962
foro conscientiæ
  veracity 543
  duty 926
  probity 939
forsake 624
forsaken 898
forsooth 535
forspent 688
forswear *lie* 544
  tergiversation 607
  refuse 764
  transgress 927
  improbity 940
fort 666, 717
fort
  le droit du plus –
  compulsion 744
  illegality 964
  un peu – 641
fortalice 717
forte 415, 698
fortelage 717
forth 282
  come –
  egress 295
  visible 446
  go – *depart* 293
  the decree has
    gone – 741
forthcoming 152,
  673
forthwith 132
fortification 717
fortify 159
fortiori, a – 467, 476
fortissimo 404
fortiter in re 171
fortitude 826, 861
fortnightly 138
fortress 717, 752
fortuitous
  extrinsic 6
  chance 156
  undersigned 621
  – concourse of
    atoms 59
fortunate
  opportune 134
  successful 731
  prosperous 734
Fortunatus's – cap
  wish 865
  spell 993
  – purse 803
fortune *chance* 156
  fate 601
  wealth 803
  be one's – 151
  clean up a – 803
  evil – 621, 735
  good – 734
  make one's –
  succeed 731
  wealth 803
  tempt –
  hazard 621
  essay 675
  trick of – 509
  try one's – 675
  wheel of – 601, 621
fortune-hunter 886,
  943
fortuneless 804
fortune-teller 513
fortune-telling 511

delight 827
globated 249
globe
sphere 249
world 318
on the face of the
– 318
– trotter 268
globule 32, 249
glomeration 72
gloom 421, 827, 837
gloomy horizon 859
glorification 884
glorify
honor 873
approve 931
worship 990
glorious
illustrious 873
tipsy 959
glory
light 420
honor 873
heaven 981
King of – 976
– in 878, 884
– be to God 990
gloss *smooth* 255
sheen 420
interpretation 522
falsehood 546
plea 617
beauty 845
– of novelty 123
– over
neglect 460
sophistry 477
falsehood 544
vindicate 937
glossary 86, 562
glossographer 492
glossologist 492
glossology 560, 562
glossy [*see* gloss]
glottology 560
glout 901a
glove 225
take up the – 720
throw down the –
715
glow *warm* 382
shine 420
appear 446
color 428
style 574
passion 821
glower
glare 443
discourteous 895
sullen 901a
glowing
[*see* glow]
orange 439
excited 824
beautiful 845
– terms 574
glow-worm 423
gloze 933, 937
glucose 396
glue *cement* 45
cementing 46
semiliquid 352
glum
discontented 832
dejected 837
sulky 901a
glut

redundance 641
satiety 869
gluttony 957
glutinous 352
glutton 954a, 957
gluttony 957
glycerine 332, 356
glyphography 558
glyptography 558
glyptotheca 557
gnarl *protuberance*
250
anger 900
threat 909
gnarled 256, 321
gnash one's teeth
839, 900
gnat *little* 193
strain at a – &c.
caprice 608
gnaw *eat* 298
rub 331
injure 659
gnawing
– grief 828, 830
– pain 378
gnome 496, 980
gnomic 496
gnomon 114
Gnostic 984
go
cease to exist 2 –
energy 171, 682
move 264
recede 287
depart 293
fade 429
disappear 449
fashion 852
come and – 314
as things – 613
– about
turn round 311
published 531
undertake 676
– across 302
– after
in time 117
in motion 281
– ahead
energetic 171
precede 280
advance 282
active 682
– against 708
– astray 495
– away 293
– back 283, 624
– bad 659
– bail 771
– before 280
– between
interjacent 228
instrumental 631
mediate 631, 724
– beyond 303
– by the board
158
– about your
business
ejection 297
dismissal 756
– by
conform to 82
elapse 109
past 122
outrun 303

subterfuge 702
give the – by to
neglect 460
deceive 545
avoid 623
not observe 773
– by the name of
564
– deep into 461
– down *sink* 306
decline 659
– down with
believed 484
tolerated 826
content 831
– farther and fare
worse 659
– forth *depart* 293
publish 531
– halves 91
– hand in hand
accompany 88
same time 120
– hard 704
– on ill 735
– in 294
– in for
resolution 604
pursuit 622
– into
ingress 294
inquire 461
dissert 595
– all lengths
complete 52
resolve 604
exertion 686
– mad 503
– near 286
– no further
keep secret 528
– for nothing
sophistry 477
unimportant 643
– off *explode* 173
depart 293
die 360
wither 659
marry 903
– on *time* 106
continue 143
advance 282
– on for ever 112
– one better 303
– out
cease 142
egress 295
extinct 385
– out of one's
head 506
– over
passage 302
explore 461
apostate 607
faithless 940
– to pieces 162
– on record 551
– round 311
– shares 778
– to sleep 683
– through
meet with 151
pass 302
explore 461
perform 599
conduct 692
complete 729

endure 826
– to *extend* 196
travel 266
direction 278
remonstrance 695
– up 305
– to war 722
– with
assent 488
concord 714
– with the stream
conform 82
servile 886
– from one's word
773
goad 615
hasten 684
goal *end* 67
reach 292
object 620
reach the –
complete 729
goat *substitute* 147
jumper 309
lecher 962
he – *male* 373
play the – 499
gob 269
gobang 840
gobbet
small piece 32
food 298
gobble *cry* 412
gormandize 957
eat 298
gobemouche 501,
547
go-between 758
goblet 191
goblin 980
go-cart 272
GOD 976
house of – 1000
kingdom of – 981
sons of – 977
–'s acre 363
– bless me! 870
– bless you
farewell 293
– forbid 766
–'s grace 906
– grant 990
– knows 491
–'s love 906
for –'s sake 765
–'s will 601
– willing 470
god 979
household –s 189
tutelary – 664
goddess *love* 897
good woman 948
heathen 979
Godhead 976
godlike 987
godly 944
godsend *good* 618
prosperity 734
Godspeed
farewell 293
hope 858
courtesy 894
benevolence 906
approbation 931
goer *horse* 271
goes [*see* go]
as one – 270

here – 676
Gog and Magog 192
goggle 441
– eyes 443
goggles 445
going [*see* go]
general 78
rumor 532
– to happen 152
– on
incomplete 53,
730
current 151
transacting 625
goiter 250
Golconda 803
gold *yellow* 436
orange 439
money 800
write in letters
of – 642
worth its weight
in – 648
gold certificate 800
golden [*see* gold]
– age
prosperity 734
pleasure 827
– apple 615
– calf
wealth 803
idol 985
idolatry 991
– dream
imagination 515
hope 858
– mean
moderation 174
mid-course 628
– opinions 931
– opportunity 134
– rule
precept 697
– season of life
127
– wedding 883
golf 840
Golgotha 363, 1000
Goliath 159, 192
goloshes 225
gondola 273
gondolier 269
gone [*see* go]
past 122
absent 187
dead 360
– bad 653
– by
antiquated 124
– out of one's rec-
ollection 506
gonfalon 550
gong 417
goniometer 244,
466
good
complete 52
palatable 394
assent 488
benefit 618
beneficial 648
right 922
virtuous 944
pious 987
as – as 197
be so – as 765
do – 906

training 537
exercise 686
contention 720
sport 840
gymnosophist
  abstainer 953
  sectarian 984
gynander 83
gynarchy 727
gynecaeum 374
gynecology 662
gyniatrics 374
gynics 374
gyp 545, 746
gyre 311
gyrate 312
gyrfalcon 913
gyromancy 511
gyrostat 312
gysart 599
gyve 752

H

habeas corpus 963, 969
haberdasher 225
habergeon 717
habiliment 225
habilitation 698
habit
  essence 5
  coat 225
  custom 613
  want of – 614
  –s of business 682
  – of mind 820
habitant 188
habitat 189
habitation 189
habit-maker 225
habitual
  unvariable 16
  orderly 58
  ordinary 82
  customary 613
habituate 537, 613
habitude
  state 7
  habit 613
habitué 613
hacienda 189, 780
hack *cut* 44
  shorten 201
  horse 271
  writer 594
  worker 690
  literary – 593
hackle 44
hackney-coach 272
hackneyed
  known 490
  trite 496
  habitual 613
Hades 982
Hadji
  traveler 268
  priest 996
hae tibi erunt artes 627
haeret lateri lethalis arundo
  displeasure 828
  anger 900
haft 633

hag *age* 128
  ugly 846
  wretch 913
  witch 994
haggard
  insane 503
  tired 688
  wild 824
  ugly 846
haggis 298
haggle *cut* 44
  chaffer 794
Hagiographa 985
Hagiolatry 984
Hagiology 983, 985
haguebut 727
ha-ha *trench* 198, 719
haik 225
hail *welcome* 292
  ice 383
  call 586
  rejoicing 838
  honor to 873
  celebration 883
  courtesy 894
  salute 928
  approve 931
  –fellow well met
  friendship 888
  sociality 892
hailstone 383
hair *small* 32
  filament 205
  roughness 256
  to a – 494
  –'s breadth
  near 197
  narrow 203
  –breadth escape
  danger 665
  escape 671
  –s on the head
  multitude 102
  make one's –
  stand on end
  distressing 830
  fear 860
  wonder 870
hairless 226
hairy *rough* 256
halberd 727
halberdier 726
halcyon *calm* 174
  peace 721
  prosperous 734
  joyful 827, 829
hale 654
half 91
  – the battle
  important 642
  success 731
  – distance 68
  – a dozen *six* 98
  several 102
  see with – an eye
  intelligent 498
  intelligible 518
  manifest 525
  – a gale 349
  – and half
  equal 27
  mixed 41
  incomplete 53
  – a hundred 98
  – light 422
  – measures

  incomplete 53
  vacillating 605
  mid-course 628
  – moon 245
  – price 815
  – rations 640
  – scholar 493
  – seas over 959
  – sight 443
  – speed
  moderate 174
  slow 275
  – truth 546
half-blind 443
half-blood
  mixture 41
  unconformity 83
  imperfect 651
half-frozen 352
half-hearted
  irresolute 605
  insensible 823
  indifferent 866
half-learned 491
half-melted 352
halfpenny
  trifle 643
half-starved
  insufficient 640
  fasting 956
half-way
  small 32
  middle 68
  between 228
  go – *irresolute* 605
  mid-course 628
  meet –
  willing 602
  compromise 774
half-witted 499, 501
hall *chamber* 189
  receptacle 191
  mart 799
  music – 599
  – of audience 588
  – mark 550
hallelujah 990
halliard 45
halloo *cry* 411
  look here! 457
  call 586
  wonder 870
hallow
  celebrate 883
  respect 928
hallowed 976
hallucination
  error 495
  insanity 503
halo *light* 420
  glory 873
Halomancy 511
halser 45
halt *cease* 142
  weak 160
  rest 265
  go *slowly* 275
  lame 655
  fail 732
  at the – 265
halter *rope* 45
  restraint 752
  punishment 975
  wear a – 874
  with a – round one's neck 665
halting

style 579
 – place 292
halve [*see* half]
halves
  do by –
  neglect 460
  not complete 730
  not do by – 729
  go – 778
ham *house* 189
hamadryad 979
hammam 386, 652
hamlet 189
hammer
  repeat 104
  knock 276
  stammer 583
  under the –
  auction 796
  between the – and the anvil 665
  – at *think* 451
  work 686
  – out *form* 240
  prepare 673
  complete 729
hammock 215
hamper *basket* 191
  obstruct 706
hamstring 158, 659
hanaper 802
hand
  measure of length 200
  side 236
  transfer 270
  man 372
  organ of touch 379
  indicator 550
  writing 590
  medium 631
  agent 690
  grasp 781
  transfer 783
  at – *future* 121
  destined 152
  near 197
  useful 644
  bad – 590
  bird in – 781
  come to – 292, 785
  fold one's –s 681
  give one's – to
  marry 903
  good –
  writing 590
  skill 698
  proficiency 700
  helping – 707, 711
  hold in – 737
  hold out the – 894
  hold up the –
  vote 609
  in –
  incomplete 53
  business 625
  preparing 673
  not finished 730
  possessed 777
  money 800
  in the –s of
  authority 737
  subjection 749
  lay –s on
  discover 480a
  use 677

take 789
rite 998
much on one's –s 682
on one's –s
  business 625
  redundant 641
  not finished 730
  for sale 796
  on the other – 468
  no – in 623
  poor – 701
  put into one's –s 784
  put one's – to 676
  ready to one's – 673
  shake –s 918
  stretch forth one's – 680
  take by the – 707
  take in –
  teach 537
  undertake 676
  time hanging on one's –s
  inaction 681
  leisure 685
  weary 841
  try one's – 675
  turn one's – 675
  turn one's – to 625
  under one's
  in writing 590
  promise 768
  compact 769
  – back 683
  – cart 272
  – of death 360
  – down
  record 551
  transfer 783
  have one's –s full 682
  – gallop 274
  – glass 445
  – and glove 709, 888
  – in hand
  joined 43
  accompanying 88
  same time 120
  concur 178
  co-operate 709
  party 712
  concord 714
  friend 888
  social 892
  – to hand
  touching 199
  transfer 270
  fight 720, 722
  – over head
  inattention 458
  neglect 460
  reckless 863
  have a – in
  cause 153
  act 680
  co-operate 709
  have one's – in
  skill 698
  keep one's – in 613
  live from – to mouth
  insufficient 640

unprepared 674
poor 804
−s off! avoid 623
leave alone 681
prohibition 761
− over
transfer 783
give 784
win −s down 731
with the −s in the
pockets 681
hand-bag 191
hand-barrow 272
handbook
travel 266
information 527
book 593
handcuff 751, 752
handfast 903
handful
quantity 25
small 32
few 103
handicap
equalize 27
inferiority 34
encumber 706
race 720
handicraft 625, 680
handicraftsman 690
effect 154
doing 680
handkerchief
clothes 225
cleaner 652
handle
feel, touch 379
name 565
dissert 595
plea 617
instrument 633
use 677
manage 693
furnish a − 937
make a − of 677
− a case 693
− to one's name
name 564
honor 877
handmaid
instrumentality
631
auxiliary 711
servant 746
handpost 550
handsel
begin 66
security 771
gift 784
pay 809
handsome
liberal 816
beautiful 845
disinterested 942
− fortune 803
handspike 633
handstaff 727
handwriting
signature 550
autograph 590
− on the wall
warning 668
handy
near 197
useful 644, 646
ready 673
dexterous 698

hang
pendency 214
kill 361
curse 908
execute 972
− about 133, 197
− back 133, 623
− in the balance
133
− in doubt 485
− fire late 133
cease 142
unproductive 169
inert 172
slow 275
reluctance 603
inactive 683
not finish 730
fail 732
refuse 764
dullness 843
− on hand 641
− down the head
837
− over the head
152
− it! regret 833
contempt 930
− out a light 420
− upon the lips of
418
− on
accompany 88
− out
display 882
entertain 892
− over
destiny 152
height 206
project 250
− out a signal 550
− on the sleeve of
servant 746
servility 886
flattery 933
− in suspense 605
− by a thread 665
− together
joined 43
cohere 46
concur 178
co-operate 709
− upon
effect 154
dependency 749
hangar 191, 273
hang-dog look 901a
hanged if, I'll be −
489
hanger
weapon 727
suspender 45, 214
pothooks and −s
590
− on
accompaniment
88
servant 746
servile 886
hanging [see hang]
elevated 307
ornament 847
− look 846
hangman
evil-doer 913
bad man 949
executioner 975

hank tie 45
hanker 865
hanky-panky 545
Hansard 551
hansom 272
hap 156
haphazard
chance 156, 621
hapless
unfortunate 735
(miserable 828)
(hopeless 859)
haply
possibly 470
(by chance 156)
happen 151
− as it may
chance 621
− what may
certain 474
reckless 863
happening 151
happiness
[see happy]
the greatest − of
the greatest
number 910
happy fit 23
opportune 134
style 578
glad 827
cheerful 836
− despatch 972
− go lucky 674
− hunting grounds
981
− returns of the
day 896
− thought 842
− valley
imagination 515
delight 827
harangue 582
hara-kiri 972
harass
fatigue 688
vex 830
worry 907
harbinger
precursor 64
omen 512
informant 527
harbor
abode 189
haven 292
refuge 666
cherish 821
natural − 343
− a design 620
in − 664
− an idea 451
− revenge 919
harborless 665
hard strong 159
dense 323
physically insen-
sible 376
sour 397
difficult 704
severe 739
morally insen-
sible 823
grievous 830
impenitent 951
blow − 349
go −
difficult 704

failure 732
adversity 735
pain 828
hit − 276
look − at 441
not be too − upon
918
strike −
energy 171
impulse 276
try − 675
work − 686
− at it 682
− bargain 819
− of belief 487
− to believe 485
− by 197
− case 735
− cash 800
− earned 704
− and fast rule 80
− fought 704
− frost 383
− of hearing 419
− heart
malevolent 907
vicious 945
impenitent 951
− hit 732
− knocks 720
− life 735
− lines
adversity 735
severity 739
− liver 954a
− lot 735
− master 739
− measure 739
− names 932
− necessity 601
− nut to crack 704
− to please 868
− pressed
haste 684
difficulty 704
hindrance 706
− put to it 704
− set 704
− tack 298
− task 703
− time 704
− up 704, 804
− upon
attack 715
severe 739
censure 932
− winter 383
− words
obscure 571
rude 895
censure 932
− work 686
− at work 682
harden [see hard]
strengthen 159
accustom 613
− the heart
insensible 823
enmity 889
impenitence 951
hardened
impious 988
− front
insolent 885
hardening
habit 613
hard-featured 846

hard-fisted 819
hard-headed 498,
739
hardihood 861, 885
hardly
scarcely 32
deal − with 739
− any few 103
− anything
small 32
unimportant 643
− ever 137
hard-mouthed 606
hardness 3°3
− of heart ग14a
hardship 735
hardy
strong 159
healthy 654
brave 861
hare 274
hold with the −
and run with
the hounds
fickle 607
servile 886
hare-brained 458,
863
harem 961
hariolation 511
hark 418, 457
− back 283
harl 205
harlequin
changeable 149
nimble 274
motley 440
pantomimic 599
humorist 844
harlequinade 599
harlot 962
harlotry 961
harm
evil 619
badness 649
malevolence 907
harmattan 349
harmless
impotent 158
good 648
perfect 650
salubrious 656
safe 664
innocent 946
bear − 717
harmonica 417
harmonics 413
harmonist 413
harmonize 178, 416
harmonium 417
harmony
agreement 23
order 58
music 413
color 428
concord 714
peace 721
friendship 888
harness
fasten 43
fastening 45
accouterment 225
yoke 370
instrument 633
restraint 752
in −
prepared 673

in action 680
active 682
subjection 749
– up 293
harp
repeat 104
musical instru-
ment 417
weary 841
Harpagon 819
harper 416
harpist 416
harpoon 727
harpsichord 417
harpy
relentless 739
thief 792
miser 819
evil-doer 913
demon 980
harquebuss 727
harridan 846, 962
harrier 366
harrow
agriculture 371
– up the soul 860
harrowing 830
harry pain 830
attack 716
persecute 907
Harry, old – 978
harsh
acrid 171
sound 410
style 579
discordant 713
severe 739
disagreeable 830
morose 895
malevolent 907
– voice 581
hart 366, 373
hartal 142, 489
harum-scarum 59,
458
haruspice 513
Haruspicy 511
harvest
effect 154
profit 618
store 636
acquisition 775
get in the –
complete 729
succeed 731
– home
celebration 883
– time
autumn 126
exertion 686
has been 122
hash mix 41
cut 44
confusion 59
food 298
make a – 699
hashish 863
hasp 43, 45
hassock 215
hastate 253
haste
velocity 274
activity 682
hurry **684**
hasten
promote 707
hasty

transient 113
hurried 684
impatient 825
irritable 901
– pudding 298
hat 225
cardinal's – 999
send round the –
765
shovel – 999
– in hand 886
hatch
produce 161
gate 232
opening 260
chickens 370
fabricate 544
shading 556
plan 626
prepare 673
– a plot 626
hatches, under –
restraint 751
prisoner 754
poor 804
hatchet
cutting 253
bury the – 918
dig up the – 722
throw the helve
after the – 818
hatchet-faced 203
hatchment
funeral 363
arms 550
record 551
hatchway 260
hate 867, **898**
hateful 649, 830
hath been, the
time – 122
hatrack 215
hatter 225
mad as a – 503
hatti-sheriff 741
hatred [*see* hate]
object of – 898
hauberk 717
haud passibus
æquis 28, 275
haugh 344
haughty
proud 878
insolent 885
contemptuous 930
haul drag 285
catch of fish &c.
789
– down one's flag
725
– in 10
haunch 236
haunt focus 74
presence 186
abode 189
alarm 860
persecute 907
– the memory
remember 505
trouble 830
haunted 980
haut
traiter de –
insolence 885
contempt 930
hautboy 417
haut-goût 392

haut-monde 875
hauteur 878
have confute 479
ken 49
possess 777
– the advantage
28, 33
– at 716
– no choice 609a
– done! 142
– to do with 9
– no end 112
– other fish to fry
135
– it
discover 480a
believe 484
– one to know 527
– some knowledge
of 490
– nothing to do
with 10
– for one's own
780
– rather 609
– one's rights 924
– the start 116
– in store 152, 637
– to 620
– up 638
– it your own way
submission 725
haven 292, 666
haversack 191
havoc
destruction 162
cry – war 722
play – spoil 659
haw 583
hawk spit 297
stammer 583
eye of a – 498
– about
publish 531
offer 763
sell 796
– at 716
between – and
buzzard 315,
828
know a – from a
handsaw 465,
698
hawker 796
hawk-eyed 441
hawking chase 622
hawser 45
**hay while the sun
shines, make** –
134
haycock 72
hazard
chance 156, 621
danger 665
at all –s 604
– a conjecture 514
– a proposition
477
haze mist 353
uncertainty 475
in a –
hidden 528
hazel 433
hazy opaque 426
he 373
head precedence 62
beginning 66

class 75
summit 210
coiffure 225
lead 280
froth 353
person 372
intellect 450
topic 454
wisdom 498
picture 556
nomenclature 564
chapter 593
direct 693
director 694
master 745
at the – of
direction 693
authority 737
repute 873
bow the – 308
bring to a – 729
come into one's –
451
come to a – 729
drive into one's –
505
gain – 175
get into one's –
thought 451
learn 505
belief 484
intoxicate 959
give a horse his –
748
hang one's – 879
have in one's – 490
from – to heels 52,
200
hit on the – 912
knock on the –
361
knock one's –
against
impulse 276
unskilful 699
fail 732
lie on one's – 926
lift up one's – 878
make – against
oppose 708
resistance 719
success 731
never entered
into one's – 458
have no – 506
on one's – 218
off one's – 503
can't get out of
one's – 505
over – and ears
deep 641
debt 806
love 897
put into one's –
supposition 514
information 527
put out of one's –
458
run in the – 505
not know whether
one stands on –
or heels
uncertain 475
wonder 870
take into one's –
thought 451
caprice 608

intention 620
turn the – 824
trouble one's –
about 457
as one's – shall
answer for 768
with – erect 878
from – to foot 200
– and front
important 642
– and front of
one's offending
provocation 830
charge 938
– over heels
inversion 218
rotation 312
– light 423
– line 591
– and shoulders
irrelevant 10
complete 52
haste 684
make neither – nor
tail of 519
hold one's – up
307
– above water
safe 664
prosperous 743
wealth 803
with a – on 353
headache 378
head-dress 225
header 310
head-foremost
violent 173
rash 863
head-gear 225
heading prefix 64
beginning 66
indication 550
title 564
headland
height 206
projection 250
headlong
hurry 684
rush 863
rush –
violence 173
headman 694
headmost
front 234
precession 280
head-piece
summit 210
intellect 450
helmet 717
ornament 847
head-quarters
focus 74
abode 189
authority 737
head-race 350
head-stone 363
heads
compendium 596
– or tails 156, 621
lay, – together
advice 695
co-operate 709
– I win tails you
lose
unfair 940
headship 737
headsman 975

high-brow 492
higher 33
highest 210
highfalutin 884
high-flavored 392
high-flier
  madman 504
  proud 878
high-flown
  imaginative 515
  style 577
  proud 878
  vain 880
  insolent 885
high-flying
  inattentive 458
  exaggerated 549
  ostentatious 822
highlands 206
high-low 225
high-mettled
  excitable 825
  brave 861
high-minded
  honorable 939
  magnanimous
  942
highness *title* 877
high-pitched 410
high-seasoned 392
high-souled 878
high-sounding
  loud 404
  words 577
  display 882
high-spirited 861,
  939
hight 564
high-toned 852
high-water
  completeness 52
  height 206
  crater 337
  – mark
  measure 466
highway 627
  –s and byways
  627
  – robbery 791
highwayman 792
high-wrought
  good 648
  prepared 673
  excited 824
hike 266
hilarity 836
hill *height* 206
  convexity 250
  ascent 305
  descent 306
  take to the –s 666
  –dwelling 206
hillock 206
hilt 633
hinc illæ lachrymæ
  155
hind *back* 235
  clown 876
  on one's – legs
  elevation 307
  anger 900
  – quarters 235
hinder 706
hindermost 67, 235
Hindooism 984
hindrance **706**
hinge *fasten* 43

fastening 45
  cause 153
  depend upon 154
  rotate 312
hinny 271
hint *reminder* 505
  suppose 514
  inform 527
  take a – 498
  – a fault &c. 932
hinterland 235
hip 236
  have on the –
  confute 479
  success 731
  authority 737
  subjection 749
  – hip, hurrah! 838
hipped [*see* hypped]
hippocentaur 80
Hippocrates 662
hippocratic 360
hippodrome
  drama 599
  arena 728
  amusement 840
hippogriff 83
Hippolytus 960
hippophagy 298
hippopotamus 192
hirdie-girdie 218
hire
  commission 755
  borrowing 788
  price 812
  reward 973
  on – 763
hireling 746
hirsute 256
hispid 256
hiss *sound* 409
  animal cry 412
  disrespect 929
  contempt 930
  disapprobation
  `932
hist! 585, 586
histology 329
historian 553
historic 594
historiette 594
historical:
  – painter 559
  – painting 556
historiographer 553
historiography 594
history *past* 122
  record 551
  narrative 594
History, Natural –
  357
histrionic 599
hit *chance* 156
  strike 276
  reach 292
  succeed 731
  censure 932
  (*punish* 972)
  good – 626
  make a – 731
  – one's fancy 829
  – the mark 731
  – off 545
  – upon
  discover 480a
  plan 626
hitch

fasten 43
  knot 45
  stoppage 142
  hang 214
  jerk 315
  harness 370
  difficulty 704
  hindrance 706
  – up 293
hither 278, 292
  come – 286
hitherto 122
hive
  multitude 102
  location 184
  abode 189
  bees 870
  workshop 691
H.M.S. 726
hoar *aged* 128
  white 430
  – frost 383
hoard 636
hoarse
  husky 405
  harsh 410
  voiceless 581
  talk oneself – 584
hoary [*see* hoar]
hoax 545
hob *support* 215
  stove 386
  – and nob
  celebration 883
  courtesy 894
hobble
  limp 275
  awkward 699
  difficulty 704
  fail 732
  shackle 751
  – skirt 225
hobbledehoy 129
hobby
  crotchet 481
  pursuit 622
  desire 865
hobby-horse 272
hobgoblin
  fearful 860
  demon 980
hobo 268
hobnail 876
Hobson's choice
  necessity 601
  no choice 609a
  compulsion 744
hoc genus omne
  876
hock 771
hock shop 787
hockey 840
hockey rink 213
hocus 545
hocus-pocus
  interchange 148
  unmeaning 517
  cheat 545
  conjuration 992
  spell 993
hod
  receptacle 191
  support 215
  vehicle 272
hoddy-doddy 501
hodge-podge 41, 59
hoe 272, 371

hog *animal* 366
  sensualist 954a
  glutton 957
  (greedy as a – 865
  go the whole – 604
hog's back 206
hogmanay 998
hogshead 191
hog-wash 653
hoist 307
  – the black flag
  722
  – a flag 550
  – on one's own
  petard
  retaliation 718
  failure 732
hoity-toity! 815,
  870
hold *cohere* 46
  contain 54
  remain 141
  cease 142
  go on 143
  happen 151
  receptacle 191
  cellar 207
  base 211
  support 215
  halt 265
  believe 484
  be passive 681
  defend 717
  power 737
  restrain 751
  prison 752
  prohibit 761
  possess 777
  retain 781
  enough! 869
  have a firm – 781
  have a – upon 175
  gain a – upon 737
  get – of 789
  quit one's – 782
  take – 175
  – aloof
  stay away 187
  distrust 487
  avoid 623
  – an argument
  476
  – authority 737
  – back *avoid* 623
  store 636
  hinder 706
  restrain 751
  retain 781
  miserly 819
  – one's breath
  wonder 870
  – converse 588
  – a council 695
  – fast 751, 781
  – forth *teach* 537
  speak 582
  – good 478, 494
  – one's ground
  141
  – in hand 737
  – one's hand
  cease 142
  relinquish 624
  – hard 265
  – up one's head
  861
  – a lease 771

  – a meeting 72
  – off 623
  – office 693
  – on
  continue 141, 143
  persevere 604a
  – out [*see below*]
  – one's own
  preserve 670
  defend 717
  resist 719
  – oneself in readi-
  ness 673
  – in remembrance
  505
  – both one's sides
  838
  – a situation 625
  – in solution 335
  – to 602
  – together 43, 709
  – one's tongue
  403, 585
  – up [*see below*]
  – oneself up 307
hold out
  endure 106
  affirm 535
  persevere 604a
  resist 719
  offer 763
  brave 861
  – expectation
  predict 511
  promise 768
  – temptation 865
hold up
  continue 143
  support 215
  not rain 340
  aid 707
  rob 791
  display 882
  extol 931
  – one's hand
  sign 550
  threat 909
  – to execration
  cures 908
  censure 932
  – the mirror 525
  – to scorn 930
  – to shame 874
  – to view 525
holder 779
holdfast 45
holding
  tenancy 777
  property 780
hole *place* 182
  hovel 189
  receptacle 191
  opening 260
  ambush 530
  – in one's coat 651
  – and corner
  place 182
  peer into – 461
  hiding 528, 530
  – to creep out of
  plea 617
  escape 671
  facility 705
holiday *leisure* 685
  repose 687
  amusement 840
  – task *easy* 705

riding 266
skill 698
horseplay 856
horse power 466
horse-shoe 245
horse-whip 972
hortation 615, 695
hortative 537
horticulture 371
hortus siccus 369
hosanna 931, 990
hose
  stockings 225
  pipe 348, 350
  extinguisher 385
hosier 225
hospice 189, 662
hospitable 816, 892
hospital 189, 662
  in – 655
hospitality
  [see hospitable]
hospodar 745
host *collection* 72
  multitude 102
  army 726
  friend 890
  rite 998
  reckon without
    one's –
  error 495
  unskilful 699
  rash 863
  – of heaven 977
  – in himself 175
hostage 771
hostel 189
hostelry 189
hostile
  disagreeing 24
  opposed 708
  enmity 889
  in – array 708
  – meeting 720
hostilities 722
hostility 889
hostler 746
hot *violent* 173
  warm 382
  pungent 392
  red 434
  orange 439
  excited 824
  irascible 901
  make – 384
  – air 482, 884
  – bath 386
  – blood *rash* 863
  angry 900
  irascible 901
  blow – and cold
  inconsistent 477
  falsehood 544
  tergiversation 607
  caprice 608
  in – haste 684
  in – pursuit 622
  – water
  difficulty 704
  quarrel 713
  painful 830
  – water bottle 386
hot air merchant
  884
hot-bed *cause* 153
  centre 222
  workshop 691

Hotchkiss gun 727
hotchpotch
  mixture 41
  confusion 59
  participation 778
hotel 189
hot-headed 684,
  825
hothouse
  conservatory 371,
    636
  furnace 386
  workshop 691
hot-press 255
Hotspur 863
Hottentot 876
hough 659
hound *animal* 366
  hunt 622
  persecute 907
  wretch 949
  hold with the hare
    but run with the
    –s 607
  – on 615
houppelande 225
hour *period* 108
  point of time 113
  present time 118
  improve the shin-
    ing – 682
  one's – is come
  occasion 134
  death 360
  – after hour 110
hour-glass
  chronometer 114
  contraction 195
  narrow 203
Houri 845
hourly *time* 106
  frequent 136
  periodical 138
house *family* 166
  locate 184
  abode 189
  theater 599
  make safe 664
  council 696
  firm 712
  before the – 454
  keep – 184
  eat out of – and
    home
  prodigal 818
  gluttony 957
  turn out of – and
    home 297
  – of cards 160
  – of correction
  prison 752
  punishment 975
  – of death 363
  – of detention 752
  – divided against
    itself 713
  bring the – about
    one's ears 699
  – of Commons
    696, 966
  – of God 1000
  – of Lords 696,
    875, 966
  set one's – in
    order 952
  – of peers 696, 875
  – of prayer 1000

– built on sand
  160
turn – out of win-
  dow 713
housebreaker 792
housebreaking 791
house-dog 366
household
  inhabitants 188
  abode 189
  – gods 189,
  – stuff 635
  – troops 726
  – words
  known 490
  language 560
  plain 576, 849
householder 188
housekeeper 637,
  694
housekeeping 692
houseless 185
housemaid 746
house-organ 531
Houses of Parlia-
  ment 191, 696
house-top 210
proclaim from –
  531
house-room 180
house-warming 892
housewife 682
housewifery 692,
  817
housing
  lodging 189
  covering 223
  horse-cloth 225
hovel 189
hoveller 269
hover *high* 206
  rove 266
  soar 267
  ascend 305
  irresolute 605
  – about
  move 264
  – over
  near 197
how *way* 627
  means 632
  – comes it?
  attribution 155
  inquiry 461
  – now 870
howbeit 30
however
  degree 26
  notwithstanding
    30
  except 83
howitzer 727
howker 273
howl
  wind 349
  human cry 411
  animal cry 412
  lamentation 839
howler 495
howling wilderness
  169, 893
hoy 273
hoyden *girl* 129
  rude 851
hub 222
hubble-bubble 392
hubbub *stir* 315

noise 404
  discord 713
huckster 794, 797
huddle
  disorder 59
  derange 61
  collect 72
  hug 197
  – on 225
Hudibrastic 856
  – *verse* 597
hue 428
  – and cry *cry* 411
  proclaim 531
  pursuit 622
  alarm 669
  raise a – and cry
    932
hueless 429
huff 885, 900
huffy 901
hug *cohere* 46
  border on 197
  retain 781
  courtesy 894
  love 897
  endearment 902
  – a belief 606
  – oneself
  pleasure 827
  content 831
  rejoicing 838
  pride 878
  – the shore
  navigation 267
  approach 286
  – a sin 945
huge 31, 192
hugger-mugger 528
Huguenot 984
huis clos, à – 528
huissier 965
huke 225
hulk *body* 50
  ship 273
hulks 752
hulky *big* 192
  unwieldy 647
  ugly 846
hull 50
hullabaloo 404, 411
hullo! 292
hum
  faint sound 405
  continued sound
    407
  animal sound 412
  sing 416
  deceive 545, 546
  – and haw
  stammer 583
  irresolute 605
  busy – of men 682
human 372
  – race 372
  – sacrifices 991
humane
  benevolent 906
  philanthropic 910
  merciful 914
humanitarian 372,
  910
humanities 560
humanize 894
humano capiti cer-
  vicem jungere
  equinam 24

humation 363
humble *meek* 879
  modest 881
  pious 987
  –r classes 876
  – oneself
  submit 725
  meek 879
  penitent 950
  worship 990
  eat – pie 725, 879
  your – servant
  dissent 489
  refusal 764
humbug
  falsehood 544
  deception 545
  deceiver 548
  trifle 643
  affectation 855
humdrum 841, 843
humectate 337, 339
humid 339
humiliate 308
humiliation
  adversity 735
  disrepute 874
  sense of shame
    879
  worship 990
  self – 950
humility 879, 987
humming-top 417
hummock 206, 250
humorist 844
humor *essence* 5
  tendency 176
  liquid 333
  disposition 602
  caprice 608
  aid 707
  indulge 760
  affections 820
  please 829
  wit 842
  flatter 933
  – (*fun* 840)
  in the – 602
  out of – 901a
  peccant –
  unclean 853
  disease 655
humorous 842
humorsome
  capricious 608
  sulky 901a
hump 250
hump-backed 243
humph! 870
Humphrey, dine
  with Duke – 956
Humpty-dumpty
  193
Hun 165, 851, 913
hunch 250, 612
hunch-backed 243
hundred
  number 98
  many 102
  region 181
  the same a – years
    hence 460
hundredth 99
hundredweight 319
hunger 865
hunger-strike 956
hunks 819

insert 300
mean 516
imply 526
be of consequence 642
importance 642
greatness 30
attach - to 642
attach too much
- to 482
of no - 643
importune 765, 830
impose order 741
awe 928
- upon
credulity 486
deceive 545
be unjust 923
imposing
important 642
exciting 824
glorious 873
imposition [see
impose]
undue 925
- of hands 998
**impossibile, credo
quia** - 486
**impossibilities,
seek after** - 645
impossibility 471
impossible 471
refusal 764
- quantity
algebra 84
impost 812
imposthume 655
impostor 548, 925
imposture 545
impotence 158
**impotent conclu-
sion 732**
impound 791
impoverish
weaken 160
waste 638
despoil 789
render poor 804
impracticable
impossible 471
misjudging 481
obstinate 606
difficult 704
imprecation
prayer 765
curse 908
**impregnable 159,
664**
impregnate mix 41
combine 48
fecundate 161,
168
insert 300
teach 537
- with 641
impresario 599
imprescriptible 924
impress cause
sensation 375
mark 550
compel 791
excite feeling 824
- upon the mind
memory 505
teach 537
impressed with
belief 484

feeling 821
impressible
motive 615
sensibility 822
impression
sensation 375
idea 453
belief 484
printing 531
mark 550
engraving 558
print 591
emotion 821
make an -
act 171
thought 451
impressionable
375, 822
impressive
language 574
important 642
feeling 821, 824
imprimis 66
imprimit 558
imprint
publisher 531
indication 550
- in the memory
505
imprison
circumscribe 229
restrain 751
punish 972
improbability 473
improbate 932
improbity 940
impromptu 612
- fait à loisir 673
improper
incongruous 24
foolish 499
solecism 568
inexpedient 647
wrong 923
unmeet 925
vicious 945
- time 135
**impropriate 777,
789**
impropriator 779
improve 658
- the occasion 134
- the shining
hour 682
- upon 658
improvement 658
improvident
careless 460
not preparing 674
prodigal 818
rash 863
improvisation
music 415
improvisatore
speech 582
poetry 597
impulse 612
improvise
imagination 515
impulse 612
unprepared 674
improviste, à l'-
508, 612
improvisatrice
612
imprudent 460, 863
impudent 885, 895

impudicity 961
impugn deny 536
attack 716
blame 932
impugnation 708
impuissance 158
impulse push **276**
sudden thought
612
motive 615
blind - 601
creature of - 612
give an - to
propel 284
aid 707
impulsive [see
impulse]
intuitive 477
excitable 825
rash 863
impunity escape 671
acquittal 970
with - safely 664
impurity 653, 961
imputation
ascribe 155
slur 874
accuse 938
in 221
go - 294
- as much as
relation 9
degree 26
- the circum-
stances 8
- doors 221
- durancevile 751
- for
- force 1
undertake 676
promise 768
- re 9
- and out 314
-s and outs 182
in : - articulo 111
- extenso whole 50
diffuse 573
- jail 751
- limine 66
- loco 23
- medias res 68
- prison 751
- propriá personá
79
- toto 52
- transitu
transient 111
transfer 270
- statu pupillari
127
- statu quo 141
- vogue 1
inability 158, 699
inabstinent 954
**inaccessible 196,
471**
inaccurate 495, 568
inaction 172, 683
inactivity 683, 172
inadequate
powerless 158
insufficient 640
useless 645
imperfect 651
inadmissible
incongruous 24
excluded 55

extraneous 57
inexpedient 647
inadvertence 458
inadvisable 647
inaffable 895
inalienable
retention 781
right 924
inamorata 897
inane void 4
unmeaning 517
unthinking 452
insufficient 640
trivial 643
useless 645
inanimate 360
- matter 358
inanition 158
inanity [see inane]
**inappetency 823,
866**
inapplicable 10, 24
inapposite 10, 24
**inappreciable 33,
193**
unimportant 643
inapprehensible
stolid 499
unintelligible 519
**inappropriate 24,
647**
inapt
incongruous 24
impotent 158
useless 645
inexpedient 647
unskilful 699
**inarticulate 581,
583**
inartificial 703
inartistic 846
inasmuch whereas 9
however 26
because 476
inattention 458
inaudible
silence 403
faint sound 405
deaf 419
voiceless 581
inaugural
precursor 64
inaugurate
begin 66
cause 153
install 755
celebrate 883
inauspicious
untimely 135
untoward 649
hopeless 859
inbeing 5
inborn, inbred
intrinsic 5
affections 820
- proclivity 601
inca 745
incage 751
incalculable 31, 105
incalescence 382
incandescence 382
incandescent 423
incantation
invocation 765
sorcery 992
spell 993
incantatory 992

incapable 158
incapacious 203
incapacitate 158
incapacity
impotence 158
ignorance 491
stupidity 499
incarcerate 751
incarnadine 434
incarnate
intrinsic 5
bodily 316
fleshly 364
vicious 945
devil -
bad man 949
Satan 978
Incarnation 976
incase 223, 229
incautious 863
incendiary
destroy 162
burn 384
influence 615
malevolent 907
evil-doer 913
bad man 949
incense fuel 388
fragrant 400
hate 898
anger 900
flatter 933
worship 990
rite 998
incension
burning 384
incentive 615
inception 66
inceptive 153
inceptor 541
incertitude 475
incessant
repeated 104
ceaseless 112
frequent 136
incest 961
inch small 32
length 200
by -es 275
to an - 494
not yield an - 606
give an - and take
an ell 789
- by inch
by degrees 26
in parts 51
slowly 275
not see an - be-
yond one's nose
699
inchoation 66, 673
incide 44
incidence 278
incident 151
incidental
extrinsic 6
circumstance 8
irrelative 10
occurring 151
casual 156
liable 177
chance 621
trivial 643
- music 415
incinerate 384
incipience 66
incircumspect 460

incision 44, 259
incisive *energy* 171
  vigor 574
  feeling 821
incisor 253
incite
  exasperate 173
  urge 615
incivility 895
incivism 911
inclasp 229
inclement
  violent 173
  cold 383
  severe 739
  pitiless 914a
inclination
  [*see* incline]
  will 600
  affection 820
  desire 865
  love 897
incline *tendency* 176
  slope 217
  direction 278
  willing 602
  induce 615
  – an ear to 457
  – the head 308
inclined
  disposed 620
  – plane 633
inclose
  surround 227
inclosure 232
include
  composition 54
  – in a class 76
inclusion 76
inclusive
  additive 37
  component 56
  class 76
incogitancy 452
incognita, terra –
  491
incognito 528
incognizable 519
incoherence
  physical 47
  mental 503
incombustible 385
income *means* 632
  profit 775
  property 780
  wealth 803
  receipt 810
  – tax 812
incoming
  ingress 294
  receipt 810
incommensurable
  10
  – quantity 84, 85
incommode 706
  hinder 706
incommunicable
  unmeaning 517
  unintelligible 519
  retention 781
incommunicado
  528
incommutable 150
incomparable 33
incompassionate
  914a
incompatible 24

incompatibility 15
incompetence
  inability 158
  incapacity 499
  unskilful 699
  dereliction 927
incompleteness 53
  non-completion
  730
incompliance 764
incomprehensible
  infinite 105
  unintelligible 519
incomprehension
  491
incompressible 321
inconcealable 525
inconceivable
  unthinkable 452
  impossible 471
  improbable 473
  incredible 485
  unintelligible 519
  wonder 870
inconceptible 519
inconcinnity
  disagreement 24
  ugliness 846
inconclusive 477
inconcoction 674
incondite 851
incongruous
  differing 15
  disagreeing 24
  illogical 477
  ungrammatical
  568
  discordant 713
inconnection 10, 44
inconsequence
  irrelation 10
inconsequential 477
inconsiderable 32,
  643
inconsiderate
  thoughtless 452
  inattentive 458
  neglectful 460
  foolish 699
inconsistent
  contrary 14
  disagreeing 24
  illogical 477
  absurd 497
  foolish 499
  capricious 608
  discord 713
inconsolable 837
inconsonant
  disagreeing 24
  fitful 149
inconspicuous 447
inconstant 149
incontestable 159,
  474, 525
incontiguous 196
incontinent 961
incontinently 132
incontrollable 173
incontrovertible
  150, 474
inconvenience 647
  put to – 706
inconversable 585,
  893
inconvertible 143
inconvincible 487

incorporate 48
  combine 48
  include 76
  materialize 316
incorporation 761
incorporeal 317
  – hereditaments
  780
incorrect
  illogical 477
  erroneous 495
  solecism 568
  vicious 945
incorrigible
  obstinate 606
  hopeless 859
  vicious 945
  impenitent 951
incorruption
  probity 939
  innocence 946
incrassate
  increase 194
  density 321
  - *fluids* 352
increase
  - *in degree* 35
  - *in number* 102
  - *in size* 194
incredible
  great 31
  impossible 471
  improbable 473
  doubtful 485
  wonderful 870
incredulity 487, 989
increment
  increase 35
  addition 37
  adjunct 39
  expansion 194
increpation 932
incriminate 938
incrust 223, 224
incubate 370
incubation 673
incubus
  hindrance 706
  pain 828
  demon 980
inculcate 6, 537
inculpable 946
inculpate 938
inculture 674
incumbency
  business 625
  churchdom 995
incumbent
  inhabitant 188
  high 206
  weight 319
  duty 926
  clergyman 996
incumber 706
incumbered 806
incunabula 66, 127
incur 177
  – blame 932
  – danger 665
  – a debt 806
  – disgrace 874
  – a loss 776
  – the risk 621
incurable
  ingrained 5
  disease 655
  hopeless 859

incuriam, per –
  458, 460
incuriosity 456
incursion 294, 716
incurvation 245
indagation 461
indebted
  owing 806
  gratitude 916
  duty 926
indecent 961
indeciduous 150
indecipherable 519
indecision 475, 605
indecisive 475
indeclinable 150
indecorous
  vulgar 851
  vicious 945
  impure 961
indeed *existing* 1
  very 31
  assent 488
  truly 494
  assertion 535
  wonder 870
indefatigable
  persevering 604a
  active 682
indefeasible
  stable 150, 474
  due 924
indefectible 650
indefensible
  powerless 158
  submission 725
  accusable 938
  wrong 945
indeficient 650
indefinite
  great 31
  unspecified 78
  infinite 105
  misty 447
  uncertain 475
  inexact 495
  vague 519
indeliberate 612
indelible *stable* 150
  memory 505
  mark 550
  feeling 821
indelicate 961
indemnity
  compensation 30
  restitution 790
  forgiveness 918
  atonement 952
  reward 973
  deed of – 771
indenizen 184
indent *scollop* 248
  list 86
indentation 252,
  257
indenture 769, 771
independence
  irrelation 10
  freedom 748
  wealth 803
Independent 984
indescribable 31,
  870
indesinent 112
indestructible 150
indeterminate
  indefinite 78

chance 156
  uncertain 475
  irresolute 605
indevotion 989
index
  arrangement 60
  exponent 84
  list 86
  sign 550
  words 62
index expurga-
  torius 761, 932
indexterity 699
Indian:
  – file 69
  – rubber 325
  – summer 126
  – weed 392
indicate
  specify 79
  direct attention to
  457
  mean 516
  mark 550
indication 550
indicative
  evidence 467
indict *accuse* 938
  arraign 969
indiction 108, 531
indifference
  incuriosity 456
  unwillingness 603
  no choice 609a
  insensibility 823
  unconcern 866
  irreligion 989
  matter of – 643
indifferent
  [*see* indifference]
  unimportant 643
  bad 649
indigence
  insufficiency 640
  poverty 804
indigenous 5, 186
indigested 674
indigestible 657
indigestion 657
indigitate 457
indign 940
indignation 900
  – meeting 832
indignity 900, 929
indigo 438
indiligence 683
indirect
  oblique 217
  devious 279
  latent 526
  circuitous 629
indiscernible 447
indiscerptible
  whole 50
  unity 87
  dense 321
indiscoverable 526
indiscreet 499, 863,
  945
indiscretion
  guilt 947
indiscriminate
  mixed 41
  unarranged 59
  multiform 81
  casual 621
indiscrimination

security 771
musical – 417
optical – 445
recording – 553
instrumental 631
– music 415
instrumentalist 41(
instrumentality 631
insuavity 895
insubordinate 742
insubstantial 4
– pageant 882
insufferable
painful 830
dislike 867
insufficiency 640
insufflation 349
insular unrelated 10
detached 44
single 87
local 181
island 346
prejudice 481
insulate 44
insulse 499, 843
insult rudeness 895
offence 900
disrespect 929
insulting 898
insuperable 471
– obstacle 706
insupportable 830
insuppressible 173
insurance 768, 771
insure
make sure 474
obtain security
771
insurgent 742
insurmountable
471
insurrection 719,
742
insusceptible 823
– of change 150
inswept 195
intact
permanent 141
perfect 650
preserved 670
intaglio mold 22
concave 252
sculpture 557
engraving 558
intangible little 193
numb 381
integer 50, 84
integer vitæ scele-
risque purus 939
integral 50
– calculus 85
– part 56
integrate 50
integrity whole 50
probity 939
virtue 944
integument 223
intellect 450
absence of – 450a
exercise of the –
451
intellectual 450
intelligence
mind 450
capacity 498
news 532
intelligencer 527

intelligentsia 492
intelligibility 518
intemperance 954
drunkenness 959
intempestivity 135
intend 620
intendant 694
intended will 600
predetermined
611
intense great 31
energetic 171
– color 428
– thought 457
intensification 35
intensify
increase 35
stimulate 171
intensity degree 26
greatness 31
energy 171
intensive culture
371
intent attention 457
will 600
design 620
active 682
– upon desire 865
resolved 604
intention 620
bad – 607
good – 906
intently, look – 441
intents and pur-
poses, to all –
27, 52
inter 363
interact 12
inter: – alia 82
– nos 528
interaction 170
interbreeding 41
intercalate 228
intercalation 300
intercede
mediate 724
deprecate 766
intercept
hinder 706
take 789
intercession
[see intercede]
worship 990
Intercessor 976
interchange 148
barter 794
– visits &c. 892
interchangeable 12
intercipient 706
interclude 706
intercommunica-
tion 527
intercommunity
892
interconnection 9
intercourse
copulation 43
friendship 888
sociality 892
verbal – 582, 58S
intercurrence
interchange 14S
interjacence 228
passage 302
interdependence 12
interdict 761
interdictive 55

interdigitate 219,
228
interest concern 9
influence 175
curiosity 455
advantage 618
importance 642
property 780
debt 806
excite 824
please 829
amuse 840
devoid of – 841
feel an – in 906
not know one's
own – 699
make – for 707
place out at –
lend 787
economy 817
take an – in
curiosity 455
love 897
take no – in
insensibility 823
indifference 866
want of – 866
interested
selfish 943
– in 457
interesting
lovable 897
interfere disagree
24
counteract 179
intervene 228
activity 682
thwart 706
mediate 724
interference
light 420
interfretted 219
interfusion 41
interim 106, 120
interior 221
painting 556
interjacence 68,
228
interject 228, 300
interlace join 43
twine 219
interlacing 41
interlard 41, 228
interleave 228
interline
interpolate 288
write 590
interlineation 39
interlink 43, 219
interlocation 228
interlocking direc-
torate 709
interlocution 588
interlocutor 582
interloper
extraneous 57
intervene 228
obstruct 706
interlude
time 106
dramatic 599
intermarriage 903
intermeddle 682,
706
intermeddling 724
intermediary 534
intermediate

mean 29
middle 68
intervening 228
ministerial 631
– time 106
intermedium
mean 29
link 45
intervention 228
instrument 631
interment 363
insertion 300
intermezzo 415
intermigration 266
interminable
infinite 105
eternal 112
long 200
intermingle 41
intermission 106,
142
intermit
interrupt 70
recur 138
discontinue 142
intermittence
time 106
intermix 41, 48
intermutation 148
intermural 278
intern 221
internal 5, 221
– evidence 467
international
reciprocal 12
sociality 892
– law 963
internecine 361
– war 722
internuncio 534,
758
interpel 142
interpellation
inquiry 461
address 586
summons 741
appeal 765
interpenetration
interjacence 228
ingress 294
passage 302
interpolation
adjunct 39
analytical 85
interpose 228
insertion 300
interpose
intervene 228
act 682
hinder 706
mediate 724
interposit 799
interplane ary 228
interpretation 522
interpreter 524
interrelation 9, 12
interregnum
intermission 106
transient 111
discontinuance
142
interval 198
laxity 738
interrogate 461
interrupt
discontinuity 70
cessation 142

hinder 706
interruption
derangement 61
interval 198
intersect 219
interspace 198, 221
intersperse 73, 228
interstellar 228
interstice 198
interstitial 221, 228
intertexture
intersection 219
tissue 329
inter-twine, -twist
unite 43
cross 219
interval
– of time 106
– of space 198
– in music 413
at –s
discontinuously
70
at regular –s 138
intervene
– in order 70
– in time 106
– in space 228
be instrumental
631
mediate 724
intervert 140, 279
interview 588, 892
intervolved 43
interweave join 43
cross 219
interjacence 228
interworking 170
intestate 552
intestine 221
inthral 749, 751
intimacy 9
intimate
personal 79
close 197
inside 221
tell 527
friendly 888, 892
intimately
joined 43
intimidate
frighten 860
insolence 885
threat 909
intitule 564
into: go – 294
put – 300
run – 300
intolerable 830
intolerance
prejudice 481
dissent 489
obstinacy 606
impatience 825
insolence 885
malevolence 907
intomb 363
intonation
sound 402
musical 313
voice 580
intone 416, 992
intort 248
intoxicant 663
intoxication
excitement 824,
825

inebriation 959
intra, ab – 221
intractable
    obstinate 606
    difficult 704
    sullen 901a
intramural 221
intransient 110
intransigeance 604
intransitive 110
intransmutable
    110, 150
intrap 545
intraregarding 221
intrench 717
    – on 303
intrepid 861
intricate
    confused 59
    convoluted 248
    difficult 704
intrigant
    meddlesome 682
    cunning 702
    libertine 962
intrigue *fascinate*
    615, 897
    plot 626
    activity 682
    cunning 702
    excite 824
    interest 829
    licentiousness 961
intrinsic 5
    – evidence 467
    – habit 613
    – truth 494
intrinsicality 5
introception 296
introduce *lead* 62
    interpose 228
    precede 280
    insert 300
    – new blood 140
    – new conditions
    469
    – to 888
introduction
    [see introduce]
    preface 64
    reception 296
    drama 599
    friendship 888
    courtesy 894
introductory
    precursor 64
    beginning 66
    priority 116
introgression 294
introit 998
intromission 228
intromit
    discontinue 142
    receive 296
introspection 441,
    457
introspective 451
introvert 218
intrude
    interfere 24
    inopportune 135
    intervene 228
    enter 294
    encroach 303
intruder 57
intrusiveness 682
intrust 755, 787

intuition *mind* 450
    unreasoning 477
    knowledge 490
intumescence 194,
    250
intwine 43, 243
inunction 223
inundate
    effusion 337
    flow 348
    redundance 641
inunderstanding
    452
inurbanity 895
inure 613, 673
inured
    insensible 823
inusitation 614
inutility 645
invade *ingress* 294
    encroach 303
    attack 716
invalid
    powerless 158
    illogical 477
    diseased 655
    undue 925
invalidate
    disable 158
    weaken 160
    confute 479
invaluable 648
invariable
    intrinsic 5
    uniform 16
    conformable 82
    stable 150
invasion
    ingress 294
    attack 716
invective 932
inveigh 932
inveigle 545, 615
invent
    discover 480a
    imagine 515
    lie 544
    devise 626
invented
    untrue 546
invention 480a
inventive
    skilful 698
inventor 164
inventory 86
inverse 14, 218
inversion
    derangement 61
    change 140
    of position 218
    contraposition
    237
    reversion 145
    language 577
invertebrate 158
invest
    empower 157
    clothe 225
    besiege 227, 716
    commission 755
    give 784
    lend 787
    expend 809
    – in *locate* 184
    purchase 795
    – money 817
    – with *ascribe* 155

investigate 461
investment 225
    – trust 712
    make –s 673
inveterate *old* 124
    established 150
    inborn 820
    – belief 484
    – habit 613
invidious
    painful 830
    hatred 898
    spite 907
    envy 921
invigorate
    strengthen 159
invigorating
    healthy 656
invincible 159
inviolable
    secret 528
    right 924
    honor 939
inviolate
    permanent 141
    secret 528
    honorable 939
invious *closed* 261
    pathless 704
invisibility 447
invisible *small* 193
    not to be seen 447
    concealed 526
    – ink 528
    become – 4
invitâ Minervâ 603,
    704
invite *induce* 615
    offer 763
    ask 765
    – the attention
    457
inviting
    [see invite]
    pleasing 829
invoice 86
invoke *address* 586
    implore 765
    pray 990
    – curses 908
    – saints 998
involucrum 223
involuntary
    necessary 601
    unwilling 603
    – servitude 749
involution [see
    involve]
    algebra 85
involve *include* 54
    derange 61
    wrap 225
    evince 467
    mean 516
    latency 526
involved
    disorder 59
    convoluted 248
    obscure style 571
    in debt 806
involvement 704
invulnerable 664
inward *intrinsic* 5
    inside 221
    – bound 294
    – monitor 926
inweave 219

inwrap 225
inwrought 5
io triumphe! 838,
    883
Ionic 597
iota 32
I. O. U. 771, 800
ipse dixit 474, 535
ipsissima verba 494
ipso facto 1
irae
    amantium – 918
    tantaene animis
    coelestibus – 900
irascibility 901
irate 900
ire 900
iridescent 440
Iris 268, 534
iris 440, 441
Irish Bull 353
Irishism 497
irk 688, 830
irksome
    tiresome 688
    difficult 704
    painful 830
    weary 841
iron *strength* 159
    smooth 255
    hard 323
    resolution 604
    rule with a rod of
    – 739
    – age *adversity* 735
    pain 828
    – cross 733
    – gray 430
    – grip 159
    – gripe 781
    – heel 739
    – necessity 601
    – rule 739
    – entering into the
    soul 828, 830
    – sway 739
    – will 604
iron-bound coast
    land 342
    danger 667
iron-clad
    covering 223
    defence 717
    man of war 726
iron-handed 739
iron-hearted 861
iron-mold 434
irons 752
    fire – 386
    put in – 751
    – in the fire
    business 625
    redundance 641
    active 682
    unskilful 699
irony
    figure of speech
    521
    untruth 546
    ridicule 856
irradiate 420
irrational
    number 84
    illogical 477
    silly 499
irreclaimable
    hopeless 859

vicious 945
    impenitent 951
irreconcilable
    unrelated 10
    discordant 24
    unwilling 603
    opponent 710
    enmity 889
irrecoverable
    past 122
    hopeless 859
irredeemable 859
irredentist 776
irreducible
    discordant 24
    out of order 59
    unchangeable 150
irrefragable 478
irrefutable 474, 478
irregular
    diverse 16a
    out of order 59
    multiform 81
    against rule 83
    – *in recurrence*
    139
    distorted 243
    combatant 726
irregularity 139
irrelation 10
irrelevant
    unrelated 10
    unaccordant 24
    sophistical 477
    unimportant 643
irreligion 989
irremediable
    bad 649
    hopeless 859
    (*spoiled* 659)
irremissible 945
irremovable 150
irreparable
    hopeless 859
irrepentance 951
irreprehensible 946
irrepressible
    violent 173
    free 748
    excitable 825
irreproachable 946
irreprovable 946
irresistible
    strong 159
    demonstration
    478
    necessary 601
irresoluble 150
irresolution 605
irresolvable 87
irresolvedly 605
irrespective 10
irresponsible
    irresolute 605
    exempt 927a
    arbitrary 964
irretrievable
    stable 150
    lost 776
    hopeless 859
irrevealable 528
irreverence 929,
    988
irreversible
    stable 150
    hopeless 859
irrevocable

stable 150
ñecessary 601
resolute 604
hopeless 859
irrigate 337
irriguous 339
irrision 856, 929
irritabile, genus –
901
irritable 825, 901
irritate violent 173
excite 824
pain 830
provoke 898
incense 900
irritation
[see irritate]
pain 828
source of – 830
irritating
[see irritate]
stringent 171
irruption 294, 716
Irvingite 984
Ishmael 83
is: that – 118
– to be 152
Isis 979
Islamism 984
island 181, 346
–s of the blessed
981
islander 188
isle 346
isobar 338
isocheimal 383
isochronal 114
isochronous 27, 120
isolate 44, 893
isolated 10, 87
isomorphism 240
isoperimetrical 27
isothermal 382
– layer 338
isotonic 413
issue distribute 73
focus 74
event 151
effect 154
posterity 167
depart 293
egress 295
stream 348, 349
inquiry 461
publication 531
book 593
ulcer 655
dénouement 729
money 800
at – discussion 476
dissent 489
negation 536
opposition 708
discord 713
contention 720
in – 461
join – lawsuit 969
– a command 741
issueless 169
isthmus
connection 45
narrow 203
land 342
italics mark 550
put in –
importance 642
itch titillation 380

desire 865
itching palm 819
item
addition 37, 39
part 51
speciality 79
unit 87
iteration 104
itinerant 266, 268
itinerary 266, 527
itur ad astra, sic –
360
ivory 430
Ixion 312

J

jab 276
jabber
unmeaning 517
stammer 583
chatter 584
jacent 213
jacet, hic – 363
jacinth 847
jack
rotation 312
ensign 550
instrument 633
money 800
Jack – Cade 742
– Ketch 975
– o' lantern 423
– in office
director 694
bully 887
– at a pinch 711
– Pudding
actor 599
humorist 844
boaster 884
before one can say
' – Robinson'
132
– tar 269
– of all trades 700
jack-a-dandy 844,
854
jackal
auxiliary 711
servility 886
jackanapes 854,
887
Jackass 271
jack-boot 225
jackdaw in pea-
cock's feathers
701
jacket 225
cork – 666
Jacobin 710
Jacquerie 716, 719
jacta est alea 601
jactitation
tossing 315
boasting 884
jaculation 284
jade horse 271
fatigue 688
low woman 876
scamp 949
drab 962
jag 257
jagged 244
jail 752

– bird
prisoner 754
bad man 949
jailer 753, 975
jakes 653
jalousie de métier
921
jam squeeze 43
crowd 72
food 298
pulp 354
sweet 396
scrape 732
– in interpose 228
jamb 215
jamboree 840
jammed in 751
jangle
harsh sound 410
quarrel 713
janissary 726
janitor 263
janty gay 836
pretty 845
stylish 852
showy 882
insolent 885
January 138
januis clausis 528
Janus deceiver 607
tergiversation 607
close the temple
of – 723
Janus-faced 544
japan coat 223
resin 356a
ornament 847
jar clash 24
vessel 191
agitation 315
stridor 410
discord 713
– upon the feel-
ings 830
jardinière 191
jargon
absurdity 497
no meaning 517
unintelligible 519
neology 563
jarvey 694
jasper 847
jaundiced
yellow 436
prejudiced 481
dejected 837
jealous 920
view with – eyes
disapprove 932
jaunt 266
jaunting car 272
jaunty [see janty]
javelin 727
jaw chatter 584
scold 932
jaw-fallen 837
jaws mouth 231
eating 298
– of death 360
jay 584
jaywalker 701
jazz 415, 840
– band 417
jealous of honor
939
jealousy 920
suspicion 485

jecur, difficili bile –
900
jeer 929
Jehovah 976
Jehu 268, 694
jejune insipid 391
style 575
scanty 640
dull 843
jell 352
jelly 298, 352
beat to a – 972
jemidar 745
jemmy lever 633
dandy 854
je ne sais quoi
exceptional 83
what d'ye call 'em
563
beauty 845
jennet 271
jeopardy 665
jerboa 309
jeremiad
lament 839
invective 932
Jericho, send to –
297
jerk start 146
throw 284
pull 285
agitate 315
jerkin 225
jerks, by – 70
Jerry Sneak 862,
941
jersey 225
Jerusalem
the new – 981
Jessamy, Jemmy –
'854
jesse 1000
jest trifle 643
wit 842
jest-book 842
jester 844
jesting-stock 857
Jesuit deceiver 548
priest 996
jesuitical 477, 544
Jesus 976
jet ship 273
stream 348
– black 431
– propulsion 267
jetsam 73, 782
jettison 782
jetty protection 250
harbor 666
jeu
le – n'en vaut pas
la chandelle
waste 638
unimportant 643
dear 814
– d'esprit 842
– de mots 842
– de théâtre 599
jeune
– premier 599
– veuve 599
Jew cunning 702
lender 787
rich 803
extortioner 819
heretic 984
worth a –'s eye

648, 814
–'s harp 417
jewel gem 648
ornament 847
favorite 899
jewelery, false –
545
Jezebel wicked 913
wretch 949
courtesan 962
jib front 234
regression 283
cut of one's –
form 240
appearance 448
jibe 140
jiffy 113
jig 840
jig-saw puzzle 840
jilt disappoint 509
deceive 545
deceiver 548
cast off 756
dishonor 940
jilted 898
jimp 845
jingal 727
jingle 408
jingo 887
jingoism 884
jinks, high – 840
jinriksha 272
jinx 649, 735
Joan of Arc 861
job business 625
action 680
unfair 940
tough – 704
Job:
patience of – 826,
830
poor as – 804
–'s comforter
dejection 837
hopeless 859
jobation 932
jobber
deceiver 548
tactician 700
merchant 797
trickster 943
jobbernowl 501
jobbery 702, 940
jobbing barter 794
jockey rider 268
deceive 545
deceiver 548
servant 746
jocose 836, 842
jocoseness fun 840
jocular 836, 842
jocund 836, 840
jocundity 829
Joe Miller 842, 844
jog push 276
shake 315
– the memory 505
– on continue 143
trudge 266
slow 275
advance 282
mediocrity 736
joggle 315
jog-trot
trudge 266
slow 275
habit 613

sad 837
- one's course 282
- an eye upon 459
- the field 722
- firm 150
- on foot
continuance 143
support 215
preparation 673
- from conceal 528
refrain 623
not do 681
restrain 751
- going
continue 143
move 264
- one's ground 141
- one's hand in 613
- one's head above
water 731, 817
- hold 150
- holy 987
- house 184
- in ignorance 528
- in restrain 751
prohibit 761
- on one's legs 654
- a good look out
for 507
- in mind 505
- moving 682
- off avoid 623
hinder 706
defend 717
resist 719
prohibition 761
- on do often 1068
continue 143
persevere 604a
- to oneself 528
- in order 693
- out
- of the way 187
- of harm's way
864
- pace with 27,
120
- the peace 714
- posted 527
- the pot boiling
143
- one's promise
772
- quiet 265
- a secret 528
- a shop 625
- in sight 459
- silence 585
- straight 944
- in suspense
uncertainty 475
irresolution 605
- in the thoughts
505
- time
punctual 132
music 416
- to 604a
- together 709
- under
authority 737
subjection 749
restraint 751
- up [see below]
- in view
attend to 457
remember 505

expect 507
- waiting 133
- watch 459
- one's word 939
keep up
continue 143
preserve 670
stimulate 824
- appearances 852
- the ball 682, 840
- a correspond-
ence 592
- the memory of
505
- one's spirits 836
- with 274
keeper 370, 753
keeping
congruity 23
in - 82
safe - safety 664
preservation 670
keepsake 505
keg 191
kelpie 979
kelson 211
kempt 652
ken 441, 490
beyond mortal -
360
kennel
assemblage 72
hovel 189
ditch 259
conduit 350
Kentish fire 931
képi 225
kérb-stone 233
kerchief 225
wave a - 550
kern quern 330
low fellow 876
varlet 949
kernel heart 5
cause 153
central 222
important 642
kerosene 356
ketch
ship 273
Ketch, Jack - 975
kettle vessel 191
caldron 386
- drum music 417
tea-party 892
- of fish
disorder 59
difficulty 704
key cause 153
opener 260
music 413
color 428
interpretation 522
indication 550
instrument 631,
633
emblem of au-
thority 747
deliver the -s of
the city 725
key-hole 260
key-note model 22
rule 80
music 413
key-stone
support 215
motive 615

importance 642
completion 729
khaki 225, 433
khan inn 189
governor 745
khedive 745
kibitka 272
kibitzer 682
kick impulse 276
recoil 277
assault 716
thrill 821
spurn 930
punish 972
- against
oppose 708
resist 719
- against the
pricks
useless 645
rash 863
unequal 28
superior 33
- up a dust
active 682
discord 713
insolent 885
- a row 900
- one's heels
kept waiting 133
nothing to do 681
- off 62
- up a row
violent 173
discord 713
- over the traces
742
kicking, alive and -
359
kickshaw food 298
trifle 643
kid child 129
progeny 167
leather 223
not to be handled
with - gloves
dirty 653
difficult 704
kidnap
deceive 545
take 789
steal 791
kidney class 75
kilderkin 191
Kilkenny cats 713
kill 361
- or cure 662
- the fatted calf
883
- the goose with
golden eggs 699
- with kindness
902
- the slain 641
- time 106
inactivity 683
amusement 840
- two birds with
one stone 682
killing 361
delightful 829
kill-joy 706
kiln 386
kilowatt 466
kilt 225
kimbo 244
kimono 225

kin 75
kind class 75
benevolent 906
- regards 894
kinder-garten 542
kindle cause 153
produce 161
quicken 171
inflame 173
set fire to 384
excite 824
incense 900
kindling wood 388
kindred 9, 11
kine 366
kinematics 264
kinetic energy 157
king 745
every inch a -
authority 737
rank 875
-maker 694
King -'s Bench
752, 966
-'s birthday 268
-'s counsel 968
- Death 360
-'s English 560
-'s evidence 529
-'s highway 627
-'s ransom 648
- of Kings 976
kingcraft 693
kingdom
region 181
property 780
- of heaven 981
kingly 737
king-post 215
kink 248, 378, 608
kiosk 189, 1000
kip 961
kirk 1000
kirtle 225
kismet 601
kiss touch 199
courtesy 894
endearment 902
- the book 535
- the hem of one's
garment 928
- in the ring 840
- the rod 725
kit class 75
equipment 191
fiddle 417
-bag 191
kitcat 556
kitchen 191, 691
- maid 746
- range 386
kitchener 386
kitchenette 691
kite fly 273
bill 800
fly a - credit 805
insolvency 808
- balloon 273, 726
kith 11
kithless 87
kitten animal 366
young 129
bring forth 161
playful as a - 836,
840
kleptomania
insanity 502

stealing 791
desire 865
kleptomaniac 504
knack 698
get into the - 613
knacker 361
knag 706
knaggy 901a
knap 206
knapsack 191
knave 548, 941
- of hearts 897
knavery
deception 545
cunning 702
improbity 940
vice 945
knead mix 41
mold 240
soften 324
stroke 379
knee angle 244
bend the -
stoop 30
submission 725
down on one's -s
humble 879
on one's -s
beg 765
respect 928
atone 952
on the -s of the
gods 121, 152
knee-deep 208, 209
kneel stoop 308
submit 725
beg 765
servility 886
courtesy 894
ask mercy 914
respect 928
worship 990
knell 363
strike the death -
361
knickerbockers 225
knicknack 643, 847
knife 253
play a good - and
fork eat 298
appetite 865
war to the - 708
knight 875
- errant
madman 504
defender 717
rash 863
philanthropist
910
-'s move 279
- service 777
- of the road 792
- Templar 71
knit 43
well - 159
- the brow
discontent 832
anger 900
disapprobation
932
knitting 847
knob pendency 214
ball 249
protuberance 250
knock blow 276
sound 406
hard -s 720

debauched 961
lichgate 363
lichen 367
licit 760, 924
lick *lap* 298
  conquer 731
  punish 972
  – the dust 933
  – into shape 240
lickerish
  savory 394
  desirous 865
  fastidious 868
  licentious 961
lickpenny 819
lickspittle 886
lictor 965
lid 223
lie *situation* 183
  presence 186
  recline 213
  falsehood 544
  untruth 546
give the – to 536
  white – 617
  – abed 683
  – in ambush 528
  – by 681
  – at one's door
    926
  – down *flat* 213
  rest 687
  – fallow 674
  – hid 528
  – in *be* 1
  give birth 161
  – low 528
  – under a neces-
    sity 601
  – in a nutshell 32
  – on 215
  – over *defer* 133
  destiny 152
  – in one's power
    157
  – at the root of
    153
  – still 265
  – to
  quiescence 265
  inaction 681
  – under 177
  – in wait for
  expect 507
  inaction 681
lief *pleasant* 829
  as – *willing* 602
  choice 609
liege 745
liegeman 746
lien 771, 805
lienteria 653
lieu 182
  in – of 147
lieutenant 745, 759
  lord – 965
life *essence* 5
  events 151
  vitality 359
  biography 594
  activity 682
  conduct 692
  cheerful 836
  animal – 364
  battle of – 682
  come to – 660
  infuse into

excite 824
  put – into 359
  recall to – 660
  see – 840
  support – 359
  take away – 361
  tenant for – 779
  – to come 152
  – after death 981
  – or death
  need 630
  important 642
  contention 720
  – and spirit 682
Life, the 976
life-blood 5, 359
life-boat 273, 666
life-giving 168
lifeguards 726
lifeless 172, 360
lifelike 17
lifelong 110
life-preserver 666,
  727
life-size 192
lifetime 108
life-weary 841
lift *raise* 307
  aid 707
  steal 791
  – cattle 791
  – up the eyes 441
  – a finger 680
  – hand against
    716
  – one's head 734
  – up the heart 990
  – the mask 529
  – the voice
  shout 411
  speak 582
lift-smoke 840
ligament 45
ligation 43
ligature 45
light *state* 7
  small 32
  window 260
  velocity 274
  arrive 292
  descend 306
  levity 320
  kindle 384
  watch 388
  luminosity 420
  luminary 423
  – *in colour* 429
  white 430
  aspect 448
  knowledge 490
  interpretation 522
  unimportant 643
  easy 705
  gay 836
  loose 961
  blue – *signal* 550
  bring to –
  discover 480a
  manifest 525
  disclose 529
  children of – 987
  come to – 529
  false – 443
  foot -s 599
  half – 422
  make – of
  underrate 483

easy 705
inexcitable 826
despise 930
  in one's own – 699
  obstruct the – 426
  side – 490
  see the – *life* 359
  publication 531
  transmit – 425
  throw – upon 522
  a – breaks in upon
    one 529
  – under a bushel
  hide 528
  not hide 878
  modesty 881
  – comedy 599
  – cruiser 726
  – fantastic toe 309
  – upon one's feet
    664
  – heart 836
  – of heel 274
  – horse 726
  – infantry 726
  – purse 804
  – and shade 420
  – of truth 543
  – up *illumine* 420
  excite 824
  cheer 836
  – upon *chance* 156
  arrive at 292
  discover 480a
  acquire 775
Light of the World
  976
lighten
  make light 320
  illume 420
  facilitate 705
lighter *boat* 273
lighterage 812
lighterman 269
light-fingered 791,
  792
light-footed 274,
  682
light-headed 503
lighthouse 550
lightless 421
light-minded 605
lightning
  velocity 274
  flash 420
  spark 423
like greased – 113
lightsome
  luminous 420
  irresolute 605
  cheerful 836
ligneous 367
lignite 388
lignography 558
ligulate 205
like *similar* 17
  relish 394
  enjoy 377, 827
  wish 865
  love 897
  do what one -s
    748
  look – 448
  we shall not look
    upon his – again
    33
  – master like man
    19

– a pin in paper 58
likely 472
  think – 507
likeness 21, 554
  bad – 555
likewise 37
liking 865, 897
  have a – for 827
  to one's – 829
lilac *color* 437
Liliputian 193
Lillith 994
lilt 416, 836
lily *white* 430
  beauty 845
  paint the – 641
lily-livered 862
līmæ *labor*
  improve 658
  toil 686
limature 330, 331
limb *member* 51
  instrument 633
  scamp 949
  – of the law 968
limber 272, 324
limbo *prison* 751,
  752
  pain 828
  purgatory 982
lime *entrap* 545
  – light 423, 531,
    599
Limehouse 908
limine, in – 66
limit *complete* 52
  end 67
  circumscribe 229
  boundary 233
  qualify 469
  restrain 751
  prohibit 761
limitarian 984
limitation [*see*
  limit]
  estate 780, 783
limited
  – *in quantity* 32
  – *in size* 393
  to a – extent
  imperfect 651
limitless 105
limitrophe 197
limn 556
limner 559
limousine 272
limp *weak* 160
  slow 275
  supple 324
  fail 732
limpid 425
lin 343, 348
lincture 662
line *fastening* 45
  continuous 69
  ancestors 166
  descendants 167
  length 200
  no breadth 203
  string 205
  lining 224
  outline 230
  straight 246
  of steamers 273
  direction 278
  music 413
  appearance 448

measure 466
mark 550
writing 590
verse 597
vocation 625
army and navy
  726
boundary – 233
draw the – 465
drop a – to 526
in a –
  continuous 69
  straight 246
  in a – with 278
read between the
  -s 522
sounding – 208
straight – 246
troops of the – 726
  – of action 692
  – of battle 69
  – of battle ship
    726
  – engraving 558
  – of march 278
  – of road 627
lineage *kindred* 11
  series 69
  ancestry 166
  posterity 167
lineament
  outline 230
  feature 240
  appearance 448
  mark 550
linear
  continuity 69
  pedigree 166
  length 200
linen 225
liner 273
lines
  fortification 717
  hard –
  adversity 735
  severity 739
  reins 752
linger *protract* 110
  delay 133
  loiter 275
lingerie 225
lingo 560, 563
lingua franca 563
linguacious 584
lingual 560, 582
linguist 492
linguistics 560
liniment 356, 662
lining 224
link *relation* 9
  connect 43
  connecting – 45
  part 51
  term 71
  crossing 219
  torch 423
  golf –s 840
  missing – 53, 729
linked together
  party 712
linoleum 223
linotype 591
linseed oil 356
linsey-wolsey 41
linstock 388
lint 223
lintel 215

lion
courage 861
prodigy 872
repute 873
come in like a –
183
as dewdrops from
the –'s mane
483
in the –'s den 665
– lies down with
the lamb 721
put one's head in
the –'s mouth
665
– in the path 706
–'s share *more* 33
chief part 50
too much 641
undue 925
lioness 374
lion-hearted 861
lionize 455, 873
lip *beginning* 66
edge 231
side 236
prominence 250
between cup and
– 111
finger on the –s
silent 581
speechless 585
hang on the –s of
418
open one's –s
speak 582
seal the –s 585
smack the –
taste 390
savory 394
– homage
flattery 933
– service
falsehood 544
hypocrisy 988
– wisdom 499
lip salve 847
lipstick 847
lipothymy 688
lippitude 443
liquefaction 335,
384
liquescence 335
liqueur 298, 396
liquid
fluid 333
sound 405
letter 561
liquidate 807, 812
liquidator 801
liquor *potable* 298
fluid 333
in – 959
– up 959
liquorice 396
liquorish [*see*
lickerish]
lisp 583
lissom 324
list *catalogue* **86**
strip 205
leaning 217
fringe 231
hear 418
record 551
will 600
choose **609**

arena 728
desire 865
enter the –s
attack 716
contend 720
listed 440
listel 847
listen 418
– in 455
– to 457
be –ed to 175
– to reason 498
listless
inattentive 458
inactive 683
indifferent 866
litany 990, 998
lite, pendente – 969
literae scriptae 590
literal
imitated 19
exact 494
manifest 525
letter 561
word 562
orthodox 983a
– meaning 516
– translation 522
literarum
homo multarum –
492
homo trium – 792
literary 560
– hack 593
– man 492
– power 569
literati 492
literatim [*see*
literal]
literature 490, 560
lithe 324
lithic 323
lithograph 558
lithology 358
lithomancy 511
lithotint 558
litigant
litigious 713
combatant 726
accusation 938
litigation
quarrel 713
contention 730
lawsuit 969
litigious 713
litter *disorder* 59
derange 61
multitude 102
brood 167
support 215
vehicle 272
useless 645
littéraire, la
morgue – 569
littérateur 492, 593
little
- *in degree* 32
- *in size* 193
darling 897
mean 940
cost – 815
do – 683
make – of 483
signify – 643
think – of 458
- did one think
508

– by little
degree 26
slowly 275
– Mary 191
– one 129
to – purpose
useless 645
failure 732
littleness **193**
littoral 342
liturgy 978
live *exist* 1
continue 141
energetic 171
dwell 186
life 359
repute 873
– apart 905
– to fight again
110
– from hand to
mouth 674
– hard 954
– in hope 858
– and let live
inaction 681
freedom 748
inexcitability 826
– in the memory
505
– upon nothing
819
– on 298
– separately 905
– by one's wits
545
livelihood 803
livelong 110
lively *keen* 375
- *style* 574
active 682
acute 821
sensitive 822
sprightly 836
– imagination 515
– pace 274
liver 83; hard –
954a
white – 862
liver-colored 433
livery *suit* 225
color 428
badge 550
decoration 877
– servant 746
liveryman 748
live wire 171
livid *dark* 431
grey 432
purple 437
living *life* 359
business 625
benefice 995
good – 957
– beings 357
–room 191
– soul 372
– thing 366
livraison 593
livret 593
lixiviate 335, 652
lixivium 335
llama 271
lo! 457, 870
load *quantity* 31
fill 52
lade 184

cargo 190
weight 319
store 636
redundance 641
hindrance 706
adversity 735
anxiety 828
oppress 830
prime and – 673
take off a – of care
834
– the memory 505
– with 706
– with reproaches
932
loads 102
loadstar [*see* lode-
star]
loaf *mass* 192
do nothing 681
dawdle 683
loafer
stroller 268
inactive 683
neglect 927
bad man 949
loam 342
loan 787
loathe 867, 898
loathing
[*see* loathe]
weariness 841
hate 898
loathsome
unsavory 395
painful 830
dislike 867
loaves and fishes
prosperity 734
acquisition 775
wealth 803
Lob's pound, in –
751
lobby 191, 615, 627
lobbying 615
lobe 51
local
– habitation 184,
189
– board 966
locale 183
locality 182, 183
localize 184
location **184**
loch 343
loci, genius – 664
lock *fasten* 43
fastening 45
tuft 256
canal 350
hindrance 706
prison 752
dead – 265
in the –up 938,
under – and key
safe 664
restraint 751
prisoner 754
– hospital 662
–out 55, 719
– the stable door
too late 135
useless 645
unskilful 699
–, stock and
barrel 50
– up *hide* 528

imprison 751
locker 191
locket 847
lock-up *prison* 752
loco, in –
agreeing 23
situation 183
expedience 646
locofoco 388
locomotion 264
– by air 267
– by land 266
– by water 267
locomotive 266, 271
locular 191
locum tenens
substitute 147
inhabitant 188
deputy 759
locus:
– *poenitentiae* 937
– *standi*
support 215
plea 617
social rank 873
locust *prodigal* 818
evil-doer 913
swarm like –s 102
locution 582
lode 636
lodestar
attraction 288
indication 550
direction 693
lodestone 288, 615
lodge *place* 184
presence 186
dwelling 189
– a complaint 938
lodgement 184
lodger
inhabitant 188
possessor 779
lodging 189
loft 191, 210
lofty *high* 206
- *style* 574
proud 878
insolent 885
magnanimous
942
log *velocity* 274
fuel 388
record 551
heave the – 466
sleep like a – 683
logarithm 84
loggerhead 501
at –s *discord* 713
contention 720
enmity 889
loggia 191
logic 476
– of facts 467
logician 476
logical acuteness
570
logography 590
logogriph 533
logolept 562
logomachy
discussion 476
words 588
dispute 720
logometer 85
logometric 84
log-rolling 709

love *desire* 865
  courtesy 894
  affection **897**
  favorite 899
  abode of – 897
  labor of –
    willing 602
  inexpensive 815
  amusement 840
  disinterested 942
  God's – 906
  make – 902
  no – lost 713
  – affair 897
  – of country 910
  – lock 256
  not for – or money
    640, 814
love-knot *token* 550
love-lorn 898
lovely 845, 897
love-making 902
love-pot 959
love-potion 865
lover [*see* love]
love-sick 897, 902
love-story 897, 902
love-token 897, 902
loving-cup 892, 894
loving-kindness
  906
low *small* 32
  not high 207
  – *sound* 405
  moo 412
  vulgar 851
  disreputable 874
  common 876
  base 940
  bring – 308
  – condition 876
  – comedy 599
  at a – ebb
  small 32
  inferior 34
  depressed 308
  waste 638
  deteriorated 659
  – fellow 876
  – life 851
  – note 408
  – origin 876
  – price 815
  – spirits 837
  – tide 207
  – tone *black* 431
  mutter 581
  – water *low* 207
  dry 340
  insufficient 640
  poor 804
low-born 876
low-brow 491
low-lands 207
low-minded 876,
  940
lower *inferior* 34
  decrease 36
  overhang 214
  depress 308
  dark 421
  dim 422
  predict 511
  sad 837
  irate 900
  sulky 901a
  – one's flag 725

– one's note 879
– orders 876
lowering 668, 859
lowly 879
lown 501, 949
lowness [*see* low]
  207
  humility 879
loy 272
loyal *obedient* 743
  observant 772
  honourable 939
lozenge 244, 662
L. s. d. 800
lubbard [*see* lubber]
lubber 683, 701
lubberly 192, 699
lubricant 332
lubrication 255, **332**
lubricity
  slippery 255
  unctuous 355
  impure 961
lucent 420
lucid
  luminous 420
  transparent 425
  intelligible 518
  – *style* 570
  – *interval* 502
lucidus ordo 58
lucifer 388
Lucifer 423, 978
lucimeter 445
luck *chance* 156, 621
  prosperity 734
  good – 858
luckless 735
lucky 134, 731
lucrative 775
lucre 775, 803
Lucretia 960
luctation 720
lucubration 451
luculent 420
lucus a non lucendo
  18, 565
lud! O – 839
ludibrious 840
ludicrous 853
luff 267
lug *pull* 285
  ear 418
luge 272
luggage 270, 780
  – van 272
lugger 273
lugubrious 837
lukewarm
  temperate 382
  irresolute 605
  torpid 823
  indifferent 866
lull *cessation* 142
  mitigate 174
  silence 403
  – to sleep 265
lullaby
  moderate 174
  song 415
  verses 597
  inactivity 683
  relief 834
lumbago 378
lumbar 235
lumbar *disorder* 59
  slow 275

store 636
useless 645
hindrance 706
lumbering 647, 846
lumber-room 191
lumbriciform 249
luminary *star* 318
  light **423**
  sage 500
luminescence 420
luminous *light* 420
  intelligible 518
  – paint 423
lump *whole* 50
  chief part 51
  amass 72
  mass 192
  projection 250
  weight 319
  density 321
  in the – 50
  – of affectation
    855
  – sum 800
  – together *join* 43
  combine 48
  assemble 72
lumpish [*see* lump]
  inactive 683
  ugly 846
Luna 318
lunacy 503
lunar 318
  – caustic 384
lunatic 503, 504
luncheon 298
lune avec les dents,
  prendre la –
  158, 471
lunette 717
lunge 276, 716
lungs *wind* 349
  loudness 404
  shout 411
  voice 580
luniform &c. 245
lupanar 961
lurch *incline* 217
  sink 306
  oscillation 314
  failure 732
  leave in the –
    outstrip 303
  deceive 545
  relinquish 624
  left in the –
    defeated 732
lure *attraction* 288,
  865
  deceive 545
  entice 615
lurid *dark* 421
  dim 422
  red 434
lurk *unseen* 447
  latent 526
  hidden 528
  lurking-place 530
luscious 394, 829
lush *vegetation* 365
  drunkenness 959
lushy 959
lusk 683
lusory 840
lust 865, 961
  – after 921
luster

brightness 420
chandelier 423
glory 873
lustily 404, 686
cry out – 839
lustless 158
lustration 652, 952
lustrum 108
lusty 159, 192
lusus naturæ 80
lute *cement* 45, 46
  guitar 417
luteous 436
Lutheran 984
luxation 44
luxuriant 168, 639
luxuriate in 377,
  827
luxurious
  pleasant 377
  delightful 829
  intemperate 954
luxury
  physical – 377
  redundance 641
  enjoyment 827
  sensuality 954
lycanthropy 503
Lyceum 542
Lydford law 964
Lydian measure
  415
lyddite 727
lying
  decumbent 213
  deceptive 544
  faithless 986
Ly-king 986
lymph *fluid* 333
  water 337
  transparent 425
lymphatic 337
lynch 972
  – law 964
lyncher 975
lynching 361
lynx-eyed 441, 498
lyre 417
lyric 415
  – poetry 597
lyrist 597

M

Mab 979
macadamize 255,
  635
Macaire, Robert –
  792
macaroni 854
macaronic
  absurdity 497
  neology 563
  verses 597
Macchiavel [*see*
  Machiavelism]
mace
  weapon 727
  scepter 747
mace-bearer 965
maceration
  saturation 337
  atonement 952
  asceticism 955
  rite 998

Macheath 792
Machiavelism
  falsehood 544
  cunning 702
  dishonesty 940
machicolation 257,
  717
machination
  trick 545
  plan 626
  cunning 702
  –s of the devil 619
machinator 626
machine 633
  like a – 698
  – gun 407, 727
  be a mere – 749
machinist
  theatrical – 599
  workman 690
macilent 203
mackerel
  mottled 440
  procuress 962
  – sky 349, 353
mackintosh 225
macrobiotic 110
macrocosm 318
macrography 441
macrology 577
mac Sycophant,
  Sir Pertinax –
  886, 935
mactation 991
macte virtute 931
macula 848
maculate
  unclean 653
maculation 440, 848
mad *insane* 503
  excited 824
  drive one – 900
  go – 825
  – after 865
  – with rage 900
madam 374
mad-brained 503
madcap
  violent 173
  lunatic 504
  excitable 825
  buffoon 844
  rash 863
madder *color* 434
made
  – to one's hand
    673
  – man 734
  – to order 673
madefaction 339
madman **504**
Madonna
  good 948
  angel 977
  pious 987
madrigal *music* 415
  verses 597
Maecenas 492, 890
Maelstrom
  whirl 312
  water 348
  pitfall 667
maestro 415
maffick 883
magazine
  periodical 53
  record 551

serve – 989
mammoth 192
man *adult* 131
  mankind 372
  male **373**
  prepare 673
  workman 690
  servant 746
  courage 861
  husband 903
  make a – of 648,
    861
  Son of – 976
  straight – 599
  to a – 488
  –at-arms 726
  one's – of business
    758
  –'s estate 131
  – in office 745
  – in the street 876
  –of-war 273, 726
  –of-war's man 269
  – at the wheel 694
  – and wife 903
manacle 751, 752
manage 693
  – to *succeed* 731
manageable 705
management
  conduct 692
  skill 698
manager
  stage - 599
  director 694
managery 693
manche après la
  cognée, jeter le
  – 859
mancible 637
mancipation 751
mandamus 741
mandarin 745
mandate 630, 741
mandible 298
mandolin 417
mandragora 174
mandrel 312
manducation·298
mane 256
man-eater 361
manège 266, 370
manes 362
manet: – altâmente
  repostum 505
  – cicatrix 919
maneuver 680, 702
manful *strong* 159
  resolute 604
  brave 861
manger 191
manger:
  cela se laisse –.394
  – son blé en herbe
    818
mangle
  separate 44
  smooth 255
  injure 659
mangled 53
mangy 655
man-hater 911
manhood 131, 861
mania *insanity* 503
  desire 865
maniac 504
manibus pedibus-

que 686
manic 503
manic-depressive
  503
manicure 847
manicheism 978
manichord 417
manie 865
maniéré 855
manifest
  list 86
  visible 446
  obvious 525
  disclose 529
manifestation **525**
manifesto 531
manifold 81, 102
manikin *dwarf* 193
  image 554
maniple 103
manipulate
  handle 379
  use 677
  conduct 692
manipulator 621
mankind **372**
manly
  adolescent 131
  strong 159
  male 373
  brave 861
  honest 939
manna *food* 396
  – in the wilderness
    aid 707
  pleasing 829
manner *kind* 75
  style 569
  way 627
  conduct 692
  in a – 32
  by all – of means
    536
  by no – of means
    602
  to the – born 5
mannered 579
mannerism
  special 79
  unconformity 83
  affectation 855
  vanity 880
mannerly 894
manners 852, 894
manor 780
  lord of the – 779
  – house 189
manorial 780
Mansard roof 223
manse 1000
mansion 189
manslaughter 361
mansuetude 894
mantelpiece 215
mantilla 225
mantle *spread* 194
  dress 225
  foam 353
  shade 424
  redden 434
  robes 747
  flush 821, 824
  anger 900
mantlet *cloak* 225
  defence 717
Mantology 511
manual *guide* 527

schoolbook 542
  book 593
  advice 695
  – labor 686
manubial 793
manufactory 691
manufacture 161,
  680
manufacturer 690
manumission 750
manure
  agriculture 371
  dirt 653
  aid 707
manuscript 22, 590
many 102
  the – 876
  for – a day 110
  – irons in the fire
    682
  – men many
    minds 489
  – times
    repeated 104
    frequent 136
many-colored 440
many-sided 81, 236
many-tóngued 532
map 234, 527, 554
  – out 626
mar 659, 706
marabou 83
marabout 1000
maranàtha 908
marasmus
  shrinking 195
  atrophy 655
  deterioration 659
maraud 791
marauder 792
marble *ball* 249
  hard 323
  sculpture 557
  tablet 590
  insensible 823
marble 440
marble-hearted 907
march *region* 181
  journey 266
  progression 282
  music 415
  dead – 363
  forced – 684
  on the – 264
  steal a –
    advance 280
    go beyond 303
    deceive 545
    active 682
    cunning 702
  – against 716
  – of events 151
  – of intellect
    knowledge 490
    improvement 658
  – off 293
  – on a point 278
  – past 882
  – of time 109
  – with 199
March, Ides of – 601
marches 233
marchioness 875
marcid 203
marconigram 523
marcor 203
mare *horse* 271

female 374
  –'s nest 497, 546
  –'s tail *wind* 349
  cloud 353
marechal 745
margarine 356
margin *space* 180
  edge 231
  redundance 641
  latitude 748
margravate 780
margrave 745, 875
marimba 417
marine *fleet* 273
  sailor 269
  oceanic 341
  soldier 726
  tell it to the –s
    489, 497
  – painter 559
  – painting 556
mariner **269**
Mariolatry 991
marionnette
  representation
    554
  drama 599
  amusement 840
marish 345
marital 903
maritime 267, 341
mark *degree* 26
  term 71
  *take cognizance
    of* 450
  attend to 457
  indication 550
  record 551
  writing 590
  object 620
  importance 642
  repute 873
  beyond the – 303
  leave one's – 873
  man of – 873, 875
  near the – 197
  overshoot the –
    699
  put a – upon 457
  save the – 870
  up to the –
    enough 639
    good 648
    skill 698
    due 924
  wide of the – 196,
    495
  within the – 304
  – down 813
  – off 551
  – out *choose* 609
    plan 626
    command 741
  – of recognition
    894
  – with a red letter
    883
  – time
    chronometry 114
    halt 265
    wait 507
  – with a white
    stone 931
marked [*see* mark]
  great 31
  affirmed 535
  well– 446

in a – degree 31
  play with – cards
    545
  – down 815
marker 550
market *buy* 795
  mart 799
  bring to – 796
  buy in the cheap-
    est &c. – 794
  in the –
    offered 763
    barter 794
    sale 796
  rig the – 794
  – garden 371
  – overt
    manifest 525
    mart 799
  – place *street* 189
    mart 799
  – price 812
  – woman 797
marketable 794,
    796
marksman 700
marksmanship 698
marl 342
marmalade 396
marmot 683
maroon
  color 433, 434
  abandon 782, 893
marplot
  bungler 701
  obstacle 706
  malicious 913
marque, letters of –
  791
marquee 223
marquetry 440
marquis 875
marriage **903**
  companionate –
    903
  ill-assorted – 904
  – bells 836
  – portion 780
marriageable 131,
    903
marrow *essence* 5
  interior 221
  central 222
  chill to the – 385
marrow-bones, on
  one's –
    submit 725
    beg 765
    humble 879
    servile 886
    atonement 952
marrowless 158
marry *combine* 48
  assertion 535
  wed 903
  – come up
    defiance 715
    anger 900
    censure 932
Mars 722, 979
  – orange 439
marsh **345**
marshal
  arrange 60
  messenger 534
  auxiliary 711
  officer 745

greater – 536
misteaching **538**
mister 373
misterm 565
misthink 481
mistime 135
mistral 349
mistranslate 523
mistress *lady* 374
   master 745
   possessor 779
   title 877
   love 897
   concubine 962
mistrust 485
misty [*see* mist]
   semi-transparent
   427
misunderstand
   misinterpret 523
misunderstanding
   495, 713
misuse **679**
mite *bit* 32
   small 193
   insufficiency 649
   money 800
   little – 129
miter *junction* 43
   angle 244
   crown 747, 999
Mithridate 662
mitigate *abate* 174
   improve 658
   relieve 834
mitigation
   [*see* mitigate]
   extenuation 937
mitraille 727
mitrailleur 727
mitten 225
mittimus 741
mix 41
   – oneself up with
   meddle 682
   co-operate 709
   – with 720
mixen 653
mixture **41**
   mere – 59
mix-up 59
mizzen 235
mizzle 348
mnemonics 505
Mnemosyne 505
moa 366
moan 405
   cry 411
   lament 839
moat *enclosure* 232
   ditch 259
   canal 350
   defence 717
mob *crowd* 72
   multitude 102
   vulgar 876
   hustle 929
   scold 932
   king – 876
   – cap 225
   – law
   authority 737
   illegality 964
mobile
   inconstant 149
   movable 264
   sensitive 822

mobility, the – 876
mobilize
   assemblage 72
   render movable
   264
   – troops 722
mobocracy 737
mobster 361
moccasin 225
mock *imitate* 17, 19
   repeat 104
   erroneous 495
   deceptive 545
   chuckle 838
   ridicule 856
   disrespect 929
   – danger 861
   – modesty 855
   – sun 423
mockery
   [*see* mock]
   unsubstantial 4
   solemn – 882
   – delusion and
   suare
   sophistry 477
   deception 545
mocking-bird 19
modal 6, 7, 8
mode *state* 7
   music 413
   habit 613
   method 627
   fashion 852
   – of expression 569
mode, à la – 852
model *copy* 21
   prototype 22
   rule 80
   form 240
   representation
   554
   sculpture 557
   perfection 650
   good man 948
   new – 658
   – after 19
   – condition 80
modeller 559
moderate
   average 29
   small 32
   allay **174**
   slow 275
   sufficient 639
   cheap 815
   temperate 953
   – circumstances
   mediocrity 736
moderately
   imperfect 651
moderation [*see*
   moderate] **174**
   mid-course 628
   inexcitability 826
moderato *music*
   415
moderator 174
   lamp 423
   director 694
   mediator 724
   judge 967
modern 123
   music 415
   art 556
modest *small* 32
modesty

humility **881**
   purity 960
mock – 855
modicum *little* 32
   allotment 786
modification
   difference 15
   variation 20a
   change 140
   qualification 469
modish 852
modulation
   variation 20a
   change 140
   music 413
module 22
modulus 84
modus: – operandi
   method 627
   conduct 692
   – in rebus 174
   – vivendi 723
mogul 745
Mohammedan 984
Mohawk
   swaggerer 887
   evil-doer 913
moiety 51, 91
moil *active* 682, 686
   exertion 686
moisture *wet* 337
   humid **339**
mokes 219
molar 330
molasses 396
mole *mound* 206
mold *condition* 7
   matrix 22
   convert 144
   form 240
   structure 329
   earth 342
   vegetation 367
   model 554
   carve 557
   decay 653
   turn to account
   677
molded 820
   on 19
molder 653, 659
molding 847
moldy 653, 659
   prominence 250
   color 432
   refuge 666
   defence 717
   spot 848
molecular 32
molecule 193
molehill *little* 193
   low 207
   trifling 643
molest *trouble* 830
molestation
   damage 649
   malevolence 907
mollia tempora 134
   – fandi 588
mollify *allay* 174
   soften 324
mollusk 366
mollycoddle 158
Molly Maguire 548
Moloch
   slaughter 361
   demon 980

heathen deity 986
molten 384
moment
   – *of time* 113
   importance 642
   for the – 111
   lose not a – 684
   not have a – 682
   on the spur of the
   – 612
momentous 152
momentum 276
Momus 838
monachism 995
monad 193
monarch 745
monarchy 737
monastery 1000
monastic 995
monasticism 984
monetary 800
   – arithmetic 11
money **800**
   wealth 803
   bad – 800
   command of – 803
   for one's – 609
   made of – 803
   make – 775
   raise – 788
   save – 817
   throw away one's
   – 818
   – to burn 641, 803
   – burning one's
   pocket 818
   – coming in 810
   – down 807
   – going out 809
   – market 800
   – matters 811
   – paid 809
   –'s worth
   useful 644
   price 812
   cheap 815
money-bag 800,
   802
money-belt 800
money-broker 797
money-changer
   797, 801
moneyed 803
moneyer 797
money-grubbing
   775
moneyless 804
monger 797
mongrel
   mixture 41
   anomalous 83
   dog 366
   base 949
moniker 565
moniliform 249
monism 984
monition 527, 668
   information 527
   warning 668
monitor *hear* 418
   oracle 513
   pupil-teacher 540
   director 694
   adviser 695
   war-ship 726
   inward – 926
monitory

prediction 511
   dissuasion 616
   warning 668
monk 996
monkey
   imitative 19
   support 215
   catapult 276
   ridiculous 857
   play the – 499
   –jacket 225
   – trick
   absurdity 497
   sport 840
   – up 900
monkhood 995
monkish Latin 563
monochord 417
monochrome 429,
   556
monocracy 737
monoculous 443
monode 445
monodrame 599
monody 597, 839
monogamist 904
monogamy 903
monogram
   sign 550
   cipher 533
   diagram 554
   letter 561
monograph
   publication 531
   writing 590
   book 593
   description 594
monolith 551
monolithic 983a
monologue
   soliloquy 589
   drama 599
monomachy 720
monomania 503
   obstinacy 606
   fanaticism 825
monomaniac 504
monomark 550
monoplane 273
monopolist 943
monopoly
   restraint 751
   possession 777
monostich 572
monosyllable 561
monotheism 983
monotonous
   uniform 16
   equal 27
   repetition 104
   permanent 141
   – *style* 575
   weary 841
   dull 843
monotype 591
monsoon 349
monsieur 370
monster
   exception 83
   large 192
   ugly 846
   prodigy 872
   evil-doer 913
   ruffian 949
monstrance 998
monstrosity
   [*see* monster]

mutable 149
mutation 140
mutatis mutandis
　correlation 12
　change 140
　interchange 148
mutato nomine de
　te &c.
　parable 521
　retaliation 718
mute *funeral* 363
　silent 403
　sordine 405,
　　408a, 417
　letter 561
　speechless 581
　taciturn 585
　dramatis persona
　　599
　deaf – 419
　render – 581
mutilate
　retrench 38
　deform 241
　injure 659
mutilated 53
mutilation 619
mutineer 742
mutiny 742
mutt 366
mutter
　faint sound 405
　mumble 583
　grumble 839
　threaten 909
mutton-chop
　whiskers 256
mutual 12, 148
mutualize 12
mutual under-
　standing 23
muzzle
　powerless 158
　edge 231
　opening 260
　silence 403
　render speechless
　　581
　restrain 751
　gag 752
muzzle-loader 727
muzzy 458
　in liquor 959
my: all – eye 546
　– stars! 870
mycology 369
mynheer 877
myology 329
myomancy 511
myopia 443
myriad 98, 102
myrmidon 726
myrrh 400
myrtle 897
myself *I* 79
　immateriality
　　317
mysterious
　invisible 447
　uncertain 475
　obscure 519
　concealed 528
mystery
　[*see* mysterious]
　latency 526
　secret 533
　play 599

craft 625
– ship 726
mystic
　uncertain 475
　obscure 519
　latent 526
　concealed 528
　sorcery 992
　puzzle 475
mystify *falsify* 477
　hide 528
　misteach 538
　deceive 545
myth 515, 546
mythology 979, 984

N

nab *deceive* 545
　seize 789
Nabob 745, 803
nacelle 273
nacre 440
nadir 211
nag *horse* 271
　quarrel 713
nager entre deux
　eaux 607
Naiad 341, 979
nail *fasten* 43
　fastening 45
　measure of length
　　200
　peg 214
　sharp 253
　hard 323
　retain 781
　on the –
　　present 118
　　pay 807
　hit the right – on
　　the head
　　discover 480a
　　skill 698
　– polish 847
naïveté 703
naked *denuded* 226
　manifest 525
　simplicity 849
　– eye 441
　– fact 151
　– steel 727
　– sword 727
　– truth 494
namby-pamby 643,
　855
name
　indication 550
　appellation 564
　appoint 755
　celebrity 873
　assume a – 565
　call –s
　　disrespect 929
　　disapprobation
　　　932
　fair – 873
　good – 873
　in the – of
　　aid 707
　　authority 737
　　due 924
　– to conjure with
　　873
nameless 565, 874

namely 79, 522
namesake 564
Nana Sahib 949
Nanny-goat 374
nap *down* 256
　texture 329
　sleep 683
　cards 840
nape *back* 235
napery 652
Napier's bones 85
napkin 652
　buried in a – 460
　lay up in a – 678
napless 226
Napoleon *food* 298
　cards 840
napping
　inattentive 458
　inexpectant 508
　dull 843
nappy *frothy* 353
　tipsy 959
narcissism 897, 943
Narcissus 845
narcosis 376
narcotic 657, 662
nard 356
narration 594
narrow
　contract 195
　thin 203
　intolerant 481
　restrict 761
　– down 42
　– end of the wedge
　　66
　– escape 671
　– house 363
　– means 804
　– search 461
narrow-minded
　481, 943
narrowness **203**
narrows 343
nasal accent 583
nascent 66
nascitur: – ridi-
　culus mus 509
　– a sociis 82
naso, omnia sus-
　pendens – 868
nasty
　unsavory 395
　foul 653
　offensive 830
　cheap and – 815
natâ, pro re – 770
natal *birth* 66
　indigenous 188
natation 267
natatorium 652
nathless 30
nation 372
national 188, 372
　– guard 726
nationality 372, 910
nations, law of 963
native
　inhabitant 188
　artless 703
　– accent 580
　– land 189
　– soil 189
　– tongue 560
nativity *birth* 66
　cast a –
　　predict 511

sorcery 992
natty 845
natura il fece e po:
　roppe la stampa
　87
naturae, vis medi-
　catrix – 662
natural *intrinsic* 5
　musical note 413
　true 494
　fool 501
　- *style* 576, 578
　spontaneous 621
　not prepared 674
　artless 703
　simple 849
　– course of things
　　613
　– death *death* 360
　– completion 729
　– impulse 601
　– meaning 516
　– order of things
　　82
　– state 90
　– turn 820
Natural – History
　357
　– Philosophy 316
　– Theology 983
naturalist 357
naturalization
　conformity 82
　conversion 144
　location 184
naturalize
　habit 613
naturalized
　inhabitant 188
naturally 154
nature *essence* 5
　rule 80
　tendency 176
　world 318
　reality 494
　artlessness 703
　affections 820
　animated – 357
　organized – 357
　second – 613
　state of –
　　naked 226
　　raw 674
　in –'s garb 226
naught *nothing* 4
　zero 101
　bring to – 732
　set at –
　　make light of 483
　　opposition 708
　　disobey 742
　　not observe 773
　　disrespect 929
　　contempt 930
naughty 945
naumachia 720
nausea 841, 867
nauseate 395, 830
nauseous
　unsavory 395
　unpleasant 830
　disgusting 867
nautch dancer 840
nautical 267
naval 267
　– authorities 745
　– engagement 720
　– forces 726

nave *middle* 68
　centre 222
　church 1000
navel 68, 222
navigation **267**
navigator 269
navvy 673, 690
navy 273, 726
　– blue 438
nay 536
　– rather 14
Nazarene 989
naze 250
N.C.O. 745
ne plus ultra
　supreme 33
　complete 52
　distance 196
　summit 210
　limit 233
　perfection 650
　completion 729
neaf 781
neap 195, 207
　– tide 36, 340
near *like* 17
　- *in space* 197
　- *in time* 121
　soon 132
　impending 152
　approach 286
　stingy 819
　bring – 17
　draw – 197
　come – 286
　– one's end 360
　– at hand 132
　– the mark 32
　– run 32
　– side 239
　– sight 443
　– the truth 480a
　– upon 3
　sail – the wind
　skilful 698
　rash 863
nearly 32
nearness **197**
neat *simple* 42
　order 58
　in writing 572,
　　576, 578
　clean 652
　spruce 845
　-'s foot oil 356
　– as a pin 58
neat-handed 698
neatherd 370
neb 250
nebula *stars* 318
　mist 353
nebular *dim* 422
nebulous *misty* 353
　obscure 519
necessarian 601
necessaries 630
necessarily 154
necessitate 630
necessity *fate* **601**
　requirement 630
　compulsion 744
　indigence 804
　make a virtue of
　　– 698
neck
　contraction 195
　narrow 203

make love 902
break one's – 360
– and crop
  completely 52
turn out – 297
– of land 342
– and neck 27
– or nothing
  resolute 604
  rash 863
neckcloth 225
necklace 247, 847
necks 980
necrology 360, 594
necromancer 548,
  994
necromancy 992
necropsy 363
necroscopic 363
necrosis 49
nectar 394, 396
need *necessity* 601
  requirement 637
  insufficiency 640
  indigence 804
  desire 865
  friend in – 711
  in one's utmost –
  735
needful
  necessary 601
  requisite 630
  money 800
  do the – *pay* 807
needle *sharp* 253
  perforator 262
  compass 693
  as the – to the
  pole
  veracity 543
  observance 772
  honour 939
  – in a bottle of
  hay 475
needle-gun 727
needle-shaped 253
needless 641
needle-witted 498
needlewoman 690
needlework 847
ne'er-do-well 949
nefarious 945
negation 536, 764
negative
  inexisting 2
  contrary 14
  prototype 22
  quantity 84
  confute 479
  deny 536
  photograph 558
  refuse 764
  prove a – 468
neglect 460
  disuse 678
  leave undone 730
  omit 773
  evade 927
  disrespect 929
  – of time 115
négligé 225, 674
negligence 460
negotiable 270
negotiate
  mediate 724
  bargain 769
  transfer 783

traffic 794
negotiations
  breaking off – 713
negotiator 724, 758
negro 431, 746
negus
  drink 298
  king 745
neif 781
neigh *cry* 412
  boast 884
neighbor 197, 890
neighborhood 183,
  197, 227
neighborly
  aid 707
  friendly 888
  social 892
  courteous 894
neither 610
  – here nor there
  irrelevant 10
  absent 187
  – more nor less
  equal 27
  true 494
  – one thing nor
  another 83
nem. con. 488
Nemesis
  vengeance 919
  justice 922
  punishment 972
**nemine contra-
  dicente** 488
**nemo me impune
  lacessit** 715
nenia 839
neogamist 903
neologism 123
neology 563
neophyte 144, 541
neoteric 123
nepenthe 662, 836
nephelogy 353
nephew 11
nepotism
  nephew 11
  wrong 923
  dishonest 940
  selfish 943
Neptune 341
Nereid 341, 979
nerve 159, 861, 885
  exposed – 378
nerveless 158
nervous *weak* 160
  style 574
  timid 860
  modest 881
nescience 491
nest
  multitude 102
  cradle 153
  lodging 189
  – of boxes 204
nest-egg 636
nestle *lodge* 186
  safety 664
  endearment 902
nestling 129
Nestor *veteran* 130
  sage 500
  advice 695
net *remainder* 40
  receptacle 191
  intersection 219

inclosure 232
snare 545
difficulty 704
gain 775
  – profit *gain* 775
  receipt 810
nether 207
nethermost 211
netting 219
nettle *bane* 663
  sting 830
  incense 900
network
  disorder 59
  crossing 219
neuralgia 378
neurasthenia 655
neuritis 378
neurology 329
neurotic 662
neuter *matter* 316
  no choice 609a
  remain –
  irresolute 605
  stand –
  indifferent 866
neutral *mean* 29
  no choice 609a
  avoidance 623
  – tint
  colorless 429
  grey 432
  peace 721
neutrality
  mid-course 628
  peace 721
  insensibility 823
  indifference 866
neutralize
  compensate 30
  counteract 179
névé 383
never 107
  – say die
  persevere 604a
  cheerful 836
  hope 858
  it will – do
  inexpedient 647
  prohibit 761
  discontent 832
  disapprobation
  932
  –dying 112
  –ending 112
  –fading
  perpetual 112
  glory 873
  – forget 916
  – to be forgotten
  642
  – indebted 807
  – hear the last of
  841
  – mind
  neglect 460
  unimportant 643
  insensible 823
  indifferent 866
  contempt 930
  – more 107
  – a one 4
  – otherwise 16
  – to return 122
  – was seen the
  like 83
  – so 31

– tell me 489
– thought of 621
– tired *active* 682
– tiring
  persevering 604a
neverness 107
nevertheless 30
new *different* 18
  additional 37
  novel 123
  unaccustomed 614
  – birth 660
  – blood *change* 140
  improve 658
  excite 824
  – brooms 614, 682
  – comer 57
  – conditions 469
  – departure 66
  – edition
  repetition 104
  reproduction 21
  improvement 658
  – ideas 537
  turn over a – leaf
  change 140
  repeat 950
  give – life to 707,
  824
  view in a – light
  658
  put on the – man
  950
New Year's Day
  138
newaub 745
new-born 123, 129
**Newcastle, carry
  coals to** – 641
new-fangled
  unfamiliar 83
  change 140
  neology 563
new-fashioned 123
new-fledged 129
Newfoundland dog
  366
Newgate 752
new-gilt 847
new-model
  convert 144
  revolutionize 146
  improve 658
newness 123
news 532
  – sheet 531
newsmonger
  curious 455
  informant 527
  news 532
newspaper 531, 551
  – correspondent
  758
newspaperman 534
newt 366
next
  following 63
  later 117
  future 121
  near 197
  – friend 759
  – of kin 11
  – to nothing 32
  – world 152
nexus 45
Niagara 348
niais 501

niaiserie 517
nib *cut* 44
  end 67
  summit 210
  point 253
nibble *eat* 298
  – at *censure* 932
  – at the bait
  dupe 547
  willing 602
nice
  savory 394
  discriminative
  465
  exact 494
  good 648
  pleasing 829
  fastidious 868
  honorable 939
  – ear 418
  – hand 700
  – perception 465
  – point 704
nicely
  completely 52
Nicene Creed 983a
nicety 466
niche *recess* 182
  receptacle 191
  angle 244
  – in the temple of
  fame 873
nicher, se – 184
nick *notch* 257
  deceive 545
  mark 550
  – it 731
  – of time 124
Nick, Old – 978
nickel
  money 800
nicknack 643
nickname 565
nicotine 392, 663
nictitate 443
nidget 862
nidification 189
nidor 398
nidorous 401
nidus 153, 189
niece 11
niggard 819
nigger 431
  – in the woodpile
  702
niggle *mock* 929
niggling 643
nigh 197
night 421
  labor day and –
  686
  orb of – 318
  – and day 136
  – school 542
night-cap 225
nightfall 126
nightingale 416
night-gown 225
nightmare
  bodily pain 378
  dream 515
  incubus 706
  mental pain 828
  alarm 860
nightshade 663
nigrescent 431
nigrification 431

nihil – ad rem 10
  – tetigit quod non
    ornavit 850
nihilism 989
nihilist 165
nihility 2, 4
nil 2, 4
  – admirari
    insensible 823
  no wonder 871
  disapproval 932
  – conscire sibi
    nullâ pallescere
    culpâ 946
  – desperandum
    858
nill *unwilling* 604
  refuse 764
nim 791
nimble 274, 682
nimble-witted 498,
  842
nimbus
  cloud 353
  halo 420
  glory 873
nimiety 641
nimis, ne quid –
  817
nimium ne crede
  colori 485
n'importe 643
Nimrod 361, 622
nincompoop 501
nine 98
  tuneful –
    music 416
  poetry 597
  – days' wonder
    transient 111
  unimportant 643
  no wonder 871
  – lives 359
  – men's morris 840
  – points of the
    law 777
ninefold 98
ninepins 840
ninety 98
ninny 501
Niobe 839
nip *cut* 44
  destroy 162
  shorten 201
  dram 298
  freeze 385
  pungent 392
  drink 959
  – in the bud
    check 201
    kill 361
    hinder 706
  – up 789
nipperkin 191
nippers 781
nipple 250
Nirwana 981
nis 980
nisi prius 741, 969
Nisus and Euryalus
  890
nisus formativus
  161
nitency 420
niter 392
nitor in adversum
  708

nitrous oxide 376
nit-wit 499, 501
niveous *cold* 383
  white 430
nixe *demon* 980
nixie *fairy* 979
nizam 745
nizy 501
N or M 78
no *zero* 101
  dissent 489
  negation 536
  refusal 764
unable to say –
  605
on – account 761
have – business
  there 83
  – chicken 128, 131
  – choice 601, 609a
  – conjuror 501,
    701
  – consequence 643
in – degree 32
at – great distance
  197
  – doubt 474, 488
have – end 112
  – end of *great* 31
    multitude 102
    length 200
  – fear 473
  – go 304, 732
at – hand 32
matter of – *import*
  4
with – interval
  199
  – one knows who
    876
  – less 639
  – longer 122
  – love lost be-
    tween them 898
  – man's land 187,
    778
  – matter
    neglect 460
    unimportant 643
and – mistake 474
  – more
    inexistent 2
    past 122
    dead 360
  – more than 32
have – notion of
  489
  – object 643
  – one 4, 187
  – other 13, 87
to – purpose
  shortcoming 304
  useless 645
  failure 732
give – quarter 361
  – scholar 493
make – scruple of
  602
  – great shakes
    small 32
    trifling 643
    imperfect 651
  – sooner said than
    done 113, 132
  – stranger to 490
  – such thing
    non-existent 2

unsubstantial 4
  contrary 14
  dissimilar 18
  – surrender 606,
    717
  – thank you 764
at – time 107
  – wonder 871
Noah's ark 41, 72
nob 210
nobilitate 873
nobility 875
noble *great* 31
  important 642
  rank 873
  peer 875
  disinterested 942
  virtuous 944
noblesse 875
nobody
  unsubstantial 4
  zero 101
  absence 187
  low-born 876
  – knows
    ignorance 491
  – knows where
    distance 196
  – present 187
  – would think 508
noctambulation 266
noctivagant
  travel 266
  dark 421
noctograph 421
noctuary 421, 551
nocturnal
  night 126
  dark 421
  black 431
nocturne 415
nocuous 649
nod *wag* 314
  assent 488
  signal 550
  sleep 683
  command 741
  bow 894
  – of approbation
    931
  – of assent 488
nodding to its fall
  162, 306
noddle 210, 450
noddy 501
node 250
nodosity 250, 256
nods and becks and
  wreathed smiles
  894
nodule 250
nodular 256
nodus, dignus vin-
  dice – 704
Noel 998
noggin 191
noise 402, 404
  – abroad 531
make a – in the
  world 873
noiseless 403
noisome
  fetid 401
  bad 649
  unhealthy 657
nolens volens 601
noli me tangere

defiance 715
excitable 825
fastidious 868
nolition 603
nolle prosequi 624
nolumus leges
  Angliae mutari
  permanence 141
  continuance 143
  preservation 670
nom de: – guerre
  565
  – plume 565
nomad 268
nomadic 266
Nomancy 511
nomenclature 564
nominal
  unsubstantial 4
  word 562
  name 564
  – price 815
nomination 564,
  755
nominee 758
nominis umbra 4
Nomology 963
non:
  – compos mentis
    503
  – constat 477
  – deficit alter 100
  – est in ventus 187
  – haec in foedera
    536, 610
  – nobis Domine
    990
  – obstante 707
  – placet 489
  – possumus
    impossible 471
    obstinate 606
    refusal 764
  – nostrum tantas
    componere lites
    471, 713
  lex – scripta 963
  – semper erit
    aestas 111
  – sequitur 477
  – sum qualis eram
    .140, 160
non-addition 38
non-admission 55
nonage 127
nonagenarian 98
non-appearance
  447
non-assemblage 73
non-attendance 187
nonce 118
  for the – 118, 134
nonchalance
  neglect 460
  insensibility 823
  indifference 866
non-coincidence 14
non-cohesive 47
non-com. 726
non-commissioned
  officer 745
non-committal 528,
  864
non-completion 730
non-compliance
  742, 764
nonconformity

difference 15
exception 83
dissent 489
sectarianism 984
non-content 489
non-cooperation
  489, 927
nondescript 83
none 101
  – else 87
  – to spare 640
  – such
    superior 33
    exceptional 83
    very good 648
  – in the world 4
  – the worse 660
non-endurance 825
nonentity
  inexistence 2
  unsubstantial 4
  unimportant 643
non esse 2
non-essential 6,
  643
non-existence 2
non-expectance 508
non-extension 180a
non-fulfilment 730,
  732
  – of one's hopes
    509
non-imitation 20
non-interference
  inaction 681
  freedom 748
nonius 466
non-juror 489, 984
non-naturals 657
nonny 501
non-observance
  inattention 458
  desuetude 614
  infraction 773
  dereliction 927
nonpareil 648
  type 591
non-payment 808
non-performance
  non-completion
    730
  dereliction 927
non-plus
  uncertain 475
  difficulty 704
  conquer 731
non-preparation
  674
non-prevalence 614
non-residence 187
non-resistance 725,
  743
non-resonance
  408a
nonsense
  absurdity 497
  unmeaning 517
  trash 643
  talk – *folly* 499
non-subsistence 2
non-success 732
nonsuch [see none]
nonsuit *defeat* 731
  fail 732
  condemn 971
nonum prematur in
  annum 133

rejection 610
refusal 764
hopeless 859
undue 925
– reach 196, 471
– one's reckoning
uncertain 475
error 495
inexpectation 508
disappointment
509
– repair 659
– repute 874
– season 135
– shape 243
put – sight
invisible 447
neglect 460
conceal 528
– sorts disorder 59
dejection 837
– the sphere of
196
– spirits 837
– one's teens 131
– time
unmusical 414
imperfect 651
spoiled 659
discord 713
– the way
irrelevant 10
exceptional 83
absent 187
distant 196
ridiculous 853
secluded 893
get – the way 623
go – one's way 629
– one's wits 824
– work 681
– the world
dead 360
secluded 893
outbalance 30, 33
outbid 794
outbrave 885
out-brazen 885
outbreak
beginning 66
violence 173
egress 295
discord 713
attack 716
revolt 742
passion 825
outburst
violence 173
egress 295
revolt 825
outcast
unconformable 83
pariah 876
secluded 893
bad man 949
outcome effect 154
egress 295
produce 775
outcry noise 411
complaint 839
censure 932
outdo superior 33
transcursion 303
activity 682
cunning 702
conquer 731
outdoor 220

outer 220
outermost 220
outface 885
outfit 225, 673
outflank flank 236
defeat 731
outgate 295
outgeneral 731
outgo 303
outgoing 295
outgoings 809
outgrow 194
outgrowth 154
out-Herod 33, 174
outhouse 191
outing 266
outjump
transcursion 303
repute 873
outlander 57
outlandish
foreign 10
extraneous 57
irregular 83
barbarous 851
ridiculous 853
outlast 110
outlaw irregular 83
secluded 893
reprobate 949
outlawry 964
outlay 809
outleap 303
outlet opening 260
egress 295
outline contour 230
form 240
features 448
sketch 554
painting 556
plan 626
outlines
rudiments 66
principles 596
outlive 110, 141
outlook view 448
outstare 885
outlying
remaining 40
exterior 220
outmaneuver
trick 545
defeat 731
outnumber 102
outpost
distant 196
circumjacent 227
front 234
outpouring
egress 295
information 527
abundance 639
output egress 295
produce 775
outrage
violence 173
evil 619
badness 649
injury to 659
malevolence 907
disrespect 929
guilt 947
outrageous
excessive 31
violent 173
scandalous 874
outrance: à –

great 31
complete 52
violent 173
guerre – 722
outrank 33, 62
outré
exceptional 83
exaggerate 549
ridiculous 853
outre mer 196
outreach 545
outreckon 482
outride 303
outrider 64
outrigger
support 215
boat 273
outright 52
outrival
superior 33
surpass 303
fame 873
outrun 303
– the constable
debt 806
prodigal 818
outscourings 653
outset 66, 873
outshine 873, 874
outside
extraneous 57
exterior 220
appearance 448
– the gates 893
mere – 544
– car 272
clean the – of the
platter
ostentation 882
outsider 57, 893
outskirts 196, 227
outspan 292
outspeak 582
outspoken say 582
artless 703
be – censure 932
outspread 202
outstanding
remaining 40
outside 220
– debt 806
– feature 642
outstare 885
outstep 303
outstretched 202
with – arms 894
outstrip 303
outtalk 584
outvie 720, 873
outvote 731
outward 220
– bound 293
outweigh 33, 175
outwit 545, 731
outwork
defence 717
outworn 124
oval 247
ovate 247
ovation 883
oven 386
like an – hot 382
over more 33
remainder 40
end 67
past 122
high 206

too much 641
all – completed 729
all – with
destroyed 162
dead 360
failure 732
adversity 735
danger – 664
get – 660
fight one's battles
– again 594
hand – 783
make – 784
set – 755
turn – 218
– and above
superior 33
added 37
remainder 40
redundance 641
– again 104
– against 237
– the border 196
– head and ears
complete 52
height 206
feeling 821
– the hills and far
away 196
– the mark 33
– one's head 208,
641
– the way 237
overabound 641
overact bustle 682
affect 855
overall 225
over-anxiety 865
overarch 223
overawe sway 737
intimidate 860
respect 928
overbalance
unequal 28
compensation 30
superior 33
overbear 175
overbearing 885
overboard, throw –
eject 297
reject 610
disuse 678
abrogate 756
relinquish 782
overborne 732, 749
overburden
redundant 641
bad 649
fatigue 688
overcast cloudy 353
dark 421
dim 422
over-cautious 864
overcharge
exaggerate 549
style 577
redundance 641
dearness 814
overcoat 225
overcolor 549
overcome
prevail 175
induce 615
conquer 731
sad 837
disgraced 874
tipsy 959

– an obstacle 731
over-confident 486,
863
over-credulous 486
over-curious 455
overdate 115
overdecorated 846
over-distension 194
overdo
redundance 641
bustle 682
affectation 855
overdose 641
overdraft 808
overdraw
exaggerate 549
misrepresent 555
prodigal 818
over-due 115, 133
over-eager 865
overeat oneself 957
over-estimation
482
overfatigued 688
overfed 957
overfeed 641
overflow stream 348
redundance 641
– with gratitude
916
overgo 303
overgorged 869,
957
overgrown much 31
large 192
expanded 194
overhang high 206
overhanging
destiny 152
over-hasty 901
overhaul count 85
attend to 457
inquire 461
censure 932
overhead 206
overhear hear 418
be informed 527
overindulgence 957
overjoyed 827
overjump 303
overlap 225, 303
overlay cover 223
exaggerate 549
excess 641
overdo 682
hinder 706
– with ornament
writing 577
overleap 303
over-liberal 818
overlie 223
overload
redundance 641
hinder 706
overlook slight 458
neglect 460
superintend 693
forgive 918
disparage 929
bewitch 992
overlooked 642
not to be – 642
overlooker 694
overlord 745
overlying 206
overmaster 731
overmastery 821

periphrase 566, 573
periplus 267
periscope 441, 445
periscopic 446
 – lens 445
perish
 cease to exist 2
 be destroyed 162
 die 360
 decay 659
 – with cold 383
 – with hunger 956
perishable 111
perissology 573
peristaltic 248
peristyle 189
periwig 225
perjured 940
perjurer 548
perjury 544
perk *dress* 225
 – *up elevate* 307
 revive 689
perked up
 proud 878
perky 880
perlustration 441
permanence
 durability 110
 unchanging **141**
 unchangeable 150
permanent
 habitual 613
permeable 260
permeate
 insinuate 228
 pervade 186
 pass through 302
 –d with 613
permissible 760
permission **760**
permissive 760
permit 760
permitting
 weather &c. – 469, 470
permutation
 numerical - 84
 change 140
 interchange 148
pernicious 649
pernicity 274
perorate
 diffuse style 573
peroration
 sequel 65
 .end 67
 speech 582
perpend *think* 451
perpendicular 212
perpension
 attention 457
perpetrate 680
 – a pun &c. 842
perpetrator 690
perpetua, esto –
 928, 931
perpetual 112
 frequent 136
 – curate 996
 – motion 467
perpetuate 112
 continue 143
 establish 150
perpetuity 69, **112**
perplex *derange* 61
 distract 458

uncertainty 475
 bother 830
perplexed 59, 248
perplexity
 disorder 59
 uncertainty 475
 unintelligibility 519
 difficulty 704
perquisite 775, 973
perquisition 461
perron 627
perscrutation 461
persecute
 oppress 649
 annoy 830
 malevolence 907
perseverance 143, 604a
Persides 215
persiflage 842, 856
persifleur 844
persist *duration* 106
 permanence 141
 continue 143
 persevere 604a
persistence
 diuturnity 110
person 3, 372
 without distinction of –s 922
persona grata 890, 899
personable 845
personae, dramatis
 – 599, 690
personage 372
personal
 [*see person*]
 special 79
 subjective 317
 – *narrative* 594
 – *property* 780
 – *remarks* 932
 – *security* 771
personality
 [*see personal*]
 discourtesy 895
 disrespect 929
 censure 932
 detraction 934
personalty 780
personate 19, 554
personify 521, 554
personnel 56, 590
perspective
 view 448
 expectation 507
 painting 556
 aerial - 428
 in – 200
perspicacity
 sight 441
 intelligence 498
 fastidiousness 868
perspicuity
 intelligibility 518
 style **570**
perspiration 295, 299
 in a – 382
perstringe 457
persuadable 602
persuade *belief* 484
 induce 615
persuasibility
 willingness 602

persuasion
 class 75
 opinion 484
 teaching 537
 inducement 615
 religious – 983
persuasive
 reasoning 476
pert
 vain 880
 insolent 885
 discourteous 895
pertain to
 relate to 9
 included under 76
 power 157
 belong 777
 property 780
 duty 926
perte de vue, à –
 196, 447
pertinacity 604a
pertinent 9, 23
pertingent 199
perturbation
 derange 61
 ferment 171
 agitation 315
 emotion 821
 excitation 824, 825
 fear 860
pertusion 260
peruke 225
peruse 539
pervade
 influence 175
 extend 186
 affect 821
 – the soul 824
pervading spirit 820
perverse
 obstinate 606
 difficult 704
 churlish 895
 sulky 901a
perversion
 sophistry 477
 misinterpretation 523
 misteaching 538
 falsehood 544
 untruth 546
 injury 659
 impiety 988
pervert 144, 607
 [*see perversion*]
perverted 495
pervestigation 461
pervicacious 606
pervigilium 682
pervious 260
pessimism
 overrate 482
 underrate 483
 dejection 837
 hopeless 859
pessimist
 [*see pessimism*]
 coward 862
pessomancy 511
pessoribus orti 876
pest 663, 830
pester 830
pest-house 662
pestiferous 657
pestilence 655

pestle 330
pet *love* 897
 favorite 899
 anger 900
 fondle 902
 flatter 933
 – lamb 266
petal 367
petard 727
 hoist on one's own
 – 718, 732
Peter to pay Paul:
 borrow of – 788
 rob – *steal* 791
 wrong 923
 –'s pence 784, 809
 peter out 142
petit-maître 854
petite dame 962
petitio principii 477
petition 765, 969, 990
petitioner 767
petrel *warning* 668
petrify *dense* 321
 hard 323
 freeze 385
 thrill 824
 affright 860
 astonish 870
petrol 388
petroleum 356
pétroleuse 384
petronel 727
petticoat *dress* 225
 woman 374
 – government
 authority 737
pettifogger 968
pettifogging
 sophistry 477
 deception 545
 litigious 713
 dishonorable 940
pettish 901
petto, in –
 mental 450
 thought of 454
 concealed 528
 intention 620
petty *little* 32, 193
 unimportant 643
 – cash 800, 811
 – jury 967
 – larceny 791
 – officer 745
 – sessions 966
 – treason 742
petulance 885, 901
petulant
 - *language* 574
peu de chose 643
peu s'en faut 32
pew *cell* 191
 church 1000
pewter 41
phaeton 272
Phaethon 423
phalanx 712, 726
phantasm
 unsubstantiality 4
 illusion 443
 appearance 448
 imagination 515
phantasmagoria 448
phantasy 453, 515

phantom *unreal* 4
 fallacy of vision 443
 imaginary 515
pharisaical 544, 988
Pharisee 548, 988
pharmacy 662
pharos 550
phase *aspect* 8
 transition 144
 form 240
 appearance 448
 have many –s 149
 assume a new –
 144
 view in all its –s
 461
phasis 448
phasma 443
phenomenon
 event 151
 appearance 448
 prodigy 872
phial 191
Phidias 559
philander 902
philanthropy 784, 906, 910
Philip drunk to
 Philip sober,
 appeal from –
 658
philippic 932
Philistine 491, 876
philologist 492
philology 560
philomath 492
philomel 416
philosopher 492, 500
 –'s stone
 impossibility 471
 perfect 650
 remedy 662
 wealth 803
philosophical
 thoughtful 451
 calm 826
philosophy
 calmness 826
 knowledge 490
 Moral – 450
 – of the Mind 450
philter 993
phiz *face* 234
 look 448
phlebotomy
 ejection 297
 remedy 662
Phlegethon 982
phlegm *viscid* 352
 insensibility 823
phlegmatic
 indifferent 866
phlogiston 382
pho! 497
Phoebus *sun* 318
 luminary 423
phoenix
 exception 83
 reproduction 163
 paragon 650
 restoration 660
phonate 402
phonetic
 sound **402**
 voice 580

color 434
perfection 650
glory 873
pink of *beauty* 845
 – fashion 852
 – perfection 650
 – politeness 894
pinnace 273
pinnacle 210
pinocle 840
pin-prick 180a
pins *legs* 266
 – and needles
 bodily pain 378
 numb 381
 mental pain 828
pinscher 366
Pinto, Fernam
 Mendez – 548
pioneer
 precursor 64
 leader 234
 teacher 540
 prepare 673
pious 987
 – *fraud* 546, 988
pip 747
pipe *tube* 260
 conduit 350
 vent 351
 tobacco 392
 sound 410
 cry 411
 music 416, 417
 weep 839
no – no dance 812
 – one's eye 839
 – of peace 721,
 723
pipeclay *habit* 613
 strictness 739
piper 416
 pay the – 707, 807
piping – hot 382
 – time 721, 734
pipkin 191
piquant
 pungent 392
 – *style* 574
 impressive 821
piquante, sauce –
 393, 829
pique *fly* 267
 excite 824
 pain 830
 hate 898
 anger 900
 – oneself
 pride 878
piqueerer 792
piquet 717, 726
pirate 773, 791, 792
piroque 273
pirouette 218, 312
 turn a – 607
Pisa, tower of – 217
pis-aller 147
piscatorial 366
pisces natare
 docere 538, 641
pisciculture 370
piscina 350, 1000
pish! *absurd* 497
 trifling 643
 excitable 825
 irascible 901
piste 551

Pistol 887
pistol 727
pistol-shot 197
piston 263
pit *deep* 208
 hole 252
 opening 260
 extract 301
 grave 363
 theater 599
 danger 667
 bottomless – 982
 – of Acheron 982
 – against 708, 713
 – against one
 another 464
pit-a-pat
 agitation 315
 rattle 407
 feeling 821
 excitation 824
pitch *degree* 26
 term 71
 location 184
 height 206
 summit 210
 erect 212
 throw 284
 descent 306
 depression 308
 reel 314
 resin 356a
 musical – 413
 black 431
 absolute – 416
 – of one's breath
 411
 – dark 421
 – into *attack* 716
 contend 720
 punish 972
 – overboard 782
 – one's tent 292
 – and toss 621
 – upon *reach* 292
 discover 480a
 choose 609
 get 775
pitched battle 720
pitcher 191
pitchfork 273, 284
 rain –s 348
pitch-pipe 417
piteous 830
piteously *much* 31
pitfall 545, 667
pith *gist* 5
 strength 159
 interior 221
 center 222
 meaning 516
 important part
 642
pithless 158
pithy *meaning* 516
 concise 572
 vigorous 574
pitiable *bad* 649
 painful 830
 contemptible 930
pitied, to be – 828
pitiful
 unimportant 643
 bad 649
 disrepute 874
 pity 914
pitiless 914a

revengeful 919
pittance
 quantity 25
 dole 640
 allotment 786
 income 810
pitted 848
pituitous 352
pity 914
 express – 915
 what a –
 regret 833
 lament 839
 for –'s sake 914
pivot *junction* 43
 cause 153
 support 215
 axis 222, 312
pix *box* 191, 998
 assay 463
pixy 980
pizzicato 415
placable 918
placard 531
placate 723, 918
place
 circumstances 8
 order 58
 arrange 60
 term 71
 situation 182, 183
 locate 184
 abode 189
 office 625
 rank 873
 give – to 623
 have – 1
 in – 183
 in – of 147
 make a – for 184
 out of – 185
 take – 151
 – to one's credit
 805
 – itself 58
 – in order 60
 – upon record 551
 – under
 include 76
placebit, decies re-
 petita – 829
placebo 933
place-hunter 767
placeman 758
placet 488, 741
placid 826
placket 260
plagiarism
 imitation 19
 borrowing 788
 theft 791
plagiarist 792
Plagiary, Sir
 Fretful – 901
plagiedral 217
plague *disease* 655
 pain 828
 worry 830
plague-spot 657
plaguy 704, 830
plaid *shawl* 225
 variegation 440
plaidoyer 476
plain
 horizontal 213
 country 344
 obvious 446

meaning 518
manifest 525
style 576
artless 703
ugly 846
simple 849
speak –ly 576
tell one –ly 527
 – English 576
 – dealing 543
 – interpretation
 522
 – question 461
 – sailing 705
 – sense 498
 – speaking 525,
 703
 – terms
 intelligible 518
 interpreted 522
 language 576
 – truth 494
 – words 703
plainness 576
plainsong 990
plain-spoken 525,
 703
plaint 411, 839
plaintiff 938
plaintive 839
plaisance
 [see pleasance]
plaisanterie 842
plaister 223
plait 219, 258
plan *itinerary* 266
 information 527
 representation
 554
 scheme 626
 according to – 82
planchette 992
plane *horizontal* 213
 flat 251
 smooth 255
 fly 267
 aeroplane 273
 soar 305
 inclined – 633
planet *world* 318
 luminary 423
 fate 601
planet-struck
 adversity 735
 wonder 870
planimeter 466
planish 255
plank *board* 204
 program 626
 path 627
 safety 666
plant *place* 184
 insert 300
 vegetable 367
 agriculture 371
 trick 545
 tools 633
 property 780
 – a battery 716
 – a dagger in the
 breast 830
 – oneself 184
 – a thorn in the
 side 830
plantation
 location 184
 agriculture 371

estate 780
planter 188
planter ses choux,
 aller – 893
plaque 204
plash *lake* 343
 stream 348
 sound 405, 408
plashy 345
plasm 22
plasma 847
plasmic 240
plaster *cement* 45
 covering 223
 remedy 662
 – up *repair* 660
plastered 959
plastic *alterable* 149
 form 240
 soft 324
 – arts 557
plastron 717
plat *weave* 219
 ground 344
plate *dish* 191
 layer 204
 covering 223
 flat 251
 food 298
 engraving 558
 – layer 690
 – printing 558,
 591
plateau 213, 344
plated 545
platform
 horizontal 213
 support 215
 stage 542
 scheme 626
 arena 728
 – orator 582
platinum-blond 430
platitude 517, 843
Platonic
 contemplative 451
 inexcitable 826
 chaste 960
 – bodies 244
Platonism 451
platoon 726
 – fire 716
platter 191
 layer 204
 flat 251
 clean the outside
 of the – 544
plaudit 931
plausible
 probable 472
 sophistical 477
 false 544
 approbation 931
 flattery 933
 vindication 937
play *operation* 170
 influence 175
 scope 180
 oscillation 314
 music 416
 drama 599
 use 677
 action 680
 freedom 748
 amusement 840
 at – 840
 bring into – 677

full – 175
full of – 836
in – 842
 – along with 709
 – one's best card
  686, 698
 – of colors 440
 – at cross pur-
  poses 59, 523
 – a deep game 702
 – the deuce 825
 – the devil 907
 – one false
  disappoint 509
  falsehood 544
  deception 545
 – fast and loose
  falsehood 544
  irresolute 605
  tergiversation 607
  caprice 608
 – on the feelings
  824
 – first fiddle 642,
  873
 – the fool
  folly 499
  clumsy 699
  amusement 840
  ridiculous 853
  ridicule 856
 – for chance 621
 – a game.
  pursue 622
  conduct 692
  pastime 840
 – the game 939
 – into the hands
  of 709
 – havoc 659
 – hide and seek
  528, 623
 – a joke 853
give – to the im-
  agination 515
 – of light 420
 – the monkey 499
 – off 545
 – a part
  false 544
  drama 599
  action 680
 – one's part 625,
  692
 – second fiddle
  34, 749
 – one a trick 509,
  545
 – tricks with 699,
  702
 – truant 623
 – upon 545, 856
 – with 460
 – upon words
  misinterpret 523
  neology 563
  wit 842
play-boy 818
play-day 840
played out
  end 67
  fatigue 688
  completion 729
  failure 732
player
  musician 416
  actor 599

– piano 417
playfellow 890
playful 836
 – imagination 515
playground 728,
  840
play-house 599
playmate 890
playsome 836
plaything
  trifle 643
  toy 840
  make-a – of 749
playwright 599
plea
  defence 462
  argument 476
  excuse 617
  vindication 937
  lawsuit 969
plead argue 467
  plea 617
  beg 765
 – one's cause 937
 – guilty 950
pleader lawyer 968
pleading, special –
  477
pleadings 969
pleasance 189, 840
pleasant
  agreeable 829
  amusing 840
  witty 842
  make things –
  deceive 545
  induce 615
  please 829
  flatter 933
pleasantry 840, 842
please 829
  as you – 743
  do what one –s
  748
  if you –
  obedience 743
  consent 762
  request 765
 – oneself 943
pleasurableness
  829
pleasure
  physical – 377
  will 600
  moral – 827
  dissipation 954
  at – 600
  at one's – 737
  during – 108a
  give – 829
  man of – 954a
  make a toil of –
  682
  take one's – 840
  will and – 600
  with –
  willingly 602
pleasure-giving 829
pleasure-ground
  demesne 189
  amusement 840
pleat 258
plebeian 851, 876
plébiscite 480, 609
plectrum 417
plectuntur Achivi
  739

pledge affirmation
  535
  promise 768
  security 771
  borrow 788
  drink to 883, 894
  hold in – 771
  take the – 771, 958
 – oneself 768
 – one's word 768
pledget 263, 662
Pleiades 72, 318
plenary 31, 52
plenipotent 157
plenipotentiary
  consignee 758
  deputy 759
plentitude 639
  in the – of power
  159
plenty
  multitude 102
  sufficient 639
 – to do 682
plenum substance 3
  matter 316
pleonasm
  repetition 104
  diffuseness 573
  redundance 641
plerophory 484
plethora 64
plexal 219
plexus 219
pliable 324
pliant soft 324
  irresolute 605
  facile 705
  servile 886
plicature 258
pliers 301, 781
plight state 7
  promise 768
  security 771
  evil – 735
 – one's faith 902
 – one's troth 768,
  902
plighted love 897,
  902
Plimsoll mark 466
plinth 211, 215
plod journey 266
  slow 275
  persevere 604a
  work 682
 – along 143
plodding 604a, 682
  dull 843
plot – of ground 181
  plain 344
  story 594
  plan 626
  reality 780
  the – thickens
  assemblage 72
plough furrow 259
  agriculture 371
 – the ground 673
 – in 228
 – the waves 267
 – one's way 266
ploughboy
  commonalty 876
ploughman 371
ploughshare 253
pluck cheat 545

resolution 604
  persevere 604a
  reject 610
  take 789
  steal 791
  courage 861
 – up courage 861
 – a crow with 932
 – out 301
plug 261, 263
 – along 143
plum number 98
  sweet 396
  money 800
plumage 256
plumb vertical 212
  close 261
  measure 466
plumber 690
plumb-line 212
plum-colored 437
plume feather 256
  ornament 847
  borrowed –s 788
 – oneself 878
plume
  coup de – 590
  nom de – 565
plumigerous 256
plummet 208, 212
plumose 256
plump
  instantaneous 113
  fat 192
  plunge 310
  unexpected 508
 – down 306
 – upon 292
plumper
  expansion 194
  vote 609
plunder 791, 793
plunderer 792
plunge
  revolution 146
  insert 300
  dive 306, 310
  immerse 337
  hurry 684
 – into difficulties
  704
 – into dissipation
  954
 – headlong 684
 – into 676
 – in medias res
  576, 604
 – into sorrow 830
plunged
 – in debt 806
 – in grief 828
plunger 621
plurality 100
plus 37
plus fours 225
plush 256
Pluto 979, 982
  realms of – 982
Plutocracy 803
plutonic 382
Plutus 803
pluvial 348
ply layer 204
  fold 258
  use 677
  exert 686
  request 765

– one's task 680
 – one's trade 625
 – a trade 794
Plymouth Brother
  984
p.m. 114, 126
pneumatics 334,
  338
pneumatology 450
pneumatoscopic
  317
poach 791, 964
poacher 792
poachy 345
pock 250
pocket place 184
  pouch 191
  diminutive 193
  receive 785
  take 789
  money 800
  treasury 802
  brook 826
  button up one's –
  808
  out of – 776, 806
  touch the – 800
 – the affront 725,
  918
pocket-book 551
pocket-handker-
  chief 225
pocket-money 800
pocket-pistol
  bottle 191
pococurante 823,
  866
pocula, inter – 959
pod 191, 223
podestà 967
podgy 201
poem 597
  book of –s 593
poenitentiae, locus -
  pity 914
  forgive 918
  vindicate 937
  repent 950
poesy 597
poet 597
poetaster 597, 855
poetic style 574
poetic frenzy 515
poetry 597
poignancy
  physical energy
  171
  pain 378
  pungency 392
  feeling 821
pogrom 361
point condition 8
  degree 26
  small 32
  end 67
  term 71
  poignancy 171
  no magnitude
  180a
  place 182
  speck 193
  sharp 253
  topic 454
  mark 550
  vigor 574
  intention 620
  wit 842

vegetation 367
praise *thanks* 916
  commendation
  931
  worship 990
praiseworthy 931,
  944
prame 273
prance 266, 315
prandial 298
prank *caprice* 608
  amusement 840
  adorn 847
prate 584
prattle 582, 584
pravity 945
praxis
  grammar 567
  action 680
Praxiteles 559
pray 765, 990
prayer 765, 990
  house of – 1000
prayer-book 998
preach *teach* 537
  speak 582
  predication 998
  – *to the winds* 645
  – *to the wise* 538
preacher
  teacher 540
  priest 996
preachment 998
preadamite 124,
  130
preamble 64
preapprehension
  481
prebend 995
prebendary 996
precarious
  transient 111
  uncertain 475
  dangerous 665
precatory 765
precaution
  care 459
  expedient 626
  safety 664
  preparation 673
precede
  superior 33
  – *in or ler* 62
  – *in time* 116
  – *in motion* 280
precedence 873
precedent
  [*see* precede]
  prototype 22
  precursor 64
  habit 613
  legal decision 969
  follow –s 82
precentor 694, 996
precept *adage* 496
  maxim 637
  order 641
  permit 760
preceptor 540
precession 62, **280**
précieuse ridicule
  855
precinct *region* 181
  place 182
  environs 227
  boundary 233
precious *great* 31

excellent 648
  valuable 814
  beloved 897
  – *metals* 800
  – *stone* 648, 847
precipice
  vertical 212
  slope 217
  dangerous 667
  on the verge of
  a – 665
precipitancy 684,
  863
precipitate
  early 132
  sink 308
  consolidate 321
  refuse 653
  haste 684
  rash 863
  – *oneself* 306
precipitous 217
précis 596
precise *exact* 494
preciosity 578
precisely
  literally 19
  assent 488
precisianism
  affectation 855
  heterodoxy 984
  over-religious 988
preclude 55, 706
precocious
  early 132
  immature 674
  pert 885
  rude 895
precognition
  forethought 490
  knowledge 510
preconceived idea
  481
preconception 481
preconcert 611, 626
preconcertation 673
precursor
  – *in order* 62, **64**
  – *in time* 116
  predict 511
predatory 789, 791
predecessor 64
predeliberation
  510, 611
predella 215
predesigned 611
predestination
  fate 152
  necessity 601
  predetermination
  611
  Deity 976
predetermination
  611
predial
  land 342
  agriculture 371
  manorial 780
predicament 8, 75
predicate
  affirm 535
  preach 998
prediction **511**
predilection
  bias 481
  affection 820
  desire 865

predispose 615, 673
predisposed
  willing 602
predisposition 176,
  820
predominant 175,
  737
predominate 33
pre-eminent 33, 873
pre-emption 795
preen 847
pre-engage 132
pre-engagement
  768
pre-establish 626
pre-examine 461
pre-exist 1, 116
preface 62, 64
prefect 745, 759
prefecture 737
prefer *choose* 609
  – *a claim* 969
  – *a petition* 765
preference 62
preferment
  improvement 658
  ecclesiastical -
  995
prefigure 511
prefix 62, 64
  letter 561
pre-glacial 124
pregnable 158
pregnant
  producing 161
  productive 168
  predicting 511
  – *style* 572
  important 642
  – *with meaning*
  516
prehensile 789
prehension 789
pre-historic 124
pre-instruct 537
prejudge 481
prejudicate 481
prejudice
  misjudge 481
  evil 619
  detriment 659
prejudicial 481, 649
prelacy 995
prelate 996
prelation 609
prelection 537, 582
prelector 540
preliminaries:
  settle – 673
  – *of peace* 723
preliminary 62, 64
prelude 62, 64
  beginning 66
  music 415
premature 132, 674
premeditate 611,
  620
prémices 154
premier 694, 759
  – *pas* 66
premiership 693
premise *prefix* 62
  precede 116
  announce 511
premises
  precursor 64
  prior 116

ground 182
  evidence 467
  logic 476
premium
  debt 805
  receipt 810
  reward 783
  at a – 814
premonish 668
premonitory 511,
  668
Premonstratensian
  996
premonstration
  appearance 448
  prediction 511
  manifestation 525
premunire 742, 974
prendre la balle au
  bond 134
prenotion
  misjudgment 481
  foresight 510
prensation 789
prentice 541
prenticeship 539
preoccupancy
  possession 777
preoccupation
  inattention 458
preoption 609
preordain 152, 601
preparation **673**
  music 413
  instruction 537
  in – 730
  in course of – 626
preparatory
  preceding 62
prepare the way
  facilitate 705
prepared *expectant*
  507
  ready 698
preparing
  destined 152
prepense
  spontaneous 600
  predetermined
  611
  intended 620
  malice – 907
prepollence 157
πρέπον, τό – 850,
  926
preponderance
  superiority 33
  influence 175
  dominance 737
prepossessed
  obstinate 606
prepossessing 829
prepossession
  prejudice 481
  possession 777
preposterous
  great 31
  absurd 497
  exaggerated 549
  ridiculous 853
  undue 925
prepotency 157
pre-Raphaelite 122,
  124, 556
pre-require 630
pre-resolve 611
prerogative 737,924

presage 511, 512
presbyopia 443
presbyter 996
Presbyterian 984
presbytery 995,
  996, 1000
prescience 510
prescious 511
prescribe *direct* 693
  advice 695
  order 741
  entitle 924
  enjoin 926
prescript 697, 741
prescription ·
  remedy 662
prescriptive *old* 124
  unchanged 141
  habitual 613
  due 924
presence
  in space **186**
  appearance 448
  breeding 894
  in the – *of*
  near 197
  real – 998
  saving one's – 928
  – *of God* 981
  – *of mind* 826,
  864
presence-chamber
  191
present
  – *in time* 118
  – *in space* 186
  offer 763
  give 784
  church prefer-
  ment 995
  at – 118
  these –s .590, 592
  – *arms* 894, 928
  – *a bold front* 861
  – *a front* 719
  – *itself event* 151
  visible 446
  thought 451
  – *oneself*
  presence 186
  offer 763
  courtesy 894
  – *to the mind*
  457, 505
  – *time* **118**
  instant 113
  – *to the view* 448
presentable 852
presentation 883,
  894
presentiment
  instinct 477
  prejudgment 481
  foresight 510
presently 132
presentment
  information 527
  law proceeding
  969
preservation
  continuance 141
  conservation **670**
  Divine attributes
  976
preserve *sweets* 396
preserver 664
preshow 511

- an inquiry 461
- the tenor of
  one's way 625,
  881
pursuer 622
pursuit **622**
pursuivant 534
pursy 194
purulent 653
purvey 637
purview 620
pus 653
Puseyite 984
push *exigency* 8
  impel 276
  progress 282
  propel 284
  essay 675
  activity 682
  haste 684
  come to the – 704
  – aside 460, 929
  – forward 682, 707
  – from 289
  – to the last 133
  – on *haste* 684
  – out *eject* 297
pushing 282, 284,
  682
pusillanimity 862
puss 366
  play – in the
  corner 148
pussy-foot 528, 958
pustule 250, 848
put *place* 184
  fool 501
  cards 840
  clown 876
  neatly – 576
  – across 484
  – about
  turn back 283
  go round 311
  publish 531
  – aside
  exclude 55
  inattention 458
  neglect 460
  disuse 678
  – away
  – *thought* 452
  relinquish 782
  divorce 905
  – back
  turn back 283
  deteriorate 659
  restore 660
  – before 527
  – by 636
  – a case 82, 514
  – in commission
    755
  – a construction
    on 522
  – on the cuff 806
  – down
  destroy 162
  record 551
  conquer 731
  compel 744
  pay 807
  humiliate 874
  – an end to
  end 67
  stop 142
  destroy 162

- *oneself* 361
- in force
  complete 729
  compel 744
- forth
  expand 194
  suggest 514
  publish 531
  assert 535
  – *a question* 461
  – *strength* 686
- forward
  suggest 514
  publish 531
  ostentation 882
  – one's hand to
    676
  – the horses to 673
  – in [*see below*]
  – to inconvenience
    647
  – a mark upon 457
  – one's nose out of
    joint 33
  – off *late* 133
  divest 226
  depart 293
  plea 617
  – on *clothe* 225
  deceive 544
  hasten 684
  affect 855
  – out [*see below*]
  – on paper 551
  – over 484, 731
  – a question 461
  – right 660
  – the saddle on
    the right horse
    155
  – the seal to 729,
    769
  – to [*see below*]
  – together *join* 43
  combine 48
  assemble 161
  – one's trust in
    484
  – up [*see below*]
  – upon 545, 649
put in *arrive* 292
  insert 300
  – an affidavit 535
  – hand 676
  – one's head 514
  – mind 505
  – motion 264
  – order 60
  – the place of 147
  – one's pocket 785
  – practice 692
  – remembrance
    505
  – shape 60
  – trim 60, 673
  – the way of 470
  – a word 582, 588
put out
  destroy 162
  outside 220
  extinguish 385
  darken 421
  *distract the atten-
  tion* 458
  uncertain 475
  difficult 704
  discontent 832

- of countenance
  874
oneself – of court
  sophistry 477
  bungling 699
  – of gear 158
  – of one's head
    458
  – of joint 61
  – of one's misery
    914
  – to nurse 707
  – of order 59
put to *attribute* 155
  request 765
  – the blush 879
  – death 361
  – the door 261
  – it 704
  – one's oath 768
  – press 591
  – the proof 463
  – the question 830
  – the rack 830
  – rights 60
  – sea 293
  – shame 874
  – silence 581
  – the sword 361
  – task 677
  – use 677
  – the vote 609
put up *assemble* 72
  locate 184
  store 636
  – to auction 796
  – for 865
  – a petition 765
  – a prayer 990
  – for sale 796
  – a shutter 424
  – the sword 723
  – to 615
  – with 147, 826
putative
  attributed 155
  believed 484
  supposed 514
putid 643
putrefy 653
putrescence 49
putrid 653
putsch 742
puttee 225
putter 683
putting the weight
  840
putty 45
puzzle *uncertain*
  475
  conceal 528
  enigma 533
  – out 522
puzzled 475, 533
puzzle-headed 499
puzzling 519
pyemia 655
pyjamas 225
Pylades and
  Orestes 890
pylon 206
pyramid *heap* 72
  height 206
  point 253
pyramids
  billiards 840
pyre 363

pyriform 249
pyrology 282
pyromaniac 384,
  504, 913
pyromancy 511
pyrometer 389
pyrotechnics 423
pyrotechny 382
Pyrrhic victory 814
pyrrhonism 487,
  989
Pythagorean 953
Pythia *oracle* 513
Python, -ess 513
pyx *vessel* 191, 998
  temple 1000

Q

Q-boat 726
Q.C. 968
Q.E.D. 478
quack *cry* 412
  imposter 548
quackery
  falsehood 544
  want of skill 699
  affectation 855
quacksalver 548
quad 189
quadragesima 956
quadrangle
  four-sided 95
  precinct 182
  house 189
  angular 244
quadrant 244, 247
quadrate with 23
quadratic 95
quadrature
  four 95
  angle 244
quadrennial 95
quadrible 96
quadrifid 97
quadriga 95, 272
quadrilateral
  sides 236
  angles 244
quadrille 840
quadripartition 97
quadrisection **97**
quadrivalent 95
quadroon 41
quadruped 366
quadruplet 96
quadruplex 96
quadruplication **96**
quaere 461
quaff 298
  – the bitter cup
    828
quaggy 345
quagmire
  marsh 345
  dirty 653
  difficult 704
quail 860, 862
quaint *odd* 83
  pretty 845
  ridiculous 853
quake *oscillate* 314
  shake 315
  cold 383
  fear 860

quakerish 826, 855
Quakerism 984
qualification
  [*see* qualify]
  power 157
  modification **469**
  skill 698
  discount 813
qualify *change* 140
  modify 469
  deny 536
  teach 537
qualis ab incepto
  141
qualities
  character 820
quality *nature* 5
  power 157
  tendency 176
  nobility 875
qualm *disbelieve* 485
  unwilling 603
  fear 860
qualms of con-
  science 950
quamdiu se bene
  gesserit 108a
quand même
  compensating 30
  opposed 708
quandary 475, 704
quantity **25**, 31, 102
quantum *amount* 25
  allotment 786
  – mutatus 140
  – sufficit 639
quaquaversum 278
quarantine 664, 751
quarrel 24, 713
  – with one's bread
    and butter
  bungling 699
  discontent 832
quarrelsome 901
quarry *object* 620
  mine 636
quart 97
quarter *cut up* 44
  fourth 95
  quadrisection 97
  period 108
  region 181
  locate 184
  abode 189
  side 236
  direction 278
  forbearance 740
  money 800
  mercy 914
  give – 914
  give no –
  kill 361
  severe 739
  pitiless 914a
  revenge 919
  – of a hundred 98
  – upon 184
quarter-day 138
quarter-deck 210
quarterly
  periodical 531
quartermaster 637
quartern 95
quarteron 41
quarters *abode* 189
  take up one's –
    184

remainder 40
corpse 362
vestige 551
organic – 357
remand defer 133
order 741
remanet 40
remark observe 457
affirmation 535
worthy of – 642
remarkable
great 31
exceptional 83
important 642
remarry 903
Rembrandtesque 160
remediable, remedial 660, 662
remediless 859
remedy 660, **662**
remembrance 505
remembrances 894
rememoration 505
remigration
regression 283
arrival 292
egress 295
remind 505
that -s me 134
reminiscence 505
remise 927a
remiss
neglectful 460
reluctant 603
idle 683
lax 738
remission
cessation 142
moderation 174
laxity 738
forgiveness 918
exemption 927a
remit
[see remission]
– one's efforts 681
remittance 807
remittent
periodic 138
remitter 790
remnant 40
remodel
convert 144
revolutionize 146
improve 658
remonstrance 615, 766, 932
remora cohere 46
hindrance 706
remorse 950
remorseless 919
remote 10, 196
– age 122
– cause 153
– future 121
remotest idea, not have – 491
remotion 270
remount 147
remove subduct 38
term 71
displace 185
transfer 270
recede 287
depart 293
dinner 298
extract 301

school 541
– the mask 529
removedness
distance 196
remugient 412
remunerate 973
remunerative 644, 775
renaissance 660
renascence 660
renascent 163
rencounter
contact 199
meeting 292
fight 720
rend 44
– the air 404, 411, 839
– the heart-strings 830
render convert 144
interpret 522
give 784
restore 790
– an account
inform 527
describe 594
– hors decombat 645
– a service 644
rendering
covering 223
rendezvous 72, 74
rendition
interpretation 522
restore 790
renegade
convert 144
turncoat 607
fugitive 623
apostate 941
renew twice 90
repeat 104
reproduce 163
recollect 505
improve 658
restore 660
– one's strength 689
reniform 245
renitence
counteraction 179
hardness 323
elasticity 325
unwillingness 603
resistance 719
renitency
light 420
renounce
recant 607
relinquish 624
resign 757
abnegate 764
– property 782
repudiate 927
renovare dolorem, infandum – 833
renovate 160, 660
renovated new 123
renown 873
renownless 874
rent tear 44
fissure 198
hire 788
purchase 795
rental 810
renter 188, 779
rent-free 815

rent-roll 780, 810
rents houses 189
renunciation
[see renounce]
exemption 927a
reorganize
order 60
convert 144
improve 658
restore 660
repair
mend 658
make good 660
refresh 689
out of – 659
– to 266
reparation
[see repair]
compensation 30
restitution 790
atonement 952
reward 973
repartee 462, 842
reparteeist 844
repartition 786
repass, pass and – 314
repast 298
repatriation 790
repay 790, 807, 973
repeal 756
repeat imitate 19
duplication 90
iterate 104
reproduce 163
affirm 535
– by rote 505
repeated 104, 136
repeater
watch 114
fire-arm 727
repel repulse 289
deter 616
defend 717
resist 719
refuse 764
give pain 830
disincline 867
banish 893
excite hate 898
repent 950
repercussion 277
répertoire 399
repertory 636
repetend
arithmetical 84
iteration 104
repetition 19, **104**
repine
pain 828
discontent 832
regret 833
sad 837
replace
substitute 147
locate 184
restore 660
replenish 52, 637
repletion
filling 639
redundance 641
satiety 869
replevin
recovery 775
borrow 788
restore 790
replica 21

replication
answer 462
law pleadings 969
reply 462, 937
répondre en Normand 544
report noise 406
judgment 480
inform 527
publish 531
news 532
rumor 532
record 551
statement 594
good – 873
through evil report and good 604a
– progress 527
reporter
informant 527
messenger 534
recorder 553
journalist 593, 758
reports law 969
repose
quiescence 265
leisure 685
rest 687
– confidence in 484
– on support 215
– on one's laurels 142
reposit 184
repository 636
repostum, manet alta mente – 919
repoussé 250
reprehend 932
reprehensible 945, 947
represent similar 17
imitate 19
exhibit 525
intimate 527
declare 535
denote 550
delineate 554
commission 755
deputy 759
– to oneself 515
representation
[see represent]
copy 21
portrait **554**
drama 599
representative
typical 79
commissioner 758
deputy 759
– government 737
– of the people 696
– of the press
messenger 534
writer 593
repress 751
– one's feelings 826
– a smile 837
reprieve
respite 133, 970
deliverance 672
release 750
pardon 918

reprimand 932
reprint
copy 21
repetition 104
reproduce 183
reprisal
retaliation 718
resumption 789
reprise 40a
reproach
disgrace 874
blame 932
accusation 938
reprobate
disapproved 932
vicious 945
bad man 949
sinner 988
reprobation 932, 988
reproduce
imitate 19
repeat 104
renovate 163
reproduction [see reproduce] 21, **163**
reproductive 163
reproof 932
reprover 936
reptile
animal 366
servile 886
knave 941
miscreant 949
republic
country 181
people 372
government 737
– of letters 560
republican
party 712
government 737
commonalty 876
republicanism 737
repudiate
exclude 55
deny 489
reject 610
abrogate 756
violate 773
not pay 808
evade 927
repugn 719
repugnance
incongruity 24
resistance 719
dislike 867
hate 898
r pulse recoil 277
repel 289
resist 719
failure 732
refusal 764
repulsion 157, **289**
repulsive
[see repulse]
unsavory 395
painful 830
ugly 846
disliked 867
discourteous 895
hateful 898
repurchase 795
reputable 873, 939
reputation 873
repute **873**

riggish 961
right *dextral* 238
  straight 246
  true 494
  property 780
  just **922**
  privilege 924
  duty 926
  honor 939
  virtuous 944
  bill of – 969
  by – 924
  have a – to 924
  set – *inform* 527
  disclose 529
  that's – 931
  – about
    [*see below*]
  – ahead 234
  – angle 212
  – ascension 466
  – away 133
  step in the – direc-
    tion 644
  – hand [*see below*]
  – itself 660
  – and left 180,
    227, 236
  – line 246
  – man in the right
    place 23
  in one's – mind
    498, 502
  hit the – nail on
    the head 480*a*,
    698
  – owner 779
  keep the – path
    944
  in the – place 23
  – thing to do 926
  – as a trivet 650
  – word in the
    right place 578
right about: to
  the – 283
  go to the – 311,
    607
  send to the –
  eject 297
  reject 610
  refuse 764
  turn to the – 218,
    279
right hand
  power 157
  dextrality 238
  help 711
  not let the – know
    what the left is
    doing 528
  – of friendship 888
righteous 944
  the – 987
  – overmuch 988
Righteousness:
  Lord our – 976
  Sun of – 976
rightful 922
  – owner 779
rightly served, be –
  972
right-minded 939,
  944
rights 748
  put to – 660
  set to – 60

stand on one's –
  748
rigid *regular* 82
  hard 323
  exact 494
  severe 739
rigmarole 517, 573
rigor 383
  – mortis 360
rigorous *exact* 494
  severe 739
  revengeful 919
rigor 494, 739
Rigsdag 696
rigueur
  de – 744
rile *annoy* 830
  hate 898
  anger 900
rilievo *convex* 250
  sculpture 557
rill 348
rim 231
rime *chink* 198
  frost 283
rimer 262
rimple 258
rind 223
ring
  fastening 45
  pendency 214
  circle 247
  loud 404
  resonance 408
  test 463
  combination 709
  clique 712
  arena 728, 840
  badge 747
  rub the – 992
  have the true –
    494
  – the changes
  repeat 104
  change 140
  changeable 149
  – in the ear 408
  in a – fence 229,
    232
  – with the praises
    of 931
  – the tocsin 669
  – up 527
ringleader
  director 694
  mutineer 742
ringlet 247, 256
rink 840
rinse 652
rinsings 653
riot *confusion* 59
  derangement 61
  violence 173
  discord 713
  resist 719
  mutiny 742
  run – *activity* 682
  excitement 825
  intemperance 954
  – in *pleasure* 742
rioter 742
riotous 173
rip 949, 962
  – open 260
  – up *tear* 44
  recall the past 505
  excite 824

Rip van Winkle
  130
riparian 342
ripe 673
  – *age old* 128
ripen *perfect* 650
  improve 658
  prepare 673
  complete 729
  – into 144
rippet 713
riposte 462
ripple *ruffle* 256
  shake 315
  water 348
  murmur 405
ripuarian 342
rire, pour – 853
rise *grow* 35
  begin 66
  slope 217
  progress 282
  ascend 305
  stir 682
  revolt 742
  – again 660
  – in arms 722
  – from 154
  – to the occasion
    612
  – in price 814
  – up *elevation* 307
  – in the world 734
risible 838, 853
rising [*see rise*]
  – of the curtain
    66, 448
  – generation 127,
    167
  – ground
  height 206
  slope 217
  worship the – sun
    886
risk *chance* 621
  danger 665
  invest 787
  at any – 604
risqué 961
rissole 298
risum teneatis
  amici? 853
rite 963, **998**
  funeral – 363
ritornello 64, 104
ritual
  ostentation 882
  rite 998
ritualism 984
rival
  emulate 648
  oppose 708
  opponent 710
  compete 720
  combatant 726
  outshine 873
rivalry *envy* 921
rive 44
rivel 258
river 348
rivet 43, 45
  – the attention
    457, 824
  – the eyes upon
    441
  – in the memory
    505

– the yoke 739
riveted *firm* 150
rivulet 348
rixation 713
Ro 560
road *street* 189
  direction 278
  way 627
  on the –
  transference 270
  progression 282
  approach 286
  on the high – to
    278
  – to ruin
  destruction 162
  danger 665
  adversity 735
road-book 266
roads *lake* 343
roadstead 154
  abode 189
  refuge 666
roadster 271
roadway 627
roam 266
roan *horse* 271
  color 433
roar *violence* 173
  wind 349
  sound 404, 407
  bellow 411, 412
  laugh 838
  weep 839
roaring *great* 31
  – trade 731, 734
roast *heat* 384
  ridicule 856
  rib – 972
  – and boiled 298
  – an ox 883
rob 354, 791
robber 792
robbery 791
robe 225, 999
  robes – of state 747
Robin Goodfellow
  980
Robinson
  say Jack – 132
Robot 554
robust *strong* 159,
  654
roc 83
rocaille 853
rock *firm* 150
  oscillate 314
  hard 323
  land 342
  safety 664
  danger 667
  build on a – 150
  founded on a –
    664
  split upon a – 732
  – ahead 665
  –bound coast 342
  – oil 356
rocket *rapid* 274
  rise 305
  light 423
  ship 273
  signal 550
  arms 727
  fireworks 840
  go up like a – and
    come down like

  the stick 732
rocking-chair 215
rococo 124, 853
rod *support* 215
  measure 466
  scourge 975
  divining 993
  kiss the – 725
  sounding – 208
  – of empire 747
  – in pickle
  prepared 673
  accusation 938
  punishment 972
  scourge 975
rodeo 720, 840
rodomontade
  exaggeration 482
  unmeaning 517
  boast 884
roe 366, 374
Roentgen rays 420
rogation
  request 765
  worship 990
rogue *cheat* 548
  knave 941
  scamp 949
  –'s march 297
roguery 940
roguish
  playful 840
Roi le veut, le –
  741
roister 885
roisterer 887
Roland for an
  Oliver
  retaliation 716
  revenge 719
  barter 794
rôle *drama* 599
  business 625
  plan 626
  conduct 692
roll *list* 86
  fillet 205
  convolution 248
  rotundity 249
  make smooth 255
  move 264
  fly 267
  rotate 312
  rock 314
  flow 384
  sound 407
  record 551
  money 800
  strike off the –
    756, 972
  – along 312
  – in the dust 731
  – on the ground
    839
  – of honour 86
  – in 639, 641
  – on 109
  – into one 43
  – in riches 803
  – up 312
  – up in 225
  – in wealth 803
roll-call 85
roller *fillet* 45
  round 249
  clothing 255
  rotate 312

roller-coaster 840
rollers *billows* 348
rollick 836
rollicker 838
rollicking
  frolicsome 836
  blustering 885
rolling: – pin 249
  – stock 272
  – stone 312
Rolls: Master of
  the – ·
  récorder 553
  judge 967
  – Court 966
Roman candle 840
Roman Catholic
  984
romance
  music 415
  absurdity 697
  imagination 515
  untruth 546
  fable 594
Romanism 984
romantic
  imaginative 515
  art 556
  sensitive 822
romanticism 515
Romanus sum,
  civis – 924
Romany 563
Rome: Church of
  984
  do at – as the
  Romans do 82
romp *violent* 173
  game 840
rondeau *music* 415
  poem 597
rondel 597
rondolette 597
rood *area* 180
  cross 998
  – loft 1000
roof 189, 223
roofless 226
rook 791, 792
rookie 726
rookery *nests* 189
  dirt 653
room *occasion* 134
  space 180
  lodge 186
  chamber 191
  plea 617
  assembly – 840
  in the – of 147
  make – for
  opening 260
  respect 928
roommate 890
rooms
  lodgings 189
roomy 180
roost 189
  rule the – 737
rooster 366
root *algebraic* - 84
  cause 153
  place 184
  abide 186
  base 211
  etymon 562
  lie at the – of 642
  pluck up by the

–s 301
strike at the – of
  716
take –
  influence 175
  locate 184·
  habit 613
  – and branch 52
  cut up – and
  branch 162
  – out *eject* 297
  extract 301
  discover 480a
rooted
  old 124
  firm 150
  located 184
  habit 613
  deep – 820
  – antipathy 867
  – belief 484
rope *fastening* 45
  cord 205
  freedom 749
  scourge 975
  give – enough 738
  –'s end 975
  – of sand
  incoherence 47
  weakness 160
  impossible 471
  – way 627
rope-dancer 700
rope-dancing 698
ropy 352
roquelaure 225
roric 339
rosá, sub – 528
rosary 990, 998
Roscius 599
rose *pipe* 350
  fragrant 400
  red 434
  beauty 845
  bed of –s 377, 734
  couleur de –
  red 434
  good 648
  prosperity 734
  hope 858
  under the – 528
  welcome as the –s
  in May 829, 892
roseate *red* 434
  hopeful 858
rose-colored
  hope 858
Rosetta stone 522
rosette 847
rose-water
  moderation 174
  flattery 933
  not made with –
  704
Rosicrucian
  sect 984
  sorcerer 994
rosin *rub* 331
  resin 356a
Rosinante 271
roster 86
rostrum *beak* 234
  pulpit 542
rosy 434
  – wine 959
rosy-cheeked 845
rot *decompose* 49

absurdity 497
rubbish 517
putrefy 653
disease 655
decay 659
rota 86, 138
Rotarian 892
rotate 138
rotation 312
  periodicity 138
rote, by – 505
  know – 490
  learn – 539
rôti 298
rôtisserie 189
rotogravure 531,
  558
rotten *weak* 160
  bad 649
  foul 653
  decayed 659
  – at the core
  deceptive 545
  diseased 655
  – borough 893
rotulorum, custos –
  553
rotund 249
rotunda 189
rotundity 249
roturier 876
roué 949
rouge 434, 847
rouge-et-noir 621
rough *violent* 173
  shapeless 241
  uneven 256
  pungent 392
  unsavory 395
  sour 397
  sound 410
  unprepared 674
  fighter 726
  ugly 846
  low fellow 876
  bully 887
  churlish 895
  evil-doer 913
  bad man 949
  cut up – 900
  – copy *writing* 590
  unprepared 674
  – diamond
  uncouth 241
  unprepared 674
  artless 703
  vulgar 851
  commonalty 876
  good man 948
  – draft 626
  – guess 514
  – it 686
  – sea 348
  – side of the
  tongue 932
  – and tumble 59
  – weather 173, 349
rough-cast 256
  covering 223
  shape 240
  scheme 626
  unpolished 674
rough-hew 240, 673
roughly
  nearly 197
rough-neck 876,
  887

roughness **256**
rough-rider 268
roughshod over,
  ride – 739
roulade 415
rouleau
  assemblage 72
  cylinder 249
  money 800
roulette 621, 840
round *series* 69
  revolution 138
  – of a ladder 215
  curve 245
  circle 247
  rotund 249
  music 415
  fight 720
  all – 227
  bring – 660
  come –
  periodic 138
  recant 607
  persuade 615
  dizzy – 312
  get – 660
  go – 311
  go one's –s 266
  go the –
  publication 531
  make the – of 311
  run the – of 682
  go the same – 104
  turn – *invert* 218
  retreat 283
  revolve 311
  – assertion 535
  – a corner 311
  – dance 840
  – game 840
  – hand 590
  – like a horse in a
  mill 613
  – of the ladder 71
  – number 84, 102
  in – numbers 29,
  197
  – pace 274
  – of pleasures
  377, 840
  – robin
  information 527
  petition 765
  censure 932
  – and round 138,
  312
  – sum 800
  – terms 566
  – trot 274
  – up 370
  – of visits 892
round about
  circumjacent 227
  deviation 279
  circuit 311
  amusement 840
  – phrases 573
  – way 729
rounded periods
  577, 578
roundelay 597
rounders 840
round-house 752
roundlet 247
round-shouldered
  243
roup 796

rouse 615, 824
  – oneself 682
rousing 171
rout *crowd* 72
  agitation 315
  overcome 731
  discomfit 732
  rabble 876
  assembly 892
  put to the – 731
  – out 652
route 627
  en – 270
  en – for 282
routine
  uniform 16
  order 58
  rule 80
  periodic 138
  custom 613
  business 625
rove *travel* 266
  deviate 279
rover *traveller* 268
  pirate 792
roving commission
  475
row *disorder* 59
  series 69
  violence 173
  street 189
  navigate 267
  discord 713
  – in the same
  boat 88
rowdy *vulgar* 851,
  876
  blusterer 887
  bad man 949
rowel 253, 615
rower 269
rowlock 215
royal 737
  – blue 438
  – highness 877
  – road 627, 705
Royal Academician
  559
royalist 737
royaliste que le roi,
  plus 33
royalty 737
Rt. Hon. 877
ruade *impulse* 276
  attack 716
ruat coelum 908
rub *friction* 331
  touch 379
  difficulty 704
  adversity 735
  painful 830
  – off corners 82
  – down *lessen* 195
  powder 330
  – down with an
  oaken towel 972
  – one's eyes 870
  – one's hands 838
  – up the memory
  505
  – off 552
  – on *slow* 275
  progress 282
  inexcitable 826
  – out 552
  – up 658
  – up the wrong

schism *dissent* 489
  discord 713
  heterodoxy 984
schismless 983a
schistose 204
scholar 492, 541
scholarly 539
scholarship
  knowledge 490
  learning 539
  distinction 873
scholastic
  knowledge 490
  teaching 537
  learning 539
  school 542
scholiast 496, 522
scholium 496, 522
school
  herd 72
  multitude 102
  system of
    opinions 484
  knowledge 490
  teaching 537
  academy 542
  painting 556
  go to – 539
  send to – 537
schoolboy 129, 541
  familiar to every –
  490
schooldays 127
schoolfellow 541
schoolgirl 129, 541
schoolman 492, 983
schoolmaster 540
  – abroad 490, 537
schoolroom 191
schooner 273
schottische 840
sciatica 378
science 490, 698
scientific *exact* 494
scientist 476, 492
scimitar 727
scintilla *small* 32
  spark 420, 423
scintillate 446, 873
scintillation
  heat 382
  light 420
  wit 842
scintillula forsan,
  latet – 858
sciolism 491
sciolist 493
sciomachy 497
Sciomancy 511
scion *part* 51
  child 129
  posterity 167
scire: – facias 461
  – quid valeant
  humeri 698
scission 44
scissors 253
  – and paste 609
scissure 198
sclerotics 195
scobs 330
scoff *ridicule* 856
  deride 929
  impiety 988
  – at *despise* 930
  censure 932
scold *shrew* 901

malediction 908
  censure 932
scollop 248, 257
sconce *top* 210
  candlestick 423
  brain 450
  defence 717
  mulct 974
scone 298
scoop
  depression 252
  perforator 262
scooter 272
scope *degree* 26
  opportunity 134
  extent 180
  meaning 516
  freedom 748
scorch
  rush 274
  heat 382, 384
scorching
  violent 173
score
  music 60, 415
  count 85
  list 86
  twenty 98
  notch 257
  furrow 259
  mark 550
  success 731
  credit 805
  debt 806
  accounts 811
  on the – of
    relation 9
    motive 615
scores *many* 102
scoria *ash* 384
  dirt 653
scorify 384
scoring board 551
scorn 930
scorpion
  painful 830
  evil-doer 913
  (*bane* 663)
  chastise with –s
  739
scorse 794
scot *reward* 973
scot free *free* 748
  cheap 815
  exempt 927a
escape –
  escape 671
  let off – 970
scotch *notch* 257
  injure 659
  – the snake
    maim 158
  insufficient 640
  non-completion
  730
  – the wheel 706
Scotsman
  canny 702
Scotticism 563
scotomy 443
scoundrel 913, 949
scour *run* 274
  rub 331
  clean 652
  – the country 266
  – the plain 274
scourge *bane* 663

painful 830
  punish 972
  instrument of
    punishment 975
  – of the human
    race 913
scourings 645
scout 234
  observer 444
  feeler 463
  messenger 534
  reject 610
  warship 726
  servant 746
  watch 664
  warning 668
  disrespect 929
  disdain 930
  (*looker* 444)
  (*underrate* 483)
  (*ridicule* 856)
scow 273
scowl
  complain 839
  frown 895
  anger 900
  sullen 901a
  disapprobation
  932
scrabble
  unmeaning 517
  scribble 590
scrag 32, 203
scraggy *lean* 193,
  203
  rough 256
scramble
  confusion 59
  climb 305
  pursue 622
  haste 684
  difficulty 704
  contend 720
  seize 789
scranch 330
scrannel 643
scrap 32, 720
  – *of* paper 158, 940
scrap-book 596
scrape *subduct* 38
  reduce 195
  pulverize 330
  abrade 331
  mezzotint 558
  difficulty 704
  mischance 732
  bow 894
  – together
    assemble 72
    acquire 775
scraper 652
scratch *groove* 259
  abrade 331
  mark 550
  daub 555
  draw 556
  write 590
  hurt 619
  wound 649
  come to the –
    720, 861
  mere – 209
  old – 978
  up to the – 861
  without a – 654,
    670
  – the head 461

– out 552
scrawl 590
scrawny 203
screak 411
scream *cry* 411, 839
screech 411, 412
screech owl 412
screed 582, 593
screen *sift* 60
  sieve 260
  shade 424
  cinema 448
  hide 528
  hider 530
  side-scene 599
  clean 562
  safety 664
  shelter 666
  defence 717
  – from sight 442
screw *fasten* 43
  fastening 45
  distort 243
  oar 267
  rotation 312
  instrument 633
  miser 819
  put on the – 739,
  744
  – one's courage to
    the sticking
    place 861
  – loose *insane* 503
    imperfect 651
    unskilful 699
    hindrance 706
    attack 713
  – up *fasten* 43
    strengthen 159
    prepare 673
  – up the eyes 443
screwed
  drunk 959
screw-driver 633
screw-steamer 273
scribble 517, 590
scribbler 593
scribe *recorder* 553
  writer 590, 593
  priest 996
  –s and Pharisees
  988
scribendi, ca-
  coëthes – 580
scrimshanker 603
scrimmage 713, 720
scrimp *short* 201
  insufficient 640
  stingy 819
scrip 191
script 590, 599
scripta, lex – 963
scriptae, literae–590
scriptural 983a
Scripture
  certain 474
  revelation 985
scrivener *writer* 590
  lawyer 968
scroll 56, 551
scrub *rub* 331
  bush 367
  clean 652
  dirty person 653
  commonalty 876
scrubby *small* 193
  trifling 643

stingy 819
  disreputable 874
  vulgar 876
  shabby 940
scruff 235
scruple
  small quantity 32
  weight 319
  doubt 485
  reluctance 603
  probity 939
scrupulous
  careful 459
  incredulous 487
  exact 494
  reluctant 603
  fastidious 868
  punctilious 939
scrutator 461
scrutiny 457, 461
scrutoire 191
scud *sail* 267
  speed 274
  shower 348
  cloud 353
  – under bare
    poles 704
scuffle 720
scull *row* 267
  brain 450
scull-cap 225
scullery 191
scullion 746
sculpsit 558
sculptor 559
sculpture 240, 557
scum *dirt* 653
  – of the earth 949
  – of society 876
scupper 350
scurf 653
scurrilous
  ridicule 856
  malediction 908
  disrespect 929
  detraction 934
scurry 274, 684
scurvy
  insufficient 640
  unimportant 643
  base 940
  wicked 945
scut 235
scutcheon
  standard 550
  honor 877
scutiform 251
scuttle *destroy* 162
  receptacle 191
  speed 274
  – along *haste* 684
Scylla and Charyb-
  dis, between –
  danger 665
  difficulty 704
Scyllam, incidit
  in – 699
scythe *pointed* 244
  sharp 253
'sdeath! *wonder* 870
  anger 900
  disapprobation
  932
se non e vero e ben
  trovato 546
sea *multitude* 102
  ocean 341

at – 341
uncertain 475
erroneous 495
go to – 293
on the high –s 41
heavy – 315
the seven –s 341
– of doubt 475
– of troubles
difficulty 704
adversity 735
seaboard 342
seafarer 269
seafaring 267, 273
sea-fight 720
sea-girt 346
sea-going 267, 341
sea-green 435
seal
matrix 22
close 261
evidence 467
mark 550
resolve 604
complete 729
compact 769
security 771
break the – 529
under – 769
– the doom of 162
– one's infamy 940
– the lips 585
– of secrecy 528
– up *restrain* 751
sealed:
one's fate is – 601
hermetically – 261
– book
ignorance 491
unintelligible 519
secret 533
sealing-wax 747
seals *insignia* 747
sealskin 223
seam 43
sea-maid 979
sea-man 269
seamanship 692,
698
sea-mark 550
seamless 50
seamstress 225,
690
seamy side 651
séance 525, 696
sea-piece 556
seaplane 273, 736
sea-port 666
sear *dry* 340
burn 384
deaden 823
– and yellow leaf
128, 659
search *inquire* 461
searching
severe 739
painful 830
searchless 519
searchlight 423,
726
seared conscience
951
searing 830
seascape 556
sea-serpent 83
seaside 342
season *mix* 41

time 106
pungent 392
accustom 613
preserve 670
prepare 673
seasonable 23, 134
seasoning 393
seasons 138
seat *place* 183
locate 184
abode 189
support 215
posterior 235
parliament 693
country – 189
judgment – 966
– of government
737
– of war 728
seated, firmly – 150
seaway 267
seaweed 367
seaworthy 273, 604
sebaceous 355
secant 219
secede *dissent* 489
relinquish 624
disobey 742
seceder
heterodox 984
secern 297
seclusion 893
second
duplication 90
– of time 108
instant 113
– in *music* 413,
415
abet 707
play or sing a –
416
– best 651, 732
– childhood 128,
499
– crop 168, 775
– edition 104
play – fiddle
obey 743
subject 749
disrepute 874
– nature 613
– to none 33
one's – self 17
– rate 659
– sight
foresight 510
sorcery 992
– thoughts
sequel 65
thought 451
improvement 658
– youth 660
secondary
inferior 34
following 63
imperfect 651
deputy 759
– education 537
– evidence 467
– school 542
seconder 711
second-hand
imitation 19
old 124
deteriorated 659
received 785
secondly 90

second-rate 651
secret *key* 522
latent 526
hidden 528
riddle 533
in the – 490
keep a – 585
– motive 615
– passage 627, 671
– place 530
– writing 590
secrétaire 191
secretary
recorder 553
writer 590
director 694
auxiliary 711
servant 746
consignee 758
– of state 694
– of the treasury
801
secrete *excrete* 297
conceal 528
secretion 299
secretive 528
sect 75
religious – 983,
984
sectarian
dissent 489
ally 711
heterodox 984
sectary 489
section *division* 44
part 51
class 75
chapter 593
troops 726
sector *part* 51
circle 247
secula seculorum,
in – 112
secular
centenary 98
periodic 138
laity 997
– education 537
secularism 984
secundum artem
82, 698
secure *fasten* 43
bespeak 132
belief 484
safe 664
restrain 751
engage 768
gain 775
confident 858
– an object 731
securities 802–805
security *safety* 664
pledge 771
hope 858
lend on – 787
Sedan
disaster 162
sedan chair 272
sedate
thoughtful 451
calm 826
grave 837
sedative 174, 662
sedentary 265
sedge 367
sedile 1000
sediment *dregs* 653

sedimentary 40
sedition 742
seduce *entice* 615
love 897
debauch 961
seducer 962
seduction 829, 865
sedulous 682, 865
see *view* 441
look 457
believe 484
know 490
bishopric 995
we shall – 507
– after 459
– daylight 480a
– double 959
– fit 600, 602
– at a glance 498
– justice done 922
– life 840
– the light
born 359
published 531
– service 722
– sights 455
– through 480a,
498
– to *attention* 457
care 459
direction 693
– one's way
foresight 510
intelligible 518
skill 698
easy 705
seed *small* 32
cause 153
posterity 167
grain 330
run to – *age* 128
lose health 659
sow the – 673
seedling 129
seed-plot 168, 371
seed-time of life
127
seedy *weak* 160
disease 655
deteriorated 659
exhausted 688
needy 804
seeing that 8, 476
seek *inquire* 461
pursue 622
offer 763
request 765
– safety 664
seek-sorrow 837
seel 217
seem 448
as it –s good to
600
seeming 488
seemingly 472
seemless 846, 925
seemliness 926
seemly
expedient 646
handsome 845
due 924
seep 295
seer *veteran* 130.
madman 504
oracle 513
sorcerer 994
see-saw 12, 314

seethe *wet* 339
hot 382
make hot 384
excitement 824
seething caldron
386
segar 392
segment 44, 51
segnitude 683
s'égosiller 411
segregate
not related 10
separate 44
exclude 55
segregated
incoherent 47
seigneur, grand –
pride 878
insolence 885
seignior 745, 875
seigniority
authority 737
possession 777
property 780
seigniory 737
seine net 232
seisin 777, 780
seismic 314
seismograph 553
seismometer 276,
314
seize 789, 791
– an opportunity
134
seized with
disease 655
feeling 821
seizure 925
sejunction 44
seldom 137
select *choose* 609
good 648
self 13, 79
–abasement 879
–accusing 950
–admiration 880
–applause 880
–appointed *task*
602
–assertion 885
–called 565
–command 604,
864
–communing 451
–complacency
836, 880
–confidence 880
–conquest 604
–conscious 855
–consultation 451
–contained 52
–control 604
–conviction
belief 484
penitent 950
condemned 971
–counsel 451
–deceit *error* 495
–deception 486
–defence 717
–delusion 486
–denial
disinterested 942
temperance 953
penance 990
–discipline 990
–effacement 879,

942
-esteem 880
-evident 474, 525
-examination 990
-existing 1
-government 748
-help 698
-immolation 991
-indulgence
selfishness 943
intemperance 954
-interest 943
-knowledge 881
-love 943
-luminous 423
-mastery 604
-opinioned 481
-possession
sanity 502
resolution 604
inexcitability 826
caution 864
-praise 880
-preservation 717
-reliance
resolution 604
hope 858
courage 861
-reproach 950
-respect 878
-restraint 953
-sacrifice 942
-satisfied 880
-seeking 943
-styled 565
-sufficient 880
-taught 490
-tormentor 837
-will 606
selfishness 943
self-same 13
sell *convince* 484
absurdity 497
deception 545
untruth 546
sale 796
- for 812
- one's life dearly
719, 722
- off 796
- oneself 940
- out 796
seller 796
selon les règles 82
selvedge 231
semaphore 550
semblance
similarity 17
imitation 19
copy 21
probability 472
wear the - of
appearance 448
semeiology 522
semeiotics 550
semester 108
semi- 91
semi-barbarian 913
semibreve 413
semicircle 247
semicircular 245
semicolon 142
semi-diaphanous
427
semi-fluid 352
semi-liquidity 352
semi-lunar 245

seminal 153
seminary 542
semination 673
semi-opaque 427
semi-pellucid 427
semiquaver 413
semitone 413
semi-transparency
427
sempervirent 110
sempiternal 112
sempstress 225, 690
senary 98
senate 696
senate-house 966
senator 695, 696
senatorship 693
senatus consultum
741
send 270, 284
- adrift 597
- away
repel 289
eject 297
refuse 764
- for 741
- forth 284, 531
- a letter to 592
- off 284
- out *eject* 297
- packing 289
commission 755
- word 527
senescence 128
seneschal
director 694
master 745
servant 746
seneschalship 737
senile 128
senility 158, 659
senior *age* 128
student 541
master 745
seniores priores 62,
380
seniority 124, 128
sennight 108
señor 373, 877
señora 374
sensation
*physical sensi-
bility* 375
emotion 821
wonder 870
sensational 574,
824
sensation drama
599
sensations of touch
380
sense 498, 516
deep - 821
horse - 498
in no - 565
accept in a par-
ticular - 522
- of duty 926
senseless
insensible 376
absurd 497
foolish 499
unmeaning 517
senses
external - 375
intellect 450
sanity 502

sensibility 375, 822
sensible
material 316
wise 498
sensitive 375, 822
sensorial 821
sensorium 450
sensual 377, 954
sensualist 954a
sensuous
sensibility 375
pleasure 377
feeling 821
sentence
decision 480
maxim 496
affirmation 535
phrase 566
condemnation 971
sententious 572,
574
sentient 375, 821
sentiment 453
sentimental
sensitive 822
affected 855
sentinel } 263
sentry }
guardian 664
watch 668
keeper 753
separate *disjoin* 44
exclude 55
bisect 91
diverge 291
divorce 905
- the chaff from
the wheat
discriminate 465
select 609
- into elements 49
- maintenance 905
separation 49
separatist 489, 984
sepia 433
seposition 44, 55
sepoy 726
sept *kin* 11
class 75
clan 166
Septentrional 237
septett 415
septic 655, 657
septicemia 655
septuagenarian 98
Septuagint 985
septum 228
sepulcher 363
whited - 545
sepulchral
interment 363
resonance 408
stridor 410
hoarse 581
sepulture 363
sequacious 63
sequacity *soft* 324
tenacity 327
sequel 65, 117
sequela 65, 154
sequence
- in order 63
- in time 117
motion 281
logical - 476
sequent 63
sequester 789, 974

sequestered 893
sequestrate
seize 789
condemn 971
confiscate 974
sequin 847
serac 383
seraglio 961
seraph 948, 977
seraphic
blissful 829
virtuous 944
pious 987
seraphina 417
seraskier 745
sere and yellow
leaf 128
serein 339, 348
serenade *music* 415
compliment 894
endearment 902
serene
pellucid 425
calm 826
content 831
imperturbable 871
- highness 877
serf *slave* 746
clown 876
serfdom 749
sergeant 745
serial
continuous 69
periodic 183
book 593
seriatim
in order 58
continuously 69
each to each 79
slowly 275
series 69, 84
sérieux, take au -
843
serio-comic 853
serious *great* 31
resolved 604
important 642
dejected 837
seriously 535
serjeant:
common - 967
-at-law 968
sermon *lesson* 537
speech 582
dissertation 595
pastoral 998
funeral - 363
sermonizer 584
seroon 72
serosity 333, 337
serpent
tortuous 248
snake 366
hiss 409
wind instrument
417
wise 498
deceiver 548
cunning 702
evil-doer 913
knave 941
demon 949
the old - 978
great sea - 515
serpentine 248
serrated 244, 257
serried 72, 321

serum 333, 337
servant *instrumen-
tality* 631
help 711
retainer **746**
- of all work 690
serve *benefit* 618
business 625
utility 644
aid 707
warfare 722
obey 743
servant 746
- an apprentice-
ship 539
- faithfully 743
- loyally 743
- notice 527
- out 972
- one right
retaliation 718
right 922
punish 972
- as a substitute
147
- one's turn 644
- with a writ 969
service *good* 618
-*utility* 644
- *use* 677
warfare 722
servitude 749
worship 990
rite 998
hold - 363
at one's - 763
press into the -
677
render a - 644,
906
serviceable 644, 648
serviette 652
servile 749, 876, **886**
servitor 746
servitorship 749
servitude 749
penal - 972
sesame, open - 260
watchword 550
spell 993
sesqui- 87
sesquipedalia verba
577
sesquipedalian 200
sess 812
sessile 46
session *council* 696
sessions *law* 966
sestet 597
set
condition 7
join 43
coherence 46
group 72
class 75
firm 150
tendency 176
place 184
form 240
sharpen 253
direction 278
go down 306
dense 321
stage 599
habit 613
prepare 673
gang 712

impose 741
lease 771, 787
make a dead - at
716
- about 66, 676
- abroach 73
- one's affections
on 897
- afloat 153, 531
- against
oppose 708
quarrel 713
hate 898
angry 900
- against one
another 464
- agoing
impulse 276
propulsion 284
aid 717
- apart
separate 44
exclude 55
select 609
- aside
displace 185
disregard 458
neglect 460
negative 536
reject 610
disuse 678
annul 756
refuse 764
not observe 773
relinquish 782
dereliction 927
- one's back up
878
- before
inform 527
choice 609
- before oneself
620
- by 636
- one's cap at
897, 902
- on a cast 621
- down [see below]
- by the ears 898
- at ease 831
- an example
model 22
motive 615
- the eyes on 441
- one's face
against
oppose 708
refuse 764
disapprove 932
- the fashion
influence 175
authority 737
fashion 852
- fast 704
- on fire
ignite 384
excite 824
- on foot 66
- foot on 294
- forth show 525
assert 535
describe 594
- forward 293
- free 750
- going
[see - agoing]
- one's hand to

467
- one's heart upon
604, 865
- at hazard 665
- in begin 66
rain 348
- on its legs 150
- on one's legs 159,
669
- in motion 264,
677
- to music 416
- at naught
make light of 483
reject 610
oppose 708
defy 715
disobey 742
not observe 773
dereliction 927
- no store by 483,
930
- off
compensation 30
depart 293
improve 658
discount 813
adorn 845
display 882
- on 615
- in order 60
- out arrange 60
begin 66
depart 293
decorate 845
display 882
- over 755
- phrase 566
- a price 85, 812
- purpose 620
- at rest end 67
answer 462
adjudge 480
complete 729
compact 769
- right
inform 527
disclose 529
teach 537
reinstate 660
vindicate 937
- to rights 60
- sail 293
- the seal on 729
- one's seal to 467
- store by 642
- straight 246, 723
- the table in a
roar 840
- one's teeth 604
- terms
manifest 525
phrase 566
style 574
- a trap for 545
- to 720, 722
- in towards 286
- up
printing 54
originate 153
strengthen 159
produce 161
upright 212
raise 307
successful 731
prosperous 734
- up shop 676

- upon
resolved 604
attack 716
desirous 865
- too high a value
upon 482
- watch 459
- one's wits to
work think 451
imagine 515
plan 626
- to work
undertake 676
impose 741
set-back 735
set down
record 551
unseat 756
humiliate 879
slight 929
censure 932
give one a -
confute 479
- as 484
- for 484
- a cause for
hearing 969
- to 155
- in writing 551
setaceous 256
seton 662
setose 256
settee 215
setter 366
settle regulate 60
establish 150
be located 184
bench 215
come to rest 265
subside 306
kill 361
decide 480
choose 609
vanquish 731
consent 762
compact 769
pay 807
- accounts 807,
811
- down 133
stability 150
moderate 174
locate oneself 184
- into 144
- matters 723
- preliminaries
673
- property 781
- the question 478
- to sleep 683
- upon give 784
- with 807, 992
settled [see settle]
characteristic 5
ended 67
account - 811
- opinion 484
- purpose 620
settlement [see
settle]
location 184
colony 188
dregs 653
compact 769
deed 771
property 780
strict - 781

settler 188
settlor 784
seven 98
-league boots 274,
992
wake the -
sleepers 404
seventy 98
sever 38, 44
several special 79
plural 100
many 102
- times 104
severalize 465
severally 44, 79
severalty 44
severance 38
severe
energetic 171
symmetry 242
exact 494
- style 576
harsh 739
painful 830
simple 849
critical 932
severely very 31
severity 739
sew 43
sewage 299, 653
sewed up
drunk 959
sewer 350, 653
sewerage 652, 653
sewer-gas 663
sewing-silk 205
sex kind 75
women 374
fair - 374
sexagenarian 98,
130
sexagenary 99
sextant 217, 244,
247
sextet 98
sextodecimo 593
sexton 363, 996
sextuple 98
seyyid 745
sforzando 415
shabbiness 34
shabby trifling 643
deteriorated 659
stingy 819
mean 874
disgraceful 940
shabby-genteel 851
shack 189
shackle
fastening 45
hinder 706
restrain 751
fetter 752
shade degree 26
small quantity 32
manes 362
darkness 421
shadow 424
color 428
conceal 528
screen 530
paint 556
ghost 980
eye - 443
in the - 528, 874
shadow of a - 32,
422

throw into the -
surpass 303
conceal 528
glory 873
throw all else into
the - 642
thrown into the -
34, 874
under the - of 664
without a - of
doubt 474
shades:
- below 982
- of death 360
- of difference 15
- of evening 422
shading 421
- off 26
shadow
unsubstantial 4
copy 21
small 32
accompaniment
88
thin 203
be behind 235
sequence 281
dark 421
shade 424
pursue 461, 622
dream 515
demon 980
fight with a - 699
follow as a - 281
partial - 422
without a - of
turning 141
worn to a -
thin 203
worse for wear
659
- of coming
events 511
- forth dim 422
predict 511
metaphor 521
represent 554
may your - never
be less
courtesy 894
respect 928
approbation 931
take the - for the
substance
credulous 486
mistake 495
unskilful 699
under the - of
one's wing 664
shadowy 4, 447
shady 874
shaft deep 208
frame 215
pit 260
missile 284
axis 312
air-pipe 351
handle 633
weapon 727
shaggy 256
shagreen 223
shah 745
shake totter 149
weak 160
vibrate 314
agitation 315
shiver 383

solfeggio 415
solicit *induce* 615
  request 765
  desire 865
  - the attention
    457
solicitor *agent* 758
  petitioner 767
  lawyer 968
solicitous 865
solicitude *care* 459
  pain 828
  anxiety 860
  desire 865
solid *complete* 52
  dense 321
  certain 474
  learned 490
  exact 494
  wise 498
  persevering 604a
  solvent 803
  - angle 244
solidarity
  party 712
solidify 321
soliloquy **589**
solitaire *game* 840
  hermit 893
solitary ⎱ *alone*
solitude ⎰ 87
  secluded 893
solmization 416
solo 87, 415
  - dance 840
Solomon ⎱ *wise*
Solon ⎰ 498
  sage 500
solstice 125, 126
soluble *fluid* 333
  liquefy 335
solus 87
solution
  liquefaction 335
  answer 462
  explanation 522
  - of continuity 70
solve *liquefy* 335
  discover 480a
  unriddle 522
solvent
  liquefier 335
  monied 803
somatics 316
somber *dark* 421
  black 431
  grey 432
  sad 837
sombrero 225
some *indefinite*
  quantity 25
  small quantity 32
  more than one
    100
  -body *person* 372
  important or dis-
    tinguished 642
  in - degree
  degree 26
  small 32
  at - other time 119
  in - place 182
  - ten or a dozen
    102
  - time ago 122
  - time or other
    119

somehow or other
  cause 155
  instrument 631
somersault 218
something *thing* 3
  small degree 32
  matter 316
  - else 15
  - like 17
  - or other 475
sometimes 136
somewhat
  a little 32
  a trifle 643
somewhere 182
  - about 32
somnambulism
  walking 266
  trance 515
somnambulist
  walker 268
  dreamer 515
somniferous
  sleepy 683
  weary 841
somnolence 683
son 167
Son, God the - 976
sonant 402
  letter 561
sonata 415
Sonderbund 769
song *music* 415
  poem 597
  death - 360, 839
  love- 597
  for a mere - 815
  no - no supper 812
  old - 643
songster 416
soniferous 402
sonnet 597
sonneteer 597
sonorous *sound* 402
  loud 404
  language 577
sons of:
  - Belial 988
  - God 977
Soofeeism 984
soon *transient* 111
  future 121
  early 132
  too - for 135
sooner:- or later
  another time 119
  future 121
  - said than done
    704
soot 431, 653
sooth 511
  in good - 543
soothe
  allay 174
  relieve 834
  flatter 933
soothing
  faint sound 405
  - syrup 174
soothsay 511
soothsayer 513, 994
soothsaying 511
sop
  small quantity 32
  food 298
  fool 501
  inducement 615

  reward 973
  - to Cerberus 458
  - in the pan 615
soph 492, 541
Sophi 745, 996
sophism 477, 497
sophist *scholar* 492
  dissembler 548
sophister 492
  student 541
sophistical 477
sophisticate *mix* 41
  debase 659
sophisticated
  spurious 545
sophistry **477**
sophomore 541
soporific 683, 841
soporous 683
soprano 410, 416
sorbet 298
sorcerer **994**
sorcery **992**
sordes 653
sordet 417
sordid *stingy* 819
  covetous 865
sordine 417
sore
  bodily pain 378
  disease 655
  mental suffering
    828, 830
  discontent 832
  anger 900
  - as a boil 901a
  - place 822
  - subject 830, 900
sorely *very* 31
s'orienter 278
sorites 476
sorority 712
sorrel 433, 434
sorrow 828
  give - words 839
sorry *trifling* 643
  grieved 828
  mean 876
  make a - face 874
  cut a - figure 874
  be - for 750, 914
  in a - plight 732
  - sight 830, 837
sort *degree* 26
  arrange 60
  kind 75
  - with
  sociality 892
sortable ⎱
sortance ⎰
  agreement 23
sortes
  chance 156, 621
  - Virgilianæ
  sorcery 992
sortie 716
sortilege
  prediction 511
  sorcery 992
sortilegy 621
sortition 621
sorts, out of -
  ill-health 655
  sulky 901a
S.O.S. 669, 707
so-so *small* 32
  trifling 643

imperfect 651
sostenuto 415
sot *fool* 501
  drunkard 959
sot à triple étage
  501
sotto voce
  faint sound 405
  conceal 528
  voiceless 581
sou *money* 800
  qui n'a pas le -
    804
soubrette 599, 746
sough *conduit* 350
  noise 405
  cloaca 653
soul *essence* 5
  person 372
  intellect 450
  genius 498
  affections 820
  cure of -s 995
  flow of - 588
  not a - 187
  not dare to say
    one's - is his
    own *subjection*
    749
  fear 860
  - of wit 572
  have one's whole
    - in his work
    686
soulless 683, 823
soul-mate 905
soul-sick 837
soul-stirring 821,
  824
sound *great* 31
  conformable 82
  stable 150
  strong 159
  fathom 208
  bay 343
  noise **402**
  investigate 461
  measure 466
  true 494
  wise 498
  sane 502
  good 648
  perfect 650
  healthy 654
  solvent 803
  orthodox 983a
  catch a - 418
  safe and - 654,
    670
  - the alarm
  indication 550
  warning 668
  alarm 669
  fear 860
  - asleep 683
  full of - and fury
  unmeaning 517
  insolent 885
  - the horn 416
  - of limb 654
  - locator 726
  - mind 502
  - the praises of
    931
  - the note of prep-
    aration 673
  - reasoning 476

- a retreat 283
- sleep 683
- a trumpet
  publish 531
  alarm 669
- of wind 654
sounding: big -
  577
- brass 517
sounding-board 417
soundings 208
soundless
  unfathomable 208
  silent 403
soup 298, 352
soupçon 32, 41
souplé 298
sour *acid* 397
  discontented 832
  embitter 835
  uncivil 895
  sulky 901
  - grapes
  impossible 471
  excuse 617
  - the temper 830
source *beginning* 66
  cause 153
sourdet 417
sourdine 417
  à la - *noiseless* 405
  concealed 528
sourdough 463
soured 832
sourness **397**
sous tous les
  rapports 52
souse 310, 337
South *direction* 278
  North and -
  opposite 237
Southern
  antipodes 237
  - Cross 318
souvenir 505
sovereign
  superior 33
  all-powerful 159
  authorities 737
  ruler 745
  - contempt 930
  - remedy 662
Soviet 696, 737
sow *scatter* 73
  pig 366
  agriculture 371
  female 374
  get the wrong -
    by the ear
  misjudgment 481
  error 495
  mismanage 699
  fail 732
  - broadcast 818
  - dissension 713,
    898
  - the sand 645
  - the seed
  prepare 673
  - the seeds of
  cause 153
  teach 537
  - one's wild oats
  improve 658
  amusement 840
  vice 945
  intemperance 954

transient 111
swift 274
gush 348
impulse 612
haste 684
exertion 686
sputa 299
sputter *emit* 297
splash 348
stammer 583
spy *see* 441
spectator 444
inquire 461
informer 527
emissary 534
watcher 664
warning 668
spy-glass 445
squab *large* 192
short 201
broad 202
bench 215
squabble 713
squad 72, 726
squadron 726
– leader 745
squalid 653, 846
squall *violent* 173
wind 349
cry 411
quarrel 713
squalor 653
squamous 204, 223
squander *waste* 638
misuse 679
lose 776
' *prodigal* 818
square
congruous 23
compensate 30
four 95
limited space 182
houses 189
perpendicular 212
form 244
sparring 720
justice 924
honorable 939
make all – 660
on the – 939
– accounts
pay 807
account 811
– dance 840
– deal 922
– the circle 471
– inches 180
– peg into a round
hole 699
– up 556
– with 23
– yards 180
square-toes 857
squash *destroy* 162
flatten 251
blow 276
soft 324
marsh 345
semiliquid 352
hiss 409
game 840
squashy 345, 352
squat 308
locate oneself 184
little 193
short 201
thick 202

low 207
squatter 188
squaw *woman* 374
wife 903
squeak ⎫
squeal ⎭ 411, 412
squeamish 655
unwilling 603
fastidious 868
squeasy 868
squeezable 762
squeeze
contract 195
condense 321
embrace 894
squeeze out 301,
784
squelch 162
squib *sound* 406
lampoon 856, 934
squiffy 959
squilgee 652
squint
peephole 260
look 441
defective sight 443
squirarchy 875
squire *aid* 707
attendant 746
gentry 875
– of Dames 897
squirm 315
squirrel 274, 682
squirt 297, 348
S.S.C. 968
stab *pierce* 260
kill 361
pain 378, 649,
828
injure 659
stabilimeter 150
stabilisator 150
stability 150, 150
stable *firm* 150
house 189
lock the – door
when the steed
is stolen
too late 135
useless 645
bungling 699
– equilibrium 150
staccato 415
stack 72, 636
staddle 215
stade 252
stadium 728, 840
stadtholder 745
staff *support* 215
music 413
measure 466
signal 550
council 696
party 712
weapon 727
chief 745
retinue 746
pastoral – 999
– of life 298
– of office 747
– officer 745
stag *deer* 366
male 373
defaulter 808
stage *degree* 26
term 71
time 106

position 183
layer 205
platform 215
forum 542
drama 599
arena 728
come upon the –
446
on the – 525, 599
go off the – 293
revolving – 599
– business 599
– coach 272
– craft 599
– direction 697
– effect 882
– hand 599
– manager 599
– name 565
– play 599
– player 599
– struck 599
– whisper 580
stager *player* 599
doer 690
old – 130
stagger *slow* 275
totter 314, 821
agitate 315
unexpected 508
dissuade 616
affect 824
astonish 870
– belief *doubt* 485
– like a drunken
man 605
staggers 315
stagirite 850
stagnant 265
stagnation 681
stagy 599, 855
staid *wise* 498
calm 826
grave 837
stain *paint* 223
color 428
dirt 653
spoil 659
blemish 848
disgrace 874
– paper *writing*
590
stained, travel- 266
stainless *clean* 652
honorable 939
innocent 946
stair 305, 627
stake *fastening* 45
wager 621
danger 665
security 771
property 780
lay down 807
execution 975
at – *intended* 620
in *danger* 665
the – *agony* 828
burn at the – 384
stalactite 224
stalagmite 224
stale *old* 124
insipid 391
deteriorated 659
– flat and unprof-
itable 645
– news 532
stale-mate 27, 731

stalk *stem* 153
support 215
walk 266
– *abroad*
generality 78
pursue 622
proud 878
stalking-horse
ambush 530
plea 617
stall *cease* 142
abode 189
receptacle 191
support 215
play-house 599
mart 799
churchdom 995
cathedral 1000
finger– 223
stallion 271, 373
stalwart 159, 192
stamina 159, 604a
stammel 434
stammering 583
stamp
character 7
prototype 22
kind 75
form 240
mark 550
engraving 558
complete 729
security 771
– the foot
anger 900
– in the memory
505
– out 162, 385
stampede 860
stanch – a *flow* 348
persevering 604a
health 654
reinstate 660
stanchion 215
stanchless 825
stand *exist* 1
rank 71
long time 110
permanent 141
support 215
quiescence 265
difficulty 704
resistance 719
brook 821
patience 826
brave 861
at a – 681
come to a – 704
make a – 708, 719
take one's –
resolve 604
resist 719
due 924
take one's – upon
reasoning 476
affirm 535
plea 617
– aghast 870
– aloof 623, 681
– of arms 727
– at attention 507
– the brunt 717
– by *near* 197
aid 707
defend 717
– a chance 470,
472

– committed 754
– at ease 458
– to one's engage-
ment 772
– fair for 472
– fire 861
– firm 150, 719
– first 66
– for *indicate* 550
deputy 759
candidate 763
– forth 446
– one's ground
preserved 670
resist 719
– the hazard of
the die 621
– one in 812
– in need of 630
– no nonsense 604
– off 287, 623
– on 215
– out *project* 250
visible 446
obstinate 606
– over 133
– the proof 648
– to reason
proof 478
manifest 525
right 922
– on one's rights
748
– in the shoes of
147
– one in good
stead 644
– still *remain* 141
stop 265
difficulty 704
– the test 494, 648
– up [*see below*]
– upon *pride* 878
– upon one's
rights 924
– in the way of 706
– well in the
opinion of 931
stand up 212, 307
– against 719
– fight 720
– for 931, 937
– to 459
standard *model* 22
degree 26
mean 29
rule 80
measure 466
flag 550
good 648
perfect 650
gold – 800
standard-bearer
726
standardize 22, 60,
466
standing *footing* 8
degree 26
long time 110
permanence 141
situation 183
note 873
– army 726
– dish *rule* 80
permanent 141
– jest *wit* 842
– order 613, 963

T

T, to a – 494
tab 39, 550, 747
tabard 225
tabby *mottled* 440
  gossip 588
tabefaction 195
tabernacle 189,
  1000
  house 189
  temple 1000
tabid *shrunk* 195
  thin 203
  disease 655
  deteriorated 659
table
  arrangement 60
  list 86
  defer 133
  layer 204
  support 215
  flat 251
  repast 298
  writing 590
  on the – 626, 673
  turn the –s 218,
    468
  under the –
    hidden 528
    drunk 959
  – of the Lord 1000
  – the motion 624
tableau *list* 86
  appearance 448
  painting 556
  theatrical 599
table-cloth 652
table d'hôte 298
table-land 213, 344
tabescent 195
tablet *layer* 204
  flat 251
  record 551
  writing 590
  remedy 662
table-talk 532, 588
tablets of the
  memory 505
table-turning 992
taboid 531, 662
taboo 762, 992
tabor 417
tabouret 215
tabret 417
tabula rasa
  inexistence 2
  absence 187
  ignorance 491
  obliterated 552
  facility 705
tabulate 60, 69
tabulation 551
tachometer 274
tachygraphy 590
tachy case 191
tacit 526
taciturnity 585
Tacitus
  concise style 572
tack *join* 43
  nails 45
  change course 140
  sharp 253
  direction 278
  turn 279
  food 289

way 627
go upon another –
  607
  wrong – 732
  – to *add* 37
tackle
  fastening 45
  gear 633
  try 675
  undertake 676
  manage 693
tacky 352
tact *touch* 379
  discrimination
    465
  wisdom 498
  skill 698
  taste 850
  want of – 851
tactful 894
tactician 700
tactics 692, 722
tactless 895
tactile &c. 379
tadpole 129
taedium vitae 837,
  841
tag *small* 32
  addition 37
  adjunct 39
  fastening 45
  sequel 65
  end 67
  point 253
  sheep 366
  – after 281
tagrag and bobtail
  876
tail *sequel* 65
  end 67
  pendent 214
  back 235
  aircraft 273
  estate – 780
  turn – 623
  – off *decrease* 36
tail-coat 225
tailor 225, 690
tailoring 225, 882
tail-piece *sequel* 65
  rear 235
  engraving 558
  ornament 847
tail-race 350
taint
  imperfection 651
  dirt 653
  decay 659
  disgrace 874
  tainted 401, 655
  taintless 652
taj 225
take *eat* 298
  believe 484
  know 490
  understand 518
  succeed 731
  receive 785
  appropriate 789
  captivate 829
  give and – 718
  – a back 508, 870
  – an account of 85
  – action 680
  – advice 695
  – after 17
  – aside 586

– away
  annihilate 2
  subtract 38
  remove 185
  seize 789
  – back again 790
  – a back seat 34
  – by [*see below*]
  – the cake 33
  – care 668, 864
  – care of 459, 664
  – no care of 460
  – off 293
  – one's chance
    621, 675
  – one's choice 609
  – things as they
    come 683, 826
  – comfort 831, 834
  – the conse-
    quences 154
  – coolly 826
  – a course 692
  – its course 143,
    151
  – no denial 606,
    744
  – a disease 655
  – down
    swallow 298
    depress 308
    record 551
    write 590
    dismantle 681
    humiliate 874
    censure 932
  – easily 826
  – effect 151, 170
  – an ell 885
  – exception 932
  – one's fancy 829,
    865
  – fire 384
  – flight 623
  – from 38, 789
  – for [*see below*]
  – the good the
    gods provide
    831
  – heart 831, 836
  – to heart 828, 832
  – heed 864
  – a hint 498
  – hold of 46, 789
  – hold of the mind
    484
  – ill 832
  – in [*see below*]
  – an infection 655
  – no interest in
    823
  – into [*see below*]
  – it 484, 514
  – the lead 62
  – a leaf out of an-
    other's book 19
  – a lease 788
  – leave of 624
  – a liberty 748
  – away life 361
  – a likeness 554
  – measures 626
  – money 810
  – no note of 460
  – no note of time
    115
  – notice 457

– one's oath 535
  – off [*see below*]
  – oneself off 293
  – on [*see below*]
  – one with an-
    other 29
  – out 301, 552
  – over 783
  – part with 709
  – pattern by 19
  – a peep 441
  – pen in hand 590
  – to pieces 44, 681
  – place 151
  – the place of 147
  – possession of 589
  – precedence 33,
    62
  – its rise 66, 154
  – root 150, 184
  – the shine out of
    33
  – ship 267
  – steps 673, 680
  – stock 85
  – time
    duration 106
    late 133
    leisure 685
  – time by the
    forelock 132
  – to *habit* 613
    pursuit 622
    use 677
    like 827
    desire 865
    love 897
  – on trust 484
  – a turn 140
  – up [*see below*]
  – upon oneself
    676, 768
  – warning 668
  – wing 293
  – one at one's
    word 769
take by
  – the button 586
  – the hand 707
  – surprise 508, 674
take for 484
  – better or for
    worse 609
  – gospel 486
  – granted 484
take in *include* 54
  shorten 201
  admit 296
  understand 518
  deceive 545
  receive money 785
  – good part
    be calm 826
    be pleased 827
    content 831
  – hand *teach* 537
  undertake 676
  aid 707
  – an idea 498
  – sail 275
take into
  – account
    include 76
    discriminate 465
    qualify 469
  – consideration
    451

– *custody* 751
  – one's head 514,
    608
take off *mimic* 19
  destroy 162
  remove 185
  divest 226
  depart 293
  discount 813
  ridicule 856
  – one's hands 785
  – the hat 894
take on
  attempt 675
  discontent 832
  melancholy 837
  – *credit* 484
  – *trust* 484
take up
  elevate 307
  inquire 461
  dissent 595
  choose 609
  undertake 676
  befriend 707
  arrest 751
  borrow 788
  censure 932
  – arms 722
  – a case 476
  – one's abode 184
  – the cudgels 716,
    720
  – an inquiry 461
  – money 788
  – one's pen 590
  – with
    attention 457
    use 677
    content 831
taken, be –
  die 360
  – ill 655
  – with 897
taker 789
taking 789
  infectious 657
  in a – *pained* 828
  angry 900
talapoin 996
talbotype 556
tale
  counting 85
  narrative 594
  thereby hangs a –
    526
  twice-told –
    diffuse style 573
    weary 841
tale-bearer 532
talent 698
  bury one's – in a
    napkin 528
  not put one's – in
    a napkin 878
talionis, lex – 718,
    922
taliped 243
talisman 747, 993
talismanic 992
talk
  unsubstantial 4
  rumor 532
  speak 582
  conversation 588
  small – 588
  – big *boast* 884

insolent 885
threat 909
- glibly 584
- nonsense 497
- of signify 516
publish 531
intend 620
- to oneself 589
- oneself out of breath 584
- over confer 588
persuade 615
- to in private 586
- at random illogical 477
loquacity 584
- together 588
- against time time 106
protract 110
inaction 681
- of the town gossip 588
fame 873
talkative 582, 584
talked of 873
talkies 599, 840
talking, fine - over-estimation 482
tall 206
- hat 225
- talk 884
tallage 812
tallies 85
tallow 356
- candle 423
tallow-faced 429
tally agree 23
list 85, 86
sign 550
credit 805
- with conform 82
tally-ho 622
tally-man 797
talma 225
Talmud 985
talons authority 737
claws 781
talus 217
tam-o'-shanter 225
tambourine 417
tame inert 172
moderate 174
domesticate 370
teach 537
feeble 575
subjugate 749
insensible 823
calm 826
tameless violent 173
malevolent 907
Tammany 940
tamp 261, 276
tamper with alter 140
seduce 615
injure 659
meddle 682
tan color 433
tandem at length 200
vehicle 272
tang taste 390

bane 663
tangent 199
angle 217
fly off at a - deviate 279
diverge 291
excitable 825
tangere ulcus 505
tangible material 316
touch 379
exact 494
sufficient 639
useful 644
tangle 61, 219
tangled 59, 704
weave a - web 704
tango 840
tank pool 343
reservoir 636
armored vehicle 726
tankard 191
tanker 273
tant: - mieux 838
- s'en faut 489
- soit peu 32
tantaene animis coelestibus irae 900
tantalize balk 509
induce 615
desire 865
tantalizing exciting 824
Tantalus: torment of - 537, 865
tantamount 27, 516
tantara 407
tantas componere lites 723
tanti 642
tantivy speed 274
tantrums 900
tap open 260
plug 263
hit 276
let out 295, 297
sound 406
turn on the - 297
tap-dance 840
tape string 205
measure 466
- machine 553
taper contract 195
narrow 203
candle 423
- to a point 253
tapestry 556, 847
tapinois, en - 528
tapis: on the - event 151
topic 454
intention 620
plan 626
tap-root 153
taps 550
tapster 746
tar cover 223
sailor 269
pitch 356a
- and feather 929, 972
taradiddle 546
tarantass 272
tarantella 840
tarboosh 225

tardiloquence 583
tardy 133, 275
tare 40a
- and tret 813
tares 645
targe 717
target 620
shield 717
tariff 812
tarmac 635
tarn 343
tarnish discoloration 429
soil 653
deface 848
disgrace 874
tarpaulin 223
tarry remain 110, 265
later 133
continue 141
- for expect 507
tart pastry 298, 396
acid 397
rude 895
irascible 901
harlot 962
tartan 440
tartane 273
Tartar choleric 901
catch a - dupe 547
unskilful 699
retaliation 718
tartar dirt 653
- emetic 663
Tartarus 982
Tartufe hypocrisy 544
deceiver 548
impiety 988
task lesson 537
business 625
put to use 677
fatigue 688
command 741
hard - 704
set a - 741
take to - 932
- the memory 505
taskmaster 694
tass 191
tassel 847
taste sapidity 390
experience 821
good taste 850
man of - 850
to one's - savory 394
pleasant 829
love 897
tasteful 850
tasteless insipid 391
tasty 394, 850
tâtonner 463
tatter small quantity 32
tatterdemalion 876
Tattersalls 799
tatters garments 225
tear to - 162
tatting 847
tattle 588
tattler 532, 588
tattoo drumming 407

mottled 440
summons 741
taught [see teach]
fastened 43
taunt 929, 938
tauromachy 720
taut 43
tautology 104, 573
tavern 189
tawdry 851
tawny 433, 436
tax inquire 461
employ 677
fatigue 688
command 741
compel 744
request 765
accounts 811
impost 812
discount 813
accuse 938
- one's energies 686
- the memory 505
taxi 266
taxi-cab 272
taxi-driver 268
taxidermy 368
taxis 60
taxonomy 60
tazza 191
Te Deum 990
te fabula narratur, de - retaliate 718
condemn 971
tea 298
teach 537
- one's grand- mother 641, 885
- one his place 879
teachable 539
teacher 540, 673
teaching 537
false - 538
teacup, storm in a - overrate 482, 549
exaggerate 549
teagown 225
team assemblage 69, 72
teamster 694
tea-party 892
tea-pot 191
tear separate 44
violence 173
move rapidly 274
excite 825
weeping 839
- away from 789
- oneself away 623
- asunder one's bonds 750
- one's hair 839
- out 301
- to pieces separate 44
destroy 162
- up destroy 162
tear-gas 663, 727
tearful 839
tearing passion 839
tears: draw - 830
shed - 839
- in one's eyes excited 824
sad 837

tease annoy 830
spite 907
teaser difficult 704
teasing 830
teat 250
tea-table talk 588
technic 698
technica, memoria - 505
technical conformable 82
workmanlike 698
- college 542
- education 537
- knowledge 698
- school 542
- term 564
technicality special 79
cant-term 563
formulary 697
technique 556, 698
technocracy 698
technology 698
techy 901
tedious 841
while away the - hours 681
tedium 841
teem produce 161
productive 168
abound 639
- with multitude 102
teemful 168
teeming crowd 72
teemless 169
'teens 98
in one's - 127, 129
teeter 314
teeth 330, 781
armed to the - 673, 717, 722
between the - 405
cast in one's - 938
chattering of - 383
have cut one's eye - 698
in the - of 704, 708
grind one's - 900
the run of one's - 815
set one's - 604
show one's - 900
in spite of one's - 708, 744
make one's - chat- ter 385, 860
set the - on edge scrape 331
saw 397
stridor 410
pain the feelings 830
tee 66
teetotalism 953, 958
teetotum 312, 840
teg 366
tegument 223
teind 99
teinoscope 445
tekel upharsin 668
telautograph 553
telegram 532
telegraph

velocity 274
messenger 534
signal 550
 – boy 534
by – haste 684
telegraphone 553
telegraphy
 publication 531
teleology 620
telemeter 200
telepathy 992
telephone 418
 inform 527
 messenger 534
telescope 445
 – word 572
telescopic 196
telesis 658
telesm 993
television 532
tell count 85
 influence 175
 evidence 467
 inform 527
 speak 582
 describe 594
 succeed 731
 let me – you 535
 who can – 475
 – one's beads 990,
  998
 – the cause of 522
 – fortunes 511
 – how 155
 – a lie 544
 – a piece of one's
  mind 529
 – of 467
 – off 85
 – one plainly 527
 – its own tale 518
 – tales
 disclose 529
 – the truth 543
teller treasurer 801
 – of tales 594
telling 175
 graphic 518
 important 642
 exciting 824
 with – effect 171,
  175
telltale news 532
 indicator 550
 knave 941
telluric 318
telum imbelle 158
temerity 863
temper nature 5
 state 7
 moderate 174
 elasticity 323
 pliability 324
 modify 469
 prepare 673
 affections 820
 irascibility 901
 command of – 826
 lose one's – 900
 out of – 901a
 trial of – 824
 – the wind to the
  shorn lamb 834
tempera 556
temperament
 nature 5
 tendency 176

musical 413
affections 820
temperance 174,
 953
temperate
 [see temperance]
 mild 826
temperature 382
 increase of – 384
 reduction of – 385
tempest
 violence 173
 agitation 315
 wind 349
 excitement 825
tempestivity 134
tempest-tossed 824
tempestuous 59
Templar 996
 Good – 958
temple house 189
 side 236
 church 1000
 – of the Holy
  Ghost 983a
templet 22
tempora:
 O –! O mores!
 lament 839
 disreputable 874
 disapprobation
  932
 improbity 940
 vice 945
 – mutantur 140
temporal
 transient 111
 laical 997
 lords – and
  spiritual 875
temporality 997
temporary 111
temporize
 protract 110
 defer 133
 cunning 702
temporizer 943
tempt entice 615
 attempt 675
 desire 865
 – fortune 621, 675
 – Providence 863,
  885
tempter 615
 Satan 978
 voice of the – 615
temulency 959
ten 98
 – to one 472
 – thousand 98
tenable 664
tenacity
 coherence 46
 toughness 327
 memory 505
 resolution 604
 obstinacy 606
 retention 781
 avarice 819
 courage 861
 – of life 357
 – of purpose 604a
tenaculum 781
tenancy 777
tenant
 present 186
 occupier 188

possessor 779
tenantless
 absence 187
 seclusion 893
tenax propositi
 204, 939
tend conduce 176
 – animals 370
 aid 707
 serve 631, 746
 – towards 278
tendence 749
tendency 176
tender slight 32
 ship 273
 soft 324
 painful 378
 color 428
 war vessel 726
 offer 763
 susceptible 822
 affectionate 897
 compassionate
  914
 – age 127
 – conscience 926
 – heart
 susceptible 822
 kind 906
 compassionate
  914
 – mercies [ironical]
 badness 649
 severity 739
 cruelty 907
 – passion 897
 – one's resignation
  757
 – to 707
tenderfoot 57, 541
tendon 45
tendril fastening 45
 offshoot 51
 infant 129
 filament 205
 convoluted 248
 plant 367
tenebrious 421
tenebrosity 421
tenement 189, 780
 – of clay 362
tenet belief 484
tenner 800
tennis 840
 – ground 213
tenor course 7
 degree 26
 direction 278
 high note 410
 singer 416
 violin 417
 meaning 516
 pursue the noise-
  less – of one's
  way 881
tense hard 323
tensile 325
tension 159, 200
tensure 200
tent abode 189
 covering 223
 pitch one's –
  locate 184
 arrive 292
tentacle 781
tentative 463, 675
tente d'abri 223

tented field 722
tenter-hook 214
 on –s 507
tenth 99
tenths
 tithe 812
tent-pegging 840
tents, O Israel, to
 your – 722
tenue, en grande –
 847, 882
tenuity
 smallness 32
 thinness 203
 rarity 322
tenuous
 shadowy 4
tenure
 possession 777
 property 780
 due 924
tepee 189
tepefaction 384
Tephramancy 511
tepid 382
tepidarium 386
ter quaterque
 beatus 827
teratology
 unconformity 83
 distortion 243
 altiloquence 577
 boasting 884
tercentenary 98,
 138, 883
terceron 41
terebration 260
teres atque rotun-
 dus 249
 in seipso – 650
tergiversation 283,
 607
term end 67
 place in series 71
 period of time 106
 limit 233
 word 562
 name 564
 lease 780
termagant 901
terminal 67, 253,
 292
terminate 67, 292
 limit 233
termination 154
termine, mezzo –
 628
terminology 562
terminus end 67
 limit 233
 arrival 292
termless 105
terms [see term]
 circumstances 8
 reasoning 476
 pacification 723
 conditions 770
 bring to – 723
 come to –
 assent 488
 pacify 723
 submit 725
 consent 762
 compact 769
 couch in – 566
 on friendly – 888
 in no measured –

574
ternary 93
ternion 92
Terpsichore 416,
 840
terra: – cotta
 baked 384
 sculpture 557
 – firma
 support 215
 land 342
 safety 664
 – incognita 491
terrace houses 189
 level 213
terrain 181
terraqueous 318
terre verte 435
terrene 318, 342
terrine 191
terrestrial 318
terrible 860
terribly greatly 31
terrier list 86
 auger 262
 dog 366
terrific 31, 830, 860
terrify 860
territorial land 342
 soldier 726
territory 181, 780
terror 860
 King of –s 360
 reign of – 739, 828
terrorem, in – 860,
 909
terrorism 860
 insolence 885
terrorist
 coward 862
 blusterer 887
 evil-doer 913
terse 572
tertian periodic 138
tertiary three 92
tertium quid
 dissimilar 18
 mixture 41
 combination 48
 unconformable 83
tesselated 440, 847
tesserae
 mosaic 440
 counters 550
test 463
testa, voce di – 410
testament 771
Testament 985
tester bedstead 215
 sixpence 800
testify 467, 550
testimonial 551
testimony 467
testy 901
tetanus 315
tetchy 901
tête: – baissée 863
 – exaltée 503
 – montée 503, 825
 –à-tête two 89
 near 197
 confer 588
tether fasten 43
 locate 184
 restrain 751
 means of restraint
  752

life hangs by a –
360
worn to a – 659
– one's way 266,
302
threadbare 226, 659
threadpaper 203
threat 909
threaten
future 121
destiny 152
danger 665
threatening
warning 668
unhopeful 859
three 93
– in one and one
in – 976
sisters – 601
go through – hun-
dred and sixty
degrees 311
– sheets in the
wind 959
– times three
number 98
approbation 931
threefold 93
three-score 98
– years and ten
128
three-tailed
bashaw
master 745
nobility 875
threne 938
threnody 839
thresh 972
– out 461
threshold
beginning 66
edge 231
at the – *near* 197
– of an inquiry 461
thrice 93
– happy 827
–told tale 573
thrid 302
thrift
prosperity 734
gain 775
economy 817
thriftless 818
thrill
physical pain 378
touch 380
feeling 821
excitation 824
thrilling
pleasing 829
painful 830
thrive 734
throat *opening* 260
pipe 350, 351
cut the – 361
force down the –
739
stick in one's –
581, 585
take by the – 789
throb 315, 821
throbbing: – heart
860
– pain 378
throe
revolution 146
violence 173

agitation 315
physical pain 378
agony 828
birth– 161
throne *abode* 189
seat 215
emblem of au-
thority 747
ascend the – 737
occupy the – 737
power behind
the – 526
– of God 981
throng 72
throttle
render powerless
158
close 261
kill 361
seize 789
– down 275
through
owing to 154
rid 278
by means of 631
get – 729
go – one 824
wet – 339
– thick and thin
complete 52
violence 173
perseverance 604a
throughout 50, 52
– the world 180
throw *impel* 276
propel 284
exertion 686
– oneself into the
arms of 664
– away *reject* 610
waste 638
relinquish 782
– back 144
– cold water on
616
– of the dice 156
– doubt upon 485
– down 162, 308
– oneself at the
feet of 725
– good money
after bad 818
– in 228
– off [*see below*]
– open 260, 296
– out [*see below*]
– over *destroy* 162
– overboard
exclude 55
destroy 162
eject 297
abrogate 756
– on paper 590
– away the scab-
bard 722
– into the shade
superior 33
lessen 36
surpass 303
important 642
– a tub to catch a
whale 545
– up [*see below*]
– a veil over 528
throw off 297
– all disguise 529
– one's guard 508

– the mask 529
– the scent .
misdirect 538
avoid 623
throw out 284, 297
eject 297
– a feeler 379
– of gear
disjoin 44
derange 61
– a hint 527
– a suggestion 514
throwing stick 727
thrown out 704
throw up *eject* 297
resign 757
– one's cap 884
– the game 624
thrum 416
thrush 416
thrust *push* 276
attack 716
– in *insert* 300
(*interpose*) 228
– one's nose in 682
– out 55
– down one's
throat 744
– upon 784
thud 406, 408a
thug *murderer* 361
thief 792
thumb *touch* 379
bite the – 929
one's fingers all –s
699
rule of –
experiment 463
unreasoning 477
essay 675
twiddle one's –
681
under one's –
authority 737
subjection 749
– over 539
– screw 975
Thumb, Tom – 539
thump
beat 276
thud 406
non-resonance
408a
punish 972
thumping *great* 31
big 192
thunder
violence 173
noise 404
prodigy 872
threaten 909
look black as –
832, 900
– against 908, 932
– of applause 931
– forth 531
– at the top of
one's voice 411
–s of the Vatican
908
thunderbolt
weapon 727
prodigy 872
thunder-clap 508,
872
thundering *great* 31
big 192

thunderstorm 173
thunderstruck 870
thurible 400, 998
thurifer 996
thuriferous 400
thurification
fragrance 400
rite 998
thus *circumstance* 8
therefore 476
– far *little* 32
limit 233
thwack 276, 972
thwart
across 219
harm 649
obstruct 706
oppose 708
cross 830
thwarted 732
tiara *insignia* 747
ornament 847
canonicals 999
Tib's eve 107
tick *graze* 199, 379
oscillation 314
sound 407
mark 550
credit 805
go on – 806
– off *record* 551
ticker 553
ticket 86, 550, 609
ticket of leave 760
– man 754, 949
tickle *touch* 380
please 829
amuse 840
– the fancy 829,
840
– the ivories 416
– the palate 394
– the palm 784,
807
ticklish
uncertain 475
dangerous 665
difficult 704
tidal wave 348, 667
tid-bit 648, 829
tide *ocean* 341
wave 348
abundance 639
prosperity 734
against the – 708
drift with the –
705
go with the – 82
high &c. – 348
stem the – 708
swim with the –
734
turn of the – 210
– of events 151
– over *time* 106
defer 133
safe 664
inaction 681
succeed 731
– of time 109
tidings 532
tidy *orderly* 58
arrange 60
good 648
clean 652
pretty 845
– up 60

tie *relation* 9
equality 27
fasten 43
fastening 45
neckcloth 225
security 771
obligation 926
nuptial – 903
ride and – 266
–s of blood 11
– down
hinder 706
compel 744
restrain 751
– the hands 158,
751
– oneself 768
– up *restrain* 751
condition 770
entail 771
tie-beam 45
tied up
busy 135
in debt 806
tier *continuity* 69
layer 204
tierce 92
– and carte 716
tiff 713, 900
tiffin 298
tiger *violent* 173
servant 746
courage 861
savage 907
evil-doer 913
bad man 949
tight *fast* 43
closed 261
smart 845
drunk 959
– grasp 739
– hand 739
– rope dancing 698
keep a – hand on
751
on one's – ropes
878
tighten 43, 195
tight-fisted 819
tights 225
tightwad 819
tigress 374
tike 876
tilbury 272
tile *roof* 223
hat 225
– loose *insane* 503
till *up to the time*
106
coffer 191
cultivate 371
treasury 802
– doomsday 112
– now 122
– the soil 673
tiller
instrument 633
money-box 802
– of the soil
agriculture 371
clown 876
tilt *slope* 217
cover 223
propel 284
fall 306
contention 720
full – *direct* 278

- a deaf ear to deaf 419
refuse 764
- down 258
- of expression 566
- the eyes upon 441
- for 698
- from repent 950
- to good account 658
- one's hand to 625
- the head induce 615
excite 824
astonish 870
vanity 880
hate 898
- on one's heel avoid 623
discourtesy 895
- the house out of window 713
- in go to bed 683
- inside out 529
- into conversion 144
translate 522
- money 796
- ridicule 856
- of mind 820
- the mind to 457
- off 972
- on the tap 297
- the other cheek 725
- out become 144
happen 151
exterior 220
clothes 225
carriage 272
eject 297
strike 719
- well 731
- ill 732
dismiss 756
display 882
- over [see below]
- a penny 775
- round
inversion 218
revolve 311
rotate 312
recant 607
- one's little finger 737
- the scale unequal 28
superior 33
change 140
reverse 145
cause 153
counter-evidence 468
induce 615
- the stomach 395, 867
- the tables 14, 718
- of the table 156
- tail go back 283
run away 623
cowardice 862
- the tide 145
- of the tide 145, 218

- topsy turvy 61, 218
- and turn about 148, 149
- turtle 218
- and twist 248
- under 258
- up [see below]
- upon depend upon 154
retaliate 718
turn over give 784
invert 218
entrust 755
- the leaves 457, 539
- in the mind 451
- a new leaf change 140
improve 658
repent 950
- to 270
turn up happen 151
chance 156
visible 446
unexpected 508
- one's eyes wonder 870
hypocrisy 988
- one's nose at aversion 867
fastidious 868
contempt 930
turn-coat 605, 607
turnover 298
turned of 128
turning-point
crisis 8
end 67
occasion 134
reversion 145
cause 153
summit 210
limit 233
turnkey 753
turnpike 706
turnscrew 633
turnspit 366
turnstile 553, 706
turpentine and beeswax 255
Turpin, Dick - 792
turpitude 874, 940
turquoise blue 438
jewel 847
turret 206
turret-ship 726
turtle savory 394
turtle-doves 897
tush silence 403
taciturn 585
trifling 643
tusk 253
tussle 720
tussock 256
tut [see tush]
censure 932
tutelage
teaching 537
learning 539
safety 664
subjection 749
tutelary safety 664
- genius
auxiliary 711
god 979

- god 664
- saint 890, 912
tutor cultivate 375
teach 537
teacher 540
tutus, cavendo - 664
tuyère 386
twaddle
absurd 497
unmeaning 517
diffuseness 573
talk 584
twain 89
in - 44
twang taste 390
pungency 392
sound 402
stridor 410
music 416
voice 583
twattle
[see twaddle]
tweak 378
- the nose 830
tweed 219
tweedle touch 379
music 416
tweedledum and tweedledee 415
tweeny 746
tweezers 781
twelfth 99
twelve 98
twentieth century 118
twenty &c. 98
- shillings in the pound 803
twice 90
twice-told tale 104, 841
twiddle 379
twig 51
hop the - 360
twilight
morning 125
evening 126
dusk 422
- sleep 376
twill crossing 219
convolution 248
fold 258
twin similar 17
accompanying 88
two 89
duplicate 90
twine string 205
intersect 219
convolution 248
- round 43, 227
twinge 378, 828
twinkle
instantaneous 113
light 420
dimness 422
twinkling of an eye, in the - 113
twins 11
twire 315
twirl convolute 248
revolve 311
rotate 312
twist join 43
thread 205
oblique 217
crossing 219

distort 243
convolution 248
deviate 279
bend 311
prejudice 481
insanity 503
fault 651
appetite 865
twit deride 856
disrespect 929
censure 932
accuse 938
twitch pull 285
shake 315
pain 378
mental - 828
twitter
agitation 315
cry 412
music 416
emotion 821
excitement 824
'twixt 228
two 89
kill - birds with one stone 682
make - bites of a cherry 629, 956
- dozen 98
- meanings 520
in - places at once 471
game at which - can play 718
- score 98
fall between - stools 732
- strings to one's bow 632
- or three 100
- of a trade 708
unable to put - words together 583
two-bits 800
two-edged 253
two-faced 544
twofold 90
twopenny-haif-penny 643
two-sided 90
two-step 840
Tyburn tree 975
tycoon 745
tyg 191
tyke 876
tymbal 417
tympani 417
tympanum 210, 218
tympany 194
type essential 5
similarity 17
pattern 22
class 75
form 240
prediction 511
metaphor 521
indication 550
letter 561
printing 591
heavy - 550
- script 21
- writing 590
typhoon 349
typical special 79
conformable 82
metaphorical 521

significant 550
typist 590
typify 511
typography 591
tyranny 739
tyrant severe 739
ruler 745
evil-doer 913
tyre 230
tyro ignoramus 493
learner 541

U

uberrima fides 484
uberty 168
ubiety 186
ubiquity 186
U-boat 726
Ucalegon, proximus ardet - 667
udder 191
ugh! 867
ugliness 846
ugly 846
- customer source of danger 667
evil-doer 913
bad man 949
- duckling 948
call by - names 932
take an - turn 732
uhlan 726
ukase 741
ukulele 417
ulcer disease 655
care 830
ulema 967, 996
uliginous 352
ullage 53, 190
ulster 225
ulterior
additional 37
extraneous 57
- in time 121
- in space 196
- motive 615
ultima ratio 744
- regum 722
ultima Thule 196
ultimate 67
ultimately 121, 133, 151
ultimatum
definite 474
intention 620
requisition 630
terms 770
ultimo 122
ultra 31, 33
- vires 925
ne plus - 729
- crepidam 471
ultramarine 438
ultramontane
foreign 57
distant 196
heterodox 984
church 995
ultramundane 196
ultra-violet rays 420
ululation 412, 839
Ulysses 702
umbilicus 222

unemployed 678,
681
unencumbered 705,
927a
unendeared 898
unending 112
unendowed 158
– with reason
450a
unendurable 830
unenjoyed 841
unenlightened 491,
499
unenslaved 748
unenterprising 864
unentertaining 843
unenthralled 748
unentitled 925
unenvied 929, 930
unequal 28, 139
inequitable 923
– *to* 640
unequalled 33
unequipped 674
unequitable 923
unequivocal
great 31
sure 474
clear 518
unerring
certain 474
tone 494
innocent 946
unessayed 678
unessential 643
unestablished 185
uneven *diverse* 16a
unequal 28
irregular 139
rough 256
uneventful 643
unexact 495
unexaggerated 494
unexamined 460
unexampled 83
unexceptionable
good 648
legitimate 924
innocent 946
unexcitable 826
unexcited 823, 826
unexciting 174
unexecuted 730
unexempt 177
unexercised 674,
678
unexerted 172
unexhausted 159,
639
unexpanded 195,
203
unexpected
exceptional 83
inexpectation 508
unexpensive 815
unexplained
not known 491
unintelligible 519
latent 626
unexplored
neglected 460
ignorant 491
unseen 526
unexposed 526
unexpressed 536
unexpressive 517
unextended 317

unextinguished
173, 382
unfaded 428
unfading 112
unfailing 141
unfair *false* 544
unjust 923
dishonorable 940
unfaithful 940
unfaltering 604a
unfamiliar 83
unfashionable 83,
851
unfashioned 241,
674
unfasten 44
unfathomable
infinite 105
deep 208
mysterious 519
unfavorable
out of season 135
hindrance 706
obstructive 708
– *chance* 473
unfeared 861
unfeasible 471
unfed 640, 956
unfeeling 376, 823
unfeigned 543
unfelt 823
unfeminine
manly 373
vulgar 851
unfertile 169
unfetter 750
unfettered 748
unfinished 53, 730
unfit
inappropriate 24
impotence 158
inexpedient 647
unskilful 699
wrong 923
undue 925
unfitted
not prepared 674
unfix 44
unfixed 149
unflagging 604a
unflammable 385
unflattering 494,
703
unfledged
young 127, 129
unprepared 674
unflinching
firm 604
persevering 604a
brave 861
unfold
straighten 246
evolve 313
interpret 522
manifest 525
disclose 529
– *a tale* 594
unforbidden 760
unforced 602, 748
unforeseen 508
unforfeited 781
unforgettable 505
unforgiving 919
unforgotten 505
unformed 241, 674
unfortified
pure 42

powerless 158
unfortunate
ill-timed 135
failure 732
adversity 735
unhappy 828
– *woman* 962
unfounded 546
unfrequent 137
unfrequented 893
unfriended
powerless 158
secluded 893
unfriendly
opposed 708
hostile 889
malevolent 907
unfrock 756, 972
unfrozen 382
unfruitful 169
unfulfilled 713, 925
unfurl
unfold 313
– *a flag* 525, 550
unfurnished 640,
674
ungainly 846, 895
ungallant 895
ungarnished 849
ungathered 678
ungenerous 819,
943
ungenial 657
ungenteel 851, 895
ungentle 173, 895
ungentlemanly
vulgar 851
rude 895
dishonorable 940
ungifted 499
unglorified 874
unglue 47
ungodly 989
ungovernable
violent 173
disobedient 742
passionate 825
ungoverned 748
ungraceful
– *language* 579
ugly 846
vulgar 851
ungracious 895, 907
ungrammatical 568
ungranted 764
ungrateful 917
ungratified 832
ungrounded
unsubstantial 4
erroneous 495
ungrudging 816
unguarded
neglected 460
spontaneous 612
unprepared 674
in an – *moment*
unexpectedly 508
unguem, ad – 494,
650
unguent 356
unguibus et rostro
686
unguided
ignorant 491
impulsive 612
unskilled 699
unguilty 946

unhabitable 187
unhabituated 614
unhackneyed 614
unhallowed 988,
989
unhand 750
unhandseled 123
unhandsome 940
unhandy 699
unhappy
adversity 735
pain 828
dejected 837
make – 830
unharbored 185
unhardened
tender 914
innocent 946
penitent 950
unharmonious 24,
414
unharness 750
unhatched 674
unhazarded 664
unhealthy 655, 657
unheard of
exceptional 83
improbable 473
ignorant 491
wonderful 870
unheated 383
unheed, –ed 460
unheeding 458
unhesitating
belief 484
resolved 604
unhewn 241, 674
unhindered 748
unhinge 61, 158
unhinged
impotent 158
insane 503
failure 732
unhitch 44
unholy 989
unhonored 874
unhook (44)
unhoped 508
unhorsed 732
unhostile 888
unhouse 297
unhoused 185
unhurt 670
unicorn
monster 83
carriage 272
unideal *existing* 1
no thought 452
true 494
unification 48, 87
uniform
homogeneous 16
simple 42
orderly 58
regular 80
dress 225
symmetry 242
livery 550
uniformity 16
unilluminated 421
unimaginable 471,
473
wonderful 870
unimaginative 576,
843, 868
unimagined 1, 494
unimitated 20

unimpaired 670
unimpassioned 826
unimpeachable
certain 474
true 494
due 924
approved 931
innocent 946
unimpeached 931,
946
unimpeded 705, 748
unimportance 643
unimpressed 838
unimpressible 823
unimproved 659
unincreased 36
unincumbered
easy 705
exempt 927a
uninduced 616
uninfected 652
uninfectious 656
uninflammable 385
uninfluenced
obstinate 606
unactuated 616
free 768
uninfluential 172,
175a
uninformed 491
uningenuous 544
uninhabit, –able,
–ed 187, 893
uninitiated 491, 699
uninjured
perfect 650
healthy 654
preserved 670
uninjurious 656
uninquisitive 456
uninspired 823
uninstructed 491
unintellectual 452,
499
unintelligent 499
unintelligibility 519
unintelligible 519
– *style* 571
render – 538
unintentional
necessary 601
undesigned 621
uninterested 456,
841, 843
unintermitting
unbroken 69
durable 110
continuing 143
persevering 604a
uninterrupted
continuous 69
perpetual 112
unremitting 893
unintroduced 893
uninured 614
uninvented 526
uninvestigated 491
uninvited 893
uninviting 830
union
agreement 23
junction 43
combination 48
concurrence 178
workhouse 189
party 712
concord 714

unpurposed 621
unpursued 624
unqualified
  incomplete 52
  impotent 158
  certain 474
  unprepared 674
  inexpert 699
  unentitled 925
  – truth 494
unquelled 173
unquenchable
  strong 159
  desire 865
unquenched
  violence 173
  heat 382
unquestionable 474
unquestionably 488
unquestioned 474,
  488
unquiet
  motion 264
  agitation 315
  excitable 825
unravel untie 44
  arrange 60
  straighten 246
  evolve 313
  discover 480a
  interpret 522
  disembarrass 705
unreached 304
unread 491
unready 674
unreal
  not existing 2
  erroneous 495
  imaginary 515
unreasonable
  impossible 471
  illogical 477
  misjudging 481
  foolish 499
  exorbitant 814
  unjust 923
unreclaimed 951
unrecognizable 146
unreconciled 713
unrecorded 552
unrecounted 55
unreduced 31
unrefined 851
unreflecting 458
unreformed 951
unrefreshed 688
unrefuted 478, 494
unregarded
  neglected 460
  unrespected 929
unregenerate 988
unregistered 552
unreined 748
unrelated 10
unrelenting 914a,
  919
unreliable
  uncertain 475
  irresolute 605
  dangerous 665
unrelieved 835
unremarked 460
unremembered 506
unremitting
  continuous 69
  continuing 110
  unvarying 143

persevering 604a
unremoved 184
unremunerated 808
unrenewed 141
unrepealed 141
unrepeated 87, 103
unrepentant 951
unrepining 831
unreplenished 640
unrepressed 173
unreproached 946
unreproved 946
unrequited 806, 917
unresented 918
unresenting 826
unreserved
  manifest 525
  veracious 543
  artless 703
unresisted 743
unresisting 725
unresolved 605
unrespected 929
unrest 149, 264
unrestored 688
unrestrained
  capricious 608
  unencumbered
    705
  free 748
unrestricted
  undiminished 31
  free 748
unretracted 535
unrevenged 918
unreversed 143
unrevoked 143
unrewarded 806,
  917
unrhymed 598
unriddle 480a, 529
unrig 645
unrighteous 945
unrip 260
unripe
  young 127
  sour 397
  immature 674
unrivalled 33
unroll evolve 313
  display 525
unromantic 494
unroot 301
unruffled
  calm 174
  quiet 265
  unaffected 823
  placid 826
unruly violent 173
  obstinate 606
  disobedient 742
unsaddle 756
unsafe 665
unsaid 526
unsaleable
  useless 645
  selling 796
  cheap 815
unsaluted 929
unsanctified 988,
  989
unsanctioned 925
unsated 865
unsatisfactory
  inexpedient 647
  bad 649
  displeasing 830

discontent 832
unsatisfied 832, 865
unsavouriness 395
unsay recant 607
unscanned 460
unscathed 654
unschooled 491
unscientific 477
unscoured 653
unscriptural 984
unscrupulous 940
unseal 529
unsearched 460
unseasonable 24,
  135
unseasoned 614,
  674
unseat 756
unseemly
  inexpedient 647
  ugly 846
  vulgar 851
  undue 925
  vicious 945
unseen
  invisible 447
  neglected 460
  latent 526
unseldom 136
unselfish 942
unseparated 46
unserviceable 645
unsettle derange 61
unsettled
  mutable 149
  displaced 185
  uncertain 475
  – in one's mind
    503
unsevered 50
unsex 146
unshaded 525
unshaken 159
  – belief 484
unshapely 846
unshapen 241
unshared 777
unsheathe
  – the sword 722
unsheltered 665
unshielded 665
unshifting 143
unship 185, 297
unshocked 823
unshorn 50
unshortened 200
unshrinking 604,
  861
unsifted 460
unsightly 846
unsinged 670
unskilfulness 699
unslaked 865
unsleeping 604a,
  682
unsmooth 256
unsociable 893
unsocial 893
unsoiled 652
unsold 777
unsoldierlike 862
unsolicitous 866
unsolved 526
unsophisticated
  simple 42
  genuine 494
  artless 703

unsorted 59
unsought
  avoided 623
  unrequested 766
unsound
  illogical 477
  erroneous 495
  deceptive 545
  imperfect 651
  – mind 503
unsown 674
unsparing
  abundant 639
  severe 739
  liberal 816
  with an – hand
    818
unspeakable 31,
  870
unspecified 78
unspent 678
unspied 526
unspiritual 316, 989
unspoiled 648
unspotted
  clean 652
  beautiful 845
  innocent 946
unstable 218
  changeable 149
  uncertain 475
  irresolute 605
  precarious 665
  – equilibrium 149
unstaid 149
unstained
  clean 652
  honorable 939
unstatesmanlike
  699
unsteadfast 605
unsteady
  mutable 149
  irresolute 605
  in danger 665
unstinted 639
unstinting 816
unstirred 823, 826
unstopped
  continuing 143
  open 260
unstored 640
unstrained
  turbid 653
  relaxed 687
  – meaning 516
unstrengthened 160
unstruck 823
unstrung 160
unstudied 460
unsubject 748
unsubmissive 742
unsubservient
  useless 645
  inexpedient 647
unsubstantial 4
  weak 160
  rare 322
  erroneous 495
  imaginary 515
unsubstantiality 4
unsuccessful 732
unsuccessive 70
unsuitable
  incongruous 24
  (inexpedient 647)
  – time 135

unsullied clean 652
  honorable 939
  (guiltless 946)
unsung 526
unsupplied 640
unsupported
  weak 160
  (unassisted 706)
  – by evidence 468
unsuppressed 141
unsurmountable
  471
unsurpassed 33
unsusceptible 823
unsuspected
  belief 484
  latent 526
unsuspecting
  hopeful 858
unsuspicious
  belief 484
  artless 703
  hope 858
unsustainable 495
unsweet 395
unswept 653
unswerving
  straight 246
  direct 278
  persevering 604a
unsymmetric 83
unsymmetrical 59,
  243
unsystematic 59
untainted pure 652
  healthy 654
  honorable 939
untalked of 526
untamed 851, 907
untarnished 939
untasted 391
untaught 491, 674
untaxed 815
unteach 538
unteachable 499,
  699
untenable
  powerless 158
  illogical 477
  undefended 725
untenanted 187,
  893
unthanked 917
unthankful 917
unthawed 321, 383
unthinkable 471
unthinking
  unconsidered 452
  involuntary 601
unthought of 452,
  460
unthreatened 664
unthrifty
  unprepared 674
  prodigal 818
unthrone 756
untidy 59, 653
untie 44, 750
  – the knot 705
until 106
  – now 118
untilled 674
untimely 135
  – end 360
untinged 42
untired 689
untiring 604a

untitled 876
untold
    countless 105
    uncertain 475
    latent 526
    secret 528
untouched
    disused 678
    insensible 823
untoward
    ill-timed 135
    bad 649
    unprosperous 735
    unpleasant 830
untraced 526
untracked 526
untractable 606,
    699
untrained
    unaccustomed 614
    unprepared 674
    unskilled 699
untrammelled 705,
    748
untransiatable 523
untranslated 523
untravelled 265
untreasured 640
untried new 123
    not decided 461
untrimmed 674,
    849
untrodden new 123
    impervious 261
    not used 678
untroubled 174, 721
untrue 495, 546
untrustworthy
    uncertain 475
    erroneous 495
    danger 665
    dishonorable 940
untruth 544, **546**
untunable 414
unturned 246
untutored
    ignorant 491
    unprepared 674
    artless 703
untwine 313
untwist 313
unused
    new 123
    unaccustomed 614
    unskilful 699
unusual 83
unusually very 31
unutterable 31,
    519, 870
unvalued
    underrated 483
    undesired 866
    disliked 898
unvanquished 748
unvaried
    continuing 143
    - style 575, 576
unvarnished
    true 494
    - style 576
    unreserved 703
    simple 849
    tale 494, 543
unvarying 16, 143
unveil 525, 529
unventilated 261
unveracious 544

unversed 491
unvexed 831
unviolated 939
unvisited 893
unwakened 683
unwarlike 862
unwarmed 383
unwarned 508, 665
unwarped judg-
    ment 498
unwarrantable 923
unwarranted
    illogical 477
    undue 925
    illegal 964
unwary 460
unwashed 653
    great - 876
unwatchful 460
unwavering 604a
unweakened 159
unwearied
    persevering 604a
    indefatigable 682
    refreshed 689
unwedded 904
unweeded garden
    674
unweeting 491
unweighed 460
unwelcome 830,
    893
unwell 655
unwept 831
unwholesome 657
unwieldy
    large 192
    heavy 319
    cumbersome 647
    difficult 704
    ugly 846
unwilling 489
unwillingness **603**
unwind evolve 313
unwiped 653
unwise 499
unwished 866
unwithered 159
unwitting
    ignorant 491
    involuntary 601
unwittingly 621
unwomanly 373
unwonted 83, 614
unworldly 939
unworn 159
unworshipped 929
unworthy
    shameful 874
    vicious 945
    - of belief 485
    - of notice 643
unwrap 246
unwrinkled 255
unwritten
    latent 526
    obliterated 552
    spoken 582
    - law 697, 963
unwrought 674
unyielding
    tough 323
    resolute 604
    obstinate 606
    resisting 719
up
    aloft 206

vertical 212
    effervescing 353
    excited 824
    the game is - 735
    prices looking -
        814
    time - 111
    - in arms
    prepared 673
    active 682
    opposition 708
    attack 716
    resistance 719
    warfare 722
    - and at them 716
    - and doing 682
    - and down 314
    - on end 212
    - in 698
    - to [see below]
all - with
    destruction 162
    failure 732
    adversity 735
up to
    time 106
    power 157
    knowing 490
    skilful 698
    brave 861
    - the brim 52
    - date 123
    - one's ears 641
    - one's eyes 641
    - the mark
    equal 27
    sufficient 639
    good 648
    due 924
    - snuff 702
    this time
    time 106
    past 122
Upas tree 663
upbear 215, 307
upbraid 932
upcast 307
upgrow 206
upgrowth 194, 305
upheaval 146
upheave 307
uphill
    acclivity 217
    ascent 305
    laborious 686
    difficult 704
uphoist 307
uphold
    continue 143
    support 215
    evidence 467
    aid 707
    praise 931
upholder 488, 711
upholstery 633
uplands 180, 206,
    344
uplift 307, 658
upon:
    - my honor 535
    - oath 535
    - which 117, 121
upper 206
    - boxes, - circle
        599
    - classes 875
    - hand

influence 175
    success 731
    sway 737
    - story
    summit 210
    intellect 450
    wisdom 498
    - ten thousand
        875
    be on one's -'s 804
    uppermost 210
    say what comes -
        612
    - in the mind
    thought 451
    topic 454
    attention 457
    - in one's thoughts
    memory 505
upraise 307
uprear 307
upright
    vertical 212
    honest 939
uprise 305
uprising 742
uproar
    disorder 59
    violence 173
    noise 404
uproarious 825
uproot 301
ups and downs of
    life 151, 735
upset destroy 162
    invert 218
    throw down 308
    defeat 731
    excite 824
    disconcert 874
    - the apple cart
        732
upshot result 154
    judgment 480
    completion 729
upside down 218
upstairs 206
upstart
    new 123
    prosperous 734
    plebeian 876
upturn 210
upwards 206
    - of 33, 100
uranology 318
urban 189
urbane 894
urbis conditæ,
    anno - 106
urceole 998
urchin
    child 129
    small 193
    wretch 949
    imp 980
urge violence 173
    impel 276
    incite 615
    hasten 684
    beg 765
urgent
    required 630
    important 642
    haste 684
    request 765
urn vase 191
    funereal 363

heater 386
cinerary - 363
usage 613, 677
usance 806
use habit 613
    waste 638
    utility 644
    employ 677
    property 780
make good - of
    658
    in - 677
    be of - to aid 707
    benevolence 906
    - one's discretion
        600
    - one's endeavor
        675
    - a right 924
    - up 677
used to 613
used up
    deteriorated 659
    disuse 678
    fatigue 688
    weary 841
    satiated 869
useful 644
    render - 677
useless 645
user,
    right of - 780
usher
    guard 263
    receive 296
    teacher 540
    servant 746
    courtesy 894
    wedding 903
    - in precedence 62
    begin 66
    precession 280
    announce 511
    - into the world
        161
usque ad nauseam
    841
U.S.S. 726
ustulation 384
usual
    general 78
    ordinary 82
    customary 613
usufruct 677
usurer
    lender 787
    merchant 797
    credit 805
    miser 819
usurious 819
usurp assume 739
    seize 789
    illegal 925
    - authority 738
usurpation
    insolence 885
usurper 737
usury 806
utensil 191, 633
uti possidetis
    permanence 141
    possession 777
    retention 781
utilitarian 677, 910
utility **644**
    general -
    actor 599

cuique – 865
voluptuary 954a,
962
voluptuous
pleasure 377
delightful 829
intemperate 954
impure 961
volutation 312
volute 248
vomit 297
vomitory 260, 295
voodoo 992, 994
voracious desire 865
glutton 957
vortex rotation 312
agitation 315
river 348
danger 667
vorticist 556
votary
auxiliary 711
devotee 865
vote 535, 609
– for 488
voting machine 553
votis, hoc erat in –
865
votive 768
– offering 990
vouch assert 535
– for 467
voucher
evidence 467
indication 550
security 771
payment 807
vouchsafe
permit 760
consent 762
ask 765
condescend 879
vow affirmation 535
promise 768
worship 990
take –s 995
vowel 561
vox:
– faucibus hæsit
voiceless 581
fear 860
wonder 870
– populi
assent 488
publication 531
choice 609
– et praeterea nihil
unsubstantial 4
powerless 158
unmeaning 517
vain 880
boasting 884
voyage 267
voyager 268
vraisemblance 472
vue d'oeil, à – 132,
446
Vulcan 690, 979
vulgar inelegant 579
low born 876
– tongue 560
vulgarian 851
vulgarity
want of refinement
851
Vulgate 985
vulgus, ignobile –

876
vulnerable 665
vulnerary 662
vulnus:
æternum servans
sub pectore –
919
immedicabile –
619
vulpine 702
vulture 739, 913

W

wabble slow 275
oscillate 314
wad 263
wadding lining 224
stopper 263
soft 324
waddle 275
wade 267
– in blood 361
– through
learn 539
exertion 686
waddle 314
wafer cement 45
thin 203
lamina 204
waft transfer 270
blow 349
wafted, be – 267
wag oscillate 314
agitate 315
joker 844
– on journey 266
progression 282
wage war 722
wager 621
– of battle 722
– of law 467
wages 973
waggery wit 842
waggish 836, 853
waggle 314, 315
wagon 272
wagoner 268
wagonette 272
wagon-load 31
waif 618, 782
waifs and estrays
73, 268
wail 412, 839
wain 272
wainscot 211, 224
waist 203
waistcoat 225
put in a strait –
751
wait 133, 681
lie in – for 530
– for 507
– impatiently 133
– on accompany 88
aid 707
– to see how the
wind blows 607
– upon serve 746
call on 894
waiter servant 746
– on Providence
neglect 460
inactive 683
content 831

waiting 507
be kept – 133
waiting-maid 746
waitress 746
waits 416
waive defer 133
not choose 609a
not use 678
waiwode 745
wake sequel 65
rear 235
funeral 363
trace 551
excite 824
amusement 840
in the – of 281
enough to – the
dead 404
– the thoughts
457
– up 824
wakeful
careful 459
active 682
Walhalla 981
walk region 181
lane 189
move 266
business 625
way 627
conduct 692
arena 728
– one's chalks
293, 623
– the earth 359
– of life 625
–ed off one's legs
688
– off with 791
– over the course
705, 731
– in the shoes of
19
walker 268
walking gentleman
599
wall vertical 212
parietes 224
inclosure 232
refuge 666
obstacle 706
defence 717
prison 752
driven to the –
704
go to the –
destruction 162
die 360
fail 732
pushed to the –
601
take the – 873,
878
wooden –s 726
–eyed 442
– in 229, 751
wallah 746
wallet 191
wallop 315
wallow low 207
plunge 310
rotate 312
– in 377, 641
– in the mire 653
– in riches 803
– in voluptuous-
ness 954

wallsend 388
Wall-street 799
– slang 563
waltz 415, 840
wamble
vacillate 149
oscillate 314
dislike 867
wampum 800
wan 429, 837
wand scepter 747
magic 993
wave a – 992
wander move 264
journey 266
deviate 279
delirium 503
the attention –s
458
wanderer 268
wandering
exceptional 83
– Jew 268
wane
decrease 36
age 128
contract 195
decay 659
one's star on the –
735
wax and – 140
wangle 943
want
inferiority 34
shortcoming 304
requirement 630
insufficiency 640
poverty 804
desire 865
wanted 187
wanting
incomplete 53
absent 187
imbecile 499
found –
imperfect 651
disapproval 932
guilt 947
wantless 639
wanton
unconformable 83
capricious 608
unrestrained 748
amusement 840
rash 863
impure 961
wapentake 181
war 722
at – 24, 720
at – with 708, 722
declare – 713
man of – 727
seat of – 728
– correspondent
534, 593
– of words 588,
720
warble 416
war-cry alarm 669
defiance 715
war 722
ward part 51
parish 181
safety 664
asylum 666
dependent 746
restraint 751

watch and – 459,
753
– off 706, 717
war-dance 715
warden
guardian 664
master 745
deputy 759
warder
perforator 262
porter 263
guardian 664
keeper 753
wardmote 966
wardrobe 191, 225
ward-room 191
war-drum 417
wardship 664
ware
warning 668
merchandise 798
warehouse 636, 799
warfare 722
discord 713
war-horse 726
warlike 722
warlock 994
warm
violent 173
hot 382
make hot 384
red 434
orange 439
wealthy 803
ardent 821
excited 824
angry 900
irascible 901
flog 972
– bath 386
– the blood 824
– the cockles of
the heart 829
– imagination 515
– man 803
– reception
repel 717
welcome 892
– up 658, 660
– work 686
warm-hearted
feeling 821
sensibility 822
friendship 888
benevolence 906
warming 384
warming-pan
locum tenens 147
heater 386
preparation 673
warmth
vigorous language
574
warn dissuade 616
caution 668
– off 761
warning omen 512
dissuasion 616
caution 668
give – dismiss 678
relinquish 782
– voice alarm 666
warp change 140
tend 176
contract 195
distort 243
navigate 267

wreck
  remainder 40
  destruction 162
  damage 659
  defeat 732
wrecker 792
wrench *disjoin* 44
  draw 285
  extract 301
  twist 311
  tool 633
  seize 789
wrest *distort* 243
  – from 789
  – the sense 523
wrestle 720
wrestler 726
wretch *sufferer* 828
  sinner 949
wretched
  unimportant 643
  bad 649
  unhappy 828
wretchedly
  small 32
wriggle 314, 315
  – into 294
  – out of 671
wright 690
wring *twist* 248
  pain 378
  clean 652
  torment 830
  – from
  extract 301
  compel 744
  take 789
  – one's hands 839
  – the heart 830
wringing wet 339
wrinkle *fold* 258
  hint 527
wrinkled 128
wrist 781
wristband 225
writ 741, 969
Writ, Holy – 985
write *compose* 54
  style 569
  writing 590
  – down *record* 551
  – music 416
  – off 624
  – out 590
  – prose 598
  – to 592
  – upon 595
  – word 527
writer 590, 593
  dramatic – 599
  pen of a ready –
    569
  – to the Signet
    968
writhe *distort* 243
  agitate 315
  pain 378
writing 590, 593
  put in – 551
  – in cipher 590

written, it is – 601
wrong *error* 495
  evil 619
  injury 649
  spite 907
  improper **923**
  vice 945
  go – 732
  in the – *error* 495,
    923
  own oneself in
    the – 950
  – box 699, 704
  wrong 923
  – course 945
  begin at the – end
    699
  – in one's head
    503
  in the – place 647
  – side out 145, 218
  – side up 218
  – side of the wall
    665
  – sow by the ear
    699, 732
  – step 732
wrong-doer 949
wrong-doing 945
wrongful 923
wrong-headed 481
wrought:
  highly:
  prepared 673
  complete 729
  – iron 323
  – out 729
  – up *excited* 824
  angry 900
wry 217, 243
  – face *pain* 378
  discontent 832
  lamentation 839
  ugly 846
  disapproval 932
wynd 189
wyvern 83

X

X-rays 420, 554
xanthic 436
Xanthippe 901
xebec 273
xenogenesis 161
xerophagy 956
xylography 558
xylophone 417
x, y, z 491

Y

yacht 273

yachting 267
yachtsman 269
yager 726
Yahoo 702
yammer 839
yap 412
yard *abode* 189
  length 200
  enclosure 232
  workshop 691
yardarm to yard-
    arm 197
yare 682
yarn *filament* 205
  story 532
  untruth 546
  exaggeration 549
  mingled – 41
  spin a long – 549
  diffuse style 573
yarr 412
yashmak 225
yataghan 727
yaup 411
yaw 279
yawl *ship* 273
  cry 412
yawn *open* 260
  sleepy 683
  tired 688
  weary 841
yawning *gulf* 198
  deep 208
yclept 564
yea *more* 33
  assent 488
yean 161
year 106, 108
  – in and – out 104
  since the – one
    124
  all the – round 110
  – after year 104
  tenant from – to
    year 779
yearling 129
yearly 138
yearn 828, 837
  – for *desire* 865
  pity 914
yearning *love* 897
years 128
  in – 128
  tenant for – 779
  – ago 122
  come to – of dis-
    cretion 131
  – old 128
yeast *leaven* 320
  bubbles 353
yell *cry* 411
  scream 839
yellow 436
  – flag 668
  – streak 862
  – and red 439
yellow-eyed 920
yellowness **436**
yelp 412
yeoman 371, 373

– of the guard 726
  –'s service 644
yeomanry 726
yerk *strike* 276
yes 488, 762
yes-man 886
yesterday *past* 122
  of – *new* 123
yet *in compensation*
    30
  exception 83
  time 106
  prior 116
  past 122
  qualification·469
yeux doux, faire les
    – 902
yield *soft* 324
  harvest 636
  submit 725
  consent 762
  resign 782
  furnish 784
  gain 810
  price 812
  – assent 488, 762
  – one's breath 360
  – to despair 859
  – up the ghost 360
  – the palm 34, 879
  – to temptation
    615
yielding *soft* 324
  facile 705
  submissive 725
yodel 580
yoicks 622
yoke *join* 43
  vinculum 45
  couple 89
  subject 749
  means of restraint
    752
  rivet the – 739
yokel 701, 876
yokemate 903
yonder 79, 196
yore 122
Yorkshireman 702
you: – don't say so
    870
  –'re another 718
young 127
  – man *lover* 897
younger generation
    127
youngster 129
younker 129
youth 127, 129
yule log 388

Z

Zadkiel 513

zambo 41
Zamiel 978
zany 501
zeal *eagerness* 602
  activity 682
  feeling 821
  desire 865
zealot *bigot* 474
  obstinate 606
  active 682
zealotry 606
zebra 440
zemindar 779
zemindary 780
zemstvo 696
zenana 374, 961
Zendavesta 986
zenith 31, 210
  in the – 873
zephyr 349
Zeppelin 273, 726
Zerdhusht 986
zero 4, 101
  – hour 66
zest 394, 827
zetetic 461
Zeus 979
zigzag *oblique* 217
  angle 244
  deviating 279
  oscillating 314
  circuit 629
  ornament 847
Zimmermann
  disciple of – 893
zinc
  – white 430
zincography 558
zircon 847
zither 412
zocle 215
zodiac *zone* 230
  worlds 318
zodiacal light 423
Zoilus 936
Zollverein 712, 769
zonam perdidit 804
zone *region* 181
  layer 204
  belt 230
  circle 247
Zoo 370
zoography 368
zoohygiantics 370
zoolatry 991
zoological 366
  – garden 370
zoology 368
zoom 305
zoonomy 368
zoophorous 210
zoophyte 366
zootomy 368
Zoroaster 986
Zoroastrianism 984
zouave 726
zounds 870, 900
zymotic 655, 657